W9-DGK-359

10⁰⁰

THE
AFRICAN METHODIST
EPISCOPAL ZION CHURCH:
Reality of the Black Church

THE
AFRICAN METHODIST
EPISCOPAL ZION CHURCH
Reality of the Black Church

By

William J. Walls

Charlotte, N.C.
A.M.E. Zion Publishing House

4

Library of Congress Cataloging in Publication Data

Walls, William Jacob, Bp 1885-

   The African Methodist Episcopal Zion Church, Reality of
The Black Church.

   Bibliography: p.
   1. African Methodist Episcopal Zion Church .
I. Title
BX8457.W34   287'.83   74-3536
Copyright © 1974 A.M.E. Zion Publishing House   Printed in U.S.A.

Acknowledgements

The lines from *East and West In Religion* by *S. Radhakrishnan,* copyright, 1933, are used by permission of the publisher, George Allen & Unwin Ltd., London, arranged with Barnes and Noble, U.S.A.—

My Life With Martin Luther King, Jr., by *Coretta Scott King,* 1970, by permission of the publisher, Hodder and Stoughton, Limited, London: U.S.A. arrangement with Holt, Rinehardt, and Winston, Inc., New York—

Excerpts from the *Letter of William Hamilton* to Governor John Jay, *March 8, 1796,* by permission of Columbia University Libraries, Division of Special Collections—

Anonymous Letter to Mayor Cornelius W. Lawrence of New York. July 12, 1834, by permission of the New York Historical Society, New York City—

By permission of the Archives and Manuscript Division of the New York Public Library, Astor, Tilden and Lenox Foundations: *The James Varick Letter* from the *Riker Collection:* The *Black Classes of John Street Church* from the Records of the Methodist Episcopal Church, by special permission of Rev. Richard Francis, pastor of John Street United Methodist Church and the New York Conference Commission on Archives and History of the United Methodist Church, Dr. C. Wesley Christman, Jr., chairman.

The Collect Pond, 1797, by permission of the Museum of the City of New York, Photograph Division.

Ancient Egypt's three main scripts; *Hieroglyphic, Hieratic,* and *Demotic,* and *Sabaean Script* used by the Ethiopians early in their history, by permission of MacMillan Publishing Co., Inc., Copyright, 1969 by Basil Davidson.

Black Civil War Soldiers. *Charge of the 54th Massachusetts Regiment* at Fort Wagner, S.C. Courtesy of the National Archives and Records Service.

LIST OF ILLUSTRATIONS

Page

This book is affectionately
dedicated to
the sons and daughters
of
James Varick
throughout the world

1750 — 1827
*Founder and First Bishop of the African Methodist
Episcopal Zion Church*

PREFACE

"Literature is the soul of action, the only sensible articulate voice of the accomplished facts of the past. The men of antiquity are dead; their cities are ruins; their temples are dust; their fleets and armies have disappeared; yet all these exist in magic preservation in the literature which they have bequeathed to us, and their manners and their deeds are as familiar to us as the events of yesterday." This quotation from *The Golden Gems of Life,** serves to remind us of the importance of recording words and deeds of every generation.

It has been my lifetime dream to write a history of my church, The African Methodist Episcopal Zion Church; a church so divinely motivated, so impregnably conscious of its religious and race obligations, composed of a people so sacrificingly devoted to the service of mankind.

Aware of how close this subject was to my heart, and my burning desire to accomplish this dream, with a realization also of the need for such a work in this age of growing solidarity; the A.M.E. Zion Church, in its Quadrennial General Conference of 1968 took a positive step in this direction. For the first time in its history it voted to finance a history project, created the post of historiographer, and commissioned your humble servant to fulfill the task. This was done upon my retirement from active duties in the episcopacy.

It was a labor of five years of massive research and assemblage of material from my own collection and writings of about seventy-five years. This included my travels as boy evangelists, pastor, general officer and bishop, in an attempt to produce a work of value. My relationship with the fathers who reached back to the founding fathers, gave me peculiar insight into our church background. I was a young disciple of our Historian, Bishop Hood who knew Father Rush, who knew the founding father, Varick; and was given personal opportunities to sit at his feet in private conferences which helped to equip me in relating the story of our church to a deserving membership and an observant public. History was also my major in college and graduate school. This training covered much of the history of mankind. This work spans the period of our church activities through 1972.

Deepest gratitude is herein expressed to the officials and delegates of the 1968 General Conference of the A.M.E. Zion Church held at Detroit, for this commission of trust; also to the officials and delegates of the 1972 General Conference held at Mobile, Alabama for their continued support and encouragement of this work, and the Board of Bishops. Bishops Raymond L.

*Author Unknown

Jones, Herbert B. Shaw, Stephen G. Spottswood, William A. Stewart, C. Ewbank Tucker, Joseph D. Cauthen, Felix S. Anderson, William M. Smith, S. Dorme Lartey, William A. Hilliard, Alfred G. Dunston, Charles H. Foggie, James C. Hoggard, James W. Wactor, Clinton R. Coleman, Arthur Marshall, John H. Miller, George J. Leake, Ruben L. Speaks.

For extensive research and secretarial work, I am indebted to my wife, Mrs. Dorothy J. Walls, who worked assiduously to consummate this work. Appreciation is tendered to intensely enthusiastic research assistants, Mrs. Willie Banks Aldrich, Head Librarian of HOOD THEOLOGICAL SEMINARY and Curator of HERITAGE HALL, LIVINGSTONE COLLEGE, and Miss Louise Marie Rountree, Head Librarian of CARNEGIE LIBRARY, LIVINGSTONE COLLEGE; both of whom gave precious time and energy in gathering facts for this volume.

I am also indebted to the following institutions and personnel for their kind assistance, diligent efforts and patient undertakings in all of our research endeavors of helping to unfold new information for this work:

NEW YORK HISTORICAL SOCIETY OF NEW YORK CITY: Mr. James Gregory, Head Librarian; Mrs. Sue Adele Gillies, Library Department; Mr. Thomas J. Dunnings, Jr., Manuscript Division, and staff members.

NEW YORK PUBLIC LIBRARY, ASTOR, LENOX AND TILDEN FOUNDATIONS: Mr. Paul Rugen, Keeper of the Records of the Manuscript and Archives Division; assistants Mr. Salvato and Mrs. Jean McNiece; Miss Elizabeth Roth of the Prints Division, and other members of the Research Library, particularly the Division of Local History and Genealogy.

SCHOMBERG COLLECTION OF NEGRO LITERATURE AND HISTORY: Mrs. Jean Blackwell Hutson, Curator and staff members.

METHODIST LIBRARY, DREW UNIVERSITY: Dr. Kenneth Rowe, Head Librarian.

GARRETT THEOLOGICAL SEMINARY LIBRARY: Dr. John David Batsel, Head Librarian.

NEWBURGH N.Y. FREE LIBRARY: Mrs. Wayhill, Genealogical Dept.

NEWARK PUBLIC LIBRARY: Mr. Charles F. Cummings, Supervising Librarian of the New Jersey Reference Department.

AMERICAN BIBLE SOCIETY LIBRARY: Miss Elizabeth Eisenhardt, Head Librarian.

MUNICIPAL ARCHIVES AND RECORD CENTER OF THE CITY OF NEW YORK: Miss Elizabeth Eilerman, Acting Director and associate, Mrs. De Angelo.

YONKERS PUBLIC LIBRARY, MAIN BRANCH: Mr. Charles Amick, Head of Reference Department.

WESLEY THEOLOGICAL SEMINARY LIBRARY, WASHINGTON, D.C.: Dr. John H. Satterwhite and library staff.

THE LIBRARY OF CONGRESS (Rare Book Division)

THE GEORGE ARENTS RESEARCH LIBRARY, SYRACUSE UNIVERSITY,

for reproducing a copy of the first Discipline of the A.M.E. Zion Church (1820); and a number of libraries and librarians throughout the country, in providing additional information. Thanks to Mr. Raymond P. Morris, Executive Secretary of the ATLA Board of Microtext, Yale Divinity School Library; and Mr. Cosby Brinkley of the University of Chicago, in making possible the microfilming of the *Star of Zion* for concentrated reference.

Lasting gratitude is expressed to a skillful and competent reading committee composed of Reverend A. McLean Spaulding, Mrs. Olivia Spaulding and Reverend George B. Thomas, who undertook the task of reading the manuscript with scrutinizing care. Also included in our deep appreciation are Mr. John H. White, Sr., prizewinning photographer of the *Chicago Daily News,* for assistance in the work of illustrations; Mr. Clarence Holte of New York City, reference person on Black History; Rev. A. N. Gibson for Memorial Church records, Rochester, N.Y. and Frederick Douglass memorabilia; Rev. Dr. Edler Hawkins, professor at Princeton Theological Seminary, for information supplied; The Tillman family for the use of the Henry Duval Tillman Collection of the A.M.E. Zion Church, and Bishop J. Clinton Hoggard, consultant on illustrative matter; also to Mrs. Annabel Addison and Mrs. Susan Shinault for secretarial services.

Special thanks to clerical assistants, Miss Eloise Boyd, Mrs. Ann Webb, and Mrs. Pauline Pharr, also to Dr. M. B. Robinson, Editor of the *Star of Zion* for cooperation in publishing my Historical Tidbits and giving constant encouragement in the long struggle, and Dr. David H. Bradley, Sr., Secretary of the Historical Society of the A.M.E. Zion Church; and all others, not only of the A.M.E. Zion Church, but of several churches and organizations, who were helpful in supplying information, illustrations and material for this work.

It is my earnest prayer that this history will serve to move forces toward everlasting peace, unity, love, and complete freedom for the black race and all mankind.

William J. Walls

CONTENTS

12

Part IV—Growth of the Church

Part V—Projection Departments

Part VI—Ministration Departments

Part VII—Faith, Hope and Charity

Part VIII—Paramount Functionalities

INTRODUCTION

In May, 1968, Bishop William Jacob Walls was commissioned to write a comprehensive history of the African Methodist Episcopal Zion Church; a church whose roots penetrate deeply into African heritage; whose beginnings were bred out of a people's relentless quest for God in a cultural milieu fraught with the shackles of slavery, sin, and servitude; and whose continuing struggles in the ensuing centuries document the triumphs and tribulations of emancipating and lifting up of a people as the Gospel is proclaimed throughout the world.

Bishop Walls brought to this task a lifetime of preparation. Nurtured in the spirit of the church fathers he emerged from the foot hills of the Blue Ridge Mountains of North Carolina as a boy preacher, and for over 75 years has stirred the souls of men at home and abroad with an electrifying proclamation of the gospel. Steeped in the tradition and mission of the church he has for almost as many years participated in its expansion, rallied to its emancipation thrusts, helped to mold and shape the development of its ecclesiastical order, and provided that kind of creative and avant garde leadership which has been felt, not only in Zion Methodism, but in the religious history of America and the ecumenical world. Disciplined as a student at Livingstone College and Hood Theological Seminary in North Carolina and through graduate pursuits of journalism, philosophy and Bible history at Columbia University and Union Theological Seminary, and earning the M.A. in Christian Education at the University of Chicago; he brings to the writing of this volume the eye of a scholar and pen of a ready writer. Sharpened by experiences which focus the vision, hone the skills, and release the talent; he brings to this writing the wisdom of a lifetime.

The writer has done a stupendous task. He has ferreted out historical facts of the church all but lost to antiquity. He has traced with candor the development of the church from fledgling beginnings to an ecumenical posture. He has placed the periods of storm and stress in perspective; seized upon the church's great moments of religious sensitivity and outreach, and challenged the church to lay claim on its heritage.

The panoramic view of the A.M.E. Zion Church in this one volume work has been structured into eight parts. Parts I and II deal with "beginnings," – a background of religious fervor in Africa, its transplantation to American shores, its manifestation in the emerging black church as it related particularly to Methodism, and inception of the A.M.E. Zion Church. The religious pioneers of these earliest days of the church — some free, some slaves, some as James Varick imbued with the spirit of the American Revolution — have been dealt with inspiringly. They emerge as men possessed with unusual talent, manifold skills, and with a vision of that identity they sought to sustain which had origins deep in ancient cultures on the shores of Africa.

Parts III-VII take the church through its "stormy splits and sunny reunions" and delineate methodically the structuring of the church to be about its business; proclamation, expansion, consolidation, nurture, social welfare, and uplift. Here the ecclesiastical structure is made vivid; bishopric, departments, and boards. But transcending and undergirding it all is the spirit of the mission of Zion Methodism to emancipate, uplift, and disseminate the Gospel.

With interwoven threads of "faith, hope, and charity" in Part VII the writer projects the A.M.E. Zion Church into efforts to implement the dream of social welfare, to participate in the continuing civil rights movements, and to launch into ecumenical movements realizing that "as long as the church is divided we will have a divided world, but the seed of uniting the church must be cultivated with indescribable and never ceasing faith and toil."

The concluding part is entitled "Paramount Functionalities." Here the writer has with succinctness and incisiveness lifted in chronological profile the church fathers,—the 76 bishops of the church elected between 1820 and 1972. The section ends with the listing of the thirty-nine general conferences held during the 178 years history of the A.M.E. Zion Church. With this the writer completes a task well done.

Hence, in the year in which this eminent churchman and leader of the race celebrates his golden anniversary as a prelate of the church, he gives to Christendom and to posterity the monumental completed work: *The African Methodist Episcopal Zion Church: Reality of the Black Church.*

A. McLean Spaulding and
Olivia T. Spaulding
Livingstone College
Salisbury, North Carolina

Part I—Genesis

CHAPTER 1

AFRICAN CIVILIZATION AND RELIGION

All civilizations and cultures have had some species of religion in their basic reasons and practices of origin and continued existence. In the ancient world, religions followed the military, and wherever conquerors reigned, their religion was imposed on the people and the conquered territory. Thus, in a sense, there has been no form of society that has not had religion in its basic principles, and to a degree in its multiple practices. All mankind has believed in a representation of God, either monotheistic or polytheistic, that is, either one God or many gods. It has radiated around material perception and images or mental conception through imagination, microscopic or telescopic, visible or invisible.

Radhakrishnan, the Indian philosopher, states: "The real character of a civilization is to be gathered not so much from its forms and institutions as from the values of the spirit, the furniture of the mind. Religion is the inside of a civilization, the soul as it were of the body of its social organization." [1] Religion precedes all movements except that of finding bread and water, and with this it is practically simultaneous. It created the desire to find the meaning of the world of the present, through work and skill, and the world to come, through revelation and faith. In a way, the religious leader was also the social discoverer, and the applier of his discoveries without knowing much of their

1. S. Radhakrishnan, *East and West in Religion*, pp.44-45.

NOTE: Complete information on all sources can be found in the Bibliography, p.629.

meaning. However, both religion and social experience were helped by working in necessary coordinate effort. For instance, bread and faith have been the concomitant watchword in the Judeo-Christian religion. Gradually prophets and breadwinners became aware of the distinction resident in these annals.

Africa is the cradle of the world's oldest civilization, and the fundamental forms and culture came originally through Africa. Asia is its proud successor. Great founders of empires in the ancient world were Africans. W. E. B. DuBois describes Africa in history:

> Africa is at once the most romantic and the most tragic of continents. Its very names reveal its mystery and wide-reaching influence. It is the "Ethiopia" of the Greek, the "Kush" and "Punt" of the Egyptian, and the Arabian "Land of the Blacks." To modern Europe it is the "Dark Continent" and "Land of Contrasts"; in literature it is the seat of the Sphinx and the lotus eaters, the home of the dwarfs, gnomes, and pixies, and the refuge of the gods; in commerce it is the slave mart and the source of ivory, ebony, rubber, gold, and diamonds. What other continent can rival in interest this Ancient of Days? [2]

We note that "the great progenitor of the Hebrew race and the founder of their religion sought refuge in Africa from the ravages of famine," when we read in Gen. 12:10: "And there was a famine in the land; and Abram went down into Egypt to sojourn there, for the famine was grievous in the land." [3]

Jethro, the priest of Midian, was head of this ancient nation before the Jews ever organized as a nation. The father-in-law of Moses, the great Jewish leader, and avowedly the greatest exponent of jurisprudence of the ages was a priest of Yahweh, and resided at the sacred mountain where the deity commissioned Moses to deliver the Israelites from Egypt. [4] Thus states Blyden:

> [In] Africa, Moses, the greatest lawgiver the world has ever seen, was born and educated. To this land also resorted the ancient philosophers of Greece and Rome, to gaze upon its wonders and gather inspiration from its arts and sciences. Later on, a greater than Moses and than all the prophets and philosophers, when in infancy, was preserved from death in Africa. "Arise," was the message conveyed by the angel to Joseph, "Arise, and take the young child and his mother and flee into Egypt, and be thou there until I bring thee word; for Herod will seek the young child to destroy him." When, in his final hours, the Saviour of mankind struggled up the heights of Calvary, under the weight of the Cross, accused by Asia and condemned by Europe, Africa furnished the man to relieve him of his burden. "And as they led him away they laid hold upon one Simon, a Cyrenian, coming out of the country, and on him they laid the Cross that he might bear it after Jesus." [5]

Africa was the scene of the basic letters, arts, architecture, and mechanics, including the hygienic sciences of the ancient world. Language was born in Africa. The Hieroglyphic, dating from before 3000 B.C., is the origin of all written languages. "*Hieratic,* a priestly 'short-hand' evolved soon afterwards; and *Demotic,* a much faster cursive developed shortly before 600 B.C." [6] Another alphabetical script was invented by the Meroites in about the third century B.C. It is said of these Kushites of Meroe, and their highly specific civilization, that

---

2. W. E. Burghardt DuBois, *The Negro,* p.9.
3. Edward Blyden, *Christianity, Islam and the Negro Race,* p.135.
4. *Encyclopedia Britannica,* 14th ed., Vol. XIII, p.29.
5. Blyden, *op. cit.,* p.135.
6. Basil Davidson, *Africa in History,* p.24.

ANCIENT SCRIPTS INVENTED BY AFRICANS

Sabaean form of script used by the Ethiopians early in their history, and from which Ge'ez was developed. Fragment of an inscription from an altar near Axum. *Used by permission of Weidenfeld and Nicholson, London.*

Ancient Egypt's three main scripts: *Hieroglyphic,* dating from 3000 B.C., *Hieratic,* and *Demotic.* By permission of MacMillan Publishing Co., Inc. Copyright 1969 by Basil Davidson.

they were people of "extraordinary diversity, creative skill, and technological success. They combined a stubborn attachment to their own traditions with the speculative and syncretic approach to new ideas and fashions that may be characteristic of all strong trading cultures." [7] Therefore, "this Kushite alphabet, and the Kushite script in which it was written, may reasonably be placed among the outstanding cultural achievements of ancient Africa." [8]

In the realm of mechanics, the wheel was born in Africa. In architecture, the keystone of the arch was born in Africa; indeed, some of the oldest buildings still existing in the world are in Africa. The Sphinx and other structures in ancient Egypt and Ethiopia are living monuments to these master builders.

Volumes could be, and have been, written of the fortitude and courage of Africans, such as Makeda, Queen of Sheba and Cleopatra, Queen of Egypt, two of the world's foremost female rulers of earliest history. The incomparable prophet, Jeremiah, was heroically saved from the dungeon and the deathly mire by the Ethiopian, Ebed-Melech (Jeremiah 38:7-13). The African, Hannibal, goes down as a symbolic general of the ancient world. He was the first man to cross the Alps with an army when there was nothing to get across but snows. Until that time, they had been sailing around the Alps on seaways, but they had not discovered the way nor did they possess the enduring courage to get over. This hero from Carthage was "one of the most renowned warriors that has ever appeared on a field of battle." [9]

7. *Ibid.,* pp.35-36.
8. Basil Davidson, *A History of East and Central Africa to the Late Nineteenth Century,* p.13.
9. J. W. Hood, *One Hundred Years of the African Methodist Episcopal Zion Church,* p.34.

[From]   the earliest period of the history of nations, the African race had been known as an industrious people, cultivators of the soil. The grain fields of Ethiopia and Egypt were the themes of the poet, and their garners, the subject of the historians. Like the present America, all the world went to Africa, to get a supply of commodities. Their massive piles of masonry, their skillful architecture, their subterranean vaults, their deep and mysterious wells, their extensive artificial channels, their mighty sculptured solid rocks, and provinces of stone quarries gave indisputable evidence, of the hardihood of that race of people. (10)

All this and much more may be said of Africa. Coupled with this stupendous record of African religion, civilization, and culture is the development of the black man's religion, not only in Africa but in the Western world, through immeasurable tribulations and miraculous faith. Therefore, as DuBois states:

The religion of Africa is the universal animism of fetishism of primitive peoples, rising to polytheism and approaching monotheism chiefly, but not wholly, as a result of Christian and Islamic missions. Of fetishism there is much misapprehension. It is not mere senseless degradation. It is a philosophy of life. . .

This then is the Gift of Black Folk to the new world. Thus in singular and fine sense the slave became the master, the bond servant became free and the meek not only inherited the earth but made that heritage a thing of questing for eternal youth, of fruitful labor, of joy and music, of the free spirit and of the ministering hand, of wide and poignant sympathy with men in their struggle to live and love which is, after all, the end of being. (11)

Everything we know about the African past, its civilization, culture, and religion in particular, confirms that African development has run in an unbroken line from its origins until the present day. The African races are numerous, and religion prevails among them in many forms. Yet, wherever those of Africa and African descent dwell upon the face of the earth, there is generally a belief, common in the bond of suffering, which is so prophetically expressed by Bishop Hood that "the black man shall not be robbed of his record which he has made during the ages." He further states that

the Holy Bible has stood as an everlasting rock in the black man's defense. . . . We acknowledge with humility and thanksgiving our great obligation to God for his goodness toward the race. At every step in this investigation we see plainly the hand divinely interposed on our behalf; and the more we investigate the subject the more deeply do we feel the obligation the race is under to love, fear, and serve that God who has so carefully watched over our destiny. (12)

10. Martin Robeson Delany, *The Condition, Elevation, Emigration and Destiny of the Colored People*, p.53.
11. W. E. Burghardt DuBois, *The Gift of Black Folk*, p.326, 340.
12. Hood, *op. cit.*, p.27.

CHAPTER 2

AFRICAN ORIGIN IN CHRISTIAN RELIGION

This chapter will discuss the origin of Christianity in Africa, how it came to America, and the sources and implications of its meanings, which have been developed in the Negro experience of the Christian church. Africa was in the absolute origin of Christianity from the days that Jesus' parents fled to Egypt for the preservation of their newborn child, Jesus, until the day the first slave was auctioned by Christians in Jamestown, Virginia.

In *The World and Africa,* by W. E. B. DuBois, Theodor Mommsen states: "It was through Africa that Christianity became the religion of the world. Tertullian and Cyprian were from Carthage; Arnobius from Sicca Veneria; Lactantius, and probably in like manner Minucius Felix, in spite of their Latin names, were natives of Africa, and not less so, Augustine. In Africa the Church found its most zealous confessors of the faith and its most gifted defenders. [1] In addition to Mommsen's statement, DuBois states: "Origen, Athanasius, and Saint Cyril were from the Nile valley. At the head of the Catholic hierarchy at Rome, three popes were African by birth: Victor I (187-198), who defended the Roman date for Easter; Miltiades (311-314), who was pope when the Emperor entered Rome as a Christian; and Gelasius I (492-496), who defended the rights of the papacy against the state." [2]

The oldest Christian Church on the African continent, representing black Africa more directly, is the Ethiopic Church, securely established A.D. 330, when Saint Athanasius, Bishop of Alexandria, consecrated Frumentius as Bishop of Ethiopia. The legend of Queen of Sheba came from a group in the highlands of Ethiopia, which had developed a culture over a thousand years before the coming of Christ. It was natural, therefore, that the pursuit of knowledge of their life's practice sent the Queen of Sheba, like her tribe, to inquire into the splendors that were advertised about Solomon.

The northern part of this continent and the western portions of Asia are the specific regions which

> saw the birth of Christianity and in which Christianity registered its first great advances. It included Palestine, where the founder of Christianity lived and taught. It embraced Syria, in whose former capital, Antioch, there had been an early center of non-Jewish Christianity. In it was Asia Minor, the first large area where Christianity became the dominant faith. It was the home of the Armenians, the first professedly Christian nation. North Africa had been the scene of an early marked development of Latin Christianity, and (as stated before) the birthplace of Augustine, the most influential of the Latin-using church fathers. [3]

The Africans did not have much affiliation in Judaism, and there was a feeling against Egypt because Jews had been held slaves by Egyptians and

1. W. E. Burghardt DuBois, *The World and Africa,* p.146.
2. *Ibid.,* p.146.
3. Latourette, *A History of the Expansion of Christianity,* Vol. 6, p.6.

Egyptians did not partake of the Jewish religion. When Christianity came, it found the Asiatic world in the hands of other religions than Judaism. The prophets had begun to open the door for other religions and to prophesy the God of Israel would become the God of nations. By the time the Christians got here, they found an atmosphere for a universal God growing and proceeded to extend the idea wherever they went that God was the Father of nations, and Jesus came to save all of the world. So the world's greatest prophetic religion is the Fatherhood of God and the brotherhood of man. It is on the wave of that prophecy, "Princes shall come out of Egypt and Ethiopia shall stretch forth her hand unto God" a rediscovery of human unity is put afloat in the world. It was a natural thing, therefore, for the prophets to say this concerning their hopes for the future of the people of Africa, as for the people of the whole world. That was expressing the extreme victory of the unity of mankind, which door would be opened by the Judeo-Christian religion.

The religion that has boldly sponsored and defended freedom (barring its corruption) is the Christian religion. The Christian religion came to America by way of Europe, although it was born in Asia and grew up in Africa and southern Europe. It was congenial to the rising intelligence of the Western world. It became paramount in America and crowded out all other species by its missionary activity. While the West originated the practice of freedom in religion, the concept was born in Africa. There were movements toward discovering the meaning of man as a social being. Africans also made discoveries of science in the environment of man, and sought to apply its objects and opportunities to man's comfort and progress.

We are considering how an infant Christian movement began in a race. The African was an ancient superstitious race like the rest when Christianity came. To a degree, many Africans did not accept it until after it had come to the Western world and gone back to Africa by way of European slavery and the slave trade. The hostility to the earliest white Christians in Africa was therefore logical, because the first act of Christianity was to exploit the African with brutal habits, degenerating economy, and the slave trade. This produced revolt of the natives. It must be remembered that slave trade was more than European; it was also African. The conquering tribes, in their internal warfares, sold their conquered brothers to the European and Asiatic slave traders, who carried them off to their colonies and made them slaves or sold them to slave traffickers. However, this hostility of the Africans involved the Christians for the most part. After Christianity had learned the lesson and began to move away from the obstacle of degeneration, cruelty, corruption, and to an extent, reduced exploitation, missionaries were admitted.

Christianity only got to the Western Negro, as a whole, through the migration to the Western world.

Slavery was first introduced in America on the island of Hispaniola [Haiti] where the aborigines of America and the West Indies had been found not sufficiently robust for the work in the mines and the plantations. Large numbers of Negroes were imported by the Portuguese, who owned the great portion of the African coast then known, into Europe a half century before the discovery of America. (4)

Beginning with its introduction in Virginia in 1619, slavery gradually made

4. John W. Cromwell, *The Negro in American History*, p.2.
5. *Ibid.*, p.3.

its way into all the thirteen colonies, and received the sanction of their several legislatures. [5]

John Wesley's *Thoughts on Slavery*, in an attempt to awaken his fellow-citizens regarding that part of Africa "whence the Negroes were brought," Guinea, states:

You know how populous, how fruitful, how pleasant it was [this country], a few years ago. You know, the people were not stupid, not wanting in sense, considering the few means of improvement they enjoyed. Neither did you find them savage, fierce, cruel, treacherous, or unkind to strangers. On the contrary, they were, in most parts, a sensible and ingenious people. They were kind and friendly, courteous and obliging, and remarkably fair and just in their dealings. Such are the men whom you hire their own countrymen to tear away from this lovely country; part by stealth; part by force, part made captives in those wars which you raise or foment on purpose. You have seen them torn away—children from their parents, parents from their children; husbands from their wives, wives from their beloved husbands, brethren and sisters from each other. You have dragged them who had never done you any wrong, perhaps in chains, from their native shore. You have forced them into your ships like a herd of swine;—them who had souls immortal as your own; only some of them leaped into the sea, and resolutely stayed under water, till they could suffer no more from you. You have stowed them together as close as ever they could lie, without any regard either to decency or convenience. And when many of them have been poisoned by foul air, or had sunk under various hardships, you have seen their remains delivered to the deep, till the sea should give up his dead. You have carried the survivors into the vilest slavery, never to end but with life. [6]

Therefore, the story of the Negro minister and Christianity among Negroes took place largely in America, where the slave trade became paramount. The European used his slave trade in his colonies in America. Incidentally and persistently, the major colonizers of the Western world who brought their brawn and endurance to the colonies were black men. Yet, there was a great departure in the formation of the United States. By a narrow margin, the vote came near putting abolition of slavery into the Constitution. It was led by Thomas Jefferson, ably assisted by John Jay, Alexander Hamilton, Quakers, and many others. At that time there was no Negro church general organization. There was only here and there a congregation sparsely organized.

We approach the period of the black ministers' and black churches' contribution in the development of their race. As we read the history of these turbulent and struggling days, we see that all the black churches were born in white congregations, East and West, North and South. Organized Christianity is the major thing the black race got out of slavery, second to which was the English language. Slavery was a big price to pay, however, especially when we remember the boon of free civilization was granted to other branches of the human race without the blighting prolongation of slavery.

The human race seems to have developed from the beginning by the strong oppressing the weak. An early great instance of universal slavery was the Greeks, who became slaves to the Romans, but it was slavery on a high order. The Romans needed the Greek culture to add to their civil polity and military prowess. They therefore gave them a status of serving, intellectually and culturally, the Roman ruling class. Greeks furnished the philosophy, the knowledge for skillful living, and all the culture the world boasted of in the days

6. John Wesley, *Thoughts on Slavery-1774*, pp.70-72.

of the Roman power. The Roman arms conquered the Greeks, but the Greek culture conquered the Romans. Fortunately the Romans were able to distribute the Greek culture to the ends of the world, and that culture still rules the unfolding and emerging cultures of man.

But even earlier, there were dim ages of developing knowledge in which one group took precedence over other groups amid the tumultuous changes of rising and evolving prehistoric nations. The earliest races and tribes were their progenitors, so that some forms of slavery were extant before the coming of the nations in recorded history. In that story are the changes and successions in such nations as Egypt, Babylon, Syria, and Persia, who at one time or another ruled the world and had conquered peoples under their thrall. The Jews were actuated by the concept of one God of all men of all nations. They suffered slavery in their development, but they freed themselves by God's guidance under Moses, and henceforth have been an indestructible element in human society.

In these times we have variations of slavery and holdovers. For instance, the African slaves of South America were absorbed, but in the United States and most of the Western islands, the distinction was cruelly persistent for three centuries. The holdover still exists in America, and that which has been removed, for the most part, has been done by friends of freedom and the black man's own organization, primarily his church organization, which first gradually awoke to the meaning of Christianity in a slave tossed world through the abolitionary efforts and the final freedom, born of the era of Lincoln. In the Western world the Africans had adhered to Christianity, and won their freedom similarly as the Hebrews did in the ancient world.

Thus says a historical sage of the A.M.E. Zion Church:

Ever since Simon the Ethiopian bore the cross of Christ, the Negro, whenever sufficiently enlightened, has stood by it. In Egypt, where Christians have been oppressed for ages, and Christianity has been almost crushed out, the Copts, the descendants of the ancient Egyptians or Mizraimites, still cling to the cross, even in that dark land. While skepticism, adventism, universalism, annihilationism, probationism, and many other pernicious isms are gaining ground among the white people, the masses of black Christians are still earnestly contending for the faith once delivered to the saints. It was probably the purpose of Jehovah in maintaining the identity of the race in this country, and forming the African Church, to make it a stronghold of pure and undefiled religion. [7]

7. Hood, *One Hundred Years,* pp.24-25.

CHAPTER 3

THE PERIOD OF ORGANIZATIONAL CONSCIOUSNESS IN AMERICA

And they made their lives bitter with hard bondage, in mortar, and in brick, and in all manner of service in the field: all their service, wherein they made them serve was with rigour.   Exodus 1:14

This quotation about the Jews in their Egyptian slavery is comprehended almost completely by the experiences of the African in American slavery. Even after the African had been on the continent over 200 years, the strong abolition journal in Ohio, founded by Benjamin Lundy [1] stated:

Altho' we have publicly declared, over and over, forty-six times, that *ALL MEN* are, by nature, free, we still have the hardihood, nay, the consummate wickedness; to hold 2,000,000 of the inhabitants of this land in unconditional bondage—a bondage more grievous than was ever suffered by any people under heaven, without affording them the most distant hope of liberation, either for themselves or their posterity!!! [2]

In the midst of this suffering, the Negro began to become conscious of his need of God. He therefore sought the means of organizing this discovery into his corporate life. Here we begin the period of self-awakening and organization in American Negro life. It started in religion, during this period of the race's severest pressure and sorrow. Man is incurably religious, and it is advantageous as a release in suffering.

There were spots of Negro membership in white churches, but the fashion of the age was to segregate them. As they grew larger, they became more and more dissatisfied with this segregation. In the intervals between their work hours, even at night until the early morning, they gathered and held worship in their own way and impulse. Characteristic, of course, was the exercise of emotions in the midst of their overall belief in God and his Son, Jesus Christ, and life after death. Their sorrow songs, as some historians have designated them, were filled with hopes of the future life and participation with God and his children in another world. In this period, there was only here and there a congregation that grew strong enough to want a self-directing organization.

As slavery grew and took stronger hold, the method was to request the privilege of worshipping between the hours of the white services. At first the only preachers permitted to serve them were white because it was feared to have Negroes meet privately under their own leadership, as there was a common fear of slave organization among the masters. However, gradually slave groups obtained permission to conduct their own worship services under white

1. Peter Bergman, *The Chronological History of the Negro in America*, p.116.
2. *The Genius of Universal Emancipation*, No. 1, Vol. II, July 1822.

guidance. But sentiment gradually changed, as the Negro persisted in organizing groups under voluntary black leadership, gaining permission from their masters to make their original efforts in church life.

The first effort of Negroes to organize independently was discovered sometime between 1773 and 1775, when a Baptist church was begun by one Mr. Palmer at Silver Bluff, S.C. This group was fortunate in having a kind master, George Galphin, who became a patron of this congregation and permitted a preacher, David George, to be ordained for this special work. They suffered misfortune when Galphin, a patriot, abandoned his slaves in his flight for refuge from the British, and the Silver Bluff Church was driven into exile. David George and 50 of these slaves went over to the British in Savannah, where they were freed in 1778. The Silver Bluff Church was revived, however, under the direction of Rev. Jesse Peter. [3] Meantime, George Liele, who had been the servant of a British officer, and a leader in the Silver Bluff Church, moved on and founded a church in Savannah, Ga.

The great promoter of the work in Savannah was Andrew Bryan, who was almost a martyr to the cause. "The greater his influence among the slaves, the more the masters were inclined to believe that his work could result only in that of servile insurrection." One time he was beaten and cut by slaveholders and their friends until the blood ran to the ground, but he lived through this and other vicissitudes almost as gruelling and died with the confidence and highest praise of the Savannah Baptist (white) Association. [4] Lott Cary was one of the first to go to Africa, where he achieved a miraculous service, living and dying among Africans. The Negro Baptist Missionary Convention is named in his memory. Many more pioneer Baptist preachers in the West and North carried on the development of this denomination during this crucial period of Negro sufferings.

The Methodists did not develop preachers who founded congregations until the coming of the National Negro Methodist Churches. There is one exception, however. The one black preacher who founded a congregation in the Methodist system in that earliest period was Henry Evans of Fayetteville, North Carolina, in 1790. The following extract, on *Henry Evans and The Evans Metropolitan A.M.E. Zion Church of Fayetteville* is taken from the *Autobiography of Bishop William Capers:*

> The most remarkable man in Fayetteville when I went there, and who died during my stay, was a negro, by the name of Henry Evans. I say *the most* remarkable in view of his class; and I call him negro with unfeigned respect. . . .I have known and loved and honored not a few negroes in my life, who were probably as pure of heart as Evans, or anybody else. . . .Remarkable. . . .I use the word in a broader sense for Henry Evans, who was confessedly the father of the Methodist Church, white and black, in Fayetteville, and the best preacher of his time in that quarter; and he was so *remarkable* as to have become the greatest curiosity of the town; insomuch that distinguished visitors hardly felt that they might pass a Sunday in Fayetteville without hearing him preach. Evans was from Virginia; a shoe-maker by trade, and I think, was born free. He became a Christian and a Methodist quite young, and was licensed to preach in Virginia. While yet a young man, he determined to remove to Charleston, South Carolina, thinking that he might succeed best there at his trade. But having reached

3. Carter G. Woodson, *The History of the Negro Church*, pp.35,36.
4. *Ibid.*, pp.37-45.

Fayetteville on his way to Charleston, and something detaining him for a few days, his spirit was stirred at perceiving that the people of his race in that town were wholly given to profanity and lewdness, never hearing preaching of any denomination, and living emphatically without hope and without God in the world. This determined him to stop in Fayetteville; and he began to preach to the negroes, with great effect. The town council interfered, and nothing in his power could prevail with them to permit him to preach. He then withdrew to the sand-hills, out of town and held meetings in the woods, changing his appointments from place to place. No law was violated, while the council was effectually eluded; and so the opposition passed into the hands of the mob. These he worried out by changing his appointments, so that when they went to work their will upon him he was preaching somewhere else. Meanwhile, whatever the most honest purpose of a simple heart could do to reconcile his enemies was employed by him for that end. He eluded no one in private, but sought opportunities to explain himself; avowed the purity of his intentions; and even begged to be subjected to the scrutiny of any surveillance that might be thought proper to prove his inoffensiveness; anything, so that he might but be allowed to preach. Happily for him and the cause of religion, his honest countenance and earnest pleadings were soon powerfully seconded by the fruits of his labors. One after another began to suspect their servants of attending his preaching, not because they were made worse, but wonderfully better. . . .

It was not long before the mob was called off by a change in the current of opinion, and Evans was allowed to preach in town. At that time there was not a single church-edifice in town, and but one congregation (Presbyterian), who worshipped in what was called the State-house, under which was the market; and it was plainly Evans or nobody to preach to the negroes. Now, too, of the mistresses there were not a few, and some masters, who were brought to think that the preaching which had proved so beneficial to their servants might be good for them also; and the famous negro preacher had some whites as well as blacks to hear him. From these the gracious influence spread to others, and a meeting-house was built. It was a frame of wood, weatherboarded only on the outside, without plastering, about fifty feet long by thirty feet wide.

Seats distinctly separated, were at first appropriated to the whites, near the pulpit. But Evans had already become famous, and these seats were insufficient. Indeed, the negroes seemed likely to lose their preacher, negro though he was, while the whites, crowded out of their appropriate seats, took possession of those in the rear. Meanwhile Evans had represented to the preacher of the Bladen Circuit how things were going, and induced him to take his meeting-house into the circuit, and constitute a church there. And now, there was no longer room for the negroes in the house when Evans preached; and for the accommodation of both classes, the weather-boards were knocked off and sheds were added to the house on either side; the whites occupying the whole of the original building, and the negroes those sheds as a part of the same house.

Evans' dwelling was a shed at the pulpit end of the church. And that was the identical state of the case when I was pastor. Often was I in that shed, and much to my edification. I have known not many preachers who appeared more conversant with Scripture than Evans, or whose conversation was more instructive as to the things of God. He seemed always deeply impressed with the responsibility of his position;. . .And yet Henry Evans was a Boanerges, and in his duty feared not the face of man.

I have said that he died during my stay in Fayetteville this year (1810).

The death of such a man could not but be triumphant, and his was distinguishingly so. I did not witness it, but was with him just before he died; and as he appeared to me, triumph should express but partially the character of his feelings, as the word imports exultation at a victory, or at most the victory and exultation together. It seems to me as if the victory he had won was no longer an object, but rather as if his spirit, past the contemplation of triumphs on earth, were already in communion with heaven. Yet his last breath was drawn in the act of pronouncing 1 Corinthians xv. 57: "Thanks be to God, which giveth us the victory through our Lord Jesus Christ." It was my practice to hold a meeting with the blacks in the church directly after morning preaching every Sunday. And on the Sunday before his death, during this meeting, the little door between his humble shed and the chancel where I stood was opened and the dying man entered for a last farewell to his people. He was almost too feeble to stand at all, but supporting himself by the railing of the chancel, he said: "I have come to say my last word to you. It is this: None but Christ. Three times I have had my life in jeopardy for preaching the gospel to you. Three times I have broken the ice on the edge of the water and swam across the Cape Fear to preach the gospel to you. And now, if in my last hour I could trust to that or to any thing else but Christ crucified, for my salvation, all should be lost and my soul perish forever." A noble testimony! Worthy not of Evans only, but St. Paul. His funeral at the church was attended by a greater concourse of persons than had been seen on any funeral occasion before. The whole community appeared to mourn his death, and the universal feeling seemed to be that in honoring the memory of Henry Evans we were paying a tribute to virtue and religion. He was buried under the chancel of the church of which he had been in so remarkably a manner the founder. [5]

One of Evans' three or four preaching points during the days he was driven into hiding was the house of Dicey Hammons, grandmother of Bishop Thomas H. Lomax, who later pastored the church and built the first brick structure on that site. [6] This church was not registered in the Methodist yearly conference records, as it was a general practice not to list black societies, especially in the South, in the printed journals of early American Methodism. In the midst of rapid growth of the African Methodist churches in the South after the Civil War, Evans Metropolitan was taken into the A.M.E. Zion Church in 1866, through the North Carolina Conference, by Bishop Joseph Jackson Clinton. James Walker Hood was sent to this charge the following year, to save an attempt to take the church out of Zion connection. Thus, this was the beginning of a new chapter in history, of national and international note for the Evans Metropolitan Church and James Walker Hood.

Circumstances for black preachers in the Methodist Church were much more crucial than the Baptists, although large numbers of Negroes joined the movement from its beginning in America in 1766. [7] The black Methodists, in the meantime, were developing ministers in the white congregations who began to organize churches. They were licensed to preach, but were denied ordination until the General Conference of 1800 passed a limited ordination rule for African preachers. It is recorded that progenitors of the Mother A.M.E. Zion Church, in New York City, were meeting privately as early as 1780. [8] The state

---

5. M. H. Moore, *Pioneers of Methodism in North Carolina and Virginia,* pp.310-314.
6. T. H. Lomax, *"Progress of the Third Quarter. . ." in* A.M.E. Zion Quarterly Review, October 1898, p.3.
7. W. E. Burghardt DuBois, *The Gift of Black Folk,* p.325.
8. J. W. Hood, *Sketch of the Early History of the A.M.E. Zion Church,* Vol. II, p.16.

law of New York had prevented Negro groups from holding open meetings since the Insurrection of 1712. [9]

At the Eighth Yearly Conference held in Baltimore, the following question appeared in the minutes: "Ought not the assistant [10] to meet the colored people himself, and appoint as helpers in his absence proper white persons, and not suffer them to stay late and meet by themselves? Answer: Yes."

Jesse Lee states that "they concluded that the preachers should meet the black people in class; and appoint white men to lead them, and not let them stay late at meetings, nor allow them to meet by themselves." [11] At the organization of the Methodist Episcopal Church in America (the Christmas Conference), 1784, the following was enacted: "Question 41: Are there any directions to be given concerning the Negroes? Answer: Let every preacher, as often as possible always appoint a proper white person as their leader. Let the assistant also make a regular return to the conference of the number of negroes in society in their respective circuits." [12]

These stiff rules coming out of the Methodist bodies were as reprehensible to the New York group as to its Southern constituents. Is it any wonder that a black organization could spring forward in New York in the eighteenth century, under both the pressure of church laws and state regulations, and of extreme poverty, with laws still enforced that prohibited Negroes to own property or have tangible assets? [13]

This earliest group of New Yorkers, led by James Varick, were members of the group which finally organized a congregation, now known as Mother Zion, in 1796, and received white preachers for a period. During that period, churches were organized in New York City, Long Island, New Haven, Connecticut, New Jersey, Philadelphia, and eastern Pennsylvania. Among the earliest pastors of the A.M.E. Zion Church were Abraham Thompson and William Miller in New York; William Carman, Long Island; Leven Smith and James Anderson, New Haven; Christopher Rush, Newark; and Simon Murray, Wesley Church, Philadelphia. [14]

The other early Methodist Church was Mother Bethel A.M.E. Church, which was organized in Philadelphia, Pa., a city and state founded by Quakers, the most forthright Protestant group in opposing slavery. The first anti-slavery society in America in 1775 had been composed largely of these Quakers, and

9. David Kobrin, *The Black Minority in New York;* pp.13-14; Roi Ottley and William J. Weatherby, eds., *The Negro in New York,* p.24.
10. The Methodist Church until 1784 was controlled by John Wesley's Methodist Movement in England, and leading missionaries of Methodist societies in other countries were known as Mr. Wesley's assistants. In this country, there were three categories: *Helpers* were the young preachers in each circuit; *assistants* were the oldest preachers in each circuit, who had charge of young preachers and the business of the circuit; *general assistants* were preachers who had charge of all circuits and appointed all the preachers to their several circuits; they were also known as general superintendents, to assist Mr. Wesley in carrying on the work of God in a general way, without being confined to one circuit. Francis Asbury was at this time Wesley's Assistant in America. (Jesse Lee, *A Short History of the Methodists in the U.S.A.,* p.72)
11. *Ibid.*
12. George A. Phoebus, "Beams of Light...," *from Diaries... of Ezekiel Cooper,* p.313.
13. Roi Ottley and William J. Weatherby, *op. cit.,* p.24; *The Colonial Laws of New York,* Vol. I, pp.764-5
14. John J. Moore, *History of the A.M.E. Zion Church,* p.94; B. F. Wheeler, *The Varick Family,* p.47.
15. Benjamin Quarles, *The Negro in the American Revolution,* p.192.

they were the foremost in the movement which led Pennsylvania to become the first state to abolish slavery. [15] Led by Richard Allen, the Bethel A.M.E. group built and dedicated their first church in 1794. This group also received white pastors and was governed by the Methodists for a while. [16] They organized churches in Baltimore, Philadelphia, Attleborough, Pa., and Salem, N.J. Some of the noted founders of the churches in Baltimore were Daniel Coker, who was elected first bishop of the church and declined in order to go to Africa and build up the religious work there, Stephen Hill, David Smith, Richard Williams, and Henry Harden. In Philadelphia, assisting Richard Allen were Jacob Tapsico, Clayton Durham, James Champion, and Thomas Webster. In Wilmington, Del., the popular Peter Spencer, and in Charleston, S.C., Morris Brown. [17] This movement of freedom in Philadelphia was divided after they left the St. George Methodist Episcopal Church in 1787, where they suffered indignities, and organized the Free African Society. The majority of the members voted to join the Church of England, and that wing, led by Absalom Jones, became the first Episcopal Church of Africans in America. [18] The first African Union Methodist Church was incorporated at Wilmington, Del., in 1807. [19]

Another instance in the preorganizational work of a Methodist minister was Harry Housier, assistant to Bishop Francis Asbury, Black Harry became known as one of the inimitable preachers of the pioneering group in America. [20]

Among these pioneers also, in North Carolina, was John Chavis, a Presbyterian who studied for a time at Princeton and was an itinerant missionary by 1801 under the General Assembly. He preached to both white and black until 1831 when Negroes were forbidden by the state legislature to function.

Famous also was Jack of Virginia, who became a licensed Baptist preacher and was noted for the high standard of conduct which he demanded of his members. [22]

Another leader in this early period was Prince Hall of Boston, who was not a pioneer in the establishment of the Negro church, but the founder of Negro freemasonry in America, when he obtained a charter from England in 1787. [23]

This was a growing race consciousness, with the church taking the lead in it as it began to make concrete structures and institutions, both at home and in the mission fields, above all in the family. In the meantime, its freedom organizations and other secret and charitable organizations were looming up. The Underground Railroad was practically a church movement. Its prime leaders were preachers, and churches were used as Underground Railroad stations.

This and other race conscious movements were being sponsored by the church, and there was a reason. The Negro people were sustaining the human trait of their religious nature. Some have tried to call this superstition and denominate our race group as superstitious people because of their intense religiousness. But we will not distinguish religion from what certain free-thinkers call superstition, for it does not originate in the five senses, but originates and influences beyond the five senses as what is called *spiritual*.

---

16. Richard Allen, *The Life Experience, and Gospel Labors of the Rt. Rev. Richard Allen,* p.20; *The Journal of Francis Asbury,* Elmer T. Clark, J. Manning Potts and Jacob Payton, ed., Vol. II, p.18
17. Daniel Payne, *History of the African Methodist Episcopal Church,* pp.13-14.
18. Woodson, *op. cit.,* p.64.
19. *Ibid.,* p.93.
20. *Ibid.,* p.48.
21. Latourette, *A History of the Expansion of Christianity,* Vol. IV, p.336.
22. *Ibid.,* pp.336-7.
23. Bardolph, *The Negro Vanguard,* p.35.

CHAPTER 4

METHODIST IDENTITY

Methodism is a spiritual movement in the temporal environment. These would be cold words if they were not built upon hearts pregnant with celestial fire and hands and bodies absorbed in a wholehearted trial to fulfill and expand the spirit and fervency of this potent reality of divine presence and meaning in the concrete environment.

It was the bold attempt of Methodism to bring to bear anew in society the eternal principles of the New Testament, mankind's only photograph of the person and action of our divine Lord in body and in character. Everything is seen by a true Methodist as stemming from the Father of the universe through this human-divine personality who trod the flint-hills of Judaea and the narrow valleys of Galilee on the Jordan.

From the time John and Charles Wesley and two associate students (later joined by George Whitefield and others) formed the Holy Club at Oxford University in 1729, "they endeavored to win fellow students to a studious and virtuous life and to obtain a thorough knowledge of the Scriptures in the original tongues. They visited the sick, took charge of schools for the poor, taught in the parish workhouses, preached in the prisons, and labored to better the conditions of the prisoners." [1] Thus we have the meaning of *Methodist*, the term applied to this group because of their "serious deportment and methodical habits of study and life;" [2] their systematic division of their time each day, allotting a period for study, another for prayer, another for work of various kinds, and another for reading the Bible. It has become the acknowledged name of one of the largest branches of the Church of Christ.

This young group "went about their new work with as much wisdom as earnestness. . and their enthusiasm was mistaken for fanaticism. . . Religion alive, moving, working, painfully disturbed the careless, gay, worldliness which was then dominant." The term for this Oxford group, "Sacramentarians," seems to have preceded Methodists, which was the name that survived. "John Wesley's definition of the word in his dictionary, published in 1753, would account for the survival. 'A METHODIST is one who lives according to the method laid down in the Bible.' " [3] The stress laid upon conversion, based upon John Wesley's experience of his heart being "strangely warm," is the primary point in Methodist experience. Thus the religion of the Methodist is centered on Christian experience. From their evangelical labors and divine influence derived what is known in Methodism as united societies.

The rise of these united societies, first in Europe, then in America, was no less than "a company of men having the form and seeking the power of godliness, united in order to pray together, to receive the word of exhortation, and to watch over one another in love, that they may help each other to work

1. Henry Wheeler, One Thousand Questions and Answers, p.2.
2. *Ibid.*
3. W. J. Townsend, H. B. Workman, George Eayres, *A New History of Methodism*, Vol. I, pp.140-143.

out their salvation." (4) This was the origin of class meetings in Methodism. John Wesley, who in 1739 began to meet with small groups who earnestly desired that he spend time with them in prayer and give them such spiritual advice as he thought needful, from time to time, (5) was the first class leader, and Methodists the world over stemmed from that class and its successors. "In the beginning there was no plan to organize a new Church. But the eighteenth century revival of religion among the common people, which swept over England, inspired by John and Charles Wesley and their associates, and the course of events that followed that great revival made the organization of a new Church necessary. The result was The Methodist Church." (6)

"Methodism is Christianity in earnest," said John Wesley. The great founder of this movement did not mean that Christianity was not originally born a religion in earnest. Nothing could be more earnest than Jesus on the cross and at the resurrection, and the apostles after the resurrection. In the infant days of the Christian movement they suffered hard work, were earnest in sacrifice, were tenacious in persecution, died in prisons or were burned at the stake, met death when tossed on the heads of bulls, or in dens of lions, or in caldrons of oil, or on crosses, or in the hellish fires of Nero's burning Rome. From under the graves and catacombs they came and went to bury their identity, and at the same time carry on their useful toil. This was indeed earnestness beyond description. Christian society is the fulfillment of deathly earnestness. But much of this is lost through organization and thinned out through efforts of ease and superficial church rules and indulgences.

In the Middle Ages the church suffered almost the death of indifference, and of social economic usurpation, or soulless formation. The church itself became the instrument of persecution, the cruel steam roller of suppression of conscience, and the iron heel that destroyed freedom. Wesley's England was heir to this progress in cruelty, and the church had practically lost its soul. The ministry had backslidden. The laity was enjoying freedom from love and service. An age of selfishness, heartless greed, and the infernal slave trade had seized the British nation and many European countries, and the Western church seemed content to have it so. Thus when the Wesleys organized the praying societies of Oxford in Britain, to restore the church as a salvation organ in England, the battle was on anew between good and evil.

Earnestness, indeed, was Methodism of this new day of Christianity's leadership and rebirth. All around Europe and the Western world the evils of Eastern medievalism were still rampant and tragic. Five million Christians had been killed by other Christians in Europe for believing in the freedom of conscience. Martin Luther's Reformation was based on the freedom of conscience. Count Zinzendorf had organized in Western Europe a little colony which still believed in the Pietism for which John Huss had died when he was burned in the streets of Prague, and the church had gloated over the destruction of Latimer, Ridley, Cranmer, and all such freedom fighters in Britain itself. Dry-eyed, cold-hearted, and nonresponsive membership in the church was the method of church membership conduct.

When Wesley and his brother were converted it was regarded as a new thing in the Anglican movement. Even his mother's heart was to be "strangely warmed" under her son's preaching in spite of her high moral life and the

4. See the *General Rules, Doctrines and Discipline of the African Methodist Episcopal Zion Church.*
5. *Ibid.*
6. Charles C. Selecman, *The Methodist Primer,* p.7.

tension in the conduct of an Anglican home. She was finally able to say, listening at her son's first sermon in the grove, that she too had found the strange warming of the heart. [7] This depth of conversion, the sense of a changed life from legalism to spirituality and into a contagion that begot spiritual sons and daughters across the globe, became the order of the Christian church of that age. Even the Roman Catholics and the high church people of England including the great theologians of the time, were forced to roost lower and to begin the re-examination of Christianity in the whole world.

Methodism, therefore, has never been a churchianity. It sought hard to change the church by staying within it, but when it saw that its people, who were changed, were not acceptable to the church, and that they were going to be disinherited, Wesley began to take steps. He defined the church as a simple organ of people who believe in God and are in love with their fellowman, and who believe that justification by faith and the witness of the Holy Spirit should continue in both individual experience and corporate formation. He led people away from all presumptuous forms that sought to put the church between man's soul and his God. Umphrey Lee wrote:

> With his conversion Wesley's High Churchmanship disappeared; and a religion of individual experience, colored strongly by emotion, took its place. Methodism became an English Pietism; and individualism, feeling, experience, freedom from ecclesiasticism became the marks of the new movement. Sometimes to this is added the revival of orthodoxy of the Reformation type. . . Pietism stressed an inward, transforming religious experience through Christ, and it was this which characterized the Christianity which Pietists propagated. [8]

"If we wonder at times whether the organization of which we are a part is in the true Methodist succession we might test it by the standard of the Methodist societies as the Wesleys held it." [9] Mr. Wesley himself often called the church "a congregation of faithful men in which the pure Word of God is preached, and the Sacraments duly administered according to Christ's ordinance." [10] He further called it "a catholic seminary of divine love," referring, of course, to the visible church as a place of association in learningship of God and divine relationship toward each other demonstrated by love—the eternal tie of Christians and of men of goodness in all history. [11]

Wesley had a burning desire for his people to maintain the basic traditions of spiritual fervor when he stated:

> I am not afraid that the people called Methodists should ever cease to exist either in Europe or America. But I am afraid lest they should exist only as a dead sect, having the form of religion without the power. And this undoubtedly will be the case unless they hold fast both the doctrine, spirit and discipline with which they first set out. [12]

Methodism went on to make the world its parish, and the general characteristics of Methodism in every age are based upon two General Advices laid down by Wesley:

7. Halford E. Luccock, Paul Hutchison and Robert W. Goodloe, *The Story of Methodism,* p.21.
8. Umphrey Lee, *John Wesley and Modern Religion,* p.13; Latourette, *op. cit.,* Vol. III, p.47.
9. Luccock *et al., op. cit.,* p.166.
10. Henry Wheeler, *History and Exposition of the Twenty-Five Articles. . .,* Article XIII, p.237.
11. Umphrey Lee, *op. cit.,* p.272.
12. Quoted in Selecman, *op. cit.,* p.28.

(1) The First General Advice which one who loves your souls would earnestly recommend everyone of you, is Consider, with deep and frequent attention, the peculiar circumstances wherein you stand. . . . Your strictness of life, taking the whole of it together, may likewise be accounted new. I mean, your making it a rule to abstain from fashionable diversions; your plainness of dress; your manner of dealing in trade; your exactness in observing the Lord's Day; your scrupulosity as to the things that have not paid custom; your abstinence from spirituous liquours (unless in cases of extreme necessity); your rule "not to mention the fault of an absent person, in particular of ministers, or of those in authority"; may justly be termed new. For we do not find any body of people who insist on all these rules together.

(2) Consider these peculiar circumstances wherein you stand, and you will see the propriety of a Second Advice. I would recommend to you: Do not imagine you can avoid giving offence. Your very name renders this impossible. And as much offence as you give by your name, you will give still more by your principles. You will give offence to the bigots for opinions, modes of worship, and ordinances, by laying no more stress upon them; to the bigots against them, by laying so much; to men of form, by insisting so frequently and strongly on the inward power of religion; to men of reason you will give offence, by talking of inspiration and receiving the Holy Ghost; to drunkards, Sabbath breakers, common swearers and other open sinners by refraining from their company, as well as by that disapprobation of their behaviour which you will be often obliged to express. Either, therefore, you must consent to give up your principle, or your fond hope of pleasing men. [13]

Thus is Methodism indeed the spirit of the saints who retreated in the Middle Ages into hills and valleys, where the monks were born and where a new movement had to rise to redeem Christianity from the neglect, lethargy, and abuses of the church.

Its fundamental qualities are characteristically expressed in the Twenty-five Articles of Faith of the Methodist Religion. Simplicity in worship, plainness of dress, pure and undefiled altars, continuous renewal of soul-salvation, as elucidated in so many of Charles Wesley's hymns; and most assuredly, the experience of that "strange warming of the heart," which led to its beginning in a prayer meeting in Aldersgate Street, London, on May 24, 1738 when John Wesley "learned what Paul had discovered, that it is not by rules and laws, nor by our own efforts at self-perfection, but by faith in God's mercy as it comes to us in Christ, that man may enter upon life and peace," [14] are all basic essentials of unique Christian people called Methodists.

The Black Race

Besides the fact that Methodism was a friend of the black race long before it was introduced on the American continent, it had the evangelical appeal to this suffering and despised race, and the system of the class meetings, to not only instruct the members for the good of their souls, but "to watch over one another in love. . .and help each other to work out their own salvation." These, along with Wesley's strong opposition to human bondage, made the strongest kind of impact upon the Negro population in the United States and West Indies during the late eighteenth and early nineteenth centuries. John Wesley baptized the first

13. James Porter, *Compendium of Methodism*, pp.66-67.
14. *Doctrines and Discipline of the Methodist Church,* Historical Statement, 1960, p.3.

converted Negro into a Protestant Church on November 29, 1758, and wrote in his diary: "I rode to Wandsworth, and baptized two Negroes belonging to Mr. Gilbert, a gentleman lately from Antigua. One of these is deeply convinced of sin; the other is rejoicing in God, her Saviour, and is the first African Christian I have known. But shall not God, in his own time, have these heathen also for his inheritance?" [15]

Also, Mr. Wesley's views on African slavery were of paramount opposition to the whole system, especially in America, during those dim days. In other words, he was a strict follower of Jesus Christ on all human questions, and slavery was uppermost in his preaching about administering the church or the nation according to the humanitarian ethic. His attitude created an atmosphere in Methodism that went all through America to the emancipation of her slaves, and is still inherent in the freedom cause. He spoke almost with his dying breath, when he declared "American slavery the vilest that ever saw the sun." [16] Dr. Thomas Coke, the first bishop of the Methodist Episcopal Church, was in full sympathy with the anti-slavery views of his chief, and got himself into trouble in America by his outspoken references to the subject in the pulpit and in private conversation. [17] It was he who gave so much time and effort to the instruction and soul-saving program of Methodism in the West Indies. Like-minded was the father of American Methodism, Francis Asbury, who wrote in his journal, in 1776: "After preaching at the Point, I met the class, and then met some black people, some of whose unhappy masters forbid their coming for religious instruction. How will the sons of oppression answer for their conduct when the great Proprietor of all shall call them to account?" [18] Four years later this entry occurs; "I spoke to some select friends about slavekeeping, but they could not bear it: this I know, God will plead the cause of the oppressed, though it gives offence to say so here. O Lord, banish the infernal spirit of slavery from thy dear Zion." [19] Freeborn Garrettson, one of the first and ablest native American Methodist preachers, was born and brought up in slave territory. Though for a time a slaveholder himself, he became so impressed with the wickedness of slaveholding that he liberated all his blacks and was known thereafter as a strong anti-slavery advocate. [20]

In American Methodism, out of which the two African Methodist Churches were born, in the late eighteenth century, there were struggles among categories of leaders while it was steadily growing; some of extreme sincerity, others of a degree of sincerity, and others quite insincere about eliminating slaves among their constituents, and particularly their preachers. The conflict within the family of Methodists on the slave question grew exceedingly until the climactic division which created the Methodist Episcopal Church and the Methodist Episcopal Church, South, in 1844, which lasted for nearly a century.

In 1786 black members were first listed in the yearly conference records, which showed that the preachers had given special attention to them. "The number reported this year was 1,869, one thousand of whom were connected with the mission at Antigua, and were soon after transferred to the care of the British Conference." In 1787, the conference said:

15. J. C. Hartzell, *Methodism and the Negro in the United States,* p.2.
16. Lucius C. Matlack, *History of American Slavery and Methodism,* p.11.
17. James Dixon, *Methodism in America,* p.6.
18. *Ibid.,* p.10.
19. *Ibid.*
20. *Ibid.*

We conjure all our ministers and preachers by the love of God, and the salvation of souls, and do require them, by all the authority that is vested in us, to leave nothing undone for the spiritual benefit and salvation of the colored people, within their respective circuits or districts. . .and to exercise the whole Methodist discipline among them. (21)

The humble beginnings of Methodism, first in England, at Oxford University in 1729, and in 1738 in Aldersgate Street; in America in 1766, at the humble home of Philip Embury in New York, our own particular branch of Zion Methodism, in 1796, in a house on Cross Street (formerly a stable), and similarly other branches; show the determination of these Christians to follow the example of the humble beginning of Christianity with the birth of Christ, our Lord and Savior, in a lonely stable, and after the resurrection, the starting of the church in the Upper Room.

21. James Porter, *A Comprehensive History of Methodism,* pp.280-281.

CHAPTER 5

ENVIRONMENTAL INFLUENCE, STATISTICS AND CAUSES

Since New York was the city of Zion's birth, and its nurturing center for the first 25 years of existence, it is important to give some background on that environment, which created the conditions of its first successful black independent organization.

Two years after 30 Dutch families settled on the island of Manhattan in 1624, 11 Negroes were imported to this new territory, which the Dutch had purchased from the Indians for "beads and trinkets," and named New Amsterdam. Servitude began immediately after their arrival when they were put to work as "company Negroes," building roads, cutting timber, clearing land, and erecting dwellings and forts. Eighteen years after their arrival, the 11 Negro pioneers, with their families, boldly demanded freedom. Official tempers flared. But the rank-and-file of colonists recalled the early labors of these black men and supported the petition. The authorities granted them land on the edge of the settlement, in a tangled swamp known today as Greenwich Village. (1)

After the war between the Dutch and the English, the British flag was hoisted over New Amsterdam in 1664 and the province became New York. Negroes then entered upon a period of sustained cruelty. The English introduced chattel slavery. They propagandized that Negroes had no souls but perished like beasts and therefore were incapable of embracing Christianity. (2) Thirty years after the English occupation of the colony there were 2,170 Negroes in New York, a little more than 13 percent of the whole colonial population. The number of slaves had increased considerably, and in 1709 a slave market was established at the foot of Wall Street. (3) Tensions began to develop between these slaves and their masters.

In 1696, a Negro named Prince angrily assaulted the mayor about some new restrictions placed on the Negroes. He was stripped to the waist, tied to a cart, and drawn through the streets, and at each corner was given 11 lashes on his naked back. (4) In 1708, an Indian man and a Negro woman were burned at the stake for killing an entire white family. During this time all wealthy whites owned slaves, some as many as 50. "Even people of moderate means had from three to six household slaves whom they regarded as impersonally as they did chairs and tables." (5)

Attempts by the blacks to either escape or revolt became more and more frequent, and finally in 1712, some of the discontented among the New York

1. Roi Ottley, *A New World a-Coming*, pp.406.
2. Ottley and Weatherby, *The Negro in New York*, p.16.
3. James Weldon Johnson, *Black Manhattan*, pp.5-6.
4. Ottley and Weatherby, *op. cit.*, p.6.
5. Edward Robb Ellis, *The Epic of New York City*, p.112.

Black Classes of John Street Church in 1795 led by white male class leaders. Note: Class No. 31, the dutch spelling of the founder of the A.M.E. Zion Church in 1796; James *Van Varck*. *The New York Public Library Manuscript and Archives Division: Astor, Tilden and Lenox Foundations. Used by permission of the John Street United Methodist Church of New York City and New York Commission on Archives and History of The United Methodist Church, Hudson, N.Y.*

slaves, angered by the many harsh treatments of them, revolted. About 1 A.M., 23 Negroes gathered in an orchard in Maiden Lane (now the heart of the Wall Street area), armed with guns, hatchets, and knives, and set fire to an outhouse. A fire alarm was sounded in the center of town. While the white inhabitants were engaged in putting out the fire, these Negroes marched toward them killing nine men and wounding six. [6]

Prior to this, about the only white person who appeared friendly toward Negroes was a French Protestant named Elias Neau, who had opened a school for them in 1704. The town began to seethe with rage and fear. Mr. Neau's school was blamed as the main cause of the barbarous plot, and Neau was accused of "putting all those wild ideas into their heads." The colonists felt that Negroes had no need for an education; they only needed to do what they were told, to work hard, and to stay in their place. Thus Neau received much abuse and persecution. [7] "Upon full trial the guilty Negroes were found to be such as never came to Mr. Neau's school; and, what is very observable, the persons whose Negroes were found most guilty were such as were the declared opposers of making them Christians." [8] The conspirators were pursued when they attempted flight, captured and executed—some hanged, some burned at the stake, some left suspended in chains to starve to death. [9]

These cruel executions were, of course, enacted for a lesson to the Negroes in general, hoping to guarantee peaceful submission and to prevent all forms of uprisings. Thus the incident had its repercussion, not only in New York, but other parts of America, causing passage of new oppressive laws, and extreme scrutiny by masters. In New York, one law in particular was designed to impoverish the entire Negro population. It ordered that "no Negro, Indian, or Mulatto made free hereafter was to enjoy, hold or possess any house, land, or tenements, or hereditaments within the colony." This law remained in effect for more than a century. Also to discourage the freeing of slaves, a master who manumitted a slave was required to pay two hundred pounds a year to the freed man during his lifetime. [10]

Twenty-nine years later the city was again thrown into a panic by the so-called "conspiracy to burn New York and murder its inhabitants." In 1741, New York had about 10,000 inhabitants, including 2000 slaves. The 1712 incident, still fresh in the minds of many citizens, and reports of Negro insurrections in the West Indies at this time, added to the general unrest and magnified suspicion in the city. "Nine fires that seemed to be incendiary came one upon another, and a robbery was committed. To escape death herself, a worthless white servant girl gave testimony against the Negroes who frequented a tavern where she was employed, declaring that a plot had been conceived whereby the slaves would kill all the white men and take control of the city. New York was aflame with fear, and evidence that at another time would have been rejected, was listened to by the judges with grave attention. The slaves were allowed no defense, and before the city had recovered from its fright, it had burned fourteen Negroes, hanged eighteen, and transported seventy-one." [11]

6. *Ibid.*, pp.112-13.
7. *Ibid.*, p.113; DuBois, *The Negro Church*, p.13.
8. W. E. Burghardt DuBois, *The Negro Church*, p.13.
9. Mary White Ovington, *Half a Man*, p.3.
10. Ottley and Weatherby, *op. cit.*, p.24.
11. Ovington, *op. cit.*, p.15.

Four whites were also executed, including a priest named John Ury. [12]

This incident also caused new and restrictive measures to be enacted against blacks with greater repression. Thus the white attitude toward the black minority was characterized by fear—both a personal fear of the black man as a strange being and a communal uneasiness over the danger of uprisings. The free Negroes in New York were hardly ever involved in slave uprisings. However, the citizens believed that the free Negroes not only joined their slave brethren in acts of violence, but that they provided the leadership for insurrection and the focal point for unrest. The citizens persistently enacted and enforced legislation restricting the rights of free Negroes, such as the right to own property and suffrage. Whites sensed that the bond of color was stronger than the bond of freedom, and given a chance to make a decision, free blacks would side with slaves rather than with other freemen. [13] This was only human and logical. "Since whites assumed that race identity was all important, they concluded that blacks, even 'free' blacks, could not be fully trusted, at least certainly as long as slavery existed. The result was an increased uneasiness among the white majority about the presence of a Negro minority—slave and free—within the white community." [14]

By the first half of the eighteenth century, New York had the largest slave population north of the plantation states, both in numbers and as a percentage of the total population. "Due to a combination of circumstances, some historical, some almost accidental, some purely economic, and some less easily defined, New York came to have the largest slave population among the nonplantation English colonies in the New World." [15]

In approaching the second half of the eighteenth century, the season of religious breakthrough for blacks in New York, one can easily observe the obstruction, the hindrance, and the barriers, which they would begin to challenge with insurmountable faith and courage, and finally make their move before the end of the century. Negroes in New York were generally kept under close watch, and could not have any meetings of any nature among themselves. The following appeared in the *New York Post Boy,* February 16, 1756:

> Nine Negroes were recently "whipt at the whipping post" for illegally assembling on Sunday, February 8. Their offense was a violation of the provincial act aimed to prevent "the Conspiracy and Insurrection of Negro and other slaves," and also of the city ordinance which required that not more than three Negroes should be seen together at one time, except in their owner's service, under penalty of being whipped.

Thus was the condition when the strange new sect from England, known by the name of Methodists, emerged on the American continent in the city of New-York, 10 years later, and near the same period on the shores of Maryland. The suspicion and fear continued to exist with very little change until the Revolutionary War period. The handicaps under these pressures and oppressive laws were severe. In spite of this, a few free Negroes managed to get enough education to read and write. Many of them were naturally skillful, full of God-given talents, and industrious in trades and occupations. I would inject here, however, that this was typical of the Africans, both slave and free, in all parts of the New Territory. Even though the strictest methods were used to keep them in

12. Johnson, *op. cit.,* p.10.
13. Kobrin, *The Black Minority in Early New York,* pp.24-25
14. *Ibid.,* p.26.
15. *Ibid.,* p.8.

ignorance and illiteracy, several incidents indicative of the skillful, tactful, and intelligent Africans in this country are depicted by noted historical writers. Most miraculous of all this is how the black man overcame a suffering handicap, long and inhumane, in comparison with the Indian whom the white man was never able to subject to slavery.

In 1766, when Irishman Philip Embury, who had been licensed by John Wesley, held the first Methodist meeting on American soil in his home in Augustus Street (then Barrack Street), exhorting to an audience of five, one black person was present. She was Betty, the slave of Barbara Heck, who had requested the meeting of her fellow countryman out of necessity to save their people from "hell." They sang and prayed while Mr. Embury instructed them in doctrines of salvation. From this meeting they formed themselves into a class, of which he became the leader, and resolved to attend regularly at his house for further instructions. As they grew, their slaves and other blacks were privileged to join the movement. As they outgrew the house, they soon obtained a more commodious facility for meeting, and a little later, moved into the Rigging or Sail Loft at 120 William Street. [16]

We observe, from journals and reports of early missionaries sent to America by Wesley, that the black membership of John Street Church, in the beginning, was principally slave. While meeting in the Rigging Loft, when the subscriptions for Wesley Chapel (the first John Street Church) were circulated, two dedicated young slave girls contributed; Rachel gave nine shillings and Margaret seven shillings of their meager belongings. Yet when the chapel was built in 1768, "a ladder stairway led to the slave gallery, thus providing for the black members." [17] A section of the gallery was also used by white male members, [18] who later crowded out the black members.

Wesley's first two missionary preachers to America, Joseph Pilmore and Richard Boardman, both pastored John Street Church for brief periods and kept Wesley well informed regarding their Negro membership in New York. For instance, John Street Church's second pastor, Joseph Pilmore, wrote Wesley on April 24, 1770, the following:

> Our house contains about seventeen hundred hearers; only about a third part of those who attend get in; the rest are glad to hear without. There appears such a willingness in the Americans to hear the word, as I never saw before. The number of blacks that attends the preaching affects me much. [19]

That Negroes in New York were still not to have any known meetings among themselves, unless otherwise supervised, was a perplexing situation, especially to the free group with a degree of education. Pilmore stated in his journal, January 27, 1771, the following: "After preaching, I met the Negroes apart, and found many of them very happy. God has wrought a most glorious work on many of their souls, and made them witnesses that he is no respecter of persons." [20] It is evident that it was a meeting to give them comfort in their unpleasant condition.

On April 23, 1771, Richard Boardman made his report to Wesley of the progress of this glorious work in New York, an extract of which we quote here:

16. *A Short Historical Account of the Early Society of Methodists,* (W. & P.C. Smith) pp.3-4.
17. Francis Bourne Upham (ed.), *The Story of Old John Street Methodist Episcopal Church.*
18. Samuel A. Seaman, *Annals of New York Methodism,* p.40.
19. Frederick Maser and Howard Maag, *The Journal of Joseph Pilmore,* p.74.
20. *Ibid.,*

We have in this city some of the best preachers both in the English and Dutch Churches that are in America, yet God works by whom he will work. I have lately been much comforted by the death of some poor negroes who have gone off the stage of time rejoicing in the God of their salvation. I asked one at the point of death, "Are you afraid to die?" "O no," said she, "I have my blessed Saviour in my heart." She continued to declare the great things God had done for her soul, to the astonishment of many, till the Lord took her to Himself. Several more seem just ready to be gone, longing for the time when mortality shall be swallowed up of life. (21)

The fact that he was comforted by their death, and the miseries of life were too much to bear, evidently caused him great concern, and he gave a vivid portrayal of these instances, both individually and collectively. This was during the period that Negroes were worshipping in the gallery and denied access to the main floor of the church for regular worship service. The civic problems of Negroes were still acute, and had their effect upon Methodism. Some of the leaders tried to improve the conditions of their black members, not only spiritually but educationally. But the itinerancy of the traveling preacher was for six months at a time, sometimes less, and, the turnover in preachers at John Street Church (the "New York Circuit") during its first 30 years of existence was part of the problem that caused the establishment of the A.M.E. Zion Church.

In the last quarter of the century, a change in sentiment regarding slavery began to make itself felt. (22) The black population had listened to the slogans of liberty, "the rights of man," and "all men are created equal," after fighting for freedom in the Revolutionary War, side by side with the colonists, and firmly believed that equality was to include *all* Americans. (23) In 1785, the New York Society for Promoting the Manumission of Slaves was founded, with John Jay as president and Alexander Hamilton as secretary, greatly stimulated by the Quakers and a few other freedom-loving people. During the next ten years the legislature relaxed its stringent laws regarding slavery in the state, and in 1799 a gradual emancipation bill was passed, signed by John Jay, providing for final abolition of slavery in New York on July 4, 1827. (24) A second emancipation act was passed in 1817. Slaves could still be brought into the state by outsiders, but after 1817 no New Yorker could own a slave. (25) These laws had very little effect or success until aided by a long series of abolition meetings, threatening and loss of lives, violent riots, and the Civil War and emancipation of slaves in the entire nation.

John Street Church reported that its membership numbered 178 whites and 25 colored in 1786—the first instance of membership tabulation on a racial basis. (26) There were six men and nineteen women in this small group. (27) Apparently the black men of New York were slowly convinced that they had any free privilege of action, even through religion. While many more black men were interested in the Methodist religion, and were holding private meetings among themselves in their homes, in the interest of the race, they refused to be a party to segregated services. Thus, several of the earliest leaders in the Zion Church movement were not members of the John Street Church or New York

21. John Atkinson, *The Beginning of the Wesleyan Movement in America*, pp.248-249.
22. Johnson, *op. cit.*, p.10.
23. Ottley and Weatherby, *op. cit.*, p.35.
24. *Ibid.*, p.45.
25. Kobrin, *op. cit.*, p.42.
26. *The Methodist Church, Inventory of the Church Archives of N.Y. City*, p.15.
27. John Street Church Records.

Circuit. They became even more suspicious of religion, and of the white man's sincere desire to accept them into the fold for the good of their souls, when in the same year, Jupiter Hammon (reputed to be the first black American poet, preceding Phillis Wheatley), servant of John Lloyd, Jr., of the Manor of Queens Village, Long Island, circulated a highly conciliatory pamphlet entitled, *An Address to the Negroes in the State of New York,* which admonished his "dear poor brethren" to be good slaves to their masters.

Let me beg you, my dear African brethren, [he wrote], to think very little of your own bondage in this life; for your thinking of it will do you no good. If God designs to set us free, he will do it in his own time and way. . . . Getting liberty is by no means the greatest thing we have to be concerned about. . . . Our liberty in this world is nothing to having the liberty of the children of God. To the free Negroes, he stated: You have more time to read God's Holy Word, to take care of the salvation of your souls. . . . Let me beg of you to spend your time this way, or it will be better for you if you had always been slaves.

He closed this devitalizing message by saying:

Let me beg of you then, for the sake of your own good and happiness, in time and for eternity, and for the sake of your poor brethren, who are still in bondage, *to lead quiet and peaceable lives* in all godliness and honesty, and may God bless you, and bring you to his kingdom, for Christ's sake. Amen. [28]

The slaves, for the most part, could neither read nor write, and these more trained Negroes could not be expected to read such a lengthy pamphlet to their nonreading sisters and brothers who were under the torture of insufferable slavery. This was an inflicting wound upon a people who were struggling to make a decision about religious affiliation with whites, where "the New York body of legislation for slaves had more in common with the 18th century slave codes in the southern colonies than with regulations enacted by New York's northern neighbors." [29]

Nevertheless, a foreboding restlessness was growing among the black race regarding their brutal status, and a more conservative reaction, common to most of the new states in the Union, was setting in among whites.

The struggle for inalienable rights had become not something which Americans had lived through and fought for, but a vicarious experience belonging to an earlier time. The passing years brought a diminution in the power of the ideas of the Declaration of Independence. By the first decades of the 19th Century the Negro was generally considered to be somehow separate from America. He was thought to be inferior, to be *different,* not really an American. Neither slavery nor the Negro fitted into the vision most New Yorkers held of the grand experiments in republicanism they believed were beginning. [30]

In 1789, John Street Church reported 290 white and 70 colored; 360 members. [31] In 1790, New York City had 3,252 Negroes, of whom 2,184 were slaves and 1,078 free. Philadelphia had 1,630 Negroes of whom 210 were slaves. Baltimore (a border city) had 1,578 Negroes, of whom 1,255 were slaves, and Boston had 791 Negroes, all of whom were free. Of the nearly 175,000 white

28. Jupiter Hammon, *An Address to the Negroes in the State of New York.*
29. Kobrin, *op. cit.,* p.14.
30. *Ibid.,* pp.43-44.
31. *Minutes of the Annual Conferences of the Methodist Episcopal Church,* 1773-1828, p.35.

families in New England, only one percent owned slaves. [32] We get a clear picture here of the high ratio of New York City slaves in comparison with other large northern cities, in the last decade of the eighteenth century.

In 1791, the revolt of Haitian slaves influenced the slaves in the states. Haiti had 40,000 whites, 28,000 freedmen, and 500,000 slaves. In April 1794, Toussaint L'Ouverture, a man of rare courage and remarkable leadership, who had attained high rank in the Spanish Army at the head of 4,000 troops, deserted the Spanish and his defection led to the surrender of the Spanish garrison in Santo Domingo L'Ouverture, Dessalines, and Christophe led the slave revolt in Haiti against French rule. Toussaint L'Ouverture issued a constitution which abolished slavery. [33] It is said that some thirteen thousand black Americans migrated to free Haiti after this revolution, where they found refuge. [34]

This incident brought about a new assertiveness among the blacks in America. Freedom was making attempts to burst from the seams. Fears became more prevalent and tensions began to mount all over America. This was the period when humanitarian consciousness among whites began to grow, and manumission societies were being formed in several cities and towns, to enhance freedom of these human beings who for nearly two hundred years had been chattel of the market. This, however, was still a vast minority against the persons who were blinded by materialistic greed, race hatred, and diabolic superiority complexes.

In New York City, members of the "New York Circuit" numbered 575 whites and 135 blacks.[35] The leading black members were beginning to lay concrete plans for the new movement of Methodism which would create a new emphasis in freedom and self-expression. They planned hard and well and reached the crest of their fondest dream in 1796. After prodding their way through numerous obstructions, they made their move to a humble house on Cross Street. Few in numbers, poor and despised, they prayerfully and zealously fought their way to victory by 1821.

Indeed, the story of the earliest period of the A.M.E. Zion Church is a romance, built on faith, hope, fortitude, and courage, inspired by God Almighty and his Son, Jesus Christ, witnessed by the Holy Spirit. Between the organization of the church in 1796 and the separation in 1821, this group passed through turbulent days. Some preachers withdrew, others wavered, and the people sometimes lost heart, but Varick stood like a rock amid some raging storms, and brought the old ship of Zion through a series of crises to freedom, and therefore was rewarded by God and his people to become the first leader of a great denomination.

32. Bergman, *Chronological History of the Negro,* p.69.
33. *Ibid.,* pp.74-75.
34. Ottley and Weatherby, *op. cit.,* p.53.
35. *Minutes of the Annual Conferences of the Methodist Episcopal Church,op. cit.,* p.56.

Part II—

The African

Methodist Episcopal

Zion Church

CHAPTER 6

DEFINITION AND ORIGIN OF
THE AFRICAN METHODIST EPISCOPAL ZION CHURCH

Defining Zion Methodism

In October 1796, the African Methodist Episcopal Zion Church was founded in New York City. The organization grew out of the well-known dissatisfaction among the people of color over the kind of treatment they received in the services of the church. Bishop Moore describes this dissatisfaction as follows:

When the first Methodist Episcopal Society was established in New York (white), among whom were several colored persons, the two races found no difficulty in the reciprocity of religious fellowship, and the equal enjoyment of religious rights and privileges, but as the church grew popular and influential, the prejudice of caste began to engender Negro proscription, and as the number of colored members increased, the race friction and proscription increased, which finally overcame the tolerance of the colored members of the M.E. Society. Again the M.E. Church in New York, licensed a number of colored men to preach, but prohibited them from preaching even to their own brethren, except occasionally, and never among the whites. The colored preachers, being thus deprived of the opportunity of improving their gifts and graces, as they then stood connected with the white M.E. Society, and prohibited from joining the annual M.E. Conference, as itinerant preachers, with their white brethren; thus restricted in their church relations, they were prompted to seek the privilege of holding meetings among themselves. [1]

Bishop Hood gives us the following general description of the state of the church during this period:

[The Negro] was wanted in the church for the support he gave it, for the numbers he enabled sectarians to claim in exhibiting their strength, and with the minority, who were truly pious, he was wanted there for the good of his soul. For these and other reasons he was not kept entirely out of the church. But in the church he was hampered and regulated. His privileges were proscribed and limited; every possible effort was made to impress him with a sense of inferiority. Preachers were selected who delighted in discoursing to him upon such texts as *"Servants, obey your masters,"* and who were adepts at impressing the Negro with inferiority in the most ingenious and least offensive way. . . . This state of things was not confined to any one particular branch of the American Church, but it was found in every denomination in every community in which there was any considerable number of the black race. [2]

In consonance with Hood's concept, Roi Ottley states that "the first independent act of Negroes was to sever all connections with the white churches, which had assigned them to sections marked 'B.M.,' meaning black members. The movement, extending to every denomination, began when Negroes broke away from the Methodist Episcopal Church and started the African Methodist Episcopal Zion Church." [3]

Wheeler states that

[The] Methodist Episcopal Church at the time that Varick and his followers withdrew from it, was a victim of circumstances. African slavery had produced its sickening effects all over the country, in Church and State. The Methodist Episcopal Church, like all other churches at the time, had been influenced by it. They did not persecute their colored brethren, however— they simply denied them certain rightful privileges which were accorded to white brethren. But this the colored brethren did not think they could stand and at the same time work out for themselves the high destiny which God holds out to all men and women who serve Him aright. [4]

In the formation of any organization that gains potency, there is practically always one who provides inspirational leadership and directional prudence, who is heavily depended upon by others to steer the ship sailing into new harbors, safely into the port. From the beginning, this independent movement of the A.M.E. Zion Church was largely influenced and structured by James Varick. He was the consistent leader and was later made the virtual pastor of this first church called Zion. Even though white preachers were in charge, black leadership among our own was a necessity.

The other leaders that became prominent in the movement were Father Abraham Thompson, June Scott, and William Miller. Thompson wavered, Scott left the movement, and Miller wandered during the birth of the movement. Varick was the most prominent name from the beginning and played the diplomat between Zion and other churches, both the Methodist Episcopal Church and the Bethel movement, but maintained the constancy and unity of the A.M.E. Zion movement.

1. Moore, *History of The A.M.E. Zion Church in America,* pp.15-16.
2. Hood, *One Hundred Years,* p.3.
3. Ottley, *New World a-Coming,* p.11.
4. B. F. Wheeler, *The Varick Family,* pp.6-7.

Father Rush, in his history, attempted to give as broad an account as possible of these happenings, most of which were related to him by others, but it was eight years after this movement officially began that he came to New York and joined the Zion Church in 1803. What occurred in the eight years of his absence is, without a doubt, one of the most vivid and heroic stories of the formation of a Christian church.

The fathers agreed that they had no fault to find with the doctrines, form of government, and evangelistic and soul-saving emphases of Methodism, but they could not endure the constant humiliation and restriction imposed by the people into whose hands Methodism had fallen. The founders were opposed to slavery and inhumane treatment of slaves, so that they could logically remain Methodists because of the spirit of the originators and the meaning of the first-born movement in England and America.

Bishop Hood who was licensed to preach in Mother Zion Church in 1856, and knew some of the founders and their direct descendants, further states:

Their teaching from the pulpit was that God is no respecter of persons. The practice was that the black people were proscribed and hindered from exercising themselves with that freedom which the form of government held out to white members. Both the masses and also those who were favored with special gifts and callings were discriminated against. The colored members were not permitted to come to the sacrament [of the Lord's Supper] until all the white members, even children, had communed. The line was also drawn at the baptismal font. [5]

He relates the story of a minister who was baptizing children. When he was through with the white children he looked up to the gallery and said, "Now you *niggers* can bring your children down." A sister brought her child and presented it. When the minister said, "Name this child," the mother said, "George Washington." The minister looked at her for a moment as though she had been guilty of some great crime, and said, "George Washington, indeed! Caesar's his name. Caesar, I baptise thee, etc." [6] They suffered many other such indignities while in John Street Church, which contributed to their final decision to withdraw. "They found it impossible to be true to their manhood and remain in this church and submit to these indignities." [7]

Thus we have the comprehensive and living definition of a small, restless, dissatisfied group, who with wholehearted determination and zeal made the giant step in eliminating brutal slavery and proscription. From then on they moved with magnifying force, not only to produce some of the world's greatest freedom fighters and advocates, but to shine as a beacon light, for individual rights and privileges, in becoming prominent and well known as "The Freedom Church."

Origin of Zion

These growing conditions of slavery, humiliation, and persecution inspired a few of the most intelligent black leaders of John Street Church to move forward. Dissatisfaction among blacks regarding their burial situation in the city was a live issue in 1795. Bishop Asbury made a visit to New York on Sunday, July 5, 1795, administered the sacraments at the New Church in the afternoon, and held a meeting with the black classes afterward. [8] There were 155 black members in

5. Hood, *One Hundred Years,* p.10.
6. *Ibid.,* p.10.
7. Wheeler, *op. cit.,* p.6.
8. Asbury, *Journals and Letters of Francis Asbury,* Vol. II, p.55.

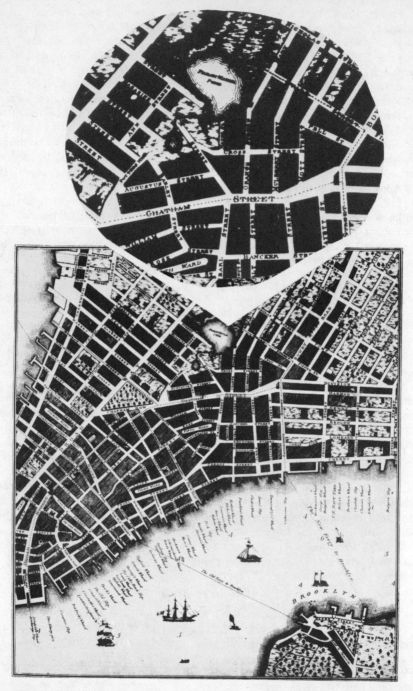

The African Methodist Episcopal Zion Church makes its debut as an independent religious organization in the fall of 1796 in a house near The Collect Pond on Cross Street between Orange and Mulberry.
Map Division, New York Public Library: Astor, Tilden and Lenox Foundations.

View of New York City from the Collect (or Fresh Water) Pond, March, 1798. Birth of the A.M.E. Zion Church where meetings were held from 1796 to 1800 in house on Cross Street opposite the pond.
The Edward W. C. Arnold Collection. Lent by the Metropolitan Museum of Art. Photo Courtesy of the Museum of the City of New York.

8 classes, only 2 of which were male classes, totalling 34. Class Number 31, led by Cornelius Warner, was the impressive class of A.M.E. Zion Church founders: James Varick, Abraham Thompson, William Miller, William Hamilton, Francis Jacobs, Thomas Miller, George Moore, George White, Thomas Cook, David Bias, Samuel Pontier, and 10 others whose names are not familiar in our history. [9]

After a group of these leading men of Class 31 held a series of meetings in the home of James Varick in number 4 Orange Street, and agreed to make firm their desire to become a separate society of Methodists, they again met with Bishop Asbury in August 1796, while he was visiting New York meeting all the classes and handling business affairs, and received permission to hold meetings separate from the Methodist Society. In October, they rented a house in Cross Street. [10]

This house, located between Mulberry and Orange Streets, was one of a group of houses on the east side of "The Collect Pond," owned by Edward Livingston, a prominent New York lawyer who became Mayor of the City in 1803, and his wife, Mary. Mr. Livingston and others had built up these houses to serve any and all purposes, for rental income. [11] In the fifth ward of the city, thickly populated with blacks, segregated not by race but by social and economic status, these two and three-story houses were used in a two-fold manner; occupants for the most part lived either above or in the rear, and

9. Ms. Record, John Street Church, Book 1B.
10. Asbury, *op. cit.,* pp.95-96; B. F. Wheeler, *op. cit.,* p.15; *New York City Directories; Star of Zion,* October 1, 1896, p.1.
11. William Smith Pelletreau, *Early New York Houses,* pp.167 & 213; 1795 Tax Book, New York City; 1796 Tax Book, NYC.

operated their businesses and trades from the front. (12) The house, on the north side of Cross Street, was originally a livery stable. William Miller had moved his cabinet-maker's shop into his living quarters at 36 Mulberry Street, just around the corner, and this was where Varick's followers had their first meeting house. (13)

The original pioneers when the separate meetings commenced were: James Varick, Abraham Thompson, June Scott, William Miller, Francis Jacobs, William Brown, Peter Williams, William Hamilton, Thomas Miller, and Samuel Pontier. (14) Their action proved to be a deliberate, determined and complete severance of relations with the Methodist denomination and a bold stroke for religious and race freedom. "Slavery still existed in New York. Every family of any pretension to affluence owned household and other servants. In all the newspapers of the period were advertisements of sales, and of runaway slaves. Many high-minded persons wished to see it abolished." (15)

For the most part, the church leaders were free, although quite a number of the members were still slave. They were possessed of unusual intellect and manifold skills. William Hamilton, like Philip Embury (who had the distinction of building his own pulpit, in the first John Street Church), was a house-carpenter. (16) Cabinet-makers in those days are known as furniture manufacturers today. They themselves fitted up the house with seats, a pulpit, and gallery. (17)

In this house, they first "held prayer meetings on Sunday afternoon in the interval of Divine Service among the white brethren, between afternoon and evening service, and also held preaching and exhorting meetings on Wednesday nights by such of their colored brethren as were licensed to preach and exhort." (18) There were three licensed preachers in New York, James Varick, Abraham Thompson, and June Scott, the first three Africans of this state to be ordained in the Methodist Church. (19)

They continued worshipping and meeting in this house on Cross Street, until they moved into their newly erected edifice on Sunday, September 7, 1800, led by these three preachers. In the beginning of the Christian movement, they were known as Apostles.

The A.M.E. Zion Church was firmly established in 1820, when the leaders voted themselves out of the Methodist Episcopal Church and published their first Discipline. The principal reasons were described in the Founders' Address of that and the subsequent Discipline:

12. Ms Record, Bancker Land Papers.
13. Wheeler, *op. cit.,* p.16.
14. Christopher Rush, *The Rise and Progress of the African Methodist Episcopal [Zion] Church in America,* p.10.
15. Martha J. Lamb, *History of the City of New York,* Vol. 3, p.419.
16. *New York City Directory,* 1797, p.195.
17. Rush, *Rise and Progress,* p.10.
18. *Ibid.*
19. Daniel Coker, *A Dialogue Between a Virginian and an African Minister,* p.40.

FOUNDERS' ADDRESS

To the Members of the African Methodist Episcopal [Zion] Church in America:

BELOVED BRETHREN: We think it proper to state briefly that, after due consideration, the Official Members of the African Methodist Episcopal Zion and Asbury Churches in the city of New York have been led to conclude that such was the relation in which we stood to the white Bishops and Conference, relative to the ecclesiastical government of the African Methodist Church or Society in America, so long as we remain in that situation our Preachers would never be able to enjoy these privileges which the Discipline of the white Church holds out to all its Members that are called to preach, in consequence of the limited access our brethren had to those privileges, and particularly in consequence of the difference of color. We have been led also to conclude that the usefulness of our Preachers has been very much hindered, and our brethren in general have been deprived of those blessings which Almighty God may have designed to grant them, through the means of those Preachers whom He has from time to time raised up from among them, because there has been no means adopted by the said Bishop and Conference for our Preachers to travel through the Connection and promulgate the Gospel of our Lord Jesus Christ; and they have had no access to the only source from whence they might have obtained a support, at least, while they traveled. Under these circumstances they believed that the formation of an itinerant plan and the establishment of a Conference for the African Methodist Preachers of the United States, who are not yet attached to any Conference of that nature, would be essential to the prosperity of the spiritual concerns of our colored brethren in general, and would be the means of advancing our Preachers (who are now in regular standing in connection with the white Preachers of the Methodist Episcopal Church), whenever it should be found necessary for the advancement of the Redeemer's kingdom among our brethren, to bring forward for ordination those who are called of God to preach the Gospel of our Lord, which may be done from time to time, according to the best of our judgment of the necessity thereof, and not according to the method which is natural to suppose our white brethren would pursue, to determine upon the necessity of such ordination. We are under strong impression of mind that such measures would induce many of our brethren to attend divine worship, who are yet careless about their eternal welfare, and thereby prove effectual in the hands of God in the awakening and conversion of their souls to the knowledge of the truth.

And whereas, Almighty God, in His all-wise and gracious providence, has recently offered a favorable opportunity, whereby these Societies may be regularly organized as an evangelical African Methodist Church, we have therefore resolved to embrace the said opportunity, and have agreed that the title of the Connection shall be the African Methodist Episcopal Church in America;* and we have selected a form of Discipline, with a little alteration from that of our Mother Church, which selection we recommend to you, for the Doctrines and Discipline of our Church, hoping that the great Shepherd and Bishop of souls, the all-wise and gracious God, will be pleased to approve of the above measures and grant that we may obtain and preserve those privileges which we have been heretofore deprived of; that thereby we may unite our mutual efforts for the prosperity of the Redeemer's kingdom among us, and for the encouragement of our colored brethren in the Ministry.

Earnestly soliciting your prayers and united endeavors for the same, we remain your affectionate brethren and servants in the kingdom of our ever-adorable Lord.

ABRAHAM THOMPSON,
JAMES VARICK,
WILLIAM MILLER.

* The word "Zion" was added to the title by the General Conference of 1848.

The Name

This first church organized in 1796 and built in 1800 was called *Zion*. The founders chose this name because "it is the name most frequently used in the Bible to designate the Church of God," [20] even Zion Hill, before there was a worship house.

Zion Church was incorporated in 1801 by the name, "The African Methodist Episcopal Church in New York." Methodist Episcopal was always in the title to exhibit the retention of the doctrine and form of church government under which the denomination originated."African was prefixed to the rest of the title of this church because it was to be controlled by descendants of Africa, in the interest of humanity, regardless of race, color, sex or condition." [21]

Therefore, these people of African descent, with an indubitable pride in the Fatherland and abiding love of kinship, desired to maintain their identity, their ancient cultures and background, for posterity. Because another organization came into existence around the same time, with the same title, and much confusion was brought about, the General Conference of 1848 voted to make Zion a part of the denominational name, henceforth to be known as *The African Methodist Episcopal Zion Church.* [22]

20. C. R. Harris, *Zion's Historical Cathechism* p.8.
21. *Ibid.*, p.8-9.
22. Hood, *op. cit.,* p.524.

CHAPTER 7

CONFLICTS AND SOLUTIONS IN THE FORMATIVE YEARS, 1796-1822

"When the Lord shall build up Zion, he shall appear in his glory. He will regard the prayer of the destitute, and not despise their prayer. This shall be written for the generation to come: and the people which shall be created shall praise the Lord." Psalms 103:16-18.

Building the First Church

A movement eventuating out of such traumatic hardships could not expect to experience anything but trial and heartaches during its first effort to build a permanent church. This small group of men and women, led by Varick, "realized that in starting out to purchase or erect a house of worship of their own, with their own poverty staring them in the face, and the prejudice of their white brethren against them, their pathway was beset with many discouragements and obstacles." [1]

In 1846, Jonathan Greenleaf wrote: "In 1796, the colored members of the Methodist Churches of the City of New York, feeling a desire to hold meetings among themselves, where they might have opportunity to exercise their spiritual gifts, and thereby, *as they hoped,* become more useful to each other, obtained permission from Bishop Asbury to hold such meetings in the intervals of the regular preaching hours of the white church." [2] These three little words, *as they hoped* retrospectively formed a key to many of the difficult experiences they subsequently endured. Unfortunately, their hopes were delayed, jarred, and in some respects smashed. At the time of our founding, the following rule existed in the Methodist Church regarding trustees and temporal affairs:

> By a law of the State of New York for incorporating religious societies, the male members of each church annually elect a *certain* specified number of Trustees for the especial oversight and management of the temporal concerns of said church. To the Trustees so elected of right belong the churches and other buildings erected for the convenience of the congregations and for the officiating ministers, they receive the revenue and satisfy all demands which may be made. The churches are erected by the Trustees, the ground is purchased by them, and all monies required for the purpose is procured by them. They are alone known in law as capable of suing and being sued. They borrow money when it is necessary, and when other security than their bond is required, they give a mortgage on the property held by them as Trustees.
> Whatever relates to the spirituality of the church, the Trustees do never interfere excepting with their advice. When a church is built, the preacher in charge has notice thereof and is requested to adopt the proper measures for opening and occupying the same, in accordance with the discipline of our

1. B. F. Wheeler, *The Varick Family,* p.6.
2. Jonathan Greenleaf, *A History of the Churches of All Denominations in the City of New York,* p.321.

church. Whatever relates to the revenue appropriated to the support of the preachers, the Trustees have no concern, that revenue comes into the hands of Stewards appointed according to the discipline, who are a body entirely independent of the Trustees, and in this matter have no connection or correspondence with them

Whenever either of the churches is required for any public celebration, other than the ordinary celebration of divine worship, particularly when a public collection is to be taken up, the consent of the Trustees must first be obtained, and without such consent the churches are not occupied. In all other respect, there is not the remotest deviation from the rules set forth in the discipline of our church, and as it regards our church in this city, the utmost harmony and brotherly feeling prevail. (3)

The first trustees selected for this African group were Francis Jacobs, William Brown, Thomas Miller, Peter Williams, Thomas Sipkins, William Hamilton, George Collins, and two others believed to be George E. Moore and George White. The first officers elected were Francis Jacobs, chairman, George Collins, secretary, and Thomas Miller, treasurer. (4) Still somewhat under the oppressive laws of Negroes not being able to own property, effective since the 1712 Insurrection, which began to break through during this period, their most well-to-do member at the time was Thomas Miller, treasurer of the Board of Trustees. According to the rules which separated the temporal affairs of the church from the spiritual, making distinct the duties of trustees, stewards, and preachers in charge, it is evident that Thomas Miller could not have been a licensed preacher, as Rush states in *The Rise and Progress.* Rather he was licensed to preach much later by the African Church Quarterly Conference, and recommended to the annual conference for deacon's orders in 1811, along with George White, another one of Zion's original trustees. They both were rejected at this time for reasons not given. However, on May 15, 1815, George White was elected by the annual conference and ordained deacon, the sixth black man in the history of New York Methodism to be so ordained. (5)

For three years, however, this little band met in a cheerful manner in their humble place on Cross Street. They were comfortable and happy in their periods of worship, vivacious in their business, and unitedly spiritual. Their leading men subsequently became the class leaders, doing away with those Methodist rules that Negroes must have white class leaders. As they grew in spiritual numbers and grace so they grew in desires and ambitions of building their own house of worship.

Having outgrown the quarters allotted to Negroes, principally the gallery in John Street Church, in 1799, they thought of building a church of their own, and of forming themselves into a body corporate, separate from the white church, according to the privilege granted to religious societies by the laws of the State of New York. They called a meeting of the leaders in their house on Cross Street. The members of this meeting cannot be given totally; however, a few of them were James Varick, Abraham Thompson, June Scott, William Miller, Francis Jacobs, William Brown, Peter Williams, Samuel Pontier, Thomas Miller, and William Hamilton of the old group, and George E. Moore, Thomas Sipkins, David Bias, George White, Thomas Cook, John Teesman, and George Collins of

---

3. Ms. Record No. 450, Methodist Episcopal Church; Porter, *The Stewards and the People,* pp.3-23; *Doctrines and Discipline of the Methodist Episcopal Church,* 1796, p.53.
4. Rush, *Rise and Progress,* p.11.
5. Ms. Record, Methodist Episcopal Church, New York Conference Journal, 1800-1820.

the new group. (6)

Major results of this history-making meeting were that they form themselves under polity of Methodist government and the creed of Methodist doctrine; that the trustees move forward, issue subscriptions, "and solicit the citizens of New York for aid to build the contemplated house for religious worship;" and that they prepare a memorial to present to the forthcoming General Conference, in 1800, granting them the privilege to secure a separate charter from the Methodist Episcopal Church.

The first hindrance was caused by the complete trust placed in the treasurer. The following article appeared in the *American Citizen and General Advertiser,* on March 21, 1800:

We hear that a subscription is on foot, for the purpose of erecting an African Church in the city. An object of such importance to the morals, and happiness of the unfortunate Africans, whom the unfeeling hand of avarice has forced from his native land, we trust will meet with the virtuous, and religious of *all* persuasions. (7)

The treasurer, Thomas Miller, an agent in the City of New York, (8) had been handling financial affairs for the trustees, paying the rent and negotiating with Edward Livingston to purchase lots for a place of worship, and other business transactions. (9) Therefore, the trustees built up a peculiar confidence in one man's ability to handle their business in carrying forth their dream of a worship house. After they had collected $80, they deposited it in the hands of the treasurer and immediately appointed him to acquire a plot of land for the worship site. The treasurer purchased a lot 25 feet wide and 75 feet long, on Orange Street, between Cross and Chatham Streets, for which he paid the $80 raised, but he obtained the deed for this lot in his own name. (10) They encountered difficulty when he refused to have the deed changed in the name of the African trustees. They soon discovered, however, that it was not a suitable place to erect a house of worship, and abandoned it. This lot was just a half block from their temporary meeting house in Cross Street.

This caused disturbance among Varick and the members, for each dollar was at a premium, especially among this slave race. The leaders and trustees "were disappointed, but not discouraged," according to Rush, and the chairman of the trustees, Francis Jacobs, who was a man of intelligence and good repute, worked with William Brown, the man they selected as treasurer replacing Thomas Miller, (11) to move forward, and with the secretary, George Collins, in procuring the worship house. The three officers were authorized to work closely together. They proceeded to negotiate with John Colvill, grocer, and his wife, Effie, for two lots on the southwest corner of Church and Leonard Streets, each 25 feet wide and 75 feet deep, at a cost of $750, fronting Church Street in a new vicinity of the Sixth Ward, spreading north, almost suburbia, according to maps and history of that era. (12)

6. Rush, *op. cit.,* p.11.
7. I. N. Phelps Stokes, *The Iconography of Manhattan Island,* Vol. 5, p.1376.
8. According to records, Thomas Miller (mulatto) and his wife, Jane, appear to be the first Negroes to purchase and own property in New York since the days of the Revolutionary War, when Samuel Fraunces, a wealthy Negro from the West Indies, owned and operated Fraunces Tavern (now a New York landmark) and entertained George Washington.
9. Ms. Record, Bancker Land Papers.
10. Rush, *op. cit.,* p.11.
11. *Ibid.,* p.12.
12. *Ibid.,* Bancker Survey Papers, Notebook No. 4.

Record of Black Classes of the New York Circuit, kept by Rev. Thomas Morrell; members received into the Methodist Society on trial by way of the "African Zion Church" in 1802-03. On right are the black class leaders who were our first preachers and trustees, with exception of two leaders.

England

1802 Blacks on trial ad forward

Nov.r   Dinah Hick ————— Cooks   read in
December Margaret Burton ———— ditto— kept on trial
1803   Peter Flemming ——— Wm Miller ditto read in
Jany   Mary Haines ————— Cooks   read in
          Stephen Church ———— Printers read in
          Charles Grinnell ——— Vanck   declined
          Polly Dunmore ———— Cooks   read in

          Abijah McCarroll ——— ditto
March 3. Christ.r Rush ————— Pontiers read in
march   Louisa Frances ——— Collins   read in
          Catharine Jackson —— ditto   read in
          Maria Suely ———— ditto   read in
          Eliz.th Ready ———— ditto   read in
          Jane Snell ———— ditto   read in
          Joseph Varnes ———— Browns   declined?
          Dolly Blakely
April   Mary Pintier ———— Myers
          Levi Brown ———————   read in
          George Johnson ———— White,   read in
          Swansey Williams ———   read in
April   Thomas Miller Jun.r — Browns   declined?
          Jane Jackson ———— Byas—   read in
          Louisa Cooly ———— Byas—   read in
          Charles Tredwell ——— Pointier read in
          Dolly Tredwell ——— Jacobs   read in
          Kitty Rutgers ——— Jacobs   member from Phila
may   Susannah Robinson —— Collins   read in
          Fanny Wilson woman — Th.s Miller read in
          John Lewis ———— Browns   read in

Note: March 3, 1803, Christopher Rush (Second Bishop of the A.M.E. Zion Church) was received on trial and assigned to the class of Samuel Pontier.
The New York Public Library Manuscript and Archives Division: Astor, Tilden and Lenox Foundations. Used by permission of the John Street United Methodist Church of New York City and New York Conference Commission on Archives and History of the United Methodist Church, Hudson, N.Y.

Working in unison, they did extremely well with their subscriptions. On Wednesday, July 30, 1800, the cornerstone was laid, after it was announced in the American-Citizen on Tuesday, July 29, 1800: [13] "On Wednesday next at 4 o'clock in the afternoon, the Corner Stone of the Church of the African Society, at the corner of Leonard and Church Streets, will be laid, and a Sermon preached on the ground, suited to the occasion." It was a hot sunny day with temperature soaring into the 90's. It was a joyous occasion, with sermon ostensibly preached by their able leader, James Varick. [14]

The building steadily progressed and was completed by early September. On Sunday, September 7, 1800, this little house of worship, so sacred in history to our members throughout the world, was dedicated to the Glory of God, by this first group heroically led by Varick, and called "Zion," commonly known at that time as "The African Methodist Episcopal Church in the City of New York." [15] They held their first business meeting in the church on Monday, September 8, 1800, and elected the trustees and officers of the board, so that they could proceed in securing a separate charter in accordance with the religious laws of the State of New York. [16]

Thomas Miller, who had been relieved from the treasurership for buying the first property in his own name and refusing to release the title, finally adjusted this matter. Rush states that he gave this property to the trustees to sell. [17] No record shows the trustees ever owned or sold this property. Another record, however, shows that Thomas Miller sold the property to William Johnson, merchant, in April 1800. [18] He seems to have satisfied the church membership by refunding the $80 he had received from the trustees, to be relieved of censorship. [19]

The Charter Story

The year 1800 was the beginning of occurrences which would shatter hopes for freely exercising "their spiritual gifts," and becoming "more useful to each other." The Methodist General Conference had been moved from the appointed time of October to May because of the "very malignant epidemic disorder called Yellow Fever in Baltimore and other seaport towns," and convened on May 6 by unanimous approval and agreement of the delegates, in the city of Baltimore. [20] They received the memorial of the African Society in New York, requesting that they be incorporated as a separate body, and made the following decision on Monday, May 19, 1800:

> Moved that the African brethren in New York be advised to apply for a charter similar to that of our African Society in Philadelphia; but if that cannot be obtained, that they apply for such a charter as is granted to the white brethren in New York, under the title of African Methodist Episcopal Church; but if the above-mentioned title be not admissible, it shall be left to the New York Conference to determine the title and all other particulars

13. Stokes, *op. cit.*, p.1378.
14. T. Thomas Fortune, "Rise of A Great Church," *The New York Sun*, Sept. 27, 1896.
15. *Who's Who in American History*, 1608-1896; Samuel A. Seaman, Annals of New York Methodism, p.157.
16. Hugh Hastings, *Ecclesiastical Records of the State of New York*, Vol. VI, p.4316.
17. Rush, *op. cit.*, p.23.
18. Evart Bancker Papers, Notebook No. 30 of Evert Bancker, Vol. IV; Liber 58, Property Conveyance Deeds, N.Y. City, p.121.
19. Rush, *op. cit.*
20. Ms. Minutes, Methodist Episcopal Church General Conference, 1800-1828.

respecting the business. [21]

Based upon this decision, they naturally expected to proceed in the normal mode, since the New York State Articles of Incorporation for Religious Societies of 1784 generally had the same pattern of language for each religious group, with the exception of name and personnel. [22] However, the glorious success of completing the house of worship commanded a more attentive eye from officials of the Methodist Church. After the Zion group held their business meeting on September 8, they made concrete plans to move forward and secure the charter. For strange reasons they were delayed nearly six months. As unbelievable as it may seem, one primary reason was an incident in Richmond, Va., which had an enormous effect upon New York and environment. It is stated that "inspirational drive was given this movement [the A.M.E. Zion Church], when a Negro slave named Gabriel Prosser led a revolt in Virginia, involving more than a thousand slaves, the reverberations of which were heard in every corner of this city." [23]

Prosser, "a Negro slave from Henrico County, Virginia, planned a slave revolt with his wife and two brothers." They organized a large number of slaves outside Richmond, and made regular and crude armaments. They also studied the location of Richmond's arms and ammunition. Governor Monroe of Virginia said that the plans for revolt embraced most of the slaves in the city of Richmond and the neighborhood. "Prosser's objective was to end slavery by seizing Richmond arsenals and killing all the whites in the city except Frenchmen, Methodists and Quakers. He planned also to attack other towns and eventually become king of Virginia. On Saturday, August 30, over 1,000 slaves, some armed with scythes, bayonets, and a few with guns, met outside Richmond. They disbanded, however, when they discovered that a storm the night before had made an essential bridge impassable." Governor Monroe had heard some rumors of a revolt, and when two slaves betrayed Prosser's plans, he called out the military. Numerous arrests were made, and Gabriel and between 24 and 35 others were tried and hanged. Governor Monroe, who had personally interviewed Prosser, reported: "From what he said to me, he seemed to have made up his mind to die, and to have resolved to say but little of the subject of the conspiracy." [24]

Fear stalked New York City once again. It shook the white citizens, and for two months dominated the press, until the last one of those involved in the incident was captured and executed. One newspaper reported that this proposed insurrection was "stated to have been the best planned and most matured of any before attempted." [25] Part of another news editorial stated:

> The conspiracy of the blacks in the southern states appears to be very general and alarming. If the modern doctrines of *liberty and equality,* and *the rights of man,* have obtained a general currency, among the slaves, they cannot be eradicated. The blacks can only be kept in subjection by rigorous punishments and a military force. The whites must constantly *lie on their arms.* [26]

The attitude of religious and civic leaders of the city now was to recede

21. *Ibid.,* Leroy M. Lee, *The Life and Times of the Rev. Jesse Lee,* p.380.
22. Hastings, Ecclesiastical Records, *op. cit.*
23. Ottley and Weatherby, *The Negro in New York,* p.56.
24. Bergman, *Chronological History of the Negro,* p.82.
25. *New York Commercial Advertiser,* Sept. 11, 1800.
26. *Ibid.,* Oct. 1, 1800.

rather than proceed with any plan to promote freedom, which the only black organization in New York would have over themselves and other Africans. With increased determination, this church group would not be deterred and thus continued its drive for independence in pursuit of incorporating.

The insurrection had such an influence upon nearby Newark, N.J., that in 1801, "at a Mass Meeting of citizens, rules were drawn up to prevent unlawful residence of free Negroes or such as falsely declared themselves to be free. To prevent Negro slaves from meeting together in an unlawful manner. To prevent the unlawful absence of Newark slaves from their owners after ten o'clock at night." (27)

According to Methodist law, the trustees had no jurisdiction over the spiritual affairs and denominational polity other than the purchase, regulation, maintenance, and sale of property subject to the will of the congregation. The spiritual and doctrinal matters, and the moral and official government of the church and its membership, belonged to the authority of the pastor and ruling elder. There was cooperative method in the system and the pastor was naturally the director of this cooperating authority in the membership. The incorporation of the entire church would certainly be a matter for the pastor and members to direct, and the trustees to work out under their direction. The skillful hand of James Varick was in the act of drawing up the Articles of Incorporation. (28)

CHARTER OF THE AFRICAN CHURCH.

In pursuance of an Act, entitled an Act to enable all the religious denominations of this State to appoint Trustees who shall be a body corporate, for the purpose of taking care of the temporalities of their respective congregations and for other purposes therein mentioned, passed the 6th day of April, 1784, public notice was given in the African Methodist Episcopal Church (called Zion Church) of the City of New York, in the State of New York, as the aforesaid law directs; and we, the subscribers, being nominated and appointed, agreeably to the aforesaid Act, Inspectors of an election held in our place of meeting, the eighth day of September, 1800, do report and declare the following persons duly elected by a plurality of voices, to serve as Trustees for the said Church, viz.: Francis Jacobs, George Collins, Thomas Sipkins, George E. Moore, George White, David Bias, Peter Williams, Thomas Cook, and Wm. Brown which said persons, so elected, and their successors in office, shall forever be styled and denominated the Trustees of the Corporation of the African Methodist Episcopal Church in the City of New York.

Given under our hands and seals, this fifth day of February, one thousand eight hundred and one.

his
PETER X WILLIAMS.
mark

FRANCIS JACOBS.

State of New York, ss. :

On this sixteenth day of February, 1801, before me personally came Peter Williams and Francis Jacobs, to me known to be the persons within described,

27. Frank J. Urquart, *A Short History of Newark, N.J.*, p.xxii.
28. *Minutes*, Nineteenth Quadrennial Session, Bishops' Quadrennial Address, 1892.

and who executed the within conveyance, who duly acknowledged the same—and there being no material erasures or interlineations therein, I do allow it to be recorded.

(Signed)   JAMES M. HUGHES,
Master in Chancery.

Recorded in the office of the Clerk of the City and County of New York, in Lib. No. 1 of Record of Incorporation of Religious Denominations, page 28, this ninth day of March, 1801.

Examined by
(Signed)   ROBERT BENSON,
Clerk.

RECORDED FOR AND AT THE REQUEST OF PETER WILLIAMS THIS 9TH DAY OF MARCH, 1801.

ARTICLES OF AGREEMENT,

Made the sixth day of April, 1801, between the Rev. John McClaskey, in behalf of the General Conference of the Methodist Episcopal Church in the United States of America, of the one part, and the Trustees of the African Methodist Episcopal Church in the City of New York, of the other part, showeth, for themselves and their successors in office:

ARTICLE I.

It is provided and declared that the style and title of this Corporation shall be "The African Methodist Episcopal Church of the City of New York, in the State of New York," and shall consist of Francis Jacobs, George Collins, Thomas Sipkins, George E. Moore, George White, David Bias, Peter Williams, Thomas Cook and William Brown, Trustees and Members of Zion Church, and their successors duly qualified, elected and appointed according to law (for the purposes and with the powers and privileges hereinafter granted and specified), of the Church called Zion Church, and of all and every such other church or churches as do now, or hereafter shall become the property of the Corporation.

ARTICLE II.

The Corporation aforesaid and their successors forever, do, and shall have and hold the said building called Zion Church, and all other churches which are now or shall become the property of the Corporation, in trust, for the religious use of the Ministers and Preachers of the Methodist Episcopal Church, who are in connection with the General Conference of the said church, and likewise for our African brethren and the descendents of the African race, as hereafter specified, and also for ministers and teachers of our African brethren, duly licensed or ordained according to the form of discipline.

ARTICLE III.

It is provided and declared that the rents, issues, profits and interests of the real and personal estate of and belonging to the said Church and Trustees and their successors shall, from time to time, be applied and laid out for repairing and maintaining their said Zion Church, and all and any other place or places of public worship, lot or lots of ground, burial grounds, or buildings which now do, or at any time hereafter may or shall belong to the said Church or Trustees, as shall, from time to time, be thought proper and expedient by the Trustees for the time being; and if the funds and revenues be sufficient, the Trustees may and shall be permitted, in their own discretion, to allow a reasonable and proportionable part for the support of the Ministers.

ARTICLE IV.

It is provided and declared that the said Trustees and their successors shall not, by deed or otherwise, grant, alien, convey, or otherwise dispose of any part or parcel of the estate, real or personal, in the said Corporation vested or to be vested, or in any other way to mortgage or pledge the said real estate for the payment of any debts by them contracted to any person or persons whatever, unless such grant, alienation and conveyance be made by and with the consent of two-thirds of the regular male members of the said church, of at least twenty-one years of age, and one year's standing.

ARTICLE V.

It is provided and declared that none but Africans or their descendents shall be chosen as Trustees of the said African Methodist Episcopal Zion Church, and such other church or churches as may or shall hereafter become the property of this Corporation, and none shall be eligible to the office of a Trustee but such as are received and acknowledged to be members of the said church by the elder of the Methodist Episcopal Church in the City of New York, who shall be appointed by the Conference of the said church, to the charge of the Methodist Society in the said city.

ARTICLE VI.

All elections for Trustees for the aforesaid Zion Church shall be by ballot of the male members, in close communion with them, or as many of them as attend, after being duly warned thereto; and no one shall have a right to vote for Trustees until he has been a member standing in full connection, one year at least; and no person shall be chosen a Trustee of the said Corporation until the said person shall have been a member in full connection and standing, at least two years. And no person shall be admitted into close connection with their classes or be enrolled on their books but Africans and descendents of the African race.

ARTICLE VII.

It is provided and declared that the Trustees aforesaid and their successors forever are and shall be empowered to have, and shall have, the entire direction and disposal of the temporal revenue of the aforesaid African Zion Church, and, after paying the ground rent of the said church, are to apply the remainder for the benefit of the said church, as a majority of the aforesaid Trustees and their successors shall, from time to time, direct. And the aforesaid Trustees and their successors forever shall have the disposal and management of the temporal concerns of the aforesaid African Methodist Episcopal Church, subject, nevertheless, to the provisions, and under the regulations made and provided in the fourth article of this instrument.

ARTICLE VIII.

It is declared that the Trustees and members of the African Methodist Episcopal Church do acquiesce and accord with the rules of the Methodist Episcopal Church for their church government and discipline, and with their creed and articles of faith, and that they and their successors will continue for ever in union with the Methodist Episcopal Church in the City of New York, subject to the government of the present Bishops and their successors, in all their ecclesiastical affairs and transactions, except in the temporal right and property of the aforesaid Zion Church, which is to be governed as herein directed, as long as the said articles and creeds of the said church remain unchanged.

ARTICLE IX.

It is declared that the elder of the Methodist Episcopal Church, for the time being, in the City of New York, appointed as aforementioned, shall have the direction and management of the spiritual concerns of the said Zion Church, or any other church or churches which may or shall be built hereafter by the Corporation aforesaid, or by any other means become their property, agreeably to the form of discipline of the said Methodist Episcopal Church, Provided, always, that the said elder shall receive no person into the African Society but such as are previously recommended by a Trustee or Trustees of the said African Zion Church. And upon complaint being made to the said African Church, or to the elder, of any of its members having walked disorderly, they shall be dealt with according to the form of discipline; provided, always, that their triers be members of their own church, and that the member, if condemned in the first trial, have an appeal to the Trustees, local preachers, exhorters and class leaders of the aforesaid Zion Church. And it is further declared that no person who may come recommended to the elder from other societies as a member of the Methodist Episcopal Church, shall be admitted or considered as a member of the African Church if he refuses to have his name registered in the books of the said Zion Church, after notice having been given him.

ARTICLE X.

It is agreed and declared that the elder of the Methodist Episcopal Church in the City of New York, appointed as aforesaid, shall, from time to time, for ever hereafter, nominate the preacher who shall officiate in said African Methodist Episcopal Church, and any, and all, other church or churches, which shall hereafter become the property of the Corporation, and shall attend to the said church or churches himself, to administer the ordinances of Baptism and the Lord's Supper, as often as he, the said Elder, can make it convenient. And the said Elder for the time being, shall license to exhort and preach any one or more of the brethren who are, or shall be, members of the said church, and shall appear, to the satisfaction of the said Elder, to be adequate to the task, and to have grace and gifts proper to appear in public: Provided, always, that such persons are previously recommended to him by a majority of the Trustees, local preachers, exhorters, and class leaders, of the aforesaid church. And if either of the said African brethren shall graduate into holy orders, it shall be done in such manner and way as the General Conference has directed. And it is provided and agreed that the said elder may claim for himself and his white brethren, and shall have and possess, a right to preach once on every Sunday, and once during the course of the week (and no more, when there is a sufficient number of African Preachers), in any or all the houses set apart and built, or to be set apart and built, by the aforesaid Trustees, or their successors, of the said African Zion Church, in the city and suburbs of New York.

ARTICLE XI.

It is provided and declared that no powers and authorities hereby given to the aforementioned Trustees shall be understood, taken, or construed, in any wise to prohibit or prevent the Elder for the time being, duly authorized and appointed as aforesaid, the religious use, benefit and enjoyment of the church known by the name of Zion Church, or of any other church or churches which, at any time hereafter, may be purchased or built by the said Corporation, or in any other way become their property, in the City of New York or the suburbs thereof, but that the same shall be, and forever hereafter continue to be, had, used, and enjoyed, by the said Elder for the time being, as heretofore, and by no other person whatever, of another denomination, unless by the particular license and consent of the Elder for the time being, with the concurrence of two-thirds of the Trustees for the time being, anything to the contrary in these articles notwithstanding.

(Signed) FRANCIS JACOBS,

THOMAS X SIPKINS, GEORGE X WHITE, PETER X WILLIAMS, WILLIAM X BROWN,
his mark   his mark   his mark   his mark

GEORGE E. MOORE,   GEORGE COLLINS,   THOMAS COOK,   DAVID BIAS.

Bishop E. D. W. Jones states that George Collins signed the charter. [29] The records show that George Collins did not sign the charter, although Francis Jacobs and George Collins were the legal persons elected by the trustees to sign the charter. The puzzling questions to members of the A.M.E. Zion Church over many years are were :

Why did not the proper officers of the Board request and sign the Charter, which included secretary, George Collins, a highly skillful and trained man, known to be a teacher in New York City? [30]

Why was the Charter secured in a secretive way without knowledge of the preachers and other trustees involved?

How did the Articles of Agreement affect full assurance of securing the Charter?

Why did the trustees sign an Article of Agreement protecting the rights of Africans to be elected trustees in Article 5, and in Articles 9, 10, and 11, sign away the rights of the African preachers to white preachers, when they were not to make decisions regarding spiritual concerns of the society?

How could the preachers freely exercise their spiritual gifts, *as they hoped*, under these conditions?

The answers to these questions, we do our best here to give according to records available.

It was obvious that the Methodists were stalling for time from the fall of 1800, in order to work out strategy to make sure this African Church would be controlled by them once the Charter was secured. They selected Rev. John McClaskey, one of the three pastors appointed to New York City at the New York Conference in June 1800, to work with the African group in securing this charter. Similar troubles are contained in the records of the African Methodist (Bethel) Church in Philadelphia when McClaskey was pastor of the Methodist Church in that city. [31] This made it necessary for our fathers to be alert when he was appointed to New York.

Reverend McClaskey, working under instruction of his conference, as implied in the action of the General Conference defining procedure in this matter, began his hindering tactics by first delaying the leaders and people who constantly kept before the Methodists the urgency of securing their charter.

On February 5 and 16, 1801, when he maneuvered Peter Williams and Francis Jacobs to apply for the charter in the City Clerk's office, it was an undercover movement of the Methodist Church. Peter Williams, sexton of John

29. E. D. W. Jones, *Comprehensive Catechism of the A.M.E. Zion Church*, p.63.
30. *New York City Directories*, 1806-1810.
31. *Doctrines and Discipline of the A.M.E. Church*, 1956, p.6; Payne, History of the A.M.E. Church, pp.4,5.

Street Church, was never a member of the A.M.E. Zion Church. He was named by the white pastor, and accepted as one of the original trustees of the African Church, and like the other trustees helped to raise subscriptions for the church building. [32] As a matter of fact, Peter Williams was not motivated to get an incorporation for a church of an independent denomination. He was acting to secure an incorporation of a church to remain within the boundaries of the Methodist Episcopal denomination. The chairman of the board of trustees was rather a pliable man, as was shown by his permitting the first effort to purchase property for the church building to get out of hand. Francis Jacobs had intelligence enough to know that the charter had to be finalized by one of the two persons designated, or both. He returned to the City Clerk's office to have it recorded, aware that he was the logical person as chairman of the board. While waiting for direction, he was by-passed by some of the powers who sent Peter Williams to the City Clerk's office, and on March 9, 1801, the Charter was recorded at the request of Peter Williams, [33] without the knowledge of Jacobs or the other trustees. (See Charter and Articles of Agreement, pp 58–62).

The trustees were informed that they must come to some agreement with the Methodist Episcopal Church as to how the African Church would be governed, before they could receive the Charter. [34] The Articles of Agreement were presented to them by Rev. McClaskey, apparently not collectively, for it would have been barely possible to hold a full meeting of trustees, and secure signatures for a document of that type, with the exclusion of the four black preachers altogether, including William Miller, the exhorter. The document was dated April 6, 1801. This ill-fated document finally had to be ignored when they made a formidable organization and withdrew from the Methodist Episcopal Church.

Two days after this grievous misstep, on April 8, the property deal for the Church and Leonard Street lots was consummated between the trustees and John Colvill and his wife, Effie, signed by the designated officers, and recorded for and at the request of Francis Jacobs on April 22, 1801. [35] The property deed, the Charter, and the Articles of Agreement were presented at a subsequent church meeting with the preachers and people getting their first knowledge of them. The inevitable happened. Instead of turning on the Methodists, they turned on themselves. A bitter dissension arose, which affected leading members of the society and their children permanently. Abraham Thompson was most deeply hurt. Being the senior licentiate, he had dreamed of becoming the first pastor of the church after it was built. The members then made use of the point in Article 6 of the Agreements, which states that "all elections of Trustees for the aforesaid Zion Church shall be by ballot of the male members. . . ." In the next election of·trustees, they voted out five and replaced them, including the chairman. Thus the trustees elected were: Thomas Edsell, chairman, George Collins, secretary, William Brown, treasurer, James Jacklin, George White, Thomas Jenkins, William Butler, Jacob Matthews, and Thomas Cook. [36]

32. J. B. Wakeley, *Lost Chapters Recovered from the Early History of American Methodism,* p.444. . . . David H. Bradley, Sr., *A History of the A.M.E. Zion Church,* Vol. I, p.44.
33. Liber 1, Record of Incorporations of Religious Denominations, p.28.
34. Rush, *op. cit.,* p.13.
35. Property Conveyance Deeds, Liber 60, N.Y. City, p.144.
36. *Minutes,* Common Council of the City of New York, 1801-1810, *City Clerk papers,* Municipal Archives and Record Center, New York City.
   See Liber 75, p.214, Property Conveyance Deed, Hall of Records, New York City.

In the midst of troubled waters, Bishop Asbury made Zion Church his first stop in his visit to the city. Indeed this was his first visit to this church ever. He states in his journal the following: "Tuesday, May 25, 1802. We came to New York, and took up our lodging at Mr. Suckley's. . . . My first public exercise in the city was in the African Church—a very neat wooden house, but by far too small: my text was Ephes. ii, 11-14.[37] ["Wherefore remember, that ye being in time past Gentiles in the flesh, who are called Uncircumcision, by that which is called the Circumcision in the flesh made by hands: that at that time ye were without Christ, being aliens from the commonwealth of Israel, and strangers from the covenant of promise, having no hope, and without God in the world: But now in Christ Jesus ye who sometimes were far off are made nigh by the blood of Christ. For he is our peace, who hath broken down the middle wall of partition between us."]

Two months later, on "Sabbath, July 25," he was in New York and preached again in the African Church at 6 o'clock in the evening, on 1 Thess. 1:5.[38] Notwithstanding, feelings worsened after the election of trustees. To shed some light on how troubles increased, in 1803, while Freeborn Garrettson was presiding elder, some of the group began to bring their grievances before the quarterly conferences. Thomas Morrell, who had been appointed to take the New York charge at the conference in 1802, manifested uneasiness over the internal problems of this congregation. In his correspondence with John McClaskey, who was serving again in Philadelphia (where one of the churches had "entered nine charges in writing against" him), [39] he apparently mentioned these troubles, for the African Church was the only society in New York, at that time, having dissatisfactions. In Brother McClaskey's reply to Morrell, from Chestertown, he said: "I received yours. . .containing the proceedings of the last quarterly meeting conference, with which I am perfectly satisfied; and at the same time I am sorry that ever there had been cause for any proceedings of the kind; but mistakes will happen, and when they do they must be made the best of." [40]

At the 1804 annual conference, Rev. William Thatcher was made presiding elder, and a group from the African Church continued to petition the quarterly conferences. The quarterly meeting of November 22, 1804, resolved that the request from the "African Brethren be laid over to the next quarterly conference for further consideration." [41] At the next quarterly conference held in the Bowery Church, February 26, 1805, they resolved the matter somewhat, by taking the following action:

ARTICLES OF AGREEMENT BETWEEN THE QUARTERLY CONFERENCE OF THE WHITE SOCIETY AND THE AFRICAN METHODIST SOCIETY

Article 1

Those 33 whose names were subscribed to a request to be taken into the white body shall be considered as members of the white society and accordingly have their names taken from the register of the African Zion Church.

37. Asbury, *op. cit.,* Vol. II. p.341,
38. *Ibid.,* p.355.
39. Thomas Morrell Letters, *Christian Advocate & Journal,* May 1, 1851.
40. *Ibid.,* July 1, 1851; also Ms. Letter of Thomas Morrell, Garrett Theological Seminary, Dec. 9, 1803.
41. Ms. Records, Methodist Episcopal Church, Quarterly Conference Minutes, 1804-1824.

Article 2

But before any other members of the African Zion Church shall be admitted into the white society, he shall, with the consent and knowledge of the leader obtain a note from the preacher. 2. And if any African in the white society wishes to remain to the Africans the same rule must be observed.

Article 3

The Africans shall have the privilege of joining on trial the white society and becoming members of the same.

Article 4

Those Africans who are in membership in the white society shall have no claim upon the poor funds of the African Zion Church, neither shall they have any vote on the privilege of holding any office in the said Zion Church.

Signed: William Thatcher
                   Joseph Smith, Secretary [42]

This seems to have straightened out the separate memberships between the two organizations, the Mother Methodist Church and the African Church.

The Ordination Of Deacons

While this group of 33 had made the decision to return to the segregated conditions in John Street Church, which existed there and in other white churches in the city of New York, [43] Zion Church was taking on phenomenal growth. In 1806, after Zion's first preachers had suffered heartaches, disappointments, and humiliations, Bishop Asbury ordained James Varick, Abraham Thompson, and June Scott deacons, at the seat of the annual conference in New York City, [44] in accordance with the legislation regarding ordination of African preachers which had passed the 1800 General Conference. He kept this action as secretive as possible because many delegates of the South stringently opposed it. This delayed, painful process was as follows:

On Tuesday, May 20, 1800, the General Conference meeting in Baltimore made the following rule "respecting the ordination of colored, or black people, to the office of Deacons:" [45]

[That] the bishops have obtained leave by the suffrages of the General Conference, to ordain local deacons of our African brethren in places where they have built a house or houses for the worship of God; provided they have a person among them qualified for that office, and he can obtain an election of two-thirds of the male members of the society to which he belongs, and a recommendation from the minister who has the charge, and from his fellow-labourers in the city or circuit. [46]

The rule "met with so much opposition, as never to have been observed, and which was, by special enactment at the time, excluded from the Discipline, and never made extensively public; so that nine years after, when compiling his *History of the Methodists,* Mr. Lee supposes it was scarcely known, as a rule of the church, to the preachers." [47] According to the General Conference rule, it

42. *Ibid.*
43. James S. Buckingham, *America, Historical, Statistic and Descriptive,* Vol. II, p.506.
44. Asbury, *Journal,* II, p.506; Coker, *op. cit.,* p.40.
45. Jesse Lee, *A Short History of the Methodists,* p.270.
46. Ms. *Minutes,* General Conference, 1800.
47. Leroy Lee, *Life and Times of Jesse Lee.,* p. 375.

was not considered that there would be more than one qualified person in an area at a specific time. This may have impeded the progress of ordination in New York for six years. Nevertheless, this accumulation of eligibles was the largest number of black preachers Asbury ordained at any one time, and the first group so ordained in the city and state of New York. The ordination at conference was unusual, considering that black Methodist preachers were not itinerants, and not allowed membership in either the annual or general conference.

Although, virtually, the Negro preachers pastored the church without pay or official status, under white pastors, the Zion congregation was constrained to pay heavy salaries to the white preachers according to Methodist Church rule and the contract which bound them. While emphatically devoted to the cause of their high calling, and utilizing, to the best of their ability, every available moment for promoting the gospel of Jesus Christ, the Zion preachers still had to maintain their various trades and occupations in order to survive. Thus, the first decade of the African Methodist Episcopal Zion Church is brought into reality with all the thrills, the joy, the sorrow, the heartbleedings, the prayers, the faith, and the insurmountable determination of continuing the cause of religion and freedom.

Permanency Attained Through Manifold Tribulations

The membership's continued growth necessitated expansion of their facilities. On April 8, 1807, the trustees purchased two additional lots fronting Church Street, and two lots 100 feet deep on Leonard St., with a small house on it, for $1,375. from the same John and Effie Colvill. [48] On March 1, 1811, they purchased additional lots, each 100 feet deep and 25 feet wide, fronting Leonard, for $2,500. [49] Therefore, Zion Church owned more than one-half of the city block between Church and Anthony (now Worth) and Leonard and Chapel (now West Broadway) Streets within this 15-year period of their existence. This sacred spot was to be their spiritual habitation until 1864, when they were forced to sell for $90,000 to allow for the business growth of the city. They then purchased a commodious church edifice, parsonage, and additional facility from the Dutch Reformed Church, at West Tenth and Bleeker Streets for $45,000, [50] and additional investment property.

In order to reasonably accommodate the large crowds, in 1807 they lengthened their original church building by 20 or 25 feet. [51] The trustees were faced with another serious problem this year regarding their burial ground, which was so small and sandy that they were obliged to build vaults for interment in their churchyard in the rear of the church building. [52]

One of the outstanding points in the history of the black race in this country is its poor, almost impossible, burial accommodations. New York Negroes confronted this condition as early as 1722, when the "dread of an uprising of blacks prompted an act providing that all Negroes and Indians should be buried by daylight. The act was amended afterward so that not more than twelve Negroes should attend a funeral. The penalty for the violation of this statute was a public flogging. Furthermore, the slave was to be buried without

48. Rush, *Rise and Progress,* p.24; Hall of Records, New York City, Liber 75, pp.214-271.
49. Liber 91, pp.26-27, Property Conveyance Records, N.Y. City.
50. Liber 811, p.564, Property Conveyance Records.
51. Rush, *Rise and Progress,* p.24.
52. *Ibid.,* p.25.

any outward signs of grief or any ceremonial tokens, such as pall, gloves or flowers." [53] 'This local ordinance tended to erode gradually. Exactly when it was totally eliminated is not known. However, the denial of a decent Christian burial for black people existed when the African Methodist Episcopal Zion Church was born. The city did not allow Negroes to be buried in white or church-owned cemeteries, although they were members of various congregations, rather in an undesirable spot north of the Alms-house and Bridewell known as the Negroes' Burial Grounds. [54] This brought the black men into political action in 1795 and they made petitions to the city government for improvement of burial places and for the privilege of observing burial rites. When Bishop Asbury met with the black classes on Sunday afternoon, July 5, 1795, this was such a live issue that the matter was apparently brought to bear upon the bishop's mind, and helped influence his decision that black members hold independent services.

After Zion Church was built in 1800, its membership continued to swell. People of the black race pined for a religious burial service with interment in a church burial ground. This being the only black church in the city of New York until the founding of the "African (Abyssinian) Baptist Church in 1808, Zion Church's burial ground by 1807 had far exceeded the number for which it was built, as had the vault built under the church, with something like 750 bodies interred in the last five years." [55] Added to this, the city was visited with yellow fever during the summer, and the city health department ordered no more burials in the church vault. [56] The trustees immediately proceeded to petition the Common Council of the city for additional burial ground, and the city granted them a section of about 50 feet in the public burial ground then called Pottersfield, later known as Washington Parade Ground, presently known as Washington Square. [57] Zion Church dedicated this ground as a sacred spot to continue the burial of their dead. Thus the history regarding religious burials for African people began in New York with the African Methodist Episcopal Zion Church. The trustees afterwards purchased some lots of ground at Yorkville, and appropriated seven lots for a burying ground. [58] This cemetery was in the neighborhood of 86th Street. [59] Later a large plot in Cypress Hills, Brooklyn, was purchased, which is still in use by this congregation. [60]

The work of the Lord prospered greatly in the church, [61] and the number of members of the society, and of the congregation, continued to increase rapidly. [62] On Wednesday, April 27, 1808, Bishop Asbury preached at the church, and ordained William Miller and Daniel Coker deacons. [63] Coker later moved to Baltimore and became one of the founders of the African Methodist Episcopal Church, was elected its first bishop and declined. [64] Two former

53. Fortune, "The Rise of a Great Church," *New York Sun,* Sept. 1903; news clippings in the New York Churches collection, Museum of the City of New York.
54. Henry Collins Brown, *Valentine's Manual of Old New York,* p.249.
55. *Minutes,* Common Council of the City of N.Y., II, pp.112, 158-159, 522.
56. *Ibid.,* Rush, *Rise and Progress,* p.25.
57. *Ibid.,* p.525; Greenwald, Ms., "Cemeteries of New York City, 1933.
58. Rush, *op. cit.,* p.25.
59. Harry Williamson, Ms., "Folks in Old New York," 1953.
60. Mother Zion Church records.
61. Rush, *op. cit.,* p.26.
62. *Ibid.*
63. Asbury, Journal, II, p.568.
64. Daniel Payne, *History of the African Methodist Episcopal Church, op. cit.,* p.14.

trustees, George White and Thomas Miller, had been licensed to preach by the Quarterly Conference in 1807, and the preachers were beginning to launch out into neighboring communities with their exhortations of faith and hope, making bold attempts in their first efforts of cultivating a denomination. [65] "The preachers held occasional conferences as early as 1812; but the first regular meeting of the New York Conference of which we have record was held in New York City, July 21, 1821." [66]

During this time, John Edwards, a former member of the Friends Society, built a church on his property at 101 Greene Street, with a meeting room, and set aside two wings of it for a free dwelling place for preachers who might be interested in a church of his creation. He incorporated this church under the name of The African Free Meeting Methodist Society, March 27, 1812, with nine trustees, William Butler being a late trustee of Zion. [67] "Abraham Thompson, being made acquainted with the supposed favorable circumstance, and hoping to have, at least a place of residence gratis, and thereby receive some compensation for his labors as a preacher, consented to become one of the preachers, and persuaded June Scott to join him." [68] When they discovered that they were mistaken in their judgment of this movement, and found that they were about to be expelled from Zion Church, Abraham Thompson came forward and pleaded ignorance in what he was doing, and thus saved his membership in the church, as did all the others that were fearful. June Scott would not return to Zion. He kept his position in the Free Meeting Society, also known as the Union Society, until it was found that the society was not able to bear its expenses, and was therefore obliged to give up the premises to John Edwards, owner. The Society consequently was broken up, and June Scott attached himself to another church. [69] From this time forward, the people looked solely to James Varick who, solid as a rock, stood steadfast and led them all the way through to independence. He never wavered, although he had a strenuous responsibility of supporting a large family.

The next manifestation of unpleasantness was when William Miller, through unstayable ambition, led some of his friends out of Zion Church and established the Asbury Church. He united with Thomas Sipkins, a former trustee of Zion Church, who had been expelled after some contentions with the church group, became lonesome, and desired company among the black Methodist group. Together they formed a church with some discordant members, [70] and received a charter from New York City on February 3, 1814. [71] Their conception that this would be an independent church of Zion ran into the problem that they could not be Methodists unless they were received into the Methodist Church through the consent of Zion. [72] This caused a series of conferences between the Methodist leaders and Zion trustees, out of which the Mother Methodist Church, in the New York Annual Conference, agreed to take in the African Asbury Church, as they named it, as a part of a circuit with the

65. George White, *A Brief Account of the Life . . . of George White,* pp.24-29.
66. Hood, *One Hundred Years,* p.213; Bucke, *History of American Methodism,* II, p.556.
67. Rush, *op. cit.,* p.28, Liber No. 1, pp.76-77, Religious Corporations.
68. Rush, *op. cit.,* p.27.
69. *Ibid.,* pp.27-28.
70. *Ibid.,* pp.28-29.
71. Liber 1, p.78, Religious Corporations, Hall of Records, N.Y. City.
72. Rush, *Rise and Progress,* p.29.

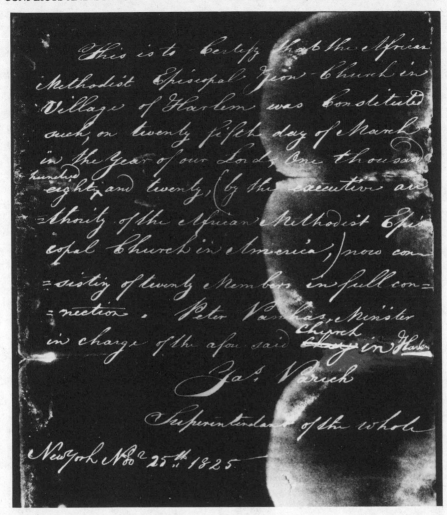

Letter of authorization by Bishop Varick, for funds for the first African Church started in Harlem, which evolved into the present Hood Memorial Church on 146th Street near Seventh Avenue.
The Riker Collection, Manuscript and Archives Division, The New York Public Library: Astor, Lenox and Tilden Foundations.

Zion Church. It was therefore placed, by a resolution of the Conference, under the same white pastorate of the Zion Church. (73) This was tantamount to uniting these churches, and they remained so when they attained independence. It therefore became the second church of the denomination in 1816. The New Haven Society was organized in 1818, the Wesley Society in Philadelphia in 1820, and subsequently, societies on Long Island. This evidences the movement of James Varick, who because of his activity of bringing these churches into a unity of procedure was leader of the group when it attained independence.

73. Ms. Minutes, Methodist Episcopal Church, New York State Annual Conference Journal, 1800-1820; June 1 & 2, 1816, pp.102, 104-105.

Meanwhile, the membership of Zion Church had prospered spiritually, and had grown so rapidly that it had an imperative need for a new building. The trustees (William Brown, chairman, George Collins, secretary, John Bias, Thomas Jenkins, Charles Tredwell, Tobias Hawkins, Philip Searing, Epiphany Davis, and Isaac Benson) met on November 25, 1818, and appointed a committee to plan for a larger church building. They contracted with master builders, James DuBois and Thompson Price, to build a worship house 55 feet wide and 75 feet long, of stone, for $11,500, on July 13, 1819. [74]

The white pastors assigned to Zion and Asbury by Bishop George, at the New York Conference, were William Phoebus in 1818, and William Stilwell in 1819 and 1820. Varick and Miller were working together as leading African preachers of these two churches. [75] On July 16, 1819, they commenced building the foundation around the old church, "which was carried up to the water table, except the front. Due to the shortage of funds, they stopped work." [76] Formerly they had received some funds from the city government to operate a school in the old church, which they were obliged to refund to the city, like the other churches operating schools. [77] The trustees petitioned the state legislature for aid toward operating a school in the new building, and were disappointed that they were denied help. Nevertheless, they proceeded to erect an extension to this new building for a school room. They were not able to finish the enterprise in the winter, and the next spring, May 1820, they took down the old building and continued their efforts for a new building. When they could not find a place large enough for this growing congregation, they rented the Riding Circus on Broadway, between Hester (now Howard) and Grand Streets. There they held meetings morning and afternoon on Sundays, and on Sunday evenings and week nights they met in the Rose Street Academy. The trustees then obtained special permission from the Master in Chancery to apply for a mortgage, which they secured on bond from James Bogert, for $3,000, and proceeded with their church building on June 5, 1820. [78]

William Stilwell, the pastor appointed in 1820, was the last pastor appointed by the Methodist Church before Zion and Asbury's withdrawal into an independent body. While these African Methodists in New York were passing through a series of crises, especially the Zion congregation, Stilwell manifested compassion.

Evidently there were further hardship and delay, for when they had raised the walls, before putting on the roof, they held their first service within these sacred walls on July 30, and William Stilwell preached. However, a strange providence befell them. It began to rain soon after the text was taken, and continued during divine service; nevertheless only a few left; "those who had umbrellas stood it out with apparent composure." [79] The weather had cleared up by the afternoon. Abraham Thompson preached, and James Varick, who was presiding with encouragement and exhortation, closed the meeting. Another service was held in the evening. John Dungy, one of the Negro preachers who

---

74. Rush, *op. cit.,* pp.29-30.
75. *Minutes,* Annual Conference, Methodist Episcopal Church, 1818, 1819, 1820.
76. Rush, *op. cit.,* p.30.
77. *Minutes,* Common Council of the City of N.Y., III, p.564, July 10, 1804.
78. Rush, *op. cit.,* p.30.
79. *Ibid.,* p.38.

later joined Zion connection, preached the sermon. [80]

Before completing this lovely stone structure, the preachers, leaders, and people passed through its severest trials. Four major problems were: the inconvenience of meeting in the Riding Circus on Broadway, which was a place for entertainment, and many of the devout members did not relish the idea of worshipping there anyhow; the procedure of withdrawing from the white church; the struggle to procure elder's orders; and the entrance of Bishop Allen's movement into New York during their precarious state. The congregation opened the new church for worship in August 1820, with solemn services led by James Varick, assisted by Abraham Thompson. They continued to hold their business meetings in the Rose Street Academy and in the homes of Varick, William Brown (chairman of the trustees Board), and other leaders. They commenced shingling the roof on Monday, September 4, and began fixing up the seats on November 2. Thus the new edifice was ready for full operation by the end of the year, and consecrated anew to the Glory of God on March 18, 1821. [81]

The Problem Of Organizing Independence

We come now to the most dangerous period of the effort to form the African Methodist Episcopal Zion Church. We will not be confused by the name. It had its historic ingredients and events before it became this full settled name, but it was our varied opinions on procedure that we had to confront and unify. There were those who wanted to be a Negro unit in the Methodist Church. There were others who wanted nothing less than separation and independence from the Mother Methodist Church. There were still others who felt a sympathy with the black groups in other areas, such as the A.M.E. Bethel Church and the African Union Church of Wilmington, Del., and preferred to see a unity of them all. The small faction, 61 of the 751 colored members that preferred the Mother Church withdrew and settled on remaining in the Methodist Episcopal Church. [82]

Those who had definitely decided on withdrawing from the white church and forming a denomination of freedom and self-assertion began a part of their action by appointing a committee of five to form a Discipline for the new church group. In a church meeting held at the Rose Street Academy on September 18, 1820, they appointed James Varick, chairman, George Collins, secretary, Charles Anderson, Christopher Rush, and William Miller the committee to draw up the Discipline of the independent church movement. It was to conform with the Methodist Church Discipline, as relating to doctrines, polity, and spiritual government. They also resolved that the preachers exert supreme energy in stimulating the other African preachers and societies in surrounding territories, with special emphasis on the Brooklyn Church. The brethren retired from this meeting "with much more satisfaction than they had done from several former meetings." [83]

The committee on Discipline met on Monday evening, September 4, at the residence of William Miller, 36 Mulberry Street, and determined on the title: The

---

80. *Ibid.*
81. *Ibid.*, pp.38, 49, 71; Greenleaf, *op. cit.*, p.322; Haride, *A Census of the New Buildings Erected in This City*, 1824, pp.25-26.
82. Federal Writers Program, Inventory of Church Archives of New York: Methodist, p.21.
83. Rush, *op. cit.*, p.43.

Doctrines and Discipline of the African Methodist Episcopal [Zion] Church in America. They requested George Collins to draw up the Preamble for the Discipline. The committee inspected and approved this preamble, then worked ardently in making the necessary selections for its contents, and on Tuesday night, September 26, 1820, they completed their selections and left the manuscript with George Collins to compile and prepare for printing. [84] Christopher Rush was chosen to assist Collins because the three leading preachers, Varick, Thompson, and Miller, were principally engaged in organizing their religious freedom society, which is evinced in their "Founders Address." [85] Twelve hundred copies of the Discipline were duly printed as a major phase of finalizing the new organization. [86]

Before the Discipline was printed, the pastor who had been assigned to Zion and Asbury Circuit, one month hence, Rev. William M. Stilwell, came to their worship service held at the Rose Street Academy on Sunday night, July 16, 1820, just before the close of the service. He informed the members present that he and several hundred of his associates had withdrawn from the Methodist Episcopal Church because of action taken at the recent General and Annual Conferences regarding the temporal concern of the churches, particularly the New York churches. "The chief resolution was to petition the Legislature of the State of New York for a special Act of Incorporation, in order to give the preachers more power over the trustees. . . ." The information was very alarming to Zion, for her preachers and trustees had been threatened and "spoken to unkindly" by elders in charge of the church, and then the circuit, from time to time, but they had some assurance with their state charter (regarding the temporalities) independent of the Methodist Episcopal Church. The Articles of Agreement had given some of the white preachers imaginary authority, which they used to maltreat the African preachers and members. This had already caused considerable dissatisfaction in the minds of the officials. Now faced with the thought of having their property controlled by the Methodist Episcopal Church, they were aroused to direct action. [87]

Another disturbing element to the preachers was the action taken at the Methodist General Conference in May, creating district conferences composed of "all the local preachers in the presiding elder's district who have been licensed two years." [88] The local preachers had been contending for a number of years for representation in the annual and general conferences. There was an uncertainty among the African preachers regarding this innovation, and the authority the conferences might attempt to exercise over them. On Tuesday, the 18th, the trustees met with Presiding Elder Peter P. Sanford of the New York District, and a committee of Methodist elders, at the John Street Church house of Peter Williams in Liberty Street, to get clarification on the new rule of incorporating churches. The preachers were meeting at the same time, in the home of James Varick, to make concrete plans. [89] After consultation with other Methodist leaders and William Stilwell, they held a members' meeting on Friday night, July 20, at the Rose Street Academy and came to some definite conclusions. Among them were:

84. *Ibid.*, pp.43-44.
85. *Ibid.*, p.48; *Doctrines and Discipline,* 1820, p.1.
86. Rush, *op. cit.*, p.48.
87. Rush, *op. cit.*, pp.34-35.
88. Emory Stevens Bucke, (ed.), *The History of American Methodism* I, p.640.
89. Rush, *op. cit.*, p.35.

That in consequence of the dissatisfaction and doubt existing in our minds, relative to the intended special Act of Incorporation, and to the conduct of the preachers in Conference requiring such an Act, we decline receiving any further services from them as respects our church government. . .and that we request William M. Stilwell to continue his services with us for the remainder of the year.

A large number of members crowded the Rose Street Academy on Wednesday, the 26th, and sanctioned all that had been done by the previous body. Thus they had totally severed themselves from the Methodist Episcopal Church.

Some of the trustees became uneasy after receiving a notice from Bishop Enoch George of the Methodist Episcopal Church, regarding their withdrawal. On Saturday morning, August 12, three trustees, William Brown, Thomas Jenkins, and Tobias Hawkins, held about a two-hour meeting with Bishop George in the home of a Morris Carter, in Church Street. [90] The bishop attempted to get them to acquiesce in the action of the Methodist Episcopal Church, to petition the New York State Legislature "for an act of incorporation which shall recognize the peculiarities of their form of church government and thereby enable them more fully and effectually to execute the Discipline of their church. [91] They explained to him that they would mention the matter to other members, as they were too small a number to make any decisions. [92]

Elders' Election and Ordination

After their withdrawal from the Methodist Episcopal Church on July 26, 1820, the preachers, leaders, and members passed through the most excruciating two years of the church's history. The struggle began with the effort of the qualified leaders to secure the order in the apostolic succession of Christianity. After finding that Richard Allen had been set apart as a bishop in his Philadelphia and Baltimore contest, certain men in our group felt that we might go on with him and advocated that we have him ordain our ministers to eldership, which the Mother Church had not done for any black preacher. Certain ones of our group sought to lead us into the direction of the Allen movement, which was organizing a competitive church in New York City when Bishop Allen of the A.M.E. Bethel group came to the city and blessed their efforts on Sunday, July 23, 1820. [93]

The feeling was high, and the Zion people had voted not to patronize Bishop Allen's visit. However, some of the more liberal leaders felt that they should sound out the bishop and visited his service, and our major leader, James Varick, who was fraternal minded, visited the service and gave the opening prayer at this Bethel Church Dedication Service. [94] Although he was criticized for this act, he went a step further. He summoned the preachers to meet at the home of William Miller, where they resolved to request a meeting of the official members of the church to consider their *present* state. The official members assembled in the Rose Street Academy on Friday night, August 11, James Varick presiding. There were two main questions put and answered at that meeting: "Shall we join Bishop Allen? Answer: No. Shall we return to the white people? Answer: No."

90. *Ibid.*, pp.37-39.
91. Ms. *Minutes*, 1820, *Journal of the New York State Annual Conference*, Ms. Division, New York Public Library.
92. Rush, *op. cit.*, p.40.
93. *Ibid.*, p.33.
94. *Ibid.*

They therefore determined to consult with the rest of the members upon "the subject of establishing a firm church government of our own, by ordinations, etc. After several brethren had given their opinions, it being late, the meeting was adjourned to the following Tuesday night." [95]

"On Tuesday night, August 15, the official members met according to adjournment at William Brown's home in Leonard Street." William Miller, representing the Asbury Church, expressed "his willingness to acquiesce with whatever the members of Zion Church should determine upon for the spiritual government of the Church." Abraham Thompson was appointed chairman and Charles Anderson, secretary. A committee was then appointed to inquire of Bishop Hobart of the Protestant Episcopal Church in the City. Abraham Thompson stringently opposed asking a white bishop to ordain men in preference to Bishop Allen who was still in the city, and as he believed, was still accessible to do this. However, there were some in the meeting who had a feeling against Allen, who they said had come into the city to establish a society in competition with our efforts, at a time when our problems were seriously threatening. Some had discovered that Bishop Allen was disposed to be friendly and wished to have a meeting with some of the preachers and trustees of Zion and Asbury churches. They then appointed a committee of four preachers and five trustees, James Varick, Abraham Thompson, William Miller and Christopher Rush, preachers, and William Brown, George Collins, Tobias Hawkins, Charles Tredwell, and Thomas Jenkins, laymen. [96]

On Thursday night, August 17, the committee met with Bishop Allen in the home of the chairman of the trustees board, William Brown. They made known to him that they would like to have him, instead of a white bishop, ordain them. He said if they would join his movement he would readily do so. When they demurred, and stated they would consider this later, but at this time they only wanted ordination he undiplomatically said to them that he *was not a child—that he knew his business,*" and that "he had no intention to assist in ordination unless we put ourselves under his charge." Father Thompson, who had been strongly advocating this, was disillusioned and made no further effort to secure favor from Bishop Allen. This effort in Zion ended there, except that George White, who had cultivated the Brooklyn society for Zion Church, took the society and joined the Allen movement. [97] He also took the Flushing, Long Island Society over to the Bethel group. William Miller and George Collins were sent to Flushing by a committee, to try to save them from the influence of White, who had deceived them by reporting to them that all the Zion group had decided to join the Bethel movement except two or three whose minds would be made up in a few days, [98] but they failed in this venture.

However, the Lord had blessings in store for Zion, as the African society in the Williamsburgh section of Brooklyn had organized November 6, 1818, and later joined our connection, and is reputed to be the oldest black church in Brooklyn. This loyal group is now known as the Varick Memorial A.M.E. Zion Church. [99] Zion also took in practically all the other African societies, from time to time, spanning the entire island.

95. *Ibid.,* p.39.
96. *Ibid.,* pp.39, 40, 41.
97. *Ibid.,* pp.41-42.
98. *Ibid.,* pp.49-50.
99. Varick Memorial Church Historical Bulletins, Dedication Program, March 30, 1952.

The committee on ordination met with the official members, Friday night, September 1, at the Rose Street Academy. Abraham Thompson made the report on behalf of the committee, who had conferred with Bishop Allen. William Miller reported that Bishop Hobart was out of the city and that the Episcopal minister would give him the message upon his return. Meantime, in the interim of these meetings, several leaders had met with William Stilwell on matters of solidifying our church government and received assurance that he would be cooperative. "The case of our Church being at this time in a very precarious state, in regard, particularly, to the want of Elders in the Church," it became necessary to do something to relieve her of this "religious pressure." (100) Discouragement had already begun to seize some of the members, and at the regular monthly meeting of the trustees, held in William Brown's home on Tuesday night, September 5, they appeared to be "rather disunited." (101) Some desired to unite with Richard Allen and others were for establishing a church government of their own. However, the decision previously made in the September 1 meeting, to proceed with a Discipline for the new organization, and the immediate course taken, eased the tension somewhat, and they continued to labor for ordination.

Reverend William Stilwell proved to be a shepherd among our people, so that he won their confidence. They consulted with him about his denomination, which had withdrawn from the Methodist Episcopal Church and formed a different organization of Methodists known as The Methodist Society of the City of New York, the nucleus finally joining in with other groups across the country in forming the Methodist Protestant Church at Baltimore in 1830. (102) He directed them on the necessity of electing an elder, and produced literature and books written by Methodist preachers to prove the "validity of such proceedings in cases of necessity." He understood the critical situation of this African church operating without an elder, among other black churches beginning to rise, some, sponsored by white churches forming a definite threat to the cause of Zion. "He advised them to pursue and adopt the plan, as it suited our case of extreme necessity." At this meeting on Wednesday night, September 13, in the Rose Street Academy, in the presence of Stilwell, they voted to accept this measure and nominated Abraham Thompson and James Varick to the office of elders in the church, to be recommended to the society for election. (103)

Bishop William McKendree of the Methodist Episcopal Church, on one of his last visits to New York City, desired to see some of the officials in order to understand their thoughts. A committee of nine met with him on Sunday, September 24, immediately after divine worship. He being ill, they met at the home of Joshua Soule, where they had a conversation about Zion's withdrawal from the Methodist Episcopal Church. He was powerless to take action without the authorization of the annual conference, and advised them to wait until the next conference. (104) However, they doubted the Methodist attitude on ordaining Negro elders, which had never been done.

On Sunday afternoon, October 1, 1820, the two men who were nominated

100. Rush, *op. cit.*, pp.41-42.
101. *Ibid.*, p.44.
102. Extracts, *Minutes* of the Sixth Yearly Conference and the State Conference of the Methodist Society, November 1826 and June 1827; John Atkinson, *Memorials of Methodism in New Jersey*, p.429.
103. Rush, *op. cit.*, p.45.
104. *Ibid.*, pp.45-46.

on September 13 to the office of elders were elected the first elders of the African Methodist Episcopal Zion Church, with much solemnity and satisfaction, with both male and female members in attendance participating. [105] With extraordinary depth and divine and orderly conduct of the Holy Spirit, it was agreed by unanimous decision that until ordination proper could be secured, these men serve the rights of elders that appertained to the position of elders in the church.

In the process of striving for their elders' orders, they began to concentrate, in the fall of 1820, on building a connection based upon their printed Discipline, with James Varick functioning as their virtual leader. On November 2, it was decided at a combined leaders' meeting and Quarterly Conference, to draw up articles of agreement on the unity of the two New York churches, Zion and Asbury, and this was signed by official members of both groups on November 30. [106] The society in New Haven, which had been set apart from the white Methodist society in 1818, [107] and was desirous of uniting with Zion connection, recommended one of their men, Jeremiah Jacobs, for license to preach. After arriving in New York on November 11, he preached his trial sermon on the 15th, which was approved, and thus he obtained his license. [108]

The Philadelphia Society, then known as the Wesleyan Church, had organized earlier that year and requested us to send them a spiritual leader. Abraham Thompson and William Miller were sent to Philadelphia and Christopher Rush to New Haven, while Varick supervised the New York churches. The preachers sent to Philadelphia and New Haven returned to New York and reported that these societies had decided to unite firmly with Zion connection. [109]

While in Philadelphia, Abraham Thompson had consulted on ordination to eldership with Ezekiel Cooper, one of the more liberal ministers of the Methodist Episcopal Church, who had pastored John Street Church in 1794-1795 and became friendly with some of our leaders during this time. In visualizing this problem, Cooper had declared:

> If we admit that every grade of office and order shall be entitled to a direct, distinct, and separate representation; then, it may be, that which all have among the several orders and grades, to the amount of ten or twelve, putting in their claim, for distinct and separate representations for *themselves*—viz. The Bishops, the Travelling elders — Travelling deacons — Travelling graduates, all distinct orders—Local elders — Local deacons — Local licenciates, all distinct grades — Then 150,000 Class leaders, — Exhorters — Trustees — Stewards, all distinct offices — Then the official laity. But what shall we do with the people of colour, especially the free part, who have Local deacons, and Licenciates, and Leaders, Trustees, etc., and have distinct houses for worship, etc. — Thus having a separate conference. [110]

After Thompson had reported, on the advice of Cooper, that the Wesleyan Church in Philadelphia and the New York churches should come to an agreement on a suitable memorial on the subject of ordination, and present it in writing to proper officials of both the Philadelphia and New York Annual Conferences, to meet the following spring, they considered it with much

---

105. *Ibid.*, p.46.
106. Rush, *op. cit.*, pp.52-54.
107. Robert A. Warner, *New Haven Negroes*, p.85; Varick Memorial Church Bulletins.
108. Rush, *op. cit.*, p.55.
109. *Ibid.*
110. *Ezekiel Cooper Papers*, Mss., Garrett Theological Seminary.

enthusiasm. They appointed a committee to draft the address: James Varick, George Collins, John Dungy, Charles Anderson, and William Miller. On February 22, 1821, they commenced work on the proposed resolution, [111] which was drawn up and presented to the respective conferences. The resolution and response from each conference follow:

To the Bishops and Preachers of the Philadelphia and New York Conferences, assembled.

RESPECTED BRETHREN:–

We, the official members of the African Methodist Zion and Asbury Churches, in the City of New York, and of the Wesleyan Church, in the City of Philadelphia, on behalf of our brethren, members of the aforesaid Churches; likewise of a small society at New Haven, and some of our colored brethren on Long Island, beg the favor of addressing you on a subject, to us, of great importance, and, we presume, not a matter of indifference to you.

In the first place, suffer us to beg you will accept of our humble and sincere thanks for your kind services to us when in our infant state, trusting that the Great Head of the Church, the all-wise and gracious God, has, and will continue to reward you for your labors among us, having made you the instruments of bringing us from darkness to light, and from the power of sin and satan, to Him, the true and living God.

In the next place we proceed to say:–When the Methodist Society in the United States was small, the Africans enjoyed comfortable privileges among their white brethren in the same meeting-house, but as the whites increased very fast the Africans were pressed back; therefore, it was thought essentially necessary for them to have meeting-houses of their own, in those places where they could obtain them, in order to have more room to invite their colored brethren yet out of the ark of safety to come in; and it is well known that the Lord has greatly enlarged their number since that memorable time, by owning their endeavors in the conversion of many hundreds. Many preachers have been raised up among them, who have been very useful in a located state; but they have hitherto been confined; they have had no opportunities to travel, being generally poor men, and having no provision made for them to go forth and dispense the Word of Life to their brethren, their usefulness has been greatly hindered, and their colored brethren have been deprived of those blessings which Almighty God might have designed to grant through their instrumentality. And now, it seems, the time has come when something must be done for the prosperity of the ministry amongst our colored brethren; and how shall this be accomplished? for we have not the least expectation that African or colored preachers will be admitted to a seat and vote in the Conference of their white brethren, let them be how much soever qualified for the work of the ministry; nor do we desire to unite with our brother Richard Allen's connexion, being dissatisfied with their general manner of proceedings (for our brethren, the members of the Wesleyan Church in Philadelphia, withdrew from them to build their present house of worship, named as above); therefore, our brethren in the City of New York, after due consideration, have been led to conclude that, to form an itinerant plan, and establish a Conference for African Methodist preachers, under the patronage of the white Methodist Bishops and Conference, would be the means of accomplishing the desired end. Believing that such an establishment would tend greatly to the prosperity of the spiritual concerns of our colored brethren in general, and would be the means of great encouragement to our preachers, who are now

111. Rush, *op. cit.,* p.56.

in regular standing in connexion with the white Methodist Episcopal Church in the United States, and also to such as may be hereafter raised among us, who may be disposed to join the said Conference and enter on the traveling plan. And, in order to commence this great work, the two Societies in the City of New York united and agreed that the title of the connexion shall be "The African Methodist Episcopal Church in America," and have selected a form of discipline from that of the mother (white) church, which, with a little alteration, we have adopted for the government of the said connexion, and to which we beg to refer you.

After the perusal of our selection and consideration of our case, should our proceedings meet your approbation, and you should be disposed to patronize the same, we will stand ready, and shall be glad to receive such advice and instruction as you may think proper to give us, through our father in the Lord, Bishop McKendree, or any other person the Conference may be pleased to appoint.

On the subject of ordination to Eldership (a privilege which our preachers have been long deprived of) permit us to say we might have obtained it from other sources, but we preferred and determined to follow the advice of Bishop McKendree, given to our brethren in New York the last time he was with them, and wait until the meeting of your Annual Conference in this and the district of New York, in order to understand what encouragement we may look for from the mother church. But, in consequence of some uneasiness in the minds of some of our members in New York, occasioned by our brother Richard Allen's determination to establish a society of his connexion in that city, our brethren there have been under the necessity of solemnly electing three of their deacons to the office of Elders, and some of their preachers to the office of deacons, to act only in cases of necessity, and to show to our people that our preachers can be authorized to administer the sacrament of the Lord's supper as well as those of brother Allen's connexion—that thereby they might keep the body together, and we believe it has had the desired effect, for very few have left the Societies there, notwithstanding the efforts made to induce them to leave us.

We expect that our first Yearly Conference will be held in the City of New York, on the 14th day of June next, at which we hope to have the happiness of hearing that our father in the Lord, Bishop McKendree, presided, and commenced his fatherly instructions in an African Methodist Conference, formed under the patronage of the Methodist Episcopal Church in the United States of America. With this hope we shall rest, waiting your answer; meanwhile praying that the great Shepherd and Bishop of souls and our most merciful Father will be pleased to bless and guide you in your deliberations on our case, so that your conclusions may be such as shall be pleasing in his sight, and tend most to the prosperity of his kingdom amongst the Africans, and consequently prove an everlasting blessing to many precious souls.

N. B. Should the above address be sanctioned by your respected body, and you should be pleased to act upon it, we will thank you to transmit the same to the New York Annual Conference, for their consideration; and should the time appointed for the sitting of the African Conference be inconvenient for the person who may be appointed to organize the same, we are willing that it should be altered to a few days sooner or later, provided you would be pleased to give us timely notice of said alteration. But should you be disposed not to favor the said address in any respect, you will please have the goodness to return it to the bearer.

Signed, in behalf of the official members of both Societies, at a meeting called especially for that purpose, March 23d, 1821, in the City of New York.

JAMES VARICK, President.
GEORGE COLLINS, Secretary.

The following is the decision of The Philadelphia Annual Conference:

The committee to whom was referred the memorial of the official members of the African Methodist Zion and Asbury Churches in the City of New York, and the Wesley Church in the City of Philadelphia, in behalf of themselves and others of their colored brethren, proposing and requesting the organization of a Conference for the African Methodist preachers, under the patronage of the Bishops and Conferences of the white Methodist Episcopal Church, having had the subject under serious and close consideration, in its various bearings and relations, ask leave now to report:

1. We view it as a subject of great importance to the colored people, demanding from us our friendly patronage and pastoral attention, so far as circumstances will admit of it. We have always acted upon the principle toward the people of color of doing them all the good that was in our power, in promoting and improving their moral and religious instruction and character, and in protecting and defending them in all their just rights and privileges, and, more particularly, we have, as instruments under God, labored much for the conversion and salvation of their souls. They know, and it is generally known and acknowledged, that our labors of good will and Christian love toward them for many years past have been crowned with gracious success and much good effect among them, as it respects both their moral and religious character, and also to the improvement, to some considerable degree, of their condition and circumstances in life.

2. There are, at this time, various societies and congregations of colored people, in different parts, who have been collected and raised under our ministerial labors, and who have erected and built themselves houses for the public worship of God, wherein they assemble separate from the white people for their religious devotions; and also, there are a considerable number of pious colored men, whom we have reason to believe are qualified to preach the word of life and salvation, and to be useful in their labors among the people of their own color; but, upon our present plan, under existing circumstances and regulations, their privileges as ministers are very much circumscribed, and their opportunities for improvement and usefulness are very limited. There exists no expectation or prospect that the colored preachers will be admitted to a vote or seat in our Conference, or participate in sundry other privileges among the white preachers, in their labors and pastoral care of the Churches and Societies generally; neither is it understood that they wish or desire it. They request a Conference themselves, in unity and friendship with, and under the patronage of, the Bishops and Conferences of the white preachers, and that our Bishops should preside among them and ordain their preachers, and extend to them their superintending protection, counsel and direction in their itinerant regulations and ministerial operations. It appears that they could obtain orders from another quarter, and become a connexion distinct from, and independent of, the white Bishops and Conferences, but they prefer and desire patronage from, and a certain degree of union with, us. They have refused to unite with Richard Allen and his African connexion, being dissatisfied with their general manner of proceedings.

3. From every view of the subject we have been able to take, we are of opinion the time has come when something must be done, more than yet

has been done, for our colored people, especially for such as are situated and circumstanced as the memorialists are, in order to enlarge their sphere of labors, and to extend their privileges and opportunities of usefulness among themselves, under our protection and direction, otherwise we shall lose their confidence in us and our influence over them, and they will become separate from, and independent of, us, and then our usefulness among them, will, in a great measure, be lost. And it appears in the present case under consideration, that they are fixed and resolved to have a Conference among themselves, whether patronized by us or not, and they have appointed the time for holding it, but they wish us to take them under our patronage: Therefore, your committee proposes the following resolutions to the Conference for adoption, viz.:

First, Resolved—That the Philadelphia Conference do advise and recommend that one of our Bishops do attend and preside in the African Conference, appointed to sit in New York, and to superintend their organization as an African Methodist Conference, under the patronage of our Bishops and Conferences, agreeably to the proper plan, (if the New York Conference concur with us,) viz.:

1. One of our Bishops always to preside in the said Conference, or in case no Bishop be present, then such white Elder as the Bishop shall appoint, is to preside.

2. Our Bishops to ordain all their Deacons and Elders, such as shall be elected by their own Conference and approved of by the Bishop as qualified for the office.

3. The Bishop, or the Elder appointed by him to preside in the Conference, with an advisory committee of three, chosen by the Conference, to make out the stations and appointments of the preachers.

4. All the other proceedings of the Conference to be as conformable to the rules and regulations generally followed in our Conferences as circumstances will admit.

5. Their discipline, doctrines, government, and rules of order in all things, to be as conformable to ours as possible, so as to secure to themselves their own peculiar rights and privileges.

6. The Bishop, or such Elder as shall be appointed by him, with his proper instructions, together with the said African Conference, to agree upon the several points, terms and considerations of unity and amity mutually to exist, as reciprocal duties and obligations between them and us. This agreement to take place and be entered into at the time of organizing the said Conference.

Secondly, Resolved—That a copy of this report be forwarded with the African Memorial to the New York Conference, and that the said New York Conference be recommended and requested to concur with us in the proposed plan of organizing the said African Conference, under our patronage, with such additions to, or alterations of, the above items as may to them appear best.

> *Committee*
> EZEKIEL COOPER,
> THOMAS WARE,
> ALWARD WHITE

The above report was adopted by the Philadelphia Conference, and the Secretary was instructed to communicate a copy of it to the New York Conference.

> SAMUEL COX, Secretary. (112)

112. Ezekiel Cooper Papers, Garrett Theological Seminary.

Rush gives us the following action of The New York Annual Conference:

The foregoing report was approved of by the official brethren, and they were encouraged to hope that their request would be granted, but they found their hope to be of short duration, when they heard from the New York Annual Conference, for that body, in their report, gave them to understand that they could do nothing for them, except they renounce the form of discipline which they had selected and adopted, and be willing to be governed by the old discipline. We shall also give a copy of their report, which reads as follows:

The committee to whom was referred the Memorial of the Africans in the City of New York and other places, together with the accompanying documents, after due consideration, reports as follows:

1. The committee conceive that humanity and religion combine to influence us to do all in our power for the instruction and salvation of colored people. To have the pure word of life preached among them, and the discipline and ordinances of the Gospel faithfully administered, is of indispensable necessity, and requisite to their happiness and prosperity. It is believed that, in these respects, we have cause to charge ourselves with too little attention to their spiritual interest, and, as though they were an inferior class of beings, they have too often been treated with unwarrantable neglect. It is to be feared that their loss of confidence in us, and the consequent measures which many of them have pursued, may, in a considerable degree, be traced to our neglect as the cause. But, painful as this consideration is, we cannot approve of the course which our colored brethren have taken, in separating themselves from us, and forming themselves under a distinct title, as an independent body. This course is the more to be regretted because it places them in a position which the constitution of our Church cannot cover. Your committee conceive that the primary object contemplated in the memorial and accompanying documents lies beyond the limits of the constitutional powers of an Annual Conference. To organize a Conference *subject to the order* and discipline of the Methodist Episcopal Church, is the prerogative of the General Conference alone. An Annual Conference, or Conferences, therefore, cannot organize even *such* a Conference, much less one acting under a distinct discipline and independent authority. In this view of the subject, your committee are of opinion that the African Conference, specified in the memorial, cannot be constitutionally organized or adopted; that it would not be advisable for our Bishops, or any one appointed by them, officially to preside at said Conference, or to ordain any deacon or Elder elected by them. But, although we judge it inexpedient to prostrate the constitution and government of the Church to accommodate any case whatever, firmly believing the evil would ultimately over-balance any good which might be supposed to result from it, we consider the condition of the Africans such as to demand every prudent exertion within our power to recover them from their wandering, and preserve them in the confidence and communion of the Church. Your committee, therefore, recommend the adoption of the following resolutions:

Resolved, 1st—That if the African brethren, who have addressed the Conference by memorial, will agree to be subject to the government of the Methodist Episcopal Church, in common with their white brethren, in such case, under the present existing circumstances, it is expedient and advisable that such colored preachers as are regularly constituted, be appointed to labor among them and take the pastoral charge of them until the next General Conference.

Resolved, 2d—That the colored brethren, submitting themselves to the order and discipline of the Church, are entitled to the same rights and privileges, with respect to the election and ordination of local deacons and Elders, as the white societies, the same form of order and discipline applying to both.

Resolved, 3d—That the organization of an African Annual Conference, on the same principles, and subject to the same order and government as other Conferences, may be effected by the General Conference, but cannot be by one or more Annual Conferences.

Resolved, 4th—That it is advisable a member or members of this Conference be appointed by the Bishop to present the above resolutions to the African brethren in New York, together with any explanations and instructions which may be thought proper, and to receive their answer. Joshua Soule was appointed to present the foregoing report, and Thomas Mason accompanied him. [113]

On June 12, the officials assembled to consider both reports. The group had planned its first annual conference for June 21, hoping by this time the two elders-elect would be ordained. The discouraging report from the New York Conference, held June 1-6, was so contrary to that of the Philadelphia Conference that it greatly agitated the Zion group, yet they remained steadfast through these perplexities. They decided to proceed according to the ideas advanced by the Philadelphia Conference, using our Discipline. Our officials later held an interview with Bishop George of the New York Methodist Episcopal Conference, and invited him to attend the first annual conference. He stated that the other two bishops were sick, and his engagements were overpowering, and "advised them to do as well as they could in their aforesaid conference." [114]

After two successful annual conferences with Varick in charge, the anxieties, bewilderment, and perturbation concerning their elders' orders had never ceased. They experienced additional difficulty when John Dungy left New York City and went to New Haven to reside. Immediately thereafter, information was received that he had applied for and received license to preach from the Methodist Episcopal Church, and he was making an effort to take over our New Haven society for that church. His attempt was unsuccessful, and the people remained steady under the pastorate of James Anderson. Before this, William Miller and his Asbury congregation had wavered, first courting the Bethel movement for friendship and favor, and later agreeing to pay $100 a year for the services of a white elder, according to a report of Bishops George and Roberts to Zion officials. However, they had returned to Zion connection by June 1822. [115]

At the Second Annual Conference held in the Wesleyan Church at Philadelphia, on May 15, 1822, it was discovered that the Wesleyan Church was greatly divided in their opinion about government and polity of the church, yet strongly united on a race church. After Bishops Roberts and George met with them to advise them to wait until General Conference in 1824, to see what action would be taken regarding separate African conferences, they boldly declared that if the government of Zion Church is established according to their printed Discipline, they would continue in union with them; "but if Zion Church returned under the government of the whites, they would not go with her, and would no longer be in connexion with her." [116] This session was

113. Rush, *op. cit.,* pp.56-67.
114. *Ibid.,* pp.67-68.
115. *Ibid.,* pp.73, 77-78.
116. *Ibid.,* 72-73.

adjourned, and continued in New York City on July 8, 1822. Meanwhile, the Philadelphia brethren arrived in New York and a meeting of the official members of the Connection was called on May 30. The officials from Philadelphia expressed a desire to move forward with the established church and suggested a mode of ordaining elders from our own ranks, as they were stringently opposed to petitioning the white conferences any further for ordination.

They took no direct action in this meeting on the Wesleyan proposal that "three of our deacons ordain an elder, or to call the assistance of an elder from some other church, who, with two of our ordained deacons, might ordain an elder, and so to be established under the Discipline we selected for the Connexion." [117] However, after Leven Smith reported that Bishop McKendree was once again in the city, and had spoken favorably respecting our situation, they appointed a committee of preachers (James Varick, Abraham Thompson, Christopher Rush, Leven Smith and James Smith) who held meetings with him concerning the ordination of elders. He finally informed them that he could not go against the will of his church. [118]

This committee continued, undiscouraged. Soon afterward they obtained the consent of three regularly ordained Methodist elders to ordain our elders-elect along with Leven Smith, (ordained deacon at the Methodist Episcopal Church, New York Conference, June 2, 1820), elders of the Church of God. [119] In addition to William M. Stilwell (who had developed true friendship with the Zion group from the time his uncle, Samuel Stilwell, was leader of one of the black classes in John Street Church), Sylvester Hutchison was the presiding elder of New York when our congregation was organized in 1796, and was an original friend of the movement.[120] James Covell was a young adventurous minister, devoted to justice and goodwill, and unlike Stilwell and Hutchison, remained in the Methodist Episcopal Church until his death in 1845. [121]

On Monday night, June 17, 1822, a planned meeting was held in the recently dedicated Zion Church, "and after an appropriate and solemn sermon delivered by Reverend James Covell, they ordained Abraham Thompson, James Varick, and Leven Smith, Elders in the Church of God, in the presence of a large and respectable audience." "Thus," states Rush, "after twenty-one months of struggling through a kind of spiritual wilderness, Zion Church obtained three ordained Elders." [122] From this highly spiritual and triumphant moment in the African Methodist Episcopal Zion Church, growth and prosperity was destined, as these first leaders, particularly Varick and Thompson, who "had patiently endured, *obtained the promise.*" (Heb. 7:15) In the following month, James Varick was elected first Superintendent and set forward as Bishop of the church.

117. *Ibid.,* p.14.
118. *Ibid.,* pp.74-78.
119. *Ibid.,* p.78: Ms. Minutes, New York State Annual Conference, 1820.
120. John Atkinson, *Memorials of Methodism in New Jersey.* p.426. . . . *Extracts From the Minutes of the Sixth Yearly Conference and the State Conference of Methodist Society,* 1826 and 1827, pp.6-24.
121. William B. Sprague, *Annals of the American Pulpit,* pp. 564-565.
122. Rush, *op. cit.,* p.78.

CHAPTER 8

JAMES VARICK

"Pioneer of Ecclesiastical Freedom"[1]

James Varick, the founder and first Bishop of the African Methodist
Episcopal Zion Church, occupies a peculiar place in the history of the Negro
race in America. Destined by Providence . . . he was to lead a few devout
men and women out of the John Street Methodist Church, New York City,
to establish an independent local church for members of his race, which
local church soon leaped the bounds of localism to be formed into a
denomination, which has grown to be one of the great religious bodies of
the world. Beginning with these few members, not more than two or three
dozen, it now numbers its members by the hundreds of thousands, and is an
important factor in the prosecution of the work of the Christian religion
among the inhabitants of the earth. [2]

Varick was born in Orange County, near Newburgh, N.Y., in 1750. [3] His
mother was a Negro slave of the household of Varicks of Dutch descent, who
settled in Hackensack, N.J., as early as 1687. His father, Richard Varick, was
born and baptized in the Dutch Church of Hackensack in 1720, and later moved
to New York with his family. [4] Members of this Varick family, with their
slaves, were from time to time in the Newburgh, Highland Falls, and the West
Point area, as well as New York City, before and during the Revolutionary War.
In some instances, the slaves of this Varick family were moved around with
them, willed to their heirs, or manumitted. [5] The Varick family figured
conspicuously in the early history of New York City, in its social, political, and
commercial life, and Varick Street, in the area where the A.M.E. Zion Church
once made itself profoundly felt in the freedom struggle, is named in honor of
the one-time mayor. [6]

Wheeler states that Varick's mother was a resident of New York City and
was visiting Newburgh, N.Y., when Varick was born. There was something of
this territory precious and dear to Varick, which caused his family to carry his

1. H. K. Carroll, *The Star of Zion,* October 8, 1896.
2. B. F. Wheeler, *The Varick Family,* p.5.
3. *Ibid.,* P.8: Bergman, *Chronological History of the Negro,* p.36.
4. Wheeler, *op. cit.,* p.5. Genealogical And Biographical Record, 1877 Vol. VIII, 1,
   pp.16-21. This Richard Varick was the uncle of the Richard Varick who was mayor of
   New York City during the time the A.M.E. Zion Church was organized. We also note
   that Mayor Richard Varick, in one of his Last Wills and Testament, dated 1782, used
   the Dutch spelling *VAN VARCK.* This is the same way James Varick's name was spelled
   in the records of the "black classes of John Street Church, of 1795."– *Cf.* Ms.
   Collection, *Richard Varick,* New York Historical Society.
5. Wheeler, *op. cit.,* p.9; Abstracts of Wills, N.Y. Historical Society, Vol. III, pp.197-198,
   Vol. IV, p.337.
6. Wheeler, *op. cit.,* p.9; Scrapbook of News Clippings of Old New York, New York Public
   Library.

remains there for burial upon his death in New York City. His mother was evidently later manumitted and returned to New York City with her son. [7] James Weldon Johnson points out that "there were a good many Negroes in New York who were the descendants of the manumitted slaves of the original Dutch settlers and who retained much of the Dutch training." He mentions the names of New York Negroes of his day bearing the names of "Van Ransellear, Van Vechten, Van Vrancken, Van Deusen, Van Dyck . . . and other such honourable Dutch names."[8]

From Varick's early life in New York City, where he grew up, he began to obtain independence and free spirit. After the effort of Elias Neau before the 1712 Insurrection, just about the only source of learning for Negro children during Varick's childhood was the Free School opened for blacks on September 15, 1760, when the following notice was published in the *New York Mercury*. [9]

> This is to inform the public, that a Free School is opened near the New Dutch-Church (Nassau street between Cedar and Liberty), for the instruction of 30 Negro children, from 5 years old and upwards . . . which school is entirely under the inspection and care of the Clergy of the Church of England in this city . . . . N.B. All that is required of their masters and mistresses is that they find them wood for the winter. Proper books will be provided for them gratis.

It is not certain that Varick attended this school; however, he being a well-trained scholar had availed himself of such school privileges as Negro children had in the city in that day. [10] There was no real plan for education of black children until the founding of the African Free School by the New York Manumission Society, in 1786, [11] and later in the early 1800's, when a school was operated in the Zion Church, where Varick taught in his spare time. [12]

"Varick was born in stirring times when the best brains and the best blood were all aflame with a desire for liberty, which was expressed twenty-six years after his birth in the Declaration of Independence of English rule." [13] As was observed by Bishop Frederick M. Jacobs:

> The history of the development of the race begins with the history of the Revolution period. The shedding of the first patriotic blood and the exposure of the first patriotic person to the bayoneted and sworded red coats of English tyranny and despotism was the opening scene of Afro-American development. From the shimmering ashes of a war which brought freedom to the colonies and sounded a bugle of patriotic defiance in the soul of every American citizen the Negro read a glorious triumph of American liberty, and at the same time saw his fated picture, blighted ambitions, and fondest anticipations, the loss of which was traced and pictured there. But little did the people who robbed him of his well-earned liberty see that there was a "divinity which shaped his end." His experience through war and carnage prepared him for the higher attainment ever toward which he, from that period, strove. [14]

7. Wheeler, *op. cit.,* p.9.
8. Johnson, *Black Manhattan,* p.26.
9. Stokes, *Iconography,* IV, p.714.
10. Wheeler, *op cit.,* p.9.
11. Ottley and Weatherby, *The Negroes in New York,* p.63.
12. *Minutes,* Common Council of NYC, III, p.564.
13. Wheeler, *op. cit.,* p.9.
14. Jacobs, *"Negro Methodism, A Factor in the Development of the Negro Race."* A.M.E. *Zion Quarterly Review,* July 1898, p.24.

"Varick caught the spirit of his age," [15] and here began his noble work of breaking down the walls of slavery and caste prejudice. "The spirit of the Revolution not only wrought in New York a humanization of sentiment regarding slavery and a softening of the condition of the slave, but also aroused and strengthened a considerable section of public opinion and set it in motion against the whole institution." [16] New York was the last Northern state (with the exception of New Jersey) to emancipate her slaves, [17] and Varick played an integral part in this tedious effort to achieve emancipation with dignity.

By the close of the war, Varick had learned the trade of shoemaking, and was operating his shop from his home at No. 4 Orange (now Baxter) Street. This whole time his devotion and dedication was toward religion and a burning desire to know the Bible. He was about 16 years of age when Philip Embury and Captain Thomas Webb began their preaching in New York City as early as 1766. He took a deep interest in the Methodist persuasion, becoming converted under their preaching and joining the famous John Street Church, the cradle of American Methodism and the place where Varick got his first religious training. [18] Varick was first privileged to exhort and then licensed to preach by the Quarterly Conference of the John Street Methodist Episcopal Church, and "because of race friction, held separate religious meetings for his people as early as 1780." [19]

Mary White Ovington points out:
While the colored people in New York started with segregated schools and attained to mixed schools, the movement in the churches was the reverse. At first the Negroes were attendants of white churches, sitting in the gallery or on the rear seats, and waiting until the white people were through before partaking of the communion; but as their number increased they chafed under their position. Why should they be placed apart to hear the doctrine of Christ, and why, too should they not have full opportunity to preach that doctrine? The desire for self-expression was perhaps the greatest factor in leading them to separate from the white church.

In 1796 about 30 Negroes, under the leadership of James Varick, withdrew from the John Street Methodist Episcopal Church, and formed the first colored church of New York. [20]

The sphere in which the local preacher, both black and white, could operate in early Methodism was exceedingly limited. He was able to preach occasionally, but could have no pastoral charge, and could exert but little influence. [21] Yet the importance attached to local preachers was brought out years later by a Rev. J. W. F. White:

In the early days of Methodism, in both England and America, local preachers were a mighty power in the Church. The great revival under Wesley was effected mainly by local preachers. Methodism in this country was planted by local preachers. They were the pioneers of our church in every state and almost every neighborhood. In the poor and neglected districts of cities, in out-of-the way villages, on the frontiers of advancing civilization, they were generally the first to preach a full salvation for all,

15. Wheeler, *op. cit.,* p.9.
16. Johnson, *Op. cit.,* p.12.
17. *Ibid.,* p.14.
18. Wheeler, *op. cit.,* pp.10-11.
19. *The Star of Zion,* Feb. 11, 1897, Historical Supplement, p.1.
20. Ovington, *Half a Man,* pp.10-11.
21. William C. Larrabee, *Asbury and His Coadjutors,* Vol. II, p.144.

and in most cases they preceded the regular itinerant in the formation of societies. They were esteemed and honored by the Bishop and traveling preachers. (22)

Thus the man Varick became distinct, first as a local preacher, leading his people through the rugged way of the faithful in the church. He had high ideals for the ministry, and no doubt dreamed of becoming an itinerant in the interest of his race, but he realized early that through previous trials and hardships, he had reached the peak for the black preacher in the Methodist Episcopal Church. The gospel, however, was in his heart, and he continued his evangelization among his people in the best manner he could under the rules of Methodism, which prevented blacks from even being class leaders of their own group. (23)

Varick met and married Aurelia Jones around 1790. "He was a man of purest morals and he placed a high premium upon the bond of sacred wedlock." (24) To this union were born seven children: four sons and three daughters, four of whom survived. (25) There is a record of baptism of the baby daughter preserved, however, in the John Street Church records: "ELIZA VARICK, Parents: James and Aurelia, colored, Born Sept. 13, 1801, Baptized, January 27, 1803 – By Rev. Thomas Morrell." (26)

The humble home of James Varick in Orange Street is where he secretly assembled small groups of his friends. For the most part they were fellow preachers, members of the black male classes of John Street Church, and other leading black men of New York City. They met in this way because of an ordinance that prevented blacks from holding meetings of any kind, in case they should plan uprisings to free themselves from oppression and their brothers and sisters from the shackles of bondage. (27) Here is where he planned the strategy of the new church movement, which he felt was of the utmost importance. "Caste prejudice had crept into the Methodism of Wesley and Coke [and Asbury] who never expected there would be any distinction in the Methodist Societies. . . . The Church had grown influential and indeed to some degree rich, and there seemed to be a disposition to push and crowd the brother in black, which soon began to impress the Negro members of the Methodist Societies that the time had come to assert their rights to worship God unhampered." (28)

After these conditions "which hindered their intellectual development and religious growth, and prevented them from engaging in the work of spreading the cause of Christ and uplifting their fellows according as they felt themselves moved by the spirit of God," and which "became so unbearable for these people of African descent, they decided to make their first move in 1796." They withdrew from the Mother Church and formed a separate organization, out of which has grown the A.M.E. Zion Church. (29) "1796 marks truly the starting point of the development of a race of people destined to become one of the

22. *The Christian Advocate*, Sept. 4, 1879.
23. Methodist Episcopal Church Annual Conference, 1780, Question 25.
24. Wheeler, *op. cit.*, pp.11, 16.
25. *Ibid.*, Dumas Malone (ed.), *Dictionary of American Biography*, Vol. X, p.225, *Who Was Who in America*, (Historical Volume), p.621.
26. Ms. Records, John Street Church, Baptisms, 1788-1820.
27. Wheeler, *op. cit.*, p.15; *The Black Minority in Early New York*, pp.13-14; Ms. Records, John Street Church, Classes; Stokes, *op. cit.*, Vols. IV & V; Jan. 5, 1755, Feb. 16, 1756, May 25, 1780, April 9, 1782.
28. J. H. White, "History of the First Twenty-Five Years of the A.M.E. Zion Church," *A.M.E. Zion Quarterly Review*, Vol. VIII, 1898, p.2.
29. *The Star of Zion*, June 11, 1896; Johnson, *op. cit.*, p.24.

most powerful on the American continent, under the special and civilizing influences of the Christian religion whose uprising marks an epoch in the rise and progress of races unparalled in the annals of history." [30]

This is the year that Varick first came to prominence, when he led a group of some of New York's leading black men, to secure permission from Bishop Asbury to hold meetings separate and distinct from the white churches. [31] Associated with Varick in this noble venture were Francis Jacobs, William Brown, Abraham Thompson, Peter Williams, June Scott, Samuel Pontier, Thomas Miller, William Hamilton, [32] and other members of Class Number 31, the black class at John Street Church, led by Cornelius Warner, in 1795.

In 1799 Varick was instrumental in leading these members into a more permanent situation; "to think about building a house of worship for themselves, and to form themselves into a corporate body separate from the white church, according to the privilege granted religious societies by the law of the State of New York." [33] During this period, Roi Ottley states, "the black population of the city had grown to seven thousand and was now concentrated in the neighborhood of Bleecker and Mercer Streets on the lower East side. On the whole, they were industrious and thrifty." [34] Wheeler gives a more detailed description of the same area:

> The city of New York was built up around the battery, and Wall Street was on the northern outskirts of the city—and this section was the place where most of the colored people lived. Strange to say that the part of New York where most of the money in America [Wall Street area] is handled today was in the days of James Varick the place where the bulk of colored people lived. . . . The corner of Church and Leonard Streets, where Varick's followers built their first church, was within a few minutes walk of Wall Street. This, then, was the battleground of Negro endeavor in the days of James Varick. If Varick were to return to the earth today he would find that his followers, so far as this section is concerned,
> "Have folded their tents, like the Arab,
> And as silently moved away." [35]

The church was dedicated to the Glory of God on September 7, 1800, and called "Zion." The disappointments and trials of these humble worshippers were many. Among their greatest disappointment at that time was the incident of the Articles of Agreement between the Methodist Episcopal Church and the trustees of Zion Church, and securing the Articles of Incorporation in 1801 (see Chapter 7). "Varick was remarkable for his prudence, energy, patience and integrity of character. By this he succeeded in firmly establishing, against much strong opposition, the church which chose him as its first leader." [36] It was a gradual, painful, heartbleeding process every step of the way. "On account of his superior talents and capacity for leadership," states T. Thomas Fortune, "James Varick became the spokesman of his brethren and the chief pioneer in this new field of church work. It is not surprising that he became the exhorter, the local preacher, the elder, by reason of his superior gifts of head and tongue." [37]

30. Jacobs, *A.M.E. Zion Quarterly Review, op. cit.,* July, 1898, p.27.
31. *Dictionary of American Biography,* X, p.225; Hyamson (ed.), A *Dictionary of Universal Biography* p.627.
32. Wheeler, *op. cit.,* p.39.
33. *Encyclopedia International,* Vol. 19, p.17; Moore, *History,* p.17.
34. Ottley, *New World A-Coming,* p.12.
35. Wheeler, *op. cit.,* pp.14-15.
36. Harris, *Zion's Historical Catechism,* p.13.
37. *The New York Age,* October 1, 1896.

There was no misunderstanding about the spiritual obligations of Varick and his colleagues, Abraham Thompson, June Scott, and William Miller an exhorter. According to Methodist rules of that day, church property matters or temporal concerns were placed squarely in the hands of trustees. It was a heavy blow when the preachers of this first black movement discovered that the trustees had been maneuvered into signing their rights to pastor their first church, away to white preachers in the Articles of Agreement of 1801. However, Varick had been through previous hardships, and when he discovered this new obstruction to their organization and freedom, he persevered. He remained steadfast while his other three colleagues either wavered or left the movement under the weight of this heavy pressure. However, after a tedious and arduous struggle, Varick, Thompson, and Scott graduated into deacon's orders by 1806, and became the first blacks ordained in New York State. [38]

Varick's activities for his race were unceasing. Free black people of New York City were normally poor, although amazingly gifted and skillful in their circumstances, just as they were in other parts of the country. Varick's fond devotion for his wife and family, and his love for religious and race freedom, impelled him into the orbit of a selfless and sacrificial life. Along with his trade of shoe-making, he labored outside his home as a tobacco-cutter to earn extra wages to care for his large family, while he also ran a classroom in his home and at his church, teaching his and other people's children the basic principles of learning. [39] But his primary interest was geared toward that which he had learned best to do in adhering to the admonition of the Apostle Paul, to "watch thou in all things, endure affliction, do the work of an evangelist, make full proof of thy ministry," and to preach the unadulterated gospel of Jesus Christ with such magnitude and power that he was requested by his and other African groups beginning to organize, to give spiritual direction in their unabating freedom cause.

In 1807, the act of the British Parliament of March 25 officially abolished the slave trade, one year before the U.S. law went into effect. In 1808, the slave population in the United States stood at the million mark, and on January 1, a federal law went into effect discontinuing the importation of slaves. It has been estimated, however, that from 1808 to 1860 approximately 250,000 slaves were illegally imported. [40] Upon learning of the abolition of the African slave trade, which was announced by the government in March 1807, the people of African descent in some large cities of the North planned thanksgiving celebrations for the momentous occasion.

In New York City, the celebration was held at Zion Church, the city's only black church at that time, and it was indeed an effective occasion. Coker was proud of those few men who had achieved for the race, and recorded these "descendants of the African Race who have given proofs of talents," among whom was James Varick who preached the "Sermon of Thanksgiving on the Occasion of the Abolition of the African Slave Trade," in the afternoon of January 1, 1808, and closed the service. [41] It was the first recorded sermon in history preached by an African on behalf of African people, Absalom Jones being the other known African to perform this same task in Philadelphia. In the

---

38. Coker, A Dialogue, p.40.
39. Wheeler, op. cit., New York City Directories, 1800-1828; Elliott's New York City Directory, 1812.
40. Bergman, op. cit., pp.89, 90.
41. Coker, A Dialogue, p.42.

New York City services, William Hamilton composed the hymns for the day, and Peter Williams, Jr. gave the oration in the morning. (42) This became an annual celebration for a period among the people of African descent, with Abraham Thompson having the honor in 1809, and William Miller in 1810. (43)

A little later this same year, a movement led by William Hamilton, the New York African Society for Mutual Relief, was begun and received a state charter two years later, March 23, 1810, with Hamilton as its first president. Its object was "to raise a fund to be appropriated toward the relief of the widows and orphans of the deceased members." (44) Its members were composed chiefly of businessmen, many of them members of the A.M.E. Zion Church, and several preachers (practically all the black preachers of the city of that day). James Varick was elected its first chaplain and functioned at the various services, especially anniversary celebrations, usually held in Zion Church. (45) This organization was still in existence in 1969, when a historic marker was placed on the site at 42 Orange (now Baxter) Street, the first building of this society.

In 1812, while Varick and the other preachers were increasing their church work and holding occasional conferences in and around the City of New York, (46) he continued active in organizations established in New York City to serve the race, locally and nationally. The black people organized numerous societies and associations during these early days, before the coming of the active abolition movements in the 1830's, in efforts to be free and recognized as citizens.

The first Lodge of Freemasonry was established in New York State in 1812, when Peter Lew, Grand Master of Prince Hall Grand Lodge, Boston, granted a warrant to nine Master Masons to open and work a Lodge of Master Masons in New York City under the title of Boyer Lodge No. 1 F. & A.M. (47) It was named in honor of General Jean Boyer, the Haitian general. Sandy Lattion, Worshipful Master, had created deep concern among the white lodges when he announced his meetings in the city newspapers. So far as is definitely known, he was the first Master. (48) Sandy Lattion was a member of the A.M.E. Zion Church, both Zion and later Asbury, where he was an original trustee. (49) None of the other eight members of the original charter have been discovered, but it is believed that Varick and Miller were associated with Lattion in this first Masonic organization of New York State, for they worked closely together in the church and other African organizations. Boyer Lodge was also known as the African Lodge, and today represents the oldest black lodge of New York State.

On January 17, 1817, The New York African Bible Society was established in William Miller's schoolroom in his home at 36 Mulberry Street, where he also operated his cabinet-maker's shop. The group met and drew up its constitution and chose the following gentlemen as managers: William Miller, president; James Varick, Jacob Matthews, and Thomas Miller, vice-presidents; George Collins, secretary; Lewis Carter, treasurer; George DeGrass, Sandy Lattion, Robert F.

42. Peter Williams, Jr. *Abolition of the African Slave Trade,* 1808, speech.
43. *Ibid.*,; Orations and Sermons on the Abolition of the African Slave Trade (Schomberg Collection, New York City).
44. John J. Zuille, *Historical Sketch of the NY Society for Mutual Relief,* pp.1-26; Annual Programs and Orations, NY Society for Mutual Relief.
45. *Ibid.,* p.25; Programs, 1809- .
46. Hood, *One Hundred Years,* p.213.
47. William H. Grimshaw *Official History of Freemasonry,* p.124.
48. Ms., *Harry* Albo Williamson papers, Schomberg Collection. Sesqui-Centennial Program Celebrating Boyer Lodge, 1812-1962, NY Historical Society.
49. Liber 1, p.78, Religious Corporations, Hall of Records, NY City.

Williams, Andrew Smith, and William Lambert. (50) It had 42 members in the beginning, and became an auxiliary society to the American Bible Society founded in 1816. By the end of the year of the American Bible Society's report for 1820, it had made donations and paid for Bibles to be distributed among its race people. The Society continued to grow, along with a sister group, "The New York Female Bible Society of People of Colour," which raised large sums for the distribution of the Bibles and reported to the American Bible Society. Its object was "to encourage as wide a circulation as possible of the Holy Scriptures amongst the people of colour in this City without note or accompanied with any comment. . . . " (51)

James Varick worked hard, also, to establish the church in New Haven, Conn., as early as 1818, with 35 members. This church later became a part of Zion connection in 1820. It was formerly the John Wesley Church on Webster Street, now the Varick Memorial Church, mother church of the New England Conference, at Dixwell Avenue and Charles Street. (52)

Varick was enthusiastically versatile in his endeavors for church and race, and "plain but orthodox in his preaching." (53) Much of his writing is lost, by decay or design, though some of it may yet be discovered. But the paucity of it need not be too surprising, for he was a man with a large family, supporting the work of his church venture and the work for his race in general, which absorbed most of his economic strength. A large number of the members of this pioneering movement, we will recall, were slaves, and generally poor. Varick's wisdom and pen were dominant and strongly directive in the documents that created the A.M.E. Zion Church and that still constitute its classic preservation. But printing was so expensive in that day, for our people in New York, that in some instances, only 100 or 200 copies of items were printed and circulated. A good instance of the difficulty of small preservation of published material is the first Discipline of the A.M.E. Zion Church of 1820. Twelve hundred copies were printed, and only three can be found in the leading libraries of the country today, including the Library of Congress. Another instance is the newspaper established by the son of William Hamilton, *The Peoples Press*, which circulated for a brief period, and no copy can be found.(54)

Varick once again came to the front in behalf of his race when a group of black ministers and businessmen met in New York City, and appointed Thomas Sipkins secretary of the committee to petition the New York State Constitutional Convention regarding their right to vote. The memorial was sent for direct action, and brought to the attention of the convention, meeting in Albany on September 12. There was much opposition on the right of suffrage, and lengthy debates. The Convention finally passed a limited law based upon age, amount of property owned, amount of taxes paid, etc. (55)

Varick figured prominently, also, in the black man's effort to start a newspaper for his race. I. Garland Penn states that: "New York State appears to have been the great fighting ground of the Afro-American abolitionists. Not only

50. *Constitution,* New York African Bible Society; American Bible Society Library.
51. Eric M. North, *Ms. History,* American Bible Society Library.
52. Robert Austin Warner, *New Haven Negroes,* p.85; Hill, *Modern History of New Haven and Eastern New Haven County,* Vol. I, p.217; *Freedom's Journal,* May 4, 1827.
53. Moore, *History,* p.349.
54. This journal mentioned by Penn in *The Afro-American Press and Its Editors;* also by James Brown of Fishkill Landing, N.Y., in his diaries. Ms. Division, New York Historical Society.
55. *Journal,* Convention of the State of New York, 1821, pp.49-51.

in New York, but throughout the whole section of New York state, papers were established, here and there, for the purpose of agitating Afro-American freedom and citizenship."[56] The Negro church helped build *Freedom's Journal,* the first black newspaper in America, and *Freedom's Journal* helped the Negro church. A group of leading men met at the home of Boston Crummell, father of the noted Alexander Crummell, who lived at 139 Leonard Street, near Zion Church and Varick's home, called by John Brown Russworm "to consider the attacks of the local paper," and "to vindicate the Negro race and unite the entire Negro people;" and there they established the *Freedom's Journal* in March 1827. [57] Russworm had the assistance of the leading preachers of that day: Samuel Cornish who was associated with him and did editorial work, James Varick, Richard Allen, Peter Williams, Jr., and others. "They exposed the contradiction of the white churches mercilessly, and challenged the sincere believer to examine the doctrines of true religion." [58] For one year, May 4, 1827 to May 2, 1828, the *Freedom's Journal* operated from the commodious and spacious facility of Zion Church at 152 Church Street. [59] An advertisement in the *Freedom's Journal* shows the interest of the leading black preachers of the city in furthering the cause of education: B. F. Hughes operated a school at St. Philip's Episcopal Church, and James Varick was one of the supporters even though there was also a school in Zion Church supported by its members. [60]

It is well known that "the church leaders influenced the thought of their time." The anti-colonization movement in New York included Rev. Samuel E. Cornish, Bishop James Varick, Rev. Peter Williams, Jr., and Rev. T. S. Wright, in its earlier period. "It was these men who saw the vicious motive of the pro-slavery men beneath the apparently innocent purpose of the colonization, and pointed it out to the gullible white abolitionists. These same men were active in the early abolition movement, as orators, writers, editors." These men formed the African Wilberforce Benevolent Society of New York, the African Clarkson Association and various organizations of that nature to fight for the cause of justice, equality, and dignity for all men, which organizations were mentioned as "the forerunners of the Urban League and National Association for the Advancement of Colored People today." [61]

When Bishop Moore gave his graphic description of Varick as a "man of great firmness, patience, perseverance, forethought, caution, and uprightness;" [62] Bishop Hood in his history, "as with the skill of a modern photographer, enlarged Bishop Moore's pen picture of James Varick." [63]

> His *forethought* is conspicuous in that he wholly avoided the difficulty that later movements had to contend with respecting the title of church property. Varick's skillful hand was in drawing up the Articles of Incorporation, and the church property of the organization, led by Bishop Varick, was all deeded to their own incorporation, viz., "The African

56. I. Garland Penn, *The Afro-American Press and Its Editors,* p.28.
57. *Ibid.,* p.28; Federal Writers Program Negroes of New York, The Negro Press, 1939-1941, Schomberg Collection; Ottley and Weatherby, *op. cit.,* p.89.
58. Federal Writers Program, *op. cit.*
59. *Freedom's Journal;* New York City Directories, African Zion Church; Property Conveyance Deeds.
60. *Freedom's Journal,*
61. Federal Writers Program New York Negroes (Churches) Schomberg Collection; Constitution, N.Y. African Clarkson Association, 1825.
62. Moore, *History,* pp.348-349.
63. C. R. Harris, "James Varick, *His Influence Upon the A.M.E. Zion Church." The Star of Zion,* Oct. 15, 1896, p.1.

Methodist Episcopal Church," commonly called Zion.

James Varick's *patience* is seen in his long waiting on the bishops of the Methodist Episcopal Church for the realization of his hopes which they held out to him. The petition of his people to grant him holy orders was deferred twenty years. . . . Varick waited and manifested his firm belief in proper procedure all along the line.

His *firmness* was not only seen in his long waiting, but in his ability to stand the tests in times of crisis, when our other leaders and people were torn asunder and wondering whether to go back to Mother Methodism, to unite with other black Methodists, or to build an independent religious movement of their own.

His *perseverance* shows he had a purpose from which nothing could turn him aside. His eye of faith rested upon a prize, and he persevered until the jewel of holy orders was handed to him by ministers whose authority was as unquestionable as history could make it.

It takes a very *cautious* man to hold his associates through a long course of years to the interest of his purpose, when they at the same time had a different purpose. Varick started out to establish an independent church. The bishop and other ministers were opposed to this and determined, if possible, to get him and his organization back into the Methodist Episcopal Church. Varick determined to maintain his own organization. [In the first Annual Conference, New York Conference, which he organized and held; Rev. Joshua Soule, who afterwards became bishop, acted as secretary.]

Varick was noted for *uprightness.* Through all the trying years of his leadership, nothing of a discreditable character is recorded of him.

To those characteristics ascribed to Bishop Varick by Bishop Moore, [Hood adds] I wish to add a few traits which I have learned are eminently characteristic of the church, which I believe are equally conspicuous in the life of James Varick. One of these traits is *humility.* Another trait of Varick and his church is *moderation,* the opposite of bigotry and sectarianism. While the fathers held to their self-prescribed course firmly and patiently, they were willing to accord another course. When Bishop Allen's missionary came to New York to organize a church of his Connection, James Varick welcomed the new organization by opening the meeting for Bishop Allen on the second or third Sunday night of the existence of the Society, then worshipping in Mott Street.

Look at the picture of Bishop James Varick. Mark his features. Do they not all stamp him as the man he proved to be, and best fitted to organize and foster a race movement, which places a grand multitude today under the guidance and religious teaching of their own race leaders? Long may his name be revered and his silent yet potent influence felt in the branch of the Apostolic Methodist Church which he did so much to found—The African Methodist Episcopal Zion Church in America. [64]

A lay person of the church expressed her views on the sainted father. Miss Maud E. Hazel of Beaufort, N.C., says of Bishop Varick:

As a man, as a leader, and as a ruler, I think him equally entitled to our praise and admiration. If I survey him as a man, I find him irreproachable in every avocation of life. His personal character was pure beyond a shadow of suspicion, and his social character was equally above the reach of blame. He was just and honorable to all men, and he infringed no unlawful rights, and exacted no undue obedience. I further regard him as a leader. I find in him everything to admire and nothing to condemn. He was brave, far-seeing, quick in insight, bold, prudent and deserving. He was just to those under his

64. C. R. Harris, *op. cit., Star of Zion,*; Hood, *One Hundred Years,* pp.162-168.

command. . . . We next notice him as a ruler. He is perhaps more remarkable still for sagacity, strong, practical wisdom, promptness, firmness, fearlessness, and unsullied justice. . . . Thus we see that we had a great and noble leader. (65)

Varick and his devoted companion toiled together in faith to produce a distinguished family of useful citizens. His time and effort were dedicated to building up his new race movement and to public service, as were those of our mother in Israel, Aurelia Varick, who used her spare time in working with the ladies of the church, particularly the Dorcas Society, and other such endeavors, while at the same time rearing a notable family. We note with particular interest their granddaughter, Aurelia Varick, daughter of Daniel and Mary Clark Varick, who taught school in the Newburgh area before she married a prominent member of the Odd Fellows and moved to New York. She was apparently proud of the fact that a Zion society was established in the town of her grandfather's birthplace, the same year in which he died, by George Matthews, and pastored later by Rev. Jacob Matthews, one of Varick's coadjutors. From a young child she took a deep interest in the work of the Newburgh Church, and the one just across the river at Fishkill Landings, where she and her mother were many times guests of James and Julia Brown. For a while Aurelia lived with the Browns, and was quite attentive to her Zion Church. Perhaps her biggest thrill was the dedication services of the new church, Sunday April 17, 1853, by Bishop Rush, while the outstanding preacher-physician, Rev. J. P. Thompson (later bishop), was pastoring there. (66)

Varick's grandson, Daniel, Jr., was quite a unique businessman in New York. He married the young widow of Zion's first record-keeper, George Collins. He was a first-class barber by trade, and "kept about the most pretentious barber shop in the city." (67) There were several other surviving descendants of Varick, who served humanity well.

William Howard Day, one of the most outstanding educators of the nineteenth century, who later became a prominent minister and general officer of the A.M.E. Zion Church, was baptized by James Varick at Zion Church, New York. His mother often entertained Varick and a host of other preachers in her home. (68)

Varick was elected first bishop during the annual conference, according to the Discipline of the A.M.E. (Zion) Church, and consecrated on Sunday morning, July 30, 1822, after which he, assisted by elders Abraham Thompson and Leven Smith, ordained six deacons: Christopher Rush, James Smith, James Anderson, William Carman, Edward Johnson, and Tilman Cornish. These same men were ordained elders in the afternoon, and appointed by Varick to go forth and commence building a strong organization in the name of Jesus Christ. He presided over the next five annual conferences of the New York Conference until his death in 1827. (69)

James Varick had lived down the mountain of jealousy and opposition, long enough to see partial achievement of his church and race people, for which he

65. Maud E. Hazel, "Our Zion, *Its Origin, Leaders, and Growth.*" *The Star of Zion*, Jan. 28, 1897.
66. *Diaries* of James Brown of Fishkill Landing; *op. cit.,* John H Nutt, Newburgh, *op. cit.* pp.128-129.
67. Ovington, *Half a Man*, p.14; Wheeler, *op. cit.,* p.22.
68. Wheeler, *op. cit.,* p.4; Hood, *One Hundred Years*, pp.321-322.
69. Rush, *Rise and Progress*, p.79; *Doctrines and Discipline*, 1820; Anderson, *Official Directory*, p.35.

had so zealously wrought. When final emancipation came to the black race in New York State, July 4, 1827, and the people assembled in heavy numbers for thanksgiving to God, and heard the major oration given by William Hamilton at Zion Church on the corner of Church and Leonard Streets, Varick sensed that this was only the beginning of their humble efforts of vigilance and protests of the evil conditions in this nation, which would continue here and elsewhere in Zion, until the black race in the entire nation, and across the world, achieved its freedom and universal dignity.

Two weeks later, Sunday morning, July 22, 1827, Varick was no more. "The Bishop of the African Zion Connexion" had passed away at his home, [70] and funeral services were held at Zion Church. Varick's remains were carried to the Colored Union Cemetery in New Windsor (now known as Woodlawn Cemetery), one mile from Newburgh, for interment. Upon the completion of the present Mother Zion Church structure, at 146 West 137th Street, in 1925 led by Rev. Dr. J. W. Brown; a committee of the New York Conference, headed by Bishop Josiah S. Caldwell had Varick's sacred ashes removed from the Woodlawn Cemetery and placed in a crypt beneath the sanctuary of the church. Dedication services of the crypt were held on February 1, 1926. "A bust and tablet to his memory are on the walls of the sanctuary, which is the shrine of Zion Methodism." [71] Above all, the greatest monument today to James Varick, sanctioned by God Almighty, and his Son Jesus Christ and the Holy Spirit, is the African Methodist Episcopal Zion Church.

> *"And in every work that he began in the service of the house of God, and in the law, and in the Commandments, to seek his God, he did it with all his heart and prospered."*   II Chron. 31:21

70. *Freedom's Journal*, July 27, 1827.
71. *The Newburgh News*, September 5, 1935; J. W. Brown, Ms. *History of Mother Zion Church*, 1927, W. J. Walls Collection.

CHAPTER 9

CHURCH POLITY AND CONNECTIONAL STRUCTURE

The Christian Church is the name and meaning of Jesus organized. It is the power of God circulated into the human organism, dispensed and defined psychologically into connections and relations. It is organized and applied spiritually, focused for broadening and knowledge; it extends to universal human society the will of God, to make goodwill between men. God brings his nature to consciousness through human personality. The individual is the contact container and society is its vehicle for distributing God's self to the mass.

In tracing the most important aspect of Methodism's "Christianity in Earnest," emphasis is placed on the individual's life and the Jesus way of expression. "Life is real, life is earnest," says Longfellow. This great exponent of life pictures it to be so real and so earnest that it cannot be bounded by earth; it cannot be contained in the dust. *Life,* for what is life? Another emphasis is that "it is even a vapor that appeareth for a little time and then vanishes away." That is James' version of the physical life and of the things that the physical life may produce of itself only But life is something that cannot be defined. Life must be lived, and the whole life is as much spiritual as physical. John Wesley's Christian religion was personal experience. "What had been to multitudes merely a formal thing, a creed remote from life, or a convention without a trace of power, became, through the conviction of Wesley's preaching (like that of the apostles), a real energy in life." [1] James Varick forcefully propagated this spiritual way of life, to spur his new movement onward in the pietistical crusade and social uplift of a much abused and broken-hearted people.

Methodism was not born in forms and structures. It was born in experience with God and the fervent desire to find his will in the whole life. But in order to carry on the group development and expansion of this concept, certain practices of church government had to be utilized. The object of church government, says Bishop Moore, "is to formulate a system of ecclesiastical rules by which the votaries of a religious sect may most effectually disseminate and practically apply the religious principles they have espoused; which system of rules is generally shaped in accordance with the force of circumstances, as are all systems established and regulated by human judgment." Writers on church government have conceded that:

> New-Testament Scriptures do not contain any formulated system of rules as a model of Church polity, or ecclesiastical economy; the integrity of which was to be perpetuated throughout the church's history, coming down from the apostles to us. Therefore, true church government has, and must mostly depend upon enlightened human judgment. . . . Each Christian denomination

1. Luccock, Hutchison and Goodloe, *The Story of Methodism,* p.166.

had been led to adopt such religious polity or form of church government as they under the force of circumstances deemed the most suitable for the propagation and the practical application of the principles of religion they had espoused. The form of church government depends primarily on the idea men entertain of the Constitution of the Church, or what constitutes the Church of Christ. (2)

The A.M.E. Zion Church, from its inception, adopted the fundamental form of polity of the American Methodist Church. "They had no fault to find with the doctrine or form of government," states Hood, "the only trouble was that they could not, in that organization, on account of their color, enjoy the privileges it offered to others." (3) This was definitely contrary to the philosophy and teachings of the Wesleys and their associates.

It was the love of righteousness, freedom, and religious liberty that prompted Varick and those fine-spirited pioneers of Zion Methodism to begin to build a firm church foundation on the American continent, in 1796. While major denominations of the Christian family have been established on ecclesiastical principles, the A.M.E. Zion Church is proud of the fact that it is established on both ecclesiastical and freedom principles. It is in accord with the passage of scripture: "And ye shall know the truth, and the truth shall make you free." The peculiar tenets and doctrines of Methodism were adopted and endorsed, with the same zeal that prompted early growth. Its personal evangelism and simplified worship with minimal ritual suited the masses, especially the slave masses of that day.

Doctrine

The Methodist Church created out of its literature 24 of the 39 Articles of Religion of the Church of England, which Wesley sent to America as a guidepost. The Christmas Conference of 1784 added the twenty-fifth, which has to do with the United States government and is numbered 23. The inexorable doctrines of Calvinism on reprobation and predestination were excluded, while the exorable doctrines of Arminianism of free grace for all, faith, repentance, and holiness were included, according to John Wesley who said: "The first of these we count as it were the porch of religion; the next, the door; the third, religion itself." (4) Along with these articles, the only formal creed adopted was the Apostles' Creed habitually used in our form of worship. These Articles of Religion, *The Nature, Design, and General Rules of Our United Societies, and Special Advices*, found in our Discipline, form the Constitution of Methodism, and are paramount facets of the fundamental meaning and original foundation of the church, based upon the teaching of Jesus and the Bible. (5)

The other prominent Doctrines of Methodism are defined as follows:

Sanctification: Belief in the doctrine of sanctification or Christian perfection; that is, that a Christian can have a conscience void of offense toward God and man, that he can order his conduct so before God and man as not to encourage his carnal nature, in opposition to his spiritual; thus his spiritual nature becomes predominant; God ruling upon the main altar of the heart; then he is sanctified, or entirely consecrated to the service of

2. Moore, *History of the A.M.E. Zion Church in America*, pp.74-75.
3. Hood, *One Hundred Years*, p.10.
4. Wesley, *The Works of John Wesley*, p.472, Vol. 8.
5. Israel Daniel Rupp, (ed.), *Religious Denominations in the U.S.*, pp.417-418; Selecman, *The Methodist Primer*, pp.31-32.

God. (6) Bishop McConnell's quotation on this is: "The Methodist ideal does not differ from the New Testament ideal, that we are to be perfect even as the Father in heaven is perfect." (7)

The Witness of the Spirit may be said to be the distinguishing doctrine of Methodism. The Spirit bears witness to those who are born again that they are children of God and joint heirs with Jesus Christ.

A Life of Joy and Obedience should follow repentance and the new birth. "If any man be in Christ, he is a new creature; old things have passed away; behold all things are become new."

Christian Experience. "A life of joy and peace should flow from fellowship with Christ and His people." It is believed that religious enjoyment or impulse should not be circumscribed by the mere feeling or customs of the common refinement of our present age. (8)

Means of Grace in practicing regular attention to all the ordinances of the Lord; such as the public worship of God; the ministry of the word either read or expounded; the Supper of the Lord; family and private prayer, and searching the scriptures. (9)

Conversion is the most essential experience of Methodism and is sometimes called the *new birth* or *regeneration.* Those who truly repent and believe on the Lord Jesus Christ, and have the experience of the presence of the Holy Spirit in their hearts, are acknowledged to be born anew.

Other Practices in Our Polity

The most essential phases in the cultivation of deep consecration and religious experience in original Methodism were class-meetings and love-feasts. These were great influences in the rapid growth of the Methodist movements. We have already seen (Chapter 4) that John Wesley organized the first class in Methodism, and gathered around him those who sought a deeper sense of grace and a better knowledge on the growth and meaning of their conversion. This class organization was duplicated over and over again, and was permitted as a practice of those who chose to be in these classes, which became known in the course of time as Methodist classes, based upon their regularity in practices. A Methodist Church is a class or collection of classes. The practice in our early church was to have a general class and love-feast once in a quarter, usually on Friday or some other week night. It always preceded the quarterly communion service. The method was for members to express themselves publicly, and not privately to the leader, as was the custom in the regular class-meetings. This kept up consistently and ardently for two or three generations. One exponent of the class-meetings and love-feasts polity was the late Bishop John B. Small, who spoke as follows:

Class-Meeting is a lawful heir of Methodism. If Methodism is intended to indicate, kept in a living state by regular methods, class-meetings and prayer meetings—to talk of God and His goodness, and to ask or pray for continuance, can never be abandoned. To abandon or neglect either, contradicts the name—Methodism: these gave it birth. (10)

Love-Feast is an ancient ordinance, instituted in the days of the apostles, when it was called, "Agapae." At the celebration thereof the early

6. Rupp, *op. cit.,* p.417.
7. Selecman, *op. cit.,* p.34.
8. *Ibid.,* pp.33-35.
9. Rupp, *Religious Denominations,* p.418.
10. Small, *Code of the Discipline of the African Methodist Episcopal Zion Church,* p.110.

Christians ate and drank together in token of Christian love and fellowship one with the other. Such a season was a time of refreshing to the hated and hunted disciples of the risen and ascended Saviour, because of their associations with tried friends and companions in sufferings.

St. John Chrysostom says: "It is a custom, the most beautiful and beneficial; for it is a supporter of love, a solace of poverty, a moderator of wealth, a discipline of humility."

Love-feasts are held in the African Methodist Episcopal Zion Church once a quarter, generally before the quarterly meeting, under the supervision of the presiding elder or pastor in charge; at which time the members of the society in general are present, and break and eat bread together, as a token of Christian fellowship with God and their brethren. This is considered an outward sign of the grace of God dwelling in their hearts, and manifested toward each other.

The reasons Mr. Wesley assigned for introducing love-feasts into the Methodist Church were: "In order to increase in them [persons in bands] a grateful sense of all His [God's] mercies, I desire that one evening in a quarter all the men in band, on a second all the women, would meet; and on a third both men and women together; that we might together "eat bread," as the ancient Christians did, "with gladness and singleness of heart." At these love-feasts (so we term them, retaining the name as well as the thing, which was in use from the beginning), our food is only a little plain cake and water; but we seldom return from them without being fed, not only with the "meat which perisheth," but with that which endureth to everlasting life. (11)

The standing rule of the African Methodist Episcopal Zion Church was admittance by love-feast tickets. Those persons who were entitled to admission into the love-feasts were all members of the church in good standing, probationers, those belonging to special classes of baptized children, and persons who were members of other Christian communions. The tickets, as a rule, bore the name of the member, the date issued, and endorsement of the preacher in charge. The tickets were renewed quarterly. (12)

The form of godliness is practiced in the following Special Advices:

In order to safeguard *marriage* and family life, every preacher is to publicly enforce the Apostle's caution; "Be ye not unequally yoked together with unbelievers," and to counsel their members upon "taking such steps in so weighty a matter without advising" with close associates and spiritual leaders.

The Ministers are to discourage procurement of *Divorce* except on Scriptural ground.

Slavery and slave-holding are against all principles of Christianity. The practice of *Temperance;* all use of spiritous liquors are prohibited except in case of necessity.

Consecration of the Christian Sabbath and observance of religious holidays are customary, with special emphasis on Passion Week, Thanksgiving, Christmas, and Watch-night meetings which are to be held on the eve of New Year, in order to thank God for past blessings and to make solemn vows.

Camp-Meeting is a specialty that grows out of our polity of evangelism and has not totally expired in Zion Methodism. They were the great outdoor revivals, not confined to Methodism. Camp meetings were born in America

11. *Ibid.*, pp.149-150.
12. *Ibid.*, p.150.

at the very end of the eighteenth century. "In the year 1800 the first camp meeting was held by Presbyterian preachers; but most Presbyterians, unwilling to countenance the attendant emotional extravagances, soon withdrew from participation in the camp meeting revivals, leaving the field free to the Baptists and the Methodists, who were less reluctant to take the gospel to the people in the form which would touch them most deeply. The result was that the latter two denominations were able to expand with the population in a way that the first was not. The fidelity of the Presbyterians and the Congregationalists to the principle of an educated ministry, their insistence on due instruction of candidates for church membership, and their 'fencing of the table of the Lord' have been valuable contributions to American church life. The Methodists and the Baptists, while not blind to the dangers of their quite different methods, deliberately persisted in them, and so became churches of the people in a remarkable way." (13)

Another section of our ecclesiastical economy embraces the *General Rules*. These appear as an abridgement in Chapter 4, in Wesley's two general advices (also see Discipline). They are "the most solemn attestations to religious sincerity and desire of salvation, by which all persons connecting or connected with our church must give."

It is intended to interpose all possible restraints upon carnal indulgences that tend to stifle the spirit of religious aspiration and Christian devotion, and alienate the heart from God, and that would chill the spiritual affections. It is intended also, to secure a distinction between the religious confessor of our church and the ungodly. It draws a line of social discrimination between the world and the church. It is to aid the professor of religion in the devotion of his soul, body and spirit to the service of God. In this form of godliness, are ritual injunctions laid, that promote religious devotional duties of the confessor in the church; that tend to perpetuate in him a constant desire for Spiritual Communion with God, and which cherish in him a perpetual religious zest. (14)

The *Member*, therefore, according to these doctrines and polity, must be orthodox in his belief. When we speak of "Orthodoxy," says Bishop Small, "we mean the creed of the Evangelical churches which embraces the doctrinal view of the divinity and atonement of our Lord Jesus Christ. . . . These are essential doctrines to members of the Methodist Church. No person can be a consistent member of the African Methodist Episcopal Zion Church who will not vow a belief in the aforesaid doctrines—without them he (or she) cannot be orthodox." (15)

The African Methodist Episcopal Zion Church has, from the beginning, held high esteem for Varick and the founding fathers, and has had symbols of freedom, independence, and iniative in enterprise and organization to which bishops, ministers and followers of Zion are inspired to direct their labors, sacrifices, objectives and ideals. All of these symbolisms and activities were, and are, subordinate to the ideals of Jesus Christ, fashioned after his life and teachings, highlighted by his glimpses of eternal life. This is all verified by the cross and resurrection and the teachings of the Apostles, who found hope for themselves and us in the personality of Jesus and his victory over the world. This hope held a suffering race together, for they believed that through him their freedom would come in this world and their salvation in the world to come. Those who died without the sight of freedom for which they fought were

13. Bucke, ed., *History of American Methodism*, Vol. I, p.246.
14. Moore, *History, op. cit.*, pp.78-79.
15. John B. Small, *Code of the Discipline, op. cit.*, p.21.

consoled by the fact that their children would be freed one day in this world. They themselves had the undefeatable comfort stemming from the blessed immortality which Christianity unfolded and promised: "These all died in the faith, not having received the promises, but having seen them afar off, and were persuaded of them, and embraced them, and confessed that they were strangers and pilgrims on the earth." (Hebrews 11:13)

This faith and the articles of their creed produced in our fathers common effort and common history. They lived under the spell of faith, and by the history of their achievements. The victories they achieved over the enemies of both body and soul caused them to shout salvation, and they embodied their strivings and assurance in songs, common strains in prayers, and a special heroic fulminating type of preaching. But most important of all was their loyalty to each other, to a connectional church, to the race, and to the country of their forefathers as well as their adopted country through slavery.

Much of our polity is practiced too partially still, and must be restored universally to our Methodism. Unless we restore the essentials of Methodism, we will destroy it. The church is not dependent upon time and human change for its movement. Its oracles are set in waters deeper than any culture, and it strikes the subcurrent of God's eternal purpose and spirit; its message is a message invincible and everlasting. Thus the motto of the Christian is *allegiance to God the eternal and not to man the temporary.* One of the major tests that defines this eternal relationship and heroic faith is expressed by Paul to Timothy: "Now unto the King eternal, immortal, invisible, the only wise God, be honour and glory for ever and ever, *Amen.*" (I Tim., 1:17)

Church Government

"Lord MaCauley declared that John Wesley's 'genius for government was not inferior to that of Richelieu,' and time shows the statement was not too strong." (16) It is interesting today to study Wesley's consciousness and his words in starting our great Methodism into organized procedure. Two paramount things stamped his words and acts in the first Methodist General Conference, June 25, 1744, in the old Foundry of London, where church government of our Mother Methodism was begun with six regularly ordained clergymen and four traveling lay preachers. His first language contained these words: "It is desired that all things be considered as in the immediate presence of God;" and following this directive, he further admonished unity with the language, "that we meet with a single eye, and as little children, who have everything to learn; that every point which is proposed may be examined to the foundation; that every person may speak freely whatever is in his heart; and that every question raised be thoroughly debated and settled." (17)

> The principles Wesley thus proposed to his Conference were foundation principles, not only of that Conference, but of genuine Methodism. With Wesley's recommendations, "that every question proposed may be fully debated and bolted to the brain," the Conference proceeded to discuss three points, namely:"1. What to teach? 2. How to teach? 3. What to do? that is, how to regulate doctrine, discipline, and practice."(18)

The inquiries and admonition of the first Methodist General Conference

16. Thomas B. Neely, *A History of the Origin and Development of the Governing Conference of Methodism*, p.1.
17. *Ibid.,* p.6.
18. *Ibid.,* pp.7-8.

seek to be at the heart of most, if not all, Methodist bodies to this day. Wesley's ideas of religion were molded for every age. He based his teachings on Jesus and his conception of God and man. The contribution Wesley made to church polity is an everlasting one. He clearly defined sin and traced it into the moral motivation and ethics tangent to his social world; and he defined righteousness in terms of self-denial, sacrifice for the growth of faith in God, and the enlargement and sanctification of human relations.

. His toleration of all men's belief, and his assurance built on love, was as everlasting as the human spirit and divine spirit wedded together to form the chain of the Fatherhood of God and the consciousness of Him by the individual between; and seized with strengthening love his brotherman.

The Methodist system began with class meetings. These continued until Wesley added conferences to its polity and included them. Individual experience with union of purpose caused the first organization of conferences, and they appropriated the organ of government as it became necessary, according to custom, on either side of the sea.

The African Methodist Episcopal Zion Church is a Methodist connection, a denomination with churches bound together with each other as congregations of the A.M.E. Zion Church, with a central form of church polity governing each congregation while each congregation maintains a separate and distinct identity. The A.M.E. Zion Church adopted the pattern of American Methodism, with modification, in the creation of its first Discipline and in development of congregations and conferences.

James Varick was God's principal instrument in shaping the destiny of the A.M.E. Zion Church government in steering its first discipline committee of 1820. Our church government was so structured from its beginning, to guard and balance the individual experience with the collective experience in its entire ecclesiastical and temporal economy. Through its principal agency, the class, the member is at once individually nurtured for his or her soul's salvation, and instructed in the obligation of the local church by way of the Doctrines and Discipline of the general organization.

Membership

Each member must enter into our Methodist fellowship by one of three methods. 1. By profession of his faith and receiving the sacrament of Baptism. 2. By transfer from an A.M.E. Zion Church or a certified letter from a Christian church. Those joining from churches other than the A.M.E. Zion Church shall be required to answer questions as to loyalty, allegiance, and practice of her Doctrines and Discipline. 3. By restoration. One who has previously been received into the fellowship of our Methodism by confessing his faith in our risen Lord, and has fallen by the wayside by neglect of means of grace, or dropped from long absence, may be restored by receiving forgiveness and coming back into the fold of the church.

Probationers: New members are received into the church on a six-months trial period by the minister in charge, who proceeds with the ritual, according to our Discipline, of the reception of new members on probation. Following this brief ceremony in the presence of the congregation, the minister assigns the probationer to a class where he must satisfy both the minister and class leader "as to the soundness of his conversion." He is afterwards received into full membership in a similar ceremony.

Membership of Children: This is recognized by the church in the ordinance of the sacrament of Baptism. Baptized children are raised up in the faith, and assigned to classes at an early age for further instruction and salvation, and the means of grace. After attaining an age sufficient to understand the obligations of religion, and giving evidence of piety, they may be admitted into full membership of the church, sanctioned by their leader and confirmed by the minister in charge. Childhood religion has been stressed by Methodism from the beginning. "Many of the great leaders of Methodism have gladly testified that they professed their love for Christ and became members of the Church at the early ages of 6, 7, and 8, and have never known a time when they did not desire to love and endeavor to serve God." [19] Dr. J. C. Price always rejoiced that he came into the church through the Sunday school, where he was discovered.

These all constitute a congregation in the A.M.E. Zion Church, known also in our economy as *the Local Church.* Class leaders, stewards, trustees, and eleemosynary organizations of the local church are composites in our personnel, headed by the pastor and assisted by other preachers.

The Ministry

Practically every Methodist minister was an evangelist, as were the apostles and disciples of Jesus Christ; and based upon him the whole spiritual and temporal machinery of the church moved forward. Three important agencies supplemented the labors of the clergy of early Methodism and prompted its growth: class leaders, stewards, and lay evangelists, known as Wesley's helpers. Laymen expounded the word and exhorted the people, "and the Holy Ghost bore witness to the validity of their ministry." [20] We see at once that the ministry is born of devout, pious laymen. Unless a person is received into our ministry from another church, in good standing, and according to the rules and regulations set forth in our Discipline, he must first exercise his gift and high calling as an exhorter.

Exhorters: These are "religious public speakers, licensed by the Quarterly Conference, a local court of the society." The prescribed method of receiving exhorters license, rules and regulations, are found in our Discipline.

Licensed or Local Preachers: "A higher order of licentiates, they are licensed by the same local court of the society, to preach as local clergymen."

Itinerant Preachers: "These are sent out by an annual conference, appointed by a bishop to their field of labor, to collect and organize societies, and to serve those already organized as pastors."

Ordained Ministers: These consist of two orders, *Deacons* and *Elders,* sacredly set apart by the church and elected by the Annual Conference, and ordained by Elders and a Bishop, by the imposition of hands. *Deacon:* "One who is elected to receive this order by the Annual Conference, (after he has travelled two years in the itinerancy), then ordained by the bishop. His duty is to preach at the requisition of the elder in whose charge he is, to assist in the administration of the Holy Communion, to baptize and administer matrimony, and to try disorderly members in the absence of the elder. *Elder:* Functionary, is the eldership (the highest of holy orders, as resting upon divine appointment of orders in the Christian Church); he is elected by the Annual Conference to receive holy orders, and then ordained by the bishop, assisted by at least two elders. His office is to take pastoral charges wherever the bishop may appoint him, to preach on the same as often as practicable, solemnize Matrimony,

19. Selecman, *op. cit.,* p.34.
20. Henry Wheeler, *One Thousand Questions and Answers,* pp.8-9.

administer the sacrament of the Lord's Supper and Baptize. Only the Elder may consecrate the elements for the Holy Communion." [21]

Supernumerary: A supernumerary preacher is one who does not have a pastoral charge, but is subject to all the duties of a minister.

Superannuate: One who is above the years of service.

Every pastor, presiding elder, superannuate, and supernumerary in good standing belongs to the itinerancy, and when able to serve may be appointed by the bishop of the district. Any minister can transfer from one conference to another, but only by his personal consent. A minister may also locate by request. The work of a conference evangelist must be in the bounds of the annual conference territory in which he or she is assigned, unless invited by the General Director of Evangelism to assist in efforts of soul-saving and recruitment of members.

These various categories of preachers have come out of the evolution of experience in the growth of the church, legalized by the General Conference. While these have been meaningful in the ongoing development of the connection, and may all be qualified elders, leadership responsibility has been designated to three classes of elders' office: the pastorate, presiding eldership, and episcopacy. This is the effectual potency of our ecclesiastical body through connectionalism.

Pastorate: The pastor is the most important person in the structure of the church. He preaches the gospel, serves the worship, leads the people to prayer, presides in the class-meetings, performs the marriage ceremony, visits the sick, cares for the bereaved, and helps to preserve the lives of the needy. During the days of slavery, A.M.E. Zion pastors were abolitionists, just as they are advocates of freedom and equality since the days of emancipation. In modern days, the pastor engages largely in the social and public enterprises of the whole people, and lays them to rest and says the word of comfort over their last remains. He is to see that the local church is properly organized and programmed for the connection's interest, and for building the ample structure.

Presiding Eldership: In the development of the church, especially in America, the districts were spread over extended territories, but not large enough to be annual conferences. When these territories became large enough to be stabilized, in the A.M.E. Zion Church organization, they were changed and named districts within the bounds of the annual conferences. The person presiding over them was changed from ruling elder to presiding elder. He is to preside over four sessions a year in the local station or circuit of his district, known as the *quarterly conference,* and one conference a year of a delegated assembly of these churches, known as the *district conference.* In the earliest history of the connection, the elder in charge of a circuit or station functioned as the ruling elder until we expanded into the presiding elder's districts, as early as 1872, after our most flourishing growth. The General Conference passed a law that "the bishop may appoint presiding elders when, in his judgment, it is necessary for the efficiency of the work of his diocese." [22] In 1888, the presiding elder system was firmly established by the General Conference when resolutions were passed defining their duties, and spelled out in the Discipline. By 1896, we had 76 presiding elder districts in the denomination. [23] In 1900,

---

21. Moore, *History, op. cit.,* pp.80-81; Rupp, *Religious Denominations, op. cit.,* pp.418-419.
22. *Doctrines and Discipline,* 1872, p.54.
23. J. Harvey Anderson, "Progress of the Fourth Quarter of Zion Methodism"*A.M.E. Zion Quarterly Review,* October 1898, p.7; *Minutes,* Eighteenth Quadrennial Session, 1888, p.113.

after the question had been debated in previous General Conferences, the position was made an appointment of the bishop, and not elective by the annual conference. (24) We now have 124 presiding elder districts.

Episcopacy: "Wesley, after due deliberation and consultation, called Dr. Thomas Coke and Reverend James Creighton, presbyters of the Church of England, to meet Richard Whatcoat, Thomas Vasey and himself at Bristol. There, on the first day of September, 1784, assisted by Coke and Creighton, Wesley ordained Vasey and Whatcoat deacons, and on the next day, elders. He also ordained Dr. Thomas Coke Superintendent or Bishop of the Methodist societies in America." (25)

The American Methodist societies, in a conference called December 24, 1784, subsequently agreed to organize themselves into a church with an episcopal form of government, thus resolving to have "superintendents, elders and deacons." They ratified Wesley's appointment and ordination of Dr. Coke by unanimously electing him superintendent. Francis Asbury was also unanimously elected superintendent on the second day of the conference, ordained deacon on Sunday, the third day, and consecrated by Dr. Coke and presbyters, Vasey and Whatcoat, on the fourth day, with Otterbein of the German Reformed Church assisting in the service. (26)

"Superintendent" is the word used by Wesley in the letter of instruction given by him to Dr. Coke: "I have accordingly appointed Dr. Coke and Mr. Francis Asbury to be joint superintendents over our brethren in North America." The words "superintendent" and "bishop" were used synonymously, as it appears in the Minutes of the Conference of 1785, where this sentence occurs: "We thought it best to become an episcopal church, making the episcopal office elective, and the elected superintendent or bishop, amenable to the body of ministers and preachers." (27)

The A.M.E. Zion Church adopted this pattern in organizing their connection as a Methodist Episcopal Church. We also used the terms "superintendent" and "bishop" synonymously in our first Discipline. While defining the duties of the superintendent, the term "bishop" was used in ordaining elders and deacons. "We believe in two orders and three offices of the ministry." (28)

The New Testament gives only two orders. Deacons and elders are episcopates. *Episkopus* and *elder* meant overseer. When they said bishop they meant elder, and when they said elder, bishop. An elder is made directly from a deacon. When the Bible says the deacon must be the husband of one wife, as must a bishop (who is an elder), and in other moral and spiritual matters, blameless; it is simply saying that a deacon and elder must be of consistent regulation. In the extreme hierarchical churches, the episcopacy is a third order. In the Methodist system two orders are only regarded as the original movement of the Christian church. The bishop is an elder elected and consecrated to the office.

Two important changes have been made in the history of the A.M.E. Zion Church episcopacy. In 1868, the General Conference changed the title of our episcopal officers from "superintendent" to "bishop." Prior to 1880, a bishop

24. *Minutes,* Twenty-First Quadrennial Session, 1900, p.107.
25. Wheeler, *One Thousand Questions and Answers,* p.21.
26. *Ibid.,* pp.23-24.
27. *Ibid.,* p.25.
28. *Doctrines and Discipline. . . ,* Alexander Walters, *Star of Zion,* Sept. 4, 1897.

was elected quadrennially. Upon adoption of a resolution presented by Rev. W. A. Foreman, the General Conference amended the law to elect and consecrate a bishop for life, so long as his conduct sustained it. After his consecration he is assigned a district. An episcopal district, which is the official territory of a bishop, is constituted of several annual conferences. It is here that he operates and enforces all the regulation of his area, subject to the general laws of the denomination, which only are enacted by the General Conference.

Organizations

Local Church Conference: The affairs of the local church are brought close to the membership by provision in our economy for the *members' meeting,* which the pastor has the sole right to call, according to necessity, and preside. The *leaders' meeting* assembles once a month and is composed of all class leaders and stewards. Its business is to report to the pastor in charge, the moral conduct of the laity of the church, and to report marriages, illnesses, and deaths. [29] *Trustees meetings* as a rule are held monthly, composed of the pastor and from three to eleven dedicated members above 21 years of age. (The original number was nine.) Their duty is to look over the temporalities of the society of their jurisdiction, to see that there is a proper disbursement of funds, and proper grants of bargains, etc. [30] Other organizational meetings are held, sanctioned by the pastor in charge, for the spiritual and social welfare of the church and its members.

Quarterly Conference: This is an established branch of our ecclesiastical system; a local court that has been commensurate with the existence of our church organization. It is composed of all the local preachers, exhorters, traveling preachers on trial, local deacons, elders, class leaders, trustees, stewards and stewardesses, superintendents of Sabbath school, [31] missionary societies, Varick Christian Endeavor Society, conference auxiliaries, and the pastor in charge of the station or circuit. It gives place of great importance in the affairs of the local church. Every three months, the presiding elder is to officiate, primarily to examine and keep regular the spiritual, moral, benevolent, and temporal concerns of members of the society, and to give an account of the same at the Annual Conference. He is also to license exhorters and preachers as prescribed by the Discipline.

District Conference: The presiding elder district plan was first established by the General Conference of 1876. The General Conference of 1880 made major improvements, outlining a specific section of this conference in the Discipline of 1881, stating that "the Annual Conference may be divided into a convenient number of districts, and one or more District Conferences may be held each year, at such time and place as may be appointed by the Presiding Elder of the District." [32] The General Conference of 1884 made revisions strengthening the definition and duties of the presiding elder. Except the customary spiritual emphasis of Methodism, the business of the district conference outlined in the Discipline was "temporal matters of the churches and schools within the District." [33] Representation of the district conference has been expanded from its origin and now includes traveling and local preachers, superintendents

---

29. Rupp, *Religious Denominations* p.419.
30. *Ibid.*
31. *Ibid.*
32. Moore, *History, op. cit.,* p.36; *Minutes,* Sixteenth Quadrennial Session, 1880, p.33;
33. *Minutes,* Seventeenth Quadrennial Session, 1884, p.142; *Doctrines and Discipline,* 1886, pp.67-72, 135-136.

of Sunday schools of the district, one lay delegate from each circuit or station, and one delegate from each Sunday school. It also includes representatives of the same organizations of the quarterly conferences within the district. The business of the district conference has been abundantly extended. It is to inquire into the spiritual life and progress of the work of the several charges; to receive local preachers and prepare ministerial candidates evangelically and literally for reception into annual conference; to stimulate the benevolent causes of the church; and to promote the program for lay members, missionaries, and children and youth through its Christian Education departments. The District Conference is therefore vitally related to the work of the laymen, children, and youth, and to the beginnings of the process of the making of the ministry, religious educators, and constituent agencies.

Annual Conference: As the name indicates, the annual conference (or yearly conference, as it was called in the days of Varick and Rush), meets once a year, at which time presiding elders, pastors, and other ministers are assigned to their work for another year, or to new work, by the presiding bishop. District missionary officers, Christian education officers, conference workers, home missions workers, and other such workers are also commissioned to go forth annually, and labor in the interest of the church, as specified in the Discipline. The annual conference is composed of the bishop assigned by the General Conference, traveling ministers and preachers, both those in full connection and on trial, with membership in the bounds of the conference, and such lay delegates as may have been legally elected to that body. Each station or circuit has the privilege of sending a lay delegate, who is elected by the quarterly conference or by members of the circuit or station it represents. These delegates are to make known to the conference the wants and wishes of their various charges. However, the district conference, which precedes the annual conference, may elect up to three delegates to represent the laity of the district in the next annual conference, and these delegates shall be entitled to all the rights and privileges of the other members of the annual conference, with the exception of the year preceding the General Conference; each station and circuit shall send a lay delegate to annual conference.

The functions of the annual conference are to examine the moral standing of ministers and their work during the year, receive men and women into the itinerancy, ordain deacons and elders, receive new societies, receive general statistics from the pastors and presiding elders, and set off new annual conference districts, according to the laws of the Discipline. [34] The conference also hears reports of boards, committees, and departmental officers. It is the principal agency for carrying out and promoting the spiritual and temporal affairs of the general church, and elects delegates of ministers and laymen to the General Conference, every four years. The annual conference is a major part of the educational system of the church, especially the ministry. While it is sometimes difficult to please both congregation and pastor, our system assures a pastor for every church and a church for every pastor in good standing.

Connectional Council: This council was established in 1900, upon recommendation of the bishops in their Quadrennial Address, that "there be instituted a Connectional Council of the Church, to be composed of the Bishops, all the General Officers, and the President, Secretary and Treasurer of all the Boards and Schools whose officers are elected by the General Conference. Said Council

34. Moore *History, op. cit.,* p.85.

to meet annually. They shall form the Board of Apportionment and make appropriations of the monies of the following departments: Education, Missionary, Church Extension, Widows and Orphans, Contingencies." The General Conference approved the recommendation with modification. On the twentieth day of the session, Bishop Alexander Walters made the motion that "Bishops, General Officers and three officers of the several boards shall constitute the Connectional Council." After the motion was seconded a discussion ensued. It was ruled that this body could codify such laws as had been recommended by the General Conference, but could not enact new legislation, as it was only an executive body. The motion carried. Therefore, the part of the bishops' recommendation regarding appropriations was ruled as legislative, and must be decided by the General Conference. [35] The Connectional Council was thus born, and the first Council was held in Indianapolis the first Wednesday in September, 1900.

Additions to its representative body have been the connectional boards and general officers created since its birth, inclusive of the officers of the Connectional Laymen's Council. [36] The chairman of the Board of Bishops is president, and the secretary is the General Secretary. Its annual meetings are held at the time and place of the summer meeting of the Board of Bishops. The council exercises executive power over the several connectional boards, and makes and enforces such rules and regulations as may be necessary for the successful operation of the several boards. Departmental reports are made, first to the board; then on behalf of the board, by the officer elected or approved by the General Conference, who must satisfy this body of its results and progress. It is an annual inspirational assemblage in our church economy, a combination of intense spiritual fellowship and strict regulatory church business.

Board of Bishops: In 1860, after 20 years of strife over assistant superintendents, three bishops were elected on equality: Joseph J. Clinton, Peter Ross, and William H. Bishop. [37] Thus Zion moved forward with its leadership when the bishops formed themselves into a Board of Bishops, and after 1868, intensely strengthened their cause to project and regulate certain interests of the connection. The General Conference of 1872 stabilized the Board of Bishops when it required them to "meet semi-annually, to counsel for the general interest of the connection, and to attend to such duties as are required by law and shall hold other meetings, as may be necessary." The only officers named were president and secretary. The Board was to have general supervision over the entire connection in the interval of the General Conference, but not to interfere in an individual bishop's work or charge. At first, it had the authority to make provision for new episcopal districts when necessary, and provide for any vacancy of the existing districts, created by death or resignation. [38] The history of this body has been altered through the years, and its responsibilities augmented, based upon changing conditions and growing needs. In addition to these existing authorities, (with exception of making new episcopal districts) it shall hear complaints, receive petitions when properly submitted by aggrieved parties in good standing, and give such advice, instructions, or corrections as the

35. *Minutes*, Twenty-First Quadrennial Session, 1900, pp.82, 107; *Doctrines and Discipline*, 1901, pp.70-72, 87.
36. *Doctrines and Discipline*, 1968, p.232.
37. Moore, *History, op. cit.*, pp.229-230; *Minutes*, Nineteenth Quadrennial Session, 1892, p.19.
38. *Doctrines and Discipline*, 1872, pp.117-119.

majority may deem necessary, or make adjustments suitable for the good of the denomination, as in their judgment considered wise and imperative. The president of the Board of Bishops is traditionally elected by rotation for a six-months term. At the mid-winter meeting of the board, it is to submit reports of the general condition of the work in each bishop's field, and to hear reports of a six-months period of general officers in charge of various departments. It is to fill vacancies that may occur among general officers and on administrative boards, in the interim of the General Conference. It is to hand down interpretations of existing church law and explanations of methods for administering the law when so interpreted. It is to make a Quadrennial Address to the General Conference, with recommendations to be in the best interest of the connection. It shall consecrate bishops upon election by the General Conference. The terms *installation* and *consecration* of superintendents and bishops were used interchangeably until the 1880 General Conference adopted the term *consecration service* when the bishops were "elected for life." [39]

General Conference: This body, which convenes every four years on the first Wednesday in May, is the one law-making body of the A.M.E. Zion Church. It enacts laws for governing the church on every level, and defines the powers and duties of the ministry, including the episcopacy. It elects all bishops and general officers and assigns them to their fields of operation, appoints the connectional boards, and regulates all spiritual and temporal affairs of the connection. The bishops and general officers report to this body on their four years labor in their field of operation. The bishops preside over the sessions by rotation.

There are five restrictive rules inherited from early American Methodism, which the General Conference cannot transform. 1. It cannot revoke, alter, or change our Articles of Religion, the only doctrinal formula which tied American Methodism forever to the evangelical form of Trinitarian Christianity; nor can it establish any new standard of rules of doctrine contrary to those existing. 2. It cannot do away with the episcopacy or the plan of itinerancy. This perpetuates a skillful design of spiritual attention to all, through peripatetic and hierarchal government. 3. It cannot abolish the right of trial and appeal by accused preachers and members. The natural democratic process is retained, giving every member due consideration in cases of conflict. 4. It cannot revoke or change the General Rules of our United Societies. This means the preservation of Methodism as a positive ethical and spiritual force. 5. It cannot appropriate the proceeds of the Publishing House or of the Chartered Fund to any purpose other than for the benefit of the traveling and superannuated ministers, their wives, widows, and children. The connectionalizing of the publishing interests and elimination of private gain in denominational enterprises are primary, [40] which are also provisions for those who labor or have labored in the preaching and teaching ministry.

Representation: Our first General Conference was held on July 10, 1820, with Varick presiding. The only delegates were ministers. The history of the development of lay representation in conferences of Methodist bodies is interesting, with the exception of the Methodist Protestant Church which included this among its principles of difference when it severed from the Mother Methodist Church, and held its first General Conference in 1830.

39. *Minutes*, Sixteenth Quadrennial Session, p.34.
40. *Doctrines and Discipline,* Townsend, Workman, Eayres, *A New History of Methodism* II, p.116.

Lay Representation: This has been a prominent feature in Annual and General Conference in Zion since 1851. The A.M.E. Zion Church held its first ten General Conferences with no lay representation. In the Reunion General Conference of Zion and Wesley Churches, held at Wesley Church, Philadelphia, May 30, 1860, nine lay delegates were included in the roll of 98 preachers and four bishops, including retired Bishop Rush, representing three of the seven annual conferences. [41] They continued this custom of representation until 1872, with eight lay delegates in 1864, and their number steadily increasing in 1868 and 1872 because of the rapid growth of the church in the south. The General Conference of 1872 adjusted lay representation in both Annual and General Conferences. It ruled that the General Conference, with the ministerial delegates, shall be composed of two lay delegates from each Annual Conference, except such conferences having but one ministerial delegate and increased it to three in 1884.[42] Bishop C. C. Pettey, in 1900, introduced a resolution granting laymen equal representation with ministers in district, annual, and general conferences, which failed to pass. This was the prevailing circumstance until the post World War I period, when surging growth in the democratic trend of the country prompted a desire for a larger share of responsibility in the growing church. This sentiment had its influence in education and all forms of economic and political life, and the Church joined the trend. The *Star of Zion,* during the editorship of W. J. Walls, and the *Quarterly Review,* edited by C. C. Alleyne, took a leading share in fomenting the sentiment for equal lay representation in the General Conference. Numbers of leading ministers and laymen made this sentiment invincible with eager pursuit.

The Board of Bishops included the importance of "increased lay representation" in their Quadrennial Address at the 1924 General Conference in Indianapolis, but would make no recommendation regarding it. Resolutions were presented at various times by Revs. Benjamin W. Swain, Thomas W. Wallace, and A. C. Cook. The General Conference voted that "lay delegates shall consist of one layman for each Annual Conference having one ministerial delegate, two laymen for each conference having from two to four ministerial delegates, and three for each Conference having five or more ministerial delegates." [43]

In 1928, at St. Louis, the Bishops' Quadrennial Address was divided on recommending equalization, but gave favorable comment on the issue and referred it to the General Conference for decision. Resolutions were presented by Revs. A. C. Cook, W. C. and W. M. Anderson, and S. W. Hamilton. The resolution presented by Rev. Hamilton [44] was passed by the revision committee and ratified by the General Conference. [45] From this time forward, the General Conference has been composed equally of ministerial and lay delegates. The other important stipulation is that the lay delegate must be a member in full connection for four consecutive years preceding his election, which law went into effect after the 1900 General Conference. [46]

In the *Ministerial Representation,* an important change was the ratio system based upon pastoral appointments within an Annual Conference, which was first introduced in the General Conference of 1872. The law stated that one

41. Moore, *History, op. cit.,* pp.221-224.
42. *Ibid.,* p.282; *Doctrines and Discipline,* p.70; *Minutes,* Seventeenth Quadrennial Session, 1884, p.146; Twenty-First Quadrennial Session, 1900, p.40.
43. *Minutes,* Twenty-Seventh Quadrennial Session, 1924, pp.30, 37, 85, 104.
44. *Minutes,* Twenty-Eighth Quadrennial Session, 1928, p.230.
45. *Ibid.,* pp.47-48, 62, 65; Bradley, *A History of the A.M.E. Zion Church,* II, pp.416-418.
46. *Doctrines and Discipline,* 1900, p.61.

delegate for every seven members of each Annual Conference shall be elected, [47] which remained in effect until 1888, when Bishop Hood offered a resolution referring to the election of delegates to the General Conference. The ratio was then changed to one delegate for every ten members, to be appointed by seniority or choice, at the discretion of the Annual Conference. [48] This rule continued until the General Conference in Charlotte, in 1912. After Bishop Harris presented a resolution on representation in the General Conference, the revision committee recommended that there be one ministerial delegate for every 10 pastoral charges up to 20, and above 20, one for every 15 pastoral charges, and one for every two-third fraction. [49] In order to qualify, the General Conference of 1900 also made the regulation that a minister shall have traveled at least four years from the time he is received into conference. [50] An elected delegate must promise to remain until the close of the session, unless excused by the General Conference. This law went into effect after the General Conference of 1884 to avoid the difficulty of running out of a quorum before the close of the General Conference. [51]

The Woman's Role

Woman's integral role in the A.M.E. Zion Church is synonymous with primitive Christianity. The strict orthodox rules of Methodism, however, prevented women from assuming certain leadership responsibilities in the church, and the A.M.E. Zion Church became the first Methodist denomination to open the door.

It was voted at the General Conference of 1876 to "strike out the word 'male' in the Discipline." This permitted women for the first time to vote for trustees in the local church, and have a greater participation in the Quarterly and Annual Conferences. [52] Duties of stewardesses were first defined when it was also voted that: "The Quarterly Conference may appoint three female members to act as stewardesses in assisting the preacher's steward in providing the necessary comfort for the minister." [53] In 1892, Miss Fannie Van Bronk of New York, a useful member of Mother Zion Church, of large influence and great capacity for successful work, was one of the first duly elected delegates to occupy a seat in the General Conference of the A.M.E. Zion Church. [54] The Centennial General Conference of 1896, therefore, included a number of lay women delegates from all parts of the country.

The highest attainment came when Bishop James Walker Hood ordained Mrs. Julia A. J. Foote, conference missionary, a deacon at the Seventy-Third Session of the New York Annual Conference, May 20, 1894, at Poughkeepsie, N.Y. The following year, Mrs. Mary J. Small, wife of Bishop John B. Small, was ordained deacon by Bishop Alexander Walters at the Sixty-Seventh Session of the Philadelphia and Baltimore Conference, May 19, 1895 at York, Pennsylvania. Mrs. Small, who had been licensed to preach in 1892 by Presiding Elder John E. Price, was the first woman of Methodism ordained an elder, by Bishop Charles Calvin Pettey at the Philadelphia and Baltimore Conference, in

47. *Doctrines and Discipline*, 1872, p.70.
48. *Minutes*, Eighteenth Quadrennial Session, 1888, pp.51, 113, 114; *Doctrines and Discipline*, 1888, p.148.
49. *Minutes*, Twenty-Fourth Quadrennial Session, 1912, pp.114, 133, 535.
50. *Doctrines and Discipline*, 1900, p.59.
51. *Minutes*, Seventeenth Quadrennial Session, 1884, p.145.
52. Harris, *Zion's Historical Catechism, op. cit.*, p.17; *Minutes*, Eleventh Session, South Carolina Annual Conference, 1876, p.9.
53. *Ibid*.
54. *A.M.E. Zion Quarterly Review*, January 1892, p.242.

1898. (55) Mrs. Foote was still listed in the roll as a deacon of the New York Conference. She transferred to the New Jersey Conference and was ordained elder by Bishop Alexander Walters before her death November 22, 1900. Thus Rev. Mrs. Small had attained the position which qualified her for the rights and privileges granted elders of the church. Other women followed, who became noteworthy ministers in the church.

Judiciary

One of the general rules of the church is that brethren should not go to law with brethren. We have prepared in our system a solution for differences or troubles that may arise among us to regulate our own matters legally as an organization. Our judicial system, which has grown apace with our church according to the fundamentals laid down in the first Discipline, is practicable and far-reaching. That "no member can be deprived of his membership without due trial by a committee," and proper process of the church law, stems from its origin, in the Discipline, Of Bringing to Trial, Finding Guilty, Reproving, Suspending, Or Excluding Disorderly Persons from Society and Church Privileges, all-inclusive of members, preachers, and leaders. (56) These courts, which are precisely defined in the Discipline, are rated as follows: Regulations in the local church congregation are encouraged by our common practice of Christianity, yet when deemed necessary, a member of the congregation may be brought before a committee appointed by the pastor, regarding his conduct or behavior. If the matter cannot be settled by the committee, it is brought to the quarterly conference. This is the highest appellate court for lay members, exhorters, and local preachers.

If the case involves a minister in full connection, the court of the quarterly conference must first attempt to settle it. If the quarterly conference does not settle it, it continues on to the district conference, and if not disposed of, it is referred to the annual conference. If it needs further trial, it is brought before a special committee appointed by the annual conference. The highest appellate of a local deacon, local elder, or preacher on trial is the annual conference. If the annual conference is unable to deal with a matter, it may be referred to an inter-conference trial committee of three representative annual conferences agreed upon by the bishops of these conferences, which shall constitute a court of appeals. This committee may recommend a solution or continuance to the General Conference. This conference shall appoint a committee to deal with it, and the decision of the General Conference may be referred to the Board of Bishops, the supreme judicial body of the general church. A bishop is accountable for his conduct to the General Conference, which has the power to order a trial according to official charges received. A bishop suspended by a trial committee of the annual conference in the interim of the General Conference may appeal to the Board of Bishops. The General Conference has the power to ratify or reverse the decisions of the lower courts. Based upon charges brought against a bishop, either from a lower court or directly to the General Conference, this body has the power to reprimand, reprove, remove, or discipline a bishop as his case may warrant. Its decision is only referable to the supreme judicial body of the general church.

55. *Minutes*, Seventy-Third and Seventy-Fourth Sessions, New York Annual Conference, 1894, 1895; *Minutes*, Twenty-First Quadrennial Session, 1900, p.261; *Minutes*, Sixty-Ninth Session, Philadelphia and Baltimore Conference, 1897, pp.83-85; Anderson, *Biographical Souvenir*, p.29; Carroll, *The Standard Historical Catechism of the A.M.E. Zion Church*, p.83.
56. *Doctrines and Discipline*, 1820, pp.30-37.

CHAPTER 10

RITUAL AND MUSIC

The black man's worship is older than his church. It is an intuitive urge which always attended his troubled soul. Along with every culture, some form of worship is born. Depth of faith and power of spirit sustained the African in persistent belief and carried him through the courageous undertaking of soul-salvation, organization of life, and racial unity. These Africans were a reasonable, peaceable people; civil and courteous, practicing justice, mercy, and truth above Europeans of the seventeenth and eighteenth centuries. But from this Eden on earth they were taken with every cruelty and sold in Europe and America. Here in America, banished from their country, from their friends and relations forever, from every comfort of life, they were reduced to a state of brutal and ruthless suffering. Debarred of the privilege of schools, the most astonishing achievement is their explicit creation of spiritual and religious fervor in their passage through exploitation and blighting slavery.

This also is their profound gift, as DuBois wrote of America: Your country? How came it yours? Before the Pilgrims landed we were here. Here we have brought our three gifts and mingled them with yours: a gift of story and song—soft, stirring melody in an ill-harmonized and unmelodious land; the gift of sweat and brawn to beat back the wilderness, conquer the soil, and lay the foundations of this vast economic empire two hundred years earlier than your weak hands could have done it; the third, a gift of the Spirit. Around us the history of the land has centred for thrice a hundred years; out of the nation's heart we have called all that was best to throttle and subdue all that was worst: Fire and blood, prayer and sacrifice, have billowed over this people, and they have found peace only in the altars of the God of Right. [1]

Hence this suffering race of Africans made its peculiar contribution to this nation's culture in spirit and songs, never to be lost or forgotten.

Ritual

While this spiritual rhythm of life was creating its throbs in the race group, his religion, like all religions, became his most universal expression. Worship is God-consciousness and dependence upon God's divine will in life. Man has lifted himself up from animism and superstition to the recognition of the Son of God who molds the manners and actuates the faith of the race. Following this religious trend in the life, worship was practiced zealously, both privately and publicly, in the home and in the church.

---

1. W. E. Burghardt DuBois, *The Souls of Black Folk*, pp.262-263.

In 1820, the following rules were adopted in the A.M.E. Zion Church for public worship:

In order for the establishment of uniformity in public worship, amongst us, on the Lord' day —

1. The best general method of preaching, is, 1. to offer Christ; 2. to invite; 3. to build up; 4. to convince; and to do this, in some measure, in every sermon.

2. Let the evening service consist of singing, prayer and preaching. . . .

Of The Matter and Manner of Preaching, and Other Public Exercises:

1. The best general method of preaching, is, 1. To convince; 2. to offer Christ; 3. to invite; 4. to build up; and to do this, in some measure, in every sermon.

2. The most effectual way of preaching Christ is to preach him in all his offices; and to declare his law, as well as his gospel, both to believers and unbelievers. Let each minister strongly and closely insist upon inward and outward holiness in all its branches.

3. There are some smaller advices, which may be of use to the preachers in general, such as these: 1. Be sure never to disappoint a congregation. 2. Begin at the time appointed. 3. Let their whole deportment be serious, weighty, and solemn. 4. Always suit their subject to their audience. 5. Choose the plainest text they can. 6. Take care not to ramble, but keep to the text, and make out what they take in hand. 7. Take care of any thing awkward or affected, either in their gesture, phrase or pronunciation. 8. Frequently read and enlarge upon a portion of scripture; and let your preachers often exhort without taking a text. 9. Always avail themselves to the great festivals, by preaching on the occasion. (2)

This simplified approach to worship showed the prophetic nature of thought of our fathers. As chief shepherd of the flock, Varick was bound by law to travel extensively over the territory, to preach and oversee the spiritual concerns of the societies, to apply these rules, and ordain according to the rules of the discipline. (3) Upon Varick's death, it became the duty of Bishop Rush, and the other bishops succeeding him, and the same rules are still in effect today (see Discipline). A Methodist historian, describing these early Methodist preachers, including Black Harry, defined them as "the eloquence of faith." Said he

Those ministers were eloquent, they were orators, just in proportion of their faith—just in the measure that they spoke from the heart. God was with them; their hearts were in the work; and when this is the case almost anybody can be eloquent. Theirs was the eloquence of faith—the oratory of the heart. (4)

They were plain in apparel. Simple neatness was the general rule. (5) "It shall be the duty of all the preachers to insist on plainness of dress. This is no time to give any encouragement to superfluity of apparel." (6) These rules were strongly enforced and vigorously encouraged through the years, in order to create a true spirit of sacrificial love. It was their deep spiritual thinking that every available sum should be preserved and shared with the society, in order to help the needy, and not spent for pomp and display. They devoutly believed in the Christian philosophy of the inner spirit and divinely guided faith, and not the outward formality. Our Methodist body, explained a noble sire of Zion,

2. *Doctrines and Discipline*, 1820, pp.56-58.
3. *Ibid.*, pp.54-55;
4. G. A. Raybold, *Reminiscense of Methodism in West Jersey*, p.202.
5. Sanuel A. Seaman, "Methodist Worship in New York City," *The Christian Advocate*, Sept. 9, 1926, 1077.
6. *Doctrines and Discipline*, 1820, p.30.

though in harmonious accord with all other systems designated to evangelize and Christianize the world, differs, in many important features, from nearly, if not quite, all others. . . .One of these is ministerial earnestness, simplicity, directness, and spirituality in administering the word; direct appeal to the heart through the medium of the understanding, and therefore, in such plain language, simple and forcible figures; as to suit the comprehension of the uninformed, and such reliance upon the aid of the Spirit as will give it unfailing effect. [7]

Simplicity of worship houses was insisted upon. The pulpit and altar were built in the most conservative manner, in keeping with Wesley's principles in building the New Room at Bristol. "The seats in the corners on each side of the pulpit, being generally occupied by the aged and prominent members who responded pretty heartily to the services, . . .were known as the 'Amen' corners." [8] This evolved from the society, to the new room and central hall in England, to the worship house in America, then the chapel, and finally into the church. Modesty in erection of church edifices and parsonages, void of elegance, embellishment, and luxurious art was encouraged, since these entailed "burdensome debt, and involved a waste of means which would well be saved and applied to far more beneficial purposes of a charitable nature." [9] Time has changed this, not only in Methodism but in most Protestant movements, and church art and architecture have dominated the concept of which the Methodist movement is heir; that is, in the United States.

Family worship was an early mode, prevalent in the nation, among church people, black and white. The old-fashioned practice was to have prayer or family devotion once a day, either at the breakfast hour in the morning or in the evening at bedtime, according to the convenience of the family. Family prayer was at first paramount in the villages and countryside, then moved to the cities. Family worship has been enhanced through channels of religious education and literature in the A.M.E. Zion Church.

These simple, comprehensive, and homogeneous features of our common Methodism constitute its singularly fascinating charm and peculiar adaptability to the lowly of the earth. . . .In its original simplicity it supplies a spiritual need, a solace and a balm. It was originally designed to bring to the hesitating a recognition which dismisses his doubts, dispels his loneliness, and makes him feel that he shares as fully as the most lofty of earth the fatherhood of God and the brotherhood of man. . . .Anything less than good Samaritanism, as taught in the New Testament, violates every principle and design of Methodism, and becomes to the lowly a cheat and snare. [10]

The worship service included in our Doctrines and Discipline has in it the necessary A.M.E. Zion Church identity, and the bishops and preachers are bound by their oath to enforce and practice this order of worship, which of course must always be authorized by the General Conference.

Other Rituals

The other rituals of significance in our church history are: the two ordinances mentioned in the doctrines, The Lord's Supper and Baptism—infant and adult (see Chapter 9)—Holy Matrimony; Burial of the Dead; The Ordination of deacons and elders, and the Consecration of bishops; consecration of local

7. S. T. Jones, *Handbook of the Discipline*, p.40.
8. Seaman, *The Christian Advocate. op. cit.*
9. Jones, *Handbook of the Discipline*, p.41.
10. *Ibid.*, pp.42-43.

church deaconesses; cornerstone laying; dedication of churches, subsidiary church buildings, and dedication of church furnishings and essentials for worship service. In all these ritualistic practices, a formula of simplicity is also encouraged, as the founder insisted upon the simple methods, which he formulated for Methodism. (11)

Music

"How shall we sing the Lord's song in a strange land?" Psalm 137:4

When the Jews were in Egypt, the Egyptians required of them to sing one of the songs of Zion, after carrying them away captive. They refused saying, "How can we sing the Lord's song in a strange land?" But the Africans in America, scattered and torn as they were, found their only consolation in creating and singing the Lord's songs. Negroes are noted for their charm in songs, both religious and secular, which were produced through manifold sufferings. Dr. DuBois called these Negro melodies sorrow songs. In the history of the black race, these songs, called *spirituals*, are among the most notable original production of American art, and the black race is accredited wholly with them. But in the midst of his religious experiences, the Negro had learned the singing of hymns of the church, particularly those of the evangelical Protestant churches. No group could sing with more joy and fulsome expression: Amazing Grace, How Sweet The Sound; God Moves In A Mysterious Way; Jesus, Lover Of My Soul; and Am I Born To Die To Lay This Body Down?

Yet his native songs, the spirituals, were more than mere songs. They were vehicles of communication and unification. A song would come to life on a slave plantation in Virginia, and in a few weeks it would be carried across to Texas and the states intervening, or it would be swirling upon the wings of the winds, as it were, from the distant northeast to the far west; and somehow all would have the same words and the same tunes. It was a solidifying and public relations method that nature and religion had utilized as a means of inventive genius. It kept a race unified, although visibly and corporately separated. From the beginning it was discovered that some of the richest voices of the world are those of black people. Paul Laurence Dunbar has an immortal line on this phase of the Negro gift. It is, "When Malindy Sings."

The utter amazement was the Southland, where slavery was fiercely blighting, and laws forbade slaves to assemble or hold worship services (which was more or less characteristic of all slave territory). They assembled behind the hills and took the risk of holding meetings with the pot turned down to muffle out the sound, worshipped God in spite of circumstances, in the late hours of the night; and were back on their jobs in early morning, on the plantation. Few could read, but when the preachers and choristers led them, their memories caught tune and word, and they became the songsters of the time, and the comforters even of their master class, when they lifted their voices upward and delivered their spirits Godward. They were the tokens of heaven and symbols of angels. There were hundreds of these sweet melodies. Among the most precious were: Swing Low, Sweet Chariot, Steal Away to Jesus, Could'nt Hear Nobody Pray, and Go Down Moses.

In our share of these great racial gifts, the African Methodist Episcopal Zion Church went forward. With no instruments but heaven-born talents and tear-soaked voices, they laid down the following rules for worship services:

11. *Ibid.*, p.40.

Of the Spirit and Truth of Singing:

In order to guard against formality in singing;

1. Choose such hymns as are proper for the congregation; do not sing too much at once, seldom more than five or six verses.

2. Let the tunes be suited to the words: and let the preacher stop occasionally and ask the people? Now! do you know what you said last? Did you speak no more than you felt? etc.

3. Do not suffer the people to sing too slow: and in every large society let them learn to sing, and let them learn our tunes first.

4. Let the women constantly sing their parts alone: let the men be silent except those who understand the notes; and sing the bass as it is composed in the tune book.

5. If a preacher needs help in singing, let him call assistance to his side.

6. Exhort every person in the congregation to sing; and when the singers would teach a tune to the congregation, they must sing only the tenor. [12]

From the above we observe the familiar practice to "line the hymns," with the preacher reading two lines, and when the congregation had sung them, reading two more. Noticeable here also is the fact that the songs were sung from the heart and soul. A veritable Methodist trait was the hymn before the sermon, a most appropriate one with the congregation seated. [13] This is maintained in the Order of Worship in the Discipline, which is specially designed, to prepare the hearts and minds of the hearers, *while seated*, in spiritual readiness and reverence toward the gospel of Jesus Christ. Another Methodist custom is the singing of the Doxology at the close of the worship service.

One of our earliest Hymn Books was published in 1839:

Preface

In consequence of the great difficulty our Societies labored under, as a denomination, in divine worship, for the want of an established Hymn Book, the following work was compiled with great care from the best of authors, under the direction of the New York and Philadelphia Annual Conferences, during the administration of Right Reverends Christopher Rush and William Miller, which was published in 1839.

Further improvement being essential, the Book Committee, by the authority of the last General Conference, has with great care improved it, by an additional number of hymns, etc., so that the work is superior to any of the previous editions.

In submitting this to you, we would recommend the laity to be more prudent, in their social prayer-meetings and similar exercises, by avoiding that irregularity in singing which destroys the harmony that should exist in this part of Divine worship. We are commanded to sing in the spirit and with the understanding: by strictly observing this precept, we cannot but be blessed under its influence.

May Almighty God make this book a blessing to all in whose hands it may fall, is the sincere prayer of your humble servants in the ministry. N.B. Should there be a surplus, after the necessary expenses of publication are defrayed, it will be placed in the fund to aid the superannuated preachers.

Jas. Simmons, Gen'l. Superintendent,
Solomon T. Scott, Assistant Superintendent [14]

This Hymn Book, published in 1858, remained in denominational use (reprinted by the office of *Zion's Standard and Weekly Review* in 1869) until

---

12. *Doctrines and Discipline,* 1820, pp.67-68.
13. Seaman, *The Christian Advocate, op. cit.*
14. *Hymns for the Use of the African Methodist Episcopal Zion Church,* p.1.

the General Conference of 1872 took action to revise it. A committee was appointed with Bishop John D. Brooks, chairman, and Rev. J. A. Jones, secretary, to publish a revised standard of *Hymns for the Use of the African Methodist Episcopal Zion Church*, in cooperation with the Methodist Book Concern. It was in essence the same book in use by the Methodist Episcopal Church, with a prefatory bishops' address admonishing the followers to make use of it, signed by Joseph J. Clinton, Samson ·D. Talbot, J. W. Loguen, S. T. Jones, John J. Moore, and J. W. Hood, Bishops. It contained well over 500 of Charles Wesley's hymns. [15] This Hymn Book was short lived. A new Hymn Book was printed in 1878 including the revised ritual of ordination services, and the additional ritual of cornerstone laying of churches, presented by Rev. J. W. Hood at the 1872 General Conference, and adopted. [16] The Hymn Book was revised in 1892, by Rev. B. F. Wheeler, editor and copyright renewed by the A.M.E. Zion Book Concern. This Hymn Book sufficed until 1909.

The General Secretary, Rev. M. D. Lee, prefaced the 1909 Hymn Book with the following statement:

At the meeting of the Connectional Council of the African Methodist Episcopal Zion Church in the City of New York, August, 1909, a resolution was adopted authorizing the change of Hymnals for use in our church, whereupon a committee on Hymnal was appointed to select a book.

The committee entered upon its work at once, and after due consideration made recommendations which were adopted.

By order and on behalf of the Board of Bishops. M. D. Lee, Secretary

This was the first Hymn Book printed by the A.M.E. Zion Publishing House in Charlotte, North Carolina, under the management of Rev. J. W. Crockett. The committee recommended the discontinuance of the hymnals then in use and the adoption of this new hymnal, bearing the imprint and containing our formula of service, special hymns and ritual; signed by J. S. Caldwell, G. L. Blackwell, A. Walters, G. W. Clinton and F. K. Bird. The Board of Bishops involved in this work were Bishops J. W. Hood, C. R. Harris, Alexander Walters, G. W. Clinton, J. W. Alstork, J. W. Smith, J. S. Caldwell, G. L. Blackwell and A. J. Warner. The Board of Bishops of 1916 unanimously approved the work, and signed the revised edition, inclusive of Bishops G. C. Clement, L. W. Kyles, and R. B. Bruce. [17]

The General Conference of 1940, at Washington, D.C., authorized a commission to work with a commission of the African Methodist Episcopal Church to produce a joint hymnal. This committee reported progress at the General Conference held in Detroit in 1944, and a resolution was passed endorsing the work and authorizing 50,000 copies of the combined hymnal with joint ownership of manuscript, plates, and sales interest on a 50% basis. It also authorized the A.M.E. Zion Church Board of Finance to pay one-half of the funds necessary for publication of this work. [18] A manuscript was prepared by this joint commission, and $6,000 placed in escrow by the A.M.E. Zion Church for the beginning of this enterprise. In spite of the fact that this was a result of an agreement that arose through an organic union proposition between the two

---

15. *A Collection of Hymns for the Use of the African Methodist Episcopal Zion Church*, 1872.
16. Moore, *History, op. cit.*, p.282; *Hymns for the Use of the A.M.E. Zion Church*, 1878; *Hymn Book*, published by the A.M.E. Zion Church, 1892.
17. *New Hymn-Tune Book for the Use of the A.M.E. Zion Church*, 1909; rev. ed. 1916.
18. *Minutes*, Thirty-Second Quadrennial Session, 1944, p.191.

churches, it was surprising to learn after some delays that the African Methodist Episcopal Church Commission had printed a hymnal for use in that church. The joint hymnal manuscript, which was in the hands of the Zion group, was practically ready for the press. The African Methodist Episcopal Zion Church excluded the African Methodist Episcopal Church's specific connectional contribution and retained the major work which the Zion Commission had prepared and submitted it to the General Conference at Brooklyn, N.Y. in 1952. After a resolution presented by Rev. J. E. McCall, that the commission work with the manager of the Publication House in finding ways and means of printing the new hymnal, the matter was referred back to the hymnal commission which had passed through numerous trials since this venture in 1940. It was composed of the following persons: Bishop W. J. Walls, chairman; Bishop C. C. Alleyne, secretary-treasurer; Dr. T. W. Tobin, recording secretary; Bishop S. G. Spottswood (who became secretary-treasurer upon the death of Bishop Alleyne in 1944); Bishop H. T. Medford; Reverends W. A. Cooper, W. E. Carrington, G. L. Fauntleroy, L. L. Boyd (manager of the Publishing House), Dr. J. Van Catledge, Dr. J. W. Eichelberger, Mr. R. W. Sherrill, and Mr. A. L. Cromwell. The sub-committee on ritual consisted of the following members: Bishops W. A. Stewart, W. W. Slade, Raymond L. Jones, J. C. Taylor, Reverends J. C. Hoggard and J. H. Satterwhite. The commission labored tirelessly to complete the manuscript with additional features.

After a statement regarding the hymnals made by Rev. J. W. Watson at the General Conference in Pittsburgh, 1956, the commission reported through its secretary, Bishop Spottswood. The General Conference approved the work and authorized its publication, which is our present official *Hymnal*, first published in 1957. The *Hymnal* was prefaced by the Bishops' Address, which admonished every department of the church to make ample use of it and appealed for uniformity in church worship throughout the church. This was signed by Bishops W. J. Walls, J. W. Martin, C. C. Alleyne, W. C. Brown, W. W. Slade, J. C. Taylor, R. L. Jones, H. T. Medford, H. B. Shaw, S. G. Spottswood, W. A. Stewart, and D. C. Pope. [19] Thus was the evolution in provision of church hymnals for use of the members of the A.M.E. Zion Church.

Also encouraged in our Methodism was simplicity in church music and singing. The organ and piano were introduced in the church in the last half of the nineteenth century, and the people of the A.M.E. Zion Church were cautioned regarding undue dependence upon them..

Instruments to assist the failing powers of the human voice may be, and doubtless are, necessary. Set pieces on special occasions may also be proper, but any wide deviation beyond these from the employment of those heart-melting, soul-stirring, and life-inspiring songs of original Methodism produced by the Wesleys, and abounding in doctrinal beauty, appropriate to every state and condition of life, robs it of its lyrical power and peculiarity, and therefore, strips it of much of its influence for good. [20]

Negro Spirituals were born without any instrumental accompaniment. Spirituals and gospel songs are now appropriate special selections of church choirs, and represent the evolution of singing in Christian congregations. These special songs have resulted in additional choirs and gospel choral groups in many churches, especially the larger churches, which are inspirational reminders of our

19. *Minutes*, Thirty-Fourth Quadrennial Session, 1952, pp.66-67; *Minutes*, Thirty-Fifth Quadrennial Session, 1956, p.127; *The A.M.E. Zion Hymnal*, 1957, pp. v, vi.
20. S. T. Jones, *Handbook of the Discipline*, p.42.

impassioned culture and unique Christian heritage.

The spirituals are the most sacred and renascent songs of the black race. "They are the music of an unhappy people, of the children of disappointment; they tell of death and suffering and unvoiced longing toward a truer world, of misty wanderings and hidden ways." [21] We are reminded by DuBois that since their day they have been imitated, sometimes well by college choral unions, sometimes ill, by straggling quartettes. "Caricature has sought again to spoil the quaint beauty of the music, and has filled the air with many debased melodies which vulgar ears scarce know from the real. But the true Negro folk-song still lives in the hearts of those who have heard them truly sung and in the hearts of the Negro people." [22] It is the responsibility of the black race of every age to keep inviolate and preserve this precious gift squeezed out of the toils and tears of our ancestral afflictions.

The gospel songs were born out of Negro singing of a later era, and brought a special message of spiritual and harmonious balm. Songs and hymns had been written by Negroes, and used as supplements to hymn books adapted from white churches. *Soul Echoes* was among the first serious and most ambitious efforts of black religious leaders to publish a song book. Charles A. Tindley would compose his songs during the week and sing them on Sunday in his worship service. His songs were published, along with other gospel songs, by a team of black Methodist churchmen, namely, Bishops J. S. Caldwell and G. L. Blackwell of the A.M.E. Zion Church, Bishop L. J. Coppin of the A.M.E. Church, and Rev. Charles A. Tindley, Methodist. Their prefatorial statement of this booklet produced in 1909 was:

A long felt desire for songs with words of Hope, Cheer, Love and Pity; for melodies that can sink to the depths of sorrow, and rise to the heights of joy, has had most to do with the publication of this book. It is the prayer of the publishers that these messages in rhyme shall float from soul to soul until the hills and valleys shall awake into joyful singing. [23]

"We'll Understand It Better Bye and Bye," "Stand By Me." "The Storm Is Passing Over." "What Are They Doing In Heaven Today," "God Has Promised to Provide for Me," and "Nothing Between My Soul and My Saviour" are but a few of these immortal productions.

Anthems and oratorios, in which the Negro has found his place with the most excellent singers of mankind, are a part of our modern church music. Church music is patently the soul's sincere desire to express itself through divine art, by God-given voices, filled with bounteous love.

21. DuBois, *The Souls of Black Folk*, p.253.
22. *Ibid*.
23. *Soul Echoes*.

Part III—

Development

CHAPTER 11

PROGRAM OF PLANNING AND EXPANSION

When the members of Zion Church in New York City officially voted themselves out of the Methodist Episcopal Church on July 26, 1820, thus operating under their Discipline published October 25, 1820, the members moved forward, continuing their first conference, June 21, 1821, and elected James Varick acting superintendent, pending the higher holy order, to function according to the Discipline. The roll of delegates numbered twenty-two:

NEW YORK:
James Varick
Abraham Thompson
Leven Smith
William Miller
Christopher Rush
John Dungy
Charles Anderson
James Smith
Timothy Eato
Samuel Bird
Peter Vanhas
Abraham Marks

Christopher Anderson
John Palmer
James Anderson
William Carman
Elijah Jackson

PHILADELPHIA:
Simon Murray
Edward Johnson
Durham Stephens
Daniel Pernal
Arthur Landford [1]

Durham Stephens, Daniel Pernal, and Arthur Landford being absent, the

1. Rush, *Rise and Progress*, pp.70-71.

conference was attended by 19 preachers, representing six churches and 1,426 members. (2)

Bishop George of the Methodist Episcopal Church sent Rev. William Phoebus and Joshua Soule, who fraternally associated them during the first two days of the seven-day conference, and on June 25, the fifth day, Rev. Freeborn Garrettson came also as a fraternal visitor. Each session was spent in joint reverence and spiritual devotion, with total awareness of their new independence. The Discipline was carefully reviewed, and these leaders seriously observed the weighty responsibilities that attended it. The superintendent, elected by ballot in the annual conferences for a period of four years, would be accorded the opportunity of re-election each succeeding quadrennium, so long as his qualification, character, and deportment sustained this highest office of the church. (3) "If a superintendent ceases from traveling, without the consent of the yearly conferences (unavoidable circumstances excepted), he shall no longer exercise the episcopal office in our church: nevertheless the yearly conferences shall finally determine the case." (4) This was a typical regulation.

It was an assembly full of thrills, trials, revelations, and adventure, accompanied by faith and prayer. The preachers were appointed by Varick as follows:

Zion Church, New York: Abraham Thompson, Leven Smith, Christopher Rush, John Dungy, Charles Anderson, James Smith, Timothy Eato, Samuel Bird, Peter Vanhas; Asbury Church, New York: William Miller, Abraham Marks, Christopher Anderson, John Palmer; New Haven: James Anderson; Long Island: William Carman and Elijah Jackson; Wesleyan Church, Philadelphia; and Easton, Pennsylvania: Simon Murray, Edward Johnson, Durham Stephens, Daniel Pernal, and Arthur Landford.

The conference adjourned on June 27 in high spirit and deep harmony, to meet in the next Annual Conference in Philadelphia, May 16, 1822, and hold the next General Conference in the spring of 1824. (5)

Because of the enormous difficulties facing this new organization, which threatened destruction in its infancy, the state of affairs in the interval of the annual conferences became critical. The variableness of a few in the New York group, who had become shaken after the negative action of the New York Methodist Episcopal Conference on their petition for conference recognition, and the determination of the Wesleyan group in Philadelphia, produced a serious difference. While the second session of the conference was being held at Philadelphia during the week of May 15, 1822, the Wesleyans were approached on the subject of returning to the Methodist Episcopal Church by Bishops George and Roberts. They boldly declared that they would in no way consider this proposal, and expressed the continued desire to be governed by the Discipline of the Zion Connection. This session adjourned to be consummated in New York, in July, and a delegation came over to New York the end of May, to encourage them to stand steady in spite of the difficulty of obtaining elders' orders.

The African Wesleyan Church of Philadelphia (now Big Wesley) was a dynamic force in the demand for freedom. In their background was a readiness

2. *Ibid.*, H. F. Kletzing and W. H. Crogman, *Progress of a Race*, pp. 430-431.
3. *Doctrines and Discipline*, 1820, pp.54-55.
4. *Ibid.*, pp.55-56.
5. Moore, *History of the A.M.E. Zion Church*, p.89.

to confront the most austere situations. A few members of this group also were a part of St. George's Church, and became charter members of The Free African Society of Philadelphia, 1787. Yet their surroundings in general were different. "The state of slavery in Pennsylvania was always of mild character, not only from the favorable and mild feelings of the Friends in their behalf, but from the common regard they found in families in general where their deportment was commendable." (6) The state also had been free long before New York's emancipation in 1827. Having this advantage over the New Yorkers, they gave the necessary boost at the right time, which proved essential in the destiny of the A.M.E. Zion Connection.

These Philadelphians had a peculiar independent air from the beginning of their church existence in 1820, which later influenced a serious schism in the denomination, and which always provided effective leadership in the church and race. Their very name, was an attraction that helped to increase the bulk of their numbers. Their selected name was actually a motivation to operate differently from American Methodism, and pattern themselves after the original Wesleyan Methodist movement of England and the West Indies. They kept up with the grand warrior against slavery, Thomas Coke, and his noble work in the West Indies, which no doubt influenced their name and independent thinking away from the American Methodist Episcopal Church, which in those days was fiercely divided on the slave question.

This group submitted a plan for ordination by A.M.E. Zion leaders, which was rejected by the New York group. Within three weeks of their arrival in New York City with their firm decision not to petition the white Methodist Conference any further, the leaders "availed themselves of the help of Dr. James Covel, Sylvester Hutchinson, and William Stilwell, who set apart Abraham Thompson, James Varick, and Leven Smith as elders, they having been previously ordained deacons." (7)

The Second Annual Conference reconvened at Zion Church in New York City, on Tuesday, July 18, 1822, to complete the business. There was much more room for rejoicing at this session. The dark cloud hovering over them for two years had been removed, and they at last had the assurance, confidence, and certainty needed to expand in the name of religion and freedom. "The work of development from this time went forward with considerable rapidity under the supervision of Right Reverend James Varick, the first regularly elected bishop of the Connection." Being the leading factor in the formation of Zion Church in 1796 and in all succeeding steps leading to the establishment of a successful itinerant system, and like Asbury, serving as superintendent of his connection before he received the highest holy order, he had conducted the efforts of the societies successfully amid great difficulties, and had shown himself equal to every emergency. Hence when he, with others, received elders orders, he was elected as first among his peers to superintend the connection. (8)

Six preachers were ordained deacons and elders at this conference, and sent out as missionaries, to take charge of societies already formed and to form new societies. Christopher Rush was assigned to the Newark charge by Bishop Varick. He rallied a group of devout, freedom-minded people around him to give this city its first black organization. An African Presbyterian Church was established

6. John F. Watson, *Annals of Philadelphia,* p.479.
7. J. M. Buckley, *A History of Methodists in the United States,* p.348.
8. Hood, *One Hundred Years,* pp.64-65.

in the early 1830's. This humble African Methodist group, led valiantly by Rush, obtained an incorporation for the society and laid the foundation (cornerstone) stone, on April 7, 1823, at Academy Street near Plane Street. [9] This church is now known as Clinton Memorial.

New York City began to expand northward, and Harlem developed under a large number of Dutch settlers. Zion kept pace with the growing city, and a third society was founded in Harlem in 1822 by Peter Vanhas, [10] called "Little Zion," and a small brick building was erected there in 1843. [11]

The connection had advanced commensurably in the northeastern section when the Third Annual Conference met at Zion Church, New York City, May 21, 1823. Three disruptions faced Bishop Varick and the preachers at the conference and during the ensuing year. First, during this session, it was learned that William Miller of the Asbury charge had connected with the Bethel Connection, and was ordained elder by them and appointed to a charge in Washington, D.C. [12] Shortly after this, the Asbury Church in New York placed themselves under the government of the Bethel connection. This same year, their church in Elizabeth Street was destroyed by fire. They then occupied for some time a room in the basement of the Broadway Tabernacle, entering from Anthony Street. They were also in a hall on the corner of Elizabeth and Grand Streets, and then occupied a hall on Howard Street. After this, they moved to Fourth Street, near the East River, and soon afterward an individual purchased for them a house of worship on Third Street near Avenue D, and in 1835 they removed to this building with a view to permanency. [13] By this time, William Miller had long since returned to Zion Connection, and was pastoring in Philadelphia. The flock had scattered somewhat, its membership had dwindled to 70 by 1846, and the congregation was still giving trouble during this schismatic period of Zion's history. [14]

Second, the Philadelphia preachers did not attend the 1823 Annual Conference, because of dissatisfaction existing from the meeting of the last Annual Conference. [15] However, they maintained cooperation with a steady growth, so much that Philadelphia was set apart as our second conference in 1829.

Third, in a continued effort at dissipation of this young connection, in 1824 a small faction of preachers of the New York group had been influenced by Methodist Episcopal Church leaders to see what their General Conference would determine for the benefit of black preachers. In order to avoid dissidence over this intervention the A.M.E. Zion Annual Conference was changed from its regular date of May 20 to July 15, to await the results of the Methodist Episcopal Conference. This was also the General Conference year of Zion Connection. When A.M.E. Zion leaders were truly convinced that nothing had been done for their advantage, they held their combined General and Annual Conferences on July 15, 1824. [16] During the year Leven Smith had established a society in Providence, R.I., and James Anderson, while pastoring New Haven,

9. Rush, *Rise and Progress*, p.79; Newark *City Directory*, 1835-1836; *Sentinel of Freedom*, April 18, 1826.
10. Varick letter, Riker Papers, N.Y. Public Library.
11. Greenleaf, *A History of the Churches*, p.322.
12. Moore, *History, op. cit.*, p.98.
13. Greenleaf, *op. cit.*, p.323; Charles H. Haswell, *Reminiscenses of an Octogenarian*, p.207.
14. Greenleaf, *op. cit.*
15. Moore, *History, op. cit.*, p.98.
16. *Ibid.*, p.99.

had founded a society at Middletown, Conn. William Carman continued his progressive work of establishing societies on Long Island.

At the Conference, James Varick was re-elected bishop. James Smith was sent to Zion Church, New York, Leven Smith to Newark, who established a society also at Elizabethtown, James Anderson to Middletown, and Christopher Rush was appointed a missionary. One of the great privileges of the preachers of that day was to be sent out as a missionary, *to do the work of evangelists, and*

CHRISTOPHER RUSH

1777 - 1873
Second Bishop

He organized four northern conferences.
Strong abolition leader and profound preacher.

make full proof of their ministry. New preachers were being received into the conference, ordained deacons and elders, and sent out to labor in the vineyard facilitating the growth of a denomination.

This year, there also arose some difficulty with the New Haven Church over the expulsion of one of its members whom many considered to be most useful to the society. "The society became insubordinate; the conference took jurisdiction of the case and by stringent steps brought them into subjection to our Discipline, and continuance in our connection." Varick nurtured this society as early as 1818 with 35 members. The interesting history behind the stabilization of this society are the efforts of two energetic women, first minister Charles Anderson, and the stamina of William H. Bishop. (17) Bishop joined Zion Church in New York in September, 1825, and joined the annual conference as a traveling preacher in May, 1826. (18) One of these founders, Mrs. Eliza Ann Galpin, the daughter of Jeremiah Paine, was employed with the family of Theodore Dwight Woolsey, a charter member of the African Improvement Society of New Haven, who became one of Yale University's most influential

17. Warner, *New Haven Negroes,* p.85; Rush, *op. cit.,* p.82.
18. Hood, *One Hundred Years,* p.531.

presidents. Mrs. Galpin's dedication was a stimulation to other members, and by 1841 they were in possession of their own building. Through all its difficulties, the church had grown to 80 members by 1848. [19] The name was changed from John Wesley to Varick Memorial. (See chapter 8.) This society had been through various vicissitudes, including a fire in 1842, which caused $500 damage, of which $350 was covered by insurance. [20] It is the mother church of the New England Conference.

Varick presided over the fifth, sixth and seventh annual conferences, from 1825 through 1827, and before the expiration of his second term "God was pleased to call him from labor to reward." [21] He had ordained a dozen deacons and elders during his seven years as first bishop, and had received twice this many traveling preachers into conference and sent them out to serve the needs of a race in despair. After Varick's death, July 22, 1827, the senior elder, Leven Smith, took on the responsibilities of the office, except ordination, according to the Discipline, until the next General Conference in 1828, when he was regularly elected by the Conference and declined. Christopher Rush was then elected the second bishop, [22] at Zion Church, New York, on May 15, 1828.

"As Joshua followed Moses, so did Rush follow Varick." Christopher Rush founded all our Northeastern conferences except the New York and New Jersey Conferences. He was truly a mighty leader. [23] He made appointments and began to lay the groundwork for expansion. On May 21, 1829, the ninth annual conference, meeting in Zion Church, not only included the preachers from the New England and New York areas but a number of preachers from Philadelphia and other parts of Pennsylvania. At this conference they set off the Philadelphia Annual Conference, to be organized June 14 following, in the city of Philadelphia. After making appointments for the regular work, the conference adjourned.

On June 13, 1829, the First Philadelphia Annual Conference met at Wesley Church, on Lombard Street, Philadelphia, with Bishop Rush presiding. There were 17 ministers in attendance including the bishop and two from New York. After a pleasant session of several days, the Conference completed its business with Rush reading the appointments, and adjourned. [24] Edward Johnson was reappointed to Wesley Church, Philadelphia, Jacob Richardson to the charge of the Western District (of Pennsylvania), and David Smith and Richard Phillips were appointed missionaries. The other preachers in attendance were Durham Stephens, David Stephens, George Stevenson, David Crosby, Jonathan Gibbs, Arthur Landford, Tower Hill, John Marshall, Samuel Johnson, and Abraham Green. [25]

The roll of the New York Conference at this time, and until 1840, was as follows: [26] Bishop Christopher Rush;

19. Warner, *New Haven Negroes*, p.85.
20. *Ibid.*
21. Hood, *One Hundred Years*, p.531.
22. *Ibid.*
23. Moore, *History, op. cit.*, p.100.
24. *Ibid.*, pp.101-102.
25. Rush, *Rise and Progress*, p.82.
26. Hood, *One Hundred Years*, pp.65-66.

Revs.:

Charles Anderson	Shadrach Golden	Abraham Miller
Jehiel C. Beman	Francis P. Graham	*William Miller
Edward Bishop	Samuel T. Gray	Richard Noyee
*William Bishop	John Jackson	*Peter Ross
David Blake	Thomas Jackson	Samuel Serrington
Nathaniel Blunt	Thomas James	William Serrington
W. L. Brown	Henry Johnson	*James Simmons
William Carman	J. B. Johnson	Benjamin Simms
John Chester	William Jones	Leven Smith
Abraham Cole	Jesse Kemble	*George Spywood
Leonard Collins	Dempsey Kennedy	*John Tappan
Henry Drayton	John A. King	John P. Thompson
John Dungy	John W. Lewis	*Joseph P. Thompson
Hosea Easton	Peter Lum	William Tillman
Timothy Eato⟩	John N. Mars	Daniel Vandevier
Adam Ford	Jacob Matthews	Peter Vanhas
William Fuller	William McFarlan	George Washington
George Garnett	Basil McKall	John Wells
		J. H. Williams

* Became bishops of the church.

Several of the others listed became quite distinguished in their day. We will note later that among the most outstanding abolitionists of the race were Jehiel C. Beman, Hosea Easton, Bishops Rush and Thompson. The above mentioned men established our first churches as far west as Jamestown, N.Y., and western points in Pennsylvania, as far north as Boston, and later Portland, Me., and as far south as Washington, D.C.

"From the years 1828 to 1840 Rush had filled the episcopal office alone, and had filled it well, and afterwards served effectively until his retirement in 1852 due to loss of sight. Every year there was an increase of members, ministers, and churches; new territory was occupied, and the connection increased in strength and influence continually." However, the General Conference of 1840 produced a disturbing element which culminated 12 years later in a split in the connection, which lasted for 8 years. [27] While the A.M.E. Zion Church was passing through its second most cataclysmic period, the Lord enabled them to reign over all difficulties, and brought the church through victoriously in 1860.

Our work was extended chiefly over the states of the north, until the emancipation of the race and the close of the Civil War, when it entered the South to organize many churches. [28] Those men who showed exceptional power which aided the development of our church were: Rev. Samuel T. Gray, who was not only a remarkable natural orator, noted for his ability to rouse enthusiasm, but was a very successful medical doctor. "He was a man of unusual acumen, easily triumphed in debate, and as a logician and parliamentarian could vanquish his opponent;" Rev. Henry Johnson who passed among his fellows as "Old Hickory" because of his strong force of character; Rev. John A. Williams was an unusual revivalist; Rev. Leonard Collins was one of the pillars of the church for a number of years, but lost his standing by yielding to the temptation of strong drink. Those who had great preaching ability and moved multitudes to

27. *Ibid.*, p.70.
28. DuBois, *The Negro Church*, p.45.

come into church were Elders Basil McKall, Abraham Cole, and especially David Stevens. (29)

Leven Smith was a dauntless pioneer, and not only established smaller societies in New England but organized our first church in Providence, in 1822. (30) Rev. Hosea Easton joined the New York Conference in 1832, and was ordained deacon and elder in 1834. He firmly established our Hartford society, now known as the Metropolitan Church, in 1836 and incorporated the church in 1841. Before 1827, the African Relief Society came into existence and

Fire breaks out at the theater on the Northwest corner of Church and Leonard Streets, September 23, 1839 and spreads across the street to the Southwest corner, totally destroying the First African Church built in the City of New York; Zion Church which was rebuilt and dedicated in 1840.
Eno Collection. Prints Division, The New York Public Library: Astor, Lenox and Tilden Foundations.

owned a building which they used for worship services. About 1833, there came about a split in the organization, out of which two black churches were formed, the Congregational and Methodist churches. For a while, both used the same building. However, Rev. Easton led the group of Methodists, which became the A.M.E. Zion Church, into purchasing land at 38 Elm Street. (31)

It was in this Elm Street Church that the New England Conference, the third conference of our connection, was organized by Bishop Rush on June 21, 1845. Among its earliest societies were Boston, New Bedford, and Nantucket, Mass.; Providence, R.I.; New Haven, Middletown, Stonington, Bridgeport, and Hartford, Conn. Its ministers were Thomas Henson, Daniel Vandevier, Leven Smith, James Simmons, George A. Spywood, Thomas James, John P. Thompson, and

29. Woodson, *History of the Negro Church*, pp.90-91; Hood, *One Hundred Years*, pp.66-67.
30. *Weekly Anglo-African*, December 15, 1860.
31. *The Hartford Daily Times*, March 21, 1936.

Dempsey Kennedy. Among the New York delegates were William H. Bishop, John A. King, Peter Ross, Henry Johnson, and J. W. Loguen. In 1856 the Hartford Church moved to a new location at 91 Pearl Street, under the eye of the state capital. (32) This church is presently located on Main Street.

"The A.M.E. Zion Church of Boston was organized June 13, 1838 with seventeen members who had withdrawn from the Methodist Episcopal Church; for more religious freedom and with a desire to become part and parcel of the A.M.E. Zion Connection which was manned and controlled by men of their own color." (33) They selected a worship hall on Cambridge Street, and petitioned the New York Conference for a minister. The right man for the right task was sent, Rev. Jehiel C. Beman. By October 5, 1840, the membership had grown to 140, and Beman's leadership was felt throughout the entire city. The church subsequently moved to Russell Street and was known as the Russell Street A.M.E. Zion church. (34) This congregation is now known as the Columbus Avenue Church, the present building having been purchased by Rev. J. H. McMullen, and dedicated on June 7, 1903 by Bishop J. W. Hood and Rev. E. George Biddle, presiding elder and member.

Zion Church (Mother Zion), which had been ravaged during the abolition riot of 1834 and destroyed by fire, September 23, 1839, (35) was rebuilt in the spring of 1840 under the leadership of Rev. Timothy Eato. It was "undoubtedly the largest and most commodious *Protestant* house of worship, owned and occupied by our people, in the world." It was dedicated on Wednesday, April 22, at 10 o'clock A.M. by Bishop Christopher Rush, with Rev. William Miller of Wesley Church, Philadelphia, and Rev. Theodore S. Wright, the noted pastor of the first Presbyterian colored church in the city, associating him. (36)

Rev. Jacob D. Richardson was quite an impressive preacher and organizer. He organized a Wesleyan society around 1826 in Middletown, Pa. George Galbraith joined that church the same year, and then joined the Philadelphia Conference in June, 1830 and was appointed to the Harrisburg circuit, under the leading minister, Rev. David Stevens. (37) From this sector, the most distinguished and exceptional leaders of the church came forth and made the greatest contribution to the development and growth of the African Methodist Episcopal Zion Church of any group in any era. These included Singleton T. Jones, who was licensed to preach at Harrisburg by Rev. George Galbraith, Joseph Jackson Clinton, John Jamison Moore, James Walker Hood, Jehu Holliday, Samson D. Talbot, all of whom became eminent bishops of the church; scores of preachers who founded churches from Philadelphia to Washington, D.C.; and William Howard Day who became the three or four renowned Negro leaders during the last half of the nineteenth century.

Under Rush's dynamic leadership, along with Galbraith, Zion had four churches in the nation's capital by 1860. The first was Zion Wesley, organized by Rev. George Galbraith in 1837, in D Street (now known as Metropolitan Wesley). (38) The Galbraith Church was organized in 1843 when six members

32. Moore, *History,* pp.140-141; *Hartford Daily Times, op. cit.*
33. Jacob W. Powell, *Bird's Eye View of the General Conference,* 1916 (History by Eliza Ann Gardner) p.21.
34. *The Colored American,* October 17, 1840.
35. Stokes, *Iconography,* Vol. V., pp.1728, 1760.
36. *The Colored American,* May 2, 1840.
37. Moore, *History,* p.356.
38. *Ibid.,* p.124.

gathered at the home of Mr. and Mrs. Samuel Payne, and a mission was established thereafter by Rev. Richard Tompkins, a local preacher of Zion Wesley Church. The first building was erected in 1853. In 1858, Rev. R. H. G. Dyson was received into the Philadelphia Annual Conference on trial, and appointed to the Washington City Mission. "He organized Galbraith Chapel (anew) in a small room with three members, but soon had to get a larger place. He secured a lot and erected a church which was dedicated March, 1862, and 390 members were enrolled." [39] It flourished also under the pastorate of Rev. Abraham Cole, who joined the Philadelphia Conference June 8, 1839, and became prominent in the growth of our early societies in Pennsylvania and Washington, especially the mother church of Washington, Zion Wesley. [40]

The Union Wesley Church was established in 1844, when a small group of men and women, chafing under oppression and longing for self-expression, withdrew from the Mt. Zion Methodist Church in Georgetown, and started this organization with black leaders in the A.M.E. Zion Church. [41] Their edifice was destroyed by fire on December 18, 1859, and rebuilt in December 1860, under the direction of Revs. Jacob P. Hamer and Charles Wallace.[42]   The John Wesley Church started out with 15 members in 1848, and was one of the fastest growing churches of that day, in spite of the prejudices against it. [43] Rev. R. H. G. Dyson, before he joined John Wesley Church in 1852, organized a choir in the church while that congregation was still worshipping at the private residence of Rev. John Brent, its pioneer pastor, on Connecticut Avenue, where the church was organized. [44] The church is known today as the "National Church of Zion Methodism."

By 1836, Zion had two churches in Pittsburgh. The first was Old John Wesley Church, organized this same year in the home of Mr. and Mrs. Edward Parker on Roberts Street. It later acquired a lot on Peru Way, with a one-story building, under the leadership of Rev. Tabbs. The second church was Avery Mission. [45]

Zion's first society in the city of Baltimore was established as early as 1842, led by Rev. Jacob M. Moore, a local preacher in the Methodist Episcopal Church, and William Johnson and Severn Johnson. It was known as the First Colored Wesley Methodist Independent Society of Baltimore. This church joined the Philadelphia Annual Conference meeting at (Big) Wesley Church, Philadelphia, in 1844. It is now known as the Pennsylvania Avenue A.M.E. Zion Church.

The Allegheny Conference stands fourth on the list, organized August 1849 by Bishop Rush, with Bishop Galbraith associating him. It was set apart from the Philadelphia Conference. The General Conference of 1848 set off the Allegheny Conference(as well as the Genesee Conference)from the Philadelphia Conference and approved their boundaries. [46] As early as 1829, the section of western Pennsylvania was referred to as the "Western District," and Rev. Jacob D. Richardson was present at the Philadelphia Conference from this district. [47]

---

39. *The Star of Zion*, July 25, 1946; Hood, *One Hundred Years*, pp.229-230.
40. J. P. Hamer, *The Weekly Anglo-African*, December 29, 1860.
41. *Souvenir Program*, Service of Church Opening, August 1, 1949.
42. *The Anglo-African*, Dec. 29, 1860; Moore, *History*, *op. cit.*, p.124,
43. Hood, *One Hundred Years*, p.229.
44. *Ibid.*
45. Moore, *History*, *op. cit.*, p.124; Ms. records, History of John Wesley Church, from Mrs. Wilhelmina Spencer.
46. Hood, *One Hundred Years*, p.524.
47. *Ibid*, p.179.

Rush organized the Fifth Annual Conference, apart from the New York Conference, known as the Genesee Conference, also in September 1849. Its first session was held in Auburn, N.Y., with Rev. W. S. Sanford, secretary-compiler, September 14-20, 1850. [48] The name was changed to Western New York Conference in 1897, while Bishop Walters presided.

Zion's work in Canada started in 1829. During the conference that year a preacher named Hamilton Johnson attended from Prescott, Upper Canada, requesting to join the New York Conference and represent a Zion society in that part of the country. [49] By the 1860 General Conference, there were five representatives from Canada. Several outstanding church leaders served in Canada. The churches, however, were later attached to the New England Conference. After Zion expanded into Michigan, a conference was then organized named the Canada-Michigan Conference, which later evolved into the Michigan Conference.

In the General Conference of 1852, an Eastern District was formed over which Bishop G. A. Spywood presided, embracing the New England, Nova Scotia, and British Guiana Conferences. [50] Our work in British Guiana survived, and the name of the conference changed, during independence of that country, in 1966, to Guyana Conference. Zion Church also had work in Haiti in 1861, when Rev. J. W. Lacey was sent there. [51]

"The Southern Conference was organized May 2, 1859, in Washington, D.C. The Conference was shortlived. It was represented in the General Conference of 1860. Its name was later changed to Baltimore Conference. In 1872, it was consolidated with the Philadelphia Conference, and since, we have had the Philadelphia and Baltimore Conference." [52]

There were a number of outstanding preachers added to the first roll; among them such notables as William F. Butler, John Williams, and Henry Dumpson of New England, William H. Decker, Samuel M. Giles, and William R. Brooks of New York Conference; J. P. Trusty, H. H. Blackson, Jacob Anderson, and George Johnson of the Philadelphia Conference; Abraham Cole, Daniel Matthews, and Joseph Armstrong of the Allegheny Conference; Hezekiah Butler, William Sanford, Jermain W. Loguen, William A. Cromwell, Thomas James, Richard Estepp, and James H. Smith of the Genesee Conference; and R. H. G. Dyson, J. D. Brooks, William T. Biddle, Jacob P. Hamer, J. A. Williams, and Joseph Sinclair of the Southern Conference.

At the end of this period just before Emancipation, there were 6 annual conferences, and 197 ministers received into the itinerancy. Of this total number of preachers, 92 were still living and in active service. [53]

> One remarkable thing about this period is that there were very few expulsions; a few recorded, but they were exceptions. . . . The ministers of the period were, as a rule, good preachers; few of them were what would be called brilliant men, but a large portion of them could preach a good sensible sermon. Some were powerful, awakening preachers; sinners could not listen without being affected to such a degree that it was impossible for them to hide it. Rev. Samuel L. Giles was a reasoner of great force; his

48. *Minutes,* One Hundred Eighth Annual Session of the Western New York Conference, 1957, p.1.
49. Rush, *Rise and Progress,* p.83.
50. Moore, *History,* p.215.
51. Hood, *One Hundred Years,* p.277.
52. Hood, *History,* Vol. II, p.28.
53. Hood, *One Hundred Years,* pp.82-83.

sermons were well arranged, logical and forcible. They were generally laid off in from three to five general divisions, with a larger number of subdivisions, and his entire discourse would have looked well in print. (54)

Rev. Giles and Dr. Gray were known as the theological instructors. Giles taught the preachers church decorum and respect for seniority in the ministry. "There were ministers then who were neither greatly endowed nor well cultured, but who had peculiarities by which they accomplished wonders. The Church, as a whole, was a power for good." (55)

"The Conferences held long sessions; they were the only theological institutes the ministers had in those days; they generally spent nearly two weeks in session." As was the Methodist custom the conferences were not held with open doors in the early days of the church, but gradually the public was admitted. "The ministers in Zion Connection, almost from its organization, were more liberal toward the laity than any other branch of the Methodist Episcopal Church." Laymen were admitted to representation in the Annual and General Conferences as early as 1851. (56)

This era of the church had elevated 13 men to the episcopacy, from James Varick to Joseph Jackson Clinton. Each made his own unique contribution to the growth of the church. A few served very short terms during the 20 years of inconstancy from 1840-1860, some served 12 and 16 years. Rush served 24 years actively, and gave a lifetime of devotion even after ill health. George Galbraith was elected for one year from 1852-1853, but he was Assistant Superintendent from 1848-1852; counting this, he had five years of service. This was the period in which Rush began to go blind, and "Galbraith did more than any other Assistant Superintendent, either before or after his time. He was the natural successor of Rush and bid fair, if he had lived, to make a glorious record." (57) The others, not listed in the roll of preachers from 1830-1840, who became bishops were Revs. D. S. Scott, Peter Ross, Samson D. Talbot, and John D. Brooks. William H. Bishop bore the brunt and passed through many trials in reuniting Zion and Wesley. That noble man, Christopher Rush, who lived to be 96 years old, was a mighty force in spirit and truth. The man who became the second bishop of the African Methodist Episcopal Zion Church sealed his fame through his versatile talent, magnetic personality, moral tenacity, far-reaching evangelical labors, and impeccable devotion to religion and freedom. He is described in brief by one of the most renowned and proficient black journalists of all times, Timothy Thomas Fortune, as follows:

Christopher Rush, a man of rare oratorical powers, deep piety, and a fine executive capacity, came North from New Bern, North Carolina, and at once identified himself with the new church. His influence was at once recognized. He knew how to organize men and wisely advise them. He was regarded as a great preacher. All classes, conditions, and races heard him gladly. To announce that he was to preach was to insure an overflow congregation. Frederick Douglass declared that he was one of the most powerful preachers he ever listened to. That he was elected as the second Bishop was no surprise to those who knew the man. (58)

The connection, passing through its second most crucial period of history, while slavery was still widespread and men and women were on fire to suppress it, made salient progress through deep faith, persistent beliefs, courageous undertakings, and freedom consciousness.

54. *Ibid.*, p.84.
55. *Ibid.*
56. *Ibid.*, p.85.
57. Hood, *History*, Vol. II, p.24.
58. *The New York Age*, October 1, 1896.

CHAPTER 12

THE RISE OF THE DAUGHTERS OF CONFERENCE

That woman, the gentler half of God's creation, was an important, even though invisible, factor in the pioneer work of the Church cannot be doubted. Since the creation of the world, woman has been a help-meet for man, and notwithstanding her power has been wrought out behind the throne, still she has been steadily at work in whatever of good the world has known. (1)

The A.M.E. Zion Church has been a prophecy of the rise of women in the church, and other affairs, all of its existence. A sort of pertinacity was bred into these women who stood by the side of the men, fought the battles of freedom, and expanded the church across the continent and across the seas. Some of the women who walked by the sides of their noble husbands and fathers in establishing the A.M.E. Zion Church in 1796 were Aurelia Varick, Sarah Thompson, Jane Cook, Jane Pontier, Pemilia Pontier, Susannah Moore, Sarah Moore, Amy Jacobs, Jane Miller, Betsy Miller, Sarah Bias, Elizabeth Brown, and a number of slave women listed in the John Street classes of black women with no surname. (2)

During this time, women in the church, as in all other public walks of life, were severely proscribed. The power women did exert was principally through advice and counsel asked of them by husband, son, or brother. Should they become inspired with ardent zeal to lift their voices in the congregation for the betterment of the church, they were met with the Pauline doctrine—"Let the women keep silence in the church." (3) Bishop Varick, Abraham Thompson, William Miller, and the other heroic pioneer workers, aware of this sentiment, did not attempt the great undertaking of establishing a separate church without wife, mother, or sister.

The Church has always had a hearty and healthful support from her women, and no doubt the women were more zealous in effecting this separation. It is probable they spent sleepless nights in this time of perplexity advising, admonishing, planning and praying over the seemingly insurmountable obstacle that confronted them. They endured discouragements thinking only of that hidden secret within their bosoms—the longing desire to worship God with freedom and ease under their own fig tree. Through patience, perseverance and prayer, they reached the goal. The independent Church was established. (4)

The parent group of all women's organizations in the A.M.E. Zion

1. Meriah E. Harris, "Woman in the Pioneer Work of the Church," *A.M.E. Zion Quarterly Review*, April, 1899, p.22.
2. John Street Church Ms. Records, New York Public Library; 1801 Census Book, New York Historical Society.
3. Meriah E. Harris, *op. cit.*
4. *Ibid.*

Connection is The Female Benevolent Society, commonly known as "The Mother Society." Their object of organization was to serve local purposes, such as administering aid to the sick and distressed, burying the dead, and assisting in supporting the orphans of their deceased members. Another "Female Branch of Zion" Society was soon organized to assist in paying the expenses of the church, "and thereby add to the declarative glory of God." (5) These stellar pillars enabled Zion to build the most complete, serviceable church edifice, both in 1820 and 1840, of the race, in the nation's largest city.

"The origin and work of the Daughters of Conference are as replete with interest as it is full of self-sacrifice and devotion to the cause of Missions and the promulgation of the Gospel." This group was organized in 1821, the year of the first Conference. Zion Church and its missionary operation were in their infancy, and the cry came from New York, New England, New Jersey, and Pennsylvania: "Send us the Gospel, send a minister; we need a church." Thus "the great need was money to aid the ministers in going to their mission fields and to assist in erecting churches." These noble and heroic women of Zion answered the call—"The preacher must go and preach; Zion churches must be erected and we will give the money—and for this grand and glorious purpose the United Daughters of Conference were organized at that early, needy time in Mother Zion Church " (6)

Noteworthy among this group was The Mite Society, composed of the aged and young. Even little children of the age of two years and upward were known as junior members, to aid in support of the gospel, and spreading it far and wide. They also organized themselves into societies for preparing the children and bringing them up in the path of duty, thus contributing their time, effort, and means for the religious and scientific training of the children of the race. (7)

The A.M.E. Zion Church, with endless gratitude, continues in remembrance of those illustrious members of this original society of the Daughters of Conference, founded by the prolific Mary Roberts of Mother Zion Church, who served as its first president for over 40 years until her decease. This organization was the greatest means of supporting preachers in establishing churches, who had no stated salaries. Mary Roberts exerted a mighty influence over the women of her day in rallying them to support and aid missions, education, and other needs of the church. (8)

Among the outstanding leaders of the Daughters of Conference in New England and New York were Sarah Ennals, Eliza Ann Gardner, Mary E. Anderson, Elizabeth A. Purnell, Sarah J. Eato, Marie Vogalsang, Matilda Busle, and Ellen Stevens. Eliza Ann Gardner of Boston, Mary E. Anderson of Worcester, and Adella Hicks Turner of Providence, "as the head and front of the Daughters of Conference of the New England Conference," were known for their "rare sagacity, untiring energy and unsparing zeal." They had, in their way, done as much for the spread of Zion and the education of her ministers as any three women anywhere; and they were more zealous in their latter days for this work, and always wore a smile of contentment and satisfaction. They were grand

5. William Thompson, "An Address Delivered Before the Female Branch Society of Zion," *The Colored American,* May 20, 1837.
6. Aurora Evans, "Origin and Work of the Daughters of Conference and Kindred Societies," *A.M.E. Zion Quarterly Review,* January 1898, pp.66-67.
7. William Thompson, *op. cit.*
8. Aurora Evans, *op. cit.;* Hood, *One Hundred Years,* p.538.

and noble women indeed. (9) Mrs. Jane Finch, who labored with Varick and testified to his sterling character in Wheeler's *The Varick Family*, also started out young and was still serving as a Daughter of Conference toward the latter part of the century. Under the leadership of Mary Roberts, Ellen Stevens organized The Young Daughters of Conference, who worked with the same enthusiasm and zeal as the older women. (10) Sometimes the societies were named for the bishops who stimulated the work, as in the following notice in *The Colored American*, September 16, 1837:

> The Juvenile Daughters of Rush, will celebrate their Anniversary, on Wednesday evening, September 20th, in Zion's Church, corner of Church and Leonard Streets. Doors open at 6 o'clock, at which time there will be speaking and singing by the young ladies of the Society. Admittance, 6¼ cents. Ann Matilda Harrington, President.

The Daughters of Conference grew rapidly and were organizing in the churches of every area. The men of the church, young and old, became interested in spreading the kingdom of God through Zion, then started organizing the Sons and Daughters of Conference. There was a strong organization at Newburgh, N.Y. under the pastorate of Rev. Joseph P. Thompson. His wife, Catherine Thompson, was an ardent worker, and was honored as the president of the Sons and Daughters of Conference before she became first treasurer of the Woman's Home and Foreign Missionary Society. She was always active in perfecting plans for the advancement of this unit of church expansion. (11)

News came from Troy, N.Y., that the "United Sons and Daughters of Zion's Benevolent Society" had organized in addition to the "Female Benevolent Society," and our A.M.E. Zion brethren and sisters "have a flourishing society," which was formed January 8, 1835, and preparing to hold its second anniversary. (12) Rev. R. Haywood Stitt organized The Sons and Daughters of Zion, which took in a large number of converts in the rapidly growing Fleet Street Church, as late as 1890, now known as The First Church, Brooklyn, N.Y. (13) This organization also proved to be a tremendous success in not only expanding the borders of Zion, but stimulating all types of benevolent causes.

The Daughters of Conference were known as "the angels of mercy of the conference, who by their presence and munificent gifts have done much to lighten the burden of the ministry." (14) Another instance was the organization at Newark known as The Daughters of Bishop. The following appeared in the *Anglo-African*, December 31, 1859:

> Newark: December 27, 1859: On Wednesday evening, the 14th inst., the Revs. Wm. F. Butler and Wilbur G. Strong, Esq. lectured in Zion Church, Academy Street, before the Daughters of Bishop, at their Anniversary. Mr. Butler's themes were "Woman and her Social Position," "John Brown Justified," and other kindred subjects. Mr. Strong's theme was, "Woman and her Influence." Both gentlemen did exceedingly well, and gave great satisfaction.

9. *A.M.E. Zion Quarterly Review*, July 1894, p.420; *The Star of Zion*, November 16, 1920.
10. Aurora Evans, *op. cit.*
11. Hood, *One Hundred Years*, p.217.
12. *The Colored American*, April 1, 1837.
13. Hood, *One Hundred Years*, p.422.
14. Aurora Evans, *op. cit.*, p.68.

Another interesting special notice appeared in the *Anglo-African,* December 15, 1860:

FAIR   The ladies of the United Daughters of Conference Society of the A.M.E. Zion Church, corner of Leonard and Church streets, intend holding a Fair for the benefit of the conference ministers, in the basement of Shiloh Church, corner of Prince and Marion streets. The Fair will open on the 17th and continue until the 28th of December. A quantity of useful articles will be offered for sale.

The ladies of the Committee solicit the patronage of their friends and all who desire the spread of the gospel. Admittance 6 cents. Donations in money or goods will be thankfully received by the Committee.

Miss Marie M. DeGrasse, Directress,	Clarissa Jefferson
Brooklyn, Long Island	Mary E. McClair
Miss Eliza A. Smith	Sarah Ennals
Mrs. Margaret Williams, Secretary	Harriet Harper
Mrs. Martha E. Varick [15]	Sarah Sands
Mrs. Sarah A. Johnson	Mary A. Forbes
Hester Howell	Elizabeth Vandevere
Elizabeth Purnell	Ann M. Dickerson
Ann R. Randall	Sarah Minen

There was a conflict here between the Daughters of Conference and the Board of Trustees. Sister Mary Roberts, the president, published an article in this same edition stating why the affair was not held in the most commodious church of the city, their own Zion Church. The society, which had been laboring over a quarter of century and had contributed over $1,000 towards sending the ministers to their different stations, "should not be forced to hold its affair in another church, when the Fair was to assist the Conference of its Connection." Also in the same edition, the trustees published their reply to the ladies, signed by T. M. Eato, Jr., secretary and Samuel J. Howard, chairman of the Board, stating that their application had been made for the purpose of assisting the trustees in paying their debts, and that is why their request was not granted to use their own church. [16] The women had insisted upon sending the proceeds from this occasion to the conference, as had been their procedure.

A more pleasant occasion immediately succeeded this one.

FESTIVAL OF PROVIDENCE—On Thursday evening, 29th ult., the Daughters of Conference of the A.M.E. Zion Church gave their annual poultry supper in Swartz' spacious hall. At 11 o'clock the company took their seats at a table plentifully supplied with all the luxuries of the season, and at the head of which was that aged soldier of the cross, Rev. Leven Smith of New York, the oldest surviving elder of the A.M.E. Zion Connection. He commenced the upbuilding of Zion in Providence in 1822, at which time it was very difficult for a colored man to walk the streets of Providence without being pushed off the sidewalk or insulted in some other way. The entertainment was a brilliant affair. [17]

These devoted church women also honored Father Rush in what was known as "The Rush Festival," held at the Masonic Hall in New York City, November 27, 1865, in his eighty-eighth year. [18]

A number of women became the main stimulaters in organizing and perpetuating church societies. This was mentioned in the case of New Haven,

15. Widow of George Collins, who married Daniel Varick, grandson of the founder.
16. *The Weekly Anglo-African,* December 15, 1860.
17. *Ibid.*
18. *Ibid.,* December 23, 1865.

and Mrs. Eliza Ann Galpin. It was also the case in Tarrytown, N.Y., where in 1864 Mrs. Amanda Foster led in organizing the society now known as Foster Memorial Church.

After Emancipation, Eliza Ann Gardner, Mary Anderson, and Adella Hicks Turner led the Daughters of Conference of New England in raising funds for sending and sustaining Revs. John Williams, J. W. Hood, W. F. Butler, and Wilbur G. Strong, in the South as missionaries, in 1863. [19] Some of these men moved into the South upon the directive of Bishop J. J. Clinton, and began to develop Zion Church with exceptional speed. Daughters of Conference were organized all over the South to aid in paying preachers' salaries and other connectional causes.

One of the grand saints who stands out prominently among women in A.M.E. Zion history is Miss Melvina Fletcher. She was a member of the first Zion congregation of Washington, D.C., Zion Wesley (now Wesley Metropolitan). It was my honor, in company with Rev. E. D. W. Jones (later bishop) to meet Miss Fletcher in her last days at her home in Washington, when she related to us the historic incident of the near relinquishment of Zion's efforts to expand in the South. She had a notable career as a governess, most of her life, in the home of Montgomery Blair, Postmaster General in Abraham Lincoln's Cabinet. She became prominent in Zion history because she was òf great help to Bishop J. J. Clinton in establishing the work in the South (see Chapter 15).

When progress had to be made, in the face of dire adversity, the women of the church were willing to sacrifice and toil, and proved to be towers of strength to the courageous men of Zion. Mrs. Frances (John J.) Moore "used to tell, with pride, the hardships with which she met in traveling with her husband, especially in California." [20] Even in our work in Africa, Rev. Andrew Cartwright was aided by the Daughters of Conference, along with the Missionary Society. [21]

Bishop Josiah S. Caldwell, elected in 1904, began to promote the conference workers throughout the areas assigned to him. It spurred on a new group of women supporters of the conference enterprises, for the most part home missions. The Daughters of Conference remained in the hands of an elderly group, who continued to work for the support of missions. The causes were so similar, that the name gradually evolved into "Conference Workers" throughout the church. With passionate zeal for spreading the kingdom of Christ, this segment of women maintain the same spirit with which they were founded.

19. *The Star of Zion*, November 16, 1920.
20. Meriah E. Harris, *op. cit.*, p.24.
21. Aurora Evans, *op. cit.*, p.69.

CHAPTER 13

GROWTH OF SOLIDARITY
IN THE STRUGGLE FOR EMANCIPATION

The pioneers of freedom in America fought to secure it when the Revolution severed the colonies from foreign dictation and tribute. Unfortunately, these fathers of the Republic neglected to move the stumbling stone of slavery from the new nation, were forced to do their first works over again, and by the 1860's met the price in blood and tears. During this severe period for black people, a mighty pressure of enforcing this new freedom came through their own creative leadership, first by way of the church.

James Varick and William Hamilton: "James Varick manifested his hatred to slavery by leading his few noble followers out of the Methodist Episcopal Church in 1796, and thus became a pioneer Negro anti-slavery leader." [1] He was resolute, and with his associates, raised and solidified the Negro's own resources and provided a platform for the nation's outstanding abolition leaders, black and white. "Zion Church had not only always been an anti-slavery church, but in the days that tried men's souls, our church was in the forefront of the battle." [2] Bishop Hood stated in his history that:

In the days of slavery the Zion ministers were generally leaders of the anti-slavery movement and their pulpits were always open to anti-slavery lectures. If no other house could be obtained for an anti-slavery meeting it was known that the Zion Church could be had. The doors of this church were never closed against one who wanted to plead for the oppressed. [3]

One of the most remarkable laymen in the formation of the A.M.E. Zion Church was William Hamilton, an original trustee. He and Varick had met in the John Street Church, and became close friends and co-workers in the freedom cause in the 1780's. They became deeply involved in freedom activities outside the church soon after American independence had been achieved. We first observe Hamilton's courageous spirit in the same year Zion Church was born, when he wrote the Governor of the State of New York. A part of that letter follows:

To his excellency John Jay, Esq.
Governor of the State of New York

From William Hamilton, A Black Man
New York
8, March, 1796

1. E. George Biddle, "The A.M.E. Zion Church and the Anti-Slavery Movement," *A.M.E. Zion Quarterly Review*, April 1898, p.74.
2. *Ibid.*, p.75.
3. *Ibid.*

Honored Sir:

. . . [In writing you] I would not have gone so far had I not believed you to be a person that would listen to the meanest persons who would want to address themselves to you. Being confident that you will not refuse to hear my simple address. . . .

I am, dear Sir, one of those whom the generality of men call Negroes. My forefathers or ancestors from Africa but I am a native of New York, worthy Sir when I behold many of the sons of Africa groaning under oppression, some laboring with difficulty to get free, and others having to bear the yoke. I cannot help shedding a silent tear at the miserable misfortunes Providence hath brought upon them, but should I blame Heaven for this when it appears from the sacred truths of the King of Heaven that his displeasure toward the perpetrators. . .of these evil deeds beheld in the spirit of (the prophecy), Solomon: (See Ecclesiastes 4:1-3)*

How falsely and contradictory do the Americans speak when this land, a land of liberty and equality, a Christian country, when almost every part of it abounds with slavery and oppression. How offended would the gentleman be that is told by another that this is not a land of liberty and equality (?) When he is asked again is this a free state with respect to the Negroes he has to answer, no kind sir. . . . Is not everyone that keeps slaves that are Negroes continually stealing, and Dear Sir, does not every [one] know that these slaves were stolen from their own country or deceived by means no better and brought here and sold. . . . In this continent or some part of Christendom(?)

When their purchasers buy them they know they were stolen property, therefore they were equal to thieves. Agreeable to this they know that [the] indisputable right of these Africans and their children is liberty and freedom but those that keep them slave take it from them against their will, for none are willing to be slaves. Just like a robber he robs them because it is in his power to do it or see that Negroes are kept slaves for nought. What harm have they done the Americans (?) Have they ever injured them in the least? . . .

> Is there as ye sometimes tell us
> Is there one who reigns on high
> Does he bid them buy and sell us
> Spreading from his throne the sky.

Has God appointed us as their slaves (?) I answer No. His word says: "he that stealeth a man and selleth him, or if he be found in his hand, he shall surely be put to death." I have already shown that every slaveholder is stealing men's labor and liberty. Some men say Negroes are like Brutes bought to be slaves, but these are unreasonable men. But may they

> Deem our nation brutes no longer
> Till some reason they can find
> Worthy of regard and stronger
> Than the color of our kind.

The intent of my writing to you was this. To know whether there can be no measures taken for the recovery of the objects of pity. Is it not high time that the scandal of the country should be taken away that it might be called a free nation in deed and in truth? Is it not time that Negroes should be free (?) Is it not time that robbery should cease (?) Is it not time that the threatening of heaven should be taken away (?) May kind heaven smile upon this nation, incline them to do unto all men as they would all men should do unto them. May Negroes be manumitted. May heaven diffuse its choicest blessings on your head. May you open your mouth and judge righteously and plead the cause of the poor and needy. May your family be blessed from above.

So no more at present but remain

Your humble servant,
William Hamilton

N. B. — an answer from you will be very acceptable by the person who gives you this. [4]

Hamilton, along with Varick and other leaders, worked in practically all of the African religious, benevolent, and freedom organizations of that day that began in New York. In a few years, the race group, at that time the A.M.E. Zion Church their only organization, had put new fire into their cause which aroused a restlessness among citizens.

A sample of the restlessness was expressed in a newspaper statement as follows: In regard to the suggestion that the freedom of the city should be more extensively granted, a citizen declares that this would result in "an addition to our present stock of Irish freemen, an insult to our citizens, and an injury to our country, the whole host of Africans that now deluge our City (already too impertinent to be borne) would be placed upon an equal with the citizens." [5]

Following these original efforts, new organizations grew. Varick and Hamilton took leading roles in organizing such groups as the New York African Clarkson Association, The Wilberforce Benevolent Society, and the New York African Mutual Relief Society to aid the cause of their race. [6] After Varick's death in 1827, Christopher Rush took up the cudgels for the freedom cause, continuing with Hamilton and others this exigence.

This prelude to the concrete efforts that began around 1830 was further stimulated by other wicked customs grasping the country before and after the abolition of African slave trade in 1808. Prior to this, "kidnappers did a flourishing business in selling captured runaways, and also freedmen whom they had seized illegally. . . . Between 1800 and 1830 a continuous stream swelled the city's [New York] black population." Many were fugitives from the Gabriel Prosser Conspiracy of 1800 in Virginia, the Denmark Vesey Uprising of 1822 in South Carolina, the Nat Turner Rebellion of 1831 in Virginia, and many other collective efforts to snatch liberty. New York was the focal point out of which several routes of the Underground Railroad Terminals led overland to Philadelphia, New Jersey, Canada, and other sections north, and by boat to New England. [7] New York and New England were also capital battlegrounds in this war against slavery. Not only did Negroes establish the first black American newspaper in 1827, but Arthur Tappan, a New York abolitionist, established the *New York Journal and Commerce* the same year to help wage the war. In 1828, "The African Dorcas Society, an organization of Negro women, held its convention in New York City. In 1830, white churches of New York which had hitherto either condoned slavery or had been silent began to agitate against it." [8]

4. John Jay papers, Columbia University Library. As we were permitted to print this letter only in part, the scripture was referenced.
5. Stokes, *Iconography*, Vol. 5, p.1397; originally from New York *Gazette and General Advertizer*, January 3, 1803.
6. Ottley and Weatherby, *The Negro in New York*, pp.60-61.
7. *Ibid.*, pp.82-83.
8. Federal Writers Program, New York Negroes, (Schomberg Collection).

Rising to prominence at this time were such notable white citizens as William Lloyd Garrison, Arthur and Lewis Tappan, Simon Jocelyn, Elias Hicks, and Benjamin Lundy; to be joined later by Wendell Phillips, Charles Sumner, Salmon Chase, Henry Ward Beecher, Harriet Beecher Stowe, the martyred John Brown, Abraham Lincoln, and many others with true freedom spirit in nation building, assisting the Negroes in their fight for emancipation. In 1827, 10,000 slaves were freed in the state of New York, and the New York Abolition Society along with the Washington, D.C. Society petitioned Congress for the abolition of slavery. By 1830, slavery in the North (north of the Mason-Dixon line) had been virtually abolished by legislative, judicial, or constitutional action. However, 3,568 Negroes still remained slaves, two-thirds of them in New Jersey. [9]

During this period Christopher Rush, Timothy Eato, Leven Smith, Jehial C. Beman, Thomas James, Hosea Easton, Samuel Giles, Joseph P. Thompson, George Galbraith, Samuel T. Gray, Peter Ross, Jermain W. Loguen, and John J. Moore, "constituted the great coterie of pulpit orators among Afro-Americans. They all stood for civil and religious liberty as enunciated in the Declaration of Independence. The African Methodist Episcopal Zion Church naturally, therefore, became to the Afro-American race what Faneuil Hall was to the Anglo-American, their Cradle of Liberty. When the doors of all the other churches and the public halls and theatres were closed to Abolitionist orators and friends of emancipation, the doors of Zion Church were always opened to them. It naturally became the forum of the proudest triumphs of Afro-American orators." [10] These men, with outstanding laymen and women of our church, figured most prominently in one venture after the other until Emancipation came in 1863, and even after the war.

One of the earliest was "The First Convention of the Colored People of these United States," which was held at Bethel A.M.E. Church in Philadelphia, on September 15, 1830. This convention of colored men was the concept of a young Baltimorian named Hezekiah Grice. After traveling through northern parts of the country from April to August 1830, in a desperate attempt to call a convention, he finally received the strong approval of leading New York Negroes with a circular printed favoring it. Grice was summoned to Philadelphia on August 11, by Bishop Richard Allen, where a meeting was in progress on the emigration matter, and near the adjournment he was called aside and requested by Allen to read the printed circular issued from New York. After the bishop left this meeting to attend a lecture in Baltimore, Grice introduced the subject of the convention. Plans were instituted to hold the first convention in Philadelphia on September 15. [11] Prominent also in assembling this first group was James Forten, "for the purpose of considering the plight of the free Negro, to plan his social redemption, and . . . to strike against the colonization idea. Forten was attempting to shift Negro opinion from emigration to abolition." [12] The convention was attended by the most outstanding men of the race: Bishops Allen and Rush, Rev. Paul of Abyssinian Baptist Church in New York, Rev. Peter Williams, Jr., Episcopal, and Rev. Samuel Cornish, Presbyterian, both of New York, James Forten of Philadelphia, William Hamilton and Thomas

9. Bergman, *The Chronological History of the Negro in America*, p.136.
10. Fortune, *The New York Age*, October 1, 1896.
11. *The Anglo-African Magazine*, Vol. 1, 1859, pp.305-310.
12. Bergman, *The Chronological History, op. cit.*, p.137.

Jennings, New York, Abraham Shadd of Delaware, J. W. C. Pennington of Brooklyn, Austin Steward of Rochester, Hosea Easton of Boston, Lewis Woodson and John Peck of Pittsburgh, Adams of Utica, Philip A. Bell and others of the Philadelphia leaders. [13]

When the convention opened, it was soon discovered that some prominent men of the city of Philadelphia had been excluded. First, Dr. Burton came in and demanded by what right the six gentlemen of Philadelphia held their seats as members of the convention.

> On a hint from Bishop Allen, Mr. Pascal moved that Dr. Burton be elected an honorary member of the Convention, which softened the Doctor. In a half an hour, five or six, tall, grave, stern-looking men, members of the Zion Methodist body in Philadelphia, entered, and demanded by what right the members present held their seats and undertook to represent the colored people. Another hint from the Bishop and it was moved that these gentlemen be elected honorary members. But the gentlemen would submit to no such thing, and would accept nothing short of full membership, which was granted them. [14]

Bishop Allen and Junius C. Morel were elected president and secretary respectively. The main subject of discussion was emigration to Canada, which took up two days. The convention recommended emigration to Canada, passed strong resolutions against the American Colonization Society, drew up a Constitution, and at its adjournment appointed the next annual convention of the people of color to be held in Philadelphia, Wesleyan (Big Wesley A.M.E. Zion) Church on the first Monday in June 1831. [15]

The national convention met twelve times from this 1830 convention to 1864 at Syracuse, N.Y.

> Emanating from these national conventions was the repeated reminder that slavery still sullied the image of a Christian democratic nation; that those blacks who were free were in all too many cases only nominally free; that the nation judged a man not by his capabilities but prejudged him by the color of his skin. During this entire era there was seldom a national conclave that did not preach the value of temperance, morality, education, economy and self-education. [16]

The next four conventions were held in Philadelphia also, from 1831 to 1834, when it assembled in New York City at the Asbury Church, June 2 to 12th. William Hamilton had been elected president at the last convention. The convention had expanded to include representatives of several other cities and states. Hamilton opened the convention with a towering address: [17]

> . . . Under present circumstances it is highly necessary the free people of color should combine, and closely attend to their own particular interest. All kinds of jealousy should be swept away from among them, and their whole eye fixed, intently fixed on their own peculiar welfare. And can they do better than to meet thus; to take into consideration what are the best means to promote their elevation, and after having decided, to pursue those means with unabating zeal until their end is obtained?. . .
>
> Cheer up, my friends! Already has your protest against the Colonization Society shown to the world that the people of color are not willing to be

13. *The Anglo-African Magazine*, Vol. 1, 1859, pp.305-310.
14. *Ibid.*
15. *Ibid.*
16. Howard H. Bell, *Minutes* of the Proceedings of the National Negro Conventions, 1830-1864, pp.i, ii.

expatriated. Cheer up. Already a right feeling begins to prevail. The friends of justice, of humanity, and the rights of man are drawing rapidly together, and are forming a moral phalanx in your defense.

The hitherto strong-footed, but sore-eyed vixen, prejudice, is limping off, seeking the shade. The Anti-Slavery Society and the friends of immediate abolition, are taking a noble, bold, and manly stand, in the cause of universal liberty. It is true they are assailed on every quarter, but the more they are assailed the faster they recruit. From present appearances the prospect is cheering, in a high degree. Anti-Slavery Societies are forming in every direction. . . . [18]

Echoes from this convention were evidently strong and widespread. New York City witnessed "The Abolition Riot"; from July 9 to 11, riots against the abolitionists occurred. The following places were sacked or damaged: Chatham Street Chapel, Bowery Theater, Dr. S. H. Cox's church and house, Zion's Church (coloured), African Baptist Church, and the residences of Arthur and Lewis Tappan. *Courier & Enquirer,* July 9,10,11,12,14,15; *Evening Post,* July 12, 1834. [19]

Mayor Cornelius Lawrence, known to be quite liberal, was threatened with both signed and anonymous letters. One such letter read thus:

Sir: I observe this morning in the cartridge boxes of a number of my military friends five pounds of ball cartridges which it appears were given out to the troops last night with which to shed the blood of their fellow citizens—As chief magistrate of this city and one upon whose head rests all the responsibility, beware this night that you act with discretion for if there is one drop of blood spilt vengeance will fall on your *devoted head.* You are a marked man and if you act with discretion you will escape, but otherwise you are a *doomed one.* Eyes that you little expect are upon you and hands raised ready to strike a blow. Again I say Your *Honor beware* July 12, 1834. [20]

The Mayor also received a letter dated July 12, 1834 as follows:

Sir: Report states that an attack will be made this Evening upon the Presbyterian Church (Dr. Cox's) on Laight and Varick Streets—and upon the African Church, corner of Leonard and Church Sts. . . . by the mob of Rioters. . . . May we request that a company of the military be stationed in the neighborhood of each of those places.

Robert C. Cornell, Ald. 5th Ward,
Robert Smith, Asst. [21]

A number of threats were received by the mayor, and Zion Church, although once sacked, was one of the centers of the threat, along with a number of Negro citizens' homes and businesses. [22] "William Hamilton, the thinker and actor, whose sparse specimens of eloquence we will one day place in gilded frames as rare and beautiful specimens of Etruscan art; . . . when met in the street, loaded down with iron missiles [during this riot], and asked where he was going, replied, 'to die on my threshold!' " [23] Two years later, December 9, 1836, William Hamilton, Sr., one of the most distinguished founding lay

17. *Ibid.,* 1834, pp.1-2.
18. *Ibid.,* pp.6-7; Hamilton, *Address to the Fourth Annual Convention of the People of Color,* pp.4, 6-7.
19. Stokes, *Iconography,* Vol. V, p.1728.
20. Mayor's Papers, Hon. Cornelius W. Lawrence, New York Historical Society.
21. *Ibid.*
22. *Ibid.*
23. *The Anglo-African Magazine,* Vol. 1, 1859, p.306.

members of the African Methodist Episcopal Zion Church, died in his 63rd year. "In recording the death of Mr. Hamilton, we are aware that we allude to no common man. He was one of sterling virtue and truth, and all his dealings thru life were marked by a strict adherence to truth and justice. 'An honest man is the noblest work of God.' " [24] When William Lloyd Garrison came on from Baltimore in 1830, Hamilton was one of the leading black men who gave him a cordial welcome and Godspeed, and subscribed largely to establish the *Liberator,* and to aid in the publication of *Garrison's Thoughts On Colonization.* [25] His chief pastor and companion in the freedom fight, Bishop Rush, gave his funeral sermon, and his beloved co-worker in New York, Henry Sipkins, elder son of Thomas Sipkins, delivered a eulogy four months later in March, 1837, at Zion Church, in a special memorial service. [26]

Christopher Rush: The influence of the abolition movements, and the aftermath of the Nat Turner Insurrection of 1831, increased repugnance among pro-slavery groups, both North and South. From 1834 on "Negro preachers were gradually outlawed in many Southern states and slaves were required to attend the church of their masters." [27] As described above, a noted pioneer in this struggle was the second bishop of the African Methodist Episcopal Zion Church, Christopher Rush, Varick's successor. He attended and participated in the National Conventions from the first one in 1830. He was "one of the Giants of the reform movement of the 1830's—one of the group of courageous militant leaders who built the Negro Convention movement, together with Bishop Richard Allen, Nathaniel Paul, Peter Williams, Jr., Samuel Cornish, and others." [28]

Rush, a full-blooded African, was born a slave in Craven County, N.C., in 1777. He escaped to New York in 1798 and joined the Zion Church in 1803, and was licensed to preach in 1815. Rush is mentioned by Samuel R. Ward in his *Autobiography* as one of the leaders "who sowed the seeds of reform and abolition," and a special account of his life and work is given. Rush's name appears in the list of executive committee members of the American and Foreign Anti-Slavery Society published in various reports from 1847-1850. [29]

Outside of expanding the A.M.E. Zion Church from Philadelphia to Washington, D.C. and Pittsburgh, Rush was best known as a prime organizer and president of the Phoenix Society of New York City, for many years after it was organized in 1833. [30]

> The Society was composed of Negro and white members, men and women, old and young, rich and poor; it was perhaps the most progressive and democratic organization in the country. Its aim was to prepare and educate the people for a new day of freedom, unity, equality and peace. Its immediate aim was "to promote the improvement of the coloured people in morals, literature, and the mechanic arts." It planned to establish a Manual Labor School of high standing, and committees were at work collecting the

24. *The Weekly Advocate (Colored American),* January 7, 1837.
25. *The Anglo-African Magazine,* Vol. 1, 1859, p.127.
26. *The Emancipator,* December 12, 1836; *The Colored American,* Jan. 7, 1837; March 4, March 18, 1837.
27. Bergman, *The Chronological History, op. cit.,* p.150.
28. Federal Writers Program, New York Negroes, Schomberg Collection (Biography).
29. *Ibid.*
30. *Ibid.*

first $10,000 early in 1838. It established a high school for Negro youth; conducted classes in adult education, organized a labor center for the training and placing in business of young Negroes to whom the doors of opportunity were, as a rule tightly closed. Phoenix Hall, on West Broadway, where the educational work was conducted, became the centre of anti-slavery activities of New York City. Many of the Anti-Slavery Conventions were held in this hall which became famous in the annals of the abolition movement. [31]

Lewis Tappan also gives an account of Rush's noble work as head of this society.

Debates, discussions, lectures and forums were regularly held and attracted a great deal of attention, according to Tappan. . . . The "Mental Feasts" became famous all over the world after travelers like Addy and Harriet Martineau recorded the romance of these great intellectual banquets where the best fruits of thought and poesy are served to all who would partake of them, in addition to crackers and cake. [32]

The society was governed by 60 directors, white and black, with Christopher Rush as president. "Negro and white worked together on a common basis. Tappan, as usual, furnished most of the funds for upkeep of the Phoenix Hall, the library, and the schools. This New York Society attracted the attention of the free Negro people everywhere in the United States. At the 1833 Convention of the Colored People, they resolved to build societies in every city where it was poss..ole to do so." [33] This society expanded and operated successfully in many northern cities as the Phoenix Moral and Reform Society. [34]

Rush had traveled all over the northeastern territory in the interest of his church and race. His acquaintance with Frederick Douglass was first formed while Douglass was in New Bedford. [35] He ordained a large number of freedom magnates, and other men of vast usefulness to the race. After Rush went blind, toward the end of the 1850's, and during and after the Civil War, he remained in the background. He passed away on July 10, 1873, in Philadelphia. [36]

In his life of almost a hundred years was symbolized the long and brilliant struggles of the Negro people to achieve their rights in the social and cultural world. But Rush will perhaps be chiefly remembered as the President of the famous Phoenix Club of New York, which, in its defiance of the slave powers, and the insidious strength of prejudice, brought together the most militant and courageous souls of the early 19th Century—the Negro and white abolitionists, the fierce fighters for freedom. [37]

Reverend Hosea Easton: "James Easton, of Bridgewater [Mass.] was one who participated in the erection of the fortifications on Dorchester Heights, under command of Washington, which the next morning so greatly surprised the British soldiers then encamped in Boston." He was a manufacturing blacksmith, and his tool factory was extensively known for its superiority of workmanship. Mr. Easton was self-educated. When a young man, stipulating for work, he always provided for chances of evening study. He was welcomed to the business

31. *Ibid.*
32. *Ibid.*
33. *Ibid.*
34. *The Colored American,* 1837; Foner, *The Life and Writings of Frederick Douglass,* Vol. II, p.21.
35. Hood, *One Hundred Years,* p.541.
36. Federal Writers Program, *op. cit.*
37. *Ibid.*

circles of Boston as a man of strict integrity, and the many who resorted to him for advice in complicated matters styled him "the Black Lawyer." His sons, Caleb, Joshua, Sylvanus, and Hosea, inherited his mechanical genius and mental ability. [38]

The early religious experience of this family is vividly portrayed by Nell as follows:

> The family were victims, however, to the spirit of colorphobia, then rampant in New England, and were persecuted even to the dragging out of some of the family from the Orthodox Church, in which, on its enlargement, a porch had been erected, exclusively for colored people. After this disgraceful occurrence, the Eastons left the church. They afterwards purchased a pew in the Baptist church at Stoughton Corner, which excited a great deal of indignation. Not succeeding in their attempt to have the bargain cancelled, the people tarred the pew. The next Sunday, the family carried seats in the waggon. The pew was then pulled down; but the family sat in the aisle. These indignities were continued until the separation of the family. [39]

The youngest son, Hosea, became quite prominent in the annals of race history of that era. He very soon made up his mind to join the freedom fight with fearless, unflinching, and unfeigned race conviction. He joined the New York Conference in 1832, and was ordained deacon and elder in 1834 by Bishop Rush. Easton was the representative from Boston to the first Colored Convention in 1830. Aside from organizing the first black Methodist church in Hartford (Metropolitan A.M.E. Zion), out of the African Religious Society in 1836, Easton had a distinguished career in religious and race activities.

In January 1832, when the editor of *The Liberator* and a faithful few met in the Belknap Street Church and organized the first Anti-Slavery Society of Boston, it influenced leading black men of the city, who had ideas of their own, to form exclusive organizations among their group. One such effective society was the "Massachusetts General Colored Association," of which "Hosea and Joshua Easton, John E. Scarlett, Thomas Cole, James G. Barbadoes, William G. Nell and others" took the lead. "The object of this Association was the promulgation of Anti-Slavery truth. In January, 1833, it made application to be received as an auxiliary to the Massachusetts (then New England) Anti-Slavery Society . . . . and the request was cordially granted; but they and their white friends soon learned that complexional Anti-Slavery societies, as such, were absurdities, to say the least, and hence, such distinctions soon melted into thin air." [40]

These were perilous times, with such noted persons as Susan Paul taking an active part in the movement. After the burning of Pennsylvania Hall, the mobbing of William Lloyd Garrison and George Thompson, and the women's meeting held "at Francis Jackson's, where Harriet Martineau consecrated herself to the cause, and historically identified herself with the colored people, colored and white have met together on one Anti-Slavery platform, where, like kindred drops, they mingle into one." [41]

Easton's consummate vigilance against prejudice kept him frequently in the anti-slavery newspapers. For instance:

38. William C. Nell, *The Colored Patriots of the American Revolution*, p.33.
39. *Ibid.*, pp.33-34.
40. *Ibid.*, pp.345-346.
41. *Ibid.*, pp.346-347.

The public (are) respectfully informed that a discussion will take place at the Baptist Meeting-house, or the old school-room in Belknap Street, on the evening of the 29th inst. at 6 o'clock, between Rev. H. Easton, of Hartford, Conn. and Mr. C. V. Caples, of this city.

Question:—Is the prejudice of the white population of the United States, as it is wrongfully exercised towards the colored people of this country, on account of their color?

Gentlemen present will be invited to take part in the discussion. The friends of the oppressed are respectfully invited to attend.

Boston, Nov. 25, 1836. [42]

One of his most remarkable contributions was the publication in 1837 of "A Treatise on the Intellectual Character and Civil and Political Condition of the Colored People of the United States; and the Prejudice Exercised Towards Them" while he was pastoring in Hartford. [43] In this document, he strongly relates to the claims of black Americans and their rights and privileges of citizenship:

In the first place, the colored people who are born in this country, are Americans in every sense of the word—Americans by birth, genius, habits, language, etc. . . . They are depending on American climate, American aliment, American government, and American manners, to sustain their American bodies and minds; a withholding of the enjoyment of any American principle from an American man, either governmental, ecclesiastical, civil, social or alimental, is in effect taking away his means of subsistence; and consequently, taking away his life. Every ecclesiastical body which denies an American the privilege of participating in its benefits, becomes his murderer. Every state which denies an American a citizenship with all its benefits, denies him his life. Every community which denies an American the privilege of public conveyances, in common with all others, murders him by piece-meal. Every community which withholds social intercourse with an American, by which he may enjoy current information, becomes his murderer of the worst kind. The claims the colored people set up, therefore, are the claims of an American. . . .

Excuses have been made in vain to cover up the hypocrisy of this nation. The most corrupt policy which ever disgraced its barbarous ancestry has been adopted by both Church and State, for the avowed purpose of withholding the *inalienable rights* of one part of the subjects of the government. Pretexts of the lowest order, which are neither witty nor decent, and which rank among that order of subterfuges under which the lowest of ruffians attempt to hide when exposed to detection, are made available. Were I capable of dipping my pen in the deepest dye of crime, and of understanding the science of the bottomless pit, I should then fail in presenting to the intelligence of mortals on earth, the true nature of American deception. There can be no appeals made in the name of the laws of the country, or philanthropy, or humanity, or religion, that are capable of drawing forth any thing but the retort— *you are a negro!* . . .

. . . Emancipation embraces the idea that the emancipated must be placed back where slavery found them and restore to them all that slavery has taken away from them. Merely to cease beating the colored people, and leave them in their gore, and call it emancipation, is nonsense. Nothing short of an entire reversal of the slave system in theory and practice—in general and in particular—will ever accomplish the work of redeeming ·the colored

42. *The Liberator,* November 26, 1836.
43. Hosea Easton, *A Treatise of the Intellectual Character and Civil and Political Condition of the Colored People. . .*

people of this country from their present condition. (44)

Reverends Beman and James: Among the other vigorous anti-slavery preachers of the earliest period were Jehiel C. Beman and Thomas James. Beman joined the New York Conference in 1830, and was appointed head of the charges of Conn. (45) "Rev. J. C. Beman gives the following account ·of the origin of his name. He says that when his father was presented with manumission papers, he was asked what name he had selected, and replied that he had always loathed slavery, and wanted to be a man; hence he adopted the name, *Be-man.*" (46) He was sent to Boston as our first pastor in 1838, where he did his major work, not only in developing the church but in the anti-slavery movement. He became president of the State Temperance Society of Colored People, and received the high acclaim of Douglass, Garrison, and other abolitionists for his cogent position. (47)

Rev. Thomas James was born a slave at Canajoharie, N.Y. in 1804. He was separated from his mother and other brothers and sisters through slave-trading. His last master worked him hard and whipped him. He escaped, made his way to freedom in Rochester, and found a home with a Lawyer Talbert. As a slave he had never been inside of a school or church, and knew nothing of letters or religion. Very anxious to learn he was taught by a Mr. Freeman who had opened a Sunday school for Negro children on Favor Street. He commenced preaching in 1830, and bought as a site for a religious edifice the lot on Favor Street and built a small church edifice (the Favor Street Church, presently known as Memorial A.M.E. Zion Church). 48)

He was ordained in 1833 by Bishop Rush. He had been called Tom as a slave and they called him Jim at the warehouse where he worked earlier. He put both together when he reached manhood and was ordained Rev. Thomas James. He also founded our church in Syracuse, New York, amid many dangers. After serving our societies at Ithaca and Sag Harbor, Long Island, he was sent to New Bedford, Mass. in 1839. It was here he first saw Frederick Douglass, who was then right out of slavery and an exhorter in the A.M.E. Zion Church, where Thomas James soon licensed him to preach. (49)

A Devoted Layman: The following is another glowing example of fidelity to church and race, on behalf of a devoted layman:

A funeral discourse was delivered in the First Wesleyan African Church (Big Wesley), on the death of JOHN JONES, by the Rev. William Miller, late of New York, a colored minister of Zion and Asbury Congregations, from the 14th. Chapter of Revelations and 13th. verse. . . .

Mr. Jones died in the 60th year of his age and left behind him an example to all his colored brethren worthy to be emulated. By his industry, he accumulated some of the comforts and blessings of this life, and when he was called to another and a better world, he gave it all back to the cause of his Lord and Master.

A few items have been extracted from his last Will and Testament, for an example to all his colored brethren,—

"First I, J. Jones, do will and bequeath in the name of God, all my

44. *Ibid.*, pp.21, 49, 33, 52.
45. Rush, *Rise and Progress*, p.85.
46. Nell, *Colored Patriots of the American Revolution*, p.143.
47. *The Colored American*, 1837, (Various issues).
48. Thomas James, *The Life of Reverend Thomas James*, pp.5-6.
49. *Ibid.*, pp.7-8.

property as follows:

> To The First Colored Wesleyan Church (A.M.E. Zion) . $150.00
> The Bethel Church (A.M.E.) 150.00
> Library Society Company 150.00
> Infant School (Sunday) 150.00

My house and lot of ground to two colored families; all the residue of my property to the Abolition Society, for the good of the poor colored people."

I would to God, that my brethren may follow his example, is the prayer of your unworthy servant in the Lord. [50]

The greatest freedom lights in the race group, practically all of whom lived and died through all their works in the A.M.E. Zion Church, were Frederick Douglass, Sojourner Truth, Harriet Tubman, Jermain W. Loguen, William Howard Day, Joseph P. Thompson, Eliza Ann Gardner, and Catherine Harris. Now that Emancipation of Negroes everywhere in the country became the goal of free black men in the North, "in this matter their philosophy was simple: slavery was wrong, any effort to end it was right." [51] Zion was a foremost anti-slavery church, "encouraging their lecturers and preachers to hold forth in the various respective meeting houses." Bishop Rush was described as "a southerner and a strong abolitionist . . . . taking a responsible lead frequently in the prominent anniversary meetings of the Anti-Slavery Society. [52] Rev. George Washington of the New England Conference was a forceful abolitionist whose voice could always be heard aloud regardless of personal consequences. Rev. John J. Moore, at Wesleyan, Philadelphia, and Rev. Joseph P. Thompson, in charge of Zion Church, New York (both became bishops), were eloquent divines of that day, active in the fight for freedom [53]

Frederick Douglass: Coincidental with the most creative era of freedom history of the A.M.E. Zion Church, "there escaped from slavery out of Maryland, a young man of native genius, with great natural gifts as an orator. But he was ignorant of his powers, and being a fugitive slave was slow in discovering them in the world." [54] Frederick Douglass, the legend of all times, began to make himself a part of the Negro community of New Bedford soon after he had settled down in their home on Elm Street. He was a member of the Sharp Street Methodist Church in Baltimore, and sought to renew his religious contacts. "He joined a local Methodist church, but remained there only a short time. He discovered that Negroes were second-class communicants, sitting in special sections of the church." [55] During a communion service, when Negroes were called on last, in disgust he walked out of the church, never to return.

At the South, I was a member of the Methodist Church. When I came north, I thought one Sunday I would attend communion, at one of the churches of my denomination, in the town I was staying. The white people gathered round the altar, the blacks clustered by the door. After the good minister had served out the bread and wine to one portion of those near him, he said, "These may withdraw, and others come forward"; thus he proceeded till all the white members had been served. Then he drew a long breath, and

---

50. From *Paulson's Philadelphia Daily Advertiser,* quoted in *The Liberator,* Feb. 14, 1835.
51. Ottley, *New World A-Coming,* p.12.
52. *A Call Upon the Church for Progressive Action,* 1848, p.9.
53. *Ibid.,* pp.7-9.
54. Fortune, *The New York Age,* October 1, 1896.
55. Philip S. Foner, *The Life and Writings of Frederick Douglass,* Vol. 1, pp.24-25.

looking out towards the door, exclaimed, "Come up, colored friends, come up! for you know God *is no respecter of persons!"* I haven't been there to see the sacraments taken since. (56)

He joined the little school-house church on Second Street, known as Zion, where he soon became a leading member of the congregation. (57) Rev. William Serrington was the minister then, in 1838. Douglass states that "I found him a man of deep piety, and of high intelligence. His character attracted me, and I received from him much excellent advice and brotherly sympathy." Under Serrington's pastorate, Douglass was extremely active in the church, serving as sexton, Sunday school superintendent, steward, class leader, clerk, and exhorter. Douglass told of Bishop Rush removing Serrington to another station, and sending Rev. Peter Ross, who stayed only a brief while, and then he sent Rev. Thomas James. Those men who pastored nearby and worked with Douglass in the anti-slavery movements were Revs. Jehiel Beman, Dempsey Kennedy, and John P. Thompson, all of whom visited and preached in the little schoolhouse on Second Street while Douglass resided in New Bedford. This is where he first met Bishop Rush. (58)

James says that upon his arrival in New Bedford, he observed that Douglass, "so to speak, right out of slavery, had already begun to talk in public though not before white people." (59) Douglass obtained a license to preach from the Quarterly Conference as a local preacher, and often occupied the pulpit by request of Rev. James. "Mr. William C. Coffin, a prominent abolitionist in those days of trial," said Douglass, "had heard me speaking to my colored friends in the little schoolhouse on Second Street, where we worshiped." Douglass was attending a grand anti-slavery convention in Nantucket during the summer of 1841, under the auspices of William Lloyd Garrison and his friends. Coffin sought him out of the crowd and invited him to say a few words to that convention.

> Thus sought out, and thus invited, I was induced to express the feelings inspired by the occasion, and the fresh recollection of the scenes through which I had passed as a slave. It was with the utmost difficulty that I could stand erect, or that I could command and articulate two words without hesitation and stammering. I trembled in every limb. I am not sure that my embarrassment was not the most effective part of my speech, if speech it could be called. At any rate, this is about the only part of my performance that I now distinctly remember. (60)

Though Douglass had a modest version of his first impression made upon this mixed audience of over 1,000 people, those who heard him "declare that he never surpassed the unexpected effort of that evening. His training in the various capacities in the little [Zion] Church . . . prepared him for that most eloquent speech. It was the outcome of the lessons of liberty he had learned in the little church." (61) Thus, says Douglass; "My connection with the little church continued long after I was in the antislavery field. I look back to the days I spent in little Zion, New Bedford, in the several capacities of sexton, steward, class leader, clerk, and local preacher, as among the happiest days of my life." (62)

56. *Ibid.; Anti-Slavery Standard,* December 23, 1841.
57. Frederick Douglass, *Life and Times of Frederick Douglass,* p.266.
58. Hood, *One Hundred Years,* pp.541-542.
59. Thomas James , *The Life of Rev. James, op. cit.,* p.8.
60. Douglass, *The Life and Times, op. cit.,* p.266.
61. *The New York Age,* October 1, 1896.
62. Hood, *One Hundred Years,* p.542.

In the summer of 1845 Douglass sailed for England, still a fugitive slave. In England and Scotland he worked and lectured on freedom. While there his friends raised money to purchase his freedom, and he became famous and a free man. He returned to America in the spring of 1847 where his prestige had greatly increased. [63] Small wonder Douglass rejoiced:

What a contrast is my *present* with my former condition? Then a slave, now a free man; then degraded, now respected; then ignorant, despised, neglected, unknown, and unfriended, my name unheard of beyond the narrow limits of a republican slave plantation; now, my friends and benefactors, people of both hemispheres, to heaven the praise belongs! [64]

Among the demonstrations of welcome, were a large gathering of Negro people in New York at Zion's (Mother Zion) Church, "to voice their joy at Douglass' success." Douglass soon made up his mind to move to Rochester, N.Y., where he founded the famous anti-slavery newspaper, *The North Star,* in the winter of 1847. [65] The very first issue of *The North Star* carried the news that its editor was already involved in the operation of the Underground Railroad. "Rochester was the last main stop on the Underground. Douglass' house on Alexander Street became an important station. By 1850, Douglass was the leader of the Railroad in Rochester, superintending all the activities and having contact with agents in the rest of the country." [66]

It was while residing in Rochester that Douglass soared in his fight against the evils of slavery. His membership in Zion and close association with the leaders and people of Zion Church, and numerous anti-slavery speeches from that pulpit, as well as the leading halls of Rochester, and his co-workers in the Committee of Vigilance, were all sources of encouragement through difficult periods. He was assisted in the critical days of his newspaper by a number of outside friends, and by friends of the church, who aided him, for a brief period, in operating the paper from the church basement. [67] In his work, he made close contact with such leading freedom fighters of the A.M.E. Zion Church as Sojourner Truth, Harriet Tubman Jermain W. Loguen, and William Howard Day. He credited Rev. Henry Highland Garnett and J. W. Loguen for his interest in meeting John Brown. [68] As important as were his services as an agent and "founder" of the Underground Railroad, he was "the first to recognize the superior contribution made by Harriet Tubman, the heroic woman who fearlessly 'carried the war into Africa.' "[69] "In his letter to the Ladies' Irish Anti-Slavery Association, Douglass referred to 'one coloured woman, who escaped from Slavery eight years. ago, has made several returns at great risk, and has brought out, since obtaining her freedom, fifty others from the house of bondage. She possesses great courage and shrewdness, and may yet render even more important service to the Cause.' " [70] This was an early stage of Harriet Tubman's Underground activities, for she kept up her courageous trips to the South and led over 300 slaves successfully through to freedom.

Douglass' long career of freedom activities was superbly described by his

63. Douglass, *The Life and Times, op. cit.,* p.74.
64. *Ibid.,* pp.74-75.
65. *Ibid.,* pp.75-77.
66. Foner, *The Life and Writings of Frederick Douglass,* Vol. II, p.42.
67. 77th Anniversary Souvenir Program, Favor St. Church, Rochester, N.Y., 1906.
68. Douglass, *The Life and Times, op. cit.,* p.337.
69. Foner, *op. cit.,* Vol. II, p.46.
70. *Ibid.,* pp.46-47.

friend and fellow church member, after his death on February 20, 1895. Said John Campbell Dancy, Sr.:

> I saw Mr. Douglass under many and varying circumstances, but he was always the same grand, peerless character in his personality. I heard him declare in a great convention, where weighty political interests were involved, and party spirit ran high, that "the Republican Party is the ship and all else is the sea"; (this was during the time that Negroes had been thoroughly convinced of this Party's interest in his behalf since Emancipation), I beheld him with cane in hand at the Columbian Exposition, at Chicago, at a great congress, tell a caustic critic of our race, in answer to his animadversions, to desist from his unfair attacks and "go home, and learn the truth, before attempting again to instruct others as to the true status of a too long maligned and oppressed race;" I heard him in a great National Republican Convention, speaking of his own race, assert that "we may be many as the waves, but we are as the sea"; I watched him before an audience made up chiefly of foreigners, at Washington, during the great Ecumenical Conference, as he rose to the loftiest pitch of overpowering eloquence and made a last appeal to them on behalf of fair play for all mankind; I sat with him an hour at the Executive Mansion, as he talked with President Harrison, portraying the greatness of the people of Hayti, whom he loved; I have seen him make merry at his home at Cedar Hill, overlooking the Potomac, as he and his grandson played in concert on violins his favorite, "The Suwannee River"; and to cap the climax, I beheld him as the orator of the day, on the occasion of the unveiling of the Lincoln monument on Capitol Hill, at Washington, in April, 1876. President Grant and his cabinet, the Vice-President, nearly all the United States Senators, and members of Congress, the Chief Justice and members of the Supreme Court, Governors of different states, the Diplomatic Corps and other notable persons were there—with an assembled mass of more than 50,000 persons, constituting the finest audience that ever heard a plain civilian in this country, speak—and Douglass never appeared to better advantage, as he addressed himself so marvelously to that surging sea of upturned faces. It was the speech of his life. But under none of these changed circumstances did he ever to our mind vary a hair's breadth from the modest, sincere, brave, true, and unaffected Frederick Douglass whom the world has known and honored for nearly a half century. . . . [71]

Frederick Douglass had two large funerals, first in Washington, D.C. (where he spent his last days), held at the Metropolitan A.M.E. Church, with a wide range of clergymen and statesmen participating. The second was held in the huge Central Presbyterian Church at Rochester, because Memorial A.M.E. Zion Church was not large enough to hold the crowd; where also a wide range of clergymen and statesmen participated. The last time this church had held such a crowd was when "Douglass sat on the platform with President Harrison on the Sunday before the unveiling of the Soldiers' Monument in May, 1892." Rev. Dr. James Edward Mason, presiding elder, and Rev. Wesley Ely, pastor of Memorial A.M.E. Zion Church, participated in these last rites. [72] Bishop Alexander Walters, Dr. Mason, and ministers of the Western New York Conference, promoted principally by J. W. Thompson, Zion's foremost laymen in Rochester of that day, steered the Rochester community in building and dedicating the Douglass Monument. Unveiling ceremonies took place at Douglass Memorial Park, June 9, 1895, with a host of outstanding persons throughout the nation

71. J. W. Thompson, *An Authentic History of the Douglass Monument*, pp.97-98.
72. *Ibid.*, pp.17-20, 28-34.

and state taking part. It was led by Governor Theodore Roosevelt, senators, congressmen, the Mayor of Rochester, the Douglass family, Susan B. Anthony, and others. [73]

Sojourner Truth: Sojourner Truth was born a slave in Ulster County, New York, about 1797, and named Isabella. Her mother was the third and last wife of an African called Baumfree, whose first two wives had been sold away from him. Elizabeth Baumfree, familiarly known as Mau-Mau Bett, had been the mother of ten or twelve boys and girls, "all but two of whom had been sold away to other plantations. Peter, age three years . . . and Isabella, a spindly, angular-boned, broad-faced, misty-eyed but imperious creature of five". . . . Whenever Mau-Mau-Bett looked at those two reminders of the others who have been taken from her, a dreadful horror convulsed her body and soul. "When will these be gone also! Alas! what will there be to look forward to in that day when Nature's course has run, and children come no more?" Isabella's mother apparently

> possessed the inevitable optimism of her race, was a perpetual moralist, believed that the God of the slave and the God of the master were one and the same—and that he was good—and finally she was endowed with an unusual intuitive sense. From her, the daughter to whom we have referred will inherit a religious zeal bordering on fanaticism, an extraordinary piety, a sense of deep devotion, and an uncanny prescience. Because of this inheritance, her journey through life will be marked with zealousness, a sublime courage, unusual experiences—and achievements far beyond anything her formal development would lead anyone to expect. [74]

As a young girl, Isabella "had experienced the ignominy of being sold three times." [75] When she was 10 years old, on account of her mistress' ill-will, she became the victim of various hardships.

> Her life was one indignity after another. The worst mishap came one Sunday morning when she received instructions to go to the barn. To her horror, when she arrived there she met her master all ready with a bundle of rods, bound together with cord, to whip her. . . . He tied her hands before her, then he proceeded to whipping. It is unthinkable that an able-bodied man would unmercifully whip a ten-year-old child for any reason, but whip her Nealy did until deep gashes were cut into her flesh, and the blood streamed from the wounds to the ground below All her life, she would carry the scars of this beating with her as a remembrance of the occasion. [76]

Isabella was a woman in her late twenties. She had been patiently waiting for July 4, 1827, when according to a law passed in 1817, she would be a free woman in New York State. Two years later she drifted into New York City, and one of the first things she did after obtaining employment was to join the church. At first she attended the class for Negroes in John Street Methodist Church, but later she transferred to the A.M.E. Zion Church on Church and Leonard Street. [77] Here, she wrote her name into fame.

> During one of the services, she walked to the altar in the front of the church, and there, while kneeling in prayer, she extended her hand to another who prayed beside her. For no reason that she could comprehend she gave a start when she grasped the woman's hand. There was something strikingly strange and yet familiar about that person whose handclasp

73. *Ibid.*, pp.120-155.
74. Arthur Huff Fauset, *Sojourner Truth, God's Faithful Pilgrim*, pp.2-3.
75. Ottley, *New World A-Coming, op. cit.*, p.16.
76. Fauset, *Sojourner Truth*, pp.12-13.
77. *Ibid.*, pp.33, 64.

symbolized the "speaking promise" of spiritual kinship.

That the hand of a woman should be bony and hard ought not to seem queer when its possessor was a Negro, but nevertheless Isabella was shocked by the mere touch. She looked up into the other woman's face. That face seemed curiously familiar also. It bore a resemblance to someone she had known very intimately.

Where, where have I seen you before, she mused to herself. She searched her mind but the answer was not there. Over and over she conjured up the woman's image, striving desperately to re-establish the bond that would bring back the association which she was confident once existed between them. But it was no use; she always just missed forming the connection. Days passed, and eventually the memory of the woman grew dim.

A while later, Isabella's sister Sophia also came to New York City to live. She sought out Isabella, who had difficulty in recognizing her in her resplendent garments. They felicitated each other on the renewal of their lives together, and then Sophia said, "I have another surprise for you."

"And what is the surprise?" asked Isabella, not entirely recovered from the shock of her sister's visit.

Your brother Michel is in the city."

"Michel!" Isabella gasped. She could not believe her ears. "You don't mean the one that Mau-Mau used to tell us about in the sleigh?" "That very one," her sister replied, and she took Isabella with her to find him.

When they reached Michel, his joy over meeting Isabella whom he had never seen before was softened by distressing news which he had to impart to his sisters. "If only you had come a little sooner," he said to Isabella. "Why?" she asked. "Then you would have met Nancy also, your sister who was shut up with me in the sleigh." "Why, where is Nancy?" inquired Isabella. "Dead," was her brother's response. "She died just a few months ago."

While the three commiserated together and bemoaned the lost sister, Michel imparted bits of information regarding Nancy. He described her manner, her dress, her appearance in general. Then he added that she formerly attended Zion Church.

"Lord God have mercy!" thought Isabella. "Why," she said, "she's the woman I've been trying to remember ever since we made the 'speaking promise' at the altar. Thank God, I did see her. That was Nancy. I have seen my sister Nancy; and it was Mau-Mau's picture written all over her face that made me know her." The two sisters and brother wept together silently. [78]

After traveling in the vicinity and passing through intensely hectic experiences, she said God had given her a new name on the road, since she was a journeying woman and her employment was proclaiming truth. She came to a religious meeting one night, and "rose suddenly and announced herself to be *'Sojourner Truth.'* The Lord had commanded her, she said, to travel throughout the land to declare Truth! She became one of the most effective antislavery speakers, and later, she took a part in the movement for women's suffrage." [79]

One of the climactic moments of her career took place at an anti-slavery convention in Salem, Ohio. After Frederick Douglass had been meeting John Brown, he became convinced that "slavery could only be destroyed by bloodshed," and was expressing this sentiment in a speech when he was, states Douglass himself, "sharply interrupted by my good old friend Sojourner Truth

78. *Ibid.,* pp.64-66.
79. Ottley, *New World A-Coming*, p.16.

FREDERICK DOUGLASS

1821 - 1895

His incomparable talents were discovered in
the New Bedford A.M.E. Zion Church
where he landed after his escape from
slavery. He was licensed to preach in Second
Street A.M.E. Zion Church, New Bedford
and held membership in Second Street
Church and Favor Street (Memorial) A.M.E.
Zion Church, Rochester, N.Y.

BISHOP JERMAIN WESLEY LOGUEN

1813 - 1872

Heroic conductor of the Underground
Railroad. Mighty originator of the first
"open city" for runaway slaves at Syracuse,
N.Y. Founder of A.M.E. Zion Churches in
Central N.Y. and Loguen Temple,
Knoxville, Tenn.

with the question, 'Frederick, is God dead?' 'No,' I answered, 'and because God
is not dead slavery can only end in blood.' " She was for nonresistance, and was
shocked by his sanguinary doctrine, "but she too became an advocate of the
sword, when the war for the maintenance of the Union was declared." [80]

Sojourner Truth was one of the greatest inspirations to her race, as she
preached freedom and pleaded the cause of justice for all. After a life well spent
in the service of mankind, she died at Battle Creek, Michigan on November 26,
1883, where she had lived during her last days.

80. Douglass, *Life and Times, op. cit.*, pp.342-343.

SOJOURNER TRUTH

The slave, Isabella, discovered a part of her family that she had never seen, at the altar of Mother Zion Church which she had joined. She went on to wage an indomitable fight for the freedom of her race throughout the country.

Harriet Tubman: "The Moses of her People" is the title given this, the bravest and most sagacious conductor of the Underground Railroad. In 1821 she was born a slave on the Eastern Shore of Maryland, in Dorchester County, as Harriet Ross; inheriting her first name from her mother, Harriet Green, and her surname from her father, Benjamin Ross, although as a slave she was not entitled to a legal name upon birth. [81] She never had a day of schooling. "She was suddenly ripped out of infancy and placed into slave labor. At five she knew what it was to have a mistress, to keep house, to take care of a baby, to labor day and night, and to feel all the callous injury that some indifferent white souls in the South of that time leveled upon their fellow humans." [82] By the time Harriet was 12 or 13, she was laboring in the field. During this time, she became the victim of her master's rage, who caught up a two-pound counter weight and hurled it toward the doorway. The block of iron struck her a stunning blow and she fell unconscious to the floor. When she regained consciousness, she took up prayer. She prayed sincerely for change. She however suffered a skull injury from the impact of that blow, causing a pressure upon her brain, from which she would suffer until death. It caused occasional sleepy spells, "but that brain which seemed so dull was full of busy thoughts, and her life problem was already trying to work itself out" at this early age. [83]

While working as a field hand in 1844, she married John Tubman, a free Negro whom she loved deeply; but he never understood her deep desire to be free. In 1849, she ran away, accompanied by two brothers. Her brothers feared capture and returned soon after they set out, "but Harriet went on, and finally arrived in Pennsylvania. It was morning when she reached freedom, and she stood on a hill and looked all about her. That was an epochal moment in the history of the Negro people." [84]

Immediately after Harriet arrived on free soil she determined to aid her family and as many of her people as possible to flee from the horrors of the

81. Earl Conrad, *Harriet Tubman*, p.7.
82. *Ibid.*, pp.7-8.
83. Sarah Bradford, *Harriet, The Moses of Her People*, p.15.
84. Conrad, *Harriet Tubman*, p.9.

slave country. "I had crossed the line of which I had so long been dreaming," she said later. "I was free but there was no one to welcome me in the land of freedom. I was a stranger in a strange land, and my home after all was down in the old cabin quarters, with the old folks and my brothers and sisters. But to this solemn resolution I came. I was free, and they would be free also. I would make a home for them in the North, and the Lord helping me, I would bring them all there." [85]

"When Harriet made her escape, the Underground Railroad was fairly well organized, both in the East and the Middle West, and was effective enough to harass the slave owners. The system had received its name from the modern industrial invention, the railroad, with its locomotives and trains, its stations and terminals." The Railroad was a network of secret routes in the Northern free states and Canada. Harriet and hundreds like her made dangerous journeys into the South, and led thousands of Negroes to freedom.

It has been estimated that during the 1850's, the period in which Harriet Tubman functioned, at least five hundred Negroes were engaged annually in going back and forth between the Northern and Southern states! Indeed, so vast did these operations become, that about 75,000 Negroes succeeded in reaching northern freedom during the existence of the Railroad. Previous to 1850, Harriet had to pilot her groups only as far as such free states as Pennsylvania and New Jersey. But in 1850, with the passage of the Fugitive Slave Law which compelled northern authorities to return fugitives to their masters, it became necessary for slaves to seek refuge in Canada. [86]

"General Tubman," as she was sometimes called, caused enraged slave-holders to offer a reward of $40,000 for her capture.

Secrecy and ingenuity characterized these operations, for agents of the slave-owners prowled everywhere. . . . Nevertheless, thousands of slaves made their escape to freedom, helped along by Negro and white persons. Runaways hid by day and traveled by night, often guided by the North Star. Sometimes it was necessary for them to hide for weeks in the woods, waiting for friendly voices to raise the signal,

Steal away, steal away,
Steal away to Jesus . . . . [87]

The Underground Railroad took concrete form in New York with the organization of the Committee of Vigilance, at a meeting held in the A.M.E. Zion Church. "It became one of the most fearless of the antislavery groups, and carried on the serious business of spiriting runaway slaves from place to place along the Underground route. Its members were called 'practical abolitionists.' Fugitives were referred to as 'parcels,' intermediary stops as 'stations,' and the committee's agents as 'conductors.' " Not only was Mother Zion Church an Underground Railroad station, but "runaways were concealed in such 'stations' as the basement of Plymouth Church, Brooklyn, and its pastor, Henry Ward Beecher, was a 'conductor.' In this manner . . . the best blood of the South drifted this way in search of freedom." [88]

Harriet had several important assistants in Philadelphia, which was one of the big "terminals." Chief among these was William Still. . . . He was head of the local Vigilance Committee which forwarded slaves to New York City. In New York, persons like David Ruggles and Oliver Johnson helped to steer

85. *Ibid.*, p.11.
86. *Ibid.*, p.12.
87. Ottley, *New World A-Coming, op. cit.,* pp.12-13.
88. *Ibid.*, p.13.

them on to Albany. From Albany, Harriet steered her charges to the home of Gerrit Smith, wealthy philanthropist and reformer who lived in Petersboro, New York. From there they were steered on to Syracuse. In Syracuse, Harriet found shelter at the home of Jermain W. Loguen a former slave (then a prominent A.M.E. Zion minister). Loguen was in favor of using stern methods against the slave power. He forwarded Harriet's bands on to Auburn, a small town nearby, which was an Abolitionist and woman-suffrage center, and in which lived Senator William H. Seward, who aspired to the Presidency, and was Secretary of State in Lincoln's Cabinet. Seward, who had coined the famous "irrepressible conflict" phrase, entered rescue work to the extent of housing Harriet's parties and in 1857 he sold her some property on very reasonable terms, and made it possible for her to settle her parents in that town. (89)

Auburn is where Harriet made her permanent home, and started a station of relief for the destitute, the lonely, and the aged. "From Auburn, Harriet's bands were delivered to Rochester, where Frederick Douglass and the woman's suffrage leader, Susan B. Anthony, housed the slaves, and paved the way for the last 'jump' to Canada." (90) In Rochester, sometimes Harriet and her slave collections took shelter inside the A.M.E. Zion Church at Spring and Favor Streets. Fugitives by the score hid in its pews. "Here also was her spiritual home while in Rochester." (91)

Harriet was always deeply religious. She joined the A.M.E. Zion Church in Auburn and devoutly worshipped there until the end of her days. Prior to Emancipation, she had courageously led 316 slaves successfully to freedom, so that she could glibly boast: "I never ditched my train, and I never lost a passenger."

By 1858 Harriet was known in progressive circles in England, Ireland, Scotland, Canada, Liberia, and South America, and she received funds from Canada and Great Britain to continue her work. In America a $40,000 ransom was on her head. This was the year John Brown, who "had long known of Harriet's work, but had never met her, greeted her in the following way when he first set eyes on her: 'The first I see is General Tubman, the second is General Tubman, and the third is General Tubman.' The name together with 'Moses' remained with her permanently." (92) Harriet Tubman's motto was "Keep Going." She was accustomed to saying to the slaves when she led them to rescue; "Children if you are tired, keep going; if you are scared, keep going; if you are hungry, keep going; if you want a taste of freedom, keep going."

Many years later, Douglass wrote to the "Moses of her people: Most that I have done has been in public, and I have received much encouragement. . . . You on the other hand have labored in a private way. . . . I have had the applause of the crowd, ... While the most that you have done has been witnessed by a few trembling, scared and footsore bondsmen. . . . The midnight sky and the silent stars have been the witnesses of your devotion to freedom and of your heroism." (93)

Harriet grew old and the 1880's and 1890's were hard years for her. Her second husband (Davis), her parents, and her old friends had passed away. However, she was still extremely active. She took an active part in the growth of

89. Earl Conrad, *Harriet Tubman, Negro Soldier and Abolitionist*, pp.15-16.
90. *Ibid.*, p.16.
91. Conrad, *Harriet Tubman, op. cit.*, p.61.
92. Conrad, *Harriet Tubman, Negro Soldier. . .*, p.23.
93. Foner, *The Life and Writing of Frederick Douglass, op. cit.*, Vol. II, p.47.

the Western New York Conference of the A.M.E. Zion Church, fought for her pension and eventually established the Home for the Aged and Indigent. She also helped to build her local church (now Thompson Memorial), addressed public meetings, and worked with the women suffragists of Auburn and the central New York region, appearing on the same platforms with its leaders, Elizabeth Cady Stanton and Susan B. Anthony, both of whom greatly admired and respected her. (94) "One of the last acts of Harriet's life was the purchase of twenty-five acres adjacent to her home." This property was deeded in her lifetime to the A.M.E. Zion Church for an old peoples' home. Harriet had become a legendary figure.

> Although awarded very late, honors were now hers. Many visitors came from all parts of the United States to meet her; from Queen Victoria she received a medal, a silk shawl, a letter congratulating her on her work for the Negro people and an invitation to come to Great Britain. Harriet was unable to go abroad, but all this made her constant "copy" for feature writers who found abundant drama in the story of her life. (95)

Thus the world still beholds

> the stupid little Negro girl, the future deliverer of hundreds of her people; the spy and scout of the Union armies; the devoted hospital nurse; the protector of hunted fugitives; the eloquent speaker in public meetings; the cunning eluder of pursuing man-hunters; the heaven guided pioneer through dangers seen and unseen; in short, as she has well been called, "The Moses of her People." (96)

Harriet died in her home at Auburn, March 10, 1913. One year after her death, the people of Auburn, N.Y., honored their great townswoman and dedicated a bronze tablet to her.

> In June, 1914, a large mass meeting was held in the town auditorium. The Mayor issued a proclamation calling for all flags on public buildings and private homes to fly at half-mast. The meeting was attended by thousands of people, Negro and white, who heard Booker T. Washington and other prominent people pay homage to Harriet and her contribution to America and to the Negro people. . . . The bronze plaque of Harriet Tubman which was then placed on the [Cayuga] County Court House entrance remains there to do everlasting honor to one of the greatest of American women. (97)

Forty years after her death, April 30, 1953, the citizens of Auburn assembled once again in large numbers, for the dedication of Harriet's Home house on South Street, which had been rebuilt and furnished by the A.M.E. Zion Church, at a cost of $30,000, led principally by Bishop W. J. Walls and the conferences of the First and Second Episcopal Districts; from 1944-1953, namely, New York, Western New York, New England, Allegheny, and Western North Carolina Conferences. People from all walks of life assembled to pay homage to this noble soldier of the cross, led by the Board of Bishops, general officers, General Missionary Society officers and members of the A.M.E. Zion Church, with Rev. and Mrs. Arthur E. May, co-directors of the Harriet Tubman Home. Mrs. Irene McCoy Gaines, president of the National Federation of Colored Women Clubs, of Chicago, guest speaker, Mrs. Howard (Sue Bailey) Thurman the outstanding leaders of Auburn, including Mayor Nelson, State Senator George Metcalf, and other statesmen. The grand parade to the Court

94. *Ibid.*, pp.44-45; Conrad, *Harriet Tubman, Negro Soldier. . .*, p.97
95. *Ibid.*, p.46.
96. Bradford, *op. cit.*, p.14.
97. Conrad, *Harriet Tubman, Negro Soldier. . .*, p.47.

HARRIET TUBMAN, Famous Underground Railroad Heroine.

PLAQUE AT ENTRANCE OF CAYUGA COUNTY COURT HOUSE, AUBURN, N.Y.
Unveiled in June, 1914. Booker T. Washington was leading speaker of Unveiling
Ceremonies.

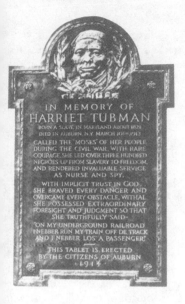

In 1953, Rev. Arthur E. May,
First Superintendent of the
restored Harriet Tubman Home, inspects an
oil painting of Harriet Tubman, by Falstat
Harris, presented at Dedication Ceremony.

Home of Harriet Tubman, owned and operated by the A.M.E. Zion Church. Rebuilt in
1952. Dedicated April 30, 1953. The famous landmark in the days of the Underground
Railroad. It is located near Auburn City line on South Street.

House ceremonies afterwards was led by the Auburn High School Band. [98]

Other persons who spoke at annual pilgrimages following the dedication of the home were Mrs. Harper Sibley, Mrs. Ruth Whitehead Whaley and Dr. Howard Thurman.

Jermain Wesley Loguen: The great "Underground Railroad King" attained this name through his daring escape to freedom and his masterly war on slavery. "There are few men whose history is so marked with stirring incidents, instructive lessons and encouraging examples as Loguen's." Here are the peculiarities of his childhood, his daring escape from bondage, the perils and hardships he endured in his passage to freedom, and the acts of subsequent manhood, which honorably connected his name with the moral and political causes for more than 20 years before Emancipation. [99]

Loguen was born in 1813. His mother was a pure African, who had passed through the intensest indignities and brutal treatment during slavery. [100] He escaped to the North; Canada and New York, from Tennessee, after passing through great trauma. He secured his only formal training at Oneida Institute. His "mistress had the temerity to write, offering to accept one thousand dollars to cancel his obligation to her, but she received only a magnificently indignant letter in reply. Long ago, when still a slave, he had scorned self-redemption, vowing that he would never pay for what was his birthright, and he was severely critical of others who used that resort particularly after they had made good their escape." [101] In carving his way to freedom, he soon identified himself with the A.M.E. Zion Church in the western and central part of the Empire State. Loguen was not only the founder of three or four of our small societies in Central New York, but he built the congregation and the church, then known as "the Abolition Church," at Syracuse, N.Y., where he made his fame as an abolitionist. [102]

Loguen was one of the principal Underground Railroad conductors, with headquarters at Syracuse.

> .... When eighteen or nineteen years of age—a slave—he formed this resolution: "I will not be a slave: henceforth I live to escape or perish; and now come death or freedom." Shortly after this noble resolution he whipped, subdued and conquered his master, and from that day to the day of his escape from slavery he was virtually his own master, and in a short time, he with two other young men escaped to Canada. . . . In a letter written to Mr. Douglass from Syracuse in 1856, he gives the following description of his arrival in Hamilton, Canada:
>
> Twenty-one years ago—the very winter I left my chains in Tennessee—I stood on this spot, penniless, ragged, lonely, nameless, helpless, hungry and forlorn—a pitiable wanderer, without a friend or shelter, or place to lay my head. I had broken from the sunny South and fought a passage through storms and tempest which made the forests crash and the mountains moan. . . . There I stood, a boy twenty-one years of age, the tempest howling over my head, and my toes touching the snow beneath my worn-out shoes, knowing nobody and nobody knowing me." There stood a lonely brave young man, the future Underground Railroad king, a future elder and Bishop of the A.M.E. Zion Church. . . . When about twenty-four

98. *The Citizens-Adertiser*, Auburn, N.Y., May 1, 1953.
99. *The Weekly Anglo-African*, Nov. 24, 1860.
100. Eber M. Pettit, *Sketches in the History of the Underground Railroad*, pp.53-54.
101. Bardolph, *The Negro Vanguard*, p.69.
102. Loguen, *op. cit.*, pp.372-374.

years of age, this young man, who was to do more towards aiding fugitive slaves to escape to Canada than any other one man, left Canada and entered these United States; Rochester, Utica, Ithaca, Bath, and Syracuse where he could better serve his Church and his people. [It was through his labors and self-sacrificing devotion in the western part of New York] that our Zion was brought and kept to the front as the leading anti-slavery church of the country. (103)

Loguen and Frederick Douglass were intimate friends. "Douglass' son married his daughter, and they both had considerable means and vied with each other in giving the young people a start in life." Loguen's heart was in emancipation of his race people. He was an abler anti-slavery lecturer than gospel preacher, though very devout and sincere in his religious activities. "He was elected bishop in 1864, but discovering that he was likely to be sent to Southern work, and thinking it too early for a fugitive to return to that land, he resigned." In 1868, he was brought forward again, and re-elected a bishop in the A.M.E. Zion Church, and assigned to the Fifth District, including the Allegheny and Kentucky Conferences and adjacent mission fields, for a two-year period. After this, he was to change with Bishop Jones and go to the Second District, including Genesee and the Philadelphia and Baltimore Conferences. He was re-elected at the 1872 General Conference, "and assigned to the Pacific coast, which appointment he did not long survive. We do not think he reached his field of labor." (104)

The world can never forget the famous Jerry Rescue, in which Loguen became prominent in his role of spiriting a slave into Canada, away from the marshal who arrested him.

Rev. J. W. Loguen, and several others, were arrested and taken to Albany, where they were tried for rescuing the slave, but the jury failed to agree upon a verdict. They were then sent for trial to Canandaigua, with the same result, and the prosecution was finally abandoned. For more than a year the Jerry rescue trials kept the State in great excitement, but no verdict was obtained against any one. The Fugitive Slave Law was brought into contempt, and Northern dough-faces were taught a salutary lesson. . . .The operations of the Underground Railroad were not suspended nor in the least disturbed by the efforts of the President to enforce the Fugitive Slave Law in Syracuse, in illustration of which fact I quote from a Syracuse paper soon after, the following card:

"TO THE FRIENDS OF THE FUGITIVES FROM SLAVERY."

"The members of the Fugitive Aid Society find it no longer convenient nor necessary to keep up their organization. The labor of sheltering those who flee from tyranny, providing for their immediate wants, and helping them to find safe homes in this country and in Canada, must needs devolve, as it always has devolved, upon a very few individuals. Hitherto, since 1850, it has been done for the most part, by Rev. J. W. Loguen. He, having been a slave and a fugitive himself, knows best how to provide for that class of sufferers, and to guard against imposition. Mr. Loguen has agreed to devote himself wholly to this humane work, and to depend for the support of himself and family, as well as the maintenance of this depot on the Underground Railroad, upon what the benevolent and friendly may give.

"We, therefore, hereby, request that all fugitives from slavery, coming this way, may be directed to him; and that all clothing or provisions

103. Biddle, A.M.E. Zion Quarterly Review, op. cit., pp.78-79, April 1898.
104. Hood, One Hundred Years, pp.180-181.

contributed may be sent to his house, or such places as he may designate.

"Mr. Loguen will make semi-annual reports of his receipts of money, clothes or provisions, and of the number of fugitives taken care of and provided for by him, and he will submit his accounts at any time to the inspection of any persons who are interested in the success of the Underground Railroad.

SAMUEL J. MAY,
JAMES FULLER,
JOSEPH A. ALLEN,
LUCIUS J. COMSBEE,
WILLIAM E. ABBOTT,
HOSEA B. KNIGHT" [105]

"That notice only affected the line through Syracuse." [106] The Underground Railroad became more public and more successful after the noted Dred Scott Decision, and the passage of the fugitive slave law. This resulted in making Syracuse the first "open city" for fugitive slaves, and the number grew to be over 400 cities before emancipation. A fugitive could not be seized in any one of these cities or towns, and returned to slavery, according to law. Thus the thirteenth bishop of the African Methodist Episcopal Zion Church was a choice of the people to serve in this high place of the church, for he had given his heart and soul in helping to free his race people.

John Jamison Moore: Bishop Moore had always taken an active part in contending for the rights of his people. His entire life is a story of thrilling interest. He was born a slave, and his freedom was procured through the bravery of his mother who, having been kidnapped, ran away from her master and carried her child with her. It was indeed a heroic flight.

She traveled till her shoes fell from her feet—till she was so foot-sore that she might have been tracked by the blood she left upon the ground. She stripped her clothing from her body and wrapped it around her boy, to keep him from freezing. A mother's love! It is the same mighty passion the world over. . . . But young Moore, though free, could not get any education. He was not allowed to look inside a school. So he resolved, like a wise youth, to educate himself; and he used to prosecute his studies by firelight. [107]

"In his youthful days he used to think with rapture of England, the Negro's friend, and when he heard it said that no bondsman could exist on British soil, he experienced an intense longing to breathe the aid and touch the soil of this great and free country." He later made that trip to England, pleading the cause of 4,000,000 freed slaves, and representing a body which had grown to a membership of 220,000 and an additional 100,000 Sunday school scholars. [108]

While pastoring Big Wesley Church, Philadelphia, in 1848, Moore was described as "one of the most eloquent divines of the present day; endowed, in a high degree, with common sense, extraordinary enlarged benevolence, elevated in his views of enlightened Christianity and religious duties; gifted with a sound education himself, and thirsting for more; he expresses the subject of moral virtue, intellectual culture of the mind, with education in general, to his people, with a dignity and zeal almost unsurpassed." [109]

105. Pettit, *Sketches in the History of the Underground Railroad,* pp.53-54.
106. *Ibid.,* p.55.
107. Moore, *History of the A.M.E. Zion Church,* pp.371-372.
108. *Ibid.*
109. *A Call Upon the Church for Progressive Action.*

While pastoring in San Francisco in the 1850's and early 1860's before emancipation, he was engaged five years in teaching school, during which time he represented a constituency of that city and county in three state conventions called for the purpose of securing the abolishment of the Black Laws, which disqualified Negroes to bear testimony against whites in criminal cases. He also took part in the agitation for the appropriation of school funds for Negro children, and became a pioneer in establishing the public school system for our race in the state. During his busy life of religious labor, Bishop Moore encountered many perils; he was three times shipwrecked at sea, and he was among hostile Indian tribes while the bullets were flying, but he came out of all mercifully preserved for further works, [110] and labored for the church and race until his death December 9, 1893.

Joseph P. Thompson: Another hard worker for freedom for his people was Bishop Joseph P. Thompson. He was born in slavery, at Winchester, Va., December 29, 1818. He ran away from his master while yet a youth, and found a home with a kind-hearted man in Pennsylvania. He was brought up in a good family, under moral and religious influences, and encouraged to improve all the advantages that could be afforded him for his future welfare. Thompson studied hard, and read theology under the direction of Rev. Dr. Mills of Auburn Theological Seminary, Auburn N.Y., "a privilege which he has often mentioned to his friends with indelible sentiment of gratitude." He was licensed to preach in 1839, "and attracted much attention and drew large crowds to hear him. His sermons were delivered with animation and zeal." Thompson also graduated from the University of Medicine in Philadelphia, and was both a competent physician and preacher. He served almost all the churches in Zion connection along the Hudson, and was three times pastor of Zion (Mother Zion) Church in New York City. [111]

Before Thompson settled in Newburgh, N.Y., and worked ardently for the betterment of the Negroes in that community, he was passionately engaged in the work of the Underground Railroad. At one time, he was one of the chief superintendents. "It is related of him that his method of transportation was to receive the runaway slaves by pre-arranged orders from his father-in-law, Mr. S. Gilchrist, of Williamsport, Pennsylvania; then take them to Harrisburg, Pa., then walk by night 130 miles to the home of Jermain W. Loguen in Syracuse." [112]

Thompson was one of the prime organizers of The African Civilization Society, which was concerned with "the Christianization of Africa, and of the descendants of African ancestors in any portion of the earth. . . .Also the destruction of African Slave trade, by the introduction of lawful commerce and trade into Africa: the promotion of products there, whereby the natives may become industrious producers as well as consumers of articles of commerce: and generally the elevation of the condition of the colored population of our own country, and of other lands." [113] He declared in an address before this group in 1861:

110. Moore, *History, op. cit.,* p.370.
111. John H. Nutt, *Newburgh, Her Institutions, Industries and Leading Citizens,* p.129; Hood, *One Hundred Years,* pp.188-191.
112. Biddle, *A.M.E. Zion Quarterly Review, op. cit.,* p.79.
113. Constitution of the African Civilization Society, Address delivered by Joseph P. Thompson, Annual Meeting, May 19, 1861; p.1. Thompson, Annual Meeting, May 19, 1861.

BISHOP JOHN JAMISON MOORE

1804 - 1893

Marvelous preacher, educator and outstanding hero of freedom. A founder of the first black school on the West Coast in San Francisco.

Go, that with your own hands you may give the death blow to slavery and the slave-trade. And because in industrial and educational appliances, in wealth, and science and art, they are poor and we are rich, they are weak and we are strong, therefore we will help them in a work whose toil shall be theirs, and theirs its honor and reward.

Oh, *Africa*! whose symbol hath been the chain and the scourge, whose soil hath been the hunting-ground of every conqueror, whose coasts the prey of every pirate, whose tribute to the wealth and civilization of other lands hath been the tears and blood of thy sons, lift up thyself at length, stretch out thy hands unto God who striketh thy shackles from thee, saying, "I will bring thy seed from the East, and gather thee from the West." The daughters of Jerusalem have scorned thee because thou art black—because the sun hath looked upon thee; thy mother's children were angry with thee, they made thee keeper of the vineyards—their fieldhand, their slave. But lo the king hath looked upon thee, and the day of thy deliverance is at hand. Thy winter is past, the rain is over and gone: the flowers appear on the earth, the time of the singing of birds is come. There is hope for thee, poor, despised, down-trodden daughter of the sun. Lift up thyself; stretch forth thy hands,

BISHOP JOSEPH PASCAL THOMPSON

1818 - 1894

Strong Abolition leader, scholarly preacher
and medical doctor. He was three times
pastor of Mother Zion Church.

reclaim thine own. "Say to the North give up; and to the South, keep not
back; bring my sons from far, and my daughters from the ends of the
earth." [114]

By precept and example he taught and encouraged his people, and was to
them a faithful friend. His faithful and efficient services did not go unrewarded;
he was consecrated to the bishopric in Louisville, Ky., July, 1876. This mark of
confidence and esteem on the part of his denomination at once commended him
to the attention and respect of all other sects and creeds, and he became one of
the most popular and honored men in the ministry of his day. Officials at
Washington frequently conferred with him on public measures, especially on
affairs in the South. [115]

William Howard Day: William Howard Day, "ripe scholar, strong abolitionist, eloquent race leader, was born in New York City, October 16, 1825. . . . He
was one of the most cultured men of our race, having graduated in 1847 from
Oberlin College. [116] Delany described him, while he was in Cleveland
preparing for the Bar, as "perhaps, the most eloquent young gentleman of his
age in the United States." [117] He was a notable minister of the A.M.E. Zion
Church while he was one of the famous leaders of the race group. He was elected
general secretary of the A.M.E. Zion Church at the General Conference in 1876;

114. *Ibid.*
115. Nutt, *Newburgh . . ., op. cit.;* Hood, *One Hundred Years.*
116. B. F. Wheeler, *Cullings from Zion's Poets,* p.117.
117. Martin Robison Delany, *The Condition, Elevation, Emigration and Destiny of the
Colored People,* p.134.

after an interval of twelve years, he was re-elected in 1892, and served until his death, March 13, 1901.

Day became prominent in race affairs when the delegates of the National Convention of Colored Freemen assembled in Cleveland, Ohio, in 1848, and elected Frederick Douglass president, and William H. Day secretary. He was very active in this Convention in subsequent years. In 1853, when the Convention met at Rochester, he and Frederick Douglass were elected vice-presidents. [118]

As the problems of the 1850's made the Negro American even more uncertain of the future, it was emigration that came to hold a very substantial influence on the minds of many strong convention men. It attracted the attention of Henry Highland Garnet, Martin R. Delany, William Howard Day, James Theodore Holly, and many others in greater or lesser degree as the dark days of the Kansas Nebraska Act, the Dred Scott Decision, and the uncertain stance of the Republican party on slavery foretold troublous times ahead. Whether they chose to remain in America, as most blacks did, or whether they chose to cast their lot beyond the borders, as a very vocal minority wished, it was obvious to most in the late 1850's that the land of promise was still far in the distance. [119]

Day, in the late 1850's, received an invitation from Rev. William King, "(the Clayton of Mrs. Stowe's work, *Dred)*, to go to England, Ireland, and Scotland, to secure the means to erect a church and four schoolhouses in the Elgin settlement at Buxton, in Canada, which Horace Greeley declared was the 'greatest problem in social science that had been wrought out on this continent.' Rev. King and Professor Day raised £7,000, or $35,000, for the purpose." While in England, Day was more directly called to the pulpit, and occupied a large portion of three years in preaching, acting for months as stated pastor of a congregation in England. When he returned from England, he was requested to serve Zion Church as editor of the *Zion's Standard and Weekly Review*. After the Virginia Conference was established, he was ordained deacon and elder by Bishop Joseph J. Clinton, in 1866. [120]

In Harrisburg, Pa., his last residence, he became president of the School Board of Control, and served the city effectively. He not only held the chairmanship of that board, he was the only black member of the board in his day. A high school was later built and named in his honor, The William Howard Day High School. In his last report as General Secretary to the 1900 General Conference, he expressed gratitude to God and the church. In 1898, after he had completed 50 years of public service, the bishops and other devoted friends tendered him a testimonial for his service to mankind as eloquent spokesman, instructive lecturer, strong abolitionist, forceful preacher, and able writer. [121]

Eliza Ann Gardner: Eliza Ann Gardner, a leading member of our first Boston church (Columbus Avenue Church), was a staunch anti-slavery leader, born in 1831, and one of the most unusual personalities of the race in the country. She was a familiar worker in the abolition movement, and shared the platform with William Lloyd Garrison, Wendell Phillips, and prominent governors and statesmen of Massachusetts and New England. Before her death in 1922, she related many of her personal experiences to the writer in his travels to Boston as a boy evangelist. She spoke not only of helping to build an

118. Bell, *Proceedings of the National Conventions, op. cit.,* pp.3, 6.
119. *Ibid.,* p.iii.
120. Hood, *One Hundred Years,* pp.320-321.
121. Wheeler, *Cullings from Zion's Poets, op. cit.; Minutes,* Twenty-First Quadrennial Session, 1900, p.176. Twenty-First Quadrennial Session, p.176.

ELIZA ANN GARDNER

Abolitionist and major leader among women of New England. Worked with William Lloyd Garrison, Frederick Douglass, Wendell Phillips and Charles Sumner. A founder of the A.M.E. Zion Missionary Movement and raised funds which sent Andrew Cartwright to Africa. She was a pioneer Vice-president of the Woman's Home and Foreign Missionary Society.

independent race church and extend its missionary borders, but of the war the people of that New England area had to wage against slavery, and aid to the oppressed, including her association with William Wells Brown, Frederick Douglass, and a number of other outstanding leaders, black and white. Miss Gardner was a blood kinswoman of Dr. W. E. B. DuBois, who told the writer that she introduced him to J. C. Price.

Catherine Harris: A devout member of our Society in Jamestown, N.Y., (Blackwell Chapel), she used her home as an Underground Railroad Station. Her basement was a congenial hiding place. The home today is the parsonage of the A.M.E. Zion Church, and marked by New York State as a memorial of Underground Railroad history.

These noble names mentioned are just a few of the daring men and women of the African Methodist Episcopal Zion Church who passed through hazardous turmoil, took great risks, and fought with all that was in them to eliminate slavery from the face of the earth.

Bishop Joseph J. Clinton and other Zion leaders suffered in jail for freedom prior to Emancipation. J. Harvey Anderson gives the following reason and account of one such incident:

The question is frequently asked, "Why did the A.M.E. Zion Church make such rapid progress in the South following the success of Federal arms and the Emancipation?" The answer to this question is to be found in the A.M.E. Zion Book of Discipline, incorporated in its first issue of 1820, and reads as follows: "*Of Slavery.* We will not receive any person into our societies who is a slaveholder. Any one who is now a member and holds a slave or slaves, and refuses to emancipate them after notice is given to such member by the pastor in charge, shall be excluded."

This pronounced position of the A.M.E. Zion Church upon the question of slavery, and which prevented her permanent establishment beyond "the Mason and Dixon Line" until 1862-63, was circulated throughout the South three decades prior to 1860, and when the success of Federal arms made way for her entrance into the South, the people knowing of her bold and pronounced liberty sentiments, for over forty years, flocked to her standard, as it was unfurled by Bishop J. J. Clinton, amidst shot and shell, fire and smoke, and gleam of sabre and shout of war.

The Southern Methodist Church in her entirety, preached, "Servants, obey in all things, your masters," the Northern Methodist Church rang clear in its pronouncements against slavery and later joined the war against it. The A.M.E. Zion Church from her inceptive organization, in her polity and pulpit insisted upon the emancipation, unconditionally of the American slave. It was this that alarmed the people of Alexandria, Virginia, and caused them to place Bishop Clinton and his coadjutors in the jail of that place, and

caused the annihilation of the A.M.E. Zion Church there and the loss of our church in Richmond, Virginia. (122)

In New York City, after the Fugitive Slave Bill of 1850, a law enforcement officer arrived to take one James Hamlet back to Baltimore, to his owner. The warrant was issued for Hamlet's arrest, and he was taken back to Baltimore after working as a porter in a store at 58 Water Street.

At the same time it was announced his owner would allow him to be redeemed for eight hundred dollars. The coloured people of the city at once took action. A mass meeting was called and advertised by a handbill which read:

"The Fugitive Slave Bill!
The Panting Slave!
Freemen to be Made Slaves!

Let Every Colored Man and Woman Attend
the Great Mass Meeting to be Held in

Zion Church

Church Street corner of Leonard

On Tuesday Evening   *October 2, 1850*

FOR YOUR LIBERTY, YOUR FIRESIDE, IS IN DANGER OF BEING INVADED! DEVOTE THIS NIGHT TO THE QUESTION OF YOUR DUTY IN THE CRISIS. SHALL WE RESIST THE PROPOSITION? SHALL WE DEFEND LIBERTIES? SHALL WE BE FREEMEN OR SLAVES?
                    By order of the COMMITTEE OF THIRTEEN."

122. J. Harvey Anderson, *Official Directory*, p.44.

Noted Landmark in Jamestown, N.Y. Home of Catherine Harris who operated Underground Railroad Station. Home is presently the parsonage of the Blackwell Memorial A.M.E. Zion Church of Jamestown.

The absence of superstitious fear in having the meeting called by a committee of thirteen was justified; Zion Church, which held about fifteen hundred, was jammed. Speeches were made and resolutions adopted denouncing the law and attacking its constitutionality. But, unlike so many mass meetings, this one did not give an occasion for speeches and resolutions. The sum of eight hundred dollars was raised; the first hundred dollars of which was given by a coloured man named Isaac Hollenbeck. Hamlet's freedom was purchased, and he was brought back to New York amidst the overwhelming rejoicing of the coloured people of the city. [123]

Union Wesley Church in Washington, D.C. served as an important station of the Underground Railroad in 1862, organized during the pastorate of Rev. J. W. Anderson. "This station was a haven for the slaves that came this way. Mr. Benjamin Franklin Grant, Frederick Douglass, and Sojourner Truth were some of the stalwart members serving this great movement. Through Mr. Grant, a contemporary of Douglass, this church established a school for colored boys." [124]

The strong action taken by the General Conference of 1856, meeting at (Mother) Zion Church, New York. expressed a positive view on behalf of its constituents:

Whereas, the whole nation is now agitated upon the great sin of American slavery, which is regarded as the "sum of all villainies," (John Wesley) it is time for every honest hearted man to define his position before the world either for or against this great moral evil. Upon this subject no neutral ground can be taken, for Christ says, "He that is not for me is against me." Therefore, the minister who evades or does not come on the side of liberty and the Gospel is not on the side of God. Therefore,

Resolved, that it is the duty of the members of this General Conference to take a Gospel stand against the sin of slavery, as against all other sins, in teaching, preaching, praying and voting; and to let the world know that so long as this sin remains, and we live, we will, through God's help, be found on the side of the slaves, whether they be white or black; and, that our motto is and ever shall be, "Freedom forever." [125]

The A.M.E. Zion Church and its leaders have always stood foremost in every movement for the advancement of the race, not only during the dark days of slavery but through the long arduous struggle for more than a hundred years afterward, working to attain equality and first-class citizenship. In fact, it continues without ceasing still.

123. Johnson, *Black Manhattan*, pp.16-18.
124. Union Wesley Church Souvenir Program, 1949,
125. Moore, *History, op. cit.*, pp.218-219.

CHAPTER 14

STORMY SPLIT AND SUNNY REUNION

The General Conference sessions were still being held in conjunction with the New York Annual Conference. On Sunday, May 24, 1840, the Sixth Session of the General Conference convened at Asbury Church, New York City, in joint session with the Twentieth Annual Session of the New York Conference. About 40 ministerial delegates "from the East, West, and North," were present, with Bishop Christopher Rush presiding, assisted by Rev. William Miller. (1) From the time Rush was made bishop in 1828 he presided at every conference, both annual and general, for 24 years, and ordained all the ministers during that period. "William Miller sat at the altar with him as senior elder for a number of years, and was made assistant superintendent in 1840, but it does not appear that he ever held a conference." The making of an assistant superintendent without having defined the office in the Discipline "was the rock upon which the church split" in 1853. "This was in line with the political idea of president and vice-president, and the four year term of office, or re-election of bishop was borrowed from the same source." (2)

The genesis of the trouble appears to have stemmed from the strong Wesleyan group, whose attitude of independence and self-assertion, and different views regarding church government, had been felt ever since the beginning of the connection in 1820. William Miller was at this time pastoring Wesley Church in Philadelphia. Even though he had been in and out of the connection at various times, he was regarded by all as senior elder, both in age and tenure, since he had been an exhorter when Zion Church was organized in 1796. In the 1840 General Conference, Rush was easily re-elected bishop for another four-year term, according to the Discipline. The General Conference then resolved to elect another bishop. "A committee of seven was appointed to make a nomination of candidates; William Miller and Edward Johnson were nominated by these, and an election was held which resulted in twenty-five votes being cast for William Miller and eight votes for Edward Johnson; whereupon William Miller was declared elected Bishop." The conference then appointed a committee of five to revise the Discipline. On the third day of the conference the committee on revision reported. The report was discussed and adopted. "After a few valedictory remarks, the conference adjourned to meet in Zion Church, New York, the third Monday in June, 1844." (3)

The delegates did not leave this General Conference unified. The revision committee, composed of Revs. Jehiel C. Beman, Jacob Matthews, Leven Smith, Solomon T. Scott, and David Stevens, went forth immediately and in 1840

1. *The Colored American*, May 30, 1840.
2. General Conference Minutes, Nineteenth Quadrennial Session, p.18.
3. Moore, *History of the A.M.E. Zion Church*, pp.206-207.

published a new Discipline for the church entitled, *The Doctrines and Discipline of the Wesleyan Methodist Episcopal Zion Church in America,* using the same title page as the previous Discipline, including the Founders' Address. Slight provisions were made in "new rules or revising thqse already made," the section on temporal economy, and other sections. No provision, however, was made for an additional superintendent, assistant superintendent, or bishop. The rule had been slightly revised regarding the election of a superintendent in the event of death, expulsion, or otherwise. [4] The revised Discipline met with stunning opposition from church leaders and members, as no action had been taken in the General Conference on changing the name of the church. The same revision committee issued another Discipline the following year, entitled, *The Doctrines and Discipline of the African Methodist Episcopal Church in America,* still with no provision for additional superintendents or assistants. The church operated under this Discipline until 1848.[5]

After the death of William Miller, December 6, 1845, Rush carried on the balance of the quadrennium. In 1848 Rev. George Galbraith was elected to the episcopal office. Some were in favor of making him a full bishop, but the majority, influenced by the example set in 1840, voted that he should be only assistant. At the 1852 Conference, there was a determined effort made to elect only full-fledged bishops. They elected three, but they failed to change the law in the revised Discipline to make it harmonize with their action. The program with some, however, included the retiring of Bishop Rush, who was both feeble and blind. Some were opposed to this part of it, but it was finally carried out, and George Galbraith, William H. Bishop, and George A. Spywood were elected on equality. George Galbraith died in 1853, and then the trouble began. [6]

"Those who had been in favor of general and assistant superintendents wanted [William H.] Bishop to take advantage of the situation and declare himself general superintendent." Others wanted him to adhere to their action of the General Conference that all of the bishops were on equality.

Finding that there would be trouble, no matter which position he took, he simply said; 'I am all that the Discipline makes me.' This satisfied one party, but not the other, hence he was called to trial by the dissatisfied party. He evaded trial, and therefore was declared suspended by one faction but continued to be recognized as bishop in good standing by the other faction. Those adhering to the suspended bishop held the territory generally from Philadelphia south and westward, and were called the Wesleyan Methodist Episcopal Zion Church; the others held the most of New York, New England, and Nova Scotia, and were called the African Methodist Episcopal Zion Church.

Zion had been added to the denominational title in the 1848 General Conference. [7]

The faction which suspended Bishop called an extraordinary General Conference in 1854, and made George A. Spywood superintendent and John Tappan assistant. At the regular session in 1856, this faction let Spywood down to the rank of elder, and made James Simmons superintendent and Solomon T. Scott assistant. The faction holding to William H. Bishop also held a General

4. *The Doctrines and Discipline of the Wesleyan Methodist Episcopal Zion Church in America,* 1840.
5. *The Doctrines and Discipline of the African Methodist Episcopal (Zion) Church in America,* 1841.
6. *Minutes,* Nineteenth Quadrennial Session. p.18; Hood, *One Hundred Years,* p.71.
7. *Ibid.,* Hood, *One Hundred Years,* p.71.

Conference in 1856, re-elected Bishop, and also elected Joseph Jackson Clinton bishop. [8] The matter was taken into court for settlement. Both sides were well represented.

The following account of that action is taken from Hood's *History:*

"BUY THE TRUTH AND SELL IT NOT."

With no small degree of satisfaction the following decision is presented to all who feel interested in the affairs of our Church, which has been hindered much in its progress on account of the pending difficulty that has existed since 1852 until now. Every effort that has been made to adjust the difficulty having been before the public, therefore we feel obligated to make public the result of another investigation, emanating from the Court of Common Pleas, Williamsport, Lycoming County, Pa., of a recent lawsuit of one of our churches there. Further preliminaries on the subject are not necessary, as the following decision and charge of the judge to the jury contain all that is necessary to satisfy an unbiased mind.

S. M. Giles.

IN THE COURT OF COMMON PLEAS, HON. A. JORDAN, JUDGE.

George Johnson, Ferdinand Capes, and Anthony Stokes, Trustees of the
African Methodist Episcopal Zion Church,

vs.

Isaac Coleman, Lewis Hill, David Thomas, Joseph Davis, Isaac Lloyd,
James Sherman, George Roach, and Isaac Thompson.
Counsel for plaintiffs, Messrs. Dietrick and Scates; counsel for defendants,
Messrs. Armstrong, Campbell, and Emery.

CHARGE.

Of all the disputes that arise those which arise among the professing Christians are most to be deplored, and are the bitterest. Strange as it may appear, it is nevertheless true that these disputes are more difficult to arrange among the disputants than any other, and perhaps more difficult to adjust, rightly and justly, before a court and jury. Each Church has its own peculiar form of government, its Discipline and creed. They are usually governed by a Constitution, each of its members either expressly or implicitly engaging to be bound by it. It is necessary for the good government of all religious organizations that there should be a form of government, without which it would not only be difficult, but perhaps impossible, to keep the members together for any length of time.

The parties to this action all profess to belong to the African Methodist Episcopal Zion Church in the United States. They are not disputing as to the doctrine of the Church, the form of worship, or the Constitution or Discipline by which the Church is to be governed. The dispute is, who has the right to the possession of the church in this place, or had at the time of the alleged trespass? If that right was in the plaintiffs at the time they would be entitled to your verdict. The action is not brought to recover damages so much as to determine the right to the property, which, under the pleadings in this action, may be done.

The suit is brought in the names of George Johnson, Ferdinand Capes, and Anthony Stokes, trustees of the African Methodist Episcopal Zion Church, Williamsport. Their election as trustees was proven by the minute book of the church.

8. *Ibid.*

The property in dispute was conveyed by Abraham Updegraff and wife to George Johnson, Ferdinand Capes, and David Thomas, trustees of the Colored Methodist Episcopal Zion Church in Williamsport, by deed, dated on the 21st of June, 1854. Both parties claim under this deed. To determine which of these parties is entitled to hold the property it will be necessary to examine the proceedings of their Conferences, with a view of ascertaining whether Mr. Coleman, the preacher recognized by the defendants and other members of the church, was properly and duly elected and appointed to take charge and oversight of this church. He, as well as his predecessors from the first organization of the church in this place, was appointed by the Philadelphia Conference. The right of this Conference to appoint was not disputed for some time, but the acts of that body were recognized as binding and were submitted to. In June, 1852, a General Conference met in Philadelphia. At that Conference a question arose whether a general superintendent should be elected in Committee of the Whole or General Conference. At that Conference it was concluded to elect a general superintendent and an assistant superintendent in Committee of the Whole, which, it is said, was contrary to the Discipline and Constitution which had been adopted for the government of the Church.

At that time Christopher Rush, the old gentleman who appeared on the stand as a witness, was general superintendent, and had been for some years before, and George Galbraith the assistant superintendent. Mr. Rush was at that time nearly blind, and wished to resign his position, that another might be elected in his place. A committee was appointed to name superintendents. They reported the names of Rush and Galbraith, and Galbraith was elected over Rush. A question arose then as to the proper mode of electing these officers. The provision in the Book of Discipline is that the superintendents were to be elected in a General Conference, not in Committee of the Whole. It was concluded that he must be elected according to the Book of Discipline. A General Conference was then entered into, a committee was appointed, who named James Simmons and William H. Bishop. Simmons resigned or declined an election, and Mr. Scott was named as the opposing candidate to Bishop. Bishop was elected over Scott for four years. Galbraith was elected assistant superintendent. Galbraith became dissatisfied, and a motion was made to have three superintendents on equal footing. The Book of Discipline provides for the election of two superintendents—one of them a general superintendent and one assistant superintendent. Bishop then put a motion, and a third superintendent was elected, namely, Spywood. Subsequently Bishop, Galbraith, and Spywood made an agreement among themselves, splitting up the connection, which the witness states they had no right to do.

Also, after the election of these three superintendents the Philadelphia Conference issued a circular to change the word "African" and insert the word "Wesleyan." The Quarterly Conference refused to receive the circulars, because they thought the General Conference had taken away the rights of the people. The Conferences would not receive the change at all. Bishop was recognized as the general superintendent, and Galbraith assistant.

Bishop went on and held a Conference at Ithaca. Galbraith held one in Pittsburg, and called it the Wesleyan Conference. A charge was preferred against Bishop for permitting it to be called by that name. A copy of the charges was given to him. In the meantime Galbraith died. Bishop appeared at the Conference, but refused to submit to the trial. While Bishop was under censure he held a Conference at Baltimore, came to Philadelphia, and held one there. When he got through at Philadelphia he came to New York Conference. He then wished to hold that Conference without submitting to be tried for his misconduct. He was then informed that he could not take the chair until he was tried. The Conference proceeded to appoint a chairman *pro tem.*, to act till Bishop was tried. Bishop refused to be tried, and denied their right to try him, holding that he could only be tried by a General Conference. Whether his position was correct or not can only be determined by referring to the Constitution or Book of Discipline. He was tried in 1853 and expelled. Before he was expelled Bishop made a motion to go to Williamsburg; a few members of the New York Conference went with him, and some of the Genesee Conference went with him, and four of the Philadelphia Conference.

When Bishop was expelled a convention was called to supply the vacancy. This convention met on July 9, 1853. All the elders were warned to attend. A General Conference was organized, the Book of Discipline adopted, and George A. Spywood elected general superintendent, and John Tappan assistant. It is stated by one of the witnesses examined that the General Conference had never before 1852 elected three superintendents.

The Philadelphia church is still attached to the General Conference. Simmons and Scott succeed Spywood and Tappan.

Mr. Thompson says Bishop was never superintendent since 1853. From the state of facts which the court submits to you, with all the other facts in the case, was Bishop, after his expulsion in 1853, a general superintendent, having the right to act as such? This involves an inquiry into the regularity of the proceedings in the Philadelphia Conference when three superintendents were elected, and the subsequent conduct of Bishop in permitting Galbraith to change the name of the Conference, the charges preferred against him, his refusal to submit to trial before the New York Conference, his right to occupy the chair, the right of the members of the Conference, while charges were pending against him, to prevent him sitting as the presiding officer, and his right to call a convention or Conference at Williamsburg. If this Conference at Williamsburg was held without authority, and in violation of the Constitution or Discipline of the Church, the members of that convention departed from the form of government of the Church, and cannot, by virtue of such act, claim to be the Church, no matter whether they were a majority or minority. The same remarks apply to other acts enumerated by the court.

Which of these parties, the plaintiffs or the defendants, adhere to the doctrine of the Church, the form of worship practiced in the Church, and the government in the Church, must be submitted to you, with instruction that your decision should be in favor of the party so adhering, and having in those respects the regular succession, no difference whether that party be in the majority or minority.

Here read from Book of Discipline and Doctrines, Section 4. Art. IV, pp. 35, 36; Art. V, p. 36; Section II, p. 53, of General Conference; p. 56, General Superintendent; p. 57, Assistant; p. 65, Yearly Conference.

Mr. Rush was the General Superintendent of the Church for twenty-four years. He appointed elders for Williamsport Church. The Philadelphia church formed part of his charge, which he visited. He, wishing to resign, being superintendent in 1852, Bishop came in after him. The church in this place was attached to the Philadelphia Conference.

It is to be hoped that your verdict will repair the troubles that exist in this breach of the African Methodist Episcopal Zion Church in the United States, and restore peace and harmony among the members. This appears to be the desire of the court. We are sure it is your wish, as it is that of the court. If Bishop, when he seceded or called a Conference at Williamsburg, should be considered as acting in violation of the government of the

Church, and was properly expelled, then, his power as general superintendent having ceased, he could not confer power upon others to officiate
in the Church. (9)

The heaviest load of the split fell upon the shoulders of Bishop William
Bishop, although he was in no way directly responsible for all that was
happening, as the foundation of the trouble was laid in 1840. Bishop distributed
the following circular, which also bears the signature of Bishop Clinton:

CIRCULAR.

In the Annual Conference of the African Methodist Episcopal Zion
Connection for the Philadelphia District, 1857, the defense of our cause
being the special order of the day, the following prevailed, to wit:

Whereas, The circular emanating from the pen of the general superintendent, William H. Bishop, presents a clear and lucid exposition of the
grounds of the difficulties which resulted in the excommunication of a
number of the ministers formerly belonging to this connection—now
following the lead of James Simmons and Solomon T. Scott (the so-called
superintendents), under the falsely assumed title of this connection;
therefore,

Resolved, That this Conference fully indorse the views therein contained and set forth, and that there be, and it is hereby ordered, that five
hundred copies of said circular be printed for circulation through this
District.

*To the Ministers, Members, and Friends of the African Methodist Episcopal
Zion Church in America, greeting:*

BELOVED BRETHREN—We doubt not you have seen and read a
circular letter sent to certain individuals, emanating from George A.
Spywood and John Tappin, calling themselves general and assistant
superintendents of the above-named connection. Dear brethren, you should
not be hasty in your conclusions in reference to so great and important a
matter, but hear both sides of the question and judge impartially, and not
suffer your minds to be prejudiced, but examine carefully and prayerfully,
with an eye single to the glory of God and the advancement of the
Redeemer's kingdom.

Beloved brethren in Christ, suffer me here to say to you that there is
some truth set forth in that circular, accompanied with a great deal of what
is not strictly true. Notice first, in regard to the Constitution in reference to
making new rules or revising those already made. See Discipline, page 68,
article 1st, 2d, and 3d, and page 69, etc. Dear friends, every section and
every article we hold sacred. Sirs, I have been a minister in this connection
for some time; I joined it, the Zion's Church in New York, in September,
1825. In May, 1826, I joined the Annual Conference as a traveling preacher.
Father Abraham Thompson, one of the founders of Zion's Church, and Rev.
James Varick, the first superintendent, were then living. He, Varick, served
the first term as superintendent; he was elected for the second term, but
before the expiration of that term God was pleased to call him from labor to
reward. We then numbered about ten Conference ministers, and of that
number there are but three living, who are of no longer standing than
myself, and here you have their names: Revs. Leven Smith, Christopher
Rush, and George Tredwell.

After the death of the first superintendent we elected Rev. Leven Smith,
who was then our choice, but he declined; we then elected Rev. Christopher

9. *Ibid.,* pp.73-77.

Rush to that office. The superintendent is elected to serve four years and no longer, unless re-elected. Rev. Christopher Rush was elected in 1828. From that time he was re-elected every four years until 1852, making twenty-four years, during which time he became destitute or deprived of his natural sight, so that he could not perform the duties of a superintendent any longer. As a matter of course, the members of the General Conference, feeling it their privilege as well as their duty, which right belongs to them, to elect to the superintendency a man of their own choice, they did elect Rev. William H. Bishop general superintendent in 1852, and did unanimously elect him general superintendent in 1856, and did also unanimously elect Rev. Joseph J. Clinton assistant superintendent.

Dear friends, I am not a stranger in the connection. Many of you know me from the time I joined the connection. I was called and owned as a worthy brother, and held in high repute up to 1852. But when I was elected superintendent, then those office seekers showed themselves to be my enemies. In their circular they inform you that we wish to deprive you of your privileges; those statements are not true, but to the reverse, for instead of depriving the Quarterly Conferences of their privileges, the intention of the General Conference of 1852 was, and still is, to give them more. It is true, we know that we cannot alter or change our rules without the consent of two thirds of the Quarterly Conferences of the entire connection, as you may see in the circular in reference to the convention.

Again they say, I lost or gave my office by putting an unconstitutional motion. Ah, how low the acts of those men are, striving to take advantage and making wrong impressions upon the uninformed and weak minds! God will, ere long, set matters right. They say that the rule was suspended to get the third superintendent, and the rule remained so. Ah, how erroneous the idea is! How often is the like done in deliberative bodies; yes, even in Congress, in Parliament, and among religious bodies. But it is so strange. The suspension of rule is part of their own doings in General Conference of 1852, when we were all together, but they (having lost their power, as they thought), when arriving in New York, called their council and there devised these low, cunning plans to effect their unrighteous designs, and to captivate weak minds, telling those innocent ones that we wanted to take their property away from them, thus flattering and deceiving them; while at the same time were they taken helpless to-morrow they would have to be sent or compelled to go to the poorhouse, the aged home, after spending their hard earnings to pay for that property. . . .

It is true that our book of Discipline knows but two superintendents, the general and assistant. The book of Discipline never knew any assistant until 1848. But C. Rush tolerated it, and it was said to be right. Much more here might be said which was unconstitutionally sanctioned by the Rev. C. Rush. Had he and his party been set at the head of affairs in 1852, all would have been right with them to-day—for the acts in that General Conference are but as ciphers compared with the General Conference of 1840. See that book signed by himself unlawfully, and in 1843, sitting in Conference with the same, asking questions out of that unlawfully revised book, and then assumed the power that was not guaranteed to him in that he told the members of the New York and Philadelphia Conferences to use either or both books of Discipline until the General Conference. This was wrong; but no one tried to remove Rev. C. Rush from office for putting that unconstitutional motion in the General Conference of 1840. I here forbear. Again to the book of Discipline. The present book knows but two superintendents, the general and assistant. We were all in General Conference assembled in Philadelphia, in 1852, and were in the act of revising the

Discipline. The sentiments of that body, even those who now strive to take the advantage, were that, in their judgment, the connection stood in need of three superintendents. But we could not get the third one unless we suspended the rule and elected one prospectively, but not to act as such, until there should be sanction given to the revised matter by a two third vote of the Quarterly Conferences of the entire connection. Here the question may arise, why was Spywood's name on the circular with Rev. William H. Bishop and Rev. George Galbraith? The answer is, that it was the expressed opinion of that body that at the next annual session the consent of the required majority of the Quarterly Conferences would be obtained, as they had already the consent of a great number of them.

The circular pointing out the defect, with the alterations which were wanting to be made, was sent out in good faith. But ah! to our surprise, the disaffected office-seeking brethren, instead of acting in good faith, ran to the old church and raised a hue and cry, saying that William H. Bishop and the General Conference were about to destroy their church, their old Mother Church, by changing the name of the connection, which caused a great excitement. They said if the name was changed they would lose their property, their beloved Zion in New York.

This game went on till 1853, when that party called a convention, as they say, while I was in Allegheny City, Pa., holding an Annual Conference, at which time, they say in their own publication, they resolved themselves into a General Conference—which is truly a new thing under the sun; and that done in Zion, called the Mother Church—with closed doors, and there elected, as they say in their own publication, three superintendents, namely, George A. Spywood, Robert C. Henderson, and John Tappan.

They elected three superintendents in open violation of the Constitution of the Church, and now that broken, disaffected party, in a circular letter, charges the General Conference proper with violating the rules of the Church. It is well known that the presidential election of these United States takes place every four years; there are two or more candidates for that office; one of these candidates, with his vice, is elected in accordance with the requirements of the Constitution of the United States. Let us suppose a case: suppose that the friends of the minority candidates, being dissatisfied, should meet in one of these United States, in one of the cities or towns, and enter into some hall, and there with closed doors should hold an election with their candidate, then come out and publish to the world that he, whomsoever he might be, was President of these United States, would that be true? The answer is at hand, No. You would look upon that party as rebels. This is a parallel case. The party now cleaving to the old house, corner of Church and Leonard Streets, New York, is the party that pursued this rebellious course, and they are making a noise before the public, claiming to be the connection proper, which is not true.

Zion was never a connectional name until 1848. At that General Conference our present book was revised, and the present name of the connection given for the first time. The book was published in 1851. Look at the 7th page, Committee's Address, page 8, the names of the said committee; see the old book of 1820, which is or was the name, the doctrine or discipline of the African Methodist Episcopal Church in America. This was the proper name of the connection until 1848, when the committee, as named on the 8th page of the present book, named the connection, which was sanctioned by the General Conference. Read for yourselves, and do not be deceived.

Spywood and Tappan, who were said to be their superintendents, did not continue their four years, but instead of four years their party was glad to get rid of them in three years; no doubt of that, for notwithstanding things as they are, there are honorable exceptions, for there are brethren and sons among them who are near and dear to me.

James Simmons and Solomon T. Scott, of the disaffected party, were elected by that party, the former general, the latter assistant superintendent, in June, 1856. He (Scott), who was an office seeker in 1852, but he being disappointed in that, he was not elected superintendent, but he received an appointment from me until the last Conference, 1855, when he (Scott) located and joined the Quarterly Conference of Wesley Church, Lombard Street, Philadelphia, held his standing as a local elder, went to work holding private council with the disaffected party in New York, and he (Scott) for less than a mess of pottage sold himself and joined them, after calling them after the names of many of his fish, as set forth in his sermon, and he called them anything but Christians and gentlemen wherever he went. After all this, thinking there was not a chance for him in the connection proper, he was determined to look out for a chance once more. Away he goes and salutes the disaffected party, and by his acts says, Hail, brethren! and kisses them. They made him their assistant superintendent. He, of course, will be a stool pigeon, to try to draw away from our beloved connection members by a refuge of lies.

Ministers, official boards, members, and friends of our beloved connection, stand together, be upon the watch, stand firm; the good Lord has enabled us to guide the ship safely through that trying term, I may say single-handed, and as the brethren have given me an assistant, under God we feel to be strong.

WILLIAM H. BISHOP, *General Superintendent.*
JOSEPH J. CLINTON, *Assistant Superintendent.* (10)

The point most against William H. Bishop was the change in the title of the church striking out "African" and inserting "Wesleyan." "This, as the court intimated, stamped him as a seceder, and as such, no matter how large his majority he could not take the Church property. This decision also tended to hasten the reunion. The fact that it went against the stronger party induced it to accept more readily the overtures which were made by the weaker side, which was more ready to offer terms." (11) After the two factions began to think seriously, there was little to keep them apart. During 1858, the subject of the union of the two factions was uppermost in the minds and conversation of both ministers and members of both sides. Rev. Jacob P. Trusty, then pastoring Newark, and Rev. Singleton T. Jones, pastor of Wesley Church, Philadelphia, were persistently sending articles and letters to the *Weekly Anglo-African,* both pleading and insisting upon union of the denomination by the 1860 General Conference. (12) Hood states:

No one could give a good reason for the split nor for the continuation of it. If William H. Bishop had met his accusers when he was called to trial it is not likely that he would have been expelled or suspended. On the other hand, the treatment he received was hasty and ill-advised. . . . A few determined men, however, made up their minds that the farce had gone on long enough, and they took steps to put a period to it. (13)

The following appeared in the *Anglo-African,* expressing public sentiment of the laymen:

10. *Ibid.,* pp.530-535.
11. *Ibid.;* . . .Hood, *One Hundred Years,* p.73.
12. *The Weekly Anglo-African,* Jan.-May, 1860.
13. Hood, *One Hundred Years,* p.78.

BISHOP SINGLETON THOMAS W. JONES

1825 - 1891

Apostle of unity of the A.M.E. Zion Church, champion debater of its history, and major authority in ecclesiastical law.

TO THE MINISTERS OF ZION

Dear Brethren:—It would be an easy matter for a body of a hundred men of intelligence all striving for the public good, to agree. The public opinion on the matter is united. There are no bitter feuds among the people. The quarrels are all confined to the ministers. The people are united on one thing though on minor points there may be a difference of opinion among them. They are opposed to our present division, and there is scarcely a church member to be found who does not regard our attempts at vindication a miserable failure. The people, generally, with hardly an exception, consider that we have done little but mischief since the split. They declare that they will not submit to men who do their utmost to array one section of the church against the other. The unanimity of feeling in the matter is astonishing and unprecedented.

Something must be done, and this right quickly. We have a decided majority in favor of immediate union. Let all such urge the approaching Annual Conference to action upon the matter, and if nothing can be accomplished then, let us select a thorough man for Superintendent—one whose interests are identified with the interests of the whole Connection—

one who will give his whole energies to the promotion of the welfare of Zion, and who will not allow private interests and personal preferences to prevent him from advocating at all times and seasons the importance of being united. The people are desirous that a man of this character should be elected. Let us elect *him*—let us have a *union.*   ZION [14]

The laity of both factions strongly influenced the reunion, and one of the plans presented by Trusty called on the lay delegates to take their place in the 1860 General Conference, and work with the ministers in effecting this union. [15] Subsequently, a convention of leading men from each faction met in Newburgh, and adopted a platform for the reunion. It was presented to the regularly scheduled General Conference held at Wesley Church, Philadelphia, May 30, led by the Bishop William H. Bishop faction. Rev. Samson Talbot read the memorial on behalf of the two separate bodies of the connection, and the matter was placed on the agenda for consideration the following day. These laymen were seated as honorary members of the Philadelphia General Conference. Thursday, May 31, was taken up in discussion of the memorial, which they finally decided to adopt in sections. On Friday, June 1, Rev. S. T. Gray, M.D. arrived with credentials from the officers of (Mother) Zion Church, and a letter informing the General Conference that "it could meet and hold its sessions in that church on and after the 6th of June, provided there should be no interference with local matters. As the other faction had appointed to meet at that time and place, this was a reminder that they had been acting like spoiled children and bickering long enough, and that the mother wanted them to come home and behave themselves." [16]

Dr. Gray's proposition was received, the discussion of union resumed, and the memorial prepared by the Newburgh convention finally adopted. It was agreed to adjourn the General Conference and meet on June 6 in Zion Church, New York. On Wednesday, June 6, 4 P M., the two factions met in Zion Church according to agreement. Bishops Bishop and Clinton presided. The organization was delayed by the absence of Bishops Simmons and Scott. Bishop Rush soon appeared, however and announced that Bishop Simmons had been taken suddenly ill. Bishop Scott's absence could not be accounted for, and it was agreed to proceed with the business. It was evident that all were anxious for the union. The basis of union prepared by the convention at Newburgh was presented as follows:

Section 1. Resolved, That all matters pertaining to former difficulties be laid aside forever.

Section 2. Resolved, That these parties agree to use both Books of Discipline* till the sitting of the General Conference of 1860, and at the assembling of the General Conference to proceed to organize under the Discipline of 1851; then to adopt or make a Discipline suitable to the wants of the people or connection.

Section 3. Resolved, That this convention recommend the General Conference under Right Rev. W. H. Bishop, which is to meet in Philadelphia, May 30, 1860, that they adjourn to meet in New York, at Zion Church, on the 6th day of June, where the union will be consummated.

Section 4. And be it further *Resolved,* That we recommend that they defer the election of superintendents and revision of Discipline till the union is effected.

Section 5. Resolved, That we cordially invite the two general superin-

---

14. *The Weekly Anglo-African,* March 3, 1860.
15. Hood, *One Hundred Years,* pp.77-78.
16. *The Anglo-African,* March 30, 1860.

tendents, with their assistants, to meet the adjourned General Conference to reassemble in New York the 6th day of June, at 4 P.M., to assist in consummating the union.

Section 6. Resolved, That nothing in the foregoing basis be so construed as to interfere with privileges of any of the members of the General Conference.

Section 7. Resolved, That as a convention we stand united on the foregoing basis.

* Both parties had revised the Discipline during the eight years they had been separated. [17]

This report was, on motion, received and adopted. "This created a great sensation. The delegates arose and embraced each other, which was followed by the entire conference, amid singing and great ecstacy and shaking of hands, lasting ten minutes." Quiet being restored, they proceeded with the business of the General Conference. [18] On motion by Dr. Gray, the words "assistant superintendent" were stricken out of the Discipline wherever they appeared. Thus after 20 years, this bone of contention had been eliminated. Three bishops were elected on equality: William H. Bishop, Peter Ross, and Joseph J. Clinton. The arrangement was that the bishops were to rotate at the end of two years. For the first two years, though, Bishop Ross was appointed to a district on which both of the other bishops had traveled before; both claimed back salary, and the General Conference permitted them to go back and get what they could. When Ross went to his new field after two years, he had difficulty raising his travel expense, resigned, and returned to pastoral work around 1863. [19]

Ross was a good man. As a pastor he had excellent qualities, not quite suited for the bishopric, however. "The same may be said of five others, who were elected during the eight years of strife. Spywood, Tappan, Henderson, Scott, and Simmons were all good preachers and strong men, and would always have appeared to advantage if they had never been elected to the episcopal chair." [20] John Tappan and S. T. Scott, like William Miller, were only assistant superintendents. George A. Spywood's status was one of the questions in dispute during the split. It was claimed by some that he was not made a full bishop in 1852, but that his election was provisional. The fact that he was re-elected by one faction in 1854 seems to have confirmed that idea. Neither he nor James Simmons were ever fully recognized by the entire connection as bishops. "They were both let down and enrolled as elders, after four years' service as superintendents of one faction." R. C. Henderson had been mentioned among the bishops, but he was only made superintendent for Demarara and died soon after. [21]

The Discipline, as finally adopted at this 1860 General Conference, was very nearly what it was made by the William H. Bishop faction in 1856, and the "hand that shaped it was that of S. T. Jones. He more than any other one man shaped the Discipline for about twelve years, from 1856 to 1868." [22] After this twenty years of struggle, passing also through a sea of troubles during slavery, the church moved forward in uniformity, making great preparations for taking the gospel to their brothers and sisters in the Southland.

17. Hood, One Hundred Years, pp.79-80.
18. Moore, History, p.228.
19. Hood, One Hundred Years, p.81; Minutes, Nineteenth Quadrennial Session, p.19.
20. Ibid.: Hood, One Hundred Years, pp.81-82.
21. Minutes, Nineteenth Quadrennial Session, 1892, p.19.
22. Ibid.

EMANCIPATION OF THE RACE

The New York Historical Society

Part IV
Growth of the Church

CHAPTER 15

THE A.M.E. ZION CHURCH GOES SOUTH AND WEST

The success of the A.M.E. Zion Church during the Reconstruction era was a marvel. "The distinguishing characteristic of our church is freedom. . . . Her very pronounced position on the subject of slavery kept her out of the South until the power of that system was broken; but she was among the first to send missionaries to our long oppressed people when the way was open, as she had been among the foremost advocates of emancipation in the dark days of slavery, and also foremost in sheltering and feeding the panting fugitive on his weary way to a land of freedom." With less than a half dozen Northern born men laboring in the entire South, her ministry was raised up almost wholly from among those who were under the iron heel of oppression. [1]

It was the famous Bishop Joseph Jackson Clinton, a man of extraordinary ability, one of the most fervent, devout, and self-sacrificing servants of the Redeemer's kingdom, who paved the way.

Noble in his personal appearance, Bishop Clinton possessed an equally noble heart. Genial in his manner, easy, graceful and commanding in his bearing, generous and jovial, kind, respectful to all, and especially to the aged; condescending toward the poorer and more unfortunate in life, it was by no means strange that he drew around him hosts of admiring friends—both in and out of the church. Large hearted, sympathetic and benevolent, he shared alike in the joys and sorrows, the sunshine and gloom, the prosperity and adversities of his brethren and companions. [2]

1. *Minutes,* Sixteenth Quadrennial Session, 1880. p. 54.
2. *Minutes,* Seventeenth Quadrennial Session, New York City, 1884, p. 89.

He was pleasant in his domestic relations, and his family was the object of his love and esteem, and understood his zeal and devotion to the cause he espoused.

No service was too hard, no sacrifice too great for that cause. . . . All good institutions had his favor and cooperation. Through his instrumentality one hundred thousand Sunday school scholars were brought into the connection. During his episcopal office he organized twelve Annual Conferences in ten years, and several others that coalesced with the conferences which continued permanent. He also took into the connection seven hundred itinerant preachers. As an executive officer he had no superior; for twenty-five years he filled the office with complete success and satisfaction to his church. [3]

Clinton was elected to the episcopal office in 1856. He had travelled extensively throughout the northeastern territory, including Canada, serving every Zion conference of the North, establishing new societies, and inspiring young men for Christian service. He was intensely enthusiastic in the struggle for freedom, and labored arduously, as president of the Freedmen's American and British Commission, to eliminate suffering of our people. [4] It was 1862 when Bishop Clinton, according to the assignment committee of the 1860 General Conference, was appointed to take charge of the district known as the Southern and Philadelphia Annual Conferences. [5] Although the district (known also as the Second District) had been designated in 1860, no bishop had gone South, and the appointment at first discouraged Clinton. But Melvina Fletcher, governess in the household of Montgomery Blair, President Lincoln's Postmaster General, and a member of Zion Wesley (Metropolitan) Church in Washington, D.C., lent great aid to Clinton, and thus made unique history among the women of Zion.

She was a loyal church woman, and had heard of the dissatisfaction that had overtaken Bishop Clinton, who had written his resignation. One memorable night, during the fall of 1863, she went to his stopping place, called him out of his sleep at 3 o'clock in the morning, and had the famous conference that changed his mind. When he complained that he had not a single minister or dollar to take a delegation as missionaries to the South, she remonstrated with him to tear up his resignation, promising that she would help raise the funds for his cause. Clinton needed $300, which she promised to raise. She took her friends in the Blair orbit and the churches of Washington and raised it, and presented the $300 in gold to him as the fulfillment of her promise, to meet the need of his mission.

Clinton selected and sent five men to the mission field during 1863-1864: James W. Hood, Wilbur G. Strong, John Williams, David Hill, and William F. Butler. [6] The New England Conference, which one time expended as much as $1,000 a year for missionary purposes, was known for starting the great work in the South. Three missionaries were sent to North Carolina by its board of missions within a year. (Before the War it sent missionaries to Nova Scotia and to the West Indies.) The New England Conference has the credit for forming the North Carolina Conference, the pioneer in our great Southern work and the mother of the conferences of the South. Miss Eliza Ann Gardner had "been the most conspicuous and the most useful woman in this Conference, if not in the entire connection." [7]

Of the above five mentioned men, John Williams was not a success. It was generally believed that he thought it not safe to go. David Hill lived only a few months after reaching North Carolina. J. W. Hood became the strong force in

3. Hood, *One Hundred Years*, pp. 172-173; Vol. II, p. 29.
4. *The Weekly Anglo-African*, Oct. 21, 1865.
5. Moore, *History of the A.M.E. Zion Church*, p. 230.
6. *Minutes*, Sixteenth Quadrennial Session, p. 19.
7. Hood, *One Hundred Years*, p. 245.

BISHOP JOSEPH JACKSON CLINTON

1823 - 1881

First Bishop to the South, organizing thirteen conferences around the realm of the country, from New Jersey to California; and hero in Emancipation. He was the youngest bishop in the history of the A.M.E. Zion Church, elected at age 33.

North Carolina, W. G. Strong in the far South, and W. F. Butler in Kentucky. [8] At the head of the column was James Walker Hood whose major work, collected and projected by a missionary appointee, is enormous in A.M.E. Zion Church history. The work in the state of North Carolina towers as his achievement. There are a larger number of members and institutions of our Zion in North Carolina than in any other state, because of the official wisdom of J. J. Clinton and the industrious skill and loyalty of J. W. Hood. Hood's work in that state reads like a miracle. He was mainly responsible for the establishment of the work in New Bern, Wilmington, Fayetteville, and Charlotte, and contributed variously to the spread of the denomination throughout the state from sea to mountain.

In June 1863, Hood was appointed to the pastorate of the church at Bridgeport, Conn. "Here he remained about only six months before Bishop J. J. Clinton, against the unyielding protest of the whole membership and community, removed and sent him to North Carolina, as the first of his race appointed as a regular missionary to the 'Freedmen of the South.'" This act of the sainted Bishop Clinton, remembered well by members of Bridgeport for a long time, was the key that unlocked the mystery of Zion's marvelous success in the Southland. Far-sighted, if not prophetic, was the vision of the man who thought out and appointed such a missionary.

> But the clash of bayonet and the roar of cannon had not ceased ere Elder James Walker Hood disembarked for the first time upon Southern soil, at New Bern, North Carolina, January, 1864; yet freighted with divine grace and chosen of God for the work—resolved as much upon success as was Paul to see Rome—wise as a serpent and bold as a lion went he forth to plant the standard of Zion Methodism and to make himself a positive factor in the amelioration of his race, for which every fibre in his heart beat, and upon which all the interests of his life focalized. [9]

The headquarters of the Confederate Army was at Kinston, only 28 miles

8. *Minutes,* Sixteenth Quadrennial Session, p. 19.
9. G. L. Blackwell, "James Walker Hood," *A.M.E. Zion Quarterly Review,* October 1890, p. 141.

away. Two battles were fought at New Bern after Hood arrived there. He was "a civilian at the very front of the Federal Army." Upon his arrival in New Bern he found a church in great confusion. Two denominations had divided the members on the matter of what church they would adopt. A Rev. J. E. Round had been sent by Bishop Baker of the Methodist Episcopal Church to take them over, but he had met a young white man working among them as a preacher, named Fitz, who tried to convince them to come into the Congregational Church. The members were greatly disturbed and agitated. Also on the day of Hood's arrival, two preachers from Norfolk, representing the African Methodist Episcopal Church, arrived and attempted to take charge, which increased the confusion. It worked out, however, through an immense struggle on behalf of Hood, who had credentials from the War Department, used this and made an extra trip to Washington at his own expense to clinch this authority and define it. When the controversy was at its height, Secretary Stanton of the War Department sent official authorization of the right of the congregation themselves to choose the way they would vote. The opinion of General Butler, who worked with Hood, caused the Secretary of War to write: "The Congregation of the Colored Methodists worshipping in Andrew Chapel, New Bern, N.C., shall have the right to decide their own church relations, and select their own pastor." [10]

This was used by Rev. Hood, who opened the church on Easter Sunday, April 1864, preaching with vitality to a packed church, and "a congregation on the outside nearly as large as that within." At the close of the highly spiritual service he announced the secretary's authorization and the people took a vote, deciding to enter the A.M.E. Zion Church. The point that weighed heavily in their decision was that they wanted a preacher and church of their own race. They had heard of old Zion Church in New York, and of Bishop Rush, who was a native of New Bern, and the missionary from that church (Hood), who had been appointed to look after them. [11]

A number of churches came into Zion at this time out of this Andrew Chapel, when Bishop J. J. Clinton, who had sent Hood and encouraged him, arrived in New Bern, May 1864. "Great was the joy of the people at being permitted to see a bishop of their own race, and especially a bishop who was willing to become all things to all men, that he might by all means gain some." At Hood's suggestion several persons were licensed to preach, most of whom made successful preachers. [12]

In the interim of the first annual conference, Hood himself went to Beaufort and Wilmington, and received those churches into Zion. His experience in Wilmington was unique and challenging. He found that the St. Luke Church and the St. Stephens Church had both adopted the A.M.E. Church as their choice. This would have given the two major churches in the largest city of the state at that time to the A.M.E. (Bethel) denomination. Hood, an adroit maneuverer and experienced mason, worked ardently and manipulated matters so that the St. Luke Church withdrew from the compact with Bethel and came with Hood into Zion. [13]

Bishop Clinton organized the North Carolina Conference on December 17, 1864 with 12 ministers and about 400 members. This first conference, like the other conferences Clinton organized in the South, was more of a school than a conference; the men were instructed how to go to work to build up the kingdom

10. Hood, *One Hundred Years,* pp. 290-291; Vol. II, p. 90.
11. *Ibid.,* pp. 291-296.
12. *Ibid.*
13. Hood's experience related to the writer personally.

BISHOP JAMES WALKER HOOD

1831 - 1918

First missionary preacher of Zion appointed South. Pioneer churchman. Established first A.M.E. Zion Church in the South, St. Peter's, New Bern, N.C. Creative race leader and Reconstructionist. Hood was the first black Assistant Superintendent of Education in North Carolina, discoverer of J. C. Price and co-founder of Livingstone College.

of God. Only three of the first 12 remained. "At this first Conference the work reported covered only that small portion of the State which was then occupied by the Union forces, including Roanoke Island, New Bern, Beaufort, and the small strip of country lying between New Bern and Beaufort. But the close of the war the following May opened up the whole state, and each of the ministers who attended the first Conference did what he could to spread the work." [14] Hood was reappointed to Andrew Chapel, New Bern, now known as St. Peter's Church, Mother Church of Zion Methodism in the South.

One of the bright stars of our connectional history was Rev. Andrew Cartwright, who organized the church at Roanoke Island, about simultaneously with the organization of Hood's work at New Bern, and went forth from North Carolina to become the founder of our work in Africa. Reverend Ellis Lavender succeeded Hood at New Bern at Hood's own suggestion to the bishop. Because of an attempt to take the church out of Zion Connection at Fayetteville, Evans Chapel, Hood accepted a reduction in salary from $800 to $300 to go there and save the situation. When the famous Henry Evans was passing through great difficulties in starting a church at Fayetteville, he had three or four preaching points: the Sandhills, the Riverside Tower, Fayetteville, and Cross Creek, and sometimes at the house of Dicey Hammons, grandmother of Thomas H. Lomax. "The Town Council interfered, and nothing in his power could prevail with them to permit him to preach. This is when he withdrew to the secluded places." Bishop Lomax recalled his experience there in the 1850's "when he built the new brick church called Evans Chapel, in 1854-1855, and placed the books, some of Evans' church records and two pieces of candle into the cornerstone." [15]

14. Hood, *One Hundred Years*, pp. 289-297.
15. Lomax, *"Progress of the Third Quarter of the A.M.E. Zion Church,"* op. cit., p. 3.

ST. PETER'S CHURCH, NEW BERN, N.C.
"The Mother Church of Zion Methodism in the South," founded as an
A.M.E. Zion Church in 1864 by Rev. J. W. Hood.

The Lord was in Hood's appointment to Fayetteville in 1866. He found a scattered membership there of 78. In three years, he increased the membership of the church to over 500. By going to Fayetteville, he was elected to the Reconstruction Constitutional Convention, and built up a good reputation among the people in 14 counties. It was the campaign in that section which made him most influential among black and white, and enabled him to establish our church as the leading church in that section, after he was set apart to the bishopric. The Reconstruction Constitutional Convention in North Carolina also laid the foundation for the public school system of that day, and he became Assistant Superintendent of Education of the State. [16]

Reverend E. H. Hill went as far west as Charlotte and organized Clinton Chapel, our first church in that city. He licensed Bird Hampton Taylor and placed him in charge of the church. When he came to conference that year, Bishop Clinton ordained him deacon and elder the same day, and sent him back to Charlotte. "He not only cared for and built up the church at Charlotte, but also went out in every direction and organized churches. He stopped not at the state line, but extended his efforts into South Carolina to the distance of fifty miles." He formed the nucleus of as many as 20 churches in that area. Hill did not live to finish his year's work, but while he was working he accomplished his task for Zion. The work was extended eastward to Edenton and Elizabeth City, and several men were licensed who organized extensively in that section.

Jeffrey Overton exhibited a license which he received in 1831, the year of Nat Turner's insurrection, after which time the Methodist Episcopal Church refused to issue or renew the license of Negro preachers. Hood, along with several other qualified ministers, renewed the license of Overton and others who had been under this limitation, and sent them forth to labor for Zion.

16. Souvenir Program, Hood Thank Offering, 1911, p. 9; Hood, *History*, Vol. II, p. 76.

One of the early organizers of the work was Thomas Henderson, who founded many of the churches in the vicinity of Salisbury, N.C. After doing missionary work for two or three years he was appointed to Fayetteville, where hundreds were converted by his labors, and afterward in New Bern. Reverend William H. Pitts joined the conference in 1865, and organized churches in Edgecombe, Pitt, and Martin counties. [17]

Reverend William J. Moore was one of the 12 members of the organizational North Carolina Conference. During the latter part of 1864 and nearly the whole of 1865 he was engaged with others in organizing societies in North Carolina. He was a stalwart leader, who made rapid progress of expansion throughout the eastern part of the state during 1865-66. Later in Charlotte, Wilmington, and New Bern, as well as Salisbury and Statesville, he made a record equal to any man who held the charges. Moore organized 68 congregations, built 11 churches and improved many others, and licensed 54 local preachers. [18]

Reverends G. B. Farmer and Daniel C. Blacknell were also among the earliest pioneer preachers of North Carolina who exhibited strength and wisdom in building this stronghold for Zion. Reverends Robert Harrison Simmons and Franklin K. Bird were forceful ministers who joined the conference in the 1870's, and continued the expansion of societies throughout the state. [19]

We must also record the fact that in 1855 "Thomas Shirden, a freeborn man, was a circuit rider in Columbus County and had the oversight of three or four hundred members, namely, Rehoboth Church and other congregations without organization, thus laying the foundation for a great church. In 1864-65 these churches were brought into the A.M.E. Zion Connection. . . . Reverend Peter McNatt, who was an active minister in 1864-65, also did a great work in bringing many souls to our beloved Zion in Bladen County, North Carolina." [20] The other ministers attending the first annual conference in New Bern were Revs. H. W. Jones, David Gray, Joseph Green, Sampson Cooper, Abel Ferribee, and Amos York. [21] Among the prominent preachers who made notable contributions in the state and connection, within this period, and became outstanding in Zion history were Revs. Robert S. Rieves, William H. Thurber, H. J. Blanks, C. T. Simmons, Joseph Charles Price, and many others. The original North Carolina Conference had furnished the connection three bishops by 1888: Thomas H. Lomax of Fayetteville, C. C. Pettey of Wilkes County, and C. R. Harris of Fayetteville. [22]

The Far South

Another one of Bishop Clinton's noble coadjutors was Wilbur Garrison Strong. Strong was a native of Hartford, Conn., where his parents resided and attended Zion Church. He moved to Newark, N.J. while a youth, and joined the Zion Church there. Clinton became deeply impressed with Strong's ability when he visited Newark, preached at the church, then extended his stay and visited the Plane Street School, where Wilbur Strong was the principal. After spending sometime listening to the children's recitations and singing, he became thoroughly convinced that Strong, and his assistant, Miss Patricia Madden, were well qualified "to impart instruction to the young." [23] Strong became the effective pioneer of

17. Hood, *One Hundred Years*, pp. 297-298.
18. *Ibid.*, pp. 285-287.
19. *Ibid.*, p. 298.
20. Lomax, "Progress of the Third Quarter . . . " *op. cit.*, p. 5.
21. *Ibid.*
22. Hood, *One Hundred Years*, p. 301.
23. *The Weekly Anglo-African*, Aug. 27, 1859, and Feb. 9, 1861.

Zion in Louisiana, Florida, and Alabama. In selecting Wilbur G. Strong for the work in the far South, "Bishop Clinton was fortunate in getting the man he wanted for that particular work. He was exceedingly well equipped—in fact, the best equipped of any man he had in the South at that time. He had a good education and was a splendid preacher. He was affable, genial, and pleasing in his manners. No one could know him and not love him." [24]

Strong's own testimony of his venture to the South is most graphic. He stated that in September 1864, he received a letter from Bishop Clinton containing the information that he desired him to go to Key West, Florida, and giving him one week to answer. When Bishop Clinton "said anything he meant business." Strong states:

> In that communication he requested me to meet him at the house of Mrs. Sarah Simmons, at Newark, New Jersey, on a certain Saturday. I was then the principal of the Fair Street Grammar School in Newark. We met, and he informed me that a minister was urgently needed at Key West, Florida, and he honored me by desiring my acceptance of the mission. I said to him: Bishop, how do you propose to send me? He replied: I propose to make you a man. I was then a local deacon. . . .
> Believing it to be my duty to labor for Zion in the field which promised the best results, I assured him that I would go. Holding a good position and thinking I might change my mind, he said that he did not want any foolishness. I gave him my hand and pledged my services to Zion. He accepted heartily, and requested me to go to Washington City, where I was ordained an elder in Zion Wesley Church, twenty years ago. The now sainted Samuel M. Giles, preached my ordination sermon. The churches in Washington gave me seventy-five dollars to defray my expenses to Key West. On the 26th day of September, 1865, I sailed from this city [New York] for Florida. I organized a church there on my arrival, with seventy-five members, which was the nucleus of all our work in the far off South. [25]

In a letter to the *Anglo-African,* Strong described the trip, which included a storm at sea. He was warmly received by the people upon his arrival the 5th of October. On October 15, the island was visited with a hurricane and much damage was done to property and fruit, but "fortunately," he stated, "no lives were lost." Said Strong: "We never witnessed such a storm and blow in our life: it was terrific. We thought at one time that our own little domicile would be blown down, but Providence preserved it and us." [26] He immediately became interested in education:

> Isaac Brown, principal of the school here having resigned his position, we have taken charge of the school for the present, and we are doing the best we can with it, and bid fair to have abundant success. . . .We purpose to continue teaching, until we find that the two-fold labor of teaching and preaching is too much for us physically. If such should be the result, we shall have to send for a teacher from the "North," for it would be detrimental to the interests of our people here to discontinue the school. If we should call for help, we hope some one will have courage and patriotism sufficient to respond.—Yours for the elevation of the colored people,

WILBUR G. STRONG. [27]

The Louisiana Conference was the second conference organized in the Southland, March 13, 1865. Soon after organizing the North Carolina Conference, Bishop Clinton went by sea to New Orleans, which like New Bern had been captured by the federal forces. Clinton sent for Wilbur Strong to meet him in New

24. Hood, *One Hundred Years,* p. 367.
25. *Minutes,* Seventeenth Quadrennial Session, 1884, p. 93.
26. *The Weekly Anglo-African,* December 9, 1865.
27. *Ibid.*

REVEREND WILBUR
GARRISON STRONG
Pioneer in the deep South after
Emancipation, particularly
Alabama, Florida, and Louisiana.

Orleans and assist him in the organization. This was the first black conference organized in Louisiana, and the last one formed before the close of the war. There were 15 preachers present. One of the strong leaders was the Rev. George Devere. [28] Others who aided in establishing Zion churches in Louisiana were Revs. P. M. Gertoux, C. Ligel, M. Greggs, and F. P. Loney. [29]

Among the conferences laid out on paper at the 1864 General Conference was the Louisiana Conference. It was to embrace the states south of the North Carolina Conference. "Starting at the James River one was to work southward, and starting at New Orleans the other was to work northward until they met. . . .However wild the scheme, the men who fixed the boundaries of the conferences, then in embryo, had faith in the success of the course of freedom, and their expectations had been quite fulfilled. They built more wisely than they knew." Five conferences were set off by the Louisiana Conference as follows: the Alabama, the Florida, the Georgia, the Texas, and the North Louisiana Conferences. Out of the Alabama Conference, the West Alabama Conference was formed, out of the Georgia, the South Georgia, and out of the Florida, the South Florida, making in all eight conferences springing from the Louisiana Conference. [30] Afterwards six other conferences sprang from these conferences.

Bishop Clinton left Wilbur Strong in New Orleans, after he organized the conference. Strong was the secretary and compiler of the minutes of this first session, and also served at the second session of the conference. Strong was to attend to Zion's interest in Louisiana while Clinton went to Mobile, Ala., where he established societies for Zion. Strong traveled with Bishop Clinton and, at his request, assisted him in organizing conferences in the Gulf states. He was once advised by Rev. E. D. Taylor not to go, as, Strong stated, "my life was in danger, but my reply was where Clinton went I would go." When Clinton organized the Louisiana Conference he thrilled the few standard-bearers around him by declaring that "it was Zion's mission to take ignorance by the throat and choke it to death." [31] Clinton had 15,000 members in Louisiana when he left that work.

28. *Minutes,* Seventeenth Quadrennial Session, p. 19; Hood, *One Hundred Years,* p. 312.
29. Moore, *History,* pp. 168-170.
30. Hood, *One Hundred Years,* pp. 312-313.
31. *Minutes,* Seventeenth Quadrennial Session, p. 93-94.

His immediate successor, by neglect and mismanagement, lost nearly all of them. [32]

Before organizing the annual conferences in the Gulf states, Clinton organized the Virginia Conference at Petersburg, in the Oak Street Church, 1866. There were 25 preachers present, most of them visitors from other conferences. The pioneer preachers of the Virginia Conference were Revs. Charles Heath, J. P. Evans, James Crocker, J. V. Givens, J. McH. Farley, Griffin Irby, Chapel Irby, Wyatt Walker, Elliston Overton, W. C. Butler, Samuel Sunderlin, and William Howard Day. The bishop's great expectation of expanding the work in Virginia was William H. Day, whom he ordained deacon and elder at that organizational conference and commissioned (for the task. Day later became involved in education in Harrisburg, and was loaned to the Philadelphia-Baltimore Conference, maintaining an interest in the Virginia Conference, though unable to expand its borders due to his involvement in race and education, as well as church causes. [33] The Virginia Conference was laid off to embrace all that portion of Virginia south of the James River, except that which was included in the Tennessee Conference, and also 14 counties in the northeast section of North Carolina. The conference grew steadily and had three presiding elders' districts by the turn of the century, all well arranged and presided over by efficient men. [34]

The third southern conference organized, four months prior to the organization of the Virginia Conference, was the Kentucky Conference, on June 6, 1866 at Center Street Church, Louisville, Ky., by Bishop Samson D. Talbot. Bishop Talbot was elected in 1864 and assigned to the Third District, Baltimore and Allegheny Conferences. Before his election, he served on the committee that planned the growth of the connection and worked out the new boundaries. [35] Talbot was a successful pastor, and equally successful episcopal leader, who after starting his ministerial career in the North, moved South during the Reconstruction era, and helped establish the work in Georgia, where he died after 14 years of service. [36] Talbot was associated by Bishop J. J. Clinton in organizing the conference. Reverend William F. Butler was specifically sent to Kentucky from New England Conference, as missionary in 1864. This was the most distinguished group of black men ever to assemble in Louisville, and made a very fine impression in that section. No conference had started off with better promise. At the first session 1,841 members were reported, and during the first year after the formation the increase was most encouraging. The other pioneer preachers of this conference besides William F. Butler were Revs. Samuel Elliott, Leroy Brannon, R. Bridwell, Anthony Bunch, R. Marshall, William Henry Miles, William Koger, E. H. Curry, Peter McCormick, Henderson First, Henry Hughes, David Cole, Henry Brown, Douglas Coward, Thomas Henry, Cicero Hazlewood, Samuel Sherman, William Corneil, Lewis Arnold, and Charles Rodman. This first session was graced with such distinguished visitors as Revs. J. A. Jones, Singleton T. Jones, Jermain W. Loguen, J. J. Whiting, James Armstrong, and J. Bowman of the Northern conferences. [37]

In spite of the fact that it did not have closeup supervision, the conference grew so rapidly the first year that the membership reported at the second conference was 3,253. Most of the men of this conference, however, had no

32. Hood, *History*, Vol. II, p. 29.
33. Hood, *One Hundred Years,* pp. 325, 353-354.
34 *Ibid.,* pp. 353-354.
35. Moore, *History,* pp. 241-242.
36. Hood, *One Hundred Years,* pp. 184-185.
37. *Ibid.,* p. 328.

experience in itinerant work, and were without knowledge of our church polity. They were sent to their appointments in many places without a church edifice, "nay, without church members; nevertheless they went trusting in God for success." In the absence of the bishop, the principal guides left to instruct the Conference were Revs. W. F. Butler and W. H. Miles. Miles was appointed general missionary and supported from Center Street Church by the Daughters of Conference. [38]

The second annual conference was presided over by Bishop William H. Bishop. He removed Butler from Center Street Church, and appointed Miles, and left the conference to be seen no more. During this time, the conference suffered from the lack of supervision, and by the sitting of the third annual conference in 1869, presided over by Bishop Jermain W. Loguen, difficulties had arisen, which resulted in the resignation of Rev. W. ,H. Miles. The creation of the schism, together with some troubles in Tennessee and Georgia, resulted in the formation of the Colored Methodist Episcopal Church a year later. Many of the leading men left the connection and the churches followed in rapid succession, leaving Zion with nine loyal men: Revs. Richard Bridwell, Samuel Elliott, Anthony Bunch, Samuel Sherman, Leroy Brannon, J. B. Stansbury, William Biddle, and E. H. Curry, in Kentucky. [39]

The next event worthy of special mention was the appointment of Right Rev. S. T. Jones, D. D., to the Third Episcopal District, which gave new life and impulse to the Kentucky Conference. The work settled to a firmer base during the twelve consecutive years of his administration, notwithstanding there was some dissatisfaction in the Board of Bishops and among leading men about organic union with the Methodist Episcopal Church, and the Conference being told by those in authority that the union would be consummated in the near future it was hard for them to tell what they were. This had much to do in shaking their faith in the firmness and stability of Zion Connection. But the fight ended, and the faithful few were seen doing what they could to build up Zion. The Kentucky Conference carried the standard of Zion into Indiana, and Missouri, and organized the Arkansas and the Missouri Annual Conferences. [40]

One of the forceful leaders of the Kentucky Conference was the Rev. E. H. Curry, a native Kentuckian. He was a member of the organizational conference, and was sent to Bardstown where he bought the ground and erected a church edifice. The following year he was ordained elder by Bishop Bishop and sent to Russellville, where he had to stand a lawsuit, and his life was threatened if he failed to leave. He stood his ground, however, and bought a lot and built a fine brick church there. From there he was sent to a mission in Louisville where he remained three years and bought a part of the lot upon which the first Jacob Street Church was built. Curry was then sent to Fifteenth Street Church, the mother church of Zion in Kentucky, after the schism, (now Hughlett Temple), where he found a membership of 300, and built up the membership to over 600 in three years. He was then sent back to Russellville for another year. However, Bishop Jones needed a strong man to go to Knoxville, Tenn. and save Loguen's Chapel, which John J. Mitchell was trying to take over to the Methodist Episcopal Church. Curry remained there four months, and handled the situation beautifully, then became seriously ill and went back home to Kentucky. His health was miraculously restored, and he resumed his work in Kentucky, where he built the Jacob Street Tabernacle (now Spradling Chapel). Curry was a successful pastor, church builder,

38. *Ibid.*, p. 329.
39. *Ibid.*
40. *Ibid.*

and presiding elder. Through all the troubled period in the Kentucky Conference, caused by the defection and withdrawal of W. H. Miles and others, Curry was the tower of strength. He was also a mighty asset in the connectional church, and helped to mold programs of progress in the General Conferences. [41]

Reverend James Bartlett Johnson was another leader of the Kentucky Conference, unforgettable in his pioneer spirit. He joined the conference in 1867, organized societies in the face of great opposition, and saved the churches at Springfield and Lebanon during the crisis. He labored ardently at Greenville and Springfield. Johnson also was a prominent connectional leader, and continuous delegate to the General Conferences. He had a family of seven children of which only one son survived, through maturity. His son, Professor Benjamin A. Johnson became the Dean of Livingstone College, after he was brought there by Dr. J. C. Price, and graduated in 1890. [42]

Another hero of the pioneer group in the Kentucky Conference was Rev. Anthony Bunch, who was noted as a man of might and great repute of character. He organized a number of churches in Kentucky. His contribution to Zion's growth was so noteworthy that his name became a household word in that state for generations.

The most distinguished organizer of conferences, Bishop J. J. Clinton, continued his rapid expansion of Zion in the South when he travelled to Chester, S.C., where he organized the South Carolina Conference on March 24, 1867. Bishop Clinton met Revs. I. C. Clinton, (later bishop) and D. I. Walker there, who aided him "in the organization of Zion's work in the Palmetto State." [43] Bishop Clinton's influence was greatly felt in this section. "His dignified and genial bearing, in connection with his executive ability, enabled him to govern that body without assistance." [44] This conference grew rapidly, led by the above mentioned men and Revs. Horace Clinton and Titus Hogans, who walked through the country from Lancaster County, S.C. to New Bern, N.C., to meet the North Carolina Conference in 1866. There they were received and ordained deacons, and sent back as missionaries, ably assisted by Rev. Barney Burton. [45]

Reverend C. A. King was a dedicated servant in building Zion in South Carolina. He joined the conference in 1867, and organized the Unity Church, southwest of Yorkville, in York County, and 16 other churches, principally in York, Chester, and Kershaw Counties. He also built most of these church buildings. "In many cases Brother King cut logs for these buildings and helped with his own hands to erect them." He was one of the four great pioneers in the building up of the South Carolina Conference. "In 1872 the Conference was divided into four presiding elders' districts (it was the first Conference in the connection in which the regular presiding elder system was established). I. C. Clinton, D. I. Walker, C. A. King, and A. M. Moore were the presiding elders. . . . During ten years, beginning with the rise of the Conference in December, 1872, they built eighty churches and paid for them." Reverend Nero A. Crockett was one of Zion's most successful builders in South Carolina also during its earliest development, along with Rev. Page R. Moore.

After organizing the South Carolina Conference, Bishop Clinton travelled

41. *Ibid.*, pp. 556-559.
42. *Ibid.*, pp. 332-336.
43. *Minutes,* Seventeenth Quadrennial Session, p. 94.
44. *Ibid.*
45. Hood, *One Hundred Years,* p. 359-360.

immediately back to Mobile, where he organized the Alabama Conference in State Street Church, April 3, 1867. He sent for Wilbur G. Strong, who served also as secretary of this first conference. The A.M.E. Zion Church was indeed blessed by Clinton's zeal and devotion in Alabama. He travelled throughout the state and organized churches in the capital and other cities. It gave Zion unusual influence in that state. "Being further south, and more affected by the blighting influence of slavery, the men who began the work there were not so well equipped as those who were nearer to the northern border," but they quickly exhibited the effects of the better opportunities in a free church. The work in this state grew so fast that, by the Centennial year, it had the largest number of churches and ministers in the entire connection. [46]

The Alabama Conference was organized during a dangerous period for black people in the South. Reverend Ferdinand H. Smith, the first minister of Little Zion Church in Mobile, was arrested and sent to the penitentiary of that state for refusing to bow to the authority of a rebel preacher. [47] Mobile became the fortress of the far South, and Big Zion Church, first known as Little Zion, grew exceedingly fast by means of conversions and revivals. [48] Among the other most "distinguished of the men whom Bishop Clinton found on the spot and ordained for the work in Alabama were Revs. Allen Hannon, Solomon Derry, Lewis Oliver, M. G. Thomas, Landy Fannin, and Miles Page. Edmund Taylor, a man of great energy, S. W. Jones, who was well equipped for the work, Samuel Wilson, a man of an excellent Christian spirit, and J. M. Butler, the great organizer, were all stalwart men of zeal, piety, and courage. [49] Those men in the galaxy who created churches for Zion also were Revs. Alfred English, E. R. Rose, Robert S. Evans, W. Higgins, S. Hilliard, Lewis Butler, Thomas Wingfield, Joseph Gomez, Hampton P. Shuford, and A. J. Rodgers. [50] An unusual layman and staunch churchman was Lewis Adams, co-founder of Tuskegee Institute, and one of the most prominent members of Butler Chapel, Tuskegee.

By 1877 the Alabama Conference had 8,954 members, and the charges were known as districts. Over 100 preachers were assigned to 39 districts, each with from three to six churches, throughout the state. The following year, the membership was 12,590, with over 400 local preachers and exhorters. [51] After organizing the Alabama Conference in 1867, Bishop Clinton had travelled from Mobile to Montgomery and organized Clinton Chapel (The Old Ship) in the capital city, and held the second and third sessions of the Alabama Conference there in 1868 and 1869, with Wilbur G. Strong, secretary. Seventy-five preachers attended, reporting a total membership of 7,320 throughout this area [52] Thus by the time the conference was 10 years old, it had spread through every section of the state, and continued to grow at a very rapid pace.

Reverends J. W. Alstork, J. W. Cooper, T. A. Weathington, R. R. Morris, and M. G. Thomas rose to prominence in collecting a number of churches in the major cities and towns for Zion. One of the outstanding pioneers previously mentioned with our work in this state was the Rev. Solomon Derry.

"In 1867 he was ordained elder by Bishop J. J. Clinton, and appointed to

---

46. *Ibid.,* pp. 362-365, 577-580.
47. *Weekly Anglo-African,* December 16, 1865.
48. *Minutes,* Twelfth Annual Session, Alabama Conference, p. 11.
49. Hood, *One Hundred Years,* p. 367.
50. *Minutes,* Twelfth Annual Session, Alabama Conference, p. 7.
51. *Ibid.,* pp. 33-35, 36-37.
52. Moore, *History,* pp. 179-180.

Union Springs, Alabama where he planted Zion and organized the following churches: Derry's Chapel at Union Springs: St. Paul at Magnolia; Lee's Chapel at Aberfoil; Zion Church at Thompson's; Mallard's Chapel at Pea River; Bascom's Cornerstone, at Bascom's Mill; Moor's Chapel at Raimer's; Ross Chapel at Hurtsboro; Henderson's Chapel and Little Zion at Orion; Anderson's Chapel at Euchee; Zion Church at Perote; Zion Church at Columbus, Georgia. [At Union Springs he taught school for a considerable time, in Derry's Chapel, with 150 pupils.] At this place he went through untold suffering for God and Zion. The Ku Kluxes were ranging that section, whipping, shooting, hanging, and burning churches and schoolhouses. He was visited by them and ordered to leave the place, but he refused to obey men, choosing rather to obey God by holding his ground; remained six years, and was the means of sending out seventy-five local and traveling preachers and brought in six hundred and twenty-five members—a total of seven hundred. [53]

Derry was known as one of the best organizers in the conference. He pastored Butler Chapel at Tuskegee as early as 1873, and built a school house out of his own pocket and gave it to the church.

Another organizer of a number of churches throughout Alabama was Rev. John Wesley Alstork (later bishop). He pastored Opelika in 1882, and in 1884 he had very great success as the young pastor of Old Ship, Montgomery, for four years. He was elected a presiding elder in 1889. In 1892 he was elected Financial Secretary of the connection and served until he was elected bishop in 1900. Alstork was National Grand Master of A.A. York Masons of the United States. His influential leadership as both a churchman and a masonic leader stimulated the growth of Zion throughout Alabama.

Another influential leader, who became presiding elder in the East Alabama Conference at Anniston, in 1893, and was appointed to the Montgomery District, was the Rev. Titus Atticus Weathington. His work of expanding the church was principally accomplished in the central part of the state. In 1888 he was elected financial secretary of the Sunday School Department of the A.M.E. Zion Church, and re-elected in 1892. [54]

Two months after organizing the Alabama Conference, Bishop J. J. Clinton travelled to Georgia and organized the Georgia Conference in Trinity Church, Augusta, June 15, 1867. "He had taken into the connection that fine Trinity Church in Augusta, said at that time to be one of the finest colored churches in the South." [55] Reverend Wilbur G. Strong travelled with him and served as secretary of that first conference. Edward West who was in charge of the church at Augusta was one of the leading men of the conference. The other leaders were Revs. Robert Brown, Simeon Beal, Jeremiah Hayes, Edward Jones, Bustee Gould, William Laws, John Roberts, H. J. Thomas, M. Broomfield, George Martin, James Whitehead, Cato Schley, Sterling Cooper, Erasemus Jones, Barriston Smith, and others. 3,472 members were reported at this first conference. However, before the second conference convened, Rev. Dr. West recanted and went to the Methodist Episcopal Church, "carrying back 1,160 members. [56] This marred Zion's hopes for becoming strong in that state. "Augusta was one of the three important points in Georgia at that time. The Methodist Episcopal Church held Atlanta, the African Methodist Episcopal Church held Savannah," and if we could have held Augusta

53. Hood, *One Hundred Yearrs*, pp. 372-374.
54. *Ibid.*, pp. 373-379.
55. Ibid., p. 364.
56. Moore, *History*, pp. 201-202; *Minutes*, Forty-Fourth Annual Session, Georgia Annual Conference, 1911, p. 3.

THE FIRST A.M.E. ZION CHURCH
OF THE WEST COAST
SAN FRANCISCO, CALIF.

Organized August 1, 1852 by Rev. John J.
Moore

Church on Stockton Street purchased
in 1864. A new church was built
in 1960.

we would have been in as good a position as any of them; but losing Augusta lost for Zion a firm hold on Georgia. All things considered, however, the few who were faithful to Zion's cause after the break struggled on like heroes and maintained the organization to keep Zion alive in Georgia. Later the North Georgia Conference was set apart, which we shall mention in turn. [57]

The second annual session of the Georgia Conference convened in Augusta, March 27, 1868, and the third session, March 17, 1869, with Bishop Clinton presiding, and Revs. A. Anderson and Peter Drayton serving as secretaries respectively. The membership of the conference was 2,032 in 1868, and continued to increase steadily. Ten years later, the membership was 4,317. [58]

The West

The A.M.E. Zion Church had missions established in California before Bishop J. J. Clinton went west and established the California Conference. John Jamison Moore, a dynamic young man who became an itinerant preacher in· the Philadelphia Annual Conference in 1839, became one of the half-dozen greatest leaders our Zion has produced. "During his connection with that Conference he traveled on numerous circuits and filled stations in various parts of Pennsylvania, Maryland, and Ohio. Crossing the Allegheny Mountains as a traveling preacher, he proclaimed life and salvation to the fugitive slaves who had found an asylum in these mountainous regions. Among the coal and iron mines he carried the gospel on foot, walking thirty miles a day and preaching at night. He left Baltimore in 1852 for California, where he established several churches, one in San Francisco worth fifty thousand dollars, the colored people in this country having none which excelled it," at that time. The whole time he was on the coast he kept his membership in the Philadelphia Conference until he was elected a bishop in 1868 and returned to the east. [59]

In the San Francisco area, the protracted meetings and revivals held under his

57. Hood, *One Hundred Years*, pp. 364-365.
58. Moore, *History*, pp. 202-204.
59. *Ibid.*, pp. 369-370.

auspices were well attended and very successful. [60] He gave himself wholeheartedly to the cause of freedom rights and education for the race during this period preceding Emancipation and immediately thereafter. He organized the first Negro school in California and the Pacific Coast.

Bishop Clinton made a brief departure from his southern work, travelled the long hard road across the continent, and organized the California Conference, in San Francisco, Jan 10, 1868. In delivering his impressive address, he mentioned God's gracious providence in bringing him safely to the Pacific Coast, and the members responded enthusiastically. The first preachers of the conference were Revs. John J. Moore, Adam Smith, Joshua B. Handy, William B. Smith, James B. Wilkinson, Edward Hall, James Lodge, A. T. Rogers, R. T. Houston, and R. Bradford. Mr. Henry M. Collins, William Brooks, and Thomas Gaines represented the laity. The three churches represented were Zion Church (now First Church), San Francisco, San Jose, and Napa, California. [61] At the General Conference in May of the same year, Bishops Loguen and Brooks were assigned this new district, to interchange after two years. Both bishops died during the following quadrennium, however, and the work on the West Coast lagged for lack of leadership. William Henry Hillery, who had represented the California Conference in the three General Conferences since its founding, was elected bishop at the 1876 General Conference and assigned the California Conference. [62] Hillery reported to the 1880 General Conference that his 15 months absence in Europe allowed the people to take advantage of the situation and flee to the A.M.E. Church. Although he reported he had been forced to go to England to solicit for the San Francisco Church, which was in jeopardy, he did not make any report of funds brought back from the trip. Only two loyal Zion ministers remained with us during his absence, Revs. J. B. Handy and A. B. Smith, and a third minister named Davis was added to the roll. [63]

Hillery was, by far, "the ablest man on the coast at that time, and if he had made the best use of natural abilities he could have planted the Church wherever there were enough of the race for the purpose. But he failed, and when the work was visited by Bishop Lomax, in 1881, there were only the original number of three churches." When Rev. Alexander Walters was sent to San Francisco, he succeeded in strengthening the things which remained, "which were ready to die"; and from that time there was a continual growth. Reverend C. C. Pettey followed with a considerable emigration from the East, especially North Carolina, which included many of his relatives, and succeeded in planting several new churches. Toward the end of the century, there were 16 preachers and 650 members. [64] Reverends J. H. Hector, Tillman Brown, George E. Jackson, H. J. Callis, and M. W. Bynum assisted Bishop Lomax and Elder Pettey in this growth.

By 1900 the California Conference embraced the states of California, Oregon, Washington, and the territory of Arizona, with 13 well-established churches. Our first church in Los Angeles was established during the Centennial year, and in 1897, Bishop G. W. Clinton found 11 members worshipping in a small hall. Reverend C. W. H. Nelson secured a lot, and the first church was built through the sacrificial efforts of Rev. H. W. Hawkins. The church at Oakland was greatly popularized by Rev. W. W. Matthews, who later became presiding elder on the coast, and afterward bishop. The man who labored the longest period for Zion in

60. *The Weekly Anglo-African*, May 11, 1861.
61. Moore, *History*, pp. 183-185.
62. *Ibid.*, (Minutes of Quadrennial Sessions, 1868, 1872, 1876).
63. *Minutes*, Sixteenth Quadrennial Session, 1880, p. 19.
64. Hood, *One Hundred Years*, p. 380.

this area was Rev. Tillman Brown. [65] Reverends W. W. Howard, W. D. Speight, and W. J. Byers also established work in Southern California and Arizona, under the leadership of Bishop J. S. Caldwell. [66] In 1916, Bishop L. W. Kyles was assigned the work on the Pacific Coast where he, with Presiding Elder E. M. Clark, bought or built nearly a dozen churches in the California-Arizona area [67] This was the beginning of the migration period of our people, north and west.

Still Advancing in the South

On October 6, 1868, the Tennessee Conference was organized by Bishop J. J. Clinton at Knoxville, Tennesee. Elder J. W. Loguen (later bishop) organized the first A.M.E. Zion Church in the city of Knoxville, and the first two annual conferences were held in this church, now known as Loguen Temple. Reverends Alfred E. Anderson, A. B. Kline, H. DeBose, Henry Rowley, John A. Tyler, John Dogan, T. A. Hopkins, who had been sent to this state earlier as a missionary, W. H. Hillery and others were among the founders. "Bishop Clinton held four annual sessions. During his episcopal stay the work increased very rapidly. More than six thousand members were added in this period mentioned." This conference, comprising East Tennessee, Western North Carolina (west of the Blue Ridge), Northern Georgia, and Southwestern Virginia, was well organized. Bishop Talbot succeeded Clinton, and during his administration hundreds were added to the church. "The bishop added, comparatively speaking, a new set of ministers to the conference. Many of the original members had transferred, and some had joined other denominations that had been created." [68]

"Reverends James A. Zachary, Robert R. Russell, Thomas Warren, Joseph Pugh, J. P. Jay, Henry Tipton, John N. Brown, D. W. Wells, W. H. Ferguson and James D. Rogers were among those who composed the Conference when Bishop Singleton T. Jones took charge in the fall of 1872." The conference flourished while he presided for the next 10 years. Large numbers were added, yet some drifted away into other denominations that offered better facilities for education. Several efforts were then made to establish a school within the bounds of the conference, and through the ingenuity of Rev. B. M. Gudger, The Greenville High School was later established.

For 15 years Zion progressed steadily in this territory. Bishops W. H. Hillery and J. P. Thompson each held one annual session of the conference, and there was no advancement during these two years in the rural districts. The larger towns and cities held their own. Bishop J. W. Hood encountered difficulty when he arrived on the scene. There was a split of over 600 members, taken from one of our churches in Knoxville, which threatened progress in surrounding areas but was overcome. Hood won the confidence of both clergy and laity, and the waste places of Zion began to rebuild. Thus in two years' time the membership nearly doubled, new churches sprang up, and confidence was once more established on the part of the people.

It was during Bishop Lomax's forceful leadership that the conference had grown to such proportions that it became necessary to divide it in 1892. Among the pioneers in building this territory were also Revs.: Samuel Sherman, J. H. Manley, J. H. Starling, M. M. Montgomery, George W. Christmas, E. J. Harris, B. J. Arnold, L. S. Baker, T. F. H. Blackman, H. Bayless, H. B. Moss, G. W. Kincaid, B.

65. *Minutes,* Twenty-First Quadrennial Session, pp. 152-153; Twenty-Third Quadrennial Session, p. 113.

66. *Minutes,* Twenty-Fourth Quadrennial Session, p. 267.

67. *Minutes,* Twenty-Sixth Quadrennial Session, pp. 124-125.

68. Hood, *One Hundred Years,* p. 336.

F. Tipton, J. T. Gaskill, D. B. Branner, F. A. Mouldin, William Walton, and M. M. Morris.

The Florida Conference was organized by Bishop J. J. Clinton at Pensacola, April 22, 1869. Its principal churches at that time were Key West, mother church in Florida, Pensacola, and Milton. There were 13 preachers present and 348 members reported. Bishop Clinton presided over the first two sessions, Rev. Edward Johnson served as secretary of the first session, and Rev. Solomon Derry of the second session. Clinton was followed by Bishop Talbot. Reverends A. C. Fisher, Joseph Sexton, and James Harris were leaders in organizing some of the churches around Key West, after Wilbur G. Strong started the first church. Reverends Simon Brown, Thomas Darley, E. Hunter, H. P. Shuford, J. M. Sims, J. H. Simons, A. L. Green, J. M. Simons, and B. J. Arnold were the early leaders who organized and built churches in other parts of the state. Presiding Elder S. L. McDonnel, Revs. M. Stokes, S. W. Jackson, J. M. Butler, Joseph and G. Sexton, W. C. Vesta, Mingo Stokes, I. L. Ferby, B. F. Stevens, Wilson Perry, and H. E. Jones later became forceful leaders in spreading the work throughout the state. (69)

The West Tennessee and Mississippi Conference was organized by Bishop J. J. Clinton in Coffeeville, Miss., October 1869. (70) Reverend T. A. Hopkins, the first missionary to the state of Tennessee, assisted Clinton. Reverends William Murphy, Grandison Simms, Alexander J. Coleman, Daniel J. Adams, I. J. Manson, and L. J. Scurlock were the leading men in spreading the borders of Zion throughout Mississippi and West Tennessee. These men, with others, expanded from this conference into Arkansas.

The last conference organized by Bishop J. J. Clinton in the South was the Arkansas Conference, set off from the West Tennessee and Mississippi Conference in January 1870, at Little Rock, Arkansas. The conference, however, was represented by members of the West Tennessee and Mississippi Conference, when an effort was made in 1879 by Bishop J. P. Thompson to revive it. Bishop Thompson stated in his report of 1880: In conformity with order, I had the honor to organize said Conference on the 13th of November last, under the name of Arkansas Conference of the A.M.E. Zion Church in America, subject to the ratification of the General Conference.   (71)

Bishop Hood writes, however, of another movement to make the Arkansas Conference permanent, but by all odds, it was done by the creative pioneership of Bishop J. J. Clinton in 1870. It was firmly established in March 1882 by Bishop Singleton T. Jones, as an offspring from the Kentucky Conference. The work was developed by men from the Kentucky Conference, especially Revs. Yarmouth Carr, Andrew J. Warner, and Jeremiah M. Washington. Other pioneers who developed the work in this state so that it was later necessary to divide it into another conference (North Arkansas) were Revs. G. W. H. Andrews, R. J. Simms, G. W. Morris, T. J. Jones, R. B. Macon, W. A. Blackwell, M. R. Williams, A. F. Goslin, J. H. Jackson, D. W. Poe, H. Bingham, A. Arnold, and S. L. Corrothers. (72)

Thus was the beginning of the African Methodist Episcopal Zion Church in the South, Southwest, and West, after Emancipation and the Civil War. The church continued to grow in its original territory, and to spread into new territory, while still swelling in numbers in the South where slavery had left ugly scars, and new programs of education and social uplift had to be begun immediately among our race people.

69. *Ibid.*, pp. 380-381: Moore, *History,* pp. 193-196; *Minutes,* Quadrennial General Conferences, 1872-1896.

70. Hood, *History,* Vol. II, p. 29.

71. *Ibid.*

72. Hood, *One Hundred Years,* pp. 433-434.

CHAPTER 16

RAPID GROWTH IN THE COUNTRY CONTINUES

Bishop J. J. Clinton's labors reached back into the North, his original land of activity. He organized the New Jersey Conference from the New York Conference, on Thursday, July 2, 1874, at Red Bank, N.J. A number of churches had been organized in the New Jersey area under his leadership, and had grown sufficiently to be made into an independent conference, embracing the whole of New Jersey and Staten Island. The first 11 appointments in the new conference were Jersey City, Paterson, Somerville, Red Bank and Eatontown, Macedonia and Mattawan, Lodi and Paramus, Rahway and Newark, Rossville and Port Richmond, Westfield and Plainfield, Greenville Station and Hackensack. The elders composing this first conference were Revs. Clinton Leonard and J. A. Roberts, Cyrus Oliver who did most of his work at Jersey City, S. J. Berry, C. W. Robinson, L. B. Henry, William H. Purnell, and J. A. Evans. These were all grand men, especially noted for their work as revivalists, which accounted for the striking success in the northern part of the state. [1] The Mother Church of the conference, Newark, organized in 1823, was having intense struggles of survival and did not become stable until 1927.

Reverend J. W. Johnson was largely responsible for our extension into Trenton, and the others who were deeply interested and resolved to organize societies for both adults and children were Revs. John P. Thompson, who labored at Paterson, Camden, Red Bank, and Asbury Park; J. S. Cowles, J. A. Wright, Nelson Turpin, Anthony Jackson, John Smith, Henry Cook, and M. G. Lansing. Other strong leaders in developing this area, and in organizing The Church Extension Board within the conference, were Revs. Benjamin F. Wheeler, William T. Biddell, M. M. Edmonson, and J. B. Saunders. Reverend C. E. Steward organized a flourishing society in Bayonne City, New Jersey; Revs. J. H. Mason, L. G. Mason Louis Hicks, J. A. D. Bloice, J. T. Tilghman, Luther Duffin, R. S. Cottene and E. M. Stanton were among the others who labored throughout the state to organize new churches for Zion within 20 years after the conference was formed. [2]

"This was the last conference organized by Bishop Clinton, the great organizer." He did his own preparatory missionary work. "He went to Louisiana alone where Zion ministers had been seen in an army transport vessel. He followed Elder Hood to New Bern in less than six months after he sent him there. He followed Elder Strong to Alabama soon after he sent him. He also followed T. A. Hopkins to Tennessee soon after he sent him. He went to Florida and Georgia to open the way for others." [3] On May 24, 1881, Clinton closed an eventful, useful

1. Hood, *One Hundred Years,* pp. 384-396.
2. *Ibid.*
3. Hood, *History,* Vol. II, p. 29.

life after long and painful affliction, [4] and the church humbly bowed to the divine mandate that bereaved it of this "bright star that scintillated in the horizon of Zion's spreading hopes.—*The Prince and great man had fallen.*" [5]

On September 11, 1879, Bishop Thomas H. Lomax organized the Canada and Michigan Conference, in Detroit, Mich. There were 32 preachers present, and 499 members were reported. After the removal of Bishop Lomax, the work suffered in this area, and was finally suspended until the coming of Bishop George Lincoln Blackwell, in 1908. [6] However, Bishop Lomax was assigned this district laid off at the 1876 General Conference as a Missionary District, and travelled and held sessions at Windsor and Grand Rapids before 1879. By 1880 he reported 14 churches and 633 members. [7]

The second conference organized in North Carolina, and the fifth offspring of the North Carolina Conference, was the Central North Carolina Conference, November 18, 1879, by Bishop J. W. Hood. "It included about twenty-five counties west of Raleigh and east of the Blue Ridge Mountains." [8] The growth in the state was so successful that it was necessary to set off the Western North Carolina Conference November 25, 1891. Bishop John J. Moore organized this conference at Lincolnton, North Carolina. [9] It was composed of the counties on the east side of the Blue Ridge Mountains, extending southeast as far as Mecklenburg County and northeast as far as Forsythe County, forming nearly one-half of the territory previously within the bounds of the Central North Carolina Conference. [10] It was reported in 1878, in five of the larger churches—Andrew Chapel (St. Peter's), New Bern; Evans Chapel, Fayetteville; Clinton Chapel, Charlotte; Zion Chapel, Salisbury (Soldiers' Memorial); and Zion Church (Zion Hill), Concord—the converts totaled over 500 during the year, and several of the rural churches had exceeded 50. [11] There were 13 presiding elder districts with from 10 to 15 churches and 202 preachers, with 26,631 members. [12] By the time these two conferences were set apart, there were nearly two dozen districts throughout the state.

Between 1888 and 1892, Bishop Lomax had doubled the number of churches in Eastern Tennessee, and organized a temporary conference known as East Tennessee, which was also referred to as East Tennessee, Virginia, and North Carolina Conference, because of extension in the western section of North Carolina and the southwestern portion of Virginia. [13] In October 1892, Bishop Lomax organized the Blue Ridge Conference at Knoxville, Tenn. The boundaries and names of these two conferences were changed several times during the next four decades, while the church continued to grow in this mountainous area. October 15, 1910, Bishop C. R. Harris organized the Southwest Virginia Conference at Asheville, N.C. [14]

Those principally responsible for the growth during the 1890's in eastern Tennessee, due to judicious management and untiring labors, were presiding elders B. M. Gudger, T. J. Manson, W. M. Anderson, and F. R. White, and Revs. F. M.

4. *Minutes,* Seventeenth Quadrennial Session, p. 89.
5. Moore, *History of the A.M.E. Zion Church,* p. 366.
6. Hood, *History,* Part II, p. 29.
7. *Minutes,* Sixteenth Quadrennial Session, p. 20.
8. Hood, *One Hundred Years,* p. 401.
9. *Minutes,* First Session of the Western North Carolina Conference, 1892.
10. Hood, *One Hundred Years,* p. 443.
11. *Minutes,* Fifteenth Session of the North Carolina Conference, p. 7.
12. *Ibid.,* pp. 40-43.
13. *Minutes,* Nineteenth Quadrennial Session, pp. 30-31; Hood, *One Hundred Years,* p. 457.
14. Hood, *History,* Vol. II, p. 30.

Jacobs, E. D. W. Jones (later bishops), B. James Jones (father of Bishop Raymond L. Jones), A. L. Cowan, W. H. Tucker, A. S. Monroe, J. W. Wright, and T. F. H. Blackman. [15] In the Blue Ridge Conference, presiding elders A. G. Kesler, Pero H. Williams, and William Lyons labored with creative earnestness; thus 10 missions were organized during the quadrennium, 1896-1900, and another 12 churches built and bought ably led by Rev. W. W. Slade (later bishop), an extraordinary and creative young preacher. Revs. William Glenn, L. V. Watson, George Rose, Jr., D. Goode, and G. W. Bell. In the Asheville area Revs. G. W. Hampton, B. J. Hill, T. B. Hacket, C. Padget, W. B. Fenderson, George W. Maize, I, J. F. Quinn, and J. W. Williams established and built new Churches [16]

By 1908, the Blue Ridge Conference had five presiding elder districts, with about 5,000 members, stretching by rail 534 miles from Gary, W. Va. to Blue Ridge, Ga. Bishop Harris then recommended the division of the conference, which was approved by the 1908 General Conference. [17] When he organized the Southwest Virginia Conference in 1910, at Asheville, N.C., the conference embraced all that part of the Blue Ridge Conference north and east of Bull's Gapp, Tenn., containing two large presiding elder districts. [18] In 1912, the seven counties lying in the Western North Carolina Conference—Polk, Rutherford, Cleveland, McDowell, Burk, Caldwell, and Watauga—were added to the Blue Ridge Conference, ranging west to Morristown, Tenn., inclusive of Blue Ridge, Ga. the present boundary of the Blue Ridge Conference. [19] While the Blue Ridge Conference, at first, comprised eastern Tennessee, today it is fundamentally the extreme western part of North Carolina eastward to Morganton, and extreme parts of eastern Tennessee.

The Southwest Virginia Conference existed until 1920, presided over by Bishop George W. Clinton. It was then known as the Southwest Virginia and East Tennessee Conference, and in 1924 the General Conference adopted the name, East Tennessee and Virginia Conference, the borders being the same, with a membership of 3,650. [20]

The fifth conference in the state of North Carolina is the West Central North Carolina Conference, set off from the Central North Carolina Conference, November 18, 1910. The boundary lines were not fixed until the following year. Each conference had three presiding elder's districts with equal assessments of connectional claims. "The improvements of this work have exceeded anything in my experience," stated Hood. In 1896 Central North Carolina Conference had 67 charges, including a number of circuits. In 1900, there were 88, in 1904 there were 107, and in 1908, 127 churches. [21]

Hood noted that the one thing above all others that enabled this Central North Carolina Conference to hold the first rank in the South was the ability of our presiding elders. [22] As a matter of fact, the presiding elders, from their inception in the church in 1872 through the period of northern migration after World War I, were the potent factor in the astonishing growth of the denomination. These men travelled the long dusty roads and became significantly responsible for organizing and bringing into Zion most of our metropolitan

15. *Minutes,* Twentieth Quadrennial Session, 1896, p. 134.
16. *Minutes,* Twenty-First Quadrennial Session, 1900, pp. 137-138.
17. *Minutes,* Twenty-Third Quadrennial Session, 1908, p. 83.
18. *Minutes,* Twenty-Fourth Quadrennial Session, p. 188.
19. *Ibid.*
20. *Minutes,* Twenty-Sixth Quadrennial Session, 1920, p. 121; *Minutes,* Twenty-Seventh Quadrennial Session, 1924, p. 235.
21. *Minutes,* Twenty-Fourth Quadrennial Session, *op. cit.,* pp. 173, 174.
22. *Ibid.*

BISHOP THOMAS HENRY LOMAX
1832 - 1908

Magnetic preacher. Molder of our Publishing
House. Organizer of conferences and
founder of schools.

churches and practically all of our present rural churches.

The Central North Carolina Conference continued to grow so rapidly, even after the Western North Carolina Conference was set off in 1891, it was difficult for the bishop to keep account of the churches. When the West Central North Carolina Conference was set apart, presiding elder John W. Thomas was conspicuous for his ability to build up the work. When he took the Concord District, it included seven counties in all. "At his death his district was composed of two counties only—Cabarrus and Union, and yet it was paying as much general claims as the whole work did when he took it. Besides this, there had been formed out of his district one other whole district, and two parts of a district; nearly three districts out of one, and he still retained the original Concord District. Out of that district the Wadesboro District was wholly formed. [23] Presiding Elders F. K. Bird and J. S. Settle built up churches on this district. The Fayetteville District was formed from a small part of Thomas' district, but a very much larger part of his district formed the Greensboro District developed largely by Rev. W. H. Graham, who also labored to build up the Carthage District. Reverend C. T. Mitchell, possessed of a missionary spirit, was regarded as one of the best missionary presiding elders of his day. His principal accomplishment was building up the Raleigh District, which was reduced three or four times. Out of his original district also about one-half of the churches made up the large Greensboro District, and other districts in surrounding areas, and later the potent Durham District was formed. Presiding Elder C. P. S. Harrison labored afterwards in continuing the growth. [24]

The other presiding elders largely responsible for building up new districts in the Central and newly organized West Central North Carolina Conferences were Reverends W. W. Slade, J. M. Hill, J. H. Mattocks, A. F. Moore, John Hooper, C. R. Harris, and T. F. H. Blackman.

23. *Ibid.*
24. *Ibid.,* p. 175-177.

Some early pioneers and expanders of the Central North Carolina Conference led by Bishop J. W. Hood and J. J. Moore (one quadrennium) were:

A. M. Barrett	Nelson Logan
L. D. Blackson	A. W. Marsh
Hilliard Blake	Jerry E. McNiel
E. C. Davidson	S. S. Mobley
J. W. Davis	R. C. Moore
J. M. Erwin	Robert S. Rieves
George Flack	Edward F. Rollins
A. F. Goslin	R. D. Russell
G. W. Grange	T. C. Simmons
G. H. Haines	S. W. Spaits
H. V. Harris	J. J. Stitt
P. J. Holmes	Henry D. Tillman
T. C. Johnson	John A. Tyler
A. G. Kesler	David Williams
William M. Little	L. H. Wyche

Leading pioneers of the West Central North Carolina Conference were:

P. L. Alexander	W. F. McKee
J. A. Barber	William McKoy
J. S. Bennett	P. A. McRae
R. Cox	G. H. Miles
A. A. Crooke	W. M. Mitchell
P. L. Cuyler	W. J. Peggans
W. C. DeBerry	N. T. Perry
C. B. Fletcher	H. W. Riddick
W. E. Foushee	J. R. Shepard
A. J. Gorham	W. J. Sides
W. H. Graham	T. C. Simmons
R. Hasty	C. K. Smith
E. J. Hawkins	W. M. Spaulding
A. S. Hubbard	R. Spruell
G. W. Hunter	T. H. Stevenson
I. S. Ingram	J. J. Stubb
W. L. Lee	Robert Taylor
J. W. Levy	R. M. Thompson
C. M. Mason	W. B. Turner
T. B. McCain	W. O. Waddell
A. McIver	E. B. Watson

Other able leaders who organized churches in the West Central North Carolina Conference were Revs. J. A. Torrence, W. J. Cotten, H. G. McLeord, A. M. Moore, George Morgan, Green W. Johnson, H. S. Hullard, Whitey Hagans, Simon Walls, J. M. Gould, C. W. Carver, R. Hasty, J. S. Settle, J. W. A. Blake, T. J. Houston, T. T. Taylor, and George Flack.

The mother Conference of the South, North Carolina Conference, continued its rapid growth in the east led by Bishops J. W. Hood, T. H. Lomax, J. P.

Thompson, Cicero R. Harris, and Alexander Walters; associated by such prominent preachers as J. H. Mattocks, S. J. Hargrave, Amos York, G. H. Hill, Joseph Charles Price, A. B. Smyer, Charles H. Smith, John B. Small, Z. T. Pearsall, William H. Thurber, S. J. Adams, A. W. Allison, John Hooper, S. B. Gaskill, A. G. Oden, H. C. Phillips, W. A. Keys, L. B. Williams, W. H. Newby, F. B. House, S. B. Hunter, O. L. W. Smith, J. E. Garrett, and such outstanding laymen as A. S. Richardson and John C. Dancy, Sr. [25]

During this period of growth, Revs. Robert Stephen Rieves, who later became deeply interested in our first educational enterprise in the South, Robert Russell Morris, founder of our Sunday School Literature, R. Haywood Stitt, J. D. McKoy, and William C. Coleman, moved steadily about this area, pastoring some of Zion's leading churches and assisting the elders in building up surrounding points. [26]

While the Western North Carolina Conference had been set off from the Central Conference earlier, it produced the leaders within its boundaries which made it the fastest growing conference of the denomination. Starting out with three presiding elders' districts, it spread so rapidly, by 1912, it was the largest conference in the denomination, and the center of Zion Methodism, which place it still holds today. Our chief educational institution, Livingstone College, and the Publishing House of our church are within the bounds of this conference. The Lincolnton District was set apart from the Statesville District, the Winston-Salem District from the Salisbury District, and the North Charlotte District from the hugely developed Charlotte District. Largely responsible for this massive growth were Bishops Thomas H. Lomax, Isom C. Clinton and George W. Clinton, assisted by Presiding Elders M. V. Marable in the Salisbury area, Henry L. Simmons around Statesville and Lincolnton, and E. L. Campbell in the Charlotte area. [27] Bishop George W. Clinton set apart the Winston-Salem District from the Salisbury District, and assigned Rev. H. B. Bennett in 1908. He increased this smallest of the five districts at that time 75% in connectional claims, and almost doubled the membership. [28] The other districts had a significant measure of success, led by Revs. H. S. Simmons, A. L. Martin, Hilliard Blake, P. A. McCorkle, and B. E. Martin. Presiding Elder Sidney D. Watkins, who succeeded Campbell, continued to expand in the Charlotte area, and Bishop G. W. Clinton made a second district called North Charlotte District by 1916. Assisting these elders in organizing churches were

Reverends:

			A. L. Newby
George S. Adams	E. D. Davidson	P. J. Holmes	S. M. Pharr
F. Archie	W. D. Dickerson	J. A. House	J. S. Settle
C. H. Ardis	W. D. Dinkens	S. W. Jackson	C. W. Simmons
L. A. Barber	J. T. L. Dunham	J. W. Jenkins	R. H. Simmons
W. J. Benjamin	A. D. Dunlap	W. M. Johnson	Mayfield Slade**
H. B. Bennett	M. R. Franklin	H. A. Keaton	J. W. Smith
J. L. Black	W. H. Goler	J. H. Love	J. W. Thomas
W. A. Blackwell	S. F. Hamilton	D. A. McCoy	J. F. Torrence
Robert B. Bruce	S. W. Hamilton	D. A. McKay	J. A. Tyler

25. *Ibid., Minutes,* First Session, Central North Carolina Conference, pp. 1-3.
26. Hood, *One Hundred Years,* pp. 403-419; *Minutes,* 16th and 17th Sessions, North Carolina Annual Conference; *Minutes,* 24th - 26th Quadrennial Sessions, 1912-1920.
27. *Minutes,* 16th-24th Quadrennial Sessions, 1880-1912.
28. *Minutes,* First Session, Western North Carolina Conference, p. 3; Twenty-Fourth Quadrennial Session, pp. 343-353.

M. Caldwell	J. L. Hendrix	H. S. McMullen	A. A. Williams
E. L. Campbell	S. Herndon	R. A. Morrissey	J. G. Williams
S. Carter	J. M. Hill	J. T. Murdock	Thomas W. Wallace
A. T. Clement*	P. C. Hilton	S. S. Murdock	J. E. Westberry
R. C. Collins		G. G. Musgrove	A. L. Wilson [29]

*Father of Bishop George C. Clement
**Father of Bishop W. W. Slade

The sixth conference formed in the state of North Carolina was the Albemarle Conference. Many churches in northeastern North Carolina were established while that part of the state was in the Virginia Conference. This section of the Virginia Conference had a steady growth since its founding in 1866. Those preachers principally responsible for organizing churches were Revs. J. McH. Farley, Alfred Newby, J. P. Evans, H. B. Pettigrew, Noah L. and E. Overton, J. A. Jones, William C. Butler, R. A. Fisher, Samuel Story, J. J. Adams, C. B. Hogans, W. H. Pitts, T. R. V. Harrison, (founder of the Norfolk District), and Andrew Cartwright (who created Zion churches at Plymouth and Jamesville, N.C.). Later Rev. B. J. Bolding came into the picture and saved the church at Petersburg, (mother church of the Virginia Conference), which had been victim of court action and almost lost to the connection. Presiding Elders C. W. Winfield, S. P. Cooke, and M. N. Levy were leaders in expanding the conference. After long tedious struggles, churches were established in Newport News and Richmond, around 1910. [30]

Bishop J. W. Smith, who had been assigned the Virginia Conference in 1908, had invited Bishop J. W. Hood to join with him in helping to organize the Albemarle Conference out of the Virginia Conference, but passed away a few months before the annual conference. The Board of Bishops authorized Bishop G. W. Clinton to take charge of the Virginia Conference. The Forty-Fifth Session of the Virginia Conference met at Edenton, N.C., on November 30, 1910, presided over jointly by Bishops G. W. Clinton and J. W. Hood. They worked in beautiful harmony in carrying out this design of Bishop Smith. Hood took charge of the Virginia Conference, and Clinton the Albemarle Conference, by authorization of the bishops until the General Conference. [31] Presiding Elders S. P. Cooke of the Edenton District and M. P. Hawkins of the Elizabeth City District carried this well begun work on into commendable history. [32]

The seventh conference organized in North Carolina was the Cape Fear Conference, on November 27, 1911, at Wilmington. Bishop Alexander Walters was assigned the historic North Carolina Conference in 1908, which he found in a flourishing condition, with 186 churches and nearly 12,000 members. Prior to the division of the conference, it had six presiding elder districts, and the work had grown considerably under Revs. W. J. Moore, William Sutton, Herbert Bell, J. H. Mosely, P. L. Lawrence, and James T. Gaskill, and continued to multiply after the division of the conference. [33]

In 1888 the South Carolina Conference was assigned to Bishop Singleton T. Jones, who passed away on April 18, 1891, when the conference was placed in charge of Bishop Charles C. Pettey. He set apart the Palmetto Conference from the South Carolina Conference in December 1891, at Spartanburg, S.C., "because

29. *Minutes,* First Session, Western North Carolina Conference, pp. 3-59.
30. *Minutes,* Ninth Session, Virginia Annual Conference, 1874, pp. 6-22; *Minutes,* Twenty-Fourth Quadrennial Session, pp. 181-183.
31. Hood, *History,* Vol. II, p. 29; *Minutes,* Twnety-Fourth Quadrennial Session, p. 181.
32. *Ibid.,* p. 349.
33. *Ibid.,* p. 192.

it was too large." [34] Bishop Isom C. Clinton was assigned to the two South Carolina conferences in May, 1892. The South Carolina Conference, which had expanded into seven large presiding elder districts, had four districts after the Palmetto Conference was set off. The growth in this state was also prompted by presiding elders, namely; Reverends F. Killingsworth, William M. Robinson, J. H. Jackson, M. Ingram, B. C. Baum, S. T. Meek, L. W. Stewart, J. H. Manley and R. K. Kearns. They were ably assisted by the following ministers: Revs. J. B. Ellis, J. R. Blake, E. Morton, Z. Belton, J. H. Jackson, W. M. Byrd, A. McLeese, E. Hinton, W. A. Blackwell, C. L. Stevenson, D. C. Covington, J. C. Lewis, James Washington Eichelberger, Sr., M. E. McClellan, L. C. Chamblin, S. R. Gatteroy, R. B. Hemphill, J. M. Erwin, T. P. R. Moore, and H. Blake. [35]

The churches in the state continued to increase, and it became necessary to set off the Pee Dee Conference from the South Carolina Conference, November 19, 1919, at Lancaster, S.C. by Bishop R. B. Bruce. The conference extended 200 miles from Cheraw to Charleston, S.C. It's first Annual Conference was held at Cheraw in 1920. Bishop Bruce recommended to the 1920 General Conference that the state of South Carolina be made an episcopal district, and assigned to one bishop so that the large part of "unoccupied territory in the southern part of this state could be built up by a thoughtful and aggressive bishop." [36]

The size of the state of Alabama and the growth of the work of the Alabama Conference, which embraced the state, was so large that it would have been necessary from the beginning to have a number of conferences, but they took a good deal of deliberation before doing so. It was not until the fall of 1880 that the territory had its first division into more than one conference. A General Conference had met on its soil when it still had only one conference. It held its first day's session in State Street, Mobile, and moved immediately to Clinton Chapel Church, known as The Old Ship Church, in Montgomery, in May 1880.

At the Fourteenth Session of the Alabama Conference, held in Montgomery, November 24, 1880, the East Alabama and West Alabama Conferences were set apart by Bishop J. P. Thompson. At this session the Alabama Conference reported 30,129 members. [37] The Central Alabama Conference evolved out of the East Alabama Conference, maintaining the same territory. It was a mere matter of changing the name. It had accomplished growth under the original name, which was reported at the General Conferences of 1896 and 1900 by Bishop Lomax, who supervised the name change and reported to the 1900 General Conference. [38]

The East Alabama Conference held its second session at Greenville, November 23, 1881, presided over by Bishop Thompson, with 153 ministers present, reporting 11,103 members. Prominent in building up the central part of Alabama besides Elders Wilbur G. Strong, Allen Hannon, Joseph Gomez, M. G. Thomas, Landy Fannin, A. J. Rodgers, and T. A. Weathington, were Revs. Franklin A. Clinton (son of Bishop J. J. Clinton), Augustus S. Watkins, William Finley, J. H. Manley, F. W. Ward, L. D. Workman, Adam White, P. J. McEntosh, J. W. Cooper, William Spencer, J. E. Sanders, Prince Caffey, Matthew Jackson, Lewis Oliver, J. T. McMillan, and W. S. Meadows. Reverends Elijah P. Mayo, March Rankins, William M. Bascom, S. L. Stinson, P. S. Samuels, J. R. Wingfield and E. L.

34. *Minutes,* Nineteenth Quadrennial Session, p. 33.
35. *Minutes,* Twentieth Quadrennial Session, pp. 162-163; Twenty-First Quadrennial Session, pp. 139-140.
36. *Minutes,* Twenty-Sixth Quadrennial Session, p. 141.
37. Moore, *History,* p. 182.
38. *Minutes,* Twentieth and Twenty-First Quadrennial Sessions.

Madison were other noted ministers who labored in this area, and many of these men served in other parts of the state and connection, with immeasurable devotion. (39)

The West Alabama Conference held its second session at Tuscaloosa, December 14, 1881, with 114 preachers in attendance, Bishop Thompson presiding. The leading pioneers in the further development of this section of Alabama were: Revs. William Spencer, A. J. Warner, J. S. Sanders, John Butler, S. S. Wales, M. W. Bynum, W. A. Murphy, A. G. Alstork, G. W. Gaines, A. B. Smyer, John W. Eason, Samuel Wilson, George Washington, Edward Hunter, H. R. Gaines, H. C. Banks, M. L. Blaylock, G. W. Johnson, S. M. Gaines, H. J. Stark, R. A. Morrisey, D. C. Davenport and Samuel Sherman.

Later leaders of this area who continued to stimulate growth were Revs. M. Rosser, J. W. Henderson, M. C. Crawford, Virgil Burk, J. C. Lodge, J. D. Donald, P. R. Pittman, L. W. Kyles, and J. W. Woods. (40)

Those men who continued to expand in the Alabama Conference were Revs. J. W. Cooper, L. S. Peterson, J. C. Laramore, P. W. Laramore, G. W. Drake, J. H. Hubbard, D. W. Wright, J. R. Gill, R. L. Boyd, Samuel Allen, J. W. Stakely, J. S. Chambliss, William M. Bascom, P. C. Alexander, S. M. Pharr, and John W. Smith, George W. Ingram, G W. Anderson, O. P. Neal, W. F. Madison, J. W. Hicks, F. W. Riley, and F. R. blakey. (41)

The fourth conference organized in Alabama was the North Alabama Conference, set apart from the West Alabama Conference in December 1894, at Scranton, Miss., by Bishop C. C. Pettey. Bishop Pettey stated that the West Alabama Conference had become so large that no small town could entertain it, and believing it to be to the best interest of the connection to hold conferences in smaller towns and villages at times, he thought best to divide the conference. The central parts of the conference, of course, were Birmingham, Tuscaloosa, Selma, and other significant cities and towns. (42) The pioneer ministers of this conference were Revs. Andrew J. Warner, Presiding Elders William Spencer, H. C. Banks and S. P. Collins, Revs. Edward Hunter, G. W. Gaines, J. H. Sylvester, H. H. Bingham, J. C. Saunders, H. J. Stark, C. H. Smith, G. W. May, W. L. Hamblin, J. C. Thompson, R. McAlpin, N. D. Crawford, and W. E. Stanton. Reverends John F. Moreland, Sr., J. S. Jackson, W. H. Mitchell, T. R. Gaines, N. R. Rhodes, William Marshall, George W. Turner, and H. R. Gaines were the other ministers giving great support to the growth of this conference. (43)

The South Alabama Conference, fifth in the state, was organized at Montgomery, from the Central Alabama Conference, December 2, 1911, by Bishop J. W. Alstork. It had three presiding elder districts. Those men who led in the beginning of this conference were Revs. F. H. Cummings, M. Rankins, J. W. Jones, L. B. Blackledge, W. W. Herring, M. S. Phinney, F. W. Ward, W. M. Burns, M. C. Glover, L. R. Johnson, G. C. Champion, S. M. Washington, B. C. Coleman, W. L. Hamblin, A. L. Trimble, J. A. Gaffney, I. A. Chance, G. W. Blake, F. L. Bell, and G. W. Hicks. (44)

The sixth conference was the Cahaba Conference, set apart also by Bishop J. W. Alstork, at Bessemer, Ala. November 20, 1912. Among the first leaders of this

39. *Minutes,* East Alabama Annual Conference Sessions, 1881-1892.
40. *Minutes,* West Alabama Annual Conference Sessions, from 1881.
41. *Minutes,* Alabama Conference Sessions, 1880-1897.
42. *Minutes,* Twentieth Quadrennial Session, p. 139.
43. *Ibid.; Minutes,* Twentieth-Twenty-Fifth Quadrennial Sessions.
44. *Minutes,* Twenty-Fourth Quadrennial Session, pp. 217-219.

new conference were Revs. H. R. Gaines, L. B. Blackledge, W. S. Dacons, J. Van Catledge, Sr., J. W.,Jones, William McGee, and W. A. Stewart. Prominent laymen were Professors T. M. Patton, M. A. Hamilton and Mr. W. A. Pitchford. [45]

Growth continued in the South, when Bishop Thomas H. Lomax, with determination and inventiveness, decided to build Zion up in areas where other denominations had gone before and established effectively as Zion had done in North Carolina, Alabama, Upper South Carolina, and Eastern Tennessee. In 1884 when Bishop Lomax was assigned to the Georgia Conference, he found the conference comprising the whole state, Georgia, in a healthy growing condition, led by Presiding Elders J. A. Peak and S. Peter Drayton; also Revs. J. L. Sympkins, E. W. Gibson, A. F. Tillman, G. W. Harris, E. L. C. Jones, G. W. Dunbar, R. I. Apostle, and J. J. Thomas. [46] He "proceeded at once to set off a new conference, known as the North Georgia Conference," [47] and called the old conference South Georgia. Reverends J. J. Moore, J. L. Tillman, J. E. Transue, N. T. Hearn, W. D. Smith, J. H. Turner, L. W. Taylor, A. W. Rice, R. I. Sings, and J. C. Dunbar labored in this territory with others, to strengthen Zion's cause. The original North Georgia Conference was organized at Summerville in 1885, as the offspring of the Georgia Conference. It included the northwestern part of the state, and the city of Atlanta, the Gate City of the South. [48]

At the 1888 General Conference, Bishop C. R. Harris was assigned both conferences in the state along with West Tennessee and Mississippi and Arkansas Conferences. "The Georgia Conference embraced the eastern part of the State of Georgia, extending from Oglethorpe County to Burke County, with a membership of about 700. The North Georgia Conference reached from Athens, in Clarke County, to Columbus, in the extreme western part of the state. It embraced the central part of the state and had a membership of about 500." The work in the state was so meaningful to Bishop Lomax, who had been assigned the Tennessee Conference, that at the first session of the Tennessee Annual Conference after the 1888 General Conference Lomax, by request, cut off "that part of the conference lying within the State of Geogia, and assigned it, with the preachers then belonging to it, to the North Georgia Conference, thus adding to the membership 200 to 300." [49]

The leaders, Bishops Brooks, Loguen, Talbot, Thompson, Lomax, and Harris, had struggled for more than a half century to develop a stronghold for Zion in Georgia. Due to inadequacy and lack of dedication of imported preachers, Zion lost ground. The men named in connection with the work in the state were exceptional and did a good job, however, but were not equal to the demands of that situation. When the decision was made to keep the two Georgia conferences (after much discussion of combining the work in the state, for more than two quadrenniums), the boundaries were adjusted in 1908. The North Georgia Conference evolved into the South Georgia Conference, and the Georgia Conference remained the mother conference of the state. [50]

45. Hood, *History*, Vol. II, p. 30; *Minutes,* Twenty-Fifth and Twenty-Sixth Quadrennial Sessions.
46. *Minutes,* Eighteenth Quadrennial Session; *Minutes,* Georgia Annual Conference, Sixteenth Annual Session, November, 1881, p. 1.
47. *Minutes,* Eighteenth Quadrennial Session, p. 31.
48. Hood, *One Hundred Years,* p. 439; *Minutes,* Fourth Session, North Georgia Annual Conference, 1888, pp. 3-12. G. L. Blackwell, I, Ms. *A Digest History of the African Methodist Episcopal Zion Church*, p. 22.
49. *Minutes,* Nineteenth Quadrennial Session, 1885-91, p. 34.
50. *Minutes,* Twenty-First, Twenty-Second, and Twenty-Third Quadrennial Sessions.

BISHOP JEHU HOLLIDAY

1827 - 1899

Inimitable preacher. Notable church organizer and builder. Founded Broadway Temple, Louisville, 1876.

There was a revival of hope when Bishop M. R. Franklin was elected in 1908 and assigned to Georgia. His grand career in New York, where he had served with significant productivity, led to the conviction that a new leader and a new day had come. He immediately moved on the scene, and was the first bishop of the generation to move on the work. He brought with him a creative vision of a new day of achievement, and "put new life in everything he touched and the Georgia Conference started on to greater success." After a most hopeful beginning, he died one year later, and the work was assigned to Bishop J. W. Alstork, who labored arduously to carry out his dream of putting a metropolitan church in Atlanta, where Zion had two smaller churches, and in other nearby cities and towns. [51]

Other outstanding preachers largely responsible for Zion's development in the state were Revs. William M. Lyons, W. J. Holland, B. J. Jones, J. A. House, A. L. Martin, P. C. Alexander, L. W. Taylor, T. M. Dumas, F. H. Hubbard, G. W. Haselrig, K. T. Thompson, W. Q. Welch, and A. M. Goodwin. [52]

Growth continued in the southeast when Bishop T. H. Lomax, assigned to the Florida Conference in 1888, became interested in the work in that state, and set off the South Florida Conference from the Florida Conference at Tampa, on January 14, 1890. [53] Although this conference was classed as entirely a missionary conference, the ministers and people had a resolute spirit, and began early excelling the Florida Conference in raising connectional claims and building new churches, under the leadership of its organizer, Lomax, and his immediate successor, Bishop C. R. Harris. [54] The prominent preachers in beginning this work were Revs. George W. Maize, I., W. C. Vesta, J. Sexton, W. A. Blaine, J. M. Sims, and J. R. Harris. Reverend Maize, known as the "prince of church builders"

51. *Minutes,* Twenty-Fourth Quadrennial Session, p. 255.
52. *Minutes,* Georgia, North Georgia, South Georgia Annual Conferences, 1881-1911.
53. *Minutes,* Twenty-Third Session, West Florida (Florida) Annual Conference, 1892, pp. 10-11; Ms. Minutes, Board of Bishops, April 30, 1890, p. 43.
54. *Star of Zion,* July 1, 1897.

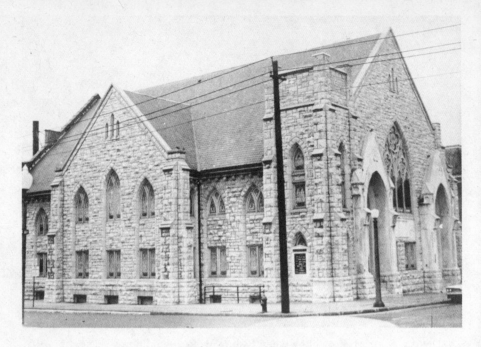

WASHINGTON METROPOLITAN CHURCH

St. Louis, Mo. Founded by Rev. Jeremiah
Washington, 1865 Above church purchased, 1915.

in this area, excelled the record of every minister that had been sent to Key West since its founder, W. G. Strong; he built one of the finest churches for Zion in the city, and a number of churches on the Keys. [55] Presiding Elder J. N. Clinton, son of Bishop J. J. Clinton, was also quite a builder and founder of churches in the Tampa District. [56] Supported by such preachers as Revs. Filmore Smith, W. J. Sanders, S. W. Cunningham, R. R. Frederick, H. H. Wells, E. D. Wood, J. T. Gaskill, W. W. Blair, W. T. Fairley, G. W. Harrell and R. H. Ottley, the work steadily grew. Reverends S. L. McDonnell, J. W. Carter and J. M. Jenkins labored to build Zion in Jacksonville. Other strong builders of the work for Zion in Florida were Elders W. H. Smith, B. F. Stevens, I. L. Ferby, James H. Manley, E. C. Simms, Henry P. Norris, N. R. Rhodes, F. Smith, C. O. H. Thomas, M. Rankin, J. H. Hall, and R. W. Houser, led by Bishops J. W. Smith, T. H. Lomax, and Andrew J. Warner.[57] Among the prominent laymen who helped to build up our churches in Florida were Aaron Brown, Sr., James H. Hannibal and Thomas Simmons. The Florida Conference, for a brief period after the organization of the South Florida Conference, was called the West Florida Conference.

Development of the church continued throughout the South and Southwest as Bishop Thomas Henry Lomax, second most outstanding organizer of conferences next to Bishop Joseph Jackson Clinton, went into Texas to establish our denomination. In organizing the Texas Conference, he ordained 18 elders and

55. *Minutes,* Twentieth Quadrennial Session, p. 135.
56. *Ibid.*
57. *Minutes,* Florida, West Florida Conferences, 1892-1897; *Minutes,* Nineteenth to Twenty-Sixth Quadrennial Sessions, 1892-1920.

TWO OF THE OLDEST
CHURCHES IN THE MIDWEST

BROADWAY TEMPLE CHURCH   Louisville, Ky. Built, 1915.

deacons and brought into the connection $18,000 worth of property. In coming upon the story of Texas, the most accurate account of its origin from Hood's history follows.

Although the African Methodist Episcopal Zion Church was founded away back in the dim vista of an almost oriental age, and, in fact, comes very near colonial times, a work which remained to be done by the resolute had long been neglected, and that is the organization of the African Methodist Episcopal Zion Connection in Texas. It remained for Bishop Lomax to explore those untrodden solitudes and gather, if possible, those rich fruits which had for so long ripened to an abundant harvest where only the footprints of other denominations had trodden. When we consider the ease and facility characteristic of the Church in the North, East, and Atlantic coast it required almost the courage of a Columbus to make a voyage to Texas, mindful of the fact that it was not only a cattle state, but a territory which has for years been the haven of all the isms save that of our beloved cognomen.

The Texas Conference was organized in November 1883, by Bishop Thomas H. Lomax, at Stoneham. Elders present, J. D. Mead, W. W. Kanna, and Barnabas Calaway. The deacons that were ordained in that year were G. R. Washington, S. Miller, Z. McKindrick, and Isaac Hambright. Preachers received were E. Carter, Henry Johnson, and G. J. Johnson.

In November, 1884, Conference convened at Bobbin, Bishop Thomas H. Lomax presiding. Elders present, J. D. Mead, W. W. Kanna; deacons G. R. Washington, S. Miller, Z. McKindrick; ordained to deacons, E. Carter, G. J. Johnson and Henry Johnson.

In November, 1885, the Conference convened at Navasota, Bishop J. P. Thompson, D.D., M.D., presiding. Elders were W. W. Kanna, V. Vincent; deacons, G. R. Washington, Z. McKindrick, I. Hambright, S. Miller, G. J. Johnson, E. Carter, Henry Johnson.

In 1886, through some misunderstanding, there was no Conference held, owing to Bishop Thompson's feebleness.

In 1887, for the above cause, there was held no Conference. In consequence of there being held no Conferences these last two years the work went down, and when Bishop Pettey was elected in 1888, and assigned to the Sixth Episcopal District (He postponed the Conferences from the fall of 1888 until February, 1889). He found in the State of Texas only one organization and thirteen members, at Stoneham. The indifference and gloomy appearances of prospects, if indeed there were any, suddenly loomed up before him as a mockery. The work at this stage required a risk of life, health, and the sacrifice of finance. It was only four weeks from the time of his arrival in the State until the convening of the Conference. There was not a minister at his post. The sacrament of the Lord's Supper had not been administered in fourteen months. The four remaining preachers who had not left Zion's fold were engaged on cotton farms and ranches. The members, becoming disheartened, lost all connectional interests and sought protection in more inviting churches. The bishop at once took in the situation, and with courage bold commenced a tour through the State. Securing the services of the distinguished Rev. F. A. Clinton, they traveled, preached, lectured, and organized churches for a month. The second Wednesday in February, 1889, found Bishop Pettey holding Conference in Stoneham. Only one elder responded to the roll call, and that was W. W. Kanna (F. A. Clinton being present). Elders ordained at Conference; G. R. Washington, S. Miller and Isaac Hambright. Deacons, G. J. Johnson, Henry Johnson, E. Carter, Z. McKindrick, and T. R. Gaines. Conference adjourned to meet the third Wednesday in October, 1889, at Hearne.

Apropos to date Conference met in October, 1889, at Hearne, Bishop C. C. Pettey presiding. Elders present responding to roll call, H. C. Philips, who had been transferred to the Texas Conference from North Carolina, W. W. Kanna, G. R. Washington, S. Miller, Isaac Hambright, Deacons, Z. McKindrick, E. Carter, G. J. Johnson, Henry Johnson, T. R. Gaines; and M.S. Jordan, who had been transferred from Alabama, was ordained to elder's orders and suceeded Philips as presiding elder, Philips being transferred back to North Carolina.

In 1890 Conference convened at Stoneham, third Wednesday in October. Elders present, M. S. Jordan, G. R. Washington, S. Miller, and W. W. Kanna. Deacons, G. J. Johnson, Henry Johnson, B. McKindrick, and E. Carter.

In 1891 Conference convened at Navasota, third Wednesday in October. Bishop Pettey presiding. Elders present, M. S. Jordan, G. R. Washington, S. Miller, W. W. Kanna, E. W. King, and R. C. O. Benjamin. Deacons, G. J. Johnson, H. Johnson, E. Carter, and Z. McKindrick. George Beard was ordained and added to the deacons' list in this conference. Preachers received, George Pugh and Giles Williams.

In 1893 Conference convened at Calvert, Texas, first Wednesday in February, Bishop Pettey presiding. Elders P. R. Pittman, G. R. Washington, W. W. Kanna, E. W. King, S. Miller, J. A. Russell, J. Steptoe, and R. E. Shelton. Deacons, G. J. Johnson, H. Johnson, E. Carter, and George Beard. Ordained, Dr. M. A. Majors. Preacher, George Pugh. Received, William Beneford. Thus ended the last Conference up to date held in Texas. For unforeseen causes the time of convening was changed from October, 1892, and hence did not meet until February 1, 1893. The redemption of Zion in Texas seems to have been assigned to Bishop Pettey. The work having almost suspended, it remained for him to restore and throw light upon the dark places, give strength to the weak, and give to the connection such an impetus, that has never before been witnessed in the Lone Star State. The force of his genius as well as the concentration of his spiritual power seems to have added to the work the long-wanting features of African Methodist Episcopal Zion expectations.

While Bishop Lomax poses as the leader and organizer of the work in Texas, Bishop Thompson the second bishop to carry farther the pioneer beginning of an undertaking destined to be great, Bishop Pettey poses as the rebuilder and restorer of the work which had grown into a state of despondency and gloom . . . *M. A. Majors, M.D., Secretary of Texas Conference.* [58]

By 1896 Bishop Pettey had organized churches in Dallas, Fort Worth, Waco, San Antonio, Dennison, and the Brazos, and made an effort to establish another conference known as West Texas and Oklahoma Conference, the result of his and Bishop Walter's united efforts of establishing work in Oklahoma. However, the Oklahoma Conference was firmly established separately the following year. He was aided in this work by Revs. A. Hokes, S. J. Walker, and P. E. Lucas. [59] Development continued in smaller towns of the state under the leadership of Bishops Jehu Holliday and J. W. Alstork, with the loyal assistance of such preachers as Revs. C. A. Steed and T. R. Simpson. When Bishop George L. Blackwell was elected and assigned to this work in 1908, Texas was greatly stimulated and growth renewed. Reverends W. A. Ray, P. R. Pittman, J. L. Lewis and H. L. Laverne assisted him in establishing churches in the state. [60] During the administration of Bishop W. J. Walls, 1924-1928, the Houston Church was organized with Rev. G. W. Smith as its founding father. He was ably assisted by his wife, who was also a gospel preacher. The church also at Dallas was re-established, having been suspended. Bishop Raymond L. Jones, from 1964 to 1968, with the support of the Church Extension Department, through Secretary D. W. Andrews, made a substantial reinforcement by purchasing three major churches and building up smaller ones.

In an attempt to swell the numbers in Louisiana where Zion had a fruitful beginning after Emancipation, the North Louisiana Conference was organized and set apart by the Louisiana Conference, November 20, 1890, in New Orleans, under the administration of Bishop C. C. Pettey. Session was held at Thompson's Chapel, near Mann's Station, in the country six miles west of Vicksburg, La., the first Wednesday in November 1891, Bishop C. C. Pettey, presiding. Reverend S. M. Morgan was elected secretary. [61] The Louisiana Conference then had nearly 3,000 members with 56 preachers. The North Louisiana Conference had 463 members and 19 preachers after its organization. [62] The pioneer preachers of this conference were Rev. H. W. Barnett, presiding elder and steward, Revs. J. H. W. Inge, J. W. Johnson, W. S. Davis, R. S. Shelton, and J. W. Eason. John Steptoe was ordained elder. Preachers received were A. I. Inge, Washington Bethany, Henry Carrell, P. C. Saunders, Peter Adams, George Carrell, Smith M. Morgan, Robert W. Williams, M. J. Roper, and Jefferson Williams. The first conference "was largely attended, and great interest was manifested by the entire community. After an interesting session of seven days, accompanied by the Holy Ghost, the conference adjourned to meet in Delhi, La., the first Wednesday in November, 1892." This conference had a promising outlook, situated as it was in the great

58. Hood, *One Hundred Years,* pp. 193, 435-439.
59. *Minutes,* Twentieth Quadrennial Session, pp. 139-140.
60. *Minutes,* Twenty-First to Twenty-Sixth Quadrennial Sessions, 1900-1920.
61. Hood, *One Hundred Years,* p. 441.
62. *Minutes,* Nineteenth Quadrennial Session, p. 32.

cotton belt of Louisiana, but able and devoted Christian ministers were greatly needed. [63] The work continued to prosper led by Bishop T. H. Lomax in 1900. assisted by Revs. D. J. Adams and J. T. Thomas.

The conference ceased to grow after the turn of the century, however, substantially manned by Bishops Alstork, J. W. Smith, Warner, and Lee, until the General Conference of 1920, when it was reported that it had only five small churches, with 500 members. Its ministerial delegate, Rev. A. C. Cook, recommended its merger with the Louisiana Conference, which the General Conference carried out. [64]

The church had an abundant growth in the Delta area. Owing to the enlargement of the work, and the fact that the West Tennessee and Mississippi Conference was very extensive, that conference was divided at its last session before the 1892 General Conference, by Bishop C. R. Harris, at Meridian, Miss., December 1891, and the South Mississippi Conference was organized. The northern portion, from Memphis, Tenn. to Greenwood, Miss. retained the original name. The southern part, from Yazoo City to Cookesville, Miss. and Sherman, Ala. was named the South Mississippi Conference, each having two presiding elder districts. The newly set off districts made rapid progress and reported several mission points organized within five months. [65] Some of the pioneers of this progress were Revs. D. J. Adams, J. E. P. Marshall, S. C. Harris, W. J. Caver, W. E. Stanton, P. Green and R. C. Nash. Led by Bishop Harris, churches were immediately organized at Jackson, West Point, Vicksburg, and other larger cities in the state. Others who followed and continued to build under the leadership of Bishops John B. Small and J. W. Alstork were Revs. J. S. Jackson, T. H. Jones, A. G. Alstork, prominent presiding elders, and Revs. F. C. Cole, J. H. Bell, Louis M. Mitchell, J. H. Hall, L. B. Blackledge, W. C. Wilcox, B. L. Stanton, M. C. Glover, William C. Pierson, William McGee, J. W. Cost, J. S. Lott, A. B. Binion, J. C. Thompson, M. F. Fulford, H. T. Henderson, J. H. McMullen (who had labored for the cause earlier in Louisiana), D. S. Williams, and T. M. McKenzie. [66]

The newly consecrated bishop at the 1896 General Conference, Jehu Holliday, known for his "wonderful powers as a preacher and organizer," was assigned to this work in the Southwest. [67] Here again, the prospects for Zion were extremely encouraging, as Bishop Holliday went into the Arkansas-Oklahoma area and prompted unusual growth in three short years. On March 2, 1899, he met his death from an accident caused by horses running away with him and breaking some of his ribs. He was a dedicated man of many talents, and saved situations for Zion, as presiding elder and pastor, in all parts of the church. He had set a noble example in the church by his last will and testament. He not only provided in it for his beloved wife, Mary, and six children, but he shared with Livingstone College, the Twelfth Street Church in Louisville (Broadway Temple), and the Dearborn Street Church in Chicago (Walters Memorial), along with two distant relatives. [68] The church suffered an unforgettable loss, as he was in the midst of giving Zion a stronghold in this Southwestern territory.

In the year of his election, he held the Arkansas Conference at Grady, Ark.,

63. Hood, *One Hundred Years,* p. 441.
64. *Minutes,* Twenty-First to Twenty-Sixth Quadrennial Sessions, 1900-1920; *Minutes,* Twenty-Sixth Quadrennial Session, pp. 152, 239, 244.
65. *Minutes,* Nineteenth Quadrennial Session, p. 34.
66. *Minutes,* Nineteenth to Twenty-Sixth Quadrennial Sessions, 1892-1920.
67. *Minutes,* Twentieth Quadrennial Session, p. 143, 204.
68. *Minutes,* Twenty-First Quadrennial Session, pp. 172-173.

and set apart the North Arkansas Conference, and held its first session at Little Rock, December 9, 1896. [69] The two Arkansas conferences were assigned to Bishop G. W. Clinton by the Board of Bishops in March 1899. Along with his regular assigned work, Clinton endeavored to carry out to the best of his ability the work so nobly begun by Bishop Holliday. Elders E. D. Washington and E. M. Martin had done valuable services in extending the work and building up churches. In North Arkansas, the work was prompted by Presiding Elders K. T. Thompson, T. H. Hanna, and D. S. Blackwell, assisted by Revs. G. W. Walters, E. B. Waul, and F. W. Riley. Bishop J. W. Alstork was assigned the two conferences in the State and continued to expand, led by Revs. R. B. Macon, A. J. Coleman, A. Miner, J. S. Lewis, J. C. Cobb, J. H. McMullen, A. Arnold, and J. R. Ward. Bishop George L. Blackwell brought new impetus to the work in this state in 1908. He established a number of new missions in both conferences. One of the most outstanding and dedicated elders during that time was Rev. W. J. J. Byers. The loyal ministers assisting him in the continued growth were Revs. W. H. Robinson, J. L. Madison, R. B. Macon, D. S. Blackwell, W. H. Howard, A. S. Jackson, J. B. A. Yelverton, J. W. Douglas, C. W. P. Mitchell, J. W. Massey, W. I. Rowan, H. C. Holly and G. E. Laston and later, Revs. W. H. Davenport, E. E. Morgan, Sr., and others. [70]

Bishop Jehu Holliday set apart the Oklahoma Conference from Texas and held its first annual conference at Guthrie, Okla., Wednesday, April 28, 1897. [71] The work in Oklahoma had its beginning four or five years earlier, through the cooperative spirit of Bishops Pettey and Walters. Bishop Pettey, who was assigned the Texas Conference, and Bishop Walters, who had the Arkansas Conference, sent missionaries from these two conferences to Oklahoma, including Rev. E. W. King of South Carolina, and established at least three churches in the state, with five or six ministers. [72] Bishop G. W. Clinton, who also succeeded Bishop Holliday after his death in Oklahoma, stated that "the untiring efforts of Bishop Holliday during the two and a half years he labored in this part of the Eighth Episcopal District did very much toward bringing Zion to the front in this section." [73] The Oklahoma Conference embraced the state of Oklahoma and the Indian Territories, Washington and Montana, with two presiding elder districts skillfully led by Revs. W. L. Brewer and L. H. Parks, with Revs. S. J. Walker, H. Jackson, A. D. Hankins, who made the first attempt to effect an organization at Oklahoma City, I. R. Hambright, and W. L. Lagrone assisting them in the spread of Zion in this territory. Bishop J. W. Alstork worked with these men for a quadrennium in this effort. Bishop George L. Blackwell was sent on the scene in 1908, and established and built new churches.

Bishop Blackwell was aided in this noble work by Revs. C. A. Hudson, J. A. Miller, R. L. Birchett, W. H. Parker, D. C. Smith, R. Wells, G. W. McMillan, J. B. Finley, and M. S. Lay. [74]

Bishop George C. Clement continued to plant churches in the state, when assigned there in 1916, as he held fond memories of the stalwart saint who started the work, Bishop Holliday. His main accomplishment was at Luther, where the Rev. J. T. Armstrong was a forceful black merchant in the town, and assisted in the organization of this and other churches. The other dedicated preachers who aided in planting Zion in Oklahoma were Revs. D. L. Dudley, I. S. Malone, and C.

69. *The Star of Zion,* October 29, 1896.
70. *Minutes,* Twenty-First to Twenty-Sixth Quadrennial Sessions, 1900-1920.
71. *The Star of Zion,* April 22, 1897.
72. *Minutes,* Twentieth Quadrennial Session, pp. 139-140.
73. *Minutes,* Twenty-First Quadrennial Session, pp. 209-210.
74. *Minutes,* Twenty-Fourth Quadrennial Session, pp. 286-290.

E. Baker, continuously led by President Elder C. A. Hudson. [75] Both the churches at Oklahoma City and Tulsa were firmly established during the tenure of Bishop W. J. Walls, 1924-1928. Reverend D. L. Dudley and Rev. Muse organized these churches for Zion.

Growth in the Midwest and West

The first conference organized in the Midwest was the Missouri Conference, set apart from the Kentucky Conference by Bishop Thomas H. Lomax, September 17, 1890, in Washington Chapel (Washington Metropolitan), St. Louis. It started off under very favorable auspices with 26 members in its organization. Reverend Anthony Bunch, one of the original members of the Kentucky Conference, headed the roll in this new conference. There were few men at that time who could equal Elder Bunch in organizing and building up a church under adverse circumstances. [76]

When the Missouri Conference was organized, it had one presiding elder, Rev. Smith Claiborne, whose first two years of labors were crowned with much success, and the work grew so fast that Bishop Lomax found it necessary to divide it into two districts under Revs. Anthony Bunch and D. J. Donohoo. [77] The Conference included the work the church had been able to salvage from the old Canada and Michigan Conference, established by Bishop Lomax in 1879, who maintained indubitable interest in the people and work of that area after he was assigned to other work in the South. Among the pioneer preachers who labored to spread the work to several adjoining states were Revs. Yarmouth Carr, Edward Jackson, Adam Wakefield, W. F. Jones, J. P. Thompson, E. Stokes, T. J. Manson, J. H. Hardin, J. U. Browder, W. H. Ealy, M. A. F. Easton, Alfred Nichols, H. W. Smith, Joseph Bunch, C. N. Payne, E. Scott, Peter Shelton, Daniel Shelton, David Jackson, Lewis Norton, Paul Shelton and Henry Parker. [78]

The greatest spirit of Zion in the Midwest, and one of the most magnetic preachers in A.M.E. Zion Church history, was Rev. Jeremiah M. Washington. Because of the magnitude of his work in the entire area, and his unusual ability for expanding the church, we give a brief description of his background and work.

Jeremiah M. Washington was born a slave in Rockville, Md., in 1852. When quite young he was bound out to a man by the name of William Braddock, who proved a cruel taskmaster. In 1861, young Jerry ran off and went to join the Union Army where he became a waiter for Captain William J. Mackery in the 28th Pennsylvania Regiment, and served two and a half years at $5 per month. He was an eyewitness of some of the most serious battles fought during that war, among them Antietam, Chancellorsville, Gettysburg, and Lookout Mountain. In the latter part of 1863 he was left at Louisville by Captain Mackery, and employed as a hotel waiter for several years. He soon became anxious to better his condition in life and learned the trade of making and packing queensware.

In 1868, he was happily converted at Old Center Street Church, Louisville, under Elder W. H. Miles who withdrew and became one of the two founders and first bishop of the C.M.E. Church. In 1873 he received an exhorters license from Rev. E. H. Curry, and received license to preach in 1874 from Rev. Yarmouth Carr. That same year he organized a congregation and built a church in Louisville. In 1875 he joined the Annual Conference at Hendersonville, Ky., under Bishop

---

75. *Minutes*, Twenty-Fifth and Twenty-Sixth Quadrennial Session, pp. 162-163.
76. Hood, *One Hundred Years*, p. 440.
77. *Minutes*, Nineteenth Quadrennial Session, p. 30.
78. Hood, *One Hundred Years*, p. 440.

Singleton T. Jones. When he joined the conference, he carried in a congregation of 180 adult members. He was appointed to Madisonville, Ky., and after 14 months, he had rebuilt the church and left it in a flourishing condition with 164 active members. In 1877, by special request of Bishop Jones, he went to St. Louis, where several fruitless efforts had been made to establish a Zion Church. On his arrival, he found 14 members worshipping in a hall over a stable. He at once took charge of this handful of people and began operations, which resulted in a most flourishing congregation. During his stay of three years and six months, he bought ground and built a large church, which at the request of the members was named Washington Chapel, and the congregation increased from 14 to 900. (Later during the pastorate of Rev. Benjamin G. Shaw, when the present edifice was purchased, the church was named Washington Metropolitan.) While pastoring in this city, he organized other churches at East St. Louis, Ill.; West St. Louis, Mo.; Codalsville, Mo.; High Hill, Mo.; and Brighton, Illinois.

He was then transferred to Knoxville, Tenn. where he labored under great disadvantage to bring our leading church out of the disastrous condition into which it had drifted, adding 160 members to its roll in his 15 months pastorate. From Knoxville he was transferred to Little Rock, Ark. at which time he found only two Zion ministers in the state. He at once set about spreading the borders of Zion in Arkansas. During his stay, he organized churches throughout the state and left more than 20 ministers in the Arkansas Conference. In 1883 he was appointed to the charge in Indianapolis, where he found a very small congregation. He built up this church, now known as Jones Tabernacle (named for Bishop Singleton T. Jones), adding 362 adult members to the roll and another 450 Sunday school scholars. In 1885, he was appointed presiding elder by Bishop J. W. Hood over the original Kentucky District (Louisville District), and served successfully for four years, establishing new churches throughout the area.

On February 9, 1889, he found himself in Chicago, where he at once set in motion plans to establish a Zion stronghold in this great city. He rented a place of worship at a cost of $45 per month, and reorganized the church, which had been established as a mission in 1875, (now known as Greater Walters Memorial), March 3, 1889, with 35 members. From this new beginning, the membership grew to nearly 800, and purchased our first metropolitan church building in the city of Chicago. He was, indeed, one of the most skillful financiers, successful revivalists and efficient pastors of the church, and a most popular singer of the race who could hold audiences spellbound under the magic influence of his sweet voice. He wrought well for Zion in this Midwestern territory. [79] He was presiding elder of the St. Louis District when he died, January 6, 1899.

The Missouri Conference then covered a lot of territory. Led by Bishops Alexander Walters, 1892-1900, George W. Clinton, 1900-1904, and Josiah S. Caldwell, 1905-1908, the work progressed rapidly in major cities and towns of the Midwest. These bishops had such outstanding preachers assisting them in building up the work in Kansas City, Missouri and Kansas; Indianapolis; Chicago; South Bend, Ind.; Jefferson City, Mo.; Northern Kentucky; Evansville, Ind.; and in the state of Iowa, as Revs. John F. Page, W. F. Jones, R. E. Wilson, D. J. Young, Andrew McCallum, J. W. Zellender, Dr. John F. Moreland, Sr., P. W. Dunauant, Jesse B. Colbert, F. H. Tipton, G. W. Register, J. A. Reeves, J. Stephens Smith, M. S. Kell, O. H. Banks, Sidney Penick, R. Farley Fisher, the outstanding presiding elder W. H. Chambers of Indiana, E. D. W. Jones, J. W. Wood and B. G. Shaw, Sr., [80] The Canada and Michigan Conference had been held in connection

79. *A.M.E. Zion Quarterly Review.* April 1892, pp. 299-301.
80. *Minutes,* Nineteenth to Twenty-Third Quadrennial Sessions, 1892-1908.

with the Missouri Conference since 1902. This made the territory inclusive of Grand Rapids and Canada, with Revs. J. R. Alexander and M. R. Williams still laboring for Zion in that region. [81]

Bishop George Lincoln Blackwell, a university man with a missionary zeal, elected and assigned to the Missouri Conference in 1908, gave a new impulse to our whole work in the West, especially the Midwest, and the Southwest. In one significant event he organized out of this territory, known as the Missouri Conference, three conferences: Michigan, Indiana, and the original Missouri Conferences, at DuQuoin, Illinois in 1909. We must surely be convinced of his wise plan and prophetic vision for our Zion in this situation from the following quote from his report to the General Conference of 1912:

> In this same territory still ought to be an Illinois, a Kansas City, a Central Arkansas and a Central Texas Conference. But from all appearances these must wait till we include such cities as Springfield, Peoria, Decatur, Champaign, Danville, Charleston, Murphysboro and Carbondale in Illinois; such cities as St. Charles, Columbia, Mexico, Lawrence, St. Joseph, Hannibal, Independence and Sedalia in Missouri; and such towns as Newport, Marianna, Forrest City, Helena, Fort Smith, Camden and Texarkana in Arkansas; such cities as Houston, Galveston, Austin, San Antonio, Corsicana, Waco, Palestine, Dallas, Fort Worth and Dennison in Texas. [82]

While presiding over these conferences, Bishop Blackwell went on to establish churches in some of the cities and towns mentioned above, and other significant cities in the conferences he served. His missionary prowess was shown by the multiplying of new missions and organizations stretched throughout the conferences assigned to him, many of which were well-nigh vacant. He followed his vision to occupy unoccupied territory for Zion. In his own deeds and work, he organized a multiplicity of churches in this new territory, and sent preachers of adventure and dedication to many places. He sacrificed even to the point of using his own salary to sustain them while building up churches for Zion. Bishop W. Sampson Brooks of the A.M.E. Church told the writer that he had seen him cash his salary check and distribute it all to his ministers to keep them able to continue service on his mission field.

In the Missouri Conference, he established two churches in Kansas City, with the assistance of Revs. William M. Johnson and G. W. Chapel; West Alton, East St. Louis, Ill. and Columbia, Mo., aided by Mrs. Dora Russell, Revs. T. B. Morris, W. H. White, J. C. Campbell, N. A. Haskins, F. D. Douglass, F. L. Overton, C. C. Cotton and G. E. Brown, and Mrs. Sallie Gaunt. Others who aided him in this mission work were Revs. C. C. Purdy, F. S. Snowden, J. H. Ellis, J. L. Butler, John Harvey, and S. Pratter. [83]

In the Indiana Conference, he organized the Indianapolis District with Rev. W. H. Chambers first serving. He was succeeded by Revs. J. H. Manley and H. M. Mickey. Associating them in spreading the work were Revs. H. J. Callis, W. I. Rowan, T. A. Fenderson, A. J. Shockley, W. J. Winfield, P. H. Wright and C. S. Holmes; and at Centralia, Revs. N. A. Haskins and D. C. Cantey. He also organized the Cairo District in Illinois, over which Rev. O. H. Banks presided, and established churches in that area assisted by Revs. R. P. Christian, C. H. Jackson, J. P. Long, E. P. Mayo, J. J. Kennedy in Terre Haute, Indiana; and Urbana, Illinois by Rev. J. A. Spurlock. Revs. J. A. Terry, S. D. Davis, A. Averitt and J. L. McDonald also aided in building this new conference. [84]

81. *Minutes*, Twenty-Second Quadrennial Session, p. 187.
82. *Minutes*, Twenty-Fourth Quadrennial Session, p. 275.
83. *Ibid.*, pp. 279-280, 288.
84. *Ibid.*, pp. 277-278, 288.

In the Michigan Conference, he organized the Chicago District, the only district at that time in the conference, with three churches, and appointed Rev. B. G. Shaw presiding elder. His leadership produced great creativity in the immediate growth of the conference. Bishop Blackwell immediately started churches in Wisconsin with the assistance of Rev. Sherman Chapman; Gary, Indiana, assisted by Rev. G. W. Henley, South Bend, Indiana, by Revs. A. M. Taylor and S. W. Weller; in Colchester, Ontario, assisted by Revs. C. A. Poole, J. U. Browder, and G. W. Claughton. He started a second church in Chicago on the south side aided by Rev. T. S. Allen. He continued organizing churches in Chicago. The Blackwell Memorial Church was established by Bishop Blackwell's brother, William A. Blackwell, I, originally named St. Catherine, in memory of their mother; and after the death of the bishop, they combined the name and called it Blackwell Memorial. Revs. G. W. Register, S. L. Smith, and S. Samuels also assisted in establishing churches in Chicago. The Bishop also planted a church in Toledo, Ohio, and several points in Michigan, Indiana, and Illinois assisted by Revs. L. P. Powell, J. M. Howard, A. J. Leggett, T. S. Allen, W. L. Barr, J. A. S. Cole, A. N. Webb, W. S. House, P. C. Wilburn, F. F. Frye, J. B. Phelps, G. W. Armstrong, J. B. Nicholson, H. R. White, J. A. Derry, W. B. Carr, and W. H. Taylor. [85]

When Bishop Blackwell went into this area we had no church in Detroit. The three churches were Walters Memorial in Chicago; Grand Rapids, Mich.; and Windsor, Canada. He first established St. Paul Church on Catherine Street, which later removed to Palmer Street. This congregation divided into two Zion Churches (St. Paul and Metropolitan). The St. Paul Church purchased a commodious edifice on Dexter Street, in 1959, and today has one of the half-dozen largest memberships in the entire denomination. Revs. M. F. Gregory, N. A. Haskins, N. C. Roundtree, T. S. Allen and L. T. Conquest were the pioneers in this first Detroit venture. The second church started in the city was Blackwell Temple by Rev. S. L. Smith and the third church was Lomax Temple. [86] One of Bishop Blackwell's greatest achievements is the Michigan Conference, which has become one of the three largest northern conferences of the denomination, inclusive of Detroit, with a dozen churches, practically created by this outstanding leader. Indeed, the whole area where he went along is strung with the enterprises of his creative missionary contribution.

The Ohio Conference, adjoining the Michigan and Indiana Conferences north and west, was organized September 16, 1891, at Cambria Chapel, Johnstown, Pa., by Bishop James W. Hood. It is the offspring of the Allegheny Conference, originally including all that part of the state of Pennsylvania lying west of the Allegheny River, and the state of Ohio. The only churches in the state of Ohio when it was organized were the Wesley Temple Church, Akron, Rev. James H. McMullen then pastor, who labored to help spread the work in the state; and churches in Salem and Massalon, Ohio. Bishop Hood expressed disappointment that the work did not grow as fast as did the other conferences organized during this same period, after Rev. Jehu Holliday had been transferred from this conference to the Kentucky Conference, and Rev. Joseph Armstrong to Washington, D.C. [87]

The first presiding elder, Rev. J. H. Trimble, began organizing churches in Ohio faster than the bishop could find preachers to hold the points he had taken in for Zion. This shortage of missionary preachers posed a problem for Zion in

85. *Ibid.*, pp. 276-277, 288-289.
86. *Ibid.*, Twenty-Fifth and Twenty-Sixth Quadrennial Sessions, p. 107.
87. *Minutes,* Forty-First Session, Allegheny Annual Conference, 1890; Hood, *One Hundred Years*, pp. 465-466.

that territory. The growth became gradual and many problems were encountered. Reverend George W. Lewis was one of the faithful pioneers, serving as first secretary of the conference and pastoring several mission points. [88] The people, however, kept the faith, and after several strenuous efforts to start churches in the metropolitan cities of Cleveland, Columbus, Dayton, Youngstown, and others, success, which had come the long hard way, was realized. Zion was quite successful, however, in establishing her first major church in Cincinnati. Dr. John F. Moreland, Sr., and a large number of members had withdrawn from the Methodist Episcopal Church and built an independent church. Through the hard work of Presiding Bishop Hood and Bishop Alexander Walters, who "travelled 1,900 miles in five days besides attending to all other work necessary to the reorganization of the church and putting it in good running order under our Discipline," the entire group voted to join Zion, and its leader and people were a big asset to the conference and connection. [89]

Reverend Martin R. Franklin was pastoring Avery Mission at that time, which was placed in the Ohio Conference, and he assisted Presiding Elder Trimble in establishing mission points. The church in Youngstown had been established as a mission point by 1894, by Revs. H. L. Jones and J. Stanard. Under our system, at that time of electing presiding elders, Rev. Martin S. Kell, also a pioneer of the conference, became the presiding elder. The elders who labored to establish churches in Ohio in its beginning were Revs. W. H. Snowden, R. E. Wilson, M. J. Snows, N. J. Watson, R. J. Strother, T. H. Slater, C. Campbell, A. H. Dorsey, E. J. Little, W. A. M. Cypress, W. H. Pollard, W. H. Hamilton, D. G. Moore, H. Butler, Jacob Skinner, and W. H. N. Tyler. In 1894, our first mission effort was started in Cleveland by Rev. M. A. Mason, with 12 members. Though it took a good while for Zion to become firmly established in this city, this was the beginning. [90]

In 1896 Bishop C. C. Pettey was assigned to the Ohio Conference, and reported the purchase of one of the finest church properties of our race people, in Cleveland, which they occupied November 15, 1899, led by Presiding Elder G. W. Lewis. The membership, however, had not grown strong enough to sustain this venture, and the property apparently was soon lost to Zion. Reverend Mrs. M. C. Brown maintained a mission group in the city in her house, under the charge of Bishop Small until 1905. Reverend Pero Williams was sent there by Bishop Caldwell, with his unique talent to construct a congregation. Reverend S. C. Harris followed Williams and held services in a storefront with his residence above it, where the writer held a revival as a boy evangelist and a number of converts were received. The mission continued its growth under Rev. Harris' pastorate. This consistently growing membership, led by Rev. E. D. W. Bell and Bishop George C. Clement, assisted by the Ter-Centenary Fund (Three Hundredth Anniversary of the Black Race in America), acquired the present edifice around 1921, which was known to be one of the finest plants in the connection. The membership increased manifold, and Zion began to blossom with other congregations and churches in and around the city of Cleveland. Like a number of churches throughout the connection, this church, our mother church of Cleveland, St. Paul, has given us some of the country's most outstanding citizens, including Carl B. Stokes, who became first black Mayor of Cleveland, and his brother, Louis Stokes, presently serving as U. S. Congressman.

The Ohio Conference at first developed so slowly that the 1900 General

Conference combined it again with the Allegheny Conference. It was known as the Allegheny-Ohio Conference until 1915, when Bishop Caldwell set it off again from the Allegheny Conference, after the Ohio District had grown sufficiently with one presiding elder district. During this time, Bishop Caldwell, also in charge of the Kentucky Conference and a conference he had set apart from Kentucky known as West Kentucky Conference, transferred the Cincinnati District of the Kentucky Conference back into the Ohio Conference, and the work in this state began to grow rapidly. The West Kentucky Conference was shortlived. Bishop Clement, who had been supervising the work for 12 years, recommended that it be reunited with the Kentucky Conference, in 1928, because of the continually decreasing Negro population in this rural, mountainous, coal-mining part of the state and in West Virginia, of which it was comprised. [91]

Before this, several churches had been developed in cities and towns throughout Ohio, under the leadership of Bishops Small, Caldwell, and Clement. Later developers of the work were Revs. S. H. Simmons, J. S. Cooper, J. E. Disharoon, P. J. McEntosh, W. A. H. Pringle, B. F. Combash, J. Harvey Anderson, Daniel F. Bradley, F. B. Leece, S. L. Newby, G. W. Kincaid, R. W. Christian, and A. D. Crockett. Those who assisted Bishop Caldwell in building up the work in the state were Revs. G. W. Johnson, H. L. Jones, Henry Durham, Paris A. Wallace J. M. Wheeler, W. L. Lee, J. C. Taylor, A. Wakefield, T. W. Mills who organized the church at Dayton, and Rev. Mrs. Mary E. Washington. Its most propitious growth came during the administration of Bishop George C. Clement. Associated by the veteran, Rev. W. J. A. Pringle, and such dedicated leaders as Revs. J. P. Foote, E. C. West, R. B. Hendricks, S. C. Harris, E. D. W. Bell, H. P. Whitehead, B. N. Henningham, J. L. Black, J. H. Williams, Thomas W. Wallace, E. L. Hogan, A. W. Settle, C. A. Leftwich and C. A. McDonald, the conference grew to a membership of over 5,000 and 35 appointments; in other words, it more than doubled in every department. [92]

The Far West

Consecrated bishop in 1888, C. C. Pettey who was assigned the California Conference wrought well his first quadrennium, as he had labored previously as pastor and presiding elder, and was familiar with the territory. The Portland Church had been established in the days of Moore and Clinton. He established churches in other parts of Oregon and in the state of Washington, and because of the vast distances of the California Conference, (which included all of California, Arizona, Oregon and Washington), he attempted to organize the Oregon Conference in 1892. The bishops succeeding him, Bishops Walters and George W. Clinton, did not attempt to hold separate conferences due to the tremendous span of territory which they were assigned; the far West was a mission field of the East and Midwest. The mode of travel and the hardships they endured made it difficult to expand according to their dreams in this western section of the country. However, progress was made in establishing new churches.

At the turn of the century, Bishop G. W. Clinton had established churches at Seattle and Spokane, Washington and Kingman, Arizona. The work in Washington was organized by Revs. G. H. W. Smith and J. E. Transue, and in Arizona by Rev. P. McEachern. He had also built up new churches in California associated by Revs.

91. *Minutes,* Twenty-Fourth to Twenty-Eighth Quadrennial Sessions; *Minutes,* Twenty-Eighth Quadrennial Session, pp. 120-121.
92. *Minutes,* Twenty-Third to Twenty-Seventh Quadrennial Sessions, 1908-1924.* A different J. C. Taylor than the Bishop elected in 1948.

J. E. McCorkle, T. Allen Harvey, A. J. Woodward, G. H. W. Smith, F. B. Moore, J. C. Taylor,* S. L. McKinney, J. W. Watlington, J. W. Wright, W. W. Howard, R. H. Hunter, S. L. Knox, and the faithful Tillman Brown. [93]

Growth continued after Bishop J. S. Caldwell was elected in 1904 and assigned to the Pacific Coast. His first quadrennium he established a conference in the Phillippine Islands, which had a bright promise. Reverend J. H. Manning Butler, a loyal Zion preacher who was employed by the government in the Philippines, became interested in building up Zion in that territory, and he and Bishop Caldwell effected plans for growth; however, the work did not survive two quadrenniums. [94] Aware of the extensive territory of this one conference, he organized the Oregon Conference, October 23, 1910. Reverend W. W. Matthews (later bishop) was at Portland, and working in that area to help extend the borders of the conference. [95] The work included the churches in the state of Washington, and in 1916 the conference became known as the Oregon-Washington Conference. By 1920, it had spread to parts of Idaho and Wyoming, and Bishop Kyles had added a few missions, including Walla Walla, Washington and Reading, California. [96] Some of these missions did not survive.

The Southwest Rocky Mountain Conference was set apart from the California Conference by Bishop Kyles, September 22, 1920 at First Church, Los Angeles. Reverends B. C. Robeson, J. B. Holmes, W. J. J. Byers, E. M. Clark, W. R. Lovell, A. C. Yearwood, E. J. McGruder, and W. E. Shaw assisted Bishop Kyles in expanding our work in this Southern part of the West Coast, during this period. [97]

By the turn of the century the church had grown to over a half million members with 3,612 church edifices and 2,500 ordained clergymen, with an average increase per year of 107 ministers, 57 church buildings, and 29,755 members. [98] While many rejoiced over the fruits of their labors in several southern states, one of the wisest men in the church, Bishop J. W. Hood, in special remarks to the 1908 General Conference, called attention to the errors of the committees on assignment of bishops in failing to make the proper appointments during seed time, which proved costly to Zion in some states. Thinking of the vast Negro population in the deep South who had just been emancipated, his remarks centered on the expired Bishop Thomas H. Lomax, second in expansion of the denomination to Bishop J. J. Clinton. Extracts of his talk follow:

In 1876, the committee on districts gave five states to one Bishop: Georgia, Florida, Alabama, Mississippi, Louisiana. And he, a bishop who did not believe it was his duty to travel over the work, went and held the conferences, and then returned to his home where he said he could make more money making pills. He said Bishops Clinton, Jones and Hood were killing themselves travelling over the country, but he was not going to do it.

At the same time, the committee sent Bishop Lomax to the Michigan and Canada Mission where there was very small possibility of accomplishing any very great results; and nothing to do with neither men nor means, except what he could gather on the mission field. Considering what was given him, he worked wonders. But if they had given him part of the five states they gave to the other bishop. . . . I think I hazard nothing in saying that we could have had from 50,000 to 100,000 (additional) members here today.

93. *Minutes,* Twenty-Second Quadrennial Session, 1904, pp. 456-458.
94. *Minutes,* Twenty-Third Quadrennial Session, p. 114.
95. *Minutes,* Twenty-Fourth Quadrennial Session, p. 268.
96. *Minutes,* Twenty-Fifth and Twenty Sixth Quadrennial Sessions, pp. 129-130.
97. *Ibid.,* pp. 41-49; *Star of Zion,* Sept. 2, 1920.
98. DuBois, *The Negro Church,* p. 131; *Minutes,* Twenty-First Quadrennial Session, 1900, pp. 236-237.

When Bishop J. J. Clinton left that work, we had a good start in Georgia, and we led all in Florida and Alabama. We had also a splendid beginning in Mississippi and West Tennessee and 15,000 members in Louisiana. When his successor left that work, I do not think we had more than 1,000 in Louisiana. Georgia, Florida and Mississippi had made but little progress. Alabama had done better because of Reverend W. G. Strong and a few good native preachers had kept the work moving. . . .

If our committee on districts, which left one bishop in charge of five states for six years, doing little more than nothing; and at the same time for the same six important years, kept Bishop Lomax where there was nothing comparatively for him to do; had turned Bishop Lomax loose in Georgia or Florida at that time when there was such a splendid opportunity for planting our beloved Zion . . . the seed time . . . the question of her strength in that field would not have come up today. The hundreds of churches and thousands of members would have been there to speak for themselves. . . .

I think these incidents in the life of Bishop Lomax show the importance of integrity, of standing firmly and doing the best we can, even under discouraging circumstance.

Notwithstanding the awkward position in which he was placed, he did not murmur nor complain, but entered upon his work with remarkable cheerfulness. And this is one of the secrets of his success. He had faith in his ability to overcome obstacles, and went forward with a determination to succeed. He has left us an example which may be studied to great benefit.

Withal, this generation of African Methodist Episcopal Zion Church members can never forget the toils and sacrificial labors of the leaders recorded in the pages of this chapter, and hundreds, nay, thousands of others of this flourishing era.

CHAPTER 17

THE CHURCH SPREADS ABROAD

Before the Foreign Missions Department and the Woman's Home and Foreign Missionary Society were formed, churches were established in several areas outside the United States. Much of it did not survive for various reasons, mainly for the lack of preachers and financial support. However, some of our early churches in foreign territory, such as Demerara and British Guiana (Guyana), were set on a firm foundation before Emancipation and continue modestly in the course of Zion history.

Efforts to establish the A.M.E. Zion Church on foreign soil began with Bishop Rush two days after the close of the New York Annual Conference session, on May 28, 1829, when Rev. Hamilton Johnson arrived from Prescott, Upper Canada, hoping to be in time to join the conference and represent a Zion Society there. From this time forward, the A.M.E. Zion Church had work intermittently in Canada. Because of the strenuous involvement of our church leaders in the abolition movement, steering a number of fugitive slaves to freedom into Canada, it was necessary to follow up with spiritual and social concern. The Canadian work remained a part of the New York Conference until the General Conference of 1856, when that body set off an annual conference in the Province of Nova Scotia, to be held on the second Saturday of September, 1857. [1]

The conference, known as the British North America Annual Conference, assembled with Bishop James Simmons presiding. Reverends John F. Loyd, Joseph G. Smith, and George H. Washington were the preachers of this conference present along with Revs. John N. Mars, Joseph P. Thompson, Samuel M. Giles, and Robert R. Morris from the New York Conference. Thomas A. Davis was received on trial. Halifax had 86 members, Mauroon Hill 9, and Liverpool 38; in addition, there were 130 Sunday school scholars and teachers. The boundary of the British North America Mission Annual Conference was set as follows: on the north by the gulf of St. Lawrence, west by Canada and the state of Maine, south and east by the Atlantic Ocean, embracing New Brunswick, Nova Scotia, Bermuda, and Cape Breton. [2]

Many of the Negroes who fled to Canada for freedom soon migrated to Africa or the West Indies, and after Emancipation, some returned to the United States because of the severity of the climate of the far North. Many of the slaves, being from the deep South, were conditioned to warmer weather; thus Canada's black population became rather sparse and our work did not grow briskly in this territory. In 1864 this conference was merged with the New England Conference, as were New Brunswick and Bermuda, while British Guiana remained a part of the New York Conference. [3] The work, which had extended westward to Ontario,

1. Moore, *History of the A.M.E. Zion Church,* p. 221.
2. *Minutes,* British North America Mission Annual Conference, 1857, p. 4.
3. Moore, *History,* pp. 240-241.

was assigned to Bishop Thomas H. Lomax after his election in 1876. Lomax wrought well in the awkward position which he had been placed; a new bishop assigned to a total missionary district, "with no mission fund in hand to aid the Bishop appointed to this field, in commencing operations." Lomax organized the Michigan and Canada Conference in October 1877 and made an incredible report of his four years labors, under existing circumstances, at the General Conference. [4] Nevertheless, that fragment of Zion in Canada later became a part of the Michigan Conference, the nucleus of which was Windsor.

One thing that hindered our work abroad was the lack of men. We did not have enough preachers after the Civil War to develop the South, to hold Canada and the distant North, and to send missionaries to new territories. [5] The church began to concentrate on spreading the borders to the West Indies and Africa, the first decade after its abundant growth in the South.

The Christianization of Africa was the dream of the Afro-American Church. The Christian churches had gone ahead and were developing missions in Africa. We felt it our responsibility as a race church to drive into the vast continent and develop our Fatherland for Christ Jesus. Bishop Alexander Walters states the following on the commencement of our work in Africa:

Our Contribution to Africa

While Scotland can boast of her David Livingstone, who stands at the head of all African explorers; indeed, who is majestic in loneliness and was so lofty in his purpose, so superb in his devotion, and who said when dying, "All that I can add to my loneliness is, may heaven's richest blessing come down on every one—American, Englishman, Turk—who will help heal this open sore of the world." And while the Methodist Episcopal Church can boast of her Melville Cox, who was so able and saintly, and who laid down his life for Africa's redemption, our Zion can boast of her rugged old hero, Andrew Cartwright, and Dudley, Arthur and Wright; nor can we forget their services, who are the connecting links between our Church and Africa. Their departed spirits whisper to us and urge us on to play our parts in the redemption of this great continent.

All honor to Bishop Small, my predecessor, who felt the burden of African redemption as no other man felt it in his day in our Church. I am afraid that there is not enough said about the work of Bishop Small; what we have in Africa today is largely due to the efforts in the interest of Africa by this sainted hero.

It is known to a good many of us that out of his own private purse he aided Frank Arthur and other African students, who matriculated at Livingstone College. Several of them he kept in his home, providing liberally for their physical needs. I consider it an honor to succeed such an eminent scholar, such an enthusiastic advocate of African redemption.

And now may I add to this closing word, I do hope that our Church will rise to the present situation and meet the present opportunity which is presented to it in Africa. . . . Let us up and be doing. Every member of the Church and race should make an annual subscription to our African Fund. [6]

After organizing and building 12 churches in 10 years, Rev. Andrew Cartwright left Plymouth, N.C., and sailed for Africa on January 7, 1876. He organized the first A.M.E. Zion Church on the continent in Brewerville, Liberia,

4. *Minutes,* Sixteenth Quadrennial Session, 1880, p. 20.
5. Hood, *One Hundred Years,* p. 96.
6. Walters, *My Life and Work,* pp. 174-176.

on February 7, 1878. and one in Clay Ashland, November 1878. [7] By 1880, he reported another church organized at Antherton, for a total of three. A formal report was sent to the General Conference assembled in Montgomery, Ala., May 1880, from Liberia, signed by Josephus Samuel Baker and others, stating the splendid beginnings of Brother Cartwright and requesting the General Conference to give Cartwright power to call a conference, and enable him to gather in more preachers for the work. [8] This is the historic General Conference which made concrete plans for our work in Africa by forming the Woman's Home and Foreign Missionary Society.

Cartwright, concerned about his position in Africa, came to America and met the Board of Bishops in session at Petersburg, Va., March 28, 1883. The Board of Bishops authorized him to hold annual conferences in Africa and appoint suitable persons to preach and teach our people there so long, states Cartwright, "as my life and conduct comported with the gospel of our Lord and Saviour Jesus Christ; subject to the ratification or modification of the General Conference. The General Conference of May, 1884 ratified the appointment." [9] Cartwright continued to serve as a missionary in Africa under the auspices of the General Conferences and Board of Bishops. In 1886 he organized another church with 40 members and 50 Sunday school scholars at Cape Palmas, but due to shortage of funds, the flock scattered and soon joined another denomination. The General Conference Committee on Districts recommended that the African Mission be left in the hands of the Board of Bishops to be supplied, and "that some one of them visit the work yearly." [10]

This same year, after passing through some difficulty in securing a woman teacher to help him start a school for Zion in this territory, he employed his wife, Carrie E. S. Cartwright, sanctioned by the Board of Bishops, for $300 per year. [11] She made a report of her labors on the organization and operation of the A.M.E. Zion Mission School at Brewerville, Liberia, to the 1892 General Conference, and the delegates were stimulated to move forward in the interest of Africa. [12] In October 1892, Bishop Walters requested Cartwright to accept the presiding eldership in Africa over his own work. He willingly did so, yet he felt that he should have been acknowledged as superintendent of African missions, with responsibilities equivalent to a bishop of the church, on the African continent. [13] He served in this capacity until the 1896 General Conference and reported his labors there. A special committee on the status of Rev. Andrew Cartwright resolved that he was a "missionary to Africa acting in the capacity of Presiding Elder by the appointment of Bishop Alexander Walters of the Seventh Episcopal District." The Committee on Episcopal Address acquiesced with the bishops of the church and recommended to the General Conference that a member of the Board of Bishops visit the work in Africa at least annually, feeling that there was not a need for the election of a missionary bishop. [14]

Cartwright had opened the door for Zion in Africa, and blessings were in store for the church on this vast continent. The General Conference elected John Bryan Small a bishop and assigned him to Africa and the West Indies with home conferences; North Alabama, West Alabama, and South Mississippi. "Previous to

7. Cartwright, "A Plea for Justice," *Start of Zion*, November 12, 1896.
8. *Minutes,* Sixteenth Quadrennial Session, pp. 15-16.
9. Cartwright, *op. cit.*
10. *Minutes,* Nineteenth Quadrennial Session, p. 175.
11. *The Star of Zion,* November 12, 1896; February 25, 1897.
12. *Minutes,* Nineteenth Quadrennial Session, pp. 176-177.
13. *The Star of Zion,* November 12, 1896.
14. *Minutes,* Twentieth Quadrennial Session, 1896, pp. 250, 253-255.

REV.   ANDREW   CARTWRIGHT,
First Missionary to Africa

the election of Bishop Small to the episcopacy, he expressed not merely a
willingness, but a desire to visit and see what there really was, and to supervise our
African work, and true to his declaration, at his first opportunity he made
strenuous efforts and so accomplished his intention." [15] In 1862, at 17 years
old, at Small's own request his father sent him to visit Jamaica and other islands,
and thence to the West Coast of Africa where he spent three years and three
months, learned to speak the Fantee language, and was present when England
crowned Quakuduo king of the Fantees.

During his residence in Africa he visited and spent his time in observing the
customs, language, etc.. at Sierra Leone, Cape Coast, Elmena, Dix Cove, Accra,
Lagos, Badagry, Bathurst, Gambia, Fort Bullin, etc. On his return from Africa
he spent five years in Balize, British Honduras, where he was engaged as
orderly room clerk, and finally became her majesty's chief clerk of the
brigade office. [16]

15. *Minutes,* Twenty-First Quadrennial Session, 1900, p. 161.
16. Hood, *One Hundred Years,* pp. 234-235.

Small's father was a strong member of the Church of England of Barbados, "and so educated his son for the ministry of that church; but while in Honduras he professed hope in Christ and joined the Wesleyan Methodist Church." In 1871, on his way to England, he came to the United States, and through the influence of Rev. R. H. G. Dyson and Bishop J. J. Clinton, he joined the African Methodist Episcopal Zion Church two weeks after his arrival. His effervescent leadership in the New England Conference, where he served several churches and was secretary of the conference, and in North Carolina won for him lofty recognition throughout the denomination. [17]

By his own efforts, Bishop Small collected $665.68, just about $150 less than the amount necessary to defray his traveling expenses to and from Africa. [18] He preached at Mother Zion Church on Sunday, June 20, 1897, and was given a reception by the people in the New York vicinity and a grand send-off prior to sailing on June 22, 1897. He had received the blessings of the entire church, and the editor of the *Star of Zion,* Rev. J. W. Smith, expressed it so beautifully that we include extracts here:

He [Bishop Small] is the first Bishop of our Zion who feels or has felt divinely called to go to Africa. Bishop James Varick one hundred years ago because of race proscription and the denial of religious liberty felt moved to quietly and honorably withdraw from the white M.E. Church in New York and establish the first Negro Church. . . . Bishops J. J. Clinton, J. W. Hood, S. T. Jones and J. J. Moore, feeling divinely impressed, tramped behind the "boys in blue," and, as the shackles of slavery fell from the limbs of our people, in the name of the God of battles, unfurled and floated to the breeze the banner of Zion in the Southland. We see and enjoy the fruits of their labors.

Africa, so vast in extent and her population; so bewilderingly great in numbers that the spots of light where mission work is done are hardly perceptible; Africa, the land that afforded the child Jesus refuge when wicked Herod sought His life; whose teeming millions are as yet hardly touched by the Christian Church, notwithstanding the fact that there are now forty missionary societies represented there by earnest, heroic missionary toilers, and the Bible has been translated in whole or in part into sixty-six of its dialects, is waiting and ready to receive from the dark sons of Ham, like Bishop Small, the glorious light of the gospel. The time is here when Zion with other denominations must capture Africa for Christ. Let us pray that the journey of Bishop Small may be one of great profit to us and that as a missionary he is but a forerunner of others who will be willing to go, live, labor and die for Zion in Africa. [19]

After visiting London, he arrived in Sierra Leone on July 16, and remained until August 3, surveying and observing the field and its situation and other connections. He left Sierra Leone and landed at Monrovia, Liberia, Saturday evening, August 7. He preached on Sunday, August 8 in the Methodist Episcopal Church, Monrovia, and left Tuesday, August 10, stopping at Virginia Landing, thence on to Brewerville where he visited the mission work established by Rev. Andrew Cartwright. [20] That field was suffering for missionary workers and pastors. There were none from America on the field but Cartwright, and the natives were confused about inadequate leadership. They saw there were bishops in other African fields and felt that Zion should have the same, but there was much division on the home base on whether to have a bishop on the field or a

17. *Ibid.*
18. *Minutes,* Twenty-First Quadrennial Session, p. 161.
19. *The Star of Zion,* June 17, 1897; July 8, 1897.
20. *Minutes,* Twenty-First Quadrennial Session, pp. 161-162.

BISHOP JOHN BRYAN SMALL

1845 - 1905

First Bishop to Africa. Founder of the
Missionary Seer and creative author.

bishop at a distance for the field. Bishop Small, however, was willing to come and go, and was willing to stay if the church had wanted a regular bishop on the field. He had background and particular interest in Africa, where he had experience prior to serving in the British Army as a member of Queen Victoria's brigade. Thus he found our church in Brewerville in need of spiritual stimulation and financial assistance. He also found a Zion mission at Johnsonville with ten members. "After remaining with the brethren and encouraging them a few days, he returned to Monrovia and awaited passage to Cape Coast." [21]

His first significant act at Cape Coast was preaching at the Christ Episcopal Church where the audience was beyond the capacity of the church. Hundreds listened from the outside as he preached with very great effect. At the close of the services he hastened to his stopping place of the Hockman brothers, accompanied by several noted gentlemen of that town; and then boarded the steamship *Loanda*, taking with him Mr. William Hockman as student to Livingstone College. They sailed the following morning to Sierra Leone, and then on to Liverpool aboard the

21. *Ibid.*

CARTWRIGHT MEMORIAL CHURCH   Brewerville, Liberia
                                    Mother Church of Africa
                                    Present edifice built in 1962

steamship *Lagos,* making several stops in other African ports. While in England, they visited London and met Rev. and Mrs. John H. Hector, who rendered them substantial aid and made their brief stay pleasant. [22] Reverend Hector was one of the well-known leaders in the A.M.E. Zion Church, and was the unanimous selection of the Centennial General Conference, 1896, to represent the African Methodist Episcopal Zion Church as fraternal delegate to the Wesleyan Conference in London. [23]

On October 14, Bishop Small and young Hockman sailed for New York and arrived on October 25. "The Bishop's trip revealed things of vital interest to the connection." First, that we had work in Africa which needed attention, and the lingering condition in which he found the work was due to the lack of substantial aid. It was then noted that:

It is really impossible to carry on successful mission work in Africa, or any foreign mission field, unless the ministers are up to the times, and aided by the mother society, and no Church can make any reasonable claim of

22. *Ibid.,* p. 163.
23. *Minutes,* Twentieth Quadrennial Session, p. 259.

fulfilling its mission which has no interest in foreign fields. Nearly all the ministers in Africa are educated men and well informed, and to send ministers to those foreign fields who are inferior to their fellow laborers, is not merely to impede their success but destroy their influence. [24]

Bishop Small had made a number of friends and contacts on this, his first trip to the Fatherland, and had attempted to bring other students over with him to study at Livingstone College, and return home equipped to extend the borders of Zion. Soon after his return home his labors began to bear fruit. While on the Gold Coast, he had offered James E. Kwegyir Aggrey and his closest friend, Kobina Osam Pinanko (Frank Arthur), the opportunity to come to America to study, but they refused. The offer was renewed. A close associate of Aggrey's, Mr. Anaman, urged Aggrey to accept it; "other friends pressed money upon him; and on July 10th, 1898, he sailed in SS. *Accra* for England and thence to America. After spending a few weeks in Bishop Small's house at York, Pennsylvania, he made his way to Salisbury, a beautiful little city in North Carolina, where Livingstone College" is situated. [25] Frank Arthur evidently arrived only a few months after Aggrey, as Aggrey and Hockman were one term ahead of him at Livingstone College by 1900. [26]

There was also an attempt to organize a Zion Society at Cape Coast by Rev. F. Egyir Asaam after Small's trip. "That society would have succeeded and grown like a bay tree," but our inadequate foreign missions program, which was in its infancy, and Rev. Asaam's ill health soon caused this work to expire. [27] Zion was more successful however, in Kwitta (now known as Keta). Reverend Thomas B. Freeman, our missionary to Kwitta, established a flourishing mission there, and had made strenuous efforts to establish similar work at Accra, Lagos, and other places. He had received very little financial assistance from the home base at this time, and Bishop Small, moved by his dedicated works, sent him $50 and persuaded the Board of Bishops in their meeting prior to the 1900 General Conference to send him $100 immediately. Reverend Dr. Owen L. W. Smith of Wilson, N.C., who had been appointed by President McKinley as Minister Resident and Consul General to Liberia in 1898, was also an asset to Zion in Africa. While serving the government, Bishop Small made him a presiding elder of the Liberian work. During this time, he also sent $50 to Rev. Freeman to help him firmly establish this and other mission work on the Gold Coast (now Ghana). [28]

Before going to Africa, Bishop Small had collected $665.68, and spent about $150 in excess of the amount collected, "but knowing the connection was in a financial struggle when urged to make his claim for the amount spent in excess, declared that he would rather lose the amount than to press the connection therefore," thus he readily surrendered the amount for the good of the connection. [29]

Much credit is due the churches in Mobile, Ala., for mothering foreign missions, just as Zion history records the noble deeds of the New England Conference in sponsoring its first missionaries to the South after the Civil War. If it had not been for the churches in Mobile, Bishop Small could not have taken either of his trips to Africa or the West Indies. The bishop was so successful in interesting these churches in foreign missions work that he recommended that the West Alabama Conference be attached to whatever episcopal district the foreign

24. *Minutes,* Twenty-First Quadrennial Session, p. 163.
25. Smith, *Aggrey of Africa,* pp. 57-58.
26. *Minutes,* Twenty-First Quadrennial Session, p. 169.
27. *Ibid.,* p. 165.
28. *Ibid.*

fields would be placed in, as they expressed willingness to assist the bishop in his visits to those fields. [30]

According to his heart's desire, the General Conference of 1900 reassigned the foreign mission work to Bishop Small along with West Alabama, South Mississippi, Allegheny-Ohio, and Western New York. These home conferences, at his request, raised additional funds to support the foreign cause. He made his second visit to the African mission work in 1902. Accompanied by William Hockman, one of the African young men whom he brought to this country, educated at Livingstone College for the foreign work, Bishop Small sailed on June 21, and arrived in Cape Coast, West Africa, on Thursday morning, July 24. [31] This journey was crowned with resolute success, as Zion was firmly planted in parts of West Africa. After delivering Hockman to his family's protection, Bishop Small remained in Cape Coast several weeks, "viewing the situation, taking observations and making friends in interest of our Zion," such as would benefit her for years to come—"knowing Africans" as Small did. The report stated:

> While in Cape Coast, at his [Bishop Small's] request, Mrs. Christine M. Selby, an educated African lady, who spends the greater part of her time in Europe, presented to him, in conjunction with her brother, Mr. Charles A. Albert Barnes, a large plot of ground, 50 feet wide and 200 feet long, in the town of Cape Coast on which to erect a church and church appliances for the African Methodist Episcopal Zion Church. The land is 10,000 square feet, valued at one guinea per square foot—a guinea is a trifle more than $5 American money—so that the land is valued at $50,000. [32]

Although the people were anxious for him to start a church in Cape Coast while he was there, he would not do so. He had no pastor to take charge of the work, and he felt it unwise to make another effort with the prospects of it falling backward and becoming unprofitable in all directions. "After his return home, on the first day of August, 1903, he sent Reverend Frank Arthur (Pinanko), who had just completed his studies at Livingstone College, to Cape Coast, and the work in this area, both churches and schools, grew abundantly under the leadership of this 'unusually sober, scholarly, and upright Christian gentleman,' and a trustworthy servant in that field." [33] So successful had been the works of Rev. Pinanko [34] the first five years in Cape Coast, that when Bishop Walters presented him to the 1908 General Conference to report on the status of the work in this area, the house gave him rousing applause over and over again, prior to his report. The report "was replete with facts and figures that called forth enthusiastic and repeated peals of applause." He paid glowing tributes to Bishop Small who had died the first part of the quadrennium, and Bishop Walters, his successor. He reported 15 churches on the Gold Coast, 527 members, 207 day scholars, and a school named Varick Memorial Institute, which had started out very successfully with $52,000 worth of property and 8 teachers. Among other recommendations, he stressed the adoption of the Varick Memorial Institute as a connectional school, and the election of a bishop for the foreign field who would have little or no work at all at home. [35]

On his African trip in 1902, Bishop Small visited Accra, Gold Coast, and felt it was very easy to establish an excellent church there. He then went to Kwitta,

30. *Ibid.*
31. *Minutes,* Twenty-Second Quadrennial Session, P. 199.
32. *Ibid.*
33. *Ibid.,* pp. 170, 200.
34. Rev. Kobina Osam Pinanko changed his name on his arrival in America to Frank Arthur. On his return to Africa, he resumed his original name.
35. *Minutes,* Twenty-Third Quadrennial Session, 1908, p. 234.

where Zion had a flourishing church organization with zealous workers and a school connected with the church. His leading missionary, Rev. Joseph D. Taylor, was engaged in a noble work assisted by William Hockman, S. F. Abban, and C. L. Acolatse.

From Kwitta the Bishop journeyed to Brewerville, Liberia, and at the request of the members of our mother church in Africa, he ordained to the order of deacon Brother Lewis B. Dudley, and placed him in charge of the church at Brewerville. Reverend Andrew Cartwright was appointed presiding elder. (36)

Cartwright was a man loyal to his church, strong in the faith, of moral integrity, and zealous for the religion of his fathers. For many years he labored unaided and almost alone in the interest of his brethren of the dark continent. In his later years the mission was greatly strengthened by Dr. Owen L. W. Smith, the American Minister at Monrovia, Liberia. Besides personal work of Dr. Smith, which he did, he contributed liberally of his means to the work of the mission. Father Cartwright was also aided in his work by his faithful wife, who assisted him as a teacher in his parochial school work. (37)

This faithful pioneer in Africa, Cartwright, died at his post on January 14, 1903. (38) He was succeeded by Rev. H. T. Wright whom Bishop Small sent from Philadelphia to Liberia with wife and child, on February 27, 1900, to take charge of the Brewerville Church. His devoted wife died at Brewerville while laboring with her husband, August 8, 1907. Reverend Wright was succeeded by Rev. J. Drybauld Taylor, a native of Africa. "He rendered most excellent service during his incumbency as pastor and presiding elder." The work in this section of Liberia became greatly stimulated when Bishop Walters appointed Rev. J. J. Pearce, during the organization of the Liberian Conference. He described Pearce as painstaking and loyal, and a most capable missionary. Eight mission points had been established, and another four or five opened up by letter, and in all these places, Americans and Liberians were working together in the best interest of Zion. (39)

Before the formation of any annual conferences in Africa, Bishop Small had received his third assignment to the foreign field at the General Conference in May, 1904. While holding the West Alabama Conference in November 1904, he had a severe attack. "One spell after another brought him to his bed, and after two weeks of painful suffering, this brave soldier of Christ laid down his weapons and went to sleep with his loved ones. His death occurred Sunday, January 5, 1905." (40) The Board of Bishops were moved not only to pay a special tribute to their beloved colleague of sainted memory, but to reaffirm their abiding interest in the cause of Africa and the foreign fields as they had not done before:

The death of a beloved colleague, Bishop John B. Small, through zealous labors, personal visits and vigilant oversight, our foreign work, especially the missions in Africa and British Honduras, which had taken on new life, was undoubtedly a stunning blow to the above named work.

We feel safe, however, in saying that the good seed which he had sown, the services he had rendered and the well-equipped workers whom he had secured and appointed to foreign work, especially our good brother and consecrated co-worker, the Rev. Frank Arthur, who is at present with us, made it possible for the work to hold its own and make some substantial progress under the oversight of Bishop Alexander Walters, who has had the

36. *Minutes,* Twenty-Second Quadrennial Session, p. 201.
37. *Minutes,* Twenty-Fourth Quadrennial Session, p. 200.
38. *Minutes,* Twenty-Second Quadrennial Session, p. 263.
39. *Minutes,* Twenty-Fourth Quadrennial Session, p. 200.
40. *Minutes,* Twenty-Third Quadrennial Session, p. 163.

cooperation of the Corresponding Secretary of Missions.

The claims of Africa upon all Christians, and particularly upon those whose ancestors came from the densely populated continent, are too great and urgent to put aside or turn over to others. Zion has hoisted her banner over the great continent whose sons made one of the largest contributions to the world's early civilization and she must see to it that the banner is neither hauled down nor lowered.

The present General Conference should, with open and attentive ears, listen to the report of those who have had the supervision of our foreign work, that such legislation may be enacted as will guarantee the continued success and early expansion of our African mission work. Four chiefs may be able to make a recommendation concerning what they believe to be the best policy to be pursued at present before we shall be called upon to plan for that important work.

We are sure we voice the feelings of our brethren on this side of the Atlantic, when we say we are greatly pleased and encouraged to have Elders Arthur and Wright among us. We congratulate Rev. Frank Arthur upon the honor he has reflected upon his Alma Mater, Livingstone College, and thank him for the untiring and fruitful services he has rendered our great church. [41]

Bishop Small, the brilliant penman, accomplished poet, conqueror of several African languages, established *The (Zion) Missionary Seer,* in 1901 to stimulate the work in foreign territory. Those famous words from his death bed: "Don't Let My African Work Fail," continue to echo throughout the entire denomination, giving fresh courage and inspiration to the members of all Zion to support vigorously the work of the church in Africa.

Bishop Alexander Walters, assigned the foreign work at the General Conference of 1908, made his trip to West Africa in 1910. Walters, who was one of the prime organizers of the Pan-African Conference in London, July 1900, was intensely interested in enhancing the cause of African peoples throughout the world. The appointment to the work in Africa had special meaning to him. He once stated:

My main object is to have our men help to civilize and Christianize non-Christian Africa, and this must be done quickly or Mohammedanism will overrun the country. The question is, which will conquer Africa—Islam or Christianity? Some very intelligent people think that Islam is better for Africa as a religion than Christianity, since it so completely emphasizes and practices the fatherhood of God and the brotherhood of man.

They say the Christian religion teaches the fatherhood of God and the brotherhood of man, but the white missionary studiously avoids it in practice. I am sorry this is true, but this does not destroy the fact that the Christian religion is the best in the world.

Mohammedanism encourages polygamy, which means the destruction of the home. Christianity stands for purity, which means the stability of the home and the nation. Now is the time for the Christian world to awake to the seriousness of this conflict and do all in its power to win Africa. . . . GOD'S PURPOSE IN ALLOWING THE NATIVES TO BE BROUGHT TO THESE SHORES.

For what other purpose were the natives brought to America and caused to pass through the crucible of slavery and now to be Christianized and trained in the best schools of the nation but to aid in the redemption of Africa. [42]

41. Episcopal Quadrennial Address, 1908, p. 11.
42. Walters, *op cit.,* p. 172.

He left New York on January 26, 1910, and arrived in Liverpool on February 1, accompanied by Bishop I. B. Scott, resident bishop of Monrovia of the Methodist Episcopal Church. They sailed for Monrovia on the 9th, stopping first at Freetown, Sierra Leone, and making a safe arrival in Monrovia around February 26. After a brief stay in the capital city, Walters journeyed to Brewerville and organized the Liberia Annual Conference, March 3, 1910. He was greatly assisted in this conference by Revs. J. D. Taylor and J. J. Pearce. [43] Missions were established in Monrovia, Po River, Roysville, Pleasant Hill, Suahn, and River Cess. Bishop Walters ordained several missionaries in each area that he visited, to carry on the work. He left Monrovia for Cape Coast, where he arrived several days ahead of his planned schedule. Reverend Pinanko, by authorization of Bishop Walters, had organized the West Gold Coast Annual Conference [44] the previous year, and on March 17, 1910, Bishop Walters presided over the second session at Cape Coast. He ordained six deacons and three elders, and organized the Zion College at Cape Coast. Bishop Walters was warmly and enthusiastically received by the people, and the work was greatly blessed. Several mission churches and training schools had been opened for the people in the towns and villages, and nearly 1,200 additional souls had been brought to Christ during this quadrennium. [45]

Bishop Walters left Cape Coast on March 28 for Kwittah, his last stop on the West Coast of Africa, accompanied by Rev. Pinanko, presiding elder, and Rev. Harold N. Kwaun, a delegate from Kwitta to the conference held at Cape Coast. He organized and held the first session of the East Gold Coast Conference at Kwitta, March 31, 1910, with five ministers and nine lay delegates present. He ordained Brothers Harold N. Kwaun and G. A. Tay deacons, and three other young men of our teaching force were admitted to this conference. He found over 300 members in Kwitta, and a day school of 270 scholars. Bishop Walters was jubilant over this work. He stated: "If our great Bishop Small were alive, who laid the foundation of this work, how his heart would rejoice, and I dare to think that he does rejoice at the wonderful progress made. Bishop Small built wiser than he knew." He was greatly assisted in this part of Africa by our staunch missionary, Rev. W. E. Shaw, who was a trained physician, "and eminently prepared by literary training and experience" to give ample service in the redemption of Africa. [46]

Bishop George C. Clement succeeded Bishop Walters as presiding bishop of the African work in 1917. Bishop Walters stated that he asked to be relieved of the African Mission Conferences owing to severe illness, at the Bishops' Meeting in January, 1917 at Concord, N.C., and Bishop Clement was assigned. He was eager to make a trip to Africa and made the necessary preparations to that end, but the rules of World War I and the difficulty of travel prevented him finally from taking the trip. The bishops praised the work and the fine coterie of consecrated workers who were serving in Africa, and stated that they were proud to send both Mrs. Henrietta Peters and Miss Lillian Tshabalala to Kwitta, and Mr. T. D. Davis to the Mt. Coffee farm in Liberia, all of whom were fine accessions to our foreign work. [47]

Reverend Pearce had returned from Liberia in 1915, and the work was without supervision until August 1919, when Rev. Thomas E. Davis was employed

43. *Ibid.,* p. 153; Hood, *History,* Vol. II, p. 30.
44. Names of the West Gold Coast and East Gold Coast Conferences established in 1910 by Bishop Walters were changed to West Ghana and East Ghana Conferences after the country's name was changed, 1957.
45. *Minutes,* Twenty-Fourth Quadrennial Session, p. 203.
46. Walters, *op. cit.,* pp. 165-167.
47. *Minutes,* Twenty-Fifth and Twenty-Sixth Quadrennial Sessions, pp. 75, 164.

by the Board of Foreign Missions and appointed by Bishop Clement to take charge of the work in Liberia, while Rev. Pinanko was still carrying on the work in the West Gold Coast Conference. The East Gold Coast Conference was being directed by Rev. R. E. Peters, who had been on the field for six years. It was felt by the natives, however, that the African work needed closeup episcopal supervision, and their sentiment was expressed by the Corresponding Secretary of Foreign Missions, Rev. W. W. Matthews, at the 1924 General Conference. He recommended that we send an American resident bishop—"one who is willing to enter heartily into their lives and problems, willing to live among them, to sympathize with them, to supervise and direct affairs and Zion's destinies in the Fatherland." [48] After operating nearly a half-century in the Fatherland, this historic General Conference answered their plea and elected the largest class of bishops in the history of the denomination, at that time, making two additional ones, and assigned to Africa a resident bishop, Cameron Chesterfield Alleyne.

Bishop Alleyne and his wife, Annie L. Washington Alleyne, made their departure within the year for their new work. Faced with discouraging situations and vicissitudes, they were successful in their four years' labors on the field. In Liberia, the bishop found Rev. and Mrs. Daniel Carleton Pope, stationed at Brewerville and Mount Coffee Farm, ardently at work for Zion. "Despite sacrifices, sickness, and the loss of their baby boy, they stuck to their post." In the West Gold Coast Conference he found the churches divided and the flock scattered. With efficacy he united the people and saved them all to Zion. He was abounding in gratitude to Professor James E. K. Aggrey, who had passed away during the quadrennium and had aided materially and helped to save Zion in the Gold Coast. [49] He found Rev. Pinanko, the pioneering, painstaking, and progressive servant for 25 years, still reliable, loyal and true. His wife, Victoria Osam-Pinanko, was working in the schools as sewing teacher to great benefit. He found Rev. Isaac Sackey to be one of our most constructive pastors and leading church builders on the coast. The missionary workers from America had also been zealous and courageous, with unquenchable enthusiasm for the African work. Reverend W. D. Francis, who had lived and preached Christ among an appreciative people, remained at his post when his devoted wife, Martha B. Francis, who was an asset to the work, broke down in health and was confined at home. Reverend and Mrs. D. G. Garland served at Mt. Coffee Mission from 1922-23. [50]

Mrs. Harriet Mae Green, the trained registered nurse who went to the field with Bishop and Mrs. Alleyne, was resplendent in her duties. While in Africa, Bishop Alleyne and our competent preaching and teaching ministry the Rev. and Mrs. R. F. Pile, Revs. P. D. Ofosuhene, D. K. Brown, Isaac Cole, G. B. Eninful, Moses D. Frans, P. O. Okyir, Alfred Eshun, Coffie, Qyason, G. B. Ado, Mr. Walter K. Dolly (later minister), and others, made vast improvements to the work and left in course of erection more than a half-dozen churches in Cape Coast. [51]

Bishop Alleyne's successor, Bishop W. W. Matthews, associated by the zealous missionaries from the home field, his wife, Alice J. Matthews, and daughter, Juanita Matthews, Oliver L. Sims, and Rev. Miss Almena Smith, made substantial enhancement of the total work in Africa. Working in close association with them were African leaders, including Revs. Henry Bassa, Henry Anaman, K. M. Medu-

48. *Minutes,* Twenty-Seventh Quadrennial Session, p. 259.
49. *Minutes,* Twenty-Eighth Quadrennial Session, pp. 154, 156.
50. *Ibid.,* pp. 163-164.
51. *Ibid.,* pp. 164-167.

Kyirpua, J. H. Phillips, and the eager and enthusiastic layman, Ben Brew. [52]

The Nigeria Conference was organized and received into the fellowship of Zion at the time of the joint sessions of the East and West Gold Coast (Ghana) Conferences, February 24-29, 1932, with 28 churches, 11 native preachers, and 2,345 members. "The Reverend J. Drybauld Taylor was the instrumental factor in bringing into our fold this new congregation of souls to march under Zion's progressive banner." By 1932, 18,000 members were reported in the conferences of West Africa. [53] Later, Miss Arwilda G. Robinson of Philadelphia, "a young woman of fine spirit, good preparation and fully devoted to the cause," was sent to Liberia, as well as Rev. and Mrs. A. W. Ricks, who took up the work at the school and farm at Mt. Coffee, Liberia. Reverend A. A. Adjahoe was sent to Keta, and served as preacher, superintendent, and school master with phenomenal success, assisted by Rev. F. K. Fiawoo, who had been trained in the United States, and returned to Keta to serve his native land. [54]

After supervising the African work for eight years, Bishop Matthews was succeeded by Bishop James W. Brown. "In his first four years of residence and service on the Foreign Field the work felt the power of his genius as an organizer and far-sighted leader. New life was in evidence everywhere on the field." [55] The small society in Monrovia organized during Bishop Walters' day had long since been lost, and Bishop Brown organized a church for the second time in this capital city, with 50 members, and erected a church building. Reverend S. Dorme Lartey became its first pastor. The Bishop's wife, Andrades Lindsay Brown, Rev. G. A. Tay of Nigeria, and Rev. and Mrs. S. W. Peacock rendered valuable services with the others on the field. After six months of strenuous labor and exposure to the intense heat and tropical diseases, Mrs. Peacock fell on sleep and was buried next to the son of Rev. and Mrs. Daniel C. Pope. [56]

Bishop J. W. Brown was reassigned to the African Conferences by the General Conference of 1940. He met with a fatal accident in New York City, when an automobile struck him down on February 27, 1941. The Board of Bishops assigned the work to the experienced Bishop Alleyne. He was prevented from visiting the field because of the emerging conditions of World War II, but through ponderous correspondence and proxies on the field, the work met with surprising success throughout the dismal war years. [57]

Bishop Edgar B. Watson was elected in 1944 and assigned the African Conferences along with two Home Missions Conferences. He and his wife, Mary J. Watson, spent considerable time in Africa, and he was given help from the Sesqui-Centennial Fund with which he did some development of the work. In 1948, the newly elected Bishop Hampton T. Medford, who served as corresponding secretary of the Foreign Missions Department, was assigned to the African work. He appointed Mrs. Cordella Medford Fauntleroy, his daughter, missionary supervisor, and she accompanied him on his first trip to Africa, because of the illness of his wife, Mrs. Mary Elizabeth Medford, who could not serve and soon passed away. His daughter, Mrs. Fauntleroy, also died five weeks after returning from their first mission, reportedly from some illness she contracted in Africa.

The work had been enhanced through the significant contributions of Dr. and

52. *Minutes,* Twenty-Ninth Quadrennial Session, 1932, pp. 152-156.
53. Ibid.
54. *Minutes,* Thirtieth Quadrennial Session, 1936, pp. 140-141, 270-271.
55. *Minutes,* Thirty-Second Quadrennial Session, p. 170.
56. *Minutes,* Thirty-First Quadrennial Session, pp. 169, 170.
57. *Minutes,* Thirty-Second Quadrennial Session, p. 170.

Mrs. J. A. Babington-Johnson of Nigeria, who later transferred to America where Dr. Babington-Johnson pastored until his death in 1971; Dr. and Mrs. S. Dorme Lartey of Liberia, and Dr. A. W. Appiah, Revs. Isaac Cole and K. O. Okyir from the Gold Coast. The notable servant, Rev. Frank Arthur Osam-Pinanko, passed away on March 15, 1946, after 43 years of dedicated services. [58]

Bishop Daniel Carleton Pope, who had done outstanding work in Liberia, was elected Secretary of Foreign Missions and subsequently elevated to the bishopric in 1952 and assigned this African territory. Soon after returning from the field around 1940, his dear wife, Louise Hudson Pope, passed away. He supervised this work unsparingly for eight years, and produced lasting results. It was during the administration of Bishop Pope, in 1954, that the First Episcopal District, under the leadership of Bishop W. J. Walls, initiated the African Memorial Banks, which raised funds specifically for African causes. Their first project was restoring the Cartwright Memorial Church at Brewerville, which had decayed and been removed entirely, the membership having temporarily joined the Methodist Church.

The African Memorial Bank Fund aggregated about $30,000 over a period of 10 to 14 years from the First Episcopal District, which included the New York, Western New York, New England, and Western North Carolina Conferences, and later the Blue Ridge Conference. The projects included $9,000 for the Brewerville Church, $10,000 for the Aggrey Memorial Church at Accra, Ghana, $6,000 for the Dorothy Walls Girls School at Po River, Liberia, $1,000 for the new hospital in Ghana, and $2,800 toward organizing a church in Lagos, Nigeria. Although the funds were presented during the administrations of Bishops Pope, Lartey, Hilliard, and Dunston respectively, construction of three of the buildings sponsored took place during the administration of Bishop Solomon Dorme Lartey, our first native African bishop, successor to Bishop Pope. These African Memorial Banks did considerable good and have the potential for doing much more. Bishop Raymond L. Jones, in his last report at the 1972 General Conference, presented $5,000 raised by the Western North Carolina Conference to Bishop Hilliard for a special project in Ghana, from these same banks, which the new bishop elected and assigned to Africa, Bishop Ruben L. Speaks, carried to Africa on his maiden trip in 1973, along with other contributions to aid the work.

The General Conference of 1960 made progressive steps in the interest of Zion in Africa. Their action was prompted by the ever-increasing need of our own church leaders on the continent, due to the rapidly growing autonomy and decolonization of African nations. The practice had been to send the last bishop elected to Africa. The 1952 General Conference changed that practice, and passed into law the following:

(1) That the Episcopal Committee shall assign to the African District without regard to seniority the Bishop who in its opinion is best suited for the work.

(2) That the Bishop assigned to Africa shall be required to reside in Africa during the period of his assignment. He shall not be given any American Conference during such period of assignment. [59]

Thus Bishop Solomon Dorme Lartey, the first African to be so elected, was consecrated bishop and assigned to the Liberia and West Ghana Conferences, and Bishop William Alexander Hilliard was elected and assigned to the East Ghana and Nigeria Conferences.

58. *Minutes,* Thirty-Third Quadrennial Session, pp. 158-160; Thirty-Fourth Quadrennial Session, p. 146.
59. *Minutes,* Thirty-Fourth Quadrennial Session, p. 393; *Doctrines and Discipline,* Paragraph 74, 1 & 2.

Bishop Lartey, residing in Monrovia, Liberia, and his faithful wife, Alecia E. Lartey, labored nine years, and he finally presided over the entire work in Africa before his death August 3, 1969. The Brewerville Church, constructed under his leadership, through funds raised from the African Memorial Banks, was the restoration of the mother church of Zion in all Africa. [60] The Aggrey Memorial Church in Accra, Ghana, was also erected through his episcopal supervision. He established the first A.M.E. Zion Mission Hospital in Ghana, and in the denomination, in 1964. He constructed and reconstructed a number of churches and schools, assisted by able African ministers and laymen. There are a number of day schools and training centers connected with our churches throughout Africa, in addition to one or two secondary schools in each conference, operated through the Foreign Missions Department, and separate from the churches. The magnitude of Bishop Lartey's constructivity, and that of his wife who is still with us, to give inspiration and encouragement to the present leaders in carrying out the hopes and dreams of the pioneers, will be far reaching through interminable times.

Bishop William A. Hilliard, accompanied by his wife, Edra Mae Hilliard, the missionary supervisor, departed for the new work assigned to him for the quadrennium, on September 23, 1960. They gave considerable stimulation to the work in both Nigeria and East Ghana. The membership in Nigeria had steadily grown to 10,500, and there was a growing interest in planting Zion Church in the capital, Lagos. [61]

To continue this program of growth, the General Conference of 1964 elected Bishop Alfred G. Dunston, Jr., and assigned him to the Nigeria Conference, while assigning the other three conferences to Bishop Lartey. The condition of the civil war in Nigeria caused great concern to the presiding bishop and the entire denomination. Nevertheless, he was able to get entree into the country, and hold three sessions of the annual conferences during the quadrennium, in the most crucial parts of Nigeria. Associating him in this work was his missionary supervisor, Miss E. Loujean Lovett. Bishop Dunston immediately purchased land in Lagos, and established an A.M.E. Zion Church with more than 80 members, which was placed on a circuit with a branch in Ikoyi under the pastorate of Rev. Emmanuel J. Ekpo. [62] The internal strife in Nigeria posed several problems for the presiding bishop; one of the most glaring was that our congregations, principally located in rural areas in Eastern Nigeria, were for the most part of the tribe of Ibos. Although a brilliant people, they were a minority, and after 31 months of one of the most bitter warfares in African history, the Biafrans finally succumbed to the stronger forces in 1970, and efforts were made on both sides to unify the country in sincere bonds of brotherhood.

Notwithstanding, Bishop Dunston was able to establish 10 new congregations during the quadrennium. One of the leaders of the Nigeria Conference, Rev. Young E. O. Eta, the field superintendent, proved a man of true grit. He had been deputized to supervise the work in the absence of the bishop, and he gave forcible leadership in this time of conflict. [63] At the 1968 General Conference, Bishop Lartey was assigned the entire African work. His death a year afterward was a stunning blow to the work in Africa. The Board of Bishops reassigned two experienced bishops to supervise the work the balance of the quadrennium, Bishop W. A. Hilliard, to the East Ghana and West Ghana Conferences, and Bishop A. G. Dunston, Jr., to Liberia and Nigeria. In consonance with Mrs. Lartey, the

60. *Minutes,* Thirty-Seventh Quadrennial Session, pp. 279-280.
61. *Minutes,* Thirty-Seventh Quadrennial Session, p. 299.
62. *Minutes,* Thirty-Eighth Quadrennial Session, p. 313.
63. *Ibid.,* pp. 308-314.

bishops and their missionary supervisors, Edra Mae Hilliard, and Dr. Armagyne G. Dunston, daughter of Bishop Dunston, with the assistance of our indigenous missionaries, teachers, and preachers, effectually projected the church in Africa through the quadrennium. Presiding Elders R. C. Barkue, Edwin M. Flowers, Sr., and B. R. Williams, are among the potent leaders continuing the work in Liberia.

The General Conference of 1972 elected Bishop Ruben L. Speaks and assigned him to the entire African field. Associating him in his new endeavor is his wife and missionary supervisor, Janie G. Speaks. A new day dawns in the Fatherland, and more than ever the African Methodist Episcopal Zion Church must give unsparingly and go willingly in the continued effort to develop our claim and rich heritage of the continent. We quote Bishop C. C. Alleyne as a reminder of our endless obligation to Africa, parent of the dusky race throughout the world:

> A million voices rise from throats of ebony, reminding us of our kinship and informing us of our responsibility. We have put our hand to the plough of African Redemption and we dare not look back. We have opened our mouths in promise to the Lord and we cannot recall the vows thus registered. [64]

South America And The West Indies

The oldest foreign work of the A.M.E. Zion Church south of the North American continent is in British Guiana, Demerara Mission. The country, discovered in 1499 by Spanish sailors, became a British possession in 1814, and African slaves and indentured servants from India were brought in to work on plantations. To this day they form the major population. After 152 years as a British colony, the country became independent May 26, 1966 (the first South American country to do so since Venezuela in 1830) and changed its name to Guyana. [65]

Demerara Mission, British Guiana, was mentioned in our history during the dark days of slavery; however, the work was suspended until Zion was able to build up her foreign missions interests beyond the Fatherland. Reverend R. C. Henderson, who once appeared in the roster of bishops of the A.M.E. Zion Church, was made superintendent only for the Demerara work. but died soon afterwards. [66] When the report for Demerara Mission was called for at the General Conference in 1856, several letters were read from the mission, in which Rev. Henderson informed the conference that he was unable to be present. [67] Even though this work and West Indies missions appeared in the records of the church, we did not become firmly established in South America until 1911, later in the Islands. While stringently laboring to spread her borders on the home field, after Emancipation and the Civil War, and endeavoring to answer the call of the exploited people of Africa, with fervent interest; looking toward her brothers and sisters in the thickly populated areas south of her American borders, Zion made several attempts in both South America and the West Indies. The impediments from within and without were manifold, but she never gave up.

Another of our earliest efforts of development was made by Rev. J. W. Lacey of the Western New York Conference who, after receiving his license to preach from Presiding Elder William Sanford in Binghamton, New York in 1858, went to Haiti in 1861.

64. *Minutes,* Twenty-Eighth Quadrennial Session, p. 154.
65. *World Almanac,* 1969, p. 518.
66. *Minutes,* Nineteenth Quadrennial Session, p. 19.
67. Moore, *History,* p. 221.

He received deacon's and elder's orders under Superintendent Clingman, and in the same year (1863), he was elected General Superintendent. During that year the two branches of Methodists, Zion and Bethel, held a convention at Gro Mound and united under the African Methodist Episcopal Zion Discipline. Superintendents Pierce and Clingman resigned at this convention, and Lacey was elected superintendent of the united societies called Zion, the headquarters being in St. Marc, where they had a fine church edifice. While holding the office of superintendent of Zion on the island of Haiti he ordained S. S. Wales and Wesley Youngs as elders, and George Evans as deacon, and several others.

Reverend Lacey returned to the United States in 1869, joined the Genesee (Western New York) Conference, was appointed by Bishop Loguen to Ithaca in 1870, and later served other churches in the conference. [68] This seems to have been the last special attention given to Haiti by the Zion group. Bishop Hood states, however, that Zion had work in Santo Domingo in 1895, along with our Bahama Island work. [69]

The General Conference of 1880, noted particularly for the advancement of missionary work at home and abroad, enthusiastically accepted the recommendations in the report of the Committee on Home and Foreign Missions and Church Extension, of not only sending the necessary supplies requested by Rev. Andrew Cartwright in Africa, but that "the Bishops give special attentions to the West India Mission in furnishing them with men and means, and any other ForeignMission that may come under their observation." [70]

At the same time Bishop John B. Small was assigned to Africa, he was also assigned to the West Indies islands, and made his first trip to the territory in August, 1899. Bishop Small reported in 1904 that Rev. Carl H. Williams had charge of our mission work on the Island of Santo Domingo. He had organized several new missions, but informed Bishop Small that the constant revolution on that island had proved a menace to material and religious work. [71] Bishop Small, on his first trip to the West Indies, made an impassioned attempt to establish Zion in British Honduras. After making several stops in other parts of the West Indies on his first trip, he arrived in Belize, British Honduras, on August 30, 1899. During his five weeks stay he had preaching engagements in the vicinity every evening. He visited Manatee—"about twenty miles from Belize by boat—the place where he started his ministry, taught public school, and built his first Church." There he preached to a large congregation and returned to Belize the next day. [72]

The bishop had made the trip at the request of Mr. A. E. Ottley, and while there received Mr. Ottley's mission work into the A.M.E. Zion connection. Upon receiving an application from the people to ordain Mr. Ottley, he refused, not feeling that Mr. Ottley measured up in collegiate training. According to the rules of the colony of British Honduras, Bishop Small issued special dispensation to marry, baptize, etc., to Ottley in the name of the A.M.E. Zion Church, and Ottley was determined to succeed with this mission work. The people, however, expressed their desire in writing for a qualified elder. Bishop Small then decided to send Mr. Ottley's brother, Charles A. Ottley, to Livingstone College to equip him for this work. [73] Thus Bishop Small was supporting five young men at

68. Hood, *One Hundred Years*, pp. 277-278.
69. *Ibid.,* p. 96.
70. *Minutes*, Sixteenth Quadrennial Session, pp. 63-64, 79.
71. *Minutes*, Twenty-Second Quadrennial Session, p. 201.
72. *Minutes*, Twenty-First Quadrennial Session, pp. 166-167.
73. *Ibid.,* pp. 167-168.

Livingstone College at the same time; the three young men from Africa, Charles A. Ottley of British Honduras, and George Bowles of his home town of York, Pennsylvania, who later became a prominent physician of this town.

This mission work suffered after the death of Brother A. E. Ottley in 1906. [74] His assistant, Rev. G. A. Ferguson, was appointed by Bishop Walters to carry on the work, as his brother, upon completing his course at Livingstone College, pastored churches in the Florida and Bahamas Island Conferences. Bishop Walters also reported that the San Pedro De Marcoris Mission in Santo Domingo was meeting with remarkable success, still managed by Rev. Carl H. Williams.

In 1908 Bishop Alexander Walters was assigned the West Indies territory and South America, including Jamaica and Demerara. He visited the work in 1911, making connection with friends in Kingston, Jamaica, and leaving them with the understanding that he would return and organize a conference, and reported on the Jamaica and Demerara Conferences in 1912. He also visited South America and made his first contact for Zion through Rev. W. A. Deane. [75] Even though he was reassigned to the work another quadrennium, 1912-1916, he was unable to make another trip because of a problem in the Financial Department, which caused a shortage in connectional funds and affected several departments and programs of the church. Reverend W. A. Deane organized the first church in South America, Walters Chapel, at Hague, Demerara in 1911, and the membership continued a steady growth. [76]

Bishop John Wesley Alstork was assigned the South American and West Indies mission work in 1916, and the work was greatly enhanced. Accompanied by the editor of the *Quarterly Review,* Dr. C. C. Alleyne, he visited this territory in the summer of 1919, and organized the British Guiana South American Conference (now known as Guyana Conference) at Walters Chapel, Hague, July 10, 1919, with seven preachers, two of them women. During the visit of the Bishop, he received the first enthusiastic congregation in Georgetown, the capital city. After the inspirational visit of the Bishop and Dr. Alleyne, Rev. Deane was instrumental in organizing several societies in the area, and was appointed presiding elder-superintendent. He was associated in this mission work by his elder son, Glasgow Deane, Rev. A. E. Mann, and Rev. James A. Agaard who was largely responsible for establishing our work at St. Croix, Virgin Islands. [77]

In our zeal for worldwide expansion, we attempted to enter Brazil the following quadrennium, during the administration of Bishop L. W. Kyles. A commission led by Bishop George C. Clement, Drs. J. W. Martin and A. A. Crooke, was sent to Rio de Janerio and Bahai, Brazil, encouraged by a Dr. Borchello "passing as a sort of envoy for those whom he claimed were waiting in large numbers to come into our communion." Dr. Borchello disappeared upon arrival of the commission, which decided to leave Rev. Crooke on the field. He remained at Bahai on a survey mission over a year and found no members; he returned home and reported that there was no place in Brazil for a race church. The church gave up the project upon recommendation of the committees and Foreign Missions Secretary. [78]

74. *Minutes,* Twenty-Third Quadrennial Session, p. 235.
75. *Minutes,* Twenty-Fourth Quadrennial Session, p. 48. The visit of Bishop Walters was reported to the writer by an old loyal members of our Zion, on his first trip to Jamaica in 1956, and lamented that "he never came back."
76. *Minutes,* Twenty-Fifth and Twenty-Sixth Quadrennial Sessions, pp. 32-33; Twenty-Seventh Quadrennial Session, pp. 197-198.
77. *Ibid,* pp. 84, 87, 88.
78. *Minutes,* Twenty-Seventh Quadrennial Session, pp. 260-261.

Bishops John W. Martin, Frederick M. Jacobs, William J. Walls, and James W. Brown served one quadrennium each in the South America and Virgin Islands territory until 1940. [79] In this 16-year period, from 1924 to 1940, Bishop Jacobs was the only one of these bishops privileged to visit the territory while supervising it. There were several reasons for this deficiency in episcopal visitation, the depression which struck the nation in 1929 being one of them. Bishop Jacobs managed to make the trip in 1930, and upon his return he recommended three young ministers who were effectively working in the area, Revs. S. F. Lewis, H. P. Hopkinson, and Henry Loaffe, to be added to the roll of missionaries. [80] The work in this area had continued under the able leadership of Rev. W. A. Deane until his death in 1935. The presiding bishop, W. J. Walls, and Dr. H. T. Medford, Secretary of Foreign Missions, paid glowing tributes to the pioneer works of Rev. Deane, and announced that his beloved widow and two sons had nobly succeeded him in the work. His son, Rev. W. F. G. Deane, who had received his training for the work at Livingstone College, became the chief leader of this South American work. [81]

In 1940, Bishop C. C. Alleyne was assigned to the territory. Principal supervision by Rev. W. F. G. Deane continued, associated by Rev. James Agaard in the Virgin Islands, during the turbulent war years. In 1947, Bishop Alleyne made his first visit to the work accompanied by his helpmate and missionary supervisor, Bettye Lee Roberts Alleyne, his first wife having expired a few years hence. He had a special interest for the people in this territory, not too far from his birthplace, and this work remained a part of his episcopal district until his death in 1955. He recommended to the General Conference of 1948 that "since the Virgin Islands are an integral part of the United States, and are more nearly accessible from North than South America, they be made a part of the Home Missions setup and attached to the Fourth Episcopal District." [82] He proceeded to set off the Virgin Island Conference from the South America Conference after his reassignment to the work in 1948. [83] The Virgin Islands Conference is the only conference in the connection which has dual recognition of home and foreign missions. Upon the death of Rev. W. A. G. Deane, the work was somewhat handicapped, and through the recommendation of another son of our pioneer, Mr. C. W. B. Deane, Bishop Alleyne and Dr. D. C. Pope, the foreign missions secretary, secured the services of Rev. Rupert Clement Rodney as chief missionary and presiding elder of the South American territory. He and his wife proved to be useful servants until their deaths, Mrs. Rita Rodney in 1966 and Rev. Rodney in 1971. [84] Reverend Samuel Bruce and Mrs. Victorrine Britton were also outstanding missionary servants of this area.

Bishop Raymond L. Jones, associated by his wife and missionary supervisor, Mabel Miller Jones, succeeded Bishop Alleyne in 1955 and served the people wholeheartedly until 1960, when the General Conference assigned Bishop William M. Smith. He and his wife and missionary supervisor, Ida M. Smith, labored one quadrennium on this field. He had just been elected a bishop and assigned nine conferences of mission status, yet he managed this foreign part as well as the home field with skill and determination. In 1964, Bishop Stephen Gill Spottswood was assigned to this work. Associated by his missionary supervisor,

79. Jackson, *Information Please*, p. 8.
80. *Minutes*, Twenty-Ninth Quadrennial Session, p. 196.
81. *Minutes,*Thirtieth Quadrennial Session, p. 121, 268-269.
82. *Minutes*, Thirty-Third Quadrennial Session, p. 118.
83. Interview, Mrs. C. C. (Bettye Lee) Alleyne, missionary supervisor of this first conference.
84. Quadrennial Reports, Secretary, Foreign Missions Department, 1968, 1972.

Mrs. Cordelia M. Elliott, he continued projection of the work in this territory.

Bishop Spottswood initiated $25 a plate missionary banquets in the home conferences assigned him to assist this foreign missions work. During his administration, the pioneer of the Virgin Islands Conference, Rev. James A. Agaard, passed away in 1965. He secured the services of Rev. John A. Parker, who had completed his studies at Hood Theological Seminary the same year, as resident missionary to Virgin Islands and presiding elder, and later, Rev. Charles C. Durant of the New England Conference who serves Zion in the Antilles. [85] After the death in 1971, of Rev. R. C. Rodney, who had given 20 years of service, Bishop Spottswood and the Department of Foreign Missions through its secretary, Dr. J. C. Hoggard, secured the services of Rev. Dr. Benjamin O. Berry, a Guianese by birth, who served Zion in America for a number of years. "He returned to Georgetown, Guyana from a pastorate in South Bend, Indiana. He and his good wife, Mrs. Hannah Berry, seem to be making rapid strides toward bringing the life and work of our denomination to a happy progressive state." [86] The General Conference of 1972 assigned Bishop William A. Hilliard to this work, who is presently associated by his wife and Missionary Supervisor, Edra Mae Hilliard.

In 1968, Bishop Spottswood and Bishop Herbert B. Shaw envisioned an expansion of our work in Barbados. Through the Foreign Missions Department, they purchased lots at Newton Terrace, Christ Church, Barbados, with the hope of building a church to the Glory of God and in memory of two noted bishops who were Barbadians by birth, John Bryan Small and Cameron Chesterfield Alleyene, who had served our foreign field productively. Also at the instance of the late Rev. C. W. B. Deane, the Guyana Conference received churches in the South Africa Republic, presided over by Bishop Spottswood, during this same period of entering Barbados. Reverend S. MacPharsumane, the correspondent, was appointed presiding elder of the South Africa District. [87] We look with favor and hope upon these laudable efforts and pray for progressive realization.

Bahamas

On December 26, 1877, a few of the ministers assembled in Nassau, for the organization of the Bahama Islands Conference. Because of the absence of the bishop, they agreed to adjourn until further information could be obtained. [88] On Friday, January 4, 1878, the first session of the Bahama Islands Conference assembled in Zion Church, Nassau, New Providence, Bahama Islands, at 10:45 A.M., Bishop Joseph P. Thompson presiding. Reverend Wilbur G. Strong, who attended the bishop in nearly all his efforts in the far South, was also present at the organization of the conference and served as secretary. Elders present were Revs. Joseph Sexton, James Harris, and D. L. Carr; deacons present were David Thomas, John A. Bain, and D. W. Martindell. This work had been stimulated by ministers of the Florida Conference, and several of them were present as fraternal visitors. The appointments made by Bishop Thompson revealed that the African Methodist Episcopal Zion Church had established churches at the following places: Nassau, Harbor Island, Tarpum Bay, Eluthera, Governor's Harbor, Andros Island, Rock Sound, and East Eluthera. [89]

The Bahama Islands Conference was organized as a home conference and

85. Quadrennial Report, Third Episcopal District, 1972.
86. Quadrennial Report Department of Foreign missions, 1972, p. 18.
87. *Ibid.,* p. 21.
88. *Minutes,* First Session, Island Annual Conference, 1877, p. 1.
89. *Ibid.,* pp. 1, 11.

remained closely associated with the South Florida Conference. 206 members were reported at this first annual conference. [90] The bishops and preachers who carried forth the work in this conference up to the twentieth century were Bishops John J. Moore, Thomas H. Lomax, and C. R. Harris; Revs. Joseph Sexton, W. C. Vesta, George W. Maize, I, T. H. Darley, R. R. Frederick, James Dudley, W. J. Sanders, H. E. Jones, A. Long, A. L. Higgs, R. W. Ballard, and J. D. Ballard, along with the original pioneers, Fathers Joseph Sexton, W. A. Baine, and James R. Harris. These preachers were highly commended by the presiding bishops, in their quadrennial reports, for their arduous labors in this mission field. [91]

The work in Bahamas, which apparently began to diminish afterward, was accounted for in the reports of the South Florida Conference by Bishop Alexander Walters in 1908, Bishop J. W. Alstork in 1912, who had been assigned after the death of Bishop J. W. Smith, and Bishop Andrew J. Warner in 1920. Bishop Warner stated that the work at Nassau was hopeful under the pastorate of Rev. L. L. Roaker. [92] We had no further account of the work in the Bahama Islands after the death of Bishop Warner. There is little known of how it failed after that; it seemed to have gone down to low ebb through lack of sufficient ministry.

The next venture in this field was made by Bishop Herbert Bell Shaw. While assigned to the South Florida Conference, he resurrected the Bahama Island Conference in 1959, and has presided over this conference and steered its growth during these 14 years. [93] He is associated in this work by his wife and missionary supervisor, M. Ardelle Shaw. After the Bahama Island Conference was revived, it became a foreign missions conference. Bishop Shaw, having knowledge of Zion's past in the Bahamas, became interested in the territory, and upon investigation found a few loyal members holding the fort, with outside forces threatening to take over the long neglected church property. He and Presiding Elder A. F. Hooper of the South Florida Conference enthusiastically pursued this matter, even to the point of court action, which declared the members of St. Jospeh A.M.E. Zion Church the rightful owners subject to the law and usages of the Discipline. [94] Some of the leading preachers in the revival of this conference are Revs. Alphaes C. Rolle, George W. Smith, Wilbert Rolle, aided by Mrs Beatrice Forbes and a number of faithful laymen. Nine churches were reported in 1965, [95] with a membership of 322. [96] The work continues to grow. The Board of Bishops held its annual meeting in Nassau in January 1967, the first time our church assembled nationally outside of the United States. The island also received its independence from the British during this same year.

Jamaica and England

One of our more recent foreign missions territory is Jamaica, West Indies. Through the instrumentality of Presiding Elder Samuel Hart Williams of the Brooklyn District, New York Conference, a native Jamaican, and his friends, Revs. Charles D. and Arnold D. Wright of the United Holy Church of Jamaica, Bishop Herbert B. Shaw received a formal invitation in 1966 from the members of this church movement expressing a desire to become united with the African

90. *Ibid.,* p. 16. 91. *Minutes,* Quadrennial Sessions, 1884-1904, Reports of Episcopal Districts.
92. *Minutes,* Twenty-Fifth and Twenty-Sixth Quadrennial Sessions, p. 118.
93. *Minutes,* Quadrennial Sessions, 1960-1972
94. *Minutes,* Thirty-Seventh Quadrennial Session, pp. 173-174.
95. Jackson, *Information Please,* p. 8.
96. *Minutes,* Thirty-Eighth Quadrennial Session, p. 167.

BISHOP HERBERT BELL SHAW
Organizer of Jamaica, West Indies
and England Conferences, and reorganized Bahamas Island Conference.

Methodist Episcopal Zion Church, their leader having died without a functioning successor. This mass movement was received into Zion by Bishop Shaw, and the Jamaica Annual Conference was organized and held its first session at Shaw Temple, Black River, Jamaica, January 19, 1967, with Bishop Shaw presiding. Five churches and pastors were represented in the first conference: Shaw Temple, Black River, Rev. C. D. Wright; Mt. Pisgah, Fyspen, Rev. Hezekiah Bailey; St. Paul, Treasure Beach, Rev. Cecil Reid; Bethany, Kingston, Rev. Beryl Gayle; and Mt. Sinai, Linstead, Rev. Stephen Thompson, and Rev. A. D. Wright, presiding elder. Several other churches had been added by 1968. [97]

The conference has recently expanded in the capital, Kingston. It is reported to be one of the fastest growing conferences in the connection during its six years existence, under the leadership of its founding bishop, H. B. Shaw. While its membership is swelling largely, the Jamaica Conference remains a heavy responsibility of the Foreign Missions Department and needs much money for its development. The bishop has initiated programs with his episcopal district to aid in promoting the work of the foreign fields assigned to his care.

The A.M.E. Zion Church expanded its border into England in 1971. Our foreign missions work in England is composed of Jamaican brothers and sisters who left the West Indies to settle in England, the head of the United Kingdom. Spilling over from this Jamaica contact led Bishop H. B. Shaw to the organization of the London-Birmingham Conference in London, England, May 15, 1971. [98] The mother church of this conference is the Ransom A.M.E. Zion Church in London. The Revs. Vincent G. Fagan and Horace G. Gordon are the pioneers of this work in England. Churches have been organized in London, Birmingham, Bristol, and Manchester, with an approximate membership of 400. [99] Bishop Shaw, associated by his wife, M. Ardelle Shaw, moves Zion Church in this newest clime, which also needs our prayers and support.

97. *Ibid.*, p. 162.
98. Quadrennial Report, Department of Foreign Missions, 1972, pp. 15-16; Quadrennial Report, Second Episcopal District, 1972, pp. 4-5.
99. *Ibid.*

CHAPTER 18

LATER GROWTH AND POST-WAR MIGRATION

The third period of extraordinary growth of the church was the time directly succeeding World Wars I and II. The church since that time has continued periodic growth in some sections of the country, especially large cities, North and South. An incessant program of expansion in large and new areas has enabled us to maintain at least a balanced condition, in lieu of the perishing state of some of the rural churches, which have diminished in membership considerably over the past 25 years.

There were three periods of large migration in the twentieth century affecting the black race in this country: the times after the two World Wars and the period of the 1950's and 1960's. All three were times of increasing tensions, racial injustices, and bad economic conditions, causing thousands to flee the South to the North and West. The black church was seized by the spirit of expansion and growth. The following quotation from the Quadrennial Address of the Bishops to the 1920 General Conference is a brief summation of the cause of the first migration:

In the years 1916, 1917, and 1918, large numbers of our people from the southern states migrated North and Northwest. The calling of the foreign reservists home to enter the armies of their respective countries caused vacancies in the factories, shops and on the railroads in the North and Northwest, hence efforts were made through agents to induce our people to fill the vacancies. Statistics say 400,000 answered the call, and among them were thousands of members of our own church. This tested the ability and resources of some of our bishops and pastors to house them. In Chicago, two churches were bought for that purpose, in Detroit two, one in Braddock, Pa., and one in the process of being purchased in Cleveland, while we profited largely in Buffalo, Pittsburgh, Cincinnati, St. Louis, Indianapolis, Philadelphia, Newark, Washington, D.C., and quite a number of other places. In view of the fact that a large majority of those who migrated will remain permanently in the North, East and Northwest, notice is served upon us to help provide for them or else we will have labored short of the demand, and others will have entered into our labor. We should say in this connection that it is very complimentary to the efficiency and adaptability of our people that they have been able to hold their jobs even though the war is closed, wherever the institution or factory has continued in business. [1]

In order to be alive with the spirit of the times and to make adequate progress in essential areas, a courageous program of expansion was innovated through the ingenuity of Bishop George L. Blackwell. The Board of Bishops, in their semi-annual meeting at Washington, D.C., January 1919, introduced the idea to the denomination, of taking notice of the 300th anniversary or tercentenary of

1. *Minutes,* Twenty-Fifth and Twenty-Sixth Quadrennial Sessions, p. 66.

BISHOP GEORGE LINCOLN BLACKWELL

1861 - 1926

First university graduate to become a bishop
in the A.M.E. Zion Church. Largest church
expander since the Reconstruction fathers.
Responsible for Zion's latter day status in
the Midwest.

the landing of the first Africans on the shores of America at Jamestown, Va. in
1619. There they inaugurated the drive for 100,000 souls and $400,000, in
commemoration of the event in a movement known as The Tercentenary
Drive. [2] The Tercentenary Drive had its origin in the Virginia Conference at
Franklin, Va., December 1918. A resolution was passed by that conference and
the Fifth Episcopal District presided over by Bishop Blackwell to celebrate the
notable event there, by initiating a drive for the improvement and social uplift of
the race at home and abroad. [3]

While the bishops were perfecting these plans, the enthusiasm of the members
and visiting ministers of the Connectional Council, meeting in August 1919 at
Paterson, N.J., was so overwhelming, they decided to increase the askings of funds
to $1,000,000, the boldest financial adventure in the 123 years history of this
black church. A central committee was appointed to conduct the campaign,
arranging for regional directors, and apportionments were made for the several
conferences adequate to reach the $1,000,000 in five years. [4] By the General

2. *Ibid.*, p. 67; Ms. Minutes, Board of Bishops, January 1919.
3. *Minutes,* Twenty-Fifth and Twenty-Sixth Quadrennial Sessions, pp. 104-105.
4. *Ibid.*, p. 67.

Conference in May 1920, seven districts had raised over $22,000 and expended $18,000 toward projection and growth. (5)

The Tercentenary Movement climaxed at the 1924 General Conference below the projected purpose. The Board of Bishops claimed, in the Quadrennial Message, that the 1920 General Conference took the teeth out of the movement by reducing it from a connectional movement to episcopal district rallies. (6) However, they rejoiced over the success and the progress made in comparison to what the church would have been without the movement and the success that had been attained in all the church, both financially and in general spiritual force and connectional morale. Growth was reflected in that General Conference, where our episcopacy was increased from 10 to 12 bishops and a larger mission and extension program than ever before was adopted for home and abroad.

Before and during the World War years, the church had made slow strides of growth in the North while growing rapidly in the South. In the thriving city of Zion's birth, there were two injurious incidents that affected the Mother Zion Church membership, though not enough to hinder its continuous growth. The first split occurred in 1870, after Bishop Talbot transferred Rev. William F. Butler from the Kentucky Conference in 1868 and appointed him pastor of Mother Zion. "His eloquence, personal magnetism and interest in all the questions of that day made him a leading pastor of that metropolitan center." Dissatisfaction arose between him and some of the leaders of the church, the disaffected members followed Rev. Butler out of the connection, and he established St. Mark Methodist Episcopal Church in 1870. (7)

The second incident occurred in 1914 when the pastor, Rev. R. M. Bolden, was brought to trial charged with "insubordination and conduct prejudicial to the peace and harmony of the Church." This action was sparked by his refusal to accept the bishop's appointment to Yonkers (The Institutional Church), and he was expelled by the conference. He also established an independent movement in New York City with some of his friends of Mother Zion Church, which finally perished. During this upheaval Mother Zion also lost all of its church property. (8) Bishop Hood forthwith appointed Rev. J. W. Brown. The church at this time was located on 89th Street, having moved from West Tenth and Beecker Streets under the administration of Rev. J. Sulla Cooper. In making the move in 1903, Bishop Hood was apprehensive and stated that "the church was moved uptown, either too far or not far enough." (9)

Reverend J. W. Brown, who was later consecrated bishop from this pastorate, was an industrious organizer, builder, and leader. He had led the people of Memorial Church, Rochester, N.Y. in the erection in 1907 of the most pretentious church structure for blacks in that city, with beautiful memorial windows of the champions of freedom: Frederick Douglass, Harriet Tubman, Susan B. Anthony, and Joseph Charles Price.

Dr. Brown won acclamation from the entire connection in guiding, the old Mother Church through the most critical period of its history. On coming to Mother Zion he found a church with a few hundred members, disorganized and leaving property mortgaged to the limit, and every available means of raising large amounts of money exhausted; and confidence and credit gone. Many who had nursed at her bosom had lifted the iron heel

5. *Ibid.*, pp. 252-253.
6. *Minutes*, Twenty-Seventh Quadrennial Session, p. 157.
7. E. D. W. Jones, Ms. History of Mother Zion Church.
8. *Minutes,* Ninety-Third Annual Session, New York Conference, 1914, pp. 29-31.
9. *Minutes,* Twenty-Fourth Quadrennial Session, p. 169.

against her, and the most conservative spoke of Mother Zion as a church of the past that could only live in history. [10]

These were some of the perplexing problems that faced Dr. Brown. He achieved much during his first year, in leading the trustees and members in purchasing the Church of the Redeemer at 151-3 West 136th Street in 1915. His first act was to borrow $1000 to do this. It was the period of the "Harlem Renaissance" of blacks, and the church began to grow led by this magnetic preacher. From the scattered 300 or 400 members in 1914, the church had grown in two years to nearly 1,000, and had outgrown its seating capacity. Thus with a vision and a grand connection supporting him and his people, Dr. Brown, in a stupendous undertaking, led in building the present massive Gothic structure on 137th Street, adjoining the 136th Street property, at a cost of $500,000. The old church facility fronting 136th Street was used for service to the community. [11]

Excavation began for the new church in July 1923, and it was completed and dedicated during the episcopal administration of Bishop Josiah S. Caldwell, on September 20, 1925. The Board of Bishops, in their Quadrennial Address in 1924, expressed the desire of the connection to aid in the building of this outstanding memorial to Zion Methodism, stating that Mother Zion Church was "rich in historic annals and inspirational in the wealth of her traditions . . . the mother of Zion Methodism and of that spirit of Christian democracy so peculiar to Zion Methodism." We quote the following also from this address:

> The increase of the colored population of the city of New York, the astounding growth of the membership of the Mother Church and her expanding needs, made it imperative that something be done immediately to help to meet the social and religious demands of the race. The Board of Bishops felt that this body would approve the effort to assist the congregation to build a temple worthy of the denomination in the largest city in the world and in the birthplace of Zion Methodism. With this end in view, on the suggestion of the Board of Bishops, the Church Extension Department pledged fifty thousand dollars toward the movement and floated bonds to raise it; thus giving the members of our denomination opportunity to participate in the erection of this great memorial to Zion Methodism. We should all rejoice in that we have finally secured a permanent home in the great city of New York. [12]

Brown's successor in 1936, Rev. Benjamin C. Robeson, led the congregation in liquidating the $160,000 mortgage on the church edifice, plus $40,000 debt on the organ and an additional mortgage on the parsonage, all by 1945, and began effecting plans for a new education building. He pastored the church until his death in December 1963. As proposed, the church is building an education and social service center on the old site of the 136th Street property, jointly with the federal government. Reverend George W. McMurray is the pastor, with a membership of approximately 6,300.

Growth in the Mother Conference had been stimulated by an experienced developer of the church. Bishop J. W. Hood, assigned to the New York Conference in 1886, found 14 churches which had pastors in charge and 12 other churches that claimed they were unable to support a pastor. By 1912 he reported 37 regular churches and 6 missions. [13] During his 30 years episcopal occupancy of the New York Conference, progress was evident. In his last episcopal address to the New York Conference, in 1915, he mentioned the churches added to the

10. *Minutes,* Ninety-Fifth Annual Session, New York Conference, p. 34.
11. *Ibid.,* E. D. W. Jones, *op. cit.*
12. *Minutes,* Twenty-Seventh Quadrennial Session, p. 107.
13. *Minutes,* Twenty-Fourth Quadrennial Session. p. 157.

EVOLUTION OF THE MOTHER CHURCH OF THE DENOMINATION
NEW YORK CITY

First Church built in 1800.
This structure built in 1820.
Destroyed by fire, 1839,

Purchased church at
West Tenth and Beecker
Streets, 1864

Artists' Concept John White

Larger edifice built in 1840.

Moved uptown to West 89th
Street. Church built, 1904

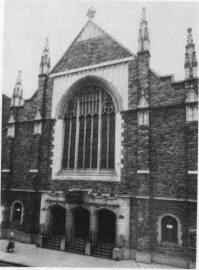

Moved to Harlem in 1914. Purchased Church
of the Redeemer on West 136th Street.

Built the above present structure on West
137th Street in 1925.

conference without any connectional aid. Three new churches in Brooklyn had been purchased, 6 in Long Island, 5 in Westchester County, and 8 up the Hudson River. He observed that Kingston and Sag Habor were the only two original churches of the conference which had not been secured, built, rebuilt, or remodelled during his tenure. 29 new churches had been built or otherwise secured. [14]

The Fleet Street Church (First Church), Brooklyn, had been organized in 1885 with 11 members. For about 10 years Bishop Hood had appointed seven pastors to that charge, but the congregation "had fluctuated, ebbed and flowed without the desirable substantial progress." He appointed Rev. Frederick M. Jacobs during the Centennial period, and the church took on phenomenal growth and expansion of church facilities. Led by Jacobs, a larger property was purchased on Bridge Street, which Bishop Hood said could seat more people at that time than any other church in the connection. [15] In 1936, Rev. William Orlando Carrington, the great pulpiteer of the church, was appointed to First Church, and in 1942 he led the congregation in purchasing the present mammoth structure at Tompkins and MacDonough Streets, one of the three largest churches in the connection. Major improvements were made on this vast property, and the congregation grew to over 6,000 during his constructive pastorate. He retired from this pulpit in 1964.

Some of the leading forces who assisted Hood in expanding the borders of the New York Conference were Revs. M. A. Bradley, L. G. Mason, F. M. Jacobs, Marshall O. Haynes, W. H. Decker, H. S. McMullen, J. H. McMullen, W. T. Biddle, John T. Matthews, Clarence Van Buren, John W. McCoy, Benjamin Judd, Charles H. Tennycke, W. H. Newby, J. J. Smyer, E. O. Clarke, W. L. Lee, A. A. Crooke, S. S. Boyd, F. J. Moultrie, H. W. Allen, A. M. Walker, William H. Coffey, Jacob Thomas, C. E McKay, C. Fairfax. A. J. Tolbert, G. H. Staton, W. H. Eley, N. E. Collins, J. F. Waters, R. H. Stitt, J. R. Smith, Alexander Walters, Josiah S. Caldwell, and Martin R. Franklin. [16]

The next period of extensive growth in this conference came after World War II. Bishop Alexander Walters, who succeeded Bishop Hood in 1916, died the following year. Bishop Josiah S. Caldwell, who served the conference from 1917 until his death in 1935, achieved greatly in persuading the Board of Bishops to secure $50,000 aid of the connection in building Mother Zion Church, and establishing two or three mission points. The first church in the Bronx was organized in 1931, with a Sunday school class led by Mrs. Anna Leftage. The most distinctive achievement during Bishop Lynwood W. Kyles' six years in New York, before his death in 1941, was salvaging the Memorial Church (Institutional), Yonkers, which was built by Rev. Redmond S. Oden and congregation during the Depression. He worked ardently to reduce a debt of more than $90,000 to less than $6,000, with the cooperative assistance of the pastor, Rev. Benjamin W. Swain, and trustees and members. Firmly establishing another church in Harlem or Manhattan was a source of trouble, and had been attempted by every bishop of New York since Varick. The Rush Memorial Church, which started out as Little Zion in 1822 in Harlem, by Rev. Peter Vanhas, was revived by Bishop Hood and Rev. J. H. McMullen, and later evolved into the New Hood Memorial Church, with a church property purchased on Lenox Avenue, led by Rev. B. J. McClelland. [17]

14. *Minutes,* Ninety-Fourth Annual Session, New York Conference, 1915, p. 29.
15. *Minutes,* Twenty-Fourth Quadrennial Session, p. 163.
16. *Minutes,* New York Annual Conference Sessions, 1872-1916.
17. *Minutes,* Thirty-First Quadrennial Session, p. 97.

Reverend J. W. Wactor later led this growing congregation into purchasing a mammoth plant on 146th Street. The New York Conference purchased the old property and established the Walters Memorial Church. Church on the Hill was organized in 1949 by Rev. William M. Poe, giving Zion four churches in Harlem and two or three missions.

During the episcopal occupancy of Bishop William J. Walls from 1941 to 1964, the pastoral appointments increased from 39 to 74. The Caldwell Temple, started in the Bronx in 1931, was holding services in a funeral home, and in 1944, led by Rev. Carnes McKinney, purchased their present site, a magnificent church structure on Stebbins Avenue and Chisholm, and in 1956 reported more than 1,000 members. Four other churches were firmly established in the Bronx, and growth became so prevalent in all areas that it enabled the bishop to set apart a third presiding elder district. Presiding Elders H. B. Norville, J. H. Tucker, H. R. Jackson, Charles C. Williams, J. W. Findley, and Samuel H. Williams were the leading forces in helping to expand the conference. New history is being made in New York under the leadership of Bishop H. B. Shaw, as we write.

The Western New York Conference greatly benefited from the migration after the wars, particularly in the city of Buffalo and vicinity, and the capital city of Albany. This was principally a conference of small towns, with most of the churches established by leaders of the abolition and freedom movement before Emancipation. Just as in our Canadian work, many of the small town churches gradually became phased out because of the sparsity of the black population. The first bold attempt to expand the borders of the conference was made by Bishop Alexander Walters. In 1896 the name of the conference was changed from Genesee Conference to Central and Western New York Conference. In 1897, the word "Central" was dropped and it became known as the Western New York Conference. He attempted to divide the conference into two presiding elder districts and appointed Rev. B. F. Wheeler, the presiding elder of the original Rochester-Syracuse District, over the new Binghamton District, and Rev. James E. Mason over the Rochester-Syracuse District. This was a perceptible move, as the boundaries of the conference extended from Schenectady (a tri-city with Albany and Troy) on the east to Jamestown on the west, as far south as Scranton, Pennsylvania, and north to Canada. Assisting Bishop Walters also were Revs. J. Harvey Anderson, S. L. Corrothers, J. J. Adams, George H. Morse, H. J. Callis, M. H. Ross, J. R. Dangerfield, C. A. Smith, E. U. A. Brooks, and G. C. Carter. [18]

The first effort to plant the A.M.E. Zion Church in Buffalo took place during the days of Bishop Rush, when he reported a society was in progress in that city. [19] The project was dormant until Bishop J. S. Caldwell was assigned the Allegheny-Ohio Conference in 1904 and attempted to start a church, with Rev. J. C. Taylor in charge. Progress was slow for Zion in this growing city. Through a friend and old schoolmate at Livingstone College, Dr. Charles Patrick, Rev. Henry Durham was invited to come to Buffalo to strengthen a mission begun in 1906. Durham was serving in the Allegheny-Ohio Conference at Sewickley, Pa., and had built a beautiful brick church structure around 1910, after 30 years without an adequate building. [20] He was a veteran of the Spanish-American War and had the spirit of courage and holy dare. He rented a storefront and lived above it, and

18. *The Star of Zion,* June 17, 1897; *Minutes,* Twenty-First Quadrennial Session, pp. 143-144.
19. Rush, *Rise and Progress,* p. 88.
20. *Minutes,* Twenty-Fourth Quadrennial Session, p. 265.

started his work in Buffalo in October 1914. The writer preached for him in that storefront and ran a revival there. Over 40 converts were taken into the church in that effort. Reverend Durham solicited funds from the citizens, and the growing membership struggled cooperatively and built the first Zion Church in Buffalo, after purchasing a $12,000 lot on Eagle near Michigan Avenue, known as St. Luke Church in 1922. Bishop George L. Blackwell, who appointed Durham to the mission, gave wholehearted support to this virgin cause. [21]

This mother church had grown so large that in 1958, led by its pastor, Rev. Hunter B. Bess, and supervised by Bishop W. J. Walls, the congregation divided, and the St. Luke congregation purchased a commodious church plant on Ferry Street. More than 200 of the members desired to remain on the sacred spot built up under the leadership of Henry Durham, which then became known as Durham Memorial Church. Its first pastor was Rev. Arthur L. Hardge. Both churches continued a steady growth.

The second church in the Buffalo area was the Lackawanna Church (St. Mark), built by Rev. N. H. Bexley and members. Bishop W. L. Lee stated that "this was an entirely new venture where we never had anything at all until several years ago when Bishop Blackwell sent Reverend Bexley to this place to gather the people and build a church." These two churches were the first churches built by people of color in Buffalo or Erie County. [22]

Today there are nine A.M.E. Zion churches in the greater Buffalo area, including Tubman Memorial, Niagara Falls, and four other churches established from 1949 to 1968. Reverend Otis Vaughn was responsible for starting both the Niagara Falls Church and Loguen Memorial Church in Buffalo. A commodious church was given to the Conference (Shaw Memorial) in 1970.

The Western New York Conference had been combined again into one presiding elder district during the episcopal administration of Bishop C. C. Alleyne. In order to stimulate growth, the conference was once again divided in 1958 into two presiding elder districts, with the new district known as the Albany District. After years of difficulty of planting a church in the capital city of the mother state of Zion, a mission was established in Albany known as Walls Temple in 1944, and Revs. V. B. Waters and A. McL. Spaulding appointed co-pastors. Rev. J. H. McMullen was sent to this point shortly thereafter who stimulated the growth. The church grew consequently under several pastors. In 1955 a second church, Sojourner Truth Chapel, was planted in Albany and nurtured for several years by its first pastor, Rev. Leslie Smith. When the new churches in Albany had reached successful stages, they and the church at Troy were transferred from the New York Conference into the Western New York Conference, adjacent to the other tri-city, Schenectady, in order to reinforce the small conference and create a competitive spirit of growth. Several new mission points were started in both the new Albany District and the Rochester-Syracuse-Buffalo District.

The New England Conference, another area where the black population is sparse (except for cities and towns such as Boston, Providence, Hartford, New Haven, Bridgeport, and Waterbury, increased from its organization in 1845 with a half dozen churches, to 25 by 1908. Following Bishop Rush in stabilizing churches in the cities and towns of New England were Bishops Bishop, Simmons, Tappan, Clinton, Talbot, Moore, and Hood (who served the conference 30 years as episcopal leader). Bishops Walters and Lee, succeeding these leaders, reported very little expansion, yet achievements in church building. The church at

21. *Minutes,* Twenty-Seventh Quadrennial Session, p. 167.
22. *Ibid.*, pp. 167-168.

Portland, Maine, established in 1895 (Green Memorial) was, and is still, the only black church in the state.

This conference has a unique history of being foremost in advocating the elevation of the race. It produced some of the strongest men of the connection during the Abolition period, such as Revs. Thomas Henson, David Vandervere, Samuel T. Gray, Samuel M. Giles, Samson D. Talbot, James A. Jones, George A. Spywood, Peter Ross, and Joseph Hicks. [23] Reverends Robert R. Morris, N. J. Green, G. H. S. Bell, George L. Blackwell, Samuel C. Birchmore, Jesse B. Colbert, William B. Fenderson, William B. Bowen, George H. Washington, E. George Biddle, John F. Lloyd, G. W. Offley, S. F. Dickson, G. W. Johnson, W. H. Coffey, J. H. Evans, J. Sulla Cooper, J. Francis Lee, C. S. Whitted, H. J. Callis, Andrew McCallum, George L. White and C. Fairfax were some of the early leaders who built up churches and congregations in the several cities and towns before the first World War. Reverends Richard R. Ball, S. W. Weller, Benjamin W. Swain, T. A. Auten, Jacob W. Powell, Felix S. Anderson and H. R. Jackson were later developers of the work. The present Columbus Avenue Church in Boston was considered a noble achievement in its day, when the people, disposing of their North Russell Street Church, purchased a Jewish Synagogue in 1903, only 15 years old at the time. It was bought at a cost of $90,000, under the direction of its pastor, Rev. J. H. McMullen. It was considered one of the finest owned by a black congregation in the city. [24]

The Metropolitan Church in Hartford was relocated from Pearl Street, and housed in its present edifice on Main Street in 1926, led by Rev. A. J. Gorham. The transition, at first, did not turn out well. All the trustees that engineered the move were white, with the exception of one Negro on the board. In the course of a very few years, the money entrusted to the trustees from the sale of Pearl Street, for the most part, disappeared. The Main Street property deal included two houses across the street from the church, one used for the parsonage and the other rented. Gross irregularities were discovered in the management by these trustees; the cash money left in their hands was discovered to be badly used, unaccounted for, and unverified. Pastor Gorham discovered this and he was directed by the bishop (Walls) to put the matter in civil court. The result was the discharge of the trustees and the ruling of the court that only members of the church could be trustees. This episode caused much hardship and grief to Rev. Gorham. It began a new day for this church, which has prospered ever since. The pastor who carried this through the court was the Rev. J. H. D. Bailey.

The period after the two World Wars produced an influx of black people into urban and industrial areas of New England. Therefore, during the episcopal tenure of Bishops Walls and Spottswood, from 1928 to 1972, several new churches were established in Connecticut and Massachusetts.

The section of Zion embracing the Philadelphia-Baltimore Conference began after the 1872 consolidation of the Philadelphia and Southern Conferences. By the turn of the century, this area had produced the largest number of Zion bishops. This historic conference, organized second in the denomination in 1829, continued its astonishing growth to become the largest conference of the denomination in the North. Spearheading this spectacular growth from 1872 through the early years of the twentieth century were Bishops J. J. Clinton, J. J. Moore, Singleton T. Jones, T. H. Lomax, J. W. Hood, C. R. Harris (who recommended that this large conference be divided in 1896), C. C. Pettey, G. W. Clinton, J. W. Smith, Alexander Walters, and J. S. Caldwell. These men were ably

23. Hood, *One Hundred Years*, p. 243.
24. *Minutes,* Twenty-Second Quadrennial Session, p. 157.

assisted by an array of devoted preachers who firmly planted Zion Church from Philadelphia and Harrisburg to Arlington, Va., and made the nation's capital a religious fort for our race people:

Reverends:

G. S. Adams	William H. Day	Z. T. Pearsall
J. Harvey Anderson	S. F. Dickerson	J. E. Price
Mark M. Bell	R. H. G. Dyson	W. A. Ray
M. L. Blaylock	J. W. Fairfax	J. B. Small
B. J. Bolding	R. Farley Fisher	J. W. Smith
George Bosley	J. P. Hamer	M. J. Snow
W. L. Clayton	J. H. Hector	William H. Snowden
J. S. Cole	W. J. Holland	E. M. Stanton
S. L. Corrothers	Logan Johnson	R. Haywood Stitt
J. S. Cowles	G. W. Kincaid	J. P. Thompson
E. H. Curry	P. J. McEntosh	G. W. A. Tolbert
P. L. Cuyler	J. H. McMullen	J. P. Trusty
R. J. Daniels	J. F. Moreland, Sr.	S. S. Wales
W. H. Davenport	W. H. Newby	A. C. Washington
J. W. Davis	G. W. Offley	B. F. Wheeler

The roster also included the noted women who made missionary history in Zion, Mrs. Mary Jones, Mrs. Mary J. Small, Mrs. Annie W. Blackwell and Miss Sarah J. Janifer, along with a number of other ministers and laymen. The fifth church in Washington, Trinity, struggled into existence against fearsome odds, around the turn of the century, led by Rev. Logan Johnson, and is one of the leading churches in the Capital City today.

The present John Wesley Church edifice, at Fourteenth and Corcoran Streets (known as the National Church of Zion), was purchased under the direction of Rev. William C. Brown. The membership continued to swell and soon became the largest Zion congregation in Washington. The Varick Church in Philadelphia was a denominational project, organized by leading bishops and general officers after the General Conference was held at Big Wesley, Philadelphia, in 1908. The present stone structure of Big Wesley Church, on 15th and Lombard Streets, was built during the pastorate of the Rev. Henry D. Tillman in 1926. This membership during the pastorate of Rev. J. S. Caldwell was the largest in the connection.

This conference continued to grow during the migration of our people North. Reverends William D. Battle, P. A. Wallace, W. H. Marshall, W. H. Ferguson, G. M. Oliver, W. D. Clinton, C. C. Alleyne, E. D. W. Jones, W. T. Beck, J. S. Shaw, C. C. Williams, George W. Gaines, J. W. McCoy, S. Q. Swann, F. R. Killingsworth, S. H. McNiel, W. O. Carrington, G. M. Edwards, and J. H. Tucker were other leaders of the conference who made outstanding contributions to house the ever-increasing crowds, after World War I. New societies were established in Philadelphia and other parts of southern Pennsylvania, Maryland, Wilmington, Delaware, Washington, D.C., and nearby communities, supported largely by home missions funds of the conference, projected by Bishop C. C. Alleyne.

The New Jersey Conference continued its growth from 1896, led by Bishops Hood, Walters, and G. W. Clinton. During the administration of Bishop Walters, the Clinton Memorial Church in Newark, which had been practically lost to the connection, moved from Astor and Sherman Streets to 98 Pennington St., the deed recovered, and the property placed in good condition in 1907-1908 by Rev. Albert P. Miller. The conference had also grown sufficiently to set apart two presiding elder districts. Largely responsible for this extension were Revs. J. R. Dangerfield, J. H. White, C. D. Hazel, S. L. Corrothers, William T. Biddle, E. M. Stanton, R. R. Ball, J. D. Meade, I. B. Walters, J. C. Temple, W. H. Davenport, G. N. Ray, I. N. Sisco, J. H. Mason, W. M. Langford, I. B. Turner, J. A. S. Cole, D. Grecian-Donowa, E. S. Hardge, Sr., S. T. Meeks, S. T. Hawkins, J. E. Rogers, W. W. Atchison, O. G. Goodwin, J. B. Kirby, and O. J. Remsen.

The cities and towns in New Jersey increased rapidly in the number of blacks after the two World Wars, and the A.M.E. Zion Church grew with the state. At Jersey City, Rev. Jeremiah M. Hoggard erected the best church owned by Negroes in the state of New Jersey in 1926, at a cost of $125,000. A few years earlier, he also purchased a commodious church in Newark, on Broadway, the present edifice of the Clinton Memorial Church. This church was saved and its debt paid by Rev. James C. Nelson. Before 1926, however, Rev. J. B. Kirby had saved the property from being sold at auction. One of the most notable among the women of our clergy, Dr. Florence Randolph, had organized the church at Summit, and secured a fine property. [25] This church developed into one of the better churches under her magnetic leadership. Zion churches in the cities of Newark, Jersey City, Trenton, Camden, Asbury Park, and Staten Island, New York, more than doubled in membership, while such places as Red Bank (birthplace of the conference), Hackensack, Paterson, Sommerville, Englewood, and Ridgewood grew exceedingly with the black population. This is one of the copious conferences in the denomination, with practically all of its churches maintaining solidly good memberships, and some continuing abundant growth.

The Allegheny Conference, embracing the great industrial region of the western part of Pennsylvania, had its most preponderant growth in Pittsburgh and vicinity after World War I, during the migration of blacks to the North. Its mother church, old John Wesley, which entertained the General Conference in 1892, worshipped in a one-story building acquired under the leadership of Rev. Tabbs in 1850, up an alleyway, known as "Little Jim." In 1886, led by Rev. Jehu Holliday, the members acquired the site on Arthur Street and proceeded to build a most impressive edifice, which was dedicated to the glory of God in October 1886. [26] Holliday afterwards became presiding elder of the only district in the Allegheny Conference, and Rev. G. W. Clinton became the inspiring pastor of John Wesley with a stimulating program of expansion. [27] After the 1944 General Conference the old John Wesley Church had no building, having lost their property by a strange twist of treacherous maneuvering. Reverend Dixon Brown gave his life to save this situation for Zion, rather than accept remunerative appointments offered him at the General Conference. He led the people in purchasing a magnificent structure on Aheron Avenue, one of the finest churches in the Allegheny Conference. After the mortgage burning, he died suddenly of a heart attack. He had cheered a discouraged congregation and wrought well for Zion for 30 years in its ministry. [28]

After the death of Bishop Singleton T. Jones in 1891, Bishop Hood filled out the unexpired term in the Allegheny Conference. The man who had done more

25. *Minutes,* Twenty-Eighth Quadrennial Session, p. 132.
26, Spencer, Ms. History, John Wesley Church, *op. cit.*
27. *Minutes,* Nineteenth Quadrennial Session, p. 25.
28. *Minutes,* Thirty-Third Quadrennial Session, p. 102.

than any other one man to increase the utility of this conference was the successful presiding elder in 1892, Rev. Holliday. He organized churches faster than the bishop was able to find men to hold the points taken in, and became the potent factor in setting off the Ohio Conference from Allegheny at that time. [29]

After the assignment of Bishop George L. Blackwell in 1920, the Allegheny Conference not only grew in Western Pennsylvania, but new mission points were established through the Southwestern section and the state of West Virginia. After his reassignment in 1924, he set apart two presiding elder districts, appointing Revs. George W. Kincaid and W. A. Blackwell to carry on expansion in growing areas of the coal mining industry. His death in March 1926 caused a stunning setback to the growth of Zion in several key areas.

The work in the Allegheny Conference was supervised by Bishop Paris A. Wallace until 1936. Zion's outstanding achievement there took place in Pittsburgh in 1927, when the congregation divided from old John Wesley Church. Led by Rev. Elijah Lovett Madison, they erected without any connectional assistance a mammoth church structure at a cost of $250,000, the Wesley Center Church, which entertained the General Conference first in 1932. [30] Dr. Madison also secured the old John Wesley Church and parsonage intact, thus giving Zion two major churches in Pittsburgh, with Rev. J. R. Respass leading Old John Wesley. [31] The Wesley Center Church was the largest black Methodist church building in the state of Pennsylvania. [32]

Bishop W. J. Walls served this conference from 1936 to 1944, after which Bishop E. L. Madison was assigned. He lived only one year, and the conference was reassigned to Bishop Walls who remained in charge of the work until 1952. In 1944, Bishop Madison converted the two presiding elder districts into one and placed Rev. C. C. Williams in charge. The West Virginia District, which had been set apart in 1938, was a source of concern by 1948. Mission work had been established earlier in Huntington, W. Va., and the church at Charleston and two other points in West Virginia were started through the sacrificial efforts of Rev. A. H. Burk, who had the assistance of Dr. William J. L. Wallace, then a chemistry teacher at West Virginia State College, son of Dr. Thomas W. Wallace.

Dr. W. J. L. Wallace hung on to this mission in Charleston with determination. He taught a Sunday school class for a number of years, and when we were able to purchase our first church in Charleston, in 1950-51, a project of the Allegheny Conference, Dr. Wallace, who had served as vice-president and later president of West Virginia State College, served as its pastor. He serves today as presiding elder of the area churches of West Virginia in the Allegheny Conference. Other churches of our denomination in West Virginia were established during an earlier period and are part of the Kentucky Conference. Though this conference is one of the small conferences today, due to another shift in population from smaller coal mining towns, it is one of the most impressive conferences of the denomination, and has produced a grand coterie of outstanding church leaders, educators, and builders.

We have related in Chapter 16 the early growth of the northern and western conferences impinging upon the original northeastern territory. However, striking growth, sometimes startling, continued through these periods of migration in Ohio, Michigan, Illinois, Indiana, Kentucky, and Missouri. California also benefited from the migration, but not as it might have. We had not developed

29. *Minutes,* Nineteenth Quadrennial Session, pp. 25-26.
30. *Minutes,* Twenty-Ninth Quadrennial Session, pp. 113-114.
31. *Minutes,* Twenty-Eighth Quadrennial Session, p. 133; Twenty-Ninth Quadrennial Session, p. 113.
32. *Minutes,* Thirty-First Quadrennial Session, p. 119.

preachers fast enough to sustain growth in California and the West.

Bishop G. L. Blackwell, the king of expansion, in setting apart new presiding elder districts during the early 1920's in the Virginia and Albermarle Conferences, stated the following:

A new presiding elder district, like a new Annual Conference, gives opportunity to a new set of men to fill new important positions. Then too, to acquire new territory or even build or buy a new church, gives new hope and kindles new inspirations. So the making of these new districts has engendered a pleasant rivalry and a holy contest among the brethren. [33]

This seems good doctrine still.

The last domestic annual conference, the Colorado Conference, was formed in December 1952 and ratified by the General Conference of 1956. Bishop Spottswood organized the Spottswood Temple Church in Denver, then a city of 20,000 blacks, a number that increased to 44,000 by 1956. He had a vision of spreading the borders of Zion from this vantage point to other cities in the state, such as Colorado Springs, Pueblo, Trinidad, Boulder, Grand Island, North Platte, Hastings, and on into Omaha, Neb. He had organized societies at Colorado Springs and Boulder, and appointed Revs. J. H. Jones and H. J. Frazier to develop this work. These two churches did not survive, yet the Denver Church grew to 125 members, led by Rev. Cajus Howell during the next four years. [34] This conference seeks still to be developed beyond its present one church. The prospect is bright as there are large numbers of our people in these areas in need of Christ, and awaiting the apostles of devotion and holy dare to lead them in this direction.

Growth Through Church Divisions

Concentric growth in some of our big cities came by way of one congregation dividing into two, and creating Christian competition for large memberships. In some instances, there is no way of designating which of the two divisions is the older church, as both congregations insist upon maintaining original history. In other instances, the so-called new congregation readily accepted the date of separation from its parent body. While some feelings of rivalry existed between congregations during the transitions, a fervent love for Christ and for the traditional church prevailed in the hearts of the people.

The first church division appears to have been the earliest development of our Zion in Louisville, Ky., after the Colored Methodist Episcopal Church formed in 1870 and took our property from us by court decisions in that state. Fifteenth Street Church was our first congregation, which Zion reorganized immediately. In 1876, under the direction of Bishop Singleton T. Jones, the Rev. Jehu Holliday, pastoring Fifteenth Street Church, bought a property on Twelfth Street and divided the congregation from the Fifteenth Street Church. Reverend Anthony Bunch was appointed to Fifteenth Street, [35] and both churches enjoyed an abundant growth. The Twelfth Street Church graduated into what is now known as Broadway Temple, leading Zion Church in that state. Fifteenth Street, the mother of Zion Methodism, is known as Hughlett Temple.

In Charlotte, N.C., after the death of Bishop Moore, trouble seized Clinton Chapel and caused much distress to his successor, Bishop Lomax, and other preachers and members of Clinton Chapel. Moore's Sanctuary, Little Rock, and

33. *Minutes,* Twenty-Seventh Quadrennial Session, p. 182.
34. *Minutes,* Thirty-Fifth Quadrennial Session, pp. 223-224; *Minutes,* Thirty-Sixth Quadrennial Session, pp. 190-191.
35. *Minutes,* Thirteenth Session, Kentucky Annual Conference, 1878, p. 30.

Biddleville (Gethsemane) had all previously sprung from this mother chruch. There was a threatening split in 1894, led by Revs. G. H. Haines and J. W. Gordon, who made an attempt to take Clinton Chapel into the Congregational Church. [36] Another faction within Clinton Chapel desired to withdraw, but when the crowd failed, they did not go with the Congregational group. When the prohibition fight came, this group went off on the temperance question and organized an A.M.E. Zion Church, known as Grace Church, giving themselves strictly a Bible name. Reverend P. A. McCorkle became its first pastor. When the church was later built by Rev. J. W. Smith, the language of their cornerstone was thus: Deo—Religio—Temperancia (God, Religion, and Temperance). Bishop Lomax and Rev. R. H. Simmons pursued the fight to the Supreme Court, along with the loyal supporters of Clinton Chapel, and won the cause for the connection. [37] Bishop Lomax organized Little Rock Church during his pastorate and presiding eldership in Charlotte in the early 1870's.

In 1943-44, guided by Bishop Benjamin G. Shaw of the Western North Carolina Conference, advised by a committee constituted of Bishops Walls, Alleyne, and Mr. Oscar W. Adams, Sr., secretary of the Church Extension Department, the Goler Memorial Church of Winston-Salem, N.C., entered into a division. [38] It resulted in two amply substantial congregations and advantageous buildings. The pastor, Rev. W. F. Witherspoon, led the congregation in purchasing a capacious church edifice, Goler Metropolitan, presently located on Fourth and Dunleith Streets, and the Rev. Hunter B. Bess steered the members of the Old Goler Memorial, remaining on its present historic site, into refinancing and greatly reducing the $72,000 debt, while liquidating the debt of the parsonage. The Church Extension Department gave $10,000 to this venture.

During 1950-51, the Hood Memorial Church in New York City, led by Rev. J. W. Wactor, purchased a $122,000 building in addition to $35,000 for remodelling the plant on 146th Street near Seventh Avenue, known today as the Greater Hood Memorial Church. The New York Conference purchased the old church on Lenox Avenue from the congregation at a cost of $37,500, with connectional assistance, and established the Walters Memorial Church for Zion in the world's largest city. Reverend Ransom Bennett became the first pastor in developing a new congregation. [39] In one of the fastest growing cities on Long Island, Rev. William H. Hogans led his congregation in purchasing a larger church home on New York Boulevard, in 1959. The New York Conference also purchased the old Calvary Church property and established the Father Abraham Thompson Memorial Church, and Rev. David Woodson became its first pastor. The conference had previously led in establishing two other churches in Jamaica. One of astonishing accomplishments and growth, Rush Temple, was organized in 1955 by Rev. Eldridge Gittens.

In Toledo, Ohio, the St. Paul Congregation was in process of purchasing an imposing stone structure, led by Rev. G. M. Oliver in 1955. Upon the death of Bishop Martin in the fall, Bishop Walls was assigned to the Michigan Conference. After the St. Paul congregation moved into their new church home, the second church of Toledo, St. James, was maneuvered into the Vance Street property formerly owned by St. Paul, assisted by the Michigan Conference, and out of these two churches were made three. The old property of St. James was also

36. *Minutes,* Twentieth Quadrennial Session, p. 137.
37. *Ibid.,* Hood, *One Hundred Years,* p. 193.
38. *Minutes,* Thirty-Second Quadrennial Session, pp. 80-81, p. 163.
39. *Minutes,* Thirty-Fourth Quadrennial Session, pp. 86-87.

retained, and the few members that were left had increased to 30 in less than six months. Reverend W. M. Cunningham led the movement of the second church, and Rev. W. G. Cochrane was placed in charge of the third church. [40] Later, during the episcopal administration of Bishop Spottswood, the two new congregations were combined, and are known today as the Walls-Friendly Chapel.

One of the most tremendous divisions in our connectional history took place in Detroit, in 1959. Under the direction of Bishop S. G. Spottswood, the St. Paul Church, led by Rev. William A. Hilliard, purchased a quarter million dollar church on Dexter Street, which has a continual flourishing growth and improvement under its present pastor, Rev. William C. Ardrey, and entertained in its building the 1968 General Conference. A remnant of some 116 persons elected to remain in the Palmer Street property, also a commodious structure, which entertained the 1944 General Conference. The old congregation is known as Metropolitan Church, and Rev. Stephen P. Spottswood became its first pastor. This church is experiencing growth in the Motor City. [41]

Another stupendous accomplishment of church division took place in Cincinnati, 1958-1960. Directed also by Bishop Spottswood, the St. John's Church, led by Rev. Joseph F. Dunn, purchased an extraordinary church plant in the Avondale section, and those members desiring not to move formed a new Zion movement, St. Mark's, and purchased land to build a new church, led by their first pastor, Rev. Novie S. Chaney. A commodious building was later erected by St. Mark's Church under the pastorate of Rev. Tecumseh X. Graham. [42]

In Knoxville, Tenn. 1958-59, the historic Loguen Temple Church, built during the pastorate of Bishop A. J. Warner, produced two profitable churches through contention and strife. Guided by Bishop H. T. Medford, one-time pastor of the church, the members entered into this division for Zion. Reverend J. A. Babington-Johnson led the congregation into purchasing a large church of multiple modern conveniences on Bell Avenue which was named First A.M.E. Zion Church. A large number of members desired to remain in the old Loguen Temple on Commerce Street, retaining its historic name in memory of the king of the Abolition movement, Bishop J. W. Loguen, and Rev. Carroll M. Felton became its first pastor. The Church Extension Department, through its secretary, Mr. D. W. Andrews, aided in bringing this project through successfully for Zion in both instances. [43]

At Norfolk, Va., under the episcopal supervision of Bishop J. D. Cauthen, during 1967-68, two Zion churches were established out of the original Metropolitan Church pastored by Rev. Richard A. Councill. Reverend Councill led the Metropolitan Church in purchasing a grand property on Springfield Avenue. That portion of the members desiring to remain at the original location on Brambleton Street, hallowed by their ancestors, entered into a program of renovation led by their first pastor, Rev. Jackson A. Browne, and named the church Greater Metropolitan Church. [44] Bishop William A. Stewart later gave tenacious support and encouragement in the adjustment of these two congregations and their property matters.

Also during this period, the leadership of Rev. A. C. Littlejohn created two congregations at Newport News; the larger movement known as Greater Walters,

40. *Minutes,* Thirty-Fifth Quadrennial Session, p. 155.
41. *Minutes,* Thirty-Sixth Quadrennial Session, pp. 194-195.
42. *Minutes,* Thirty-Sixth Quadrennial Session, p. 192; Thirty-Seventh Quadrennial Session, p. 206; Thirty Eighth Quadrennial Session, p. 196.
43. *Minutes,* Thirty-Sixth Quadrennial Session, p. 151.
44. *Minutes,* Thirty-Eighth Quadrennial Session, p. 240.

pastored by Rev. Littlejohn, and the remaining group, Old Walters, pastored by Rev. P. N. Shannon.

Not singled out in this chapter are numerous churches of average strength, from coast to coast, to which our Zion has given birth. Some started out as missions with the determined "two or three gathered together," and others started with more advantageous situations and grew into sturdy churches. This is a result of productive missionary-minded bishops, ministers, and laymen. Churches mentioned, for the most part, are those whose memberships have skyrocketed from small missions and sparse congregations into the thousand mark, or congregations in principal cities where Zion had a late start and kindled unusual growth. Our church growth has continued, and should and will doubtless continue more.

Part V
Projection Departments

CHAPTER 19

RECORDS DEPARTMENT, AUDIT, AND PUBLIC RELATIONS

Promotion of our connection in system and records has been a normal procedure. At the beginning of our organization, Zion had the eminent George Collins recording the actions and deeds of the movement. He was a man of brilliance, a schoolteacher of his own race group. Because of the inadequacy of education for blacks in that age, he also had to earn his living by other trades. Therefore, in addition to teaching, he was a painter and operated a grocery store on the side. [1] He was the first secretary of the trustees board of the mother church, and served in this capacity a number of years. In fact, he was for 50 years one of the most prominent men in the church.

George Collins in effect, was our first General Secretary. The committee of five, led by James Varick, selected Christopher Rush and George Collins to edit the first Discipline in 1820, and Collins served as secretary. He was an expert record keeper and zealous church worker, and "amanuensis to Bishop Rush" most of the Bishop's years of service, especially when the Bishop wrote *The Rise and Progress of the African Methodist Episcopal (Zion) Church.* [2] Unfortunately, the first church records were destroyed in a disastrous fire in 1839.

Since laymen were not a part of the Methodist Annual and General Conference structure, after the organization of the A.M.E. Zion Church into a connection Rev. Christopher Rush of New York served as secretary of the next General Conference held in 1824 at Old Zion (Mother Zion Church) in New York City, and was elected bishop in 1828. [3] Reverend Jacob Matthews of New York served as secretary of the next two General Conferences held in 1828 and 1832 at Old Zion in New York City. [4] Reverend John A. King of New York served as secretary of the General Conference held at Old Zion in 1836, and Rev. John P. Thompson of New York was secretary of the 1840 General Conference held at Asbury Church in New York City. [5]

1. Directories of New York City, 1800-1820.
2. Wheeler, *The Varick Family,* pp. 22-23.
3. Ms, "Negroes of New York," Federal Writers Program.
4. Blackwell, Ms. A Digest History of the A.M.E. Zion Church, pp. 12-13; Moore, *History,* p. 284.
5. Moore, *History of the A.M.E. Zion Church* p. 105,295.

These first six General Conferences were held in joint session with the New York Annual Conference, as were the two successive General Conferences, held in 1844 and 1848. Reverend Samson Talbot of New York served as secretary of the 1844 General Conference, and Rev. John J. Moore of Philadelphia was secretary in 1848, Reverend John D. Brooks of Baltimore was elected secretary of the General Conference held at Big Wesley Church, Philadelphia, in 1852 and Reverend Daniel Vandervier of New York, recording secretary. Reverend Samuel M. Giles of New York was chosen to serve the General Conference meeting in New York, as secretary in 1856. Reverend William F. Butler, serving in New York, New England and Kentucky, was elected secretary of the General Conference in 1860, 1864, and 1868. [6] These men kept the records faithfully of all proceedings of quadrennial sessions, local statistics, Sunday school pupils, finances raised, important records of church property, and annual conference records before the church began to organize a records department connectionally. They also helped to revise the Discipline, keep up correspondence with fraternal organizations, and issue resolutions on important church action. These men, along with the annual conference secretaries, labored gratuitously, for the most part, in helping to build a great denomination.

At the General Conference in 1872, Rev. William H. Hillery of San Francisco was elected secretary, a layman, from North Carolina, Robert Harris recorder of the minutes, and Rev. James A. Jones of Philadelphia, compiler of the minutes. This General Conference enacted that a general secretary should be elected at the time the bishops were elected, to serve four years, or until his successor was elected. This was the first general office created in the A.M.E. Zion Church. His duty was

> to record the proceedings of the ensuing General Conference, take charge of all the books and papers, and other property of the General Conference not otherwise provided for, to issue certificates to the Bishops, which certificates shall be countersigned by the Senior Bishop; and also, shall provide certificates to the active Bishops for Deacons' and Elders' orders. [7]

Elder James A. Jones was elected General Conference Secretary (or first General Secretary), and served with perserverance until his death in 1875. The Board of Bishops then selected Dr. William Howard Day of Harrisburg, Pa. [8] One of the first-line race leaders in the history of our church, Day was known for his great mental capacity and inventive ability. He was once described as follows:

> As a scholar, he easily ranks as one of the broadest, most thorough and polished American sons of Liberal Art. As a theologian, he is erudite, deep and profound. As an orator, he has but few peers on this continent. As a debater, he is ever ready to discuss all living issues on Church or State; and on all such occasions seems to be a walking encyclopedia.
>
> As a writer, he is versatile, with diction pure and chaste. His logic is always clear and convincing; and whatever emanates from his pen is sought as precious dew-drops from an intellectual sky. As an educator, he is a recognized guide. For many years he has labored as a director of youthful minds; and today there are scores of stalwart intellectual men and women transmitting unto others precepts and examples, ever reflecting the inner life of William Howard Day. [9]

6. *Ibid.*, pp. 208, 210, 212, 216, 222, 231, 247.
7. *Ibid.*, pp. 273, 280-281; *Doctrines and Discipline*, 1872, p. 74.
8. Moore, *History*, pp. 281-282, 293; Simmons, *Men of Mark*, p. 933.
9. *The Star of Zion*, January 27, 1898.

REV. WILLIAM HOWARD DAY

1825 - 1901

First black graduate of Oberlin University. Assembled the first black international convention. President of the School Board of Control, Harrisburg, Pa. First General Secretary of the A.M.E. Zion Church and lived to be the last person in our church who was baptized by James Varick.

Day served with exceptional proficiency, during the year and at the 1876 General Conference. He nominated as his assistants of the 1876 General Conference Revs. C. R. Harris, W. H. Ferguson and L. J. Scurlock; Revs. J. H. McFarley and Mark M. Bell, statistical secretaries, all of whom the General Conference confirmed. [10] Day was re-elected in 1876, General Secretary. Further, at his instigation, a journal was adopted, *National Standard and Zion Church Advocate,* and he was appointed editor-in-chief. Bishop J. W. Hood, in his episcopal address to the South Carolina Conference, stated that Professor W. H. Day "is peculiarly suited to the work, and you may expect a good paper." [11]

The heavy responsibilites placed upon the talented Dr. Day by this General Conference, and the educational program in which he was engaged for both race and church in Pennsylvania, along with his ministerial duties, proved to be too much, and trouble began between the General Secretary and the general church mid-quadrennium. In a special report on the deportment of the General Secretary, which was placed in the hands of a committee on complaints at the General Conference in 1880, the following case was stated:

> Professor William Howard Day, Secretary of the General Conference and compiler of the Minutes, having failed to publish the minutes up to January, 1878, the Board of Bishops resolved to publish them. We were informed by good authority that Professor Day had them compiled, and as two years had passed and he was paid $25 for compiling them, we had no thought to the contrary. . . . Therefore, having resolved to publish the Minutes, we sent to Professor Day for the *Manuscript Minutes.* . . . After considerable delay, he sent the journal of the General Conference through a party whose pledge he took that it should be returned to him. . . .

10. Moore, *History,* pp. 290, 295.
11. *Ibid.,* pp. 331-333; *Minutes,* Eleventh Session, South Carolina Annual Conference, 1876, pp. 9-10.

It was not what we wanted; we had no use for it; we dispatched repeatedly for the manuscript. In our last dispatch we told him he would be held in contempt. . . . He did not say that he had not the manuscript written. As we could not get the manuscript, and had not the time, if we had the authority, to prepare a compilation, nor were we willing to pay someone else to do the work for which Professor Day had been so well paid; therefore we had to give up publishing the Minutes. [12]

It was further stated that Professor Day had been working against the Zion Hill Collegiate Institute (a school in Middletown, Pennsylvania, highly favored by Bishop J. J. Clinton, for becoming a Connectional School;–see Chapter 22) and that he otherwise appeared disaffected toward the connection. Bishop Clinton was instructed to hold the journal until further developments. Clinton was also instructed to prepare charges against Day and place them in the hands of a committee. Day was subsequently suspended from the Virginia Conference, thus vacating the office of General Secretary.

Professor Day did not make his appearance at the General Conference held in Montgomery, in 1880, and his case was taken up there. "In Professor Day's defense sent to the Conference, he expressed a doubt of the committee's right to call him, took issue with the composition of the committee, and stated that one member of the committee was not fit to sit upon his case." He claimed also that a portion of the committee had prejudged the case and were not competent to try him.

The Committee, using the information it had in hand, found Professor Day guilty of contempt in refusing to send the Board of Bishops the manuscript minutes of the preceding General Conference, "and recommended that he be suspended from all official standing and church privileges until he *meets* the General Conference and *answers* to the charges preferred against him." The report, submitted by A. Paxton, W. H Pitts, W. Jones, S. Story and H. H. Whidbee of the Committee on Complaints, was adopted by the General Conference. [13]

At the opening session of the General Conference, Rev. C. R. Harris was elected secretary, Rev. Alfred Day assistant secretary, Rev. C. C. Pettey journal secretary, Revs. J. B. Small and C. Max Manning statistical secretaries. Reverend C. R. Harris had been elected the first General Steward at this General Conference, and he served the quadrennium in the dual capacity of General Secretary and General Steward. [14] At New York in 1884, Rev. C. C. Pettey was elected General Secretary, and Rev. J. Harvey Anderson, Statistical Secretary. Also elected to assist Rev. Pettey in compiling the records were Rev. Alexander Walters, Nathaniel J. Green, Joseph Gomez, and George W. Clinton, and Gen. T. M. Chester, stenographic reporter. [15] Reverend Pettey served as General Secretary for the quadrennium, and in 1888 at New Bern, Rev. G. W. Clinton was elected to act as secretary of the General Conference for Rev. Pettey, who was late arriving. [16] At this General Conference, Rev. C. C. Pettey was elected bishop.

Reverend William Howard Day, who had before and afterward proven a faithful servant in the interest of his beloved church, settled the matter of clerical concern with the Board of Bishops and reconciliation with Bishop Clinton on the

12. *Minutes,* Sixteenth Quadrennial Session, pp. 45-46.
13. *Ibid.,* pp. 46-47.
14. Ibid., pp. 8, 55.
15. *Minutes,* Seventeenth Quadrennial Session, p. 11.
16. *Minutes,* Eighteenth Quadrennial Session, pp. 10, 12.

Zion Hill Collegiate Institute. He was soon reinstated in the Virginia Conference, [17] and afterwards transferred to the Philadelphia-Baltimore Conference, and had been reactivated in General Church service by 1884. Professor Day was elected delegate to the 1888 General Conference from the Philadelphia-Baltimore Conference and was active in its deliberations. Here he was elected once again to serve as General Secretary of the denomination. [18] He was re-elected at the General Conferences of 1892, 1896, and 1900, and served with immense efficiency until his death on December 3, 1900. He was greatly assisted in his last days of illness by Rev. George L. Blackwell whom the Board of Bishops selected to succeed him on Wednesday, March 13, 1901. [19]

The revised rules in existence from 1888 to 1900 made it imperative for the General Secretary and the General Steward to work in consonance in the operation of financial affairs of the connection. This legislation was prompted by the insufficient verbal report made at the General Conference in 1888, by its secretary, Rev. C. C. Pettey of New Bern, N.C. He felt that his duties were not well-defined, and that there was not enough work involved to merit the salary of $300 allowed the General Secretary. Thus out of his generous spirit and love for the church, he contributed one-half of his salary to the Board of Bishops and the other half to the Board of Trustees of Livingstone College. Bishop J. W. Hood and Dr. Joseph C. Price tendered warm expressions of thanks on behalf of each group. [20]

In addition to the record making and keeping duties, the General Secretary's office became the clearing house for church finances. While the General Steward's duties were still to receive general claims throughout the connection, the 1888 legislation directed that he transmit all funds to the General Secretary, whose responsibility it was to make the disbursements to the various departments, Livingstone College, African missions, bishops' salaries, and General Secretary and General Steward salaries. [21]

In 1892 the General Conference introduced the Bureau of Statistics and elected Revs. N. J. Green, chairman, J. H. White, secretary, and J. S. Caldwell. It included the General Statistician in the Discipline as an officer of the General Conference. [22] Statistical work had not been a part of the official duties of the General Secretary, and those persons elected by the General Conferences willingly gave their valuable services to this vital system. Reverend James Harvey Anderson serving in Philadelphia and Baltimore, Western New York and New Jersey Conferences, was elected Statistician in 1896 and rendered incalculable service until 1916 (when he was elected editor of the *Star of Zion*), and a denominational Board of Statistics was introduced. Anderson compiled the statistics from annual conference records, caused an enlargement of the statistical report forms which are still in use today for local church, annual conference, and connectional use, and in 1895 produced the first *Handbook of the African Methodist Episcopal Zion Church*, prior to the Centennial, which was an indispensable work. He also produced other literature about the A.M.E. Zion Church while serving as Statistician.

17. *Minutes,* Seventeenth Session of Virginia Annual Conference, 1882, p. 2.
18. *Minutes,* Eighteenth Quadrennial Session, p. 73.
19. *Minutes,* Twenty-First Quadrennial Session, p. 16.
20. *Minutes,* Eighteenth Quadrennial Session, pp. 16-17.
21. *Ibid.,* pp. 110-113; *Doctrines and Discipline,* 1888, 1892, 1896.
22. *Minutes,* Nineteenth Quadrennial Session, pp. 3, 122; *Minutes,* Twenty-First Quadrennial Session, p. 289.

At the 1900 General Conference, Dr. William Howard Day made his last report, and expressed heartfelt gratitude to the bishops and devoted friends of the A.M.E. Zion Church who sponsored a testimonial in his honor in April 1898, for 50 years of devoted service to the General Public. The office of General Secretary was largely transformed at that conference. All matters but one pertaining to the finances of the church were placed in the custody of the Department of Finance and the secretary and Finance Board for its administration. Many of the rules set forth defining the duties of the General Secretary apply today, with a few revisions and alterations. Prior to this, the election of the General Secretary was designated to take place on the last day of the General Conference, but the election was changed to follow immediately the election of bishops. In addition to recording proceedings of the General Conference, the General Secretary was to record the proceedings of the newly instituted Connectional Council. His duties also were to "record the names of all the delegates-elect to the ensuing General Conference, which names shall be sent him immediately upon their election, by the secretary of each Annual Conference," which rule went into effect in 1884. [23]

Some of the new duties of the General Secretary were: to record a brief historic statement in the journal of the connection of official acts of the Board of Bishops and Connectional Council; the deaths, resignations, and changes occurring among the officials of the church; to edit and issue all necessary blanks, receipt books, credentials, and certificates for the use of the bishops, presiding elders, pastors and conferences; to issue certificates of appointments for bishops' use; to keep the seal of the connection and see that all official papers issued by him bear its stamp; to keep in his ledger a record of all the indebtedness of the connection; to make an annual publication in the church organ of the aggregated statistical table of the whole connection. [24]

As General Secretary, Dr. George L. Blackwell was methodical and very meticulous in gathering and systematizing the facts of our history and literary achievement in the church. He was re-elected to this office in 1904 and served until 1908, at Philadelphia, when he was elevated to the bishopric. In 1900, as a result of the assistance of Dr. Blackwell to Dr. Day during his illness, the office of Assistant General Secretary was created, whose duties were to "assist the General Secretary wherever the services were needed." In case of death, resignation or otherwise of the General Secretary, the assistant secretary was to assume the responsibilities of General Secretary. [25] Reverend F. M. Jacobs of Brooklyn, N.Y., was elected Assistant Secretary by the Board of Bishops in 1901, when Dr. Blackwell was elected General Secretary. [26]

Since 1872, each General Conference had appointed an audit committee, which thoroughly examined the records of the various departments, as they were created, and made its reports before the close of the General Conference. Auditing reports of General Officers semi-annually was initiated in 1908, and was the duty of the Assistant General Secretary, also named auditor. His salary was set at $300 plus traveling expense. [27] This office was soon abolished, and auditing the departmental reports became the responsibility of the General Secretary under the

23. *Doctrines and Discipline,* 1884, p. 124.
24. *Doctrines and Discipline,* 1900, pp. 178-180.
25. *Ibid.,* p. 180.
26. *Minutes,* Twenty-First Quadrennial Session, pp. 249-250.
27. *Doctrines and Discipline,* 1908, p. 181.

direction of the Board of Audit. Reverend M. D. Lee of Rock Hill, S.C., who was elected General Secretary in 1908, utilized the services of Rev. Frank H. Hill of Charlotte, N.C. as Official Auditor. [28] Inasmuch as the General Secretary was yet performing one important financial obligation for the connection, "to make out the pro rata monthly, and issue all orders upon the Financial Secretary for the payment of Claimants on the General Fund," the work was actually a follow-up of the detail work of the Financial Secretary. The system of having nearly duplicate reports compensated for a lack of strict accounting of records until the audit system was enforced. This method was abolished in 1916 when the Board of Bishops, in its Episcopal Address, recommended "that the duties of General Secretary in connection with the Financial Department be discontinued and that the safeguard of the Financial Department be entrusted to the Board of Finance," and the General Conference passed this into law. [29]

Reverend W. L. Hamblin of Montgomery, Ala. served as Official Auditor from 1916 to 1924. At this time, the Board of Bishops recommended in its Episcopal Address that the duties of Auditor and General Secretary be combined, in which the General Conference acquiesced, and the officer thus became known as General Secretary-Auditor, with total responsibilities defined in the Discipline. [30] However, as the church grew and the departments expanded, there was a demand for more scrutiny of departmental records. It was therefore enacted that the reports of every fiduciary department of the connection be examined periodically by a certified public accountant, as well as by the General Secretary-Auditor, under the direction of the Board of Audit, who shall report his finding to the Board of Bishops in its semi-annual meetings.

Reverend M. D. Lee, the productive educator, was re-elected as General Secretary in 1912 and 1916. The office was declared vacant in 1917; Rev. Lee becoming principal for the second time of Lancaster Normal and Industrial School, Lancaster, S.C., and the Board of Bishops elected Rev. Frederick M. Jacobs to fill out the unexpired term at the Connectional Council in 1917. [31] Reverend Jacobs, a medical doctor and enterprising spiritual leader, was re-elected to this office in 1920 and 1924, and in 1928 he was elected bishop. Reverend Henry C. Weeden of Louisville, Ky., was elected at the General Conference, and re-elected in 1932 and 1936. He died in 1937, and the Board of Bishops, in its January meeting, 1938, elected Attorney Samuel Madison Dudley who had succeeded Dr. J. H. Anderson as Official Statistician in 1916, and was named by the General Conference of 1920 as Official Census Representative of the A.M.E. Zion Church. [32] He administered the office with precision from Washington, D.C., which at this time became the permanent national headquarters of our denomination for this department.

Attorney Dudley was re-elected by the General Conferences of 1940 and 1944, and served until his death, January 6, 1947. Reverend Robert Farley Fisher, an ascribed thorough record keeper, was elected by the Board of Bishops on January 17, 1947 to serve the balance of the quadrennium. [33] His effective

28. *Minutes,* Twenty-Fourth Quadrennial Session, p. 329.
29. Quadrennial Episcopal Address, Twenty-Fifth Quadrennial Session, (1916) p. 13.
30. *Doctrines and Discipline,* 1920, p.366; *Minutes,* Twenty-Seventh Quadrennial Session, p.5.
31. Henry Weeden, *A.M.E. Zion Church Yearbook,* 1930-31, p. 32.
32. Ms. Minutes, Board of Bishops, January 12, 1938; *Minutes,* Twenty-Sixth Quadrennial Session, p. 122.
33. Ms. Minutes, Board of Bishops, January 17. 1947.

work motivated his re-election at the General Conferences of 1948 and 1952, and he served until his death, March 19, 1953. Reverend F. Claude Spurgeon, entrusted correspondent, was elected to fill the post by the Board of Bishops in special session at Salisbury, N.C., June 1-2, 1953. [34] Dr. Spurgeon, of Knoxville, Tenn. was elected by the General Conference in 1956 and served until his death, June 2, 1959. During the Connectional Council in August 1959, the Board of Bishops elected Mrs. Willie G. Alstork, a clerk in the office, to fill out the unexpired term of Dr. Spurgeon. Highly competent and versatile, as were her predecessors, Mrs. Alstork was the only woman to head a general department in the A.M.E. Zion Church, other then the Woman's Home and Foreign Missionary Society.

The General Conference of 1960 elected another layman of unswerving loyalty to this post, Edward M. Graham of Chicago, who was re-elected in 1964, and passed away June 20, 1967. At the Connectional Council held at Brooklyn, N.Y., July 1967, Rev. R. H. Collins Lee, a conformable officer, was selected by the Board of Bishops to fill this post. Dr. Lee was re-elected at the 1968 and 1972 General Conferences.

Public Relations

The work of the office of General Secretary has always been correlative with public relations of the church. These persons serving throughout the history of our church as general secretaries were also charged with keeping the general public informed of the religious and social action of the A.M.E. Zion Church as a leading Christian organization, in the forefront of world and national affairs. By the Sesqui-Centennial years, our international organization had reached the point of needing a qualified officer to interrelate with other great bodies of the world in its continuous effort of promoting the kingdom of Christ.

At the General Conference in 1952, a resolution was presented by Rev. G. W. McMurray for the establishment of a distinct Public Relations Department, and referred to the revision committee. The matter was presented by the revision committee on the last day of the General Conference, and was referred to the Board of Bishops for action. A budget was recommended for this part-time general office of $3,000 per year operational expenses, and $1,200 annual salary of the director. [35] By virtue of the authority vested in it, the Board of Bishops immediately established a part-time general office, the Bureau of Public Relations, which name was changed to the Public Relations and Social Service Department in 1956.

Reverend J. W. Findley, with the office set up at New York City was known for his perennial alertness and skill in making contacts with heads of government, heads of state, city officials, federal judges, outstanding church leaders, national radio companies, and other groups. He was elected the first director of this department by the Board of Bishops in August 1952, and served for the entire quadrennium. [36] In 1956, the General Conference elected Alexander Barnes, of Durham, N.C., an experienced news reporter and reference man. He is presently serving the church in this office, having been re-elected by the General Conferences of 1960, 1964, 1968, and 1972.

---

34. *Ibid.*, June 2, 1953; Alstork, *A.M.E. Zion Handbook,* 1956-1960, p. 18.

35. *Minutes*, Thirty-Fourth Quadrennial Session, pp. 74, 78, 399.

36. Ms. Minutes, Board of Bishops Meeting, Columbus Avenue Church, August 1, 1952; *Minutes,* Thirty-Fourth Quadrennial Session, p. 91.

CHAPTER 20

STEWARDSHIP AND FINANCIAL DEPARTMENT

While our founding fathers were still busy in the effort to spread the borders of the church, they early discovered the necessity of organizing the forces they had gathered to more intelligently perpetuate the institution to which they were giving their lives. In promoting the kingdom of Christ, chief among the many concerns of our leaders was the spiritual welfare of their people, and the cultivation of their souls and lives for righteousness. Our Discipline today governing the spirituality of each member has not been fundamentally changed from the first Discipline. Thus foremost in the tradition of the A.M.E. Zion Church is the expectation for each member, as far as possible, to live the righteous life and strive for perfection.

In the well-laid scheme of the fathers to project the church into areas of greater service to mankind, their manner of temporal concern was based on spiritual premises and remained within this realm, following as closely as possible the New Testament doctrines of performing services through financial support of constituents. The temporal economy of the church was the last chapter included in our first Discipline. Our first temporal economy was exceedingly small and barely regulated. It was designated to be raised through the quarterly conference arrangement and supported the most stringent necessities, such as the ministry, including the bishop, pastors, and superannuated preachers. The churches were principally missions, with the exception of the mother church, and the people were slaves for the most part. Slavery and poverty almost hopelessly handicapped their development. In most instances we had both trustees and stewards; where there were no trustees, the stewards served, and vice versa.

The rule of that day for trustees and stewards was no less than three and no more than five (stewards) on a board, "men of solid piety, who love the Methodist doctrine and discipline, and able to transact the temporal business of the circuit or society." [1] The first connectional project other than the support of the preachers, and support of local church, was raising assessments for the poor. To show how early our missionary consciousness came alive, the following rule obtained:

> Every preacher having charge of a circuit or station shall make a yearly collection in every congregation where there is a probability that the people will be willing to contribute, for the propagation of the gospel amongst our African brethren; and the money so collected shall be lodged with the trustees or stewards to be sent to the ensuing yearly conference. [2]

We came to this country with an interest of our Fatherland in our hearts, and any Afro-American today that does not have that consciousness is an abnormality.

---

1. *Doctrines and Discipline*, 1820, pp. 126-127.
2. *Ibid.*, p. 129.

Every succeeding General Conference dealt with this matter of temporal economy and made improvements according to growth and change. The five ensuing general conferences grappled with the problems of supporting the bishops, traveling preachers, their wives and children, and providing traveling expenses for these itinerants. When the book committee was established at the 1840 General Conference, providing for a profit from sale of denominational literature, support of the ministry was extended, and for the first time specific allowances were stipulated in the Discipline. The allowance of superintendents or bishops was $200 plus traveling expenses; for traveling preachers, $100 and traveling expenses; for the wives of traveling preachers, $100. Each child of the traveling preacher was allowed $12 annually to the age or 7 and $20 from the age of 7 to 14 years; "and those preachers whose wives are dead shall be allowed for each child annually, a sum sufficient to pay the board of such child or children, during the above term." Similiar provisions were also made for the widows of traveling preachers, superannuated, worn out and supernumerary preachers, and orphans of all these preachers, by the annual conferences. This General Conference also made the first effort to establish parsonages, when it recommended that friends in general "hire or rent houses for the married preachers, on their circuits or stations," and further recommended that they furnish the houses according to their ability. [3]

Although the denomination for the next 20 years was divided on the leadership issue, it continued to extend its temporal program in the General Conferences into areas of improved ministerial support, charity and education. In 1856, it established the Home and Foreign Mission Fund in the annual conferences. Until 1872, the church continued to operate in the same general manner, with annual conferences receiving funds reported by local churches, according to the rules of the Discipline. This was done on a larger scale, however, as the program included missionary funds to assist in the rapid growth of the South and attempted expansion into foreign territory. For instance, the General Conference directly after Emancipation, in 1864, reported $2,883.13 expended for missionary purposes. [4]

After spreading the church and increasing its numbers to 300,000 members and Sunday school pupils, from about 5,000 members in the northeastern section in 1863, [5] the fathers forthrightly faced the situation of our temporal economy in their Episcopal Address to the delegates in 1872. They pointed out the financial embarrassments of having to suspend our connectional journal for two years. Also the missionary work had been greatly hindered, and they were "prevented from making the desired progress in the work of the establishment of educational institutions for training of the ministers." A new handicap had come upon them. In spite of ecumenicity and organic union, the Methodist Episcopal Church, (North), and the Methodist Episcopal Church, South, had been proselytizing our preachers and members, offering them financial advantages to decoy them away from Zion. The financial problems, therefore, became serious. This had also slowed down any ideas of Methodist union, for the fathers felt that the distraction which they created among us, and sometimes ruptures in our churches, "which course no Christian body could sanction, in the light of the golden rule," could not produce a satisfactory result on behalf of our people. However, even barring this, it became necessary for us to support plans for

3. *Doctrines and Discipline,* 1840, pp. 152-154.
4. Moore, *History of the A.M.E. Zion Church,* p. 246.
5. *Ibid.,* p. 285; Hood, *One Hundred Years,* p. 85.

financing the onward going and development of our church. In their recommendations they therefore stated: "We must adopt a general practical financial system; such a system as will secure a general support of our connectional institutions." [6]

Facing this crucial demand, the 1872 General Conference made drastic efforts to improve the system, but maintained the scheme of annual conferences receiving the appropriations from local churches and making disbursements directly. The general claims concept was born in this General Conference. It was here that an annual assessment was levied upon each member for the support of our bishops, of not less than 25 cents or more than 50 cents per member annually, "to be collected by the preacher in charge and paid over to the Bishop who shall give credit for the same." They also stipulated that any member neglecting to pay such tax as the General Conference and Quarterly Conference impose, in order to meet the lawful demands of the societies, could be deprived of his or her membership. This law was flexible, in order to exempt the unfortunate and handicapped member. [7]

The General Conference of 1876 strengthened the laws regarding church property, fixed the salary and expenses of bishops from $1,200 to $1,500 per year, made provisions for appointments of committees in the annual conferences to apportion local churches for this support, and set annual salaries of preachers in charge of circuits and stations to be $700 plus parsonage, with definite arrangements for collecting this support from the local societies. [8]

The first concrete connectional plan of temporal economy was born in the General Conference of 1880. The first report submitted by the Committee on Financial System, read by Rev. Mark M. Bell, secretary, was rejected by the delegates; being strongly opposed by Revs. C. R. Harris and C. C. Pettey, who said that it was not in accord with the instructions given to the committee. On the eighteenth day of the General Conference, May 24, the committee on finance made its well-defined report, which was adopted. The General Conference then proceeded to make appropriations. [9] It provided for the following:

(1) Fifty cents per annum to remain the assessment of each member.

(2) Initiation of Annual Conference Stewards with full responsibility to put forth every effort in collecting the whole amount of general claims, with complete cooperation of each minister of the connection, in charge of a circuit or station, prior to the assembling of the annual conferences.

(3) Obligation of the presiding bishop to see that each minister faithfully perform the above described duty.

(4) Each annual conference to enforce the prescribed rules and regulations by which a preacher could neither willfully nor wrongfully neglect his responsibility to the connection of collecting claims and reporting same. Failure to submit reports promptly to the Annual Conference Steward, upon conviction, could result in suspension or location, as the conference shall determine.

(5) Election and duties of the annual conference Steward defined, with specific rules of keeping up with the collection of connectional funds through correspondence and contact, and reporting to the Episcopal District Steward immediately upon receiving financial reports; and to keep the presiding

6. Moore, *History*, pp. 285-287.
7. *Doctrines and Discipline*, 1872, p. 112.
8. *Doctrines and Discipline*, 1876, pp. 100-116.
9. *Minutes*, Sixteenth Quadrennial Session, *op. cit.*, pp. 33-34, 45.

bishop informed of failure or negligence of ministers to make proper remittances.

(6) Election by the General Conference, upon nomination of the bishop, of an Episcopal District Steward designated from the ranks of elders. His duties were to receive all annual conference funds and issue receipts for same; to pay the salary of the bishop of the district from funds received, and to forward the balance of these funds semi-annually to the General Steward, also to make a quarterly report to the General Steward of the amount received and expended and balance in hand.

(7) The Secretary of the General Conference to become the General Steward. His duties were defined: mainly to receive reports from Episcopal District Stewards for the support of connectional causes and institutions, and to meet with the Board of Bishops and render full reports of Episcopal District Stewards to them, and preserving strict records, correspondence and papers as the property of the General Conference. He was also commissioned to send each annual conference a report of the condition of the General Treasury and actions of the Board of Bishops, and make a full report of his transactions to the general conferences.

(8) Arrangements were made for an Executive Board constituted of the Board of Bishops. The duties of the Board were to see that the General Steward kept strict records, and to direct the funds collected by him and apply the same toward the support of Education, Book Concern, Foreign Missions, Home Missions, Literature, Retired preachers, and salaries of general officers.

It was directed that this report be printed in its entirety, in pamphlet form, and sent to each church through the pastor in charge.

By the guiding hand of Bishop J. W. Hood and Rev. C. R. Harris, the committee, who wrought faithfully to give Zion her first connectional planned budget was composed of Rev. George H. Washington, chairman, Revs. S. W. Jones, Joseph Sexton, A. Tasker, R. H. Simmons, A. Paxton, G. F. Smith, Z. T. Pearsall, E. W. Gibson, C. C. Pettey, Alfred Day, F. A. Hopkins, J. P. Hamer, M. L. Gale, J. F. Page, and C. Max Manning, secretary. [10] Reverend C. R. Harris, the secretary of the 1880 General Conference, principal and one of the first teachers of Zion Wesley Institute, subsequently Livingstone College, was a meticulous mathematician and highly competent bookkeeper. He became the first General Steward in 1880, with headquarters at Salisbury, N.C., and served with efficiency until his elevation to the bishopric in 1888. This was the beginning of effectively carrying through a connection wide budget.

The new system was by no means sufficient for a growing denomination. The General Conference of 1884 made a few improvements by dissolving the Executive Board and making the Board of Apportionment, which consisted of the Board of Bishops, the General Steward, and three of the annual conference stewards residing nearest to the meeting place of the semi-annual sessions of the Board. This was the time all reports were brought to summation. The bishops, who took the responsibility themselves of collecting the general funds on the field, turned over their money to the General Steward, and the apportionments were made during these semi-annual meetings, to the schools and colleges and departments. They were never, however, successful in raising the full assessment any one year during the existence of this system. The General Conference of 1884 was the first to make provisions for General Conference delegates' expenses by levying an assessment upon the local church through the annual conference held

10. *Ibid.*, pp. 67-70.

the year preceding the General Conference. [11]

Dr. Isom Caleb Clinton of Lancaster, S.C., was elected General Steward in 1888. The first salaries were stipulated for General officers; $600 for the General Steward and $300 for the General Secretary annually. He made an encouraging report of nearly $70,000 raised through annual conference stewards, together with the traveling expenses of the bishops, representing the total amount of general funds for the quadrennium in 1892. [12] He was elected bishop at this General Conference and Rev. J. W. Alstork of Montgomery, Alabama, was elected General Steward. The Children's Day had been established in the 1884 General Conference, to be observed the fourth Sabbath in June, in order to supplement the amount raised for Livingstone College. An attempt was also made at this General Confernce to observe Sunday-School Day, with special collections to be raised through the Sunday schools to support the Sunday School Department, but it did not succeed. [13]

In 1896, the Board of Bishops recommended that an additional 25 cents for education purposes and 25 cents for church extension and missionary causes be levied upon each member of the connection, with specified appropriations for bishops' and general officers' salaries and departments, and Rev. Eli George Biddle made extensive proposals along these same lines. [14] All of these proposals were weighed, and the General Conference made impressive changes. They divided the Children's Day Fund to support five schools by episcopal districts. For the first time, assessments were levied upon the nine episcopal districts, aggregating $37,500 annually. If the 50 cents *per member* proved insufficient to furnish this amount, the Discipline provided for special collections to make up the deficiency. This was the beginning of the designation of connectional days in which these offerings were annually raised. [15]

In 1900, Rev. John W. Alstork was elected bishop and Rev. Josiah S. Caldwell was elected General Steward, and the name was changed here to Financial Department with headquarters at Philadelphia, Pa. The General Conference added 30 cents per member to the general claims and called it special assessment for support of our benevolent institutions. [16]

In 1904 the name of the officer was changed from General Steward to Financial Secretary. [17] Reverend Josiah S. Caldwell was elected bishop and Rev. Martin R. Franklin was elected Financial Secretary maintaining the office at Philadelphia. At this time was appointed a Board of Connectional Trustees, the duty of which was to control and administer the property owned by the general church, which board was duly incorporated at Washington, D.C. The special assessment for benevolent causes was changed from 30 cents to 50 cents per member, which made the total assessment one dollar general claims. [18]

In 1908, Rev. M. R. Franklin was elevated to the bishopric, and Rev. John Simpson Jackson was elected Financial Secretary. He was from Birmingham, Ala.,

11. *Minutes,* Seventeenth Quadrennial Session, pp. 145-147.
12. *Minutes,* Nineteenth Quadrennial Session, pp. 67-68; *Doctrines and Discipline,* 1888, p. 112.
13. *Doctrines and Discipline,* 1892, p. 45.
14. *Minutes,* Twentieth Quadrennial Session, pp. 114-115, 245-247.
15. *Doctrines and Discipline,* 1896, pp. 45, 108.
16. *Doctrines and Discipline,* 1900, p. 185.
17. *Minutes,* Twenty-Second Quadrennial Session, p. 406.
18. *Doctrines and Discipline,* 1904, pp. 367-378. 348-349.

where the office was then moved. He was also re-elected at the General Conference of 1912. Here the general claims were specifically set at one dollar per member annually, the term *general fund* was changed to *general claims* and the funds were partly centralized. The church suffered its first major setback during this quadrennium. The budget fell short about $20,000 the second year of the quadrennium due to short crops made by the inroads of the boll weevil and a general financial depression. The third year of the quadrennium (December 1915) through mismanagement by the Financial Secretary, the budget fell short about $15,000. He loaned out funds promiscuously, and placed $9,000 of the funds in the Alabama Penny Prudential Savings Bank without authority, and the bank suspended. [19] He was tried by a competent committee for these illegal deeds, and removed from office. The Board of Bishops confirmed this at their January meeting in 1916 at Montgomery, Alabama, and placed John C. Dancy, Sr. in charge of the department until the General Conference of 1916.

The General Conference of 1916 elected Dr. William Harvey Goler, who had served Livingstone College as its second president, the Financial Secretary. The office had been moved to the headquarters building at 420 South 11th Street, Philadelphia, by Dr. Dancy, and Dr. Goler operated, according to a directive of the denomination, from this office. He skillfully supervised this department through some very crucial years, from World War I through the Depression until 1932. The Board of Finance was instituted in 1916, to have supervision over the finance department in the interim of the General Conference. [20]

In 1924 the most progressive connectional budget legislation since 1880 went into effect. The participants in thrusting forward "The Budget System," were Bishops L. W. Kyles and P. A. Wallace, and Revs. P. R. Flack, E. M. Argyle, J. S. Campbell, James E. Mason, W. W. Blair, A. C. Yearwood, G. F. Hall, H. T. Medford, F. D. Douglass, W. C. Brown, and G. W. Brown. [21] The practice of bishops collecting funds on the field and giving receipts was discontinued, and the funds henceforth were sent directly to the Financial Secretary. The annual assessment per member was doubled to $2, and the general claims apportionment totalled $220,000, equally divided between general claims and benevolent causes. The Finance Department was made the clearing house for all the departments of the church, and provision was made for raising extra funds for support of annual conferences, and for committees within the annual conferences to collect and disburse funds according to the Discipline. [22]

The church's economy, like practically all organizations in the nation, suffered during the Depression years. After the General Conference of 1932, Zion began to rebuild her economic program. The Board of Bishops in their Quadrennial Address commended Dr. Goler for the splendid way he handled the finances of the church during the crisis, and the Finance Board for its faithful services. It was observed that Dr. Goler, as secretary and custodian, many times came to the rescue of the church with his own money and credit to meet payments of the budget. [23] The General Conference reverted back to the $1.00 per member general claims annually. Dr. E. L. Madison, a skillful financier, was elected Financial Secretary at this General Conference administering the office

19. *Minutes,* Twenty-Fourth Quadrennial Session, p. 525; Twenty-Fifth, pp. 32, 33.
20. *Doctrines and Discipline,* 1916, pp. 177-180.
21. *Minutes,* Twenty-Seventh Quadrennial Session, pp. 55-57, 85, 89, 96.
22. *Ibid., Doctrines and Discipline,* 1924, pp. 171-189.
23. *Minutes,* Twenty-Ninth Quadrennial Session, p. 91.

from Pittsburgh, Pa. He served until 1936 when he was elected bishop. Reverend J. W. Younge was then elected Financial Secretary and operated the office trustfully from the A.M.E. Zion headquarters in Charlotte, N.C. This has been the headquarters of this department ever since. He passed away in 1939. The Board of Bishops, in their semi-annual meeting January 1940, authorized the Board of Finance to organize for the purpose of carrying on the routine work of the department until the May General Conference. Bishop L. W. Kyles, the chairman, and members of the board, Mr. Oscar W. Adams, Sr., Revs. W. J. J. Byers, E. S. Hardge, C. J. Henderson, L. P. Powell, H. B. Shaw, B. C. Robeson, W. A. Stewart, and F. A. Osam-Pinanko diligently steered the operation of this department until the General Conference, at which time Rev. W. W. Slade, a reliable entrepreneur, was elected Financial Secretary. [24]

In 1944 Rev. W. W. Slade was elected bishop and Rev. George Frederick Hall, unremitting administrator, was elected Financial Secretary. Dr. Hall was re-elected at the General Conference in 1948. This General Conference revised the law regarding duties of members, deleting the $1 per member obligation. The new rule emphasized that every member should pay an annual amount commensurate to the general claims apportionment for the support of the connection. [25] Dr. Hall expired a few months prior to the 1952 General Conference, and the Board of Bishops authorized the chairman of the Board of Finance, Bishop W. W. Slade, to complete the work of the department. Ably assisted by the following members of this board, Revs. M. C. Williams, H. R. Jackson, Elias S. Hardge, Sr., W. A. Cooper G. W. Beard, C. C. Coleman, W. O. Carson, S.P. Perry, Executive Secretary, Ford G. Ratcliffe, J. E. McCall, E. M. Graham, Mr. H. T. Fonville, and the office staff member, Mrs. Madie Simpson, the activities of the quadrennium during the administration of Dr. Hall were brought successfully to a close. [26]

In 1952, Richard Wadsworth Sherrill was elected Financial Secretary the first time in the history of the church a laymen was elected by the General Conference to fill this most trustful office. This is a tribute to his great integrity. He is the son of noble parents of Rowan County, North Carolina, James and Rosa Sherrill, and the son-in-law of Dr. Joseph Charles Price. He has been re-elected to this office in each succeeding General Conference for the past 20 years. The Finance Department operated with minimal change in its structure until 1964.

The Budget and Apportionment Committee of the 1964 General Conference presented to the delegates a new Budget plan. It was composed of the following members:

Rev. M. C. Williams, chairman, Rev. E. Franklin Jackson, secretary, Revs: George J. Leake, J. E. Spruill, S. P. Spottswood, R. A. Councill, L. R. Rogers, J. W. Wactor, O. D. Carson, C. R. Thompson, George A. Brooks; Margaret J. May, M. Ardelle Shaw, Elizabeth Davis, Carrie Spaulding, Abbie C. Jackson, Mrs. E. B. Patton, Mattie D. Eagan, Eugene Williams, Chief Brown Nyenfuah, Marvin Mobley, and Richard Gray.

The delegates ratified the plan, which included an entire restructuring of the budget program of the denomination, with a stipulated apportionment of $1,250,000. All funds raised through the annual conferences were centralized and channelled through the Connectional Budget Department, with the various annual

---

24. *Minutes,* Thirty-First Quadrennial Session, pp. 72, 173.
25. *Doctrines and Discipline,* 1948, p. 165.
26. *Ibid.,* pp. 366-367; *Minutes,* Thirty-Fourth Quadrennial Session, pp. 155-163.

conferences requisitioning headquarters or specific departments for the projects of missions and social services they were sponsoring, and for support of the annual conferences. Stringent rules were enforced that local churches or ministers were not to receive assessments from any authority for any additional purposes, except in case of emergency. It provided for a Connectional Budget Board of 25 members; 3 bishops, an executive committee of 12 members, one from each episcopal district, and members at large representing each episcopal district. The first officers of the Connectional Budget Board were Bishop S. G. Spottswood, chairman, Bishops H. B. Shaw and R. L. Jones, vice-chairmen, Rev. E. Franklin Jackson, secretary. These served until the General Conference of 1972, with Mr. R. W. Sherrill continuing as financial secretary. The General Conference, which has the sole power to assess the denomination, increased the budget to $1,450,000 plus an additional $200,000 for education supplement, at the 1972 General Conference, in order to keep abreast with the times, its program of supporting education, missions, benevolent, and other causes. The same general rules, however, which were passed by the 1964 General Conference, of projecting the connectional budget program, are still in effect.[27]

27. *Doctrines and Discipline,* 1968, pp. 114-130.

CHAPTER 21

EDUCATION—CHURCH PROGRAMMING

Jesus Christ gave the command to his disciples to Go . . . Teach, and this He made commensurate with Go . . . preach. The door for teaching anything is opened in childhood, St. John Chrysostom once declared that "the corruption of the world remains unchecked because nobody guards his children, nobody speaks to them of chastity, of despising riches and glory, of the commandments of God." He urged "parents to regard the education of their children as the highest and holiest of tasks and to provide them with the true riches of the soul rather than with worldly wealth." [1]

Chrysostom said this on the very outer edge of pagan society. Even now in this so-called Christian era, the same laxity and weakness are threatening the social salvation and welfare progress of mankind.

From its beginnings the African Methodist Episcopal Zion Church has stressed training through the church process by emphasizing the preparation of its children and leaders, and implementing it to the greatest possible degree. Our founding fathers had the concept during the days of destitution, and were perceptive in issuing their first mandate, based upon the Pauline doctrine that the leader should be "apt to teach." It is as follows:

Of the Instruction of Children:

1. In order to benefit the rising generation, let him who is zealous for God and the souls of men begin now, and where there are ten children whose parents are in society, meet them an hour once a week; but where this is impracticable, meet them once in two weeks.

2. Procure the Methodist instructions for them, and let all who can, read and commit them to memory.

3. Explain and impress them upon their hearts; and talk with them every time you see them at home.

4. Pray earnestly for them; and diligently instruct and exhort all parents at their own houses.

5. Let the elders, deacons and preachers take a list of the names of the children; and if any of them be truly awakened let them be admitted into society.

6. Let the preachers preach expressly on education. [2]

To be certain that this branch of the church work was fully projected, the pastors were placed under obligation to report the progress of Sabbath schools annually. The earliest annual conference records included the number of Sunday schools, teachers, scholars and libraries in local churches, and the number of

---

1. Johannes Quasten, *Patrology,* Vol. III, pp. 465-466.
2. *Doctrines and Discipline,* 1820, pp. 69-70.

Sunday school scholars were kept separate and distinct from the general membership, so that toward the close of the nineteenth century, the General Statistical Secretary reported 497,845 members and an additional 124,227 Sunday school scholars.[3]

Before the spread of the church South, and the birth of the Education Department in the church, there was a cooperative effort in the six northern conferences on the education or training of their ministry and people. To have reasonable assurance that the preacher was suitably equipped for his task, the conferences early adopted courses of studies for graduates to holy orders. For deacons' orders, the courses included grammar, arithmetic, geography, rules and doctrines of Discipline, scripture doctrine, historical events of scripture, isms, Baptism, and sacrament or the Lord's Supper. For elders' orders; a review of the previous studies, theology, church government, ancient and modern history and rhetoric were the prescribed courses of study. Textbooks were recommended in pursuing these studies. [4]

As early as 1858, the Genesee (Western New York) Conference resolved that it would not recommend any person for holy orders who had "not a sufficient knowledge of the English language to speak with tolerable accuracy, and whose knowledge of Theology does not enable him to distinguish between Arminianism, Calvinism and Universalism." [5] At the organization of the British North American Mission Annual Conference in 1857, these same general rules applied. [6] The bishops, beginning with Varick, and the men who served on the committees on education, both in the general and annual conferences, had been trained under adverse circumstances, and were potent in their ability to foster tremendous character-building and scholastic advancement in the church. The committees on education and Sabbath schools of the general conferences continued to improve standards proportionate to the needs following the general archetype of the American Sunday School Union which had been formed in 1824.

The Sunday School Department

After the International Sunday School Convention was organized in 1869, the General Conference of 1872 approved the organization of The Sunday School Union of the A.M.E. Zion Church, and the Constitution inclusive of preamble and ten articles, was published in the Discipline. It was also decided by this General Conference to publish the four-year course of study to be pursued by candidates for the ministry. [7]

In 1873, the International Uniform Lessons were made official for Sunday school use by the International Sunday School Convention, and the General Conference of 1880 through its committee on Sunday schools, reconstructed the Constitution of the Sunday School Union, making multiple improvements, and voted to endorse the "International Series" of lessons. [8] The officers of local Sunday schools were to consist of the minister in charge who was required to be present and nurture the superintendent, secretary, assistant secretary, treasurer

3. Moore, *History;* Anderson, "Progress of the Fourth Quarter of the A.M.E. Zion Church," *A.M.E. Zion Quarterly Review,* October 1898, pp. 7-8.
4. *Minutes* of the New York and New England Annual Conferences, 1857, p. 45.
5. *Minutes,* Genesee Annual Conference, 1858, p. 15.
6. *Minutes,* British North America Mission Conference, 1857, p. 6.
7. *Doctrines and Discipline,* 1872, pp. 218-226.
8. *Minutes,* Sixteenth Quadrennial Session, pp. 74-77.

and librarian, and each officer's duty was carefully outlined. Rules for the schools were set forth, and the basic lessons were "to consist of Scriptural instruction, pursued on some given plan adapted to the scholars minds, and the Catechism of the A.M.E. Zion Church." This action was stimulated by Rev. Mark M. Bell's resolution, which was unanimously adopted, that the revision committee report on an article to be placed in the Discipline, "defining the relation of baptized children to our Church, and also for their religious instruction and training." Sunday school conventions were being held by annual conferences; and annual proceedings of Sunday school conventions were being published as early as 1880. [9]

Dr. Robert Russell Morris, a studious minister of the gospel (See Chapter 23), was elected the first General Superintendent of Sunday Schools, and editor of the Sunday School Literature, by the Board of Bishops in its meeting at Asheville, N.C., September 1888, and Rev. Titus A. Weathington at the same time was elected first Financial Secretary of the Sunday School Department. These officers went on to project the Sunday school work of the A.M.E. Zion Church with prolific results.

The following resolution passed the General Conference of 1888:

On Sunday School Conventions:

Whereas, The need of stirring Sunday School work is indispensable in these years of grace, both for the moral and spiritual advancement of Christ's Church: and,

Whereas, The real necessity of Quarterly and Annual Conferences gives evidences of the effectual operation of organic motive power for the uniform prosperity of the great work of evangelization.

Resolved, That be it now enacted by the General Conference, that in each Annual Conference District there shall be held annually a State Sunday School Convention of that Conference District, place and date of meeting to be fixed first, by said Annual Conference; and others by the preceding Convention.

That all ministers of the Conference District, Superintendents of schools, and one delegate for every fifty scholars or fractional part, shall be the constituted members of the Convention.

That every pastor, holding a charge, shall give his special presence to Sunday School work; and failing to attend the State Sunday School Convention shall give satisfactory reasons—as would be legal for absence from Annual Conference—or in default shall be dealt with for "gross neglect of duty." The true hope of our Church is in the care of the children.

J. B. Small

R. H. G. Dixon

W. H. Day [10]

Dr. R. R. Morris served until his death in 1895, and Rev. Dr. Robert Blair Bruce filled out his unexpired term until the 1896 General Conference. When the headquarters were moved from Montgomery, Ala., to the newly purchased Publishing House in 1894, Rev. A. T. Weathington, the Financial Secretary, did not move. The Board of Bishops directed that both officers of the Sunday School Department move to Charlotte.

In 1896, the Constitution for Sabbath Schools of the A.M.E. Zion Church was revised. The Sabbath School Union was placed under the direct management of the Board of Publication, with the General superintendent of the Union to be

9. Ibid., p. 39, *Minutes,* Eighteenth Quadrennial Session, p. 106.
10. *Minutes,* Eighteenth Quadrennial Session, p. 106.

REV. RICHARD HAYWOOD STITT

REV. ROBERT RUSSELL MORRIS

First Secretary of the Varick Christian
First Editor of Sunday School Literature   Endeavor Society

elected by the General Conference. It intensified the Sunday school program of the annual conferences and local churches, and provided for Sunday school conventions and normal institutes within the districts. Easter Sunday was made a special day for Sunday school programs throughout the church, to be promoted by the general superintendent, and the collections arising from these special services to be sent to the general superintendent of the Sunday School Department for promoting the program on the annual conference, district conference, and local level. (11)

The provision of the office of General Superintendent had not been utilized until 1916. The editor of the Sunday school literature, Rev. R. B. Bruce, 1896 to 1916; propelled the Sunday school program of the denomination during these years, in the heightening and effectual distribution of the Sunday school literature, along with the unified connectional activity through annual conferences and presiding elders' districts. The office was revived in 1916 when Professor James W. Eichelberger was elected General Superintendent of the Sunday Schools while serving as principal of Walters Institute. The program of the Sunday School Department was greatly enhanced and departmentalized more thoroughly. The headquarters subsequently moved to Chicago, and Mr. Eichelberger was re-elected Superintendent in 1920, serving in this capacity until the coming of the Christian Education Department in 1924; he was then elected Corresponding Secretary of the Christian Education Department.

The Education Department

At the General Conference of 1892, considerable time was spent in discussion and debate, after which two significant laws became effective for the advancement of religious education. The first recommendation passed by the General Conference was submitted by the Board of Bishops as follows:

For insertion in our Book of Discipline, Paragraph 38:–*"On The Sunday-Schools and Instruction of Children,"*–

1. It shall be the duty of every pastor in charge of a circuit or station to organize the local and itinerant preachers and the exhorters residing in his charge into a Preachers' Institute.

11. *Doctrines and Discipline,* 1896, pp. 206-210.

MR. SIMON GREEN ATKINS

First Secretary of Education

MR. JAMES WILLIAM EICHELBERGER

First Secretary of the combined Christian Education Department.

2. The object of the Institute shall be: (1) To cultivate Christian fellowship and helpfulness between its members. (2) To aid its members in gaining such knowledge as shall be of use to them in the discharge of the duties required of them by the Discipline of the Church. (3) To pursue a course of instruction or reading for the purpose of cultivating their moral, spiritual, and intellectual powers.

3. One night in every week shall be set apart in every charge, when the exhorters and local preachers shall conduct services in succession, under the supervision of the pastor, who shall privately give them such friendly criticism and instruction as may be of benefit to those officiating in said services.

4. A report on the condition of the Preachers' Institute shall be submitted by the pastor at each Quarterly Conference. (12)

The second recommendation, to establish an education department had been conceived by the Board of Bishops in its meeting March 6, 1892 at Wilmington N.C. It was drafted and presented to the General Conference by the Committee on Education. "Professor Atkins read with great force and animation the report of the Committee on Education. Bishop Hood moved that the report be adopted. The motion was seconded by Rev. J. S. Caldwell. After discussion, Bishop Hood amended his motion to read, 'that the report be adopted by sections,' and the motion thus amended prevailed."

Speeches were made by the following, for the most part favoring the new department: Revs. J. T. Williams, Jehu Holliday, John P. Thompson, J. C. Price, W. H. Goler, R. H. Simmons, Honorable J. C. Dancy, and Rev. T. A. Weathington. "Dr. Price thought that if we could get this Board of Education organized, it would help not only Livingstone College, but all our institutions of learning." Professor Atkins read the first part of the report recommending the existing appropiation and $1,000 additional, which was adopted. The second part of the report was then read:

12. *Minutes,* Nineteenth Quadrennial Session, pp. 40-41; *Doctrines and Discipline,* 1896, pp. 38-39.

In order that our entire field of educational work may be encouraged, especially that our various institutions in our episcopal and conference districts may be fostered in their noble efforts to honor the connection, and far and wide raise the standard of intelligence in Zion, we recommend that a department of education be, and is hereby created by the General Conference; that the scope of its operations shall include the working up and development of the Children's Day, the raising of funds for educational purposes everywhere, and in every way possible, as well as representing the Church in everything that pertains to the work of education, not in conflict with the legitimate and peculiar functions of the Board of Trustees and Faculty of Livingstone College. [13]

Four other sections of the report with an amendment passed the body, and the Constitution of the Education Department was drawn up and placed in the Discipline. Its chief officer was the General Secretary of Education, and it provided for an executive board composed of one member from each episcopal district, which had power to locate headquarters with the consent of the secretary and approval of the bishops who were managers of the department. The functions of the General Secretary of Education were defined as follows:

> The General Secretary of Education shall report at each meeting of the Board, and shall receive a salary of not less than $800 per annum, to be taken from the Children's Day Fund (*provided,* that the Children's Day Fund be reimbursed to the amount of his salary from funds collected by him), and traveling expenses (*provided,* that such traveling expenses shall be raised by himself). *Provided,* further, that when not in conflict with some special arrangement of pastors and congregation all the churches in our connection shall be open to his appeals in the aid of this cause in any way. [14]

Bishop C. C. Pettey was elected first chairman of the Board of Education.

While the innovation was definitely a stimulus to the schools and colleges, the Education Department, directed by its first elected General Secretary, Dr. Simon Green Atkins of Winston-Salem, N.C., also quickened the education program in the local churches, and by his inspirational projection gave a rebirth to Christian education in the A.M.E. Zion Church. He was "a man of deep, pure consciousness, keen scholarship, eloquent and exhaustive in speech, constructive and economic in educational spheres," [15] Atkins was the most aggressive stimulator for education in the church after J. C. Price. He was a major force on the faculty with Dr. Price at Livingstone College. After one quadrennium of service in this department, he was again elected in 1904 and served until 1916, a total of 20 years.

The General Conference of 1896 elected Benjamin Franklin Wheeler of Mobile, Alabama, whose propensity for education was conspicuous. He was re-elected in 1900 and served until 1904. Wheeler, already engaged as principal of the Zion Institute in Mobile, and in creative writings for the church, was succeeded in this office by his predecessor, Dr. Atkins. In 1916, Rev. John William Martin of Atkinson College, Madisonville Ky.; "a scholar of marked ability," was elected. [16] He filled this post with efficiency and inaugurated some expansion in the schools until 1924 when he was elected bishop. Professor J. W. Younge of Greenville, Tenn., was then elected and served with continued effectiveness until 1932. The Department of Education was then merged into the Christian Education Department.

---

13. *Minutes,* Nineteenth Quadrennial Session, pp. 71-75.
14. *Doctrines and Discipline,* 1892, pp. 215-216.
15. J. Harvey Anderson, *Biographical Souvenir Volume of the Twenty-Third Quadrennial Session of the General Conference of the African Methodist Episcopal Zion Church,* p.2
16. *Ibid.,* p. 58.

The Varick Christian Endeavor Society

The Christian Endeavor Society was established in 1881 by Rev. Francis E. Clark of Portland, Me. It is a promotional and devotional movement for youth that spread throughout the Congregational churches and several other denominations throughout the world. The A.M.E. Zion Church adopted it because of its freedom, inspirational expressions, and development of young people. Overall, the great influence and example of Father and Mother Clark was shed over the youth of the country and around the world.

Through the efforts of Rev. Richard Haywood Stitt, provision of a uniform organization for the young people, through Christian Endeavor, was made. In 1893, while pastoring the Fleet Memorial (First Church), Brooklyn, he organized a young people's society of Christian Endeavor with 85 members. He represented the A.M.E. Zion Church in the first and organizational International Convention of Christian Endeavor Societies at Montreal in 1893, serving on an important committee which issued a circular to the Methodist churches of the world.[17] While there, he nominated Bishop Alexander Walters to be placed on the Board of Trustees of the International Christian Endeavor Society, on which this Bishop continued as a member until his death. Bishop Walters was a powerful element in the development of Christian Endeavor of the country and the world. He was one of the speakers on the main program in Alexandra Palace when the International Christian Endeavor Society assembled in London; and Father Clark leaned much on him for support and helpful leadership. Reverend Stitt became the strongest advocate of organizing a Christian Endeavor Society denominationally, while pastoring Big Wesley Church, Philadelphia. In the course of his plans for submission to the General Conference, he died at Philadelphia, March 15, 1896. The Board of Bishops recommended ". . .The Christian Endeavor Society to your consideration, and also recommend a distinct organization of our own to be known as the 'Varick Alliance.' " The General Conference adopted the recommendation, thus founding the Varick Christian Endeavor Society.[18]

Reverend Jesse Beauregard Colbert of St. Louis, Mo., was elected, and the undeveloped work was taken up by him and pushed on successfully. The V.C.E. movement was unique and became a very essential part of the Christian education system. [19] Reverend Colbert built up and strengthened the organization by working vehemently. He carried a weekly column in the *Star of Zion* to help build societies in local churches, while Reverend J. S. Caldwell, editor of the *Varick Christian Endeavorer,* publicized the infant organization through this medium. Bishop Walters in a written message to the "Endeavorers" stated:

Above all things we must develop our young people. Strict attention must be held for their education. Our bishops can aid in the work by insisting that a local V.C.E. Society be organized in each church. The Presiding Elder can help by seeing that the orders of the bishops are enforced and the pastors in their turn can assist by the appointment of capable young men and women to take charge and successfully operate the societies. All the members . . . can assist by contributing to the cause. "Let us all to the work." [20]

The Society first emphasizes loyalty on the part of the individual members. Then it emphasizes loyalty to the church; the local church and the denomination,

17. Hood, *One Hundred Years,* p. 422.
18. *Minutes,* Twentieth Quadrennial Session, pp. 115, 241, 253.
19. Jesse B. Colbert (Ed.), *History of the Varick Christian Endeavor Society,* p. 21.
20. *Ibid.,* p. 31

and above all, loyalty to Jesus Christ. There were three recognized plans in the Varick Christian Endeavor Society. The *Three-Society Plan,* recommended for churches with less than 250 members, included a Junior Society, ages 9-11 years; an Intermediate-Senior Society, 12-17 years; and the Young People's Society, 18-23 years. The *Five-Society Plan* and the *Seven-Society Plan* were recommended for larger memberships, additional societies with flexibility in age groups and inclusive of older people. [21]

After eight years of service, Rev. Colbert was succeeded in the position at the General Conference of 1904, by Rev. John T. McMillan, also a pioneer in the V.C.E. movement. He served as presiding elder of the Tuskegee District in the Alabama Conference, and manifested an abiding interest in the youth of the church. Reverend McMillan also served eight years, and an earnest layman, Aaron Brown, Sr., of Pensacola, Fla., was elected in 1912. Mr. Brown was a United States Customs Inspector, and the efficient secretary of the Florida Conference. Besides being a sagacious officer, he was noted as a good speaker and first class clerical scribe. [22]

Mr. Brown was re-elected at successive general conferences and served in this office 20 years. His cogitative individuality made him a progressive administrator of this promotional and devotional work of our young people. Under him the story of the Varick Christian Endeavor Society reached its highest point. In the correlation of the Christian Education movement in 1924, the Varick Christian Endeavor Society became a separate and distinct part of the Christian Education Department, and Dr. Brown continued to serve as General Secretary of the V.C.E. The *Varick Christian Endeavorer* and the *Sunday School Journal* were combined and Dr. Brown and Dr. Eichelberger became joint editors of this journal, *The Church School Herald.* [23] After considerable discussion and debate, the General Conference of 1932 merged the V.C.E. with the total Christian Education Department under one general officer. [24] Dr. Brown was thus left without a general office. His heart was in the work of youth until the end. He passed away during the quadrennium.

The Christian Education Department

During the interval of the death of the first Superintendent of Sunday Schools, Rev. R. R. Morris, in 1895, and the election of Professor J. W. Eichelberger, Jr., in 1916, the church did not fill the position of General Sunday School Superintendent as provided in the Constitution, and thereby caused lethargy in connectional unity in the enterprise of the Sunday School Department. The Sunday school movement was left entirely in the hands of the editors of the Sunday school literature for the scanty promotion it had. The A.M.E. Zion Church, however, had leaders and members aflame for prompting a first class Sunday school program in the church. Our church had been ably represented in the international Sunday school meetings as early as 1889, when Rev. Alexander Walters attended the first World's Sunday School Convention at London. He was appointed by the Board of Bishops to represent the A.M.E. Zion Church at this meeting, and also elected as one of the delgates of the Sunday School Union of the State of New York, during his first year's pastorate at Mother Zion Church. [25]

21. W. H. Davenport, *Membership in Zion Methodism,* pp. 86-87.
22. Anderson, *Biographical Souvenir,* pp. 24, 56.
23. *Minutes,* Twenty-Eighth Quadrennial Session, pp. 217, 223.
24. *Minutes,* Twenty-Ninth Quadrennial Session, pp. 61,75,78.
25. Walters, *My Life and Work,* p. 56.

Bishop George Wylie Clinton was elected "Vice President for the Negroes" at the International Sunday School Convention at Louisville, Ky. in 1908, and also elected one of the three on the official register for blacks at the San Francisco Convention in 1911. "He was one of the seventy-five leaders, white and black, invited who attended the Clifton Conference in 1908, which recommended the change in program and policy of the International Sunday School Association with reference to its Negro work." There were five delegates of the A.M.E. Zion Church present among the 74 black delegates who attended the International Sunday School Convention at Toronto, in 1905: Dr J. S. Jackson of Birmingham; Miss Emma E. Andrews of Williamston, N.C.; Miss Nettie C. Crockette and J. S. Stanback of Chester, S.C.; and James W. Eichelberger, Jr., of Columbia, S.C. Since this time, the delegates and members attended each subsequent International Sunday School Convention in increasing numbers. [26]

While the church was adequately represented in these early national and international Sunday school bodies, it was in desperate need of an improved program throughout the denomination. James W. Eichelberger, Jr. and the writer manifested grave concern while they were students at Livingstone College. After Mr. Eichelberger's graduation in 1904, he went to Rock Hill, S.C. to teach at Clinton Junior College, and in 1905, after attending the Toronto meeting, returned with the idea of holding a Sunday school convention. He and the other delegates from South Carolina who attended the meeting planned a Convention at Rock Hill, S.C. Reverend W. J. Walls, who made the principal address, and a few other friends of North and South Carolina constituted the first supporters of this convention, held in the fall of 1905 at Mount Zion Church, Rock Hill. Prime supporters were Bishop George W. Clinton, Presiding Elders W. M. Robinson, F. Killingsworth and M. Ingram, Eichelberger's father and stepmother, Rev. and Mrs. James W. Eichelberger, Sr., and several other ministers and concerned Sunday school superintendents. This was the rivival of annual state conventions and new impulse into the Sunday school movement.

The day had arrived when Christian education demanded a new emphasis and greater promotion. This was the same era when the philosophy of John Dewey, a disciple of Hegel, the early nineteenth century German philosopher, was sweeping America and exercising great influence upon educators and the entire education system in the country. He did not deal with religion in his education system, and stated that he found no place for it in his program. Dewey was the acknowledged great educator of the country and was then reigning in this field. The religious people became challenged by his thin religious assertions.

Mr. Eichelberger and Rev. Walls began to work incessantly for an improved religious education program. Mr. Eichelberger wrote articles and editorialized in the paper then operated by the Sunday School Department, *The Sunday School Headlight*. Reverend Walls wrote a series of articles to *The Star of Zion* in the interest of this cause and circulated a pamphlet entitled *What Youth Wants*. They aroused dissatisfaction and fomented sentiment to produce the necessary changes and greater projection of the religious education movement. In 1913, Mr. Eichelberger attended the World's Sunday School Convention at Zurich, Switzerland, where he became enthusiastically involved in the religious education program upon returning home. He and a number of other leaders then requested the Board of Bishops to appoint a Sunday School Commission to study the program of the A.M.E. Zion Church and its needs. A study commission of twelve was appointed. This commission recommended to the Board of Bishops, meeting

26. *Minutes,* Thirty-Third Quadrennial Session, p. 197.

at New Bern, N.C., in 1914 that a General Sunday School and Varick Christian Endeavor Convention be convened. By this time, each annual conference was holding an annual Sunday School convention.

The recommendation was approved, and the First General Sunday School and Varick Christian Endeavor Convention was held in connection with the General Convention of the Woman's Home and Foreign Missionary Society at Washington Memorial Church, St. Louis, August 5-10, 1915. At the General Conference of 1916, Professor Eichelberger made his first report on behalf of the commission, which was referred to the Sunday School Commission. Progress was clear as one Sunday school office became two, and Mr. Eichelberger was elected General Superintendent of Sunday Schools and Dr. J. Francis Lee elected Editor of the Sunday School Literature. In addition to this a Sunday School Board was appointed. [27]

A Second General Sunday School and Varick Christian Endeavor Convention was held in Atlantic City, N.J., Price Memorial Church, August 2-6, 1919, after the Connectional Council. In order to augment these conventions throughout the connection, the General Conference at Knoxville, Tenn., passed legislation giving the Sunday School Board the power to convoke a General Sunday School Convention. The First General Convention under the auspices of the Sunday School Board was held at Hopkins Chapel, Asheville, N.C. in 1922. Another Sunday School Convention was held at St. Paul Church, Cleveland, August 1-5, 1923, entertained by Rev. Ether D. W. Bell. The Cleveland meeting was held to finalize plans for continuing General Conventions quadrennially. Staff leaders associating Mr. Eichelberger in these first conventions were Dr. Jacob W. Powell, Malden, Mass., superintendent of Teacher Training; Miss Sarah J. Janifer, superintendent of Elementary Division; Professor J. W. Myers of St. Louis and Mr. W. J. Trent, Sr., of Atlanta, superintendents of Young People's Division; Mr. Daniel J. Hughlett, Louisville, Ky., superintendent of Adult Division; Miss Mary A. Lynch of Salisbury, N.C., superintendent of Temperance and Purity; and Mrs. John C. Taylor of Pittsburgh, superintendent of Missionary Education. Frank A. Ray of Brooklyn, N.Y., and J. Henry Warren of Charlotte, N.C. served as General Sunday School Convention presidents.

In projecting Christian Education on a broad scale, Bishop G. W. Clinton, in addition to his leadership in the International Sunday-School movement, was lecturer at Tuskegee Institute 26 consecutive years until his death in 1921. He served as president of the Young Peoples' Negro Congress, evinced deep interest in this movement, and dynamically supported it. The bishops of the church and members of the commission observed with serious concern the change that took place in 1922 in the Sunday school movement of the world. It was generally conceded that the church must move in progression with the program, after the dramatic merger of the International Sunday School Association and the Sunday School Council of Evangelical denominations, which new organization became known as The International Council of Religious Education. The movement had been closely supervised and carefully studied, and the new day of Christian education in the A.M.E. Zion Church took place at the General Conference of 1924, in Indianapolis. The bishops led in influencing the legislation by making a lengthy discourse on the subject in their address, a part of which follows:

... The Church has delegated its sacred obligation of teaching to several

---

27. *Minutes,* Twenty-Fifth Quadrennial Session, p. 25; Ms. records, Christian Education Department.

unrelated organizations with fragmentary, incomplete programs, duplications and confusion of aims, functions and activites. The Church as a teacher has seriously failed in developing even among its members a clear conception of the meaning of Christianity for human life. The child must be placed in the midst. A comprehensive program from the capacities, needs and interests of the pupil must be formulated and executed. In other words the need of the pupil should be the law of the school. The Church should correlate all of its educational agencies for the sake of economy; of unity of aims, function, and activity, of educational efficiency: and of the pupil and the kingdom.

For a long time educational theory has insisted upon the unification of the religious education program as offered in the Sunday School, Christian Endeavor and Missionary Societies. The fact that the International Lesson Committee has a sub-committee at work now relating all the elements of the entire program of religious education, carries the matter beyond the pale of theory. The Correlation conferences held under the auspices of the Federal Council of Churches at Garden City, L.I., in 1923 was attended by executives of religious education departments of more than thirty denominations and a score of interdenominational and extra church organizations to form a correlation program. Six of the largest denominations have correlated, or are in the process of correlating their religious education organizations. These significant actions confirm us in the opinion that within the next quadrennium correlation will be forced upon us whether we elect it or not.

Correlation as here used means that the departments concerned will formulate definite aims to the several stages of child development for the church's education program; that the leadership courses, lesson courses, activities and other means be selected in consonance with that aim; that the functions be divided between the Sunday School, Varick Christian Endeavor, and any other agencies that overlapping may be reduced to the minimum; that the officers in charge of the respective departments be empowered to inquire into the work of both organizations and advise the officiary in each in whatever territory they are visiting. [28]

Mr. Eichelberger, the General Superintendent of Sunday Schools, in making his quadrennial report, took time to present the entire new program and its different facets, and wholeheartedly recommended its adoption by the delegates. The delegates were thoroughly convinced after the bishops' declaration, a resolution presented by Rev. W. J. Walls, and the following magnetic summation made toward the close of Mr. Eichelberger's report:

The genius of Zion Methodism has driven her forth through the years in new paths. A first in withdrawing on account of proscription, first in seeking organic union, first in granting women equality within the church, first in quickening a freedman—Frederick Douglass—who startled the world as an abolitionist orator, first in starting a college in the Southland, first in sensing the need of a national industrial school, first in the Christian Endeavor movement, first in the recent venture for cooperative Christianity, she has a glorious record of achievement. Timorous souls that tremble and quake at new ventures for God are untrue to her noble traditions.

Therefore, I call upon you men and women, who are happy to follow the train of the fathers and to magnify the glorious deeds of Varick, Rush, J. J. Clinton, (S. T.) Jones, Moore, Hood, Lomax, Walters, G. W. Clinton, Alstork, Price, Harris, Small, Cartwright, Dancy and Mrs. Annie W. Blackwell and the hosts of others, to justify your right to this heritage by meeting the present-day challenge as did they. . . .

I have faith in the intelligence of this body and the passion of its

28. *Minutes,* Twenty-Seventh Quadrennial Session, pp. 113-114.

delegates for the kingdom to believe that we shall seek the upper room to know the mind of Christ and not be disobedient to His vision. [29]

The entire religious education program of the church was thus centralized at this General Conference, the Department of Christian Education was reborn, and the Board of Religious Education, which later became the Home and Church Division, was created. As a compliment to two of the prime promoters of the movement, Dr. James W. Eichelberger was elected Corresponding Secretary of the Christian Education Department and served over 42 years until his death in January, 1967, and newly elected Bishop W. J. Walls was made Chairman of the Board, and served 44 years until his retirement in 1968.

This was one of the most significant and constructive movements in the A.M.E. Zion Church of the twentieth century. It placed in entity a brand new emphasis, creating hundreds of new positions of local, district conference, annual conference, episcopal district, and national officers. It became interrelated with practically every department of the church, and rendered valuable service in programming of church organizational meetings. It developed an affiliation with the Department of Foreign Missions, which fosters separately the denominational schools on the foreign field but works cooperatively on matters of curriculum, programming. literature, etc. It is the program which remains in effect today, though greatly enlarged.

The Christian Education Department afterward purchased a headquarters building at 128 East 58th Street, Chicago, and continues its operational program from there. The Department of Education, established in 1892, was incorporated into the Christian Education Department, along with the Varick Christian Endeavor Office, at the General Conference of 1932 as a means of economizing in the operation of departments after the Depression. The department was then governed by two boards: Board of Christian Education—School and College and the Home and Church Board, which was the original Religious Education Board.

The operation of the Home and Church Division includes all "Christian Education curriculum material, methods, facilities, programs, and promotion used in homes, churches, districts, conferences by Sunday Church Schools, Varick Christian Endeavor Societies, Leadership Education, Vacation and Week-Day Church Schools, Boy Scouts and by all other educational organizations utilized in the denomination." The Home and Church Division is subdivided into two sections, Editorial, and Education and Promotion.

One of the bright and encouraging movements of the Home and Church Division is the National Christian Youth Council, which extends to and connects with councils in local churches, district and annual conferences. It elects its own youth officers during the Quadrennial Christian Education Convention, in the interim of the Quadrennial General Conference. Its supervisory officer is the international director of youth of the church.

Dr. James William Eichelberger made a connection wide impression, and in some respects he became a symbol for black Protestants in the field of Christian Education. After his death, the Board of Bishops met in February 1967 and elected to this post one who had come up through its ranks and implanted Christian character in our youth, Rev. George Lincoln Blackwell, II. He has continued in a modern and more tensely organizational way projecting the program.

The leadership training institutes held annually on the various school campuses, assembly grounds, and camps of the denomination are making a vital

29. *Ibid.*, 233-234.

contribution to the continued success and progress of Christian teaching. There is an earnest desire on the part of the writer to tell the complete story of the entrusted servants of the church, who have toiled almost sacrificially in many capacities of this diversified program. For the most part, men, women and youth have exhibited dexterity, cognition, and cohesion in keeping the Christian Education Department in the progressive succession. Some of the foremost projectors of this new movement however, in our history were the national directors of the Christian Education Divisions. Reverend Jacob W. Powell of Boston, Mass., continued to conduct the Leadership Training Conferences at the General Conventions held in Asheville, N.C., 1922, Washington D.C., in 1926, and in Detroit, 1930.

The pioneer Director of Children was Miss Sarah J. Janifer of Washington, D.C., who was suceeded by Miss Elizabeth Tucker of Pratt City, Alabama; Mrs. Ida Hauser Duncan of Salisbury, N.C.; Miss Edith M. Kemp of Asbury Park, N.J. and Mrs. Willie Lee Aldrich of Salisbury, N.C.

Directors of Youth: Martin L. Harvey, Hempstead, N.Y., Rev. J. Clinton Hoggard, Yonkers, N.Y., Rev. George L. Blackwell, II, Hackensack, N.J., Miss Lina L. Culbreth, Dunn, N.C., Rev. Enoch B. Rochester, Hackensack, N.J., Rev. C. R. Thompson, Little Rock. Ark.

Directors of Adults: Miss Bess Hunter Robinson, Mr. Charles G. Lawson, Miss Margaret L. Lewis, Associate Director Dr. J. Van Catledge, Jr., Salisbury, N.C., Rev. Daniel J. Hughlett, Louisville, Ky., Mrs. Josephine Riggins, East Chicago, Ind., and Mrs. Willie M. Stone, Montgomery, Ala.

Serving as the Director of the Vacation and Weekday Church School through the years was Mrs. M. Irene Moore of Indianapolis. The Director of Leadership Education and Administrative Assistant to the General Corresponding Secretary since 1938, Dr. David Henry Bradley, Sr., and the Director of Social Education and Action, also since 1938, Mrs. Josephine Humbles Kyles; have been assets to the development of the Christian Education program. Effectual in the movement also were the following presidents of General conventions: J. Henry Warren, Charlotte, N.C., Elliot S. Peters, Mobile, Ala., F. A. Ray, Brooklyn, N.Y., E. C. Harris, Los Angeles, Calif., George A. Moore, New Bern, N.C., Charles H. Anderson, Washington, D.C., R. B. Henderson, New York, N.Y., William H. Moore, Kinston, N.C., John H. White, New York, N.Y., John Shaw Talley, Detroit, Mich., Victor J. Tulane, Washington, D.C., Arthur E. Brooks, Washington, D.C., Samuel E. Besteda, Jr., Mobile, Ala., and the longest-term vice-president, Mrs. Senora B. Lawson of Richmond, Va., Mrs. Ola W. Crawley of Madisonville, Ky., Mrs. Mattie D. Singleton Eagan of Pensacola, Fla. and D. D. Garrett of Greenville, N.C.; also the Executive secretaries: Dr. Victor J. Tulane, Washington, D.C. and Mrs. DeVera Johnson Lockhart of Flushing, N.Y.

The other vice-presidents and members of the Executive Committee of the conventions are all long-standing members of the church and Sunday school work and contribute uniquely to the success of this powerful element of the church.

Quadrennial Christian Education Conventions

FIRST: Hopkins Chapel Church, Asheville, N.C.–August 2-6, 1922. Hosts: Bishop Lynwood W. Kyles, William Anderson, presiding elder, S. J. Howie, pastor.

SECOND: John Wesley Church, Washington, D.C.–August 3-8, 1926. Hosts: Bishop Josiah S. Caldwell, Martin Luther Blaylock, presiding elder, Hampton T. Medford, pastor.

THIRD: St. Paul Church, Detroit, Michigan—August 5-11, 1930. Hosts: Bishop John W. Martin, L. P. Powell, Presiding elder, P. R. Flack, pastor.

FOURTH: Loguen Temple, Knoxville, Tennessee—August 7-12, 1934. Hosts: Bishop Paris A. Wallace; S. E. Dixon, Presiding elder; Shepard H. Marion, pastor.

FIFTH: St. John Church, Cincinnati, Ohio—August 9-14, 1938. Hosts: Bishop Paris A. Wallace; W. S. Dacons, presiding elder; J. E. Kennedy, pastor.

SIXTH: Livingstone College Salisbury North Carolina—August 11-16, 1942. Host: President William Johnson Trent, Sr. **Mrs. Eleanor Roosevelt, wife of the United States President, Guest Speaker.

SEVENTH: Mother Zion Church, New York City—September 8-22, 1946. Hosts: Bishop William J. Walls; J. H. Tucker, presiding elder; Benjamin C. Robeson, pastor.**

EIGHTH: Hood Temple, Richmond, Virginia—August 1-6, 1950. Hosts: Bishop Hampton T. Medford; Watt J. Bailey, presiding elder; C.W. Turns, pastor.

NINTH: Broadway Temple, Louisville, Kentucky—July 31-August 6, 1954. Hosts: Bishop William C. Brown; B. N. Henningham, presiding elder; Felix S. Anderson, pastor.*

TENTH: Caldwell Temple and State Fair Grounds, Columbus, Ohio—July 20-25, 1958. Hosts: Bishop Stephen G. Spottswood; I. B. Pierce, presiding elder; J. Dallas Jenkins, pastor.

ELEVENTH: Livingstone College, Salisbury, North Carolina—August 5-10, 1962. Host: President Samuel Edward Duncan.

TWELFTH: Livingstone College, Salisbury, N.C. July 31-August 5, 1966. Host: President Samuel Edward Duncan.

THIRTEENTH: Livingstone College, Salisbury, North Carolina August 2-7, 1970. Host: President Furney George Shipman. [30]

Giving inspirational leadership to the youth through their own organization since 1930 were the following elected presidents of Zion's National Christian Youth Council: Martin L. Harvey, Hempstead, N.Y., Joseph N. Michael, Knoxville, Tenn., Charles M. Campbell, New York, N.Y., Miss Rena L. Weller, Waterbury, Conn., James W. Eichelberger, III, Chicago, Ill., Miss Marjorie Stiggers, Detroit, Mich., Miss Marian Marsh, Richmond, Va., Miss Helen C. Scott, Washington, D.C., George A. L. Gantt, Midland, Mich., Curtis Crockett, Detroit, Mich., James A. French, Salisbury, N.C. There has been a continuous increase in official responsibilities of qualified men, women, and youth in this agency, which has made it a practical contribution to the people of this emerging age.

Representation in National and International Organizations

Before the Christian education movements were combined in one department in 1924, the most outstanding leaders of the A.M.E. Zion Church making remarkable contribution to the cause of Christian education, in international Sunday school and Christian Endeavor conventions were Rev. Richard Haywood

---

30. Information compiled from Corresponding General Secretaries of Christian Education Reports to the Quadrennial General Conference; Powell, *Echoes of Christian Education*, pp. 32-34.

*Attorney Thurgood Marshall, (first Black man to become Supreme Court Justice) addressed this Convention after leading in the struggle which eventuated in the historic Supreme Court Decision on Desegration of Schools, May 17, 1954.

**Sesqui-Centennial Observance of the denomination.

Stitt, Bishop Alexander Walters, Bishop George Wylie Clinton, and Mr. James W. Eichelberger. A.M.E. Zion youth participation has been considered of the utmost importance from the beginning of the ecumenical Sunday school movement. The A.M.E. Zion Church has membership in every significant interdenominational Christian education organization on the national and international levels. "The outreach and influence of our Christian Education Department are extensive and increasingly effective." [31]

The International Christian Endeavor Conventions

In the early part of the twentieth century, though there was an International Christian Endeavor Society movement, there was also the World Christian Endeavor movement, which graduated into the International Society of Christian Endeavor. It is well known that Reverend Daniel A. Poling became the world renown leader in helping to spread this united movement around the world. The A.M.E. Zion Church was represented in these separate conventions by its General Secretary of Christian Education, Mr. James W. Eichelberger, and the faithful Secretary of Christian Endeavor, Mr. Aaron Brown, Sr. Mr. Brown served as a member of the International Christian Endeavor faculty in 1929. After the demise of Bishop Alexander Walters, another methodical denominational spokesman, Bishop Lynwood W. Kyles, took up the cudgels attending meetings in Europe and North America, and became a voice of significance in the International Christian Endeavor Conventions. He was a trustee at large of the International Christian Endeavor Society, and sustained a place of distinction by his masterly contributions to the program. [32]

Mr. Eichelberger became a noted spokesman in this organization. He served on executive committees and as a trustee and became a potent voice for Christian action in serving the needs of youth throughout the world. Succeeding him in faithfully attending these conventions and executing the work of Christian Endeavor is the present General Secretary of Christian Education, Dr. George Lincoln Blackwell, II, who is presently a trustee of this Society along with Bishops W. J. Walls and H. B. Shaw.

The youth representation has always been far-reaching from the A.M.E. Zion Church. In 1947, Rev. William H. Coleman, Jr., attending the International Christian Endeavor Convention at San Francisco and was the official youth representative of the A.M.E. Zion Church. "He was selected by the youth to preside over their deliberations and later by them as a trustee of the International Society." [33] The youth representatives are continuously chosen from among the officers of the A.M.E. Zion Church National Christian Youth Council.

The International and World Sunday School Conventions

In 1924, Dr. James W. Eichelberger and Miss Sarah J. Janifer, superintendent of the Galbraith Sunday School in Washington, D.C., represented the A.M.E. Zion Church at the World Sunday School Convention held at Glasgow, Scotland. In 1936, our church was represented by Bishop William J. Walls and Dr. J. W. Eichelberger in Oslo, Norway. Mr. Eichelberger was elected vice-president of the

31. *Minutes,* Thirty-third Quadrennial Session, pp. 197-198.
32. *Minutes,* Twenty-Eighth Quadrennial Session, p. 225; Twenty-Ninth Quadrennial Session, p. 207.
33. *Minutes,* Thirty-Third Quadrennial Session, p. 203.

World Sunday School Convention Pilgrims, and Bishop Walls made a major address to this assembly. At the International Sunday School Convention, held in Des Moines, Iowa in 1947, the A.M.E. Zion Church was signally honored when Mr. E. S. Peters, Superintendent of Big Zion Sunday School, Mobile, Ala. was awarded an engraved chain for having served 44 years as Sunday school superintendent. Bishop John W. Martin presided over one of the plenary sessions, and Mr. J. S. Stanback, a pioneer in A.M.E. Zion and world Sunday School work, received a citation for conspicuous service by the International Council of Religious Education. [34]

Meaningful contributions have been made by Revs. George Lincoln Blackwell, I, J. Francis Lee, B. F. Gordon, J. S. N. Tross and scores of young people of Zion in the deliberations of these organizations.

The International Council of Religious Education Conventions

"The World's Sunday School Association which became the World Council of Christian Education in 1947, was organized at London, England, in 1889 during the first World's Sunday School Convention. The World's Association is a federation of national interdenominational organizations. 'In 1934 the name World Council was given to the governing body of the Association.' The membership of the World Council is composed of 'direct representatives of constituent organizations of the Association.' "

"The International Council of Religious Education is the constituent organization in North America." It had 23 representatives in the World Council, of which Dr. J. W. Eichelberger was a member in 1948. [35] Long before this he was a member of its executive committee and attended the meetings faithfully. In 1925 when it was decided to hold the convention at Birmingham, Ala., "and it was evident that Negro members would be segregated in the International Council, no delegate was certified to this Convention from the A.M.E. Zion Church," therefore Dr. Eichelberger did not attend. [36] This has been the spirit of our leadership in the whole ecumenical story—many times rebuffing experiences in the struggle of working towards equality and race rights. At the convention held at Toronto, Mrs. Josephine H. Kyles proficiently served as resource leader.

At present Drs. George L. Blackwell, David H. Bradley, and L. J. Baptiste are Zion's leading representatives along with the youth delegates in the International Council.

Youth Representation, World Christian Education, and World Methodism

Our first Director of Youth, Mr. Martin L. Harvey, was elected as one of the two black delegates, constituting the North American delegation to the International Missionary Council at Madras, India in 1938. In 1939, Mr. Harvey was one of the youth representatives of the A.M.E. Zion Church, along with Mr. Charles M. Black and Miss Margaret L. Lewis, at the World Conference of Christian Youth at Amsterdam, Holland. Mr. Harvey was on the program at this convention. The Editor of Church School Literature, Dr. B. F. Gordon, also

---

34. *Minutes,* Thirty-First Quadrennial Session, pp. 83, 194; Thirty-Third Quadrennial Session, p. 204.
35. Ibid., p. 205.
36. *Minutes,* Twenty-Eighth Quadrennial Session, p. 224.

attended this meeting. [37]

At the Second Assembly of Christian Youth at Oslo, Norway, the A.M.E. Zion Church was represented by Miss Rena J. Weller (Mrs. Karefa-Smart) and Mr. James W. Eichelberger, III. The talented Miss Weller was a member of the planning committee, having been sent to Europe in 1946 to participate in the committee's deliberations and a presiding officer in this conference. "At Oslo, she was a member of the Conference Committee and was the only one of the 227 American delegates to preside over the Conference. This she did with becoming ability and grace." [38]

"Another youth from Mother Zion Church, Miss Violet Gaskin, was a delegate chosen by the Greater New York Protestant Youth Council. After the Oslo Conference, Mr. Eichelberger, III attended the consultative churches at Lund, Sweden. Miss Weller attended the post-Oslo meeting of the World's Student Christian Federation at Lundsberg, Sweden." [39] Another incident regarding one of these youth delegates was that the name of Mrs. Rena Weller Karefa-Smart was submitted as a candidate for one of the six presidents of the World Council of Churches at the Fourth Assembly in Uppsala, Sweden in 1968. Had the nomination been successful, she would have been the first Afro-American and first woman to attain this post; however she was not elected.

Rev. George L. Blackwell, II and Miss Mary Macon Lindsay also attended an International Youth Meeting in Havana, Cuba and brought echoes of this meeting during the Sesqui-Centennial Program of the A.M.E. Zion Church in 1946.

The Third World Conference of Christian Youth held at Travancore, India, December 1952 had as the A.M.E. Zion Church representative Miss Marjorie Stiggers (Mrs. Lyda), who made "a splendid representative." [40]

In August 1958, at the World Convention of Christian Education meeting in Tokyo, Japan, the youth representative of the A.M.E. Zion Church was Miss Marian Marsh, who was popular in the institute, convention and on the youth tour. The adult delegates, Bishops W. J. Walls and H. B. Shaw, Dr. J. W. Eichelberger, Rev. Clinton L. Wilcox, Sr., and Mr. and Mrs. David P. Wisdom, were active participants among the 4,200 members from 64 nations.

Reverend Enoch B. Rochester was the able youth representative of the A.M.E. Zion Church at a number of ecumenical meetings during the 1960s.

At the World Methodist Youth Conference in Oslo, Norway, in 1961, the A.M.E. Zion Church was first represented by Miss Belinda Benson of Englewood, N.J. Larger emphasis was placed on the next meeting, and the A.M.E. Zion Church had more than a dozen representatives from three episcopal districts present at Bath, England, in 1966, and a like representation in 1971 at Denver, Colo.

The Boy Scouts' World Jamboree was held at Moissons, France, in 1947, and three boy scouts from the A.M.E. Zion Church were among the large attendance; Ira A. Daves, Jr. of New Bern, N.C., a representative of Lancaster, S.C., and one of First Church, Brooklyn. The denomination through its Christian Education Department has been well represented. [41]

A.M.E. Zion youth participation continues to be wide and varied in a large

37. *Minutes,* Thirty-First Quadrennial Session, p. 194.
38. *Minutes,* Thirty-Third Quadrennial Session, pp. 202, 207.
39. *Ibid.*
40. *Minutes,* Thirty-Fifth Quadrennial Session, p. 285.
41. *Minutes,* Thirty-third Quadrennial Session, p. 207.

number of ecumenical Christian fellowship and religious councils around the world.

So we have J. C. Price's immortal words to remind all generations that:
Christian Education is the most indispensable element in the progress of civilization of the world. The church must be abreast if not in advance of the times. It occurs to me that this imperative feature of the work of the church is second only to personal consecration. [42]

42. W. J. Walls, *J. C. Price Educator-Race Leader*, p. 211.

Frame building where the school, then known as Zion Wesley Institute, originated at Concord, N.C., 1879, now Livingstone College, Salisbury, N.C.

CHAPTER 22

EDUCATION—BIRTH OF SCHOOLS AND COLLEGES

The African Methodist Episcopal Zion Church has sponsored institutional education practically since its beginning. The first little frame church built and dedicated to God in 1800 also had accommodation for a school. The schools of New York City operated from the churches, and funds were granted the city by the state legislature for such encouragement. The other school for blacks which received support from this fund was the African Free School founded by the New York Manumission Society. According to the following, there was evidently some provision in the law for refunds from schools operated in churches:

Returns were received from the following churches of the monies given to them for the use of schools agreeably to law, to wit the German Lutheran Church, the Methodist Episcopal Church, the Reformed Protestant Dutch Church, the Scotch Presbyterian Church, and the African (A.M.E. Zion) Church. [1]

As noted before, early among the teachers were a few A.M.E. Zion Church leaders: James Varick, George Collins, and William Miller. Miller also made use of his home at 36 Mulberry Street for a classroom.

When a larger building was erected in 1820, an additional school facility was added to the church building. In the course of erection, July 1819, the "trustees petitioned the Legislature of the State for aid towards the schoolroom, hoping to obtain from them a small part, at least, of the amount of money which was allowed, according to a law of the State; to be appropriated for the use of public schools; but they did not succeed." [2] These were the small days, when the sparsest accommodation was made for giving a degree of education to black people.

This education arrangement continued to a small degree among free and slave until the Nat Turner Uprising in 1831. A law was then created throughout the slave system that no slave could be taught to read or write. By this time, however, slavery had been abolished in some of the northern states, and blacks continued to get a meager amount of learning. Some ardent students among them became proficient scholars. The only facility which the Board of Education of Rochester, N.Y., for instance, offered for blacks was the basement of the A.M.E. Zion Church. Frederick Douglass made a blazing attack on this arrangement in his fight for integrated schools, through *The North Star*. He said there was no reason founded in justice why they should be shut out of the fine, airy schoolhouses of the districts, and driven into the dull, damp, dark and badly ventilated

1. *Minutes*, Common Council of the City of New York, Vol III, p. 564 July 10, 1804.
2. Rush, *Rise and Progress*, p. 30.

celler of Zion Church. . . . If we yield willingly to this encroachment, perhaps the next demand will require us to live in a certain part of the city—our children are to go to a particular school—colored people are to attend their own meeting; and it may, by and by, follow that we are to occupy a given place in the town. For one, we say, most distinctly, to the Board of Education, that *in no emergency*, will we send a child of ours to the miserable cellar under Zion Church. [3]

It is certain that Douglass' unrestrained protests were effectual in improving the education system for blacks, not only in Rochester, but in other sections of the country.

Our second bishop, Christopher Rush, was founder and first president of The Phoenix Society in 1833, in New York City, which spread through other urban areas of the North. These societies made proposals and worked for the improvement of the moral welfare of blacks, and instructed them in literature and mechanical arts. [4]

Reverend John J. Moore, who later became bishop, established the first African Methodist Episcopal Zion Church west of the Mississippi River, in San Francisco, August 1, 1852. He was endowed with special educational qualities (see Chapter 13), and became the first teacher of a school for black children in California. "In the 1850's and 1860's, children of racial minorities were not allowed to attend public school with white children, nor were they permitted a school of their own except through a limited provision." J. B. Sanderson, a stalwart abolitionist from New Bedford, Mass., travelled to California in the interest of promoting education for blacks in the state, and organized schools in San Francisco, Oakland, Sacramento, and Stockton; and Rev. John J. Moore became the first teacher of the first school founded for blacks, in the state, in the basement of St. Cyprian A.M.E. Church at San Francisco. Moore also took an active part in the fight for appropriation of funds to educate black children. [5]

The first movement in the A.M.E. Zion Church to establish a connectional institution of learning was an action taken by the General Conference of 1844, in New York City. A committee of five was appointed to draft a constitution, as a basis for the establishment of a connectional manual labor school, under the supervision of the General Conference. The committee members were Rev. Jehial C. Beman, John P. Thompson, Leonard Collins, Abraham Cole, and Peter Ross. "This action resulted in the calling of a Literary Connectional Convention at York, Pa., to be composed of delegates from the New York and Philadelphia Conferences to convene in 1847." Reverends David Stevens, S. T. Scott, Leonard Collins, and John J. Moore represented the Philadelphia Conference at this convention. [6]

The convention took initial steps to present to the General Conference of 1848 the plan for the establishment of the Connectional Manual Labor School in Essex County, N.Y., and proceeded to draw up a Constitution with preamble for operating the institution to be known as Rush Academy. [7] The preamble gave explicit reasons to establish educational institutions:

Whereas, We the ministry of the African Methodist Episcopal Zion Church in America, feeling as we do that many of the difficulties against

3. Foner, *The Life and Writings of Frederick Douglass*, Vol. I, pp. 415-416;
4. *Ibid.*, Vol. II, p. 21; Federal Writers Program Negroes of New York, Biography—Rush.
5. Sue Bailey Thurman, *Pioneers of Negro Origin in California*, pp. 28, 37-38.
6. Moore, *History*, p. 307.
7. *Ibid.*

which we have to labor, grow out of the fact that there is a great lack of education among us; and,

Whereas, Man viewed as a being susceptible of happiness and capable of responsible action, sustains a thousand relations, involving as many duties; whatever, therefore, tends to increase this susceptibility and enlarge this capacity, must exalt his nature and promote the benevolent purpose for which he was created, and as such is the tendency of a well directed education, of virtuous example, of sound philosophy and theology, indeed, of everything which gives the understanding a controlling influence over the grosser passions, of everything which purifies and regulates the feelings without diminishing their order or depriving them of their appropriate objects; and since among the many causes which conspire to produce this effect, none is so efficient as a well directed education; therefore, these persons whose names are here connected do agree to form an institution, having for its objects the establishment of prominent schools of education preparatory to the ministry, and for other useful information calculated to elevate our whole people, do agree to be governed by the following Constitution and By-Laws, which seem to be found necessary for carrying out or effecting the object set forth in this preamble. [8]

The Constitution was broad, including 13 articles outlining responsibilities of governors and officers of the school. The General Conference of 1848 approved the plan and the committee was authorized to draw up a plan of the buildings for the school and estimate their cost. [9] During the 1840's, Gerrit Smith contributed land in New York State to several leaders of black organizations, specifically for institutional development. He contributed large plots of land in Essex County to three outstanding black leaders: Rev. Charles B. Ray, prominent journalist and clergyman who died in 1886; Dr. James McCune Smith, physician and writer, who graduated from the University of Glasgow in 1832; and Bishop Christopher Rush, of the A.M.E. Zion Church. He deeded four 160 acre lots to Christopher Rush, and in 1849 Rush deeded the property to the trustees of Rush Academy. [10]

The trustees appointed an agent to raise funds for the institution, but little progress had been made in development. Rush Academy was incorporated by the Board of Regents of the State of New York in 1864, but the trustees, consisting of Bishops John Tappan, J. W. Loguen, Revs. Joseph P. Thompson, J. H. Smith, William Sanford, John Thomas, Edward V. Clark, John Durnell, Henry Travis, Samuel J. Howard, Christopher Brown, and James Stockley, moved too deliberately. When the project was presented at the General Conference of 1872, at Charlotte, N.C., it was discovered that nothing had been effected further than the procuring of the property, incorporation of the Board of Trustees to manage the institution, and collection of some funds to erect suitable buildings and to make all necessary provisions for the establishment of the school. [11]

"In an action on the subject of education at the General Conference of 1872, the Rush Academy was turned over by the trustees into the hands of the General Conference, and the General Conference authorized Rev. Thomas H. Lomax to sell the land belonging to the Rush Academy, and purchase land at Fayetteville, N.C. Reverend Lomax did not sell the land." However, Rev. J. McHenry Farley was appointed agent and sent out to collect money with which to purchase land

8. *Ibid.*, pp. 308-309.
9. *Ibid.*, p. 313.
10. Author's papers, File on Rush Academy, Lake Placid, N.Y.
11. Moore, *History*, pp. 242-243, 313.

there and establish an institution, to be known as Rush University. Funds were collected and a lot purchased at Fayetteville, but the project did not materialize. [12]

Before our successful venture in the South, there was one other attempt to establish a university in the north, at Middletown, Pennsylvania, around the same time of the Fayetteville venture, in 1871, by Bishop Joseph J. Clinton. Zion Hill Collegiate Institute was an enterprise embraced by Bishop Clinton and his friends, who became interested in purchasing the school, and began raising money for it. The Pennsylvania legislature was prevailed upon to make a $5,000 appropriation for the school, and the bill passed the House of Representatives while the Philadelphia and Baltimore Annual Conference was in session, May 15-22, 1878, and was on its way to the Senate, which it subsequently passed. [13] This was a bit encouraging, but it did not reach fulfillment.

"For some reason the governor of the state vetoed the appropriation bill. This seems to have been a fatal blow to the school." [14] William Howard Day had a strong philosophy against segregated schools in the North, and Bishop Clinton became convinced that Day was behind the veto. The following year Bishop Clinton, in his annual address to the Philadelphia and Baltimore Conference, stated the precarious condition in which the school had been placed. Josiah King, holder of the mortgage, asked that the General Conference pledge itself as a corporation to maintain a school at the location of Zion Hill Institute in perpetuity, and give him a mortgage for the property for $8,000. He made the condition that if the church defaulted in maintaining the school, or in the event of private or forced sale for other uses, the mortgage would be to him a lien, and could be enforced only in such contingency. Since the General Conference was not meeting that year, he decided to transfer the mortgage to the American Missionary Association of New York, and suggested that this organization transfer the property to the A.M.E. Zion Church on the same conditions. Bishop Clinton recommended pursuance of acquiring the school, and stated that the New Jersey Conference had resolved to raise $100 annually for the project. The Philadelphia and Baltimore Conference acted favorably, and voted that "Bishop J. J. Clinton be requested to repair to New York and meet the American Board of Missions in the interest of the Zion Hill College." [15]

Partly because of hard times then being experienced by colored people in America, and partly because they did not wish to run it under obligation to an outside party . . . the bishops passed a resolution in 1879 "that we cease attempting the institution at that place. . . and that we tender Mr. King a vote of thanks for interest taken in our behalf in the matter." . . . Bishop Clinton suspected that some men in his own connection. . . prevailed upon the

---

12. Ibid., pp. 313-314. ** The State of New York claimed title to property by tax deeds from three tax sales in 1877, 1881, and 1885, but this was against the law because it was church owned property. Someone operated timber-cutting on the land and caused taxation to be levied. This was without the consent of the church. During the administration of Bishop W. J. Walls in the Western New York Conference, this property matter was placed in the hands of a lawyer, with retainer, to pursue the church claim, and decision is pending.
13. *Minutes*, Fiftieth Annual Session, Philadelphia-Baltimore Conference, 1878.
14. Rufus E. Clement, *History of Education in the A.M.E. Zion Church*, Ms. thesis; Walls, *Joseph C. Price*. p. 230.
15. *Minutes*, Fifty-First Session of the Philadelphia and Baltimore Annual Conference, 1879, pp. 10, 38.

governor of Pennsylvania to veto the bill appropriating $5000.00 to the school, and now had influenced the general church through its Board of Bishops to decide to give up the school altogether. [16]

The General Conference of 1880 took similar action, voting not to purchase the property as a connection, but referred the matter to the Allegheny Conference, within whose bounds it was located, for it to decide on purchasing it and making it a conference or district school. [17]

The Allegheny Conference was not strong enough to undertake such a project. Senior Bishop J. J. Clinton had his heart set on procuring this school for the connection. When the venture failed, he became greatly depressed in mind, and subsequently declined in health and never recovered. "We shall never forget the forlorn appearance he presented when we visited him after the disaster," stated Hood. "We soon found it would not do to talk to him on the subject of the college." [18]

Livingstone College

The urgent necessity for a theological and collegiate institution had been increasingly felt throughout the connection for several years. This need found a voice in the North Carolina Conference which met in Salisbury in November 1877. At this time, the conference included the whole state of North Carolina, with the exception of the churches set off to form the Virginia Conference and churches in the extreme western part of the state which were then a part of the Tennessee Conference. The North Carolina Conference with its 16 presiding elder districts, and 362 pastoral appointments, varied personnel and determined component, moved in the same creative spirit to establish a permanent education center as it did to establish a permanent journal, while it continued in abundant growth.

This concept of establishing an institution of learning, which had concerned the denomination for years, was put into activity by the Twelfth Annual Session of the North Carolina Conference held in Zion Chapel, Concord, November 1875. During this session, Revs. Thomas H. Lomax, William H. Thurber, and Robert S. Rieves went to the Scotia Seminary for girls to visit students who were members of churches which they pastored. President Darlington, founding president of Scotia, denied them the privilege of visiting their member students. This humiliated the ministers, and they met afterwards, on a log across the road in front of the school and the church. Seated on this log, they recalled that the word was out that some were leading the public to believe that the A.M.E. Zion Church was an ignorant church, and they resolved that "we must get a college of our own and destroy this false impression."

The Fayetteville venture sponsored by Zion connection had practically failed, due to the appointment of Professor Robert Harris, brother of Cicero R. Harris, as principal of the State Normal School there. Robert Harris had been instrumental in establishing the school in Fayetteville, and he was also the choice of the conference to organize a school for Zion. In the meantime, Zion was developing Rev. C. R. Harris, an apostle of lore; serving also as principal of the High School in Charlotte, and when the school was eventually started at Concord, he became the first principal.

16. Clement, Thesis; . . . Walls, op. cit., p. 231.
17. *Minutes*, Sixteenth Quadrennial Session, p. 83.
18. Hood, *One Hundred Years*, p. 111.

After Thomas H. Lomax helped to conceive the plan of the school at Concord, he was elevated to the bishopric in May 1876, and placed in charge of a total mission district. Yet deeply interested, he was not always on the scene in the continual planning for the school by the North Carolina Conference, presided over by Bishop J. W. Hood. However, he associated Bishop Hood in the historic conference of 1877. Reverend William Henry Thurber, the pastor of the church at Concord, N.C., was more deeply affected, and led in the pursuit.

In conjunction with Professor A. S. Richardson, member of his church and nephew of Rev. Cicero R. Harris, then teaching in the public school, Thurber prepared papers for enlisting the North Carolina Conference in an attempt to establish the proposed institution. "This was done in the Conference which met in Salisbury, N.C., in November, 1877, and efforts at once began to carry out the plans proposed. Mr. Richardson was appointed agent and traveled extensively in the bounds of the Conference." [19] At this conference session, C. R. Harris presented the paper signed by Thurber, Harris, and Rieves, on the establishment of a theological seminary in this state, which was adopted. The plan was thus:

1. Provides for the election of trustees, who, after the incorporation of the Seminary, are to devise the form, and have charge of the printing and distribution of the building stock.

2. Shares to be $10 each; minimum limit to be sold, 500; each church to be allowed at least one share.

3. Each share entitles its representative to a year's tuition in Seminary, and may be purchased by individuals.

4. Provides for the final returns of Elders, and the time and place of trustees annual meeting, to frame, and to present to the Annual Conference, a report of the progress of the work.

Trustees were then elected, viz: C. R. Harris, W. H. Thurber, Wm. J. Moore, Bishop J. W. Hood, R. H. Simmons, Bishop T. H. Lomax, Z. T. Pearsall, Amos York and A. B. Smyer.

Bishop J. W. Hood, E. H. Hill and H. C. Phillips were selected to attend to the incorporation of the Seminary.[20]

At the instance of Elder Thurber, the trustees of Zion Chapel, Concord, N.C., donated seven acres of land to the use of the Seminary known as the Zion Wesley Institute. Warren C. Coleman, chairman of the trustees board and superintendent of Sunday schools, and incidentally, the only black owner of a cotton mill in the United States business, presented the property at the 1880 General Conference. [21] "Still, money was lacking. On the 9th of May, 1878, a meeting of the trustees was held in Concord, at which Bishop J. W. Hood was elected President, Bishop T. H. Lomax, vice-president, C. R. Harris, secretary and treasurer." The project moved slowly. In the following annual conference held at Goldsboro, only two churches had contributed anything. [22]

Bishop Hood forthrightly confronted the plight of Zion Wesley Institute in his annual episcopal address. In climaxing, he inquired:

Were you in earnest when you gave that vote? I supposed you were. If you were not, I hope you will say so, and we shall know what to do. Let us not trifle any longer.

Hood stated further in his history that "the Conference having voted to issue shares of stock, it was necessary to set the idea clearly before the churches; very

19. Walls, *op. cit.*, p. 485.
20. *Minutes*, Fourteenth Session, North Carolina Annual Conference, pp. 22-23.
21. W. J. Walls, *Joseph Charles Price*, p. 485; *Minutes*, Sixteenth Quadrennial Session, p. 82.
22. *Ibid.;* Moore, *History*, p. 314.

BISHOP CICERO RICHARDSON HARRIS
Founder of Zion Wesley Institute, first principal
and one of four teachers at opening session, December, 1879.

few of the ministers of that time were sufficiently intelligent to do it." [23]

Professor A. S. Richardson, a fine lecturer who had volunteered to give 60 days to the cause, submitted his report as lecturing agent for Zion Wesley Institute, and also made an eloquent speech in behalf of the institution. "He gave an itemized account of the shares he had distributed, and congratulated the members of the Conference on the prospect of soon having an institution of our own to reflect its light over the whole country. He counseled united and vigorous action." Said he:

> We must deny ourselves and set the example of taking scholarships and aiding pecuniarily in the work. Votes are powerful, they declare war and command peace, but votes will not build Zion Wesley Institute. . . . Presbyterians have schools of their faith, Baptists of theirs, Catholics of theirs; we should have one of ours. We shall never firmly establish ourselves as a connection until we have a good seminary of learning. We want a supply of good ministers, and a good institution alone will give them to us. Our people are yearly becoming better educated, and we must have a ministry to instruct and assist them. Education will secure this, and education we must have. [24]

Richardson, with his saguine sacrificial spirit and courageous undertakings, is affectionately remembered in Zion history as the most heroic layman in establishing our first institution of learning. After Bishop Hood's and Mr. Richardson's addresses, the conference was invigorated, and the promotion of the institution continued in its struggle.

23. Hood, *One Hundred Years,* p. 114.
24. *Ibid.,* pp. 114-115.

MRS. MERIAH GION HARRIS, pioneer teacher in 1879 and became first matron of
Livingstone College. First Secretary of the Woman's Home and Foreign Missionary
Society, 1880-1892.(1.)

MISS VICTORIA RICHARDSON, niece of Bishop Harris, also a pioneer teacher, with her
brother, Professor A. S. Richardson, in 1879. Miss Richardson also organized the Young
Woman's Department of the Woman's Home and Foreign Missionary Society in 1912.(r.)

A fresh effort was made; Diplomas of Honor provided for, which were to be
given to every donor of five dollars to the institution; and an agent was
appointed to distribute the diplomas, and stir up an interest among the
churches. The Board of Trustees was enlarged so as to include all the bishops
of the connection and several elders from each of the annual conferences.
Honarary trustees were appointed in most of the counties of the state, who
also, it was hoped, would work for the success of the cause. [25]

In 1879 an appeal was made to the ministers to raise funds for the
construction of a building, but up to the assembling of the North Carolina
Conference, "none had responded to the appeal but Jerry M. McNeil, who sent
two dollars from Swan's Station." [26] The appeal seemed in vain, but at the
North Carolina Conference meeting in Lincolnton, November 1879, proceeds
were brought in which, with donations from Bishops Hood and Lomax, amounted
to $155. [27]

To stimulate interest and so increase the revenues of the Institute, it was
agreed at this Annual Conference in Lincolnton to open a school under the
principalship of Rev. C. R. Harris. [28] Zion Wesley Institute subsequently held its
first session in December 1879, in the frame house across the road from Scotia
Seminary, with three students in attendance and four teachers, on the first day.
The teachers were Principal C. R. Harris; his wife, Meriah E. Harris; his niece, Miss
Victoria Richardson, and his nephew, A. S. Richardson. After a brief recess,
classes resumed the first Monday in January 1880. At this school session over 20
pupils were enrolled, some of them preachers in the traveling connection. [29]

The General Conference of 1880 readily accepted Zion Wesley Institute as
the chief institution of the connection. It also voted, in accordance with a
resolution received from the North Carolina Conference, that the Rush University

25. Moore, *History*, p. 315.
26. Simon G. Atkins and Thomas W. Wallace, *The Twenty-Fifth Annual Commencement and
    Quarter Centennial Livingstone College*, p. 32.
27. Moore, *History*, p. 315.
28. Walls, *op. cit.*, p. 485.
29. *Ibid;* Walls, *The Romance of a College*, p. 21.

property in Fayetteville be turned over to the trustees of Zion Wesley Institute, and that the property be transferred to said trustees. The Fayetteville property was later sold and the cash transferred to Zion Wesley Institute. The trustees had planned for a brick building to accommodate 200 students at Concord, and reported on this at the General Conference. The deed for the property at Concord was presented here, and the conference ordered a special collection to be raised in all the churches for the support of the institution. [30]

In the fall of 1880, A. S. Richardson was chosen principal and taught throughout that session, which lasted eight months. During this year very little had been collected for the institution. Thus the school suspended for lack of funds before the end of the 1881 session, and Mr. Richardson accepted a government position in Washington, D.C.

In the meantime, the delegates of the A.M.E. Zion Church to the Ecumenical Conference held in London, England, September 1881, Bishops J. W. Hood, J. P. Thompson, Revs. J. McH. Farley, and J. C. Price, "presented an opportunity of bringing the needs of our education work before the people of Great Britain–a people who have ever listened with sympathetic ear to the appeals of the American Negro for the amelioration of his unfortunate condition." [31] On the· boat crossing the Atlantic, Bishop Hood induced J. C. Price, a young man of 27 years, to become an agent for raising funds in England to help establish the school. [32]

Bishop Hood had discovered Price as a young boy in his wife's Sunday school class in New Bern, North Carolina, about 1866, and a little later found that he was the most promising student in a day school taught by a Miss Merrick. Before that Price had been discovered by Mr. Thomas Battle, superintendent of Sunday school of St. Peter's A.M.E. Zion Church, who invited him into the Sunday school. Hood followed Price through Shaw and Lincoln Universities, giving him aid from the conferences of his episcopal district. After Price was licensed to preach in 1876, he was admitted into the North Carolina Conference, ordained deacon and elder, by Hood, and elected delegate to the 1880 General Conference, all by 1879 while he was a student and had not met the annual conference. "The beauty of it was that Brother Price had no part whatever in his rapid advancement; he simply acquiesced in what was done." [33] Price's extraordinary talents were necessary to the church and race at that time. Several leaders encouraged his rapid advancement, though others were somewhat critical.

Price accepted the urgent appeal of Bishop Hood to become the agent of the school, and remained in England lecturing for one year. He was vigorous at the Ecumenical Council in London. While the subject of foreign missions was being discussed, Price digressed to say, "the work that presents itself to the American Negro is to go there (to Africa) to save the immortal souls of his people," and continued that this can be better assured "by preparing those in America." He further stated:

> Six or seven million Negroes in America are the instrument to elevate their brethren in Africa, and since they have not the training schools in Africa, my idea is that we encourage the schools that we have in America and send the people . . . intelligent, moral, and well prepared men, to preach the gospel of Christ in Africa. [34]

30. *Minutes*, Sixteenth Quadrennial Session, p. 82; Moore, *History*, p. 316.
31. *Ibid*, Walls, *Joseph Charles Price*, pp. 485-486.
32. W. J. Walls, *The Romance of a College*, p. 22.
33. Hood, *One Hundred Years*, pp. 459-461.
34. Walls, *Joseph Charles Price*, p. 51.

At this meeting in City Road Chapel, London, in a five-minute speech, he secured the attention of the delegates of the world. Speaking also on other vital issues, the *London Times* published him as "the world's orator."

It was Price's original intention to spend several months in Europe seeing the Old World and lecturing. There would have been more money in it for him, but he made the wisest choice in serving his own church and race. "His action in this case was the more honorable because the connection had furnished no money to send him. The money he received from Mr. William E. Dodge for his temperance work in North Carolina supplied him the means for this trip, which he thought he was taking for his own personal benefit." [35]

Price returned from England after one year lecture trip, with $10,000 above his expenses. "Never was a choice more judicious or opportune." [36] At long last, success had supervened upon our educational trials. Professor A. S. Richardson had worked up the sentiment which induced the white citizens of Salisbury to give $1,000, and this had influenced the decision of the trustees to move the school from Concord. [37] The additional funds raised by Dr. Price were used to remove the school to Salisbury, and the present property was purchased with a well-built farmhouse on it. The trustees elected Dr. Joseph Charles Price president in September, and the college resumed classes in early October 1882. Reverend C. R. Harris and Dr. Edward Moore were chosen as Price's assistants, and Mrs. Meriah E. Harris as matron. [38]

The immortal J. C. Price planted the school on a firm foundation, toiling the remaining 11 years of his life to build a creditable race institution. At Dr. Price's suggestion, the board voted to change the name of the institution to Livingstone College in 1885, in memory of the great explorer and missionary to Africa, David Livingstone, and a charter was procured. Thus the adeptness of Price, his resonant skill, resolute and sacrificial determination, afford him the place in history as founder and first president of Livingstone College. He made indelible impressions in his oratory and works. One noted historian of the late nineteenth and early twentieth centuries wrote:

> It is doubtful if the nineteenth century produced a superior or more popular orator of the type that enlists the sympathies, entertains and compels conviction than Joseph C. Price. In little more than a brief, decade he was known in Great Britain and the United States, both on the Pacific and the Atlantic, as a peerless orator. In 1881 he first rose to eminence as a platform speaker; in 1893 his star sank below the horizon. Yet he was more than orator: he was a recognized race leader; a most potential force in politics, though not a politician; a builder of a great school—a most conspicuous object lesson of "Negro Capabilities."

> His fame rests not alone upon his popularity within his own church or his own race, for the evidence is conclusive that though unmistakably identified with the Negro, Democratic whites and whole communities recognized his worth, highly esteemed him, honored him in life and mourned him in death. [39]

Livingstone College was growing like a mushroom under Price's leadership. W. E. B. DuBois said that: "The star of achievement which Joseph C. Price, a black boy of those days, hitched his wagon to was the founding of a school for colored

35. Hood, *One Hundred Years*, pp. 465, 467-468.
36. Walls, *Joseph Charles Price*, p. 485.
37. Hood, *One Hundred Years*, p. 114.
38. Walls, *Joseph Charles Price*, p. 485.
39. Cromwell, *op. cit.*, p. 171.

REV. JOSEPH

CHARLES PRICE

Founder and First
President of Livingstone College,
Salisbury, N.C., 1881-2.
World known orator,
philosopher and race leader.

youth, a sort of black Harvard. . . ." [40] DuBois also said, had Price lived,
Livingstone would have become a black Harvard. He was in touch with the leading
philanthropists and received their support for the college. Livingstone College,
from its beginning, had a broad charter with no discrimination of race, creed or
color.

It was brought out in the Education Committee Report at the General
Conference of 1884 that:

> This institution is under the auspices of the African M. E. Zion Church in
> America. But persons of all denominations are welcome, and respectful
> deference is given their denominational proclivities. Members of the various
> branches of the Christian church are already included in our list of students.

It is emphatic that: "Livingstone College was the sole gift of a race church to
the whole people. It was never provincial nor circumscribed. It was begun by
altruists, once slaves for the most part, who had experienced some denominational
interference with religious freedom and choice in some sectarian philanthropic
schools, and the policy of whose boards was unprescribed service and many of
whose faculties were so, but whose particular teachers and presidents had often
been guilty of coercion and proselytism. But this could never be said of the
A.M.E. Zion Church in its schools, and certainly by no means of this
college." [41]

There was a growing conception when Livingstone College was established,.
that it was time for an institution of learning by blacks for blacks. This
self-creation of Livingstone College was to be a concrete justification of the
educational enterprise of northern whites for leadership training of blacks. In
opening the school at Salisbury, Price immediately secured funds for the
enlargement of the building on the property purchased, from Collins P.
Huntington of New York, a philanthropic supporter of Dr. Price. The building was
used as a dormitory for both teachers and students, auditorium-chapel, library and
classrooms, and a kitchen and dining room in the basement, and named
Huntington Hall. It was later destroyed by fire.

Subsequent buildings were erected through the help of philanthropic
supporters. The first men's dormitory, Dodge Hall, was a gift of William E. Dodge

40. Walls, *Joseph Charles Price*, pp. 102, 185; *Crisis Magazine*, March 1922, pp. 1-3.
41. Walls, *Joseph Charles Price*, p. 250.

HUNTINGTON HALL—FIRST BUILDING, LIVINGSTONE COLLEGE, SALIS-
BURY, N.C. Destroyed by fire in 1918. After removal of Campus from Concord to
Salisbury, in 1882, the name was changed from Zion Wesley Institute to Livingstone
College and incorporated in 1885.

THE PRICE MEMORIAL ADMINISTRATION BUILDING, Built, 1930.

who expressed his desire to see the experiment of an African college, and the faculty as well as the undergraduates, wholly within their own control. [42] Built in 1888, it is today the oldest building on the campus. Stanford Seminary for young women was given by Leland Stanford, Senator from California, builder of the Southern Pacific Railroad Company and donor of Stanford University of California. Ballard Hall was a gift of Stpehen Ballard of New York, and was used, in those days, for industrial education. Withal, the A.M.E. Zion Church, through its meager means, has done its utmost from the beginning. Bishop Hood recalls:

When the Bishops met in Petersburg in February, 1883, Reverend Price came and asked the Board to give the College one-fourth of the General Fund. This was asking very much of the Bishops, for at the close of the preceding year, the Bishops for the first time in the history of the church, had each received his full fifteen hundred dollars salary. The calculation was that if one-fourth was given to the school, they could not· get more than two-thirds of their salary. Nevertheless, the Bishops agreed to the proposition. Just as was anticipated at the end of five years, the Bishops had each received exactly two-thirds of their salary, and $2,500 was due each. [This amount was still due three of the bishops in 1914.] [43]

The General Conference of 1884 first instituted the Children's Day Fund when the school was known as Zion Wesley College. It adoped the rule that "the appropriation from the General Fund in aid of Zion Wesley College being insufficient, the fourth Sunday in June shall be instituted as 'Children's Day,' throughout the connection, and the collections during the day shall be appropriated for the benefit of the said institution." It also adopted a $6,000 annual appropriation for the school. [44] The Children's Day arrangement remained in effect for Livingstone College until 1896, when it was voted that the fund be distributed among other schools of the connection by episcopal districts. The Children's Day Fund later evolved into the support of the Christian Education Department and other schools and colleges, while the church continued to seek other ways and means of supporting its chief institution.

Livingstone College, under the sponsorship of President William H. Goler, led by Dean Ben A. Johnson, began to observe J. C. Price's birthday, Founder's Day, on February 10, 1901, by holding a farmers' conference at the college, and it held two annual sessions. Congressman George H. White of North Carolina, the last black Congressman of the Reconstruction Era, made the address at the first conference. After Mr. Johnson's death, the farmer's conference was discontinued. An earlier attempt had been made when the denomination decided to institute Livingstone College Founder's Day as an income day to help support the college. February 10th, or the Sunday nearest it, was to be observed in the churches as Livingstone College Day, and a collection taken for the college and sent to the treasurer of the college. [45] This action was never implemented. It was not until 1936, when the college had reached a precarious state and its rating was threatened, that a resolution passed the General Conference, signed by Bishops L. W. Kyles, W. J. Walls and Dr. J. W. Eichelberger, to implement Founder's Day financially.

Each member of the denomination was asked to pay 25% of the general claims in an annual Founder's Day Rally. [46] Subsequent General Conferences

42. *Ibid.,* p. 228.
43. Hood, *History,* Vol. II, p. 34.
44. *Doctrines and Discipline,* 1884, p. 50.
45. *Doctrines and Discipline,* 1896, p. 49.
46. *Minutes,* Thirtieth Quadrennial Session, pp. 47, 52.

increased the percentages, and this movement grew until over $100,000 was reported at the annual Founder's Day observances at Livingstone College. Since the 1964 General Conference, when a centralized budget was passed and $270,000 appropriated for Livingstone College in the budget, the Founder's Day observance and program at Livingstone College has been modified. Though the General Conference of 1972 increased the support to nearly a half million dollars, and proposed to revive Founder's Day enthusiasm, the church is still gravely concerned, inventing various means of support, in the midst of the crisis facing education today; especially the black private colleges. The alumni have also become a potent factor in raising funds for the school.

J. C. Price had directed his efforts for the education of all races in the South, and had a passionate belief in its efficacy for helping in all human relations. He was founding president of the first magazine published in the South in the interest of Afro-Americans, known as *The Southland,* with Dr. Simon G. Atkins, editor. [47] He also led a delegation from North Carolina to Washington, D.C., to petition the government for the founding of A. & T. College at Greensboro, N.C. He built Livingstone College, the oldest black liberal arts college totally owned and manned by members of the race. [48] Price was valedictorian of his graduation class at Lincoln University, Pennsylvania, and selected his classmates, William H. Goler and Edward Moore, to be associated with him in establishing Livingstone College.

His chief associate in building the college was Dr. W. H. Goler. All the buildings placed on the campus during the Price administration were constructed by Dr. Goler, a brick mason-contractor who utilized the skill of the students to erect them. Price nominated Goler to be his successor when he learned from his physician that he had about three weeks to live. He made this request to Bishop Hood, chairman of the Board of Trustees. Price died October 25, 1893. Dr. James Edward Mason of Rochester, N.Y., was the virtual successor of Price in the field of philanthropy. He served as financial secretary of the school, and for a long time, secretary of the Trustees Board, giving full measure of devotion to this institution for more than 50 years until his death, April 16, 1946.

Dr. William Harvey Goler was elected to succeed Price, and will be remembered as having secured $50,000 from the Rockefeller Foundation, which aided in building a woman's dormitory, Goler Hall, and funds from Andrew Carnegie, with the assistance of Dr. Booker T. Washington and Bishop George W. Clinton, for the Carnegie Library. He also built the first auditorium on the campus. The Goler administration represented the most constructive period in the founding days of our educational work, extending the creativity of Joseph Charles Price. Dr. Goler, a native Canadian, had a great mentality. He taught the philosophies and rhetoric of the college, and became the reference man of the graduates throughout the country and the world as well as the noted preacher of the church. He served as head of the institution for 23 years, and resigned in 1916, at which time he was elected Financial Secretary of the A.M.E. Zion Church.

The Board of Trustees elected to succeed Goler, Dr. Simon Green Atkins, noted educator and builder of the North Carolina Teachers College at Winston-Salem, but he declined, and Goler was succeeded by Daniel Cato Suggs in 1917. He had been president of the State College of Georgia, and for more than

47. Penn, *The Afro-American Press,* p. 124.
48. Walls, *Joseph Charles Price,* p. vi.

40 years a teacher in the public school system. Dr. Suggs, a very frugal man, was a millionaire as listed by Dunn and Bradstreet. He made some improvements on the property. The school ran into some very heavy problems, and after eight years, President Suggs was relieved of that situation, and a stronger, more practical administration was sought.

In 1925, William Johnson Trent, Sr. was the first graduate of Livingstone College to be secured as president. He placed the school in the A Class column with national rating boards, erected the Price Memorial Building, and several other buildings on the campus, and raised the educational status of the school.

Prior to this, the graduates matriculated in universities for graduate and professional courses, by taking examinations. We have no record of any ever failing. The first bachelor of arts to enter a graduate school, J. A. D. Bloice, went to Boston University, and the president told Dr. Price, "If you have more like him, send them to Boston University." Trent's administration was also blessed with philanthropic increased support. We recall, a heart-rending experience in Durham, N.C., during the earliest years of Dr. Trent's administration, when it was announced that the $75,000 conditional offer of the Rockefeller Foundation for the Price Memorial Building had been cancelled because the A.M.E. Zion Church was unable to raise the funds to match it.

As we walked back to our hotel, Mr. Trent and the writer were bemoaning the loss when Trent came forth with the remark: "I just do not believe Livingstone College is going to fail. There is too much blood and tears of the fathers stored up in the brick and mortar of those buildings for God to let it fail."

He continued heroically, to work on this proposition, and two years afterwards, the gift of $75,000 was made, without any condition. Julius Rosenwald had already given $30,000; the denomination rallied, and the Price Memorial Administration Building was completed. Livingstone College was one of the originial schools included in the organization for support through the United Negro College Fund, during Mr. Trent's tenure. He retired in 1957 owing to ill health, and Dean J. H. Brockett, Jr. was placed in charge until a permanent president was elected.

The trustees selected Samuel Edward Duncan. He was the second graduate of the school elected, and maintained its classification with continuous improvements. He erected the largest number of buildings of any president of the school during his ten-year tenure. The Theological School got its highest consideration under his administration. Imbued with the Pricean spirit of sacrifice, he labored successfully among philanthropic organizations. Trent and Duncan achieved great loyalties among the alumni across the country, after this group had grown large enough to be of consequence. Dr. Duncan died in July 1968, at the top of his career, leaving some of his dreams for Livingstone College incomplete. A committee composed of the chairman of the Board of Trustees, Bishop W. J. Walls, the assistant to the president, Dr. Victor J. Tulane, Dean J. C. Simpson, and the registrar, Miss Julia Bell Duncan, were placed in charge until the election of a president.

Furney George Shipman, another Livingstone College graduate, was elected in 1969. He began promisingly toward a constructive administration, and has inaugurated a program that proposes to keep the standard of Livingstone College achievements high. Three of the buildings provided in the Duncan administration have been completed and dedicated recently.

HOOD THEOLOGICAL SEMINARY
Built, 1910

The faculty members of this institution, have been quite varied from its beginning; for the most part eminent men and women of rare ability, able teachers of several races, who have sacrificed and worked for small salaries in order to serve a struggling race. They have brought out the highest expression of religion, culture, art, civilization, and genuine character. The positions and intellectual contributions of its students in every profession have been felt and recognized around the world since its first Commencement, June 5, 1883. One of the most distinguished graduates of the school and the most noted African of the first half century was James Emman Kwegyir Aggrey of the Gold Coast (Ghana); co-founder of Achimota College in Ghana. The spirit of Livingstone College is the spirit of Joseph Charles Price.

Hood Theological Seminary

Though the primary object of establishing Livingstone College was religious training, it had also soon developed courses in the classical arts and trades. There were efforts of having a religious department in the school. Dr. George Lincoln Blackwell, a graduate of Livingstone College and Boston University School of Theology, became the first to head the theological department of Livingstone College, and was recognized as dean of the theological department. [49] The need of a regular theological department at Livingstone College and other schools had been voiced strongly throughout the denomination. The administration had been criticized, "and sometimes maligned, for not sustaining a first-class Theological Department" at Livingstone College. The General Conference of 1900 gave the matter serious attention, and pledged to raise $6,000 annually to establish and operate a full-fledged theological department. At the Board of Bishops Meeting in Rock Hill, S.C., March 13, 1901, a committee of 33 was appointed to devise a plan for the complete establishment of the theological

49. *Minutes,* Twenty-Eighth Quadrennial Session, 1928. p. 38.

DR. WILLIAM HARVEY GOLER

Theologian and Philosopher. Companion with the great Price in building Livingstone College and became its second president.

DR. JAMES E. KWEGYIR AGGREY

One of the students brought from Africa by Bishop J. B. Small and graduate of Livingstone College. He served as a teacher of the college. While a student at Columbia University, he was chosen by the Phelps-Stokes Fund to tour Europe and America to propagate the cause of African Education. He became Co-founder of Achimota College, Ghana.

department. After much urgency on the part of the bishops and others, a regular organized theological school, for which theological teachers were selected, was begun in the fall of 1903 by President W. H. Goler, [50] Dr. Goler showed that he had been aware of this need in the following explication:

> The dominant idea on the minds of the fathers of the Church in their effort to found an institution of learning, was to meet the necessity of a growing church for a well-prepared and trained ministry.... From the beginning of the work we have had in mind a trained ministry as a necessity absolute for the perpetuation and edification of the Church, and we have for nearly all these years conducted such a department with some considerable success. The young men who have gone out from us are acquitting themselves creditably, many of the churches having testified to their hearty and helpful influence, some of them are occupying the largest and most influential charges in the Connection, and other high and important offices, and they are among the most loyal and energetic workers in the church.... [51]

The Board of Trustees voted to name the newly established department in honor and appreciation of the services of Senior Bishop J. W. Hood, first chairman of the Board of Trustees of Livingstone College, and plans got immediately on the way for a new building. "It would be a source of gratification and no little pleasure to great numbers in our Connection," said Goler, "to have it built and in thorough operation during the lifetime of our most worthy and distinguished Bishop." [52]

Dr. Goler was able to secure the full-time service of Dr. W. H. Hebrew, a graduate of Livingstone College and Boston University School of Theology,—"a man of rare fitness and ability," for this special work. He was also able to get Dr. R. B. Bruce, while he was Editor of the Sunday School Literature, to commute

50. *Minutes,* Twenty-Second Quadrennial Session, 1904, pp. 143-144, 253, 327.
51. *Minutes,* Twenty-Third Quadrennial Session, 1908, p. 211.
52. *Minutes,* Twenty-Second Quadrennial Session, p. 329.

from Charlotte and teach on a part-time basis. There were four instructors the first year with 50 students, divided into two classes. At that time, the course of study of the Hood Theological Seminary was planned to cover four years, along the same line as the leading theological seminaries. Thus the aim was to make "Hood Theological Seminary equal to any Theological Seminary in the South, so that the students may not only be well informed as to Armenianism, but also rooted and grounded in Zion Methodism," and to give a broad view of the entire Christian religion. [53]

The denomination rallied to the cause, and the first Hood Theological Seminary building was completed and opened for operation in October 1910. It was dedicated to the Glory of God with impressive ceremonies in May 1911. President Goler rejoiced:

> It stands an imposing structure on the campus of the College, not only as a lasting testimony and demonstration of the appreciation of our Connection in general of the labors and life work of Bishop Hood for the Church in all its departments, but also to the self-sacrifice of our laity and the determined effort of our ministers to erect this building for the special training of men for the pulpit service of our Church. Bishop Hood, with all the bishops except Bishop Walters who was absent in Africa, was present, and conducted as master of ceremonies, the dedicatory exercises. [54]

After the General Conference of 1912 voted to make Hood Theological Seminary a graduate school of religion, with provision for a full-time dean, under the sponsorship of Livingstone College, Dr. William Orlando Carrington was elected dean. This noted imperturbable scholar served 10 years productively. The Theological School subsequently ran into difficulty during the administration of President Suggs and was suspended indefinitely. The committee on Hood Theological Seminary of the 1932 General Conference recommended that the General Conference make provision for reopening and reorganizing the Hood Theological Seminary, and that a dean be elected by the Board of Trustees, with an effort to resume classes beginning the second semester in February 1933, which was approved. [55]

President Trent put into effect this action and subsequent recommendations for reopening the School of Religion, presented by the trustees in their 1934 meeting. A versatile scholar, Dr. William Edward Carrington, was elected dean. During the first year, 1934-35, students had met the requirements under the improved curriculum, and the three years prescribed theological study, after earning the bachelor degree, was reinforced. Dr. Trent, Dean Carrington, and the staff had worked out exclusive plans for seminary expansion, with an outline of the universal standard theological courses. [56] After serving three years, he transferred to the School of Religion at Howard University, and Professor N. W. Hoffman was placed in temporary charge. The services of Dr. John Henry Satterwhite were secured in 1938. Dean Satterwhite, polished theologian, travelled extensively throughout the church in the interest of the seminary, and won a reputation for recruiting many young men for the ministry of Zion, and training in Hood Theological Seminary.

After 15 years, Dr. Satterwhite went on a sabbatical year of study, and Dr. Frank R. Brown, Sr., was made acting dean. Dr. Satterwhite later removed to

53. *Ibid.*, p. 327.
54. *Minutes,* Twnety-Fourth Quadrennial Session, p. 422.
55. *Minutes,* Twenty-Ninth Quadrennial Session, p. 222.
56. *Minutes,* Thirtieth Quadrennial Session, pp. 296-297.

Washington, D.C., where he became subsequent pastor of the Trinity A.M.E. Zion Church and part-time professor of Wesley Theological Seminary. Dr. F. R. Brown, the acting dean since 1953, was elected dean in 1955. This highly trained, conscientious, hard-working dean increased the student enrollment beyond any previous record.

Classified naturally as sectarian, the Hood Theological Seminary has not had the good fortune of philanthropic assistance like the college department, except in latter days through some of its interested alumni, and in a meager way a few philanthropic friends. Its support has come from the A.M.E. Zion Church. Its enlarged and adequate facility was the result of a denominational rally in 1963 in observance of one hundred years Emancipation. The church raised over $400,000 in this special effort, and one-half went toward the erection of the building known as Walls Center of Hood Theological Seminary, on the site presented to the trustees by Bishop and Mrs. W. J. Walls, plus a donation of $5,000. Under the direction of President Duncan and Dean Brown, the $400,000 building was completed and dedicated to the glory of God in 1965.

Clinton Junior College

Around the same time Livingstone College was established, efforts were made to establish schools in every section of the country where the A.M.E. Zion Church had a large or average following. This movement betokened the universal desire of the black race for knowledge to become useful freedmen. Their first resolve was to have a school in each presiding elder's district, and later, a school in each bishop's district. Some of these schools had promising beginnings and survived several decades. Others were shortlived. Only three of them have remained and are still grappling with the situation. Aside from Livingstone College, the A.M.E. Zion Church sponsors two junior colleges.

History presents an interesting delineation of two endeavors of the A.M.E. Zion Church in the state of South Carolina to establish institutions of learning. Charles Calvin Pettey deserves credit for beginning and promoting the whole program of school building in the state of South Carolina, as well as in Alabama, where he was the father of our education movement. A brief picture of Bishop Pettey's zeal for education from the beginning of his ministry is given here:

He was licensed to exhort August 4, 1968, by Reverend George Frost, at Wilkesboro, N.C.; licensed to preach by Bishop Hood, August, 1872. On December 11 of the same year he was ordained deacon by Bishop Hood. From that time until he graduated he had charge of country circuits in the vicinity of Biddle University. His summer vacations were spent in teaching. By this means he made his way through college, frequently walking fifty miles from Friday evening until Monday morning in order to fill his appointments. Immediately after graduating he was elected principal of the city school in Charlotte, N.C., which position he resigned four months later, was ordained elder by Bishop J. W. Hood, at Chester, S.C., and sent to take charge of the African Methodist Episcopal Zion Church at Lancaster Court House, S.C. While there he founded the "Pettey High School," and was its principal for three years in connection with his church work. Many of his students, of whom he feels justly proud, are now conspicuous race leaders. . . . [57]

He opened the Pettey High School on November 17, 1879, with 50 students, 20 of them boarders, and it was accepted by the General Conference of 1880 as a

57. Hood, *One Hundred Years*, pp. 198-199.

LOMAX-HANNON JUNIOR COLLEGE, GREENVILLE, ALA.
Administrative Building
Founded 1893

connectional school. It soon became the Lancaster High School, and was incorporated in 1898 as the Lancaster Normal and Industrial Institute. During its 45 years of existence (1879-1924), this school produced a large number of reputable and influential citizens. Succeeding Rev. Pettey as its principals and giving splendid service through many vicissitudes were Professors J. A. Cunningham, Wade R. Douglas, R. J. Crockett, and M. D. Lee. Reverend Lee, who also served the church as General Secretary from 1908 to 1917, served two terms at the school, from 1900 to 1912, and from 1916 until the school suspended. After Professor Lee's debilitation, and the rigors of supporting multiple institutions with conformity and standardization, the school was taken over by the public school system, and Zion turned her attention toward her other institution in the state, Clinton Junior College.

This school was founded in Rock Hill, S.C., in 1894 as Clinton Institute, by Presiding Elder Nero A. Crockett of the Yorkville District, and his leading pastor, Rev. W. M. Robinson of Clinton Chapel, Rock Hill. It was named in honor of their presiding bishop, Isom Caleb Clinton, and received as a connectional institution in the 1896 General Conference. Traditionally, a large number of its trustees have been composed of influential members of the church residing in the state, and both schools, as well as other connectional schools, depended largely on state constituents for early support, while the denomination passed through several experimental stages of improvisation.

Its first president was Professor Robert J. Crockett, an energetic and enthusiastic tutor. [At] "The Clinton Institute, at Rock Hill, S.C., the character of his [Professor Crockett's] work and the deportment of his students command the respect and favorable comment of the people in whose midst the institution is doing its praiseworthy work," declared Dr. Goler, who also pointed out that Clinton Institute was a large school controlled and managed satisfactorily by Professor Crockett. (58) He served until 1908, when he became principal of Lancaster Normal and Industrial School. He was succeeded by Professor Robert James Boulware, a good man and laudable educator, who served until his death in

58. W. H. Goler, "Our Educational Institutions. . .," *A.M.E. Zion Quarterly Review*, April 1898, p. 13.

CLINTON JUNIOR COLLEGE, ROCK HILL, S.C.
Administrative Building
Founded 1894

1931. The school lapsed for a brief period after the death of Professor Boulware. In this emergency, Professor James Stephen Stanback was drafted as president by the Board of Christian Education.

Stanback was an ardent reader, with a deep interest in the education program of the church, and conducted this institution with anxious solicitude without a fixed salary, until his health forced him to resign, and he soon passed away. "Reverend C. T. Hinton served as acting President after President Standback's resignation, and until called by death" around 1940. "He brought to the work understanding and enthusiasm." [59]

The school had a resurgence under Hinton's successor, Edward Warner Brice, Jr., who intensified the scholastic standards, and Clinton Junior College received accreditation from the South Carolina State Department of Education and the American Association of Junior Colleges; it also granted State Teachers' Certificates. [60] Professor Brice served with effulgence for two years until called to the United States Army. "Mr. E. P. Gist, an alumnus and trustee of the institution served as acting President for several months until the Reverend James W. Shaw was elected in August, 1942." [61] This devoted churchman-educator served with a high degree of efficiency and success for two years, and was succeeded by Revs. W. J. Campbell and Booker T. Medford, acting presidents. Assiduous in their brief tenure, they were followed by Mrs. Sallie V. (John F. Jr.) Moreland, who was first requested to serve as acting president in 1946, and afterwards elected by the joint Board of Education—Schools and Colleges and the Board of Trustees. Dr. Moreland, who still serves with resplendence, has imbued many scholars with accurate and well-disciplined learning. She is a dedicated, sacrificial worker who has improved the school in many ways, with the well directed assistance of her regents.

59. *Minutes,* Thirty-First Quadrennial Session, p. 190.
60. *Minutes,* Thirty-First Quadrennial Session, pp. 190, 234.
61. *Minutes,* Thirty-Second Quadrennial Session, p. 141.

Lomax-Hannon Junior College

There were three school ventures of the A.M.E. Zion Church in Alabama; first in Tuscaloosa, second in Greenville, and third in Mobile. The oldest school, Tuscaloosa, lasted until 1900 and was merged by the General Conference with the Lomax-Hannon School effort. The Mobile School became a local project principally to serve Zion in that city and southern Alabama. Lomax-Hannon Junior College remains the A.M.E. Zion Church institution of learning in the state.

One of the most promising prospects in the early years of our educational undertaking was the establishment of Jones University at Tuscaloosa, as a connectional school, by Bishop Charles C. Pettey, within the bounds of the old West Alabama Conference, prior to the setting off of the North Alabama Conference. Jones University, named in memory of Bishop Singleton T. W. Jones, was founded by Presiding Bishop Pettey and members of the conference in December 1890. [62] By May 1892, it had secured ample property, with seven instructors and 175 students. It continued to carry a large enrollment under the management of its first president, Professor David Williams Parker, who emanated rare academic skill. He was known as one of the ablest educators of the church and race. Professor Parker operated the school, with the meager support the church was able to give, until 1900 when Jones University was absorbed with Lomax-Hannon High School. [63]

In 1896 there were instituted the patronizing conferences, that is, the assignment of annual conferences to schools by the General Conference for their support, in addition to denominational appropriation. The conferences embracing Alabama, Louisiana, and Florida were designated to support Jones University, while Lomax-Hannon was being formed, and in 1900 these same conferences were assigned to support Lomax-Hannon School. [64]

Lomax-Hannon Junior College was first conceived at the East Alabama (presently Central Alabama) Annual Conference in 1889, at the newly built Mt. Zion Church, Montgomery. In the report of the Committee on Education, it was stated that:

> The remarkable fecundity of our people however, with their strong inherent religious tendencies, call for a constant increase of preachers and fears are entertained that the demand in this large professional field, with the necessity for men which constantly presents itself will induce many to enter without the necessary preparation, thereby crippling their own influence and retarding the progress of, and reflecting discredit on the general church. . . . Let us endeavor to further our advantages for education by the establishment of a preparatory and high school within the bounds of this Conference as soon as the outlook for its support will justify the effort to organize. A. J. Rodgers, L. A. Oliver, J. W. Drake, W. H. Goler, Committee. [65]

Lomax-Hannon Junior College was organized in 1893 as Greenville High School by Bishop Thomas H. Lomax and leading elders of the East Alabama Conference, (after the 1892 General Conference) at Butler Chapel, Greenville, Ala. Reverend Allen Hannon, a dedicated pioneer in Alabama and past presiding

---

62. *Minutes,* Nineteenth Quadrennial Session, pp. 32-33.
63. Goler, *op. cit.,* p. 13.
64. *Minutes,* Twenty-First Quadrennial Session, pp. 84, 95-96; *Doctrines and Discipline,* 1896, p. 49; 1900, p. 189.
65. *Minutes,* Twenty-Second Annual Session, East Alabama Annual Conference, 1889, p. 27.

elder of the Montgomery District, helped to acquire the first land on which the school was located. It is reputed to be the first high school, black or white, in Butler County. Other stalwart and unyielding leaders associating Bishop Lomax and Rev. Hannon in establishing the school were Presiding Elders John W. Alstork, W. G. Strong, J. W. Cooper, H. P. Shuford, M. G. Thomas, and Revs. L. S. Peterson, Joseph Gomez, Titus A. Weathington, A. J. Rodgers, and T. L. Holt, and the pastor of Butler Chapel, Greenville, Rev. Augustus S. Watkins. (66)

The church was creditably represented at Lomax-Hannon by the nurturing and promotional work of Bishop John Wesley Alstork, a staunch friend of education, who lifted its level to a junior college and purchased more than 200 additional acres of land. Financing was a constant problem, and Bishop Alstork engineered more finance for the school than the connection had been able to give it before his administration as bishop of the area and long-term chairmanship of the trustees board. It will be remembered that he served in that district the entire 20 years of his episcopacy. He toiled ardently for the advancement and perpetuity of the institution until he died in 1920, and willed his home to the Lomax-Hannon Junior College. Sometime later, Bishop Buford F. Gordon directed an intensely constructive program for the school.

First principal of the high school was Miss Rosebud Simpson, who was succeeded by Rev. S. B. Boyd in 1900; both were pioneers in converting a theory into practice. Reverend J. R. Wingfield was elected president in 1908, served judiciously for 10 years, and in 1918 was succeeded by the head of the theological department, Rev. W. M. McGee, who served more than a year.

Professor W. N. Rakestraw was elected in 1920; he died in 1922 and was succeeded by Professor T. M. Patton, who served about four years. Professor W. A. Johnson was then elected, serving a brief period, and Rev. Solomon S. Seay followed, serving about 10 years. Mrs. Maud E. Leak served as president from 1938 to 1942, and went on to become president of Walters-Southland Institute in Warren, Ark. From 1942-1943, Rev. O. J. Remsen became acting president, and Professor W. J. Longmire was elected in 1943 and served until 1947 when Professor T. M. Patton was again elected and served until his voluntary retirement in 1968. These presidents were all of exceptional caliber, with such training as the colleges of that day were giving to our inspired and rising people.

Professor Patton's resourceful administration spanned 25 years, and Mrs. Ellenbell Patton, all these years, was a valued and brilliant assistant of the presidents. Professor B. M. Montgomery, who was elected in 1968, continued to inculcate the principles of knowledge until his decision to retire in 1972, and the sedulous Rev. C. Mifflin Smith, Sr. was elected. The institution is governed by a Trustees Board of 30 and the Board of Christian Education—Schools and Colleges.

Zion Institute or Josephine Allen Institute

The other school endeavor in Alabama began shortly after the closing of Jones University. Bishop John B. Small, and a number of faithful brethren cooperating with him, secured a very desirable piece of property at Mobile. At the General Conference of 1900, following a debate on appropriation of funds for Alabama schools involving Bishop Small, Rev. Jesse B. Colbert, Professor Ben A. Johnson, and Dr. S. G. Atkins, Dr. W. H. Goler moved that the money formerly

66. *Ibid.; Minutes,* Twentieth Quadrennial Session, pp. 135, 193; Anderson, *Biographical Souvenir,* pp. 8, 46.

given to Jones University be equally divided between the Lomax-Hannon High School and the Zion Institute; the motion carried. [67] Although it was intended for a connectional institution from this time on, it eventually became a project supported by the A.M.E. Zion Church in Mobile and surrounding territory, serving southern Alabama.

The first principal was Rev. R. A. Morrisey, M. A.; an efficacious guide, who served from 1900 to 1904 and was succeeded by Rev. Benjamin F. Wheeler, noted author and outstanding poet of the A.M.E. Zion Church. After the death of Dr. Wheeler in 1909, Mrs. Josephine Allen, a devoted member of State Street Church in Mobile, a musician and educator, and director of its music, became principal, and maintained the Zion Institute for more than a quarter of a century. She had an unusual personality and incessant loyalty. The school became known as the Josephine Allen Institute. Henry Louis (Hank) Aaron of the Atlanta Braves graduated from this school.

Several other schools came into existence around the same time. Sensing the extreme necessity of education of the race, the General Conference of 1892, through its Committee on Education, took the following positive action:

Whereas, We feel that education among the people whom we represent cannot be too strongly encouraged, and that too many schools for such education cannot be established, offering such advantages to the subjects of our common Church; and,

Whereas, it seems to us that it is the disposition of the Church to enlarge upon the advantages given the youth in all the parts of this land and *Whereas*, The Tennessee Conference has established the Greenville High School; Arkansas Conferences, the Arkansas High School; the Central North Carolina Conference, the Carr Academy at Norwood, N.C.; the Florida Conference, the High and Normal School at Barton, Fla; the South Carolina Conference, the Lancaster High School, the Kirkwood Manual Training School; the West Alabama, the Jones University, Tuscaloosa; the East Alabama, Lomax High School, the Kentucky High School of Madisonville, Ky; and

Whereas, The trustees of said schools and property have desired to transfer the same to the General Church, provided that such property shall be deeded to the Connection, and operated by it as such, and not till then shall it receive help from the Church, be it

Resolved, 1. To encourage, help, and stimulate such, and this General Conference accept and adopt these schools as connectional schools. 2. That the trustees of those institutions be elected by the General Conference, and that their powers be defined provided, first that the majority of said Board shall be elected from the Conferences in which these schools are situated. 3. That these schools receive special consideration in the distribution of connectional help from the Board of Education. F. M. Jacobs, W. H. Ferguson, B. M. Gudger, J. W. Wright, F. J. Manson, J. H. Manley. [68]

This action gave others incentive and stimulation to continue the progress of establishing schools. Bishop C. R. Harris stated in his report at the 1896 General Conference that:

It has been the policy of the Bishop to encourage the establishment of a parochial school in each presiding elder's district to operate in the interval of public school terms, for the purpose of preparing students for the Normal department of Livingstone College, or, in course of time, for a Normal School within the bounds of the conference.

67. *Minutes,* Twenty-First Quadrennial Session, pp. 84, 95-96.
68. *Minutes,* Nineteenth Quadrennial Session, p. 118.

By the turn of the century the A.M.E. Zion Church was fostering 17 institutions of learning, [69] though some of them were soon discontinued owing to lack of funds. A few others were taken over by the Negro public school systems in the various communities. A few, however, came into existence and flourished a while. giving years of enrichment and equipping youth for service and leadership. An account of some of these institutions follows.

Greenville College

During the quadrennium of 1884-1888, when the rotation of bishops after two years was in effect, in 1886, Bishop Thomas H. Lomax assumed the responsibility of the large and progressive Tennessee Conference, which he afterward divided into the East Tennessee Conference. The Greenville High School was organized in 1887 and soon became a fixture. Reverend B. M. Gudger is known in history as the originator of this school. He secured acres of land in Greenville, Tenn., and had a two-story frame building erected to accommodate 300 students. Because of the tenacity of Bishop Lomax, Revs. Gudger, W. H. Ferguson, B. F. Tipton, and R. E. Toomey, the school was soon developed into a college for those who could not afford to attend more distant institutions. [70]

This work found propitious encouragement in that section of the country, due to the zeal of its first president, Rev. R. A. Morrisey, and the hearty cooperation of Bishop T. H. Lomax and the leaders of the Tennessee, East Tennessee, and Virginia Conferences. [71] Reverend F. R. White, Professors William J. Trent, Sr., J. A. Chandler, T. C. Irwin, H. V. Taylor, E. P. Mayo, Arthur A. Madison, J. W. Younge, and Vivian R. Campbell, all served as presidents of this institution with indubitable literary skill, enhancing the minds of a number of scholars who completed their higher education there. It began a financial struggle before the Depression, and did not recover. After 1932 the Greenville College buildings and grounds were leased to the Greenville School Board for use as a public school. The prospect of reopening the school was quite remote, and the property was subsequently sold. [72] Mrs. Roberta Hastie, mother of Judge William H. Hastie, was a prominent member of the faculty at Greenville during the administration of Dr. Younge, while the judge was growing up. He once shared an apple with a friend in the presence of Dr. Younge, and gave his friend the larger part. Dr. Younge inquired of him why he gave his friend the larger part. He answered, "mother always taught me to give the other fellow the bigger half." This type of character education by his mother was instrumental in helping to raise the judge to a top place in the service of his people and country.

Atkinson College

This was the education project of the Kentucky Conference, to fill a long-felt need in that section of our church and was at first, directly under the patronage of the Conference. Atkinson College was established in 1889 at Madisonville, Ky., as Madisonville High School, by Presiding Bishop Thomas H. Lomax, Revs. E. H. Curry, James B. Johnson, and G. B. Walker. It first had difficulty in maintaining

---

69. *Minutes,* Twentieth Quadrennial Session, pp. 160, 193.
70. Hood, *One Hundred Years,* pp. 194, 337, 560; Anderson, *Official Directory,* p. 60; *Minutes,* Twenty-Fourth Session, East Tennessee Annual Conference, 1889, pp. 51-53.
71. Goler, *op. cit.,* p. 13.
72. *Minutes,* Thirtieth Quadrennial Session, p. 230.

its existence, but in 1894 John B. Atkinson, a prominent wealthy white citizen of Earlington, Ky., with a deep interest in the elevation of the Negro race, helped to relieve the pressure and place it upon a sure foundation. From the establishment of the school until his death, Mr. Atkinson contributed substantially to this work, "for the development of Negro youths in literary and industrial attainment." The school was incorporated January 26, 1896 under the title of Atkinson Literary and Industrial College. [73] Reverend E. H. Curry was its first principal, and he was succeeded by Rev. G. B. Walker. There was augmentation in 1900 when Bishop George Wylie Clinton, chairman of the trustees, also worked as financial agent, and lectured in history, logic and Bible studies, and Reverend Samuel Edward Duncan, Sr., served as president. He was succeeded by Rev. John W. Martin, who served until he was elected Secretary of Education in 1916. Professor James Muir served for a brief period. Reverend H. V. Taylor was then elected president and served until it became difficult to operate as a full-fledged institution after the 1936 General Conference. These presidents with pedagogical skill made broad contributions to producing meaningful scholars for society.

The school was then utilized by the Kentucky Conference and surrounding areas as a summer religious training institute. The property, still owned by the Christian Education Board of the connection, consists of nearly 34 acres of land with approximate value of $150.000. [74]

Eastern North Carolina Academy

In 1904 Rev. William H. Sutton founded this Industrial Academy in New Bern, N.C., with the patronage of the North Carolina Conference presided over by Bishop Thomas H. Lomax. Dr. Sutton, its president, accomplished a significant task in starting this school. He took his own money and bought a lot, built the first house upon it, and deeded it to the connection. He afterward made available the use of two other buildings for girls' and boys' dormitories. He was known for his economy and ability to successfully operate the school with the assistance of dedicated teachers. A fine spirited administrator and instructor, he operated the school under the auspices of the Christian Education Board—Schools and Colleges until the Depression. The General Conference of 1932 sustained the Committee on Schools and Colleges in their recommendation that this school be discontinued, along with the Macon Industrial School of Macon, Ga., where Professor W. M. McGee was principal, preceded by Professor B. J. Bridges, also the Edenton High School of Edenton, N.C. [75] The Zion High School of Norfolk, Va., which once numbered several hundred pupils under its first principal, Professor E. C. Simms, had been discontinued some time before. Palmetto Institute at Union, S.C.; Lloyd Academy at Elizabethtown, N.C.; Hemphill High School at Crockett, Ga.; Pettey Academy at New Bern, N.C.; Lomax and Rutledge Academy at Tampa, Fla.; Carr Academy, N.C.; and Pettey Institute at Calvert, Tex. were other schools started by annual conferences and had brief existences. Reverend C. D. Hazel, dean of the Correspondence School and Theological Circle, operated this institution for Zion at Atlantic City for more than 25 years.

73. *Minutes,* Twenty-Seventh Quadrennial Session, pp. 356-362; . . . Anderson, *Official Directory,* p. 61.
74. George L. Blackwell, II, Christian Education Dept., Six Months Report, January 4, 1972, p. ii.
75. *Minutes,* Twenty-Ninth Session, p. 227.

Walters–Southland Institute

Bishop C. R. Harris' effort to establish the Arkansas High School at Parkdale, Ark., in 1891, did not succeed. However, this same year, prior to the 1892 General Conference, he founded the Ashley County High School at Wilmot, Ark., out of which evolved the Walters Institute. "Reverend A. J. Coleman was one of the foremost promoters of it. Reverends A. J. Sims, G. W. Morris, T. J. Jones, H. H. Bingham and others were with him in the work. Reverends A. Arnold and J. R. Ward gave the land for the school, and Bishops Jehu Holliday and Alexander Walters labored for its improvement along with Reverends R. B. Macon, James Smith and A. W. Weekly." The name was changed to Walters Institute, to honor the sacrificial work of Bishop Walters, and Bishop J. W. Alstork continued to promote the work at Wilmot. [76]

In 1906, through the influence of Professor Simon G. Atkins, secretary of education, and Rev. J. W. Murray, Walters Institute was moved to Warren, Ark., where the citizens had donated three acres of ground and subscribed $1,000 for an enlarged school. Here in Warren, Rev. J. W. Murray, a gifted religious poet and writer, became its principal, and the enrollment began to increase. [77] His tenure ended in 1909, and in September of that year, Professor James W. Eichelberger, Jr. was elected principal. Following this promoter of education were Rev. C. W. P. Mitchell, Professor L. O. Grady, Professor Allen S. Meacham, Rev. W. T. Rieves, and Professor T. R. Wright.

When the work of this institution had so expanded as to need more land, and after all available adjacent property had been purchased, the white citizens of Warren gave a 50-acre site in another section of the city, and also gave toward the rebuilding of the school on the new site. Additional land was later purchased by the institution. In 1935, upon the inspection of the secretary of the Board of Education, Dr. J. W. Eichelberger, and recommendation of trustees of the school and officers of the board, Walters Institute purchased the Southland College site from the Free and Accepted Masonic Lodge of Arkansas, and the joint school opened on January 20, 1936. The school was then known as Walters-Southland Institute. [78]

The new campus was relocated near Lexa, Ark. and was manned by Professor J. H. Hammond, and later Mrs. Maud E. Leak. In 1948, the school experienced a setback after the presiding bishop, W. W. Matthews, who had been chairman of the Trustees Board for a number of years, was disciplined by the church, and a controversy ensued with the Board of Christian Education and the dismissed bishop. After this episode the school was removed back to Warren, and the principal, Rev. J. W. Hatch, skillfully managed the situation directed by the Board of Trustees and Board of Christian Education jointly. The Institution was afterward placed in the custody of Rev. Stephen P. Spottswood who was succeeded by Rev. C. R. Thompson. The school finally closed down. The Southland property in Lexa has been sold, and the church, through the Christian Education Department. maintains the property at Warren, approximately 82 acres.

---

76. *Minutes,* Twenty-Second Quadrennial Session, pp. 218, 240.
77. *Minutes,* Twenty-Third Quadrennial Session, pp. 253-254.
78. *Minutes,* Thirtieth Quadrennial Session, pp. 228-230.

TUSKEGEE INSTITUTE IS BORN IN THE A.M.E. ZION CHURCH

THE ORIGINAL BUTLER CHAPEL CHURCH (founded, 1865 by Rev. J. B. Butler) AND "SHANTY" WHERE BOOKER T. WASHINGTON TAUGHT HIS FIRST CLASSES.

DR. BOOKER T. WASHINGTON

MR. LEWIS ADAMS Superintendent of the Sunday School, taught crafts in the church building. He was desirous for a Normal School for Colored to be located at Tuskegee, and wrote General Armstrong of Hampton, Virginia who responded by sending Booker T. Washington. Mr. Washington started classes in the church on July 4, 1881.

MARKER IN FRONT OF THE PRESENT CHURCH
INDICATING SPOT WHERE SCHOOL WAS FOUNDED.

PRESENT BUTLER CHAPEL CHURCH WITH MARKER (Extreme Left) INDICATING
FOUNDING SITE OF TUSKEGEE INSTITUTE.

Dinwiddie Institute

The splendid school property at Dinwiddie, Va. came into the possession of the church as a gift from Mr. Alexander Van Rensaler of Philadelphia. Professor Simon G. Atkins, secretary of the Board of Education, and the General Secretary, Dr. George L. Blackwell, acting for the special committee appointed by the Board of Bishops, at Washington, D.C., February 1908, completed the agreement for the property, located 15 miles north of Petersburg. [79] Dinwiddie Agricultural and Industrial School of the A.M.E. Zion Church was opened January 1, 1910 with Professor T. C. Irwin as its first principal. Both the Virginia and Albermarle Conferences, presided over by Bishops Hood and G. W. Clinton respectively, gave vital support, which continued through the years. In 1912 Professor W. E. Woodyard was elected principal and served faithfully over 30 years before the school became inoperative in 1944. By arrangements with the State and County Board of Education, a county training school was placed near our property, and the principal was working with this school and at the same time, serving his own institution. This property of about 240 acres was also used for a summer religious training institute by the Virginia, Albermarle, and other surrounding conferences. A building is in course of erection, replacing one destroyed by fire, under the direction of the Board of Trustees and Board of Christian Education—Schools and Colleges, for continual projection of vicinal religious training.

Johnson Memorial Institute

The founding of Johnson Rural High School at Batesville, Miss., was an emboldening incentive for our people in the Delta. The following extract from the report of Bishop George C. Clement to the General Conference of 1920 is a picturesque account of this beginning:

> ... Credit must be given to the lamented Albert J. Johnson who fell asleep October 5th last for this school. Mr. Johnson was the wealthiest Negro in Mississippi, and one of the richest in the A.M.E. Zion Church. At the time of his death he owned and operated a three thousand acre planation with seventy-two families living and working upon it . . . Beginning life as an illiterate cotton field hand he struggled hard with wonderful success. Around him were poor school facilities and his heart yearned for the dawn of light for his people. This moved him two years before his death to give to the A.M.E. Zion Church five acres of land, and $1.00 in cash as an impetus to the West Tennessee and Mississippi Conference towards establishing a Rural High School. The Conference and community rallied and a total of over $7,000 was raised. Two modern buildings, among the best appointed in our educational system, were erected at a cost of $15,000. Mr. Johnson loaned all that was needed for their completion. On the very day the school was to have opened, Mr. Johnson was buried from its Chapel. Peace to his name.
>
> Under the direction of Professor G. W. Vance [its first principal], B. S., and with the assistance of Professor F. D. Cooper and three lady teachers we have conducted a very successful term of the Johnson High School. There were fifty-five boarding students and one hundred forty-nine day students. The school closed April 30th without owing a dollar to teachers or leaving a penny of current indebtedness.
>
> We commend it as the beacon for 40,000 Negroes who live in a radius of thirty miles and who otherwise have no school above the sixth grade. [80]

79. *Minutes,* Twenty-Third Quadrennial Session, p. 156; *Minutes,* Twenty-Fourth Quadrennial Session, p. 463.
80. *Minutes,* Twenty-Sixth Quadrennial Session, p. 162.

Professor J. H. Hammond succeeded Professor Vance as principal; however, he soon became principal of another connectional school, Price Memorial Institute at Macon, Ga. Other leading preceptors of this institution were Professors P. C. Moore, G. C. Sylvester, M. M. Leak, A. S. McCord, Rev. J. J. Wells, Professors J. H. A. Shaw, Claudius C. Scott, and upon Scott's death, Miss Annie M. Valentine, faithful secretary of the Trustees Board, served a brief period. Reverend D. F. Martinez became principal in 1952 and served until his death in April 1958. He was succeeded by Rev. G. Sims Rivers. Mr. Tom Cooper has served as treasurer of the institution over 20 years. The high school closed around 1960, and the modern classroom building presently accommodates the community Headstart Program. Annual conference and district religious leadership training institutes are also held there.

The Institute of Black Ministries in Philadelphia, directed by one of the rising sons of Zion, Rev. Vaughn T. Eason, was considered at the 1972 General Conference, and endorsed by the Board of Bishops for denominational support at the Connectional Council at Philadelphia, in July 1972.

The struggle to organize and support our schools and colleges, and a number of other institutional ventures whose existences were too short and have not been mentioned in this work, exhibits our intrepid spirit in overcoming the calamities of slavery, and gives abundant evidence and concrete proof of the uncompromising stand of the African Methodist Episcopal Zion Church in favor of education.

Tuskegee Institute at Butler Chapel

The Tuskegee Institute was founded in the Butler Chapel Church, fostered in its beginning by Mr. Lewis Adams, the superintendent of Sunday schools and loyal member of the church. Dr. Booker T. Washington expressed it as follows in his address at Livingstone College during its Quarter-Centennial Celebration:

> The Tuskegee Institute extends most hearty congratulations and good wishes to Livingstone College on the occasion of the celebration of its twenty-fifth anniversary. These two institutions were founded at about the same time and are therefore practically of the same age. There is, however, another connection between Tuskegee Institute and Livingstone College, and the great church which stands behind Livingstone, which makes Tuskegee feel very near to the African M. E. Zion Church, for Tuskegee Institute had its birth in a church of your denomination in 1881. Mr. Lewis Adams, one of the most prominent members of your church, had begun to lay the foundation of the Tuskegee Institute before I went into Alabama, and it was in the church of which he was a member that Tuskegee Institute was born, and I might add, that during all the years of this life I never found a wiser counsellor in all the affairs of the institution than I did in Mr. Adams. [81]

Adams, a master craftsman of leather making, teaching trades; harness and shoe-making, etc. was running the school himself. When it expanded, he consulted with Bishop Singleton T. Jones about taking over the enterprise for the A.M.E. Zion Church, and Bishop Jones regretfully declined because of the effort then being made to establish Livingstone College. He subsequently communicated with General Samuel Armstrong, who founded Hampton Institute with the American Missionary Association in 1868, to send a teacher for his school venture. The answer was Booker T. Washington. Mr. Washington formally opened Tuskegee

81. Atkins and Wallace, *Quarter-Centennial of Livingstone College,* p. 107.

MR. WILLIAM JOHNSON TRENT, SR.

Fourth President of Livingstone College. Led in expanding the campus and his outstanding achievement was raising the rating of the college to the A Class. (l.)

MR. SAMUEL EDWARD DUNCAN

Fifth President of Livingstone College. This constructive educator erected nine buildings and began the building of three more in ten years to the campus of the college. (r.)

W. J. Walls Center of the Hood Theological Seminary Built, 1965.

Institute on July 4, 1881, with one teacher (Lewis Adams), and 30 students. The school operated for two years in Butler Chapel and then moved to its present location, [82] though miraculously expanded.

Some other educators of the first rank of achievement produced in the A.M.E. Zion Church were Rev. William Hooper Councill, founder of Huntsville Normal Institute, in 1875, now Alabama A & M College, Normal, Ala.; William Johnson Trent, Jr., first Executive Director of the United Negro College Fund and later, Personnel Director of Time-Life Magazine; Aaron Brown, Jr., who served as president of Albany State College, Albany, Ga., and later elected member of New York City Board of Education; and Roy D. Hudson, President of Hampton University.

A noteworthy feature in the A.M.E. Zion Church's interest in ecumenicity is the black ecumenical education complex established in 1959 through the distinguished achievement of Dr. Harry V. Richardson, the Interdenominational Theological Center at Atlanta. This project has continued to make a significant contribution under the leadership of his skillful successor in 1968, President Oswald P. Bronson.

82. *The Star of Zion,* December 23, 1897, p. 1.

CHAPTER 23

THE PUBLISHING INTEREST AND LITERATURE

"And now for a little space grace hath *shewed* from the Lord our God, to leave us a remnant to escape, and to give us a nail (a pin that is a constant and sure abode), in his holy place, that our God may lighten our eyes, and give us a little reviving in our bondage." Ezra 9:8

This is a description of the encouragement the A.M.E. Zion Church imbibed from God and his word in the midst of its efforts to create literary means and to light the way. The struggle to launch the enterprise of a permanent connectional journal and other literature gives a chapter in history as varied and almost as heroic as the founding of the denomination. Before our denominational efforts, our first two bishops were integral parts of the effort to give renewed strength, courage, and understanding to a people of serfdom, in uniting with other black leaders to promote the race's earliest journalistic movement. [1]

The part James Varick and a few other potent leaders had in the founding of the first black newspaper, *Freedom's Journal* with John Russworm and Samuel Cornish, brought forth the following declaration in their first publication, March 16, 1827:

Useful knowledge of every kind and everything that relates to Africa, shall find a ready admission into our columns: and as that vast continent becomes daily more known, we trust that many things will come to light, proving that the natives of it are neither so ignorant nor stupid as they have generally been supposed to be.

And while these important subjects shall occupy the columns of the *Freedom's Journal*; we would not be unmindful of our brethren who are still in the iron fetters of bondage. They are our kindred by all the ties of nature; and though but little can be effected by us, still let our sympathies be poured forth, and our prayers in their behalf, ascend to Him who is able to succour them. From the press and from the pulpit we have suffered much by being incorrectly represented. [2]

The fact that *Freedom's Journal* operated from old Zion Church at 152 Church Street from May 4, 1827 to May 2, 1828, attests to the passionate concern of our leaders and people in efforts to keep this first black American journal alive. It began waning after Mr. Russworm assumed sole editorial control, in September 1827, and the name of the paper was later changed to *Rights of All;* Russworm's later interest in the African colonization movement caused him to go to Africa, and finally, to suspend the newspaper. [3]

1. Federal Writers Program, New York Negroes.
2. *Freedom's Journal,* March 16, 1827.
3. Federal Writers Program; Penn, *The Afro American Press,* p. 30.

The second journalistic effort on behalf of the race was the New York based *Weekly Advocate,* started in January 1837, which changed its name two months later to *The Colored American.* Appearing in its first issues was a lengthy circular letter from the ministers and pastors of the several congregations of colored people in the city of New York, to the free colored citizens of the United States and to all their Christian brethren and friends. It was a stringent appeal for developing high intellectual, moral, and spiritual propensities, with vital statistics on the people of color in slave and free states, including a stalwart statement on *Prejudice Against Color,* and calling upon its people to mightily support anti-slavery societies and similar agencies. It climaxed as follows:

There is a work which the most exalted and untiring philanthropy cannot effect for us. Religion may prompt, intelligency may devise, and moral heroism may accomplish, but if we remain inactive or indifferent, the work cannot be done. The breach will be wide, and not only wide, but most dishonorable to ourselves.

But, beloved, we believe better things of you, though we thus write—and that you may be able to comprehend the work in its entire magnitude, and be inspired to embark in it, by the bright prospects which are opening before you and to the *millions of our land in chains,* we commit you to God and to the work of his grace.

CHRISTOPHER RUSH, Superintendent, Zion's Church Methodist Connection

ISAAC BARNEY, Elder, African Union Methodist Church

TIMOTHY EATO, Elder, Asbury Methodist Church, Zion's Connexion

JAMES SIMMONS, Elder, Zion Church, Zion Methodist Connexion

JOHN T. RAYMOND, Elder, Zion's Baptist Church

WILLIAM A. CORNISH, Elder, Methodist Church, Bethel connexion

THEODORE S. WRIGHT, Pastor, Presbyterian Church, Frankfort St.

SAMUEL E. CORNISH, Presbyterian[4]

In 1840, Charles B. Ray became the editor of *The Colored American.* After making a brilliant record, the journal was suspended in the early part of 1842. [5]

The first effort of the A.M.E. Zion Church toward establishing an independent church journal and its own literary concern was in 1841, prompted by actions of the 1840 General Conference and the New York Annual Conference, May 22, 1841, at Mother Zion Church. A resolution was passed by the conference, and a committee composed of Revs. Jehial C. Beman, Jacob D. Richardson, and Nathan Blunt was appointed to draft a prospectus for a connectional monthly newspaper, to be known as *The Zion Wesley.* The Philadelphia Annual Conference of the same year concurred with the movement and appointed Revs. David Stevens, George Galbraith, and Leonard Collins to represent them. The venture was not a success. [6] Our people were afterwards encouraged to support the *North Star,* established by Frederick Douglass in Rochester, N.Y. in 1847, and later called *Frederick Douglass' Paper.* Frequent contributions were made by Revs. Jermain W. Loguen and William Howard Day. [7]

The subject of a journal was taken up again at the General Conference of 1860, which resolved that some plan be adopted to start a monthly periodical for

4. *The Weekly Advocate,* February 18, 1837.
5. Penn, *The Afro-American Press, op. cit.,* p. 47.
6. Moore, *History of the A.M.E. Zion Church,* pp. 323-324.
7. *The North Star & Frederick Douglass' Paper,* various issues, 1847.

the benefit of the connection. The General Conference further resolved to give its wholehearted support to *The Weekly Anglo-African,* a journal founded in 1859, and edited by Thomas Hamilton and his brother, Robert Hamilton, the chorister of Mother Zion Church. The Conference recommended it to our churches, as being worthy of the highest regard and meriting the influence of every minister of the connection. [8] In 1864 the General Conference resolved to enlarge its support of *The Anglo-African,* and to appoint a committee to consult the editor concerning the purchase of a press. This committee was composed of Revs. W.F. Butler, R. H. G. Dyson, J. W. Hood, J. H. Smith, and Benjamin Pulpress, a layman from the Allegheny Conference. [9]

The Anglo-African soon failed. "It lived to see the Afro-American a freedman, and to enjoy the awarded—'Well done, good and faithful servant,' in the Abolition fight. It lived to see the Afro-American on the march to an intellectual position and to civil citizenship; and with this consciousness it died peacefully in the arms of its promoters." [10] During the quadrennium between 1864 and 1868, the trustees and some members of Mother Zion Church in New York, under the auspices and editorial management of their pastor, Rev. Singleton T. Jones, and William Howard Day, secular editor, established a most creditable paper known as *Zion Standard and Weekly Review.* It was a weekly journal serving the race, under the auspices of Zion Church, New York, with its business management and publication under Samuel Howard and M. B. Coss. Much of the news was published in the interest of Zion connection. The General Conference of 1868 entered into an agreement with the trustees of Mother Zion Church to purchase the *Zion Standard* for $8,750, including all appurtenances (all outstanding debts, obligations or encumbrance), from June 1, 1868, and to take possession on this date. Mother Zion Church, in compliance with the terms of payments to extend over a period of two years with 7% interest, agreed to donate $4,500 out of the $8,750 contract price. Reverend J. N. Gloucester was elected editor. [11]

"From the action of the General Conference in the purchase of the paper, its fate was soon sealed and soon *Zion Standard and Weekly Review* was defunct, leaving the Connection without an organ." In the next quadrennium, 1868-1872, a newspaper was started by Revs. Jacob P. Hamer and John E. Price, assisted by Rev. Jacob B. Trusty, in Washington, D.C., published semi-monthly in the interest of the connection, titled *Zion Church Advocate.* The journal was adopted by the General Conference of 1872, but it also became defunct in the interim.

The delegates to the General Conference of 1876 were determined to establish a permanent connectional journal. The committee on journal or church organ worked out a detailed plan for projection and operation, submitted by Revs. William T. Biddle, secretary and William Howard Day, president. The plan was adopted by the General Conference to publish the *National Standard and Zion Church Advocate,* and William Howard Day was made editor-in-chief, with an assistant from each annual conference. Harrisburg, Pa., was to be the place of publication. [12]

At the close of this General Conference, the delegates returned home with

8. Moore, *History,* p. 325.
9. Ibid.; Walls, Ms. History, *The Star of Zion* 1921, p. 1.
10. Penn. *op. cit.,* p. 88.
11. Moore, *History,* pp. 264, 326-328.
12. *Ibid.,* pp. 329-333.

high hopes of success. "It had been agreed that each minister should pledge $4.50, the price of three copies per year, but for some cause, not a copy was issued after the General Conference." Tired of being harassed by persons who had sent their money and could get no paper, within a few months after the General Conference Bishop Hood went to New Bern, N.C. to arrange with Rev. John Tyler to publish a newspaper. The paper was started also to supply a need resulting from the failure of *Zion Church Advocate* the previous quadrennium. [13] After 35 years of earnest endeavor, our journalistic effort met with success, though marked by continuous strife; thus the *Star of Zion* was born in 1876, and the church continued its pursuit in establishing a publication house for this and other church literature.

The Book Concern and Publication House

Another movement in the direction of furnishing literature for the church was The Book Concern of the A.M.E. Zion Church, established in New York City by the New York Conference in 1841. Reverend Jacob D. Richardson was appointed first general book steward, and supervised the Book Concern until his death in 1844. Reverend Nathan Blunt associated him, and from the beginning they formed a publishing committee. They published hymn books for our church use, disciplines, minutes, and other connectional matter. After the death of Richardson, the General Conference of 1844 appointed a management committee, composed of Revs. J. P. Thompson, William H. Bishop, and Timothy Eato. Because of the unfortunate schism in the connection between 1848 and 1856, it was difficult to obtain an account of the Book Concern and its operation. [14]

The General Conference of 1856 appointed Bishop Christopher Rush and Revs. Joseph P. Thompson and Samuel M. Giles a general book committee, with entire supervision over the Book Concern. This committee published a Hymnal for the use of our church in 1858. It reported at the General Conference of 1860 that the Book Concern had a stock in the hymn books valued at $327.38. In the course of reuniting after the split, the General Conference appointed a Board of Trustees of the Book Concern consisting of Revs. Singleton T. Jones, Samuel M. Giles, John P. Thompson, J. D. Brooks, and Joseph P. Thompson. Reverends Henry Johnson, Abraham Cole, and Jermain W. Loguen were appointed Book Stewards for the several annual conferences, to improve the means of circulating the literature. [15]

In an effort to improve the system, the General Conference of 1864 elected general officers immediately after the assignment of bishops. Reverend Isaac Coleman of the New York Conference was chosen General Book Steward, and Revs. Singleton T. Jones, William H. Decker, William H. Pitts, and Jeptha Bancroft as trustees of the Book Concern. Faced with perplexities, at the General Conference of 1868 the book steward and trustees reported embarrassment and debts. The connection was in need of Disciplines and hymnals and they were unable to supply them. [16]

The connection, which at this time was without an organized financial system, and had no funds for promoting this cause, elected Rev. Jacob Thomas at the 1868 General Conference as general book agent. Depending largely upon his

13. Hood, *One Hundred Years,* pp. 108,109.
14. Moore, *History,* pp. 317-318.
15. *Ibid.,* p. 318.
16. *Ibid.,* pp. 237, 242, 318-319.

ingenuity and skill, he was authorized by this body to publish the old Hymn Books and Disciplines, "without any means except his own with which to accomplish the work." Reverend Thomas, however, went forward and published, but in small amounts, which increased the price of printing. The sales were small, and "the proceeds did no more than meet the outlays." [17]

At the General Conference of 1872, after the committee reported unsuccessful operation during the four years, the constitution of the Book Concern was totally revised, and its object stated in the Discipline: "To furnish means for the support of education insitutions, our Press, Book Concern, and Missionary interests." The new constitution provided for a board of officers consisting of a president, vice-president, secretary, treasurer, corresponding secretary, a finance committee of five, and two collecting agents, which the General Conference proceeded to elect. [18] The Conference manifested confidence in Rev. Thomas' ability to manage the Book Concern, and re-elected him general book agent, with authorization to secure hymnals and other literature for the denomination. [19]

At the General Conference of 1876, the Book Concern, which Bishop John D. Brooks had presided over the past four years, with Revs. J. Harvey Anderson, J. B. Trusty, J. E. Price, J. P. Hamer, and George Bosley, all connected with the Board of Book Concern, the Connectional Journal, and the *Zion Church Advocate*; "reported the Book Concern being without funds or stock, and in debt $287.80." The General Conference appointed a new board, and Rev. Jacob Thomas was re-elected General Book or Publishing Agent. From this General Conference, for the first time since the death of the founder of the Book Concern, Rev. Jacob Richardson, our publishing venture started on an upward trend.

The denomination was greatly in need of literature and new hymnals, and the forward move made by the 1876 General Conference, projecting a permanent church organ and ways and means of publishing it, began to produce concrete results. Reverend Thomas, who was also the treasurer of the joint Mission Board of the New York and New Jersey Conferences, contracted with that board to come to the aid of the Book Concern, and publish the neccessary books. They did this and received the profits of the sale until the Board of Bishops met the following year. The Board of Bishops, in its semi-annual meeting in 1877, reorganized the Board of Book Concern, "appointing Bishop J. J. Moore, president, Reverend Jacob Thomas, vice president, Reverend Henry M. Wilson, Secretary, Reverend Clinton Leonard, treasurer, Reverend C. W. Robinson, corresponding secretary, and Bishops Hood, Jones, Thompson and Lomax a financial committee to supervise the Book Concern." [20]

The bishops contracted, through the executive board of the Book Concern, to purchase from the New York and New Jersey Conferences Joint Mission Board, the capital stock it held in the literature it had published for the Book Concern, and thus proceeded to direct the Book Concern under its new setup. In 1879 a fund raising campaign was devised for the successful operation of the Book Concern by the delegates of the various annual conferences of the First Episcopal District (Bishop J. J. Clinton, presiding). They called a district convention at Jersey City, N.J. and decided that Bishop John J. Moore be appointed agent to

17. *Ibid.*, p. 319.
18. *Ibid.*; *Doctrines and Discipline*, 1872, pp. 213-217.
19. Moore, *History*, pp. 319-320.
20. *Ibid.*, pp. 320-321.

England to raise funds to relieve the needs of our financial insitutions. At a subsequent meeting of the Board of Bishops, this action was sanctioned, and Bishop Moore was deputized to travel to England as agent of the denomination. His trip was propitious in every way. He collected $2,300 in all and turned over $1,100 to the Book Concern, which gave it the necessary boost for accomplishing its goal. [21]

Reverend Jacob Thomas, the general agent, made an astonishing report at the 1880 General Conference, in which he gave the historical struggle, especially from 1872 to 1879 when the Book Concern passed through its most crucial period, practically suspending. From March 1879, the business was conducted totally in the interest of the connection as General Conference property. He reported several agents set up within the bounds of annual conferences, and supplietl with books, and the Book Concern operating under very favorable financial circumstances. He gave credit to Bishop Moore. [22]

Bishop Moore, on the other hand, praised the forcible leadership of Rev. Thomas, calling him one of the most faithful sons of Zion, "who had given for many years his service without pay to save our Book Concern from utter failure;—when he could do no better, he would carry it in his trunk from conference to conference." [23] The committee on book concern of the 1880 General Conference submitted a revised plan of the Consitution, which was approved, and enlarged the system of operation. Its publishing department was to be located in New York City, and a book room was provided at 183 Bleecker Street. It had a fine stock of A.M.E. Zion Church literature and a general assortment of religious books. It began to yield income at this time toward the support of worn-out preachers and their families, according to the regulation of the Discipline. A catalogue of the publications of our church was published and distributed by Rev. Thomas, the general agent. The list of materials printed for the use of our denomination was quite varied. [24]

At the 1884 General Conference, Rev. Thomas reported the increased need of church membership patronage to make the Book Concern ultimately a success. It had been able, for the first time, to send throughout the connection a Sabbath school paper for the benefit of the children. The report was one of hope for future growth and progress. The *Star of Zion,* during this time, was being operated in North Carolina under separate management. It had the united encouragement of the church leaders, and began to increase in strength and utility. [25] On the last day of the General Conference a resolution prevailed which authorized the Board of Bishops to overhaul the Book Concern. A petition was granted, upon examination of the Constitution of the Book Concern by a special committee, to give this committee power to make such revision of the Consitution and By-Laws as would enable them to carry on the business of the Book Concern with the greatest possible advantage to the connection. [26]

At the General Conference of 1888, reports were made by the committee on Book Concern; the General Agent, Rev. Thomas; and the auditors of the Book Concern, and it was evident that the Book Concern was depreciating. Elder

21. *Ibid.,* p. 322.
22. *Minutes,* Sixteenth Quadrennial Session, pp. 58-60.
23. Moore, *History,* p. 322.
24. Jacob Thomas, *Catalogue* of the Publications of the A.M.E. Zion Book Concern, 1882.
25. *Minutes,* Seventeenth Quadrennial Session, pp. 26, 127-128.
26. *Ibid.,* pp. 112-113,149

Thomas had assumed heavy responsibilities in keeping it afloat. A resolution was presented by Rev. L. J. Scurlock to remove the Book Concern from New York. "Reverend Alexander Walters made a motion which authorized the bishops to appoint a Board of Publication; and the following were appointed, viz; Bishop J. W. Hood, Reverends J. B. Small, W. H. Goler, Jacob Thomas, and Alexander Walters." [27] The action taken by the General Conference four years previously had not been enforced, and immediately after the 1888 General Conference, the committee proceeded to reconstruct the Book Concern with Bishop J. P. Thompson as chairman and Rev. Alexander Walters, pastor of Mother Zion Church, was placed in charge as agent, October 15, 1889. Due to the financial embarrassment and outstanding debts of the Concern, Elder Thomas resigned as agent. The first thing they did was to remove the Book Concern from the basement of 183 Bleecker Street into comfortable quarters at 353 Bleecker Street, which had been fitted up for the purpose. The debt of $1,080 was cancelled by a loan from Bishop Thompson. [28]

Both the Book Concern committee and the agent stressed the necessity of larger patronage from our own members, which was reiterated by the chairman, Bishop Thompson. The agent, Rev. Walters, recommended the following, almost in consonance with the recommendations of the committee, at the General Conference of 1892:

The continuation of the Book Room in New York, and in addition to this, *The Star of Zion*, thus making a publishing house for us in New York. This is the only way we will ever have a publishing house, for the trade will more than pay for itself.

The renumbering of the hymnal and the renumbering and repaging of the hymn book. . .

The continuation of the appropriation. . .

That a Bishop, the pastor of Zion Church (Mother Zion), and one member from each episcopal district compose the Committee of Management.

That said member of each episcopal district be the authorized book agent for that district, and be held responsible for the books committed to his charge.

The General Conference approved these recommendations. It was also voted that the Board of Managers of the Book Concern be the bishops and one member from each of the five conferences nearest the location. [29]

Dr. Alexander Walters was elected bishop in 1892, and Rev. Dr. Jehu Holliday was elected agent of the Book concern. Bishop Walters became the chairman of the Board of Managers, and the operation of the Book Concern met with decided success the next few years. The Book Concern was declared by several leaders, in reports and general articles, as well as articles appearing in *The Star of Zion*, as one of the finest book businesses of any black church in the United States. Bishop Walters and Rev. Holliday were largely credited with this new success. [30]

Dr. Jehu Holliday, who was elected bishop in 1896, made the report as general agent of the Book Concern. He had passed through a quadrennium of arduous toils and sacrifice. At the request of Bishop Walters, he left the Book Room in New York and accepted the pastorate of the Twelfth Street Church

27. *Minutes,* Eighteenth Quadrennial Session, pp. 51, 75, 104.
28. *Minutes,* Nineteenth Quadrennial Session, pp. 29, 134.
29. *Ibid.,* pp. 98, 137.
30. *Star of Zion,* Sept. 24, 1896; Jan. 21, 1897; Nov. 18, 1897.

(Broadway Temple), Louisville, Ky., and was criticized for this by some of the brethren. He explained his situation in his report, and the decision made to save the Book Concern. "As a result of my giving up my salary," stated Holliday, "we have today Bishop Hood's *History of the A.M.E. Zion Church,* published at a cost of over $1,500, a first class Hymnal and Hymn Book that we are proud of, and all other kinds of literature in abundance. Besides this, we have seven sets of plates which could not be duplicated." It was a highly commendable report, exhibiting $4,033.73 assets. [31]

This, however, was a decisive General Conference for the publishing concern of the denomination. As early as 1885 the industrial department of Livingstone College established a printing press. Here the *Star of Zion* and a variety of other A.M.E. Zion Church literature were published. At the beginning of 1893, the office was placed under the management of Professor George L. Blackwell, who was instrumental in gathering large patronage. Nearly all of the male students had been taught type-setting, press work, binding, etc., and each year several of them were employed in the printing office. [32] Through the instrumentality and influence of Bishop Thomas H. Lomax, the Publishing House was secured in Charlotte, N.C. in 1894. [33]

The Board of Bishops had made the decision to move the Publication Department to Charlotte in its semi-annual meeting, January 1894, and immediately set out to purchase the property at a cost of $6,000, with Bishop Lomax serving as chairman, and Dr. G. L. Blackwell first business manager. The property, located at 206 South College Street, was a large and spacious four-story brick building, including basement, with the purchase of $2,500 worth of press equipment added. The building was named the *Varick Memorial Building,* in honor of the founder of the connection. [34]

The Bishops, in their quadrennial episcopal address in 1896, recommended that *The Star of Zion,* the *Quarterly Review,* the Sunday school Literature, and all other literature of the church be, as far as possible, published at the Publication House at Charlotte, N.C. They further recommended that the Board of Managers of the Varick Memorial Publishing House be the bishops, the general business manager of the Publishing Department, and the editors of the several departments located therein. Instead of a book agent, they recommended a business manager be elected to run the publishing department, "who shall be the General Steward." They also recommended that we have a book depository in New York, tha $1,000 a year be appropriated to sustain it, that it be under the management of the Board of Bishops, and the Business Manager of the Publishing Department, with a clerk employee to look after the sales, and that such provisions be made to put the Varick Memorial Publishing House in condition to do all our publishing.

The recommendations were submitted by the Committee on Episcopal Address, and adopted by the General Conference, with one addition; that there be a representative from each episcopal district on the publishing board. [35] After the action taken by this General Conference, the book depository in New York gradually declined, and after the removal of Mother Zion Church from West Tenth and Bleecker Streets, it ebbed away, leaving Charlotte as the headquarters for sale

31. *Minutes,* Twentieth Quadrennial Session, pp. 204-208.
32. Ibid., p. 189; Walls, *J. C. Price,* p. 488.
33. Hood, *One Hundred Years,* p. 194.
34. A.M.E. Zion *Quarterly Review,* April, 1894, p. 313.
35. *Minutes,* Twentieth Quadrennial Session, pp. 70-71, 114, 251-252.

EVOLUTION OF THE

A.M.E. ZION PUBLISHING HOUSE

VARICK MEMORIAL BUILDINGS

(1) A.M.E. Zion Book Concern. This was the beginning of publishing interest of the A.M.E. Zion Church in New York City, 1840, Rev. Jacob Richardson, first Book Agent. *Above*: 353 Bleeker Street, New York City, Rev. Jacob Thomas, Book Agent.

(2) 206 S. College St., Charlotte, N.C. Purchased in 1894 by Bishop T. H. Lomax, for the A.M.E. Zion Church at a cost of $6,000. Interior remodelled and fitted up for a first-class printing office in 1898 by Rev. G. L. Blackwell, Business Manager, at a cost of $2,500.

(3) Second and Brevard Streets, Charlotte, N.C. Built in 1911. Rev. F. K. Bird, General Manager, Bishop G. W. Clinton, Chairman of Board of Publication.

(4)

Second and Brevard Streets, Charlotte. Built in 1966. Rev. D. L. Blakey, General Manager, Bishop W. A. Stewart, Chairman of Board of Publication.

of literature and books.

The duties of the Board were "to supervise the publication of the papers, periodicals, Sunday School matter and all other general interests authorized by the General Conference and the Board of Bishops, and incidental matters created in the interval, and private publications of authors of the church." A complete set of printing machinery was owned by the church, and the work done totally by black compositors. [36] Consolidation of the publishing interests and placement of the same under one management was considered by all of the editors as a very progressive step.

The remodelling and full equipment of the Publication House was observed as the first notable achievement of the quadrennium, in the Bishops' Episcopal Address of 1900. They stated that; "the printing and sending out from our own Sunday School Department a first class and large quantity of Sunday School and other literature, the product of Negro brains and Negro brawn, belong distinctly to the past quadrennium." [37]

Dr. J. M. Hill was elected manager of the Publishing House by the Board of Bishops in 1901, succeeding Dr. G. L. Blackwell who had been made General Secretary. He had proven a competent manager, and "more than justified the favorable prophecies of his most sanguine friends." The bishops of the church were justly proud of the Publication Department, stating that: "It is a monument to the intelligence, thrift, and frugality of the Negro. It furnishes employment to a large number of men and women. We can truthfully say, as we believe no other Negro Church in America can say, that upon neither building, nor machinery do we owe a penny." They recommended the purchase of modern printing equipment. Dr. Hill died just before General Conference and Bishop G. W. Clinton, the manager at the time of the General Conference, made the quadrennial report at the 1904 General Conference.

Dr. John F. Moreland, Sr., was elected manager at the 1904 General Conference, [38] and rendered expert service. He strongly advocated the plan of having an assistant in training in each of the departments, especially in the Publication Department. [39] He was commended by the editor of the *Quarterly Review,* Dr. John C. Dancy, Sr., for his keen ability and sharp insight in managing the department. Every department of the Publication House was reported as furnishing some revenue to the church independent of salaries paid by the General Church, which was decidedly encouraging. [40]

In 1908, Dr. Moreland was elected secretary of the Brotherhood, and Dr. F. K. Bird was elected manager of the Publishing House. Because the church had outgrown the facility and the building had deteriorated, this General Conference also "ordered that the old property be disposed of to the best advantage and the money accruing from the sale be used in purchasing or building a more desirable place." [41]

The old property was sold at a cost of $12,000, and the new property, situated on the corner of Second and Brevard Streets, was purchased for $11,000. It had a rental income of about $80 per month at purchase. The new property had

36. Anderson, *Offical Directory,* 1895, p. 27.
37. *Minutes,* Twenty-First Quadrennial Session, p. 95.

38. *Minutes*, Twenty-Second Quadrennial Session, pp. 87, 135, 137-138.
39. *Minutes,* Twenty-Third Quadrennial Session, pp. 198-205.
40. *A.M.E. Zion Quarterly Review,* Fourth Quarter, 1906, p. 96.
41. *Minutes,* Twenty-Fourth Quadrennial Session, p. 146.

one store building, nine tenant houses, and a large vacant lot on which to build. The commodious new Publication House was built by a black contractor, W. W. Smith, at a total cost of $16,500. All of the difference of $5,500, except a loan of $1,000 made by Thad L. Tate, a prominent laymen on the Board of Publication, and member of Grace Church, Charlotte, came from the Publishing House funds. Thus, by the summer of 1911, "the first *Publishing House* in the country built by Negroes" graced the city of Charlotte in structure, finish and beauty, and was known as the Negro Skyscraper of the city. The imposing building with its white pressed-brick front trimmed in stone, displaying the bold letters, *The Varick Memorial Building,* was interiorly equipped with the most modern printing facility and office equipment.

This was accomplished through the masterly business skill and unusual initiative of Bishop George W. Clinton, chairman of the Board, and particularly, general manager F. K. Bird. The house was blessed with successful operation. The other members of the board who made themselves active in committee work and useful advice, and helped to steer the transition to glorious success, were Rev. George C. Clement, secretary, Mr. S. B. Washington, treasurer, Rev. J. T. Williams, Rev. R. B. Bruce, Rev. S. D. Watkins, Mr. Thad L. Tate, and Mr. C. S. Smith. [42]

Dr. F. K. Bird, "the noble hero and financier," was re-elected manager at the General Conference of 1912, and died in the interim (1914), having magnificently achieved for the church and race. The printed report of the operations of the quadrennium was distributed at the General Conference of 1916 by Rev. George C. Clement, editor of the *Star of Zion.* The business had continued under the direction of the Publication Board, chaired by Bishop G. W. Clinton. "The late Dr. Bird had acted more wisely than he knew," in purchasing the plant owned by Zion in Charlotte. J. W. Crockett, the first layman General Manager, was elected in 1916. He had continued the business for four years "in a way highly creditable to himself and those whom he represented." Soaring prices had put the manager to his wit's end to keep the business going, and it became necessary to increase suscriptions of the *Star of Zion,* to help balance situations, and aid with contributions for certain other relief. It was a quadrennium of financial difficulty, and Brother Crockett operated under stress and strain and was forced to borrow funds to keep up salaries and expenses. However, every interest of the House had been cared for with great painstaking. [43]

At the General Conference of 1920, Rev. S. D. Watkins was elected manager, and re-elected in 1924. His administration inspired confidence and a degree of creative venture in the midst of a difficult financial period. Growth of industry after the war, and business competition in religious publications, along with rising prices, caused vexation. In the Quadrennial Episcopal Address, the bishops requested the General Conference to consider restructuring, and electing or appointing a governing board for this department, with power to employ management as necessary to guarantee better security and progress. The Publishing House had faced a crisis in 1922, which made it necessary for the General Church to come to its rescue. After supplying the help needed and placing it on better basis for operation, the bishops placed at the disposal of the management business counsel and encouragement, to tide the department over until the convening of the General Conference. [44]

42. *Ibid.,* pp. 399-409.
43. *Minutes,* Twenty-Fifth Quadrennial Session, p. 27; *Minutes,* Twenty-Sixth Quadrennial Session, p. 76, 169-170, 177.
44. *Minutes*, Twenty-Seventh Quadrennial Session, pp. 107-108.

Through vigorous participation of Revs. W. F. Witherspoon, R. Farley Fisher, E. M. Argyle, E. B. Watson, W. L. Hamblin, and Mr. Oscar W. Adams, Sr., the 1924 General Conference adopted a scheme of reorganization, instituting a Board of Governors which was given extensive power in operating the Publishing House. The General Manager, whose duties were constricted by the Board of Governors, was still to be elected by the General Conferences, and accountable to both the Board of Governors and General Conference for conduct of operation. [45]

In 1928, Richard W. Sherrill was elected Manager, the second laymen to serve. He was re-elected the next four quadrenniums, thus serving 20 years with nobility and business acumen. During this time, the bishops and members of the Publishing House Board of Governors continuously stressed increased patronage in order to supplement the support of effective and retired ministers, their families, and families of deceased ministers. In 1948, Mr. Sherrill submitted recommendations on behalf of the Publishing Board, for consideration of the General Conference, which became effective. Recommendation number four was: "Inasmuch as the Publishing House is a monument to James Varick, that we adopt a 'Varick Day' to be observed as a celebration and funds accruing therefrom be given to the Publishing House." [46] This appeared to be a creative action of this General Conference; however, this day was originated by the fathers directly after the first Publishing House was purchased in August 1894. "The second Sunday in August, 1894, was set apart by the Board of Bishops as 'Varick Day,' to raise a collection in all the churches for the purchase of this fine building" [47] The observance, which was to be annual, had not been placed before a General Conference until 1948, and afterwards was placed in the Discipline as follows:

Varick Day

The first Sunday in October of each year shall be known as Varick Day. A suitable program shall be carried out during the following week to commemorate the work of James Varick, our Founder and first Bishop, and our other founding fathers, in order to inspire a greater interest in our history and doctrine, and to disseminate historical knowledge through the distribution of our literature, and our belief in freedom, race enterprise and church socialism. [48]

This action was also prompted by the recommendation of the bishops.

The compiling committee of 1948, in revising the Discipline, brought up to date the matter of the Board of Publication, which had been effective since 1932, which affected all connectional boards. The Board, consisting of one bishop as chairman, and a member from each episcopal district, replaced the Board of Governors, and its duties were similarly defined, though placing a larger portion of responsibility back into the hands of the management. [49]

Dr. William A. Blackwell, II, was elected manager in 1948. He wrought four years with genuine competence under prevailing circumstances. Once again, the property was beginning to depreciate considerably. The high cost of labor and equipment made management difficult, especially with the limitations of our

45. *Ibid.,* pp. 82-83; *Doctrines and Discipline,* 1924, pp. 203-209.
46. *Minutes,* Thirty-Third Quadrennial Session, p. 179.
47. Anderson, *Official Directory,* 1895, p. 53.
48. *Minutes,* Thirty-Third Quadrennial Session p. 320; *Doctrines and Discipline,* 1948, p. 170.
49. *Minutes,* Twenty-Ninth Quadrennial Session, pp. 63, 75-76, 92; *Doctrines and Discipline,* 1932, p. 346; 1948 pp. 198-203.

budget and the inability to sufficiently supplement the operation of the House. Dr. Leonard L. Boyd was elected Manager in 1952, under these pressing circumstances. He was re-elected in 1956, and served eight years faithfully, carrying it, some of the time, with his own salary. The General Conference of 1960, upon recommendations of the Board of Bishops through its Episcopal Address, and the Publishing House Committee, made major revisions in the law affecting the operation of the Publishing House. The church has been determined through the years to succeed in this department, in spite of the competition of other religious publication firms of larger means. Operating for years without the anticipated profit and desired success, the General Conference made two major resolutions among others:

(1) That the Manager of the Publication House be nominated by the Board of Publication and nomination confirmed by the Board of Bishops.

(2) Inasmuch as the city of Charlotte planned redevelopment and expansion in the area where our Publication House was located, that we build a new publication house to conform with city regulations of buildings in the area where our present publication house is located.

Although he is to give an account of his labors quadrennially to the General Conference, and semi-annually to the Bishops and Connectional Council, the manager's tenure of office is for one year, and he is accountable only to the Board of Publication and Board of Bishops for his conduct of operation. [50]

Upon recommendation of the Board of Publication, the Board of Bishops confirmed the appointment of Lennie A. Barnes as acting manager after the 1960 General Conference. Early in the quadrennium, the Board of Bishops initiated a centennial freedom rally, in honor of the One Hundredth Anniversary of the Emancipation Proclamation (1963), to raise $400,000 throughout the denomination. Funds were to be equally divided between the new Publishing House building at Charlotte and the new Hood Theological Seminary Building at Livingstone College, Salisbury. The rally, which terminated in 1963, was a glowing success. However, problems of operation at the Publishing House had become extremely critical and severely affected our patronage. While building a new plant, the departments were forced to move into temporary quarters. This and other administrative problems caused interruption of printing, and the schedule ran nearly a year behind. It had to catch up subsequently, to fill the gap made by this cessation of publishing material. [51]

Bishop William A. Stewart, chairman, worked tirelessly in steering the Publication Department through the most turbulant period of its history, as did the following members of the Board of Publication; Bishops Raymond L. Jones, H. B. Shaw, Revs. George J. Leake, Edgar F. Jones, Bennie Mallette, William C. Ardrey, J. W. Watson, D. S. Williams, C. J. Jenkins, Damon A. Gaines, Charles H. Banks, Arthur Marshall, D. U. Udafa, and Mrs. Samuel Besteda.

The Publishing Board soon secured the services of Rev. Durocher L. Blakey as interim manager. Sufficient funds were borrowed to provide for the extreme emergency. Reverend Blakey came into this office in 1963, during very dark days for our publishing interest. With dexterity he directed the Publishing House through this period of transition. He led in the construction of the new Varick Memorial Publishing House, which was built at a cost of $550,000, and formally opened on October 30, 1966. [52] The chairman of the Board of Publication worked

50. *Minutes,* Thirty-Sixth Quadrennial Session, pp. 79, 438, 474.
51. *Minutes,* Thirty-Seventh Quadrennial Session, pp. 315-320.
52. *Minutes,* Thirty-Eighth Quadrennial Session, p. 333.

ardently, side by side with the manager, to attain this success for Zion. Both men served until 1972. Mr. Lem Long, Jr., acuminate Church Extension Secretary, was placed in charge as interim Manager by the Board of Publication, under the direction of Bishop Arthur Marshall.

The Star of Zion

At the close of the General Conference of 1876, the delegates returned home with high hopes of the success of the journal project adopted. Some of the preachers went forth collecting subscriptions according to the plan proposed. It was agreed that each minister should pledge $4.50 for three copies per year, and the chief architect of the plan, Rev. William Howard Day of Harrisburg, was made editor-in-chief of the paper, to be known as *The National Standard and Zion Church Advocate*. While this project did not succeed, Bishop James Walker Hood and Rev. John A. Tyler, the efficient secretary and compiler of the published minutes of the North Carolina Conference and the first sessions of the Central North Carolina Conference, became the heroes of the permanent establishment of a journal for the African Methodist Episcopal Zion Church. [53]

Reverend Tyler had this matter so much on his heart, he personally campaigned for its support throughout the North Carolina Conference during the summer and fall of 1876, and generated much enthusiasm among the members. The *Star of Zion* was born at the Thirteenth Session of the North Carolina Annual Conference, held in Phillips Chapel, Washington, N.C., in 1876, Bishop James W. Hood presiding. On the fourth day of the session, November 25, "the hour of 2 o'clock arrived, and the Church organ being the special order of that hour, J. A. Tyler offered the following resolution:

Whereas, the General Conference in June last, to publish a paper for the Connection, provided that any minister or person might take stock in said paper, and whereas, many of the ministers wishing to do something in that way, but are not able to take stock to the amount required in a stock:

Resolved, That this Conference take stock in said paper to the amount of its ability, and said stock be raised by each member of the Conference contributing fifty cents and upward: further, this stock shall be called the stock of the North Carolina Annual Conference; also that the following brothers, R. H. Simmons, E. H. Hill, and William H. Pitts be appointed as the Annual Conference stock committee, and said committee be appointed annually.

The resolution prevailed, and a list of members of the conference contributed to the stock totalling $50, of which J. A. Tyler paid the largest amount, $13.50. Reverend Tyler became the "local editor of the paper for the North Carolina Conference," and on the fifth day of the conference, he announced that he was prepared "to enroll the names of all who were ready to subscribe for the paper, and he hoped everyone would do his duty as required by the General Conference." [54] He commenced publishing monthly issues of the *Star of Zion,* at the close of the session, which he sent to a number of ministers throughout the connection. The following year, interest became manifest, stimulated by the presiding bishop, J. W. Hood. [55]

Before this session, Tyler had suffered embarrassment for accepting subscriptions for a paper which did not succeed in operation. Reverend C. R.

53. Moore, *History,* p. 333; Hood, *One Hundred Years,* p. 108.
54. *Minutes,* Thirteenth Session of the North Carolina Annual Conference, pp. 17-18, 20.
55. Hood, *One Hundred Years,* pp. 108-109.

Harris, in an effort to "quiet those whose money he had received, subscribed for the *Weekly Witness* a paper published by Tyler in the interest of several conferences of the Carolinas, for them, paying for it out of his own money. Elder Tyler could not thus pay off all whose money he had taken, for the number was too great; yet something had to be done to quiet the claim." During this critical time, Bishop Hood journeyed to New Bern and met with Rev. Tyler, and they compared notes and found that "they had hit upon the same plan." Circulars were sent out asking persons to pay a dollar per month for the support of a monthly paper until it could become self-sustaining. They soon expressed regret that they had not sent the circulars to a larger number of members, as only about 25 persons responded. [56]

They therefore secured their first stockholders and subscribers at the North Carolina Annual Conference in 1876. They spent considerable time and effort to increase the number of stockholders, during the quadrennium, but the *Star* remained primarily a North Carolina project until the General Conference of 1880. In advancing this organ during its infancy, the North Carolina Annual Conference of 1877 took substantial steps. First it passed a resolution to perpetuate this plan and intention of the 1876 General Conference, by giving its hearty support to the paper. The *Star* was established through the wisdom of Bishop J. W. Hood, who appointed Rev. J. A. Tyler editor, a man of superior learning and artistic skill, with unshrinking love and zeal for the advancement of the kingdom of Jesus Christ and the A.M.E. Zion Church. The *Star of Zion* which started as a one page journal, had been published the first year by Mr. A. S. Richardson of New Bern, N.C., who had manifested consuming interest in the *Star*. The conference resolved to tender deep gratitude to him for his sacrifical helpfulness. It also elected a stockholders' board of managers to aid in the support of the *Star of Zion,* and Rev. W. J. Moore became the first business manager by virtue of his appointment at Andrew Chapel (St. Peters), New Bern, N.C. The first officers of stockholders were elected as follows: Bishop J. W. Hood, president; W. J. Moore, vice-president; J. McH. Farley, secretary; the pastor of Andrew Chapel, business manager; and J. A. Tyler, editor and treasurer.

The conference added a number of stockholders to its list and raised $216.50 for the purchase of a press. Reverend J. A. Tyler was authorized to travel North during the winter in behalf of the *Star of Zion.* [57] All of these significant actions on the part of one conference solidified the *Star of Zion,* within one year of its founding.

A strong disposition was shown at the next two annual conferences to continue a hearty support of the *Star of Zion.* In 1878 several prominent ministers and laymen of the conference made strong appeals in its behalf. It was brought out that some northern members had attempted to disparage the *Star,* claiming it was a sectional paper, but the conference stressed the fact that it was for the benefit of the entire connection. The conference voted to desist from purchasing a press at that time, as it was less expensive to print the *Star* by contract. However, the press and other equipment had been purchased in 1879, and the annual conference prepared to present the *Star of Zion* to the forthcoming General Conference. [58]

56. *Ibid.*; Moore, *History*, p. 334; Anderson, *Official Directory,* p. 32.
57. Hood, *One Hundred Years,* pp. 109-110; *Minutes,* Fourteenth Session, North Carolina Annual Conference, 1877, pp. 19, 21, 43.
58. *Minutes.* Fifteenth Session, North Carolina Annual Conference, 1878, pp. 14, 36.

"The South Carolina and Virgina Conferences also took an active part in supporting the paper, and several leading men in different parts of the connection gave it their influence and support, so that by the meeting of the General Conference in 1880 it had a considerable circulation and was known in every section." [59]

The *Star of Zion* was readily received by the delegates to the 1880 General Conference. During the election of General Conference officers, John C. Dancy, Sr. was elected reporter to the *Star of Zion*. The conference, anxious to avoid the predicament of 1876 of not having the General Conference proceedings published, voted to have the General Conference Minutes published by the *Star of Zion*. (However, the minutes were actually published by the A.M.E. Zion Book Concern in New York). In addition to Revs. J. A. Tyler and W. J. Moore, Bishop Hood mentioned in his report that Revs. C. R. Harris and C.C. Pettey were due much credit for the editorial and business management of the paper, as were the stockholders who paid $12 or more to sustain the paper. [60] The report on church organ, which follows, was read by Rev. J. A. Tyler and adopted:

Report of Committee on Press
Dear Brethren:

We your committee on press and publication have interviewed the stockholders of the *Star of Zion* by proxy; and desire to report as follows:

Sec. 1. The stockholders of the *Star of Zion,* have as machinery for printing purposes, press, type, cases, racks, galleys, composing sticks, and ink slabs; total value, $247. Liabilities to subscribers one year, $225.

Sec. 2. Amount paid in by stockholders, $290. And on offering this paper to the General Conference, the stockholders are willing to make 25 per cent, discount on this amount, thus $72.50. This deduction of 25 per cent leaves due the stockholders $217.50.

Sec. 3. We would recommend that the General Conference do not assume the entire obligations of the *Star*, but that the General Conference appropriate a certain amount annually, and working conjointly with the stockholders, until the said stockholders, at their proposed discount, are reimbursed; the paper then coming entirely into the hands of the Connection.

Sec. 4. That the General Conference, on its behalf, appoint an Auditing Committee, of nine, whose business it shall be to audit the account of the stockholders when properly notified, and report to the party authorizing it thus to act.

Sec. 5. We recommend that the General Conference appoint a corresponding editor in each Annual Conference district, whose business it shall be to give all items of interest for that district.

Sec. 6. That by proper efforts in each Annual Conference, we will put forth every energy to raise the subscription list, to not less than twelve hundred subscribers at once. We recommend that each pastor and presiding elder act as an agent for the paper; that he be allowed twenty per cent on all yearly subscriptions, but where the pastor wishes and can find an agent from his congregation, he may appoint such an agent. Also, that the Annual Conference shall make it the duty of its ministers to act as above mentioned. Respectfully submitted. [61]

On motion of Rev. J. A. Tyler it was resolved that nine trustees be appointed by the General Conference to represent its stock in the *Star of Zion.* They were appointed as follows: Revs. Alfred Day, Mark M. Bell, S. W. Jones, Thomas

59. Hood, *One Hundred Years,* p. 110.
60. Minutes, Sixteenth Quadrennial Session, pp. 14, 21.
61. *Ibid.,* pp. 88-89.

Darley, Jacob Thomas, E. H. Curry, Landa Fanning, Isom Nicholas, and J. S. Cowles. [62] J. A. Tyler was offered as editor of the *Star of Zion* for the ensuing quadrennium. He refused to serve unless he could be assured that he would receive his salary. Tyler had received a small stipend of appreciation for his services from the North Carolina Conference each year. He was a faithful servant in the vineyard, until his death at Charlotte, N.C., in 1893.[63] Mr. A. S. Richardson, teacher and literatus, was offered and elected the editor of *The Star of Zion.* Reverend C. R. Harris was appointed business manager. Hence, the *Star of Zion* became the official organ of the African Methodist Episcopal Zion Church, and *operated weekly.*

Both Richardson and Harris resided at Concord, and were engrossed in establishing Zion Wesley Institute (Livingstone College), and Dr. Harris had also been elected first General Steward of the church at the 1880 General Conference. The *Star of Zion* was published in Charlotte by Mr. W. C. Smith, who quit work by the end of October 1880 because his wages were in arrears. Unwilling to suspend the paper, Harris engaged the services of a young printer in Concord "to get out succeeding issues." [64] The subscriptions were not sustaining the debts incurred. A publisher was then secured in Salisbury. The responsibilities of operating and editing the *Star* were too cumbersome for Harris and Richardson, since during the same time the college was undergoing transition and relocation to Salisbury. They both resigned in 1882, and the Board of Bishops, at their semi-annual meeting in Chester, S.C., in September 1882, appointed Rev. J. McHenry Farley, editor and publisher. The *Star* was removed to Petersburg, Va. [65]

Rev. J. McHenry Farley, businessman and illuminating writer, rendered tangible services with little means, and kept the *Star* operating successively while performing the editorial duties enthusiastically. The General Conference of 1884 appropriated $1,200 for the *Star of Zion.* It also elected Rev. A. L. Scott of Alabama, editor. He was a new man who was but little acquainted with the rules of composition, and was not qualified to serve. [66] The General Conference had previously elected Rev. J. McH. Farley as business manager. After it voted that funds coming from the *Star of Zion* appropriation should be paid on the $925 debt of the *Star*, which had incurred by Farley, Rev. Scott soon withdrew. Dr. Farley edited the paper again until Dr. John C. Dancy was elected by the Board of Bishops in 1885.[67]

Dr. Dancy, a rising young layman of religious zeal, had been the successful editor of the *North Carolina Sentinel* at Tarboro, N.C. Statesman, silver-tongued orator and inimitable writer of the *king's english,* he challenged the nation's notice in these columns, and though a layman, was sound on every issue of the Church.

It was observed by the Virginia Conference, presided over by Bishop Hood, that the *Star of Zion* had been greatly improved and established upon firm bases "and was gaining in popularity every day as an organ of a great church with the

62. *Ibid.,* pp. 44, 56.
63. *Ibid.,* p. 44; *Minutes,* North Carolina Annual Conferences, 1876-1879; *Minutes,* Twentieth Quadrennial Session, p. 241.
64. *Minutes,* First Session, Central North Carolina Annual Conference, 1880. pp. 28-29.
65. Moore, *History,* p. 335; *Minutes,* Quadrennial Session, p. 131-133.
66. *Minutes,* Seventeenth Quadrennial Session, p. 107; Hood, *One Hundred Years,* p. 126-7.
67. *Ibid.;* Ms. Walls, History of *The Star of Zion,* p. 8.

REV. JOHN A. TYLER,
Founding Editor, The *Star of Zion*, 1876

prospect of being enlarged to a seven column paper the beginning of the new year, 1888." Dancy accomplished this goal the next quadrennium. It was voted to cooperate with Dancy in every way to help make the *Star of Zion* one of the leading church organs of the black race in America. [68] The *Star* was published from Ballard Industrial Hall, Livingstone College, Salisbury, N.C. Much of the work was done by the class in printing, J. C. Dancy, instructor. [69]

Mr. Dancy was unanimously re-elected editor in 1888, and served until 1892. He was then elected editor of the *Quarterly Review,* which was founded in 1890 by Rev. George W. Clinton, and Rev. Clinton was elected editor of the *Star of Zion* at this 1892 General Conference. The *Star* continued its publication from Livingstone College, under the management of Dr. George L. Blackwell. It was during the editorship of Dr. Clinton that the *Star of Zion* moved into its permanent home, the first A.M.E. Zion Publishing House (Varick Memorial Building), Charlotte, N.C., in August 1894. Since this time the *Star of Zion* has been edited from this headquarters. Clinton was a pointed systematic editor of profound vocabulary. A lofty coiner of living phrases and marshaller of facts in eloquent strains, for four years he molded the sentiment of church and race through the *Star,* and was elected bishop in 1896.

Reverend John W. Smith, called "the left-handed Benjaminite," was elected editor in 1896. He was known as the prophet of the common people. With his left hand, he sounded all their longings and made them vocal in strange words, living wit, and bristling shrewdness. He was elevated to the bishopric at the General Conference of 1904. In 1897, the *Star of Zion* was changed from a four page seven-column paper to an eight-page five-column one. [70]

Bishop J. W. Smith was succeeded by Rev. George C. Clement. The Negro Church had not had a more widely informed editor. He served productively for 12 years and pushed the influence of the *Star* into every press association, national

68. *Minutes,* Twenty-Second Session, Virginia Annual Conference, 1887, p. 17.
69. Walls, *Joseph Charles Price,* p. 488.
70. *A.M.E. Zion Quarterly Review,* July, 1898, p. 86.

JOHN CAMPBELL DANCY, SR.

REV. BENJAMIN FRANKLIN WHEELER

Noted Official Layman. Twenty-five years Editor of the *Star of Zion* and *A.M.E. Zion Quarterly Review,* and Secretary of Church Extension Department. He was appointed by four presidents as U.S. Collector of Customs at Wilmington and Recorder of Deeds in the District of Columbia.

Noted Zion Author and Poet. Founder of Zion Institute (later Josephine Allen Institute), Mobile, Alabama and first superintendent of the Harriet Tubman Home for the Aged, Auburn, N.Y.

convention, and race institution, and had the happiness to reach the hearts of classes and masses alike. Dr. Clement was elected bishop in 1916.

Reverend James Harvey Anderson, elected editor in 1916, had already made a monumental record in gathering statistics and facts of the denomination. He was a tireless gatherer of news and molder of startling phrases, and a scarred veteran of national and ecclesiastic battles, blending both rugged experience and brillant culture; he fulfilled the glory of a ripe experience and a good old age. He gave four years of faithful service. [71]

The writer occupied the editorship of the *Star* from 1920 to 1924, boosted circulation from 3,000 to 9,000, and placed the *Star of Zion* on the largest exchange list in its history. Elected bishop in 1924, he was succeeded by Rev. William H. Davenport, one of the most brilliant editors the *Star of Zion* ever had, with broad perception. He was re-elected at the next three general conferences. His sudden death, after his re-election at the 1936 General Conference in Greensboro, ended 12 years of incisive journalistic service.

A special election became necessary at the close of the General Conference, and Rev. William A. Blackwell, I, was elected. He was one of the best-read men of our church and race, and almost a genius as a pulpiteer. He carried on the work in an admirable way for nearly three-years, and passed away on March 17, 1939. Following his demise, a committee was named by the Board of Publication, consisting of Mr. R. W. Sherrill, Revs. Buford F. Gordon; J. W. Younge, J. S. N. Tross and H. E. Wilson, to edit the *Star of Zion* until the ensuing Board of Bishops meeting. The Board of Bishops, meeting at Salisbury, N.C., June 6, elected Rev. Walter R. Lovell, editor. [72]

Dr. Lovell keen thinker and flexible rhetorician, was active in his concern for the issues of the church and developed a popular following. In 1955, he was disciplined by the Board of Bishops for permitting a scurrilous reflective article to

71. Walls, Ms. History of the *Star of Zion*, 1921.
72. *Minutes,* Thirty-First Quadrennial Session, p. 176; MS. Minutes, Board of Bishops, June 6, 1939.

pass through the paper, and an editorial committee composed of Bishop W. W. Slade, Revs. F. R. Blakey and P. L. DeBerry, and Mr. J. H. Brockett, Jr., served until the 1956 General Conference. Dr. Lovell was pardoned and restored to the editorship at this General Conference. Being elected by successive general conferences, he served the office a little more than 29 years, and passed away in November 1968. At the direction of the Board of Publication, his wife, Hera Blakey Lovell, continued to edit the *Star of Zion* until the ensuing Board of Bishops meeting.

The Board of Bishops, in its semi-annual meeting at Jersey City, January 10, 1970, elected Rev. Milton B. Robinson editor. Re-elected by the General Conference of 1972, he now holds the position with accredited popularity due primarily to his broad scope, unquestionable loyalty, and wise surveillance. He has implemented ways and means of increasing the circulation of the *Star* (which had periods of declination due to the Depression, world wars, and intermittent strife in the operation of the publication department) by more than 2,000 during his tenure of office.

The *Star of Zion,* conceived by a persecuted and oppressed people born of a steadfast spirit in sounding forth the everlasting truth of Jesus Christ, and proclaiming equality of all, has been blessed by Almighty God and strengthened in its growth and sustenance by the expression of its founding bishop, J. W. Hood, who adopted the motto: "I commend the *Star* to your heartiest and most earnest consideration. Let us make it a power in this land—a *Star* so bright that no cloud can hide the beauty of its rays." [73]

The Western Star of Zion

In the same spirit of spreading the church west, there was an effort to expand our publicity in the denomination. Therefore, the General Conference of 1912 created the Western Star of Zion, which was sponsored largely by Revs. William A. Blackwell I and Thomas W. Wallace; Dr. Wallace was elected the editor. [74] His report at the General Conference four years later "was more than encouraging and showed that a printing plant worth about $1,500 had been installed" at headquarters in East St. Louis, Ill. The Bishops recommended "that the *Western Star of Zion* be put on par with the *Star of Zion* and *Quarterly Review* as one of the official organs of the Church, and that its editor receive $1,000 per year, and travel expenses limited to $200.00 per year," which the General Conference adopted. [75]

This bright prospect met with tragedy. During World War I, "stories of race riots and lynchings filled the front pages, rivaling only the war news in death and violence. In July 1917, a massacre occurred in East St. Louis, in which many Negroes were burned alive in their homes, 6,000 driven from the city and $400,000 worth of property destroyed." [76] Entire Negro settlements were burned. Though the lives of Dr. Wallace and his family were miraculously spared, the office of the *Western Star of Zion* was destroyed by fire, and all the equipment lost, including major material collected by Dr. Wallace on the life of Dr. Joseph Charles Price from Price's widow. He had contemplated writing the life

73. Hood, *One Hundred Years,* p. 109.
74. *Minutes,* Twenty-Fourth Quadrennial Session, pp. 130-131.
75. *Minutes,* Twenty-Fifth Quadrennial Session, p. 12; Quadrennial Address, Board of Bishops, *op. cit.,* p. 16.
76. Langston Hughes and Milton Meltzer (eds.), *A Pictorial History of the Negro in America,* p. 266.

of Dr. Price, and carried the material there.

After this incident, Dr. Wallace accepted a commission as chaplain in the United States Army. Though there were several attempts to resurrect the *Western Star of Zion* in subsequent General Conferences, by other interested persons in the West, these all proved fruitless.

Sunday School Literature

In the beginning, our race church was an education center for children and adults who were denied this privilege during slavery. Catechizing was the primary teaching method of reading, writing, and religious training in the African Methodist Episcopal Zion Church. The advanced Sunday school literature simplified interpretation of the Bible with a view to applying it to life. The Book Concern, established in 1841, became the distributor of Sunday school literature throughout the connection, and the rapidly growing Sabbath schools were encouraged to build libraries, all of which were included in the statistical reports of local societies at the annual conferences. [77]

Reverend Robert Russell Morris of the North Carolina Conference, was the father of our Sunday school literature, and named first General Superintendent of Sunday schools by the Board of Bishops after the 1888 General Conference. At the same time, Rev. Titus Atticus Weathington of Montgomery, Ala. was elected Financial Secretary of the Sunday School Department.

Dr. Morris, a native of Halifax, Nova Scotia, was a brillant scholar. While attending Gorham College at Liverpool, N.S., he decided to enter the ministry of the A.M.E. Zion Church. During his pastorate at Halifax, he attended the Presbyterian Theological School, studying mental and moral science, church history, theology, Greek Testament, Hebrew, and Syriac. Sometime afterward he tried to do missionary work in Haiti, but returned after one year when he discovered the climate was not agreeable to his health; he had buried his wife and two children there.

He returned to Canada, and later transferred to the New England Conference, pastoring Bridgeport and Hartford, before transferring to the North Carolina Conference after the 1884 General Conference, from which he was elected head of the Sunday School department. [78]

At the General Conference of 1888, Dr. R. R. Morris served as secretary of the committee on revision of ministerial studies. In addition to the recommendations naming theology, church history, and other specified literature and books for ministerial candidates, the report adquately provided for Sunday school scholars as follows:

> ...We have examined the catechisms written by Rt. Rev. J. J. Moore, D.D., for the use of the A.M.E. Zion Sunday Schools, and in consideration of their (depth and breadth) submit the same to the Board of Bishops, with a view of the work being simplified and published.
>
> Furthermore, we also submit at the same time to the Board of Bishops, R. R. Morris' Infant Catechism, for the use of the A.M.E. Zion Sunday School.
>
> Furthermore, whereas, we, your committee upon considering the letter forwarded by P. Austadt & Sons, publishers of our Sunday-School literature, recognize the fact that the present arrangements are not satisfactory to either party; but recommend that the contract remain until something better can be

77. Moore, *History*, (Annual Conference Proceedings).
78. Hood, *One Hundred Years*, pp. 414-419.

made by the general agent of our book concern at New York.

J. B. SMALL, G. W. OFFLEY, W. H. DAY, J. W. BROWN, C.R. HARRIS, R. R. MORRIS, Secretary. [79]

This matter was taken into serious consideration by the Board of Bishops which, immediately after the General Conference, created the Sunday School Department, in their semi-annual session, September 1888, Asheville, North Carolina; appointed Morris and Weathington officers, and placed its general headquarters at Montgomery, Ala. [80]

The following year, Dr. Morris reported to the Board of Bishops, in session at Louisville, Ky., during September, that 173 schools were taking the literature of the department. He explained the delay in supplying publications of the department, and stated that "he asked not for salary but for assistance and suggested that a portion of the Book Concern General Fund could be applied to their work. He suggested also that a Press was very much needed," and expressed a desire for further cooperation of the bishops. The bishops strongly interrogated Dr. Morris on improving ways and means of furnishing our Sunday school literature, after which Bishop Hood suggested that there ought to be a Publishing Company established, and explained how it could be done. Dr. Morris had considered the idea, and was pleased that the Board of Bishops "would view an effort of that kind." Thus the action began here which created our first publishing house in 1894. [81]

Dr. R. R. Morris had succeeded in securing plates to illustrate the lessons, and added many other important improvements to the quarterlies and catechisms, and Rev. T. A. Weathington, a well prepared and loyal churchman, was eagerly promoting distribution and sales. [82] The first quadrennial report of the Sunday School Department at the 1892 General Conference exhibited ongoing vision and determination, and both men were re-elected to their positions unanimously. [83]

The Board of Bishops directed that the Sunday School Union Department move its headquarters from Montgomery into the newly purchased Varick Memorial Publication House at Charlotte, in its meeting held in the building, October 4, 1894, and appointed Bishop T. H. Lomax to supervise the transition and work out details of expense and operation. "Bishop Walters moved that the *Star of Zion* and the *Quarterly Review* be ordered to remove to this building not later than January 1st, 1895, and that when they come they shall be assessed in a similar manner to that of the Sunday School Department. Adopted." These departments thus moved forward. [84] The Sunday school literature editors have served from this headquarters ever since.

Dr. Robert R. Morris died at Charlotte, N.C., October 25, 1895. The Board of Bishops elected Rev. Robert Blair Bruce acting superintendent to serve until the ensuing General Conference. The General Conference of 1896, however, altered the arrangement and elected Rev. George Lincoln Blackwell both editor of the Sunday school literature and manager of the Publication House. [85] Dr.

79. *Minutes*, Eighteenth Quadrennial Session, p. 115.
80. Ms. Minutes, Board of Bishops, September 29, 1889, pp. 33-34; *Minutes*, Nineteenth Quadrennial Session, p. 169.
81. *Ibid.*
82. *A.M.E. Zion Quarterly Review*, Vol. 1, p. 134.
83. *Minutes*, Nineteenth Quadrennial Session, pp. 92, 169-171.
84. *Minutes*, Twentieth Quadrennial Session, p. 251; Ms. Minutes, Board of Bishops, October 5, 1894.
85. *Minutes*, Twentieth Quadrennial Session, pp. 65, 81, 97-98, 101, 241.

Blackwell mentioned that we were using other publishing companies for our literature with our imprint, and Zion printed the literature on its own press for the first time in July 1898. [86] In the fall of 1898, finding himself overloaded with responsibilities of both offices, he requested and secured the services of Rev. R. B. Bruce, who began writing the senior and junior comments, and in 1899 took over the responsibility of editing the beginner's literature, while the manager continued to edit both the picture card and teacher's journal. Both Blackwell and Bruce, who had attributes of literary finesse, served with a high degree of satisfaction. Dr. Bruce, a graduate of Payne Divinity School of Petersburg, Va., which prepared ministers for the Protestant Episcopal Church, and a profound theologian, was elected by the General Conference of 1900 as editor of the Sunday school literature, and continued his scrupulous work in this office until he was elected bishop at the General Conference of 1916. Reverend J. Francis Lee was then elected editor. The department expanded during the leadership of this versatile writer and poet. In 1920, the Board of Bishops took occasion to observe the editorial skill of our writers;

> To be able in a half century of citizenship to produce men capable of writing literature of a high grade, and editors whose pens record sentences of perfect grammatical construction, is well nigh a marvel, when you reflect that little over fifty years ago not a thousand of us could read or write. The quality of literature sent out through the Sunday School periodicals, *Star of Zion, Quarterly Review, Missionary Seer,* and the *Sunday School Bulletin,* is highly commendable and is a credit to our race. [87]

Up to 1916, the department produced the *Picture Lesson Card,* the *Junior Quarterly,* the *Senior Quarterly* and the *Teacher's Journal.* During his first quadrennium in office, Dr. J. Francis Lee added the *Primary Quarterly,* and greatly boosted the circulation of the Sunday school literature. [88]

After Professor James W. Eichelberger, Jr., principal of Walters-Southland Institute, was elected General Superintendent of Sunday Schools in 1916, he created a journal for promotional purposes, *The Sunday School Bulletin,* edited monthly from his office at Warren, Ark. In 1924, the name of the journal was changed to *The Church School Herald Journal,* and continued under the editorship of Dr. Eichelberger and Professor Aaron Brown, Sr. until 1928. The *Church School Herald Journal* was then made a quarterly, and the responsibility of editorship became that of the Editor of the Church School Literature. [89]

The general scope of Christian education in the Protestant Church had broadened; thus the entire education department of the A.M.E. Zion Church was restructured at the 1924 General Conference. Our responsibility, like that of other churches, was enlarged. Departmentalization of the Sunday school literature, with an expanded curriculum to suit the particular need of every age level, accelerated the work of this department. The Church School Literature Department, known also as the editorial section, one of the three sections of the newly created Christian Education Department, was made responsible for editing all church school literature in 1924. [90] A closer relationship of the churches with the national and international Sunday school movements was demanded, and annual

86. *Minutes,* Twenty-First Quadrennial Session, p. 199.
87. *Minutes,* Twenty-Fifth Quadrennial Session, pp. 76-77.
88. *Ibid.,* pp. 245-246.
89. Ms., "Journalism in the A.M.E. Zion Church," 1946; *Minutes,* Twenty-Eighth Quadrennial Session, p. 223.
90. *Minutes,* Twenty-Eighth Quadrennial Session, pp. 218-219.

national meetings of the Sunday School councils required the presence of our Editor of Church School Literature. It became necessary to secure the services of writers to assist the editor, each with appropriate preparation, and employ them on a stipend. After serving 14 years, and passing through these innovations, Dr. J. Francis Lee passed away in 1930 with a fine reputation of constructive loyalty.

Reverend Buford F. Gordon who authored a booklet, *Pastor and People,* was elected to fill the vacancy by the Board of Bishops in its meeting, January 14, 1931. This capable writer was re-elected by the General Conference of 1932, and served until he was elevated to the bishopric in 1944. He was succeeded at this General Conference by Rev. Dr. J. S. Nathaniel Tross, controversial philosophic scholar, and author of *The Meaning of Education,* and *The Challenge of the Hour.* He served until the General Conference of 1952 when Rev. Dr. John Van Catledge, Jr. was elected. This painstaking industrious theologian published an essential work *Know Your Church,* (also *Improving Youth Worship in the Church School,* while teaching at Livingstone College), and after ten years in office he passed away, March 26, 1962. Reverend Dr. Louis J. Baptiste was elected to fill the position in June 1962, re-elected in the last three General Conferences through 1972, and presently serves. Author of the book, *Basic Beliefs,* he moves in confrontation with the changing age and its illumination. All of these men were highly trained in the major colleges and universities.

The Quarterly Review

George Wylie Clinton attended the common school in Lancaster, S.C., and entered the University of South Carolina at Columbia, an institution that had graduated the first men of color of the South. When he had completed the sophomore year in 1876, the election of Wade Hampton as governor threw out the black students from the University. "He began to read law under lawyers of his native town and while reading the Bible for his legal data, he became impressed with the call to the ministry and thus the lawyer died in him that the preacher might live." He pastored the church at Chester, S.C., and completed his college work at Brainerd Institute. He later studied theology at Livingstone College. [91] He was then transferred to John Wesley Church, Pittsburgh, by Bishop Singleton T. Jones, succeeding Rev. Jehu Holliday who built the church. While pastoring there, he founded the *Quarterly Review,* in 1890. He entertained the General Counference of 1892, was elected editor of the *Star of Zion* at this General Conference and was elected bishop in 1896. The following is the history of the establishment of the *Quarterly Review.*

PROSPECTUS OF THE CHURCH QUARTERLY–THE CHURCH QUARTERLY IS DESIGNED TO REPRESENT THE HISTORY, CHARACTER, RELIGIOUS THOUGHT, DEVELOPMENT AND GENERAL PROGRESS OF THE COLORED CHURCHES OF AMERICA:
PUBLISHED UNDER THE AUSPICES OF THE A.M.E. ZION CHURCH.

REV. GEORGE W. CLINTON, Editor

The Quarterly will contain from time to time, papers, sermons and reports from representatives of the various denominations throughout the country. It is our object to give an insight into the pulpit and church work as represented by the Negroes of America and other lands. The need of some source of information as to the work being done by our people in their respective denominations is acknowledged by all.

91. *Minutes,* Twenty-Seventh Quadrennial Session, pp. 146-147.

1. Much has been done for religious work among the Negroes, and there is now a growing desire to see some of the tangible results of their endeavors. Young men have been educated for the ministry, churches have been built, school houses have been erected, and money spent in various ways to further the religious development of the race. The question has been repeatedly asked, "What have these young men done? Where are they working? What is the prospect in the fields in which they have labored?" In other words: Have the ends justified the means? *The Quarterly* shall aim to afford an opportunity for an answer to all such questions. It will further represent the best phases of our pulpit work. Unfortunately for the colored pulpit, it has been too often represented by the "Lime Kiln Club" class of sermons while the better class of pulpit efforts have been kept back by those who were not very anxious to see the race appear to its best advantage; but there is a growing necessity for the proper representation of the better side of our pulpit and church work. This we hope to furnish in the columns of *The Quarterly.*

2. This endeavor will stimulate the Negro clergy to more definite lines of thought and more careful preparation for the pulpit work. It will also encourage the laity in the church in the very important work which they are doing by having that work intelligently before the public and those interested in it. We further desire to give the laity an opportunity to be heard on the different phases of the work in their respective churches.

3. *The Quarterly* will be open for discussions on church work to all denominations, but the management reserves the right to pass upon the merit of the papers in their hands: for it shall be our purpose to secure the best thought of the foremost men and women of various denominations throughout the country. *The Quarterly* must be first class in every particular. But nothing we have said above must be construed that we bar any other race the privileges of our columns. We not only desire, but invite and gladly welcome articles and reports of church work from the pens of any other race. We shall gladly publish statements and reports from the secretaries or other officers of the different denominations having colored churches identified with them.

4. The biographical section will be of special interest to all Negroes from a race standpoint. We shall seek out and strive to obtain historical sketches and cuts representing the brain and merit of men of the race, both living and dead. There is now no work extant which gives a fair and impartial biographical account of the men and women who have done and are doing so nobly in the work of solving the race problems. We propose to obtain the best representatives of the various lines of work and give the public the benefit of the methods, work and accomplishments of the race.

The work will be divided up into the following sections:—

I. A Review Section

II. A Sermonic or Religious section which will contain one or more religious contributions.

III. An Editorial Section in which may be found brief editorials and comments on current topics, also clippings and excerpts from standard periodicals.

IV. The Biographical Section, as before said, will furnish brief historical sketches and cuts of leading race representatives, both living and dead. We invite special correspondence relative to this department of the work.

V. The Miscellaneous Section will contain articles on a variety of subjects and give general information on matters which concern the race and the public.

Trusting to have the earnest and hearty cooperation of all who wish to see the race attain to its desired standard of religious and intellectual prosperity and success, I beg to subscribe myself.

Yours for progress along every line,

Geo. W. Clinton, Editor, [92]

Dr. John Campbell Dancy, Sr., of Wilmington, N.C., who goes down in our church history as one of the towering laymen, became *The Quarterly's* second editor in 1892, following tradition. He showed mastery, thoroughness, and glowing subtlety in 16 years' editorship of the *Quarterly Review* and 7 years of the *Star of Zion*. After a close race between Dancy and Rev. L. W. Kyles for editor of the *Quarterly Review* in 1908, the General Conference re-elected Dr. Dancy that he might complete at least 25 years (by 1910), as the brillant scribe of these two religious publications of prominent distinction. Reverend Kyles was elected editor of the Homiletic Department of the *Quarterly Review,* which was created at this General Conference, and received $200 of the $500 per year salary appropriated for the editor of the *Quarterly Review.* [93]

In 1912, Dr. Lynwood Westinghouse Kyles was elected. He eminently edited the *Quarterly Review* in its entirety four years, and was elected bishop in 1916. He was succeeded by Rev. Cameron Chesterfield Alleyne, of Charlotte N.C., whose erudition was evident during his eight years' editorship. After his election to the bishopric in 1924, he was succeeded by Rev. William Orlando Carrington of New Rochelle, N.Y., profound scholar and veritable pulpit genius, who also served eight years.

In 1932, Rev. Polk Knox Fonvielle, from Worcester, Mass., was elected editor. This concrete thinker of a contributive family of writers (whose brother W. F. Fonvielle, was the noted author) served one quadrennium. In 1936, Rev. James Clair Taylor, at Paterson, N.J. a pellucid writer, was elected and served until 1948 when he was elevated to the bishopric. Succeeding Bishop Taylor in this post was Rev. David Henry Bradley, Sr., of Bedford, Pa., of theological, educational, and editorial concomitance. He has been re-elected in successive general conferences, and in 1973 reaches a milestone of a quarter of a century of effectiveness as editor of the *Quarterly Review.*

The Missionary Seer

Bishop John Bryan Small was the founder of the *Missionary Seer* in 1901. It was adopted at the Connectional Council in Price Memorial Church, Atlantic City, N.J., July 31, 1901, and Bishop Small was chosen editor. Small, the first bishop of our church assigned to foreign territory, travelled throughout Africa and the West Indies promoting our work. He experienced agonizing hardships, not only in extending the church abroad amid grim obstacles but in communication with our members at home to gain their support for this work in a larger measure. The reason for starting the *Missionary Seer* was given by Bishop Small, in 1904:

In order to bring before the Connection the work and working of the Foreign Mission fields, the Bishop having charge of that work, found it necessary to establish a missionary paper, so as to give to the Connection the correct condition of the work—its progress, working, and minute state of missionary operations, as heretofore we knew little or nothing of our work in the foreign fields.

92. *A.M.E. Zion Quarterly Review,* Vol. I, pp. i-ii.

93. *Minutes,* Twenty-Third Quadrennial Session, p. 44; *Minutes,* Twenty-Fourth Quadrennial Session, pp. 494-495.

... We knew that it takes money to run a paper, secular or religious; that we determined to give to, at least, a part of the Connection—for there are many persons you cannot interest in anything—news fresh and direct from the various parts of the mission fields; and for three successive years we have published the paper without a line of patent matter, and have not omitted but one number, and then we gave a double number in the following issue.

The paper costs between twenty-five and thirty dollars per issue, and is constantly sent to those whose names are on the list; but it is to be regretted, the amount received by subscription, has not reached an average of twenty eight dollars per month or three hundred and thirty-eight dollars per year—one thousand and eight dollars for the three years [94]

In this the General Conference delegates could readily see the sacrifice made by this God-sent servant to perpetuate foreign missions. The delegates voted to adopt the *Missionary Seer* as the organ of the Missionary Department, and that the price of subscription be 50 cents per year.[95] Reverend George L. Blackwell was elected secretary of the Missionary Department (a title and office that later became Corresponding Secretary of the Department of Foreign Missions) and editor of the *Missionary Seer.*

During the next four years, the *Missionary Seer* became well-founded and revitalized our foreign missions cause. The Board of Bishops gratefully acknowledged this at the General Conference of 1908, stating that Dr. Blackwell had

kept the cause of missions so steadily before the Church and presented the claims thereof in such a way and with such vigor, both by voice and pen, through the columns of that sprightly organ, *The Missionary Seer,* which he has edited in connection with his other duties, that no other department will be able to make a more creditable and satisfactory showing, or report larger results than the Missionary Department. . . . [96]

General secretaries of the Foreign Missions Department, served as editors of the *Missionary Seer.* Each made his own peculiar contribution with clarity of language, persuasive diction, and unswerving love and devotion for kindred Africans and all mankind in other lands; convincing the adherents of the continual necessity to help raise the level of these less fortunate, who are children of the Heavenly King. These men included Revs. Richard Albertus Morrisey, 1908-1912, John Wesley Wood, 1912-1920, William Walter Matthews, 1920-1928, Hampton Thomas Medford, 1928-1948, Daniel Carleton Pope, 1948-1952, James Clinton Hoggard, 1952-1972, Harold A. L. Clement, since 1972.

Other Publications and Literature

Ever since the birth of the A.M.E. Zion Church, creative writings and production of books and literature of all types and forms have shown our quest for knowledge and exemplifying the equality of the races. Printing was costly and the race was poor, without printing press or apprenticeship, but it sacrificed, particularly through its church, to gather records from its ancestry, facts from the knowledgeable and data from the informed, and paid the price to put them in print. The books and literature written by leaders, both men and women, of the A.M.E. Zion Church, for and about our church, from its earliest years of existence, are too numerous to mention here. Aside from the printed material

---

94. *Minutes,* Twenty-Second Quadrennial Session, p. 203.
95. *Ibid.,* p. 110.
96. Quadrennial Episcopal Address, Twenty-Third Quadrennial Session, p. 15.

used by the writer as sources for this work, we mention here a few other publications of our church, growing out of movements within the church, which rendered most valuable service in their day.

Practically indispensable to our denominational progress were the catechisms. In 1889, Bishop John Jamison Moore issued *The Graded Catechism for the Use of the A.M.E. Zion Church.* In 1888, Dr. Robert R. Morris issued *The Children's Catechism,* and also authored *The Minister's Handbook* in 1892. In May 1892, Rev. J. H. Trimble issued *The Historical Catechism of the A.M.E. Zion Church,* and in 1919 Rev. Richard Alexander Carroll issued *The Standard Historical Catechism of the African Methodist Episcopal Zion Church.*[97] The most widely used catechism today in our church is the *Zion's Historical Catechism,* edited by Bishop Cicero Richardson Harris in 1898 along with *The Beginner's Catechism.*[98] *The Comprehensive Catechism of the A.M.E. Zion Church,* was produced by Bishop E. D. W. Jones in 1934. The *Handbooks* published by general secretaries are also important works.

Prior to the organization of our Sunday School Literature Department, Bishop John J. Moore edited the *A.M.E. Zion Sunday School Banner,* published at York, Pa., for several years. During the days of our serious efforts to establish an official connectional church organ, several regional newspapers were established. Some existed for long periods as annual conference newspapers, others sought to become connectional periodicals and were suspended within a few years. Mentioned previously in this chapter was the *Zion Advocate,* published in the interest of the Philadelphia and Baltimore Conference by Revs. Jacob Hamer and John E. Price. "It was turned over to the General Conference of 1872, and adopted as the connectional organ, and being placed under the supervision of the Book Concern, suffered the fate of the *Zion Standard and Weekly Review*." *Zion's Banner,* founded in 1880 was published by Rev. W. H. Ferguson, and later by Rev. E. H. Curry at Louisville, Kentucky. The *Charlotte Messenger* was founded in 1880 and edited by Rev. W. C. Smith, at Charlotte, N.C., Rev. M. G. Thomas edited the *Southern Spokesman* in the interest of the West Alabama Conference, and *The Watchman* was published at Athens, Tenn., by Rev. W. H. Ferguson. The *New England Enterprise,* edited by Rev. E. George Biddle, was founded in 1886. The *Zion Methodist* was a brillant pamphlet published at Washington, D.C. by Rev. R. C. O. Benjamin. It was presented to the General Conference of 1904 and adopted as a connectional organ, as was *Zion's Trumpet,* founded at New Haven, Conn. in 1889 by Rev. E. George Biddle.[99] There were several other journals which started at later dates, but they were shortlived.

The Varick Christian Endeavorer

There were two efforts to establish a Christian Endeavor paper in our church. The first effort was made by Rev. R. Haywood Stitt, who founded *The Christian Endeavor Advocate,* around 1893. He died in the midst of its development, and thus the paper was lost. The second attempt was made by Revs. Josiah S. Caldwell and Jesse B. Colbert. After the General Conference of 1896 approved an official journal of the Varick Christian Endeavor Society, the journal known as the *Varick*

---

97. Anderson, *Official Directory,* 1895, p. 32.
98. Louise Rountree, *An Index of Biographical Sketches and Publications of the Bishops of the A.M.E. Zion Church.* p. 10.
99. Anderson, *Official Directory,* p. 32.

Christian Endeavorer was launched in less than three months by these two religious educators. At the General Conference held in Washington, D.C. in 1900, the journal was separated from the Varick Christian Endeavor Union. Drs. Caldwell and Colbert, co-editors, declined to continue as editors, and Rev. B. J. Bolding was elected editor. At the General Conference of 1904, Rev. John McMillan was elected editor of the *Varick Christian Endeavorer* and president of the Varick Christian Endeavor Society. [100] Professor Aaron Brown, Sr. was elected to this position in 1912 and served until 1924. The office was later absorbed in the Christian Education Department.

The Varick Christian Endeavorer was successful for a long time, and filled a need among our youth, "serving as a medium through which the best and purest sentiments affecting our young people" were expressed.[101] It lived until the transformation took place in the Christian Education Department in 1924, and was interrelated when the *Church School Herald Journal* was established, which became the organ of the combined department.

The Strength of My Life

This daily meditation booklet was introduced into the A.M.E. Zion Church by Bishop Raymond L. Jones in December, 1962. A firm believer in family prayer, he always had a desire to produce a devotional meditation magazine for A.M.E. Zion Church families. After tribulations seized him and his family, loss of his last brother and of his daughter in childbirth, both in the same week and in the midst of presiding over annual conferences, the faith of his family members was shaken and he was put to a great test. Compelled to stand the test like Job, he renewed his strength and made a decision to write prayers and meditations, which would be helpful to others in times of affliction, distress, and trials. He immediately went forth, after strengthening his family through prayer, and published 100 copies of the devotional booklet known as *The Strength of My Life,* and mailed them throughout the church and to friends in lieu of Christmas cards.

Bishop Jones then conferred with President Samuel E. Duncan of Livingstone College and Dean Frank R. Brown of Hood Theological Seminary, on receiving editorial and publishing assistance for the booklet which had been published each month by the bishop, for nearly a year. *The Strength of My Life* was then placed under the sponsorship of Hood Theological Seminary, with proceeds from subscriptions and sales to go toward support of students at Hood Theological Seminary, and issued monthly from this office in Salisbury, N.C.

The Strength of My Life, which had given Bishop R. L. Jones and his family "a spiritual storehouse and sustained them in their darkest hours," was produced for morning devotions among A.M.E. Zion Church families and for the daily strengthening of family life.[102]

100. Jesse Colbert, *History of the Varick Christian Endeavor Society,* pp. 17-18.
101. *Ibid.*
102. Interview, Mrs. Mable Miller Jones, 1972.

Part VI

Ministration Departments

CHAPTER 24

HOME MISSIONS AND CHURCH EXTENSION

Home Missions and Church Extension have been separate and distinct departments in our church economy for a number of years, but because of the interrelation of their program and their conjugation during one period of our history, it is appropriate to combine these two efficacious departments in a single chapter.

Home Missions

In the beginning of the denomination, it was necessary for the fathers to define a local circuit or station and plan for its growth and extension as follows:

A circuit is a city, town, distance or circle, taking in several societies, whose temporal concerns are transacted by separate bodies of trustees or stewards, according to their different charters or constitutions, and consequently requiring separate trustees and leaders' meetings. A station is a city or town where there is but one society (tho' having several houses for divine worship) whose temporal concerns are transacted by one body of trustees or stewards, and consequently do not require separate trustees nor leaders' meetings. [1]

Included in the duties of an elder having the charge of a circuit or station, were:

... To choose a person, in the interval of the quarterly conference, (where there are no trustees nor stewards) to take charge of the money collected for the preachers, church or poor; and to choose a committee of lay members to make a just application of the same.

To raise a yearly subscription in his circuit or station (if they can bear it) for the purpose of building houses for divine worship, and paying debts of those already erected. [2]

1. *Doctrines and Discipline,* 1820, pp. 53-54.
2. *Ibid.,* p. 52.

In the spirit of connectionalism, this small band of believers moved forward in spreading the church throughout the North and West. Slavery still rampant, the strong sentiment expressed in the Discipline against it caused a blockage in spreading the A.M.E. Zion Church South until Emancipation. [3] At the General Conference in 1840, the Committee on Condition of the Church reported favorable conditions in general embracing the two annual conferences, New York and Philadelphia, and an encouraging increase of preachers and laymen. The General Conference of 1848, which set off the Allegheny and Genesee Conferences, reported in its statistics from the four established annual conferences, (New York, Philadelphia, New England, and Baltimore) 90 itinerant preachers, 6,352 members, and two bishops. [4]

Soon afterwards, missionary societies or Home and Foreign Missions Boards were established in the annual conferences, and constitutions were adopted. For instance the following constitution and by-laws were adopted by the Genesee (Western New York) Conference in 1858:

1. This institution shall be known by the name of the A.M.E. Zion Church Connectional Missionary Society of the Genesee Conference. The object of this Society shall be to send out and support Missionaries in those places where the gospel is most needed, and can do the most or greater good to mankind.

2. It shall be the duty of every preacher appointed by this conference, to hold missionary meetings in all the appointments given him. The object of the meetings shall be to interest our people in the great subject of missions, and to raise money by subscriptions, collections, or otherwise, for the institution. The money shall be brought to the Conference by said preachers.

3. It shall be the duty of the Annual Conference to lay out all such monies in raising new societies, and for the support of the same.

4. No money shall be paid or go out of the Annual Conference District, except that part given to the General Conference Committee.

5. It shall be the duty of the Annual Conference to elect by vote five officers to take charge of the monies and divide the same as directed by the vote of the Annual Conference, provided, in all cases, any church having fifty members and a meeting house paid for, shall not be entitled to any of the mission fund.

6. The Annual Conference may give to the General Conference of this Connection one-third of the money thus raised, provided the other Conferences will adopt a similar course, for general purposes. Officers, William H. Bishop, Superintendent, Joseph J. Clinton, Associate Superintendent, William Sanford, Secretary, John Thomas, Treasurer. Committee: —R. T. Estepp, William A. Cromwell, John Anderson, George Bosley. [5]

The constitution of the Home and Foreign Mission Fund of the New York and New England Annual Conferences was somewhat broader, although also controlled by a board of officers of the annual conferences. Their principal object was to sustain and aid those preachers engaged as missionaries, "when necessity may require." [6]

When the church began to spread its borders throughout the South after Emancipation, the northern conferences, which had been engaged in missionary work, prepared the way, furnishing leadership and funds. Leading in raising funds

3. Anderson, *Official Directory,* p. 44.
4. Moore, *History,* pp. 207, 211.
5. *Minutes,* Genesee Annual Conference, 1858, pp. 8-9.
6. *Minutes,* New York and New England Annual Conference, 1857, p. 41.

was the New England Conference, which had the best established Home and
Foreign Missions Board of the church, ably led by Miss Eliza Ann Gardner of
Boston and other dedicated women of the conference. The rapidly growing
church soon began to make plans for a connectional home missions organization,
to continue its spread of the kingdom of Christ. Though the term home and
foreign missions was used in our earliest development, foreign missions received
nominal support for Canada and the West Indies Islands while home missions was
the principal beneficiary until the coming of the Woman's Home and Foreign
Missionary Society, which started out as an auxiliary in the principal interest of
foreign missions.

In articles 49 and 50 of the revised Discipline of 1872, the following rule
prevailed:

Of Home And Foreign Missions:
Section I. What shall be done in order to defray the expenses of our
home and foreign missionaries?
Ans. Each Annual Conference shall organize a missionary society, the
members of which shall pay such sums as shall be determined, from year to
year, by the Conference.
Section II. It shall be the duty of each minister in charge to organize
missionary societies, wherever it is convenient in his charge, the same to be
auxiliary to the Annual Conference society for that district.
Of The Maintenance Of Ministers In Charge:
Section I. What can be done toward relieving the pecuniary
embarrassments of our ministers in charge?
Ans. Let the great importance of their maintenance be peremptorily
urged and enforced in each society by the Bishops, until a favorable change is
effected, and the membership perform their duty in this respect. . . . [7]

The church had spread with such rapidity, it increased its number of bishops
from three to four in 1868, and 1876, "in consequence of the growth of the
work," the number of active bishops was increased to seven, more than double
over four quadrenniums. In General Conference legislation, two of them were
made missionary bishops, and "five cents per member" was to be collected for
their support. The amount was to be deducted from the 50 cents provided by law
for the support of the bishops. [8]

The results of the missionary work on the home field were astonishing.
Strenuous efforts had begun to fill the apertures for God and Zion in the
Southwest and Northwest territories, with similar success to that attained in the
Southeast. A poor people for the most part, proud of its origins, yet volitive in
spirit, moved in their impecunious condition as sacrificing servants of Christ,
establishing, building, and buying churches and parsonages, and making every
provision possible in the best manner they could to support the ministry. Many of
the churches not being able to meet the requirement of the Discipline for
supporting ministers, the connection began to move in, devising ways and means
of supplementing ministerial support through the home missions funds.

At the General Conference of 1880, there was coordination in the Bishops'
Address and the home missions segment of the committee report on home and
foreign missions and church extension. The bishops stated: "For a view of the vast
mission fields open before us, we refer you to the reports from the Third, Fourth,
Fifth and Seventh Districts; not only have we the missionary district of Canada,

---

7. *Doctrines and Discipline,* 1872, pp. 114-115.
8. *Minutes,* Eleventh Annual Session, South Carolina Annual Conference, 1876, p. 10.

and the great northwest, but Kansas at this time presents one of the finest openings for missionary effort that can be desired." [9]

We quote the following from the committee report:

The Territory or State of Kansas opens to us a good field for missionary labor, for thousands of our people are emigrating there, and among them a large number of our members, and

Whereas, We your committee, believe it would be conducive to the good of our beloved Zion, we further recommend that our bishops appoint competent missionaries for that work, also any other mission referred to in the Episcopal Addresses of the Bishops. [10]

The division of the annual conferences into presiding elders' districts, with provision for its structure and operation in 1876, was one of the encouraging and stimulating facets of the church's growth. The presiding elders were at first elected by the annual conference, and they created a vigorous type of competition and emulation among themselves. The positions were held by some of the most potent men of the church, who gave great assistance to the bishops in every phase of the work, their greatest contribution being the establishment of churches. This era produced our largest number of new annual conferences with growing presiding elders' districts, and our greatest period of membership growth.

In 1884 the presiding elder system was amplified by the General Conference, to keep pace with the growth of the denomination. The annual statistical report blanks for pastors in charge were vastly enlarged for compilation of details for denominational use. [11] The General Conference of 1888 revised the Discipline, making provision for each annual conference to organize boards for receiving and distributing connectional funds. One such board was for home missions, "to be composed of three members, to receive the appropriation from the General Mission Board, and to dispose of the same by direction of the Annual Conference." [12] For more than a quarter of a century, the church moved in this sphere of missions, with the anticipation that all dedicated church members were missionaries and expected to share in the program of expanding the church. The bishops expressed their feelings in this matter in 1908, in relating the conditions of the home missions field, stating that some home missions conferences needed assistance in their upward struggles and endeavors.

A better class and larger number of workers are needed.

It is unnecessary for us to tell what the securing and maintenance of such workers implies.

We admonish you now that you have an eye single to the requirements and the demands of our mission work at home and abroad; if you expect to see the great Church of Varick and the sainted fathers, do your part of the work in winning souls for Christ, and do your full quota of the work to be done in Christianizing and advancing the race in upward struggles and endeavors.[13]

Home Missions was not departmentalized until 1916. It was then placed with the Church Extension Department, and the Honorable John C. Dancy, Sr., was re-elected Corresponding Secretary of the Church Extension and Home Missions Department. It was generally conceded by the majority of church leaders at that time that home missions and church extension were synonymous; church

9. *Minutes,* Sixteenth Quadrennial Session, p. 48.
10. *Ibid.,* p. 79.
11. *Minutes,* Seventeenth Quadrennial Session, pp. 143-145.
12. *Minutes, Eighteenth Quadrennial Session,* p. 114.
13. Episcopal Quadrennial Address, 1908, pp. 11-12.

extension assisting the conferences in building and buying churches in new and expanded territories, and home missions making provision for ministerial support of mission preachers, especially in new fields where churches were planted through the church extension appropriation.

Home missions placement continued to be a source of contention for several quadrenniums. The leaders and concerned members of the church had different views regarding its connectional status. Some desired a separate Home Missions Department, others wanted to combine it with the Department of Foreign Missions, while some others felt that if it were a part of the department already in operation for the support of aged ministers and their families and the relief of mission preachers, it would be more effective.

At the General Conference of 1932, the matter was placed in the hands of a special committee on consolidation and elimination of departments. The Board of Bishops had recommended "that there be a Department of Relief which shall conduct and control all denominational operations for the relief of our Superannuated Preachers, Widows, Orphans, the Brotherhood and Home Missions preachers and that there be an executive secretary in charge of this department." The committee thus made the same recommendation to the General Conference, and on motion by Rev. F. R. Blakey, seconded by Rev. E. A. Abbott, this recommendation was adopted. [14] Reverend Thomas W. Wallace, who had been serving as secretary of Ministerial Relief and Brotherhood, was elected corresponding secretary of this three-division department. Since Dr. Wallace's death in 1942, the department has been served by Revs. Herbert Bell Shaw, Solomon S. Seay, and Austin Paul Morris, present incumbent (see Chapter 27).

The first quadrennium, 1932-1936, Dr. Wallace operated the Home Missions Department with very limited means. In 1936, the financial secretary, Dr. E. L. Madison, included the following in his recommendations to the General Conference:

> ... To stimulate and strengthen Home Mission work, we recommend that all conference workers, daughters of education or special agents appointed to raise money for the annual conference shall be required to give an account of their stewardship at the annual conference, and monies raised by them shall be turned over to the finance committee only and used to assist churches and mission preachers in the conference, and a complete report of the same sent to the Home Missions Department. [15]

The General Conference concurred, and the annual conferences began to utilize home missions committees, and dedicated Home Missions Workers were appointed in some episcopal areas and annual conferences, which proved greatly beneficial in spreading sections of the church. So successful was the arrangement in some annual conferences that a renewed effort was made at the General Conference in 1944 to have a full-fledged Home Missions Department with a concentrated connectional program. The bishops were divided in opinion and unable to make a specific recommendation; thus they made the following statement:

> We forebear to recommend definitely on the matter of Home Missions. There were three minds in our body on the subject. Some are of the opinion that the Home Missions could be committed to one board on all Missions, Home and Foreign in the church. There are two bureaus to function, and the

14. *Minutes,* Twenty-Ninth Quadrennial Session, pp. 64, 245.
15. *Minutes,* Thirtieth Quadrennial Session, p. 209.

money . equally divided. Others strongly desired a separation of Home Missions from any and all departments and that it be made independent as other departments with a Home Missions Board, Home Missions Secretary, and the law on the Woman's Home Missions Society now in the Discipline be oriented to fit in as auxiliary to Home Missions Department. Others still were of the opinion that Home Missions should be kept within the status quo in the Department of Relief, and monies boosted through Home and Foreign Missions budgets for the cause. In every case the opinion was that something radically new and dynamically motivative must be done for Home Missions to meet the needs of our Zion in the spread of missions, supporting Mission Preachers and carrying forward a program of Social Service of our pastors and people in the churches to open the way to receive the returning women and men now in the service of the Army.[16]

This precipitated a debate on whether to have a separate department or to divide the funds raised by the Woman's Home and Foreign Missionary Society, inasmuch as the society was carrying the name but organizational funds were used primarily for foreign missions. Strongly advocating the separate home missions department were Bishops B. G. Shaw, W. J. Walls, Revs. I. B. Turner, D. C. Pope, H. J. Callis, J. E. McCall, and S. S. Seay. Those expressing opposite views were Bishop E. L. Madison, Mrs. Abbie Clement Jackson, and other missionary women. A compromise was reached, and 40% of the Woman's Home and Foreign Missionary Society budget was voted for home missions.[17] These funds are supplementary to the support the Home Missions Department received from the connectional budget. Missions, however, home and foreign, are everlasting extremities of Christianity, and the desire for fulfillment is far beyond the scope of satisfactory provision. The department is governed by the Board of Home Missions, appointed quadrennially by the General Conference upon nomination of the bishops.

The primary function of the Department of Home Missions is to help mission churches support their ministers and presiding elders. While the department is engaged in this phase of ministerial relief, the General Conference of 1964 adopted the ministers minimum salary. This fund has not been utilized because it must reach a certain level before it is regarded as sufficient to operate. It is being held in custody of the Connectional Budget Board until it reaches an amount to become operative.

Church Extension

As early as 1872, church extension committees were formed in annual conferences with objectives similar to those of Home Missions. However, they were more directly concerned about church property; conditions, evaluation, extension, etc., within the bounds of the annual conference. The committees made their reports according to conditions and needs, and for the most part introduced creative methods of expansion. The church extension segment of the committee report on Home and Foreign Missions and Church Extension at the General Conference of 1880 began a connectional interest in safeguarding and expanding church property. It recommended to the General Conference that pastors and trustees see that a clear title be given for church property, and that the deed be in accordance with our Discipline.[18] The General Conference of

16. *Minutes,* Thirty-Second Quadrennial Session, pp. 240-241.
17. *Minutes,* Thirty-Second Quadrennial Session, pp. 57, 62-63, 189; *Doctrines and Discipline,* 1944, p. 294; Jackson, *Information Please,* p. 16.
18. *Minutes,* Sixteenth Quadrennial Session, p. 80.

1888 made this a legal part of our economy and incorporated the following in the Discipline:

It shall be the duty of the pastor in charge, and the Presiding Elder, to see that the property is deeded according to our Book of Discipline, and duly incorporated in accordance with the laws of the State in which they are situated. [19]

The successful work of the church extension committees in the annual and general conferences animated the spirit of the connection, and in 1892 the Church Extension Department was established by the General Conference when the Board of Bishops recommended a Constitution for the Board of Church Extension and the Committee on Church Extension reported:

. . . A review of the work of church extension within the pale of our beloved Zion during the last four years furnishes cause for rejoicing and great encouragement. It is quite possible that we have never since the days of reconstruction accomplished so much for God as we have done during the last four years. All over our land, from North to South, from East to West, beautiful and stately churches have gone up and are today pointing their spires heavenward, betokening the ushering in of a more glorious condition of things in our Zion than we have hitherto enjoyed.

The conquests for God through the earnest, energetic, and self-sacrificing spirit of our bishops, ministers, and loyal members have been simply marvelous. The glowing report of our General Secretary gives us conclusive evidence of our wonderful success financially. And we have but to look over the minutes of the several conferences at the great number of souls saved to note the success spiritually. While our work has increased all over the connection, the results we have accomplished in our Western and Southwestern fields are especially encouraging. In the extreme South the work has been blessed by God, and the borders of our beloved Zion have been greatly enlarged. In the northern part of our work, many new churches have been built or remodeled. . . . In every direction we look there are signs of improvement. All glory to the apostolic fire and zeal burning in the hearts of our bishops and ministers, which urges them on to such herculean deeds for God and our Zion!

But, vast as have been our accomplishments, there still remains the inviting field; the world before us. That we must follow up the rapid flow of migration toward the West land and there plant the colors of our beloved Zion, especially in the Oklahoma Territory, must be clear to all. Our work in the far South, Southwest, and extreme West must be pushed with unabated zeal, to say nothing of the far-off land of Africa, which has such peculiar claims upon us.

Now, to do this, to further this grand work, it is clear to your committee that some new steps must be taken in this direction. We therefore recommend the establishment of General and Sub Church Extension Boards. [20]

The Connectional Board was composed of the bishops of the church, the General Secretary and General Steward, "to hold in trust monies and property for the ministers and members of the African Methodist Episcopal Zion Church." The object of these monies were to aid in the erection and improving of churches and parsonages of the denomination. The Constitution also provided for sub-boards in each annual conference, consisting of five elders to be nominated by the presiding bishop and elected by the conference. Provisions for making loans from the General Board were outlined, and the officers and their duties specified. The

19. *Minutes,* Eighteenth Quadrennial Session, p. 114.
20. *Minutes,* Nineteenth Quadrennial Session, pp. 42-43, 147-150.

committee recommended that each bishop "be requested to furnish the General Statistician the number of churches erected or repaired on his district during the quadrennium; also the number of souls converted on his district during the four years, and the number of new societies organized."[21]

Working in consonance with the Board of Bishops, the members of the committee responsible for our first connectional plan of church extension were:

C. H. Smith, chairman	J. H. McMullen
B. F. Wheeler, secretary	J. P. Meacham
C. C. Allison	G. H. Miles
S. L. Corrothers	J. W. Mills
W. H. Chambers, M.D.	T. P. R. Moore
Y. J. P. Cohen	J. C. Price
J. H. Dennis	Scott Robinson
H. B. Derritt	J. C. Saunders
J. M. B. Holmes	J. Seals
Adam Jackson	W. G. Strong
J. H. Jackson	J. E. Transue
F. M. Jacobs	J. A. Tyler
Logan Johnson	A. Wakefield
James E. Mason	G. B. Walker
F. E. McCorrico	J. T. Williams, M.D.[22]

The General Conference of 1896 amended the Constitution upon recommendations that a General Secretary of Church Extension be elected, whose salary would be paid from the general funds. His principal duties were to travel to the annual conferences and arouse an interest among the brethren and urge renewed zeal; also to visit the several churches as far as possible, so as to work up a greater enthusiasm among the laity. The connectional board was extended to include one member of each episcopal district, with the new secretary of Church Extension to replace the General Secretary and General Steward.[23] From these foundations of 1892 and 1896, and revisions in 1900, the Board and Department of Church Extension have operated through the years, with a few alterations in method and procedure, and some progression in order to keep pace with the changing times.

Reverend Andrew Jackson Warner was elected the first Church Extension and Missionary Secretary, as it was then called, of the denomination in 1896.[24] The General Conference of 1896 had made provision for support of church extension by requiring every pastor to make an annual collection in his congregation for church extension purposes, to be reported to the annual conference. The General Conference of 1900 enlarged upon this plan of fund raising by adding an appropriation from the general funds, and effecting solicitations of bequests and donations.[25] It was several quadrenniums later, however, before these plans met with feasible success. The first two secretaries pioneered under strenuous

21. *Doctrines and Discipline,* 1892, pp. 224-229.
22. *Minutes,* Nineteenth Quadrennial Session, p. 150.
23. *Minutes,* Twentieth Quadrennial Session, pp. 240-241; *Doctrines and Discipline,* 1900, pp. 239-248.
24. *Minutes,* Twentieth Quadrennial Session, p. 81.
25. *Doctrines and Discipline,* 1900, p. 241.

conditions to implant the Church Extension Department of the A.M.E. Zion Church. Dr. Warner, a magnetic preacher and speaker, remained at his pastorate at Birmingham, Alabama for nearly two years after he was elected. He then left for his work in the field on January 21, 1898, travelling over 12,000 miles and delivering 263 sermons and lectures in less than a year. He attempted the organization of "Mite societies" in churches throughout the connection to assist needy and mission churches.[26] The societies were not established on a firm foundation connection wide, and soon vanished.

At the General Conference of 1900, Rev. Elijah H. Curry was unanimously elected Corresponding Secretary of the Church Extension Department. Reverend George W. Maize, I, expressed to the General Conference his grievance; being a candidate for the office, no opportunity had been given him to be considered in the vote. On a later date Maize made explanation to the body that he had not been dealt with fairly, and then moved the unanimous election of Dr. Curry.[27] Dr. Curry did not serve as secretary. He chose to remain in the pastorate. Therefore in essence, the second secretary of the Church Extension Department was Rev. William Henry Coffey, who operated the office from the A.M.E. Zion Headquarters, in Philadelphia, Pa.

At the Connectional Council in August 1901, at Atlantic City, N.J., it was voted that Drs. Curry and Coffey change places; Curry becoming president of the Church Extension Board and Coffey the secretary.[28] The Board of Bishops, being members of the Church Extension Board and the executive authority in the interim of the General Conference, agreed to this arrangement pending ratification of the ensuing General Conference. In June 1902, in the financial secretary's office (Dr. J. S. Caldwell), Philadelphia, Pa., the Church Extension Department was reorganized. Dr. Coffey first trembled and feared for the life of the department; he told how Bishop J. W. Hood became the man of the hour for Church Extension: In the reorganization, Bishop Hood became "responsible for $300 to tide us over the summer months. In August, of the same year, we were about to go adrift; and Bishop Hood threw out the life boat of $100, and rescued us from drowning. That $100, some day, will be worth millions to Zion. It was 'Bread cast upon the water.' " [29]

Bishop Hood dedicated his fortieth anniversary in the episcopacy to programs of thank-service and a debt-paying rally in 1912, and the proceeds were dedicated to paying debts on churches throughout the connection.

Since the General Conference of 1904, bishops have been elected chairmen of administrative boards, and Bishop George W. Clinton became the first chairman of the Church Extension Board. The corresponding secretary, Dr. W. H. Coffey, was the most constructive secretary in the history of the denomination. He soon began taking Zion churches out of alleys in cities and major towns, and placing them on avenues and streets. He was a magnificent preacher and had a style on the order of Bishop Bascom of the Methodist Episcopal Church. He reminded the General Conference of 1912, in his farewell report, that he had started out 10 years ago without a penny. He said: "We must drill the world to keep step with the church, and not the church to keep step with the world." Coffey made several

26. *Minutes,* Twenty-First Quadrennial Session, p. 219.
27. *Ibid.,* pp. 69-70, 77.
28. *Minutes,* Twenty-Second Quadrennial Session, pp. 204, 365-366.
29. *Ibid.*

recommendations to that body to strengthen the department; they were referred to the revision committee, and some were implemented. He created the system which taught the church how to secure loans from the department, and built up a larger system of securing loans to build and buy churches and parsonages throughout the connection. From the 1912 General Conference, he became presiding elder in the New England Conference, and died during the quadrennium. [30]

One of Zion's foremost laymen of the era, the Hon. John C. Dancy, Sr., was elected Corresponding Secretary of the Church Extension Department at the 1912 General Conference. He continued to administer the affairs from the headquarters in Philadelphia. Although he encouraged the building and buying of churches, he was not as gifted in this field, for he was more the editorial and public relations type. However, he made a positive contribution by encouraging the work. Dancy was trustworthy in any position he held for the connection or the country.

As previously mentioned, from 1916 to 1932, the Church Extension Department and Home Missions Department functioned as a unit. The Board of Bishops, in 1920, gave a brief account of its works as follows:

> The uniting of the Church Extension and Home Missions at the last quadrennial session was a happy blending of two closely related interests. This department has furnished relief in a very satisfactory way, commensurate with the funds it has handled. The ten per cent it receives from the general claims should not be its main income. The amount received on Easter should be doubled if the department is to furnish the relief so largely expected of it. It is regrettable that some pastors have not allowed or encouraged their churches to raise their quota on that day for the department, and yet they make application to the department for help. It ought to be seen that help can only be given as the churches combined make the department strong. Despite this handicap, this department has been the source of relief and a very present help in the time of trouble to many struggling churches. We think it would prove an admirable plan to transfer the church obligations from the General Claims department, and then legislate to put a larger revenue with the department for the discharging of its obligation.[31]

The Board of Bishops inaugurated a Debt Paying Campaign in 1917, and initiated plans for raising larger sums through the Tercentenary Observance of the black race in America, by 1919-1920. These two campaigns relieved the church of some heavy pressures and invigorated the spirit of the people, and produced the second largest era of growth in the church since the Reconstruction and post-Reconstruction eras. The secretary, Dr. Dancy, noted that the church had never before had so many grand rallies resulting in the collection of large sums for the individual churches as during the four years from 1916 to 1920. Dr. Dancy was re-elected to the position by the General Conference of 1920, and passed away July 15, 1920. The Board of Bishops elected Dr. Simon Green Atkins of Winston Salem, N.C. at the Connectional Council in August 1920, and he served effectively until the General Conference of 1924. The advocacy for the separation of Home Missions and Church Extension began at this General Conference when the Bishops declared:

> . . . We have had eight years of experiment with the Combination Theory (Home Missions and Church Extension Departments) and ample opportunity

30. Bishops' Quadrennial Address, 1916, p. 12.
31. *Minutes,* Twenty-Sixth Quadrennial Session, pp. 73-74.

to determine its merits. It is a question in the minds of many as to whether or not it has been conducive to the best interest of the Church. There are many who feel that the success of the Church Extension Department has been secured at the expense of the Home Missions Department and the sacrifice of the interest of the mission preachers. Whatever may be the facts in this case, we your Chief Pastors feel that beginning with the General Conference some definite arrangements should be made for the care and protection of the mission preachers.[32]

The bishops also spoke forcefully of the great importance of the Church Extension Department:

Our Church has profited by this system. Before the introduction of the departmental system in the conduct of the affairs of our Church we drifted along in a methodless manner, fighting the resistances at a great disadvantage. The Church Extension Department was perhaps the first well ordered department established by our church, and for the organization of this department, the credit is due the late Reverend W. H. Coffey. It is true that the Church has all along established and developed many influential churches. But we have seen our most phenomenal growth in the large congested cities in every section of the country since the establishment of the Church Extension Department. This department has been the means of encouraging and helping the struggling churches in every section of the country and of greatly strengthening the confidence of the members in the integrity of the general church. [33]

There was a desperate attempt on behalf of several leading delegates of this General Conference to separate these two departments. After two entire sessions were devoted to the issue prior to the election, the effort failed, and Attorney Samuel Madison Dudley of Washington, D.C. was elected Corresponding Secretary of the Church Extension and Home Missions Department.[34] Mr. Dudley, a loyal church leader who had been employed in the nation's capital by the federal government, labored eight years to relieve the department of some of the heavy debts it had incurred. The adversity of the nation's Depression caused serious problems, and this department was affected by the legislation of the General Conference in 1932. When the Committee on Elimination and Consolidation reported, an attempt was made to merge the Church Extension Department with another department under one secretary. Participating in the discussion and debate on this matter were Dr. Ernest A. Robinson, S. M. Dudley, Simon G. Atkins, Revs. S. W. Hamilton, H. E. Wilson, John F. Moreland, Jr., T. Allen Harvey, and Bishop L. W. Kyles. Due to the intricacies of this department, it was voted that the department be operated by the Board, with no salaried secretary. [35]

The Board of Church Extension administered the department for one quadrennium, with its chairman, Bishop Josiah S. Caldwell, the reliable figure. His able assistants of the board who worked diligently for the maintenance of the department were Revs. Frank W. Alstork, B. W. Swain, John F. Moreland, Jr., W. D. Battle, J. P. Foote, S. E. Dixon, D. C. Crosby, S. S. Seay, J. H. Chase, Attorney S. M. Dudley, and Rev. Fred D. Douglass.[36] Administering the department was

32. *Minutes,* Twenty-Seventh Quadrennial Session, pp. 110-111.
33. *Ibid.*
34. *Ibid.,* pp. 68-71, 74.
35. *Minutes,* Twenty-Ninth Quadrennial Session, p. 62.
36. *Doctrines and Discipline,* pp. 342-343.

cumbersome, for these men were heavily engaged in their regular church work. The General Conference of 1936, therefore, decided to restore the office of corresponding secretary, and Oscar W. Adams, Sr. was elected to fill the post. Adams was an industrious and highly intelligent layman from Birmingham, who combined editorial skill with business acumen. He moved the office to Birmingham, Ala. and also operated a black secular newspaper. He was also Grand Master of the Masonic Lodge, and was widely known. He travelled extensively in the interest of church extension, and administered the department trustworthily for 10 years until his death in 1946. Reverend C. W. Lawrence of Greensboro, N.C., was elected by the Board of Bishops at the Connectional Council in August 1946 to complete Mr. Adams' unexpired term. Reverend Lawrence, a high-grade presiding elder and dedicated public servant, known for his lore and resourcefulness, served with reliance and dependability for two years.

To continue the work of extending the borders of Zion, the General Conference of 1948 elected an enterprising layman of Winston-Salem, N.C., Daniel Webster Andrews. He was a scientific businessman and very methodical in his conduct of affairs. He was re-elected by successive General Conferences, and served with assiduity for 20 years. Perhaps the most difficult years of this departmental work, since the days of Rev. W. H. Coffey, were 1964-1968, after the reconstructed connectional budget was adopted by the General Conference of 1964. The Church Extension Department was allotted $130,000. All annual conference expansion projects and conference supported camps with existing mortgages became the obligation of the Church Extension Department, in addition to the regular program of building and buying churches in new areas. The system of requisitioning for existing conference obligations and new church extension projects met with serious limitations and vicissitudes. The demands of some areas were much greater than others, according to the size, obligations, and needs of particular conferences. The anomaly of operation made it almost impossible for the department to avoid indiscriminate practices, or to satisfy the diverse remittances of the various conferences. Remedial plans were enacted after the General Conference of 1968, when the Board of Church Extension voted to apportion each episcopal district which functioned or handled its obligations within the bounds of the appropriation.

The General Conference of 1968 elected to this position Lem Long, Jr., a trustworthy talented layman of untarnished record and scrupulous mentality, whose life is consecrated to God and the affairs of the A.M.E. Zion Church in the high interest of his race and country. He was re-elected by the General Conference of 1972. He moved the Church Extension Office into the Varick Memorial Publishing House Building, Charlotte, N.C. The Department of Church Extension continues to serve in a very fruitful way.

CHAPTER 25

FOREIGN MISSIONS

Soon the Ethiop's hand will rise,
Shouting praise to God all-wise,
Soon he will his portion claim
Join in chorus with the train.

Rev. George W. Clinton, 1879 [1]

In her infant years, the African Methodist Episcopal Zion Church stressed another projection of the precious commands of Jesus: "Go ye into all the world. . . ." It was through foreign missions. Needless to say that our specific first attack in executing this command is Africa. Our maiden efforts, however, were the West Indies islands, Canada and Haiti (see Chapter 17).

By 1856, the Home and Foreign Missions Board of the New York Conference had established a church in Demerara. A letter addressed to Bishop James Simmons on behalf of the African Methodist Episcopal Zion Church, Friendship, East Coast, Demerara, expressed the gratitude of the members to the bishop, the New York Conference and Mother Zion Church for granting their request and sending them a missionary. They reported 141 members besides the general congregation.

> We rejoice to inform you that the Holy Spirit has been remarkably poured out upon us: every week some more or less are added to the church. But what cheers us most in this glorious refreshing season from the Lord, is that the majority of *the converts*, as well as those who are seeking for salvation by the cross of Jesus Christ, never before made any profession of religion whatever, but were in the world doing the works of the devil. We now are scarcely able to accommodate the congregation; in fact, our church accommodation is utterly inadequate to our present necessities. May the Lord of the harvest ever continue to be mindful of us.

The lengthy letter, in the form of a report, was signed on behalf of the trustees by Mindas August, president. [2] When the report for the Demerara Mission was called up at the General Conference of 1856, several letters from the mission were read, "in which Reverend R. C. Henderson informed the conference that he could not be present. His term having expired, he was not re-elected Superintendent of the mission." [3] The work suspended for some time here, but later became our first established foreign missions work of the church in the Western Hemisphere.

1. B. F. Wheeler, *Cullings from Zion's Poets,* p. 47.
2. *Minutes* of the New York and New England Conferences, 1857, pp. 39-41
3. Moore, *History, p. 221.*

There were a number of recorded experimental missionary attempts in the Caribbean by the annual conference missionary boards, but they were shortlived, or lost from Zion. These annual conference boards first began to function connectionally after the General Conference of 1872, as the work of home and foreign missions of local churches and annual conferences was outlined in the Discipline. From this time forth, there were those among us with unyielding determination who began to take serious thought and concrete steps in the redemptive work of Africa. The most persevering among this group was the Rev. Andrew Cartwright. His pioneer work in Africa led to the first organization of a connectional missions board, a missionary society in 1880, and eventually the Foreign Missions Department.

Cartwright was a member of the Virginia Conference, head elder of churches on a circuit which he had founded: Plymouth, Jamesville, Bethel, and Macedonia, N.C. During this period, the subject of African colonization had become rife again, as it had been in the days of Varick and Rush, Allen and Coker, and Lott Cary. This subject constantly divided the black people. Northerners gaining their freedom in the early part of the nineteenth century were suspicious, with just cause, that whites had used them in every brutal way to build up the nation, and were now attempting to banish them from the country. This deep sensitivity continued among blacks, and became even stronger after Emancipation and the revival of the campaign among leading whites, many of whom had the firm intention of relieving the country of the black race. Yet in the midst of confusion and division, there were those of the race who constantly expressed the desire to go to Africa and serve their people in the name of missions. Those who boldly ventured forth, and helped to restore faith when they were in need of faith and hope, made everlasting impressions in our race history.

Cartwright had been projecting his dream of starting work in Africa for Zion among his friends in the conference and throughout the church. He had been greatly encouraged by some, while others did not give it much serious thought. By 1875, he had made his decision. He was going to Africa and start mission work. At the Virginia Annual Conference in November 1875, Presiding Bishop Hood, who stringently opposed African colonization, clarified his position in his episcopal address as follows:

> There is much excitement at this time on the subject of the colonization of our people in Africa. The colonization society, the old and untiring enemy of our race, is unusually active at this time. I have ever been opposed to the schemes of this society. It has done more to impede the progress of our people than any other agency except slavery, and caste prejudice. . . .
>
> Since our people have all been made free, this society is constantly sending agents and mischevious documents among them, to render them discontented, and to prevent them from settling down and building up their fortunes here. It has prophecied that we cannot live here except as slaves or inferiors, and it has determined to have its prophecy fulfilled. It bears upon its face, in infamous characters, the dogma of Negro inferiority. He who lends his aid to it, helps to degrade our race. . . .
>
> I would not be understood as opposing the evangelization of Africa. If men feel moved upon to go to that far off, pestilential land, to carry the glad tidings of salvation, I say to them,
>
> > "Go, ye messengers of God—
> > Like the beams of morning, fly!"
>
> I bid them God's speed in their God-like work, but any general

colonizing of our people, I shall oppose. [4]

The following morning Elder Andrew Cartwright asked leave of absence from the conference, "to be absent during the day on business, as he was getting ready to go to Liberia, Africa. The Bishop granted him his wish, by stating to him that as he was going, the Conference would make of him a missionary to that country, and that he would commission him for that purpose." The conference voted that "thirteen dollars and ninety cents, in the mission board, be donated to Elder Cartwright, Missionary to Liberia." [5] The ultradetermined Cartwright turned to the leading missionary woman in the denomination, Eliza Ann Gardner, who solicited funds throughout the New England Conference. She also enlisted the assistance of the Board of Missions of the New England Conference, and raised the funds that determined the adequacy of Cartwright's and his family's trip to Africa. [6]

Reverend Cartwright set sail for Liberia on January 7, 1876 and landed in Monrovia in February of the same year with his mother, Mary Cartwright, first wife, Rosanna, and two daughters, Anne Maria and Lucy. "They made their way to the New Commer Settlement of Brewerville, as the place was then called, and here planted the first flag of Zion in Africa in 1878." [7] The reports of his labors by correspondence, to the 1880 General Conference moved this body to permanent action on behalf of our mission work in Africa and other fields.

The Home and Foreign Missions Board and the Woman's Home and Foreign Missionary Society were conceived at the same time by Rev. Mark M. Bell. He drew up the plans and presented the Constitution of the Home and Foreign Board to the General Conference of 1880, made the motion for its passage, and worked vehemently to enforce it. Though the term "Home and Foreign Missions" was first used for the board and society, these two organizations labored principally for foreign missions. The home missions phase of the work was left largely with the Daughters of Conference, where the concept had originated 'and was in practice, guided by the bishops and annual conferences. By 1888, both the board and the society were supporting home as well as foreign missions until guidelines were better established from 1912 to 1916. The society continued raising only nominal support for home missions until 1944, when the General Conference voted 40% of the society's budget for home missions. It was afterward equalized for home and foreign missions. In both instances, the Woman's Home and Foreign Missionary Society supplements and increases the Connectional Budget projectional program of missions. [8]

The first articles of the Constitution of the Home and Foreign Missionary Board of the A.M.E. Zion Church (the governing board of the Woman's Home and Foreign Missionary Society) were:

Article I

Title

This Board shall be known as the General Home and Foreign Missionary Board of the A.M.E. Zion Church of America.

---

4. *Minutes*, Tenth Session, Virginia Annual Conference, 1875, pp. 39-41.
5. *Ibid.*, pp. 9, 17.
6. This was related to the writer by Miss Gardner, when he was entertained in her home on his first trip to Boston as a boy preacher.
7. *Minutes*, Thirty-Seventh Quadrennial Session, p. 279.
8. *Doctrines and Discipline*, 1948, p. 266.

Article II

Object

The object of this Board, shall be to receive from the General fund of our Church and Missionary Society, all moneys collected for Home and Foreign Missions, and by such other means as it may deem proper, and disburse the same for the aforesaid purposes.

The Board shall also have power to employ missionaries from any of our conferences, who are willing to labor in Foreign Missions Fields, with the consent of the Bishop of said Conference.

Article III

Officers

The officers of this Board shall be a President, (who shall be one of the Bishops), Vice-President, Treasurer, and Secretary, together with one ministerial member from each Episcopal District.

Article IV outlined the duties of the officers; article V, the time and place of meetings; and article VI stated that the Constitution was not to be altered or amended except by a majority of the General Conference. The first officers of this board were Bishop Singleton T. Jones, president; Bishop James W. Hood, vice-president; Bishop Joseph P. Thompson, treasurer; and Rev. Mark M. Bell, secretary. [9] The other members of this first board were Revs. Jacob Thomas, Stephen S. Wales, William J. Moore, S. W. Jones, E. H. Curry, and J. B. Handy, representing six episcopal districts. Rev. Bell administered the affairs from Philadelphia.

Reverend Bell, first secretary of the Foreign Missions Board, was a man of undaunted spirit. He was born in Anne Arundel County, Md. He moved to Washington, D.C. and joined Galbraith Church in 1863. He was licensed to preach in 1866, joined the Philadelphia and Baltimore Conference in 1867 and spent the major part of his ministry in that conference. One of his unusual characteristics was his versatile intinerant practice, which demonstrated his fundamental zeal for missions. He pastored Baltimore (Pennsylvania Avenue) on a circuit embracing also Brightwood and Rock Creek, Washington, D.C. He built a Zion Church at Rock Creek, which was lost to the connection some years later. After two years, he was appointed to Arlington, Va. He transferred the following year to Allegheny Conference and served Avery Mission, Allegheny City (Pittsburgh), three years. He organized a society at Jack's Run, Pa., later called Bellevue Church, and by 1875 he was transferred back to the Philadelphia and Baltimore Conference and stationed at Big Wesley Church, Philadelphia. [10]

During his three-years pastorate here, two societies were organized in Philadelphia, and the church at Wilmington, Del. received into the connection with 35 members. In 1877, he purchased ground and built a church at Frankford, Pa. In May 1878, "he was appointed to the Philadelphia Mission;" adding members to the St. Mark's, Mount Olive and Frankford churches, and reducing the debt on the Frankford Church. In May 1880, around the time he introduced the new missionary program in the church, he was appointed to York, Pa., and "resigned on account of declining health and sought a more southern climate; but God overruled his plans, and he spent the year preaching and lecturing wherever

9. *Minutes, Sixteenth Quadrennial Session,* pp. 24, 35-36, 56, 65-66.
10. Hood, *One Hundred Years,* pp. 544-545.

he found an open door." He held services in his own house at Burrville, Washington, D.C. and organized the Burrville Mission and Sunday school, January, 1881. [11]

He was next appointed to Union Wesley, Washington, D.C., and served one year. He then served the church at Carlisle, Pa., for three years, and in 1885 he was appointed presiding elder of the Philadelphia District. In May 1886, he was appointed missionary agent. In May 1887, he transferred to the Tennessee Conference, and was appointed presiding elder of the Georgia District of that conference, "which he was compelled to resign before the year expired, owing to sickness and death in his family." He then returned to the Philadelphia and Baltimore Conference and pastored the Rockville, Md., circuit. In 1889, he was appointed to the Arlington circuit. In October 1891, he was appointed to the Washington City Mission and began building up a Sunday school membership and a few adult members. This mission was finally merged with central mission. [12]

He was again transferred to the Allegheny Conference and appointed to Uniontown, Pa., in 1892. He served five years and transferred back to the Philadelphia and Baltimore Conference, returning to the pastorate of Zion Church (Pennsylvania Avenue), Baltimore in 1897. After serving five years, he went to Williamsport, Pa. He died during the quadrennium of 1904-1908, a member of this conference. [13]

Reverend Bell was a minister of marked piety and an excellent pastor. He served as secretary of the General Mission Board from 1880 to 1888. [14] The close relationship between the Foreign Missions Board and the Woman's Home and Foreign Missionary Society began with the first secretary of this board, who steered the women on to great success. It is fortunate for the church that Rev. Bell had experience in various fields, from the smallest missions to the largest metropolitan churches. He made a special study of its mission cause and therefore evolved its first workable plan. In this he won immortality.

The creation of the annual Foreign Missionary Day was as follows in the General Conference of 1888:

> Bishop Singleton T. Jones made a statement relative to the Home and Foreign Missionary Society. He said he thought the Board should be empowered to make such changes in the Constitution as the officers suggested, and such other changes as would tend to success and better government of the Society He read a proposition setting apart a Sabbath in September of each year for a special collection for our mission cause. The proposition was adopted. [15]

The fourth Sunday in September was adopted as Missionary Day. In 1904, the term Woman's Day was used. In 1916, it became known as Foreign Missionary Day, and has traditionally been observed throughout the church to promote the cause of foreign missions. [16]

In 1888 the General Conference decided that "the General Secretary be secretary of the Home and Foreign Missionary Society (Board)." [17] Therefore, the successor to Rev. Mark Bell in foreign missions work was Rev. William Howard Day. Dr. Day executed his duties in connection with foreign missions and kept in

---

11. *Ibid.*, pp. 546-547.
12. *Ibid.*
13. *Ibid.*; *Minutes*, Philadelphia and Baltimore Annual Conference, 1897, 1901, 1911.
14. Hood, *One Hundred Years*, p. 547.
15. *Minutes*, Eighteenth Quadrennial Session, p. 75.
16. *Doctrines and Discipline*, 1904, 1916, 1968
17. *Minutes*, Eighteenth Quadrennial Session, p. 76.

close contact with Rev. Cartwright and his second wife, Carrie. Cartwright's first wife, Rosanna had passed away in Liberia, after the General Conference of 1880. In 1882, he engaged Sister Clementina Barker as a teacher in Liberia, but was unable to keep up her salary. He married Carrie while in this country reporting his labors to the Board of Bishops, and she was employed as a missionary teacher by the missionary department in 1886. The first foreign missions school of the A.M.E. Zion Church, the A.M.E. Zion Mission School, with both male and female students, was started in 1888 by Rev. and Mrs. Cartwright. [18]

The bishops made an attempt to arouse greater interest in the African work in 1892:

> In regard to our actual mission work in Liberia, West Africa, under the superintendency of Rev. A. Cartwright and wife, we learn that we have about one hundred members, and about seventy-five pupils in the day school. Much more might have been done had we possessed the means to have followed up the American settlements with our Church. We note, just here, that upon these settlements depends the progress of our Church in Africa. So long as we send them the ordinary American preacher, and neglect the work of the school room, we may not hope to convert the nations. By far the greatest part of this work must be done through educated natives called to the ministry.
>
> This work in Liberia, like that at home, has suffered from lack of means. The superintendent has received not more than half of his salary, and Mrs. Cartwright but very little for her four years' service as teacher. The Board of Bishops is helpless in this matter and can do nothing to further strengthen these missions, unless the people are first aroused to the duty of supporting them. [19]

The General Conference elected a trusted and highly competent leader, Rev. James H. Manley, missionary secretary. Reverend Manley was voted into the

18. *Minutes*, Nineteenth Quadrennial Session, pp. 175-184; *Minutes*, Virginia Annual Conference, 1882, p. 16.
19. *Minutes*, Nineteenth Quadrennial Session, pp. 38-39.

THE AGGREY MEMORIAL A.M.E. ZION SECONDARY SCHOOL AT BRAFO YAW NEAR CAPE COAST, GHANA.

THE A.M.E. ZION SCHOOL, NYA ODIONG,
Eastern Nigeria.

A.M.E. Zion connection as an elder from the Protestant M.E. Church. At the Virginia Annual Conference in 1884, the president of the Ladies Home and Foreign Missionary Society, Mrs. Mary J. Jones, was introduced and made an impressive address to the body. Every member seemed to feel that he or she would be careless no longer about the missionary cause. In concluding her address she said, "any amount will be thankfully received." Reverend J. H. Manley being appointed to receive what the conference would give, took his seat at the table, and about one-half of the members contributed $1.00 each and more towards the missionary cause. [20]

Manley was a progressive servant of the church. He organized several societies. At the next annual conference, he made a motion to divide the conference of 82 churches into two presiding elders' districts. The motion caused a heavy discussion and several leading preachers opposed it at that time; however it was soon divided, and Rev. Manley served two years as one of the presiding elders of the conference. [21] His eloquence as preacher and lecturer was a remarkable asset to our missionary cause. Operating the office from Pensacola, Fla., he traveled extensively, lecturing and preaching, in addition to captivating audiences with his singing, for he was also known for his magnetic voice and singing ability. His four years labors for missions were uplifting but apparently not conformable to the original machinery set up for the board and missionary society.

The missionary reports at the 1896 General Conference showed a conflict in procedure. Mrs. Mary J. Jones, the president of the Woman's Home and Foreign Missionary Society, had passed away during the quadrennium, and the secretary, Mrs. Katie P. Hood, reporting in behalf of both offices, stated that "by reason of

20. *Ibid.; Minutes*, Nineteenth Session, Virginia Annual Conference, 1884, p. 12.
21. *Minutes*, Twentieth Session, Virginia Annual Conference, 1885, p. 11; Hood, *One Hundred Years*, pp. 356-357.

THE ALLEYNE A.M.E. ZION SECONDARY SCHOOL,
Georgetown, Guyana.

the fact that the last General Conference elected a Missionary Secretary, we have not done so well during the last four years as we had during the preceding quadrennium." She continued:

> The presence of the General Secretary in the field cut off some of our means of supply. Of course we shall not know what the actual gain or loss to the connection has been until we learn how much the Home and Foreign Mission Board has received through his effort. Our effort is for the purpose of raising money to meet the demands upon that Board, and therefore if they get the funds they need by other means, the end to which we are working is reached. But if the efforts of the Secretary have simply resulted in a hindrance to us, without making up the deficiency caused by his presence in the field, then the loss is irretrievable. . . .

Reverend Manley's report was very broad and encouraging, however. [22]

The Board of Bishops recommended that the Church Extension Department and Missionary Department be consolidated. When the recommendations were presented Bishop Hood moved their adoption. Reverend J. F. Moreland, Sr. offered a substitute motion that the offices remain separate and distinct. Bishop I. C. Clinton spoke in opposition to the substitute motion. Bishop Hood, Dr. B. F. Wheeler, and Rev. A. J. Warner spoke in favor of combining the departments. "Dr. Manley sternly opposed separation, since he knew from experience whereof he spoke." Reverends W. H. Coffey, S. L. Corrothers, H. B. Pettigrew, and W. H. Davenport made speeches on the matter pro and con. The recommendation was finally adopted. This was the beginning of an experimental Board of Foreign Missions, until the Department of Foreign Missions was firmly established in 1904 and a full-time corresponding secretary elected in 1908.

On the sixteenth day of the General Conference in 1896, Reverend Andrew J. Warner was elected Church Extension and Missionary Secretary for the

22. *Minutes,* Twentieth-Quadrennial Session, p. 79, 196.

quadrennium. [23] As stated by the bishops at the 1900 General Conference, the following adjustment was made in administration:

Dr. Warner travelled extensively and laid the claims of these departments before the people, in a way they had not been previously presented. It soon became evident that he could more easily develop one department than he could develop two, therefore he tendered his resignation to the Board of Bishops, at the semi-annual meeting, held at Asbury Park, in August, 1898, and the Rev. Jesse B. Colbert, . . . the President of the Varick Christian Endeavor work of our church, was appointed by the bishops to fill out the unexpired term of Dr. Warner as Missionary Secretary. It is almost, if not quite, the universal verdict that the department has greatly improved under the management of Elder Colbert. His work in the way of organizing and educating our young people for Christian service and Church loyalty through the Varick Christian Endeavor Societies and his keeping the cause of missions before both Endeavorers and other church members, have made these features of our Church work better understood. His report will represent his work fully, and, we hope, to the satisfaction of all. [24]

Reverend Colbert of Charlotte N.C., recommended a reconstruction of the Missionary Department. He made his report, however, in conjunction with his duties as secretary of the Varick Christian Endeavor Society, and created some confusion. The General Conference adhered to some of his recommendations regarding the Missionary Department, but did not elect a missionary secretary during the session. The first bishop elected for the foreign field, Bishop John B. Small, had made glowing progress in both Africa and the West Indies, and was deeply concerned about the operational procedure. Based upon all facts presented, the committee on foreign missions recommended for the African work, that instead of sending ministers from this country as missionaries, an appropriation from the Foreign Missions Board, $2,000 per year, be placed at the disposal of the presiding bishop to secure native missionaires to carry on our work on the continent and to encourage the Rev. Thomas B. Freeman, who was working earnestly on the field. The General Conference favored the report. [25]

The foreign missions work was faithfully supervised and scrutinized during the quadrennium of 1900-1904 by the Board of Missions, consisting of all the bishops and a member from each episcopal district. The officers, Rev. C. W. Winfield, chairman, William H. Chambers, secretary, and M. R. Franklin, treasurer, associated by Revs. J. W. Smith, S. T. Meeks, William Finley, B. J. Jones, S. Sherman, and S. P. Collins, administered the affairs according to the Discipline, but it was evident that an officer was needed for the heavy responsibilities of carrying on the work in foreign fields. [26]

In 1904, the General Conference made the following revisions governing the Missionary Department:

That the money appropriated from the General Fund for foreign missions be paid to the Secretary of missions for distribution.

That all foreign missionaries be placed under and paid by the missionary department direct. . . .

That money collected for missions be used solely to help missionaries and mission stations and to sustain the department. . . .

23. *Ibid.*, pp. 71-72, 81, 115.
24. *Minutes*, Twenty-First Quadrennial Session, p. 96.
25. *Ibid.*, pp. 56-57, 245-246, 290-291; *Doctrines and Discipline*, 1900, pp. 248-254.
26. *Ibid.*, p. 364.

That we put the missionary department in full fledged operation with headquarters at No. 420 S. 11th Street, Philadelphia, Pa. [27]

That the recommendation of the Board of Bishops in attaching the duties of the missionary secretary to those of general secretary be adopted.

That ministers and all the general and local officers of the Woman's Home and Foreign Missionary Society be required to subscribe for the organ of the missionary department (*The Missionary Seer*).

Resolved that the Missionary Secretary shall be secretary of the Board of Missions and shall be the operating officer thereof. [28]

At this time, the Missionary Department was coming into its most constructive era. Reverend George Lincoln Blackwell was elected to the dual positions of Missionary Secretary and General Secretary of the Church. Blackwell was one of the most creative men in the story of the A.M.E. Zion Church. He laid the foundations of the present Foreign Missions Department. He and his wife, Annie W. Blackwell, the corresponding secretary of the Woman's Home and Foreign Missionary Society, formed a strong partnership in this era of permanent development and organization of foreign missions.

In 1908 when Dr. Blackwell was elected bishop, Rev. Richard Albertus Morrisey was elected corresponding secretary of the Missionary Department with office at the headquaters, Philadelphia. He was a keen educator and pastor of some of our largest and most influential churches, including Big Wesley, Philadelphia. He entered upon the work in regular order and did well for a while. He took on some unreasonable obligations (which he thought was right), and increased the obligations of an overburdened and handicapped department, which made it impossible to meet the claims of the department. "Finding that the department would not be able to make any show toward satisfying the claimants unless some retrenchment was made to relieve the situation, the Secretary agreed to serve without salary until the meeting of the General Conference. This method made it possible to greatly relieve the embarrassment of the situation." [29] This unfortunate overreach concluded his administration by the Board of Bishops just before the 1912 General Conference. The Board of Missions, led by Bishop J. W. Hood and Reverends W. H. Chambers and S. L. Corrothers, managed the affairs of the missionary department, and made the report at the 1912 General Conference. [30] Dr. Morrisey left the church for a while and returned in subsequent years, serving as presiding elder of the Knoxville District in the Tennessee Conference before he died.

Reverend John Wesley Wood of Indianapolis was elected Missionary Secretary in 1912, and re-elected in 1916, thus serving until 1920 when he was elevated to the bishopric. He had visited the work in Africa while pastoring in Mobile, with great advantage to the denominational cause, at his own expense. Foreign Missions became explicit in 1916, as Home Missions was detached and placed with Church Extension. The name Foreign Missions was permanently fixed upon the Board which started in the 1850 s. The secretary had assumed the responsibility of treasurer of the department when Dr. Blackwell was elected secretary. Since 1916 this officer has been known as corresponding secretary-treasurer of the Board and Department of Foreign Missions.

27. Both the General Secretary and Financial Headquarters of the A.M.E. Zion Church were in Philadelphia at this time.
28. *Minutes*, Twenty-Second Quadrennial Session, pp. 406-407.
29. *Minutes*, Twenty-Fourth Quadrennial Session, p. 143.
30. *Ibid.*, p. 89; *Doctrines and Discipline*, 1908, p. 362.

Dr. Wood, genial and capable servant of the church, came to the office when there were no effective methods employed for collecting funds and operating successfully. He was able to bring together the various programs for operation and effectively enforce them. He began to place greater stress upon Missionary Day to be properly observed the fourth Sunday in September. "In short," he stated in 1920, "We started out without purse or scrip, but we bring back to you an incorporated institution and a full-fledged mission department that functions in common with all other missionary societies in the country." [31] The Foreign Missions Board was first incorporated on May 5, 1920 in Indianapolis, Indiana.

Dr. Wood pointed out in his report that the A.M.E. Zion Church controlled 2,000 acres of Liberia's best soil, and made a plea for the ultimate development of these lands for agriculture. This property had been given to the church by the American Colonization Society of New York, with the stipulation that the church develop and maintain a school at Mt. Coffee.

Our missionaries were, for the most part, conscientious sacrificial men and women who loved the cause of Christ and the A.M.E. Zion Church, and placed them above all else. Through the years, the church has employed both missionaries from the home base and natives, who have served with reliability and proficiency. Dr. Wood was resistless in his appeals for the foreign work. Training centers and day schools were opening up in Africa and South America, and the demands were growing. He had established a good relationship with the workers on the field, and with the Woman's Home and Foreign Missionary Society. He then moved into the episcopacy, leaving the field wide open for further growth in this redemptive service to mankind.

Succeeding Bishop Wood was Rev. William Walter Matthews. He executed the multiform duties of the Foreign Missions Department with penetrating skill, for eight years. He, too, called the church's attention to one of its most precious possessions, the Mt. Coffee Plantation near Monrovia, Liberia, where Rev. and Mrs. Daniel C. Pope were then laboring to begin a development project. "At the Mt. Coffee farm," he stated, "everything grows luxuriantly. There, besides fine coffee, we find mahogany, rubber, dyewood, ebony, cocoa, cassava, groves of palm trees for palm oil, the kola bean and all the tropical fruits and vegetables. . . . in abundance." Matthews pointed out that the A.M.E. Zion Church was the only church, black or white, engaged officially in doing missionary work in Gold Coast (Ghana), West Africa, and in 1928 had just a few less than 100 mission stations, which were manned, for the most part, by native missionaries. [32]

Aside from the glorious work the Rev. W. A. Deane was doing in South America and the Virgin Islands of expanding the church work, an A.M.E. Zion Mission school was in operation, headed by Mr. H. A. Norman Niles, in South America. After eight years concomitance with the workers on the foreign field and the missionary society, Dr. Matthews was elected bishop in 1928.

His immediate successor, Rev. Hampton Thomas Medford, served 20 years, and had a wide range of experience in foreign missions when he was elected bishop in 1948. Dr. Medford was essentially a businessman, particularly gifted in real estate. During the first quadrennium of his administration, Bishop Matthews and Rev. D. C. Pope centered on projecting Annie W. Blackwell's dream, and

31. *Minutes*, Twenty-Sixth Quadrennial Session, p. 212.
32. *Minutes*, Twenty-Eighth Quadrennial Session, pp. 205, 207.

building the Annie W. Blackwell Memorial School at Mount Coffee, Liberia. They had soon erected six buildings, one a mammoth granite structure. [33] In 1932, the vast mission work of Nigeria became a part of the A.M.E. Zion Church, with its churches and training centers. A few of the secondary schools and training centers had the assistance of native governments.

By 1930, the A.M.E. Zion Church had 23 day schools in the Gold Coast Colony (Ghana), with an enrollment of 2,270 boys and girls. Five of these schools were on the government assisted list, and for 1928 they earned a grant in aid from the government of $30,000. [34] One of the earliest school projects in the Gold Coast, with over $1,000 raised toward it, was the Eliza Ann Gardner Day School. A little later, the Mary Jones, Daisy V. Johnson and Annie Lucille Alleyne Girls' Schools were organized. Some of the schools were utilized by the governments of the countries. During the episcopal administration of Bishop E. B. Watson, two independently organized and operated schools were taken over by the church. They were the Zion College of West Africa at Angola, founded by Rev. F. K. Fiawoo of the East Gold Coast, and the Aggrey Memorial College of Cape Coast, organized by Rev. A. W. E. Appiah. [35]

A bookstore was started while Bishop Alleyne was serving as resident bishop, 1924 to 1928, with A. W. E. Appiah as book steward. This not only met a long-felt need but was also another source of self-help. The revenue from this enterprise was intended to aid the mission work. [36]

During the 20-year span of Dr. Medford's administration as corresponding secretary-treasurer, the work improved in the foreign field. He maintained a sound relationship with the missionaries and used his business genius to carry forward the foreign missions enterprise to an admirable degree of progress.

The 1948 General Conference elected Rev. Daniel Carleton Pope to succeed Bishop Medford. Dr. Pope's experience was far-reaching. He and his late wife, Louise Hudson Pope, had dedicated themselves to foreign missions as early as 1924, and did notable work at Mt. Coffee. Their first baby boy was born in Liberia and died prior to the 1928 General Conference. Dr. Pope had missionary enthusiasm, especially for Africa. He did some of our most meaningful work in that field. Affable and much beloved, he was an asset of enlightenment. The denomination felt a need for his guidance and direct supervision of the African work, and after one quadrennium of service as secretary, he was elected Resident Bishop to Africa, and spent 8 of his nearly 12 years of episcopal life in Africa, the work so close to his heart.

In 1952, Rev. James Clinton Hoggard, Sr. was elected to succeed Bishop Pope. This vigilant young leader was both missionary and ecumenically minded, and had a beginning of real experience in youth ecumenical organizations. He was the first Corresponding Secretary to visit all the foreign missions fields of the A.M.E. Zion Church. His administration witnessed the revolutions of the independence of black nations, involving our A.M.E. Zion Church territory in Africa, South America, and the West Indies Islands. Ever since the secretaryship of Dr. Matthews in 1920, the office had been located in Washington, D.C. The Board of Foreign Missions was thus incorporated in Washington, D.C. on May 20, 1958.

33. *Minutes*, Twenty-Ninth Quadrennial Session, p. 195; Thirtieth-Quadrennial Session, p. 269.
34. Cameron C. Alleyne, *Gold Coast at a Glance*, p. 95.
35. *Minutes*, Thirty-Fourth Quadrennial Session, p. 276.
36. *Ibid.*, pp. 96ff.

Upon completion of the Interchurch Center building in New York City, the Board of Bishops and General Conference agreed that the office of Foreign Missions be located in this building, and the transition took place after the 1960 General Conference. The Board of Foreign Missions is the holder of the deeds for many school and church properties and land overseas, and upon its removal of headquarters to New York City, a house was purchased in Mount Vernon, N.Y. by the Board, which is used as residence for the Secretary of Foreign Missions, with accommodations for missionaries or church officials when traveling to or through New York. [37]

A cooperative spirit prevailed in the Department of Foreign Missions, encouraged by the secretary, Dr. Hoggard, in maintaining and developing the mission work, and helping to promote the works of bishops expanding into new foreign territories. His administration also witnessed the election of our first native bishop, Bishop Solomon Dorme Lartey, and his assignment and progressive works in Africa from 1960 until his death in 1969. Dr. Hoggard was thorough in his purveyance of funds and supplies to speed the cause. He was the second secretary-treasurer to serve the Foreign Missions Department 20 consecutive years. Throughout these years he maintained compatibility with the workers on the field and close alliance with the officers of the Woman's Home and Foreign Missionary Society. In 1972 he was elevated to the episcopacy.

The Rev. Harold A. L. Clement was elected by the General Conference to fill the post. He was an educator and successful pastor from coast to coast and served on a commission of San Francisco State College which toured and studied conditions in India. He manifests a concrete interest for the mission cause. He is genial and deeply interested in the total advancement of the black people; therefore, he may cultivate much support for the total redemption of Africa and her people throughout the world.

The educational institutions supported by the Foreign Missions Department today are as follows: In Ghana: The A.M.E. Zion Educational Unit in Ghana; The Aggrey Memorial A.M.E. Zion Secondary School, Brafo Yaw, and Tafo Teacher Training College, Old Tafo, where our Livingstone College trained J. Aggrey Smith serves as president of the College; the Zion College of West Africa and Small Memorial Theological Seminary, Angola, under the guidance of its founder, another Livingatone College graduate, Reverend F. K. Fiawoo.

In Nigeria, the federal government has taken over all public education at the elementary through high school levels. This will cause adjustments in the parochial schools. Our teacher training center no longer exists. "The former site is now the location of the Commercial Secondary School. The government gave approval for it to begin classes on January 17, 1972." Though a large commitment of funds will be necessary to carry on the A.M.E. Zion Church identification with this school, it is the intention of the denomination to continue to support this enterprise. [38]

In Liberia: This conference has approximately 20 schools, most of them receiving government aid. The Barfowin-Sinoe District School, the Greenville District School, and the Annie W. Blackwell School (recently merged with the Dorothy Walls Girls School at Po River) are A.M.E. Zion Church whole

37. *Minutes*, Thirty-Seventh Quadrennial Session, pp. 343-344; *Foreign Missions Department Quadrennial Report*, 1972, pp. 53-55.
38. *Ibid.*, pp. 27, 77.

enterprises. In 1972. Rev. Miss. B. Margheretta Jones contributed $1,000 to the Foreign Missions Department to aid in establishing a school in Liberia in memory of her sister, Edna Earl Jones Wright, the wife of Rev. H. T. Wright, who served as missionary from 1904 to 1908 in Liberia, where she died and was buried. [39]

In South America is the Alleyne High School and Domestic Science Center at Georgetown, Guyana. [40] A good number of students have been brought here, sponsored by the Foreign Missions Department and the Woman's Home and Foreign Missionary Society, educated in various vocations, and returned to serve our people in their native lands. Some, however, did not return, but the practice overall is successful.

Foreign missions is one of the beloved endless causes of the A.M.E. Zion Church. It is her concrescence in continuous faith, her personal symbolism of love, and her persistent evidence of closer ties to needy people (especially kith and kin), and an everlasting reminder of her spirit to share in world Christianization.

"We are rising with the changes of our state,
While Afric's sunny fountain cries out, we are not too late!"[41]

39. *Ibid.*, pp. 24-25, 77.
40. *Ibid.*, p. 18.
41. C. C. Pettey, *Ethiopia,* in *Minutes* Twelfth Annual Session, North Carolina Conference, 1875, p. 29.

CHAPTER 26

THE COMING OF THE
WOMAN'S HOME AND FOREIGN MISSIONARY
SOCIETY

The organization of the Woman's Home and Foreign Missionary Society of the African Methodist Episcopal Zion Church was the extension of the spirit that organized the denomination itself. The difference was that it transferred more responsibility to women in their own right, and utilized their gifts as servants in spreading the kingdom of God. From the beginning women have been indispensable in spreading the borders of the church. Cartwright's missionary voyage to Africa made it clear that the time had arrived for an independent women's movement for advancing missions, closely allied with church officials.

The revisions and amendments to the Discipline included the resolution presented by Rev. Mark M. Bell at the General Conference of 1880:

Whereas, The progress of our Church in Home and Foreign Missions has been much impeded through the want of sufficient means to send missionaries thereto, and to support those who have been already sent, and that the call for more missionaries in Africa (Liberia), and in other distant lands (as well as in our own), has been heard and,

Whereas, We have found the ladies of our church always willing to do all in their power to forward the Gospel, in a benighted land and whose willingness has been and is now being demonstrated by them, in their liberal contributions, annually received for the support of our Conference and Home Missions, therefore, be it

Resolved, That the General Conference do constitute a fund to be known as the "Ladies' Home and Foreign Missionary Society of the African Methodist Episcopal Zion Church."

Resolved, That the officers of this society shall be chosen from among the wives and daughters of our bishops and elders, and other influential ladies of our churches, in the several Episcopal Districts; further

Resolved, that this General Conference do organize a Board to be known as the "General Home and Foreign Missionary Board of the A.M.E. Zion Church of America."

Resolved, That the following Constitutions be adopted for the government of the General Missionary Board and Ladies Home and Foreign Missionary Society herein before mentioned." [See Chapter 25 for Board Consitution]. [1]

1. *Minutes*, Sixteenth Quadrennial Session, pp. 63-64.

The first Constitution of the General Home and Foreign Missionary Board included the substance which would govern the Ladies Home and Foreign Missionary Society. The first officers, as the society was then structured, were elected by the General Conference, and these pioneers of promoting the cause of missions throughout the world were thus listed:

OFFICERS OF THE LADIES' HOME AND FOREIGN MISSIONARY SOCIETY

(Amenable to the General Home and Foreign Missionary Board)

Mrs. Bishop S. T. Jones, President, Washington, D.C.
*Rev. Mrs. C. R. Harris, Secretary, Concord, N.C.
Mrs. Bishop J. P. Thompson, Treasurer, Newburgh, N.Y.
*Rev. Mrs. N. H. Turpin, Corresponding Secretary, Newburgh, N.Y.

Vice-Presidents

1. New York Conference: Mrs. Ellen Stevens, New York City
2. Philadelphia and Baltimore Conference: *Rev. Mrs. J. P. Hamer, Washington, D.C.
3. New England: Miss Eliza Ann Gardner, Boston, Mass.
4. Genesee (Western New York): *Rev. Mrs. J. A. Wright, Auburn, N.Y.
5. Allegheny: Mrs. Catherine Williams, Franklin County, Pa.
6. Virginia: Miss P. Delia Farley, Petersburg, Va.
7. California: Mrs. Bishop W. H. Hillery, San Francisco, Calif.
8. Kentucky: Mrs. Nannie J. Demby, Coridon, Ky.
9. North Carolina: Mrs. Sarah Freeman, Washington, N.C.
10. South Carolina: *Rev. Mrs. I. C. Clinton, Lancaster, S.C.
11. West Alabama: Mrs. Adelia Johnson, Mobile, Ala.
12. East (Central) Alabama: Mrs. Sarah Hale, Montgomery, Ala.
13. Georgia: Mrs. Esther Harris, Augusta, Ga.
14. East Tennessee: Mrs. Lavenia R. Hopkins, Newport, Tenn.
15. Louisiana: *Rev. Mrs. Isum Nicholas, New Orleans, La.
16. West Tennessee and Mississippi: Mrs. Mary Williams, Batesville, Miss.
17. Florida: *Rev. Mrs. Thomas Darley, Key West, Fl.
18. New Jersey: Mrs. Hannah Jackson, Burlington, N.J.
19. Arkansas: Mrs. M. McMary, Little Rock, Ark.
20. Michigan and Canada: Mrs. Elizabeth Johnson, Windsor, Ont.
21. Central North Carolina: Mrs. Bishop J. W. Hood, Fayetteville, N.C.
22. Bahama: Cecelia Wilson, Nassau, New Providence

For effective operation, the following rules were also adopted, signed by Bishop Singleton T. Jones, president, and Rev. M. M. Bell, secretary of the General Mission Board:

Each elder, deacon and preacher in charge of a church is requested, (in addition to his regular missionary collections, which his Conference directs to be taken), to form a Missionary Society in his church as soon as practicable, to meet monthly, and contribute what its members can afford; say three or five cents per member monthly, or more, to forward on the Gospel of the Kingdom of our blessed Redeemer. Each preacher will see that said Society makes returns to the Vice-President of the Ladies' Home and Foreign Missionary Society, appointed in his Conference District, once in every three

*In these instances, titles and names of the husbands were used for ministers' wives, which was the customary practice.

months, prior to the quarterly meetings of the L.H. and F. Missionary Society, when each Auxiliary Society shall have proper credit for the amount of money paid over. If the above course be adopted by the preachers in charge, each Vice-President will be greatly encouraged and aided in performing her duties, and the work of missions largely increased, and the borders of God's Zion will spread more rapidly and His name be glorified.[2]

The first quadrennium of this well-devised organization was motivated by a powerful faith in the women, the standard-bearers for missions. These first officers encountered multiple difficulties in the assertion of their leadership programming and raising funds for missions. As we can see from the above machinery, the success of this new movement depended heavily upon the cooperation of leaders and ministers. The district conference system, adopted in 1876, had not been well enforced, and the presiding elders were utilized through the process of election by annual conferences in a few annual conferences. The presiding elder districts' construction, therefore, is almost synonymous with the beginning and growth of the Woman's Home and Foreign Missionary Society.

In projecting the society's program, the women found that some men were slow to cooperate. Some were not responsive at all, but a few had wholeheartedly given the society the necessary injection to thrust it onward. In New York, in 1884, reporting their labors of the quadrennium to the General Conference, some of the vice-presidents revealed that they had become disheartened. Some were unable to accept the disparagement of their leadership efforts, some became apprehensive and despairing, but the leading officers and a few vice-presidents of the conferences were never daunted by adversity. With indomitable wills, they came forth to give an account of their stewardship, and to make bold attempts to change the conditions which impeded their progress.

The Secretary of the Home and Foreign Missions Board, Rev. Mark M. Bell, interposed:

> The constitution of the Missionary Board requires that we should report to the General Conference, and in connection with this report I have to announce that Mrs. Mary J. Jones, the President of the Ladies Home and Foreign Missionary Society, and several of the Vice-Presidents are here, who are desirous of making some remarks and to have some letters read, which are important in this connection. [3]

The women had raised $486.64 the first quadrennium and expended $100 for society expenses. Mrs. Jane Hamer of the Philadelphia and Baltimore Conference reported $115.80; Mrs. Delia Johnson of West Alabama, $108.60; Miss Eliza Ann Gardner of New England, $93.44; Mrs. Ann Hale of East (Central) Alabama Conference, $80.80; Mrs. Thomas Darley of Florida, $47.53; Mrs. Esther Harris of Georgia, $14.20; Mrs. P. Delia Farley of Virginia, $8.00; Mrs. Katie P. Hood of Central North Carolina, $7.65; Mrs. Isum Nicholas of Louisiana, $7.00; Mrs. Nannie Demby of Kentucky, $2.00; and the East Tennessee Conference, $1.62. Philadelphia and Baltimore Conference, through the efforts of Rev. Bell, had remitted to the missions board an additional $50. Reverend Bell reported two missionary expenditures: to Rev. Andrew Cartwright, $200.10 and to Sister Minch, $13.26. His other expenditures were the Book Concern, $99.18 and the *Star of Zion*, $49.60, leaving a balance in treasury of $74.30. Reverend Bell then presented the officers of the Ladies' Home and Foreign Missionary Society for remarks; first the President, Mrs. Mary J. Jones, who stated:

2. *Ibid.*, pp. 57-58.
3. *Report of the Ladies' General Conference Home and Foreign Missionary Society, of the A.M.E. Zion Church in America*, 1884, pp. 3-4.

I am pleased to meet the General Conference as the President of the organization created by the General Conference of 1880, at Montgomery, Alabama, and to present the report of our efforts. I hope you will be satisfied with our good intentions. We have done the best we could in an humble way; we would have done better if more of the ministers had given us their cooperation. If they could become active or honorary members of our Society they would stimulate us and help our operations. If they would set the example by taking an active interest in our work, they would enable us next year to increase our results. We hope and pray that each minister will do his duty, which will strengthen us in the missionary work. [4]

Her address was received with applause. Bishop Singleton T. Jones, her husband, was presiding, and commented upon his wife's statement as follows:

The President of the Home and Foreign Missionary Society says that they were greatly hindered last year in consequence of a want of cooperation on the part of the brethren, who created this society; that is, to come down to plain English, they did not encourage their sisters in their praiseworthy effort. They did the best they could under all the circumstances. While they keenly felt what seemed to be indifference, they are glad that their success, humble as it is, is the beginning of a great work. I am agreeably surprised at the result. The first effort of the Methodist Episcopal Church in this direction, did not much exceed our operations for the same period. I look upon this Society with great hopefulness. Under God it is destined to do good. [5]

Bishop Jones then introduced the treasurer, Mrs. Catharine Thompson. Her address was one of the most dynamic and forceful appeals coming from the women, full of historic interludes, such as,

I remember when Zion Conference met in New York, when Father Rush urged the members on; we could not then go South and bring up our brethren as now. When Brother Thompson went down under the reign of terror, he had to be passed through by others; he could not go on his own merit. But now these brethren have come up here from the far off South to mingle with us. My heart has been thrilled since I have been here witnessing your proceedings. You are a mighty host going up; you are the servants of the most high God. Go on! We are going up together, brethren; we have got a free pass through the land; a free ticket to the end of the journey; all you have to do is to show it at the stations along the line. . . .Help us! Help us! dear brethren, by your cooperation, and we will try, under God, to do what we can to make the missionary work of our church a grand success. Will you say one dollar each for yourselves? [Many voices, Yes! yes!] If you will favor and support our missionary work you will soon see what we shall be able to accomplish. With your assistance our results in the future will be more successful than in the past. You well know we cannot carry on this work ourselves; but we can succeed with your aid. What little is in our power we shall do for God and Zion. Help us, brethren, in our work. [6]

"The remarks of Mrs. Thompson were delivered in an earnest and pathetic tone, which thrilled the conference and produced a profound impression upon all present. Almost every sentence was received with applause and exclamations of delight." Bishop Jones then presented the vice-president of the Philadelphia and Baltimore Conference, Mrs. Jane P. Hamer, who also stringently appealed to the conference as follows:

4. *Ibid.*, pp. 4-5.
5. *Ibid.*, p. 5.
6. *Ibid.*, pp. 5-6.

. . . What we as Vice-presidents want in our several districts, as our worthy President has informed you, is the cooperation of the ministers. The absence of that has been the great difficulty which we have experienced in our work. With the assistance of the brethren, we are now moving along very nicely in the Second Episcopal District, and we expect to do still better in the future. I hope and pray that each minister will go to his respective place to labor with strength and energy for the missionary work; that is really all that is wanted. The ministers created us, and we do hope that they will look after the Vice-presidents and encourage them in their operations. I am for Zion. [7]

Bishop Jones then presented Miss Eliza Ann Gardner, Vice-president of New England Conference. Miss Gardner, "one of the brightest, most earnest and self-sacrificing women in behalf of her race," was always "pointed and convincing in speech, winning in manner, overpowering in appeal, and gentle as the zephyrs of spring in her devotions to the sick, oppressed, or distressed in ministering unto them." [8] She courageously summed it all up as follows:

. . . I hardly know what to say, only to reiterate what my sisters have uttered. Were it not that I might be accused of showing the white feather I might refuse to say anything. Probably if I had been called upon a few days ago, when the brethren seemed at a loss to determine our status in the conference, when the spirit of rebellion was rife within me, I might have been able to express myself more freely. Then for a few moments I thought that my hands would hang down. I do not think I felt quite so Christian-like as my dear sisters. I come from old Massachusetts, where we have declared that all, not only men, but women, too, are created free and equal, with certain inalienable rights which men are bound to respect. [Loud applause]

I am inclined to think that some of my brethren here will regard this as rank heresy. But you will remember that I come from a state where such sentiments prevail. Not only this heresy, but temperance reform, the anti-slavery cause, and many other good movements had their birth in the old Bay State; God bless her. [Applause]. I have been thrilled with inspiration from the lips of William Lloyd Garrison and Wendell Phillips; I have sat at the feet of Edna Cheney, Abbie May, and Julia Ward Howe, whose names are household words in many of the school houses of the South. You should not wonder if a little of their spirit is within me. If I would go back to Boston and tell the people that some of the members of this conference were against the women, it might have a tendency to prejudice our interests in that city with those upon whom we can rely for assistance.

Zion has ever been very dear to our family; my sainted mother was a member of this church some fifty years ago, and I am so earnest for its progress and success, that I could not let my hands hang down if I wanted to. We are in earnest in this work. If you will try to do by us the best you can; if you will encourage the hearts of the Vice-presidents in your respective districts, you will strengthen our efforts and make us a power; but if you commence to talk about the superiority of men, if you persist in telling us that after the fall of man we were put under your feet and that we are intended to be subject to your will, we cannot help you in New England one bit. We assure you that we will pray for you; and when we go up to make our report next year to the Annual Conference, if you will assist us with your influence and by your cooperation, we will be able to do the work committed to our care.

The great educational work of the church should receive our earnest attention and material support. You will remember during your proceedings

7. *Ibid.,* pp. 6-7.
8. *A.M.E. Zion Quarterly Review,* January 1894, p. 500.

there was some objection raised to appropriating the proceeds of the Children's Day to Zion Wesley Institute; but instead of discouraging the work the women of the Home and Foreign Missionary Board in Boston have been active in advancing its interests. I heard during your discussions, Professor Price charging some of the brethren with failing to raise the annual collections for the support of the college, as ordered by authority, but in New England, at the Annual Conference held at Boston in 1883 by Bishop Jones, the question was asked; What would the Vice-president of the district do toward a scholarship? I responded that I would be responsible for half a scholarship, which is $40. The amount is already raised, and just as soon as New England selects the scholar the full amount will be forthcoming. I do not know that I have anything more to say. My heart and my sympathies are with you all. May eternal God bless you and yours. [9]

Miss Gardner's address was received with loud applause. Afterward, Bishop Hood attempted to make explanations for the vice-president of the Central North Carolina Conference. However, Bishop Jones explained that Mrs. Katie P. Hood had sent a written report, also expressing a desire for deeper interest on behalf of the ministers in this organization. She had sent out a circular through the columns of the *Star of Zion,* urging the organization of societies for mission purposes, and many had failed to comply.

Reverend W. T. Biddle made explanations for the work in Western New York, in behalf of Mrs. J. A. Wright who was absent. He stated that some funds had been raised, but some misunderstanding arose on the process of channelling them to denominational personnel, and it was decided that the funds remain in the conference for missions work. Reverend C. C. Pettey made remarks in behalf of Mrs. Sarah Hale, vice-president of the Alabama Conference, in her absence, stating; "While our Vice-president enjoys the full confidence and respect of all who know her, she is not as successful as she is earnestly devoted to the cause." He also appealed for greater support. Reverend I. C. Clinton told of his wife's death soon after she was elected vice-president of the South Carolina Conference. The position had just been filled that spring and he expressed hope for great success, since quite a number of auxiliaries had been formed. [10]

This vibrating report with all its stirring appeals was well received by the members of the General Conference and produced a revitalization in the women's work for missions. From this first quadrennium, with $436.44 raised for mission work, the society has soared to over $100,000 in budgeting, in addition to their projection programs which almost doubles their annual budget.

Structuring the Society

The reports of the officers of the Ladies Home and Foreign Missionary Society at the General Conference of 1888 exhibited marked improvement. The societies had expanded with the annual conferences and presiding elders' districts, and a number of new vice-presidents were elected to fill the vacancies in old annual conferences and to serve the new annual conferences. Reverend Mark M. Bell made some timely remarks on his conception of the Ladies Home and Foreign Missionary Society. He suggested that the society be called The Woman's Home and Foreign Missionary Society (W.H. & F.M. Society), instead of Ladies' Home and Foreign Missionary Society (L.H. & F.M. Society), and the new name

9. *Report of the Ladies' General Conference Home and Foreign Missionary Society,* pp. 8-10.
10. *Ibid.,* pp. 11-14.

was adopted. [11]

At this same General Conference, later in the week when Rev. Bell was making his report on behalf of the General Home and Foreign Missions Board, he read a proposed constitution of the Woman's Home and Foreign Missionary Society, which was referred to the Committee on Missions. A few days later, Rev. S. S. Wales brought the matter of the constitution of government of the Woman's Home and Foreign Missionary Society before the body, where it was discussed and recommitted. Finally, on the last day of the General Conference, after the impelling appeal by Bishop Singleton T. Jones, in connection with his plea for annual observance of Missionary Day in September, the first Constitution of the Woman's Home and Foreign Missionary Society was adopted.[12] The ultimate language of the Constitution first placed in the Discipline was that "no amendment shall be made . . . except by a majority of the General Conference." The Constitution went through a series of major amendments each quadrennium until 1904. By this time its expansion had necessitated putting into effect three constitutional provisions on national, district, and local levels.

The object of the first Constitution was to raise funds for home and foreign missions. The society continued its relationship to the Home and Foreign Missions Board, as paragraph three of *Name* and *Object* specified that the society was subject to the Board, and must make returns to this board at its semi-annual meetings, of all money received for missionary purposes. In the second section, *Officers and their Duties,* the Constitution provided for the following officers: "President, one Vice-President from each Annual Conference district, a Secretary, a Corresponding Secretary, a Treasurer, and an Agent, all of whom shall be appointed by the General Conference immediately after the election of the Home and Foreign Missions Board."

The constitutions and by-laws of the General, District, and Local Woman's Home and Foreign Missionary Societies of the African Methodist Episcopal Zion Church, as they exist today, were painstakingly and adroitly built from this first Constitution of 1888. The president's duties encompassed the projectional work of the denominational societies with supervision of its temporalities. She had equal responsibility with the treasurer to see that all money collected be paid over to the Board of Home and Foreign Missions at its semi-annual meetings. Her travels were widespread, for she was to preside over the semi-annual meetings held on the third Wednesday of February and July (the annual meeting being in July), at the home of a Vice-President who would request it; and to call special meetings when she deemed it necessary for the good of the cause. [13]

The vice-presidents of the annual conferences were the connecting link between the General President and the officers of the local church societies. The duties of the vice-presidents were defined as follows:

. . . to raise funds in their respective districts for the aforesaid purpose by subscription, donations and collections. They shall insist upon the organization of auxiliary societies, and the money thus raised shall be forwarded to the Secretary of the Society once a quarter through the Vice-president of the said Annual Conference district, according to the blank hereinafter provided. . . .

To attend each session of the Annual Conference of her district, and shall be a member of the same. She shall urgently request every minister to become a

11. *Minutes,* Eighteenth Quadrennial Session, p. 21.
12. *Ibid.,* pp. 53, 64, 75.
13. *Doctrines and Discipline,* 1888, pp. 209-212.

member of the Society and that he take an active part in its meetings. [14]
The vice-presidents were also responsible for receiving the annual missionary offering from the pastor in charge of local churches, after the fourth Sunday in September, and remitting it also to the secretary.

The movement was blessed with salubrious growth and prosperity for missions. More organization had become necessary, and a well-defined Constitution of the Local Woman's Home and Foreign Missionary Society was adopted in 1892. Persons who were not members of the church were permitted to be members of the local society. It was explicit that the officers must be members of the A.M.E. Zion Church, and be amenable to the Quarterly Conference. [15] While this Constitution provided for a well-organized society in the local church in conformity with the General Church Society, it did not interpret obligations of local officers in channelling funds to the annual conference vice-presidents.

The Constitution of the local W.H. & F.M. Society was revised in 1896, and included the following language:

It shall be the duty of the Society to devise various means to increase its funds. All moneys raised in the Church or by enterprises in the name of the Society shall be disposed of by each representative Society as follows:

1. One third to be at the disposal of each Society for missionary purposes.

2. One third to be sent to the Treasurer of the Annual Conference Missionary Board in which said society is organized.

3. One third to be sent to the Treasurer of the Woman's Home and Foreign Missionary Society.

The Society shall report to each Quarterly Conference, a copy of which report, when approved by the Conference, shall be sent to the Secretary of the Annual Conference Mission Board, who shall make an annual report to his Conference. [16]

In 1900, both constitutions of the General W.H. & F.M. Society and the Local W.H. & F.M. Society were slighty amended. The organization of the local society as it exists today was enforced, to wit: "The officers of the local Woman's Home and Foreign Missionary Society shall consist of President, Vice-President, Secretary, Corresponding Secretary and Treasurer, who shall be members of the African Methodist Episcopal Zion Church, and shall be elected annually by the Society, a notice of the election to be given at least one week before the time they are to be elected." [17]

After the implantation of presiding elder districts, which necessitated an improved system, major revisions were made in the Constitution of the General Society, and the District Missionary Society was born in 1904. The district president replaced the vice-president of annual conferences, and became the principal wheel in the structure between the General Society and the Local Society. The Executive Board of the General Society was established at the Connectional Council in 1902, at Louisville, Ky., constituted of the general missionary officers, and these general officers were made members of the Connectional Council. [18] The three divisions of officers began to develop into a cooperating structure throughout the church.

14. *Ibid.*, pp. 210-213.
15. *Doctrines and Discipline*, 1892, pp. 217-220.
16. *Doctrines and Discipline*, 1896, p. 217.
17. *Doctrines and Discipline*, 1900, pp. 254-260.
18. *Doctrines and Discipline*, 1904, pp. 255-260; *Minutes*, Twenty-Second Quadrennial Session, p. 256; *Information Please*, p. 4.

The bishops' wives, who had been among the originators of the General Missionary Society, began losing their official positions to other missionary-minded women who felt the need to broaden the leadership. In order to guarantee them a principal position in the society, a law passed in 1912 that "the Bishops' wives and widows shall be Vice-Presidents and active members of the Executive Board. They shall have power to organize Missionary Societies in all of its branches anywhere in the General Church." [19] They were members of the Executive Board without a vote. They continued in this way until the General Conference of 1928, when the W.H. & F.M. Society made its report through Mrs. S.D. Davis and Mrs. Lizzie Pierce, and Section Two was adopted, which stated:

> That District Supervisors be appointed or elected to organize and execute the work of missions instead of Bishops' wives being automatically Vice-Presidents of the W.H. & F.M. Society. It was so moved. Reverend R. E. Clement offered as amendment that the Vice-Presidents of the W.H. & F.M. Society be appointed by the Bishop of the District upon recommendation of the missionary officers of the annual conferences. Rev. W. L. Hamblin seconded the motion. The amendment was approved.

The bishop's wife, or a woman appointed by the bishop at his discretion, did the promotional work throughout the episcopal district assigned to the bishop, and became known as missionary supervisor still maintaining a place on the Executive Board without full privileges in 1932. After the action of the General Missionary Convention of 1943 with ratification of the 1944 General Conference, the missionary supervisors became full-fledged members of the Executive Board along with general officers and chairmen of standing committees. [20]

The Woman's Home and Foreign Missionary Society is one of the best organizational concinnities of the denomination. It is a well-constructed component of local, district, and national departments and offices with connecting and interconnecting links, continuously generating missional effulgence. It would take a volume almost as large as this to give details of the evolution and the hundreds, nay thousands of people involved in it, spanning nearly 100 years and including bishops, presiding elders, and pastors. It is our endeavor to be as succinct as possible in presenting the high spots in history and creative personnel that brought this organization to its present status.

Meetings

The successful operation of the organization centers around the quarterly district mass meetings and quadrennial missionary conventions. Both were concepts of the pioneers that have been altered and enlarged upon several times for greater effectiveness. The quarterly district mass meetings held in each presiding elder's district are the most potent elements of the society's operation. In the original structure of the L.H. & F.M. Society in 1880, the machinery was set in operation with the quarterly meetings. The society functioned largely through this medium with interchangeable systems until the district quarterly mass meetings were adopted in 1912, and guidelines ameliorated with the growing organization. [21] The quarterly district mass meetings, with district officers in

19. *Minutes,* Twenty-Fourth Quadrennial Session, p. 540.
20. *Minutes,* Twenty-Eighth Quadrennial Session, p. 95; *Minutes,* Twenty-Ninth Quadrennial Session, p. 236; *Doctrines and Discipline,* 1944, p. 284.
21. *Doctrines and Discipline* 1884-1916 (1916, p. 262); *Minutes,* Twenty-Fourth Quadrennial Session, p. 541.

charge, is the connecting link between the local society and officers and the general society and officers in every phase of the work; in conjunction with the annual conference, missionary supervisor, and presiding bishop.

A major milestone in the history of the Woman's Home and Foreign Missionary Society was the attainment of its own solid organization within the church. Before the First Quadrennial Convention, there were several key meetings or conventions leading to the establishment of the Quadrennial Convention. The first Missionary Convention was held in connection with the Second Annual Connectional Council at Price Memorial Church, Atlantic City, N.J., July 31, 1901. It was at this meeting that the council ordered the expenses of the general officers of the W.H. & F.M. Society to be paid by the treasurer of the Missionary Board. It was here also that the *Missionary Seer,* edited by Bishop John B. Small, was adopted as the organ of the Missionary Department. [22]

The following year a convention was held jointly with the Connectional Council at Louisville, Ky., in August. The Executive Board was organized, and Mrs. Annie W. Blackwell was appointed assistant corresponding secretary of the W.H. & F.M. Society, and editor of the woman's column of the *Star of Zion* for the society. [23] At the convention held jointly with the Fourth Connectional Council at Hopkins Chapel, Asheville, N.C., "important legislation was enacted to put the W.H. & F.M. Society in improved running order, and a most healthy and beneficial meeting was held by the officers of the Society." [24]

At the General Conference held at Washington Memorial Church, St. Louis, in 1904, the Board of Bishops expressed concern over a report of the assistant corresponding secretary, Mrs. Annie W. Blackwell, that the church had only 420 missionary societies after 107 years of existence. "We must change this state of affairs," they declared. ". . . We urge that the women have full control of the Woman's H. & F.M. Society, and that it be distinctly understood that it is an auxiliary to the Missionary Department of the A.M.E. Zion Church." [25] This General Conference took forward steps in this direction. Among its significant action was the following: "A General Connectional Convention may be held at least once a quadrennium, and its membership shall consist of the general officers of the Society and District Presidents." [26]

Upon the twenty-fifth anniversary of the W.H. & F.M. Society, in 1905, some very interesting and progressive moves were made for the improvement of the missionary work. At the Connectional Council held at Avery Memorial Church, Allegheny City (Pittsburgh), Pa., several innovations took place. The president, Mrs. Katie P. Hood, stated that "the election of a missionary secretary (Dr. G. L. Blackwell) brought about new conditions, and it was necessary for us to adjust ourselves to these new conditions." [27] The women held their first separate meeting presided over by Mrs. Hood at this Connectional Council—Missionary Convention. The Board of Bishops referred to the progress of this convention as follows:

> When our last General Conference closed, the Woman's Home and Foreign Missionary Society was a subordinate branch of our General Missionary

22. *Minutes,* Twenty-Second Quadrennial Session, p. 255.
23. *Ibid.,* p. 256; *Information Please,* p. 4.
24. *Minutes,* Twenty-Second Quadrennial Session, p. 258.
25. *Ibid.,* p. 145.
26. *Ibid. p.* 406-407; *Doctrines and Discipline,* 1904, p. 257.
27. *Minutes,* Twenty-Third Quadrennial Session, p. 223.

Department. By compliance with the request of the officers and working missionary women of our Church, the council which convened in Allegheny City, Pa. . . . arranged that this helpful adjunct of our great Church should be operated and controlled solely by the women of the Church. They held their first general meetings at Boston, Mass., and Lousiville, Ky., in August and September of last year. They have adopted devices and put into service plans and achieved such a measure of success as have fully justified their action in asking, and the Council in deciding the present plan be put in force. Nothing has done more to give the Church a more vigorous and healthy growth and awaken the men to take a deeper interest in its forward movements for mission work and the general amelioration of the human family than the great awakening which has been given its most powerful momentum by consecrated and self-sacrificing women. . . .

We are convinced from the success of the first general effort made by our own women from the increased activity and results following the efforts of our missionary women workers and from the benefits which the Church is receiving, and the larger benefits it is destined to receive because of the organization and zeal of our women, and because of the organization and training of the children of the Church for systematic, intelligent and charitable service, that the future outcome of this department furnishes showers of spiritual blessings, and at the same time, greatly increases the missionary funds of the Church. We advise the General Conference to hear the women attentively and give them such legislation and encouragement as will enable them to do what their devoted hearts seem desirous of doing to further our missionary work. . . .

Only time and the cooperation of the ministers are needed to give Zion one of the most excellent and successful woman's organizations in our land. The capable and earnest women now in the lead, and the many who are aiding them, deserve the thanks of the entire Church for what they have done during the quadrennium in extending the influence of their organization and for the funds they have raised.[28]

The 1905 Convention definitely reasserted the relationship of the W.H. & F.M. Society to the Missionary Board, and the position of the Missionary Board as chief board for all home and foreign missions operations in the A.M.E. Zion Church. Thus the W.H. & F.M. Society, the auxiliary organization "to the Parent Missions Board of the A.M.E. Zion Church," maintained its relationship when this parent board became known as the Board of Foreign Missions in 1916. This relationship was reaffirmed in the first convention held separate from the General Conference in 1931 in the amendment of the Constitution and By-Laws, approved by the 1932 General Conference. [29]

The Missionary Society continued to hold annual conventions in connection with the Connectional Councils, placing emphasis upon a Quadrennial Convention as provided in the Constitution and Discipline. The annual Missionary Conventions held at Metropolitan Church, Norfolk, Va. in 1906 and Columbus Avenue, Boston in 1907, gave impetus to the the society for carrying forth the plan after their first Quadrennial Session in 1908 at the General Conference. They held Quadrennial Missionary conventions in 1911 at Loguen Temple, Knoxville, Tenn., and 1915 at Washington Memorial, St. Louis, Mo., but the General Conferences were the focalizing assemblies in all reports, legislative matters and election of general officers. The Quadrennial General Conventions were held

28. *Episcopal Quadrennial Address,* 1908, pp. 16-17.
29. *Doctrines and Discipline,* 1908, p. 256; 1932, p. 244.

officially in connection and simultaneously with the General Conferences until the General Conference of 1928 when Section 5 of the resolutions presented was approved on motion of Bishop G. C. Clement: "That the General Convention shall be held once in every Quadrennium in the year preceding the meeting of the General Conference, and that the Convention elect their own officers." [30]

By the time the society held its first convention at Birmingham in 1931, the Constitution had been so revised as to provide representatives in the convention of Executive Board members, district presidents, district secretaries of the Young Woman's Department, and district superintendent of Buds of Promise, one delegate from each presiding elder's district, and one delegate from each annual conference. The Supply and Life Members departments were in operation without convention representation. Subsequent conventions provided for district representatives of these departments, and altered the arrangement of the delegate from the presiding elder's district, in order to have youth representation. This particular delegate must be elected from the ranks of the Young Woman's Department, and must be between the age of 17 and 26. All Life Members and Matrons are honored as associate members of the convention. The convention is the legislative body of the Woman's Home and Foreign Missionary Society, in that it participates in making its own laws, ratified by the General Conference, and elects its general officers.

The society received a new incentive from the Board of Bishops in 1928, in the message to delegates as follows:

The rapid growth of the Woman's Home and Foreign Missionary Society in recent years, has been especially gratifying. No department of the Church has shown larger gains than this one under the direction of our noble womanhood. The first quadrennium ending in 1908 showed collections and disbursements of about Two Thousand Dollars. How steadily and grandly has been the advance when it is seen that the present quadrennium shows a total of over Eighty Thousand Dollars collected and disbursed. It would be a grave mistake to measure the growth in mere dollars and cents. More than this, are the advantages and opportunities which our women have used to develop themselves as leaders and workers in the Church, and for the race and Kingdom. Women in all parts of the land have been trained and advanced until many of them take rank with any others in the social and spiritual uplift of the nation. To them and to all the ministers and laymen who have unstintedly supported their unselfish labors we offer the thanks of the Church. [31]

The W.H. & F.M. Society moved forward from here and planned their first separate and distinct convention in three years, which proved to be one of the most constructive and decisive conventions for the good of the missions cause. The Constitution was altered considerably after 10 days of deliberations beginning August 16, 1931. Articles 2 and 3 underwent total changes so that foreign missions would be greatly emphasized. The two articles, still in effect today, thus read:

Article II - *OBJECT:*

The object of the organization shall be to promote the Cause of World Evangelization, and by systematic means, raise funds for the promotion of the work.

Article III - *ORGANIZATION:*

The Board of Foreign Missions of the A.M.E. Zion Church shall

30. *Minutes,* Twenty-Eighth Quadrennial Session, p. 96.
31. *Ibid.,* p. 48.

constitute the point of official contact and relationship between the Woman's Home and Foreign Missionary Society and the General Church. The General Officers of the Society shall be members of the Connectional Council. [32]

The Foreign Missions Board therefore has the detailed responsibility of all purveyance and communicative activities of the foreign field, and the W.H. & F.M. Society is represented by the executive members of the Executive Board who are members of the Foreign Missions Board.

Zeal and inspiration prompted the organization also in adopting the Motto; *The World for Christ,* and the general theme song, *Lift Him Up.* Each department began to adopt colors, mottos, and themes for projecting missions and stimulating growth in the different departments. The colors adopted for the parent society were purple and gold. By way of the pioneering annual conventions and the 17 quadrennial conventions held, has come one of the most thoroughgoing, creative, and inspirational international women's groups.

Quadrennial Missionary Conventions:

FIRST: May 6-21, 1908 (see General Conference, Chapter 35) *Loguen Temple, Knoxville, Tenn.: August 11-15, 1915. Hosts: Bishop and Mrs. Andrew Jackson Warner; B. J. Jones, presiding elder; Robert S. Rieves, pastor.

SECOND: May 1-22, 1912 (see General Conference, Chapter 35) *Washington Memorial Church, St. Louis: August 5-10, 1915. Hosts: Bishop and Mrs. George L. Blackwell; M. S. Kell, presiding elder; B. G. Shaw, pastor.

THIRD: May 3-17, 1916 (see General Conference, Chapter 35) *St. Paul Church, Asbury Park, N.J.: August 8-11, 1919. Hosts: Bishop and Mrs. George W. Clinton; James H. White, presiding elder; S. D. Conrad, pastor. (At this assembly, plans for the Fortieth Anniversary of the society was made.)

FOURTH: May 5-19, 1920 Observance of Fortieth Anniversary

FIFTH: May 5 27, 1924
SIXTH: May 2-21, 1928 (see General Conference, Chapter 35)

SEVENTH: Metropolitan Church, Birmingham, Ala.—August 16-25, 1931. Hosts: Bishop and Mrs. B. G. Shaw A. E. Hudson, presiding elder; Edgar B. Watson, pastor.

EIGHTH: Jones Tabernacle, Indianapolis, Ind.—August 3-9, 1935. Hosts: Bishop and Mrs. C. C. Alleyne; James L. White, presiding elder-pastor.

NINTH: St. Paul Church, Detroit, Mich.—August 5-11, 1939. Hosts: Bishop and Mrs. John W. Martin; Lott P. Powell, presiding elder; P. R. Flack, pastor.

TENTH: First Church, Brooklyn, N.Y.—August 7-13, 1943. Hosts: Bishop W. J. Walls; Mrs. Abbie Clement Jackson, missionary supervisor; Henry B. Norville, presiding elder; William Orlando Carrington, pastor.

ELEVENTH: St. Luke Church, Wilmington, N.C.—August 2-8, 1947. Hosts: Bishop and Mrs. John W. Martin; S. J. Howie, presiding elder; A. J. Kirk, pastor.

TWELFTH: Goler Metropolitan Church, Winston Salem, N.C.—August 4-10, 1951. Hosts: Bishop B. G. Shaw (Deceased, April, 1951), Bishop W. J. Walls; Mrs. Maybelle Shaw, Mrs. Rose Weller, Missionary supervisors; Claude E. Norment, presiding elder; William F. Witherspoon, pastor.

THIRTEENTH: First Church, Los Angeles, Calif.—August 6-12, 1955. Hosts: Bishop and Mrs. William A. Stewart; Theodore P. Headen, presiding elder; Shepard H. Marion, pastor; The Diamond Jubilee of the W.H. & F.M. Society.

*Not legislative assemblies.

32. *Minutes,* Twenty-Ninth Quadrennial Session, p. 163; *Doctrines and Discipline,* 1932, p. 244; 1968, pp. 209-210.

FOURTEENTH: Metropolitan Church, Hartford, Conn.—August 1-7, 1959. Hosts: Bishop and Mrs. W. J. Walls; H. B. Norville, presiding elder; Robert T. Hunter, pastor.

FIFTEENTH: Washington Metropolitan Church, St. Louis, Mo.—August 3-9, 1963. Hosts: Bishop and Mrs. Joseph D. Cauthen; James F. Gray, presiding elder; Arthur Marshall, Jr., pastor.

SIXTEENTH: First Church, Brooklyn N.Y.—August 5-11, 1967. Hosts: Bishop and Mrs. Herbert B. Shaw; Samuel Hart Williams, presiding elder; Ruben L. Speaks, pastor.

SEVENTEENTH: Shaw Memorial Church, Buffalo, N.Y.—July 31-August 7, 1971. Hosts: Bishop and Mrs. Herbert B. Shaw; Milton A. Williams; presiding elder-pastor.

Aside from the mass meetings and conventions, the Constitution is broad in the provision of promotional meetings of the society. Anniversary programs, missionary convocations, workshops, and institutes are among the meetings designed to carry on the work effectively. A more recent innovation is the regional summer conference held annually, with a program of missionary leadership training planned by a special committee appointed by the Executive Board.

Officers and Departments

The W.H. & F.M. Society began with four general officers and 22 annual conference vice-presidents. It has taken many routes through the years, and finally developed into 11 general offices, 5 being departmental officials and one a representative editor of the missionary organ. The district and local societies have developed along these same lines. Many times the society experienced anguish and discouragement in promoting missions, which motivated it to adventure in several directions for salvation and progression, through its conventions. The story of effecting these offices and departments is the core of the entire movement.

The Convention of 1935 set into effect the limited tenure of general officers for four years with no person elected more than two consecutive terms. In 1943 the Convention made a ruling that after the lapse of one quadrennium, the officer may aspire for the same office or another office. No general officer shall serve as missionary supervisor while serving her term in office. [33] The district officers are appointed annually at the discretion of the presiding bishop of the annual conference. The local officers are elected annually, and confirmed by the pastor in charge.

Parent Body—The President

The organization which started out with a small band of women in 1880, determined by the will of God to diffuse its mission work at home and abroad, laid a solid foundation for growth, and by 1892 provisions were made in the Constitution for a juvenile society. Continuous growth naturally spurred departmentalizing of the society. The first organization became known as the

33. *Minutes,* Thirtieth Quadrennial Session, p. 150; *Doctrines and Discipline,* 1936, p. 247, *Doctrines and Discipline,* 1944, p. 284.

Senior Society in 1892 while making provision for local juvenile societies.[34] The society was later known as the Woman's Home and Foreign Missionary Society, or the Woman's Society, with age groups designated which varied from time to time; however, not less than 23 years of age. The 1943 Convention decided upon two groups within this parent society: women from 23-36, and from 35 to an unlimited age. The younger group was changed in 1959 from 26 to 36, and in 1963, from 27 to 36, where it presently stands. [35] The chief officer of the Woman's Society or parent body is the President of the W.H. & F.M. Society, whether it be the local, district, or general society, and the President of the general society is head of the entire organization.

The General W.H. & F.M. Society has been blessed with competent and deeply interested leadership. Some of the earliest leaders were extremely sacrificial and able women of the church and race. Among several women who worked ardently in the preorganizational movement for missions were two unassuming but exceptionally devoted bishops' wives.

Mrs. Letitia Sisco Clinton, the wife of Senior Bishop J. J. Clinton, was not only a model wife and great helper to her husband, but an earnest hardworking member of the church, notwithstanding the fact they they had ten children (one son, Joseph N. Clinton, was serving as presiding elde'r in Florida when she died in 1894). "Mrs. Clinton was well known for her good works and kindly ways; and had therefore a large circle of friends. She was deeply interested in the success of African mission work, and raised money which she sent as private contributions to Mrs. Carrie E. S. Cartwright, with whom she kept up a regular correspondence." Prior to 1870, she organized the first Zion Church in Atlantic City, N.J., at which time there was no church for black people in that city.

Mrs. Clinton served as the vice-president of the W.H. & F.M. Society of the New Jersey Conference for a number of years until her death. She was considered the mother of the church work, as well as of the Sunday school and missionary work. After the death of Mrs. Clinton in 1894, the editor of the *Quarterly Reveiw,* Dr. John C. Dancy, related the fact that Mrs. Mary J. Jones, "the only surviving widow of our bishops, was her companion in youth, a true and trusted friend through life, and in death remembers only the beautiful picture of-a pure and consistent Christian character that caused a long and patient sufferer to bear her afflictions with the most exemplary resignation." [36] Mrs. Frances Moore of Salisbury, N.C. wife of Bishop John J. Moore, who preceded him one year in death, was also a dedicated sacrificial servant in helping her husband spread the church. She labored more in the field of home missions, and endured numerous hardships in pioneering across the continent and working side by side with her husband to plant Zion firmly on the West Coast. [37]

Mrs. Mary Jane Talbert Jones, Washington, D.C. 1880-1895: The first President, elected by the 1880 General Conference, was born in Brownsville, Pa., in 1831. She was a highly resourceful, energetic, and diligent worker. After her marriage to Singleton T. W. Jones at Allegheny City (Pittsburgh), Pa., in 1846, the couple moved harmoniously in stamping their perpetual imprint upon the A.M.E. Zion Church and the black race. Mr. Jones had embraced religion in 1842 and

34. *Doctrines and Discipline,* 1892, p. 219.
35. *Doctrines and Discipline,* 1944, p. 287; 1964, pp. 209-210.
36. *A.M.E. Zion Quarterly Review*, January 1894, p. 195.
37. *Ibid.,* April 1899, p. 24.

MRS. MARY JANE TALBERT JONES
Founding President of the Woman's Home and Foreign Missionary Society, 1880–1895.

Born—Brownsville, Pa., 1831.

Married to Singleton T. W. Jones (Bishop), Nov. 29th, 1846.

Died: July 18, 1895, Washington, D.C.

Buried in Harmony Cemetery, Washington, D.C.

joined the A.M.E. Zion Church in Harrisburg, Pa., in February of that year. He was 21 years of age when he and Mary were united in holy wedlock, and had been "reared in the hard school of adversity." He was licensed to preach in 1846, and entered the Allegheny Conference as one of the founders in' 1849, was subsequently ordained deacon and elder by Bishop Galbraith, and met his first General Conference in 1852. He was elected bishop at the General Conference in 1868, and moved vivaciously about the country expanding the borders of Zion.[38]

During this time his beloved companion, who had borne twelve children, was attentively raising her family and tenaciously laboring for the success of her husband's ministry. Bishop and Mrs. Jones had wrought valorously in destroying slavery and working for the elevation of the race after Emancipation. The obstacles experienced by them in this hard struggle made a determined, courageous, and adventurous woman of the first missionary president.

"Mrs. Mary Jones was devoted to the mission cause and labored untiringly for its furtherance." Notwithstanding the hard task of introducing a new society, as first president of the W.H. & F.M. Society, "she wrought in patience and humility the missionary work of the church, it being her particular field. In spite of the fact that woman was debarred from so many privileges, she has silently and steadily worked on," stated her companion in the cause, Mrs. Meriah E. Harris, first treasurer of the society. [39] Mary J. Jones was a woman of many virtues, persevering initiative, and noble characteristics, and rendered 15 years of effective service. [40] She died at her home in Washington, D.C., July 18, 1895. Her successor opened her report in 1896 as follows:

> By an allwise and inscrutable Providence the dear sister who for so many years faithfully guided the affairs of the Woman's Home and Foreign Missionary Society has been taken from us. Sister Mary J. Jones is laid at rest. I will not anticipate the tender services which this General Conference may decide to hold in memory of her excellent and useful life; I may simply now say that we knew her only to love her. Her devotion to the cause of missions and to every other interest of the church she loved so dearly, is known to all who were favored with her acquaintance. [41]

38. *A.M.E. Zion Quarterly Review*, October 1891, pp. 335-336; Moore, *History*, p. 373.
39. *A.M.E. Zion Quarterly Review*, April 1899, pp. 24-25.
40. Memorial tributes by G. W. Clinton and John C. Dancy, *Minutes* Forty-Fifth Session, Genesee Annual Conference, 1895.
41. *Minutes*, Twentieth Quadrennial Session, p. 195.

Mrs. Katie P. McCoy Hood, Fayetteville, N.C. 1895-1912: When the president died, Mrs. Katie P. Hood was serving as corresponding secretary, and was requested by the Board of Bishops to function in the dual capacity until the 1896 General Conference, when she was elected second president of the society. A native of Wilmington, N.C., she was married to Bishop James W. Hood, June 6, 1877, and moved to Fayetteville where she became interwoven in the work at Evans Metropolitan. Mrs. Hood became the pioneering vice-president of the W.H. & F.M. Society of the Central North Carolina Conference, in 1880, and was elected corresponding secretary of the society in 1892.

Mrs. Hood was "the embodiment of highest and purest womanhood, quiet, modest, industrious, lofty ideals, strong force of character, deeply pious, strong faith in God, self-reliance . . . good administrative ability, and influential in the higher councils of the Church." [42] She was a perspicacious leader for 16 years. "To secure the best results," she once stated in a dynamic report, "the person who fills this office must be inspired by the spirit of sincere benevolence; not for gain nor for fame, but with a desire to do the best that can be done for the Master on this line." [43] She failed to receive the majority vote in 1912.

Rev. Mrs. Mary Julia Blair Small, York, Pa., 1912-1916: The third president of the W.H. & F.M., elected at the General Conference in 1912, was a woman of extraordinary talent and ability. Mary Julia Blair was married to Rev. John Bryan Small while he was pastoring Bridgeport, Conn., October 23, 1873. She was born in Murfreesboro, Tenn., October 20, 1850. The mission work of this widow of the first foreign missionary bishop of the A.M.E. Zion Church was indubitably progressive. She dared to break down the barrier in all Methodism and became the first woman ordained an elder. Her four years administration was significant. [44] She passed away September 11, 1945, at 95 years of age.

Rev. Mrs. Florence Spearing Randolph, Jersey City, N.J., 1916-1920: This woman, who chose the ministry after she had become distinguished as a social leader, organized and built a church at Summit, N.J. and became the fourth president of the society in 1916. She was born in 1866, and married Hugh Randolph, May 1886; one daughter, Lelia (Johnson). In 1915 she organized the New Jersey State Federation of Colored Women's clubs, and prior to this she labored ardently to enhance the missionary program of the A.M.E. Zion Church. After her office terminated in 1920, she continued her very effective missionary work, making trips through West Africa, the Holy Land, and Europe, returning each time with broad programs and added inspiration. Reverend Dr. Florence Randolph was awarded the Doctor of Divinity from Livingstone College in 1933. She died December 28, 1951.

Mrs. Daisy V. Winfield Johnson, Birmingham, Ala., 1920-1932: The fifth president, Mrs. Daisy V. Johnson, was elected at the 1920 General Conference. She was an extremely successful organizer and a very competent person, in charge of the society when the Missionary Convention was set apart from the General Conference. In 1931, she presided over the first Quadrennial Convention separated from the General Conference. She built a large following among the people of the deep

42. Anderson, *Biographical Souvenir*, p. 25.
43. *Minutes*, Twenty-Third Quadrennial Session, p. 222.
44. *A.M.E. Zion Quarterly Review*, April 1892, p. 292; Anderson, *op. cit.*, p. 29.

South, both east and west. "A woman of great devotion to her church and its cause of missions, possessed with even temper, unusual poise, a good heart and splendid executive and leadership ability," died at the helm one month after attending the 1932 General Conference, June 12, 1932. [45]

Mrs. Henrietta M. Davis, St. Louis, Mo., 1932-1943: The Executive Board, which has the power to fill all vacancies of office occurring during the interim of the quadrennium, elected its vice-president to complete the unexpired term of Mrs. Johnson. At the Convention in 1935, Mrs. Davis, widow of Rev. S. D. Davis, was re-elected president and served two terms. She had considerable knowledge in parliamentary procedure, due principally to her prominence in secret society organizations. This coupled with her missionary work resulted in an administration of stimulative missionary projection. She died October 31, 1962.

Mrs. Mary Anna Steas Hauser, Salisbury, N.C. 1943-1951: This zealous worker was a lucid thinker and skillful administrator, whose heart was ingrained in the cause of missions. She served the two full terms allotted after her election in 1943, giving full measure of loyalty to the mission field.

After proposing in her president's message to the Convention in 1947 that an accredited missionary training program at Hood Theological Seminary, Livingstone College, be sponsored by the W.H. & F.M. Society and making the motion, the legislation passed at this Convention that the society place in reserve a fund for the support of a chair of missionary education from funds raised through the Life Members' Council.

Mrs. Rosa Lee Weller, Waterbury, Conn. 1951-1953: With her amiable personality and constructive leadership, Mrs. Weller rose to the head missionary position, bringing a wealth of experience as devoted pastor's wife (of Rev. S. W. Weller), cherished mother, and diligent missionary supervisor. In two years, the will of God prevailed, and the enterprising missionary program which she began was left for the society to carry forth, as she was gloriously crowned in August 1953. The vice-president, Mrs. Missouri Moore, predeceased Mrs. Weller in April of the same year, and the society was left in need of leadership. This act of Providence prompted the Convention of 1959 to create the office of second vice-president. Meanwhile, the W.H. & F.M. Society, destitute of a leader, filled the vacancy through its Executive Board in September 1953.

Mrs. Elsie Gray Keyes, Washington, D.C. 1953-1955: Modesty and humility were the most remarkable virtues of Mrs. Keyes. She came from the ranks of district officer with a notable record of missionary accomplishments in her Union Wesley Church and Washington District, and envisaged calmly the responsibilities placed upon her. She served the unexpired term of Mrs. Weller with the utmost perspicacity. She died September 4, 1962.

Mrs. Abbie Clement Jackson, Louisville, Ky. 1955-1963: The tenth president of the W.H. & F.M. Society grew up in the knowledge of every phase of the work. She was the youthful supervisor of two bishops with the guidance of her missionary-minded father, Bishop George C. Clement, and her painstaking mother, Mrs. Emma C. Williams Clement. She served eight years as executive secretary. Her ecumenical activities were broad, connecting with several world and national organizations. In 1948, she was elected recording secretary of the United Council of Church Women. She was the first president to visit the entire foreign field, and did a great deal of work in the home territory while in office. Dr. Jackson was

45. *Minutes,* Thirtieth Quadrennial Session, p. 268.

awarded the Doctorate of Humane Letters at Livingstone College in 1961. Her widespread church activities continue since her office terminated in 1963.

Mrs. Emma Brown Watson, Fayetteville, N.C. and Pittsburgh, Pa., 1963-1971: Coming up with her husband, Rev. James W. Watson, through several pastorates, she became a steady local and district missionary worker. She was elected in 1951 and served 8 years as executive secretary. She became the eleventh president of the society, and went the rounds, visiting our foreign work fully and several points of the home field, and eventuated a presidency that received the commendation of the denomination. She continues in the wake of promoting the cause of missions since her tenure ended in 1971.

Mrs. Willa Mae Anderson Rice, Pittsburgh, Pa. Elected 1971: The twelfth president, a sedulous worker, brought to this high office more than 25 years of dedicated service in home and foreign missions. Her specialty of projecting home missions within the bounds of the Allegheny Conference, and promoting the total program as district president, missionary supervisor, and member of the Foreign Board, gave her insight and practice. Her versatile capacities and zealous spirit should be the impetus of vast creative planning for missionary expansion as the Woman's Home and Foreign Missionary Society approaches its centennial. A new program of advancing missions will be placed largely upon the shoulders of this president, if God wills her to serve the full two terms, and her multifarious organization will give renewed courage and inspiration to needy people throughout the world.

Vice-Presidents

The vice-president system of the W.H. & F.M. Society initiated in each annual conference was an important position for the success of the organization in the formative years, depended largely upon the ability of this officer to travel throughout the territory of the annual conference and organize local societies with the assistance of the ministry. In 1900 the Constitution provided for a general vice-president. It continued in this way until 1904 when the district president system was introduced and the Constitution provided for two general vice-presidents. The society operated two quadrenniums with this system, and in 1912 voted that bishops' wives, before adopting the name missionary supervisor, be vice-presidents in numbers according to their husbands' seniority. However, a regular vice-president among general officers had been created at the same time as the customary adjutant to the president. [46] The society functioned with one vice-president until 1959, when the office of second vice-president was created.

A few of the vice-presidents of the early society who labored in the field to help organize societies, working side by side with their husbands, were faithful bishops' wives who were not general officers. Mrs. Katie Knox Walters died December 22, 1896, after walking by Bishop Walters' side 19 years. Miss Emeline Virginia Bird, the competent secretary for many years in the office of the A.M.E. Zion Book Concern in New York, became the second wife of Bishop Walters and labored ardently as vice-president of his area. She soon passed away February 27, 1902. He later married Lelia Coleman, who promoted the work of missions throughout his episcopal district until his death in 1917.

Mrs. Mary S. Holliday served in the field with her husband, Bishop Jehu Holliday, until his death in 1899. The first wife of Bishop Isom C. Clinton, Winnie

---

46. *Doctrines and Discipline.* 1904, p. 255; 1916, p. 261; *Minutes,* Twenty-Fourth Quadrennial Session, pp. 4-5, 540.

Thompson Clinton, had just begun to develop the work in the South Carolina Conference before her husband was elected a bishop, and died shortly after the 1880 General Conference. His second wife, Mary Ivy Clinton, was a glorious asset to missions in her husband's field after he was elected bishop until his death in October 1904, and continued her effective service in accordance with the Constitution, which provided for the services of bishops' widows as vice-presidents. Mrs. Eliza Clinton, first wife of Bishop George W. Clinton, served as vice-president in the Allegheny Conference before he was elected bishop, and died August 26, 1892. His second wife, Annie Kimball Clinton, served as vice-president during his early episcopacy, and died June 1, 1899. Mrs. M. R. Franklin, wife of Bishop M. R. Franklin served. (See missionary supervisors also).

The first general vice-president of the Woman's Home and Foreign Missionary Society was Mrs. Robert Russell Morris of Charlotte, N.C., appointed by the General Conference of 1896, who remarried and became Mrs. Morris A. Walker. She had projected the missionary cause in her annual conference, but was unable to make the general office effectual. Her fondest interest was the Sunday school work, projected by her late husband, Dr. Morris. In 1900, when the general vice-president first became one of the constitutional offices of the society, Rev. Mrs. Mary Elizabeth Washington of New Albany, Ind., Kentucky Conference, received the majority vote, and on motion of her opponent and predecessor, Mrs. M. A. Walker, it was voted to make her election unanimous. [47]

Reverend Mrs. Washington was the most prominent woman in Zion Methodism in Indiana. She was companion in the mission work in the West with Mrs. Annie C. Vance Tucker, who had a long administration as president of the Louisville District, W.H. & F.M. Society, while lady principal and matron of Livingstone College, and was responsible for molding the lives and character of many notable missionaries, both laymen and ministers, including students from the foreign field. These two women with high intellectual qualities, Mrs. Tucker a saintly personality and Mrs. Washington a gifted evangelist, gave great impetus and spiritual ozone to the missionary cause in the Midwest and throughout the denomination.

Reverend Mrs. Washington served this position for 16 years, from 1900 to 1912 and 1916 to 1920, building it to efficacy. In 1920 she entered the full time pastorate in the Ohio Conference. This is where she did her last work. She made the ingression for her competent and skillful missionary vice-president successors as follows:

Mrs. Daisy V. Johnson, Birmingham, Ala., 1912-1916. [48]

Mrs. Henrietta Davis, Mobile, Ala. and St. Louis, Mo., 1920-1935.

> (She served three years, from 1932 to 1935, as both president and vice-president, after the death of President Daisy V. Johnson.)

Mrs. M. Anna Hauser, Salisbury, N.C., 1935-43.

Mrs. Delacy Grecian-Donowa, Asbury Park, N.J., 1943-1951.

Mrs. Missouri A. Moore, Brooklyn, N.Y., 1951-1953 (deceased).

Mrs. Elsie Gray Keyes, Washington, D.C., 1953-1962.

> (She served the first two years dualistically, filling the unexpired terms of the

47. *Minutes,* Philadelphia and Baltimore Annual Conferences, 1896, 1897, 1898; New York Annual Conference, 1898; 1899; *Minutes,* Twenty-First Quadrennial Session, pp. ii, 14, 70.

48. *Minutes,* Twenty-Fourth Quadrennial Session, p. 131; Twenty-Fifth and Twenty Sixth Quadrennial Sessions, p. 233; *Doctrines and Discipline,* 1916, p. 361.

president and vice-president caused by death. In 1959, she was elected the first vice-president after two vice-president offices were created.)

Mrs. Rosanna Nelson, Newark, N.J., 1963-1971.

Mrs. Mary Gaither Meeks, Chicago, Ill., elected in 1971.

Second Vice-Presidents

For three quadrenniums, 1904 to 1912, the Constitution provided for two vice-presidents of the society. Mrs. Elizabeth Lomax was elected second vice-president in 1904, after serving a number of years as Western North Carolina Annual Conference vice-president. [49] She served effectively until 1912 when the office was transformed to appointment of bishops' wives and widows. The office was re-created in 1959, and Mrs. Alcestis McCollough Coleman, former supervisor and widow of Bishop Charles C. Coleman, was elected and served eight years. She was succeeded in 1967 by Mrs. Elizabeth Arnold Michael, who was re-elected for another four-year term in 1971.

General Corresponding Secretary, or Executive Secretary

The fundamental success of the W.H. & F.M. Society has centered on this office from the inception of the organization. When the term corresponding secretary was adopted for the office, it was equivalent in duties and responsibilities to corresponding secretaries of the other general departments of the church. Transmutation of corresponding secretary to executive secretary in 1935 was masterly planned, restructuring the administrative duties to encompass accurate management in every particular of the enlarged and growing society. Every woman who has served the church in this position has served with the deepest devotion to the furtherance of missions and a broad vision of the need of others. Our race church has not been able to keep the salary pace of the growing society's responsibilities and complexities of office. Every important circumstance of each department must be channelled through the office of the executive secretary. The total promulgation of the missions program is reliant upon this office. An account is herein given of the veracious women who have been entrusted with this office.

Mrs. Meriah Elizabeth Gion Harris, Salisbury, N.C.: Mrs. Turpin, wife of Rev. Nelson H. Turpin of Newburgh, N.Y., though named to this office, did not serve. The responsibilities were transferred to Mrs. Meriah Harris, the first recording secretary, who made her maiden quadrennial report at the 1884 General Conference. [50] Mrs. Harris was unusually competent for her task as pioneer secretary of the Missionary Society. Born in Lincolnton, N.C., March 10, 1856, and graduated from Atlanta University with high honors in 1879, she married Cicero R. Harris the same month he opened Zion Wesley Institute (Livingstone College), and became a teacher and first matron of the school. She was a "consummate model of pure womanhood," keen, conscientious, and trustworthy in all her work and an ideal bishop's wife. She served 12 years as secretary with efficiency, contributing to the growth of the society. [51] Following in the succession were:

49. *Minutes,* Twenty-Second Quadrennial Session, p. 92.
50. Ladies' General Conference H. & F.M. Missionary Report, p. 3.
51. Anderson, *Biographical Souvenir,* p. 28.

Mrs. Katie P. Hood, Fayetteville, N.C. of virtuous loyalty, was elected in 1892 and served until 1896 when she was elected president. Mrs Sarah E. C. Dudley Pettey, prudent and industrious wife of Bishop Pettey, was elected and served until 1900. Miss Eliza Ann Gardner, a valiant zealot for Zion from Boston, Mass. was elected at the 1900 General Conference, and gave one quadrennium of service. In 1904, the W.H. & F.M. Society had a rebirth. The woman who did more in the history of the Society to construct the organization connectionwide than any other one person, was elected corresponding secretary at the General Conference:

Mrs. Annie E. Walker Blackwell, Philadelphia, Pa.: She was born in Chester, S.C., August 21, 1862, the oldest daughter of the pioneer presiding elder of our work in that state. Reverend D. I. Walker was once imprisoned in South Carolina for reasons of malice and design to ruin his good name because of his advocacy of race rights and full freedom. [52] His daughter was possessed of that same intrepid spirit. The "highly cultured and accomplished lady; talented, forceful and graceful speaker and writer, and worker in the Missionary Department of untiring zeal," completed Scotia Seminary at Concord, N.C., and was married to Rev. George Lincoln Blackwell on December 7, 1887.[53] By the active energy of Mrs. Blackwell, the plan of Life Membership and Life Matron was put into operation. "Several names were enrolled as Life Members" at the Missionary Convention held in Metropolitan Church, Norfolk, Va., in August 1906, "Presiding Elder J. W. Thomas having the honor of raising the first $20 to make a life member." A large number was enrolled at the following Missionary Convention held at Columbus Avenue Church in Boston, August, 1907. [54] It was at this convention that Mrs. Blackwell was made a Life Member of the W.H. & F.M. Society by her friends. [55]

Her executive ability and administrative works were so powerful and continuously creative that she was re-elected in the five successive General Conferences, and after 26 years of dedicated service, died on the mountaintop of love and admiration of old and young, of her church and race. It was in the service of this department as corresponding secretary, declared the Board of Bishops, "that she appeared to best advantage, as she appealed for a higher type of Negro womanhood in America and for the redemption of our Fatherland. She rendered the best service of which she was capable. . ." [56]

With a keen, perceptive mind, a genial and gracious manner, an attractive, winning personality, with innate faith and optimism, and with unique organizing and oratorical gifts, Mrs. Blackwell could easily have succeeded in any calling or vocation to which she might have devoted her time and her talents. But that gifted woman consecrated her remarkable talents and personality to the Master's cause. In the school room, on the lecture platform, or on the floor of the Annual Conference, Mrs. Blackwell was ever keen, alert, resourceful, tactful persuasive and sympathetic. Her judicial mind, poise and serenity enabled her to smooth over many difficulties and spread an atmosphere of peace and joy wherever she went. Her passing away [was] a great loss to the race, to humanity, and Zion Methodism, but she left a memory which will inspire many who climb the rugged heights of achievement. Her greatest forte, however, was in the missionary work. And in

52. *Minutes,* Tenth Session, South Carolina Annual Conference, 1875, p. 22.
53. Anderson, *op. cit.,* pp. 26-27; A.M.E. Zion, *Quarterly Review,* October 1892, p. 93.
54. *Minutes,* Twenty-Third Quadrennial Session, p. 225.
55. Anderson, *Biographical Souvenir,* p. 27.
56. *Minutes,* Twenty-Seventh Quadrennial Session, p. 98.

MRS. ANNIE WALKER BLACKWELL

Corresponding Secretary of the Woman's Home and Foreign Missionary Society, 1904-1922. The most forceful personality in constructing a permanent and ample organization of the society.

Born—Chester, S.C., August 21st, 1862

Married to George L. Blackwell (Bishop), December 7th, 1887.

Died on her 35th wedding anniversary, Dec. 7th 1922

Buried in Eden Cemetery, Phildelphia, Pa.
    Her motto was: "Keep everlastingly at it."

that, she excelled. [57]

It was on her thirty-fifth wedding anniversary, December 7, 1922, that she suddenly passed away while faithfully attending her stricken husband. [58] Thus this is the date in which the denomination holds sacred to the memory of Annie Walker Blackwell, and her renowned husband who also toiled ceaselessly for the cause of missions, home and foreign.

Mrs. Anna L. Anderson, serving as a national organizer of the general society, was elected by the Executive Board in 1923, and re-elected by the General Conferences of 1924 and 1928 and Missionary Convention in 1931. She did creative work for the Life Members' Department while in office, and administered the affairs with lucidity, until 1935. At the Convention in 1935 the office was restructured, and Mrs. Creola B. Cowan an inveterate missionary worker, was elected the first executive secretary, giving eight years of earnest promotional service. Mrs. Anderson, who had been indisposed for several months, declined to run for re-election, and the convention "by unanimous vote, elected her corresponding secretary-emeritus." [59]

Mrs. Cowan was succeeded by Mrs. Abbie Clement Jackson of Louisville, Ky., in 1943, an articulate and thorough executive. After eight years tenure, she was succeeded by Mrs. Emma B. Watson, a staid and dependable administrator who served from 1951 to 1959. Mrs. Margaret Atkinson May of Auburn, N.Y., a woman of notable intelligence and assiduity, was elected. She was re-elected in 1963, and on November 21, 1964, met with a fatal accident in an automobile, leaving the society and denomination bereft. The president, Mrs. Emma B. Watson of Lancaster, S.C., executed the affairs for two months, and in January 1965, the Executive Board elected Mrs. Grace Lou Holmes of Knoxville, Tenn., to fill the

57. *Ibid.,* p. 249.
58. *Ibid.,* p. 181.
59. *Doctrines and Discipline,* 1924-1932; *Minutes,* Thirtieth Quadrennial Session, p. 150.

unexpired term of Mrs. May. This genial and lovable character, with steadfast loyalty, was elected executive secretary by the conventions in 1967 and 1971, presently conducting the affairs of this essential office of the W.H. & F.M. Society with skillful determination and a spirit of goodwill toward all.

Recording Secretary

In 1880, the organization of the society providing for two secretaries, became void when Mrs. Meriah Harris and her successors served the dual position as corresponding and recording secretaries.

The office of recording secretary was placed in the Constitution in 1904. The duties of this officer gave justification of the need of the office. She was to keep a roll of the officers of the Executive Board, the roll of all Life Members and Matrons; keep the business proceedings of Executive Board meetings and general conventions and read the same on demand. Her responsibility also was to "draw up and sign all orders on the treasurer for the payment of money." This obligation was eliminated, and provisions otherwise made at the first separate convention in 1931. [60]

Miss Sarah J. Janifer, Washington, D.C.: The first recording secretary, elected at the General Conference, May 21, 1904, was born in 1862. She was a useful servant in every aspect of the church, particularly Christian education and missions. She began teaching in the public schools of Washington at age 20. This early world traveler and Sunday school superintendent of Galbraith Church "braved the Pacific alone"; went to Japan to the World Sunday School Convention in 1920 and "brought back laurels taken for her splendid participation in the deliberations." She represented the A.M.E. Zion Church at the World Sunday School Convention in 1924, at Glasgow, Scotland. [61]

She was specifically known "as an adept scholar, experienced teacher (later becoming principal), skilled musician, spirited and forceful speaker, efficient scribe, and indefatigable worker in her local church and the missionary field." [62] Her usefulness as the first recording secretary was decidedly a beneficent acquisition to the A.M.E. Zion Church, and became an inspiring example for that office. Those who walked this way in the history of the society, and efficiently sustained its glow were:

Mrs. Lizzie B. Evans Pierce, Louisville, Ky. 1912-1939,
Miss Amelie R. Harris, Washington, D.C., 1939-1947.
Mrs. Cynthia Martin Waff, Philadelphia, Pa., 1947-1955.
Mrs. Sallie V. Moreland, Rock Hill, S.C., 1955-1963.
Miss Susie M. Moore, Washington, D.C., 1963-1971, and presently,
Mrs. Ida M. Francis, Sacramento, Calif., elected in 1971.

General Treasurer

With high degree of integrity, the treasurers have coupled missionary perception with business zeal. The Missionary Society has had its recesses but in spite of handicaps, it has made steady progress in building and maintaining its work on the home and foreign fields.

60. *Doctrines and Discipline,* 1904, pp. 257-258; 1932, p. 248.
61. E.D.W. Jones, *Comprehensive Catechism,* p. 37; *Minutes,* Twenty-Eighth Quadrennial Session, p. 225.
62. Anderson, *Biographical Souvenir,* p. 28.

MRS. CATHERINE GILCHRIST THOMPSON

First Treasurer, Woman's Home and Foreign Missionary Society, 1880-1893
(Wife of Bishop Joseph P. Thompson)

Mrs. Catherine Gilchrist Thompson, Newburgh, N.Y.: The pioneer treasurer
was an "exceptional woman in many respects—amiable, pious devout."[63] She
was born February 7, 1817 at North Hampton, Lehigh County, Pa. Her father was
a noted Underground Railroad operator in Pennsylvania. She married Joseph P.
Thompson, November 16, 1841, who was consecrated Bishop in 1876. Bishop
Hood includes in his history a lucid account of her remarkable career as follows:
        She was a great organizer, and had wonderful executive ability. Her
greatest delight was in the Sunday School work. She devoted hours of earnest
thought and prayer to the most effective means of attracting the youthful
mind to the truths of the Scriptures. In the work she was earnest and
persevering, and by her winning manner captivated the hearts of the children,
drew them together, and her labors were almost always bountifully rewarded.
        In Church society work Mrs. Thompson occupied the highest place
among her sister laborers. . . . No sacrifice seemed too great for her to make
for the good of the cause. She was long honored as the president of the Sons
and Daughters of Conference of her Church (African Methodist Episcopal
Zion), and always active in perfecting plans for its advancement. The Bible
was her book of books, and her familiarity with its contents was as
remarkable as her many faculties. Indeed, in depth of learning she ably coped
with many of the clergy of her day. She was a valuable helpmate to her
husband, and many long hours found them together discussing intricate
scriptural doctrines.
        During the dark days of slavery her mind was riveted on the work of
allaying the suffering of her unfortunate fellow-creatures. Many clever

63. Hood, *One Hundred Years,* pp. 216-218.

schemes she devised in effecting their escape from bondage. The incidents she and the bishop have related have been most thrilling in detail. [64]

One can perceive from her first report to the 1884 General Conference that Mrs. Thompson was a dynamic personality. She gave efficacious service to this office for 12 years and paved the way for systematic manageability of our missionary harvest. She died March 4, 1893, at Newburgh, N.Y. Succeeding treasurers of sincere probity were:

Mrs. Sarah E. C. Dudley Pettey, New Bern, N.C. 1892-1896,

Mrs. Meriah Elizabeth Harris, Salisbury, N.C. 1896-1912.

(Mrs. Harris' 12 years as pioneering corresponding secretary and 20 years as trustworthy treasurer of the society; a total of 32 years in general office, betokened her unequivocal fealty to A.M.E. Zion Church missionary work.)

Mrs. Ida V. Thompson Smith, Washington, D.C., 1912-1939.

(The widow of Bishop John W. Smith was a woman of high veracity and deep religious sincerity with fervent fidelity to her church and its connectional interests. She served faithfully 27 years, the longest term treasury of the missionary society. She was the daughter and inheritance of a man of affluence. Many times she helped the organization to tide over in its strenuous efforts; often salvaging crucial situations. $6,000 had even been borrowed by Bishop Caldwell for Mother Zion Church building program, for which she had given a mortgage against her home.

After the death of Mrs. Ida V. Smith in 1943, the denomination faced an entanglement. The loss of records of the deceased General Secretary-Auditor, which the church felt contained settlement of loans with Mrs. Smith before she passed, caused a concession on behalf of the church. Being unable to produce the records, there was a difference on the opinion of the settlement with Mrs. Smith's family, but the adjustment was peaceably made.)

Mrs. Ida V. Houston Jackson, St. Louis, Mo. 1939-1947,

Mrs. Julia Baum Shaw, Columbia, S.C., 1947-1954.

(In 1954 a shortage was found in the report. It was settled by relieving the treasurer of her position and requiring her to make restitution, releasing funds from her estate to fulfill the gap left in the handling of funds.)

Mrs. Willie G. Kemp Alstork, Washington, D.C. 1954-1963,

Mrs. Minnie DeHaven Hurley, New York, N.Y., 1963-1971, and at present,

Miss Evelyn M. Harris, New York, N.Y., elected in 1971.

The immense growth in the administrative program of the society stimulated exactitude in financial affairs. Since the 1955 convention, the services of a certified public accountant have been utilized.

Other Departments

The W.H. & F.M. Society grew into other departments after the organization of the parent body. The four additional departments are integral working components of the parent body, and well structured in the local, district, and national societies.

The Young Woman's Department

This department is a derivation of both the parent body and Buds of Promise. Its founder, Miss Victoria Richardson, became intensely interested in effecting the

---

64. *Ibid.*, ("From Ringwood's Journal.")

missionary work of the church through a specific age group not adapted to the adult society or the juvenile society, and took upon herself the responsibility of organizing this intermediate group of women to advance our missionary work while being trained in the more definite efforts of missionary service. There are three age groups constituting the Young Woman's Department: Junior Y's, age 13-16; Senior Y's, age 17-20; and the Young Adult, age 21-26. They are led by an experienced adult officer known as the secretary of the Young Woman's Department. In the local society, however, a competent officer is elected by the Young Woman's Local Missionary Society for this special work, and confirmed by the pastor. (65)

Miss Victoria Richardson: Born January 12, 1856, at Cleveland, Ohio. After receiving her education, she moved away to South Carolina with her uncle, Robert Harris, where she taught for a brief period; and then came to Concord, N.C., with her uncle, Cicero R. Harris, and began teaching. In 1879 she started as one of the four pioneer teachers at Livingstone College and dedicated her life to teaching at this institution. This exemplary, effusive, and keenly literary life also included shaping the religious destiny of young women through the W.H. & F.M. Society. She was instructional and interpretive, and a finely trained musician who composed the music for the Livingstone College Song: "Oh Livingstone, My Livingstone, Thy dear old name we sing" (the words being composed by W. F. Fonvielle).

The Young Woman's Society had its humble beginning in 1909 in the home of Miss Richardson, across the street from the College on Monroe Street, Salisbury, N.C., when she called a meeting of young women of the A.M.E. Zion churches in Salisbury to interest them in missionary work. She was then requested by the executive officers of the society to effect the work generally. At the General Conference in 1912, when her first report was made before the department was officially adopted, she had fortified the young women in character building, munificence, charity, and goodwill. She made a financial report for the cause of missions of $830.48, raised by these young ladies in less than three years. (66) In her report to the General Conference of 1920, many of these good deeds were revealed from the following account:

> It was at Charlotte, N.C., during the sitting of our General Conference (1912), that the young women of our church were adopted into the missionary family. Previous to said time your humble servant had been requested by the President, Mrs. K. P. Hood, through the Corresponding Secretary, Mrs. Annie W. Blackwell, to begin to effect organizations among the young women of our church.
>
> The women and the Buds of Promise were doing splendid work, but the young women were not included; so, while in attendance upon a convention at Landis, N.C., the request came to organize, so at this very opportune time and at this meeting, organization began. By the time of the meeting at Charlotte, N.C., in 1912, a report was rendered which so pleased the General Conference that it at once set apart the young women of our church as a branch of our Missionary Society.
>
> Since the beginning, the number of societies has rapidly increased, and each year finds our dear girls moving onward and accomplishing much for God and Zion. Their report blanks and letters to me show that they are making themselves felt at home. In the church, they are indispensable and the ministers have long since fully realized their value as aids to the church.

65. *Constitution and By-Laws,* W.H. & F.M. Society.
66. *Minutes,* Twenty-Fourth Quadrennial Session, p. 117.

During the war they took an active part in giving cheer and comfort to our soldier boys who were going to camp and overseas. In the influenza epidemic they proved themselves heroines, indeed. In one town where the disease was raging, twenty young women (missionaries), offered their services and served where needed. They have given useful service among the sick, visiting almhouses, relieving the suffering, giving garments to the needy, bringing children into the Sunday school, and aiding the minister in his efforts to secure his assessments. These are some of the things that our missionary young women are doing at home.

They are enthusiastic over the foreign work and have evinced it by their activity in the drives and other devices put forth in order to secure funds. The Mission Study Class is still being conducted in many of our organizations. *Daybreak in the Dark Continent* is a favorite textbook, the careful study of which thoroughly acquaints one with the true condition in Africa.

Since our recent acquisition of a large number of churches in South America, our curriculum will be enlarged and our study classes will take on new interest. Some of our societies have adopted girls in our schools at Kwittah (Keta) and are paying $30 per year for the education of each. If we could but adopt the system of tithing in our societies, we believe there would be little doubt about our raising all the money necessary for education and missions. . . .

The Buds represent the tiny mountain streams, or brooklet flowing gently down the slope; the Young Women the onward flowing river fed by the little singing stream, and the Women represent the great ocean fed by the rivers, while rounding out its life for eternity. . . ."[67]

Miss Richardson had firmly planted this department in the society, and continued to animate it until her death, August 1, 1928. The theme of the department is "Africa's Redemption." Its colors are blue and gold, and young men of the same age level may be honorary members. Other capable women elected to the office of general secretary of the Young Woman's Department to carry on the heritage were:

Mrs. Ada H. Battle, Boston, Mass., 1928-1939.

Mrs. Daisy Caldwell Tucker, Peekskill, N.Y., 1939-1944.

(Mrs. Tucker was re-elected for a second term at the convention in 1943. She accepted the position of missionary supervisor of Bishop W. J. Walls' episcopal district in 1944, which created a vacancy in this office. Mrs. Willie M. Bascom was elected at the Connectional Council at Louisville, Ky., in 1944.)

Mrs. Willie M. Bascom, Montgomery, Ala., 1944-1955.

Mrs. Hildred Henry Wactor, New York City and Mobile, Ala., 1955-1963.

Mrs. Lonia M. Gill, Whistler, Ala., 1963-1971, and at present.

Mrs. Maggie K. Beard, Rockingham, S.C., elected in 1971.

It was during the term of Mrs. Willie Bascom, upon her recommendation at the Convention at Wilmington, N.C., 1951, which was passed and ratified by the 1952 General Conference, that Victory Day, an annual observance on January 12 in memory of Miss Victoria Richardson, its founder and first secretary, was introduced in the Society. [68]

The Buds of Promise Department

In 1892 the Constitution provided for the formation of juvenile departments in local societies, "having the proper officers, providing the Treasurer shall be

67. *Minutes,* Twenty-Sixth Quadrennial Session, pp. 253-254.
68. Interview, Mrs. W. M. Bascom; *Minutes*, Thirty-Fourth Quadrennial Session, p. 399.

MRS. MARIE CLAY CLINTON   MRS. SARAH JANIFER

Organized the Buds of Promise.   First Recording Secretary

elected from the Senior Society, and also two to act as instructors." [69] The juvenile society developed according to specifications, and in 1904 became a general department. The young lady who worked ardently to advance this movement, Mrs. Marie L. Clinton was elected the first "Superintendent of the Juvenile Missionary Department," when it was adopted at the 1904 General Conference. By her conception, the department became permanently known as The Buds of Promise Department, in 1908. It consists of three age groups: Beginners, 3 to 6; Primary, 6 to 9; and Junior, 9 to 12. Boys may be honorary members.

Mrs. Marie Louise Clay Clinton: She was born in Huntsville, Ala., in 1871 to Alfred and Eliza Clay. "She passed successfully the Alabama State Normal Course, Central Alabama Academy and Clark University for literary training and voice culture, graduating in each with high honors." As a soloist she won many prizes and lofty compliments. [70] She was vice-principal of a school in Huntsville, when she married Bishop George Wylie Clinton of the Fourth Episcopal District at Huntsville, February 6, 1901. This same year she accompanied her husband to London, attending the Third Ecumenical Conference. She was one of the early Fisk Jubilee Singers and was known throughout Protestantism when she sang before this world body with great favor. [71]

Mrs. Clinton was a good speaker, talented writer, and a woman of queenly dignity and cordial disposition. [72] She loved children and children's work. Having none herself, she spent her life in blessing the orphans and children of

69. *Doctrines and Discipline,* 1892, p. 219.
70. Anderson, *Biographical Souvenir,* p. 27.
71. *Ibid.,*; Caldwell, History of the American Negro, p. 12.
72. Anderson, *op. cit.*

others. She persistently set forth the value of the child in the kingdom of God and the necessity and importance of saving and training children for service. There was a continual efflorescence in the department of Buds of Promise during her 28 years of service. "Like Dorcas of the Holy Writ, with a life 'full of good works and alms deeds which she did,' left us in full triumph of faith from Tuskegee Hospital, Tuskegee, Alabama," on January 9, 1932. [73] She lived in Charlotte, N.C., after her marriage to Bishop Clinton, and administered the department from this city.

The Buds of Promise motto is "Blooming All for Jesus." Its colors are green and white. The names of those who have walked in this historic path are:

Mrs. Hattie Neal Flack, Detroit, Michigan, 1932-1939
Mrs. Elizabeth Tucker Smith, Pratt City, Ala., 1939-1946
Mrs. Edra Mae Hilliard, Detroit, Michigan, 1946-1955,
  (Mrs. Hilliard was elected by the board at the Connectional Council of 1946, to fill the unexpired term of Mrs. Smith, and re-elected two terms by the conventions.)
Mrs. Charlotte T. Haslerig, Chicamauga, Ga. 1955-1959,
Mrs. Josie E. Fuller, Cleveland, Ohio, 1959-1967
Mrs. Willie Heath Bobo, Spartanburg, S.C., elected in 1967; re-elected, 1971.

During the tenure of Mrs. Edra Mae Hilliard, the convention held at Wilmington, N.C. in 1951 voted that a day be set aside in our denominational calendar known as "Marie L. Clinton Day," to honor the founder of this department, which the 1952 General Conference sanctioned. A set program for Buds of Promise is to be circularized and used throughout the connection by this unit of the W.H. & F.M. Society, and funds accruing from this program are to be sent to the office of the executive secretary of the W.H. & F.M. Society, earmarked and used for the salary of a foreign missionary teacher in any of our foreign schools. [74]

The Bureau of Supplies

This department, essential to missions, is often called the supply department. Its head officer is the secretary of the Bureau of Supplies in the three connectional phases, (local, district, and national). Rev. Mrs. Florence Randolph was the mother of this mission of benevolence. At the Missionary Convention held jointly with the Connectional Council at Knoxville, Tenn. August 1911, she presented her dream for progress in the Missionary Society, which was brought before the General Conference of 1912 and adopted as follows:

There shall be a Bureau of Foreign Supplies, to which all donations of clothing, medicine, literature, etc., shall be sent. The chairman of this department shall be designated Secretary of this Bureau, and she, with the Bishop of the Foreign work and a committee of five, shall have charge of all articles to be sent to the foreign field and make annual reports to the Board of Missions. All money for this department shall be sent to the General Treasurer. [75]

Reverend Mrs. Randolph was born and educated in Charleston, S.C. She was elected the first Secretary of the Bureau of Supplies at the Connectional Council

73. *Minutes,* Twenty-Ninth Quadrennial Session, p. 198.
74. *Minutes,* Thirty-Fourth Quadrennial Session, p. 399; *Constitution and By-Laws of the W.H. & F.M. Society.*
75. *Minutes,* Twenty-Fourth Quadrennial Session, p. 540; *Doctrines and Discipline,* 1916, p. 264.

in Poughkeepsie, N.Y., August 1912, by the Executive Board. [76]

This highly public spirited woman gave four years of creative service as secretary of the Bureau of Supplies, and was elected president of the society in 1916. She was ever sponsoring new causes for the foreign work, stimulated by her travels. She was programmed with Mrs. Eleanor Roosevelt on two occastions, at the A.M.E. Zion Church General Sunday School Convention in 1942 and at the New Jersey State Federation of Colored Women's Clubs, Convention in 1942. She faithfully attended the meetings until the end. Her death on December 28, 1951, [77] was mourned by the race and church. She left the work of this department to be carried on by the following resourceful secretaries:

Mrs. Martha Hill Brown, New York, N.Y., 1916-1928
Mrs. Nancy Jones, Yonkers, N.Y. 1928-1929
Mrs. Missouri A. Moore, Brooklyn, N.Y., 1929-1939
Mrs. Minnie D. Hurley, New York, N.Y. 1939-1947
Mrs. Martha Biggs Francis, Bronx, N.Y. 1947-1955
Mrs. Juanita G. Adjahoe, Westbury, L.I.,N.Y., 1955-1963
Mrs. Laura E. Small, Washington, D.C., 1963-1971
Mrs. Josephine T. Morris, Charlotte, N.C., elected in 1971

Because of the accessibility of the New York port in the earlier period, for shipping supplies to the foreign field, all the secretaries until Mrs. Small were elected from the New York vicinity. The method of purveyance of goods to the foreign field and more convenient means of shipment have adjusted this condition. Pink is the representative color of this department. "Florence Randolph Day" was adopted in 1959. A program is to be arranged by the secretary of the Bureau of Supplies, and circulated throughout the church.

Life Members Council

Life members and matrons were included in the first Constitution of the W.H. & F.M. Society presented by Rev. Mark M. Bell in 1888. as follows:

Membership:

1. Any lady paying the sum of $100 may be a Life Matron; the payment of $20 shall constitute one a Life Member.

2. Any lady may be a member of this Society by paying annually the sum of one dollar.

The revised Constitution in 1900 abridged the language: however, the corresponding secretary, Mrs. Annie W. Blackwell, began to revive interest, and in 1916 Mrs. Anna L. Anderson presented a working plan for making life members, life matrons, and patrons. We have previously mentioned the emphasis placed upon making life members between the quadrennium of 1904 and 1908, and the Missionary Convention at Norfolk in 1906 where Presiding Elder J. W. Thomas raised the first $20 to make a life member. The treasurer, Mrs. M. E. Harris, reported $297.74 in a reserve fund of Life Members and Red Letter, and $316.00 for Life Members and Matrons. [78]

At a meeting in the ladies' parlor of Broadway Temple Church, Louisville, Ky., during the 1916 General Conference, the women's attention focused upon a 2,000 acre site at Mt. Coffee, Liberia, given to the church by the American Colonization Society of New York for 100 years. The conditional requirements

76. Laura E. Small, *Handbook for Supply Secretaries,* p. 5.
77. *Minutes,* Thirty-Fourth Quadrennial Session, p. 224.
78. *Doctrines and Discipline,* 1888, p. 212, *Minutes,* Twenty-Third Quadrennial Session, pp. 225, 233.

MRS.   FLORENCE
SPEARING   RANDOLPH
Organized the Supply Department

MRS. ANNA L. GREEN ANDERSON
Formed the Life Members Council

for possession of the land were to develop and maintain it for a school. The president, Rev. Mrs. Small, and other leading missionary women became seriously concerned about this matter, as no previous effort had been made for its implementation. The sprightly district president of the Pittsburgh District, Allegheny Conference, Mrs. Anna L. Anderson, introduced the idea of building a department and projecting a program of fund raising through life members, matrons, and patrons, and use of these funds to help carry out the condition of the grant. [79]

A Life Members' Council was organized with the original constitutional purpose restored and enlarged to entreat women and men to become Life Members and Honorary Life Members of the society, by paying into the general treasury the sum of $20, and Life Matrons and Patrons and Honorary Life Matrons and Patrons, the sum of $100. At this meeting, the scope of this plan was broadened to train missionary women to serve in the foreign field. The amounts raised through "Life Members, Matrons, Memorial Members, Patrons fees and Red-Letter Day exercises" were to be placed in the bank in a reserve fund on interest by the general treasurer, "to be used as an educational fund to prepare and support missionary women in the foreign field." [80]

As an additional stimulus to this cause, each Life Member and Honorary Life Member, Matron and Patron, was to pay one dollar annual dues. This new program added impetus to the life membership program of the society, and gave a broader and more specific undertaking to the group. The Life Members Council was

79. Medis G. Warren, *Guidebook for Life Members Council.*
80. *Doctrines and Discipline,* 1916, p. 266.

organized, and the following officers were appointed: Rev. Mrs. Mary E. Washington, president; Mrs. Florence Auten, vice-president; Mrs. Anna L. Anderson, recording secretary; Mrs. Henrietta M. Davis, corresponding secretary; and Mrs. Nellie A. Callis, treasurer. This Life Members Council had arranged for mission study classes at annual conferences and quadrennial conventions, and the organization of study classes throughout the local and district societies. The Life Members Council, with its officers, was discontinued at the Executive Board meeting at Indianapolis, August 1917; as the Executive Board declared it "an organization within an organization." Mrs. Callis, the treasurer, reported $54 annual dues collected and turned over this amount to the general treasurer, Mrs. Ida V. Smith. [81]

This did not deter or destroy the spirit of the life members program. The membership arrangement remained in the Constitution, and its principal infusion was continuously goaded by the society's two corresponding secretaries from 1916 to 1935, Mrs. Annie W. Blackwell and Mrs. Anna L. Anderson. A practicable number of Life Members, Matrons and Patrons were recorded each quadrennium, and the program, though it needed an organizational plan for enlarged success, was proving greatly beneficial to the society and the missions field. One of the noteworthy contributions of this department today, is the sponsoring of a chair for missionary education and maintenance of a student loan fund at Livingstone College and Hood Theological Seminary.

The woman who had introduced the plan in 1916, Anna L. Anderson, never yielded, and in 1928 the Executive Board elected its first general chairman of Life Members Council, but her duties were not defined in the Constitution until 1935. At the Missionary Convention that year, the Life Members Council was permanently established. The general chairman of the Life Members Council continued to be selected by the Executive Board until the Convention in 1943 when the office became elective by the General Convention, and the Life Members Council became the fifth full-fledged department of the society throughout the denomination, with duties of the national, district and local chairmen defined for successful operation. [82]

Mrs. Anna Lucille Green Anderson: Anna Lucille Green was born in New York City on June 25, 1867, and manifested an early talent for music and church work. She served as a Sunday school teacher, president of the Varick Christian Endeavor, and leader of the choir in Zion Church. She was married to Charles Anderson in October 1893, and the couple moved to Pittsburgh. This gifted musician immediately joined Old John Wesley A.M.E. Zion Church by transfer, and was selected a member of the choir the following week. In 1899 she became organist of the church, serving for 18 years, and was local president of the Missionary Society. In 1908 she became district president of the Pittsburgh District, Allegheny Conference, an office she held until she was elected corresponding secretary in 1923, after the death of Mrs. Annie W. Blackwell.

Mrs. Anderson was the only founder of a missionary department who never headed it. She worked tirelessly for its salvation and fundamental rootage, and watched it come to fruition in 1935 at the convention held in Indianapolis. She had consecrated herself for missions in early childhood and was a resolute worker

---

81. Warren, *Guidebook for Life Members Council.*
82. *Doctrines and Discipline,* 1932, p. 246; 1936, pp. 247-248; 1940, pp. 274-276; 1944, pp. 284-292; *Minutes,* Twenty-Eighth Quadrennial Session, p. 96.

until the end. She died in Pittsburgh, August 23, 1940, and had selected her funeral text which was expounded by Bishop E. L. Madison at Wesley Center Church, August 26—"*She Hath Done What She Could*". [83]

The Life Members Council Department is one of the many-sided inspirational aspects of the Missionary Society, which continuously generates support through membership growth with a durable impulse of training missionaries for the field. Its color is red, which was apparently selected from its past Red-Letter Day exercises. Continuing in the wake of Mrs. Anderson's noble work were the following daughters of virtue and diligence:

Miss Lillian I. Browder, Chicago, Ill., 1928-1938

> (For a few quadrenniums, the Executive Board selected a Parliamentarian to serve on the Board and at Conventions as an officer. Miss Browder served in this position from 1939 to 1943. Mrs. Mary B. Douglass served from 1931 to 1939.) [84]

Mrs. Emma Clarissa Williams Clement, Louisville, Ky., 1939-1947

Mrs. Anna F. Fields, Los Angeles, Calif., 1947-1951

Mrs. Daisy Rand Rudd, New Haven, Conn., 1951-1959

Mrs. Medis Gholson Warren, Portsmouth, Va., 1959-1967

Mrs. Ann Walker, Arlington, Va., elected 1967, re-elected 1971.

In. 1943, the Convention voted that October be set aside as Life Members' Month, in memory of Anna L. Anderson. On this occasion, each member is asked to contribute one dollar annual dues.

Editors, Woman's Column—Missionary Seer

The W.H. & F.M. Society has always had its means of publicity. Mrs. Sarah E. C. Dudley Pettey was the pioneer missionary journalist who wrote the weekly woman's column for the W.H. & F.M. Society in the *Star of Zion* as early as 1896. [85] She was succeeded by Mrs. Annie W. Blackwell in 1902. The office became an integral part of the society in 1912 when the General Conference passed a resolution that "Mrs. J. S. Jackson be editor of the Woman's Department of the *Missionary Seer* for the W.H. & F.M. Society." [86] The editor of the woman's column of the Missionary Seer (the official organ of the W.H. & F.M. Society) was selected by the Executive Board until the Constitution was revised in 1960, stating that "the Editor of Woman's Column of the *Missionary Seer* shall be elected by the Convention." [87] Mrs. Pauline H. Jackson of Birmingham was a very intelligent woman and gifted in public relations who served until 1916. The successive editors listed have combined missionary enthusiasm with illuminating composition to keep the columns enlivened with the concrete results of the Home and Foreign Missions Departments and W.H. & F.M. Society:

Mrs. M. B. Stinson, 1916-1920

Reverend Mrs. Mary E. Washington, New Albany, Ind., 1920-1928

Mrs. Pauline H. Jackson, Birmingham, Ala., 1928-1932

Mrs. Cora E. Burke, Knoxville, Tenn., 1932-1939

Mrs. Missouri A. Moore, Brooklyn, N.Y., 1939-1947

---

83. Warren, *op. cit.*
84. *Doctrines and Discipline,* 1940, pp. 274, 379; Jones, *Comprehensive Catechism*, p. 68.
85. *Star of Zion*, 1896-1902.
86. *Minutes,* Twenty-Fourth Quadrennial Session, p. 540.
87. *Doctrines and Discipline,* 1960, p. 203.

Miss Eula M. Brown, Kansas City, Mo., 1947-1955
Mrs. Idonia Elizabeth Rogerson, Winfall, N.C., 1955-1963
Mrs. Maggie E. Shepard, Los Angeles, Calif., 1963-1971
Mrs. Frealy M. Garrison, Perry, Iowa, elected in 1971
 At the 1912 General Conference, Mrs. Ada L. M. Hall of Tuscaloosa, Ala. and Mrs. Lena Harris of Johnstown, Pa., were appointed National Organizers of the Society and served several quadrenniums, with Mrs. Anna L. Anderson promoting the movement. Mrs. Ida Barber of Charlotte, N.C., was appointed in 1920.

Missionary Supervisors

 Since 1912, when the bishops' wives and widows were first made vice-presidents of the W.H. & F.M. Society, the bishops' wives had been the most active promoters of the program on the field. This remained so in almost every instance, and the persons designated by the bishops to do this constructive work within their episcopal districts became known as missionary supervisors. The supervisor was appointed by the bishop, of course, and was usually his wife or some dedicated missionary of prominent usefulness. Through the years these women have carried the burden of this work within their respective episcopal districts and brought the organization through with a degree of increased success. The following women have served since 1912:

Bishop J. W. Hood—Mrs. Katie P. McCoy Hood
Bishop C. R. Harris—Mrs. Meriah E. Gion Harris
Bishop Alexander Walters—Mrs. Lelia Coleman Walters
Bishop George W. Clinton—Mrs. Marie Clay Clinton
Bishop J. W. Alstork—Mrs. Mamie M. Lawson Alstork
Bishop J. S. Caldwell—Mrs. Ella J. Melchor Caldwell
Bishop G. L. Blackwell—Mrs. Annie Walker Blackwell
Bishop A. J. Warner—Mrs. Annie Weddington Warner
Bishop L. W. Kyles—Mrs. Lou Ella M. Bryan Kyles (deceased)
 Mrs. Josephine Humbles Kyles
Bishop R. B. Bruce—Mrs. Henrietta Foster Bruce
Bishop William L. Lee—Mrs. Nettie Tillman Lee
Bishop George C. Clement—Mrs. Emma C. Williams Clement
Bishop John W. Wood—Mrs. Janie Edmond Wood (honorary)
 Mrs. Inez Wood Carter (Smith)
Bishop P. A. Wallace—Mrs. Ida L. Bannister Wallace
Bishop B. G. Shaw—Mrs. Garnett Wilkins Shaw (deceased)
 Mrs. Maybelle Leona Gunn Shaw
Bishop E. D. W. Jones—Mrs. Maggie E. Jones (honorary)
 Mrs. Mary M. Bryant
 Mrs. Abbie Clement Jackson
Bishop W. J. Walls—†Mrs. Harriet Edgerton Walls (honorary)
 Mrs. Abbie Clement Jackson (elected executive secretary)
 Mrs. Daisy Caldwell Tucker (deceased)
 Mrs. Rosa L. Weller (elected president)
†Mother

Mrs. Margaret J. Atkinson May
Mrs. Dorothy L. Jordon Walls
Bishop J. W. Martin—Mrs. Ola Mae Ecton Martin

Bishop C. C. Alleyne—Mrs. Annie Lucille Washington Alleyne (deceased)
 Mrs. Creola B. Cowan
 Mrs. Bettye Lee Roberts Alleyne
Bishop W. W. Matthews—Mrs. Alice Johnson Matthews (deceased)
 Mrs. Etoria Dryer Matthews
Bishop F. D. Jacobs—Mrs. Laura Etta Lomax Jacobs
Bishop E. L. Madison—Mrs. Lucille Madison Cuthbert
 Mrs. Andrades Lindsay Brown
 Mrs. Creola B. Cowan
Bishop W. C. Brown—Mrs. Gertrude Capehart Brown (deceased)
 Mrs. Willa Mae Rice
Bishop J. W. Brown—Mrs. Andrades Lindsay Brown
Bishop W. W. Slade—Mrs. Sallie Watson Blake Slade
Bishop B. F. Gordon—Mrs. Thelma Ruth Pierce Gordon
Bishop F. W. Alstork—Mrs. Willie Gertrude Kemp Alstork
Bishop E. B. Watson—Mrs. Mary Hedgepath Watson
Bishop J. C. Taylor—Mrs. Ann Pate Taylor
Bishop R. L. Jones—Mrs. Carrie Lena Smith Jones (deceased)
 Miss Raymona L. Jones
 Mrs. Mabel Miller Jones
Bishop H. T. Medford—Mrs. Mary Elizabeth Camp Medford (deceased)
 Mrs. Cordelia Medford Fauntleroy (deceased)
 Mrs. Savannah Jones Medford
Bishop H. B. Shaw—Mrs. Mary Ardelle Stokes Shaw
Bishop Spottswood—Mrs. Viola Booker Spottswood (deceased)
 Reverend Mrs. Mildred G. Pait
 Mrs. Cordelia Marie Elliott
 Mrs. Mattie Johnson Elliott Spottswood (Honorary-1970)
Bishop W. A. Stewart—Mrs. Sula Ruby Cunningham Stewart
 Mrs. Ruby C. Stewart Romao
 Mrs. Alta E. Howard
Bishop D. C. Pope—Mrs. Willie G. Alstork (elected treasurer)
 Mrs. Andrades Lindsay Brown (deceased)
 Mrs. Anna Mary Pope Moore
 Mrs. Charlotte T. Haslerig
Bishop C. E. Tucker—Reverend Mrs. Amelia Moore Tucker
Bishop J. D. Cauthen—Mrs. Georgia Little Cauthen (deceased)
 Mrs. Eliza Edwards Walker
Bishop C. C. Coleman—Mrs. Alcestis McCollough Coleman
Bishop F. S. Anderson—Mrs. Bessie Bernice Bizzell Anderson
Bishop W. M. Smith—Mrs. Ida Mae Anderson Smith
Bishop S. D. Lartey—Mrs. Alecia Ethel Smith Lartey
Bishop W. A. Hilliard—Mrs. Edra Mae Estell Hilliard
Bishop A. G. Dunston, Jr.—Miss E. Loujean Lovett
 Dr. Armayne Garrinetta Dunston, M.D.
Bishop C. H. Foggie—Mrs. Madelyn Sharpe Foggie

Bishop J. C. Hoggard—Mrs. Eva Stanton Hoggard
Bishop J. W. Wactor—Mrs. Hildred Anita Henry Wactor
Bishop C. R. Coleman—Mrs. Ethel Gillis Coleman '
Bishop A. Marshall, Jr—Mrs. Mary Ann Stotts Marshall
Bishop J. H. Miller—Mrs. Bernice Frances Dillard Miller
Bishop G. J. Leake—Mrs. Vilma Louise Dew Leake
Bishop R. L. Speaks—Mrs. Janie Angelyne Griffin Speaks

Other Yearly Observances

The 1943 Convention adopted the Anniversary Day of the Woman's Home and Foreign Missionary Society, to be observed the first week in May annually. With the adoption of other special days of departments, this day has become a day set apart for special programs of the parent society. The Converrtion of 1959 adopted the "Emma Clarissa Clement Day," to be observed annually on Mother's Day, in memory of the first black American mother, named in 1946. A program is distributed for this observance by the office of the executive secretary.

And thus onward and upward moves the cause of missions in the African Methodist Episcopal Zion Church through the general officers, missionary supervisors, and faithful corps of district and local officers of the Woman's Home and Foreign Missionary Society.

Chapter 27

CONCERN FOR AGED MINISTERS, WIDOWS AND CHILDREN

The history of the black church in America is also highlighted by the effort to achieve its objectives free of any outside assistance. The A.M.E. Zion Church has always had a consistent concern for the poor, and the orphans, for aged ministers and families. It is almost miraculous that a poor race, striving to free itself from the shackles of slavery, could plan at all in this direction. During its vigorous struggle for Emancipation, projection of its ideals for the needy never ceased. While their passion for freedom was rife, they were imbued with the realization that serving the needy was the first mission of the church of Jesus Christ.

In 1810, the African Marine Fund was formed in the Mother Church, our only society at that time to assist the poor members of the race in general. Its Constitution was as follows:

Preamble

The present subscribers have for some time considered the situation of our poor Africans, and descendants of our mother country. Also, considering the calamities that mankind in general are liable to fall into, more especially the Africans and their descendants,

Article I

It is agreed, that both male and female members, on their joining this society, paying the sum of *one dollar*, shall be entitled to vote for the officers of the said fund, which shall consist of a Treasurer, a President, and Secretary, with four Trustees, who shall be chosen by ballot, and the election to be adjudged by the Elders of the fund, who shall be one or each of the elder ministers of the African Zion Church in this city.

Article II

It shall be the duty of the Trustees of this fund at all meetings to make a collection, and to give a strict account of the same to the treasurer the day or evening after such collections are made.

Article III

It shall be the duty of the Secretary to make an entry of such monies collected by the Trustees, and give an account of it to the President and members, provided always one of the elders be present, once every month.

Article IV

It shall be the duty of the President to be present at all meetings; and should any difference be among the members respecting their upright walk and behaviour during their membership, he shall with the elders have a casting vote.

Article V

All monies paid in by the members, and made by collection, is to be appropriated to the use of schooling the poor African children, whose parents are unable to educate them. And as the fund increases, to give them such clothes as the Elders, President, and Trustees may think in council necessary.

Article VI

It shall also be understood that each member shall pay *twenty-five cents* every month, towards the schooling of the poor children, and the support of the sick members of the said fund. And furthermore, if any member is sick, according to this constitution they must be supported during their sickness; provided they make application to the Elder or Elders of this fund, and satisfy them respecting their circumstances.

Article VII

There shall be also a Committee appointed to visit our African brethren, and the descendants of our mother country, to give information of their several distresses and wants; and on the report of the same to the Elders, with sufficient satisfaction, the Elders may, without the consent of the Trustees, send an order to the Treasurer for such amount as in their judgment may seem sufficient to their relief.

Article VIII

It is agreed, that if any of the members of this fund should die, the Committee must immediately give notice to the Elders, who shall call a meeting and see the situation of the fund; and should the fund be not altogether sufficient to inter him or her, the members shall make a collection sufficient to bury him or her decent, and defray all the burial expenses.

(Signed) Rev. June Scott
Rev. Abraham Thompson
Simon Hackett
Joseph Harman [1]

From the organization of the connection in 1820, and printing of the first Discipline, the rules were made to correlate with the publishing interests of the church in order to guarantee some type of support to the needy while building a new movement. One of the laws in the Discipline (see Chapter 9) restricts the General Conference from appropriating the proceeds of the Publishing House or Chartered Fund to any purpose other than the benefit of the traveling and superannuated ministers, their wives, widows, and children. In an early Discipline the Bishops' or Superintendents' Address read as follows:

---

1. Constitution of the African Marine Fund, pp. 3-7.

... This present edition is small and cheap, and we can assure you that the profits of the sales of it shall be applied to the relief of the distressed and worn out preachers, or their widows or children. We remain your very affectionate brethren and Pastors, who labour night and day both in public and in private for your good. [2]

It is striking to note how concerned the connection became with this aspect of its church program during its days of development in slave times. The following conditions were set forth as early as the 1840 General Conference:

Of the Allowance to Ministers and Preachers, their wives, widows; and children:

1. The annual allowance of the superintendents shall be two hundred dollars and their traveling expenses.

2. The annual allowance of the traveling preachers shall be one hundred dollars, and traveling expenses.

3. The annual allowance of the wives of traveling preachers, shall be one hundred dollars.

4. Each child of a traveling preacher shall be allowed twelve dollars annually, to the age of seven years, and twenty dollars annually from the age of seven to fourteen years; and those preachers whose wives are dead, shall be allowed for each child annually, a sum sufficient to pay the board of such child or children, during the above term of years.

5. The annual allowance of a superannuated, worn out, and supernumerary preachers, shall be one hundred dollars.

6. The annual allowance of widows of traveling, superannuated, worn out, and supernumerary preachers, shall be one hundred dollars.

7. The orphans of traveling, supernumerary, superannuated, and worn out preachers, shall be allowed by the annual conference, the same sums respectively, which are allowed to the children of living preachers.

8. The General Conference do recommend to our friends in general, that they hire, or rent houses for the married preachers, on their circuits or stations; and they further recommend them to furnish the houses as far as they can, according to their ability. . . . [3]

This was a bold attempt growing out of the eagerness to provide adequately for the ministry and its components. The effects of this arrangement naturally resulted in disappointment in the requirements of a striving race church to keep this pace of ministerial support. One year earlier, the New York Conference had given momentous consideration to the matter, Meeting at (Mother) Zion Church in May 1839, the conference made a decision to establish the *New York Annual Conference Fund.* It made the following resolution:

On account of the people's delinquency in many of our stations and circuits, our preachers fail to get means to support their families and are compelled to neglect their duties as ministers, or suffer. We have therefore agreed in our associated capacity as ministers, to establish a fund to be used in relief of our brother ministers connected with this conference, when they are in want of relief or help.

A constitution was drawn up and adopted which directed that the bishop be the president of the fund. [4] This was the first brotherhood plan in the history of the church.

The church continued its compelling effort to provide for the needy and the ministry. The General Conference of 1848 changed the procedure and made it the

2. Doctrines and Discipline, 1848, p. 9.
3. Doctrines and Discipline, 1840, pp. 152-154.
4. Moore, History, pp. 107-109.

obligation of the quarterly conferences to aid in supporting the ministry. Quarterly collections were to be made in all the classes by class leaders "at the time of giving out love-feast tickets." The fund was to be kept separate from the funds collected for the poor of the church and lodged with the trustees or stewards for the support of the ministry.

In some states there was a regulation regarding support of the ministry, for the Discipline from this time to 1900 specifically stated that:

> In such places where the state legislature does not interfere, the money collected as aforesaid shall be distributed according to the judgment of the Yearly Conference, to the best interest of the ministers, their wives, widows, and children.
>
> In those places where the acts of the state legislature has pointed out the mode, and makes it the business of the male members of the society to determine upon the allowance to be made to the ministers, it must be done accordingly; nevertheless the advice of the Yearly Conference shall be taken, through the medium of the Quarterly Conference, previous to the determination of the male members on the subject. [5]

In 1888, the General Conference made a slight revision in this rule, stating that: "There shall be a public collection made in all our congregations every year, which money shall be sent to the Annual Conference for the benefit of the widows and orphans of our worn-out ministers." [6] In an effort to fortify this program, it also made provision for the support of "the superannuated and worn-out ministers, and widows and orphans of deceased ministers," in constructing a connectional financial plan. A pro rata plan was adopted for ministerial relief, church extension, educational institutions, local missions, and conference expenses after the regular budgetary requirements had been met, with an apportionment over and above $700 per presiding elder's district. [7]

Thus the brotherhood or ministerial relief of the A.M.E. Zion Church has always been a dream of interested leaders. Their most earnest vision was the proposed supplementary support as specified in the establishment of the Book Concern and Publishing House, which did not produce the expected revenue. The diversified voluntary plan of ministerial relief, which from the beginning was scattered around the church, supported for the most part by local congregations, according to emphasis and strength, began its organizational structure between 1896 and 1900. The ministers themselves had spent years before and after Emancipation sacrificing and building up a church to serve the needs of its oppressed race, neglecting their own means of support. The gravity of this situation was faced at the 1896 General Conference when the Committee on Worn-out Preachers made its report. It related a situation in which a widow of a deceased superannuated minister, Mrs. S. S. Murdock of Statesville, N. C., had been unable to complete the burial expense of her late husband. Reverend Murdock was the founder of the A.M.E. Zion Church at Statesville now known as Center Street Church. The following extract of this report caused the General Conference to adopt the report signed by Revs. N. A. Crockett and W. J. Sides, chairman and secretary, "with but few changes."

> We note that by a careful study of the law of our Church that the money now paid for the support of our superannuated ministers is still inadequate. . . .

5. Doctrines and Discipline, 1848, pp. 124-125.
6. *Minutes,* Eighteenth Quadrennial Session, p. 113; *Doctrines and Discipline,* 1888, p. 79.
7. *Minutes,* Eighteenth Quadrennial Session, p. 112; *Doctrines and Discipline,* 1888, pp. 87-89.

As all other great institutions encourage those who founded them upon permanent basis, so do we mean to foster the same idea. The A.M.E. Zion Church is one of the Christian influences that is making powerful strides to make the world better. And as she is a distinct and separate organization of the world, and we are now reaping the fruits of the efforts of the fathers of our great Church, therefore

Your committee do recommend that the superannuated ministers receive for their support for their services in our church the money, as the law now provides, by the pro rata plan.

We further recommend that each annual conference shall make such arrangement as may be necessary for the sustenance of the superannuated ministers in the respective annual conferences. . . . [8]

By 1900, the matter had become crucial. The Committee on Worn-out Preachers presented a plan to the General Conference which had been drafted by Rev. J. T. Gaskill, a member of the committee, and read by Rev. F. H. Hill, who made the motion for its passage. Bishops T. H. Lomax, J. W. Hood, Revs. E. H. Curry, T. B. McCain, H. H. Bingham, W. H. Goler, and J. T. Gaskill entered into a lengthy discussion on this plan, which was not accepted. An alternate plan submitted by Dr. J. S. Caldwell was endorsed by the conference with provisions as follows: [9]

The Ministerial Brotherhood is instituted to cultivate a more benevolent spirit toward and mutual interest in the temporal welfare of the Traveling Ministry of the African Methodist Episcopal Zion Church.

Each Bishop, General Officer (who is a minister), Presiding Elder, and Traveling Minister of the African Methodist Episcopal Zion Church shall be eligible to Membership in the Ministerial Brotherhood.

Its officers shall be a President, who shall be the Senior Bishop; a Secretary, who shall be the General Secretary; and a Treasurer, who shall be the General Steward.

Each Bishop, General Officer (who is a minister), Presiding Elder, and Pastor receiving a salary from the local or general church, shall pay into the funds of the Ministerial Brotherhood each year as hereinafter provided, one per cent, of the salary he receives; provided that no member, whether he holds an appointment or not, shall pay into the fund less than One ($1.00) Dollar per year. . . .

The Ministerial Brotherhood fund shall be used as follows:

1. Twenty-five per cent shall be appropriated as the Relief Fund for Superannuated Ministers. On the fourth Wednesday in December and May of each year, the General Secretary shall prorate, and the General Steward shall pay to the Superannuated Ministers twenty-five percent of the funds that have been received for the six months preceding.

2. Twenty-five percent of the funds shall be kept in the treasury as a permanent fund. Whenever a Superannuated Minister dies twenty-five dollars out of this fund shall be allowed for his burial expenses.

3. Fifty per cent of the funds shall be kept as an Endowment Fund for effective ministers. Whenever an effective minister dies fifty per cent of the amount he has paid into the funds shall be allowed for his burial expenses.

4. The one percent of salary money shall be paid at the Annual Conference to the Conference Treasurer before the characters are passed, and the Presiding Bishop shall see that the whole amount received, together with the names of those who paid, is forwarded by the Treasurer to the General Steward before the close of the Conference; provided, however, that each

8. *Minutes,* Twentieth Quadrennial Session, pp. 87-88, 260.
9. *Minutes,* Twenty-First Quadrennial Session, pp. 75-76.

Bishop shall pay his apportionment at the first conference named in his Episcopal District. . . .

The General Secretary and General Steward shall report the condition of the Brotherhood to the semi-annual meeting of the Board of Bishops, to the Connectional Council and to the General Conference. [10]

This plan had not met with the desired success during the quadrennium. At the 1904 General Conference the general steward stated in his report, that it took two years after the close of the 1900 General Conference to get the institution into actual operation, and the next two years to test its strength.

We think the great drawback to the Institution has been on account of its attempt to benefit the active ministers, when it was intended by its originators to benefit only the Superannuated Ministers. It offers such small returns to the active minister until it is regarded by many as mockery at giving assistance. Several of the conferences have not given any support at all to the Institution, others supported it one year and dropped out; and still others have stood loyally by the Institution each year from the time the law governing it was declared. [11]

Meanwhile, the church had in operation a board of widows and orphans. The treasurer of this board, Rev. H. H. Bingham, reported $738 raised for all purposes. It was the plan of the denomination that the annual conferences raise and distribute the major portion of funds for widows and orphans while the General Board supplement their efforts through amounts provided in the general budget and additional means of collections. During this same time a plan was presented, "The Volunteer Board for Ministerial Aid," which was not accepted. Dr. J. H. Manley, chairman, and Rev. J. H. Branner, secretary of the Committee on Superannuated Ministers submitted a resolution to increase the annual appropriation from $1,000 to $2,000, and to continue to receive one-sixth of the special assessment. They further recommended that whatever change be made in the ministerial brotherhood, "that the sum of $25 shall be given to each superannuated minister for burial expenses." [12] This plan was adopted: however, the Discipline was restructured on the entire method of ministerial support. It specified the legislation which had been effected for the support of effective ministers, relief of superannuated ministers, relief of widows and orphans, and relief of the poor. The action of the ministerial brotherhood was explained by the Board of Bishops in the next General Conference as follows:

After dealing this important department a most stunning and almost fatal blow, the last General Conference proceeded to elect the Reverend Dr. Henry L. Simmons, secretary, to operate it, and put life in it, if he possessed such power.

Dr. Simmons has made it possible for this General Conference to have an organization duly chartered and intact as a basis for devising ways and means by which the Brotherhood may be made what it was intended to be, viz: a helpful agency to our superannuated and worn-out preachers, their widows and orphans also a protection to the families of active ministers, who may die and leave their families without adequate support. The present secretary has had the Brotherhood chartered, prepared such literature as is needed to conform to the requirements of the charter, and has kept the organization constantly before the Church. His report will show the number of active supporters composing the Brotherhood, also its financial status.

10. *Doctrines and Discipline*, 1900, pp. 278-281.
11. *Minutes*, Twenty-Second Quadrennial Session, pp. 412-413.
12. *Ibid.*, pp. 91, 109.

We have examined the charter and literature and desire to express our approval of the course which has been pursued by the secretary.

We wish also to again impress upon the General Conference the urgent need of such an organization, both as a means of strengthening the meagre stipend already provided for the class of persons the Brotherhood is designed to benefit, and as an evidence of gratitude to those whose labors have helped give to us and preserve the goodly heritage which we now enjoy.

We believe that the weak should be helped by the strong, therefore we regard the Brotherhood as an agency that gives every loyal son of Zion an opportunity to contribute to that end. We ask the General Conference to make such provisions for the future operation of the Brotherhood as will enlist the sympathy and hearty cooperation of our ministry throughout the entire connection. [13]

Reverend Henry L. Simmons of Lincolnton, N.C., was the successful presiding elder in the growth of the Lincolnton and Statesville districts of the Western North Carolina Conference. He was "one of Zion's most faithful, painstaking, and successful men" who could be depended upon to take care of and manage with proficiency the trust committed to his charge. [14]

The General Conference of 1908 elected Rev. John Franklin Moreland, Sr., who had built a commendable church in Chicago (the Walters Memorial Church) supplementing the building fund from his own personal funds. Dr. Moreland was quite a business genius and capitalist. The Ministerial Brotherhood Department was placed in a prosperous condition by him. He travelled throughout the connection, visiting almost every annual conference, and many of the churches, almost annually to promote this cause. [15] He administered the office from the headquarters at Charlotte, N.C. The department was regenerated and enlarged in 1912 when he made the following statement and recommendations:

If sane legislation be given to this much needed department of our Zion, your Secretary will give the department this $2,215.38 (deficit reported), and start the new quadrennium with $2500.00 cash, and 460 financial members. *Recommendations:*

We pray your honorable body to give us a law "that all whose name is on the Annual Conference Roll shall pay on the Bishop's table not less than $2.50 a year and that he or she shall at no time in the quadrennium be in arrears more than $2.60." This shall entitle the claimant to $50 at death. We pray (that because the two interests are so akin) that you will divorce the contingencies from the "Benevolences" and put that interest representing the superannuated and wornout preachers, widows and orphans in the Brotherhood Department and thus make the two combined a fullfledged department with a regular Secretary. We would further pray that none of this money be left in the Annual Conference, but that every cent be sent to the Secretary whose duty it shall be to send it out monthly to the claimants. [16]

The committee on ministerial brotherhood, signed by Revs. B. G. Shaw, chairman and E. U. A. Brooks, secretary, working with Dr. Moreland, made its report containing identical recommendations, which was adopted by the General Conference. [17] Dr. Moreland was re-elected and inaugurated the new program of this department. The division of the widows and orphans fund was not placed with this department, however, until 1916.

13. Quadrennial Episcopal Address, 1908 *op. cit.,* p. 18.
14. *Minutes,* Twenty-Third Quadrennial Session, pp. 153-154.
15. *Minutes,* Twenty-Fourth Quadrennial Session, p. 455.
16. *Ibid.,* p. 456.
17. *Ibid.,* p. 541.

REV. HENRY L. SIMMONS
Father of the Brotherhood Fund

REV. JOHN F. MORELAND, SR.   BISHOP WILLIAM CORNELIUS BROWN
Augmented the Brotherhood and Relief Funds   Father of the Pension Fund

Dr. Moreland was the adventurous type, who would stake his own funds on making his ventures a success. He used his funds to the advantage of the department, and upon his death in 1915, the church owed his estate more than $23,000 which it settled with his widow, Mrs. Grace Moreland, over a period of years. [18] The Editor of the *Quarterly Review*, Rev. Lynwood Westinghouse Kyles, of Winston-Salem, N.C., was selected by the Board of Bishops to carry on the work of this department until the General Conference. Dr. Kyles was an alert churchman and capable preacher, and successful in the pastorate and general officership or whatever he was entrusted to do in the church. He directed the two general offices until 1916, when he was elected bishop.

The 1916 General Conference created the Relief Department, organizing support of ministers' widows and orphans in a connectional way, and combined it with the Ministerial Brotherhood Department. Reverend Calvin S. Whitted was elected and executed the office affairs in Philadelphia, Pa. Dr. Whitted was a skillful businessman and a highly creative secretary. He had built churches at Waterbury and New Haven, Conn., and Attleboro, Mass. He had placed the ministerial brotherhood department in a healthy condition with smooth operation to the satisfaction of the church, and stabilized the relief department in a way that caused the following response from the bishops in 1920:

The establishment of the Relief Department in a regular way at our last session has proven to have been wise legislation. At no time in our past

18. *Minutes,* Twenty-Fifth and Twenty-Sixth Quadrennial Sessions, p. 184; Twenty Seventh, Quadrennial Session, p. 403; Twenty-Eighth Quadrennial Session, p. 174.

history have we been able to give our superannuated ministers, widows and orphans, the support that has been given them this quadrennium. This is very gratifying from every point of view. The law was so fixed that there accrues a larger revenue than ever before for this purpose, and we hope that nothing we do at this session will lessen the stipend now available. [19]

After his re-election to the office the third time, Dr. Whitted died, in June 1928. At the Connectional Council in August 1928, the Board of Bishops elected Rev. Thomas Walker Wallace, Sr., who administered the office in Washington, D.C., from the A.M.E. Zion Church headquarters. Dr. Wallace was a profound scholar, scientist, universal historian, and publicist, and an inventive industrious officer. The departments grew with great permanent results during his administration. He was able to effect the combination with the third department, Home Missions, in 1932. The Home Missions Department became permanently established with the two departments upon his recommendation in 1936: "Inasmuch as Home Missions is essentially a form of relief to mission preachers. . . . missions should be continued as a part of the Department of Relief and Home Missions." His persistent desire to improve the condition of the ministers' widows and orphans was brought forth in another recommendation this same year: "For the relief of superannuated ministers, widows, and orphans an amount equal to five percent of the pastors' salary be placed upon the certificate of appointment, reported at the session of the annual conference and sent in to the department." This method was not accepted, but a slight increase was made in the general budget, with additional legislation passed on the improvement of superannuated ministers, widows, and orphans support. [20] The pension plan for ministers which the denomination adopted eight years afterward was conceived at this General Conference. The father of this plan had been assiduously engaged in convincing ministers of its importance, and thus introduced it:

Bishop-elect W. C. Brown offered the following resolution: "Whereas, the industrial organizations have compensations for their workers, the states have relief and old age pensions, and some religious organizations have age and disability securities for their ministers, therefore be it—

"*Resolved,* that a commission be appointed to study a pension plan for ministers of the A.M.E. Zion Church and present the same to the Connectional Council in 1937 for its consideration:

"*Resolved,* the Bishops shall present the plan as approved by the Connectional Council to the Annual Conference for consideration:

"*Resolved,* that a vote shall be taken in each annual conference, on the plan, the results of which shall be signed by the Bishop, presiding elders, and Secretary of the Conference, and presented to the Connectional Council in 1938 for further consideration:

"*Resolved* further, that if the Annual Conferences affirming the plan represent fifty-five percent of the membership of our Connection, that the Board of Bishops shall immediately arrange for the operation of the Pension Plan as adopted by the Annual Conference of the A.M.E. Zion Church for the ministers of said church."

Bishop-elect W. C. Brown made a motion that the resolution be adopted, which was seconded by Bishop Kyles. Dr. B. C. Robeson offered as a substitute motion that this General Conference take action now. The substitute was adopted. [21] The intricacy of this plan brought about a delay in execution. The

19. *Minutes,* Twenty-Sixth Quadrennial Session, p. 77.
20. *Minutes,* Thirtieth Quadrennial Session, pp. 58, 63, 266.
21. *Ibid.,* pp. 56-57.

bishops and the General Conference expressed their desire for pursuit. The following declaration of the bishops in 1940 kept the committee at work for a plan:

> This department under the direction of Dr. Thomas W. Wallace, has been able only to give a gesture in trying to meet the needs of the many calls of our worn-out ministers and widows. It is a known fact that the small amount given to our disabled ministers is far inadequate for their needs. While we know the A.M.E. Zion Church for many generations will be unable to meet the needs of all of the ministers and to satisfy the widows and orphans of deceased ministers according to their desires nor will we be able to come up to our desires, but this General Conference ought to go on record in working out a more feasible plan than what we have at this time. In connection with our present set-up, your Chief Pastors feel that the plan as outlined by Bishop W. C. Brown, should be carefully studied with prayer and deep devotion, that a more satisfactory plan might be inaugurated so that our disabled ministers, widows and orphans of our church might not be ashamed of what they shall receive from time to time. . . . [The bishops recommended the] adoption of a workable pension plan for the ministers. . . . and the taking out of a Group Insurance as a means of supplementing our relief funds, so as to more adequately care for our retired ministers, widows and orphans. (22)

In the midst of the committee's work on this plan for presentation at the next General Conference, Dr. Wallace passed away in September 7, 1942. His wife, Lauretta J. Wallace, faithfully held the office intact and made the six months report to the Board of Bishops in January 1943, when a new officer was chosen.

Reverend Herbert Bell Shaw, presiding elder of the Wilmington District, Wilmington, N. C.; was elected by the Board of Bishops, and the office was moved to Wilmington. A businessman, he executed the office with business acumen. At the General Conference of 1944, after eight years of earnest and tenacious labor, the A.M.E. Zion Church adopted the Pension Plan as follows:

Brotherhood Pension Service Plan

> Offered for adoption in the 1944 session of the General Conference of the African Methodist Episcopal Zion Church.
>
> A commission headed by Bishop W. C. Brown was appointed at the General Conference in Greensboro, North Carolina, (1936) to devise plans of compensation for aged and debilitated ministers in the A.M.E. Zion Church. This Commission under the direction of Bishop Brown has continued its work and now submits the following pension plan to this General Conference for adoption.
>
> This Pension Plan has been submitted to insurance experts and actuaries and has been approved by them as being safe and capable of providing a sound method of giving security to the ministers of the A.M.E. Zion Church. The plan assures a definite income and guarantees a definite protection. The element of uncertainty is eliminated because we know the number of ministers who will be paying members, therefore, we know definitely how much our income will be per year. We know that we must be able to measure and determine our income before we can honestly make promises about what the Pension Plan will be able to pay.

---

22. *Minutes,* Thirty-First Quadrennial Session, pp. 89, 218.

"The Pension Plan"

Resources and Plan for Building the Fund:

We must enroll every Pastor in the A.M.E. Zion Church in the Pension Plan. At the present time we have enrolled in our Ministerial Brotherhood approximately 1500 Ministers. We are of the opinion that every minister pastoring in our church is not connected with the Ministerial Brotherhood. We ask that every minister who holds a certificate of appointment in the A.M.E. Zion Church shall be enrolled and pay a minimum of $25.00 per year to the Brotherhood Pension Service. Assuming that we can enroll from our total ministerial body 1500 members who will pay into the Pension Fund $25.00 per year, the total annual amount paid in would be $37,500.00.

Eligibility and Dues:

Every pastor who is a member of the Ministerial Brotherhood of the A.M.E. Zion Church automatically becomes a member of the Brotherhood Pension Service by the payment of his first annual dues of $25.00. Any preacher who is not a member of the Ministerial Brotherhood may become a member of the Brotherhood Pension Service by paying $1.00 joining fee plus his annual dues of $25.00. Your membership may be sustained by paying $25.00 per year. A minister who desires to carry a double benefit may do so by paying a double premium of $50.00 per year. The organization of which the minister is a compensated or salaried servant shall pay half of his annual dues. Payment should be made to the Annual Conference of which the preacher is a member, or to the Secretary-Treasurer.

Each Bishop may sustain a membership in this organization by the payment of $10.00 per year and not receive pension, either pay $25.00 or $50.00 per year and become a regular participating member.

Any minister who is retired or superannuated prior to 1944, may continue to pay the annual premium of $2.50 or $5.00, and thus maintain his original Ministerial Brotherhood status. Persons who are not holding pastor's certificate of appointment, may maintain their original Ministerial Brotherhood status by the payment of $2.50 or $5.00 per year, of if they should so elect, they may become members of the Brotherhood Pension Service by the payment of $25.00 per year.

Brotherhood Pension Service dues may be paid annually ($25.00); semi-annually ($12.50); or quarterly ($6.25). When the dues are paid annually they are to be paid in the Annual Conference; when paid semi-annually or quarterly they are to be sent to the Secretary-Treasurer. The same ration obtains for members paying $50.00.

Retirement:

1. If a minister is permanently incapacitated by reason of sickness or accident he is eligible for retirement and pension.

2. The pensioner will not be permitted to receive a pension and hold a pastoral charge at the same time.

3. All pension claims must be approved by a quorum of the Brotherhood Service Pension Board.

4. The minister must be duly superannuated or retired by the Annual Conference of which he is a member before his case is reviewed by the Pension Board.

Compensation:

Every member of the Brotherhood Pension Service who is superannuated or retired according to our regulations because of length of service, or total and permanent disability who pays an annual premium of $25.00, shall receive from the Brotherhood Pension Service $300.00 per year to be paid at the rate of $25.00 per month.

Every member who pays an annual premium of $50.00, shall receive from the Brotherhood Pension Service after retirement or superannuation $600.00 per year to be paid at the rate of $50.00 per month.

All persons who pay annual dues amount to $2.50 or $5.00 per year shall not receive any pension from the Brotherhood Pension Service.

The Pension Service immediately after its enactment shall begin paying the hereinafter specified death benefits.

The Pension Service shall begin paying "Pensions" at the time agreed upon by the Board of Bishops, and the Brotherhood Pension Service Board.

Death Benefits:

The death benefit of the Brotherhood Pension Service shall be $200.00, payable to the beneficiary or estate of deceased members who have not been superannuated or retired from active duty and who pay the annual premium of $25.00. The death benefit payable to the beneficiary or estate of members who die after retirement or superannuation who pay an annual premium of $25.00 shall be $100.00.

The death benefit payable to the beneficiary or estate of deceased members who have not been superannuated or retired who have paid annual premiums of $50.00, shall be $400.00.

The death benefit payable to the beneficiary or estate of members who die after retirement or superannuation who have paid annual premiums of $50.00, shall be $200.00.

All persons who maintain their original Ministerial Brotherhood status by paying annual premiums of $2.50 or $5.00 the death benefit payable to the beneficiary or estate shall be $50.00, and $100.00 respectively.

The death benefit payable to the beneficiary or estate of a deceased Bishop shall be $150.00 if he pays $10.00 per year.

Death benefits shall be paid within thirty days after proof of death has been received in the office of the Brotherhood Pension Service.

Machinery for Operating Fund:

That in each Annual Conference the Bishop shall nominate a committee which shall be elected by the conference. The committee shall receive all money at the Conference for the Brotherhood Pension Service directed and supervised by the Bishop of the Conference. That a corresponding secretary shall prepare and send blanks to the Bishops for the use of this committee. Three shall be made out for the following: One to be sent to the Secretary of the Brotherhood Pension Service; one given to the Bishop of the Conference; one kept by this committee. At the close of the Conference all dues collected for the Brotherhood Pension Service shall be sent to the Secretary-Treasurer. That the funds should be directed by a board composed of one person from each Episcopal District, a corresponding secretary and two bishops who shall be president and vice-president of the board. The Board shall meet the day before the meeting of the Connectional Council and five members, including the corresponding secretary, and one Bishop shall constitute a quorum for the transaction of business.

The secretary's duties to be hereafter definitely defined.

That a reputable company or companies shall be selected as trustee or trustees of the fund who shall receive monthly remittances from the corresponding secretary during the time of accumulation.

Name and Union:

That the Ministerial Brotherhood be converted into a Pension Plan to be known hereafter as the Brotherhood Pension Service of the African Methodist Episcopal Zion Church.

That all members of the present Ministerial Brotherhood, on becoming members of the Brotherhood Pension Service shall be entitled to all benefits in the new organization promised to them by the payment of the annual dues.

That the Brotherhood Pension Service go into effect immediately upon the close of the General Conference in 1944, and that the above measures be put into law and effect and all other laws in conflict be hereby repealed.

BISHOP W. C. BROWN,
Chairman Pension Board.
REVEREND H. B. SHAW,
Secretary-Treasurer Department of
Home Missions, Brotherhood and Relief.

Participating in the discussion when the plan was presented for illumination, were Revs. M. C. Glover, H. D. Tillman, H. B. Shaw, and H. R. Jackson. Rev. P. C. Wilburn made the motion for its passage, seconded by Rev. J. W. I. Tunstall, which was adopted. Mrs. Queenie A. Catledge and Senator Robert L. Brokenburr made speeches of commendation for the progress in this area. [23]

Dr. Shaw worked perseveringly to effectuate the new pension plan throughout the church. He performed the duties of these interlocking departments with estimable accountability until 1952 when he was elected bishop.

Elected to succeed Bishop Shaw was Rev. Solomon Snowden Seay of Montgomery, Ala., an ardent churchman and race advocate. In 1955 some unsatisfactory procedures and necessary adjustments caused the Board of Bishops to move the office back to North Carolina, where the departments were incorporated. A committee directed by Bishop H. B. Shaw, associated by Bishops R. L. Jones, S. G. Spottswood, Rev. G. L. Fauntleroy and Mr. D. Caffey, with the cooperation of presiding Bishop W. A. Stewart of the Montgomery area, and acting secretary, Rev. Edgar N. French, administered the departments until the 1956 General Conference. [24]

Dr. Austin Paul Morris of Charlotte, N.C., was thus elected. This methodical, veracious, and painstaking servant of the church was re-elected at each General Conference through 1972. He has administered complex responsibilities of the departments of Brotherhood Pension, Ministerial Relief and Home Missions with admirable concern for the needy preachers, widows and orphans, and mission churches from the headquarters at Charlotte.

The Everline Barber Memorial Home

On February 14, 1893, George W. Barber, the only child and legal heir of Everline Barber, deeded a 360-acre plot situated in Granville, Mass. to J. W. Hood of Fayetteville, N.C.; Cicero R. Harris and John J. Moore both of Salisbury, N.C.; I. C. Clinton of Lancaster, S.C.; T. H. Lomax of Charlotte, N.C.; C. C. Pettey of New Bern, N.C.; Alexander Walters of Jersey City, N.J.; and Joseph P. Thompson of Newburgh, N.Y.; the Board of Bishops of the A.M.E. Zion Church in America; and their associates and successors in office.

23. *Minutes,* Thirty-Second Quadrennial Session, p. 60.
24. Ms. Minutes, Board of Bishops Meeting, July 30-August 2, 1955; January 10-15, 1956.

The property, which had been owned by Everline Barber, a white citizen of Granville, was given in trust for the following uses and purposes:

> Said premises shall be used, kept and managed, improved and maintained as and for a residence and home for the aged, infirm and incapacitated ministers of said church, their widows and orphans and such other needy and worthy persons as said Bishops and their successors in office may from time to time permit to reside there, and said home shall be known as "The Everline Barber Memorial Home." [25]

The property had two large frame buildings on it, and the church began to utilize this gift through the New England Conference, for the purpose for which it was given, Reverend Alfred Day, pastor of the A.M.E. Zion Church, Hartford, Conn., church was commended by the conference for his influence in getting Mr. Barber to give this valuable land to the church. [26] The New England Conference, directed by Presiding Elder S. C. Birchmore, attempted to operate the home in the beginning. The conference requested Rev. W. L. Moore to move there and become the first manager, which he did, but died soon afterwards. His wife, Mrs. Emma Moore, then had charge for a while. [27]

The property passed through a period of neglect until Rev. C. S. Whitted was made secretary of the Ministerial Brotherhood Department. He discovered intruders cutting timbers, picking berries every summer, and tapping trees for maple syrup; capitalizing from its resources, which had been permitted by one of our ministers, Rev. Lowe. After Dr. Whitted's demise, Dr. Thomas W. Wallace, who succeeded him in office, passed through great perplexities to save the property for Zion. The property had been neglected by the connection and became laden with taxes and liens, because people in the area had become squatters and had been allowed to utilize it for money-making purposes. Dr. Wallace, associated with Bishop W. J. Walls and the General Secretary, Dr. Henry C. Weeden, confronted the struggle of reclaiming the property for Zion free of encumbrances.

Being a graduate of Tuskegee Institute, with some of the trades, Dr. Wallace had industrial education. As a Livingstonian, he was steeped in religious education, and his experience as a chaplain in the Army helped him in courageous and creative oversight. Dr. Wallace had to pursue the matter through the court, and was successful in exempting the church from these obligations. He became fervently interested in this property and spent considerable time there. He was instrumental in getting the church to borrow $5,000 to build roads and other facilities. Through much of his own labor he placed several frame buildings on the grounds. The original buildings had been destroyed by fire. As it was difficult to arrange for a home for the aged ministers and their families, the church began to utilize the property for camp purposes. The New England Conference, led by Bishop W. J. Walls, held annual religious training institutes there in the summer, and Dr. Wallace began holding regular camp programs. These programs continue until the present day. Dr. Wallace was successful in getting the denomination to include this institution in the denominational home missions budget for annual operation.

Bishop Walls, who served as chairman of the Board of Home Missions, cooperated with Dr. Wallace in getting the institution in operation. He supervised the contiguous area of New England, New York, and Western New York

---

25. Conveyance Deed, February 14, 1893.
26. Minutes, Forty-Eighth Annual Session, New England Conference, p. 49.
27. Minutes, Fifty-Second Annual Session, New England Conference, p. 21.
28. Bradford, *Harriet Tubman, The Moses of Her People*, p. 6.

Conferences for nearly a quarter of a century, and stimulated support among the people of these conferences for this cause. Through special observances of his thirtieth and fortieth anniversaries in the episcopacy, and episcopal district rallies, $60,000 with accrued interest was accumulated for further development of this property. In 1966, through a hasty and unstudied decision, over $17,000 of this fund was ordered paid as an architect's fee for an abortive plan. Later, $20,000 was put into a multi-purpose building placed on the grounds by Bishop Stephen G. Spottswood, director James M. Hubert, and the people of the New England Conference, and $1,300 was sent to conference and camp officials for the erection of a chapel. The balance of more than $21,000 has been placed in custody of the Board and Department of Home Missions to be used in the erection of a chapel to be named for Bishop J. W. Hood, the bishop through whom the land was bequeathed by George W. Barber.

After Dr. Wallace's death, the secretaries of the department, Dr. H. B. Shaw and Dr. A. P. Morris, representing the Home Missions Board, continued to manifest staunch interest in this institution. This 310-acre plot in the beautiful Berkshire Mountains is still a source of great natural wealth as well as real estate property, and has in it the potential for enhancing a refulgent future in our church for the Everline Barber Memorial Home for old preachers and old people and their families, the main incentive of the gift.

The Harriet Tubman Home

The origin of the property in Auburn, N.Y., acquired by the immortal Harriet Tubman, and her dream for its development, are almost as dramatic as her pathetic, eminent, and incomparable life. For her courageous services in the Civil War, Secretary of State William H. Seward "exerted himself in every possible way to procure her a pension from Congress, but red-tape proved too strong even for him, and her case was rejected, because it did not come under any recognized law." [28] From Sarah Bradford we learn:

In 1857 she made her most venturesome journey, for she brought with her to the North her old parents, who were no longer able to walk such distances as she must go by night. Consequently she must hire a wagon for them, and it required all her ingenuity to get them through Maryland and Delaware safe. She accomplished it, however, and by the aid of her friends she brought them safe to Canada, where they spent the winter. Her account of their sufferings there—of her mother's complaining and her own philosophy about it—is a lesson of trust in Providence better than many sermons. But she decided to bring them to a more comfortable place, and so she negotiated with Mr. Seward—then in Senate—for a little patch of ground. To the credit of the Secretary of State it should be said that he sold her the property on very favorable terms, and gave her some time for payment. To this house she removed her parents, and set herself to work to pay for the purchase. It was on this errand that she first visited Boston—we believe in the winter of 1858-59. She brought a few letters from her friends in New York, but she could herself neither read nor write, and she was obliged to trust her wits that they were delivered to the right persons. [29]

One of the letters was to Sarah Bradford. After she received it, she called on Harriet Tubman at her boarding house and wrote:

It was curious to see the caution with which she received her visitor, until

29. *Ibid.*, pp. 115-116.

she felt assured that there was no mistake. One of her means of security was to carry with her the daguerreotypes of her friends, and show them to each new person. If they recognized the likeness, then it was all right.

Pains were taken to secure her the attention to which her great services of humanity entitled her, and she left New England with a handsome sum of money toward the payment of her debt to Mr. Seward. Before she left, however, she had several interviews with Captain (John) Brown, then in Boston. He is supposed to have communicated his plans to her, and to have been aided by her in obtaining recruits and money among her people. At any rate, he always spoke of her with the greatest respect, and declared that "General Tubman," as he styled her, was a better officer than most whom he had seen, and could command an army as successfully as she had led her small parties of fugitives. [30]

Harriet did not receive any government aid until 1890. After her husband died in October 1888, and a pension act was passed in 1890 granting relief to widows of Civil War veterans, Harriet applied for such a pension. She was put through a series of trials and red tape. Finally in the late 1890's when the pension was awarded her as the widow of Nelson Davis, $5 was whittled off the $25 a month which had been requested, "and she was granted twenty dollars a month for the duration of her life." It was her resolute spirit for continuing her service to humanity that induced her to acquire additional property.

For years Harriet had looked from the porch of her residence over a 25-acre expanse of adjoining terrain, dreaming of what a fine community farm it would make. She was desirous of presenting this to the Negro church of Auburn, for that institution to operate collectively. At last, in June of 1896, by sheer audacity, she did come into possession of this property. The lot was to be sold at auction, and on the day of the sale Harriet appeared at the scene with very little money, but a determination to have the land, cost what it might.

Harriet has described the circumstances of her purchase: "They were all white folks but me, there, and I was like a blackberry in a pail of milk, but I hid down in a corner, and no one knew who was bidding. The man began down pretty low, and kept going up by fifties. At last I got up to fourteen hundred and fifty, and then others stopped bidding, and the man said, "All done. Who is the buyer? Harriet Tubman, I shouted."

They turned to her in astonishment, wondering where she would obtain the money to make the purchase, but Harriet went down to a bank and secured the money by mortgaging the land. But it was not easy to operate an enterprise like this, and because of lack of funds the permanent incorporation of what Harriet wished to call the "John Brown Home," was not achieved until 1903 when she deeded the 25 acres and her home to the African Methodist Episcopal Zion Church. [31]

The General Conference of 1904 gave this matter of Harriet Tubman's bequest serious concern. Reverend B. F. Wheeler, pastor of the A.M.E. Zion Church at Auburn, N.Y.; Harriet Tubman's home church, became the superintendent of the Home and gave the following account of the bequest to the General Conference:

Early in the year 1902 Professor Robert W. Taylor, financial agent of Booker T. Washington's school and a loyal member of the A.M.E. Zion Church, who is a good friend of Aunt Harriet Tubman Davis, secured a deed

30. *Ibid.*, pp. 116-117.
31. Conrad, *Harriet Tubman*, pp. 218-221.

from her of the property known as the Harriet Tubman Home in Auburn, N.Y.; for the Western New York Conference.

There were present at the time of the drawing of the will Prof. R. W. Taylor, Dr. J. E. Mason, Lawyer E. U. A. Brooks and others. They were all to meet later by appointment to close up the conveyance of the property. I had been asked by Dr. Mason to be present at the meeting, but could not arrange to be present. At the second meeting, when all the details of the transactions were to be completed, I, by invitation, was present. I had not seen Aunt Harriet since the summer of the previous year, nor had I heard from her. . . .

At this second meeting we had hoped to get her to sign a new deed as there was found to be some defect in the one she had given us. We met in the home of Rev. C. A. Smith. Those present were Revs. J. E. Mason, J. J. Adams, Lawyer E. U. A. Brooks, Harriet Tubman and myself.

When Aunt Harriet came in and found that we wanted her to sign a new deed, she refused to do so and said that she would do business only with Wheeler. I was surprised at this turn of affairs. I did not know what her object was for taking this stand.

To give myself time to consult her alone, I decided that it would not be advisable to go further in the matter until a later date and so named February 26th for the next meeting. The fact that there was a second mortgage on the property to the amount of $575.00 greatly worried her. By the terms of the deed she had given us we were to pay off the second mortgage, as well as resume the responsibility of the remaining indebtedness of the property.

Through the efforts of Rev. Dr. J. E. Mason and Prof. Taylor the sum of $200.00 was secured from the Church Extension Society to help pay off this second mortgage. The property was then formally turned over to us. When the brethren saw the stand taken by Aunt Harriet, they turned the money over to me.

Prof. Taylor raised $161.00 from a sale of "A Brief Sketch of the Life of Aunt Harriet," which he had gotten out at a personal expense of $96.00. The balance of $214.00 on the second mortgage was donated by the following named brethren: Rev. J. E. Mason, $64.00; Rev. C. A. Smith, Rev. B. F. Wheeler, and Mr. R. J. Frazier $50.00 each. I gave each of these brethren notes, with interest at six percent for one year.

On the 26th of February, Rev. C. A. Smith accompanied me to the place of meeting with Aunt Harriet to see about securing a deed for the property. I assured her that I could not have the property deeded to me personally as she had suggested. I told her that I had communicated with Prof. Taylor and had been informed by him that he would not consent to her deeding the property to him as she had also suggested. I urged her to deed it to the A.M.E. Zion Church; this she refused to do at first, but finally upon my telling her that in case she did deed it to the church, I would superintend it until other arrangements could be made, she reluctantly consented to do so. . . . When she became willing that I should select my own lawyer, I telegraphed to Utica to Lawyer E. U. A. Brooks to come at an early hour next morning.

Early next morning, accompanied by Rev. C. A. Smith and Lawyer E. U. A. Brooks, I went to see Aunt Harriet again. As some of Aunt Harriet's white friends were bitterly opposed to her deeding the property to us, we had to make generous provisions for her in drawing the deed. I stipulated in the deed that she had a life interest in the property. That is to say, she is to have a life interest in all money accruing from rents, on conditions that she pay the taxes and keep up the insurance, but that these rents should cease when we needed the property. As soon as the deed was drawn, we hastened it to Little Rock, Ark., where the Board of Bishops were in session. The property was deeded to the A.M.E. Zion Church Trustees in consideration of our assuming the following financial obligations:

First mortgage, 5 per cent interest	$1,000
Second mortgage, held by Geo. F. Bell	575
Third mortgage of $350 with interest 1 yr.	371
Total	$1,946

The sum of $371.00 was due William H. Stewart, a brother of Aunt Harriet. On forwarding the deed to the Board of Bishops at Little Rock, Ark., I requested that they arranged to pay off the third mortgage to William H. Stewart. . . . This request was complied with. They also appointed me superintendent of the home. I have held this position ever since as well as pastoring our church at Auburn, N.Y.

On April 10, 1902, the Church Extension Society met in Philadelphia . . . and several of the bishops and general officers being present, the Board of Bishops appointed the following board of trustees to serve until General Conference: Bishops J. W. Hood, A. Walters, G. W. Clinton, J. B. Small, Hon. J. C. Dancy, Rev. Drs. M. R. Franklin, J. S. Caldwell, J. E. Mason, C. A. Smith, Profs. R. W. Taylor, J. H. Osborne, R. J. Frazier, Revs. E. U. A. Brooks and B. F. Wheeler. The board of trustees thus appointed met and organized with Bishop A. Walters president; Rev. B. F. Wheeler, secretary and J. H. Osborne, treasurer. The board agreed that the superintendent should receive a salary of $400.00 per annum. June 10, 1903, the board of trustees met on the grounds of the home in one of the buildings known as "John Brown Hall." . . . In the absence of the president Bishop Hood was appointed president pro tem on motion by Bishop Small. The superintendent then read his report, which was adopted. The treasurer also read his report. . . .

An appeal was made to the board for funds for the home and the sum of $110.00 was paid in cash subscriptions by different members of the board, and a goodly sum was subscribed. . . .

With no money coming from the church to the home, and the sentiment in Auburn being so strong against agents collecting on shares, we were left to get on as best we could until General Conference. The condition of the church at Auburn was of such as required all my time, and hence it was difficult for me to collect funds from the public for the home. I sacrificed Tuesday and Wednesday of each week visiting the neighboring towns, soliciting in the interest of the home. The public are in great sympathy with the work, and if the General Conference can arrange to let the superintendent give his whole time to the work, this home will soon be developed into a great institution for the aged and infirm colored people, who are constantly seeking shelter under its roof. It is not intended by the superintendent that this home shall be a heavy expense to the church; it simply needs a start and it can live and thrive by the help that comes from the public.

The deed conveying the property to the church stipulates that when the trustees see their way clear to do so, they shall establish on the grounds, besides the home, a school of domestic science where girls may be taught the various branches of industrial education. This feature of the work is particularly popular with the white people in this western part of the state of New York.

This property, as is generally known, is situated in Auburn, N.Y., on South Street, the most aristocratic street in the city. It consists of 25 acres of land, with a large orchard, two houses of ten rooms each, one brick and one frame, together with two large barns and other out-houses.

Aunt Harriet Tubman is a remarkable character. Born a slave, she escaped to the North, and after several years' residence, returned to the southland and succeeded in smuggling hundreds of slaves from the South by means of the Underground Railroad. She served various troops in the Federal army, and from the time the war closed she opened her doors to unfortunate colored people, which act of charity she continues until today. The founding of this home for aged and infirm colored people is the crowning work of her remarkable and eventful life. Mr. Frank J. Garrison, the son of the great William Lloyd Garrison of Boston, told me recently in his office at Boston, that Harriet Tubman came nearer exemplifying the spirit of Christ than any person he had ever seen. She is about ninety years of age and is as active as a woman of fifty years. It would be well for the Conference to tender a vote of thanks to Aunt Harriet for her gift of $10,000 worth of property to the church. [32]

The ten bishops, Revs. B. F. Wheeler, J. E. Mason, J. J. Adams, Dr. J. C. Dancy, and members of the Western New York Conference were elected trustees at the General Conference. Dr. Wheeler presented the deeds of the property to the General Secretary, and the church commenced operating the home in the best manner they could. [33]

In 1908 the center was formally opened, and the first inmates settled there. That had been the chief aim of her latter years, and now it was realized. From that time on until Harriet's death, and long beyond her passing, ten or twelve persons were constantly sheltered there. The white people of Auburn were astonished at this place, for it had no specific character: it housed the sick and the well, the young and the old, sightless and seeing, whoever was in need. A young colored woman named Frances Smith became matron, doing the cooking, and much of the other hard work, and watching out for Harriet.

Once she broke off active participation in behalf of the home. "When I gave the Home over to Zion Church, what do you suppose they did? Why, they made a rule that nobody should come in without a hundred dollars. Now I wanted to make a rule that nobody could come in unless they had no money. What's the good of a Home if a person who wants to get in has to have money?" Harriet was eminently philanthropic, as usual, but she may have been a bit impractical by now. The colored community of Auburn deemed itself unable to support a completely free institution. On another score, though, Harriet was correct. She came to grips with the colored leaders about the composition of the executive board of her home. She was in favor of a board combining membership of both white and Negro communities, but the colored advisers overruled her, and kept the directorship of the home exclusively in Negro hands. [34]

Aunt Harriet was up against a condition which she could not control. Her despair elicited a repining statement to her friend Dr. E. U. A. Brooks: "If I had the privilege of bequeathing my property again, I would not give it to my church." [35] She was part of an impoverished race which had not overcome the ineffectuality and inability of slavery, but her people had the dream of independence and so sought to practice it. This produced a condition that went on for some time after the death of Harriet until her home house, in which she

32. *Minutes,* Twenty-Second Quadrennial Session, pp. 97-102.
33. *Ibid.,* pp. 102-103.
34. Conrad, *op. cit.,* p. 221.
35. Related to the writer by Rev. E. U. A. Brooks before his death.

herself was an occupant when she died, was finally forced to be closed down. The church for a time retreated to her old residence, and finally was not able to keep it in habitable condition. Bishop Alexander Walters, Dr. James E. Mason, and other friends had passed on, and the home itself, which had been waived by the connection to the Western New York Conference, finally fell into devastation.

When the writer became the episcopal custodian of the Western New York Conference in 1944, everything was in decay. Some 20 years before this, the Federation of Colored Women's Clubs of New York State had appealed to the A.M.E. Zion Church to deed this property to them for a girls' home in memory of Mother Tubman, and the church refused the petition. We induced the denomination during its Sesqui-Centennial observance to raise a special fund to aid in the restoration of the home house as a shrine. The Sesqui-Centennial rally, under the leadership of Miss Lillian I. Browder of Chicago who sponsored a "Miss A.M.E. Zion Church" Contest, raised $1,300 for this special project.

The present Harriet Tubman Home house was constructed at a cost of $23,000 and an additional $7,000 for equipment. Except for $2,500 from the Home Missions Department through its secretary, Dr. H. B. Shaw, funds were principally furnished by the Second Episcopal District, supervised by Bishop W. J. Walls. Mrs. Daisy Caldwell Tucker of New York introduced a resolution at the 1948 General Conference to place the Tubman Home on the connectional budget, it being deeded to the A.M.E. Zion Connection, which the General Conference passed into law. [36] It was not, however, placed in the general budget until 1952. During this time, the Second Episcopal District continued raising funds and constructing the home.

Reverend James C. Brown, the presiding elder who had the management of the home while it was under construction, lived in the Auburn Church parsonage and had a local pastor to assist him in responsibilities. After the Harriet Tubman Home was built in 1952, Rev. Arthur E. May was appointed presiding elder of the Rochester-Syracuse-Buffalo District, and Superintendent of the Harriet Tubman Home, which became a national shrine after its dedication in April 1953. He and his wife, Margaret J. May, gave full measure of devotion in supervising the property for 12 years. After the tragic death of Mrs. May, in November 1964, Rev. May retired. The Home was directed by the bishop of the conference, assisted by a nephew of Harriet Tubman, Clarence Stewart of Auburn. Reverend Samuel L. Brown was appointed presiding elder and superintendent of the Home in 1965 and served until 1972, at which time Rev. Guthrie Carter was appointed superintendent of the home by the new chairman of the Harriet Tubman Foundation Board, Bishop H. B. Shaw.

Since 1952 this landmark for tourists has been operated from connectional funds, mortgage paid, and funds saved for the envisioned Old Peoples Home. Bolstered by projects of the First Episcopal District from 1952 to 1968 an amount exceeding $107,000 had been salvaged for development by 1972, and placed in custody of the Board of Ministerial Relief by Chairman Walls of the Harriet Tubman Foundation Board. Two faithful women of the New York Conference worked ardently for this cause. Mrs. Hattie M. Leak and Mrs. Margaret P. Persons were raising funds through the years. They and their successors are the custodians of these funds for carrying out Harriet Tubman's dream. There should be no variableness in the expectation of the A.M.E. Zion Church, the race, and the country to develop a fitting memorial on these grounds to this universal personality.

36. *Minutes,* Thirty-Third Quadrennial Session, p. 291, also pp. 82-83.

CHAPTER 28

EVANGELISM

"From the incipiency of the Christian church there has been need of evangelistic efforts to convert men to the principles of Christianity and to deepen the life of piety in those professing Christianity." [1]

Methodism was born in an evangelistic crisis and it has had a gospel and a movement which have been adequate to meet the crisis which Christianity has been forced to confront in the world ever since. All over our church territory, like the rest of the world, this civilization has found Methodism's message necessary at the very heart of the revolutionary situation. Its service has been necessary to point the way out of confusion and to nerve the heart of the Christian movement to meet and demonstrate the power of Christianity in bringing salvation to mankind. Other Christian churches, in particular those of Protestantism, have profited by the Methodist evangel as Methodism has received impetus from them.

The African Methodist Episcopal Zion Church, characteristic of Methodism, has shown a consummate zeal in this revival, and goes forward with Methodism in leading evangelism of the modern world.

For a number of years the A.M.E. Zion Church felt the need of concentrating on the evangelistic phase of the work because of the growth of departmentalism in the church as a whole, and the tendency toward absorbing the spiritual phase of the church in economic and mechanical structures of the general organization. It was felt that efforts of the soul-saving and spiritualizing forces, and the interesting of persons in these phases, were fading, and the meaning of our A.M.E. Zion Church needed refreshment through more specific organization and development. Thus was the realization when the African Methodist Episcopal Zion Church established the Bureau of Evangelism at the General Conference in 1920, with the following decree on General Evangelism:

> With all the sermons preached, even true religion often becomes dimmed and intermittent and often needs rekindling by revival influence. The ministry of Jesus Christ was of a revival type. He preached repentance, so did the Apostles. The tendency of the Church today is to expand itself through finance and fine edifices. These we must have, but reliance upon them alone produces spiritual declension and bareness. A genuine revival of religion fills the Church with members, arouses its activities, quickens its sympathy, and increases its moral and spiritual power by shaking off its lethargy; increases ministerial power by invigorating the soul of the minister; makes church work easy and enjoyable, produces a spirit of benevolence among the people, and proves to be a harvest season for gathering in the fruits of pastoral seed-sowing. [2]

1. *Minutes,* Twenty-Sixth Quadrennial Session, p. 68.
2. *Doctrines and Discipline,* 1920, pp. 268 n-o.

At the 1912 General Conference, Rev. A. McLeese of Rock Hill, S.C., and Rev. W. M. Lyons of Asheville, N.C., were elected connectional evangelists. In 1916 Rev. W. M. Lyons was re-elected and Rev. Fred D. Douglass of Indianapolis was elected. [3] These men served the church with promising results for eight years. The General Conference then decided to organize a department and elect a general officer.

The Bureau of Evangelism was organized on the general, annual conference, and local church level, with a national Board of Evangelism governing the affairs of the department. In its objective it was stated:

> In order that the African Methodist Episcopal Zion Church may conform more closely to the spirt and mission of the ministry of our Lord and employ the most effective means for the accomplishment of the chief end of the Gospel—the salvation of souls; and that the Church may more vigorously promote and apply the moral and spiritual agencies by which men are rescued from sin and trained for Christian life; and that a more inviting opportunity may be given our ministers to use their evangelistic talent more frequently in conducting revivals; and to systematize the work of evangelism among the ministry, the General Conference directs that there shall be an organization in our Church known as the Bureau of Evangelism, and for the general control of which there shall be elected by the General Conference, upon the nomination of the Board of Bishops, a Board of Evangelism consting of one Bishop and one member from each episcopal district, whose officers shall be a President, Vice-president, Secretary and Treasurer. . . ." [4]

The officer elected for a four-year term was styled the director of the Bureau of Evangelism. In the specification of the director's duties, he or she must have a constructive organization, survey the fields from time to time, assign evangelists to certain territories by direction of the board corroborated by the missions program of the church, supervise meetings of outlining the best methods for conducting evangelistic campaigns, and direct other matters pertinent to the attention of the soul of individuals. [5] The department started out as a part-time general office, with the director's salary supplemented through his labors on the field. It later grew into a full-fledged department of the church.

The Bureau of Evangelism, which had been established by the 1920 General Conference, did not receive a director until 1921. Reverend Benjamin Garland Shaw, Sr., who had led the congregation in purchasing the mammoth Washington Memorial Church in St. Louis, a magnetizing preacher and incomparable evangelist, was elected by the Board of Bishops on February 12, 1921 at Salisbury, N.C. For the next three years, he travelled across the country, crowding churches and having grand success in conversions and accessions of members. The connectional evangelists associated with him were Revs. F. D. Douglass, W. M. Lyons, W. T. Beck, A. J. Shockley, L. W. Wood, and Rev. and Mrs. Deener. With the help of these evangelists and pastors, he had been successful in gaining over 35,000 additional souls for the A.M.E. Zion Church, and helping others to find the way to Christ and connect with some Christian movement. [6] Dr. Shaw was elected bishop at the next General Conference in 1924. He kept a supervising eye on this department for four years, and in 1928, Rev. Walter William Slade was elected director. [7]

3. *Minutes,* Twenty-Fourth Quadrennial Session, p. 134: Twenty-Fifth, p. 40.
4. *Doctrines and Discipline,* 1920, p. 268-j.
5. *Ibid.,* pp. 268 k-l.
6. Minutes, Twenty-Seventh Quadrennial Session, pp. 234-239.
7. *Minutes,* Twenty-Eighth Quadrennial Session, p. 93.

BISHOP BENJAMIN GARLAND SHAW
Founder of the Department of Evangelism

Reverend Slade had served as presiding elder nearly 20 years in the conferences of North Carolina and was the successful presiding elder of the Asheville District when he was elected director of this department. A dynamic pulpiteer, keenly interested in the spiritual welfare of the connection, he was sent to Wesley Center Church, Pittsburgh, in 1932, and served both this pastorate and the Bureau of Evangelism until 1936. He was elected in 1940, as financial secretary of the denomination, and bishop in 1944.

The General Conference of 1936 elected Dr. William S. Dacons, who was a characteristic preacher of the group and could stir the natives. He was serving as presiding elder of the Cincinnati District, Ohio Conference, and holding revivals all over the connection when he was elected. [8] He then pastored St. Paul Church in Little Rock, Ark., while serving as presiding elder of the Little Rock District. In 1944, the Bureau of Evangelism was moved to the headquarters at Charlotte, N.C. where he served until 1960. His 24-year tenure as director was the longest in the history of the church. After giving concern to the operation of the evangelistic department in 1944, the General Conference voted that the Bureau of Evangelism be made a bureau of the Home Missions Department. [9] This is the apparent time, upon its removal to the headquarters in Charlotte, N.C., that the decision was made to make the Bureau of Evangelism a more stabilized department. It was in 1956 when this officer became a full-time salaried general office. [10]

The General Conference of 1960 elected Rev. Elias S. Hardge, Sr., who was by nature an active exponent of the religion of his people, with a pithy evangelistic style. He was elected from the pastorate of the Goler Metropolitan Church, Winston-Salem, N.C. During Dr. Hardge's administration, the office was moved to the national headquarters building of the A.M.E. Zion Church in Washington, D.C., where it is today.

8. *Minutes,* Thirtieth Quadrennial Session, pp. 59, 118.
9. *Minutes,* Thirty-Second Quadrennial Session, p. 66.
10. *Doctrines and Discipline,* 1956, p. 119.

In 1968, the General Conference elected to this office Rev. John Dallas Jenkins, Sr., from the pastorate of the Blackwell Memorial Church in Chicago. Dr. Jenkins is a resourceful preacher with considerable dramatic forcefulness. He was re-elected by the 1972 General Conference.

It is a serious question whether Methodism is maintaining its old place in the evangelistic front line, and the A.M.E. Zion Church suffers the same tendency toward spiritual lethargy. However, our organization is setting itself towards a new day of sacrifice, courage, and creative undertaking in Christian evangelism. We are attuning the hearts in our Department of Evangelism of our younger men and women in this field, both in the organization and in our emphasis on Christian attitude at the altar and in the whole community, and the social needs of people in our social world.

CHAPTER 29

EXTRA-DENOMINATIONAL PROGRAMS

The African Methodist Episcopal Zion Church has always been engaged in benevolent causes and programs. These have not become departmentalized, however organizational, but have been worked in the structure with denominational cohesion to bring about a more humane imprint on the spiritual and social concerns of Christianity.

The Health Center

In 1952 a constant minister-medical doctor in our church, Rev. Dr. Samuel C. Coleman of Hot Springs, Ark., induced the Ministers' and Laymen's Association to present a resolution to the General Conference to establish a connectional convalescent home for the A.M.E. Zion constituency in Hot Springs. It was suggested that the support for the proposed convalescent home would be by gifts, annuities, and solicitations throughout the connection by duly authorized persons. The committee on revision concurred with the resolution, but the house voted nonconcurrence. [1]

Dr. Coleman has always been mentally adapted to the health and social welfare of his people. He had been a long-standing physician in the community; pastored churches, served as presiding elder of the Crossett District, Arkansas Conference, served as medical examiner and advisor of Walters-Southland Institute at Warren, and a useful participant in the A.M.E. Zion Church General Conferences and National Medical Association (Negro) Conventions, since 1920. Hot Springs being one of the country's noted health resorts, Dr. Coleman had built a health clinic by his initiative which he proffered to operate for Zion. In August 1956, the Board of Bishops voted to accept the project and issue a certificate of appointment to Dr. Coleman as health director. [2] It soon became known as the A.M.E. Zion Health Center at Hot Springs. In addition, he rendered invaluable service of medical attention at the connectional meetings of the church.

Determined not to be deterred in promoting this serviceable facility for Zion, Dr. Coleman, supported by the Board of Bishops and friends in general, acquired a stipend from the connectional budget at the 1972 General Conference, to supplement his program of health service in administering the A.M.E. Zion Church Health Center at Hot Springs. This advanced step is an incentive to Dr. Coleman and the people of the community to continue the effort of projecting this noteworthy cause of serving humanity.

1. *Minutes,* Thirty-Fourth Quadrennial Session, pp. 319-392.
2. Ms. Minutes, Board of Bishops, August 25, 1956.

The Laymen's Council

The church which is the body of Christ is a unit of Christian service and fellowship. It is a well-organized body of many parts and activities to serve divine ends. An organ of this body is the laity. The role of laymen since primitive Christianity through every age has been diversified and highly significant in its spiritual function, yet adjunct to the representative head of the church, Christ's chosen apostle.

The integrality of ministers and laymen of the African Methodist Episcopal Zion Church was simultaneous with the foundation of the church. Subsequently, as the ministry and the church grew together connectionally, the laymen required a definite organization of their expression and helpful thrust. The effort has been to organize helpfully and not competitively with the whole church. This has practically produced a degree of competition short of government within the structure of the church. The purpose is to move in congruous and parallel efforts without conflicting with the structural organization.

The first connectional laymen's organization was established at the 1916 General Conference. Upon presentation of the report of the committee on constitution; (B. T. Parsons, W. M. Bradley, R. McN. Williams, J. T. Hamilton, D. L. Gaines, Mrs. Anna L. Anderson, D. R. Corrothers, H. C. Wright, and Jacob W. Powell the organization of *The Lay Members Association of the African Methodist Episcopal Zion Church* was adopted on May 18, 1916.[3] The organization issued a four-page printed Constitution and By-Laws to take effect throughout the denomination. J. H. Johnson was the president, and the other members of the committee were vice-presidents, with the exception of Mrs. Anna L. Anderson and Rev. Jacob Powell. In addition, Cephus McPhaul, M. A. Bonner, and W. T. Abrams were vice-presidents; Oscar W. Adams Sr., corresponding secretary and reporter; Alonzo A. Rieves, recording secretary; and Mrs. E. H. Badhams, treasurer. Its objects were as follows:

To support the Bishops, general officers, pastors and all officers of the connection, and to cooperate with them in all their plans for the advancement of the kingdom of Jesus Christ.

To work especially for the missionary cause.

To give expression to the opinions of the laity on all matters relating to the ideals, principles, policies and servants of the church, and to secure proper consideration of the wishes of the laity.

To work for an increase in lay membership in the General conferences and boards, to the end that equal lay representation may soon become an established fact. (Achieved in 1928)

To promote progressive legislation in the councils of the church, and to encourage only the best ideals, principles, policies, and people.

To encourage the increased use of approved business methods of conducting the affairs of the church; and to bring to the attention of the church such laymen and others whose training and experience, especially qualify them to serve in elective or appointive positions.

To keep the lay interest in connectional affairs, during the intervals between the various conferences, and to promote unity of action for the welfare of the church.

To carry out the wishes of the lay electoral colleges, annual and general. [4]

---

3. Jacob W. Powell, *Echoes of Christian Education,* p. 32.
4. *Constitution,* Lay Members Association, pp. 1-2.

This organization made attempts to carry out its dynamic aims and did well for a while. But for want of interested lay leaders and support of the clergy to build on this foundation, it became dormant. The spirit of reviving the laymen connectionally remained rife among several noted laymen of the denomination, through the years. Finally with the aid of interested bishops and ministers, the lay members began to build a concrete organization.

It was in 1948 when Dr. Victor J. Tulane and Arthur E. Brooks, both of Washington, D.C., presented a recommendation to the General Conference in behalf of the Laymen's Association, "to set up organizations known as the Laymen's Association in each Annual Conference throughout the Episcopal areas," and moved that the Conference adopt it. A discussion arose for clarification of its objectives, and the type of organization the laymen desired to project, with Rufus Clement, Mrs. Helen McClinton, J. T. Ellebee, and James W. Eichelberger speaking on unreadiness. Bishop Frank W. Alstork and Rev. C. L. Wilcox offered that the recommendation be referred back to the committee for clarification. Bishop W. J. Walls and Dr. Victor J. Tulane expressed differences of opinion on its definition. Reverends S. G. Spottswood and Arthur Marshall, Jr. moved to proceed with the previous motion. Later in the session Revs. H. R. Hawkins and A. P. Morris made motions to adopt the Laymen's Council. "The General Conference sustained the concurrence of the Laymen's Committee, with an order to the Committee to bring to the next session of the General Conference proposed Constitution and By-Laws by said General Conference." [5]

On the fourteenth day of the 1952 General Conference, "Dr. Victor J. Tulane submitted the Constitution and By-Laws of the Connectional Laymen's Council of the A.M.E. Zion Church. Each article was adopted separately. It was moved by Dr. Tulane and seconded by Reverend J. A. Harris that the Constitution and By-Laws be adopted as a whole. The motion prevailed." [6] The Laymen's Council thus became a part of the constitutional structure of the denomination to be projected throughout the church in local churches, annual conferences, and connectionally, with the connectional officers of the Laymen's Council leading the forces. Its prime objects, as the General Conference directed, are:

> for the purpose of deepening the spiritual life of the laymen of the Church, to disseminate information and cultivate denominational loyalty, to expand the denomination through methods of education and evangelism and to promote any other interest of the Kingdom of God. [7]

The Laymen's Council was placed under the control of a new administrative board known as the Board of Lay Activities, composed of a representative from each episcopal district, appointed by the bishop and confirmed by the General Conference. The Laymen's Council as structured in 1952 has been an active and responsive organization in the life of the church. Its connectional officers and interested members have participated in lengthening the cords of our membership and deepening its spirituality and social concern. The officers for the past twenty years have been dedicated men and women with high attribute of religious conviction.

The first president, elected in 1952, was Dr. Victor J. Tulane of Washington, D.C. and later, Salisbury, N.C., who served until 1964. Arthur E. Brooks was elected as his successor in 1964, re-elected in 1968 and 1972, and presently leads the connectional movement. The other officers serving from 1952 through 1972:

5. *Minutes,* Thirty-Third Quadrennial Session, pp. 77, 83 292.
6. *Minutes,* Thirty-Fourth Quadrennial Session, pp. 76, 396-398.
7. *Doctrines and Discipline,* 1952, p. 288.

Vice-presidents; Dr. Ashley L. Cromwell of Winston Salem, N.C., D.D. Garrett of Greenville, N.C., and Mrs. Betty V. Stith of New Rochelle, N.Y., who was elected in 1972. Mr. Garrett was elected second vice-president in 1972.

First secretary was D. Oliver Francis of Bronx, N.Y., who helped to draw up the present constitution. He was succeeded by Mrs. Betty V. Stith, of New Rochelle, N.Y. and Mrs. Essie Robinson McDaniels, of Salisbury, N.C., elected in 1972, who had previously served as assistant secretary. Mrs. Rosemarie Holmes of White Plains, N.Y. was elected the assistant secretary in 1972.

Richard J. Harris, Sr., of Statesville, N.C., was elected treasurer in 1952 and re-elected in 1972 for the fifth term. Guy Mayzck of Durham, N.C. was elected chaplain in 1952 and also re-elected in 1972 for a fifth term. Mr. James Duke was elected regional vice-president of the West Coast in May, 1972. [8]

The Ministers' and Laymen's Association

The Ministers' and Laymen's Association of the A.M.E. Zion Church was organized in January 1938. After the Board of Bishops decided to hold closed sessions during its mid-winter session held January 13-15, 1937 at First A.M.E. Zion Church, Paterson, N.J., the ministers and laymen who customarily attended these meetings became imbued with an exhilaration for connectional causes. They therefore organized themselves into a body for the purpose of stimulating interest in general church affairs. Meeting simultaneously with the mid-winter sessions of the Board of Bishops, the new group formed their organization January 12, 1938 at St. Peter's A.M.E. Zion Church, New Bern, N.C., and elected Rev. Hilliard R. Jackson of Brooklyn, N.Y. (serving as presiding elder of the Hartford District, New England Conference) its first president. [9]

The organization began to chart its course with rudimentary procedure, and it developed tenaciously. Although not a constitutional organization of the church, it is one of the cooperative movements within the church which seeks to help in the execution of plans and purposes of the denomination, and to apply its forcefulness to the trends and needs of the times. Its method of electing officers has varied somewhat through the years; especially its vice-presidency. In addition to the president, its roster includes two administrative vice-presidents; an executive secretary, financial secretary recording secretary, assistant recording secretary, and treasurer.

From 1938 through 1972 the organization has been led by four ministers of stalwart denominational stature. Successors to Dr. H. R. Jackson were Dr. Stephen Gill Spottswood, while serving the pastorate of John Wesley Church, Washington, D.C.; Dr. Edward Franklin Jackson, pastor of the same church; and Dr. Eugene E. Morgan, Jr., pastor of Wesley Temple Church, Akron, Ohio. The officers and members of this organization have been and are a noble variegation in the field of Christian service, and know the full meaning of sharing in the responsibility of religious and social uplift.

The Historical Society

At the General Conference of 1944 a resolution written by Rev. James Clair Taylor on organizing a Historical Society in the A.M.E. Zion Church was

---

8. List of officers secured from Arthur E. Brooks, president; also *Star of Zion*, Directory, p. 8.
9. Ms. Minutes, Board of Bishops Meeting, January 13, 1937; January, 12-13, 1938.

presentéd by the Revision Committee. A discussion ensued, led by Bishop W. J. Walls, President W. J. Trent of Livingstone College, and Rev. S. S. Seay. Bishop C. C. Alleyne suggested that this organization should be set up at Livingstone College in connection with the Department of History and proceeded to make the motion for adopting the Historical Society, which was seconded by Bishop Walls. Dr. Rufus E. Clement suggested that it should be connected with the division of history in the Theological Department of Livingstone College, and the motion was adopted including this amendment. After the Historical Society was adopted by this General Conference, plans were formulated for a historian to write a history of the denomination upon approaching its Sesqui-Centennial in 1946, and for an officer of the Historical Society. "Bishop Walls moved that a non-salaried historian be appointed for the time being until plans can be worked out, seconded by Senator R. L. Brokenburr. Rev. H. R. Jackson stated that because of the importance of the position, a salary should be paid. Bishop Walls expressed himself as agreeable to this if a plan could be worked out for compensation. The motion was adopted. Bishop J. W. Martin moved that Dr. Rufus E. Clement be elected to head this society, seconded by Reverend J. W. I. Tunstall. The motion prevailed." The resolution on alloting $5,000 to Bishop Walls for writing a history of the A.M.E. Zion Church was voted unfavorable by the body. [10]

In passing the legislation, the two parties involved—a historian to write a denominational history, and the officer of the Historical Society—were both left without budgets. Also guidelines for effectuation of the Historical Society had not been offered. Thus Dr. Rufus E. Clement, President of Atlanta University, was handicapped in projecting the new movement and the matter was dormant until the General Conference of 1956.

At the 1956 General Conference, almost identical resolutions were presented by Rev. David H. Bradley, Editor of the *Quarterly Review,* and the Ministers' and Laymen's Association. The only difference was that the Ministers' and Laymen's Association, which had approved the recommendation at its meeting at Durham, N.C., January 1956, presented its resolution with a prefatory statement as follows:

Whereas, the establishment of a Historical Society was authorized by the action of the Thirty-Second Quadrennial Session of the A.M.E. Zion Church General Conference meeting at Detroit, Michigan, 1944 . . . and whereas that action has not been to this date implemented, be it resolved: That the following be entered in our book of Discipline as Paragraph 548:

1. In order that valuable historical records and history of the denomination may be kept and maintained, the General Conference shall establish a Historical Department in which shall be gathered the original minutes of the several annual conferences, the said minute books to be turned over periodically by the conference secretaries.

2. The General Conference shall further direct the maintenance at a place designated of Annual and General Conference minutes or copies, published books and pamphlets of interest to the denomination, and any other work which may have a bearing on Denominational, Church, or Annual Conference history.

3. A secretary of this historical department shall be elected and shall hold office for four years or until his successor is elected. He shall devote at least half-time to this service. He shall report semi-annually to the Board of Bishops, annually to the Connectional Council, and every four years to the General Conference.

10. *Minutes,* Thirty-Second Quadrennial Session, pp. 57-58.

4. The General Conference shall provide a budget whereby the Secretary of the Historical Department shall be able to maintain an office, travel, purchase aforementioned books and pamphlets, provide the annual conferences with a standard minute book, best suited for filing, and he shall maintain reasonable relationships with the World Methodist Historical Society.

Signed,
E. FRANKLIN JACKSON, President
G. W. McMURRAY, Corresponding
Secretary

[The fifth section presented by Dr. Bradley stated that:]

Any pamphlets or books written or edited by the Secretary of the Historical Department shall be the copyrighted property of the denomination provided the denomination assumes publication responsibility either through the General Conference, the Board of Bishops, or Connectional Council. [11]

The above resolutions were edited and placed in the Discipline as Paragraph 548, after the General Conference of 1956 had passed upon them. It further stated that, "The Historical Society shall operate under the Board of Public Relations, Social Service and Historical Society." [12]

On Monday evening, May 14th, the General Conference voted: "To restore the Historical Society with its depository at Hood Theological Seminary," during the report of the revision committee. [13] It seems by general agreement, this part-time office was placed with the editor of the *Quarterly Review* after the Connectional Council held at Hopkins Chapel, Asheville, N.C., August 1956. Dr. David H. Bradley, the secretary of the Historical Society, in making his report to the Board of Bishops in its semi-annual meeting held in January 1957 at Oklahoma City, related important history working up to the Society. "He was given permission to select certain books of history for our historic library . ." [14] According to the rules set forth in the Discipline, he has been elected by successive General Conferences through 1972. Dr. Bradley has written a two-volume history of the denomination, produced other historical literature, and built up denominational archives at Bedford, Pa., manifesting ardent concern for this consequential need in the church.

The Chaplaincy and Patriotism

. . .True type of the warrior sons of God—active pastors who have left their flocks in quiet meadows to take charge of others surrounded by murders—church bells, pealing organs and vested choirs will be drowned by the sound of rifle, booming of cannon and shout of men who struggle in death grips to uphold rule and order against the miscreants who have deluged the world with blood.

Noble men worthy of a noble race and devoted to a grand cause. Their nobility is all the more marked and distinctive for they go to give to the world the rights and privileges from which they themselves are debarred. Glorious Race, Christlike Race, giving its blood to heal the hurt that the rapacity, cupidity, ambition, jealousy and envy of the white man inflicted on the world.

11. *Minutes,* Thirty-Fifth Quadrennial Session, p. 460-461, 463.
12. *Doctrines and Discipline,* 1956, p. 217.
13. *Minutes,* Thirty-Fifth Quadrennial Session, p. 120.
14. Ms. Minutes, Board of Bishops Meeting, August 22-23, 1956; January 9-13, 1957.

Self-forgetting Race that leaves its men and women at home to be lynched while it goes abroad to curb and destroy the passions of wolf-like men, worse than the wolves . . . .

We pray for the purification of our nation and the return of our men and of our chaplains. They are in the hands of God. [15]

The African Methodist Episcopal Zion Church, even in the earlier days of its existence, figured conspicuously in the wars of the United States of America furnishing chaplains to its official staff and brave men and women to its ranks. Thus the church demonstrated to the world the patriotic spirit that burned in the breasts of those lovers of freedom who believed it would be attained through democracy. Of the thousands of men and women of the black race in America, who have been perilously involved in this country's wars since the Revolutionary War, the A.M.E. Zion Church has had its copious share, most of whose names are recorded on plaques and scrolls in their local churches across the country, for their bravery and sacrifice.

The heroism demonstrated by these people since Crispus Attucks, the first martyr in the Boston Massacre, March 5, 1770, has always been vividly and endurably marked. The earliest recorded heroes of the A.M.E. Zion Church were those who fought to procure the freedom of their people in the Union Army of the Civil War. Long will the deeds of our loyal church member, Harriet Tubman, perhaps the greatest heroine since Joan of Arc, be remembered. She served as nurse, spy, and scout in the Union Army during the Civil War, and not only continuously exhibited rare valor but endured manifold hardships.

Bishop Hood, in his history of the A.M.E. Zion Church, gives accounts of those men who saw action in the Civil War, some becoming severely wounded, and some left with blemishing experiences. These men afterward became some of our most outstanding pioneer preachers in expanding the borders of Zion across the country. Reverend Eli George Biddle enlisted in Company A of the 54 Regiment, Massachusetts Colored Infantry, and served with the famous Sergeant William H. Carney of Company C, who was awarded the Congressional Medal of Honor for his bravery in the Battle of Fort Wagner, S.C. When the standard bearer was killed, Carney picked up the regimental colors and led the attack to the fort. He was badly wounded on two occasions during the fighting. [16] At the end of the battle, he said the historic patriotic words.—"The old flag never touched the ground." E. George Biddle was also severely wounded at the battle of Fort Wagner, July 18, 1863. [17] No less courageous in their march for freedom and salvation of the Union were Zion's following men of nobility:

Reverends James Harvey Anderson, Mark Anthony Bradley, William B. Bowen, Alexander Johnson Coleman, Nathaniel James Green, James Bartlett Johnson, William J. Moore, Major A. G. Oden, H. B. Pettigrew, J. H. Trimble, Andrew Jackson Warner, and Jeremiah Washington. Zion men who served as Army chaplains during the Civil War were Revs. David Stevens, John N. Mars, and A. A. Smith.

To the Brave Men Who Commanded the Black Phalanx:

—As a mark of esteem and respect for your patriotic devotion to the cause of human freedom [stated Joseph T. Wilson], I desire to dedicate to you this record of the services of the Negro soldiers, whom you led so often and successfully in the struggle for liberty and union during the great war of 1861-65.

---

15. Charles Martin, "Our Chaplains," in *A.M.E. Zion Quarterly Review*, April 1918, p. 60.
16. Bergman, *The Chronological History of the Negro*, p. 233.
17. Hood, *One Hundred Years*, pp. 480-481.

E. George Biddle

BLACK CIVIL WAR SOLDIERS

Charge by the 54th Massachusetts Regiment at Fort Wagner, S.C. Rev. E. George Biddle saw action in this battle.

Your coming from the highest ranks of social life, undeterred by the prevailing spirit of caste prejudice, to take commands in the largest Negro army ever enrolled beneath the flag of any western country, was in itself a brave act. The organization and disciplining of over two hundred thousand men, of a race that for more than two centuries had patiently borne the burdens of an unrequited bondage, for the maintenance of laws which had guaranteed to them neither rights nor protection, was indeed a magnificent undertaking.

You were outlawed by the decrees of Jefferson Davis, criticised by many friends at home, and contemptuously received by brother officers at headquarters, in the field, in the trenches, and at the mess table; yet, you did not waver in your fidelity to principle or in your heroic leadership of those whose valor was denied until it was proven in carnage and victory. [18]

The noble A.M.E. Zion chaplains appointed by the Governor of North Carolina and serving in the Spanish-American War were Revs. Henry Durham and

18. Joseph T. Wilson, *The Black Phalanx*, p. ii.

Henry Western Morrison. Those worthy and efficient representatives of our Zion in the expeditionary forces during World War I were Revs: Thomas E. Davis, George Marion Edwards, Alexander Huntingdon Hatwood, Benjamin Congelton Robeson, Thomas Walker Wallace.

The following noteworthy ministers of Zion were commissioned chaplains during World War II, and served their country with utter devotion:
Reverends: Walter David S. Barrett, Frank Reginald Brown, Sr., Julius Caesar Carter, David Cecil, James Addison Clement, Rufus A. Cooper, Thomas O. Diggs, Alfred Gilbert Dunston, Jr., Edward Wesley Gantt, Ervin Eugene Grimmett, Simmie P. Holland, Cajus B. Howell, Robert H. Collins Lee, C. A. Leftwich, Harlee H. Little, Johnson W. Littlejohn, Jr., Charles H. Mack, Phillip Rudolph McCurdy, Booker T. Medford, Edmund J. O'Neal, Theodore R. Owens, Isaiah Benjamin Pierce, William Mitchell Poe, Thomas E. Roach, James E. W. Stewart, James Wesley Wactor, John R. Wesley.[19]

Reverend William J. Jiles served as army chaplain for a brief period after the Korean war. After leading the people in building a capacious structure, Rev. Charles E. Quick relinquished his pulpit at East Stonewall Church, Charlotte, in 1968, to give his service as chaplain of the Veteran's Hospital at Augusta, Ga. Rev. Raymond E. Tinsley of marked distinction is presently serving in the armed forces, and after the 1972 General Conference which he attended, became engaged in a practical and essential mission in the human concerns of the armed services in Viet Nam.

Chaplain James E. W. Stewart, who remained in the service for a number of years and became a major before his return to the pastorate, introduced an important resolution in the 1952 General Conference, which produced considerations as follows:

> *Whereas* the Chaplains of the A.M.E. Zion Church who are on active duty, serving in the armed forces of our land, should be counted among the frontier pastors of our church, who follow and serve our men and women in the armed forces at home and abroad:
>
> *Whereas*, our Chaplains in the services are the representatives of the A.M.E. Zion Church in the armed forces of our land:
>
> *Be it resolved*, that they will be carried on the rosters, and in the minutes of the Annual Conference of their last Conference Appointment as Chaplains on active duty;
>
> *Be it further resolved*, that the Chaplains on active duty be required to submit periodic reports of their labors in the field, that the church may be kept abreast of the labors of its Frontier pastors in the services;
>
> *Be it further resolved*, that these periodic reports be given publicity in summarized form through the *Missionary Seer* and the other Church publications;
>
> *Be it further resolved*, that the Chaplains on active duty be automatically seated as members of the General Conference, with the question of voting power being left to the discretion of the General Conference in session;
>
> *Be it further resolved*, that a limited supply of the *Missionary Seer* and other church periodicals be made available to Chaplains for distribution among service men;
>
> *Be it further resolved*, that the Bishops of the several Annual Conferences, formally request that the Chaplains whose memberships are within the bounds of their conferences and who are stationed within

19. *Sesqui-Centennial Souvenir Program*, 1946, pp. 41-44.

continental United States be placed on temporary duty during the sitting of the Annual Conference, that they might be in attendance at the same. [20]

After Chaplain Stewart read the resolution, he moved that the rules be suspended and the resolution be voted upon immediately. "It was moved by Bishop W. J. Walls and seconded by Rev. L. R. Bennett that the resolution be adopted with the exception of that portion relating to the seating of Chaplains in the General Conference. The motion prevailed." [21]

With the shortage of pulpiteers in every age, the A.M.E. Zion Church has sounded forth the tocsin, sharing with the nation our ministerial support of inspirational chaplains' service. Of course, that which prompts universal inspiration is the continued bravery and patriotism of the many young laymen of the A.M.E. Zion Church who serve in the armed forces today.

20. *Minutes,* Thirty-Fourth Quadrennial Session, pp. 63-64.
21. *Ibid.,* p. 64.

Part VII
Faith, Hope and Charity

CHAPTER 30

ZION AND ECUMENICITY

Christian unity is the way to a peaceful world. The rave of agnostics and skeptics is that Christianity has failed and the church is impotent to bring peace. We answer: God's hand is in human history today no less than in the great eras of the past, but it is incumbent upon us to follow that Hand in the unity of His world. The Christian church has the seed of peace and the mighty force of world control, but it must be worked out through the unity of the gospel. As long as the church is divided we will have a divided world, but the seed of uniting the church must be cultivated with indescribable and never ceasing faith and toil.

This principle has its root in the scriptures of God. In the hands of man it has suffered harm, but the democratic spirit in its essence is of God, and in its ultimatum it is the consummate flower of Christianity. There are good signs of Christian unity in overall efforts of councils, local and general, which have mankind, the world over, in profound thinking and serious undertaking..Naturally, theological and doctrinal differences have posed a problem for Christian unity since the first division of the Christian church, Eastern Orthodox and Roman Catholic, in 1054. It is remembered, however, that Jesus went to the cross staking everything on the coupling of humanity's love of God and love for each other in one great commandment; thus it is the duty of his apostles to take the lead in bringing about the oneness of humanity.

Organic Union

The African churches in America, born out of oppressive circumstances, have always felt the providential and environmental need to furnish leadership to its people in America, Africa, and other parts of the world. When almost two centuries ago, the Negro began to unite his members and give form to a church organization of which he was to be the arbiter, there was much misgiving concerning the wisdom and durability of the project. Stormy and tedious days have marked the painful progress of these years. While we confess to many faults and failures, the wonder is that they are not more, and that we have made the progress we have. It is interesting to imagine what would have been the black man's condition without his church.

In American Christianity a very large proportion of the black race is registered in the membership of black oriented churches. Scores of schools dotting the country have been built under the direction and by the foresight of these churches, attesting to faith in the power of Christian education to aid in the solving of all the ills of humanity. The finest buildings in this neighborhood, like the temple of Solomon among the chosen people, is the Negro's church, and this sacred property can be found in every corner of the world.

The Negro established his church in reaction against segregation of the most rabid sort in the mother churches of Protestantism. It is sufficient to say that the Baptist Church grew faster in multiplying congregations because of its unlimited congregational nature. The A.M.E., A.M.E. Zion, and later the C.M.E. Churches took from Asbury's church the limited episcopal form of organization which, indeed, has been the primary teacher of connectional cohesion and country-wide cooperation of the Negro. The burden of this chapter, however, is organic union, which is the first point of attack in bringing the churches most alike together.

The A.M.E. Zion denomination and the A.M.E. (Bethel) denomination, although many times classified together by outside groups in their earliest history, have been separate and independent of each other since their severance from white Methodist denomination. There remained some confusion about these separate denominations operating under the same name until 1848, when the A.M.E. Zion Church attached *Zion* to its denominational title. "Compare the autonomy of the various Orthodox Byzantine churches, the Greek, the Russian, etc.," stated H. B. Hoffman of New York City. "Both the A.M.E. Zion and A.M.E. denominations originated at the end of the eighteenth century, the Zion Church in this city (New York), and the A.M.E. (Bethel) Church in Philadelphia." [1]

From the beginning, competition between these two organizations demonstrated feeling from which they never became wholly healed. In their work of stabilizing their organizations against prejudicial forces, the indecisiveness of a few leading men in both denominations intensified the situation. George White and Thomas Miller, two original trustees of Zion Church who had become licensed preachers in Zion Church, went over to the Bethel connection, and White became forceful in turning over to the Bethel group Zion's proposed societies at Brooklyn and Flushing, Long Island. William Lambert, also an original trustee of the Asbury Church in New York, went over to the Bethel movement and assisted them in establishing their first society in New York. [2] Jacob Matthews, who had become

1. Henry B. Hoffman, "Transformation of New York Churches," *New York Historical Society Quarterly Bulletin*, January 1938, p. 7.
2. Payne, *History of the A.M.E. Church*, pp. 34-37; Rush, *Rise and Progress*, pp. 41, 49-50.

a trustee and later a licensed preacher in Zion Church, afterward Asbury Church, New York, withdrew from Zion and Asbury, for reasons unknown, went over to Bethel, and became a powerful force in structuring its connection. He was even elected general superintendent in the A.M.E. Church. Matthews returned to Zion Connection, August 15, 1827, and became equally potent in establishing new societies up the Hudson River, serving devotedly until his death. [3]

Reverends Jacob Richardson and David Smith, founders of the A.M.E. Bethel Connection at Baltimore, later came over to Zion Connection and proved to be unusually effective in promoting the work of Zion in Pennsylvania and Washington, D.C. Another early A.M.E. minister, Rev. Henry Drayton, also joined Zion Connection. [4] The loss of these strong leaders and development of societies by their skill against opposite forces caused deeper estrangement between these two churches, and the competition grew throughout the country.

The struggle for freedom, which had united both groups in bonds of affliction, was culminating, and the sentiment on behalf of the people of these two movements began to change. The initial effort was made soon after Emancipation.

On May 24, 1864, the Twelfth Quadrennial Session of the General Conference of the A.M.E. Zion Church convened at Wesley Church, Philadelphia.

Preceding the sitting of the General Conference the subject of union between Zion and Bethel had been much talked of. The union of the two factions of Zion four years previous had made the impression with many that it might be an easy matter to unite the African Methodist Episcopal (Bethel) and African Methodist Episcopal Zion Churches, and make them one. Ministers in both churches had preached on the subject, and it was thought that the people were pretty well prepared for it, and, in fact, many were, but there were also those who were bitterly opposed to union. . . .

The first formal proposition for union came from the African Methodist Episcopal (Bethel) Church, and was presented to this General Conference.

The following was taken from the Minutes of the second day's session, May 26, 1864:

A special committee from the General Conference of the African Methodist Episcopal Church, consisting of Revs. A. McIntosh, M. Sluby, and Dr. Watts, were introduced to the Conference and were cordially received. Business was suspended to give them audience.

Rev. McIntosh, the chairman of the committee, after some congratulatory remarks, presented and read a document emanating from that body as to its action and provision made for consolidation of the two connections, namely, African Methodist Episcopal Church and the African Methodist Episcopal Zion Church: That in order to duly consider the matter a committee of nine had been appointed, with two bishops, to meet a similar number from this General Conference as a joint committee, in the event they deem such consummation possible, shall call a convention consisting of such number of delegates as may be determined by said joint committee. When the convention shall have assembled they shall determine the conditions upon which the union shall be consummated; and said conditions shall be submitted to all the Annual Conferences of each connection. If the terms agreed upon by the convention be ratified by a majority of all the Annual Conferences above mentioned, that the two connections from that date shall be one.

After a brief interchange of sentiment with the committee touching the subject the following prevailed:

3. Payne, *op. cit.,* p. 32; Rush, *op, cit.,* p. 82.

Resolved, That we cordially receive the representation made to this Conference by the subcommittee from the Committee on Church Union appointed by the African Methodist Episcopal General Conference, and that we promise to give the subject presented a Christian and fraternal consideration which its importance so justly demands at the earliest opportunity.

The committee withdrew. The subject was further deliberated upon which resulted in the following resolution:

Resolved, That a committee of three be appointed to present the Christian greetings and resolutions of the African Methodist Episopal Zion General Conference to the African Methodist Episcopal General Conference.

The following were appointed: Revs: S. T. Jones, J. B. Trusty, S. M. Giles. This committee, having filled its mission, returned and reported through the chairman, Rev. S. T. Jones, the cordial reception they met with and the feeling evinced upon the subject of consolidation; that they were upon the point of adjourning that evening, but upon hearing of our approval of their proposition suspended the adjournment until our Conference could get a sufficient quorum to consider the matter properly. He corrected an error in the report of the committee from that body, namely: Instead of two bishops as was reported, it is the Bench of Bishops to be united with nine from that body, and the same from us or an equivalent in members.

On the following day, May 27, the following preamble and resolutions, offered by S. T. Jones, were adopted:

Whereas, By the working and control of an all-wise and gracious Providence, circumstances and events have so conspired during the present great struggle as clearly to indicate that the set time to favor Zion was fully come; and,

Whereas, This is specially manifested as relates to that portion of the Church composed of colored Methodists in America; and,

Whereas, We should prove ourselves false alike to the principles of our holy religion, our obligations as the representatives of Christ, and our duty and responsibilities as the leaders of a weak because divided people, should we fail, from any minor consideration, to improve the present favorable opportunity with a view to the future peace and prosperity of the Church, and the moral, social, and political interest of the race with which we are immediately identified; therefore,

Resolved, That in the great principle of Christian union and brotherhood we fully indorse all proper measures employed in furtherance of that principle, and that our warm sympathies are with those who are heartily engaged in the effort to unite in one body the African Methodist Episcopal Zion and African Methodist Episcopal Churches.

Resolved, That as an evidence of our sincerity, and with a view of facilitating the consummation so ardently desired, this Conference appoint a committee of nine with the Bench of Superintendents forthwith, who shall be authorized and empowered to confer with a similar committee in connection with the Bench of Bishops chosen by the General Conference of the African Methodist Episcopal Church on all matters touching a consolidation of the bodies represented. [5]

A committee of three appointed by the A.M.E. Zion General Conference informed the General Conference of the A.M.E. Church that "in compliance with

---

4. Payne, *op. cit.,* pp. 27, 34-37; Rush, *op. cit.,* pp. 83-86; Moore, *History,* pp. 101-107.
5. Hood, *One Hundred Years,* pp. 88-90.

their wish a committee had been appointed to confer with them on consolidation of the connections. Six o'clock that evening was agreed upon for the joint committee meeting." Bishops W. H. Bishop and J. J. Clinton and Rev. S. T. Jones, J. W. Loguen, P. G. Laws, Samson D. Talbot, G. H. Washington, J. Coleman, J. W. Hood, J. D. Brooks, J. P. Hamer, S. M. Giles, and W. F. Butler constituted the committee on our part. [6]

On the third day of the A.M.E. Zion Church General Conference, the joint committees met accordingly at 6 P.M., in Bethel Church, Sixth Street. The meeting was organized by Bishop J. J. Clinton, and Revs. J. M. Brown (A.M.E.) and J. P. Hamer (A.M.E. Zion) were chosen secretaries. "After deliberation it was decided that this should be a formal meeting." [7] Subcommittees were appointed from both churches. They reported to the conference on Saturday, May 28, that it had been agreed to submit the subject of consolidation to a convention composed of 25 on each side, and their action to be submitted to all the annual conferences for confirmation.

The convention met in Philadelphia, June 14 and 16, 1874, and formulated a platform for consolidation.

> Zion carried out her part of the agreement. To make the final consolidation the more convenient she agreed to meet in Washington, where the other body had agreed to meet; she also changed the date of sitting of the General Conference, as may be seen by the following resolution (p. 50, *Minutes of the General Conference,* 1864):
> *Resolved,* That the rule for the sitting of the General Conference on the "last Wednesday in May" be suspended, and the "first Wednesday in May" be substituted. [8]

The A.M.E. Zion people ratified the platform and the General Conference of 1868 confirmed it. At the A.M.E. Zion General Conference of 1868, a resolution on this matter was offered by Rev. J. J. Moore and adopted, after this body had been officially informed by a committee of the A.M.E. Church that they were not prepared to unite with Zion on the plan agreed upon by the convention of the two connections held at Philadelphia:

> ... *Whereas,* They decline uniting on the basis agreed upon, but now ask us to meet with them to unite on some other basis or plan; and
> *Whereas,* Our people in adopting the plan proposed by the said convention did it in good faith and did not authorize us to offer or accept any other plan; therefore
> *Resolved,* That we deem it inexpedient to meet with them according to their proposal. [9]

The A.M.E. Church sent a committee of five ministers to the A.M.E. Zion General Conference, who subsequently reported on the action of their church, stating in substance that:

> ... *Whereas,* There are certain propositions laid down by said convention which were submitted to the people, giving the interval of four years to canvass and take the votes of the people in the several portions of both connections; and
> *Whereas,* There has not been that fullness of the members of our church which is their right; and

6. *Ibid.,* pp. 90-91.
7. Moore, History, pp. 234-235.
8. *Ibid.,* pp. 91-92.
9. Moore, *History,* p. 258.

Whereas, Those congregations which have voted on the subject have expressed a willingness for union, but are averse to the general plan put forth by the convention; therefore be it

Resolved, That this body do not deem it politic or wise in us to form a consolidation on the basis laid down by the conventions of 1864, lest we interfere with the interests of our church and create dissatisfaction among our own members. [10]

They expressed a willingness to meet with the members of the A.M.E. Zion Church and arrange a new plan of union that they felt would be agreeable to both connections. After the completion of the A.M.E. Church Committee report, the A.M.E. Zion General Conference took the following action:

Whereas, The A.M.E. Bethel General Conference say in their communication or document that while they are willing for a union, they are not ready to unite upon the platform agreed upon by the convention in Philadelphia in 1864; therefore,

Resolved, That the whole matter lay on the table until 1872. [11]

This action, which had taken place on Tuesday, May 19, prompted a sinewy editorial in the official organ of the A.M.E. Zion Church, *The Zion's Standard and Weekly Review,* on May 20, 1868, an extract of which stated:

The A.M.E. Zion Connection, having carefully kept within the bounds of the Platform as agreed upon by the two Connections, comes forward to make good her agreement and say—"we are *ready,*" ready to unite upon one common platform. We are ready to make common cause with you for the upbuilding of the Church of Christ. *We are ready* to meet the demands of the People; for the good of the People, *we are ready* to sacrifice all our own interests, views, differences and mode of electing Executives, that the cause of Christ and His people shall be advanced here on earth. *We are ready* to meet with you and to sacrifice our connectional name, that we may present to the world a UNITED AFRICAN METHODIST CHURCH IN AMERICA, and the response is for THE ADOPTION OF A NEW PLATFORM": to this we demur; to this our Connection demurs. We now leave the matter, and let it never be said, that Zion was the cause of the future division between the A.M.E. and A.M.E. Zion Connections, for WE WERE READY. [12]

The 1868 General Conference was practically devoted to matters of union. From this action, the General Conference entered immediately into consideration of a plan of union between the Methodist Episcopal Church (northern division) and the A.M.E. Zion Church. The apostle of Christian unity of the A.M.E. Zion Church, bishop-elect Singleton T. Jones, was the spearhead in effecting efforts of union between Zion and Bethel, and afterwards between Zion and the Methodist Episcopal Church. He was sent as the delegate of the A.M.E. Zion General Conference to the General Conference of the Methodist Episcopal Church, on a mission requested of the A.M.E. Zion General Conference and the acceptance of the Methodist Conference by telegraphic communication. He was elected a bishop in his absence, while he was on this mission in Chicago. Before making his own spellbinding address to that body, he presented the address of the African Methodist Episcopal Zion Church as follows:

To the Bishops of the Methodist Episcopal Church—Greetings:

I am instructed by the General Conference of the African Methodist Episcopal Zion Church in America to say, that the M.E. Church is still

10. *Ibid.,* pp. 259-261.
11. *Ibid.,* p. 261.
12. S. T. Jones, *Report Made by the Delegate on Affiliation and Union Between the M.E. Church and the A.M.E. Zion Church. . .and the Failure of the Union Project,* p. 16.

regarded the mother of our organization, and that, as we were induced to leave her, simply because she made a distinction among her children which seriously affected our interests, we are ready to return, if we can be assured that no invidious distinction will be made in regard to us.

We are ready, therefore, to enter into arrangements by which to affiliate on the basis of equality, and to become one and inseparable, now and forever.

Aside from the condition of full equality with the most favored of the Church, we desire the further stipulation that a sufficient number of those whom we may select to exercise the Episcopal oversight of the colored element of the body may be set apart to that office, on the basis of perfect equality with all other bishops of the Methodist Episcopal Church.

As we have practically demonstrated that a lay representation, especially in the law-making department of the Church, is at once sound, safe, and productive of harmony among the people, we hope, if at all compatible with your views of religious progress, that you will adopt the same as the rule of the Church. [13]

Bishop Jones' address was felicitous and was received with marked enthusiasm. The *Chicago Daily Republican* stated:

One of the most interesting incidents in connection with the Methodist General Conference, now in session in this city, was the speech of Bishop Jones before the Conference. . . . His remarks elicited the most enthusiastic applause. Mr. Jones' proposition is that his church is ready to come into communion with the Methodist Episcopal Church on terms of perfect equality. It is difficult to see how the M.E. Church can refuse to accept these colored brethren on the terms they propose. It cannot, in conscience or reason, ask them to come in on any other terms if it believes in the language of Bishop Jones, that a man is a man, and a Christian is a Christian, irrespective of the color of the skin. [14]

Two committee meetings were held on this matter at the General Conference following bishop-elect Jones' address. At the third committee meeting, Bishop Jones presented a five-point manifesto of "Stipulations of Affiliation and Union Between The M.E. And A.M.E. Zion Church." A report was to be made later in the session in harmony with these stipulations. In the report presented to the body on Monday, May 25, it was evident that time was needed to study the plan. They therefore resolved the following:

. . . That this Conference entertain favorably the proposal of union between the two bodies aforesaid. . . .

That whereas the time of the sessions of these two Conferences is so far spent that it will be impracticable to have the necessary negotiations and to discuss and determine the details of the terms of union before their adjournment, that eight members of this Body be appointed, who, with the Bishops, shall constitute a Commission to meet and confer with a similar Commission of the A.M.E. Zion Church, and report to the next General Conference. . . .

That a copy of the foregoing action of this body be given to the delegate, and by him be forwarded to the General Conference of the A.M.E. Zion Church. [15]

There was opposition to the report; however, on May 26 it was adopted by a very larger majority. On returning to the A.M.E. Zion General Conference still in session at Washington, D.C., bishop-elect Jones made his report on May 29. "The

13. *Ibid.,* p. 6.
14. J. W. Smith, *Sermons and Addresses of Bishop S. T. Jones,* p. xiv.
15. S.T. Jones, *Report on Affiliation. . .* p. 9.

Report was unanimously adopted; the thanks of the Conference was voted to the Delegate for his highly successful mission, and a Commission consisting of eight members of the Conference and Board of Bishops was ordered and appointed." The names of the two Commissions were to be published in the *Zion Standard and Weekly Review,* with the time and place of meeting, as soon as they could be obtained from the secretary of the Board of Bishops of the M.E. Church. [16]

The A.M.E. Zion Church at that time was the only Methodist body, with the exception of the Methodist Protestants, that had lay representation in its law-making body, which could have been a hindrance, in both instances, to immediate union. However, this plan of union with the Methodist Episcopal Church failed principally because of the crisis through which the black race and church were passing during this Reconstruction era. The Board of Bishops so expressed its sentiment against union with the M.E. Church in its Episcopal Address of 1872. The bishops afterwards stated in 1880:

> The propositions coming from leading men in that church looked so fair and honorable, that we did not guard our people sufficiently against being misled by them; the result was that they took advantage of the situation to proselyte our people, and we found ourselves worse off at the end of this negotiation than at the beginning, with nothing gained except a little dear bought experience. [17]

African Methodism then encountered stiff competition. The public concern of the unsettled South after Emancipation had its eye on the race in politics, business, education, and religion. Religion, as in all ages, was one of the deep concerns of the movements affecting the relationship of the races and the destiny of the black people in general. The rapid success of both the Bethel and Zion Connections, both African church movements from the North, were not a little disturbing to Southern church people, particularly nationally governed bodies. A number of black leaders of the Methodist Episcopal Church in the South came in on this wave of Southern unrest. The white Southerners were not satisfied to have these organizations headed by Northern blacks working in the South, over whom they had little or no influence or control.

Some of the black leaders in the Southern wing of Methodism, themselves desiring to be leaders of their own people in the South, conferred with leaders of the Methodist Episcopal Church, South, whom they knew to be susceptible of organizing a Negro branch of Methodism in the South. They coveted such control of Southern Negroes upon a segregated basis, such as Mother Methodism had retained by keeping the Negroes in their membership in this circumscribed form, especially in their Southern missions.

In 1966, provision was made by the Methodist Episcopal Church, South for organizing these free Negroes into a separate and distinct body, if they so desired, over a four-year period. "It was further determined that should the time arrive when the Negro members should be so set apart, all the property intended for the use of such members, held by the trustees of the Methodist Episcopal Church, South, should be transferred to duly qualified trustees of the new organization." [18] Meanwhile, many of the black congregations were voting themselves into the A.M.E. and A.M.E. Zion churches, which property they felt they had more than paid for through "blood, sweat and tears." Bishop Lomax

16. *Ibid.,* pp. 9-12; Moore, *History,* pp. 271-272.
17. *Minutes,* Sixteenth Quadrennial Session, p. 52.
18. Woodson, *The History of the Negro Church,* p. 173.

brought out the fact in the 1892 General Conference that there were "colored Methodist churches in the South organized by and deeded to free colored people long prior to the organization of colored Methodist churches in the North, and these churches now formed a part of Zion connection." [19]

The new Negro group secured 80,000 members and was set apart as a separate and distinct organization, known as the Colored Methodist Episcopal Church, by the Methodist Episcopal Church, South, in December 1870. They selected a man from the A.M.E. Zion Church, William Henry Miles of Kentucky, and another from the A.M.E. Church, R. L. Vanderhorst of South Carolina, to be consecrated their first bishops. The territories of the African churches from which these men broke their denominational ties were deeply affected. Church divisions and property losses ensued. The two African churches in particular felt it because of the specialized basis of the Colored Methodist Episcopal Church.

The organization and protracted growth of the C.M.E. Church was one of the major influences that fomented a second serious effort of church union on behalf of the two African Methodist churches, in 1884. Both the A.M.E. and A.M.E. Zion General Conferences, and other official bodies, had continuously advocated union between the churches since 1872, either by way of bishops' episcopal addresses, committee reports, or conference discussions.

T. Thomas Fortune, a remarkable journalist and member of Mother Zion Church, made an effort to boost the cause in these two churches. On the second day of the A.M.E. Zion General Conference, meeting in New York City, he addressed the body, stating:

> ... Methodism is the same the world over, that being true and without disparaging other religious sects. . . . Religion is religion, but Methodism is the religion I believe in. . . . I believe in it, and have some enthusiasm on the subject of union of all branches of this faith.
>
> I urged recently, in the *Globe,* a union of all the colored Methodist bodies. I would like to see the General Conference in Baltimore (A.M.E.), impressed with that spirit, and I wish you would seriously consider the matter. I have come to the conclusion that our moral and religious interests are to be advanced by ourselves. Just as Africa is to be civilized from within and not from without, when it is done, as it will be in the divine providence of God. Solidify your forces. Talk the matter over among yourselves and others. . . . Our forces are divided and we should unite them, because our people generally are poor. . . . When we divide our strength, we weaken our efforts. I would like for you to consider the question of union. . . .[20]

The Hon. John C. Dancy, Bishops Singleton T. Jones, J. W. Hood, J. P. Thompson, Revs. Jehu Holliday and N. H. Williams all responded illuminatingly to Mr. Fortune's speech, favoring union in general, and with the A.M.E. Church in particular. Bishop Jones stated that if stepping down from a bishop to a probationer would unite the colored Methodists, he would be willing to become a probationer "tomorrow"; for the man "who could not sacrifice his official position for the union of this people, strong as it would make them, has been wrongly selected and is not the man for the place." [21]

Mr. Fortune then left the Zion General Conference and journeyed to Baltimore, where the A.M.E. General Conference was in session. On May 21, 1884, a telegram was read by Bishop Hood from T. Thomas Fortune while

19. *Minutes,* Nineteenth Quadrennial Session, p. 87.
20. *Minutes,* Seventeenth Quadrennial Session, pp. 13-14.
21. *Ibid.,* pp. 14-17.

attending the A.M.E. General Conference, "stating that the said General Conference had appointed a committee of ten on Organic Union with the A.M.E. Zion Church." Whereupon the General Conference ordered a similar committee to confer with the Committee of the A.M.E. Conference. The A.M.E. Zion Committee was appointed as follows:

Rev. J. C. Price (North Carolina Conference)
Rev. R. R. Morris (New England Conference)
Rev. Jehu Holliday (Allegheny Conference)
Rev. Jacob Thomas (New York Conference)
Hon. John C. Dancy (North Carolina Conference)
Rev. C. C. Pettey (East [Central] Alabama Conference)
Rev. I. C. Clinton (South Carolina Conference)
Rev. S. S. Wales (East Alabama Conference)
Rev. J. S. Cowles (Philadelphia and Baltimore Conference)
Rev. A. J. Warner (Kentucky Conference)

Bishop Singleton T. Jones and Bishop J. W. Hood were added to the committee upon the request of the chairman, Rev. J. C. Price. [22] This was the beginning of nine years onerous labors of what seemed to be an unrestrained attempt between churches to unite.

The two committees worked out a plan. "In 1885 the union was prevented by the failure of the Bishops to submit to the people the platform agreed upon by the Joint Commission of the two churches." [23] The action of the A.M.E. Zion General Conference of 1888 on union was positively affirmed in the committee's report, deliberative sessions, and the Quadrennial Episcopal Address. Bishop Lomax read the Episcopal Address, "which was heard with continued attention until the paragraph was reached referring to Union, which called forth prolonged applause and numerous calls for second reading. The Bishop repeated the paragraph with much emphasis, and continued until the very able document was completed, the strength of which can be better realized by its careful perusal." This section of the address was evidently mistakenly omitted in the printed minutes by the compilers. "After the entire address was read, "a motion was made by Dr. J. C. Dancy that the part of the address referring to union be adopted, and the remainder referred to appropriate committees. [24]

From this General Conference the commissions appointed by the 1884 General Conferences of both churches continued their rational efforts to effect union. The meetings which took place between the two commissions while gathered together for the Second Ecumenical Conference in Washington, D.C., October 1891, was of the most compatible and thriving nature. "Twenty-three out of twenty-four agreed on a basis of union, which was submitted," stated the chairman of our Commission, Dr. Price at the A.M.E. Zion General Conference of 1892; "but the Board did not agree on a name, and hence the whole matter fell into a prolonged silence until the meeting of the Ecumenical Conference." [25] It was agreed, however, at this conference, that unification was necessary. Stimulated by the progress of this meeting, Bishop C. R. Harris offered a resolution signed by him and Bishop J. W. Hood at the 1892 General Conference as follows:

22. *Ibid.*, pp. iii, 103.
23. *Minutes*, Forty-Third Session, Allegheny Annual Conference, pp. 29-30.
24. *Minutes*, Eighteenth Quadrennial Session, pp. 27-40, 68-69, 102-103.
25. *Minutes*, Nineteenth Quadrennial Session, p. 58.

Whereas, A large majority of the African Methodist Episcopal Zion and of the African Methodist Episcopal Churches are desirous for the union of these two great bodies of Methodism; therefore, be it

Resolved. 1. That we send a delegate to the General Conference of the African Methodist Episcopal Church now in session in Philadelphia, Pa., to express our readiness to confer with them as to the appointment at once of a Commission on Organic Union, if they favor such a movement; said commission to consist of seven members (or more), together with a similar commission to be appointed by this body, which shall arrange a basis of union between the two Churches aforenamed.

2. That said commission, if appointed, shall sit in Harrisburg, Pa., or at some other place convenient of access, for a period not exceeding six days from the time of their appointment, at the end of which time the basis of union, if agreed upon, shall be presented to the two General Conferences now in session.

3. In case both of the General Conferences shall adopt the basis of union thus presented, or as it may be modified by concurrent action of both bodies, the said basis shall be submitted to all the Annual and Quarterly Conferences of both churches; and upon being ratified by a majority vote in all the Annual Conferences, and by three fourths of all the Quarterly Conferences in each connection, the union shall be declared effected and a United General Conference called by a joint session of the Board of Bishops of the two Churches. [26]

Bishop Hood moved that the rules be suspended in favor of immediate consideration of the subject. After some discussion on the matter of union, the Conference voted 92 to 49 in favor of the resolution. [27] The plan met with complete favor of the A.M.E. General Conference. After each General Conference exchanged correspondence by telegrams, it was voted by the A.M.E. Zion General Conference to extend its session until May 25, "in order to carry out the proposition made by the A.M.E. General Conference," and to give a chance for both General Conferences to act upon the report of the commissioners. The commissioners met at the Wesley Union A.M.E. Zion Church in Harrisburg, May 20, while the General Conferences were still in session, and harmoniously agreed upon total conditions of union to be submitted to their respective church bodies.

The A.M.E. Zion Commission presented the basis of union to the General Conference, which was adopted by this body, and then submitted the following report:

In view of the proceedings and action of the joint commission of the two churches, the African Methodist Episcopal and the African Methodist Episcopal Zion, we, the members representing the latter, do recommend that, as in all constitutional elements the commission decided the two churches are virtually one, all statutory provisions be relegated to the United General Conference for adjustment.

"Since it was also agreed, by a vote of twenty-two to two, that the name of the united body be "The African-Zion Methodist Episcopal Church," we agree upon the basis of union already adopted by both General Conferences. [28]

(Signed: C. R. Harris, chairman, J. C. Dancy, secretary, F. Killingsworth, N. J. Green, E. H. Curry, W. H. Goler, F. M. Jacobs, A. Walters, C. C. Pettey, G. W. Offley, A. J. Warner, commissioners.)

26. *Ibid.,* p. 57.
27. *Ibid.,* pp. 57-58.
28. *Ibid.,* pp. 114-115, 128.

From all indications of minutes and records available, the bishops of the A.M.E. Zion Church were in full accord with the plan, and presented the matter, as agreed upon, within the year to their various annual conferences and churches for action. We note from several annual conference minutes, the bishops for the most part were enthusiastic in presenting the matter to the annual conferences, usually through their episcopal addresses. For instance, at the California Annual Conference meeting at San Jose, January 11-14, 1893, Bishop Alexander Walters made the following statement in his Episcopal Address:

> One of the most important questions which has ever been presented to Colored Methodism is the organic union of the A.M.E. Zion and A.M.E. Churches. This matter was submitted to the general conferences of the two churches at their last sessions. By an almost unanimous vote they agreed to submit to the Annual-Quarterly Conferences and churches the following name as the title of the United Church: "African—Zion Methodist Episcopal Church." A Joint session of the Boards of Bishops of the two churches met in Washington, D.C., in July, 1892, and prepared terms of union, etc., which will be submitted to this conference ere it adjourns. When an affirmative vote has been taken by a majority of all the annual and quarterly conferences, and two-thirds of all the churches, these two churches shall be declared one. A joint meeting of the Bishops will then be called to issue a call for a United General Conference, which shall consummate the Union. I am glad to inform you that every annual conference of both churches that has met since the joint meeting of the Boards has voted in favor of such a union. God grant that the good work may go on. I believe the Lord is in the movement hence, I believe in its final consummation. [29]

The results of the votes, 1892-1893, were published in the 1896 A.M.E. Zion General Conference minutes by churches, quarterly conferences, and annual conferences. A vast majority in every instance voted to unite with the A.M.E. Church. By churches, out of 6,891 votes, 6,048 voted in the affirmative while 843 voted negatively. By quarterly conferences, 2,616 voted affirmatively and 363 voted negatively. In the annual conferences, out of the 1,569 registered members, 1,512 voted in the affirmative while 57 voted in the negative. [30]

Most likely the constituents of the A.M.E. Church, wherever submitted, voted in the affirmative, according to Bishop Walters. Our Bishop Hood states that the responsibility for the failure of this union plan lies with the bishops of the A.M.E. Church, who divided on the subject. He felt that Bishops Daniel A. Payne, Wesley J. Gaines, James A. Handy and Abraham Grant were sincerely in favor of the union and made cogent efforts, however some other bishops and delegates strongly opposing it seemed to have been the forceful and decisive factors. [31]

Although there were similar attempts on behalf of the A.M.E. Church to lay the blame on Zion, neither group could present *bona fide* or justifiable reasons for the actual failure. So disenchanted was the A.M.E. Zion Church over the failure that she refused to make any pronouncement whatsoever on the subject of union at her 1896 General Conference, even though she had fraternal delegates of the mother and sister churches and received their speeches cordially. This seems to be the only General Conference since the beginning of these talks where the subject of organic union was not mentioned. Perhaps the most disillusioned leader was

29. *Minutes,* Twenty-Fifth Annual Session, California Conference, p. 5.
30. *Minutes,* Twentieth Quadrennial Session, pp. 229-234.
31. Hood, *One Hundred Years,* pp. 92, 153.

Bishop C. R. Harris, introducer of the idea, chairman of the new A.M.E. Zion Commission, and ardent promoter who made a lengthy plea for union in the Allegheny Conference prior to taking the vote of the conference. He said:

> Thus far well. We have avoided the rocks upon which other schemes of Union have split. But we have not yet reached the Port. . . . I entreat you to work zealously in favor of Union and allay whatever of strife may exist in any part of this Conference District. When this Union is effected, we shall doubtless soon be joined by the C.M.E. Church and by the large number of colored members in the Methodist Episcopal Church. [32]

J. Harvey Anderson predicted that it would not be likely that the A.M.E. Zion Church would take the initiative in proposals for organic union again unless "the profoundest impulses are aroused by a most favorable prospect for success. As regards the recent efforts to secure the Organic Union of the A.M.E. and A.M.E. Zion churches," he stated, "a profound and ominous silence has taken the place of sensational enthusiasm and wild Union desire." [33]

Striking was the urgency for union in spite of our disappointment. At the 1900 General Conference there began a courtship of the African Methodist Episcopal Zion Church and the Colored Methodist Episcopal Church on organic union.

The severe need and self-defense of the freedman's growth in the battle for full citizenship, education developments, and economic enterprise warranted race solidarity and unity on behalf of its strongest force, the black church. The three major black Methodist churches had the potential of unity, being of one doctrine and the same polity, but lacked the vision of what unity in religion would do for the race.

The appointment of an A.M.E. Zion Commission of 18 members at the 1900 General Conference was the result of a suggestion on the part of Rev. M. T. Jamison, the fraternal messenger to the General Conference from the C.M.E. Church. At the General Conference of the C.M.E. Church, which convened in Nashville, Tenn., May 1902, a similar commission was appointed. The joint commissions of these two churches met in Israel C.M.E. Church, Washington, D.C., October 7, 1902, and drew up Articles of Agreement to be submitted to the next two general conferences. The Board of Bishops of the A.M.E. Zion Church presented the Articles of Agreements to the General Conference of 1904 and stated that: We believe that we voice the sentiment of the General Conference when we assert that we are prepared to stand by the articles as signed by our commissioners and recommend them to your most favorable consideration. [34]

However, while this negotiation was in process, the fraternal messengers: Rev. R. R. Downs of the A.M.E. Church to the A.M.E. Zion General Conference, and Rev. W. H. Anderson of the A.M.E. Zion Church to the A.M.E. General Conference made impassioned speeches in behalf of unity in the 1904 General Conferences. Bishop C. R. Harris' vital expressed interest on the subject, and a proposition of the A.M.E. General Conference of producing a joint hymn book and catechism for Negro Methodists sent to the A.M.E. Zion General Conference and signed by Bishops W. B. Derrick, Bynum W. Arnett and L. H. Reynolds, all opened the first door of unity among the three families of black Methodists. [35]

32. *Minutes,* Forty-Third Session, Allegheny Annual Conference, 1892, pp. 32-33.
33. Anderson, *Official Directory,* p. 45.
34. *Minutes,* Twenty-Second Quadrennial Session, pp. 148-150.
35. *Ibid.,* pp. 258, 411-412, 413-423.

The Board of Bishops of the A.M.E. Zion Church stated the situation to the General Conference of 1908 as follows:

Since we last met, the subject of Church Federation has received more than usual attention among all denominations, and in every stronghold of Protestantism. After correspondence and an interchange of views as to the advisability as to holding a joint council of the Bishops of the C.M.E., A.M.E., and A.M.E. Zion churches, which originated with Bishops C. R. Harris of our church and R. S. Williams of the C.M.E. Church, and later the Senior bishops of the above named churches, an agreement was reached which resulted in a joint meeting of all the Bishops of the C.M.E., A.M.E., and A.M.E. Zion churches in the Metropolitan A.M.E. Church, Washington, D.C., February 12-17 of this year.

All of the bishops of the above named churches were present except Bishop James A. Handy of the A.M.E. Church and Bishop Thomas H. Lomax of the A.M.E. Zion Church.* The meeting was a most harmonious and a fruitful one, and the proceedings thereof received the hearty approval of your chief pastors and the many brethren of our church who were present. A report of said joint Council of Bishops will be submitted to you by Bishop Alexander Walters, the Secretary of our Board. We commend the same to your favorable consideration and we hope that you may take such action as this important matter demands. [36]

Elsewhere in the same address, the bishops stated the objectives as follows:

The joint meeting of the bishops of the A.M.E. Zion, A.M.E., and C.M.E. Churches resulting in a plan of federation among the chief pastors of these energetic branches of the great Methodist family, and the adoption of an agreement which provides for a common hymnal and catechism and a uniform service and other commendable propositions stand out among the notable doings of the quadrennium. [37]

This meeting was the formal organization of the Tri-Federation Council of Bishops of the A.M.E., A.M.E. Zion, and C.M.E. Churches, as it was later called. The goals set forth in this and subsequent meetings of this black Methodist triumvirate, with careful, painstaking, gradual undertakings aroused a large number of its constituents into believing this would most assuredly terminate in a triumphant union.

This tri-federation held its second meeting at Big Zion A.M.E. Zion Church, Mobile, Ala., February 9-12, 1911. "A declaration strongly favoring organic union was adopted." [38] The A.M.E. Zion bishops reported in their address of 1912:

Concord and peace dwelt in our midst. Fraternal ties are being drawn closer and closer. These three churches understand each other as never before. Let us hope that we shall ever go on in this good way. We still intend to bring out the common hymn and tune book.

That we will not receive preachers from other churches unless they come recommended by the Bishop. That the *Christian Recorder, Star of Zion,* and *Christian Index* be exchanged with the Bishops of each church gratis. That we shall get out a common form of service and catechism. [39]

Progress continued. Therefore, when the third Tri-Federation Council of Bishops met at Chestnut Street C.M.E. Church, Louisville, Ky., February 16-17, 1918, it appointed a commission of three bishops, three elders, and three laymen

36. Episcopal Quadrennial Address, 1908, p. 27; *Both bishops were absent due to illness.
37. *Ibid.,* p. 9.
38. Roy W. Trueblood, "Union Negotiations. . .," *Methodist History,* July 1970, p. 23; Smith, *A History of the African Methodist Episcopal Church,* p. 289.
39. *Minutes,* Twenty-Fourth Quadrennial Session, pp. 145-146.

from each church to formulate plans for effecting union and set the commission meeting for Birmingham, Alabama the first week in April.[40] The commission met accordingly and proceeded to draw up concrete plans for uniting the three churches. "The Birmingham Plan of Organic Union" had met the approval of all concerned, and was to be voted upon by the General Conference of the C.M.E. Church in Chicago, May 1918, and the General Conferences of the A.M.E. and A.M.E. Zion churches in St. Louis and Knoxville respectively, in May 1920. The A.M.E. Zion Board of Bishops presented the matter to the General Conference, first by way of its Episcopal Address as follows:

    . . . A committee was appointed on ways and means composed of three bishops, three elders, and three laymen from each church, which met in Birmingham, Alabama, April 7, 1918, and unanimously agreed on the basis for the union. Their report will be represented at this session of our General Conference for action. The C.M.E. General Conference meeting in Chicago in 1918 adopted the basis and agreed to unite. It remains to see what action will be taken at our General Conference and the General Conference of the A.M.E. Church which is meeting at this time at St. Louis, Mo. In February of this year, the bishops of the A.M.E. and A.M.E. Zion churches met in Baltimore in their semi-annual meeting, Episcopal courtesies were extended on the part of our Board by a formal visit, and these courtesies were reciprocated by the A.M.E. bishops. There was no attempt at holding a joint meeting, and yet the sentiment created in favor of organic union was more potential than on any previous occasion. The frank and clerical greetings, the recognition of each other as equals, the general repudiation of the ideas of the old school which have prevented union hitherto, the forceful enthusiastic speeches made in favor of the union, the minimizing of the reasons why we should not, and the cogency of the reasoning why we should be united, culminated in a veritable love-feast and an informal wedding of the two great Methodist bodies together. The sentiment formulated in favor of organic union became so irresistible that it obliterated what little pessimism there was, and every bishop on both sides was convinced of the feasibility of unification of these three large bodies of Negro Methodists. Your Board of Bishops hold the opinion that organic union of the A.M.E., and A.M.E. Zion and C.M.E. Branches of the Methodist family should be effected:—

    First, because our doctrines are the same, and the little difference in polity can easily be adjusted.

    Second, because in a very large measure we cover the same territory, and thus it would obviate the overlapping of areas.

    Third, for economic reasons in running the machinery of the church.

    Fourth, because of the increased efficiency it would add in the crystalizing sentiment politically in favor of our race.

    Fifth, for the salutory effect it would have upon the economic, religious, and business life of the Negro in America, in the Isles of the seas and in Africa. [41]

After the Episcopal Address had been read, Bishop J.S. Caldwell read a telegram from the A.M.E. General Conference in session at St. Louis, "to the effect that the plan for Organic Union had been adopted without a dissenting vote. On motion by Bishop Caldwell it was decided that on Friday at 11 o'clock the vote be taken on the plan for Organic Union." On the following day, Bishop G. W. Clinton presented Dr. S. G. Atkins to read the plan for organic union of the

40. *The Star of Zion,* February 28, 1918, p. 2.
41. *Minutes,* Twenty-Sixth Quadrennial Session, pp. 61-62.

three churches. A motion was then offered by Dr. F. M. Jacobs seconded by Dr. W. L. Hamblin that the document as read be adopted. "Bishop L. W. Kyles, representing the Commission and speaking for the adoption of the plan, delivered an able, eloquent and convincing address. Drs. T. J. Moppins, B. G. Shaw, and G. L. White spoke briefly. The motion to adopt the plan was passed by a vote of 378 for and 5 against." [42]

The plan thus being voted favorably by the three General Conferences was sent to the annual conferences of the three churches to be voted upon. The plan was voted by a large majority of both the A.M.E. and A. M. E. Zion Churches, and decisively defeated by the C.M.E. Church. Here again, the bishops of the A.M.E. Zion Church refused to discuss the basis of the failure in 1924, but only stated that:

> The A.M.E. Zion Church has never varied in her attitude or defaulted in her obligations regarding organic union. We had even hoped that the Negro Methodists of America might lead the Methodists of the world in organic union and set the example for other religious bodies. That organic union of Negro Methodists in America has not been effected is no fault of the A.M.E. Zion Church.[43]

After the C.M.E. General Conference in 1918, Bishop C. H. Phillips led the opposition toward the Birmingham plan by drawing up 14 objections to it, printing and circulating them throughout the church, and travelling across the country preaching against it. His chief objection was that "the so-called plan was no plan at all. The denominations were asked to sign a blank check, to agree to unite and trust the negotiators to work out the terms of agreement later. Phillips wanted the terms of agreement worked out before union was negotiated. He was convinced that no valid plan for union could be produced in one day. . . . He was not willing to see the efforts of his spiritual forebears go down the drain. He also feared the power of the A.M.E. Church, largest of the three. . . . The rights of the minority in such a union must be protected and the Birmingham Plan offered no such guarantees."[44]

Bishop Phillips was aware that the two sister churches would place the blame on him and the C.M.E. Church for the failure of the union plan and wrote:

> . . . the author entertains the opinion that the failure at unification was far more pleasing than displeasing to the other two churches, and so the way out is just to make the Colored Methodist Episcopal Church the scapegoat, place the failure for union upon her symbolical head and dismiss the subject without remorse or tears.[45]

The leaders of the A.M.E. Zion Church, in a determined attempt to carry through the union plan, continued meeting with leaders of the A.M.E. Church, and the bishops of the A.M.E. Zion Church submitted its alternate proposal for union with the A.M.E. Church to the 1928 General Conference, and a recommendation to be passed upon by this body. In the address they stated:

> . . . Our Zion has never refused the proffered hand of a sister denomination. Our annual conference registered a large majority for the union as did the annual conferences of the African Methodist Episcopal Church. Unfortunately the conferences of the Colored Methodist Episcopal Church saw fit to turn down the proposed union, and have not shown interest

42. *Ibid.*, pp. 80, 94.
43. *Minutes,* Twenty-Seventh Quadrennial Session, pp. 115-116.
44. Trueblood, *op. cit.,* pp. 24-25.
45. *Ibid.;* C. H. Phillips, *The History of the Colored Methodist Episcopal Church in America* p. 537.

since. Not so with Zion and Bethel, for each has continuously and consistently appointed commissions authorized to treat with others looking toward organic union. In the present quadrennium these two commissions acting with the knowledge and consent of their respective Boards and Councils of Bishops, and in the full glare of public scrutiny, and we believe with Divine approval have formulated and do now submit the most advanced and comprehensive basis and plan for unification ever to come before our General Conferences. Said plan will be duly presented to this august assembly, and we ask for it your most careful and prayerful action. We commend it as a great forward step for the good and safety of the African race in America and in Africa, as a beacon light for the Methodist family in the world, and as a most heartening and convincing call to the divided family of Christ everywhere. We see in it the harbinger of racial recognition in the United States, and we offer it as our answer to the Saviour's prayer for a united Church.

Recommendation:

We recommend the Organic Union of the African Methodist Episcopal and the African Methodist Episcopal Zion Churches as provided in the plan submitted by the Joint Commission on Organic Union of said churches. We consider this the logical and Providential step toward a United Negro Methodism. We ask such careful and prayerful consideration as will bring about this action.[46]

The 1929 Depression slowed down the effort. The A.M.E. Zion Church, however, continued its interlocution with the A.M.E. Church, and at the 1932 General Conference, called the delegates' attention to this recession of the plan. The organic union committee thus recommended the following:

We are advised that the Bishops of the African Methodist Episcopal Church recommended the completion of the vote by their local congregations on said Organic Union. In view of the fact that our local congregations did not vote on the propositions, we recommend that the Board of Bishops authorize the Commission on Organic Union to submit the proposition of Organic Union with the African M.E. Church to the local congregations in accordance with the action taken by the General Conference on this proposition in 1928.[47]

The General Conference voted affirmatively to unite with the A.M.E. Church, after the bishops made a similar plea, and the matter was once again submitted to the annual conferences of the two connections for consideration. The A.M.E. Zion Church again voted for it by a majority, but it was not acted upon by the ensuing General conference. [48] From this time forward, the three churches made only sympathetic expressions of organic union, keeping up compatible relationships through continuous fraternal association and messages, but not enlivening union ideas again until 1964.

During some preliminary meetings of the executive committee of the World Methodist Council, the senior bishops of these three churches (Sherman L. Greene, A.M.E.; William J. Walls, A.M.E. Zion; and Bertram W. Doyle, C.M.E.) counselled and suggested renewal of the organic union plan. In 1964 the matter was presented to the bishops of the respective churches, who received it with much cordiality and studious attention. On March 31-April 1, 1965 another organization of the Tri-Council of Bishops was revived, with 39 bishops of the

46. *Minutes,* Twenty-Eighth Quadrennial Session, pp. 47-52.
47. *Minutes,* Twenty-Ninth Quadrennial Session, p. 232.
48. *Ibid.,* p. 93.

triad present in St. Louis at Lane Temple C.M.E. Church. A structure similar to that of 1908 was approved; mainly the senior bishops of the three churches were given authority to convoke meetings whenever necessary, as expressed by the leaders of the three denominations. The principal object was to work for an ultimate plan of union of these three churches by spring of 1972. A general commission of 20 members of each church was named. Three meetings were held, similar to those leading up to the Birmingham Plan of 1918. The first meeting was held at Big Bethel A.M.E. Church, Atlanta, December 14-15, 1965. This meeting had as its invited visitor the presence of the martyred Dr. Martin Luther King, Jr., who brought general greetings to the mass assembly on the evening of December 14. Candid discussions on the past present and future of organic union took place, and the bishops and commissions left Atlanta with a general impression of advancement, all looking forward to the next steps which would bring us closer to union.[49]

The Christian Methodist Episcopal Church (which had changed its name from Colored Methodist Episcopal Church in 1954) passed through a General Conference in 1966, and issued its ultimatum to move forward with union of the three churches. The second meeting took place at John Wesley A.M.E. Zion Church, Washington, D.C., December 5 and 6, 1967. The tri-council of bishops, the commissioners, and the committees assembled in large number to continue their work. The entire assembly expressed lamentation over the passing of the esteemed senior bishop of the A.M.E. Church, Bishop Sherman Lawrence Greene, the last of July, 1967. Working committees were appointed by the three churches. An executive committee was made here. Chairmen of the Joint Commission were named instead of senior bishops. Bishops Frederick D. Jordan (A.M.E.), William J. Walls (A.M.E. Zion), and Bertram W. Doyle (with B. Julian Smith, acting in the absence of Bishop Doyle) constituted the approved chairmen of the commission. The two General Conferences of the A.M.E. and A. M.E. Zion Churches met in 1968 and gave their blessings to the work which had been done, and also supported the actions of the tri-council of bishops and commissioners to work out a plan of union for approval by the ensuing General Conferences, ending in May 1972.[50] The A.M.E. Zion General Conference reappointed the following commissioners: Bishops William J. Walls (chairman), Raymond L. Jones, Joseph D. Cauthen, C. Ewbank Tucker. Revs: John H. Miller, John H. Satterwhite, Ruben L. Speaks, Eugene E. Morgan, Jr., John D. McArthur, Mr. W. Mance Gilliam, Revs: John W. Hatch, R. M. Richmond, Charles E. Bourne, Alton C. Hunnicutt, Arthur Marshall, Jr., George L. Blackwell, Durocher L. Blakey, Mrs. Farris A. Williams. Reverends J. Aggrey Smith and Young E. O. Eta, Co-operatives. [51]

The third meeting of the tri-council of bishops, joint commissioners, and committees assembled at Carter Temple C.M.E. Church, Chicago, January 28-29, 1969. Progress reports were made, and there was a quickening spirit on behalf of each group present. Since this time the three churches have continued to talk in amicable terms on the subject, but there have been no further meetings.

Each church is on record with the majority strongly favoring organic union. On one word this entire subject hinges: *Readiness.* Are we ready to give and take, to sink ambitions, and to become Christian in spirit enough to bring these

49. Papers, W. J. Walls files, 1961-1970.
50. *Ibid.*
51. *Minutes,* Thirty-Eighth Quadrennial Session, p. 619.

churches together so that they shall stay together? Is it our intention to try for the advantages of each other or to use each other to obtain advantages of and from each other? The historic answer to these questions has always proven the latter. We have differed, only at points, where one felt that he had the advantage of the other by some point of superiority, or was suspicious each of the other on the insincertiy of leadership.

Can we believe in each other firmly enough? Can we love each other deeply enough? Can we associate amicably with each other persistently enough? Can we treat with each other fairly enough to bring to pass the happy outcome of three connections which have gone their different ways; two for more than a century and three-quarters, and one for more than a century? There is only one thing that can do it, and that will be to center our structures of experience around the Christian myth, which is love and faith combined with God and his Son, Jesus in the midst, and the Holy Spirit giving the guidelines.

Ecumenical Organizations

The seven ecumenical councils held at Nicea, 325; Constantinople, 381; Ephesus, 431; Chalcedon, 451; Constantinople, 553 and 681; and Nicaea, 787 aimed to bring together the different factions in Christendom for the purpose of promoting church unity long before the Protestant movement was born. Then came this ecclesiastical revolution in 1529, initiated by an Augustian monk, Martin Luther, by which a considerable number of European states severed themselves from the Roman Catholic Church and adopted the Protestant beliefs and free church organizations.

In the latter part of the nineteenth century, a modern ecumenical movement originated with Protestant missions, the purpose of which has been cooperation in unity of her capacity and means to serve the kingdom of God more effectively. Though the movement is primarily European and white American dominated, the A.M.E. Zion Church and three or four other independent black churches exemplified a broad spirit of ecumenicity by affiliating and contributing to the ecumenical movement since the beginning of these organizations in the Protestant churches. Black Africa and the West Indies have been widely represented in some organizations from their beginnings, by independent churches, such as the ancient Ethiopic Church, as well as by European-American based churches.

World Methodist Council

When denominations across countries joined in federation and world alliance, the Methodists became the third to so organize; the first being the Anglican Lambeth Conference in 1867; second, the Alliance of Reformed and Presbyterian Churches (now known as World Alliance of Reformed Churches or World Presbyterians) in 1875. The Methodist bodies of the world organized and held its first assembly under the title, Ecumenical Conference, in 1881.

In an assessment of the First Ecumenical Conference held at City Road (Wesleyan) Chapel, London, the *London Times* stated:

The Pan-Anglican Synods at Lambeth probably suggested the Methodist Ecumenical Conference. . . . The Conference is, however, at once narrower and deeper in its basis than the Synod. . . . By the theory of an Episcopal church an assembly of bishops such as has more than once responded to the invitation of the Archbishop of Canterbury has sovereign rights. . . . The four hundred delegates of Methodism disclaim all pretension to be legislators. . . . They are gathered simply to "confer and not consult," as the programme of their convocation stated, "for co-operation, not for consolidation." A Lambeth Synod desires uniformity as its ideal; the Methodist Conference desires, 'not uniformity, but unity. . . . [52]

The following were the representatives of the A.M.E. Zion Church attending this meeting:

Bishop J. W. Hood (Fayetteville, N.C.)
Bishop W. H. Hillery (Pittsburgh, Pa.)
Bishop Joseph P. Thompson (Newburgh, N.Y.)
Prof. William Howard Day (Harrisburg, Pa.)
Rev. J. McH. Farley (Petersburgh, Va.)
Rev. J. C. Price (N.C.)

Bishop S. T. Jones, Revs. J. B. Small, Samuel Wilson, and Wilbur G. Strong were named delegates, but did not attend this meeting. [53] The conference was considered majorly progressive in its proceedings, and exhibited deep Christian courtesy as far as black church leadership was concerned. Bishop L. H. Holsey of the C.M.E. Church, Bishop J. P. Thompson and Rev. J. McH. Farley of the A.M.E. Zion Church, and Bishop Daniel A. Payne of the A.M.E. Church were invited speakers, and Bishop Payne assisted in administering the Lord's Supper and served as one of the secretaries of the conference. [54] Other black church leaders became active participants in the discussions and debates. Bishop J. W. Hood (A.M.E. Zion) made a striking plea for unity in Home missions efforts, [55] and the noted Dr. J. C. Price won his fame as a "world orator" in his eloquent responses and general remarks on vital issues brought forth for the betterment of Methodism. [56] Dr. Price particularly stressed education and missions for blacks in Africa and America. Dr. Price remained in Great Britain a year, lecturing and raising the funds which established Livingstone College.

The Second Ecumenical Conference meeting in Washington, D.C., in October 1891, had increased representation from every communion, as well as additional bodies of Methodists from around the world. [57] Of the 20 named delegates of the A.M.E. Zion Church, 15 were in attendance: Bishops C. R. Harris, J. W. Hood, Thomas H. Lomax, J. J. Moore, C. C. Pettey, Revs. G. W. Clinton, J. S. Cowles, W. H. Day, N. J. Green, R. H. G. Dyson, I. C. Clinton, J. C. Price, Alexander Walters, T. A. Weathington, and the Hon. John C. Dancy. [58]

Participation of black churchmen in the Second Ecumenical Conference was varied, and it appeared that the Conference endeavored to practice comity and equitable relationship on a broad scale. Of the A.M.E. Zion Church, Bishop J. W. Hood was the presiding officer of the first session on the fifth day. Reverend William Howard Day made a major address, Bishops Hood and Harris, Revs. J. C. Price, Alexander Walters, and G. W. Clinton took part in debates and discussions, and John C. Dancy, addressed the Conference on secondary education and was

52. *Proceedings of the Ecumenical Methodist Church, 1881, pp. 619-620.*
53. *Ibid.,* p. xxviii.
54. *Ibid.,* pp. 20, 78-80, 82, 168-170, 290-293, 587.
55. *Ibid.,* pp. 433-434.
56. *Ibid.,* pp. 81-82, 186-187, 219, 511-512.
57. *Official Program and Handbook,* Ecumenical Methodist Conference, 1891, pp. 9-22.
58. *Proceedings of the Second Ecumenical Methodist Conference,* 1891, p. xx.

BISHOP GEORGE CLINTON CLEMENT

Chairman of the Race Relations
Commission of the Federal Council of
Churches of Christ and one of the most
literary men of the church's history.

placed on the Wesley Statue Committee. [59] In this Conference Bishop Hood forthrightly defended the rights of women in church, declaring that:

> The word male was stricken out of our Discipline many years ago, and at a more recent period every restriction removed. So that as far as our church is concerned, woman can go to a General Conference as delegate in common with man. All she needs is to get votes enough to elect her, and she goes. That is the position our Church takes and because it is a fact I wanted it to be stated here,—that there is one Methodist Episcopal Church that guarantees to women all rights in common with men.[60]

At the successive Ecumenical Methodist Conferences (Third, 1901 in London; Fourth, 1911 at Toronto; Fifth, 1921 at London; Sixth, 1931 at Atlanta; and Seventh at Springfield, Mass., 1947, the time of which was changed from the 1941 Conference due to the turbulent conditions of World War II) the three leading black Methodist churches were represented by forceful and able leaders:

A.M.E. Zion: Bishops J. W. Hood, C. R. Harris, I. C. Clinton, T. H. Lomax, Alexander Walters, G. W. Clinton, John B. Small, J. W. Alstork, Josiah S. Caldwell, George L. Blackwell, Andrew J. Warner, Lynwood W. Kyles, George C. Clement, J. W. Wood, P. A. Wallace, E. D. W. Jones, C. C. Alleyne, F. M. Jacobs, W. J. Walls, and Revs. W. O. Carrington, S. G. Spottswood, William A. Blackwell, I, Thomas W. Wallace, M. A. Bradley, Jesse B. Colbert, John F. Moreland, Sr., Raymond L. Jones, James C. Taylor, H. T. Medford, Dr. Simon G. Atkins, John C. Dancy, E. S. Peters, Mrs. Cora E. Burke, Mrs. Annie W. Blackwell, James W. Eichelberger, Mrs. Abbie Clement Jackson, Aaron Brown, Jr.

59. *Ibid.,* pp. 109, 209, 217, 222, 313-314, 319, 645-646.
60. *Ibid.,* p. 313.

A.M.E.: Bishops B. W. Arnett, Henry McNeil Turner, B. T. Tanner, Alexander W. Wayman, Abraham Grant, Benjamin F. Lee, Levi J. Coppin, James A. Handy, Henry B. Parks, C. S. Smith, Joseph S. Flipper, William H. Heard, Cornelius T. Shaffer, Evans Tyree, John F. Hurst, William T. Vernon, Archibald J. Carey, William S. Brooks, Abraham L. Gaines, John H. Clayborn, Reverdy C. Ransom, John A. Gregg, Richard R. Wright, Jr., W. D. Fountain, A. J. Allen, and Sherman L. Greene; Revs. J. C. Embry, Charles H. Wesley, W. W. Wilkes, Prof. J. R. Hawkins, Prof. D. J. Jordan, Rev. J. G. Robinson, and Mrs. Fannie J. Coppin.

C.M.E.: Bishops L. H. Holsey, Isaac Lane, R. S. Williams, Elias Cottrell, Nelson C. Cleaves, Charles H. Phillips, Randall A. Carter, William Y. Bell, H. P. Porter, J. A. Martin, W. A. Womack, J. A. Bray, J. Arthur Hamlett, Luther C. Stewart, B. W. Doyle; Professor C. W. Lane, and Dr. Channing Tobias.

Also attending were such black leaders in the Methodist Episcopal Church as Bishops Isaiah B. Scott, Robert E. Jones, Matthew W. Clair, Alexander P. Shaw, Willis J. King, Robert N. Brooks, and Edward N. Kelly. [61]

These were some of the mighty men and women of the black race in religious, social, and freedom action they were by all means the vanguard of black Methodism in the ecumenical Methodist conferences. At the 1947 Conference, serious efforts were made to establish a permanent structure for the Ecumenical Methodist Council, and the decision was made to hold the conferences every five years instead of every ten years.

At the Eighth Ecumenical Methodist Conference held at Oxford, England, a reorganization was completed and a Permanent Secretariat was set up. The name of the Ecumenical Methodist Conference was changed to the World Methodist Conference, and to give stability and permanence to the organization a World Methodist Council was formed, with an Executive Committee to carry on its functions by annual meetings. [62]

As far as the black race was concerned, the Eighth Ecumenical Methodist Conference retrogressed in its program. While Sherman L. Greene, William J. Walls, and Bertram W. Doyle, bishops of the A.M.E., A.M.E. Zion, and C.M.E. churches respectively were placed on the newly organized Executive Committee to represent these three churches annually at the World Methodist Council meetings, in planning the program of the conference, black church leaders were sidelined. So resentful were the black delegates of the three major black denominations (American based), that they held a protest meeting at Wesley Chapel in the afternoon of September 5, led by Bishops John Gregg, W. J. Walls, and W. A. Womack. Bishop D. Ward Nichols and Dr. Frederick D. Jordan also bitterly protested against the program. Attention was called to this by the writer during the meeting, and when he returned home, he issued a statement to the press:

> The 1951 Ecumenical Methodist Conference, which met at Oxford, England, completely ignored representatives of the Negro churches, according to Bishop W. J. Walls, a delegate to the conference.
>
> He made this statement here in Chicago last week as he returned home from England.
>
> Bishop Walls branded this conference the most segregated of any. He pointed out that at the preceding conference in 1947 two Negroes, Dr.

61. *Proceedings* of the Third, Fourth, Fifth, Sixth, and Seventh Ecumenical Methodist Conferences.
62. *Proceedings of the Ninth World Methodist Conference*, p. 1.

Channing Tobias and Dr. Charles Wesley, were principal speakers. However, during the past meeting, there were no colored persons asked to take a major part in the discussions.

Bishop Walls said:

"The Black world was silent in the World Conference." It was true that there were two leaders of color on the morning worship series: Bishop John Gregg and Bishop B. W. Doyle. But all the social, historical, theological, political and general message interpretations were spoken by white men except one from India.

"It was the most segregated program that the Methodist Ecumenical Conference ever had and created the most general dissatisfaction among people of color who attended."

"The conference this time did not see need to use men and women of color in significant places although we had some of the ablest of race groups present."

On discussing a resolution condemning racial prejudice, Bishop Walls asserted that many delegates felt America and England were against this because of their color problem.

"This conference had not only fallen down in placing the Negro in places of significance, but attempted to smother his achievements for the church by passing over any mention of the black race churches—in speeches assumed to cover fields of American Methodist achievements through its whole history," Bishop Walls added.

"However, the bishop commented, a white delegate, seeing this, made a motion that hereafter Negroes be placed on the program on par with other groups, and asked that it be put in the record so that it would not be forgotten." [63]

At the Ninth World Methodist Conference held at Lake Junaluska, N.C., in 1956, and in the annual Executive Committee meetings, the writer was expressive, with others, on seeking to guarantee untramelled rights for all minorities in the delegation.

At the Tenth World Methodist Conference, Oslo, Norway in 1961, an attempt was made by the nominating committee (the only change proposed among black churches) to drop the writer from the Executive Committee and place another delegate from the A.M.E. Zion Church in the vice-presidency and on the Executive Committee. But the house voted to correct this while the report was being made and the writer was placed back on the Executive Committee for the ensuing quinquennium. [64]

Since this conference there has been no trouble in obtaining fair representation of the black race in the official family of the World Methodist Council, and representation of program participants in the World Methodist Conferences has been satisfactory, barring the neglect of the 1951 Conference.

At Oslo in 1961, Bishop Herbert B. Shaw of the A.M.E. Zion Church was made one of the vice-presidents, representing the black churches, and served two terms in this capacity until 1971. At the Eleventh World Methodist Conference in London, 1966, Bishop Stephen G. Spottswood was placed on the Executive Committee as an additional representative of the A.M.E. Zion Church.

At the Twelfth World Methodist Conference held in Denver, 1971, the World Methodist Council was reconstituted. An eight-member presidium was formed, of

63. *The Chicago Defender,* October 27, 1951; p. 21; *The Afro-American,* September 22, 1951, p. 5; October 27, 1951, p. 18.
64. *Proceedings of the Tenth World Methodist Conference,* p. 57.

which Bishop Herbert B. Shaw was elected a member, the representative of the black American churches. Bishop Prince Taylor, a black bishop of the Methodist Church, was elected President of the World Methodist Conference, and several black leaders were placed in strategic positions of trust.

Representing the A.M. E. Zion Church with adeptness on the programs of the latter conferences were Revs. David H. Bradley, John H. Satterwhite, Arthur Marshall, Jr., Bishops S. G. Spottswood, H. B. Shaw, S. D. Lartey, and Dr. J. W. Eichelberger. Several members of our communion are now serving on strategic permanent committees of the World Methodist Council. [65]

> By reason of its historic and essential nature World Methodism had within itself a truly ecumenical spirit from the first. It was at the beginning of the Methodist movement that John Wesley declared, "I look upon all the world as my parish," and within his lifetime saw Methodist life and work extending beyond national frontiers. But John Wesley also gave expression to the truly Catholic spirit and declared the Methodists to be the "friends of all and the enemy of none." Thus the World Methodist Council has ever in mind the concept of the World Church. [66]

The World Federation of Methodist Women

This organization, which had been in existence a few years, held a special session prior to the World Methodist Conference at Lake Junaluska, N.C., on August 29, 1956, with Mrs. Ottila De O. Chaves presiding. A new proposal had been sent to the different units of Methodist women for their consideration of joining the restructured World Federation of Methodist Women, who voted to become an affiliated organization of the World Methodist Council. This proposal underwent thorough discussion by the delegates and all the explanations necessary were given. It was then put to a vote and voted favorably by the house.

> After the doxology was sung and the President extended an invitation to the duly authorized representatives of other groups to express their desire to become members of the World Federation of Methodist Women, if they care to do so.

> "The representative of the African Methodist Episcopal Zion Church, Mrs. Abbie Clement Jackson, was the first one to rise and, presenting the document that authorized her to vote at this occasion, she declared that the women of her church were ready to join this world-wide fellowship. Others followed and the women of eight Methodist bodies. . . . became members of the World Federation of Methodist Women. They were recognized by the President as voting members of the present Assembly." [67]

The World Federation of Methodist Women is a fellowship of such officially recognized groups of Methodist Women organized on a national basis as will affirm the purpose "to know Christ and make Him known." Aside from the duly consituted officers, the organization included eight area vice-presidents. In 1956, Mrs. Ernst Scholz of Germany was elected president, and Mrs. T. Otto Nall was elected vice-president of the North American area. At the next conference of the World Federation of Methodist Women held in Oslo, Norway, Dr. Abbie Clement Jackson was elected area president for North America, and served one term until the following Conference held in London, 1966.[68] Mrs. Mable M. Jones was

---

65. *Proceedings,* Tenth and Twelfth World Methodist Conferences.
66. *Proceedings of the Ninth World Methodist Conference,* p. 48.
67. *Ibid.,* pp. 50-51.
68. *Ibid.,* p. 57; *Proceedings of the Tenth World Methodist Conference.*

elected by the Executive Board of the Woman's Home and Foreign Missionary Society, as the Official Correspondent of the A.M.E. Zion Church to this world body, and served until 1972. The President of the Woman's Home and Foreign Missionary Society from 1963 to 1971, Mrs. Emma B. Watson, became the official representative of the A.M.E. Zion Church in this organization from 1966 to 1971. Mrs. Willa Mae Rice, the present president of our W.H. & F.M. Society, has been representing the church since the World Federation of Methodist Women Conference in Denver, September 1971. Mrs. Artishia Jordan of the African Methodist Episcopal Church became the second black North American area president at this conference. [69]

The American Bible Society

Much of the distribution of the Bible has been in the hands of Bible societies throughout the world. Many of these societies were organized in the nineteenth century. The American Bible Society was organized May 8, 1816, with Joshua M. Wallace of Burlington, N.J. presiding and Rev. Lyman Beecher of Cincinnati, secretary of the convention. The Hon. Elias Boudinot of New Jersey was elected president, John R. Mason, secretary, for foreign correspondence, and Rev. J. B. Romeyn, first secretary for domestic correspondence. [70] The African Methodist Episcopal Zion Church has had some type of interrelation with the American Bible Society since its existence. Our earlier history has been traced with the formation of the New York African Bible Society, by William Miller, James Varick, and others in 1817 (see Chapter 8). Our church, historically, has felt its responsibility to cooperate with this important agency in the distribution of the Bible. The position of the A.M.E. Zion Church was best expressed by the American Bible Society Committee of the General Conference of 1928 as follows:

> We, the Committee on American Bible Society, ask leave to submit our report. The American Bible Society . . . New York City, was organized, May, 1816 . . . . It was a three-fold purpose as an objective; that of translation of the scriptures into the various languages and dialects of the world, totalling to date more than 800 tongues. Special emphasis and business foresight have been applied to the publication of the Bible in order that individuals, churches and nations may secure it at the lowest possible cost. Then comes the sacrificing task of distributing the scriptures.

> The distribution of the scriptures is carried on under the supervision of ten home and twelve foreign agencies. The work of the American Bible Society is interdenominational, touching the diverse countries of the earth. It is fostered by the Christian peoples of the world. Its program is strictly missionary in endeavor, and benevolent as to manipulation.

> The Bible must not cease to be translated, published nor distributed because it is the seed corn of the kingdom, as well as the missionary's chief weapon.

> More than a quarter of a century ago the American Bible Society organized an agency for the colored people of the United States, with Dr. J. P. Wragg, Agency-Secretary. The work of this Agency is now carried on under four sub-agencies, Atlanta, Georgia, Rev. H.W.B. Wilson, Secretary, Houston, Tex., Rev. S. L. Lucas, Secretary, and Charlotte, N.C., Rev. D. H. Sansom, Jr., Secretary. These sub-agencies represent the following denominations respectively: Methodist Episcopal, Colored Methodist Episcopal, African

69. *Ibid., Proceedings of the Twelfth World Methodist Conference.*
70. W. P. Strickland, *History of the American Bible Society,* pp. 28-35.

Methodist Episcopal and African Methodist Episcopal Zion.

For the universal service as rendered by the American Bible Society whose task it is to translate, publish and distribute the Holy Scriptures, including a number of editions for the blind, our plea is that the interest and support of the A.M.E. Zion Church be not lessened. The work is a great one, too important to be retarded.

The following recommendations are offered:

First: That the A.M.E. Zion Church cooperate one hundred per cent in the observance of universal Bible Sunday which is the first Sunday in December of each year, as a means of education showing the purposes of the American Bible Society, thereby emphasizing the meaning and the importance of the Bible, to the individual, to the nation and to the world.

Second: That the A.M.E. Zion ministers send to the nearest Sub-Agency, Secretary, or to the Bible House, Astor Place, New York City, for free literature prepared yearly for Bible Sunday observance.

Third: That the ministry and laity of the A.M.E. Zion Church endeavor to participate in the world wide Annual Bible reading campaign during the months of January and February, for the purpose of enlightening and evangelizing Christian workers.

Special prepared scriptures may be secured at the nearest depository for one cent each.

Respectfully submitted,
T. H. Stevenson
F. R. Killingsworth
L. C. Williams [71]

The American Bible Society has had manifold growth and momentous changes in operation since that time. By its sesquicentennial year, 1966, it had translated and distributed more than 750 million of the Holy Scriptures in portions of the Bible or total Bibles, and moved into its newly built headquarters at Broadway and 61st Street in New York City. Although the Bible is the most widely read of all books, the American Bible Society, adopting as its theme, "God's Word For A New Age," set its goal of reaching 10 million new Bible readers in what was termed, "The Year of the Bible." It thus moved in this direction of lifting the Spirit of humanity through his own enlightenment of the word; a task to which the organization had dedicated itself 150 years before. "1967—Urgent needs for Scriptures all over the world demand that the American Bible Society distribute at least 75 million copies a year. This means that the Society must do as much in the next ten years as it has done in its first 150 years." [72]

The African Methodist Episcopal Zion Church continues to dedicate a part of its program in this direction. Reverend D. H. Sansom, Jr., was a faithful agent on behalf of our church. He was followed in this work by Revs. J. S. N. Tross, J. W. I. Tunstall, and Oscar D. Carson. The system was changed, and in 1948, the American Bible Society was included in the annual appropriation of our church budget. The Advisory Council of the American Bible Society was established in 1919. Bishop L. W. Kyles became the first A.M.E. Zion Church representative on the Advisory Council and served until his death in 1941. Bishop W. J. Walls served from 1941 to 1969. Representing the A.M.E. Zion Church since 1970 are Revs: J. Dallas Jenkins, Bishop J. Clinton Hoggard, Revs. E. Raphael Michael and H. A. L. Clement.

71. *Minutes,* Twenty-Eighth Quadrennial Session, pp. 235-237.
72. 150th Anniversary Literature, American Bible Society, 1966.

The Federal Council of Churches of Christ in America
and
The National Council of Churches of Christ in the U.S.A.

In 1905 the Inter-Church Conference on Federation, leading up to the organization of the Federal Council of Churches, held its first meeting at Carnegie Hall, New York City, November 15-21. Bishop Alexander Walters was the leading force of the A.M.E. Zion Church present and served as a member of the executive committee.

A prominent journalist in a report of this Conference . . . says: No one could come away from that assemblage in New York without the largest hopes. Men's faces there were forward, away from the weakly divided past, toward the strong and united future. Men's voices there were learning to say, "We are one"; better their hearts were coming to know it; and the goal of that union was, and will be more and more "that the world may believe." [73]

The group met faithfully for three years, led by its permanent chairman of the executive committee, who became its first presiding officer at the uniting assembly held in Philadelphia, 1908, the Rev. William Henry Roberts of the Presbyterian Church, Philadelphia. The large family of Protestant Americans assembled at Philadelphia, December 2-8, 1908, adopted as its theme: "Above All the Cross of Christ." Delegates of the A.M.E. Zion Church present were Bishops George W. Clinton, C. R. Harris, Alexander Walters, and Andrew J. Warner.

Among the newly elected officers were Bishop E. R. Hendricks, Methodist Episcopal, of Kansas City, Mo., president; Bishop C. R. Harris, a vice-president representing the A.M.E. Zion Church; the noted corresponding secretary who had worked so ardently for this movement, Rev. E. B. Sanford, Congregational, of New York City. Bishops J. S. Caldwell and J. W. Smith were elected members of the Executive Committee and Bishop A. J. Warner served as a member of the Family Life Committee.

Leading forth in projecting this organization were some of the most distinguished men in American ecumenicity: Dr. Samuel Parkes Cadman, Dean Haile R. Mathews of Chicago University, Dr. Frank Mason North, and Bishop Francis J. McConnell, serving as its earlier presidents; and succeeding Dr. Sanford; becoming the General Secretaries were Rev. John Milton Moore (Baptist) of New York, Rev. Charles S. McFarland, Congregational of Yale Divinity School, and Dr. Samuel McCrea Cavert, who served the longest term and helped to make the transition into the new organization in 1950. Leading the forces of Zion Methodism in this organization, on the General Assembly programs and the Executive Committee were Bishop Alexander Walters, Revs. Henry J. Callis, James E. Mason, Thomas W. Wallace, and Dr. Simon G. Atkins. Vice-presidents of the organization representing the A.M.E. Zion Church were: Bishop C. R. Harris, 1908-1915; Rev. W. A. Blackwell.I1915-1917; Bishop L. W. Kyles, 1917-1932.

The organization was restructured after 1932, and only one vice-president was elected. Our Board of Bishops summed up our history in the Federal Council, and its meaning to our church and society, as follows:

At the initial meeting held in Cooper Union in 1905 which looked toward the organization of the Federal Council of Churches as well as in 1908

---

73. Elias B. Sanford, *Report of the First Meeting of the Federal Council of Churches of Christ in America,* pp. 2-3.

Bishops William J. Walls (A.M.E. Zion) and Sherman L. Greene (A.M.E.) lead the procession of signers to the Charter establishing the National Council of Churches of Christ, U.S.A., 1950.

at Philadelphia when the organization was perfected, and in all the succeeding years, the A.M.E. Zion Church has actively and heartily participated in the Federal Council of Churches in America. We are one of the Twenty-nine Protestant bodies of which the Council is composed. The scope and influence of this federated body in an advisory and cooperative way have grown and strengthened, and we count it a privilege to share in all that has made for fellowship and service in its activities. Missionary enterprises, national and international peace and good will and other major questions have engaged the attention of the Federal Council. (74)

Bishop George C. Clement, who became a towering figure in this organization, served as chairman of the Commission on Race Relations of the Federal Council of Churches. The General Secretary, Rev. Dr. Samuel McCrea Cavert, constructive ecumenist, and Dr. George E. Haynes, Secretary of Race Relations of the FCC, noted black advocate of privilege and freedom for his people, and founder of the National Urban League, both attended the 1932 General Conference representing the Federal Council of Churches. Dr. Cavert in his address "expressed his great pleasure at being present and his gratification of the fact that our own church had been a member of the Council since its organization in 1908. He paid a tribute to the worth and work of our representatives in the Council. If there was any one word which gathered up the aims and ideals of the Federal Council it was Brotherhood, and he undertook to show how it was endeavoring to make that Brotherhood a reality: (1) between the churches, (2) between the nations, and (3) between the races." (75)

Dr. George E. Haynes was presented later in the afternoon session, and spoke at length on the work being done by the Federal Council of Churches through the

74. Minutes, Twenty-Eighth Quadrennial Session, pp. 45-46.
75. *Minutes,* Twenty-Ninth Quadrennial Session, p. 44.

Race Relations Commission. The A.M.E. Zion Church, as usual manifesting concern in the affairs of the whole race, took liberty to clear up points with Dr. Haynes.

> Reverend J. T. Daniels asked Dr. Haynes why did the Federal Council of Churches retract its preliminary investigation into the Salisbury lynching as reported by the daily press?
> Answer: The press report was untrue and was falsely released by the *Salisbury Times* and later by Mr. (Carl) Murphy, editor of the *Afro-American.*

> Dr. J. W. Brown asked: If the farmers mentioned in the address getting bank relief in Arkansas and Mississippi were members of the Negro race. Answer: They are all members of our race . . . Reverend W. A. Blackwell, I moved that the Board of Bishops appoint a Committee of twelve looking forward to a Social Service Commission to study the problems enunciated through the Federal Council of Churches in America and all social problems. The motion was seconded by Reverend J. E. Garrett and approved by the Conference. [76]

Continuing to lead in representation of the A.M.E. Zion Church in the Federal Council of Churches were Bishops L. W. Kyles, J. S. Caldwell, J. W. Wood, W. J. Walls, C. C. Alleyne, J. W. Martin, H. T. Medford, Dr. J. W. Eichelberger, Mrs. Abbie Clement Jackson, Rev. Thomas W. Wallace, John F. Moreland, Jr., R. Farley Fisher, B. C. Robeson, W. R. Lovell, and Dr. William J. Trent, Sr.

The Federal Council of Churches, working toward an amplified movement of Christian unity, began work through its Commission on the Study of Christian Unity in 1937. The new movement took a decade of preparation. Dr. Luther A. Weigle, dean emeritus of Yale University Divinity School, was elected chairman of the planning committee and was given credit as the principal constructor of the enlarged new ecumenical organization which combined its forces with seven other Christian movements and became known as "The National Council of the Churches of Christ in the United States of America."[77] It enlarged its scope to meet the changing demands of the nation and world, and set in motion a more definite and inclusive capacity for attaining cooperation and unity of Christian churches. It included virtually all of the leading Protestant and Eastern Orthodox churches in America, as did its parent organization, which extended to 34 member churches. [78] It also kindled its program toward ambitious efforts to fraternize and have consortia with the Roman Catholic Church. "The member communions, responding to the gospel revealed in the Scriptures, confess Jesus, the incarnate Son of God, as Savior and Lord. Relying on the transforming power of the Holy Spirit, the council works to bring churches into a life-giving fellowship and into common witness, study and action to the glory of God and in service to all creation." [79]

The representatives of the A.M.E. Zion Church attending the Constituting Convention at Cleveland, Ohio, November 28 to December 1, 1950 were:

Bishop Cameron C. Alleyne, Philadelphia, Pa.

Rev. H. J. Callis, Washington, D.C.

---

76. *Ibid.,* p. 45.
77. Robbins W. Barstow (ed.), *Christian Faith in Action,* pp. 25-30.
78. The Triennial Report of 1969-1972 lists 32 member churches, even though other communions have joined in recent years; this is due to the uniting of some of the member churches, etc.
79. Preamble, Constitution, NCCUSA, 1972 p. 123.

Rev. Rufus E. Clement, Atlanta, Ga.
Mr. A. L. Cromwell, Winston-Salem, N.C.
Mr. Samuel E. Duncan, Reidsville, N.C.
Mr. J. W. Eichelberger, Chicago, Ill.
Rev. Robert F. Fisher, Washington, D.C.
Rev. George F. Hall, Charlotte, N.C.
Mrs. M. Anna Hauser, Winston-Salem, N.C.
Rev. J. Clinton Hoggard, Yonkers, N.Y.
Bishop J. W. Martin, Chicago, Ill.
Rev. A. A. Perry, Roxbury, Mass.
Rev. J. H. Satterwhite, Salisbury, N.C.
Rev. S. G. Spottswood, Washington, D.C.
Bishop James Clair Taylor, Memphis, Tenn.
Bishop William J. Walls, Chicago, Ill.
Bishop Edgar B. Watson, Greensboro, N.C.
    Alternate representatives attending were:
Rev. C. C. Coleman, Mobile, Ala.
Mrs. Abbie Clement Jackson, Louisville, Ky.
Mr. B. M. Montgomery, Charlotte, N.C.
Mr. Victor J. Tulane, Washington, D.C.
    (Bishop B. F. Gordon of Charlotte, N.C., and Rev. E. J. Hayes, Williamston,
    N.C. were unable to attend.)

The Right Reverend Henry Knox Sherrill, Bishop of the Protestant Episcopal
Church, became the first president, and Dr. Samuel McCrea Cavert, who had been
General Secretary of the Federal Council since 1930, served as the first General
Secretary. Mrs. Abbie C. Jackson was named one of the four vice-presidents at
large for the triennium, and Bishop W. J. Walls signed the compact of agreement
on behalf of the A.M.E. Zion Church. [80]

In its problematic procedures, representatives of the A.M.E. Zion Church,
during the Triennial General Assemblies, General Board (now Governing Board) and
Divisional Commission meetings, contribute salubriously for better conditions
along many lines in our nation and world. Many other A.M.E. Zion Church leaders
have been industriously engaged in their various communities, and have become
leading officials in local, state, regional, and the National Council of Churches. The
two succeeding General Secretaries, Rev. Drs., Roy G. Ross and R. H. Edwin Espy,
have been the embodiment of spiritual goodwill and genuine cooperation for the
ongoing success of the organization. At the Triennial Assembly in December,
1972, the NCCUSA elected its first black president, Rev. W. Sterling Cary, of the
United Church of Christ, New York City.

The A.M.E. Zion Church has cooperated with the ascribed spirit of this
organization as expressed in one of its messages in 1957:

    As judgment begins in the house of God, so also must reformation begin
    there. Organizational complacency, statistical self-assurance or the running of
    successful programs must not be confused with the achieving of a holy
    purpose. We are called to become the proving ground of God's will for a
    fellowship that is universally human just because it is ultimately divine.

    Racial discrimination and segregation, though repeatedly condemned by
    many church bodies, still prevails. We pledge ourselves to more devoted and

---

80. *Christian Faith in Action*, pp. 159-160, 207, 219; *Minutes*, Thirty-Fourth Quadrennial
    Session, p. 152.

creative effort toward a more neighborly and brotherly America. May God grant us the forbearance of those who understand, and the eagerness of those who love.

The local congregation is utterly basic to the ecumenical movement. Here if anywhere our unity becomes operative and effective. The congregation should serve the religious needs of its own neighborhood in full cooperation with other congregations. Furthermore, it should explore new ways to express its ecumenical character—returning to more authentic modes of worship, giving greater opportunity for laymen and laywomen to take part, studying afresh the basis, aim, and nature of church membership itself.

Oneness in Christ is a reality, known and lived, which constitutes the very being of the church. It is not a thing of this world, after the fashion of some chummy humanism or militant collectivism. We know that it is of God, who has disclosed His will and poured out his spirit in Jesus Christ our Lord. In this assurance we move forward together. May God perfect our unity and grant us all His blessing and His peace! [81]

Church Women United

Church Women United has had two names since it became allied with the National Council of Churches in 1950: United Church Women and Church Women United. (The United Council of Church Women preceded these groups.) The presidents and executive secretaries of the Woman's Home and Foreign Missionary Society of the A.M.E. Zion Church—Mesdames M. Anna Hauser, Rosa L. Weller, Elsie G. Keyes, Abbie C. Jackson, Emma B. Watson, Willa Mae Rice, Margaret J. May, and Grace L. Holmes—have been able and effective representatives in the deliberations and on various committees of these organizations. Several women of the A.M.E. Zion Church have participated also locally, regionally, and nationally, and some have become heads of Church Women United in their respective communities and sections. Mrs. Claire Collins Harvey (Methodist) wife of A.M.E. Zion Rev. Martin L. Harvey, was the first black woman to head the national organization of Church Women United in 1971 and she is presently serving a three-year term.

The Interchurch Center

Another striking move of interaction in ecumenicity of the A.M.E. Zion Church was its role in helping construct the Interchurch Center, from the concept through its completion. This 19-story imposing structure at 475 Riverside Drive, New York City, constructed principally as headquarters of general departments of a number of Protestant churches and missionary organizations, was formally dedicated May 29, 1960. Prior to this, the cornerstone laying ceremonies were led by the President of the United States, Dwight D. Eisenhower; October 12, 1958, and the writer was a program participant on both historic occasions.

The African Methodist Episcopal Zion Church set the pace for black churches, and became the donor of a fund-raising effort on behalf of the NCC to aid in completion and equipment of the building. The church through its Board of Bishops voted $10,000 to this project for a memorial conference room. "It was agreed by vote to memorialize Bishop James Varick, founder and first bishop and to honor Bishop W. J. Walls, a contemporary representative in ecumenical affairs for our church." [82]

81. Ms. Papers, Excerpts from the National Council Message, General Board Meeting, NCCUSA, Sept. 4, 1957.
82. Ms. Minutes, Board of Bishops, January 12, 1961, p. 4.

The A.M.E. Zion Church also resolved that the Foreign Missions Department maintain its office in this building, which manifests the two-fold purpose of the spirit of unity in our Protestantism and full convenience of international communication and transportation of the foreign fields of our church.

The National Fraternal Council of Churches

This organization began as the Negro Fraternal Council of Churches at Chicago, in 1934. It later comprised 12 black denominations, representing 7,000,000 members; the A.M.E., A.M.E. Zion and C.M.E. churches, the Central Jurisdiction of the Methodist Church, the two leading National Baptist Conventions, the African Orthodox Church, the Freewill Baptist, the Church of God in Christ, the Apostolic Churches, the Bible Way Church of Washington, D.C., Church of God and Saints of Christ, and the Metropolitan Community Church of Chicago.

The purposes of the organization were:
1) To develop cooperative relations among all member denominations, and to take appropriate collective measures to strengthen this bond of Christian Unity, so that they may work together as one United Church to bring about racial and economic justice, progressive measures of non-partisan political legislation and social reform. 2) To afford a center for coordinating the actions of the denominations in the achievement of their common goals. 3) To cooperate with other organizations of like nature in seeking to foster the world-wide program of Christ. [83]

This organization was a necessity long before it began, since the Negro was still almost universally proscribed. In relating to this cause of Negro organization in an earlier period, Bishop Hood states:

I am fully convinced that this necessity is Providential. Without this the Negro's development would be slow. As the spreading oak dwarfs the grass which grows beneath its boughs, so does superior advantages of the white race dwarf the efforts of the black man and prevent him from rising to eminence in the white organization. At a religious convention some years ago, there was a man of African descent who delivered an address which was regarded as one of the best productions of that memorable session. If he had been a white man that one speech would have given him a start which would have brought him to the front, but outside of a limited circle he has not been heard of since that night . . . .

A race is distinguished by its great men, but where there is no opportunity for development nor for the exhibition of the capacity for development, it is impossible to tell what that race can do . . . The Negro church offers the race the opportunity it needs . . . . [84]

The National Fraternal Council of Churches was an assertion of the black religious leader on the same platform of Christian unity as other ecumenical movements. It gave him opportunity to express himself on vital issues, especially those appertaining to the rights of the black people of America and their deepest concerns. It also proved a ground for the use of his own talent and an area of living service.

This organization was created by some of the most forthright leaders of the Negro pulpit, and a few of its genuinely determined freedom constructivists

---

83. Revised Constitution, The National Fraternal Council of Churches, U.S.A., April 26-27, 1950.
84. *Minutes,* Fourth Session Ohio Annual Conference, Sept. 26 - Oct. 1, 1894, p. 10.

among our laymen. It was a vigilante group on all the issues that pertained to the well-being, the freedom, the religious and political equality, and the outstanding fight for a balanced and progressive social activism in the nation's whole life, especially in education, religion and civil rights.

Among the names of its original vigilante were its founding president, Bishop Reverdy C. Ransom (A.M.E.), Bishops R. R. Wright, Jr. (A.M.E.) Lynwood W. Kyles (A.M.E.Z.) William J. Walls, (A.M.E.Z.) J. W. Golden, (Methodist) Alexander P. Shaw, (Methodist) Randall A. Carter, (C.M.E.) Revs. William H. Jernagin (Baptist), George W. Lucas (Baptist) J. H. Peters (Baptist), William D. Cook, (Community-Chicago) J. C. Austin, Sr. (Baptist), Dr. James W. Eichelberger (A.M.E.Z.), and Douglas Greer (Baptist). These were succeeded by a group of men

who seemed equally determined, and the National Fraternal Council of Churches seemed for a time to have a perpetually enduring foundation. Bishop E. P. Murchison, (C.M.E.) an activist for the cause of Church Union, was elected the president in December 1965.

It appeared to be the expanding voice of an upward and ongoing united effort in the black church of America. But the multiplication of organizations has caused it to have a somewhat persistent slowing down. It owns headquarters property in Washington, D.C., and has an officer in charge of this project, but its activities are rather unimpressive at this writing.

However, the need is still great for an organization of this prestige, of the unity and cooperation of the grand and prophetic leaders of the black church in the United States, for we are far from having attained the power, significance, and recognition of this great resource that is due in the universal church and the country at large. Besides that, the day has come when this people must have an incentive and inspiration that has hitherto been denied it, if all continues to go well in the striving toward a full realization of the success that American democracy foretokened in the oncoming restlessness of this age. To keep us from becoming involved in a caste system or in a "conflict which the country has not hitherto witnessed," as Dr. Price once uttered on a like subject, the leaders of the black oriented churches must have similar recognition according to qualification and service, as leaders produced by other churches.

The World Council of Churches

The initial step taken toward forming a world Protestant ecumenical organization was in 1910, when a World Missionary Conference was convened at Edinburgh, Scotland. The A.M.E. Zion Church sent Professor W. B. Crittendon of Livingstone College as its representative, to share in the origin of what was then considered world unity in the promotion of Christian missions by the Protestant movement. The voice which rang around the world from that meeting was that of Bishop Charles Brent, first Anglican missionary Bishop of the Phillippine Islands, who had a vision "that a world conference should be convened to consider matters of faith and order."[85] The men present that took up this refrain were Bishop William Temple, Anglican (Great Britain), Dr. John R. Mott, Methodist Episcopal (U.S.A.), and Dr. J. H. Oldham, Anglican (Great Britain).

The two commissions which came out of this meeting were Faith and Order and Life and Work: one was seeking a way to think together theologically, and the other was finding ways to work together. These leaders were joined by others and

85. George K. A. Bell, *The Kingship of Christ*, pp. 20-21.

a series of meetings were held by the organized commissions. By 1937 it was decided that the two groups should become one and the World Council of Churches was first proposed. It was organized provisionally at Utrecht, Holland in 1938, Archbishop William Temple was elected first chairman of a provisional committee to be responsible for all work preliminary to the meeting of the First Assembly, and Dr. W. A. Visser 't Hooft was appointed General Secretary. An earlier meeting of the Provisional Committee had fixed August 1941 as the date for the First Assembly. "But once again preparations for this new and great advance in Christian unity were interrupted by war," as it had been by World War I.[86]

According to the first Constitution drawn up in 1938, its purposes are:

1) to carry on the work of the two world movements of *Faith and Order* and *Life and Work:* 2) to facilitate common action by the churches; 3) to promote co-operation in study; 4) to promote the growth of ecumenical consciousness in the members of all churches; 5) to establish relations with denominational federations of worldwide scope and with other ecumenical movements; 6) to call world conferences on specific subjects as occasion may require, such conferences being empowered to publish their own findings. [87]

On Sunday, 22 August 1948, at 3 P.M. the delegates of 147 Churches assembled for the opening session of the First Assembly of the World Council in the Nieuwe Kerk, Amsterdam. It was a thrilling moment, for here at last the hopes and prayers of years were to be fulfilled. Some of the oldest Churches in the world were represented—the Church of Ethiopia and the Orthodox Syrian Church of Malabar, for example; and some of the youngest, like the Presbyterian Church of Korea. Well-known leaders of the principal Churches in the United States and Canada were side by side with leaders of the Lutheran and Reformed Churches in different countries of Europe. Bishops of the Orthodox Church, the Anglican, and Old Catholic Churches, leaders of the Church of Scotland, and of the Evangelical Free Churches of Britain, with their colleages in every continent, were there. Almost every grade of denomination was to be found: and more striking still, lay men and women and ministers of every color and race. It was a truly international and inter-racial gathering, ecumenical in the largest sense; and all had come together as belonging to a fellowship of Churches which acknowledge our Lord Jesus Christ as God and Saviour.[88]

Representing the African Methodist Episcopal Zion Church as delegates, alternates and official visitors were Bishops B. G. Shaw and W. J. Walls; Rev. D. P. Thomas, Sr., and George F. Hall, Mrs. Abbie Clement Jackson, and Dr. James W. Eichelberger; Rev. J. Clinton Hoggard was one of the youth observers. [89]

The opening service was

the prelude to the acceptance of the Constitution of the World Council on the following day by the official delegates, in the main hall of the Concertgebouw. The effective resolution was carried without a dissentient vote. The World Council, which had been for so long in process of formation, was now formed. The Archbishop of Canterbury, who was chairman for the occasion, asked all to stand in silent prayer, and invoked God's blessing on

86. *Ibid.,* p. 33.
87. Constitution, World Council of Churches, First Assembly, 1948; from ms. papers, author's collection.
88. Bell, *op. cit.,* p. 50.
89. Ms. Minutes, Board of Bishops, March 12, 1948.

the solemn decision. [90]

Dr. John R. Mott, the noted 83-year-old Methodist layman and the only living pioneer who in 1910 planned the organization of the World Council, delivered one of two opening messages. He said: "Our ecumenical gathering here at Amsterdam has assembled at one of the most fateful moments of the life of the world. There has been no time like it, not only in point of danger but also of opportunity. Never did my heart beat so high with hope as it does here and now." He included J. E. Kwegyir Aggrey of Africa and of Zion Methodism among those to whom "we would pay our grateful tribute to many colleagues and master builders of different lands, races, and communions who have passed on into the Land of Large Dimensions." [91]

One of the last acts of this assembly, representing 147 Protestant and Orthodox member communions, comprising more than 150,000,000 members in some 45 countries, was to elect joint presidents and appoint the 90 members of the Central Committee, the important policy making committee which was to meet annually in the interest of promoting the cause of the church universal. "It is obvious, therefore, that the responsibility of the Central Committee is great, and that on its conduct of the business of the World Council, and above all on the wisdom and ability of the officers whom it appoints, under God, the well-being of the Council depends." [92]

When the nominating committee made its first report, Bishop W. J. Walls, delegate representing the A.M.E. Zion Church, obtained the platform and stated that there were member churches of this body containing memberships of about 15 million people in America who had no representative on the Central Committee and made the motion that representation should be placed on the committee. The presiding officer, the Archbishop of Canterbury, put the motion immediately, and it carried. The Assembly thus approved the Central Committee which included the first two black Americans, Dr. Benjamin E. Mays representing the National Baptists and Bishop W. J. Walls representing the three black Methodist denominations. [93]

These two men served for six years, attending committee meetings in different parts of the world, to help make a creative organization, to bring the church forward in the largest possible usefulness, and to make Jesus felt and emulated in every way in all areas. On the race question, they were both vigorously engaged opposing discrimination in America and other countries, and apartheid in South Africa. [94]

After the Second Assembly held in Evanston, Illinois in 1954, they were succeeded by Dr. Joseph H. Jackson (Baptist) and Bishop D. Ward Nichols (A.M.E.). The writer was privileged, by the good offices of his denomination, to serve as delegate to the Third Assembly held at New Delhi, India in 1961, and the Fourth Assembly held at Uppsala, Sweden in 1968; becoming one of the few in the 20-year history of the World Council of Churches to be an official representative in all four assemblies.

The World Council of Churches has received into its fold several new member communions, East and West, and World Christian organizations since its inception. The Central Committee has enlarged to 120 members. The World Council has had

90. Bell, *op. cit.,* p. 51.
91. *Minutes,* Thirty-Fourth Quadrennial Session, 1952, pp. 211-212.
92. Bell, *op. cit.,* p. 81.
93. W. A. Visser 't Hooft (ed.), *The First Assembly of the WCC,* pp. 216-217.
94. Bell, *op. cit.,* p. 136; Minutes, Central Committee Meetings, 1949-1954.

three General Secretaries: Dr. W. A. Visser 't Hooft, Reformed Church of the Netherlands, Dr. Eugene Carson Blake, United Presbyterian, U.S.A., and the newly-elected secretary in 1972, Dr. Phillip Alford Potter, Methodist of Jamaica, West Indies and London. All of these have been friends to a common doctrine to facilitate a united effort in bringing the kingdom of Jesus Christ into helping regulate human affairs the world over. The six-member presidium represents men and women from around the world who give great impetus to the cause, and make possible the effectiveness of the organization. They rotate in presiding over the assemblies and Central Committee meetings; however, the real spirit and leader that carries forward the World Council of Churches is the General Secretary. In the organization of the WCC, with headquarters at Geneva, Switzerland. Dr. Robert S. Bilheimer, first secretary of the American section and Miss Eleanor Kent Browne, two staunch ecumenists, worked zealously for the welfare of the organization as pioneers, with others, in establishing headquarters in the U.S.A. Dr. Eugene Smith became the Second Secretary of the American Section.

At Uppsala in 1968, Rev. Andrew E. Whitted (A.M.E. Zion) became one of the members of the central committee, representing the black Methodist churches, succeeding Bishop B. Julian Smith (C.M.E.). At this assembly several American black churchmen and women were named on the Central Committee, representing leading denominations in this country. Reverend John H. Satterwhite presently represents our church on the important Commission on Faith and Order.

Among all the questions facing the world, the race question is still predominant. "As 'a fellowship of Churches' within which all the races of mankind are represented, and as a body the very *raison d'etre* of which is to render witness to the unity and universality of the Church of Christ, the World Council is bound to be concerned with the relationship between races."[95] Since its assembly at Amsterdam the World Council of Churches has taken vigorous stands and worked exceedingly hard against racial injustice and oppression, discrimination and segregation.

The World Council of Churches has been especially progressive in aiding humanitarian improvements and potential forces of the kingdom of Jesus Christ in South Africa and other parts of the world. The Central Committee meeting held in Addis Ababa, Ethiopia, January 1971, made bold and unprecedented decisions, in appointing a special commission and assuming large budgetary responsibilities for its program to combat racisim which new concerns had been first projected by the World Council in 1966. [96]

We live in a day when the ecumenical trend is attaining a manifest vitalization. In 1960, the Christian world was thrilled when Pope John XXIII announced his intention to verge upon church unity in practical approaches, and created a new interfaith climate by convoking Vatican Council II, in 1962. After his death in 1963, Pope Paul VI persisted in enlarging and defining these policies. June 10, 1969 was a dramatic moment in history when the Pope paid a courtesy visit to the World Council of Churches headquarters at Geneva, Switzerland. [97] Our Protestant and Orthodox units in Christendom, already in agreement looking toward cooperation in the pursuit of unity and unified efforts in the salvation of society, have developed fraternal relationship with the Roman Catholic Church

95. Bell, *op. cit.,* p. 136.
96. *The Christian Century,* February 17, 1971, pp. 214-216; February 24, 1971, p. 247; March 22, 1972, pp. 329-330.
97. William H. Nault (ed.), *The World Book,* 1970, p. 483.

through the World Council. They have begun rapprochement to the matter of a universal ecumenical movement, with caution. Some of our groups are even daring to undertake the study and pursuit of organic union, and a few others are forming mergers. The World Council of Churches has sufficient prophets and leaders of the various types under the power of Christ our Lord, to continue to chart the way toward catholicity.

Delegates, Official Visitors and Advisors of the African Methodist Episcopal Zion Church to the other Assemblies:

SECOND ASSEMBLY, Evanston, Illinois, August 1, 1954

Bishop H. T. Medford }
Bishop W. J. Walls,   } Delegates

Dr. James Eichelberger }
Rev. J. W. Findley   }
Mrs. Martha B. Francis } Accredited Visitors
Mrs. Josephine H. Kyles,}

THIRD ASSEMBLY, New Delhi, India, November, 1961
Bishop W. J. Walls,
Bishop Herbert B. Shaw,
Dr. James W. Eichelberger,
Rev. Enoch B. Rochester, Youth Participant

FOURTH ASSEMBLY, Uppsala, Sweden, July, 1968
Bishop W. J. Walls
Rev. Andrew E. Whitted
Mr. Arthur E. Brooks
Rev. J. Clinton Hoggard, Advisor
Rev. John H. Satterwhite, Advisor

The Consultation on Church Union

During the National Council of Churches Triennial Assembly in 1960 at San Francisco, Dr. Eugene Carson Blake and Bishop James A. Pike proposed the concrete union of three churches (Episcopal, Presbyterian, and Congregational-Christian), for the first time, with dissimilar theologies, which had been accomplished only in South India and Canada. It progressed into a study commission that moved American Christianity into new experiences of organic union, resulting in the Consultation on Church Union. The A.M.E. Zion Church became interested at first as an observer-consultant church. While augmenting interest of major denominations, the A.M.E. Zion Church looked favorably upon this movement and became a participating member in 1966. By 1967 there were ten-participating churches in COCU. Merger of the Methodist and United Brethren churches brought the number of churches to nine.

Representatives of the nine member churches, including the three major black Methodist churches, have been engaged in various committee meetings and plenary sessions. We have had several propositions submitted and have been contemplating them studiously and seriously. Serving on the Executive Committee of COCU from the A.M.E. Zion Church through 1972 were Bishop W. J. Walls and Dr. John H. Satterwhite, with the rotating chairmen of the Board of Bishops as alternates. Bishops J. Clinton Hoggard and Arthur Marshall became the representatives on the Executive Committee in 1972.

Representatives of the A.M.E. Zion Church named to attend the last plenary sessions, 1971-1972, were Bishops W. J. Walls, R. L. Jones, H. B. Shaw, Stephen G. Spottswood, Revs. William C. Ardrey, J. Clinton Hoggard, George J. Hill, John H. Satterwhite, Mr. W. Mance Gilliam, Dr. E. Warner Brice, Mr. Alexander Barnes, Mrs. Willa Mae Rice, and George Mason Miller representing the youth. Mrs. Vopi Dell Morley and Mr. Curtis Sewell, both of Denver, served as delegates in place of Mrs. Rice and Mr. Gilliam, at the Denver Plenary, September 1971. [98] George Mason Miller had been elected secretary of the Consultation on Church Union in 1970, and served through this plenary session.

In April 1970, the Consultation on Church Union participated in a worldwide Conference on Church Union Negotiations at Limuru, Kenya. Bishop Alfred G. Dunston, Jr. was the able representative of the A.M.E. Zion Church along with leading churchmen and theologians of the world, meeting in serious efforts of bringing the Christian church closer together.

A dedicated group of churchmen are continuously studying the methods of union plans, analysis for constructing, and methods for manning a new church. The General Secretary of COCU, Dr. Paul A. Crow, Jr. is one of the most optimistic, serious, diligent, and patient servants of the union cause. The COCU organization had set a target date but has had to change that date while it continues to delve deeper into organic union, and to grapple with the problems which arise in the conversations. Most of us have hopes for its success, but we do not dare to predict how soon it will be.

Naturally, the black church has its old reservation on whether the time is right for equitable treatment in the close association in organic union, but there are denominational difficulties such as polity problems, and by all means, doctrinal hills to climb. Nevertheless, faith will not down in the power of Jesus Christ to make his people one, and to make the steps that will bring such a finalization in the structure we call the Christian church.

Other Ecumenical Organizations

The A.M.E. Zion Church is affiliated with several other ecumenical and interfaith organizations, and supports their causes and purposes to the fullest extent, in the nation and around the world. Representatives among our ministry and laity are continuously sent to multilateral meetings; they participate well in these movements of unity and ecumenicity, and upon returning home, make their reports to our official bodies. (We have discussed the role of the A.M.E. Zion Church and its leaders and representatives in the various world Sunday school movements, international and national Christian Endeavor and Christian Education organizations in Chapter 21.)

98. *Digest of the Proceedings of the Tenth Meeting of the Consultation on Church Union,* September 27-30, 1971, pp. 208-210.

CHAPTER 31

EQUAL RIGHTS AND CITIZENSHIP

The value, usefulness and stability of institutions largely depend upon the character and motives of the men who are the founders thereof. It is therefore but fitting as we pause here to arrange for the future of our great Church, to give at least a passing consideration to the founders of the African Methodist Episcopal Zion Church. One hundred and four years ago, a band of God-fearing and liberty-loving men and women of African descent prompted by the prevailing spirit of the times and inspired by the teachings and precepts of God's revealed word, formed an organization of humble beginners and modest pretentions. The conditions then prevailing made such a movement a necessity for men and women of African extraction—who would maintain and defend their manhood rights, and worship God as they felt the Holy Spirit dictated.

. . . Whoever has marked the progress and achievements of the African Methodist Episcopal Zion Church cannot doubt that the men who founded this branch of God's moving militant host, were men raised up for the times and work which resulted in the formation of one of the greatest religious organizations and most potent forces for race uplifting and development in existence. The founders of the A.M.E. Zion Church were men of devout piety, sterling integrity and noted for their devotion to the principles which stand for untrammeled manhood and unrestrained religious freedom of every being who bears the image of his Creator, whether that image is beneath a covering of ebony or ivory hue.

They represented and stood for all that was best in the race, and that which was in harmony with the highest thought and noblest purpose of the founders of the new republic.

Their attitude and achievements forcibly demonstrated the fact that the same fires that had kindled and blazed in the breasts of the founders of American civilization and American Christianity had caught hold of and illumined their souls; and that they were both capable and ready to keep step with the progress of the times. Their untiring and self-sacrificing labors laid the foundation and reared the goodly supersturcture which had come down to us as a religious heritage and heirloom which we shall do well to highly appreciate and labor zealously to perpetuate with all the powers which a gracious God may give us.

Let it be our daily prayer to God to give us such gratitude, wisdom and consecration as will ever prove us to be worthy sons of such noble and godly sires. [1]

The two most powerful black organizations in the nation prior to the Civil War were the A.M.E. Bethel and A.M.E. Zion churches. They had organized conferences and pushed their work throughout the North, so that up to the war they were found in nearly every free state in which there were any considerable number of black people. Even those who had migrated West had established and perpetuated churches in the name of these two organizations.

The forces awakened by Harriet Beecher Stowe in her immortal *Uncle Tom's Cabin*, and the able speeches against slavery in the Senate by Charles Sumner, for which he was subsequently beaten into insensibility by a South Carolina representative, had produced, by this time, concrete results in the onward movement of freedom. The struggle of the black man in the onward movement of freedom, supported by sacrificial and sincere abolitionists, was verging upon a new day.

Meanwhile, the two leading Methodist churches, which had split over the slave question in 1844, were deeply involved in the political struggle on opposite sides in the agitation of the war. The Methodist Episcopal Church was known to be such a strong force in the struggle against slavery that the bishops and ministers not only preached, lectured, and exhorted against it wherever they went, but they produced strong sentiment among their consitutents in their publications. So impelling was the Methodist Episcopal Church for the downfall of slavery and support of the Union that President Lincoln declared it "no fault of other denominations that the Methodist Episcopal Church furnished more money and men to suppress the Rebellion."

The Methodist Episcopal Church, South, which had led in the secession movement in favor of slavery, patronized the Confederacy so forcefully that "it was natural therefore, for the Southern Confederacy to adopt it, and grant it a kind of supremacy above every other denomination." [2]

The Methodist Episcopal Church, South, had developed some leaders who devotedly directed their attention to mission work among its black members, such as Bishop William Capers and Dr. Atticus G. Haygood, later bishop. Bishop Capers, who labored in North Carolina, South Carolina, and Georgia, believed in the relation of slave and master by the Bible, and had presented the series of resolutions proposing the division of the Methodist Episcopal Church in 1844. He emphasized "the necessity of the masters' being kind to their bondsmen, and especially in providing for their spiritual needs." [3]

Bishop Haygood, who did his missionary work among slaves in Eastern Tennessee, represented in a large measure the best thought in the South concerning the race. "He boldly endeavored to impress upon the South the claims of the Negro on the 'sympathy and helpfulness of all who were more fortunate, especially those who called themselves the followers of Jesus Christ.' This sentiment he set forth in a book entitled *Our Brother in Black,* which struck the North with agreeable surprise and led the South to think more seriously of

1. *Minutes,* Twenty-First Quadrennial Session, (Bishop's Address) pp. 88-89.
2. L. M. Hagood, *The Colored Man in the Methodist Episcopal Church,* pp. 118, 116-117.
3. Emory Stevens, Bucke, (ed.) *The History of American Methodism* Vol. II, p. 59; Woodson, *History of the Negro Church,* p. 139.

another solution of the so-called Negro problem," after Emancipation. [4]

Nevertheless, due to the suspicion and fear of leaders and people of Southern white churches since the Nat Turner uprising, which had caused reprisals, suppression, and surveillance of Negro worshippers, accompanied by the debarring of Northern black churches, there prevailed a natural consensus that if and when freedom were attained, the Negro would become a threat to the South. The U.S. Congress and public servants of every profession were preaching, teaching, and writing on both sides of the slave question, and in one way or the other the entire nation had become involved. This produced an embranglement in the cause of freedom and threw the nation into utter confusion with the predominant issue of one of the bloodiest, severest, acrimonious, and relentless warfares in the history of civil wars being the preservation of the union of the states. By his Emancipation Proclamation, President Abraham Lincoln made the abolition of slavery the cornerstone of the salvation of the nation.

In the South, the Negro Baptist Church, which could organize congregationally without leaders or headquarters, got the advantage of establishing churches before Emancipation, and was able to do considerable work in the freedom cause. However, connectionalism of Methodism enabled it to prove a stronger force in the politics and Emancipation processes because it was led by bishops and organized conferences. Methodist bishops and leaders invaded the doorsteps of governors and presidents. This, however, could not obtain until the race was free and could establish its own general institutions throughout the South.

The effort to spread the A.M.E. Zion Church South began directly after Emanciaption in the midst of the Civil War. The principles upon which the church had been founded, surviving slavery and oppression, were giving new incentive in the creative work of the men who were to brave every danger in taking their church movement to their emancipated brothers and sisters. From the beginning of Emancipation, a new struggle for citizenship began, and the black church was the chief agency in leading the way through. The story of this struggle in the North starts with an early incident of martyrdom in the membership of the A.M.E. Zion Church.

Naturally the readjustments of Emancipation that the war had made in the nation, particularly in black-white relationships, were not received without some trouble, and even bloodshed, in the midst of the war, before they were settled. During this period serious incidents occurred, in the North and South. Anti-savery riots broke out in the northern cities of Detroit and New York. "In 1863 the Union government passed a conscription act, which exempted those who were wealthy enough to pay $300 or hire a substitute." [5] This met with open hostility in New York City. The draft riot which occurred on July 11, 1863 and raged out of control for three days before the police and federal troops quelled it, left more than a thousand dead and wounded, and a million dollars worth of property destroyed. "After demolishing draft headquarters the mob proceeded to wreak vengeance upon Negroes wherever found. They were chased and beaten and killed—hanged to trees and lamp posts." [6] One such incident affecting our church which became historical happened to a member of Mother Zion Church.

4. Woodson, op. cit., pp. 191-192.
5. James M. McPherson, *Anti-Negro Riots in the North*, p. iv.
6. Johnson, *Black Manhattan*, pp. 51, 53.

Abraham Franklin: This young man who was murdered by the mob on the corner of Twenty-seventh St., and Seventh avenue, was a quiet, inoffensive man, 23 years of age, of unexceptionable character, and a member of Zion African Church in this city. Although a cripple, he earned a living for himself and his mother by serving a gentleman in the capacity of coachman.

A short time previous to the assault upon his person, he called upon his mother to see if anything could be done by him for her safety. The old lady, who was noted for her piety and her Christian deportment, said she considered herself perfectly safe; but if her time to die had come, she was ready to die. Her son then knelt down by her side, and implored the protection of Heaven in behalf of his mother. The old lady was affected to tears, and said to our informant that it seemed to her that the good angels were present in the room. Scarcely had the supplicant risen from his knees, when the mob broke down the door, seized him, beat him over the head and face with fists and clubs, and then hanged him in the presence of his mother.

While they were thus engaged, the military came and drove them away, cutting down the body of Franklin, who raised his arm once slightly and gave a few signs of life.

The military then moved on to quell other riots, when the mob returned and again suspended the now probably lifeless body of Franklin, cutting out pieces of flesh and otherwise mutilating it. [7]

In the South, Senior Bishop Joseph J. Clinton was in the throes of the freedom strife while planting Zion connection in new territories. "His heart, in its natural prompting, went out after the common and special well-being of his fellowmen; this was evidenced in his early engagement in the work of the Christian ministry. The further attestation of the strength of his philanthropic nature, was his connection with the Underground Railroad (in the palmy days of slavery), in which he was frequently exposed to great personal dangers." [8] His bold stand for justice, and his experience of being thrown in jail with some of his preachers at Alexandria, Va., in 1863, also attest to his strength to endure hardships for his race. [9] As president of the Freedmen's American and British Commission, he constantly importuned the race leaders to advance their own cause. He was often misunderstood and received much abuse, but seldom did he attempt to defend any of his statements or actions.

In one such instance, after the close of the Civil War in 1865, while church and race leaders found themselves engaged in the social uplift and moral advancement of their people, Bishop Clinton had been attacked in the press on one of his speeches and replied that he was diametrically opposed to newspaper controversy, but felt that the gentleman's able letter necessitated a reply. He said that his address delivered before the Freedmen's American and British Commission in Zion (Mother Zion) Church, New York, "a synopsis of which was reported in the *New York Herald*," had been erroneously interpreted in four statements, to which he countervailed, and stated:

You admit that the African Civilization Society is doing much good. And the Zion and A.M.E. Churches are doing much for the Freedom. And I will add that the Freedman's American and British Commission is contributing its part in forwarding on the good work.

Now suppose our people, generally, East, West, North and South, would rally to the help of these institutions and give them their co-operation. I tell

7. McPherson, *op. cit.*, p. 14.
8. Moore, *History*, p. 364.
9. Anderson, *Official Directory*, p. 44.

you we would soon find ourselves fully adequate to the task.

... The time has come when we must get off the white man's back and do something for ourselves. We must go down among our brethren, the Freedmen and teach them to help themselves. In conclusion, permit me to say that it is my candid opinion that we can only be elevated in this country by the blessings of God and our own endeavors. [10]

Bishop Clinton's attitude of the black race forcefully uniting and independently working his way out of the devastating condition in which the war had left him was prophetic indeed. His chief coadjutor and missionary to the South during the turbulent days of the war, Rev. J. W. Hood, proved by his valiant deeds to be a tower of strength to his constitutents and a mighty race leader.

Hood went to North Carolina in January, 1864. Aside from founding the first A.M.E. Zion Church in the South, he bacame engaged in many activities to benefit his people upon his arrival at New Bern. "During that year, in the absence of the chaplain, he preached to the colored troops and was often called 'chaplain,' but he never held the commission as such. He went there as missionary under General Butler's invitation to the churches to send missionaries into his department. New Bern was twice attacked after he went there, so that he understands what it is to be under Confederate fire," stated Dr. Simmons. [11]

Among the "first" conventions, if not the first of them all, of colored men in the South, was the one in October, 1865, in Raleigh. In this meeting he was elected president as the "dark horse." Three other candidates had packed delegations as it appears, and thus defeated each other. The opening speech in that convention was the subject of much comment from the press, some not very complimentary to the speaker. He was reminded "that hemp grew in that part of the State." It was the first time that a black man had so publicly stated that the Negro was among those who came from one blood, and among those whom the Declaration of Independence included as endowed with inalienable rights, liberty and the pursuit of happiness; a right to the jury-box, cartridge box, and ballot box, were among the demands which he said the colored people would contend for, and that with the help of God. He was reminded in some of the bitter papers at that time that he would get all these in one box. [12]

Hood was a leader in assembling this Convention, and his address also contended for education "for our children that they may be useful in all the relations of life." [13]

Hood was, without a doubt, one of the most influential and creative black leaders of the Reconstruction era. He moved to Fayetteville, and while pastoring Evans Memorial Church, in 1867 he was elected as a delegate to the Constitutional Convention of the State of North Carolina. The Constitution then adopted was called the "Hood Constitution."

He took an active interest in matters pertaining to education, serving on the Committee on Education. This constitution of 1868 established the public school system in North Carolina for all the children of all the people. James Walker Hood in 1868 was made Assistant Superintendent of Public Instruction by the State Board of Education. His duty was to supervise the public schools of the colored children. Hood urged the need of one or more normal schools for the training of colored teachers and other institutions of

10. *The Anglo-African*, October 21, 1865, pp. 1-2.
11. William J. Simmons, *Men of Mark*, p. 135.
12. *Ibid.*,
13. C. H. Hamlin, *Ninety Bits of North Caroline Biography*, p. 107.

learning for Negroes. By 1870, he had 49,000 colored children in school and he had established a school for deaf, dumb, and blind. [14]

He had received, unsolicited, a commission from General O. O. Howard, as Assistant Superintendent under the Freedmen's Bureau, without pay, except that he was allowed three dollars a day, when traveling in the interest of the Bureau, to cover expenses.

At the Convention in 1867, "he made a speech which was full of sarcasm and ridicule of his opponent, a gentleman who had opposed some measure in which he was interested. He said:

After all I am compelled to acknowledge that I feel myself to be under some obligation to the secessionists. I am compelled to acknowledge that to their folly, in a great measure, we owe our present enfranchisement. The gentleman from Orange remarked last night that his race has always occupied a position more elevated than the rest of mankind. I am astonished at that young man that he has no more regard for his reputation as a historian than to assert such a ridiculous fallacy in the hearing of intelligent gentlemen in the noonday splendor of the nineteenth century. Does he not know that his ancestors, the ancient Britons, were in bondage in ancient Rome, in the days of Julius Caesar, and ever since that day? Mr. Chairman, the worst that has ever been said of my people was that they were too ignorant to be anything but slaves; but of the Britons it was said that they were too ignorant even to be slaves. A friend of Julius Caesar, writing to him, urged him not to bring slaves from Britain, for they were so ignorant that they could not be taught music. Now I have never heard it said of colored people that they were too ignorant to sing. I admit that this is not very flattering to the ancestors of the gentleman from Cleveland and Orange. Ancestry is something that they should not go back into, except with their mouths in the dust; but I don't blame them for this. It is something they cannot help. I am sorry for them, but I don't blame them for springing from such a low origin. I only think hard of them for making mouths at me. [15]

"In 1868 he demanded and obtained cabin passage on the Cape Fear steamers. The agents told him that nothing but the fact that the city was under military authority caused the company to yield to his demand. He advised the bishop not to attempt to take advantage of this, as it would be the worse for him when the military was withdrawn. The answer was characteristic of the man. He said he would enjoy it while he could, and trust the Lord for the balance. His right, however, has never been questioned on that river since. This proves what we have often said." wrote Simmons, "that, if colored men would demand what belongs to them they could very many times get it, but because of their indifference and littleness of soul, they are often shoved into places where it is a disgrace to go." [16]

Hood worked for total equality of mankind. The State Constitution of North Carolina of 1868 was illustrative of his labors. The Constitution first provided "a school system for all the children of all the people; political rights were made independent of property, race, or creed; the death penalty was reduced from seventeen crimes to four crimes; imprisonment for debt was prohibited, and the whipping post was abolished." [17]

14. *Ibid.*, p. 108; *The Star of Zion*, August 13, 1896.
15. Simmons, *op. cit.*, p. 137.
16. *Ibid.*, pp. 135-136.
17. Hamlin, *op. cit.*, p. 108.

"In 1872, Hood was offered the Republican nomination as their candidate for Secretary of State of North Carolina. He declined and that year became bishop of the African Methodist Episcopal Zion Church." [18] "He never desired a purely secular office and did not regard his educational position in that light. He was made temporary chairman of the Republican State Convention in 1876, and gave such satisfaction that the gentleman who was selected for permanent chairman wanted to decline in his favor." [19]

During this period before Hood's election to the bishopric, the 4,000,000 free men and women, who had been the center of controversies in Congress and throughout the country since Emancipation, were still the center of the storm. The unsettled state of the South was a source of continuous trouble. The "scalawags," as the Southern whites were called, the "carpetbaggers," as the Northern whites were known, and the Negroes shared governing power in the ex-slave states. "The scalawag managed the Negro, the latter did the voting, while the carpetbagger held the office. And when there were 'more stalls than horses' the Negroes and scalawags occasionally got an office." [20]

After the inauguration of President Rutherford B. Hayes in 1877, who favored civil service reform and sought to heal the wounds of the Civil War, and principally the Southern white supremacists by withdrawing federal troops from the South along with the so-called "carpetbaggers," efforts of readjustment for the Negro became problematic. These conditions were always blamed upon the Negro freedmen because they had been left in charge of the government of Southern states before they had governmental experience, and therefore, did a well-timed job punctuated by mistakes because the Southern group would not cooperate while they were in charge. The black man was always blamed for the retardation of the development of the South after the war, even though his situation was a natural consequence of the damage that the war had done and the new responsibility of finding a just place and relationship for the freedmen.

Hence there grew up a doctrine among Southern whites of anathematization and disfranchisement of Negroes. Events of unpleasantness and sometimes violence were practiced, all in the interest of what was said to be the necessity of partitioning these racial groups with disfranchisement, segregation, etc. More and more this condition grew upon the politics and the public practices of the entire group of the ex-slave states. The stimulation of segregation and practice of disfranchisement aggravated the situation, so that unpleasantness became the vogue and often flared into violence, such as lynching, the practice of peonage, intimidation, and terrorism of the Negro by such groups as the Ku Klux Klan and other peace-breaking organizations.

In spite of the Thirteenth, Fourteenth and Fifteenth Amendments to the Constitution and the Civil Rights Bill of 1875, disfranchisement, segregation, and Jim Crow conditions had been accomplished gradually by legislation, and finally completed throughout the South by the first part of the twentieth century. And Jim Crow practices continued in the North in disparateness and disguise. Therefore, the so-called Negro problem, for more than 100 years, was one of education and economics. Education was the major solution and the chief weapon to wage war on this new suppression which had overtaken the Negro after slavery. Northern white churches, the black churches, and the Freedmen's Aid Bureau

18. *Ibid.*
19. Simmons, *op. cit.*, p. 140.
20. George W. Williams, *History of the Negro Race in America*, pp. 381-382.

grasped the opportunity and began their work of establishing schools in the South. Wilberforce University in Ohio, which served primarily Southern blacks, was established in the North.

The A.M.E. Zion Church, in the process of building up its membership in the South, was education-minded but very limited in means. Most of its 21 educational institutions in history were forcibly discontinued. Coupled with the education efforts was the contention for justice, equality, elimination of discrimination, and full citizenship according to the nation's written mandate. This new struggle to break down the walls of a democratic nation living in deception since the Declaration of Independence, was carried on by many of the same people who agitated and suffered for the destruction of slavery, such as Frederick Douglass, William Wells Brown, Harriet Tubman, Sojourner Truth, Isaiah C. Wears, William Lloyd Garrison, Harriet Beecher Stowe, Henry Highland Garnett, Martin Delaney, and John Mercer Langston.

Black men were spurred into action and new leaders continued to come forward. Blacks and whites were becoming deeply involved for the sake of justice. Thus thousands of incidents developed, recorded and unrecorded, significant and many times overlooked. However, all were of the most courageous, forthright, enterprising, and audacious nature, even in defiance of Klansmen, mobs, and riotous race-haters in general, spanning more than 100 years, to help bring about rights of citizenship for the freedmen as much as for the rest of the nation.

Continuing his involvement in the struggle for the rights of his people was Bishop J. W. Hood. By 1876 he had discovered Joseph Charles Price, the incomparable young orator and brilliant genius. Hood and C. R. Harris worked inseparably with Price to give the South its first college organized and manned by blacks. While the first two had labored incessantly to organize the school, the latter traversed the British Isles in 1881 with his rare oratorical gifts, and raised the funds which re-established Livingstone College at Salisbury, North Carolina, and he continued to work for its perpetuity until his death in 1893. Price had made the trip with Hood, delegate to the First Ecumenical Methodist Conference, representing the A.M.E. Zion Church.

On his return to America he was no longer Reverend Joseph C. Price, the popular orator of his denomination, but he was hailed as a new leader, verifying the prophecy that Frederick Douglass made in 1867, of "men rising up under the fostering wings of freedom and education all over the South, surpassing in eloquence and oratorical power" himself who "had been complimented as the great black man of the North." During the remaining twelve years of his life no other Negro enjoyed greater popularity nor seemed destined by the consent of the people to be their acknowledged leader. [21]

During these days, "what the colored people needed most of all was a wise and unselfish leadership, not only politically but in every walk of life—in education, in religion and in industry. They had developed some of these leaders, but their need was still obvious and most acute when Joseph C. Price grew to manhood. . . .It was as a public speaker that he won distinction and was able to find the means to carry on constructive work along other lines." [22] Within a decade Price had led the North Carolina delegation of black people to the inauguration of President James A. Garfield, refused the office of

21. Cromwell, *The Negro in American History,* p. 173.
22. Charles W. Chestnutt, *Joseph C. Price, Orator and Educator* (unpublished ms.); Walls, *J. C. Price, Educator and Race Leader,* pp. 379, 381.

Minister and Consul General to Liberia, even after his name had been sent to the Senate by President Grover Cleveland, to continue developing Livingstone College; and through his acquaintance with President Benjamin Harrison, aided his close friend and associate, John C. Dancy, in securing the position of collector of customs at Wilmington, N. C. [23]

In 1890 a promising move was made, when the Afro-American Council was organized "for a renewed fight for equal rights." J. C. Price was elected president, and New York editor T. Thomas Fortune, secretary. [24] Alexander Walters, the pastor of Mother Zion Church in New York, gives the following historical background of this organization:

WHAT must we do to be saved?

This was the serious inquiry proposed at the close of the Civil War. The answer came quickly and decisively—Educate—Improve our morals—Get Money—and the Party of Lincoln that has added the thirteenth and fourteenth and fifteenth amendments to the Federal Constitution will see that we get our Civil and Political Rights. For it had promised them to us. We forthwith proceeded to educate; to improve our morals; and to get money. And we, indeed, made astonishing progress.

In the midst of this progress, we were suddenly awakened to the fact that the party of Lincoln had sold us out in 1876 in order to secure the presidency. The protection which had been given us in the South and without which it was utterly impossible for us to retain our Civil and Political rights, had been withdrawn; hence we were left exposed to the wrath of our enemies.

It was apparent to all that something must be done by way of organization, if the race was to be saved. Mr. T. Thomas Fortune, one of the ablest and bravest of our leaders, in a series of articles in the *New York Freeman* (now *Age*), called attention to the deplorable state of affairs and urged the Negroes to organize for their self-protection.

He finally issued the following Appeal:

"To the Colored Citizens of the Republic: Being convinced that the time is ripe for the organization of the National Afro-American League, proposed by me two years ago, to successfully combat the denial of our Constitutional and inherent rights, so generally denied or abridged throughout the Republic, and being urged to do so by members of branch leagues all over the country, I, by these presents, issue a call to all the branches of the Afro-American League, and invite all clubs and societies organized to secure the rights of the race, to meet by their representatives in National Convention at Chicago, Ill., Wednesday, January 15, 1890, for the purpose of organizing a National Afro-American League; the basis of Representation to be four delegates for every one hundred members, or one delegate for every twenty-five members, constituting the branch league, club or society, desiring to co-operate in the movement for National organization.

Correspondence from all organizations desiring to join this movement is requested.

Very respectfully,
T. Thomas Fortune." [25]

Several men concurred in the call. Reverend Walters, Mr. Fortune's pastor, was the first to respond. In accordance with the call, the league convened in Chicago, January 15, 1890, and was an enthusiastic gathering. "At the next meeting Price was succeeded in the presidency by Mr. Fortune, but for lack of

23. Walls, *op. cit.*, pp. 29, 93, 385; Cromwell, *op. cit.*, p. 175.
24. Ottley, *New World A-Coming*, p. 23.
25. Walters, *My Life and Work*, pp. 95-96.

interest on the part of the masses as well as leaders of the race, there was not another meeting of the league called." [26]

Meantime after J. C. Price had been elected president of the Afro-American Council, which was composed of a young group of black Republican leaders, later that same year the "old guard" Afro-American Republicans held a convention in Washington, D.C., which Price attended only as a fraternal representative.

"Frederick Douglass, in thunderous tones spoke only as Douglass could speak when aroused." He was followed by the greatest Negro debater of his day in the country, Isaiah Wears of Philadelphia, "who by force of logic enthused and delighted his hearers." Senator Blanche K. Bruce, first black U.S. Senator, still wearing with pride the honor of his distinguished and eminent position," addressed the convention also. Also addressing the convention was John Mercer Langston, keen magnetic platform orator, who had been elected to the Fifty-First U.S. Congress over a Virginia white man, at first had his seat contested, and received his seat in the last days of the first session. J. C. Price was the last speaker. "In his persuasive manner, he entered upon the subject still in question before the meeting, 'Proper Racial Political Adjustments.' " [27] This convention had chosen "Bishop Alexander W. Wayman as its presiding officer, but because of factional differences between Bishop Wayman and former Lieutenant-Governor P. B. S. Pinchback of Louisiana, Mr. Price, who had not arrived when the Convention was called to order, was subsequently elected president amidst great enthusiasm." [28]

"In 1891 Mr. Price was appointed Commissioner-General of what was to be the Grand Southern Exposition to be held at Raleigh. In the discharge of this duty he traveled extensively through the South, journeying in the interior as well as in the larger cities, and learned much at first hand of the material conditions of the masses at the South." [29]

In what is known as the interim between Frederick Douglass and the rise of Booker T. Washington, Joseph Charles Price was chief of all Negro race leaders in our land. While his brief life of 39 years was ebbing away, Frederick Douglass made a substitute speech in the absence of the invited speaker, Price, at the World's Congress of Races at the World's Fair in Chicago in 1893. Little did he dream that he would survive the invited speaker. The famous race advocate, Ida B. Wells Barnett, who had been terrorized and victimized for her courageous leadership, was present and related the words spoken by "old man eloquent" who began:

> This is Price's day. I am here as a substitute. Since I have grown old I was one time disturbed about the cause of my people on the American platform, in leadership and organization. Since the rise of Joseph C. Price, I have dismissed all fears. I am willing to die and leave the race in his hands. [30]

Three weeks after Douglass made this speech, Price died, and Douglass sent Mrs. Price a telegram stating—"The Race Has Lost its Ablest Advocate."

Frederick Douglass, who had denounced "the so-called emancipation as a stupendous fraud," lived nearly two years longer in the continual battle for race rights. In 1888, after visiting South Carolina and Georgia, he was deeply shocked by what he discovered and said in a speech April 10, 1888:

26. *Ibid.*, pp. 97-98.
27. Walls, *op. cit.,* pp. 350-351; Cromwell, *op. cit.,* pp. 159, 163.
28. Cromwell, *op. cit.,* p. 175.
29. *Ibid.*
30. Walls, *op. cit,* p. 86.

EQUAL RIGHTS AND CITIZENSHIP

I have of late seen enough, heard enough and learned enough of the condition of these people in South Carolina and Georgia to make me welcome any movement which will take them out of the wretched condition which I now know them to be. While I shall continue to labor for increased justice to those who stay in the South, I give you my hearty "Godspeed" your emigration scheme. I believe you are doing a good work. [31]

He delivered one of his most effective addresses a few days later at the twenty-sixth anniversary of Emancipation in the District of Columbia. "In earnest tones, he told the nation: 'I here and now denounce his so-called emancipation as a stupendous fraud—a fraud upon him, a fraud upon the world.' He drew a terrifying picture of exploitation of the Southern Negro, and he denounced the national government for having abandoned the black man, ignored his rights as an American citizen, and left him "a deserted, a defrauded, a swindled, and an outcast man—in law, free; in fact a slave." [32] He further asserted:

I have assisted in fighting one battle for the abolition of slavery, and the American people have shed their blood in defense of the Union and the Constitution, and neither I nor they should wish to fight this battle over again; and in order that we may not, we should look the facts in the face today and, if possible, nip the evil in the bud. . . .

I am, however, not here to name men. My mission now, as all along during nearly fifty years, is to plead the cause of the dumb millions of our countrymen against injustice, oppression, meanness and cruelty, and to hasten the day when the principles of liberty and humanity expressed in the Declaration of Independence and the Constitution of the United States shall be the law and the practice of every section, and of all the people of this great country without regard to race, sex, color or religion. [33]

February 20, 1895 Douglass was no more, but his spirit hovered over his people. By 1897, the two leaders who had become senior bishops of the A.M.E. and A.M.E. Zion Churches, Bishops Henry McNeil Turner and James Walker Hood, had been placed in positions to exert wonderful influence, and were continuing to give vivid and constructive leadership for race justice. It was recalled by an A.M.E. Zion preacher that during Reconstruction, "these two great men could be heard in the pulpit and on the platform thundering through North and South Carolina, Georgia, Virginia and other Southern states in behalf of their people. They counted not their own lives dear unto themselves, but went forward, often facing death itself, laboring in the interest of their race." [34]

The work done in North Carolina by Hood, and in Georgia by Turner, for the betterment of their people, was being utterly smashed by continued interventions of Jim Crowism and violent terrorism. Yet the two men continued to fight uncompromising battles without flinching. Both lived long and fought hard. Toward the end of his years, Turner had become so disappointed over the cruel treatment of the race without civil protection, that he made a statement that he would never die on American soil, and when he felt his last days near, he made his way to Canada and gave up the ghost. Hood, although equally disappointed over the conditions of the race, remained on the battlefield, and died in his 87th year at Fayetteville.

Over a 10-year period from 1882 to 1892 more than 1,400 Negroes had been lynched. An additional 564 known lynchings had taken place in another five years,

31. Philip S. Foner, *The Voice of Black America*, pp. 520-521.
32. *Ibid.*, p. 521.
33. *Ibid.*, pp. 522, 536.
34. A. J. Warner, *The Star of Zion*, August 12, 1897.

2,000 blacks had been lynched, and an additional number prior to 1882, known and unknown. The race was suffering all kinds of abuse and martyrdom. On March 10, 1898, Bishop Alexander Walters published the following article in the *New York Age:*

Fellow Citizens: The late outrages perpetrated against Postmasters Loften of Hogansville, Ga., and Baker of Lake City, S.C., for no other reason than their race and color, and having no reason to believe from past experience that the perpetrators will be brought to justice; and further, because there is a determined effort on the part of the white labor unions of the country to exclude the Negro from the industrial avenues in which he can make an honest living, it becomes absolutely necessary that we organize for self-protection.

I therefore move that T. Thomas Fortune, president of the National Afro-American League, call a meeting of the leaders of the race at an early date, to take in consideration the present condition of affairs and suggest a remedy for the same. All who will unite with me in this request please send their names to this paper.

Respectfully,
A. Walters,
Bishop of A.M.E. Zion Church [35]

Over a hundred black leaders from all walks of life and every corner of the country joined in the call, and on August 24, 1898, President T. Thomas Fortune issued the call, through the *New York Age*, for the delegates to assemble at Rochester, N.Y., September 15. A hundred and fifty prominent representatives of the black race in the United States assembled to consider the advisability of reviving the old Afro-American League. "After thoroughly discussing the need of the organization in order to fight everything that is antagonistic to the race, it was decided not to reorganize the old league, but to form a new one under the name of the National Afro-American Council."

T. Thomas Fortune was made chairman and presided over this historic assembly. When the nominating committee reported, it was in favor of him being named president, but "Mr. Fortune acknowledged that he had not confidence enough in the race to carry the council on to success, and consequently his name was withdrawn." [36] Fortune had expressed his strong sentiment in the first Afro-American League meeting, and "urged the black man to 'fight fire with fire' and 'face the enemy and fight inch by inch for every right he denies us.' " [37] Fortune was a courageous fighter for the cause, but, he felt he could fight more freely as a writer and agitator. Thus the officers agreed upon were as follows: "President, Bishop Alexander Walters, Jersey City, N.J.; Vice-President, J. C. Dancy, Wilmington, N.C.; Secretary, Mrs. Ida B. W. Barnett, Chicago; Financial Secretary, John E. Bruce (Bruce's Grit), Albany, N.Y.; Treasurer, John W. Thompson, Rochester; Executive Committee: Bishop B. W. Arnett, Joseph P. Peaker, Chris Perry, H. T. Kealing." The committee on address presented a manifesto which represented the objects of the council, which was adopted in toto, reviewing and denouncing lynchings, the convict lease system, the separate car law, and actions of the Labor Commission, with added expressions on the Paris Exposition and the Cuban immigration. [38] This council of potent race leaders began its work to alleviate racial conditions in the country.

35. Walters, *op. cit.,* p. 98.
36. *Ibid.,* p. 106.
37. Stephen R. Fox, *The Guardian of Boston*, p. 46.
38. Walters, *op. cit.,* pp. 106-109.

Nine days after the council issued its second call to chart its course of action, that which has been termed by some as the Wilmington riot took place on November 10, 1898. Actually it was the Wilmington massacre, for blacks were harmless and defenseless. ("Charles W. Chestnutt's novel, *The Marrow of Tradition*, includes a vivid description of the Wilmington Massacre.") [39]

On November 9, 1898, a mass meeting of white citizens was held at Wilmington, N.C., in an effort to redeem the city from Negro rule ... who outnumbered the whites 17,000 to 8,000. It was demanded that the editor of the Negro newspaper remove himself and his press by 7 o'clock the next morning. When this demand was not met, 600 armed whites destroyed the printing material, and the building "took fire" and burned to the ground. A race riot followed, with some ten Negroes being killed and three whites wounded. The coroner ruled that the Negroes came to their death by gunshot wounds at the hands of unknown parties. All of the city officials resigned and were superseded by white Democrats. [40]

The A.M.E. Zion Church was deeply affected. The printing office burned down was in the same block as St. Luke A.M.E. Zion Church and the pastor, Rev. Martin L. Blaylock, had to run for his life and made his escape passing as a white man, hiking out of the state, and safely landed in Harrisburg, Pa. [41] John C. Dancy, collector of customs, also managed to flee for his life, and came to New York with T. Thomas Fortune expressing wonderment as to why he left the beseiged city, while others of the race were in need of his leadership. Another refugee, Rev. Charles S. Morris, delivered an address in Boston, January 1890 stating:

NINE NEGROES were massacred outright; a score wounded and hunted like partridges on the mountain; one man, brave enough to fight against such odds would be hailed as a hero anywhere else, was given the privilege of running the gauntlet up a broad street, where he sank ankle-deep in the sand, while crowds of men lined the sidewalks and riddled him with a pint of bullets as he ran bleeding past their doors; another Negro shot twenty times in the back as he scrambled empty-handed over a fence; thousands of women and children fleeing in terror from their humble homes in the darkness of the night, out under a gray and angry sky, from which falls a cold and bone-chilling rain, out to the dark and tangled ooze of the swamp amid the crawling things of night, fearing to light a fire, startled at every footstep, cowering, shivering, shuddering, trembling, praying in gloom and terror; half-clad and barefooted mothers, with their babies wrapped only in a shawl, whimpering with cold and hunger at their icy breasts, crouched in terror from the vengeance of those who, in the name of civilization, and with the benediction of the ministers of the Prince of Peace, inaugurated the reformation of the city of Wilmington the day after the election by driving out one set of white officeholders and filling their places with another set of white officers—the one being Republican and the other Democrat. All this happened, not in Turkey, nor in Russia, nor in Spain, not in the gardens of Nero, nor in the dungeons of Torquemada, but within three hundred miles of the White House, in the best state in the South, within a year of the twentieth century, while the nation was on its knees thanking God for having enabled it to break the Spanish yoke from the neck of Cuba. This is our civilization. This is Cuba's kindergarten of ethics and good government. This is Protestant religion in the United States that is planning a wholesale missionary crusade against

---

39. Foner, *op. cit.*, p. 604.
40. James Truslow Adams (ed.), *Dictionary of American History*, Vol. V, p. 469.
41. This story related to the writer by Reverend Blaylock.

Catholic Cuba. This is the golden rule as interpreted by the white pulpit of Wilmington. [42]

While whites attempted to justify the incident to "end Negro domination," Morris gave contrasting statistics on white office holders throughout the city and state representing Wilmington, from the white Mayor to the white Superintendent of garbage. [43]

These atrocious and useless outrages were growing all over the South. Five months after the Wilmington massacre, on March 16, 1899, "the white citizens of Palmetto, Georgia, broke into the town jail and killed four Negroes and seriously wounded another four, all of whom had been accused of having set fires in town. During the next few weeks the outrage was discussed at meetings of black people all over the country. The contrasting reactions of two of America's leaders were presented in speeches during the last week of April, 1899." [44]

Still chafing over the murder of black South Carolina postmaster Baker and his baby, the shooting and maiming for life of his wife and three daughters, and the wounding of his son, which prompted the reorganization of the National-Afro-American Council, Bishop Walters said:

> The real cause of our trouble is race hatred. Some years ago it was thought that as the Negroes became intelligent and cultured this race prejudice would disappear; but in some sections of the country it has only intensified this feeling. The passing of the Jim-Crow-car laws in several of the Southern states; the disfranchisement of Negroes, regardless of qualification; the shutting-out of them from hotels, restuarants, and places of amusement, are all manifestations of race hatred. We are censured as a race for not exhibiting manly qualities and are considered "impudent niggers" if we presume to assert our manhood. We are truly between the upper and nether millstone. I have come to the conclusion that nothing but manly resistance on the part of the Afro-Americans themselves will stop these outrages. President McKinley and the federal government have shown themselves impotent to convict the murders of federal officials. The governors of certain states in the South have acknowledged their inability to protect their colored citizens. In the name of almighty God, what are we to do but fight and die? [45]

Booker T. Washington expressed the following opinion on these murders:

> As a rule, the men guilty of these outrages are ignorant individuals who have had no opportunity to secure an education and moral restraint. The only permanent remedy for such crimes as have been recently perpetrated in Georgia, and the only permanent remedy for the mob violence, is in the thorough education of all the people in the South—education that shall reach the head, the hand, the heart, so that, in discussing the educational needs of my people this evening, after all, we are considering the problem which is fundamental in the salvation of the whole South. [46]

In 1901, "W. E. B. DuBois stated that there were many Negro intellectuals who refuted Booker T. Washington as a popular leader, refusing to accept his position that the Negro was to give up social equality for the time being. George Forbes and William Monroe Trotter began publishing *The Guardian* (Boston), which demanded full equality for Negroes, and opposed the ideas of Booker T.

42. Foner, *op. cit.*, p. 605.
43. *Ibid.*, pp. 606-607.
44. *Ibid.*, pp. 611-612. ·
45. *Ibid.*, p. 612.
46. *Ibid.*, p. 613.

Washington." [47]

While Price, Walters, DuBois, Fortune, and Trotter all often expressed opposite views from those of Booker T. Washington on the race problems, each of them had a part of the general solution. The first set were of the complete freedom idealist group working along the line of unlimited freedom. The other was a long term creative worker through the process of education and the patient plodding of economic success through industry and agriculture.

President Theodore Roosevelt was inaugurated in 1901, and for the first time since Emancipation, the head of the country openly denounced human sufferings of the race. He was a great advocate and courageous fighter for the rights of common people, and a man of firm conviction of equality up against an inmovable government.

The Board of Bishops of the A.M.E. Zion Church, which had been clear in its advice and encouragement of the race as it passed through the ordeal of Emancipation and oppression which they later endured, came forward in its message to the church at the General Conference of 1904 with the following clarion ring:

> . . . Notwithstanding our efforts to become worthy citizens, producers as well as consumers, we are still discriminated against and in many instances, unjustly and barbarously outraged; as was the case a few days ago in Mississippi where a woman whose only crime was the remaining with her hunted husband, who was being pursued by a mob for taking the life of a white man in self-defense. She was brutally mutilated, fingers, nose and breasts cut off and holes bored in her flesh, and finally burned at the stake. Such cruelties force us to cry to Almighty God for vengeance and ask, How long, O Lord, are we to suffer such inhuman treatment? While lynchings are becoming more fiendish, public sentiment against them, both in the North and South, is on the increase which will eventually stop them. We believe firmly in agitation and urge our people everywhere to take advantage of the press and other legitimate agencies to create sentiment against lynchings, disfranchisement, Jim Crow car laws and other discriminations.
>
> Since we are in the right, we know that God is on our side, and we shall prevail. [48]

At the next General Conference, in 1908, the bishops in their message to the church stated:

> In view of the unique and rather anamolous position occupied by the Negro population of the United States, and the treatment that is meted out to them in many parts of the country, we deem it expedient to call attention to some matters which affect our civil and political statutes of the country. . . . In view of the fact that we have a National Constitution guaranteeing civil, political and equal rights to every law abiding citizen, it is reasonable that we should expect that the government of the nation and each State composing a nation give such a just and impartial administration of the laws as would carry out the principles and purposes of the nation.
>
> We are grieved, however, to observe that subordinate States are permitted to nullify the provisions of the National Constitution and trample down the rights of industrious, faithful and valuable citizens.
>
> We regard the disfranchisement of Constitutional amendments, the class legislation, unjust treatment, the disregard of the law and other acts which are perpetrated to humiliate the Negro as being no less detrimental to the good

47. Bergman, *The Chronological History of the Negro*, p. 333.
48. *Minutes,* Twenty-Second Quadrennial Session, pp. 151-152.

BISHOP ALEXANDER WALTERS

1858 - 1917

The most influential black churchman of his generation. One of the organizers of the National Association for the Advancement of Colored People. Served as President of the Afro-American Council, President of the Pan-African Congress, and an original trustee of the International Christian Endeavor Society.

name of our common country and inimical to the welfare of other citizens, than a great injustice and gross wrong to the Negro population of the country, and therefore calculated to finally undermine the very foundation of the government and our institutions unless these evils are checked.

Inasmuch as we are required to support the government of the State and nation with our taxes and willingly obey the laws, and we stand ever ready as in the past to defend the flag under which the brave men of the race have fought to preserve the Union and give liberty to their fellowmen at home and abroad, and we believe it to be the duty of the State and nation to make us secure in the enjoyment of every citizen's privilege and constitutional rights now enjoyed by any other good citizen . . .

We appeal to the friends of justice everywhere, as well as to the States and nation, that manhood and merit shall be the standard by which citizenship shall be relegated. . . .

We insist that if laws are to be enacted regulating the rights to vote, that they be made to apply to all citizens alike, and we pledge ourselves to be willing to abide by the result.

Until this is done and fair treatment and decent accommodations are offered our people on the public carriers, where we are required to pay equal fares, we feel it to be our uncompromising duty to agitate and appeal to every known authority until our cry is heard and our petition is granted.

In face of unfavorable conditions, such as we have named above, we rejoice that our people are neither discouraged nor are they allowing themselves to stand still or cease their earnest endeavors to make steady and substantial progress along every line of honorable effort. [49]

49. Episcopal Quadrennial Address, 1908, pp. 23-24.

BISHOP GEORGE WYLIE CLINTON

1859 - 1921

He opposed the Governor Wade Hampton regime and was a victim of the racial outward political thrust in South Carolina. He was a general crusader for the black race in America, a friend of Booker T. Washington, and lectured 26 years at Tuskegee Institute. He was advisor during the administrations of Presidents McKinley and Theodore Roosevelt.

This message to the people had been in circulation no more than three months when the nation was reawakened by another bloody incident. One of the members of the Board of Bishops, Alexander Walters, had ably kept pace with the movements to combat racial evils. Since 1903 he supported W. E. B. DuBois in the work of establishing the Niagara Movement in 1905, and William Monroe Trotter in radical moves to eliminate racial conditions. In 1906, Atlanta had been hit by the biggest race riot of the decade. The year before, Booker T. Washington's control of the organization had weakened it, and it gave up its support of a restrictive franchise. As a result of the Atlanta riot, the council "became more militant and less amenable to Booker T. Washington's direction." [50] However, the Afro-American Council had not fully realized its aim since its beginning.

It found it impossible to arouse the sort of spirit and response on the part of the coloured people of the country necessary for the real growth of the organization; nor was it able to raise sufficient funds to create a permanent and efficient machine; so after a somewhat languishing existence of several years longer. But . . . it had accomplished something; it had pointed the way—not a new one but the old one—and it was to be followed by a similar effort made in what was more nearly the fullness of time. [51]
The Afro-American Council was the black unit in the formation of the N.A.A.C.P.

Birth of the National Association for the Advancement of Colored People

In August 1908, a race riot in Springfield, Illinois—home of Lincoln—in which several Negroes were lynched and killed, several Negroes and whites

50. Bergman, *op. cit.*, pp. 345, 347-348.
51. Johnson, *op. cit.*, p. 131.

TIMOTHY THOMAS FORTUNE

Member of Mother Zion Church, New York City. Founder of the New York *Globe,* later the *Age.* This skillful and courageous writer was one of the first blacks to work on editorial staff of a white daily, the New York *Sun.*

wounded, and thousands of Negroes driven from the city, horrified white liberals and brought them into action in the interest of justice as they had not been involved since Emancipation. "William English Walling, a radical white Southerner, sounded the alarm with an article in *The Independent.* The article, 'Race War in the North,' appeared September 3, 1908. 'Either the spirit of Lincoln and Lovejoy must be revived and we must come to treat the Negro on a plane of absolute political and social equality, or Vardaman and Tillman will soon have transferred the race war to the North.' " [52] Oswald Garrison Villard, grandson of abolitionist William Lloyd Garrison, and publisher of the New York *Evening Post,* spoke out editorially, and Mary White Ovington, a white humanitarian who had worked among Negroes in New York City and had studied conditions of Negroes North and South, and even attended the 1906 meeting of the Niagara Movement at Harpers Ferry, became deeply concerned.

Miss Ovington wrote to Mr. Walling and later talked with him about the matter, together with Dr. Henry Moskowitz, early in January 1909. Plans were discussed for making a demonstration on February 12, the hundredth anniversary of Abraham Lincoln's birth. Oswald Garrison Villard joined with the movement, and on Lincoln's birthday a call for a national conference on the Negro question, drafted by Mr. Villard, was issued: "We call upon all believers in democracy to join in a national conference for the discussion of present evils, the voicing of protests and the renewal of the struggle for civil and political rights." Among the liberal whites who signed the call were Charles Edward Russell, Jane Addams, John Dewey, Lillian D. Wald, Rabbi Stephen S. Wise, Rev. John Haynes Holmes and William Dean Howells. Among the black liberals who signed were W. E. B. DuBois, Bishop Alexander Walters, Ida B. Wells Barnett, and Rev. Francis J. Grimké. [53]

52. Lerone Bennett, Jr., *Before the Mayflower,* p. 281.
53. *Ibid.,* p. 54; Johnson, *op. cit,* pp. 140-141; Ottley, *op. cit,* p. 35; Bergman, *op. cit.,* p. 357.

Between May 30 and June 1, the National Negro Conference met in New York in the United Charities Building. The biracial group had expanded. Members of the Niagara Movement attended, and afterwards merged with this organization at the second conference in May 1910. William Monroe Trotter, suspicious of the aims of the whites, refused an invitation. Rather he started his own organization known as the National Equal Rights League, which several leaders and members of the A.M.E. Zion Church supported, especially in the East. Moorfield Storey, a prominent white Boston lawyer was elected president of the NAACP, and offices were established in New York City. At the conference in 1910, when joined by the forces of the Niagara Movement, the platform adopted was practically the same as that which had been adopted by the Niagara Movement in 1905. "It was commented upon as being extremely radical." [54]

The National Association for the Advancement of Colored People—the organization which was to fully dedicate its forces to securing "inalienable rights" for all—had thus been born with A.M.E. Zion Bishop Walters one of the central figures, and he became one of three vice-presidents. Dr. W. E. B. DuBois, already an outstanding figure, resigned his professorship at Atlanta University and came to New York to become director of publicity and research. Bringing with him his old magazine, *The Voice of the Negro* (1905), he became the founder and first editor of the organization's official organ, *The Crisis,* "considered the most effective and best-written propagandist periodical in the United States." [55] Around this same time, "two other strong friends became allied with the movement, Joel E. Spingarn and Arthur B. Spingarn." [56]

The black church in general and preachers in particular have bolstered this movement through the years, in its local, state, and regional chapters and the national organization. Many of the subordinate chapters in cities and towns were founded by black preachers. The black preacher has served as president of city, town state, and regional chapters, and the A.M.E. Zion Church preachers have been many among those deeply involved for citizenship, in building and maintaining this organization. There are other prominent leaders of the A.M.E. Zion Church who helped pave the way to justice and equality through this national organization.

In 1910 Moorfield Storey was elected president, William E. Walling, chairman of the Executive Committee, Frances Blascoer, national secretary, Walter E. Sachs, treasurer, Oswald Garrison Villard, assistant treasurer, and W. E. B. DuBois the only Negro officer, director of publicity and research. Succeeding Miss Blascoer as secretary were Mary White Ovington, May Childs Nerney and Royal Freeman Nash. Nash resigned in 1917 and was succeeded by John R. Shillady who went to Texas in August 1919 to defend the NAACP as a civic and educational organization and was beaten unconcious in the streets of Austin. He afterward resigned and in 1920 James Weldon Johnson became the first black executive secretary of the NAACP. He was succeeded by Walter White and Roy Wilkins. The title has been changed from executive secretary to executive director. Each of these men has had his experience in leadership of the organization into eras of achievement, and each worked and suffered peculiar hardship, ostracism and humiliations of his period. Each executive made his own inimitable reputation as

54. Johnson, *op. cit.,* p. 141.
55. Ottley, *op. cit.,* p. 35; John E. Bruce Ms. papers, Schomberg Collection.
56. Johnson, *op. cit.,* p. 141.

creative leader: Shillady through his peculiar daring and suffering; Johnson, invincible poet, thinker, writer and author of the National Negro Anthem; White, who uncovered the horrors of lynching and led with Thurgood Marshall in the situation that brought about desegregation of schools; and Wilkins who has chief credit of general disegregation and re-enfranchisement. (Note outstanding work of other A.M.E. Zion Church leaders of this movement later in chapter).

The National Urban League

The A.M.E. Zion Church became a cooperative factor in another movement of that time. In April 1910, the perfervid young scholar, George Edmund Haynes, founded the Committee on Urban Conditions Among Negroes in New York City. In 1911 it combined with the National League for the Protection of Colored Women founded by Mrs. William Baldwin, Jr. and Frances Keller, in 1905, and several organizations which had been formed to improve conditions of black men, women, and children. This total organization, which opened opportunities in industry, trained young Negro social workers, and assisted black migrants from the South in adjusting to life in Northern cities, became known as The National Urban League. George Edmund Haynes and Eugene Kinckle Jones were its first executive officers. Some years afterwards Jones became the enterprising Executive Director. This interracial movement began with a conservative program, but was gradually impelled into boycotts and other measures according to conditions of the times, for the advancement of the race cause. It continued to develop and actuate job and position placement of blacks, led by Jones and his perservering successor, Lester Granger. It took on its most aggressive program of combating racism under the directorship of Whitney Young, Jr. The present executive director, Vernon Jordan, moves forth with determination and zeal in the total involvement of complete equality of all minorities.

As this movement began its growth nationally, leaders and members of the A.M.E. Zion Church again figured prominently in local, state, and regional organizations as head executives and chairmen or members of the boards of directors. One influential leader of the Urban League was John C. Dancy, Jr., member of John Wesley A.M.E. Zion Church, Detroit, who served as Executive Director of the Detroit Urban League for 42 years, 1918 to 1960. The relationship of the A.M.E. Zion Church with this and other civil rights organizations through the years is one of total unity for the cause of the minority.

The Struggle Continues

The next decade, from 1910 to 1920, was one of slim improvement and great disappointment for the black race. When Southern whites discovered that organizations of defense were accomplishing goals, their threatening tactics became increasingly flagrant in many ways. Terrorism by secret groups became rampant and a story of a Negro lynching appeared in the papers on an average of every six days in 1911. Southern and border states continued to pass segregation laws in the face of these protestations, for example, housing segregation in Louisville, Baltimore, Richmond, and Atlanta in 1912, "and Negro ghettos sanctioned by law became well established in many parts of the country." [57]

Some had felt the progressive results of the NAACP, which had engaged a battery of some of the nation's best lawyers, including Clarence Darrow, and won constitutional cases of segregation, peonage, and the ballot. It had a big hand in

57. Bergman, *op. cit.*, pp. 366, 367.

winning the decision of the "Grandfather clause" case.

"Grandfather clauses" began to be adopted in the constitutions of Southern states in 1898. They were disfranchising devices, in that they laid down as necessary to the right of suffrage a list of property, literacy, and character qualifications; and then provided that none of these qualifications need to be met by any person who had the right to vote or had an ancestor who had the right to vote at the time of the close of the Civil War . . . [58]

Rejoicing over this decision of 1915, the Board of Bishops of the A.M.E. Zion Church, in its continued pursuit of racial justice, stated:

Lawlessness or disregard for the majesty of the law from which our country and especially our people have suffered so long, has not shown itself in so many forms in recent years as hitherto, but the venomous serpent of prejudice which shows itself in the form of segregation, lynching, discrimination and oppression is not by any means dead. It is for this reason that we hail with feelings of joy the decision of . . . the Supreme Court, the Court of last resort—that the Grandfather clause in many State Constitutions, . . . is unconstitutional and therefore null and void. This decision more firmly fixes our status as a part and factor of this great nation. We regard it as the most far-reaching and important deliverance emanating from that body, so far as we are concerned, in the last forty years. It is a fitting answer to the decision handed down by the same Court in the famous Dred Scott case, by Chief Justice Taney, nearly sixty years ago, in which it was held that we had no rights at all that other people were bound to respect. [59]

The A.M.E. Zion Church was not alone in its expressions of joy. The entire race rejoiced over what it considered a big victory. This however, boomeranged, as southern state governments continued to pass disfranchisement laws. The Board of Bishops in this same message firmly protested against the attitude of the administration of President Wilson:

in declaring his intention not to appoint men of our race in the list of Presidential appointments, because of expressed opposition to such appointments by some Southern Senators who would fight their confirmation. This attitude seems the more unfair, unreasonable and untenable in view of his appointment of an Indian, who is also colored, and a Jew, who appeared equally objectionable. He risked their confirmation, and in justice to our numbers and our loyalty to the flag at all times, he ought to be fair, and at least make the appointment and take a chance as to the confirmation. We feel humiliated and chagrined by this treatment, since every President since Hayes, without distinction of party affiliation has cheerfully accorded us the Recordership of Deeds, and to deny us such paltry consideration we regard as an affront and an open insult to ten millions of the most loyal and patriotic part of our population. [60]

Our loyal member, John C. Dancy, Sr., had held this position under Presidents McKinley and Theodore Roosevelt. Mr. Wilson had also removed Negroes from government common laboring jobs in the South, especially those who worked on the wharfs or seafronts. One of the hardest hit by Mr. Wilson's actions was Bishop Walters. He and several other liberal black leaders had succeeded in securing a sizable black vote for the Democratic candidate on the thesis that the time had come for the Negro to divide the vote and on the basis of the campaign promises of Wilson for justice—"not mere grudging justice but justice executed with liberality and cordial good feeling" [61] as he stated to

58. Johnson, *op. cit.*, p. 142.
59. Quadrennial Episcopal Address, Twenty-Fifth Quadrennial Session, p. 10.
60. *Ibid.*, p. 11.
61. *Dictionary of American Biography*, Vol. 19, pp. 398, 399.

Bishop Walters in a letter. Directly after Mr. Wilson was elected president he permitted, and thereby encouraged, segregated signs, *white* and *colored*, to be placed in government public facilities, not only in other parts of the country, but in the nation's capital where the world came to see democracy in action; the democracy of the man who entered into the biggest war in history "to make the world safe for democracy."

Bishop Walters became the object of criticism at church gatherings and other groups. He journeyed to the White House and had a private encounter with the president on this matter, to no avail. The president by this time had built up a compact understanding in prejudicial procedures, deceiving thoroughly the blacks who had voted for him. Bishop Walters died in 1917, having not recovered from the affect that this had upon him.

Both Bishops Hood and Walters having passed away this quadrennium, the church moved into the 1920's with the nation and the world having passed through a reputed decisive war, and not much accomplished for the race. The Bishops thus volleyed forth in 1920:

American sympathy appears to be active in helping the oppressed in other lands and allowing the smaller groups the right of self-determination, but unfortunate for her own territory, the spirit of democracy is not universally allowed or encouraged. Four hundred and fifteen thousand Negro boys were in the great conflict, wore the American uniform, and about half of them were in the thick of the fight and a large number breveted for bravery. We had officers there, captains, lieutenants, chaplains, engineers, sergeants and the like, and they were among the bravest of the brave. With the conflict over, the Negro logically looked for a fairer opportunity—a man's chance in a democratic country. The blood he shed in Flanders, on the Marne, at Chateau Thierre and elsewhere, has not mitigated, nor has it reduced the number of lynchings, nor prevented unequal accommodation in public carriers, nor granted him the free exercise of the right of franchise in every state in keeping with the spirit of our Constitution and the laws safeguarding it. . . . The foreigner coming to our shores who is the instigator of all strikes and anarchy is preferred to us while our existence here is coeval with the white American and our record for loyalty cannot be questioned.

We protest against such unjust and undemocratic treatment. We are full-fledged American citizens, loyal and true, and we are opposed to any organization at home or abroad which makes murder, anarchy and ruin its chief stock in trade and announces them as its propaganda. We ask for full protection for ourselves against these threatening evils, and are ready to stand by the Government in suppressing them. [62]

The resurgence of the Ku Klux Klan influence, racial hatred, open lawlessness, and the most notorious race riots of the nation's history after the war, produced a current of general unrest among the race. It began to appear to some Negroes that decisive and heroic measures should be taken to change the trend of worsening conditions nearly six decades after Emancipation.

Three months after our 1920 General Conference, Marcus Garvey founded the Universal Negro Improvement Association (UNIA) in New York City, inventing his pervasive slogan, "Africa for Africans!" and beginning his preachments to blacks on a "Back to Africa" campaign. The latter implied the former: that Westerners of African descent must go by way of its original continent (which was also being exploited by Europeans, though thickly populated with natives), consolidate its numbers, push for economic retrieval of Africa, and govern the

62. *Minutes,* Twenty-Sixth Quadrennial Session, pp. 63-64.

universe. Without a doubt, the race was being heavily impressed by his universal doctrine, and the UNIA became a powerful unit of black solidarity. Garvey had prophesied that there comes a great world change once every thousand years, and that this new era was the beginning of the thousand-year change. Thus the black man must seize his opportunity, for if he failed it would be another thousand years before he would have the opportunity. The Garvey movement had a noticeable existence in this country for a period of time. In 1927 Garvey was deported back to English territory by way of his home, the West Indies Island, and his movement was finally suppressed. He had, however, made an indelible impression.

In pursuit of full rights continuously sought by the A.M.E. Zion Church, one of its bishops later encountered a shocking experience. In the East, every state south of Pennsylvania practiced Jim Crowism by approval or legality, except, as the world little believed, the public spot in the nation's capital—Union Railroad Terminal, through which thousands of passengers of all walks of life embarked and disembarked, from around the world.

On the morning of September 26, 1925, Bishop W. J. Walls, and the wife of his episcopal classmate, Mrs. Annie Lucille Alleyne, entered the dining room of Union Station and took their seats to be served, after the bishop had debarked a train from the South en route to Boston. They were told to go sit in the rear of the dining room, and when they refused to move, the waiters refused to serve them. The bishop and his guest staged a three hour sit-in, missing several connecting trains to Boston. When the bishop appealed to authorities and they refused to respond, he remonstrated and called for officers of the local NAACP who sent the president, Neval H. Thomas, with a delegation. Bishop E. D. W. Jones and Mr. William O. Walker, (then editor of the *Washington Tribune*), came to the scene. Representatives of the Civil Rights Committee of Standard Oil Company, led by its agent, James A. (Billboard) Jackson also came. They entered into a conference with the manager of the Washington Terminal Company and Bishop Walls, who insisted on being served on equal terms, and after undue humiliation the bishop and his guest were finally served. This was the first major breakthrough in desegregation of restaurants in the Washington, D.C. area. He returned from Boston a week afterward, and engaged in conferences with the same civil rights committees and the manager of the Washington Terminal Company, who ordered that segregation in that dining room be discontinued, which was done permanently. "Twelve years later, as far North as Portland, Maine, where he had gone to address the Interracial Fellowship of America, Walls found hotels closed to him until a white judge, Max Pinanski, intervened privately in his behalf." [63]

Supporting the Washington Terminal Dining Room remonstrance wholeheartedly was the Associated Negro Press, headed by Claude Barnett of Chicago. The editor, Rev. L. H. King of the *Southwestern Christian Advocate*, who did a full page editorial on the incident, expressed the comprehensive and universal sentiment of the race:

. . . In refusing to be segregated in the Washington Terminal, Bishop Walls was right, because such segregation is wrong. Nothing sanctions it but its enforcement by a prejudiced majority. To those who cajole themselves on their ability to enforce segregation against the Negro, we must urge that "might is right." Just as the highwayman at the point of a gun holds up his helpless victim and strips him of his prized possessions, so the prejudiced preachers of white supremacy, moved by colorphobia, armed with the weapon of social control, hold up the colored American, stripping us of all

63. *The Washington Post,* October 1, 1925, p. 2; Bardolph, *The Negro Vanguard,* p. 159.

our citizenship rights to free and unhampered concourse in the pursuit and fulfillment of our public duties and responsibilities in the body politic. But those who highhandedly do such things must and will some day discover that there are moral foundations underlying all real prosperity, national and individual, and that any infringement of these laws by the community will result as disastrously as similar infringement by the individual.

Segregation is the national sequence of nervous paroxysm induced by fears of social contacts on the part of many folk who cannot risk themsleves against the probably easy collapse of certain superficial barriers thrown up by belabored effort, between existing social groups, with a view to maintaining a certain traditional social theory that has its roots in other days—those days long since, and forever, gone by. By statute law, by moral law, and biological law the colored American is entitled to the same equities and freedom of movement, social and political, in American life, as is any other group of citizens in our American population. This determined effort to segregate him in public life will but prove abortive unless it resorts to crass force and might to uphold it. Our national institutions will not stand the strain of a dual social order. American public institutions are not the products of any one race group. All of us, directly and indirectly, have contributed to their establishment. No one group has the right, nor should have the temerity to try to delimit any other American group from the fullest enjoyment therefore of the benefits and use of our American public institutions. The bishop, by the history, genius, and rightful spirit and purpose of American public institutions, had every right to expect and receive first-class service at the lunch counter of the Washington Terminal Company, with all the jim-crow features eliminated. He went there not to "socialize" with white patrons. He went there to eat, because he was hungry. And he was right to insist, by every honorable and legal method, for the best service for which that lunchroom stands for every citizen of this country.

Otherwise Bishop Walls would clearly have appeared to be acquiescing in the segregation principle for our American institutions. To have done this would have been a gratuitous insult to 12,000,000 colored Americans and their friends, who are aware of the wrong of segregation and who tolerate it only because of their minority numbers. Without an adequate, relentless protest, had Bishop Walls accepted the proposed and proffered jim-crow service, he would thus, in the eyes of our group, have suffered gross impairment of his Christian dignity, and his leadership would have been repudiated by the majority of colored Americans of all religious persuasions.

Bishop Walls was right. Among the many efforts being put forth by colored Americans against the insults, injustices, and indignities we are suffering is the very outrage of segregation, and that, too, right in the nation's capital and in the government's public buildings. It would have weakened the efforts of loyal and public-spirited men and women of our group and their many fair-minded white friends, had the bishop yielded the point involved. But he didn't; thereby helping out in the anti-segregation campaign being waged by colored people throughout the country. In Washington, Brooklyn, Detroit, Cleveland, Baltimore, Chicago, and a score of cities north and south, this silly segregation sentiment is growing bolder in its un-American aggression. And everywhere it must be protested against. Every colored organization, political, educational, industrial, fraternal, and religious, must meet this issue with preachment, protest, and plan, until all the public institutions of our land shall reflect the spirit of true Americanism—equalization of opportunity for all Americans, the color barrier being broken down. For the net value of segregation is mental satisfaction for those who impose it; and mental dissatisfaction for those on whom it is imposed. [64]

Despite these stalwart denunciations from the black press, both church and secular, against America's foremost evil; the rampage continued. The Ku Klux Klan had grown to approximately four and a half million members by 1924, [65] and its principal object was terrorism and subjugation of the Negro. Besides the *Southwestern Christian Advocate*, official publication of the Central Jurisdiction of the Methodist Episcopal Church, the united forces of black journalism pugnaciously revolting against racial injustices included such church organs as The A.M.E. *Christian Recorder,* The A.M.E. Zion *Star of Zion,* The C.M.E. *Christian Index, The Baptist Voice*; and other influential secular papers such as T. Thomas Fortune's *Globe* or *Age* of New York, George L. Knox's *Freeman* of Indianapolis, C. A. Scott's *Atlanta Daily World* (the first black daily paper published since Reconstruction), John H. Murphy's *Afro-American* of Baltimore, Chris J. Perry's *Tribune* of Philadelphia, Robert S. Abbott's *Defender* of Chicago, Robert L. Vann's *Courier* of Pittsburgh, P. B. Young's *Journal and Guide* of Norfolk, William O. Walker's *Call-Post* of Cleveland, and James H. Anderson's *Amsterdam News* of New York. Several other black newspapers and journals were looming up across the nation, chiefly to join the protest against indignity and injustice.

On October 29, 1929 the stock market crashed and the nation passed through its worst Depression, affecting all alike; black and white, rich and poor, high and low. In its attempt to survive the crisis, it elected as president Franklin Delano Roosevelt, who began his rehabilitation program. The Negro began to renew his faith and build up hope for a new America, with justice for all. It was not easy, for though this liberal Democratic administration appointed many Negro advisers in various government departments (more than had ever before served in high official capacities), a horrifying incident of racial injustice occurred in 1931, in Scottsboro, Ala., (The Scottsboro Case), involving nine black boys. It caused a convulsive reaction throughout the world, with total justice never accomplished.

During this same time, Mussolini and his Italian Fascist army began their invasion in Ethiopia. Black Americans still passing through their own torment, were aroused to the point of organizing, raising funds, and utilizing other sympathetic means to aid this only ancient African country, which had hitherto been unconquered. The A.M.E. Zion Board of Bishops asserted in 1936:

The dictator snapped contemptuous fingers in the face of the League of Nations, whose members registered but feeble and vacillating protests, as their fears pictured the victorious Italian army sweeping over their African colonies, and engulfing all Europe in war as in the days of Napoleon. The plea that Italy needs more territory for her growing population fell upon many sympathetic ears. It never once occurred to Italy that both England and France held large possessions near Ethiopia which they might have shared with her if necessary, and thus have left the ancient Christian Empire of Ethiopia in peace. As we meet here today, the carnage of blood and death goes on, regardless of treaties or the laws of so-called civilized warfare. E. Stanley Jones, one of God's modern prophets recently said: "We created a class society, and now we are on the verge of paying for it. The battering ram which is thundering at the gates of civilization is a class war." [66]

Through his own fortitude, and prayers and concern of black people all over

64. *The Southwestern Christian Advocate,* October 22, 1925.
65. Bergman, *op. cit.,* p. 411.
66. *Minutes,* Thirtieth Quadrennial Session, pp. 72-73.

the world, Emperor Haile Selassie later succeeded, with the League of Nations, in dispelling the occupants.

The bishops also made observation that though lynchings had been condemned from the Negro pulpit and press, and had met with resistance and even retaliation, a habit of enduring silence had prevailed in the nation's government. A ray of hope was voiced to our people as the Bishops' decreed

.... President Franklin Delano Roosevelt declared that lynching is collective murder and that those who take part in it should be punished as any other murderer. The crime never before reached enough importance to attract national attention, and an honest effort has been made by certain congressmen to have legislation passed making it a federal offense. An endorsement of the Costigan-Wagner Anti-Lynching Bill should go from this General Conference, and all our churches and prominent citizens should send petitions to congressmen and the President urging its early passage. [67]

These processes by no means called a halt but began somewhat to palliate abominations. Bolstering this and other causes of the Negro was Oscar DePriest of Chicago, the first black Congressman since George H. White of North Carolina in 1901, who had "predicted in a moving valedictory that the Negro would return." [68] A year after his election in 1928 in a Harlem rally of 2,500 at Abyssinian Baptist Church, DePriest said: "You will never be able to get what you want politically unless you elect leaders who will fight for your interest. . . . White people, as a rule, elect Negroes that they can control. Negroes will never get a square deal unless you elect your own leader. [69] Remember that no one can really lead you but one who had been Jim-Crowed as you have." Indeed this speech had its impact upon young Adam Clayton Powell, Jr., who was to become Harlem's first black U.S. Congressman in 1945. DePriest served two terms in the House of Representatives, and was defeated by a conservative Negro of the Democratic party. DePriest "spoke out bluntly, not only in Congress, but to Negro audiences in the Deep South and at such peril that he carried pistols on the lecture platform while he denounced race-baiting whites and timid Uncle Toms alike." [70]

The state of the Negro in the nation warranted additional organizations for the continued combat against racial strife. Leading black churchmen assembled in Chicago and organized the Negro Fraternal Council of Churches in 1934 (see Chapter 30). In 1936 another group of black leaders assembled at Howard University and organized The National Negro Congress. It was a coalition of religious, educational, labor, fraternal, and civic groups to work for better economic situation and protect the rights of foreign-born Negroes. The first meeting was held in Chicago with over 800 delegates attending. A. Philip Randolph was elected president and John P. Davis, executive secretary. The writer and several A.M.E. Zion Church leaders were participants, as well as Mary McLeod Bethune, Mordecai W. Johnson, Lester Granger, Ralph Bunche, Walter White, Paul Robeson, Langston Hughes, and most of the noted race leaders of that day. The work started out with bright prospects, and all seemed to be encouraged. However, by 1940, communist influence had dwarfed the organization and the majority of members, who had become disillusioned, continued their works for citizenship otherwise.

67. *Ibid.*, pp. 75-76.
68. Bardolph, *op. cit.*, p. 196.
69. Bergman, *op. cit.*, pp. 441-442.
70. Bardolph, *op. cit.*, p. 197.

In 1940 America was steadily becoming involved in the war raging in Europe. Asa Philip Randolph, polished philosophical orator and dynamic leader, began planning a movement for a March on Washington to protest against job discrimination in government and defense industries, and the NAACP began a coordinated drive for desegregation of the armed forces. In 1941 Randolph, supported by the organization he founded in 1925, the Brotherhood of Sleeping Car Porters, the black churches, and the NAACP, planned a march of 100,000 blacks on Washington. President Roosevelt felt that the march would be embarrassing to his administration and made concessionary agreements with Mr. Randolph, which were accepted for the time being, and the march, planned for July 1, was called off. By the president's directive, the Fair Employment Practices Commission (FEPC) was given birth as a result of the planned march. Six months later came Pearl Harbor.

Once again, as has been so since the Revolutionary War, the Negro proved his valor. Not allowing the heinous injustices and brutal slayings of families and friends to deter him in the least, but with the spirit of a Dory Miller (messman on the USS Arizona, untrained for military combat, shooting down four Japanese planes in the Pearl Harbor attack), he helped wage the war against double odds: prejudiced allies and bitter foes.

In the midst of the battle, in 1942, an enterprising young black man in Chicago, John H. Johnson, founded a magazine called *Negro Digest, (Black World)*. He established *Ebony* magazine in 1947, and later added the weekly magazine, *Jet*, to his flourishing publishing concern. This was not the first such venture of the race. There is a history of Negro magazines and periodicals of all types in America, which served noble purposes in the onward pursuit for justice. However, this was the beginning of a unique promulgation of black race interests—its churches, businesses, education enterprises, African and Caribbean affairs, politics, economics, arts and sciences, and every other aspect of life, nationally and internationally, in enlightening and bringing the black race closer together throughout the world.

Also in 1942 another civil rights organization was born. The Congress of Racial Equality (CORE), headed by James Farmer, who passed through almost intolerable trauma in the deep South in efforts to improve racial conditions. In 1966 he was succeeded as national director by the grandson of an A.M.E. Zion preacher; Floyd B. McKissick, who after serving a brief term, accepted a position in the federal government, and was succeeded by the present incumbent, Roy Innis. This organization was also interrelated with black churches in its work. Reverends Martin L. King, Jr., Ralph D. Abernathy, Howard Thurman, Gardner Taylor, Bishops W. J. Walls and Frederick D. Jordan, and the famous white missionary to India, Rev. E. Stanley Jones, were among church leaders who served on its National Advisory Committee and encouraged it in its actions.

While the war was raging, the A.M.E. Zion Church expressed concern at its 1944 General Conference over the war, the lives lost and marred in combat, the chaplains who had left their parishes, the growing race problems in the North and South, and another degradation in Africa. A member of the delegation, state Senator R. L. Brokenburr of Indiana, presented a resolution on a protectorate by the United States over the Belgian Congo. Joe Thomas of Kentucky had given illumination on the condition of the Congo Free State and the fact was disclosed that Belgium had 14,000,000 Negroes in slavery in the Congo State. A discussion ensued for complete clarification. Dr. Rufus E. Clement suggested that the General Conference should petition the United States government to appoint a Negro in the American delegation to whatever peace conference was planned in the general interest of the oppressed. The entire matter was referred to the Board of Bishops to pursue the proper course in behalf of these suffering people. [71] Reverend William H. Shepard, the first black missionary to the Congo of the Presbyterian Church in the U.S., had labored around the turn of the century, in the hottest times of Belgium's brutality, made great sacrifices and won universal acclaim in helping to break the notorious oppression perpetrated against the natives of Belgian-Congo.

The war ended in 1945. A year later, President Harry S. Truman placed into action far-reaching civil rights measures, and also integrated the armed forces. The spirit of the Negro after the second war was positive. Having done their share in helping to win two world wars, blacks of America began developing a strong attitude of demanding equal status in American citizenship. They began to assert themselves in a new way.

The Editor of the *Star of Zion*, Dr. Walter R. Lovell, lashed out the sentiment of the church and race in the following editorial, October 25, 1945:

Prejudice Dies Hard. The despicable and hateful fact of unreasonable prejudice has again raised its ugly head in the refusal of the Daughters of the American Revolution to permit Hazel Scott to play the piano in Constitution Hall. If more than a million Negro Americans in the Armed Forces of the nation had dreams that race prejudice would be removed (they probably did not), when they returned from their sacrifices to preserve or win American freedom, they are in for a lot of cruel, painful disillusionment.

For those proud and haughty ladies of the D.A.R., who glory in rich legacy of American patriotism, which rose up to destroy tyranny and depotism, are not yet civilized enough to concede that "all men are created equal" and although many of them probably delude themselves into believing they are good American Christians, they are still blind to the tenets that are inherent in true democracy. While insisting that their marbled temple shall be for "white artists only," they remain blissfully ignorant of the fact that the rich, noble and proud blood of African kings probably flows in the veins of members of their un-American cult, which heaps ignominy upon itself by an exhibition of race prejudice that smells to high heaven.

America never produced an artist in its history that brought greater glory to the nation than Marian Anderson, but she too, like Hazel Scott, because her skin is a rich and gorgeous brown, so blinded the eyes of the elegant ladies of the D.A.R., that their ears were deaf to the sweetness of "a voice that appears only once in a hundred years," and their hearts were like stone to the pleas of those who wanted America, even the nation's capital, to be "the land of the free."

One hundred and sixty-nine years after Boston Commons the soul of Crispus Attucks marches on, but the gates of ignorant, un-Christian, un-American race prejudice still bar the progress of his descendants. Prejudice dies hard, but thanks to a few real Americans, it dies nevertheless, and perhaps in another century and a half it will lie lifeless, the hideous monster that once stalked triumphantly throughout the land.

The A.M.E. Zion Church was admonished by its bishops in 1948 as follows:

71. *Minutes,* Thirty-Second Quadrennial Session, p. 60.

It must never appear that a race is willing to get over behind a log and lie hidden while someone else goes forth to contend for it. There is always the danger that they may say, "Let my conscience be your guide." It will be more profitable if we can strike the first blow in the fight for our freedom; others may not be able to see just what concerns us most. We know what we have in mind, what we consider our just dues; what we have earned by the sacrifices we have made in order to make the United States of America the outstanding nation it is. We will never forget that we did the rough work in the beginning of this nation; we will always remember that our backs bore the burden, and that we suffered the heat of the day. We are now demanding to share in the fruits of our labor. [72]

By 1950 there were over 15,000,000 Negroes in the United States representing 10 percent of the population. Over 200,000 were working in the federal government and several thousands in municipal and state employment, while an increasing number had struggled up the ladder of time, winning great distinction in the nation's history; such as Jack Roosevelt Robinson, first to break the color barrier in baseball in 1947, and Ralph Bunche, first black American Nobel Peace Prize winner. In the first line of men and women of achievement for the race produced in the A.M.E. Zion Church were: Dr. Solomon C. Fuller, noted pathologist and educator, and his wife, Meta Warrick Fuller, one of America's most outstanding sculptresses; Paul Robeson, world famous concert artist and freedom advocate; Selma Burke, nationally known sculptress; Ruth Whitehead Whaley, who as an attorney fought and won national legal battles for the sake of justice in New York, and later served as Secretary of the Board of Estimate of New York City under four mayors: Rufus Early Clement, President of Atlanta University, elected to the Board of Education in Atlanta by an 8,000 vote margin: and John B. Duncan, former Recorder of Deeds, Washington, D.C.

The decade of the fifties was ushered in with a new scarecrow against freedom. "Senator Joseph McCarthy of Wisconsin headed the post-World War II witch-hunt against Communists and all Americans of progressive thought, black and white, and gave the word McCarthyism to the language as an expression for wild charges of disloyalty." He blew the effort to intimidate all freedom lovers of the country out of proportion, and by 1954, he was censured by the Senate "for conduct unbecoming a member."

"In 1953, as the intensity of the McCarthy era mounted and more and more black Americans came under atttacks as 'subversives' because they dared to speak up for freedom, the Committee to Defend Negro Leadership was established," headed by an unyielding black Methodist clergyman, Rev. Edward D. McGowan. McGowan began his fearless defense of black leaders of the period who were persistently under attack by the press and House Un-American Activities Committee for their militancy and courage. "He linked persecution of black leadership in the United States with that against leaders of the African peoples in their struggles for freedom and independence." [73] There was hardly a leader of note, especially men and women in official position, who had not been included in this villainous smear. Some were placed under secret surveillance and treated as though they had done a great injustice to the country in contending for race

72. *Minutes,* Thirty-third Quadrennial Session, p. 307.
73. Foner, *The Voice of Black America,* p. 860.

rights; sometimes they were abused publicly or in the press. The black queen of peace and race relations, Mary McLeod Bethune, was refused the privilege of speaking in at least one, if not more, public halls. Even Bishop G. Bromley Oxnam of the Methodist Church was dragged through a hearing of the House Un-American Activities Committee in attempts to debauch and intimidate religious leadership.

Speaking out in the keynote address delivered at the annual meeting of the National Fraternal Council of Churches in Detroit, April 1953, McGowan vehemently defended black religious leaders and African leaders who had been under the hammer of these tyrannical assaults. He condemned insults and abuses hurled at the Baptist minister of Detroit, Rev. Charles A. Hill; the attempt to impugn the leadership of Bishop W. J. Walls, Chairman of the Board of Religious Education of the A.M.E. Zion Church, and Vice-Chairman of the N.A.A.C.P.; "the attempt of the U.S. State Department to deny passport rights to Reverend James H. Robinson of New York City," black Presbyterian leader of Harlem, "because he insisted on voicing the Negro and colonial peoples' demands against racism as practiced at home and exported abroad"; the denial of entry of Bishops Frederick D. Jordan and Howard T. Primm of the A.M.E. Church by the "neofacist Malan government of South Africa" to administer the work assigned them; and the character assassination of such nationally known leaders as Bishops Reverdy C. Ransom (A.M.E.), C. C. Alleyne (A.M.E. Zion), A. W. Womack (C.M.E.), Rev. W. H. Jernagin (Baptist), and Mrs. Mary Church Terrell. [74]

McGowan also called for an effective protest "against the persecution of those leaders in South and East Africa—Dr. Dadoo, Dr. Z. K. Matthews, Jomo Kenyatta and the five other leaders who were sentenced to seven years' hard labor—because they oppose the exclusion of the African people from the political and economic life in a country which belongs to them." [75] It was an established fact that the oppressed people of America were forming a close alliance and compact with the oppressed people of Africa, more than any other time since the African had landed on the American continent, and including India, which produced anxiety and fear in the white world.

This was the decade of the commencement of change, both in America and Africa. In America, migration and immigration after the two world wars had multiplied populations of both races in Northern cities, and an increased number of whites had drawn the color line. Steps taken by blacks to cross the lines of demarcation, especially in housing and labor, repeatedly caused bloodshed, riots, and tragedy. By this time the so-called Negro problem was prevalent, North and South, and the real test was on the way.

On May 17, 1954 the Supreme Court of the United States unanimously ruled that school segregation was unconstitutional since "separate educational facilities are inherently unequal." Thurgood Marshall, head of Legal Defense of the NAACP, was the legal genius who led in winning this case, with the opinion written by Chief Justice Earl Warren. It was the high-water mark of the black freedom struggle since Emancipation.

Delay tactics began immediately, and by 1955 the desegregation of schools battle was in full force. The year was marked with tragic lynchings, especially in Mississippi (one of a 14-year-old Chicago boy named Emmett Till), which brought

74. *Ibid.*, pp. 862-865
75. Ibid., p. 863

on stormy mass meetings and stern protests of blacks and liberal whites in every corner of the nation.

Near the end of the year, the first significant incident, which was to move the world in the name of American Negro freedom, took place in Montgomery, Alabama. The ministers and members of the A.M.E. Zion Church shared indomitably in the incident and the following struggle. A black woman, a bus, and an arrest ignited the revolution.

On Thursday, December 1, 1955, Mrs. Rosa Parks, weary from her full day's work at a leading department store, boarded the Cleveland Avenue bus and took a vacant seat directly behind the section reserved for whites. When additional white passengers boarded the bus which had become crowded, she refused to give her seat to a white man and stand up, as the driver had ordered, and was arrested. Mrs. Parks thus became the "victim of both the forces of history and the forces of destiny." [76]

The black people swiftly became aroused, not only over the arrest but the indignities and rough treatment of Mrs. Parks. The next day a meeting was called of local black leaders; predominantly ministers, chaired by the Rev. L. Roy Bennett, pastor of Mt. Zion A.M.E. Zion Church and president of the Interdenominational Ministerial Alliance. The leaders decided to call a bus boycott for the following Monday, December 5. Reverend Martin Luther King, Jr., pastor of Dexter Avenue Baptist Church, accepted the job of seeing that the Negro community of over 50,000 was informed of the boycott. Normally 75 percent of the Montgomery bus riders were Negro. It was agreed to get the Negro taxi companies of the city (18 with about 200 taxis) "to transport the people for the same price that they were currently paying on the bus. A committee was appointed to make this contact, with Reverend W. J. Powell, minister of the Old Ship A.M.E. Zion Church, as chairman."

With the cooperative black unit, from the elderly to the child, the boycott was a startling success. The boycott took place the same day Rosa Parks was tried for "disobeying the city segregation ordinance." The judge found her guilty and fined her ten dollars and court costs, and she appealed the case. This caused a continuation of positive action on behalf of the race.

Leaving Mrs. Parks' trial, Ralph Abernathy, E. D. Nixon (fearless foe of injustice and the signer of Mrs. Park's bond), and Rev. E. N. French—then minister of the Hilliard Chapel A.M.E. Zion Church—discussed the need for some organization to guide and direct the protest. Up to this time things had moved forward more or less spontaneously. These men were wise enough to see that the moment had now come for a clearer order and direction. [77]

After Rev. Bennett had called several people together that afternoon to make plans for an evening mass meeting, the group proceeded to organize. Reverend Martin L. King was elected president, Rev. L. Roy Bennett, vice-president, Rev. U. J. Fields, recording secretary, Rev. E. N. French, corresponding secretary, Mrs. Erna A. Dungee, financial secretary, and Mr. E. D. Nixon, treasurer. Upon the suggestion of Rev. Ralph Abernathy it was agreed that the new organization should be known as The Montgomery Improvement Association. [78]

Henceforth began another "idea whose time had come." In pursuit of justice, the Negroes had tested their strength through unity and their power through

76. M. L. King, Jr., *Stride Toward Freedom*, p. 44.
77. *Ibid.*, pp. 53-55.
78. *Ibid.*, pp. 56-57.

BISHOP STEPHEN GILL SPOTTSWOOD

Steadfast Civil Rights Leader. Chairman of the Board of Directors of the National Association for the Advancement of Colored People since 1961.

MONTGOMERY BUS BOYCOTT

A.M.E. Zion ministers involved in protest. L. to R.: *Revs. H. H. Hubbard, Ralph D. Abernathy, Martin Luther King, Jr. (Baptist), Solomon S. Seay (A.M.E. Zion), B. D. Lambert (Baptist), W. J. Powell (A.M.E. Zion), and A. W. Wilson (Baptist).*

non-violent protests in the face of racial flare-ups, numerous arrests (of several leaders), cruel harassments, and diabolical bombings; even the bombing of Rev. King's home, jeopardizing the lives of his wife and baby. It had organized car pools and subsequently succeeded in driving the adamant municipal bus company out of business. It later developed into a chain of non-violent protests throughout segregated parts of the nation.

The A.M.E. Zion Church ministers who had figured conspicuously in·this local struggle were Rev. J. H. Cherry, "a chief dispatcher—stationed at the downtown parking lot [who] proved to be of inestimable value," Revs. S. S. Seay, J. W. Hayes, and a little later, H. A. L. Clement, who were members of the executive board along with those already mentioned. [79] Concerning this struggle, King stated:

> W. J. Powell and S. S. Seay, like Bennett, were ministers of the A.M.E. Zion Church. Powell brought a cool head and an even temper to the problems that confronted the strategy committee in these tempestuous days. S. S. Seay's was one of the few clerical voices that, in the years preceding the protest, had lashed out against the injustices heaped on the Negro, and urged his people to a greater appreciation of their own worth. A dynamic preacher, his addresses from time to time at the weekly mass meetings raised the spirits of all who heard him.[80]

In the thick of the struggle there was a ray of pleasure for world blacks. The Gold Coast, the country with the largest A.M.E. Zion membership of foreign territory, formally celebrated its Independence, March 6, 1957; changing the name of the country to Ghana and premier Kwame Nkrumah becoming its first President. Bishop Walls had been delegated by the A.M.E. Zion Church to attend this jubilant occasion in Africa, but he requested Bishop William A. Stewart to substitute for him. Bishop Stewart brought back news of the triumphant entry of this country's Independence of English rule among modern states. Following in this line, black nations of Africa, the West Indies and South America gradually secured their independence, some by way of violence and bloodshed, and some by other means.

Back in America, inflictions and pressure borne by blacks in school desegregation breakthrough against hard core authorities, prompted new civil rights organizations. These included the cases of Autherine Lucy in the University of Alabama at Tuscaloosa; Daisy Bates and the Little Rock, Arkansas nine high school students; James Meredith in the University of Mississippi; and others, in addition to continued tortures, brutal killings, and persistent threats. The Leadership Conference on Civil Rights, of which the A.M.E. Zion Church became a charter supporting member, Martin Luther King's Southern Christian Leadership Conference (S.C.L.C.), The Student Non-Violent Coordinating Committee (SNCC), also established by King; and Ella Baker in 1960, and led on by King, James Forman, John Lewis and Stokely Carmichael; and the National Council of Negro Women led by Miss Dorothy Height (which was already receiving support from the Woman's Home and Foreign Missionary Society of the A.M.E. Zion Church), formed an instinctive coalition with other established civil rights organizations and the leading black churches in order to enhance the power of the race in the midst of an intensified struggle. Thus the decade from 1960 to 1970 was one of notable victories but through violence and tragedy. It was the most violent period for freedom advocates (including the assassination of prominent leaders) in the history of the nation.

The decade opened in February 1960 with students of A & T College of Greensboro, N.C., staging sit-ins at lunch counters and other public facilities, demanding equality of service. This was followed through by students in many of the Southern black colleges. It led to the arrest of participants and mass protest demonstrations, with some places yielding to the new day while others held out. At Salisbury, N.C., Livingstone College students were jailed for attempting to break up the Jim-Crow lunch counters and theater arrangements, and young

79. *Ibid.*, pp. 79, 225.
80. *Ibid.*, p. 73.

preachers were jailed for joining in the protest. Throughout the country the protests and arrests continued. Then came the Freedom Rides. Participating were several A.M.E. Zion ministers and laymen (men, women, and youth) of the North and South, who were manhandled by civic officers, some beaten, thrown in jail, and harshly abused on these perilous journeys of adventure in desegregation. Testimonies were made in our various meetings by the Freedom Riders, who endured insurmountable sufferings with unmatched courage in the pursuit of justice.

January 21, 1961 the liberal Democrat from Massachusetts, John Fitzgerald Kennedy became president, and soon afterward he appointed Robert Weaver Administrator of the Federal Housing and Home Finance Agency, the highest post held by an American Negro up to this time. President Kennedy later attempted to create a new cabinet post on Housing Development, which Congress vetoed. However, in 1966, President Lyndon B. Johnson succeeded in creating the post and appointed Robert Weaver Secretary of Housing and Urban Development, the first and only black Cabinet member in United States history, to this date. Weaver who was serving as chairman of the Board of Directors of the National Association for the Advancement of Colored People, resigned his post when he accepted the position under Kennedy in 1961.

Elected to succeed Weaver as Chairman of the NAACP Board of Directors was Bishop Stephen Gill Spottswood of the A.M.E. Zion Church, April 19, 1961. Spottswood, born and raised in a restrictive New England town, when a child discovered from his playmates that he was different. This molded his attitude to be equal. Closely akin to his interest in his church was his zeal for the welfare of his race. He worked ardently in local and state chapters of the NAACP in every city and town which he had pastored. He was courageous both as a pastor and a bishop. While serving as bishop in the deep South, he encountered opposition in Mississippi and Arkansas, and had some dangerous experiences. It was logical that this adventurous, fearless leader would be considered for this chairmanship. He has followed in the wake of heroic leaders of the church in that same area, and made contributions of commendable proportion. Some of his hardest blows against racial injustices are to be found in his several keynote addresses delivered at the annual conventions of the NAACP. As chairman who became deeply involved, he suffers the scars of the turbulent sixties which practiced nefarious brutality against freedom lovers, in defiance of justice.

Another apostle of justice is Rev. Kenneth L. Buford of the A.M.E. Zion Church, who desired to be totally involved in the struggle and relinquished his pastorate of Butler Chapel, Tuskegee, Ala., to become field secretary of the NAACP in Alabama during this crucial period. Buford had led in assembling a crowd estimated at 3,000 in and around Butler Chapel on June 25, 1957, and successfully organized boycott procedures against the segregated community. This again proved Negro unity and power in the face of white business pressures. The blacks won out, to the point of finally electing a black mayor.

The Negro faced his Centennial of Emancipation with mixed emotions, amidst a conglomerate national situation in freedom's cause. In May 1963, demonstrators in Birmingham, led by King, against practices of discrimination, encountered police dogs and high-powered water hoses used by the notorious police chief, Eugene "Bull" Connor and company, and more than 2,400 suffered arrest. In June, the field secretary of the NAACP in Mississippi, Medgar Evers, was stealthily killed by long-range bullet on his doorstep. In August, 250,000 citizens (about 60,000 whites), converged upon the nation's capital in *The March on Washington*, led by A. Philip Randolph.

The first week in September, the A.M.E. Zion Church held a mass Emancipation Centennial Celebration in New York City, and a delegation of the bishops and leading members, led by Bishop W. J. Walls, was received by President Kennedy at the White House in honor of the occasion. This was followed by the message from the President and the participation of such notables as Mayor Robert F. Wagner, Roy Wilkins, James Farmer, A. Philip Randolph, Monroe Work, Rev. Eugene Carson Blake, Bishop Sherman L. Greene, Rev. R. H. Edwin Espy, Rabbi Marc H. Tannenbaum, Monsignor Flynn representing Francis Cardinal Spellman, and Arthur B. Spingarn.

On Sunday morning, September 15, four black Sunday school children were killed and 21 persons injured when a bomb was thrown into the 16th Street Baptist Church in Birmingham. As a climax, in November, the President of the United States, known to be a friend and supporter of freedom and justice for all, was assassinated at Dallas, Texas. Thus was the outcome at the end of a hundred years of so-called freedom in the United States.

Courage of the blacks heightened, white friends of justice increased, and protests continued. In 1964 "Reverend K. L. Buford and Stanley Smith were elected to the Tuskegee City Council, the first Negroes elected to public office in Alabama in the twentieth century." [81] This same year, however, the country became alarmed over the murders of two white civil rights workers from New York, Michael H. Schwerner and Andrew Goodman, and a black Mississippian, James E. Chaney, by local whites of Philadelphia, Miss.

In 1965 there was a massive march from Selma to Montgomery, Ala., in protest of the killing of a black man and the arrest of about 1,000 demonstrators in the voter registration of Selma. Thousands marched, with 4,000 rallying to the cause in Montgomery four days later. Viola Liuzzo, a young white civil rights leader, wife and mother, from Detroit, paid the price with her life, and three white Unitarian ministers were beaten mercilessly. Riots later broke out in Watts (Los Angeles) and Chicago, and it began to appear that gradual disorders were replacing the successful Non-violent protests.

Civil rights legislation and mechanization of farms caused great suffering in the latter 60's, in the Delta section of Mississippi, and hundreds of black families were evicted from plantations. Bishop and Mrs. C. E. Tucker were instrumental in gathering support and with the assistance of Rev. R. M. Richmond, distributed over 60 tons of clothing, together with food and money.

Terrorism and violence were still practiced against the race as the Supreme Court, during the administrations of Presidents Kennedy and Johnson, had ruled in favor of general rights and desegregation, and the government utilized protective measures in voter registration campaigns. The door that had been locked for so long was opening for blacks in America. The following year, after America received its first black Cabinet Member, in 1967 Thurgood Marshall was the first black man named to the United States Supreme Court by President Lyndon Johnson.

The latter 1960's produced social problems, aggravated by the large ratio of

81. Bergman, *op. cit.*, p. 583.

President John F. Kennedy greets A.M.E. Zion Church leaders at the White House, September, 1963; Centennial of black Emancipation in America.

Clockwise (l to r) Bishops W. M. Smith, H. B. Shaw, Mr. John B. Duncan, Bishops J. D. Cauthen, S. D. Lartey, H. T. Medford, D. C. Pope, W. A. Hilliard, (far left) Mrs. Ruth Whitehead Whaley, Mrs. Dorothy Walls, Dr. E. Franklin Jackson, Mr. Alexander Barnes; Mr. William J. Trent, Bishops W. A. Stewart, C. E. Tucker, F. S. Anderson, President Kennedy, Bishops R. L. Jones and W. J. Walls

black Americans critically wounded and killed in the Viet Nam War and the quest for peace. The chief agitator for complete citizenship and peace, demonstrating many times in the North as well as the South, was Martin Luther King, Jr. King's life had been many times threatened, first attempted soon after the Montgomery Bus Boycott by a near fatal stabbing in the midst of a crowd, and accomplished finally in the shot that carried him away in Memphis, Tennessee, April 4, 1968. His contribution was incalculable and indescribable in helping to bring about the change for the better in his race group and country. King's thesis was "peace and goodwill among all men," and he cast an influence throughout the world in this area. Within two months, Senator Robert F. Kennedy, friend of the black race as all the Kennedy family is, became the victim of an assassin's bullet in June 1968. These murders precipitated violence and unrest; and a series of other kinds of murders began in the name of police brutality, civil disobedience, and even innocent students on college campuses were slain. The decade of the 1970's ushered in racial discord, and the turmoil continues to exist while leaders, black and white, search for new methods of achieving harmony and peace.

In the latter part of the freedom struggle were men and women of distinction who rendered invaluable service, and continue in the wake of full freedom, and peace. Some are products of the A.M.E. Zion Church, for example, the virtuous and patient wife of Martin Luther King, Jr., Coretta Scott King. Her paternal grandfather, Jeff Scott, who "either led or played an important role in everything involving the uplift of the people" in their community, was the preacher's steward and chairman of the trustees of Mt. Tabor A.M.E. Zion Church in Marion, Ala., and also superintendent of the Sunday school. [82] Her father, Obadiah Scott, "a born leader" and "unusual person" of faith and courage, and other members of the family are faithful, hardworking members of Mt. Tabor Church. Mrs. King states that her first experiences of social life were happy. "They centered around the Mount Tabor A.M.E. Zion Church. Most of the congregation were kinfolk, so it was almost a family affair." [83]

In 1955-56, State Senator Robert L. Brokenburr, member of Jones Tabernacle, Indianapolis, served as alternate delegate to the United Nations. [84] Carl B. Stokes, first black mayor of Cleveland, serving two terms, is member of St. Paul A.M.E. Zion Church of that city. His brother, U.S. Congressman Louis Stokes, is an ardent church member of St. Paul, and was elected trustee during the pastorate of Rev. Albert L. Fuller. Alfred L. Edwards, deputy assistant secretary of the Department of Agriculture (HEW), is a faithful member of Trinity Church, Washington, D.C.

Angie Elizabeth Brooks, elected President of the Twenty-Fourth United Nations General Assembly in September 1969, was one of five girls among nine children of a rural minister of the A.M.E. Zion Church in Liberia. [85] A large number of contemporary international and national leaders for total justice, are products of the A.M.E. Zion Church.

The story of the struggle of the black race to achieve full citizenship is the story of the African Methodist Episcopal Zion Church. Through the years, we tenaciously held back the bitterness and preached the gospel of non-violence. The prayers, faith, tears, toils, bloodshed, loss of life, organizing, mass meetings, negotiating, sit-ins, arrests, marches, fund-raising rallies, tortures, warfares, freedom-rides, defeats, disappointments, harrassments, threats, and victories, bespeak the total involvement and desire to practice our love, love which "worketh no ill to his neighbor: therefore love is the fulfilling of the law."

The Pan-African Congress

The American Negro began to turn his eyes toward worldwide black race cooperation in the fight for status in the universal striving of mankind. The first assembly of Africans and descendants of Africa throughout the world was held in Westminister Town Hall, near the House of Parliament, London, July 23-25, 1900. It attracted such leaders as M. Benito Sylvian, aide-de camp to Emperor Menelik II, Abyssinia; Hon. F. S. R. Johnson, former Attorney-General of Liberia; W. E. B. DuBois, Bishops Alexander Walters and B. W. Arnett and J. F. Loudin, director of the Fisk Jubilee Singers; Rev. H. Mason Joseph of Antigua, B. W. I.; A. F. Ribero, barrister-at-law of the Gold Coast, and nearly two dozen other leaders from all parts of the world.

82. Coretta Scott King, *My Life with Martin Luther King, Jr.*, p. 35.
83. *Ibid.*, pp. 37, 43.   84. Bergman, *op. cit.*, p. 525.
85. Charles Moritz, (ed.), *Current Biography Yearbook,* 1970. p. 48.

A permanent organization was formed, and among its officers and members of the executive board, Bishop Alexander Walters was elected president, and Dr. W. E. B. DuBois, a vice-president representing America. One of their chief objects was to start a movement looking forward to the securing of all African races their full rights, and to promote their business interests. [86]

At this conference,

a Memorial setting forth the following acts of justice directed against Her Majesty's subjects in South Africa, and other parts of her dominions, was prepared and sent to Queen Victoria—

"1. The degrading and illegal compound system of native labor in vogue in Kimberley and Rhodesia. 2. The so-called indenture i.e., legalized bondage of native men, women and children to white colonists. 3. The system of compulsory labour on public works. 4. The 'pass' or docket system used for people of colour. 5. Local by-laws tending to segregate and degrade the natives of the use of the footpaths; and the use of separate public conveyances. 6. Difficulties in acquiring real property. 7. Difficulties in obtaining the franchise." [87]

Her Majesty replied through her official agencies, who promised not to overlook the interests and welfare of the native races.

This organization dreams of the articulation of the black races of the world upon a basis of peace, science, and merit. Whatever is said and done, there will always be a sympathetic heartbeat in the people of the world according to their ethnological origin and intuitive sympathies, even in the midst of the most peaceful situations that could be imagined. This will happen nationally as well as racially.

Nations and races will always be proud of their kith and kin, when they do well and excel, and will always be in sympathy to a tangible degree with these same ethnical relations when they are in trouble or fail. The ultimate dream is not the obliteration of nations and races, but the alteration of relationships to include universal empathy and unimpeachable "peace and goodwill on earth."

The woeful condition that the natives of South Africa have suffered under for generations is beginning to open toward the light of day.

"Any social arrangement that denies the integrity of the birthright is not merely unfair, unjust, undemocratic, but it is evil and against life and against God. He who indulges in it *sins* and in his sinning becomes an agent of wickedness in the world." [88]

Just as the black race in America kept the faith through all the tortures of gaining citizenship (and the pursuit continues for full rights and privileges), a similar hope is rising upon South Africa. The time is fast approaching when no such cruelty as that which enshrouds South Africa can continue upon the face of the earth, and the African races of the world are moving in the phalanx of this human current that is sweeping through the world.

86. Walters, *op. cit.,* pp. 253-254, 260
87. *A.M.E. Zion Quarterly Review,* Second Quarter, 1901, p. 166.
88. Howard Thurman, "Christ's Message to the Disinherited," *Ebony Magazine,* September, 1963, p. 62.

CHAPTER 32

SOCIAL ACTION AND ENTERPRISE

The Negro Church is the only social institution of the Negroes which started in the African forest and survived slavery; under the leadership of priest or medicine-man, afterward the Christian pastor, the Church preserved in itself the remnants of African tribal life and became after emancipation the center of Negro social life. So that today the Negro population is virtually divided into church congregations [which form the majority of the units of race life]. [1]

The African Methodist Episcopal Zion Church like all black American denominations, for the most part has had more of the dream of social welfare for its people than it has been able to implement. Only 20 years younger than the American republic, the A.M.E. Zion Church began with the vision to provide centers for the sick, homes for the orphans, shelters for the aged, havens for the lonely, and refuge for the needy, but slavery and economic suppression obstructed our efforts and retarded our goals. Despite these circumstances, we have made some effective social progress.

Besides taking collections and making distribution among the poor and sick, there were early fragmental attempts to establish children's homes. These were followed by endeavors to provide homes for the aged, while local churches sought to establish community welfare centers and programs of uplift.

Inasmuch as the black church represented the only organized social existence of the race outside of the family, its leaders became assertive and its people cooperative in forming other types of social programs and clubs within the church. The earliest and most cooperative were benevolent organizations and the vigilance committees in the North during slavery.

In providing a structured social life in which the Negro could give expression to his deepest feeling and at the same time achieve status and find a meaningful existence, the Negro church provided a refuge in a hostile white world. For the slaves who worked and suffered in an alien world, religion offered a means of catharsis for their pent-up emotions and frustrations. Moreover, it turned their minds from the sufferings and privations of this world to a world after death where the weary would find rest and the victims of injustices would be compensated . . . . For the Negro masses, in their social and moral isolation in American society, the Negro church community has been a nation within a nation. [2]

The Negro church, with its peculiar forms of religious worship, was a world which whites regarded in wonderment, from the standpoint of the Negro's

1. W. E. Burghardt DuBois, *The Negro American Family*, p. 130.
2. E. Franklin Frazier, *The Negro Church in America*, pp. 44-45.

mysticism and godly enthusiasm in the midst of suffering.

The A.M.E. Zion Church, a cradle of free institutions, naturally had a lion's share of molding the life and character of the race through the advancement of other institutions and causes. It was, like other black churches, the meeting place for business organizations. It was the platform of our first teachers. It was the only classroom that black children ever knew in a number of cities and towns. It was the advertising point of our first professional men and women. It gave the black businessmen and professionals their send-off, as many of them appeared before large gatherings and smaller church meetings to establish a business or set up an office to help carry forth the material progress of the race.

The benevolent societies in Varick's day, organized to provide assistance in time of sickness, death, and other extreme conditions, were connected with the church. The African Marine Society was the chief organization of Zion for this purpose, while the New York African Society for Mutual Relief, founded by William Hamilton, was established on a community basis and largely bolstered by Zion Church. The societies continued developing with the denomination throughout the North. The Female Benevolent Societies of Zion were particularly active in Elmira, Ithaca, and Troy, N.Y., New Haven and Middletown, Conn., and in Zion Church in New York City, prior to the Civil War. The African Dorcas Society of Mother Zion Church, organized in the later 1820's, made clothing for poor children, assisted in their education, and later gathered the necessary food and clothing for passing fugitives of the Underground Railroad in aiding the Vigilante Committee.

Reverend J. W. Loguen had mentioned the flourishing school sponsored by the Ithaca congregation (St. James), pastored by Rev. George H. Washington, and the two Benevolent and Moral Improvement Societies, "in which they manifest a deep and becoming interest" as far back as 1841. Loguen said: "They are, for the most part, endeavoring to become possessed of property, and all have some honest occupation which they pursue with commendable industry."[3]

Organizing simultaneously with the benevolent societies were the Zion African Literary Societies, established in local churches, highly encouraged by Bishops Varick, Rush, Bishop, and J. J. Clinton, who were the outstanding social service types of the early bishops. These local societies were organized as a means of self-training in the face of educational neglects to the slave race, conversant with and preparatory for the needs of the time. The benevolent societies continued organizing in the church while the literary and educational organizations took on a more encouraging process of development and service after Emancipation. The societies had also organized conference wide, and reported the progress of their labors through this medium. The New England Conference "was regarded as the strongest intellectually of any in the connection, and was foremost in the advocacy of whatever tended to the elevation of the race . . . . There was a literary society connected with the Conference, and young men were encouraged to improve their minds by the offer of rewards for the best essays." [4]

While pointedly engaged in working for their own freedom and social improvement, and the freedom of their brothers and sisters in the South, individuals and groups within congregations aimed at establishing serviceable institutions; but due to economic status, the most they could do successfully was

3. *The Colored American,* March 13, 1841.
4. Hood, *One Hundred Years,* p. 243.

build and maintain simple church edifices.

In New Haven, Miss Hannah Gray "found time from her hard daily labor to collect money for the support of a Negro missionary worker among the fugitives in Canada," and to establish a home for indigent, aged colored females in her home house. [5] After her death in 1861, she left her property in the hands of white trustees, but the Varick Memorial A.M.E. Zion Church "cared for the house and sometimes sought charity for the old ladies from the 'white folks,' but more needed to be done." The Women's Twentieth Century Club, oldest black community organization, founded in 1900, soon became interested in the conditions of the frame house which still had several infirm inhabitants, and undertook repairs and improvements. The home, under the guidance of the Women's Twentieth Century Club, later became a Community Chest agency, with pleasant accommodations for ten beneficiaries. [6]

In the South, the glowing point of success was autonomous education after Emancipation. Forceful social action was a predominant factor among church leaders in the political arena. It was a must that black church leaders become involved in not only the spiritual welfare, but every phase of their peoples' lives for their betterment. In 1896, success had attended their labors, and the bishops' address to the people pointed up the following:

> As we trace evidences of design in all material structures, so find we most abundant evidences of divine sovereignty overruling the doings of men, whether as individuals or in organized society . . . .
>
> The history of materiality teaches us that each and every event is a link or a component part of some link making up a great chain of a divine universal administration of human affairs. The more we attempt to trace the hand of God in the administration of human government, the more and more profound becomes the study of universal theocracy. It makes very little difference as to the variety of forms of government or mode of administration; they all seem to be overruled by God with one common upward trend.[7]

The bishops continued to trace religious and political history from Old Testament times and cited incidents of changes throughout the centuries, of God's mighty hand ruling the universe. They further stated:

> In such a new world of thought and aggressiveness God reserved a place for a large portion of Negroes that Africa through them might be redeemed. Thus He brought the Negro to this Continent in chains, as he would come no other way. In this we see the many links constituting the great chain of divine providence. Everywhere we can trace the footprints of God walking around in nature's laboratory providing first for man and then overruling man's acts of His glory . . . . In fact our religion is largely based upon the idea of divine providence including a universal administration. In nothing less could we trust . . . .
>
> But of all the changes, none are more marked than those wrought in American sentiment, and no transition greater than that of the American Negro. Even our little Zion on the corner of Church and Leonard Streets has

5. Warner, *New Haven Negroes,* p. 97; DuBois, *Efforts for Social Betterment Among Negro Americans,* p. 65.
6. Warner, *op. cit.,* p. 284.
7. *Minutes,* Twentieth Quadrennial Session, pp. 105-106.

changed into spires and steeples, bedecking thousands of temples where millions of people sing praises unto God and ofttimes some of these persons are ex-masters listening to the gospel expounded by ex-slaves. We have reason also to be thankful for the rapid growth of the Church.

In 1863, when the proclamation of freedom was issued, we could only claim six small conferences, ninety-two preachers, and five thousand members. And we owned no other connectional interest. In the same year Elder J. W. Hood . . . was sent to North Carolina; Elder Wilbur G. Strong was sent to Key West, Florida, and a little later Elder Wm. F. Butler was sent to Kentucky. These three great missionaries and able divines followed in the wake of the cannons of liberty, with the gospel of peace, and ere the smoke of battle had cleared away, they had established our Zion upon the ruins of slavery . . . . With courage bold and faith undaunted they traveled, preached, and lectured as pioneers when even their hearers trembled with fear for their safety. The sentiment of the country and the new conditions of the South made it unsafe for such men and they frequent¹ had to walk by faith and not by sight, and that too, at times, in great haste . . . .

The early Negro preachers have been criticised for political affiliations; but it ought to be remembered that the conditions of the South at that time were such that these men had not merely to deal with a new born race of illiterate people along church lines, but frequently found it necessary to be their leaders as well in all matters pertaining to the interest of the race . . . .

Elder Hood, for instance (now bishop), who did more for the betterment of his race during and since the days of reconstruction than any other citizen of his state, and possibly more for his race than any other man in the South, found it necessary to accept the position of Assistant State Superintendent of Education, in order to establish schools for the education of his people and thus prepare them for the responsibilities of citizenship.

The same may be said of Dr. I. C. Clinton (now bishop) who by force of circumstances found it necessary to accept the position of county treasurer, which place he filled acceptably for eight years. Such examples, however necessary then, have been misinterpreted by many of our ministers of a later day, who have mingled local politics with their church work to the injury of themselves and all concerned . . . .

We say to those who are disposed to speak unkindly of the Negro ministry and its unfitness to lead the race, that the Negro ministry of early days has been charged with manifold responsibilities and constituted the largest proportion of true race leaders for the first twenty years after the war. And whatever good has come to the race came mainly through its church and ministry. [Because the church was the only universal organization of the race group].

And whatever may be said of our lawyers, doctors and other professional guides, even our Douglass, they are but the products of the Church, and largely of Zion Church, guided by our ministry. They have not, and are not likely to rise higher than the level of the Church. We would, however, advise more of our young men to study law, medicine, agriculture, and mechanism and thus provide the race with suitable guides along all professional lines and thereby relieve the ministry of much responsibility.[8]

Four years prior to this message, at the General Conference held in Pittsburgh, an explicit report by the state of the church committee on the social thinking of the A.M.E. Zion Church was passed upon by the delegates for implementation. High moral standards and strict temperance, which for many years received the unstinted support of church organizations, was projected with

8. *Ibid.*, pp. 106, 110, 112-13.

great force through pronouncements of church leaders, and cooperation with the Women's Christian Temperance Union founded by Frances Willard, and the Young Men's and Young Women's Christian Associations, which had their origin in England and spread throughout the world. In 1892 our Committee on State of the Church said:

> ... Our pulpits, instead of being continually on the defensive, are in a position to wage aggressive warfare against sin and offer abundant grace to all seeking penitents ....

Foremost among the gigantic evils that afflict society is the liquor traffic. Wasting and destruction are in its paths, and its fruit is unto everlasting death. While corporations bow submissively to its will, and political parties court its favor, and eccleciastical assemblies are often dumb in its presence, our Church is distinctively committed to uncompromising hostility to it. She regards it as a monster of iniquity deserving the hatred of all good men. The proposition to sanction it by legal enactment she denounces as impolitic and criminal, an offense against wisdom and righteousness. Your committee finds reason for satisfaction in this radical position and urge upon all preachers a fearless maintenance of it.

On all humanitarian and ethical reforms there is no need to apologize for the attitude of our denomination. We have always taken advanced grounds in these matters. Gambling, the social evil, related vices of every variety, have received unqualified condemnation. Whatever militates against the New Testament ideal of life and character has been reprobated in unsparing terms.

We reaffirm our traditional position, and call on all who bear our name to strictly observe the requirements of personal integrity.

The family is properly viewed as the foundation of society. The rapid increase of divorces is an alarming feature of modern life. Our attitude as a Church on the question of divorce has always been conservative. There appears no sufficient reason for changing opinion or practice. We believe the Scripture rule puts the proper limit on the grounds of divorce and we advise conformity thereto ..

Intelligent concern for the extension of the kingdom of heaven on earth calls for attention to social agitation. The Bible clearly teaches that rich and poor should dwell together in peace, for the Lord is the maker of them all. The arraying of capital against labor and the division of society into conflicting classes are to be deplored, and, as far as possible, prevented. The Church should emphasize the duty of mutual forbearance and charity. It should be her aim to exalt the dignity of labor and to sanctify wealth and culture. The ministers of the Lord's house ought to be of such a nature that lines of social distinction should disappear, and the wholesome truth be universally accepted that God is no respector of persons. [9]

The A.M.E. Zion Church commenced with these high moral standards based upon New Testament interpretation and Methodist doctrines, of the Orthodox order, to which it has sought to adhere in the midst of conflicting social changes. The church has held intelligent attention on the conditions of the nation and world, particularly that which concerned the African peoples. These matters have been appraised through the annual and general conferences, and concerted action taken by committees on state of the country and state of the church, and by delegates voting from time to time. The leaders have kept the church up front on all issues affecting the race throughout the nation and the world, and have participated and encouraged participation for the social betterment of our people.

In early 1900, Mary White Ovington, in her study of social conditions of New

9. *Minutes,* Nineteenth Quadrennial Session, pp. 150-151.

York metropolis, observed the oldest black churches, inclusive of Mother Zion Church, stating that:

> The church is a busy place and retains its members, not only by its preaching, but by midweek meetings. There are the class meetings of the Methodists, the young people's societies, the prayer meetings, and the sermons preached to the secret benefit organizations. Visiting sisters and brothers attend to relief work, and standing at a side table, sometimes picturesque with lighted lantern, ask for dole for the poor.[10]

This has been a general practice, not only in urban churches, but in rural churches. In the A.M.E. Zion Church, this program extended on a connectionwide basis and reached across the seas to Africa, and a little later to the West Indies, South America, and England.

While the church has strongly voiced its sentiment on vital issues and kept in contact with head statesmen, world and national, it has also taken occasion to commemorate historical events on a broad scale which made immeasurable impressions upon community, state, and nation. An early instance of this was at the General Conference in Washington, D.C., May 9, 1900. The evening session was dedicated to the centennial anniversary of the birth of John Brown. Bishop Walters presided, and Dr. Andrew J. Warner first spoke in glowing terms of the heroism of John Brown. Dr. J. H. Hector, well-known temperance lecturer throughout England and North America and an A.M.E. Zion minister, then spoke.

> He had associated with one of the sons of John Brown in a lecturing tour to save the latter's home .... He delivered a most impressive and instructive speech, detailing in vivid terms the life struggle of the hero John Brown ....
> Dr. Archibald Grimke was introduced and made an eloquent address, using as a basis of his remarks the influence of an idea. Bishop Walters read a letter of conversation between John Brown and Governor Wise, of Virginia, before his execution, of which the Governor said John Brown is no fool, and the Nation will see it one day. Prof. Kelley Miller, of Howard University was introduced, and read a well prepared paper on the subject: "The Negro as a Religious and Social, and Political Factor of the Race" ... The financial agent of the Afro-American Council was introduced in the person of Prof. J. Lawson. He made a brief address, and appealed to the audience for aid. He spoke of the cases now docketed in the Supreme Court of the United States. Rev. J. J. Adams made a statement concerning the meeting in Rochester [that same evening] for the purpose of money to prosecute these cases.[11]

Generally, sessions of this type are held in A.M.E. Zion Church meetings to bolster the cause of the black race.

In 1904 the President of the United States sent the following telegram to our General Conference through Bishop Alexander Walters:

Bishop Walters,

> My Dear Bishop:—Permit me, through you, to extend my hearty greeting to the General Conference of your Church, and I wish you all success in your work for the uplifting of the people whom you represent. With best wishes,
>
> Sincerely yours,
> THEODORE ROOSEVELT [12]

In 1908, the Bishops addressed the church stating that:

10. Ovington, *Half a Man*, p. 65.
11. *Minutes,* Twenty-First Quadrennial Session, pp. 46-47.
12. *Minutes,* Twenty-Second Quadrennial Session, p. 33.

We note with pleasure that the administration of President Roosevelt has ever stood for that which tends toward the highest and most progressive advancement of individuals and nations. The present administration deserves the commendation of every good citizen for the part it has taken in promoting peace among the nations and a satisfactory adjustment of conflicts between capital and labor.

Notwithstanding this, we deplore the hasty action by which the one hundred and sixty-seven Negro soldiers were dismissed without first making a thorough investigation according to the customary form of law usually employed in such cases, and it is our fond hope that since the evidence produced after a full investigation has not been sufficient to prove the soldiers guilty, that the said soldiers be restored to their former ranks and record, and that they be allowed their back pay. [13]

The bishops went on to express their gratitude to two Senators who had joined in the effort to secure justice for the Negro soldiers, and better treatment for the entire race.

Dr. Booker T. Washington had opened Tuskegee Institute in Butler Chapel A.M.E. Zion Church in 1881, delivered the last speech before his death, in Varick Memorial Church, New Haven, Conn., October 25, 1915. His subject was: "How the North can Help the South." [14]

A social spirit in the church continued as the first World War, President Wilson's policy on peace and democracy, the large migration of blacks from the South to the North and Northwest, and national prohibition comprehended the next two decades. The A.M.E. Zion Church, in each General Conference, forcefully reaffirmed her convictions on raising the low economic status of the race, temperance and sobriety, and the never-ending search for peace. In the Bishops' Message to the church in 1920, the following sentiment was voiced:

Ministers who desire to participate in the new propaganda of a larger church on a more advanced scale, and with a higher and more divine prospective, must rise up to a larger and fuller vision of a world to be saved for Christ. They must be real church engineers who will survey the needs of humanity and be able to inaugurate methods and means of supplying those needs . . . The social, racial, political, civic and industrial questions which prevent the peace of the world cannot be settled alone by legislation. A League of Nations and Treaties of Peace will amount to but little unless the leaven of Christianity penetrates them, and at least the name of the Lord be written in them. Education alone cannot do it, for the best educated nation on earth led the world astray. Democracy alone cannot do it, for it is not general in its application. The doctrine of sociology will not solve these problems, for it deals principally with the laws controlling human intercourse in society. Nothing but the teachings of the Son of God can permanently settle the differences of men, races and nations. Since the church is the custodian of the oracles of God, she must assume the responsibility of arbitrating the differences of men, predicating her actions upon the Golden Rule, and assert her right to do so. [15]

In the latter 1920's the country was hit with the "oncoming tides and youthful self-expression and self-assertion that tread down the barriers of parental restraint and conventional standards." Despite the continuous warnings and attack of our church and other leading churches against violence, "adult depravity and

13. Episcopal Quadrennial Address, 1908, p. 23.
14. Colbert, *General Conference Handbook,* Twenty-Fifth Quadrennial Session, p. 136.
15. *Minutes,* Twenty-Sixth Quadrennial Session, pp. 70-71.

youthful delinquency" had brought about an almost uncontrollable crime wave in the nation, which affected innocent victims by the thousands. [16] The A.M.E. Zion Church, through its Department of Christian Education, had set up its own programs for youth in order to combat this evil, and work in cooperation with other forces and government agencies to improve conditions in changing society.

The 1940 General Conference began to think seriously about a department of social service. The matter was brought to the attention of successive General Conferences, until 1952, when the General Conference passed into law a part-time General Office of Public Relations and Social Service. The Social Service Committee of the 1940 General Conference expressed strong views on improving social conditions of the Negro, in health, recreation and housing, and lifted up the fact that: "Recreation should form a part of church activity inasmuch as leisure time is the most dangerous time in the lives of children, young people and adults:—and the prosperity of the nation depends upon the social well-being of all the people. Good health, good homes, opportunity to labor in chosen lines of endeavor, proper education along all lines are assets of a prosperous nation and the church has a definite part in the development of these assets." The committee recommended that the General Conference appoint a permanent commission on social service and outline a social service program for the. A.M.E. Zion Church. [17]

Since this General Conference was held in Washington, D.C., Bishop W. J. Walls, representing the General Conference visited the White House, and expressed views to President Franklin D. Roosevelt on behalf of the church, stating:

Mr. President: May 3, 1940
    I bring you the greetings of the Board of Bishops of the General Conference of the African Methodist Episcopal Zion Church, with conferences in America, Africa, South America, and the West Indies. We are aware of how tremendous must be the duties of the President of the United States in the present situation of the country and the world. I deeply appreciate the honor of this brief conference.
    People of my race always have liked the name Roosevelt.
    The human race is indebted to you for the great social emphasis you have given to the statesmanship of our times. I congratulate you upon the affection and the confidence which your name inspires everywhere.
                                                    Bishop W. J. Walls, Chicago, Ill.
The President responded with the following message to the General Conference.
THE WHITE HOUSE
WASHINGTON

                                                                              May 3, 1940
My dear Bishop Walls:
    It was a great pleasure to see you this morning and to receive from you the greetings of the Bishops and the Delegates attending the General Conference of the African Methodist Episcopal Zion Church.
    I trust that all your deliberations concerning the missionary, educational and social problems before the Conference will be fruitful of wise counsels and constructive action to make real the highest ideals of the A.M.E. Zion Church. I was particularly glad to hear of plans to extend your missionary work in Panama and in Liberia.

16. *Minutes,* Twenty-Eighth Quadrennial Session, p. 40.
17. *Minutes,* Thirty-First Quadrennial Session, pp. 220-222.

May I reiterate what I have previously stated, that in establishing the rights of a minority in a democracy we must always bear in mind that the political, social and economic well-being of the whole people depends upon the achievement of that well-being for all sections of the population regardless of color, creed, or geography. I shall appreciate it if you will extend to the members of the conference my greetings and assurance that I heartily reciprocate their cordial sentiment.

Very sincerely yours,

Franklin D. Roosevelt[18]

Social conditions improved slightly with the beginning of the Federal Fair Employment Practice Commission (FEPC) initiated by the Roosevelt administration. Unemployment for the black race had been unjustly practiced in the North as well as the South since World War I. In 1944, in its message to the church, the Board of Bishops stated:

We strongly insist that the F.E.P.C., which has done a notable work in balancing industry with justice for race minorities, be continued. In that form some interracial implementation of Government for fair practices should be set up for post war adjustment and continued in peace time.[19]

From 1944 to 1948, a black woman, Anna Arnold Hedgeman, served as executive director of the National Council of the F.E.P.C. From 1949 to 1953, she was assistant to the director of the Federal Security Agency.[20]

The Bishops also spoke out in 1944 firmly on other problems facing the nation and world during World War II:

Other problems such as home-breaking, disorganization of the mores, liberalism, drink and many other bi-products will flow out of this social upheaval.

To illustrate, it is predicted by Burgess, using his method of judging by the trend line of past decades, that the ratio of one divorce to every six marriages, at present, will increase to one to three. This will come in the after-war confusion, and he thinks will be caused in part by the hasty war marriages. The maladjustment of war period separation will be another phase of this growth of divorce.

New ideas of sex, incident to changing post-war mores, and to the abolishing of the red light district after the last war, liberties between women and the soldier element, based on the idea that it is patriotic to indulge those who lay their lives on the country's altar, the changed and independent status of women economically, and public service opportunity, thrusts womanhood into both new privileges bearing with it new social peril.

And so: the Church, especially its youth agencies, will be thrust, yea, is already under a great and burdening responsibility to enter into the solution of these problems. If the church and religion fail, the State is bound to fail. President Coolidge once said to an A.M.E. Zion delegation at the White House, which invited him to address its General Conference. "If you succeed, we here can succeed. If you fail, I see no hope for us here."

It was an irony of neglected religion when three years before the Munich Conference, David Lloyd George, writing in the Hearst papers, said, "The world has the jitters and the politicians cannot save it. I am turning it over to the preachers, and if they fail, I have no hope to save it from the oncoming calamity."[21]

18. *Ibid.,* pp. 33-34
19. *Minutes,* Thirty-Second Quadrennial Session, p. 235.
20. Bergman, *Chronological History of the Negro,* p. 506.
21. *Minutes,* Thirty-Second Quadrennial Session, p. 235.

And so came the postwar problems as religious leaders and others had prophesied. In 1948 the Board of Bishops appealed for world order and international cooperation. "To be sure we believe in World Order and International Cooperation" the Bishops stated, "that is, we believe if it stands for full and complete equality down to the last man in the last nation. We will pray for this, we will contend against anything short of this. Bishop Oxnam remarks: 'Men may kneel in repentance, but they must stand upon their feet to march. The day of marching is upon us.' We are ready and willing to go into action for One World provided it is one world with Christ at the center, with all eyes fixed on Him and with all hearts in tune with the command: 'Thou shalt love the Lord Thy God with all thy heart, and with all thy soul, and with all thy strength, and with all thy mind: and thy neighbor as thyself."[22] This was the church's fitting cooperative answer to the United Nations, which had been born in 1945.

In the next six quadrenniums, the A.M.E. Zion Church voiced strong opinions and became incisively active through leadership and delegated representatives in the causes for a just and durable society. Some church leaders participated in the demonstrations and marches for freedom, some went to jail, some, such as Rev. Felix S. Anderson (later bishop), and Rev. Mrs. Amelia M. Tucker, desired to enter the political arena, like the fathers after the Civil War, in efforts to bring about social justice and reform. Both leaders served in the state legislature of Kentucky and fought for desegregation in that state. Reverend E. Franklin Jackson served as national committeeman of the Democratic Party. The bishops continued to speak out vehemently against the destructive forces in our civilization, increasing crime, colonialism, the racist program of the government of South Africa, atomic power, the degeneration and decadence of American society, and growing immorality.

The pillaging civil war in Nigeria of the late 1960's was deeply disturbing, as the A.M.E. Zion Church had an abiding concern for the people of Nigeria and its members, largely in the rural section, and largely Biafrians. The strife in other African countries, such as Kenya, to win independence was also of large concern. The hunger and conditions of underdeveloped countries, especially Asiatic and African countries, increased our concern, and the church searched for new ways to alleviate sufferings, by joining in programs of relief through the National Council of Churches and the World Council of Churches. Our Foreign Missions Department cooperates with Church World Service of the National Council of Churches, and similar organizations.

At home, there have been hurricanes, cyclones, floods and earthquakes, which have left many places practically destitute and others in total ruin. Thousands upon thousands of lives have been lost, and homes and fields alike swept away, while many more have been stripped of all their possessions. We have always deemed it opportune to express for these and others our sympathy; to raise special funds of relief through our local churches, annual conferences, and sometimes appropriation of our General Fund; and to cooperate with the Red Cross and other national agencies, which are more competent to care for stricken areas. We have not only endeavored to come to the aid of the needy financially, but when necessity calls, our church buildings, parsonages, ministers, missionaries, members, schools, and other facilities and personnel are utilized to the fullest extent.

The A.M.E. Zion Church has helped to wage the War on Poverty. Its leaders

22. *Minutes,* Thirty-Third Quadrennial Session, p. 308.

have lauded the civil rights stands taken from time to time by Presidents Truman, Eisenhower, Kennedy, and Johnson, and especially the latter in his drastic measures of eliminating injustices between 1964 and 1968. The leaders have also expressed themselves openly against President Nixon's conservative administration; his attitude on school busing for balancing integration of schools and equal education opportunities, Supreme Court appointees, and no appointment of a black cabinet member after President Johnson paved the way for a new America along these lines.

On "The Church and Human Welfare," the Board of Bishops stated in 1961:

> The most compelling Christian action is relief and social welfare economy. This helping of the needy and finding and protecting adequate living employment, are upon the church today as in no previous period since the coming of democracy. We must no longer lag on this action in our Zion. Let our present provision on our law be set going by the officers of the Social Service Department.
>
> The protection of the aged legislation and the relief of the people who suffer in unemployment areas, proposed by President Kennedy and the platform of the national administration, we endorse heartily. We admonish our people to support it, and thus add the weight of the government to the efforts of the church, to give our people social salvation and sustained Christian living.[23]

The National Conference of Black Churchmen (NCBC) was established to help balance racial situations, and in 1967 Bishop Herbert Bell Shaw of the A.M.E. Zion Church was elected chairman of the board of directors and was still serving in this office through 1972.[24]

Acording to our interpretation of biblical teaching, the A.M.E. Zion Church, through its leadership, in an age of social change, has been pronounced against abortion. It has family planning under study, and has continued to stress development of full-fledged family life. Serving as chairman of the National Commission on Family Life of the A.M.E. Zion Church through the Christian Education Department was Rev. George B. Thomas. He was succeeded by Mrs. Evelyn S. Wilcher. The church has become concerned, in numerous ways, over the worsening conditions of racial strife, tensions, civil disorders, chaos, dope traffic, and corruption in high government offices. Study commissions have been appointed to cooperate with other churches and agencies in finding a way out.

At the 1972 General Conference, the Board of Bishops declared:

The A.M.E. Zion, through its Ecumenical relationships, viz; the World Council of Churches, the National Council of Churches, Consultation on Church Union, by resolutions passed, has expressed its attitude not only on the war in Vietnam, but also, concerning the conflicts in the Far East, South America, Ireland, South African Rhodesia and elsewhere, deploring the war-like philosophy that plunges nations into economic, caste, civil, religious, social, racial, political and territorial conflict, all destructive to the welfare of humanity. Our Church renews its efforts to eliminate violence in the lives of individuals, nations and communities . . . .

In the realm of freedom and justice it is always the right time for the "establishment" to do right. But the establishment will not move without pressure, so, we must use what we have, or lose what we want. Full and complete freedom is not ever given—it must be won or achieved. The right sort of political action, and the wise use of the ballot; buttressed with an

23. Ms. Message, Board of Bishops, January 1961 p. 15.
24. Report of Second Episcopal District, 1972, p. 1.

impregnable faith in God, we can overcome. [25]

In social enterprises, the A.M.E. Zion Church was born with an eagerness to provide homes and health care centers, as well as education facilities. In some respects, we have had a more improved program of institution building in Africa and other foreign fields than at home. There are a large number of A.M.E. Zion Church training schools and educational centers, and one hospital, in Africa. In the latter part of the nineteenth and beginning of the twentieth century, while annual conferences were giving great concentration to education in this country; at least three persons in Zion managed to establish other social institutions. Harriet Tubman established and operated a home for the elderly, and needy wayfarers, on her property at Auburn, N.Y., before bequeathing it to the A.M.E. Zion Church. While she was engaged in this noble work, she helped to build the Thompson Memorial A.M.E. Zion Church at Auburn. She participated in temperance work and was most active, speaking at woman suffrage meetings, appearing on the same platform with such leaders as Elizabeth Cady Stanton and Susan B. Anthony, both of whom greatly admired and respected her. [26]

It was at such a suffrage meeting in a Rochester church, presided over by these two ladies, that Harriet was presented as the Underground Railroad Conductor by Miss Anthony who led her to the platform, after she had awakened out of a deep sleep, and in awesome wonderment of why so many white ladies were gathered there. She then uttered her immortal words: "I was the conductor of the Underground Railroad for eight years, and I can say what most conductors can't say—I never ran my train off the track and I never lost a passenger." [27]

In Montgomery, Ala., another noble woman, one of the pioneers of the Woman's Home and Foreign Missionary Society in East (Central) Alabama Conference, Mrs. Ann Hale, founded The Hale Infirmary or Home for the Aged. [28] She gave the building for the inmates, and the home received assistance of her church and clubs in the city. Mrs. Hale was cited as one who "never tires in her efforts to help the needy and provide for them. She is a true benefactress." [29]

Around the first part of the century, Rev. James H. Manley established the Oxford Orphanage at Oxford, N.C., which operated with illuminating success with the assistance of the local church at Oxford and community friends.

After the death of Bishop Clement, there was an effort to establish and maintain the George C. Clement Memorial Old Peoples' Home, by the Relief Department of the Church, on a part of the Atkinson College plot in Kentucky, with Rev. C. C. Ellis in charge. Insufficient staff and budget ceased operation.

That which began to concern the church greatly was the problem of amusement for black youth in America after Emancipation. First, they were "frankly shut out of most places of public amusement and most Negro Parents" were "afraid to send their children where they would be admitted for fear that some veiled action or word would poison their pleasure. Secondly, these naturally, joyous, . . . singing people," had "received a puritanic training which continually thundered against 'worldly' amusements." [30]

25. Quadrennial Message, Board of Bishops, Thirty-Ninth Quadrennial Session, pp. 3, 24.
26. Conrad, *Harriet Tubman, Negro Soldier and Abolitionist*, p. 45.
27. Conrad, *Harriet Tubman*, pp. 213-214.
28. W. E. Burghardt DuBois, *Efforts for Social Betterment*, p. 57.
29. *A.M.E. Zion Quarterly Review*, April 1894, p. 333.
30. W. E. Burghardt DuBois, *Morals and Manners Among Negro Americans*, p. 90.

BARBER MEMORIAL CAMP,
West Granville, Mass.
Established in 1934.

The Bishop
John J. Moore Chapel
A.M.E. ZION
ASSEMBLY-CAMP
DOROTHY WALLS
Black Mountain, N.C.
Founded, 1958.

VIOLA BOOKER
SPOTTSWOOD
MEMORIAL CAMP
Grovesport, Ohio,
Founded, 1962.

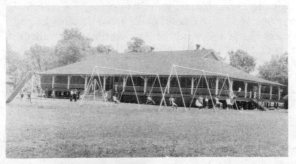

M. ARDELLE SHAW CAMP
Burlington, N.Y. Accepted
in New York Conference,
late 1960's.

Dr. Thomas Walker Wallace
Pioneer of our church camps.

In seriously awakening to the need of wholesome recreation and amusement for children and youth, the church first coupled it with education and Sunday school training; naturally the indoor-outdoor games, then the encouragement of the Y.M.C.A. and Y.W.C.A. programs. Later according to the demands of the times, the church in the 1920's utilized complete programs of training and recreation through its Christian Education Department and Varick Christian Endeavor Society (afterward the Home and Church Division), working with the National Boy Scout and Girl Scout organizations of America.

In New York City, Mother Zion Church, under the leadership of Rev. J. W. Brown, was the first in the connection to initiate a week-day community program. More and more this became a part of urban church life. Concern increased for summer outdoor programs, especially for children in crowded cities.

In the summer of 1934, Dr. Thomas W. Wallace decided to utilize the 310 acre property with two lakes, owned by the A.M.E. Zion Church in the Berkshire Mountains, for children's recreation, since the church had been slow in developing the Barber Memorial Home there. With his industrial training and skillful techniques, he built cabins, a chapel and dining hall, mainly from timber developed on the grounds, and commenced operating the Barber Memorial Camp. As secretary of home missions and relief, he was able to interest the connection, which placed the camp under the auspices of the Home Missions Department. It was largely supported through the years by the children and youth of the New England, New York, and Western New York Conferences, especially for development led by Bishop W. J. Walls who helped to make this a permanent success. After the death of Rev. Thomas W. Wallace, his son, Thomas W. Wallace, Jr. operated the camp one summer. The camp was then managed for a brief period by Rev. C. C. Ellis. He was succeeded by Rev. Ralph W. Gullette and Rev. J. H. French, and Rev. Gullette later became manager for the second time. Reverend James Hubert, the present manager, is a tireless worker in the interest of continuing the development for the health and recreational welfare of the children of Zion in the Northeast.

The Columbus Avenue Church of Boston came into gift possession of its own Camp Nippernicket, under the pastorate of Rev. W. D. Battle around the time Dr. Wallace opened Barber Camp for summer sessions. The camping interests were divided somewhat, with the largest church of the New England Conference owning its separate camp facility.

In the Southland, blacks were still deprived of camp facilities owned by churches and private concerns. In 1957, the presiding bishop of the Western North Carolina Conference, Bishop W. J. Walls, appointed a committee of the conference to investigate purchase of a campsite. By the persistent efforts of some of the missionary women of the Western North Carolina Conference, a 66-acre plot was purchased by the conference in 1958 at Black Mountain, N.C., in the Blue Ridge Mountains. These women included Mrs. L. Barbara Jones Taylor and Makepeace Long, who had been taking children to a small summer camp which had been phased out after the owner's death, and others: Mrs. Delacy Grecian-Donowa, Estelle Norment, Mary Gladden, Watty L. Blakey, and Celelah Lohr; and the missionary supervisor, Mrs. Dorothy J. Walls, with the full cooperation of presiding elders, ministers, and leading laymen, most of whom worked without ceasing. The plot, purchased from the Royal League of Illinois with one significant major building and other smaller buildings, encompassed the area of major religious assemblies.

Upon the suggestion of several missionary women, Rev. E. R. Michael made the motion that the newly acquired property be named in honor of the missionary supervisor, which was unanimously voted by the conference. The A.M.E. Zion Church Assembly-Camp Dorothy Walls was formally opened and dedicated in September 1958, with President Samuel E. Duncan of Livingstone College delivering the dedicatorial address. It made unusual progress and continued to develop under the Western North Carolina Conference Board of Trustees, chaired by Rev. L. C. Clark, and its managers: Rev. K. Melvin Taylor, Mr. Douglas Mallory, Rev. W. J. Campbell, Rev. and Mrs. W. L. McDaniels, Rev. Richard Stewart, Rev. and Mrs. C. W. Anthony, Mr. Lonnie Paul Davis, and a committee of Rev. J. D. Armstrong and Mr. Thomas Banks. The enterprising and trustworthy custodian of this property through the years has been Mrs. Hettie Petty. In 1964, the Blue Ridge Conference, in which the assembly-camp is located, became interested and associated the Western North Carolina Conference in advancing this cause for summer retreats in the Southeast. [31]

In 1961 the Ohio Conference purchased a 30-acre park from the Ohio Council of Churches, for camping purposes, and dedicated it to the memory of Viola Booker Spottswood, late wife and missionary supervisor of the presiding bishop of Ohio, Stephen Gill Spottswood. The camp opened officially during the summer of 1963, with Rev. Earl Peterson as camp director. [32]

At the General Conference of 1964, the A.M.E. Zion Assembly Ground-Camp Dorothy Walls at Black Mountain, N.C. and the Viola Booker Spottswood Memorial Camp near Columbus, Ohio were placed under the auspices of the Church Extension Department, while Barber Memorial Camp remained a part of the Home Missions Department.

Members of the New York Conference have invested in a camp in the Catskill Mountains at Burlington, N.Y., which they named M. Ardelle Shaw Memorial Camp, in honor of their missionary supervisor, led by Bishop Herbert B. Shaw. Its debt was liquidated from the Sesqui-Centennial Celebration of the New York Conference in 1971. "The Western New York Conference also contributed toward the acquiring of the camp, of which they are co-owners." Reverends Belvie H. Jackson, Jr., Andrew E. Whitted, and Eldridge Gittens served as co-managers through 1972. [33]

The property at Dinwiddie, Va., under the ownership of the Christian Education Department, was largely improved for summer camping, and a swimming pool added, under the leadership of Bishop W. A. Stewart and the Virginia Conference during the early 1960's.

All of these properties have provided facilities for summer leadership training schools as well as recreation and outlet for underprivileged and ghetto children.

In the increasing demands of the sixties and seventies, to fulfill the need of adequate housing, through federal and state government assistance, churches have received long-term loans and grants for building housing projects for low and middle income families. All over the country, projects are being sponsored by black churches as well as white, and the A.M.E. Zion Church has been involved in the program. Among the housing projects completed or near completion by 1972 were the Varick Apartments, led by the Washington Street A.M.E. Zion Church in Newburgh, N.Y., Rev. Frank E. Jones, pastor; the Carrington Arms, New

31. *Minutes,* Western North Carolina Annual Conference, 1958-1970.
32. *Minutes,* Thirty-Seventh Quadrennial Session, p. 206.
33. Report of the Second Episcopal District, Thirty-Ninth Quadrennial Session, p. 3.

Rochelle, N.Y., in memory of Rev. William E. Carrington, led by St. Catherine Church, Rev. A. E. Whitted, pastor; the Zion Hill Apartments, Salisbury, N.C., under the directorship of Soldiers Memorial Church and Moores Chapel Church, Revs. Herman L. Anderson and Vernon A. Shannon pastors; The Little Rock A.M.E. Zion Church Apartments in Charlotte, N.C., directed by the pastor, Rev. George J. Leake; The Goler Metropolitan Apartments, Winston-Salem N.C., led by Rev. H. C. Walser. The Churchill Towers under the sponsorship of Hood Memorial A.M.E. Zion Church in New York City, Rev. Frank E. Churchill, pastor; the St. Stephens A.M.E. Zion Church Apartments, under the directorship of the church at Asbury Park, N.J., Rev. W. J. Powell, pastor; and the Caldwell Apartments in the Bronx, N.Y. under the sponsorship of the church and pastor, Rev. Carnes McKinney. The St. Paul A.M.E. Zion Church of Detroit has a senior citizens project under construction by 1972, led by Rev. William C. Ardrey, and several other family dwellings and senior citizen projects are in process at this writing.

The day care centers provided in a number of churches to assist working mothers in care of their children and kindergartens operated in the churches are also salubrious programs in helping to mold the lives and character of pre-school age children.

With all of these programs and facilities of social service, and several more, however, the church finds itself today, as never before, in a challenging situation. Particularly in the United States, the black church has come into a diversified responsibility. The A.M.E. Zion Church, as an integral part of this social concern, comes into major influence in the moving up and the balancing of judgment in a tumultuous period of restless ambition, striving for a new citizenship with a better status of freedom than has been accorded the race before around the world, especially in Africa and on this continent.

This nation is in the midst of change: scientifically, politically, economically, and socially. Our youth are vacillating between the last season and the present. There were more furor and upheavals in the schools a year or two ago. At present, it appears that furor has turned to serious constructive thinking and resolute attitude. Study for permanent change is now the vogue.

The questions are asked: What shall we do to define and satisfy the causes of fomenting revolutionary attitudes in the colleges and areas of education? What can we do with science, which defies much of the tradition in the social mores, and actually seeks to taboo much of our religious standpat beliefs and practices in pretentious regulation?

Things are brought to test and trial regularly these days, but through methods of study as well as protest and unprecedented designs, they are daily unfolding among us. The A.M.E. Zion Church, like many American churches, is at work reconstructing its literature, undoing old thought, and seeking creation of new thoughts. All religion is brought to a new attention and recreative action. Ministers are altering their messages. Teachers are thrusting scientific methodology into their instruction. Old methods are being tested, and untried methods are thrusting into the situation pressures that must be reckoned with. Prophets are now reconstructing their thinking in the light of unfolding new visions. Everything has become more expensive and still the building of new structures, the adoption of more particularized and analytical propositions, filling our homes and our hearts with countless tomes of printed matter so that everything now has become a matter of study and challenge.

Reorganization has seized every department of the church and created new ones; home life, human relations of various sources and types, and the word has gone forth—less talk and more deeds. Our churches are therefore reorganizing, and we find ourselves in the midst of raising funds to compete in far more than property and the building of worship cells. We are forced to consider the whole gamut of human needs.

While the demand seems great, the A.M.E. Zion Church is awakening, and to an encouraging extent making some progress. It tends to legislate in the interest of the progress of the church. It continues to take definite and onward thrusting interest in the cause of freedom, and in the espousal of movements and organizations that mean progress, creativeness, and freedom.

Nevertheless, the social gospel and programs in our church are not enough. The foremost projection of evangelism must head church programming. The place of assembly of which the church has been the center must have more prepared leadership because the competition has come upon us with other forms of organizing, assembling more intelligence and greater demands of the people for varied expressions of rights. Their powers have caused variations and competing organizations, and secularistic assertiveness in the face of what has been mostly religious prevalence in organization. By growing intelligence and rising tide of learning the church will be forced to produce adequate leadership of both ministers and laymen to stay at the forefront. This brings to bear the importance of laymen to not only give reason for the faith in themselves, but to become effective in its expression and dissemination, and the power of organizing and promoting, through all the agencies of societies, these immortal principles.

Reforms are born in extreme situations, and this country is now ripe for moral reform. Deeper thinking and better living are the demands of the hour.

CHAPTER 33

THE CENTENNIAL AND SESQUI-CENTENNIAL OBSERVANCES

Hallow the past—Consecrate the present—Have
Faith in the future—and above all—Protect
the Heritage.

When the A.M.E. Zion Church was organized in 1796 the pulpits were not generally supplied with Afro-American clergymen.

The wielding of the gavel was out of the question. The rule was to submit to authority rather than to exercise it. Afro-Americans had not then ascended to the proud dignity of rising to questions of privilege, making points, and all the rest of the parliamentary tangle. All this was left as a sacred right to the Anglo-Saxon brother. The new Church suggested new responsibilities, new duties, and new spirit of self-reliance. The exercise of their religious rights opened their eyes to all their rights. Religious liberty suggested civil liberty. The right and privilege to preach aroused the ambition to make an effort in other professional lines. Physicians, lawyers, and teachers followed in the wake of the new preacher. [1]

In the next 25 years the infant church had envisaged its way into a separate and distinct denomination through countless obstacles. By 1846 this denomination was in the midst of a life and death struggle. While preaching an unadulterated gospel of deepening and strengthening Christian faith, it was engaged in the business of smuggling slaves from the South and shielding fugitives.

This denomination had developed inner strife which would soon split it asunder for the next dozen years. The time was not ripe, thus it was unable to "hallow the fiftieth year and proclaim liberty throughout the land unto all the inhabitants thereof."(Lev. 25:10)

The A.M.E. Zion Church, a pioneer in the movement for the abolition of human slavery, continued to preach against this invidious evil and work for its downfall. "Scarcely was a sermon of any of its ministers considered complete without reference in some form to this 'sum of all villainies.' " [2] The church paved its way through the throes of division in 1860 and pangs of slavery in 1863, and moved like a rushing stream into the Southland to unite in Christian bonds with the rejoicing freedmen and assist in building churches and institutions. It made remarkable gains in some Southern states and lost in others, while it failed to make the necessary inroads in some other largely populated areas because of the incapacity to develop leadership at the necessary pace and overcome obstructions. Notwithstanding the obstacles, fears and frustrations, race aversions, threats

1. Fortune, *The New York Age,* October 1, 1896, p. 1.
2. *Ibid.*

and malicious outrages following Reconstruction, the race had been proclaimed free more than 30 years. The church had weathered severe storms and safely made it to 1896 with nearly a half million members in a hostile land. By this time it had reached across the seas to Africa and rejoined with its ancestral inhabitants from whom its people had been separated by shackles, and stretched its arms into ethnical West Indies. It had given birth the hard way to institutions. It had helped prepare leaders to withstand oppressions heaped upon the race and race church daily. It had rejoiced over success and lamented over failures. It had reached a new day, and it was time to tell the story. It was truly "A Year of Jubilee."

1796–The Centennial–1896

Four years previously, in Pittsburgh during the General Conference, the fathers of the church had decreed 1896 a Year of Jubilee in the African Methodist Episcopal Zion Church, and began with themselves and members of the General Conference planning the commemoration. In summarizing the history of the church in their Episcopal Message, the bishops emphasized the meaning of our church and the preponderance of its founder as follows:

> The Afro-American Church is the one great developing and elevating agency, in comparison with which all others sink into insignificance. There is one name connected with this movement, of which comparatively little is now said, which coming generations will rescue from the obscurity in which we have permitted it to rest. Our children's children, in their search for information respecting this movement which has done so much to develop the race, will find the name of James Varick, and will discover that to him is due the credit of starting a Church organization for the race. [3]

The next segment of preparation came on the eleventh day of the General Conference when previous arrangement had been made for Bishop J. W. Hood to read extracts of his proposed *History of the Connection,* or *One Hundred Years of the African Methodist Episcopal Zion Church,* which was done with the assistance of John C. Dancy. A strong resolution favoring the publication of the proposed history was read by Rev. E. George Biddle and enthusiastically passed with Revs. E. H. Curry, J. C. Price, W. H. Day, Bishops C. C. Pettey and T. H. Lomax heartily endorsing it and expressing appreciation and high confidence in the ability of Bishop Hood to produce a genuine reflector of the demonination. [4] Committees were subsequently appointed to meet and work the quadrennium in efforts to crown the 100 years of labor with blessed events.

A giant promotional step came in 1894, when editor John C. Dancy wrote:

> Zion Methodism is all aglow with hope and enthusiasm and jubilation over the prospects of her Centennial Jubilee just two years hence. It will be the completion of a hundred years journey–a journey fraught with toil and sacrifice and endeavor and triumph–a journey from a cabinetmaker's shop with a little more than a dozen worshippers, to a splendid edifice of architectural design and finish known as the "Mother Church" with more than two hundred thousand children dotting two continents, and nearly a half million worshippers.
>
> A stupendous progress. One can hardly realize its truth. This journey has been pursued through sufferings and heart-burnings and tears;–through oppression and servitude and death. The transformations and reformations

---

3. *Minutes,* Nineteenth Quadrennial Session, p. 2.
4. *Ibid.,* p. 87.

have been wonderful, almost incredible, but Zion has contributed her quota to pioneers and heroes who led in them all. . . .

The time is therefore at the door when we are to take a reckoning of our achievements and plan for the future. There must be rallying all along the line. Every out-post must be carefully looked after, and a free will offering be made in every place of worship, in thanks to the God of battles Who has sustained, protected and strengthened us, and enabled us to come forth with songs of rejoicing bringing our sheaves with us.

Let the work of preparation for that greatest event in our history begin at once. Let no man prove a drone in this great hive of industry and activity. Zion *must* let her light shine in the year 1896. . . .

Begin to talk over the matter now, and don't stop until the jubilee is over and the most satisfactory results are realized. [5]

Principal leaders of the proposed celebration were Bishop Alexander Walters, general chairman of the centennial committee; Bishop J. W. Hood, senior and host bishop; Dr. John C. Dancy, general manager, and Rev. Martin R. Franklin, host pastor. Hundreds of other persons were named to serve on various centennial committees. Two remarkable persons who started out a part of the planning died before the Centennial, namely, Dr. Joseph Charles Price and Hon. Frederick Douglass.

At the first meeting of combined committees to "plan, devise means and make arrangements for the proposed Jubilee of Zion Methodism, " held at Metropolitan Zion (Wesley) Church in Washington, D.C., January 24, 1895, Bishops Hood and Walters presided over the four-day meeting. Dr. Dancy said of this meeting:

We never observed more enthusiasm for any cause than was displayed at this gathering by the large number of delegates in behalf of the Centennial. They were there, even in mid-winter, from all parts of the country, and in larger proportion than any one even dreamed they would be. The work was begun and pushed with a zest and zeal which at once evinced a determination to plan for a great event and then make the event a fitting close of the first hundred years' work. . . .

On the afternoon of the first day Hon. Frederick Douglass, in company with Miss Ednorah Nahar, visited the meeting and Mr. Douglass never made a more comprehensive, significant and inspiring address. His description of John the Baptist's introduction of Jesus Christ was as fine a piece of eloquence as we ever heard. His renewed declaration that he began his "life work in Zion Church at New Bedford, Mass., as sexton, exhorter, class-leader, local preacher, preacher's steward, Sunday school superintendent and financial agent." and that he "owed whatever he was to the fact of his training in this severe school of adversity," evoked warm and unstinted applause. Mr. Douglass has repeatedly made this statement, and when it was drawn out again just three weeks prior to his lamented death it possessed new significance and inspiration. Mr. Douglass gave Ten Dollars cash and asserted that he would be pleased to give largely, when called upon to the Centennial Jubilee Fund. Editor Dancy jocosely remarked that he "would be pleased to make him as happy as possible by the size of the contribution he would ask," and Mr. Douglass nodded his assent and laughed heartily. Dr. Jehu Holliday and Dr. Wm. Howard Day responded warmly to Mr. Douglass' address and for it he was tendered a hearty vote of thanks. The address proved an inspiration. [6]

5. *A.M.E. Zion Quarterly Review,* April 1894, pp. 314-15.
6. *A.M.E. Zion Quarterly Review,* April 1895, pp. 81-82.

The editor of the *New York Age,* Timothy Thomas Fortune, attended this committee meeting along with other noted lay members throughout the church. The body paused to pay tribute to the memory of Senior Bishop John Jamison Moore, Bishop Joseph P. Thompson, Rev. Joseph C. Price, Nathaniel J. Green, John A. Tyler, and others who had begun the plans and looked forward to the occasion with glowing anticipation.

Many in the group recalled how Dr. J. C. Price had captivated the large assembly at the Methodist Episcopal Church Centennial of the Christmas Conference held in Lovely Lane Methodist Episcopal Church, Baltimore, in 1884, when he responded to the opening address of Bishop E. G. Andrews. His oratory was described as "peculiarly his own—not much of the dash and show, but. . .with a combination of rhetoric and logic, poured forth in such masterly strains of eloquence, chains his hearers as if influenced by magic or under some peculiar spell." [7]

The committees proceeded to work and found themselves fully pepared to celebrate the occasion by the time the General Conference was held in Mobile, Ala. in May 1896.

The Year of Jubilee had arrived. The hour was at hand. On Thursday, October 1, the most stimulating, inspirational, spectacular, extolling, solemn event in the history of the A.M.E. Zion Church commenced and lasted through Monday evening, Ocotber 12, in the city of its birth, New York. Represented on the occasion were outstanding leaders of both races, church and state, business and professional. At the oldest black church in the city of New York, Mother Zion, general chairman Bishop Alexander Walters presented Bishop James W. Hood at 10:30 Thursday morning to preside over the opening session. After Bishop I. C. Clinton led the huge congregation in singing a centennial hymn, "Hail the Church that Varick Started," the opening sermon was delivered by Bishop C. H. Fowler of the Methodist Episcopal Church.

At the afternoon Communion Service presided over by Bishop Lomax, the sermon was delivered by Bishop Benjamin F. Lee of the African Methodist Episcopal Church, Wilberforce, Ohio. On Thursday night, the Governor of the State of New York, Honorable L. P. Morton, who was scheduled to preside over the Welcome Program, was absent due to illness. Bishop B. W. Arnett of the African Methodist Episcopal Church, "who was for several years an active member of the Legislature of the State of Ohio, and (is) one of the most gifted and pleasing orators of the race," presided. Reverend H. K. Carroll of the New York *Independent,* Rev. E. Lyons of the Methodist Episcopal Church, and Bishop W. B. Derrick of the African Methodist Episcopal Church made welcome addresses.

A diversified program of far-reaching application by distinguished leaders of the A.M.E. Zion Church and other church and race leaders followed. On Woman's Day, Mrs. Victoria Earle Matthews, noted black social worker of New York, Miss Eliza Ann Gardner, and Mrs. Katie P. Hood presided over the sessions. Among the array of program participants were Bishop Isaac Lane of the C.M.E. Church; Rev. W. P. Thirkield, President of Gammon Theological Seminary; Bishop J. H. Cook of the Union African Methodist Episcopal Church: Rev. J. M. Henderson, M.D., A.M.E.; Rev. F. H. Grimké, Presbyterian Church, Washington, D.C.; Bishop G. F. Galloway, Methodist Episcopal Church, South; Rev. Walter Brooks, Washington,

7. Simmons, *Men of Mark,* pp. 756-57.

D.C., Baptist; Rev. J. M. Buckley, editor, New York *Christian Advocate;* Father Francis E. Clark, founder of the World-wide Christian Endeavor Society; Rev. C. H. Phillips (later bishop) of the C.M.E. Church; Rev. Alexander Crummell, Protestant Episcopal Church, Washington D.C.; Rev. William Hayes Ward, editor, *Independent,* Congregational Church, N.Y.; Bishop Henry McNeil Turner of the African Methodist Episcopal Church; Bishop E. G. Andrews of the Methodist Episcopal Church; T. Thomas Fortune; and a large number of bishops, ministers, general officers, and laymen of the A.M.E. Zion Church.

Presiding over the closing session, the Grand Jubilee Meeting at Carnegie Hall, was Mayor W. L. Strong of New York City. Toastmaster of the Jubilee Concert and Banquet at Carnegie Hall that same evening was Mr. C. H. Lansing, Jr. Guest speakers were such notables as the Honorable P. B. S. Pinchback, Washington, D.C.; Mrs. Frederick Douglass, Washington, D.C.; Counselor D. Macon Webster, Brooklyn, N.Y.; Mrs. S. J. S. Garnett, Brooklyn, N.Y., Mr. T. Thomas Fortune and Hon. John C. Dancy, other noted laymen; Mr. E. V. C. Eato and Dr. P. W. Ray of Brooklyn N.Y.; Rev. H. A. Monroe of Philadelphia; the Honorable C. H. J. Taylor of Washington, D.C. and Dr. Booker T. Washington, Tuskegee, Ala.

The outstanding black concert artists of that day provided the music that evening: Mme. Marie Selika, Mme. Sissieretta Jones (Black Patti), Mme. Flora Batson Bergen (Queen of Song), and Mr. Harry Thacker Burleigh. Also a chorus of 100 voices from the National Conservatory of Music, and Prof. J. A. Lively associated by Mme. V. Adele Montgomery. Music was also rendered during the Centennial by the Mother Zion Church Choirs, the Fleet Street (First Church), Brooklyn Choir; Abyssinian Baptist Church Choir; Bethel A.M.E. Church Choir of New York; Bridge Street A.M.E. Church Choir of Brooklyn; and the Famous Boys Choir of St. Philip's Protestant Episcopal Church of New York.

Booker T. Washington said in his address:

> One hundred years in the life of a state means much; one hundred years in the life of any church means more; one hundred years in the life of a religious body born in poverty, in the midnight of bondage, amidst the throes and groans of slavery, surrounded and penetrated by oppression and lack of opportunity, furnishes an occasion for supreme thanksgiving and congratulation. Then $80 in property, now $3,500,000; then 20 in church membership, now 500,000; then one minister of the Gospel, now 4,000 besides 9 bishops.

> But the record is not complete; blot out this property and these members and the church with such a birth that could within a century produce a Price, a Dancy, a Hood, or a Walters, and set the world an example in its ability for self-dependence and self-government would have with these achievements alone more than justified its existence.

> The crucial test for a race as for an individual is the ability to stand upon its own feet and make progress. In demonstrating to the world that the Negro has legislative and executive ability of a high order, your great Christian body has helped the entire race.

> But what of the present? Religion is supposed to be the first business of a church. In proportion to our numbers, intelligence and wealth, I do not speak irreverently when I say that we have more religion than anything else, and in many sections this seems to be the only article of possession. . . .

Besides, the ministry—the Church—must help the educators bring about such a change in the education of the black man that there will be a more vital and practical connection between the Negro's educated brain and his means of earning a living. . .

We must, as a race, enter business; for we are constantly being required to measure ourselves by the side of the business world, and by this test, we rise or fall. . . .

Reverend and honored sirs, grand as has been the past, inspiring as is the present, the future holds for your church still greater achievements, if it seizes, as I believe it will, upon the opportunities that are about it and lead our people into the promised land of business, educational and religious development. [8]

Ex-Governor P. B. S. Pinchback of Louisiana stated that:

First, in the greatest, most important and best of organizations, not only of this race, but of all races, the church, we have men whose incessant efforts to advance the interest of their people in the fields of their endeavor pre-eminently entitle them to this distinction. The A.M.E. Zion Church, which is completing its Centennial Jubilee on this pleasant occasion, is the product of our leaders in that denomination, and its marvelous growth attests their worth and efficiency. When we consider the peculiar condition of the colored people in this country and the extraordinary difficulties they have had to overcome in every undertaking during the past century, it seems almost incredible that the small number of inexperienced men, who in defense of their manhood, and to preserve their self-respect, withdrew from the M.E. Church a century ago, could have organized and planned so wisely as to perpetuate an institution destined to reach such splendid proportions in numbers and wealth, and whose influence in all that tends to elevate and improve its people, intellectually and morally, as the A.M.E. Zion Church presents to the world today with its 1,500 organizations, 1,600 churches, 497,845 members, 17 educational institutions, Book Concern, *Quarterly Review*, and $3,500,000 of property. Its founders laid a sure and enduring foundation and it has been transmitted to the care and keeping of safe, competent and trustworthy successors, the present bishops and general officers who control and manage its affairs so efficiently and successfully. [9]

The Centennial closed in a blaze of glory. The editor of the *Star of Zion*, Rev. J. W. Smith, stated:

Mayor W. L. Strong presided in a most felicitous manner and seemed to enter heartily into the spirit of the occasion. His genial air of interest and appreciative approval of the many good points made by the speakers indicated that his presence was not without an educational effect. This was clearly shown in his closing remarks, when he paid a graceful tribute to the characters of the exercises he had listened to and predicted greater possibilities for the race in the next century of progress. [10]

There had been the financial rally accompanying the celebration, which assisted in the debt of the Varick Memorial Publishing House at Charlotte, and connectional schools. The denomination salvaged enough to sponsor one project of note. The Centennial A.M.E. Zion Church of Mt. Vernon, N.Y., organized December 18, 1895 by Rev. William H. Eley, was placed on a firm foundation by the denomination as a memorial of the Centennial Celebration. [11] Annual conferences sponsored other mission projects within the bounds of their conferences.

8. *The Star of Zion,* November 19, 1896; Booker T. Washington, "Address on Industrial Education," *Centennial Souvenir Program,* p. 1.
9. *The Star of Zion,* November 5, 1896, p. 1.
10. *Ibid.*
11. The *Star of Zion,* December 10, 1896.

The celebration had been efectually led by Bishops J. W. Hood, T. H. Lomax, C. C. Pettey, C. R. Harris, I. C. Clinton, Alexander Walters, George W. Clinton, Jehu Holliday, and J. B. Small. The host pastor, Rev. Martin R. Franklin and local committees and the massive general committees of the denomination had labored commendably in unison. There had been the Centennial banners, the posters and buttons bearing the likeness of the founder, James Varick, the special literature, the Centennial poems and songs, the special Varick Christian Endeavor badges, city and state cooperation, and in the midst of the celebration, a visit to Major William McKinley's home in Canton, Ohio, by a delegation of 50 of the church. The delegation visited Major McKinley on October 9, and extended greetings on behalf of the centennial, and prayers and best wishes for his presidential candidacy. One month later, Mr. McKinley was elected President of the United States. Bishop George W. Clinton had read a statement from Senior Bishop Hood on behalf of the A.M.E. Zion Church, who remained at the celebration in New York, and then added:

We have come to join with the thousands of our fellow citizens from every part of our great country to give you assurance that we believe in the principles of which you are the foremost exponent, and that we are willing to support the platform upon which you so firmly and unfalteringly stand—a platform that stands not only for protection to American industries and institutions, but for protection to liberties and lives of American citizens, regardless of race, color or previous condition. We find that a man who was not afraid as Congressman to advocate such legislation as would promote the interests and secure the rights of all the people, a man who as governor of the great State of Ohio had the moral courage to protect the life of even a criminal, thereby guaranteeing to all the full protection of law, and a man who is not ashamed to stand upon the platform that condemns the most atrocious crime of the age, is a man that we as people and church can safely follow in this call from the patriots of our great country to come to the front to save its National honor.

Major McKinley responded as follows:

That you should have journeyed so great a distance to give me your assurances of goodwill and to express your devotion to the Republican cause and principles is an honor which I shall always value. I cannot refrain from congratulating you as members of the African Methodist Episcopal Zion Church upon the splendid progress you have made in the first century of your existence. I bid you God-speed in the noble work in which you are engaged, and I trust that future years will bring to all of you love, contentment, peace and prosperity.

Your race has made wonderful progress since it was made free. Progress in all that goes to make men better, all that goes to make better citizenship, better husbands, better fathers, better men. In one of the battles near Baton Rouge, the first black brigade was engaged. The colonel, a white man, called the color-bearer to his side, and in the presence of the regiment handed to him this glorious banner of the free, and said to him: "Color-bearer, take this flag. Fight for it, yes, die for it, but never surrender it into the hands of the enemy." And that color-bearer, whose face was as black as my hat, said to his colonel: "Colonel, I will bring this flag back to you in honor, or I will report to God the reason why."

I thank you for this call most heartily and sincerely, and I bid you bear back to your venerable bishop my personal good wishes and my desire for his long life and continued health. [12]

12. *The Star of Zion*, October 15, 1896.

The sermons, worship, discourses, distinguished personnel, concerts, banquet, youth programs, rallies and songs had greatly blessed the triumphal occasion. Thus the Bishops observed later that:

This was the crowning event of our first hundred years' growth, and the one great agency which set our Church more fully and properly before the world in its true light than any and all other previous efforts. The centennial set in motion and gave impetus to the strides of progress which began during the celebration and have gone forward with increasing momentum since that time.

It was the occasion which enabled us to discover and bring to light the varied, resourceful and brilliant intellects of the Church and race... In addition to the valuable literary products which were called into service upon that occasion from our own ranks, we were able to draw upon some of the strongest and most cultured men of many of our sister denominations and the professional men of the race throughout the country. [13]

The Centennial of the A.M.E. Zion Church

Oh God, our Father, come we now,
And In Thy presence humbly bow
In thanks that for one hundred years,
Thy church has stood through blood and tears.

We bless Thee for thy early care
To help Thy people do and dare,
When foes without blasphemed Thy name,
And friends within were clad with shame.

To recognize Thine image here,
Because 'twas cut in ebon clear,
We thank Thee for our color now,
We bless Thee that we did not bow.

To the behest of slavery,
Nor spurn the price of Liberty —
And thank Thee for the friends who stood,
In early days and sought our good.

William Howard Day [14]

The Sesqui—Centennial

Succeeding generations were definitely challenged, and continued in the spirit of their progenitors. In 50 years, the church and race had passed through many kinds of strife; the church had extended its borders in Africa and West Indies, and again into South America, while continuing its growth in the nation, especially during the migration North after World War I.

1946 was another "Year of Jubilee" for the A.M.E. Zion Church. There were five steps in launching the Sesqui-Centennial Observance, which began in 1844 at the General Conference held in Detroit, Michigan. First, in its Episcopal Address, the Board of Bishops strongly recommended an appropriate celebration of the

13. *Minutes,* Twenty-First Quadrennial Session, pp. 93-94.
14. B. F. Wheeler, *Cullings from Zion's Poets,* p. 122.

150th Anniversary. Following this, a resolution authorizing a celebration to be called *The Sesqui-Centennial* was passed by the General Conference, and a commission appointed to work out the details. The General Conference adopted a plan that included the objectives to win a half million souls to Christ and his church and raise $2,000,000 for church expansion. [15]

The second step was taken in a meeting held at Jacob Street A.M.E. Zion Church, Louisville, Kentucky, August 1944. "A staff of officers was elected as follows: Bishop W. J. Walls, general chairman, Bishop W. C. Brown, First Vice-chairman, Mrs. Creola B. Cowan, Second Vice-chairman; Bishop B. F. Gordon, Secretary, Reverend H. T. Henry, Assistant Secretary, Reverend H. B. Shaw, Treasurer. Tentative plans were adopted." [16]

The third step was the meeting held in the St. Paul Church, Cleveland, Ohio, October 17-18, 1944. "Further details of the plan of operation were considered. Functioning committees were appointed. The completion of the setup by the election of Reverend A. H. Hatwood as Business Manager, directions for the setting up of a temporary headquarters office in the Clinton Building, Washington, D.C., November 1, 1944, and an inspirational public meeting with enthusiastic addresses. New York was selected as the place of the celebration and September 8-22, 1946 as the time." [17]

The fourth step was taken at a meeting held in Loguen Temple Church, Knoxville, Tenn., January 8-11, 1945. "The opening of the meeting was highlighted by the Chairman's profound inspirational and elucidating address, excerpts of which are printed in the *Historical Review*. Reports were heard from the Business Manager and Treasurer, and further details worked out. A grand banquet in which nearly five hundred participated at $10.00 per plate was given and a local broadcast over Station WNOX, Knoxville, in which Dr. S. G. Spottswood and Dr. James W. Eichelberger delivered telling speeches." At this time the Sequi was considered connectionally launched and March 4, 1945 set as the day for the launching of the Sesqui in every church of the denomination.

"In the fifth step, the first Sunday in March (March 4, 1945), the Sesqui was proclaimed by pastors from their pulpits and an offering taken which was reported to the treasurer following the observance, and our Sesqui-Centennial celebration was fully launched." [18] The Mother Church had moved for the fourth time since 1796. It had built an imposing structure during 1925-26, led by Rev. J. W. Brown. Located in Central Harlem, 140-46 West 137th Street, it was again chosen the host church for the jubilee, Rev. Benjamin C. Robeson, pastor. Official headquarters for the Sesqui-Centennial had been established in the Mother Zion Church. Other task force members of the celebration were Bishops Paris A. Wallace, J. W. Martin, W. W. Matthews, and E. B. Watson, and the chairmen of the following committees: Evangelism, Bishop B. G. Shaw; Headquarters, Bishop C. C. Alleyne; Pilgrimages, Bishop Frank W. Alstork; Home Missions—Church Extension, Bishop W. W. Slade; Program, Dr. James W. Eichelberger; Publicity, Dr. S. G. Spottswood; Young Peoples' Work, Dr. J. Van Catledge, Jr.; Woman's Missionary Auxiliary, Mrs. M. Anna Hauser; Foreign Missions, Dr. H. T. Medford; Devising Contests, Mrs. Ola M. Martin; Pageants, Mrs. Minnie D. Hurley; Philanthropy, Dr. Victor J. Tulane; Operating Field Officer of History and Literature, Dr. E.

15. *Minutes,* Thirty-Second Quadrennial Session, pp. 230, 246-47; *Official Souvenir Journal,* Sesqui-centennial, 1946, p. 12.
16. *Ibid.*
17. *Ibid.*
18. *Ibid.*

President Harry S. Truman greets A.M.E. Zion Church Leaders during the Sesqui-Centennial of the Church, 1946, at the White House.

Mrs. Emma C. Williams Clement,
American Mother of 1946,
is greeted by Mayor O'Dwyer
of New York City.

Franklin Jackson; Miss A.M.E. Zion Church Contest, Miss Lillian I. Browder. Bishop E. L. Madison, who served as chairman of the ways and means committee, died two months before the opening of the Sesqui-Centennial program.

One of the striking events leading up to the Sesqui-Centennial observance was the naming of Mrs. Emma Clarissa Williams Clement as the American Mother of 1946, during Mother's Day in May, by The Golden Rule Foundation. Mrs. Clement, the widow of Bishop George C. Clement, and mother of seven children, principally religious leaders and educators, was the first black woman to be so honored. After presentation of the award to Mrs. Clement during impressive ceremonies at the Waldorf-Astoria Hotel, the A.M.E. Zion Church took occasion to pay high tribute and give suitable honors from the Sesqui-Centennial of the grand old church, to its member who was receiving national recognition of fine character and exemplary motherhood.

Mrs. Clement accompanied the special committee of the Sesqui-Centennial to the White House, led by the chairman, Bishop W. J. Walls, and received the best wishes of the denomination on behalf of the country from President Harry S. Truman on September 18, 1946. Truman also sent a message of felicitation to the celebration by Senator James M. Mead of New York. Mrs. Clement was tendered a banquet during the Sesqui-Centennial Celebration.

Once again, the A.M.E. Zion Church was thrown into the limelight before the American public and the church press throughout the Protestant world. In the Bishops' Proclamation, they had stated:

... James Varick, the first bishop, won a high place in the history of his country by his unselfish motives, sterling sagacity and sacrificing leadership. By the example of him and his associates who refused to remain in a condition where people of color worshipped from the gallery, were forced to wait for the Holy Communion until white members were served and where no persons of their race were ordained elders; this race self-enterprise and self-expression in America was begun. . . .

The picture of this noble brigade of freedom-seeking, race conscious Christians, planting the units of their organization with its humanitarian principles, courage and faith, into communities ranging over thousands of miles, north, south, east, and west and pushing into the fatherland, Africa, singing, praying, preaching, cheering and saving the souls of their fellowmen, most of whom were slaves, forms an epic in the history of the western hemisphere. . . .

We the chief pastors, do here and now proclaim this celebration for our church and to our sister churches of all races and denominations, and to all men who love the progress of righteousness, peace and goodwill of mankind. . . .

Ordered and proclaimed by the Board of Bishops: B. G. Shaw, W. J. Walls, J. W. Martin, C. C. Alleyne, W. W. Matthews, E. L. Madison, W. C. Brown, W. W. Slade, B. F. Gordon, F. W. Alstork, E. B. Watson, P. A. Wallace (Retired). [19]

A strong appeal came forth from the Proclamation of the Sesqui-Centennial Committee as follows:

Whereas the A.M.E. Zion Church was founded in New York City in 1796, and *Whereas* this was the first independent Negro organization in New York and in the United States, save one other (in Philadelphia), and *Whereas* this organization has spread throughout America to Africa, South America and the Southern Islands and is now approaching its 150th anniversary . . . and *Whereas* this great church has been a blessing to hundreds of thousands of race people in creative living, soul saving and practical race work such as; education, home building and general social uplift and political and business leadership, and *Whereas* it has led the race in establishing character, erecting churches and institutions, and making opportunity for the better life, and *Whereas* this is a day of reconstruction and looking forward toward the expansion of freedom under its new interpretation and Christian evolution, the issue from the bloodiest war of history, and *Whereas* the needs of our church are growing increasingly great for the manning of these institutions to meet the expanding demands and competition of our time upon the helpful influence of this most useful Negro Christian organization; Be it resolved that we celebrate the 150th Anniversary including a period of two years approaching thereto, in crusading emphasis of evangelism, religious education, missions and social service enterprise. . . .

Upon this glorious effort we invoke the blessings of Almighty God while we commend this cause and undertaking to the active and liberal support and enthusiasm of our members and friends everywhere.

We are your servants, The General Committee: W. J. Walls, Chairman, W. C. Brown, Vice-Chairman, Creola B. Cowan, Second Vice-chairman, B. F. Gordon, Secretary; A. H. Hatwood, General Manager; H. B. Shaw, Treasurer. [20]

The response of the proclamations and the committees' work had made an enrapturing impact upon the Protestant world. The two weeks program, inclusive of the Quadrennial Christian Education Convention, comprised ennobling men and women of church and state, national and international, and a glorious array of participants in a highly diversified commemoration.

19. *Ibid.*, p. 8.
20. *Ibid.*, p. 9.

Again, the most puissant leaders of church and state came and participated with the A.M.E. Zion Church in her jubilee. Bishop Walls and President W. J. Trent, Sr., of Livingstone College, introduced the historic celebration over "the seventy-one key stations of Columbia Broadcasting System" Radio. Commissioner Samuel J. Battle of New York City, member of Mother Zion Church, was Grand Marshal of the Parade, associated by Oscar W. Adams, Sr., of Birmingham (who passed away in May, 1946), Colonel Woodruff Chisholm, J. Finley Wilson, Councilman Benjamin Davis, A. Philip Randolph, Henrietta M. Davis, Cora E. Burke, Samuel E. Duncan, J. Otis Smith and John King who worked as the committee on parade. It was a grandoise event, depicting the history in colorful floats and massive motorcade from 110th Street up Seventh Avenue, turning at 135th Street, proceeding west to St. Nicholas, then north on St. Nicholas to 145th Street, east on 145th Street, back to Seventh Avenue, and south on Seventh Avenue to the 136th Street entrance of the Mother Zion Church.

Additional participants included Mayor William O'Dwyer of New York City; Senator James M. Mead, New York; J. Finley Wilson, Grand Exalted Ruler of IBPOE (Elks); Captain Grant Reynolds; Congressman Adam Clayton Powell, Jr., Mrs. Mary McLeod Bethune; Walter White and Roy Wilkins of the NAACP; Governor William H. Hastie; Judge Hubert T. Delany; Mrs. Jackson Davis of the General Board of Education; Dr. Frederick Douglass Patterson, President of Tuskegee Institute; Dr. Max Yergan of the National Negro Congress; and Mrs. Pauline Meyers of the African Academy of Arts. Dr. Ozumba Mbodiwi and Congressman Vito Macantino also addressed the assemblage. Leading the religious forces were Methodist Bishops G. Bromley Oxman of New York and Lewis O. Hartman of Boston; A. J. Allen of the A.M.E. Church, Luther C. Stewart of the C.M.E. Church, Dr. Tollie L. Caution of the Protestant Episcopal Church, Dr. Robert Bruce Moss of historic John Street Church, Rev. Alfred Saburo Akamatua; Dr. Eric M. North of the American Bible Society; Dr. Forrest L. Knapp of the World Sunday School Association; Dr. Henry Smith Leiper representing the proposed World Council of Churches; Dr. Roy G. Ross, International Society of Christian Education and Mr. Carroll M. Wright, International Society of Christian Endeavor; Dr. Franklin D. Cogswell, Missionary Education Movement; Dr. F. Ernest Johnson, Religious Education Association; Bishop Richard R. Wright, Jr., President of the National Fraternal Council of Negro Churches; Drs. Samuel McCrea Cavert and George E. Haynes of the Federal Council of Churches; Dr. Daniel A. Poling, President of the International Society of Christian Endeavor and Editor of the *Christian Endeavor Herald;* Mrs. Harper Sibley, President of the United Council of Church Women, a number of our own distinguished church personnel, and other civic, state, and national leaders.

Mr. James A. Mundy of Chicago directed the Sesqui-Centennial Choir of nearly 1,000 voices, composed of leading choirs of the A.M.E. Zion churches and the New York community. This occasion, after assembling in Mother Zion Church, First Church, Brooklyn, New York's Town Hall, Manhattan Center, climaxed at Madison Square Garden. This closing session placed emphasis on freedom, and was highlighted by some of the noted speakers previously mentioned, and the singing voice of Paul Robeson and the Sesqui-Centennial Choir. It had been announced that this particular program would be "dedicated to the ideals of defense, justice, relief, and brotherhood, and the net proceeds would be contributed to the rehabilitation of war-torn Africa and the National Defense Fund."

Other leading features were the historic pagaent led by Miss E. Marie Coleman of Pittsburgh, "Varick's Children in Freedom's Land;" the Miss A.M.E. Zion Contest, sponsored by Miss Lillian I. Browder and leading women of the church, the proceeds of which went toward erecting the shrine at Auburn, N.Y. to Harriet Tubman; the Oratorical Contest, chaired by Mrs. Ola Martin, which awarded a scholarship to Livingstone College to the winning youth contestant. The first prize was won by Miss Nian Laurel Beidelman of Bristol, Tenn., second prize by Miss Louise Toland of Schenectady, N.Y., and third prize by Miss Ellaleon Carson, Mobile, Ala. Reverend R. A. G. Foster was a leading force also on national radio, in keeping the public apprised of the black church which had made it through 150 years of struggle in America, Africa, the West Indies, and South America.

The bishops, each general officer, the Woman's Home and Foreign Missionary Society, thousands of ministers and laymen throughout the entire church, had all worked faithfully to help make the Sesqui-Centennial the largest possible success. Over $2,500,000 was raised in efforts to fortify our missions program and move our church forward in the freedom, social, and economic trials. We had the complete cooperation and goodwill of sister denominations, the press and communication annuals. The editor of the *Star of Zion,* Dr. Lovell, summarized the occasion as follows:

> Only those who had the good fortune to be there and see it for themselves can have an adequate conception of the impact and implications of so mammoth an affair. Naturally, the attendance was not as large as we desired, for we simply wished that every Zion Methodist in the world could have witnessed that impressive demonstration. But, of course, that could not be. However, the thousands who were there and those who came day after day from nearby communities and cities constituted a fine cross section of our great communion. [21]

Some of the very young who attended this celebration will remember, with glowing impressions, and will very likely be on hand at the Bicentennial in 1996; aware that we will have made greater progress toward union, to give witness to another jubilee of a church that fought the way of a race out of bondage, and contending at the time of the Sesqui-Centennial for first class citizenship in a country which they had helped to mold, under God..

21. *The Star of Zion,* September 5, 12, 19, 26, 1946. (Editorial, Sept. 26)

Part VIII
Paramount Functionalities

CHAPTER 34

THE BISHOPS

Wherever the standards of religion as set forth in the Articles of Faith and General Rules governing the A.M.E. Zion Church have been discarded or disregarded, the power of the Church working under such rules has become of little spiritual force in the community. Let it be heard all along the line—"Remove not the ancient landmarks, but rather lift up a higher moral and more potent spiritual standard among and for the people." [1]

In American Methodism, for no other purpose was the form of episcopal government adopted but for men of deep piety, godly judgment, and irrefutable ability to enforce and maintain regulations and standards regarded by the founders to be the sure foundation of the organization. Bishops are elected by the people through the General Conference. In the beginning it was left purely to the judgment of the ministry to make the best possible selection of leaders among men. The A.M.E. Zion Church was the first among Methodists to grant this and other privileges to laymen, paving the way for broad representation in high council in the spirit of the prophet who expressed the common rule for every human being; especially Judeo-Christian, when he uttered: "And what doth the Lord require of thee, but to do justly and love mercy, and walk humbly with thy God?"

By this it is absolutely unnecessary for an aspirant to this holy office to sound forth vainglorious trumpets; rather he must let the light of his good works shine throughout the church. The spirit of the aspirant and the spirit of the voter must be directed by the Holy Spirit, through prayer and dedication of both. In the eyesight of God the voter is held accountable just as the aspirant, for the moral standards and character of the church of Jesus Christ when electing the man for "holding fast the faithful word as he hath been taught, that he may be able by sound doctrine both to exhort and to convince gainsayers."

1. *Minutes,* Twenty-First Quadrennial Session, p. 103.

The A.M.E. Zion Church, from 1820 to 1972, has elected 76 bishops. For a man to have reached this milepost is a remarkable attestation of glorious works among people. Being of the human race, none can profess perfection. It is gratifying, however, to note that in most instances, these men have been the symbols of piety, dignity, and order and the image and exemplar of virtuous, pure, and upright conduct, which has continuously occasioned reverence and veneration for the church in inner and outer circles.

At this writing, only two among this number have been disciplined by the church for laxity in character and failure to live up to the standards by which they were elected. Both were disqualified, William H. Hillery by the General Conference of 1884 and W. W. Matthews by the 1948 General Conference.

This chapter will record the fathers chronologically, with background information on each, and condense in cases where they have been mentioned explicitly in the history. The largest number consecrated to the office of bishop at one time (seven) was at the General Conference of 1972. It would be illogical and quite improbable to attempt to give historic synopses of the twelve effective bishops who are in the process of making history, except where the deeds have become history.

The writer shall do his best to give faithful, accurate, and dispassionate delineations of these church fathers according to available records and personal knowledge.

1. *JAMES VARICK:* Born, Newburgh, N.Y. 1750; Ordained Deacon, May 18, 1806; Elder, June 22, 1821; Elected President (Organizational Meeting of the Connection) July 21, 1820; Consecrated Bishop, July 22, 1822.

The life's works of this trailblazer of Zion Methodism are found in Chapter 8. Among the creative progenitors of the greatest black organizations, he is listed in a large number of national and international biographies and encyclopedias. Some are:

Who's who in American History, A Dictionary of Universal Biography of All Ages and All People, Dictionary of American Biography, Volume 10, Appleton's Encyclopedia of American Biography, Vol. VI, Encyclopedia International, 1963-64 Negro Makers of History (Carter G. Woodson and Charles Wesley), The Chronological History of the Negro in America, Ebony Pictorial History of Black America, Volume I. His sacred ashes rest in the famous crypt at Mother Zion Church (Harlem), New York City.

2. *CHRISTOPHER RUSH:* Born, Cravens County, near New Bern, N.C., 1777; Ordained Deacon and Elder, July 23, 1822; Consecrated Bishop, May 18, 1828; Died, July 16, 1873.

He was spared to see the spreading of Zion's borders over a large portion of the United States—east, west, north and south—which he served as its second bishop for the term of twenty-four years, which office he filled with great dignity. His life was marked with filial devotion, to the prosperity of the church and an answering confidence in God, and the spread of the Gospel and the elevation of his race, morally and intellectually; and until the hour of his death, he was an educator and upholder of the principles of Christianity. [2]

Father Rush was celibate. He is buried beneath an imposing monument at Mother Zion Church's Cypress Hill Cemetery, Brooklyn, N.Y.

2. *Minutes,* Twenty-Seventh Session, New England Annual Conference, p. 33.

3. *WILLIAM MILLER:* Born, August 23, 1775 in Queen Ann County, Md.; Ordained Deacon, April 27, 1808; Elder (A.M.E. Church, 1823); Consecrated Bishop, May 25, 1840; Died, December 6, 1845

Wm. Miller was an example to the Christian community, in Christian ardor and zeal; as a preacher he was simple, but clear and pathetic, commanding great precision, always evincing the highest Christian affection. His beneficent hand was always ready to be extended; his treatment of the subordinate ministers was highly commendable, impartial and unprescribed; council was always in wait for the humble solicitant among the ministry—. [3]

Bishop Miller was celibate. He died in Philadelphia and was buried in that city after funeral services at Wesley Church.

4. *GEORGE GALBRAITH:* Born, March 4, 1799 in Lancaster County, Pa.; Ordained Deacon and elder, June 16, 1830; Consecrated Bishop, May 30, 1848; Died, 1853.

His parents were slaves owned by Dr. Galbraith. George was raised in the family of Moses Williams of Hanover Township, Pa., who sent him to school with his own children. He learned the carpenter's trade and later cabinetmaking in Middletown, Pa., where he embraced religion and joined the Winebrenarians in 1826. He later joined the A.M.E. Zion Church founded by Rev. J. D. Richardson in Middletown. He joined the Philadelphia Annual Conference in June 1830, and was ordained that year by Bishop Rush and appointed to the Harrisburg Circuit.

As a man, Bishop Galbraith possessed a vigorous, active, firm and benevolent mind. He thought with energy and quickness, and he dreaded not the labor of thinking. In promptitude of conception and readiness of utterance few were his equals . . . . The firmness of his mind was a leading trait; a prominent feature of his whole character. It enabled him in all vicissitudes and under the severest trials of life—and he was familiar with them—to maintain an equanimity of conduct which seemed to flow from the fortitude of the philosopher mingled with the patience and resignation of the Christian. His kindness and benevolence was great and extensive; they were the ornament of his other virtues. As a husband, a father, a brother, a friend, he was singularly indulgent, tender and affectionate; but his benevolence was not confined to these limits; it led him to be in a peculiar manner the friend of the oppressed; he espoused their cause and advanced their interests with the warmest zeal . . . . It was this part of his character which led him to connect himself with certain humane institutions, and which rendered him one of their most active, attentive and valuable members.

His desire and study was to do all possible good to mankind in general, yet, without breaking in upon this plan, some were the objects of his peculiar attention. This may be justly said of his younger brethren who served with him in the itinerancy, who always experienced in him the kindness of a father. His seniority and his superior influence gave him frequent opportunities of doing them good offices which he never failed to improve with as much pleasure to himself as they produced to them. His own improvement as a scholar and as a clergyman abundantly qualified him for the direction of his younger brethren, and none ever followed it without finding it to his advantage to do so. [4]

Bishop Galbraith died in Philadelphia, and last rites were held at Wesley Church.

3. Moore, *History*, p. 354.
4. *Ibid.*, pp. 356-361, passim.

5. *WILLIAM HAYWOOD BISHOP:* Born in Maryland in 1793; Ordained Deacon, May 21, 1827; Elder, May 18, 1828; Consecrated Bishop, July 4, 1852; Died, June, 1873.

Bishop joined the New York Conference, May 18, 1826 and was ordained deacon and elder by Bishop Varick before his death. He was a man of deep Christian faith and unusual tenacity. He passed through the crisis of the denominational split bearing the major burden after the death of Bishop Galbraith in 1853. With stern loyalty he furnished a strong hand in restoring the harmony of the dissenting groups in 1860. He served 16 faithful years as an active bishop until 1868, presiding over every northern conference of that day. "He filled this office with great honor, and he labored ardently for the general diffusion and spread of the connection, which he lived to see and fill as a ripe shock of corn for the harvest." [5]

6. *GEORGE ALFRED SPYWOOD:* Born at Mashpee, Mass., in 1802; Ordained Deacon, May 24, 1843; Elder, May 23, 1844; Consecrated Bishop, July 9, 1853; [6] Died, January 15, 1875.

Bishop Spywood was a man of extraordinary force of character; he had a happy blending of the Indian and the African; he had the veneration of the African united with the reckless daring of the Indian, which made him every inch a man. He was rigidly honest and feared none but the Maker. He was retired from the bishopric in 1856 because there were more bishops than could be used to advantage. For the remainder of his life he was employed as agent of the New England Mission Board, in which position he had very great success—far beyond that of anyone who has succeeded him. [7]

His life was marked with devotion to the prosperity of Zion and the spread of the gospel of the kingdom of his Father and God. As an elevator of his people, he was always on the alert for opportunities to aid them, either morally or financially, and so as an upholder of the principles of Christianity he was unflinching in opinions, and grand as a counselor. Like John, the beloved disciple of Christ, declining in age, resting upon his staff he could say, "be faithful, be truthful, and the everlasting God, the mighty Captain of your salvation, will lead you on to victory."

As an Agent he was energetic, traveling night and day for the success of Zion and her cause. His success was great as an agent, having collected more money than any other missionary for the cause .... A good man, a true friend, a bright and cheerful Christian, a heroic standard-bearer, a veteran of the cross. [8]

5. *Minutes*, Twenty-Seventh Session, New England Annual Conference, p. 33
6. At the commencement of the turbulent split in the A.M.E. Zion Church, the East faction called a General Conference in July 1853 and elected Spywood and Tappan bishops, and later Simmons and Scott, whom we acknowledge in the apostolic succession in history. See Hood, *One Hundred Years*, p. 76.
7. *One Hundred Years*, p. 68.
8. *Minutes*, Twenty-Eighth Session, New England Annual Conference, p. 30.

BISHOP WILLIAM MILLER

BISHOP GEORGE GALBRAITH

BISHOP WILLIAM HAYWOOD BISHOP

BISHOP GEORGE ALFRED SPYWOOD

7. *JOHN TAPPAN:* Born in North Carolina, June 1799; Ordained Deacon, May 20, 1834; Elder, May 15, 1835; Consecrated Bishop, July 9, 1853; Died, 1870.

He was born of slave parents and came to New York and joined the Conference in May 1833. He spent most of his ministry in this conference. "He was a very plain but spirited and forcible preacher. [9]

At the General Conference in 1856 when Spywood and Tappan failed to be re-elected, the following resolution passed:

Whereas, justice and truth is our motto, it is due then to every one who labors with us, and with pure motives for the advancement of the Redeemer's kingdom. We are taught in the Scriptures that it is our duty to do justly and render to everyone his due; then we should remember with regard the Reverends G. A. Spywood and John Tappan, who have labored hard for the good of the connection, amid the series of difficulties that have occurred the last three years; they were firm in their minds and true to their trust. During this long interval they have suffered much, with respect to both pecuniary embarrassments and strong opposition. There have been expressions made to other brethren who labored for the benefit and good of the Connection; it is considered essential, also that some expression should go forth from this conference to these brethren, as a tribute of the respect and regard we have for them;

Resolved, that we are under great obligation to Revs. George A. Spywood and John Tappan for their indefatigable labors and faithful service rendered the last three years, as the executive officers of the Connection, amid so many trying circumstances, that they are worthy of our highest esteem and regard, for we believe they did their best for the good of the Connection.

Resolved, that we tender to them a hearty vote of thanks for their ardent labors in the connection during their administration. We shall ever pray for their prosperity, that the blessing of God be upon them and that they be rewarded by the Higher Hand. [10]

8. *JAMES SIMMONS:* Born in Accomac County, Md., December 3, 1792; Ordained Deacon and Elder, May 22, 1833; Consecrated Bishop, June 30, 1856; Died, February, 1874.

He joined the New York Conference in May, 1832. "He was a man irreproachable in his character, of stern demands in his requirements in Christian duty, and very rigid in exacting the requirements of church government. He was plain in his style, and simple in his preaching; gentlemanly in his bearing and very self-reliant. He served his connection faithfully . . . ." [11]

Simmons served only one quadrennium as Bishop, but went on to give very effective service in the New York and New England Conferences. "He was a man of religious integrity, and a devoted Christian by all who knew him and labored many years with great acceptability which endeared him in the hearts of the members of the New England Conference," which he presided over and of which he was a member when he died. [12]

9. Moore, *History,* p.367.
10. *Ibid.,* pp. 219-220.
11. *Ibid.,* p. 367.
12. *Minutes,* Twenty-Seventh Session, New England Annual Conference, p. 34.

BISHOP
JAMES
SIMMONS

BISHOP
JOHN
TAPPAN

BISHOP SOLOMON
TIMOTHY SCOTT

BISHOP PETER ROSS

9. *SOLOMON TIMOTHY SCOTT:* Born at Smyrna, Del., August 20, 1790; Ordained Deacon, June 20, 1834; Elder, June 18, 1835; Consecrated Bishop, June 30, 1856; Died, January 4, 1862.

He joined the Philadelphia Annual Conference in June 1833. Bishop Scott "was distinguished for preaching from metaphors. The announcement that he would preach his *fish* sermon always drew a crowd." This popular sermon was printed in pamphlet form; and "though it was read by many, yet people never seemed to tire of hearing it preached . . . . He had also an anti-slavery sermon, intended to encourage his people to help fugitives who were making their escape from bondage. He was regarded as a great preacher, had a very gentle and humble disposition, and seemed hardly at ease in the bishopric. The period of his bishopric was the most stormy that the church has known; and considering his peculair temperament it is not strange that he felt deeply the responsibility of his position. He was retired in 1860." [13]

10. *JOSEPH JACKSON CLINTON:* Born in Philadelphia, October 3, 1823; Ordained Deacon, May 6, 1845; Elder, June 30, 1846; Consecrated Bishop, June 30, 1856; [14] Died, May 24, 1881.

The youngest bishop elected in the history of the church at age 32 years and 9 months, was also the most progressive in behalf of the connection. It would be hard to visualize today how a man could select a helpmate possessed with untrammelled love for the church, produce ten children (six of whom survived

13. Hood, *One Hundred Years,* p. 69
14. Clinton was elected during the split by the faction of the west in 1856 with Bishop W. H. Bishop, and the two were re-elected in 1860 with Peter Ross when the church united.

them), of culture and ability, one Rev. Joseph N. Clinton, a presiding elder in Florida; add over 100,000 Sunday School Scholars to the church, organize 13 annual conferences; take in over 700 itinerant preachers; and become the grand prince of Zion. "As an executive officer he had no superior. For 25 years he filled the office with complete success and satisfaction to the church."

He was a champion of freedom and an unconquerable churchman. He died at his home in Atlantic City, N.J. after a protracted illness. His widow, Mrs. Letitia Sisco Clinton, who added so much to Zion, and passed away September 23, 1893, sleeps by his side at Mt. Olive Cemetery in Philadelphia. [15] Bishop Clinton goes down as the incomparable expansionist in the history of the church.

11. *PETER ROSS:* Born in New York City, 1809, Ordained Deacon, May 22, 1840; Ordained Elder, 1842; Consecrated Bishop, June 12, 1860; Died, July 25, 1890.

He joined the New York Conference in May 1834, and was sent as a missionary to Providence, R.I. Prior to this he was converted in Mother Zion Church, New York,

> and he was wont to say he was but a lad. Here in the great metropolis with mental and physical forces unimpaired, he commenced that career that was so long and useful and ended so gloriously. He commenced to exhort soon after his conversion. In 1828 we see him with gospel trumpet in his hand . . . .He was ordained to the Diaconate by Bishop William Miller in New York City in 1840, and an Elder by Bishop C. Rush in Middletown, in 1842. In 1860 his brethren elevated him to the bishopric. He took no small part in the early establishment and making our Zion the great connection it is. He was sent as a Missionary to Nova Scotia and New England when it was a mission field. For more than a half century he stood in the front rank with Zion's trumpeters. He was a man of unsullied character, rich in experience, matured in knowledge, having served his God and church sixty-two years and lived to the ripe old age of 81. [16]

Ross was a man of great force, of character pure and upright. He was a forcible and logical preacher. He served only one quadrennium as bishop, assigned annually to the First, Second and Third Districts by the rotation system with Bishops W. H. Bishop and J. J. Clinton. He died at Providence, R.I.

12. *JOHN DELAWARE BROOKS:* Born in Baltimore, Md., October 7, 1803; Ordained Deacon, June 11, 1843; Elder, May 4, 1845; Consecrated Bishop, May 30, 1864; Died, 1874.

Brooks was one of the most serious men we ever made a bishop. He joined the Philadelphia Conference in 1842. He was one of our very well preapred men, and his character was above reproach. He was a sound preacher of the gospel and unalterable advocate of Methodist rules and standard. Some of his practices were extremely rigid and he stressed the highest point of discipline and execution of laws. He believed more in justice than he did in toleration or patient training. This caused misunderstanding in his pastorates, loss of some members, and in one case, a church split at Zion Wesley Church at which time St. Paul A.M.E. Church was established in Washington, D.C.

15. Biographical Sketch of Mrs. Letitia Clinton, *A.M.E. Zion Quarterly Review,* January 1894, pp. 193-197.
16. *Minutes,* Forty-Sixth Session, New England Annual Conference, 1891, p. 44.

His good, however, was that of a standard-maker, although he did not have the evangelistic patience, nor was he as successful in helping as he was in disciplining. Taking him in toto, he was brave, steady, and contributed to the highest realities of the church in a generation which doubtless needed his more inflexible contribution in a developing young church.

He served in the active episcopacy until 1872 and was retired and made chairman of the Book Concern. At the Philadelphia and Baltimore Annual Conference in 1874 he associated Bishop John J. Moore, at Carlisle, Pa., Just as the Conference was about to adjourn on Thursday morning, May 14, "Bishop Brooks arose and said that he heartily thanked the Lord for undeserved and unexpected mercies bestowed upon him in his severe affliction, especially since our last annual conference. He stated that he felt grateful to the members of the Conference for their kind treatment to him. He thought that in view of his frail condition of health he would never meet them in another Conference. He invoked the blessings of God upon the assembly and hoped they would prepare to meet him in heaven. He announced the 1122 hymn, commencing, 'Christian brethren, ere we part,' which was sung by the Conference."[17] Before the year had gone, he passed away in his home at York, Pa.

13. *JERMAIN WESLEY LOGUEN ("Jarm"):* Born in Davidson County, Tenn., in 1813; Ordained Deacon, May 21, 1843; Elder, May 23, 1844; Consecrated Bishop, May 30, 1864 (Did not serve this quadrennium); Consecrated Bishop, May 29, 1868; Died, September 30, 1872.

Loguen was born about 16 miles from Nashville. His mother was a slave. She had been born free in Ohio, but when she was seven she was kidnapped and sold to a Tennessean who ran a whisky distillery with slave labor. His father, of the white master class, threw aside the slave girl a few years after Jermain's birth. When hard times came, the father, David Logue, sold his son and the boy's mother to an owner who treated them brutally. As a child he saw his mother whipped by the white master almost mercilessly. Young Jermain determined to be free and to do all within his power to later free his mother. Thus he and two other slaves crossed the Ohio River and followed the North Star to Canada.

After remaining in Canada for a while as lumberjack and farmer, Loguen recrossed the border and settled in Central New York. In his early twenties he studied at the Oneida Institute at Utica for three year. Later, he opened the first school for Negro children in Utica, N.Y. In 1840 he married Caroline Storum. "This connection was a fortunate event in the life of Mr. Loguen. Mrs. Loguen was about twenty years of age when married—of pleasing person and address, amiable, and of the best of breeding which undervalues the shining and superficial, and highly esteems the intellectual and substantial, the useful and good—qualities which fitted her to instruct her household, and even her husband, in some things—and to receive comfort and bless the hundreds of fugitives from slavery who found an asylum at her house,—which, therefore acquired the eminently appropriate appellation of the Underground Railroad Depot at Syracuse."

During his lifetime it is estimated that he aided over 1,500 slaves to escape to freedom.

Loguen started his ministry in 1841. He joined the New York Conference in May 1842, and was ordained by Bishop Christopher Rush. He founded and

17. *Minutes,* Forty-Sixth Session, Philadelphia and Baltimore Annual Conference, p. 25.

stablized nearly a half dozen churches in the central part of New York. While his point of concentration was at Syracuse, he labored in the preaching and teaching ministry at Bath,; Courtland, Troy, Ithaca, Utica, Schoharie, and Canajoharie, N.Y. Perhaps his hardest struggle was building our first church at Syracuse. Some of the largest white churches in the Syracuse area would not utter a word against the evil of slavery. Loguen, however, brought about a change. He even converted to the abolition movement the leading pastor of the town. "These newly-won converts among the whites joined with the Negroes in making Syracuse one of the principal 'depots' of the Underground Railroad."

The Fugitive Slave Law of 1850 was a threat to the safety of all runaway slaves. Some of them fled to Canada, while others remained to fight it out with slave catchers. One of the most dramatic cases occurred when he and other abolitionists showed courage in the rescue of the runaway slave Jerry. Crowbars and a battering-ram were used to break into the Syracuse courthouse and free the fugitive under the guns of the marshals, and the episode became a national sensation.

> Having become a reader, after two years hard labor for good wages, and after acquiring the character of an able, faithful, and judicious farmer, in good repute as a man and citizen, he assumed the name he now bears. His paternal name was Logue—but he disliked that name, and added to it the letter *n*, to suit his taste. The name Jarm, which his master gave him, was an abbreviation of Jarmain. His Methodist friends insisted he should adopt the name of Wesley for his middle name, which he did—and from this time forward was known only by the name of Jarmain Wesley Loguen. [18]

His and Douglass' was one of the closest relationships in the work of the Underground Railroad, and they shared a passionate desire for freedom of their people from their suffering in slavery. Loguen's daughter, Amelia, thus married Douglass' son, Lewis, which family relationship helped to strengthen and quicken the abolition work among them.

Bishop Loguen labored four years and four months actively in the episcopacy, serving Kentucky, Tennessee, Western New York, Allegheny, and Philadelphia and Baltimore Conferences. In 1872, he was appointed to the mission work on the Pacific Coast. In four months' time he had died; thus it is believed that he never reached that field of labor. In his native state, he established the renowned Loguen Temple, the first church of the A.M.E. Zion Church in Tennessee, at Knoxville. Bishop Loguen died at Saratoga Springs, N.Y. [19]

14. *SAMSON DUNBAR TALBOT:* Born in West Bridgewater, Mass., in 1819; Ordained Deacon, May 21, 1843; Elder, May 23, 1844; Consecrated Bishop, May 30, 1864; Died 1878.

> Bishop Talbot, like Loguen, joined the New York Conference in May 1842. He was regarded as one of the best men as well as one of the best preachers of his day. During his pastorate he had charge of the most important churches in the connection, including New York and Boston; and the man who was a success in either of those churches was considered a strong man. Bishop Talbot was always a success as a pastor, and was equally so as a bishop. He had charge of the First District, including the New York, New England and

---

18. Loguen, *The Rev. J. W. Loguen.* . . , p. 355.
19. *Ibid.,* p. 341; *Negro History Bulletin,* October 1941, p. 40; Hood, *One Hundred Years,* pp. 180-181; *Dictionary of American Biography,* Vol. II, pp. 368-369.

BISHOP JOHN DELAWARE BROOKS

BISHOP SAMSON DUNBAR TALBOT

Genesee Conferences, for two years, and then went to the Fourth District, including the Georgia, Alabama, and Louisiana Conferences. After fourteen years' service he died at his home in Georgia. He will long be remembered in that section as one of the pioneer bishops. Respected by all classes, and considering that he lived in the hottest region during the hottest period of the Reconstruction, and he a Northern man; this speaks volumes for his sagacity and Christian bearing. [20]

At his death his colleagues stated:

We have been called to witness the taking down of the tabernacle; we have seen human nature in ruins; we have visited the house appointed for all living; we have stood at the gate of eternity; we have seen the lifeless form deposited in its last resting place; we have heard the earth rattle upon the coffin; we have dropped the silent, parting tear upon the grave of our fallen colleague, BISHOP SAMSON D. TALBOT IS NO MORE!

We all remember the whisper which cast a cloud over his reputation and brought sadness to our hearts, how anxiously we awaited his anticipated coming at the last General Conference, and how, he failing to reach the General Conference, the case was not investigated, but he was left without work. Thank God, the cloud was lifted from his reputation. Candor compels us to say that we think his marriage was not good taste for a Bishop, and we hope no other Bishop will marry a divorced woman under any circumstance. Yet our investigation satisfies us that the woman he married was divorced on Scriptural grounds. One of our members has seen the document, and so reports to us.

It gives us joy, thus to be able to speak in his defense, and to clear his memory from the cloud which hung over it. We recommend that a suitable tribute be paid to his memory. [21]

20. Hood, *One Hundred Years,* pp. 184-185
21. *Minutes,* Sixteenth Quadrennial Session, pp. 48-49

15. *JOHN JAMISON MOORE (D.D.):* Born in Berkeley County, W.V., about 1804 of slave parents. Ordained Deacon, June 10, 1842; Elder, June 12, 1843; Consecrated Bishop, May 27, 1868; Died, December 9, 1893.

His mother was born free, but at the age of fifteen years was kidnapped in Maryland and sold into slavery in West Virginia, where she married the Bishop's father.

Her maiden name was Riedoubt and her husband's name was Hodge, but a change of owners caused him to adopt the surname of Moore. When the Bishop was six years old, his parents, by the advice and assistance of friendly Quakers, attempted a flight from slavery with their six children, of whom the Bishop was the youngest. They were recaptured, however, and the oldest four children sold South. A second attempt to gain their liberty was successful, and the Bishop's parents with their remaining two children after many hardships and sufferings reached Bedford County, Pa. [22]

He was taught to read and write, and acquired a knowledge of farming, for which he showed a fondness long after his strength to perform it, forsook him. The man to whom he was bound robbed him of two years or more, and would have continued the robbery, but for another friendly Quaker who informed him that his time was out, advised him to leave and agreed to stand by him if the man claimed longer time. The fact that the man made no effort to get him back, he regarded as evidence that the information was correct.

The Bishop embraced religon while in Harrisburg, Pa., in 1833, and was soon after impressed with his call to the ministry, and was licensed to preach in the same city in 1834. He felt his lack of the education necessary for the ministerial work, with the importance of which he was deeply impressed. During his minorhood, he had only received instruction for a few weeks each year, from the time he was bound to service.

In 1836 he employed private tutors, and took lessons in the English branches and also in Latin, Greek and Hebrew, thus acquiring knowledge in all of these languages, enabling him to pursue his calling so well that he soon became one of the ablest and most noted of black preachers of his day. He was soon designated the "silver tongued" orator. He wrote a most legible hand up to the time of his death. [23]

In 1839, he became connected with a body of itinerant ministers composing the Philadelphia Annual Conference of the A.M.E. Zion Church." He joined the conference in 1841, and continued a member until 1868, when he was elevated to the bishopric. He served as assistant secretary of the conference in 1843, and was elected secretary in 1844. "He left Baltimore in 1852 for California, where he established several churches." [24]

Moore was nearly 90 years of age when he passed. These "years bore lightly upon him, so that he felt the vigor of youth even though he had long passed his allotted fourscore of years, which came by reason of his marvelous strength and vitality. He was universally acknowledged to be one of the greatest preachers of his time . . . . His knowledge of the Scriptures was remarkable; and to the time of his death he could quote passages, without notes or manuscript, with an ease and facility that were astonishing . . . .

Bishop Moore loved his men and took great interest in young men of promise . . . .He delighted to be in the company of young men and encourage them and laugh with them, and urge them to make themselves men in the highest

22. Moore, *History*, pp.367-368.
23. *A.M.E. Zion Quarterly Review*, April 1894, p. 321; Hood, *One Hundred Years*, pp. 174-175.
24. Moore, *History*, pp. 126, 370.

sense of that term."

This remarkable man died on the train, after closing the Western North Carolina Conference, at Greensboro on his way home to Salisbury; "having preached to within a few days of his death in the full triumph of the Christian faith." [25] He was laid to final rest at Salisbury, after services at Zion Chapel (Soldiers Memorial) Church.

16. *SINGLETON THOMAS WEBSTER JONES, (D.D.):* Born in Wrightsville, York County, Pa., March 8, 1825; Ordained Deacon, August 12, 1850; Elder, August 15, 1851; Consecrated Bishop, May 31, 1868; [26] Died, April 18, 1891.

He was a charter member of the Allegheny Conference when it organized the second Saturday in August, and joined the conference, August 23, 1849, after he had been licensed to preach by Bishop Galbraith in September, 1846. "When he entered the ministry, he had scarcely the rudiments of an English education, but he was sensible of the importance and responsibilities of his calling, and he went to work to prepare himself . . . . He so acquainted himself with the English language that he could select the most choice and fitting words to express his ideas, and could form most beautiful and expressive sentences." [27] Bishop Jones was one of the strong men; distinguished as an energetic worker, a pulpit orator, an eloquent and impressive preacher. He was a great disciplinarian, a most rigid constitutionalist; clear in his preaching, in his dealing with antagonisms; his irony was keen and withering. [28] As a presiding officer he was able, as a counselor he was reliable, as a pulpit orator he was eloquent and finished, as a writer he was broad and lucid. A Christian for 49 years, an elder 17, a bishop 23 years. [29]

He exemplified that modest and unostentatious disposition all through life. It was mainly through his efforts that the Kentucky Conference stood out as one of the strongest bodies of the connection or black race. He was ever on the alert in planning for the extension and upbuilding of his connection. He was a friend and devoted advocate of all her institutions. [30]

He was one of the founders and religious editor of *Zion's Standard and Weekly Review,* which was published in New York City early in the sixties. His associates on that paper were such men as the gallant and tried man of God, Elder William H. Decker, and the polished, scholarly, and highly cultured gentleman, Rev. William H. Day.

As a preacher he was justly ranked as the foremost "black preacher" of America. and the equal of any preacher of his day . . . . The pulpit was his forte and there he was content. He could have been a success and achieved renown as a lecturer. As an author, his *Handbook of the Discipline* is his most substantial work. He composed several poems . . . . Besides the Handbook and the poems . . . the Bishop has several published addresses and papers which were compiled and published by Reverend J. W. Smith.

Bishop Jones was a man of many accomplishments. Besides wielding a facile pen, being an able preacher, debater and orator and very successful pastor, he was a sweet singer, and could play upon the instrument with such ease, grace and excellence as would do honor to almost any organist. He

25. *A.M.E. Zion Quarterly Review,* January, 1894, pp. 187-89.
26. Moore, *History,* p. 267.
27. Hood, *One Hundred Years,* p. 178.
28. Moore, *History,* pp. 373-374.
29. *Minutes,* Forty-Sixth Session, New England Annual Conference, p. 45.
30. *A.M.E. Zion Quarterly Review,* October, 1891, pp. 28-29.

could speak French, converse with the German in his native tongue, and use Latin to advantage. As a presiding officer and expounder of the law he stood first among equals. At sixty-six years of age his sun went down and left its reflecting light to fall upon the rising stars, and to illuminate every section in the church for which he lived to honor and to extend, and from which he went out all covered with glory. [31] Funeral services were held at John Wesley Church and he was buried in Harmony Cemetery, Washington, D.C.

17. *JAMES WALKER HOOD (M.A., D.D., LL.D):* Born in Kennett Township, Chester County, Pa., May 30, 1831; Ordained Deacon, September 2, 1860; Elder, June 15, 1862; Consecrated Bishop, July 3, 1872; Died, October 30, 1918.

He was principally self-educated. "His mother taught him grammar, and interested him in the act of public speaking. He delivered his first Abolitionist speech at the age of fifteen years. In this speech he predicted the emancipation of the slaves, and this in the face of Judge Taney's unjust decision (Dred Scott), the Fugitive Slave Law and the Missouri Compromise."

Hood was distinguished for his coolness and deliberation in excitment. He was a great projector of measures in council; a conciliator, a deep reasoner, and a self-sacrificer for the cause to which he was devoted . . . . His Christian integrity stood unimpeached. He was a tireless worker, and of an invulnerable spirit, very discerning, genial and affable in his personal bearing, and kind to friend and foe, aged and young. [32]

Bishop Hood was first married October 4, 1852, to Miss Hannah L. Ralph of Lancaster, Pa., who died April 15, 1855; he then married Miss Sophia J. Nugent of Washington, D.C. She died September 13, 1875. He afterwards married Katie P. McCoy, June 6, 1877.

"After forty-six years of the highest quality of service in the office of bishop, he yielded up the ghost . . . . His very busy life, his untold sacrifices for his church, rich contribution to the uplift of his race, and his long tenure of service, entitled him to the foremost place among his peers in the advancement of the church of his choice." [33] Hood served 44 active years, being retired by the General Conference of 1916. He died in his home town of Fayetteville, N.C., and was buried in that city after funeral at Evans Chapel.

18. *JOSEPH PASCAL THOMPSON (D.D.):* Born at Winchester, Va., December 20, 1818; Ordained Deacon, May 17, 1846; Elder, May 2, 1847, Consecrated Bishop, July 4, 1876; Died, December 21, 1894.

Thompson was born in slavery, ran away from his master while yet a youth, and found a home with a kind-hearted man in Pennsylvania. He acquired a good common school education in early life. At the age of 15 he experienced religion, and at the age of 20 he was licensed to preach. He joined the New York Conference in May 1844. He held the pastoral charge of all the prominent churches in the New York Conference, and was a missionary to Nova Scotia. [34]

---

31. *Ibid.,* pp. 23-31
32. Moore, *History,* p. 375; Souvenir Programme, *HOOD THANK OFFERING,* 1911, p. 7.
33. *Minutes,* Twenty-Sixth Quadrennial Session, p. 55.
34. History has sometimes confused Bishop Thompson with Rev. Joseph P. Thompson, who also pastored successfully in New York state and was a staunch freedom fighter. He died in the pastorate at Elmira, N.Y., November 14, 1895.

In connection with his ministry, he had studied and practiced medicine in Newburgh, N.Y., where he became one of its most prominent citizens. He had experience in aiding fugitives in the Underground Railroad, and married Catherine Gilchrist, the daughter of a conductor. He read theology under the direction of Rev. Dr. Mills of Auburn Theological Seminary, Auburn, N.Y. [35]

In his personal character he [was] self-reliant, independent, generally guided by his own judgment, scrutinizing and dogmatic with contestants, generous in helping a good cause, especially in the interest of his connection; eccentric in his demeanor, prompt and reliable in his engagements; he [was] a lover of Christian principles, and stood respected and honored by his Connection as one of its worthy sons.[36]

By precept and example he has taught and encouraged his people, and had been to them a benefactor and faithful friend . . . . Officials at Washington have frequently conferred with him on public measures, especially on affairs in the South. In 1881 he was invited to England and by special request read a paper before the Ecumenical Conference of Methodist churches convened in London from all parts of the world. [37]

Bishop Thompson was bold in utterance, magnificent in physique and devoted to every interest of his race, his church, his country and his God. [38]

He was a historian, preacher, organizer, one who loved the church of his choice. He was in the church in her several troubles, and was ever ready to give his counsel and financial support. [39]

He passed away at Newburgh, N.Y., and was buried in that city.

19. *WILLIAM HENRY HILLERY (D.D.):* Born in Virginia, May 1839; Ordained Deacon November 10, 1864; Elder, November 16, 1866. Consecrated Bishop, July 4, 1876; Disrobed, May 12, 1884; Died, July 22, 1893.

He moved to Wilkes Barre, Pa. when very young. He commenced preaching at 18 years old, and later joined the Genesee (Western New York) Conference under the inspiration of Bishop J. J. Clinton, September 6, 1862. He was sent as a missionary to Tennessee and labored ardently in the eastern Tennessee area, from Strawberry Plains to Wheeling, W. Va., establishing several societies with hundreds of members amid perils and threats of violence during the reign of terror. He afterwards transferred to Washington, N.C.

In 1868 he served as one of the assistant secretaries of the General Conference. He transferred to the West Coast this same year and became presiding elder. He served several annual conferences for eight years after he was elected to the episcopacy in 1876. He developed a weakness which finally overtook him and caused his failure. He was disrobed by the General Conference of 1884 on charges of intemperance and immoral conduct, and final action on his case was taken by the Genesee Conference. [40]

35. Hood, *One Hundred Years,* pp. 188-191.
36. Moore, *History,* p. 376.
37. Nutt, *Newburgh,* p. 129; Hood, *op. cit.,* pp. 188-191.
38. *Minutes,* Seventy-Fourth Session, New York Annual Conference, pp. 45-46.
39. *Minutes,* Forty-Fifth Session, Genesee Conference, p. 46; *Minutes,* Twenty-Second Session, New Jersey Annual Conference, 1895; pp. 49-50.
40. Hood, *One Hundred Years,* pp. 122-126; *Minutes,* Seventeenth Quadrennial Session, pp. 35-80.

20. *THOMAS HENRY LOMAX (D.D.):* Born in Cumberland County near Fayetteville, N.C., January 15, 1832; Ordained Deacon, November 25, 1867; Elder, December 1, 1868; Consecrated Bishop, July 4, 1876; Died, March 31, 1908.

The son of Enoch and Rachel Hammons Lomax joined the Methodist Episcopal Church, South at 14. In 1850 he connected himself with a night school, in which he learned to read and write. He had been told the story of Henry Evans by his forebears. When Evans first arrived in Fayetteville there was no church in town. He had three or four preaching points; one was the home of Dicey Hammons, grandmother of Bishop Lomax. His grandfather, William Lomax, came to America with General LaFayette from the French colony in Africa, and joined the Revolutionary War under George Washington and LaFayette, fighting faithfully to the close of the war to secure the liberty of Americans.

At the close of the Civil War, he and other brothers, employed a Dr. Sanford, a learned gentleman, to teach them privately; thus he aimed to prepare himself for some usefulness in life. He joined the A.M.E. Zion Church, and in 1864 he was licensed to preach by Bishop J. W. Hood, ordained deacon by Bishop J. J. Clinton and elder by Bishop J. J. Moore.

He was a strong preacher, aggressive organizer, energetic and successful episcopal officer for 32 years, and one of the most thrifty and enterprising businessmen the race had produced. He was in his personal character open and frank; as a preacher he was plain, practical, orthodox, unpretending, and earnest. He loved Christian honesty, and lived above reproach and was loved and respected by all. [41]

His was a most fruitful life, whether we consider him as a tradesman, businessman or churchman. For thirty-six years he was a citizen of Charlotte, where his life and example in various spheres of activity furnished an inspiration to men of his own race, and a forceful illustration of the capabilities and possibilities of the Negro when given anything like a fair chance in the race of life. He was held in high esteem and honored by the best citizens of North Carolina for what he was and what he did. He was beloved and reverenced throughout the borders of our great church . . . . [42]

Funeral services were held at Clinton Chapel, Charlotte.

21. *CHARLES CALVIN PETTEY (M.A., D.D.):* Born in Wilkes County, near Wilkesboro, N.C., December 3, 1849; Ordained Deacon, December 11, 1872; Elder, November 10, 1878; Consecrated Bishop, May 22, 1888; Died, December 8, 1900.

Bishop Pettey had just reached mature manhood when his summons came. He was born a slave amid disadvantageous environments for mental culture, and the development of the higher faculties with which he was endowed. But in the providence of God freedom came when he was yet a youth and with it came the schoolhouse and college. He heard of these and soon learned what they could do for one seeking light and striving to grow into useful manhood. After utilizing the limited advantages offered by the common and night schools of his native Wilkesboro, N. C., he made his way to Biddle on foot where he began the struggle for higher education.

41. Moore, *History,* p. 377; Hood, *One Hundred Years,* pp. 191-195.
42. Episcopal Quadrennial Address, 1908, p. 6.

BISHOP CHARLES CALVIN PETTEY

BISHOP WILLIAM HENRY HILLERY   BISHOP ISOM CALEB CLINTON

He served Zion faithfully as preacher in North and South Carolina, Alabama, Tennessee, and California. He became General Secretary in 1884, and bishop in 1888, and entered upon his career as chief pastor in the South and West, where he did much to more strongly establish and widen the borders of Zion and lift up the race. He was a man of many excellent qualities; he was an able and eloquent preacher whose descriptive powers, fertile imagination, and forceful presentation of gospel truths were irresistible at times and impressive always.

As a presiding officer he distinguished himself on more than one occasion and was beloved and honored by ministers and laymen in all the conferences where he labored. He was aggressive along many lines, tenacious in his convictions, ambitious to excel as a leader, and always a bold defender of his opinions, his Church and his race when the occasion demanded. He was an ardent student of scientific subjects, especially as they related to Christianity and he sought to utilize his knowledge gained in investigating such subjects to make the gospel more effective and adapted to the progress of the age. As a man he was ever friendly and obligingly kind; as a citizen he was progressive and conservative; as a preacher and churchman he was always thoughtful, zealous, aggressive, eloquently able and forceful. In his home he was a most devoted and self-sacrificing husband, a kind and indulgent father . . . . He was one of the best prepared men of Zion's ministerial forces and one of the ablest of her prelates. [43]

22. *CICERO RICHARDSON HARRIS, (M.A., D.D.):* Born in Fayetteville, N.C., August 25, 1844; Ordained Deacon, January 4, 1874; Elder, December 6, 1874; Consecrated Bishop, May 22, 1868; Died, June 24, 1917.

Bishop Harris was the youngest of a family that had made its mark in the various fields of theology, medicine, teaching, and technical industry, thus representing an unusual degree of versatility and success. His father died when he was three years old and at six years of age he, with the rest of the family, was

43. *Minutes,* Seventy-Fourth Session, Philadelphia and Baltimore Conference, 1901, pp. 44-45; *Minutes,* Twenty-Second Quadrennial Session, p. 135; *A.M.E. Zion Quarterly Review,* April 1894, pp. 324-27.

taken to Chillicothe, Ohio, where his education immediately began. "His narrow escape from drowning, about a year afterward, may be construed as a special manifestation of providential care." In 1854 the family moved to Delaware, Ohio, and in 1857 to Cleveland. He finished Cleveland Central High School, and took training of the superior schools in Ohio, although he was in a notable degree a self-taught man. He moved back to Fayetteville in 1866 and began teaching with his brother, Robert, under the commission of the American Missionary Association. He joined the A.M.E. Zion Church in 1867, removing his membership from the American Wesleyan Church, Cleveland.

He received his license to preach in 1872, and the same year joined the North Carolina Conference. He was a pious, cultured educator. His style was lucid, elegant, forceful, and scholarly. His mind was systematic and well poised. As a preacher he was persuasive and forceful, never losing confidence in the power of "the word." As a Methodist he was strictly orthodox, and believed in evangelical religion pure and simple. He had a genial personality. He was a friend and confidante and devoted and constant husband and father. [44]

Harris and his beloved companion, niece, and nephew, pioneered with unquestionable faith in founding Zion Wesley Institute. Bishop Harris was awarded the Doctor of Divinity by Howard University in 1891, and the honorary A.M. degree by his own Livingstone College. He was a rare man of rare attainments. His traits of Christian character were always unquestionable, and his life of usefulness, in the schoolroom, the general office, and the bishopric, endeared him to all who knew him. Bishop Harris was retired at the 1916 General Conference along with Bishop Hood. After 29 years of service in the episcopacy, he fell asleep. He is buried in Salisbury, N.C., after last rites at Soldiers Memorial Church.

23. *ISOM CALEB CLINTON (D.D.):* Born in Cedar Creek Township, Lancaster County, S.C. May 22, 1830; Ordained Deacon and Elder, March 24, 1867; Consecrated Bishop, May 18, 1892; Died, October 18, 1904.

This godly nobleman, who was one of the most beloved men of our church, the first citizen of his home town and county, and ideal man of the race wherever he was known, was born the slave of Irvin Clinton, who owned his mother, Camie Clinton; his father, Lewis McDonald, was free. His owner was a leading lawyer and did not debar his human chattels from the privilege of gaining knowledge from books. Thus he learned to write and cipher before Lincoln's Proclamation and Grant's sword vouchsafed such privileges to the millions of his race who wore the shackles of bondage as he did. Being a man of splendid presence and rare traits, even while yet a slave, he became the trusted foreman and confidante of his master and continued in the management of his master's business after emancipation.

"In addition to his splendid service in the Church he also held the position of County treasurer for eight years. He was licensed to preach while yet in bondage and had the privilege of preaching to the people of his race on the Sunday afternoon in the church where his master had heard the Gospel from the lips of a white minister in the forenoon."

In 1866 he organized the Mount Carmel Church, about eight miles from Lancaster, where he established a public school. "One of the first colored schools

---

44. Hood, *One Hundred Years,* pp. 202-07; Anderson, *Biographical Souvenir,* pp. 8-9; *Minutes,* Twenty-Sixth Quadrennial Session, p. 55.

opened in Lancaster County outside of the town was that opened by him in a private house on his former master's place. Here he taught his own and many other children the first rudiments of a common school education." When Bishop J. J. Clinton went to South Carolina to organize the Conference, he found the then preacher, I. C. Clinton, ready to take hold of the work, and anxious to join him in spreading the borders of Zion. Bishop Clinton ordained I. C. Clinton deacon in the morning and elder in the evening of the same day he organized the South Carolina Conference. He was made presiding elder in 1872, and continued in that office until he was elected bishop. He was also made General Steward in 1888, and served both positions until his elevation in 1892.

"Starting at the foot of the ladder he speedily won his way upward, until in 1892 he was chosen one of the chief pastors of the A.M.E. Zion Church. Before his promotion he had been a successful pastor and organizer," and had greatly expanded the work of Zion in South Carolina. He had been the consistent friend of the poor and keeper of the needy, and known for his philanthropic deeds. "He lived a beautiful consistent life and died a serenely peaceful death," in his home city of Lancaster, S.C. [45]

24. *ALEXANDER WALTERS (M.A., D.D.):* Born at Bardstown (Nelson County), Ky. August 1, 1858; Ordained Deacon, July 3, 1879; Elder, April 10, 1881; Consecrated Bishop, May 18, 1892; Died, February 1, 1917.

The second youngest bishop elected in the history of our church was a man of extraordinary ability. "At an early age he manifested deep concern about spiritual things. At the age of eight he became a pupil under Mr. Brown of Wickliffe, and at twelve years of age he joined the church." He busied himself in Louisville in early life, removed to Indianapolis, Indiana, and began the study of theology under private tutors. "His wonderful pastoral career embraced Corydon, Ky., Clovesport, Ky., Fifteenth Street (Hughlett Temple), Louisville, Ky., and was made secretary of the conference, and of *Zion's Banner,* a popular journal of the conference and episcopal district. In 1883 he took charge of the leading Negro Church on the Pacific Coast—Stockton Street (First) A.M.E. Zion Church, San Francisco, Calif.; then Chattanooga, Tenn., Knoxville, Tenn., Mother Zion Church, New York City, where, as general agent he resuscitated and fully developed the Book Concern, and was the leading factor in local affairs of the city concerning his race . . . . He traveled extensively through European countries, Egypt and the Holy Land," and also Africa.

As a man, Walters was "sympathetic, liberal, conscientious, industrious, affable, painstaking and thorough. As a preacher—scholarly, brilliant, logical, eloquent, enthusiastic, fiery. As an orator—popular, captivating, pleasing and forceful. As an executive—strong, persuasive, parliamentarian, graceful, easy." Participating in all popular movements of the race, he was the best known of the younger black bishops of his day, "a real race leader."[46] Walters was laid to rest at Mother Zion's Cypress Hill Cemetery in Brooklyn.

45. Hood, *One Hundred Years,* pp. 207-09; *A.M.E. Zion Quarterly Review,* July 1891. pp 347-352; Episcopal Quadrennial Address, 1908, pp. 4-5.
46. Hood, *One Hundred Years,* pp. 209-212; Anderson, Op. cit., pp. 9-10; *Dictionary of Americal Biography,* Vol. 19, p. 398.

25. *GEORGE WYLIE CLINTON, (M.A., D.D., LL.D.):* Born in Cedar Creek Township, Lancaster County, S.C., March 28, 1859; Ordained Deacon, November 5, 1882; Elder, November 8, 1885; Consecrated Bishop, May 21, 1896; Died, May 21, 1921.

He was born a slave, son of Jonathan Clinton and Rachel Patterson. His mother was a slave, and according to the law the condition of the son followed that of the mother. Young Clinton was very much devoted to his mother, "and this devotion was largely the natural result of the pious training which she had given him. The death of his father when he was so young necessarily brought him more fully under the care and training of his mother and more constantly in her association." He received his education under adverse circumstances in private and public schools of his native home, the South Carolina University, Brainard Institute, and Livingstone College. He received the Honorary D.D. and LL.D. degrees from Wilberforce University, and A.M. from Livingstone College.

Clinton was licensed to preach February 14, 1879 and joined the South Carolina Conference in November 1880. He pastored successfully several leading churches, including Old John Wesley, Pittsburgh, where he built a magnificent parsonage, introduced a new pipe organ, and entertained the 1892 General Conference. By projecting, founding, and operating the A.M.E. Zion *Quarterly Review,* he showed not only his genius for organization, but his ability to manage successfully a large and important literary venture. "He ran the *Quarterly* on his own resources for two years, and then turned it over to the General Conference in Pittsburgh without a cent of cost to the Connection." He then became editor of the official organ, *The Star of Zion,* and after four years, he became bishop. (47)

He was of "splendid physique, strong debater, noted scholar, eloquent speaker, polished and popular preacher, able writer, author and well equipped executive. The Bishop's rise was rapid, symmetrical and steady, therefore, permanent. (48)

Through his wide travel, close study and personal contact, not only with the leaders, but with the rank and file of the people all over the country, Bishop Clinton concluded that the best interests of the race were to be promoted by the formation of business concerns directed by responsible men and women of the race; by joint action of white and black for peace, uplift and community welfare; by the best possible training and higher education in industrial and technological schools and by the investment and conservation of race means in enterprises that would furnish employment to the youth of the race. (49)

Bishop G. W. Clinton, magnanimous in spirit, lovable in disposition, heroic in deeds, eloquent in speech, one of God's noblemen, passed away in his home city, Charlotte, N.C. and last rites were held at his Little Rock Church, where he once pastored. (50)

26. *JEHU HOLLIDAY (D.D.):* Born in Goshen township, Columbia County, Ohio, December 25, 1827; Ordained Deacon and Elder, July 27, 1862; Consecrated Bishop, May 21, 1896; Died, March 2, 1899.

47. Hood, *One Hundred Years,* pp. 269, 273.
48. Anderson, *op. cit.,* p. 10.
49. A. B. Caldwell, *History of the American Negro,* p. 13.
50. *Minutes,* Twenty-Seventh Quadrennial Session, p. 98.

Holliday joined the church under the administration of Rev. Joseph Armstrong, the great pioneer preacher of Zion in Ohio, and joined the Allegheny Conference in July 1861, and was ordained the following year by Bishop J. J. Clinton, deacon in the morning and elder at night. He pastored several important charges from this time to 1892, and was a glowing inspiration to people everywhere he served. He either salvaged or made astonishing improvements in all his pastorates, some of which were Fifteenth Street Church (Hughlett Temple), Louisville, Ky.; Russellville, Ky.; Bedford, Pa.; Johnstown, Pa.; Avery Mission, Pittsburgh, Pa.

After he was appointed for the second time to Fifteenth Street Church in Louisville, by Bishop S. T. Jones in 1876, he entertained the Fifteenth Session of the General Conference that year. At the close of the General Conference he founded the Twelfth Street (Broadway Temple) Church, purchased the property, enlarged it, and paid all debts but $1000. He pastored it one year, taking in more than 200 members, and was appointed to Blackford Street (Jones Tabernacle) Church, Indianapolis in 1878.

In 1880 he was appointed to John Wesley Chapel in Pittsburgh, and purchased an unusually commodious church in which the General Conference of 1892 was held. From this point he went to Avery Mission for one year, and then to Johnstown, Pa., "to rebuild our church which the great flood had washed away." In 1890 he was appointed presiding elder of the Allegheny Conference, and in 1892, elected General Agent of the Book Concern, succeeding Bishop Walters. He left New York in September 1892, with the consent of the Board of Bishops and by request of Bishop Walters, presiding over the Kentucky Conference, to help save the deteriorating situation of the Twelfth Street Church, which he had given birth, and so reported his dual labors at the General Conference of 1896 where he was consecrated bishop. [51]

His particular characteristic was attachment to and interest in young men aspiring for the ministry and other Christian work.

The inspiration and zeal of this heroic pioneer bishop in the South was felt by the church of his choice. Personally he possessed the utmost dignity of character, and a sweet tender nature. He was a warm and sympathetic friend, always ready to advise in difficulty and assist in need. He was a man of deep research and rare intelligence, sound judgment and acute executive ability. Broad in Christian ideas, liberal in ecclesiastic association; and yet, an uncompromising defender of the church he loved and for which he gave his life. As a preacher, he possessed simplicity of style and force of utterance, which frequently ended in eloquence of expression. His doctrine was practical, manner earnest and appeals persuasive. His voice was musical and of extensive compass. He was a power in prayer, and, having unanswering confidence in his Maker, he fearlessly marched to his death. He was known and appreciated from the East to the West and from the North to the South. He erected his own monument in the hearts he gladdened, the churches he built, and the souls he pointed to the haven of eternal rest. [52]

He died in Little Rock, Ark., and was funeralized at John Welsey Church, Pittsburg and buried in that city.

In 1900 the Bishops stated:

51. Autobiography of Jehu Holliday, 1892 (W. J. Walls Collection).
52. *Minutes,* Seventy-Eighth Session, New York Annual Conference, pp.73-74.

We are called upon to lament our sainted colleague and your chief pastor, the Right Rev. Jehu Holliday, . . . whose labors during the short period of his episcopate proved him to be one of the most profitable selections Zion ever chose to fill the office of Bishop.

The accident which befell him in the active and zealous discharge of his duty, his patient resignation while sick, his acts of charity while battling with the last enemy, the stipulations in his will and his glowing testimony for the Master are matters about which you will hear more fully when the Committee on Memoirs shall report, and during the services accompanying the report. He died as he lived, a brillant and outspoken witness for Christ. His sun went down in the full evening of his mortal existence, but the rays of his increasingly lustrous character rises still higher here and will ever shine while Zion has work to do in bringing men to Christ by the preaching of the Gospel. [53]

27. *JOHN BRYAN SMALL (M.A., D.D., LL.D.):* Born at Frazer, St. Joseph's Parish, Barbados, British West Indies, March 14, 1845; Ordained Deacon, May 26, 1872; Elder, June 1, 1873; Consecrated Bishop, May 21, 1896; Died, January 15, 1905.

Bishop Small died a few days before his colleagues met in semi-annual session at Fayetteville, N.C.. He was "a princely servant of the heavenly king, and an untiring workman of our Church."

In early life he gave evidence of the brightness and studiousness which in later years became distinguishing traits of his life. He was given the best advantage within reach of his father to secure his education and fit him for usefulness. After good home training and special instruction, under a well-equipped instructor, upon the recommendation of Bishop Parry of the established Church of England, he matriculated at St. John's Lodge where he spent the ensuing four years and graduated at the head of a class of fifty-six, composed of both white and colored students. He later entered Codrington College, an institution of his native land, won distinction and carried away first honor, leaving with favorable prophecies and kindest wishes from his instructors. [54]

In 1862 he spent six months in Jamaica, West Indies, and in 1863 he traveled to many points in Africa. In 1871 he decided to visit Europe, passing through the United States. He thus left Balize, Honduras, and in 28 days, landed in Boston, Mass. On Saturday, August 5, 1871, he preached in Zion Church, North Russell Street (presently Columbus Avenue). Passing through New York, he spent some time in Philadelphia, and preached at Wesley Zion, then on Sixth and Lombard Streets. He then visited the nation's capital, and attended a camp meeting given by the Zion churches of Washington. "It was there, Rev. R.H.G. Dyson met Rev. Small and persuaded him to stay in this country, telling him he was needed, and could accomplish much good. Elder Dyson dispatched to Bishop J. J. Clinton who immediately answered by telegram, saying: 'Detain him; letter coming.' " He was sent to Springfield, Mass.; Worcester, Mass; New Bedford, Mass; Norwich, Conn;

and Bridgeport, Conn.; where he met and married Mary Julia Blair. "Elder Small was elected secretary of the New England Conference the first time he met it (in 1873), and furnished well-arranged minutes until he transferred to the New York

---

53. *Minutes,* Twenty-First Quadrennial Session, pp. 92-93.
54. Episcopal Quadrennial Address, 1908, p. 5.
55. *A.M.E. Zion Quarterly Review,* April, 1892, pp. 289-293.

Conference, and was sent as a transferee to the Central North Carolina Conference and stationed at Fayetteville by Bishop Hood." After serving nine years in North Carolina, he transferred to the Philadelphia and Baltimore Conference and was appointed to John Wesley Church on Connecticut Avenue, Washington, D.C., by Bishop S. T. Jones. He was among the first group of four to receive the Honorary Doctor of Divinity Degree from Livingstone College in 1887. [55]

It was while he was serving as presiding elder of the Philadelphia and Baltimore Conference that he was elected to the bishopric, and upon his own suggestion, the mission work of our church in Africa was made a part of his district. "He was the first A.M.E. Zion bishop to make an offical visit to Africa, and under his administration the work in Africa took on new life, made steady and substantial progress, both in the forming of new organizations and in the establishment of parochial schools." A voluminous author, dignified theologian, and creative thinker, he passed away in his home town of York, Pa. [56]

28. *JOHN WESLEY ALSTORK (M.A., D.D., LL.D):* Born at Talladega, Ala. September 1, 1852; Ordained Deacon, November 26, 1882; Elder, November 30, 1884; Consecrated Bishop, May 20, 1900; Died, July 23, 1920.

"The grand old state of Alabama, that has next to North Carolina, the largest membership of our Zion," produced its first bishop in the election of Bishop Alstork on May 14, 1900. "He was a massive man in heart, mind and body." He became known in his lifetime throughout the country. Before he was Grand Master of the York Rite Masons, he was bishop of the A.M.E. Zion Church. He was licensed to preach in 1878, and joined the Alabama Conference in 1879. He was ordained in the East Alabama Conference, deacon by Bishop Pettey and elder by Bishop Hood. [57] He was appointed to Opelika Station in 1882. "The most prominent church that he pastored was Old Ship Church at Montgomery. He was a brillant scholar with an ever-increasing quest for education of himself and others. He became presiding elder in 1889, during the time elders were elected by the annual conferences; in which office he served in several of the conferences and won the love of all his brethren. He was elected General Steward of the denomination and in 1900 at Washington, D.C., he was made bishop; his election was the first by acclamation in our church.

"Bishop Alstork was a beloved leader and in Alabama his name became a name to conjure with. His chief work was the building of Lomax-Hannon College in which he was able to command the support and loyalty of Alabama and the Southwest. No more enduring monument could be erected to a man than a school." He passed away while addressing a Sunday School Convention at Searcy, Alabama, and laid to rest at Montgomery, after funeral services at Mt. Zion Church in Montgomery, July 27, 1920. [58]

29. *JOHN WESLEY SMITH (M.A., D.D.):* Born in Fayetteville, N.C., January 27, 1862; Ordained Deacon, November 21, 1881; Elder, September 4, 1882; Consecrated Bishop, May 19, 1904; Died, October 14, 1910.

Bishop C. R. Harris was his first teacher in the grade school of Fayetteville. He finished the state normal school and took a private course in higher studies. He

---

56. Episcopal Quadrennial Address, 1908; *Cullings from Zion's Poets,* p.49.
57. *Minutes,* East Alabama (Central) Annual Conference, 1882, 1884.
58. *Minutes,* Twenty-Seventh Quadrennial Session, p. 146; *The Star of Zion,* July 29, 1920, p. 1.

BISHOP JOHN WESLEY ALSTORK

BISHOP JOHN WESLEY SMITH

BISHOP JOSIAH SAMUEL CALDWELL

was licensed to preach October 4, 1880. He was admitted on trial in the Central North Carolina Conference held at Charlotte, in 1881, "and acted as assistant secretary of the Conference. He also passed the examination, and was ordained deacon at the conference. The New Haven pulpit having been left vacant by the transfer of Elder Dyson, Bishop Hood . . . found much difficulty in finding a man for that church. After several unsuccessful efforts he concluded to try Smith; the church was consulted, and was found willing to take him, young and inexperienced as he was, if he were ordained elder. The bishop consented to this, called a council of elders to meet him in Hartford where Smith passed a satisfactory examination and was ordained elder . . . ." [59]

His other pastorates were Little Rock, Ark., Fifteenth Street Church, Louisville; Baltimore, Md.; John Wesley Church, Washington, D.C., Wesley Union, Harrisburg, Pa., and Carlisle, Pa., from which he was elected editor of the *Star of Zion* in 1896. Bishop Smith was known as an eloquent, graphic, soaring, inspiring pulpiteer; brief but pointed in debate; pleasing and able presiding officer; a fearless writer, hospitable, communicative and extremely friendly. In 1888 he

59. Hood, *One Hundred Years*, pp. 241-242;

married Miss Emma Thompson, who passed away and later he married Miss Ida. V. Thompson. "His short life of forty-eight years was employed to the glory of God and to good of mankind." He labored faithfully six years in the episcopacy before summoned to answer the call from labor to reward. He was laid to rest in Carlisle, Pa. [60]

30. *JOSIAH SAMUEL CALDWELL (M.A., D.D.):* Born in Charlotte, Mecklenburg County, N.C., August 2, 1862; Ordained Deacon, November 21, 1886; Elder, November 9, 1888; Consecrated Bishop, May 19, 1904; Died, April 7, 1935. He joined the A.M.E. Zion Church under the inspiration of Rev. J. M. Hill at a camp-meeting of Zion Hill, Concord, N.C. at 19 years of age. Night study largely contributed to his primary education, and he completed the course graduating with excellent attainments from Livingstone College in 1888.

At the age of twenty-one he felt divinely called to preach, and he entered the sacred ministry where he was to lay the foundation of his future fame. He preached his trial sermon in Concord, N.C.; and was licensed as a local preacher. Feeling his inefficiency, he entered Livingstone College, during the fall of 1883. Entering college almost penniless, and with the tender care of a wife and child entrusted to him, he did not find it easy sailing. With these environments his time alternated very evenly between the college and the farm, until May 1888, when he completed his curriculum with great credit to his persevering and untiring efforts. On the day of graduation his oration was; "Christ the Example of true Greatness."

He joined the Central North Carolina Conference 1884; was ordained deacon by Bishop J. W. Hood at Lincolnton, N.C.; ordained elder in Augusta, Ga., and stationed in 1888 by Bishop C. R. Harris. He served Pineville, N.C., China Grove, N.C.; Mt. Lebanon, Elizabeth City, N.C.; Oak Street, Petersburgh, Va.; and Mother Zion, New York and Big Wesley, Philadelphia. For a three-months period, he pastored both Mother Zion and Big Wesley as a circuit, until the New York Conference held session and released him from Mother Zion. He served as a most effective financial secretary from 1900 to 1904.

For 31 years "the Bishop ranked well with his official peers, beautiful, impressive and inspiring songster; pleasing, powerful, eloquent preacher; able, decisive executive; good parliamentarian; strong in debate, quick and far-seeing," he loved to be much alone, yet companionable. "At the time of his passing, he was strong in faith, wise in counsel, resourceful, courageous in the discharge of duty, invincible in leadership; a strong and powerful gospel preacher, while engaged in his routine daily tasks. 'A mortal arrow pierced his frame; he fell but felt no fear.' " [61] With last rites held at Big Wesley Church, he was laid to rest in the city of Philadelphia.

31. *MARTIN ROBERT FRANKLIN (D.D.):* Born January 8, 1853 near Macon, Ga.; Ordained Deacon, November 21, 1886; Elder, November 27, 1888; Consecrated Bishop, May 20, 1908; Died, May 13, 1909.

His parents were sold from him when he was an infant, and he had never seen nor heard from them . . . .He followed Sherman's army, and reached the North in 1865, and resided in Illinois, near Chicago, for several years. He

---

60. Anderson, *Biographical Souvenir,* pp. 11-12; *A.M.E. Zion Quarterly Review,* April 1892, pp. 306-307; *Minutes,* Twenty-Fourth Quadrennial Session, pp. 149-150.
61. Anderson, *op. cit.,* p. 12; *A.M.E. Zion Quarterly Review,* April 1892, pp. 294-297; W. J. Walls, Ms. *Bishop J. S. Caldwell and Twenty-five Years in the Episcopacy, Minutes,* Thirtieth Quadrennial Session, p. 70.

entered Wayland Seminary in Washington, D.C., in 1879 where he studied for two years. While there he embraced religion in the Asbury Methodist Episcopal Church. He moved to Boston, Mass., and in 1881 joined North Russell (Columbus Avenue) Street A.M.E. Zion Church, and was licensed to preach the same year. He was ordained both deacon and elder in this conference by Bishops Hood and Moore respectively. His first appointment was at Laurinburg, N.C.; where he erected a church and gave new life to work which had been languishing for some years. His other appointments in that Conference were Manley, Carthage, and Statesville.

He then transferred to Allegheny Conference and pastored Avery Mission, Allegheny City, five years, and to Mother Zion, New York City, where he was entertaining pastor of the Centennial Observance. After five years, he was made presiding elder of the New York Conference, and elected Financial Secretary of the denomination in 1904.

Bishop Franklin headed the trio elected in 1908 by polling the highest vote of the three. He was consecrated and assigned to the Eighth Episcopal District, embracing the Georgia, South Carolina and Palmetto Conferences. At the time of his election he lived at his own home in Brooklyn, N.Y., but believing he could render the church better service by living on his district, he packed his household goods, took his family and moved to Atlanta, Georgia. The work took on new life. The city of Atlanta rejoiced at the coming of that good and great man, who denied himself and family of privileges and comforts and went South (where most colored men were afraid to go), in order that the borders of Zion might be extended and the kingdom of Christ built up. He started off nobly. Everything he touched prospered. As badly as we needed him on earth, God needed him more in heaven. Therefore . . . the Lord called him from labor to reward.

He was an impressive preacher and safe administrator, of pious character and manner.

The history of his life as a successful laborer and pastor will be found interesting and read with inspiration. As a man he was tender, gentle and urbane; and having an unassuming and unselfish vein spoke out loud accents—"Behold the Man." His bearing was one of modesty; being honestly devout, his Christian life was made up of such inherent qualities, which made him an embodiment of Christian force and exemplary character. Bishop Franklin was funeralized from Mother Zion Church and interred in Cypress Hill, Brooklyn, N.Y. [62]

32. *GEORGE LINCOLN BLACKWELL (M.A., D.D.):* Born in Henderson, N.C., July 3, 1861; Ordained Deacon, February 18, 1884; Elder, February 22, 1885; Consecrated Bishop, May 20, 1908; Died, March 21, 1926.

He joined the Union A.M.E. Zion Church under the inspiration of Rev. M. V. Marable in 1876, and advanced rapidly in his church work. He served as superintendent of Sunday school, preacher's steward, class leader, and exhorter during the second year of his religious experience, and in 1880 he was licensed to preach and recommended as a suitable candidate for admission into the North Carolina Conference, which he joined in 1881. He pastored with remarkable success at the prominent charges of Moore's Chapel, Lincolnton, N.C.; Mt.

62. Hood, *One Hundred Years,* p 597; Anderson, *op. cit.,* p. 14; *Minutes,* Twenty-Fourth Quadrennial Session, p. 149; *Minutes,* Thirtieth Session, Central North Carolina Annual Conference, 1909, p. 115.

Pleasant (Center Street), Statesville, N.C.; Bridgeport, Conn.; Cambridgeport, Mass,; North Russell Street, Boston; and Big Wesley, Philadelphia: and was a productive general officer.

This noble sire of the Church had made his way to the very front of the Christian ministry by years of diligent study. In the rural school and afterwards in Livingstone College, where he enrolled in the early 80's where he was recognized as a faithful and apt student. Having graduated with honors at Livingstone (1888), he entered Boston University and received his degree from the School of Theology with high rank. Meanwhile, he served with great usefulness and credit churches in North Carolina, Connecticut and Massachusetts. Later as Dean of the Theological Department of Livingstone College, Manager of the Publication House, and then as both General and Missionary Secretary, he won for himself a place in the forefront of the leadership of the denomination, and made a signal contribution to his race and country. As a bishop . . . George Lincoln Blackwell kindled afresh the fires of pioneer missionary endeavor. With the zeal of Wesley, the self-sacrifice of Asbury, and the devotion of Varick and Rush, he went everywhere preaching Jesus and gathering the flock of Christ. No man among us had combined the qualities of preacher, publicist and administrator in so pronounced a degree and with such substantial accomplishments, as he. His eighteen years as a chief pastor were full and fruitful.

He passed away at his home in Philadelphia, and was laid to rest in Eden Cemetery after funeral services at Big Wesley Church. [63]

33. *ANDREW JACKSON WARNER (D.D.):* Born in Washington, Ky., March 4, 1850; Ordained Deacon and Elder, September 9, 1857; Consecrated Bishop, May 20, 1908; Died, May 31, 1920.

He was born a slave, and at the age of thirteen years, he ran away from his owners, and crossing the Ohio River one night he found himself in Ripley, Ohio, a stranger and knowing not where to go, he went to headquarters. where colored soldiers were being enlisted, and enlisted as a drummer boy. After serving in the Union Army until the close of the war, and being honorably discharged with the rank of sergeant, he returned to his old Kentucky home.

Feeling the need of an education, and there being no good colored schools at the time in Kentucky, he went to Ohio and attended the high school in Cincinnati. From there he went to Wilberforce in Xenia, Ohio. . . . He also read law in the office of Honorable W. H. Wordsworth of Marysville, Ky. . . . [64]

He joined the A.M.E. Zion Church while still in his teens, and was called to the ministry before he was twenty. "His formal schooling ended with his boyhood, but he continued to study both men and books, attended lectures, read and thus by patient endeavor equipped himself for his great work in life." He was licensed to preach in 1874 and joined the Kentucky Conference under Bishop S. T. Jones, at Greenville, Ky., who also ordained him in the morning and evening, and sent him to Wesley Chapel, Greenville, in 1877. He remained there two and a half years and added more than a hundred to the membership. He was then transferred to Little Rock and built the first Zion Church in Arkansas. He lived to see that small beginning grow into two conferences. From Little Rock he went to

63. *A.M.E. Zion Quarterly Review,* October 1892, pp. 90-94; Anderson, *op. cit.* p. 13; *Minutes,* Twenty-Eighth Quadrennial Session, p. 38.
64. Hood, *One Hundred Years,* pp. 553-554.

BISHOP ANDREW
JACKSON WARNER

BISHOP MARTIN ROBERT FRANKLIN   BISHOP   LYNWOOD
                                       WESTINGHOUSE KYLES

Russellville, Ky., and from there to Washington Metropolitan, St. Louis, for five years. While here he founded St. John Church in South St. Louis, Centralia, and DuQuoin , Ill. He went to Knoxville and built Loguen Temple Church. He successfully pastored Big Zion, Mobile, Ala.; Tuscaloosa for one year; and Metropolitan, Birmingham. His success was remarkable here as he left after seven years a church with more than a thousand members.

In 1896 he was instrumental in organizing the Board of Church Extension and was made Secretary. Two years later he was appointed to the work at Clinton Chapel, Charlotte, and in a ten years' pastorate so organized its forces and developed its resources as to make it one of the best stations in the connection. . . . His sympathy with his men and their loyalty to him caused him to be known as the "Swamp Angel." . . . He was married three times. His first marriage was to Alice McNeil (two children); she passed away around 1891. His second marriage was to Mary Eliza Delmor (four children), who died in 1908. On July 10, 1910, he married Annie Weddington of Charlotte (one child), who served as his missionary supervisor. [65]

His fame as a ready talker, witty debater and gospel preacher was national. His popularity as an able speaker brought to him unsought, the nomination for Congress in the first Alabama District. He was twice chosen Presidential Elector and one time ran for Governor of the State. Bishop Warner was a big brother and a man of astute political sense, of a strong countenance, tall and massive body, magnificent in gracefulness and musical in voice. As a Bishop he stamped his impress on the states of Mississippi, Louisiana, Tennessee, North Carolina, South Carolina and Florida. [66] After funeral services at Big Zion (Clinton Chapel), Charlotte, he was laid to rest in the city.

65. Caldwell, *History of the American Negro*, pp. 213-217.
66. *Minutes,* Twenty-Seventh Quadrennial Session, p. 145.

34. *LYNWOOD WESTINGHOUSE KYLES (D.D., LL.D.):* Born at Ivy
Depot, Albermarle County, Va., May 3, 1874; Ordained Deacon, May 2, 1897;
Elder, May 20, 1901; Consecrated Bishop, May 19, 1916; Died, July 8, 1941.

In general efficiency and actual accomplishment in the various avenues of
church service, Lynwood W. Kyles ranked as one of the leading characters,
not only of Zion Methodism, but of Negro Methodism generally. In spite of
the fact that he was born in the country at a time and under conditions not
far removed from slavery, he showed at an early age, unusual mental alertness
and a strong tendency in moral and religious directions.

Rising above the environments incidental to rural life, he made his way
to Hampton Institute when but a boy of fifteen, completing the English
course, and graduating from the Industrial department as a wheelright and
blacksmith. After working at these trades a number of years, he entered the
ministry in the New Jersey Conference in 1895, and received his first
appointment to the pastoral charge of Englewood, New Jersey in 1896. He
was ordained in the conference by Bishop Walters. Not content with this
educational qualification he entered Lincoln University in Pennsylvania,
remaining seven years and graduating from both the College and Theological
departments with honor (1901, A.B.; 1904, B.D.). He worked his way
through both of these institutions and endured hardships and privations to fit
himself for the ministry such as few men of any race had undergone. Thus,
through self-denial, devotion to duty and unyielding persistency, he won an
enviable place in the estimation of his fellowmen.

He was a great success as pastor, forging his way from a circuit rider to
some of the largest pastorates in the connection, and demonstrating in each
of them his ability to marshall forces and handle large propositions.

After Englewood, N.J., he pastored Media, Pa.; afterward John Wesley
Church, Washington, D.C.; Center Street Church, Statesville, N.C.; Goler
Memorial, Winston-Salem, N.C., and Big Zion, Mobile, Ala. During his six years'
pastorate of Big Zion, he built the largest and most conveniently arranged
parsonage owned by Negroes in the United States at that time.

He married Jenny Smith (deceased) in 1897, Louella Marie Bryan, December
18, 1908 (deceased), and Josephine Humbles, 1926.

He made good in the general official work of the church. As secretary and
treasurer of the Ministerial Brotherhood, he permanently established this
department and gained for it the confidence of the entire connection. As editor
and manager of the *Quarterly Review,* he helped to make it the foremost
magazine by the race, especially the homiletics department. [67]

He was a magnetic spokesman of any cause he espoused. He was not bounded
in his activities to the church of his choice, but was a leader in the
interdenominational and interracial movements, and felt in political leadership in
the nation. "He was a gifted financier and a sagacious leader, and wielded a strong
hand in manipulating the general affairs of the connection. Being a man of
forceful conviction and strong will, his name was significant of one who built up a
great following which he was able to call upon on all occasions." [68] His last rites
were held at Goler Memorial Church, and he was buried in Winston-Salem, N.C.

67. Jesse Colbert, *General Conference Handbook 25th Quadrennial Session of the A.M.E.
Zion Church,* p. 66.
68. *Minutes,* Thirty-Second Quadrennial Session, p. 215.

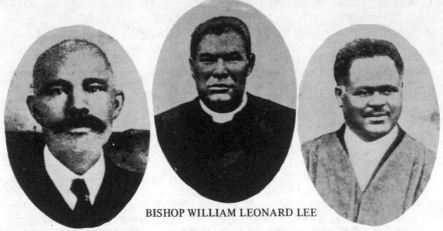

BISHOP WILLIAM LEONARD LEE

BISHOP ROBERT BLAIR BRUCE

BISHOP JOHN WESLEY WOOD

35. *ROBERT BLAIR BRUCE (D.D.):* Born at Charlie Hope, Brunswick County, Va., June 26, 1861; Ordained Deacon, September 5, 1886; Elder, November 20, 1892; Consecrated Bishop, May 19, 1916; Died, July 9, 1920.

Bruce grew up on a farm in his home town and was permitted to go to school on rainy days.

His grandmother and an uncle raised him. At an early age he aspired to a more liberal education than his environments promised. The nearest school of importance was Lawrenceville, seven miles away. Something of his eagerness is understood when it is stated that he walked that distance back and forth each day until the foundation of a good education was laid. Incidentally, these hard years of his youth did other things for him. They developed a vigorous body which was able to stand the strain of the years remarkably well. They also taught him lessons of thrift and economy which played their part in life. . . . They created in him a bond of sympathy with all struggling youth.

Bishop Bruce was scarcely more than ten years of age when he was converted and joined Solomon's Temple at Charlie Hope, Va. He early turned to the ministry and was an active minister of the gospel for almost 40 years when he died. He joined the Virginia Conference in 1884 and was ordained by Bishop Hood at Petersburg, while he was there attending Payne Divinity School. After completing his work at Petersburg, he transferred to the Western North Carolina Conference, and for two years pastored in Winston-Salem. In 1894 he went to Grace Church, Charlotte, where he served five years and began the building of its present edifice. He pastored Little Rock Church in Charlotte for one year, and Soldiers Memorial, Salisbury, two years.

Early in his ministry he saw the tremendous advantage in every way which must accrue to the denomination by producing its own literature, especially its Sunday School periodicals. He was a pioneer in that field and was largely instrumental in the establishment and building up of the publishing interests of the denomination. For more than twenty years he was Editor of the A.M.E. Zion Sunday School periodicals. . . . Though never formally appointed presiding elder, he virtually served in that capacity for a number of years in and around Charlotte. [69]

69. Caldwell, *History of the American Negro,* pp. 284-287.

He was, for a time, Dean of Theology at Livingstone College and graduated one class. In both of these positions he built himself into the affections of the youth of the church. Bishop Bruce was a fine thinker and a preacher of pathos and power. His eloquence was rugged and keen. He could cut like a scythe at one time and at another heal like Gilead's balm. As a Bishop he had begun to do constructive work in Georgia and South Carolina. [70]

He believed that the permanent progress of the race must ultimately rest on hard work, common sense, and economy. His final rites were held at Grace Church and his body laid to rest in Cedar Grove Cemetery, Charlotte, N.C.

36. *WILLIAM LEONARD LEE (D.D.):* Born in Madison County, near Canton, Miss., August 8, 1866; Ordained Deacon, November 12, 1893, Elder, November 10, 1895; consecrated Bishop, May 19, 1916; Died, October 3, 1927.

Bishop Lee early took every advantage of the common schools, then set himself to personal study which he pursued without relenting. After joining the Middleton Grove Church in Madison County in 1888, and joining the West Tennessee and Mississippi Conference in 1889, he became an able preacher and pastor. He was subsequently ordained in the conference by Bishop Walters. "After pastoring successfully several minor points he was apointed to Batesville and Coffeeville, Miss.: Monroe and Wadesboro, N.C.; then Rock Hill, S.C., and afterwards, St. 'Luke, Wilmington, N.C. In 1908, he was appointed to John Wesley, Pittsburgh and Fleet Memorial (First Church), Brooklyn, in 1914." [71]

From the fertile wilds and dense mazes of Dutch Guiana, there rises the mighty Con Con tree, higher of crest and larger of girth than any other, the very loftiness of which dwarfs the surrounding forest; so the magnificent form and striking personality of Bishop Lee loomed upon the ecclasiastical horizon and diverted the gaze of all. He could be fittingly called the maker of himself—self-made he was from the cotton field and railroad grade, to the pulpit and the episcopacy. A craving for knowledge, a thirst for the Pierian waters, urged him on and despite the handicaps of his youth, he came into the flay of the mighty full panoplied to emerge victorious. As a homely philosopher, a quaint humorist, a preacher of the glorious gospel, and a friend and brother he ranked with the noblest of them. Whether tramping the red hills and rich deltas of his own Mississippi or holding high the flag in the Carolinas, or yet leading the marching hosts of Zion in a northern clime, he was ever loyal, tried and true. Eleven years and more he stood at the helm a bishop and master of the craft. . . In the annals of those who died in the faith, respected, honored, and remembered, will ever stand the stalwart figure of Bishop Lee. [72]

He married Amerial Aurillia Dunn in 1891, who soon passed away, and in September 1900, he married Nettie E. Tillman. His service of triumph was held at Fleet Memorial Church and he was buried in Brooklyn, N.Y.

70. *Minutes,* Twenty-Seventh Quadrennial Session, pp. 145-146; *The Star of Zion,* July 15, 1920.
71. Anderson, *op. cit.* p. 92; *Who's Who in Colored America,* 1937.
72. *Minutes,* Twenty-Eighth Quadrennial Session, pp. 38-39.

37. *GEORGE CLINTON CLEMENT (M.A., D.D., LL.D.):* Born at Mocksville, N.C., December 23, 1871; Ordained Deacon, December 10, 1893; Elder, December 9, 1895; Consecrated Bishop, May 19, 1916; Died, October 23, 1934.

Bishop Clement was educated primarily in the public schools of Mocksville and graduated with prominent honors from Livingstone College, receiving his B.A. in 1898, and honorary M.A. and D.D. in 1904 and 1906 respectively. He entered the ministry September 18, 1888 at Mocksville, N.C., and became a charter member of the Western North Carolina Conference, and was ordained by Bishop Lomax. He pastored with striking success the Second Creek Circuit, China Grove Church and Grace Church, Charlotte, N.C.; Soldier's Memorial, Salisbury, N.C.; and transferred to Louisville, Ky., and became pastor of Twelfth Street Church. He purchased the valuable property on Broadway, on which the Broadway Temple Church was later built. He became editor of *The Star of Zion* in 1904.

He was deeply pious and conscientious, and he and his wife, Emma Clarissa Williams Clement, produced a noted family of religious leaders, public servants, and educators, which later won his widow the laurels of becoming the first black American Mother.

Bishop Clement, "scholarly, brilliant, tireless in action, decisive, resolute, fearless in the discharge of duty, was stricken on the field of action, and after a long and wasting illness in the early morning was summoned to the Father's house and to his eternal reward." [73] He was funeralized from the Broadway Temple Church in Louisville, his home city, and buried in the city.

38. *JOHN WESLEY WOOD (D.D.):* Born in Tolbert County, Ga., May 10, 1865; Ordained Deacon, December 17, 1888; Elder, December 14, 1890; Consecrated Bishop, May 20, 1920; Died, April 17, 1940.

He secured his education through the public schools of Troy County and LaGrange Academy in La Grange, Ga., completing his work there in 1882. He later attended Morris Brown College, Atlanta, in 1896 and the Moody Bible Institute in Chicago, 1911-12. He joined the West Tennessee and Mississippi Conference at Kosisko, Miss., in 1888, and pastored several points in the conference, including Memphis, Tenn. He transferred to the Virginia Conference and pastored Norfolk, Berkley, Va.; and Ahoskie and Edenton, N.C., and afterwards Jones Tabernacle in Indianapolis. He then pastored State Street Church, Mobile, Ala., and became Foreign Missions Secretary from this pastorate.

During his early pastorate, he was a diligent teacher. He served two years as president of Edenton High School and taught three years in the public schools of Lincoln, Ala. "He was a man of splendid physique, an able preacher and pastor, imposing and strong personality, of rather quite mien but strong and decisive when the time demanded it." [74]

> Bishop Wood served well for nineteen years, eleven months and seventeen days. He was a leader, and his followers rejoiced in his leadership. He was one of Zion's notable spiritual leaders ... greatly beloved by the entire bench of Bishops and the Connection. He possessed many rare qualities, among them the quality of meekness, the quality of making friends and holding them. . . . He knew the value of love, and it was demonstrated in his love for God, for his church, his colleagues; and his superb love and devotion for his family was one of his glowing assets. He was a student of the

73. *Minutes,* Thirtieth Quadrennial Session, p. 70.

Bible and of human nature. . . . [75]

Bishop Wood passed away in his home city of Indianapolis, and after final rites held at Jones Tabernacle, he was buried in the city.

39. *PARIS ARTHUR WALLACE (M.A., D.D.):* Born in Maryville, Tenn., April 17, 1870; Ordained Deacon, September 20, 1896; Elder, May 23, 1897; Consecrated Bishop, May 20, 1920; Died, February 21, 1952.

He was licensed to preach in Maryville by Rev. E. D. W. Jones in 1894. He was a local preacher for three weeks and joined the Tennessee Conference. He was ordained deacon at St. Louis and elder at Chambersburg, Pa. Some of his pastorates embraced Thompkin's Chapel, Chattanooga, Tenn.; Jacob Street, Louisville; Metropolitan Zion, Washington, D.C.; Gettysburg, Pa.; and Fleet Street (First Church), Brooklyn. He graduated from Maryville (Tenn.) College in 1895. He received his A.B. and B.D. degrees from Lincoln University, Pa., and honorary degree of A.M. from Lincoln and D.D. from Livingstone College.

He was an all-around pastor, polished scholar, lively companion and family man, pulpit master, with an imposing personality. He possessed the elements of either science or theology, and was genial and sincere. In 1944 he celebrated his fiftieth anniversary in the ministry. He was retired at the General Conference.

His record was one of distinguished service, devoted labor and brilliant achievement. He excelled in scholarship, and was a noteworthy preacher. . . . In the pastorate he filled many of our leading pulpits, and always gave a good account of his stewardship. The days of the years of his pilgrimage were 83. In those years he attained scholastic, pastoral, and episcopal honors, all of which he richly deserved. He did not have greatness thrust upon him. His was a great soul, a prodigious intellect, and a burning zeal for his church. [76]

After a long and trying illness, he passed away at Brooklyn, N.Y. Funeral services were held at First Church, and he was laid to rest in Brooklyn.

40. *BENJAMIN GARLAND SHAW (D.D):* Born at Pope (Panola County), Miss., August 26, 1878; Ordained Deacon, November 13, 1898, Elder, November 19, 1899; Consecrated Bishop, May 20, 1924; Died, April 14, 1951.

He attended public schools in Pope County; continued his studies in Greenwood College, Greenwood, Miss., and earned the B.A. degree at Philander-Smith College. He took a correspondence course in theology, Oskaloosa, Iowa, and studied at the Louisville Medical College, completing the course in 1907. He started his ministry in the West Tennessee and Mississippi Conference in 1898, and pastored the following churches: Greenwood Mission, Greenwood, Miss.; Sharkey Circuit, Miss.; Payne Chapel, Little Rock, Ark; St. John's Chapel, New Albany, Ind.; Hood Temple, Evansville, Ind.; served as presiding elder of the Chicago District, and pastored Washington Metropolitan Church, St. Louis, from 1910 to 1920. Through his dynamic evangelistic appeal he won many members for Zion in these areas. He led the congregation in purchasing the present mammoth structure in St. Louis, in which has been held quadrennial sessions of the General Conference, Missionary Convention and Christian Education Convention and connectional councils and bishops' meetings.

He was a passionate, dynamic preacher, with an evangelistic emphasis, and

74. Anderson, *op. cit.,* p. 64.
75. *Minutes,* Thirty-First Quadrennial Session, pp. 79-80.
76. *Minutes,* Thirty-Fourth Quadrennial Session, p. 420.

BISHOP PARIS ARTHUR WALLACE

BISHOP EDWARD DERUSHA WILMOT JONES

served as the first Director of Evangelism from 1920 to 1924. He pioneered in home missions areas as a bishop. " Perhaps his greatest single contribution as a bishop is the New Goler Metropolitan Church at Winston-Salem, N.C.," a division of the old Goler Memorial Church.

He was, without doubt, a leading religious psychologist and inimitable soul winner. "His gifts and graces made him a versatile character. He was a builder in every sense of the word. His was a burning desire to acquire imposing houses of worship—and also to build the characters of men in his own unique way. The Word of God was both potent and cogent when he preached it. . . . His was a life of aggressiveness and achievement. Despite circumstances, he kept marching forward, never doubting that ultimately God would 'perfect that which concerneth me.' " [77] Bishop Shaw died on the job at Salisbury, was funeralized at the Livingstone College Auditorium in Salisbury, and Metropolitan Church, Birmingham, and was buried at Birmingham, Ala.

41. *EDWARD DERUSHA WILMOT JONES (D.D.):* Born in Washington, D.C., September 11, 1871; Ordained Deacon, October 6, 1891; Elder, October 15, 1893; Consecrated Bishop, May 20, 1924; Died June 16, 1935.

The son of the famous Bishop Singleton T. W. Jones and missionary pioneer, Mary J. Jones, attended the schools at Washington, D.C. and graduated from Livingstone College with high honors. He joined the John Wesley Church in Washington, D.C., and was licensed to preach in 1891. He joined the Western North Carolina Conference at Hickory, and was ordained deacon the same year.

---

77. Colbert, *General Conference Handbook,* (1916) pp. 70-73; *Minutes,* Thirty-Fourth Quadrennial Session, p.420.

BISHOP JOHN
WILLIAM MARTIN

BISHOP WILLIAM
WALTER MATTHEWS

BISHOP CAMERON
CHESTERFIELD ALLEYNE

He pastored Moore's Sanctuary in Charlotte; Maryville, Tenn.; Jacob Street Tabernacle, Louisville; Avery Church, Allegheny, Pa.; Walters Memorial, Chicago; Memorial Church, Rochester, N.Y.; First Church, San Francisco; and Union Wesley Church, Washington, D.C., from which he was elected bishop. "He was distinguished as scholar, preacher, orator, writer, and pastor of an advanced order."

Bishop E. D. W. Jones was a personal friend and admirer of Dr. Mordecai Johnson, first black president of Howard University, who attended and paid high tribute to the bishop at his funeral. His methodical and industrious characteristics come to life in his *Comprehensive Catechism of the A.M.E. Zion Church,* and his sermons and addresses. His powerful personality was indeed a gift of God, which created lasting impressions among the people he served.

Bishop Jones, richly gifted by nature, versatile with his pen, superbly eloquent on the platform and in the pulpit, a prodigy of industry, many-sided, possessing in an unusual degree the rare gift of making and retaining friends; was one of the ablest and most voluminous writers of the church. A few days after closing one of his annual conferences, he received the summons to drop his weapons of warfare and come home, and his militant soul felt the thrill of the dawn of the eternal morning.

His service of triumph was held at Union Wesley Church, Washington, D.C. and he was laid to rest in the city. [78]

42. *WILLIAM JACOB WALLS (D.D., LL.D):* Born at Chimney Rock, Rutherford County, N.C., May 8, 1885; Ordained Deacon, October 20, 1903; Elder, October 16, 1905; Consecrated Bishop, May 20, 1924.

78. Anderson, *op. cit.,* pp. 63-64; *Minutes,* Thirtieth Quadrennial Session, p. 70.

Attended Allen Industrial School of Asheville, N.C.; transferred to Livingstone College, and completed the grammar and normal schools. Received B.A., Livingstone College, 1908, B.D., Hood Theological Seminary, 1913, studied journalism and philosophy at Columbia University, 1921-22, and received his M.A. in Christian Education, University of Chicago, 1941. He was licensed to preach at Hopkins Chapel, Asheville, September, 1899 and joined the Blue Ridge Conference at Johnson City, Tenn., October 6, 1902, and was ordained by Bishop C. R. Harris. Bishop J. W. Smith assisted during the illness of Bishop Harris in the ordination to eldership. He pastored Cedar Grove Circuit, Cleveland, N.C.; Miller's Chapel and Sandy Ridge Circuit in N.C.; Moore's Chapel, Lincolnton, N.C.; Soldier's Memorial, Salisbury, N.C., and Broadway Temple, Louisville, Ky., where he led the congregation in erecting the present edifice in 1915. He was elected editor of the *Star of Zion* in 1920 and served until 1924 when he was elected bishop. After 44 active years in the episcopacy, he was retired in 1968 and commissioned Historiographer by the General Conference, to construct, edit, and publish a comprehensive history of the denomination.

43. JOHN WILLIAM MARTIN (D.D., LLD.):

Born in Russell County, near Lebanon, Va. June 30, 1879; Ordained Deacon, May 21,1905; Elder, September 8, 1907; Consecrated Bishop, May 20, 1924; Died, October 16, 1955.

He had his early training in schools of Johnson City, Tenn., and after finishing Langston High School, he moved on to Lincoln University in Pennsylvania, and earned the A.B. and B.D. degrees. While attending school he joined the Philadelphia and Baltimore Conference, and was ordained both deacon and elder. He pastored Wooderville Circuit on the Washington District, and after completing his education at Lincoln University, he transferred to the Kentucky Conference and was appointed to the pastorate of St. Mark Church, Indianapolis. While serving St. Mark Church, Bishop G. W. Clinton insisted that he become head of Atkinson College in Madisonville, Ky., where he was also teaching; and he remained there for the next 10 years. He was elected secretary of education in 1916 and served in this capacity until he was elevated to the episcopacy.

Bishop Martin was a scholar of marked ability and a profound thinker. He was a philosopher and witty, "whose observations as he traveled throughout the connection as Secretary of Education gave him insights into denominational needs, and made a rich contribution to our Zion. Quite a number of our churches on the Pacific Coast were acquired while he was our first resident bishop in the area. He was a steady, painstaking, ruggedly honest adminstrator." [79] Bishop Martin served as bishop for more than 30 years. "He was a preacher of extraordinary ability, an administrator of great wisdom and courage, and a much beloved servant of the church." Funeral services were held at Greater Walters Church in Chicago, and he was laid to rest at Lincoln Cemetery in that city.

44. CAMERON CHESTERFIELD ALLEYNE (D.D., LL.D.):

Born in Bridgetown, Barbados, British West Indies, September 3, 1880; Ordained Deacon, October 5, 1904; Elder, December 12, 1905; Consecrated Bishop, May 20, 1924; Died, March 24, 1955.

79. J. C. Taylor, "Tribute to the Episcopal Class of 1924," *A.M.E. Zion Quarterly Review*, July 1949, p. 113.

He was educated at Naprima College, Port of Spain, Trinidad, B.W.I., having matriculated there between 1889 and 1903. He came to the United States in 1903 and attended Tuskegee Institute, 1903-1904. He received the honorary M.A. and D.D. from Livingstone College, and LL.D. from Howard University. He pastored Anniston, Ala.; Elmo, Tenn.; John Wesley Church, Washington, D.C.; People's (First Church—now Hood Memorial), Providence, R.I.; Grace Church, Charlotte, N.C.; and St. Catherine, New Rochelle, N.Y. He was elected editor of the *Quarterly Review* in 1916, and served in that capacity until 1924 when he was elevated to the bishopric.

He was a man of rare qualities and much brilliancy of mind; a reliable pastor, keen scholar, industrious disposition and wide-awake preacher. [80] Bishop Alleyne was also a dedicated missionary, particularly to the foreign work, and a noted author. "He was our first resident bishop to Africa, and later served as bishop of South America and Virgin Islands. Returning to America from Africa in 1928, he devoted his thought, energies and skills to expanding our work in the areas he superintended. He did a phenomenal job of expansion." [81] He was one of the most progressive leaders in the history of our Zion, in both church and state affairs. "The visible signs of his stewardship in churches and schools will remind us at home and abroad, of his glowing contribution to our church cause." [82] He passed away in his home city of Philadelphia, and last rites were held at Big Wesley Church, Philadelphia, and St. Catherine Church, New Rochelle. He was laid to rest in Beechwood Cemetery, New Rochelle, N.Y.

45. *WILLIAM WALTER MATTHEWS (D.D.):* Born in Batesville, Miss. October 28, 1871; Ordained Deacon, December 12, 1904; Elder, November 30, 1906; Consecrated Bishop, May 20, 1928; Retired and divested of the Episcopacy, May 12, 1948; Died, March 15, 1962 at Washington, D.C.

He attended school at Branch Normal College, Pine Bluff, Ark., 1890-1900, and New Orleans University, 1898 to 1901. He joined the Arkansas Conference in 1904 and was ordained deacon that year. He pastored Cooper Church, Oakland, Calif.; First Church, San Francisco; Cherry Street Church, Pine Bluff, Ark.; Zion Temple, McCloud, Calif.; and The Old Ship, Montgomery, Ala. He served as Foreign Missions Secretary, and when elected bishop, served as resident bishop to Africa. Bishop Matthews had made noted contributions in the episcopacy; however, he grossly violated the Discipline on rules governing the episcopacy which resulted in his divestiture in a judiciary action taken by the 1948 General Conference. [83]

46. *FREDERICK MILLER JACOBS (D.D., LL.D.):* Born in Camden, S.C., Ordained Deacon, May 24, 1886; Elder, May 20, 1888; Consecrated Bishop, May 20, 1928; Died, December 31, 1931.

Bishop Jacobs attended the normal schools, Jackson College and South Carolina University. His course of education being interrupted, he took private tutoring in the Carleston Military College. He entered Howard University in 1884 and received the A.B. degree in 1888, attended Illinois Wesleyan College in 1896, and received the M.D. degree from Long Island Medical College in 1901. He joined the A.M.E. Zion Church in Charlotte, N.C., in 1882 and was licensed to preach,

80. Anderson, op. cit, p. 133.
81. *A.M.E. Zion Quarterly Review,* July, 1942, p. 113.
82. *Minutes,* Thirty-Fifth Quadrennial Session, p. 41.
83. *Minutes,* Thirty-Third Quadrennial Session, pp. 301-303.

and joined the North Carolina Conference that fall. He transferred to the Philadelphia and Baltimore Conference where he was ordained.

He pastored successfully Baltimore; Harrisburg, Pa.; Chattanooga, Tenn; Hopkins Chapel, Asheville, N.C.; Loguen Temple, Knoxville, Tenn.; returned to Hopkins Chapel for another year; and then to Fleet Street Church, Brooklyn. He was professor of Latin, Greek, literature, and higher mathematics at Greenville College, Greenville, Tenn., 1895. Bishop Jacobs completed a thorough course in medicine and surgery in the New York Medical College, and was one of the most noted physicians of Brooklyn, and well-to-do in real estate and business. He was a powerful preacher, excellent speaker, generous and model pastor. He served as General Secretary-Auditor of the connection from 1918 until he was elected bishop in 1928. "Bishop Jacobs was in every sense, loyal to all the intimate relations of life. He was an ideal husband, father, friend and churchman. Like Abraham, he went where he was called and was faithful in all things. Like Jonathan, he met many a discouraged brother and cheered him, by giving him strength from God. . . . He was a versatile man and in his passing," church and society were keenly conscious of the loss which they had sustained of the minister-physician, friend and counsellor, and prophet of God. [84] He passed away in Brooklyn, and after final rites at Fleet Street Church, he was buried in the borough of Brooklyn.

47. *ELIJAH LOVETTE MADISON (D.D.):* Born at Madison Park, near Montgomery, Ala., May 20, 1876; Ordained Deacon, November 6, 1898; Elder, November 11, 1900; Consecrated Bishop, May 20, 1936; Died, June 26, 1946.

He joined the Western North Carolina Conference at Lincolnton, N.C., in 1898, and entered Livingstone College where he earned his A.B. Degree. He pastored Cedar Grove and Second Creek Circuit, Hopkins Chapel, Asheville; Clinton Chapel, Charlotte; St. Stephens, High Point; Trinity, Greensboro; St. Luke, Wilmington, all in North Carolina, and transferred to the Allegheny Conference and the pastorate of John Wesley Church, Pittsburgh in 1920. His first wife, Julia Moseley Madison of New Bern, N.C., was the second woman graduate of the college department of Livingstone College in 1902, where she won high honors in scholarship and conduct. She was the mother of eight of his nine children, and died in childbirth while he was pastoring Wilmington, N.C. He later married Lucy Coleman, which union produced one child.

At Pittsburgh, "he found a people who 'had a mind to work,' and who already had dreamed dreams and begun plans for a new Zion there." And so, in harmony with them and with the desires of the general church, he led the John Wesley congregation into creating an additional congregation and the construction of Wesley Center Church which stands today as a monument to his memory. "He was elected Financial Secretary in 1932 and to the bishopric in 1936. He was the presiding bishop of the Sixth Episcopal District when he was suddenly stricken. . . . He had a passionate devotion to what he believed to be the right and no influence could divert him from his course once he had chosen it. In his own words, he had 'a covenant with his conscience and with his God,' therefore, he knew no compromise." He passed calmly and peacefully into eternal rest with scarcely a sigh, as though weary of his long suffering. He was funeralized from Wesley Center Church and buried in Pittsburgh. [85]

84. *Minutes,* Twenty-Ninth Quadrennial Session, p. 89.
85. *Minutes,* Thirty-Third Quadrennial Session, p. 309.

BISHOP ELIJAH LOVETTE MADISON

BISHOP FREDERICK MILLER JACOBS   BISHOP JAMES WALTER BROWN

48. *WILLIAM CORNELIUS BROWN:* Born in Chowan County, near Edenton, N.C., June 24, 1877; Ordained Deacon, May 5, 1901; Elder, June 12, 1904; Consecrated Bishop, May 20, 1936; Died, January 2, 1964.

Bishop Brown attended grade schools in his home county, and later moved to Portland, Maine. He attended the Westbrook Seminary there from 1900 to 1904, completing the course while pastoring the Portland Mission. He had started as a lay preacher in Canaan's Temple Church, Chowan County, N.C., and joined the New England Conference in 1901 at Providence, R.I., where he was ordained deacon and later, at Cambridge, elder, by Bishop Hood. He attended Yale University in 1912. He afterwards pastored Creswell Circuit in the Virginia Conference; Kadesh Chapel, Edenton, N.C.; Walters Memorial, Bridgeport, Conn.; Varick Memorial, New Haven, Conn.; John Wesley Church, Washington, D.C., where he led in purchasing the present edifice; and Fleet Street Church, Brooklyn.

His pastorate was eminently successful. He saved the situation in the only black church in Portland, Maine, after it was begun by the presiding elder; he built the Columbia Mission, Columbia, N.C. paid debts and improved situations otherwise. An exegete, seer, keen executive, who labored ardently to give our church its improved efficiency in the pension plan. Bishop Brown was retired in May, 1960. He passed away in his home city of Brooklyn, was funeralized from First Church, Brooklyn and Kadesh Chapel, Edenton, and laid to rest in Edenton, N.C.

49. *JAMES WALTER BROWN (D.D.):* Born, July 19, 1872 at Elizabeth City, N.C., Ordained Deacon, May 17, 1903; Elder, May 21, 1905; Consecrated Bishop, May 20, 1936; died, February 27, 1941.

Bishop Brown received his early training in Elizabeth City and at Shaw University where he earned the A.B. degree in 1893. He taught at the State Normal School, Elizabeth City, from 1893 to 1899. He entered the ministry through the Philadelphia-Baltimore Conference, and pastored Media and South Bethlehem, Pa. after attending Lincoln University where he earned the M.A., and in 1903 the ST.B. degree. In 1905 he transferred to Western New York Conference, becoming the pastor of Memorial Church, Rochester, and was appointed by Bishop Hood to Mother Zion Church in 1913. He was a constructive pastor, deeply imbued with the history of the church. He built the church at Rochester as a memorial to church and race pioneers. He salvaged a critical situation at Mother Zion, which had been wounded by a church split, and practically left them out of doors. He led in purchsaing the church property on 136th Street in which the congregation worshipped until he led them in building the gigantic gothic structure, which stands today as a monument to the glory and honor of God and in memory of J. W. Brown.

He was a silver-tongued preacher, illustrious social thinker, and dynamic scholar. His brief five years in the episcopacy, serving with profound devotion; Africa, South America, and in the United States, ended when he was struck down by an automobile in the vicinity of Mother Zion Church where his funeral services were held, and he was buried in the Mother Zion Cemetery, Cypress Hills, Brooklyn.

50. *WALTER WILLIAM SLADE (D.D.):* Born at Newton, N.C., July 4, 1875; Ordained Deacon, November 10, 1896; Elder, November 13, 1898; Consecrated Bishop, May 14, 1944; Died, May 19, 1963.

He was the son of an outstanding pioneer in the Western North Carolina and Blue Ridge Conferences, Rev. Mayfield Slade. He joined the Blue Ridge Conference, and was ordained deacon his first year. He finished Livingstone College in 1901. He pastored the Lebaum Circuit: Greenville, Tenn. during the time his father was presiding elder of the Greenville District in the Blue Ridge Conference, and transferred to Central and West Central North Carolina, pastoring several points and serving as presiding elder. He then pastored the Wesley Center Church in Pittsburgh, and afterwards was elected Secretary of Evangelism and Financial Secretary of the denomination. He married Miss Mildred Burgen, who passed away in 1927, and in 1931 he married Mrs. Sallie Mae Blake.

Bishop Slade was an ardent evangelistic preacher, financier, and magnetic congenial leader. His episcopal labors were confined principally to North and South Carolina, and he nurtured Clinton Junior College at Rock Hill, S.C. He was retired at the General Conference in May 1960, and passed away early on a Sunday morning. His triumphant service was held at Grace Church, and he was laid to rest in the city of Charlotte, N.C.

51. *BUFORD FRANKLIN GORDON (D.D.):* Born in Pulaski, Tenn., August 24, 1893; Ordained Deacon, June 27, 1920; Elder, June 18, 1922; Consecrated Bishop, May 14, 1944; Died, January 19, 1952.

He received his rudimentary training at home then attended Fisk University where he earned the A.B. Degree in 1917. He studied at Yale University, 1917-18. In 1920 he received his B.D. degree from the University of Chicago. He entered the ministry in 1917, joined the Michigan Conference June 24, 1920, and was ordained deacon the same year. He pastored Branford, Conn., First Church, South Bend, Ind., where he built the church and John Wesley, Akron, Ohio where he also built the church. From the Akron pastorate he became editor of the Church School Literature in 1931 and served productively until elected bishop. Bishop Gordon had also attended the Officers Training School during World War I, 1818-19.

An author, educator, intellectual force, and noble family man, he served his church and race efficiently and faithfully. He passed away in his home city of Charlotte, and was funeralized from Little Rock Church (his home church, Gethsemane, being too small), and was laid to rest in Charlotte, N.C.

BISHOP BUFORD FRANKLIN GORDON

BISHOP WALTER WILLIAM SLADE

BISHOP FRANK WESLEY ALSTORK   BISHOP EDGAR BENTON WATSON

52. *FRANK WESLEY ALSTORK (D.D.):* Born at Coatopa, Ala. June 16, 1885; Ordained Deacon, December 1, 1907; Elder, November 28, 1909; Consecrated Bishop, May 14, 1944; Died, July 5, 1948.

He first joined Big Zion Church, Mobile, then Little Hope Chapel in Mobile, where he was licensed to preach at 20 years of age. He joined the West Alabama Conference, and completed his studies at Talladega College while holding his first pastoral appointment at Talladega, Ala. He then pastored Midland City, Hurtsboro, Ala. St. Mark, St. Louis; Smith Memorial, DuQuoin, Ill; served as presiding elder in the Missouri Conference, then pastored Metropolitan, Birmingham, Union Wesley, Washington, D.C. and Big Wesley, Philadelphia, from which he was elected bishop.

Bishop Alstork was a defender and promoter of education. He labored earnestly in behalf of Lomax-Hannon Junior College, following in the footsteps of his sainted uncle, Bishop John Wesley Alstork. He was a splended preacher, habitual Zionite and loyal active leader in race rights, especially in Alabama. "He was in the forefront of the fight against police brutality and was known to have added greatly in combating this evil." After last rites held at Galbraith Church, Washington, D.C., he was laid to rest in Lincoln Cemetery in the nation's capital. [86]

53. *EDGAR BENTON WATSON (D.D.):* Born in Chatham County, N.C., February 7, 1874; Ordained Deacon, November 24, 1907; Elder, November 21, 1909; Consecrated Bishop, May 14, 1944; Died, January 17, 1951.

Bishop Watson was admitted to the Central North Carolina Conference in 1905, and became a charter member of the West Central North Carolina Conference when it was organized in 1910. He pastored the following churches: Mt. Pleasant Circuit, N.C.; Norwood Station, N.C.; Zion Hill, Concord, N.C.; Trinity, Greensboro, N.C.; Metropolitan, Birmingham; Oak Street, Petersburg;

86. Interview with Mrs. Ellenbelle A. Patton, sister of Bishop Alstork., *Star of Zion,* July 22, 1946, p. 1.

Hood Temple, Richmond; and Metropolitan, Norfolk, Va. In 1911 he was married to Miss Margaret Morrow, who passed away. He later married Miss Mary Jane Hedgepath. Watson graduated from Livingstone College in 1911, and earned the B.D. degree from Hood Theological Seminary in 1915.

He was a man of wide-experience in church matters, and of broad culture. For four years (his first quadrennium as bishop), he served in Africa admirably, presenting a challenging program. He was wise, patient, and diligent in God's business, and demonstrated successful leadership in the episcopacy. His passing was sudden and a distinct loss to Zion Methodism. His last rites were held at Trinity Church, and he was buried in Greensboro, N.C.

54. *JAMES CLAIR TAYLOR (D.D.):* Born at Cambridge, Massachusetts, May 3, 1893; Ordained Deacon, June 16, 1918; Elder, June 20, 1920; Consecrated Bishop, May 16, 1948; Died, July 23, 1954.

Bishop Taylor completed the elementary and high school in Cambridge. He entered the ministry through his native New England Conference, and his first pastorate was Meriden, Conn. He later served churches at Goldsboro, N.C.; Moore's Chapel, Salisbury, N.C.; St. John's, Rutherfordton, N.C.; Memorial, Rochester, N.Y.; Wesley Union, Harrisburg, Pa.; and First Church, Paterson, N.J. He was elected editor of the *Quarterly Review* in 1936, and served in this capacity with extraordinary distinction, until his elevation to the episcopacy. He was married in 1912 to Alma Jackson of Boston and had one son. She later passed away. He married Ann Pate of Goldsboro, N.C. [87]

Bishop Taylor was a well prepared, competent leader of unusual dedication to his ministerial task. During the six years of his episcopacy, he spent time and energy in the furtherance and development of our work in Alabama and Mississippi, and the West Tennessee and Mississippi Conference, where he had an episcopal residence. He passed away quite suddenly at Birmingham, and was funeralized at Old Ship, Montgomery, and laid to rest in that city.

55. *RAYMOND LUTHER JONES (D.D.):* Born in Chattanooga, Tenn. April 7, 1900; Ordained Deacon, November 12, 1922; Elder, November 16, 1924; Consecrated Bishop, May 16, 1948; Died, May 12, 1972.

This son of a faithful A.M.E. Zion minister of the Tennessee Conference received his elementary and normal training in Knoxville, Tenn., and earned his A.B. from Livingstone College and B.D. from Hood Thelogical Seminary. He was converted in 1906 at Loguen Temple, Knoxville, and began to think seriously of the ministry. At the age of 17 he preached his trial sermon in Loguen Temple and joined the Tennessee Conference soon afterward. He successfully pastored Second Creek Circuit near Salisbury, N.C.; Marable Memorial, Kannapolis, N.C.; Grace Church, Charlotte, N.C.; St. Paul, Johnson City, Tenn.; Hopkins Chapel, Asheville, N.C.; and Broadway Temple, Louisville, Ky., from which he was elected bishop, while serving as host pastor of the General Conference.

Bishop Jones had lofty aspirations for the church and labored 24 years in the episcopacy, devoting himself to the high ideals of Christian practice and teaching. His home at Salisbury was a haven for needy students who came from distant lands to attend Livingstone College. He was hospitable, friendly, understanding,

---

87. David H. Bradley, Sr., *History of the A.M.E. Zion Church*, Vol. II, pp. 436-37; *Minutes, Thirty-Sixth Quadrennial Session*, p. 41.

BISHOP RAYMOND
LUTHER JONES

BISHOP JAMES
CLAIR TAYLOR

BISHOP HAMPTON
THOMAS MEDFORD

and deeply sympathetic with problems of others. He was a noble representative of the church in ecumenical, race, and social organizations, nationally and internationally, a beloved servant of God and a dedicated family man. He died at his post on the final day of the 1972 General Conference in Mobile. Funeral services were held at the Varick Auditorium, Livingstone College, in lieu of his home church, Moore's Chapel, and he was buried in Salisbury, N.C.

56. *HAMPTON THOMAS MEDFORD (D.D.):* Born at Marion, N.C., January 29, 1885; Ordained Deacon; November 17, 1907; Elder, November 13, 1910; Consecrated Bishop, May 16, 1948; Died, September 14, 1964.

From a youth he possessed a studious business mind. He joined the Western North Carolina Conference in 1906, when he decided to leave his home town and attend Livingstone College. He earned his A.B. in 1912 and the B.D. from Hood Theological Seminary in 1915. He pastored in Western North Carolina while attending school. His pastorates included the Cherryville Circuit, N.C., China Grove, N.C.; Cleveland Circuit, N.C.; Moore's Chapel, Salisbury, N.C.; Grace Church, Charlotte, N.C.; Jacob Street Tabernacle, Louisville, Ky.; Loguen Temple, Knoxville, Tenn.; and John Wesley Church, Washington, D.C. From this last pastorate he was elected secretary-treasurer of the Department of Foreign Missions, and editor of the *Missionary Seer.* While he was attending Livingstone College he served as editor of *The Piedmont Advocate,* official organ of the Masons.

Bishop Medford was unassuming and quietly aggressive. His style was scholarly yet simple, cautious and positive, well balanced in judgment, and his manner was commanding. He was a skilled executive and a man of the utmost trustworthiness. He served in Africa his first quadrennium in the episcopacy with enterprising skill. He was retired at the General Conference in 1960, and passed away in Washington, D.C. Funeral services were held at John Wesley Church, and he was buried in the city.

BISHOP WILLIAM ANDREW STEWART

BISHOP DANIEL CARLETON POPE

57. *HERBERT BELL SHAW (D.D.):* Born in Wilmington, N.C., February 9, 1908; Ordained Deacon, April, 1928; Elder, November 16, 1930; Consecrated Bishop, May 18, 1952.

He was named for a noteworthy pioneer Zion preacher in the Cape Fear Conference, Rev. Herbert Bell. He received his early training in the public schools of Wilmington and St. Emma's Preparatory School, and later attended Fisk University and Howard University School of Religion. He entered the ministry through the Cape Fear Conference in November, 1927, and afterwards transferred to the Philadelphia and Baltimore Conference where he served as associate pastor of Union Wesley Church in Washington, D.C., and was ordained deacon. He returned to his home conference, and served as pastor from 1920 to 1937 at Bowen's Chapel, St. Andrews, and Price Memorial, in and near Wilmington, N.C.

He then served as presiding elder of the Wilmington District of the Cape Fear Conference from 1937 to 1943 when he was elected secretary-treasurer of the Department of Home Mission, Pension, and Ministerial Relief. He served effectively in this department until his elevation to the bishopric in 1952.

Bishop Shaw is an able executive of business method, industrious and cautious, and a consummate evangelist. He has taken a passionate interest in expanding the borders of the A.M.E. Zion Church into new foreign territories where our people are settled in considerate numbers. He is an impressive representative in several ecumenical organizations.

58. *STEPHEN GILL SPOTTSWOOD (D.D.):* Born at Boston, Mass., July 18, 1897; Ordained Deacon, February 5, 1920; Elder, June 20, 1920; Consecrated Bishop, May 18, 1952.

He earned the B.A. Degree from Albright College, Reading, Pa., in 1917, and Th.B. from Gordon Divinity School in Boston in 1919, and did graduate study at Yale University in 1923 and 1924. He entered the traveling ministry through the New England Conference, in 1919, and was appointed to West Newton and Lowell, Mass. He was ordained deacon by Bishop W. L. Lee and elder by Bishop George W. Clinton. He afterward pastored the Green Memorial Church in Portland, Maine, which remained the only black church since its founding in that city. His other pastorates included Varick Memorial, New Haven, Conn., Goler Memorial, Winston-Salem, N.C.; Jones Tabernacle, Indianapolis; St. Luke, Buffalo; and John Wesley Church, Washington, D.C., from which he was elected bishop. His first quadrennium as bishop he presided in the deep South and Southwest. During this time he was serving as a member of various local branches, on executive committees, and President of the Washington Branch of the NAACP, and labored vividly in the interest of both church and race. He became a member of the National Board of Directors in 1951.

Bishop Spottswood was a noted champion of equality and first-class citizenship throughout his ministerial career, which was prevalent when he was elected to the chairmanship of the Board of Directors of the NAACP in 1961. He is effective and diligent in administrative affairs, entertaining one General Conference as pastor and two as bishop, and serving with tractability as publicity chairman of the Sesqui-Centennial Celebration. He is a dutiful churchman, affectionate family man; hospitable and generous. His son, Rev. Stephen Paul Spottswood, serves as an A.M.E. Zion pastor. He gave 20 years of fervent service in the active episcopacy and was retired at the 1972 General Conference.

59. *WILLIAM ANDREW STEWART (D.D.):* Born in Burntcorn, Alabama, August 20, 1890; Ordained Deacon, November 18, 1917; Elder, November 16, 1919; Consecrated Bishop, May 18, 1952.

A sedulous and painstaking youth, he graduated from Phelps Hall Training School and Tuskegee Institute, and taught school in Macon County and Tuskegee, Ala., for several years, even after he had entered the ministry. He entered the ministry through the South Alabama Conference in 1915, and pastored Pineapple Circuit, River Falls, Ala. He later transferred to the Western North Carolina Conference and pastored People's Choice, Winston-Salem, N.C. and Center Street, Statesville, N.C., while pursuing his studies at Livingstone College and Hood Theological Seminary, where he earned his A.B. and B.D. degrees. He also pastored Hill Street (Varick) Chapel, Asheville, N.C. He afterward pastored Loguen Temple, Knoxville, Tenn., and Old Ship, Montgomery, Ala. He was an adroitly successful pastor, and reached his acme at Union Wesley, Washington, D.C., where he built a grand and glorious church, and was elected to the bishopric from this achievement. While pastoring in Washington, he pursued his studies further at Howard University.

He is a positive leader, serious churchman, and enterprising executive. He also labored in the episcopacy 20 years, from the West Coast to the deep South and Southeast with glowing success, and retired in 1972. He is a methodical thinker, impressive preacher, and a man of deep piety and genuine character.

60. *DANIEL CARLETON POPE (D.D.):* Born at Theodore, Mobile County, Ala., 1887; Ordained Deacon, November 30, 1913; Elder, November 28, 1915; Consecrated Bishop, May 18, 1952; Died, March 4, 1964.

He was educated in the public schools of Mobile County, Tuskegee Institute, and received his A.B. and B.D. at Lincoln University, Pa. He entered the traveling ministry through the Alabama Conference, and pastored Butler Chapel, Tuskegee, Ala. He served as a missionary in Liberia from 1924 to 1930 and returned to America in 1930 because of the illness of his wife, Louise Hudson Pope, who passed away ten years later, November 1940. Upon his return to America he pastored Wesley Union, Harrisburg; Galbraith, Washington, D.C.; Trinity, Southern Pines, N.C.; Evans Metropolitan, Fayetteville, N.C.; and Old Ship, Montgomery, Ala.; prior to his election as secretary-treasurer of Foreign Missions. Upon his election to the bishopric, he was assigned to the African field where he served willingly and venerably for eight years. The following quadrennium he labored in Georgia, South Carolina, and the East Tennessee and Virginia Conference.

Bishop Pope was a devout, sincere and able leader who possessed a passion for all Africa. He was a succinct preacher and speaker, and a brother beloved by all who knew him. He passed away in Bristol, Tenn., and after funeral services at Bristol, his body was carried to Sparta, Ga., (next to his beloved wife), for final rest.

61. *CHARLES EWBANK TUCKER (D.D. LL.D.):* Born in Baltimore, January 12, 1896; Received on credentials; Ordained; Elder, July 2, 1916, Consecrated Bishop, May 13, 1956.

He received his education at Beckford and Smith's College in Jamaica, West Indies graduating in 1913, and completed studies at Lincoln University, Pa., in 1917, and Temple University in 1919. He read law under the Hon. Charles Gogg at Point Pleasant, Va., and began practicing law in Louisville as early as 1929. His father, Rev. W. H. Tucker, was a clergyman of the Jamaica branch of the English Baptist Union. Charles Ewbank, along with D. Grecian-Donowa and C. J. Henderson, also of the Baptist Church, joined the Philadelphia and Baltimore Conference in 1915. He pastored Middletown, Pa.; Delta, Pa.; Salem Church, Williamsport, Pa.; Hillard Chapel, Montgomery, Ala.; Sharon, Miss.; Mt. Zion, Augusta, Ga.; Cornish Temple, Key West, Fla.; and Stoner Memorial, Louisville, Ky. He served as presiding elder in the Philadelphia and Baltimore Conference, 1923-27; and Kentucky Conference, from 1931. He was elected bishop from the presiding eldership of the Indianapolis District, Indiana Conference. While he supervised other areas, much of his 16 active years in the episcopacy was spent in the Delta area of Mississippi and in the West Tennessee and Mississippi Conference. He was retired at the 1972 General Conference.

Bishop Tucker was an aggressive leader in advancing and lending popular prestige to the A.M.E. Zion Church in Mississippi, Tennessee, Alabama, and other Southern states. He is a clergyman of recognized capacity and a highly industrious scholar, coupling the profession of law with his ministry and activity in the political arena.

62. *JOSEPH DIXON CAUTHEN (D.D.):* Born in Kershaw County, S.C., February 21, 1887; Ordained Deacon, November 26, 1916; Elder, November 14, 1920; Consecrated Bishop, May 13, 1956.

He attended Lancaster Normal and Industrial School, Lancaster, S.C.; Clinton Junior College, Rock Hill, S.C.; Livingstone College where he earned his A.B. degree; and Hood Theological Seminary, earning his B.D. degree. He entered the

BISHOP JOSEPH
DIXON CAUTHEN

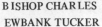
BISHOP CHARLES
EWBANK TUCKER

BISHOP CHARLES
CECIL COLEMAN

ministry and joined the South Carolina Conference in 1912, and was ordained deacon in his home Conference, and elder in the Western North Carolina Conference. He was an effectual pastor at the following churches: Gethsemane, Charlotte, N.C.; State Street, Mobile, Ala.; Varick Chapel, Philadelphia; and Metropolitan, Norfolk, Va. In 1921 he married Miss Ruth Smith of Concord, N.C., who passed away in 1929. In 1940, he married Miss Georgia Little of Mobile, Ala., who passed away in 1964.

Bishop Cauthen is an impressive gospel preacher, orderly and dignified churchman, with a high sense of Christian character. He has an affable personality in which he adds humor and wit, and contains himself at all times in a most graceful and composed manner.

63. *CHARLES CECIL COLEMAN (D.D.):* Born in Key West, Fla., February 22, 1906; Ordained Deacon, November 30, 1924 Elder, November 26, 1926: Consecrated Bishop, May 13, 1956; Died, July 17, 1958.

He had an early indication of becoming a minister, entered Livingstone College in 1925, and earned the A.B. degree with highest honors in 1929. He entered the traveling ministry through the West Central North Carolina Conference and received his first appointment at Cedar Grove Circuit, Gold Hill, N.C. Afterward he pastored St. James, Southport, N.C.; Clinton Chapel, New Bern, N.C.; Metropolitan, Atlanta, Ga.; Monticello, Ark.; St. Paul, Little Rock, Ark.; Clinton Chapel, Union, S.C.; Metropolitan, Clinton, S.C.; and State Street, Mobile, Ala., from which he was elevated to the bishopric.

Bishop Coleman brought to the episcopacy a wide-ranging and resourceful experience of ministering the needs of people. He was assigned to the Southwest territory and set up episcopal residence at Oklahoma City. Again, a man was laboring on the field who had the vision of pervading that territory in a new day of growth for our church, but like Holliday, who had moved into Arkansas with a broad vision 60 years before, his administration ended in two years and two months. God had called him home. He was an effective preacher, creative thinker, and translucent writer. Last rites were held at First Church, Brooklyn, and he was laid to rest in Evergreen Cemetery, Brooklyn.

BISHOP FELIX
SYLVESTER ANDERSON

BISHOP SOLOMON
DORME LARTEY

BISHOP WILLIAM
MILTON SMITH

64. *FELIX SYLVESTER ANDERSON (D.D.):* Born in Wilmington, N.C., October 3, 1893; Ordained Deacon, November 15, 1915; Elder, November 17, 1917; Consecrated Bishop, May 15, 1960.

He had his early religious and educational training in Boston, at Rice and Dwight elementary schools and English High School. He earned his A.B. from Livingstone College in 1920 and studied at Hood Theological Seminary, 1921, and Western Theological Seminary at Pittsburgh, 1922-1924. From Columbus Avenue Church in Boston, under the inspiration of Rev. Green W. Johnson, he was called to preach in 1910, and was licensed in 1912 by Rev. P. A. McCorkle. He then entered the traveling ministry through the Western North Carolina Conference and pastored the following churches: Rocky Creek Circuit, N.C.; Maineville Circuit, N.C.; Cedar Grove, N.C.; First Church, Providence, R.I.; Mt. Washington, Pittsburgh, Pa.; Trimble Chapel, Oakdale, Pa.; Mt. Lebanon, Elizabeth City, N.C.; Kadesh, Edenton, N.C.; Hunter Chapel, Tuscaloosa, Ala.; Shaw Metropolitan, Atlanta, Ga.; Union Chapel, Athens, Ga.; St. Peter's, Southern Pines, N.C.; Big Zion, Mobile, Ala.; and Broadway Temple, Louisville, Ky. While pastoring at Broadway Temple he served three terms, from 1954 to 1960, in the Kentucky Legislature, representing the 42nd District. In 1954 he presented to the Legislature and fought through to victory an immutable desegregation bill.

Bishop Anderson gave 12 years of venerable service in the active episcopacy in the South and in Kentucky. His every personal quality is of the highest grade. His preaching and teaching ministry was a blessing to hundreds. He and his wife produced an admirable family, including an A.M.E. Zion minister, Rev. Herman Anderson. His ministerial career has been far-reaching. He is a representative executive and a man of work and worth. He was retired at the General Conference of 1972.

65. *WILLIAM MILTON SMITH (D.D.):* Born at Stockton, Baldwin County, Ala., December 18, 1915; Ordained Deacon, November 14, 1937; Elder, November 12, 1939; Consecrated Bishop, May 15, 1960.

He completed his normal training at Lomax-Hannon Junior College, and earned the B.S. degree from Alabama State College at Montgomery. He pursued his studies at Tuskegee Institute, Hood Theological Seminary, and Perkins School of Theology at Dallas, Tex. He entered the ministry at an early age and soon joined the South Alabama Conference. All of his pastorates were in the state of Alabama: St. Thomas, Perdita; Zion, Atmore; Zion Star and Zion Fountain, Brewton; Ebenezer, Montgomery; and Big Zion, Mobile, from which he was elected bishop.

Bishop Smith was a highly successful pastor, and always labored in civic and community affairs for the betterment of his people. He has had a variegated task in the episcopacy which began with the assignment of nine mission conferences, including South America and Virgin Islands. He is an earnest evangelistic preacher, and his religious life runs in deep channels of pious thought. He exerts strong force of character, painstaking methods, and constructive leadership, full of plans and good works.

66. *SOLOMON DORME LARTEY (D.D., Litt.D, Ph.D.):* Born, September 12, 1898, at Christiansborg, Accra, Ghana; Ordained Elder, 1940; Consecrated Bishop, May 15, 1960; Died, August 3, 1969.

He received his education from the Presbyterian Mission School in Accra, (the Gold Coast), and ordained a minister in the Presbyterian Church in 1933. He moved to Liberia, and joined the A.M.E. Zion Church in 1939 under Bishop J. W. Brown, and was ordained elder and appointed presiding elder in 1940, and reappointed by Bishop Alleyne after the passing of Bishop Brown. He became the chief representative of the A.M.E. Zion Church in Liberia and supervisor of the Mt. Coffee mission during World War II, at which time he extended the work to Sinoe County. Our work in Liberia had been previously limited to Montserrado County. He was appointed bishop's deputy by Bishop E. B. Watson, and served in the absence of the bishop from the field during the administrations of Bishops Watson, Medford, and Pope. He organized the A.M.E. Zion Church in the capital, Monrovia, and built the Brown Memorial Church and Zion Academy, of which he was pastor and general manager respectively. Upon this record of solid achievement, Bishop Lartey became the first native African consecrated bishop in the A.M.E. Zion Church. He had served as Inspector of Internal Revenue in Liberia and was appointed by President Tubman as postmaster of Monrovia.

Bishop Lartey, a Christian statesman distinguished both in church and state for his ardent advocacy of the highest ideals of freedom and justice, reliable and able, passed away after a brief illness and after funeral services in Monrovia, he was interred at Po River Station, Liberia.

67. *WILLIAM ALEXANDER HILLIARD (D.D.):* Born, Greenville, Tex., September 12, 1904; Ordained Deacon, July 8, 1924; Elder, September 7, 1927; Consecrated Bishop, May 15, 1960.

At an early age his parents moved to Kansas City, Kansas, and then to Des Moines, Iowa where he received his elementary training. He completed High

School in Kansas City, and studied at Western University in Quinders, Kan., and later at Wayne University, Detroit. He entered the traveling ministry through the Missouri Conference in 1922, and pastored the following churches: St. Matthew, Kansas City; Mt. Zion, Argentine, Kan., Metropolitan, Kansas City, Mo.; Metropolitan Church, Chester, S.C.; St. John, Wilson, N.C.; and St. Paul, Detroit, Mich., where he made one congregation into two and led the St. Paul congregation in purchasing the mammoth edifice on Dexter Street.

Bishop Hilliard is an enterprising administrator and an attractive and industrious attendant in the affairs of the church, with exceptional traits of affability and friendliness. He has already served in the episcopacy, the foreign field Africa and the home field, on the West Coast, and South America and Virgin Islands became a part of his district in 1972.

68. *ALFRED GILBERT DUNSTON, JUNIOR (D.D., LL.D.):* Born at Coinjock, N.C., June 25, 1915; Ordained Deacon, June 1, 1937; Elder, June 1, 1938; Consecrated Bishop, May 21, 1964.

He received his elementary and high school training at Elizabeth City, N.C., where he also entered the ministry and preached his trial sermon at Mt. Lebanon Church in 1935. He earned the A.B. degree from Livingstone College, and furthered his studies at Hood Thelogical Seminary and Drew University. He joined the Western North Carolina Conference in 1936, and began his pastorate at Mt. Sinai, Advance, N.C. He subsequently pastored Wallace Temple, Bayonne, N.J.; Price Memorial, Atlantic City, N.J.; Wallace Chapel, Summit, N.J.; Loguen Temple, Knoxville, Tenn.; Big Wesley, Philadelphia; and Mother Zion Church, New York. He was married to Miss Permilla R. Flack in 1940. He served in the 92nd Infantry Division as Chaplain in World War II, and won a citation for meritorious service in support of combat troops.

Bishop Dunston has unusual powers of expression and is capable of attracting considerable support of a cause that he espouses. He was assigned to Nigeria upon his election, and served the country during the blighting Civil War. He is a rhetorical poetic stylist in the pulpit, a lucid, impressive thinker and studious administrator.

69. *CHARLES HERBERT FOGGIE (D.D.):* Born at Sumter, S.C., August 4, 1912; Ordained Deacon, June 10, 1934; Elder, June 14, 1936; Consecrated Bishop, May 15, 1968.

He was raised in Boston, Mass., and became affiliated with the Columbus Avenue Church in his early youth. He joined the traveling ministry through the New England Conference in 1932. He earned his A.B. degree from Livingstone College in 1936, A.M. from Boston University in 1938, S.T.B. in 1939 and S.T.M. in 1944 from Boston University School of Theology. He pastored the Second Church (Wadsworth Street). Providence, R.I.; Rush Church, Cambridge, Mass.; and Wesley Center, Pittsburgh, from which he was elected to the episcopacy.

Bishop Foggie is a polished systematic scholarly churchman of deep humility. He is a pulpit orator and has qualities of a litterateur. He is a member of the University of Pittsburgh Fellowship, and a prominent leader of church and race.

BISHOP WILLIAM
ALEXANDER HILLIARD

BISHOP ALFRED
GILBERT DUNSTON, JR.

BISHOP CHARLES
HERBERT FOGGIE

BISHOP JAMES
CLINTON HOGGARD, SR.

70. *JAMES CLINTON HOGGARD, SENIOR:* Born in Jersey City, N.J., August 9, 1916; Ordained Deacon, November 4, 1940; Elder, June 21, 1942; Consecrated Bishop, May 12, 1972.

This son of Rev. Jeremiah M. Hoggard of the A.M.E. Zion Church, inspired by both parents, entered the ministry, and joined the New York Conference in June 1939. He earned his A.B. degree from Rutgers University in 1939 and B.D. from Union Theological Seminary in 1942. He pastored St. Francis Church, Mt. Kisco, N.Y.; Institutional Church, Yonkers, N.Y.; and Little Rock Church, Charlotte, N.C.; and was elected in 1952, secretary-treasurer of the Department of Foreign Missions. After 20 years of faithful service in this department, he was elevated to the bishopric.

Bishop Hoggard is a thoroughly studious generalizing thinker, engaging preacher, and able orator. He is perseveringly active in the cause of church progress with ecumenical zeal.

BISHOP JAMES WESLEY WACTOR   BISHOP CLINTON REUBEN COLEMAN

71. *JAMES WESLEY WACTOR (D.D):* Born, Hoke County, N.C., September 13, 1908; Ordained Deacon, July 30, 1933; Elder, November 17, 1935; Consecrated Bishop, May 12, 1972.

He entered the ministry through his home church, Fair Promise, Sanford, N.C. and later pastored in the Western North Carolina Conference which he joined in 1931, while he studied at Livingstone College where he earned the A.B. degree in 1935. He continued his studies at Hood Theological Seminary, Union Theological Seminary in New York, and Harvard University School for Chaplains. He had an interesting career of success and building in the pastorate as follows: Maineville Circuit near Salisbury, N.C.; White Rock, Granite Quarry and New Hope, Salisbury, N.C.; Young's Chapel, Morristown, Tenn.; Kesler Temple, Henderson, N.C.; Mattocks Memorial, Fayetteville, N.C.; St. James, Red Springs, N.C.; Barry Ave., Mamaroneck, N.Y.; Hood Memorial, New York City, Big Zion, Mobile; and Metropolitan, Birmingham from which he was elected bishop. He was a dutiful patriotic chaplain during World War II. During the post-war period, his overseas tours of duty included North Africa, Italy, France, and Germany. He and his wife labored in occupied Europe where he worked and became a member of the Board of Directors of the German Youth Activities Program for Kaiser Wilhelm, Mannheim, Germany. [88] He had a commendable and steadily progressive pastorate.

Bishop Wactor is a veteran administrator, genial and well-liked, and is making significant progress as a bishop.

72. *CLINTON REUBEN COLEMAN (D.D.):* Born in Coden, Ala., December 4, 1916; Ordained Deacon, November 28, 1937; Elder, February 10, 1938; Consecrated Bishop, May 12, 1972.

He made his way to North Carolina to attend Livingstone College, and entered the traveling ministry through the West Central North Carolina Conference in 1936. His first pastorate while in school was Parker's Chapel Circuit, Concord, N.C. He earned the A.B. degree at Livingstone College in 1939, and attended Hood Theological Seminary, earning the B.D. degree at Howard University School of Religion in 1971. He also pastored Union Chapel, Albermarle, N.C.; St. Stephen, Hamlet, N.C.; Evans Metropolitan, Fayetteville,

88. Ethel L. Williams, *Biographical Dictionary of Negro Ministers,* p. 519.

BISHOP ARTHUR MARSHALL, JR.   BISHOP JOHN HENRY MILLER, SR.

N.C.; and Pennsylvania Avenue, Baltimore, Md., from which pastorate he was elected bishop. Perennial success attended his ministry, and he became a well-known civic and community leader in the cities and town where he pastored.

Bishop Coleman is thoroughly interested in the betterment of society, race progress, and the welfare of the needy people. Among his family of four children, (two sons), he and his wife have produced one young rising minister of the church, Rev. Gordon Ray Coleman, and the youngest son who is attending Livingstone College, has strong inclination of following in the footsteps of his father and older brother. The prospects for this impressive, convincing, and somewhat humorous preacher-orator are bright for a glorious record of episcopal achievement.

73. *ARTHUR MARSHALL, JUNIOR (D.D.):* Born at High Point, N.C., March 2, 1914; Ordained Deacon, November 25, 1934; Elder, November 15, 1936; Consecrated Bishop, May 12, 1972.

He began his early ministry at his home church, St. Stephen, High Point, and joined the West Central North Carolina Conference in 1933. He pastored St. Philip Circuit in Greensboro, N.C., and in 1938 became dean at Walters-Southland Institute at Lexa, Ark., and served as presiding elder of the Pine Bluff District, Arkansas Conference. Prior to this he had earned his B.A. degree at Livingstone College in 1937; S.T.B. from Boston University in 1941 and M.A. also from Boston University, while pastoring in the New England Conference, at Wadsworth Street, Providence, R.I. He also pastored Ansonia, Conn.; Peoples Church, Syracuse, N.Y.; John Wesley, Pittsburgh; and Washington Metropolitan in St. Louis, and was elected bishop from the St. Louis pastorate. [89]

Bishop Marshall is a brilliant pulpit orator and hard student, gifted with vivid eloquence. His record in administrative affairs gives radiant hope of constructive episcopal leadership.

74. *JOHN HENRY MILLER, SENIOR, (D.D.):* Born in Ridgeway, S.C., December 3, 1917; Ordained Deacon, November 27, 1939; Elder, December 3, 1940; Consecrated Bishop, May 12, 1972.

He received his elementary training in his hometown, and had early aspirations to become a minister. He came to Livingstone College and while

89. *Ibid.,* pp. 345-46.

BISHOP RUBEN LEE SPEAKS

BISHOP GEORGE JUNIUS LEAKE, III

preparing himself for the larger service, he joined the West Central North Carolina Conference, November 30, 1938. He earned the A.B. degree from Livingstone College, and the B.D. degree from Hood Theological Seminary with highest honors. He pastored the following churches: Peoples Church, Syracuse, N.Y.; Seventh Street, Troy, N.Y.; New Britain, Conn.; Mt. Olive, Waterbury, Conn.; Goler Metropolitan, Winston-Salem, N.C.; and Broadway Temple, Louisville, Ky. From this pastorate he was elevated to the episcopacy.

Bishop Miller, modern-minded theologian and man of conviction, was an assiduous pastor. His diversified activity in religious and social concerns destines him to be a useful leader.

75. *GEORGE JUNIUS LEAKE, III (D.D.):* Born in Wilson, N.C., November 21, 1929; Ordained Deacon, November, 1951; Ordained Elder, November 15, 1953; Consecrated Bishop, May 12, 1972.

He entered the traveling ministry in 1950, came to Salisbury in quest of greater preparation, and finished Livingstone College in 1957. He earned the B.D. degree from Hood Theological Seminary, in 1960. His pastorate started while in school, and included the following churches: Shelby, N.C.; Pleasant Ridge, Gastonia, N.C.; Durham Memorial, Buffalo, N.Y.; and Little Rock Church, Charlotte, N.C.; from which pastorate he was elected bishop.

Bishop Leake, the ninth youngest bishop in the history of our church, was a constructive pastor and leader in community and race affairs. He was one of the freedom riders in the turbulent era of our race history in this country just before the centennial of Emancipation. He is a talented orator and gifted in handling situations.

76. *RUBEN LEE SPEAKS (D.D.):* Born at Lake Providence, La., January 8, 1920; Received on Credentials, May 20, 1946; ordained Elder, June 8, 1947; Consecrated Bishop, May 12, 1972.

He received his early training in his hometown, and earned his A.B. degree from Drake University, Des Moines, Iowa, in 1946; the B.D. degree from Drew University, 1949; S.T.M. at Temple University, Philadelphia, 1952, and pursued his studies at Duke University at Durham, N.C. He entered the traveling ministry of Zion through the New Jersey Conference. He pastored the following churches: St. Thomas, Sommerville, N.J.; Wallace Chapel, Summit, N.J.; Varick Chapel, Philadelphia; St. Mark, Durham, N.C., and First Church, Brooklyn, N.Y. [90] From this pastorate he was elected bishop. He gave creditable service as a teacher of Hood Theological Seminary while pastoring at Durham.

Bishop Speaks is a scholarly pulpiteer and absorbing leader. He has a vision and zeal to make a decidedly improved situation in the field to which he was assigned by the General Conference; Africa. His ability and experience will be in his favor in new accomplishments in a new day of progress of the Fatherland.

90. *Ibid.,* p. 479.

For the bishops' wives, (vice-presidents and missionary supervisors), see Chapter 26; unless otherwise mentioned in this chapter.

Record of birth, ordination and consecration of bishops 1-24 procured from J. Harvey Anderson, *A.M.E. Zion Handbook,* 1895, p. 35. Information for bishops 1-49, from Samuel Madison Dudley, *Handbook of the A.M.E. Zion Church,* p. 147.

HISTORIC LANDMARKS

North Carolina State Highway Markers
prompted by the late Rev. Lafayette Williams

B 44

ANDREW CARTWRIGHT

Agent of the American
Colonization Society in
Liberia, founded the
A.M.E. Zion churches in
Albemarle area. His first
church, 1865, near here.

Manteo, N.C.

Highway 17
Elizabeth City, N.C.

A 61

JOSEPH C. PRICE
(1854-1893)

Negro orator and teacher.
A founder and president
of Livingstone College.
Born in Elizabeth City.
House was 2 miles S.

C 33

JAMES WALKER HOOD

Asst. Superintendent Pub-
lic Instruction, 1868-70; a
founder Livingstone Col-
lege, 1885; Bishop A.M.E.
Zion Church; founded St.
Peters, 1864. One blk. N.

Highway 17
New Bern, N.C.

CHAPTER 35

THE GENERAL CONFERENCES

The lawmaking body of Zion Methodism meets every four years. The bishops preside in rotation and the delegates elect bishops and general officers of the denomination and promote the necessary legislation for the progress of the church. The African Methodist Episcopal Zion Church has held thirty-nine general conferences in its 176 years history, to wit:

		Date	Days in Session
FIRST:	ZION CHURCH, NEW YORK CITY Presiding Officer:—James Varick Host Pastor—Abraham Thompson	July 10, 1820	6
SECOND:	ZION CHURCH, NEW YORK CITY Host Bishop—James Varick Host Pastor—Leven Smith	July 15, 1824	6
THIRD:	ZION CHURCH, NEW YORK CITY Presiding Officer, Christopher Rush Host Pastor—James Smith	May 15, 1828	6
FOURTH:	ZION CHURCH, NEW YORK CITY Host Bishop—Christopher Rush Host Pastor—Peter Vanhas	May 19, 1832	6
FIFTH:	ZION CHURCH, NEW YORK CITY Host Bishop—Christopher Rush Host Pastor—Peter Vanhas	May 14, 1836	6
SIXTH:	ASBURY CHURCH, NEW YORK CITY Host Bishop—Christopher Rush Host Pastor—Timothy Eato	May 28, 1840	3
SEVENTH:	ZION CHURCH, NEW YORK CITY Host Bishop—Christopher Rush Host Pastor—William H. Bishop	May 18, 1844	6
EIGHTH:	ZION CHURCH, NEW YORK CITY Host Bishop—Christopher Rush Host Pastor—John P. Thompson	May 29, 1848	6

		Date	Days in Session
NINTH:	WESLEY CHURCH, PHILA-DELPHIA Host Bishop—Christopher Rush Host Pastor—Jacob Trusty	May 26, 1852	20
TENTH:	ZION CHURCH, NEW YORK CITY Host Bishop—James Simmons Host Pastor—Dempsey Kennedy	June 26, 1856	15
ELEVENTH:	WESLEY CHURCH, PHILA-DELPHIA Host Bishop—William H. Bishop Host Pastor—Singleton T. Jones	May 30, 1860	12
TWELFTH:	WESLEY CHURCH, PHILA-DELPHIA Host Bishop—William H. Bishop Host Pastor—John A. Williams	May 25, 1864	25
THIRTEENTH:	WESLEY ZION (METROPOLITAN), WASHINGTON, D. C. Host Bishop—Samson D. Talbot Host Pastor—John Tappan	May 6, 1868	20
FOURTEENTH:	CLINTON CHAPEL, CHARLOTTE, N. C. Host Bishop—John D. Brooks Host Pastor—William J. Moore	June 19, 1872	14
FIFTEENTH:	FIFTEENTH STREET CHURCH (HUGHLETT TEMPLE), LOUISVILLE, KENTUCKY Host Bishop—Singleton T. Jones Host Presiding Elder—E. H. Curry Host Pastor—Jehu Holliday	June 1, 1876	17
SIXTEENTH:	CLINTON CHAPEL (The Old Ship) MONTGOMERY, ALA. Host Bishop—Joseph P. Thompson Presiding Elder—Wilbur G. Strong Pastor—Allen Hannon	May 5, 1880	18
SEVENTEENTH:	MOTHER ZION CHURCH, NEW YORK CITY Host Bishop—Singleton T. Jones Presidng Elder—Abram Anderson Pastor—R. H. G. Dyson	May 7, 1884	25
EIGHTEENTH:	ST. PETER'S, NEW BERN, N. C. Host Bishop—Joseph P. Thompson Presiding Elder—Abram W. Allison Pastor—C. H. Smith	May 2, 1888	18

| NINETEENTH: | JOHN WESLEY CHURCH, PITTSBURGH | May 4, 1892 | 21 |

NINETEENTH: JOHN WESLEY CHURCH,   May 4, 1892   21
PITTSBURGH
Host Bishop—Singleton T. Jones
  (deceased) James W. Hood
Presiding Elder—Jehu Holliday
Pastor—George W. Clinton

TWENTIETH: STATE STREET CHURCH,   May 6, 1896   20
MOBILE   ALA.
Host Bishop—Charles C. Pettey
Presiding Elder—Wilbur G. Strong
Pastor—P. J. McEntosh

TWENTY-FIRST: METROPOLITAN WESLEY   May 2, 1900   23
CHURCH, WASHINGTON, D. C.
Host Bishop—Charles C. Pettey
Presiding Elder—W. H. Snowden
Pastor—P. J. McEntosh

TWENTY-SECOND: WASHINGTON MEMORIAL   May 4, 1904   15
CHURCH, ST. LOUIS
Host Bishop—Alexander Walters
Presiding Elder—Jesse B. Colbert
Pastor—E. D. W. Jones

TWENTY-THIRD: BIG WESLEY, PHILADELPHIA   May 6, 1908   16
Host Bishop—George W. Clinton
Presiding Elder—E. H. Curry
Pastor—R. A. Morrissey

TWENTY-FOURTH: CLINTON CHAPEL, CHARLOTTE   May 1, 1912   22
Host Bishop—George W. Clinton
Presiding Elder—S. D. Watkins
Pastor—P. A. McCorkle

TWENTY-FIFTH: BROADWAY TEMPLE,   May 3, 1916   15
LOUISVILLE
Host Bishop—Josiah S. Caldwell
Presiding Elder—R. B. Hendricks
Pastor—William J. Walls

TWENTY-SIXTH: LOGUEN TEMPLE, KNOXVILLE   May 5, 1920   15
Host Bishop—George C. Clement
Presiding Elder—W. H. Mitchell
Pastor—J. L. Black

TWENTY-SEVENTH: JONES TABERNACLE,   May 5, 1924   23
INDIANAPOLIS
Host Bishop—Paris A. Wallace
Presiding Elder—L. D. Davis
Pastor—S. D. Davis

		Date	Days in Session
TWENTY-EIGHTH:	WASHINGTON METROPOLITAN CHURCH, ST. LOUIS Host Bishop—John W. Wood Presiding Elder—S. D. Davis Pastor—H. H. Jackson	May 2, 1928	20
TWENTY-NINTH:	WESLEY CENTER CHURCH, PITTSBURGH Host Bishop—Paris A. Wallace Presiding Elder—D. H. Thomas Pastor—Elijah L. Madison	May 4, 1932	14
THIRTIETH:	TRINITY CHURCH, GREENS-BORO, N. C. Host Bishop—W. W. Matthews Presiding Elder—T. J. Houston Pastor—William F. Witherspoon	May 6, 1936	15
THIRTY-FIRST:	JOHN WESLEY, WASHINGTON, D. C. Host Bishop—C. C. Alleyne Presiding Elder—A. A. Crooke Pastor—Stephen G. Spottswood	May 1, 1940	16
THIRTY-SECOND:	ST. PAUL CHURCH, DETROIT Host Bishop—John W. Martin Presiding Elder—Fred D. Porter Pastor—Lott P. Powell	May 3, 1944	13
THIRTY-THIRD:	BROADWAY TEMPLE, LOUIS-VILLE Host Bishop—William C. Brown Presiding Elder—B. N. Henningham Pastor—Raymond L. Jones	May 5, 1948	16
THIRTY-FOURTH:	FIRST CHURCH, BROOKLYN Host Bishop—William J. Walls Presiding Elder—J. H. Tucker Pastor—William Orlando Carrington	May 7, 1952	15
THIRTY-FIFTH:	WESLEY CENTER CHURCH PITTSBURGH Host Bishop—William C. Brown Presiding Elder—Alexander L. Pierce Pastor—Charles H. Foggie	May 2, 1956	15
THIRTY-SIXTH:	ST. LUKE CHURCH, BUFFALO, N. Y. Host Bishop—William J. Walls Presiding Elder—Arthur E. May Pastor—Hunter B. Bess	May 4, 1960	15

THIRTY-SEVENTH:	JONES TABERNACLE, INDIANAPOLIS	May 6, 1964	15
	Host Bishop—Stephen G. Spottswood		
	Presiding Elder—J. Humphrey Lee		
	Pastor—I. Benjamin Pierce		
THIRTY-EIGHTH:	ST. PAUL CHURCH, DETROIT	May 1, 1968	15
	Host Bishop—Stephen G. Spottswood		
	Presiding Elder—William M. Poe		
	Pastor—William C. Ardrey		
THIRTY-NINTH:	BIG ZION CHURCH, MOBILE	May 3, 1972	10
	Host Bishop—William M. Smith		
	Presiding Elder—Leon W. Watts, Sr.		
	Pastor—Marshall H. Strickland		

There were eight delegates present at the first General Conference. The official roll of delegates now numbers more than five hundred.

APPENDIX

FREDERICK DOUGLASS—One of His Last Significant Letters

LETTER FROM THE LATE HON. FREDERICK DOUGLASS.

A BEAUTIFUL TRIBUTE AND PARTING FAREWELL—A SENSE OF HUMOR RADIATE HIS DELIVERANCE

Washington, D. C.,
December 17, '94

My dear John C. Dancy:

I have just laid down your A.M.E. Zion QUARTERLY for the month of December, and cannot, with any sort of justice to myself or to you or to Bishop Hood, allow the incident to pass without some feeble expression of the happiness I felt while perusing its well filled pages. I can do but little reading or writing now and my reading is mostly confined to the magazines and papers by colored individuals and associations, and I have read none with more interest than the monthly of which you are the honored editor, but I did not set out to say so much of this. The fact is, however, that some people cannot talk about any thing without talking about everything, including themselves, and this, perhaps, is my case. Well, my honored brother, what I want to say in this letter is that I set a very high value upon the able paper giving a history of Negro education in North Carolina, contributed to the pages of your magazine by Bishop J. W. Hood, D. D., LL. D. That paper is worth the price of your Zion QUARTERLY for more than one year. I have read much on the subject of the progress of education amongst our people, but I have seen no such succinct, calm, quiet, and candid statement, one giving credit to whom credit is due, and honor to whom honor in any of our race papers or periodicals to match the one now before me. The Rev. Bishop has given us this history happily free from all attempts at fine writing. He is too great to attempt anything like that. The paper is edifying as well as cheering. It contains just the information which both the country and ourselves need. It will help us in the formation of any intelligent judgment of what may be the future of our people.

If such things can be done in North Carolina, the same can be done in other states. It would be greatly to the advantage of our cause if we could have some such history of the rise and progress of Negro education in each of the other late slave states. Of course, we cannot hope to find a Bishop Hood in each of those states. There are far too few of his variety in any of the states, North or South. He evidently possesses high intelligence, remarkable self poise, elevation and dignity of thought. These combined with his earnestness of purpose and signleness of aim make him preeminently a leader. He has traced with painstaking fidelity and research the rise and progress of Negro education in North Carolina. He made no account of the political opinions of men from whom we have derived any aid in this important department of our progress. Few writers, I apprehend, can match him in the possession of judical candor and calm impartiality. It is not my purpose to eulogize Bishop Hood. He needs no eulogy from me. His works here and elsewhere speak for him. You may have seen long ago that I am not much of a hand for praising men while they are alive, and I am commending Bishop Hood now more for the sake of his example to others than for any purpose of giving special pleasure to him. I am glad to see that he writes in plain English, so that a child can understand him. There are no labyrinthian mazes or metaphorical confusions in his composition. He has something to say, and says it. In this he is entirely unlike some of our young fledglings, whose delight seems to be to display their linguistical knowledge, rather than the knowledge of the subjects upon which they write. Their writings are a good deal like my penmanship which, at times, I am not able to understand myself. Many men of moderate intelligence can understand a learned professor more readily than they can understand a student. The words of the latter are bigger than those of the former.

Long ago I remarked the intelligence of colored men coming from North Carolina, and I desired much to know the secret of their intelligence. This, Bishop Hood, in his article, has divested of mystery. I am not sure, however, that he hasn't given a higher claim to the Negroes in North Carolina to intelligence, and especially in comparison with those of other states, than they deserve. I am somewhat afraid that he forgot in his paper the existence of the state of Maryland. He should not forget that one Henry Highland Garnett; one Samuel Ringgold Ward; one J. W. Pennington; one Bishop Wayman, and I was going to say, if I dared, one Frederick Douglass, came from the state of Maryland.

I have been writing of late somewhat of my thoughts and recollections of slavery. Old men, you know, are much in the habit, not only of talking about themselves, but of talking about the past. Things which occurred yesterday fade and vanish from their minds very quickly, but incidents of their childhood and youth follow them to the verge of the grave. It is well. The child is father to the man; the present stands upon the shoulders of the past. Institutions, like individuals, have the power of transmission. Slavery had that power in large measure, and I am inclined to think it has bequeathed some of its worst habits to the present generation.

I have heard much, and the country has heard much, of what is popularly called the "New South." Please tell me if you have seen any such south in your travels. I fear that the New South is but a slightly revised edition of the Old South. It is said at a town meeting in some remote part a series of resolutions were adopted to build a new jail. The first resolution was,

"Resolved, That we will build a new jail.

"Resolved, 2nd, That we will build it out of material of the old one.

"Resolved, 3rd, That the new jail shall stand on the site of the old jail, and the prisoners shall remain in the old jail until the new jail is built."

I think there is some resemblance to this in the so-called New South, and shall continue to think so until I hear less of lynch law and lawless violence in general in that section.

Do you know, my dear Sir, I am often blamed for not going South, and many even think that I am afraid to do so. This certainly is not the case. I have visited many places in southern states, and I would gladly visit more of them, but the boys must permit me to grow old. They should not expect me, after more than fifty years of travel, to keep up my journeying as I once did. They write me from all parts of the South to come and visit places a thousand miles from Washington, and can hardly understand why I do not. I have no prejudice against the South. I wish I could visit every section of it. But to do so requires more time, more money, more strength than I can wisely expend in that way. All that my dear southern brethren should require of me at my time of life is to keep at work on such lines as I can, and which, in my judgment, is the best disposition I can make of my remaining resources. No day finds me entirely idle. My pen is not still and my voice is not silent. Wherever a word can be written or otherwise uttered in our cause I am ready to supply pen and voice. I want you to say to such friends as you have at the South that it is useless to send letters requesting a visit from me. Some such word will save me the trouble of writing letters, and save those who request them the pain of disappointment.

I have found my limits, and my friends in the South have a right to know this fact. I am, dear friend,

Very truly yours,

Frederick Douglass [1]

[1]*A.M.E. Zion Quarterly Review*, April 1895, pp. 59-62.

BIBLIOGRAPHY

1. Reference Works
2. General Bibliography
3. Catechisms, Discipline and Hymnbooks
4. Manuscripts and Unpublished Material
5. Published Minutes and Official Proceedings
6. Newspaper Articles
7. New York City Directories
8. Periodicals
9. Constitutions, Reports and other Published works

*Source widely used but not cited in this work

1. Reference Works:

Adams, James Truslow, ed., *Dictionary of American History* (Vol. V). New York: Charles Scribner & Sons, 2nd ed., 1940.
*Burr, Nelson R., *A Critical Bibliography of Religion in America*. Princeton, N.J.: Princeton University Press, 1961.
Cornish, George A., ed., *Encyclopedia International.* 20 Vols., New York: Grolier Publishers, 1963-64.
Ebony Pictorial History. Introduction by Lerone Bennett, Jr., 3 Vols., Chicago: Johnson Publishing Company, Inc., 1971.
Encyclopedia Britannica, 14th ed. (Vol XIII) 24 Vols. London: The Encyclopedia Britannica, 1929.
Fleming, G. James and Burckel, Christian E., *Who's Who in Colored America*. Yonkers, N.Y.: Christian E. Burckel Associates, 1950.
Hyamson, Albert Montefiore, *A Dictionary of Universal Biography of All Ages and of All People*. London: Routledge & Kegan Paul Ltd., Rev. Ed., 1951.
Long, Luman H., ed., *The World Almanac and Book of Facts*. New York: The New York News, 1969.
Malone, Dumas, ed. *Dictionary of American Biography.* _____ Vols., New York: Charles Scribner, 1936.
Moritz, Charles, ed. *Current Biography Yearbook.* 1970. New York: The H. W. Wilson Co. 1970.
Nault, William H., ed. Dir. *The World Book* (1970). Chicago, London, et. Field Enterprises Education Corp., 1971.
New York Genealogical and Biographical Record. Vol. VIII, New York: Published by the New York Genealogical and Biographical Society, 1877.
*Porter, Dorothy Burnett. "Early American Negro Writings: A Bibliographical Study," *Papers of the Bibliographical Society of America*. Vol. 39 (Third Quarter, 1945).
*Rountree, Louise M., *An Index to Biographical Sketches and Publications of the Bishops of the A.M.E. Zion Church*, Salisbury, N.C.: Copyright by Louise M. Rountree, 1963.
Thomas, Jacob. *Catalogue of the Publications of the African Methodist Episcopal Zion Book Concern*. New York: 1882.
Who Was Who in America, Chicago: The A. N. Marquis Company, rev. ed. 1967.
Who's Who in America (Various Editions).
Who's Who in American History, (16-7-1896), 1963.
Williams, Ethel L. *Biographical Dictionary of Negro Ministers*, Metuchen, New Jersey: The Scarecrow Press, Inc., 1970.
Wilson, James Grant and Fiske, John, ed. *Appelton's Cyclopedia of American Biography*, Vols. V & VI, New York: D Appleton & Co., 1889.
Yenser, Thomas, ed., *Who's Who in Colored America*, 4th Ed. Brooklyn: Thomas Yenser, 1933, 1937.

2. General Bibliography:

Allen, Richard, *The Life Experience and Gospel Labors of the Rt. Rev. Richard Allen, Written by Himself.* Philadelphia: The A.M.E. Book Concern, 1887.

Alleyne, Cameron C., *Gold Coast at a Glance.* U.S.A.: Cameron C. Alleyne, 1931.

Alstork, Willie G., *A.M.E. Zion Handbook.* 1956-1960. Washington, D.C.: 1960.

Anderson, J. Harvey, *Biographical Souvenir Volume of the Twenty-Third Quadrennial Session of the General Conference of the African Methodist Episcopal Zion Church.* Published by the author, 1908.

_____, *The Official Directory of the African Methodist Episcopal Zion Church in America*, New York: A.M.E. Zion Book Concern, 1895.

Asbury, Francis. *The Journal and Letters of Francis Asbury*, ed. Elmer T. Clark, J. Manning Potts, and Jacob S. Payton. 3 vols. Nashville: Abingdon Press, 1958.

Atkins, Simon G. and Wallace, Thomas W., *The Twenty-Fifth Annual Commencement and Quarto-Centennial of Livingstone College.* 1907. Salisbury, N.C.: Livingstone Press, 1910.

Atkinson, John, *The Beginning of the Wesleyan Movement in America.* New York: Hunt & Eaton, Cincinnati: Cranston & Curtis, 1896.

_____, *Memorials of Methodism in New Jersey.* Philadelphia: Perkinpine & Higgins, 1860.

Bardolph, Richard, *The Negro Vanguard.* New York: Vintage Books (Random House), 1959.

Barstow, Robbins, W. Chmn., ed., comm. *Christian Faith in Action—The Constituting Convention Of The National Council Of Churches Of Christ In The U.S.A.* Published by the Central Department of Publication and Distribution, National Council of Churches of Christ in the United States of America, 1951.

Bell, George A. K., Bishop of Chichester, *The Kingship of Christ.* Penguin Books Ltd., Hammondsworth, Middlesex, Great Britain: The Campfield Press, 1954.

Bennett, Lerone, Jr., *Before the Mayflower.* Chicago: Johnson Publishing Company, Inc., 1961.

Bergman, Peter M., *The Chronological History of the Negro in America.* New York: Harper and Row, 1969.

Blyden, Edward W., *Christianity, Islam and the Negro Race.* London: W. B. Whittingham & Co., 1888.

Bradford, Sarah H., *Harriet the Moses of Her People.* New York: George R. Lockwood & Son, 1886.

Bradley, David Henry, Sr., *A History of the A.M.E. Zion Church.* 2 Vols. Nashville: The Parthenon Press, 1956 & 1971.

Brown, Henry Collins, ed., *Valentine's Manual of Old New York.* New York: Valentine's Manual Inc., Baker & Taylor, 1924.

Bucke, Emory Stevens, gen. ed., *The History of American Methodism*, 3 Vols. Nashville: Abingdon Press, 1964.

Buckingham, James S., *America, Historical, Statistic and Descriptive.* 2 Vols. London and Paris: Fisher, Son and Co., 1841.

Buckley, James M., *A History of Methodist in the United States—American Church Series.* New York: The Christian Literature Co., 1896.

Caldwell, A. B. *History of the American Negro*, North Carolina Edition. Vol. IV. Atlanta, Georgia: A. B. Caldwell Publishing Co., 1921.

Coker, Daniel, *A Dialogue Between a Virginian and an African Minister.* Baltimore: Printed by Benjamin Edes for Joseph James, 1810.

Colbert, Jesse B., *General Conference Handbook, 25th Quadrennial Session of the A.M.E. Zion Church.* Louisville, Ky.: Jesse B. Colbert, Editor and Publisher, 1916.

_____, *History of the Varick Christian Endeavor Society, A.M.E. Zion Church*, n.p., 1905.

The Colonial Laws of New York (1664-1776), 2 Vols. Albany: James B. Lyons, State Printer, 1894.

Conrad, Earl, *Harriet Tubman.* Washington, D.C.: The Associated Publishers, Inc., 1943.

_____, *Harriet Tubman, Negro Soldier and Abolitionist.* New York: International Publishers, 1942.

Cromwell, John W., *The Negro in American History.* Washington, D.C.: The American Negro Academy, 1914. Reprinted, New York & London: Johnson Reprint Corporation, 1968.

Davenport, W. H., *Membership in Zion Methodism.* Christian Education Department, African Methodist Episcopal Zion Church, 1935.

Davidson, Basil, *A History of East and Central Africa to the Late Nineteenth Century.* Garden City, New York: Doubleday & Company, Inc., 1969.

_____, *Africa in History.* New York: The MacMillan Company, 1969.

Delany, Martin Robison, *The Condition, Elevation, Emigration, and Destiny of the Colored People of the United States.* Philadelphia: Published by the Author, 1852. Reprint, New York: Arno Press and The New York Times, 1968.

Dixon, James, *Methodism in America.* London: John Mason and James Peart. Birmingham: 1849.

Douglass, Frederick, *The Life and Times of Frederick Douglass.* Boston: De Wolfe, Fiske & Co., 1893.

DuBois, W. E. Burghardt, *The American Negro Family.* Atlanta, Georgia: Atlanta University Press, 1908.

_____, *Efforts for Social Betterment Among Negro Americans.* Atlanta, Ga.: Atlanta University Press, 1909.

_____, *The Gift of Black Folk.* Boston: The Stratford Co., Publishers, 1924.

_____, *The Negro.* New York: Henry Holt and Company. London: Williams and Norgate, 1915.

_____, *The Negro Church.* Atlanta: Atlanta University Press, 1903.

_____, *The Souls of Black Folk.* Chicago: A. C. McClurg & Co. 1903.

_____, *The World and Africa.* New York: Viking Press. 1947.

Dudley, Samuel Madison, *Handbook of the A.M.E. Zion Church.* Washington, D.C.: 1944.

Easton, Hosea, *A Treatise of the Intellectual Character, and Civil and Political Condition of the Colored People of the United States: and the Prejudice Exercised Towards Them.* Boston: Isaac Knapp, 1837.

Ellis, Edward Robb, *The Epic of New York City.* New York: Coward-McCann, Inc., 1966.

Fauset, Arthur Huff, *Sojourner Truth, God's Faithful Pilgrim.* Chapel Hill: The University of North Carolina Press, 1938.

Federal Writers' Project of the Works Progress Administration for the City of New York: Inventory of the Church Archives of New York City (Methodist). New York: The Historical Records Survey, December, 1940.

Foner, Philip S., *The Life and Writings of Frederick Douglass,* 4 Vols. New York: International Publishers, 1950.

_____, *The Voice of Black America.* New York: Simon and Schuster, 1972.

Fox, Stephen R., *The Guardian of Boston.* New York: Atheneum, 1970.

Frazier, E. Franklin, *The Negro Church in America.* New York: Schocken Books, 1963.

Greenleaf, Jonathan, *A History of the Churches of all Denominations in the City of New York.* New York: E. French, 136 Nassau Street, Portland, Hyde, Lord and Duren. 1846.

Grimshaw, William H., *Official History of Freemasonry Among the Colored People of North America.* Montreal, New York, London: Broadway Publishing Co. 1903.

Hagood, L. M., *The Colored Man in the Methodist Episcopal Church.* Cincinnati: Cranston & Stowe, New York: Hunt & Eaton, 1890.

Hamilton, William, *Address to the Fourth Annual Convention of the People of Color of the United States.* New York: S. W. Benedict & Co., 1834.

Hamlin, C. H., *Ninety Bits of North Carolina Biography,* n.p., C. H. Hamlin. 1946.

Hammon, Jupiter, *An Address to the Negroes in the State of New York.* New York, 1786. Reprinted, Philadelphia: Daniel Humphreys, 1787.

Hardie, James, *A Census of the New Buildings Erected in This City in the Year 1824.* New York: Samuel Marks, 1825.

Hartzell, J. C., *Methodism and the Negro in the United States.* Cincinnati: Cranston & Curts, New York: Hunt & Eaton, 1894.

Hastings, Hugh, *Ecclesiastical Records of the State of New York,* 7 Vols. Albany: J. B. Lyons Company, 1905.

Haswell, Charles H., *Reminiscenses of an Octogenarian.* New York: Harper and Brothers Publishers, 1896.

Hill, Everett G., *Modern History of New Haven and Eastern New Haven County,* 2 Vols. New York and Chicago: The S. J. Clark Co., 1918.

Hood, J. W., *One Hundred Years of the African Methodist Episcopal Zion Church.* New York: A.M.F. Zion Book Concern, 1895.

————, *Sketch of the Early History of the African Methodist Episcopal Zion Church*, Vol. II, n.p., J. W. Hood, 1914.

Hughes, Langston and Meltzer, Milton. eds., *A Pictorial History of the Negro in America*. New York: Crown Publishers, 1956 & 1963.

Jackson, Abbie C., *Information Please*. n.p. Woman's Home and Foreign Missionary Society, A.M.E. Zion Church, Literature Committee, 1945.

James, Thomas, *The Life of Reverend Thomas James*. n.p. Rochester: 1886.

Johnson, James Weldon, *Black Manhattan*. New York: Atheneum, reprint, 1969.

Jones, Singleton T., *Handbook of the Discipline of the African Methodist Episcopal Zion Church*. New York: Hunt and Eaton, 1888.

Kletzing, H. F. and Crogman, W. H., *Progress of a Race*. Atlanta, Naperville, Ill., and Toronto, Ont.: J. L. Nichols and Co., 1898.

King, Coretta Scott, *My Life with Martin Luther King, Jr.* Great Britain: Hodder and Stoughton, 1970.

King, Martin Luther, Jr., *Stride Toward Freedom*. New York: Harper and Brothers, 1958.

Kobrin, David, *The Black Minority in Early New York*. Albany: The University of the State of New York, State Education Department, 1971.

Lamb, Martha J., *History of the City of New York: Its Origin, Rise and Progress*, 3 Vols. New York: A. S. Barnes and Company, 1896.

Larrabee, William C., *Asbury and His Coadjutors*, 2 Vols. Cincinnati: Swormstedt and Poe, 1853.

Latourette, Kenneth Scott, *A History of the Expansion of Christianity*, 7 Vols. New York: Harper & Brothers, 1937.

Lee, Jesse, *A Short History of the Methodists in the U.S.A.* Baltimore: Magill and Clime, 1810.

Lee, Leroy M., *The Life and Times of the Rev. Jesse Lee*. Louisville: Published by John Early for the Methodist Episcopal Church, South, 1848.

Lee, Umphrey, *John Wesley and Modern Religion*. Nashville: Cokesbury Press, 1936.

Loguen, J. W., *The Rev. J. W. Loguen as a Slave and as a Freeman*. Syracuse: J. G. K. Truair & Co., Office of *The Daily Journal*, 1859.

Luccock, Halford E., Hutchison, Paul, and Goodloe, Robert W., *The Story of Methodism*. Nashville: Abingdon Press, 1949.

Maser, Frederick and Maag, Howard, *The Journal of Joseph Pilmore, Methodist Itinerant*. Philadelphia: Message Publishing Co., 1969.

Matlack, Lucius C., *History of American Slavery and Methodism*. New York, 1849.

McPherson, James M., *Anti-Negro Riots in the North*. New York: Arno Press and *The New York Times*, 1969.

Moore, John J., *History of the A.M.E. Zion Church in America*. York, Pa.: Teachers Journal Office, 1884.

Moore, M. H., *Pioneers of Methodism in North Carolina and Virginia*. Nashville: Southern Methodist Publishing House, 1884.

Neely, Thomas B., *A History of the Origin and Development of the Governing Conference of Methodism*. Cincinnati: Cranston & Stowe, New York: Hunt and Eaton, 1892.

Nell, William C., *The Colored Patriots of the American Revolution*. Boston: Robert F. Wallcut, 1855. Reprint, New York: Arno Press and *The New York Times*, 1968.

Nutt, John H., *Newburgh, Her Institutions, Industries and Leading Citizens*. Newburgh, N.Y.: Ritchie & Hull, 1891.

Ottley, Roi, *New World A-Coming*. Cleveland and New York: The World Publishing Company, 1943.

————, and Weatherby, William J. (eds.), *The Negro in New York*. Dobbs Ferry, New York: Oceana Publications, Inc., 1967.

Ovington, Mary White, *Half a Man*. Reprint, New York: Hill and Wang, 1969.

Payne, Daniel A., *History of the African Methodist Episcopal Church*. Nashville: Publishing House of the A.M.E. Sunday-School Union, 1891.

Pelletreau, William Smith, *Early New York Houses*. New York: Francis P. Harper, Publisher, 1900.

Penn, I. Garland, *The Afro-American Press and Its Editors*. Springfield, Mass.: Willey & Co., 1891.

Pettit, Eber M., *Sketches in the History of the Underground Railroad*. Fredonia, N.Y.: W. McKinstry & Son, 1879.

Phillips, C. H., *The History of the Colored Methodist Episcopal Church in America*, 3rd ed. Jackson, Tennessee: 1935.

Phoebus, George A., *Beams of Light on Early Methodism in America*. From *Diaries, Letters, etc., of Ezekiel Cooper*. New York: Phillip & Hunt, 1887.

Porter, Dorothy Burnett, *Negro Protest Pamphlets, a Compendium*. New York: Arno Press and *The New York Times*, 1969.

Porter, James, *A Comprehensive History of Methodism*. Cincinnati: Hitchcock & Walden, New York: Nelson & Phillips, 1876.

————, *Compendium of Methodism*. New York: Carleton & Porter, 1851.

————, *The Stewards and the People*. New York: Carleton & Porter, 1863.

Powell, Jacob W., *Bird's Eye View of the General Conference of the A.M.E. Zion Church at Louisville, Kentucky*, 1916. (Eliza Ann Gardner, *Historical Sketch of the A.M.E. Zion Church, Boston Mass.*) Boston: Lavelle Press, 1918.

————, *Echoes of Christian Education*. Malden, Mass.: 1934.

Quarles, Benjamin, *The Negro in the American Revolution*. Chapel Hill: The University of North Carolina, 1961.

Quasten, Johannes, *Patrology*. Utrecht/Antwerp: Spectrum Publishers, and Westminister, Maryland: The Newman Press, 1960, 1963.

Radhakrishnan, S., *East and West in Religion*. London: George Allen & Unwin Ltd., 1933.

Raybold, G. A., *Reminiscense of Methodism in West Jersey*. New York: Lane & Scott, 1849.

Rupp, Israel Daniel (ed.) *Religious Denominations in the United States: Their Past History, Present Condition, and Doctrines*. Philadelphia: Charles Desilver, 1871.

Rush, Christopher, *The Rise and Progress of the African Methodist Episcopal (Zion) Church in America*. New York: The Author, 1843.

Seaman, Samuel A., *Annals of New York Methodism*. New York, Hunt & Eaton, 1892.

Selecman, Charles C., *The Methodist Primer*. Nashville: Tidings, 1945.

A Short Historical Account of the Early Society of Methodists. New York: Printed & Published by W. & P. C. Smith, 1824.

Simmons, William J., *Men of Mark*. Cleveland: George M. Rowell & Co., 1887.

Small, John B., *Code of the Discipline of the African Methodist Episcopal Zion Church*. York, Pa.: York Dispatch Print, 1898.

Small, Laura E., *Handbook for Supply Secretaries*. n.p., 1967.

Smith, Charles Spencer, *A History of the African Methodist Episcopal Church*. Philadelphia: 1922.

Smith, Edwin W., *Aggrey of Africa*. New York: Doubleday, Doran and Co., Inc., 1929.

Smith, J. W., *Sermons and Addresses of Bishop S. T. Jones*. York, Pa.: P. Anstadt & Sons, 1892.

Sprague, William B., *Annals of the American Pulpit: Commemorative Notices of Distinguished Clergymen*. Vol. VII, *Methodists*. New York: Robert Carter and Brothers, 1861.

Stokes, I. N. Phelps, *Iconography of Manhattan Island*. 6 Vols. New York: Robert H. Dodd, 1928.

Strickland, W. P., *History of the American Bible Society*. New York: Harper & Brothers, 1849.

Thompson, J. W., *An Authentic History of the Douglass Monument, Biographical Facts and Incidents in the Life of Frederick Douglass*. Rochester, N.Y.: Rochester Herald Press, 1903.

Thurman, Sue Bailey. *Pioneers of Negro Origin in California*. San Francisco: Acme Publishing Company, 1952.

Townsend, W. J., Workman, H. B., George Eayres, *A New History of Methodism*, 2 Vols. London: Hodder and Stoughton.

Upham, Francis Bourne, *The Story of Old John Street Methodist Episcopal Church, 1766-1934*. New York: 1934.

Urquart, Frank J., *A Short History of Newark, N.J*. Newark: Baker Printing Co., 1916.

Visser 't Hooft, William H., *The First Assembly of the World Council of Churches*. New York. Harper and Brothers, 1949.

Wakeley, J. B., *Lost Chapters Recovered from the Early History of American Methodism*. New York: Published for the Author by Carleton and Porter, 1858.

Walls, William Jacob, *Joseph Charles Price, Educator and Race Leader*. Boston: The Christopher Publishing House, 1943.

————, *The Romance of a College*. New York: Vantage Press. 1963.

Walters, Alexander, *My Life and Work*. New York, Chicago, Toronto: Fleming H. Revell Company, 1917.

Warner, Robert Austin, *New Haven Negroes*. New Haven: Yale University Press, 1940.

Warren, Medis G., *Guidebook for Life Members Council*. n.p., 1963.

Watson, John F., *Annals of Philadelphia*. Philadelphia: E. L. Carey and A. Hart. New York: G. & C. & H. Carvill, 1830.

Weeden, Henry C., *Handbook of the A.M.E. Zion Church, 1930-31*. n.p.

Wesley, John. *The Works of John Wesley, A.M.*, ed. Vol. 8, 3rd ed. London: J. Mason, 1830.
————, *Thoughts on Slavery—1774*. New York: Published by the American A.S. Society, 1839.

Wheeler, B. F., *Cullings from Zion's Poets*. n.p. B. F. Wheeler, D.D.: 1907.
————, *The Varick Family*. Mobile, Alabama: 1906.

Wheeler, Henry, *One Thousand Questions and Answers Concerning the Methodist Episcopal Church*. New York: Eaton & Mains, Cincinnati: Curts & Jennings, 1898.

————, *History and Exposition of the Twenty-Five Articles of Religion of the Methodist Episcopal Church. Article XIII (of the Church)*. New York: Eaton and Mains, 1908.

White, George, *A Brief Account of the Life, Experience, Travels and Gospel Labours of George White*. New York: John C. Totten, 1810.

Williams, George W., *History of the Negro Race in America*. New York and London: G. P. Putnam's Sons, The Knickerbocker Press, 1882.

Williams, Peter, Jr., *Program and Oration Delivered by Peter Williams Jr., Abolition of the African Slave Trade, at the African Church, New York City, January 1, 1808*. New York: Printed by Samuel Wood, 1808. (Schomberg Collection, New York Public Library).

Wilson, Joseph T., *The Black Phalanx*. Hartford, Conn.: American Publishing Company, 1890.

Woodson, Carter G., *The History of the Negro Church*. Washington, D.C.: The Associated Publishers, 1921.

————, and Wesley, Charles, *Negro Stars in American History*.

Zuille, John J., *Historical Sketch of the New York Society for Mutual Relief*. n.p., n. pub.

3. Catechisms, Discipline and Hymnbooks.

Carroll, Richard Alexander, Sr., *The Standard Historical Catechism of the African Methodist Episcopal Zion Church*. Providence, R.I.: 1919.

Harris, C. R., *Zion's Historical Catechism*. Charlotte, N.C.: A.M.E. Zion Publishing House, rev. ed., 1972.

Jones, E. D. W., *Comprehensive Catechism of the A.M.E. Zion Church*. Washington, D.C.: Bishop E. D. W. Jones, 1934.

Discipline (Chronologically).

1796—*The Doctrines and Discipline of the Methodist Episcopal Church in America, Revised and Approved at the General Conference Held at Baltimore, in the State of Maryland, in November, 1792*. Philadelphia: Printed by R. Aitken, sold by John Dickins, 1790.

1820—*The Doctrines and Discipline of the African Methodist Episcopal [Zion] Church in America, Established in the City of New York*, October 25, 1820. First Edition. New York: Published By Christopher Rush and George Collins, for the African Methodist Episcopal Church in America. J. C. Totten, printer, 1820.

1840—*The Doctrines and Discipline of the African Methodist Episcopal [Zion] Church in America, Established in the City of New York, October 25, 1820*. New York: Joseph M. Marsh, Printer, 1841.

1840–*The Doctrines and Discipline of the Wesleyan Methodist Episcopal Zion Church in America, Established in the City of New York, October 25, 1820.* Second Edition. Revised and Adopted in the City of New York, June 8, 1840. New York: J. M. Marsh, Printer, 1840.

1848–*The Doctrines and Discipline of the African Methodist Episcopal Zion Church in America.* Revised In The City of New York, June 3rd, A.D., 1848, Second Edition. New York: Published for the African Methodist Episcopal Zion Connexion in America, 1851.

1868–*The Doctrines and Discipline of the African Methodist Episcopal Zion Church in America.* Revised In The City of Washington, 1868. New York: The A.M.E. Zion Book Concern, 1869.

1872–*The Doctrines and Discipline of the African Methodist Episcopal Zion Church in America.* Revised By The General Conference In Charlotte, N.C., 1872. Washington. D.C.: Published by the General Book Concern. 1872.

1876 Through 1968–*The Doctrines and Discipline of the African Methodist Episcopal Zion Church* published quadrennially, following the General Conferences, By The A.M.E. Zion Book Concern of New York (until 1892), and the A.M.E. Zion Publishing House of Charlotte, North Carolina.

1956–*The Doctrines and Discipline of the African Methodist Episcopal Church.* Nashville, Tennessee: The A.M.E. Sunday School Union, 1957.

*1958–*The Doctrines and Discipline of the Christian Methodist Episcopal Church.* Revised 1958. Jackson, Tennessee: C.M.E. Church Publishing Department, Grover H. Carter, Agent, 1958.

1960–*The Doctrines and Discipline of the Methodist Church.* Nashville, Tenn.: The Methodist Publishing House, 1960.

Hymnals.

A Collection of Hymns for the Use of the African Methodist Episcopal Zion Church. Published by the Committee by Order of the General Conference of 1872. New York: Methodist Book Concern, 1872.

The African Methodist Episcopal Zion Hymnal, Charlotte, N.C.: A.M.E. Zion Church Publishing House, Charlotte, N.C. 1957.

Hymnbook Published by the A.M.E. Zion Church (Rev. B. F. Wheeler, Editor). New York: A.M.E. Zion Book Concern. Recopyright, 1892.

Hymns for the Use of the African Methodist Episcopal Zion Church. Published by Samuel M. Giles, Christopher Rush and Joseph P. Thompson. New York: D. Fanshaw, 1858.

Hymns for the Use of the African Methodist Episcopal Zion Church. New York: Nelson & Phillips, 1878.

Hymns for the Use of the African Methodist Episcopal Zion Church. New York Office of Zion Statesman & Weekly Review, 1869.

New Hymn–Tune Book for the Use of the African Methodist Episcopal Zion Church. Charlotte, N.C.: African Methodist Episcopal Zion Church Book Concern, 1909. Rev. ed., 1916.

Soul Echoes, ed. Philadelphia: Soul Echoes Publishing Co., 420 South Eleventh Street, 1909.

4. Manuscripts and Unpublished Material.

Bancker, Evart, *Bancker Land Papers.* New York Historical Society Manuscript Division, also New York Public Library, Manuscript and Archives Division.

————, *Bancker Survey Papers.* New York Historical Society.

Barber Memorial Home Conveyance Deed, February 14, 1893.

Blackwell, George L., I., *A Digest History of the A.M.E. Zion Church.* Author's Collection. n.d.

Brown, James, *Diaries of James Brown (A Negro) of Fishkill Landing, N.Y., 1827-1866.* 4 Vols. New York Historical Society Manuscript Division.

Brown, James W., *History of Mother Zion Church.* By the Pastor, 1927. Author's Collection.

Bruce, John Edward, Mss collected as the John Edward Bruce papers, Schomberg Collection, New York.

Chestnutt, Charles W., *Joseph C. Price, Orator and Educator*. Author's Collection. Cleveland, 1928.

Clement, Rufus E., *History of Education in the A.M.E. Zion Church*, Ms. Thesis, Northwestern University, 1920. Author's Collection.

Cooper, Ezekiel. Mss collected as the Ezekiel Cooper papers, Garrett Theological Seminary, Evanston, Illinois.

Federal Writers' Program of the Works Project Administration. Negroes of New York. Schomberg Collection of Negro Literature and History, New York Public Library, 1939-41.

Greenwald, Frank. Prize Winning Essay, *Cemeteries of New York City*. New York Historical Society MS. Division, 1933.

Hamilton, William, *Letter to Governor John Jay, March 8, 1796*. John Jay Papers, Columbia University Libraries Special Collection.

The John Street Methodist Episcopal Church Records. Books 1 and 2. New York Public Library Manuscript and Archives Division.

Jones, E. D. W., *History of Mother A.M.E. Zion Church*, n.d. Author's Collection.

Journalism in the A.M.E. Zion Church. Ms. Historical Records of the Sesqui-Centennial of the A.M.E. Zion Church, 1946.

Letter to Mayor Cornelius W. Lawrence (Anonymous). Mayor's Papers, New York Historical Society MS. Division.

Memorial A.M.E. Zion Church Historical Records. Rochester, N.Y. 77th Anniversary Souvenir Program, 1906.

Message of the Board of Bishops, A.M.E. Zion Church. First A.M.E. Zion Church, Knoxville, Tenn., 1961.

MS Minutes, Board of Bishops Meetings, A.M.E. Zion Church:

September 29, 1889	Twelfth Street Church, (Broadway Temple) Louisville, Ky.
April 30, 1890	Gaspee Street Church, Providence, R.I.
October 5, 1894	Varick Memorial Building, Charlotte, N.C.
January 10, 1919	Metropolitan Wesley, Washington, D.C.
January 14, 1937	First Church, Paterson, New Jersey
January 12-13, 1938	St. Peter's Church, New Bern, N.C.
June 6, 1939	Livingstone College, Salisbury, N.C.
January 17, 1947	Cooper Memorial, Oakland, California
March 12, 1948	Home of Bishop Matthews, Washington, D.C.
August 1, 1952	Columbus Avenue Church, Boston, Mass.
June 2, 1953	Livingstone College, Salisbury, N.C.
July 30, 1955	Martin Temple, Chicago, Ill.
January 10, 1956	St. Mark, Durham, N.C.
August 25-30, 1956	Hopkins Chapel, Asheville, N.C.
January 9-13, 1957	Walls Chapel, Oklahoma City, Okla.
January 12, 1961	First Church, Knoxville, Tenn.

Ms. Minutes, Methodist Episcopal Church General Conferences, 1800-1828. Methodist Library, Drew University, Madison, New Jersey.

Ms. Minutes, Methodist Episcopal Church, *New York State Annual Conference Journal*, 1800-1820. New York Public Library Manuscript and Archives Division.

Morrell, Thomas, Mss collected and letters of Thomas Morrell, Garrett Theological Seminary.

Mother Zion Church Records.

National Council of Churches—Excerpts from the National Council Message, General Board Meeting, National Council of Churches, U.S.A., September 4, 1957.

New York City Records:

1801 Census Book, MS Division, New York Historical Society.

City Clerk papers, Municipal Archives and Record Center of New York City, 1801-1810.

Property Conveyance Deeds, Hall of Records, New York City.

Religious Corporations, Hall of Records, New York City.

1795 Taxbook, Municipal Archives and Record Center.

1796 Taxbook, New York Historical Society.

North, Eric M., *History of the American Bible Society*. Ms. Collection, American Bible Society Library, New York City.

Rush Academy, Lake Placid, New York Farm Plot, Ms. Records, Author's Collection.

Spencer, Wilhemina, Ms. *History of John Wesley Church*, Pittsburgh, Pa., 1972.

Varick, James, Ms. Letter, Riker Papers, Division of Archives and Manuscripts, New York Public Library.

Walls, W. J., *Bishop J. S. Caldwell and Twenty-Five Years in the Episcopacy*. 1929.

_____, *History of the Star of Zion*, 1921.

Williamson, Harry A., *Folks in Old New York*, New York Historical Society, 1953.

Williamson, Harry Albo. MSS collected as the Harry Albo Williamson Collection of Negro Masonry in the Schomberg Collection, New York Public Library.

5. Published Minutes and Official Proceedings:

AFRICAN METHODIST EPISCOPAL ZION CHURCH ANNUAL CONFERENCES:

Twelfth Session, Alabama Conference, Held December 12th to 18th, 1877, At State Street Church, Mobile, Ala. Montgomery, Ala.: Smith, Allred & Beers, Printers, 1878.

Thirty-First Session, Alabama Annual Conference Held in Butler Chapel, Tuskegee, Alabama, December 8-14, 1897. Charlotte, N.C.: A.M.E. Zion Publication House, 1898.

Forty-First Session, Allegheny Annual Conference, Convened in Washington, Pa., September 17, 1890. Johnstown, Pa.: H. M. Benshoff, Printer, 1890.

Forty-Third Session, Allegheny Annual Conference, Bedford, Pa., September 21, 1892. Salisbury, N.C. Livingstone College Print, 1892.

British North America Mission Annual Conference of the African Methodist Episcopal Zion Church, Halifax, N.S., Sept. 12-27, 1857. Worcester: Henry J. Howland.

Twenty-Fifth Annual Session, California Conference, Jan. 11-14, 1893. San Jose, Calif. San Francisco: Brunt & Co., 1893.

First Session, Central North Carolina Conference, Fayetteville, North Carolina, November 10 to 18, 1880. Monroe, N.C.: Printed By W. J. Boylin At The Express Job Office, 1881.

Twenty-Fourth Session, Central North Carolina Annual Conference, November 17-23, 1909, Mt. Calvary Church, Monroe, N.C.

Third Session, East (Central) Alabama Annual Conference, Clinton Chapel, Montgomery, Ala. November 22-19, 1882. Montgomery, Ala.: Barrett & Co., Printers, 1883.

Fourth Session, East Alabama Conference, Zion Church, Talladaga, Alabama, November 21 to 25th, 1883. Montgomery, Ala.: G. W. Beers & Co. Printer, 1884.

Fifth Session, East Alabama Conference, Mt. Zion Church, Montgomery, Alabama, November 26 to 30, 1884. Montgomery, Ala.: Allred Bros, Job Printers, 1885.

Seventh Session East Alabama Conference, Union Springs, Alabama, November 24 to 29, 1886. Tuskegee, Ala.: Normal School Print, 1887.

Twenty-Second Session, East Alabama Conference, Mt. Zion Church, Montgomery, Alabama, Nov. 28-Dec. 3, 1889. Tuskegee, Ala.: Normal School Print, 1890.

Twenty-Third Session, East Alabama Conference, Thompson Chapel, Opelika, Alabama, Nov. 26 To Dec. 3, 1890. Montgomery, Ala.: W. E. Allred, Steam Power Printer, 1891.

Twenty-Fourth Session, East Tennessee Annual Conference, A.M.E. Zion Church, Asheville, N.C., Oct. 16-23, 1889. Asheville, N.C.: Citizens Publishing Co., 1889.

Twenty-Eighth Session, Florida Annual Conference, Isaiah Chapel, Milton, Fla.: Feb. 24 - Mar. 1, 1897. Charlotte, N.C. A.M.E. Zion Publishing House, 1897.

Thirty-Sixth Session, Florida Conference, Talbot Chapel, Pensacola, Florida, October 26-31, 1904. Charlotte, N.C., A.M.E. Zion Publishing House, 1904.

Genesee Annual Conference Convened at Montrose, Pa., September 1, 1858. Ithaca, N.Y.: Andrus, Gauntlett & Company, 1858.

Forty-Fifth Session, Genesee, Gloversville, New York, September 25-30, 1895. Charlotte, N.C.: A.M.E. Zion Publishing House, 1895.

Sixteenth Session, Georgia Annual Conference, John Wesley Chapel, Social Circle, Walton County, Georgia, Nov. 16-21, 1881. J. A. Peak and E. W. Gibson Publishers.

First Session, Island Annual Conference, A.M.E. Zion Church, Nassau, N.P., December 26, 1877 - January 8, 1878. n. pub., n.d.

Thirteenth Session, Kentucky Annual Conference, Jones Tabernacle A.M.E. Zion Church, Indianapolis, Indiana. September 4-12, 1878. Louisville, Ky.: I. C. Asa Printer, 1878.

Twenty-Seventh Session, New England Annual Conference, Zion Church, New Haven, Conn., May 6-14, 1874. New Haven: Judson Grenell, Steam Printer, 1874.

Twenty-Eighth Session, New England Conference, Elm Street Church, New Bedford, Mass., May 5 - May 13, 1875. Bridgeport: The Standard Association, Printers, 1875.

Forty-Sixth Session, New England Conference, Foote Street A.M.E. Zion Church, New Haven, Conn., May 6-11, 1891. Cambridge, Mass: Harvard Printing Co, 1891.

Forty-Eighth Session, New England Conference, Russell Street Church, Boston, Mass., June 10-15, 1893. Cambridge: Harvard Printing Company, 1893.

Fifty-Second Session, New England Conference, Second A.M.E. Zion Church, Providence, R.I., June 3-9, 1896. Charlotte, N.C.: A.M.E. Zion Publication House, 1896.

Twenty-Second Session, New Jersey Annual Conference, Clinton, A.M.E. Zion Church of The Strangers, Newark, New Jersey, April 24-29, 1895. Salisbury, N.C.: Livingstone College Press, 1895.

Twenty-Fourth Session, New Jersey Conference, Red Bank, New Jersey, April 28, 1897. Charlotte, N.C.: A.M.E. Zion Publication House, 1897.

Minutes of the New York and New England Annual Conferences, A.M.E. Zion Church In America, 1857. New York: D. Fanshaw, 1857.

Fifty-First Session, New York Annual Conference, Zion Church, New York City, April 17-27, 1872. Published by the Missionary Board of the New York Annual Conference. New York: John J. Reed, Printer, 1872.

Fifty-Sixth Session, New York Conference, A.M.E. Zion Church, Catherine Street, Poughkeepsie, New York, May 16-22, 1877. Brooklyn, N.Y.: Brooklyn Daily Times Print, 1877.

Seventy-Third Session, New York Conference, Poughkeepsie, N.Y. May 16-21, 1894, n. pub.

Seventy-Fourth Session, New York Conference, A.M.E. Zion Church, Newburgh, N.Y. May 8-13, 1895. Salisbury, N.C.: Livingstone College Press, 1895.

Seventy-Seventh Session, New York Conference, Troy, New York, May 11, 1898. Fishkill -On-Hudson, N.Y.: Press of Henry King, Jr., 1898.

Seventy-Eighth Session, New York Conference, Mother Zion Church, New York City, May 10, 1899. Fishkill-On-Hudson, N.Y.: Henry King, Jr., 1899.

Ninety-Third Session, New York Conference, Centennial A.M.E. Zion Church, Mt. Vernon, N.Y., June 10-15, 1914. Poughkeepsie, N.Y.: Wm. V. Maar, 1914.

Ninety-Fourth Session, New York Conference, Fleet Memorial Church, Brooklyn, N.Y., June 9-14, 1915. Poughkeepsie, N.Y.: Wm. V. Maar, 1915.

Ninety-Fifth Session, New York Conference, Seventh Avenue A.M.E. Zion Church, Troy, New York, June 28-July 3, 1916. Poughkeepsie, N.Y.: Wm. V. Maar, 1916.

Eleventh Session, North Carolina Annual Conference, Andrews Chapel, New Bern, N.C., November 25-December 2, 1874. Raleigh: John Nichols & Co., Book and Job Printers, 1875.

Twelfth Session, North Carolina Conference, Zion Chapel, Concord, N.C., November 24-December 1, 1875.

Thirteenth Session, North Carolina Conference, Phillips Chapel, Washington, N.C. November 22-28, 1876.

Fourteenth Session, North Carolina Conference, Zion Chapel, Salisbury, N.C., November 28-December 6, 1877.

Fifteenth Session, North Carolina Conference, Zion Church, Goldsboro, N.C., November 27-December 4, 1878.

Sixteenth Session, North Carolina Conference, Moore's Chapel, Lincolnton, N.C., November 26-December 3, 1879.

Fourth Session, North Georgia Annual Conference, Stone Mountain, Dekalb County, Georgia, November 31-December 5, 1888. Atlanta, Ga.: Clark University Press, 1888.

Second Session, Ohio Annual Conference, Mt. Zion Chapel, Akron, Ohio, September 28-October 2, 1893. New Castle, Pa.: News Company's Job Rooms, 1893.

Fourth Session, Ohio Conference, Y.M.C.A. Hall, New Castle, Pa., September 26-October 1, 1894. Salisbury, N.C.: Livingstone College Press, 1894.

Forty-Sixty Session, Philadelphia and Baltimore Conference, Wesley Zion Church, Carlisle, Cumberland County, Pa., May 6-14, 1874. Harrisburg, Pa.: J. P. Hammer, Compiler and Publisher, 1874.

Fiftieth Session, Philadelphia and Baltimore Annual Conference, Wesley Union Church, Harrisburg, Pa., May 15-22, 1878. Philadelphia, Pa.: M. M. Bell, Compiler and Publisher, 1878.

Sixty-Eighth Session, Philadelphia and Baltimore Conference, Metropolitan Zion Church, Washington, D.C., June 17, 1896. Harrisburg, Pa.: Wm. Howard Day, Publisher, 1896.

Sixty-Ninth Session, Philadelphia and Baltimore Conference, The A.M.E. Zion Church, Chambersburg, Pa., May 19, 1897. Harrisburg, Pa.: Wm. Howard Day, Publisher, 1897.

Seventy-Fourth Session, Philadelphia and Baltimore Conference, A.M.E. Zion Church, York, Pa., May 15-20, 1901. Charlotte, N.C.: A.M.E. Zion Publishing House, 1901.

Tenth Session, South Carolina Annual Conference, Zion Church, Lancaster, S.C., October 27-November 2, 1875. Raleigh: John Nichols & Co., Book and Job Printers, 1875.

Eleventh Session, South Carolina Conference, St. Augustine Church, Unionville, S.C., October 25-28, 1876. Raleigh: John Nichols, Book and Job Printer, 1876.

Twenty-Seventh Session, South Carolina Conference, Mt. Zion Church, Chester, South Carolina, November 22-28, 1894. Salisbury, N.C.: Livingstone College Press, 1894.

Thirty-Third Session, South Georgia Annual Conference, Mt. Zion Church, Augusta, Georgia. November 8-13, 1899. Augusta, Ga.: The Augusta Journal Print, 1900.

Thirty-Second Session, Tennessee Conference, Thompkins Chapel, Chattanooga, Tenn., October 13, 1897. Charlotte, N.C.: A.M.E. Zion Publication House, 1897.

Ninth Session, Virginia Annual Conference, Petersburg, Va., November 11-18, 1874. Raleigh: John Nichols & Co., Book and Job Printers, 1874.

Tenth Session, Virginia Conference, Mount Lebanon, Elizabeth City, N.C., November 10-17, 1875. Raleigh: John Nichols & Co., Book and Job Printers, 1875.

Seventeenth Session, Virginia Conference, Kadesh Church, Edenton, N.C., November 15-21, 1882. Petersburg, Va.: Wm. I. Zimmer & Co., Book and Job Press, 1882.

Twenty-Second Session, Virginia Conference, Mosley Street Church, Norfolk, Va. November 23-28, 1887. Petersburgh, Pa.: Mitchell & Co., Steam Printers and Binders, 1887.

Second Session, West Alabama Annual Conference, Zion Church, Tuscaloosa, Ala., December 14-21, 1881. Tuscaloosa, Ala.: Tuscaloosa Gazette Print, 1882.

Third Session, West Alabama Conference, Little Zion Chapter, Mobile, Alabama, December 13-21, 1882. Mobile: Geo. Matzenger, Printer, 1883.

Ninth Session, West Alabama Conference, Zion Chapel, Selma, Alabama, December 12th, 1888. Selma, Ala.: Bryant Publishing House, 1889.

Tenth Session, West Alabama Conference, Little Zion Chapel, Mobile, Alabama, December 11-19, 1889. Tuskegee, Ala.: Normal School Print, 1890.

Eleventh Session, West Alabama Conference, Zion Church, Tuscaloosa, Alabama, December 10th, 1890. Mobile: Thomas J. PaPrade, Printer, 1891.

Twenty-Third Session, West Florida Annual Conference, St. Luke Chapel, Jacksonville, Florida, March 10-16, 1892. Milton, Fla.: The Milton Clarion Book and Job Print, 1892.

One Hundred and Eighth Session, Western New York Conference, St. Luke Church, Buffalo, May 14-19, 1957.

First Session, Western North Carolina Annual Conference, Moore's Chapel, Lincolnton, N.C. November 25-30, 1891. Winston, N.C.: Stewarts Printing House, 1892.

Eighth Session, Western North Carolina Conference, Soldiers Memorial Church, Salisbury, N.C., November 3-9, 1897. Charlotte, N.C.: A.M.E. Zion Publishing House, 1897.

Twenty-Second Session, Western North Carolina Conference, Moore's Chapel, Lincolnton, N.C. November 12-18, 1912. Gastonia, N.C.: Loftin & Co. Printers, 1912.

Sixty-Eighth Session, Western North Carolina Conference, Little Rock Church, Charlotte, N.C., November 10-16, 1958.

GENERAL QUADRENNIAL SESSIONS:

Minutes or Daily Journal of the Sixteenth Quadrennial Session of The General Conference Clinton Chapel, Montgomery, Alabama, May, 1880. Published by The Book Concern of the A.M.E. Zion Church, Rev. Jacob Thomas, Agent. New York: William Knowles, Printer, 1880.

Minutes or Daily Proceedings of the Seventeenth Quadrennial Session of The General Conference, New York City, May, 1884. New York: A.M.E. Zion Book Concern, 1884.

Minutes or Daily Proceedings of the Eighteenth Quadrennial Session of The General Conference, St. Peter's Church, New Bern, N.C., May 2d, 1888. Wilmington, N.C.: Jackson & Bell, Printers and Binders, 1888.

Minutes or Journal of the Nineteenth Quadrennial Session of the General Conference, John Wesley Church, Pittsburg, Pa., May 4-24, 1892. New York City: A.M.E. Zion Book Concern, 1892.

Minutes or Daily Proceedings of the Twentieth Quadrennial Session of the General Conference, Big Zion, Mobile, Alabama, May 6th, 1896. Charlotte, N.C.: A.M.E. Zion Publishing House, 1896.

Minutes or Official Journal of the Daily Proceedings of the Twenty-First Quadrennial Session of the General Conference, Metropolitan Church, Washington, D.C., May 2-22, 1900. York, Pa.: Dispatch Print, 1901.

_____, Twenty-Second Quadrennial Session of the General Conference, Washington Metropolitan Church, St. Louis, Missouri, May 4-19, 1904. n. pub. Compiled by Rev. G. L. Blackwell, A.M., D.D.

_____, Twenty-Third Quadrennial Session of the General Conference, Wesley Church, Philadelphia, May 6-21, 1908. Salisbury, N.C.: Livingstone Press, 1911.

_____, Twenty-Fourth Quadrennial Session of the General Conference, Clinton Chapel Church, Charlotte, N.C., May 1-22, 1912. Charlotte, N.C.: A.M.E. Zion Job Print, 1912.

_____, Twenty-Fifth Session of the General Conference, Broadway Temple, Louisville, Ky., May 3, 1916 Also of the Twenty-Sixth Session of the General Conference, Loguen Temple, Knoxville, Tenn., May 5, 1920. Charlotte, N.C.: A.M.E. Zion Publishing House, n.d.

_____, Twenty-Seventh Quadrennial Session of the General Conference, Tomlinson Hall and Jones Tabernacle, Indianapolis, Ind., May 5-27, 1924. Charlotte, N.C.: A.M.E. Zion Publishing House Print. n.d.

_____, Twenty-Eighth Session of the General Conference, The New Coliseum and Washington Metropolitan Church, May 2-21, 1928, n. pub., n.d.

_____, Twenty-Ninth General Conference, Wesley Center Church, Pittsburg, Pa., May 4-17, 1932. Charlotte, N.C.: A.M.E. Zion Press n.d.

_____, Thirtieth Quadrennial Session of the General Conference, Trinity Church, Greensboro, N.C., May 6-20, 1936. Charlotte, N.C.: The A.M.E. Zion Publishing House.

_____, Thirty-First Quadrennial Session of the General Conference, John Wesley Church, Washington, D.C., May 1-16, 1940. Charlotte, N.C.: The A.M.E. Zion Publishing House.

_____, Thirty-Second Quadrennial Session General Conference, St. Paul Church, Detroit, Michigan, May 3-15, 1944. Charlotte, N.C.: The A.M.E. Zion Publishing House.

_____, Thirty-Third Quadrennial Session General Conference, Broadway Temple, Louisville, Ky., May 5-20, 1948. Charlotte, N.C.: A.M.E. Zion Publishing House.

_____, Thirty-Fourth Quadrennial Session General Conference, First Church, Brooklyn, New York, May 7-21, 1952. Charlotte, N.C.: A.M.E. Zion Publishing House.

_____ Thirty-Fifth Quadrennial Session General Conference, Wesley Center Church, Pittsburgh, Pa., May 2-16, 1956. Charlotte, N.C.: the A.M.E. Zion Publishing House.

_____, Thirty-Sixth Quadrennial Session General Conference, St. Luke Church and Buffalo Memorial Hall, Buffalo, New York, May 4-18, 1960. Charlotte, N.C.: A.M.E. Zion Publishing House.

_____, Thirty-Seventh Quadrennial Session General Conference, Jones Tabernacle and Farmers Building Indiana State Fairgrounds, Indianapolis, Ind., May 6-20, 1964. Wilmington, North Carolina: Carolina Print Company.

_____, Thirty-Eighth Quadrennial Session General Conference, St. Paul Church, Detroit, May 1-15, 1968.

Bell, Howard H., *Minutes* of the Proceedings of the National Negro Conventions, 1830-1864. New York: Arno and *The New York Times*, 1969.

Digest of the Proceedings of the Tenth Meeting of the Consultation on Church Union, Denver, Colorado, September 27-30, 1971. Princeton: Consultation On Church Union, 1971.

Extracts from the Minutes of the Sixth Yearly Conference and the State Conference of the Methodist Society, November, 1826 and June, 1827. New York: Aaron G. Brewer, 1827.

Journal of the Convention of the State of New York, Held at the Capitol in the City of Albany, on the 12th of August, 1821. Albany: Cantine & Leake, 1821.

Minutes of the Annual Conferences of the Methodist Episcopal Church for the Years 1773-1828. Vol. 1. New York: T. Mason & C. Lane; J. Collard, printer, 1840.

Minutes of the Common Council of the City of New York, 1784-1831. 21 vols. New York: M. B. Brown Printing and Binding Co., 1930.

Proceedings of the Ecumenical Methodist Conference, 1881. London: Wesleyan Conference Office, 1881.

Proceedings of the Second Ecumenical Methodist Conference, 1891. New York: Methodist Book Concern; Hunt and Eaton, Agents, 1892.

Proceedings of the Third Ecumenical Methodist Conference. New York: Eaton and Mains, 1901.

Proceedings of the Fourth Ecumenical Methodist Conference. New York: Eaton and Mains, 1911.

Proceedings of the Fifth Ecumenical Methodist Conference, London, Sept. 6-16, 1921. New York and London: The Methodist Book Concern, 1921.

Proceedings of the Sixth Ecumenical Methodist Conference, Atlanta, Ga., Wesley Memorial Church, Oct. 16-25, 1931. New York, Cincinnati, Chicago: The Methodist Book Concern, 1931.

Proceedings of the Seventh Ecumenical Methodist Conference, Springfield, Mass., Sept. 24-Oct. 2, 1947. New York, London: The Methodist Publishing House.

Proceedings of the Eighth Ecumenical Methodist Conference, Oxford, Aug. 28-Sept. 7, 1951. London: The Epworth Press, 1951.

Proceedings of the Ninth World Methodist Conference. . . . 1956. (Edited by Elmer T. Clark and E. Benson Perkins). The Methodist Publishing House, 1857.

Proceedings of the Tenth World Methodist Conference, Oslo, Norway, August 17-25, 1961. Ed. E. Benson Perkins and Elmer T. Clark. London: The Epworth Press; New York and Nashville: Abingdon Press, 1961.

Proceedings of the Twelfth World Methodist Conference, Denver, Colo., U.S.A., 1971. Nashville and New York: Abingdon Press, 1971.

6. Newspaper Articles:

The Afro-American, Baltimore, Maryland, September 22, 1951; October 27, 1951.

The Anglo-African (Weekly), New York City: August 27, 1859; January through May, 1860; November 24, 1860; December 15, 1860; December 29, 1860; February 9, 1861; May 11, 1861; October 21, 1865; December 9, 1865; December 16, 1865; December 23, 1865.

Carroll, H. K. "James Varick—Pioneer of Ecclesiastical Freedom." *The Star of Zion*, October 8, 1896.

Cartwright, Andrew. "A Plea for Justice." *The Star of Zion*, November 12, 1896.

The Chicago Defender, October 27, 1951.

The Colored American, also *The Weekly Advocate*, New York City: January 7, 1837; February 18, 1837; March 4, 1837; April 1, 1837; May 20, 1837; May 2, 1840; May 30, 1840; October 1, 1840; March 13, 1841.

The Commercial Advertiser, New York City, September 11, 1800; October 1, 1800.

The Emancipator, New York: December 12, 1836.

Fortune, T. Thomas, "Rise of a Great Church," *The New York Sun*, September 27, 1896.

_____, *The New York Age*, October 1, 1896.

Freedom's Journal, New York: March 16, 1827; May 4, 1827; July 27, 1827.

Harris, C. R. "James Varick, His Influence Upon the A.M.E. Zion Church," *The Star of Zion*, October 15, 1896.

The Hartford Daily Times, March 21, 1936.

Hazel, Maud E., "Our Zion, Its Origin, Leaders and Growth," *The Star of Zion*, January 28, 1897.

The Liberator, Boston. November 26, 1836.

The Newburgh News, Newburgh, New York. September 5, 1935.

The North Star and Frederick Douglass' Paper. Various issues, 1847.

The Sentinel of Freedom, Newark, New Jersey, April 18, 1826.

The Star of Zion: September 24, 1896; October 1, 1896; October 29, 1896; November 5, 1896; November 19, 1896; December 10, 1896; January 21, 1897; February 11, 1897; February 25, 1897; April 22, 1897; June 17, 1897; July 8, 1897; September 4, 1897; November 18, 1897; December 23, 1897; January 27, 1898; February 28, 1918; July 8, 1920; July 15, 1920; July 29, 1920; September 2, 1920; November 16, 1920; October 25, 1945; July 18, 1946; September 5, 1946; September 12, 1946; September 19, 1946; September 26, 1946.

The Washington Post, October 1, 1925.

Thompson, William, "An Address Delivered Before the Female Branch Society of Zion at Zion Church, New York City." *The Colored American*, May 8, 1837.

"Zion Visits McKinley," *The Star of Zion*, October 15, 1896.

7. New York City Directories:

Duncan, William. ed., *The New York Directory and Register for the Years 1791 to 1795*. New York: Printed for the Editor By T. and J. Swords, 1791.

Elliot, William, *Elliot's Improved New York Double Directory*. New York: Printed and Sold By William Elliot, 1812.

Franks, David C. ed., *The New York Directory*, 1787. New York: Printed for the Editor,1787.

Longworth, David. ed., *Longworth's Almanac, New York Register and City Directory*. New York: Printed for the Editor by T. J. Swords, 1797.

_____, *Longworth Directories*. 1815-1819.

Longworth, Thomas, *Longworth's Almanac and New York Register and City Directory*. 1820 to 1842.

Low, John, *The New York Directory*. New York: John Bull, 1796.

The New York Directory and Register for the Year(s) 1789, 1790. New York: Printed by Hodge, Allen and Campbell. M,DCC,XC.

The New York City Directory, 1842 to 1851. New York: John Doggett, Jr., Publisher and Proprietor.

Rode, Charles R., *The New York City Directory*. New York: Doggett and Rode, 1851.

Wilson, H. Compiler, *Trow's New York City Directory*. New York: John F. Trow, Publisher. 1852-1881.

8. Periodicals:

The A.M.E. Zion Quarterly Review: Volume I, 1890; October 1891, "*Memorial Issue— Bishop Singleton T. Jones*"; April 1892; October 1892; April 1894; January 1894; July 1894; April 1899; April 1901; October 1906.

Anderson, J. Harvey, "Progress of the Fourth Quarter of the A.M.E. Zion Church," *The A.M.E. Zion Quarterly Review*, October 1898.

Biddle, E. George, "The African Methodist Episcopal Zion Church and The Anti-Slavery Movement," *The A.M.E. Zion Quarterly Review*, April 1898.

Biographical Sketch, Mrs. Letitia Clinton, *The A.M.E. Zion Quarterly Review*. January, 1894.

Blackwell, George L. I., "The Rt. Reverend James W. Hood," *A.M.E. Zion Quarterly Review*, October 1890.

Bloice, John A. D., "The Progress of the Second Quarter of Zion Methodism," *The A.M.E. Zion Quarterly Review*, July 1898.

The Christian Advocate, September 4, 1879.

The Christian Advocate and Journal, "Thomas Morrell Letters," May 1, 1851.

The Christian Century, February 17, 1971; February 24, 1971; March 22, 1972.

The Crisis, March, 1922.

Douglass, Frederick, "Letter from the Late Honorable Frederick Douglass," *The A.M.E. Zion Quarterly Review*, April 1895.

Evans, Aurora, "Origin and Work of the Daughters of Conference," *The A.M.E. Zion Quarterly Review*, January 1898.

The Genius of Universal Emancipation, No. 1, Vol. II, July, 1822.

Goler, William H., "Our Educational Institutions and Their Needs," *The A.M.E. Zion Quarterly Review*, April 1898.

Harris, Meriah E., "Woman in Pioneer Work of the Church," *The A.M.E. Zion Quarterly Review*, April 1899.

Hoffman, Henry B., "Transformations of New York Churches," The New York Historical Society *Quarterly Bulletin*, Vol. XXII, January 1938. No. 1.

Jacobs, Frederick M., "Negro Methodism a Factor in the Development of The Negro Race," *The A.M.E. Zion Quarterly Review*, July 1898.

Lomax, T. H., "Progress of the Third Quarter of the A.M.E. Zion Church," *The A.M.E. Zion Quarterly Review*, October 1898.

Martin, Charles, "Our Chaplains," *The A.M.E. Zion Quarterly Review*, April 1918.

The Negro History Bulletin, Vol. 5, No. 1. October 1941.

Seaman, Samuel A., "Methodist Worship in New York City One Hundred Years Ago," *The Christian Advocate*, September 9, 1926.

The Southwestern Christian Advocate, October 22, 1925.

Taylor, James C., "A Tribute to the Class of 1924," *The A.M.E. Zion Quarterly Review*, Vol. LIX, No. 3, 1949.

Thurman, Howard, "Christ's Message to the Disinherited," *Ebony Magazine*. September 1963.

Trueblood, Roy W., "Union Negotiations Between Black Methodists in America," *Methodist History*, July 1970.

White, J. H., "The History of the First Twenty-Five Years of the African Methodist Episcopal Zion Church," *The A.M.E. Zion Quarterly Review*, July 1898.

9. Constitutions, Reports and Other Published Works:

A Call Upon the Church for Progressive Action to Elevate the Colored American People. n. pub. Fall River, 1848.

Annual Reports, Federal Council of Churches of Christ, U.S.A., 1908-1932.

Blackwell, George L., II. Secretary, Christian Education Department. *Six-Months Report, St. Mark Church, Dallas, Texas*. January 4, 1972.

Centennial Program of the African Methodist Episcopal Zion Church, 1896.

Constitution of the African Marine Fund, for the Relief of the Distressed Orphans and Poor Members of This Fund. New York: John C. Totten, 1810.

Constitution, Lay Members Association of the African Methodist Episcopal Zion Church. Louisville, Kentucky, 1916.

Constitution, New York African Bible Society. Ms. Collection, American Bible Society Library, New York City.

*Constitution of the New York African Clarkson Association. New York: Printed By E. Conrad, 1825.

Constitution of the Woman's Home and Foreign Missionary Society, African Methodist Episcopal Zion Church. Issued by The Executive Secretary, Harriet Tubman Home, Auburn, New York. 1960.

Constitution, World Council of Churches, Ms. Papers, First Assembly, Amsterdam, Holland, 1948. Author's collection.

Episcopal Quadrennial Address to the Delegates of the Twenty-Third Quadrennial General Conference of the African Methodist Episcopal Zion Church. Philadelphia, Pennsylvania, May 6, 1908.

Eichelberger, J. W., *Report of Secretary of Christian Education Department, Minutes, Thirty-Fourth Quadrennial Session*, 1952.

Holliday, Jehu, *Printed Autobiography*, 1892. Author's Collection.

Hood Thank-Offering Fortieth Anniversary Souvenir Program, 1911.

Jones, S. T., Report Made by the Delegate to the M.E. General Conference in Chicago, Ill. on the Subject of Affiliation and Union Between the M.E. Church and the A.M.E. Zion Church in America, and the Failure of the Union Project (A.M.E. & A.M.E. Zion Church). Washington, D.C. Printed by W. H. Moore, June, 1868.

Official Program and Handbook, Ecumenical Methodist Conference, Washington, D.C., October, 1891. New York: Methodist Book Concern; Hunt and Eaton, Agents, 1891.

Official Program, First Assembly World Council of Churches, Amsterdam, Holland, 1948.

Official Souvenir Journal of the Sesqui-Centennial, African Methodist Episcopal Zion Church, New York, 1946.

150th Anniversary Literature of the American Bible Society, New York, 1966.

Quadrennial Message by the Board of Bishops to the Thirty-Ninth A.M.E. Zion General Conference, Mobile, Alabama, May 1972.

Quadrennial Report of the Corresponding Secretary of the Foreign Missions Department, African Methodist Episcopal Zion Church, (Reverend J. C. Hoggard), 1968-1972. Mobile, Alabama: 1972.

Quadrennial Report of the Second Episcopal District, African Methodist Episcopal Zion Church (Bishop H. B. Shaw), Mobile, Alabama: 1972.

Quadrennial Report of the Third Episcopal District, African Methodist Episcopal Zion Church (Bishop S. G. Spottswood), Mobile, Alabama: 1972.

Report of the Ladies' General Conference Home and Foreign Missionary Society of the A.M.E. Zion Church in America. York, Pa.: Teachers' Journal Office, 1884.

Revised Constitution, The National Fraternal Council of Churches, USA, Inc. April 26-27, 1950.

Sanford, Elias B., *The Federal Council of Churches of Christ in America. Report of the First Meeting of the Federal Council of Churches, Philadelphia, 1908.* New York: The Revell Press, 1909.

Sesqui-Centennial Celebration Program, Boyer Lodge No. 1, F. & A.M. (Free and Accepted Mason of Prince Hall Lodge) 1812-1862. New York Historical Society, New York City.

Sesqui-Centennial Souvenir Program of the African Methodist Episcopal Zion Church. 1946.

Thompson, Joseph P., *Constitution of the African Civilization Society ... Also The Anniversary Address Delivered by Rev. Joseph P. Thompson, D.D., Annual Meeting, May 19, 1861.* New Haven: Thomas J. Stafford, 1861.

Triennial Report, National Council of the Churches of Christ in the United States of America, 1972. (Preamble of The Constitution).

Varick Memorial Church Historical Bulletin, Dedication Program, Brooklyn, New York. March 30, 1952.

Williams, Milford. ed. *Union Wesley African Methodist Episcopal Zion Church Souvenir Journal, Washington, D.C., 1949, Service of Church Opening, August 1, 1949.* Rev. W. A. Stewart, Pastor.

INDEX